निघण्टुसमन्वितं निरुक्तम्

THE NIGHAṆṬU
AND
THE NIRUKTA

श्रीयास्काचार्यप्रणीतं

शब्दव्युत्पत्ति-भाषाविज्ञानार्थविज्ञान-विषयकं

निघण्टुसमन्वितं निरुक्तम्

पञ्चनदीय–प्राच्यमहाविद्यालये संस्कृताचार्येण

डॉ. लक्ष्मणसरूप इत्येतेन

संहिता–ब्राह्मण–प्रातिशाख्याष्यादिग्रन्थान्तरैः साकं निरुक्तसम्बन्ध–प्रदर्शिना परिशिष्टेन, तथा विस्तृतेनोपोद्घातेन, आङ्लभाषानुवादेन, टिप्पण्या, अनुक्रमणीभिः परिष्टिैश्च समलङ्कृत्य सम्पादितम्

भाग १ः प्रस्तावना,
भाग २ः आङ्गलभाषानुवादः,
भाग ३ः संस्कृतमूलम्

मोतीलाल बनारसीदास पब्लिशर्स
प्राइवेट लिमिटेड • दिल्ली

THE NIGHAṆṬU

and

THE NIRUKTA

of Śrī Yāskācārya

The Oldest Indian Treatise on Etymology, Philology and Semantics

The First Critical Edition, Translation, showing relation of the Nirukta to Saṁhitā, Brāhmaṇa, Prātiśākhya, Aṣṭādhyāyī, Mahābhāṣya etc., Exegetical and Critical Notes, Indexes and Appendices.

LAKSHMAN SARUP

Part I: Introduction
Part II: English Translation
Part III: Sanskrit Text

MOTILAL BANARSIDASS PUBLISHERS
PRIVATE LIMITED • DELHI

5th Reprint: Delhi, ***2015***
First Edition: 1920-27

ISBN: 978-81-208-1381-6 (Cloth)
ISBN: 978-81-208-3993-9 (Paper)

MOTILAL BANARSIDASS

41 U.A. Bungalow Road, Jawahar Nagar, Delhi 110 007
8 Mahalaxmi Chamber, 22 Bhulabhai Desai Road, Mumbai 400 026
203 Royapettah High Road, Mylapore, Chennai 600 004
236, 9th Main III Block, Jayanagar, Bangalore 560 011
8 Camac Street, Kolkata 700 017
Ashok Rajpath, Patna 800 004
Chowk, Varanasi 221 001

Printed in India

by RP Jain at NAB Printing Unit,
A-44, Naraina Industrial Area, Phase I, New Delhi–110028
and published by JP Jain for Motilal Banarsidass Publishers (P) Ltd,
41 U.A. Bungalow Road, Jawahar Nagar, Delhi-110007

TO

PROFESSOR A. A. MACDONELL

AS A HUMBLE MARK

OF RESPECT

॥ श्रीः ॥

॥ समर्पणम् ॥

॥ षट्पदी ॥

शशिकरशुचिगुणगणपरिगुम्फितजनतामनसः
नीतिप्रतिभाशालिशीलसम्पन्नसुमनसः ।
देवगिरारसिकस्य लोकदृक्शीतलमहसः
पञ्चनदीय "गवर्नेर" वरनरमञ्जुलमहसः ॥
ग्रन्थ उपायनमस्त्वयं दोषकृतामवहेलिनः ।
गुणगृह्यप्रवरस्य "सर् विलियम् मल्कम् हेलिनः" ॥ १ ॥

TABLE OF CONTENTS
PART I

TABLE OF CONTENTS

PART II

निघण्टुविषयानुक्रमणी

भाग ३

निरुक्तविषयानुक्रमणी।

PART I

INTRODUCTION

PREFACE

WHEN I first came to Oxford in the autumn of 1916, I undertook, on the suggestion of Professor A. A. Macdonell, to collate the hitherto unutilized *Nirukta* Manuscripts, contained in the Max Müller Memorial and the Chandra Shum Shere Collections, and to see if some new light could be thrown on the text of the *Nirukta*. A careful examination of the materials at my disposal has led me to the conclusion that the text of the *Nirukta* has been gradually expanded by the addition of short passages, chiefly in the etymological explanations which easily lent themselves to such interpolations. At present the history of this gradual expansion can be traced only down to the thirteenth century A.D. There is a lack of reliable evidence going further. But I have reasons to suspect that even up to the thirteenth century, the text of the *Nirukta* has not been handed down with a uniform and unbroken tradition. A few remarks of Durga scattered here and there in his commentary open up the possibility that the interpolators were already busy with their nefarious work. There is no doubt that the text had already been tampered with. Thus one should be cautious in making Yāska responsible for many passages, and the numerous absurd derivations contained therein, now commonly attributed to him. All such passages have been pointed out in my edition of the text, which sets forth as clearly as possible the history of the gradual expansion by means of square brackets and foot-notes.

I have also produced, for the first time, a complete English translation of the whole of the *Nirukta*. I have added numerous exegetical and critical notes with a view to extract as much information as possible from Yāska. And in order to make my work further useful, I have also prepared the following Indexes and Appendices: (1) An Index to the words of the *Nighaṇṭu* with meanings; (2) An Index to the words of the Quoted Passages occurring in the *Nirukta* with meanings; (3) an Index

Verborum to the *Nirukta* minus the Quoted Passages with meanings; (4) An alphabetical list of the Quotations occurring in the *Nirukta*; (5) An alphabetical list of the Untraced Quotations occurring in the *Nirukta*; (6) A list of Vedic Quotations arranged in the order of the *Saṁhitās*; (7) A list of the Authorities mentioned by Yāska; (8) A list of Stories related by Yāska; (9) The Relation of the *Nirukta* to other texts, i. e. a collection of parallel passages from the *Brāhmaṇas, Prātiśākhyas, Mahābhāṣya*, &c.; (10) An alphabetical list of the etymologies to be found in the *Nirukta*; (11) A list of the *Nirukta* passages quoted by Sāyaṇa. The whole work being embodied in the form of a dissertation was presented to, and accepted by, the University of Oxford, for the degree of Doctor of Philosophy. Notwithstanding the Statt. Tit. VI, Sec. v, § 5. (8), which requires an Advanced Student to publish his thesis *in extenso* before supplicating for the said degree, the Committee for Advanced Studies very kindly permitted me—taking into consideration the very high cost of printing at present—to publish the Introduction alone. I think I need make no apology for bringing out this part only at present, in the hope that the rest will follow in course of time.

If my labours have borne any fruit, it is simply due to the guidance which I have received in the course of my work, and which it is my very pleasant duty to acknowledge.

I owe a great debt of gratitude to Professor A. A. Macdonell. The inception of this study is, as I have already mentioned, due to his suggestion. The whole work was done under his supervision. His guidance and encouragement have been of invaluable help to me. And through his recommendation the Administrators to the Max Müller Memorial Fund have voted a sum of £50 for the publication of my dissertation—my thanks to them for this generous help. I am much indebted to Dr. F. W. Thomas, Librarian, India Office, and to Dr. J. Morison, Librarian, Indian Institute, Oxford, for granting me facilities in the use of books, and for their readiness to help me in every way whenever I had the occasion to seek their advice. I desire to put on record my special thanks to Mr. Madan, ex-Librarian of the Bodleian, for permission to work on valuable manuscripts during the dark days of air-raids, when the manuscripts had been carefully stored away. Professor A. B. Keith has placed me under great obligation by giving me his valuable opinion on many difficult points. Dr. T. W. Arnold, C.I.E., Educational Adviser to the Secretary of State for India, has taken a good deal of interest in my work and has supported me in almost every obstacle to the completion of my studies.

It has been my privilege to interpret an ancient Indian author, who, as far as Etymology and Semantics are concerned, is far in advance of the greatest of ancient Greek writers like Plato and Aristotle, and if he comes to be better appreciated, my labour will be amply repaid.

LAKSHMAN SARUP.

BALLIOL COLLEGE, OXFORD.
July, 1920.

INTRODUCTION

THE NIGHAṆṬU

The following manuscripts have been collated for this edition of the *Nighaṇṭu*:

1.	Max Müller Memorial MS.	e. 5	= M 1
2.	„ „ „ „	e. 6	= M 2
3 and 4.	„ „ „ „	e. 7	= M 3 and M 4 respectively
5.	Chandra Shum Shere MS.	d. 184	= C 1
6, 7, 8.	„ „ „ „	e. 62	= C 2, C 3, C 4 respectively
9.	MS. Sanskrit	e. 17	= S
10.	MS. Wilson	379	= W 1
11 and 12.	„ „	502	= W 2, W 3 respectively
13.	„ „	503	= W 4

a. Detailed Description of the Manuscripts.

M 1.—This is a neatly-written manuscript in *Devanāgarī* characters on paper. It originally consisted of 13 leaves, but the first two are missing. The accent has been marked in yellow ink. The text is not bounded on either side by double lines.

The size of the paper is $9\frac{1}{5}'' \times 3\frac{3}{4}''$.

The number of lines on each page varies from 9 to 10. The date given on f. 14 r. as *Śak.* 1455, is not reliable, and has obviously been added at a later period by a different hand, as the evidence of the writing indicates. The manuscript is well preserved, but neither its general appearance nor the condition and the colour of its paper, nor its spelling lend the least support to the date given above. It is on the whole accurate. It belongs to the longer recension. The scribe seems to have been a devotee of Kṛṣṇa, for he says: **श्री कृष्णार्पणमस्तु**. Neither the name of the scribe, nor of the owner, nor of the place of its origin, is known.

M 2.—This is perhaps the oldest of all the manuscripts of the *Nighaṇṭu*. It is written in *Devanāgarī* characters on paper, but is not well preserved. In many places it suffers from illegibility, partly caused by the smudging of the ink.

It begins: **ॐ नमो गणेशाय ॥ ॐ ॥ अथ शिक्षां प्रवक्ष्यामि** . . . , &c. It gives the *Śikṣā Catuṣṭaya* in 26 leaves. The different treatises are not bodily separated from each other, all the four, i. e. *Śikṣā*, *Jyotiṣa*, *Chandas* and *Nighaṇṭu* being written continuously without a break. The end of each is found on f. 4 r., f. 7 v., f. 12 r., and f. 24 v. respectively. The accent is not marked. The text is bounded on each side by double black lines.

The size of the paper is $9\frac{4}{5}'' \times 4\frac{4}{5}''$.

The number of lines on each page varies from 10–13.

It has preserved the archaic spelling in many cases, especially in the case of श्री ; कौरयाणः is written ञकोरयाणः and तौरयाणः as ञतोरयाणः on f. 22 v. Ff. 15–26 are slightly worm-eaten. It was copied in the month of *Phālguṇa*, *Saṃvat* 1778, by a scribe named Śivānanda. It belongs to the shorter recension.

M 3.—This is a paper manuscript, neatly written in *Devanāgarī* characters. In this manuscript also the *Śikṣā*, *Jyotiṣa*, *Chandas*, and *Nighaṇṭu* are written without a break between them. The accent in the *Nighaṇṭu* is not marked. The size of the paper is $9'' \times 4''$, and the number of lines on each page is 7. The text is bounded on each side by double red lines. The name of the owner is Āśārāma Kedāreśvara, son of Śrī Nandarāma. It was copied for private study at Benares. The date given is *Saṃvat* 1801: (*sic*) संवत् १८०१ नामिति श्रावणमासे शुक्लपक्षे पंचमीयं बुद्धवासरे ग्रंथसमाप्तिः ॥ शुभमस्तु ॥ The manuscript ends: (*sic*) सर्वेषां खण्डिकासंख्या ॥ १०० ॥ श्लोकसंख्या ॥ ३७५ ॥

तैलाद्रक्षेज्जलाद्रक्षेद्रक्षेत्सिथिलबन्धनात् ।
मूर्षहस्ते न दातव्यं एवं वदति पुस्तकम् ॥
शुभं भवतु ॥ कल्याणमस्तु ॥

It belongs to the shorter recension.

M 4.—This contains the *Śikṣā*, &c., without a break between them, and gives, in 23 leaves, the *Śikṣā*, *Jyotiṣa*, *Chandas*, and *Nighaṇṭu*, which end on f. 5 v., f. 8 r., f. 13 r., and f. 23 v. respectively. The five *adhāyās* of the *Nighaṇṭu* end on f. 15 v., f. 18 v., f. 21 r., f. 22 v., f. 23 v. respectively. It begins: श्री गणेशाय नमः ॥ श्री दुर्गादेव्यै नमः ॥ ॐ अथ शिक्षां प्रवक्ष्यामि, &c. It ends: इति नैघंटुके पंचमोध्यायः समाप्तः ॥

The size of paper is $8\frac{2}{5}'' \times 3\frac{2}{5}''$; the number of lines on each page is 8. The text is bounded on either side by double red lines. The accent is marked in the *Nighaṇṭu* with red ink. No date is given, nor the name of the scribe, nor the place.

It belongs to the longer recension.

C 1.—It consists of three different manuscripts. The first manuscript, which gives the *Nighaṇṭu* in full, seems to be a fragment, for the first folio is numbered 10. It appears that originally it gave the *Śikṣā Catuṣṭaya*, and that now the *Nighaṇṭu* alone survives. It begins on f. 10 r., and ends on f. 22 r. The text is bounded on each side by double red lines. The accent is marked. The size of the paper is 9″ × 4⅕″; the number of lines is 11. It ends: (*sic*) **इति निघंटौ पंचमोध्यायः ॥ श्री तीक्ष्णभांडेश्वरार्पणमस्तु ॥ श्री गंगा प्रसन् ॥**

The date *Śak.* 1875, and the name of the then owner, Gopāla Ānanda Sarasvatī, are added in a different, probably later, hand. It belongs to the longer recension.

C 2.—Is the first of five different manuscripts bound in one volume [e. 62]. It contains the *Nighaṇṭu* in 17 leaves, marking the accent with red ink in the first *adhyāya* only.

It begins: **॥ श्री गणेशाय नमः ॥ हरिः ॐ ॥** It ends: (*sic*) **इति निघंटे पंचमोध्यायः ॥ समाप्तः ॥** Neither the date nor the name of the scribe is given.

The size of the paper is 8⅕″ × 3½″. The number of lines on each page is 7. Ff. 15, 16, 17 are slightly worm-eaten.

It is written in *Devanāgarī* characters on paper, and is fairly accurate. It belongs to the longer recension.

C 3–C 4.—Are contained in the same volume, each being a *Śikṣā Catuṣṭaya*, of which the *Nighaṇṭu* forms a part. The text of each of these *Śikṣā Catuṣṭaya* is written continuously, and is bounded by double red lines. The size of the paper is 8⅕″ × 4, and the number of lines on each page is 10. The first two sections of the first *adhyāya* are missing in the first manuscript. The other manuscript is dated *Saṃvat*, 1852.

Both are written in *Devanāgarī* characters and represent the longer recension.

The other manuscripts are a *Śikṣā* attributed to Pāṇini, and a *Śikṣā* attributed to Yājñavalkya. The latter begins: (*sic*) **डों श्री गणेशाय नमः याज्ञवल्क्य उवाच अथातस्त्रैस्वर्य्यलक्षणं व्याख्यास्यामः उदात्तश्चानुदात्तश्च स्वरितश्च तथैव तत् लक्षणं वर्णयिष्यामि दैवतं स्थानमेव च**, &c. It ends: **इति श्री याज्ञवल्क्यमुनिकृता वाजसनेयीशिक्षा समाप्ता संवत्? ३० माघमासे . . . . समाप्ता रामः विश्न विश्न विश्न वि.**

Another manuscript bound in the same volume gives in seven leaves the *Śikṣā* of the *Sāma Veda*, attributed to Lomaśa. It begins: **ॐ नमः सामवेदाय.** It has preserved some old spellings; for instance, it writes **वेद** as **ावद.**

The last manuscript gives the *Chandomañjarī* in 5 leaves. It begins: (*sic*) **श्री गणपतये नमः ॥ प्रणम्य वेदं पुरुषं छन्दःशास्त्रेषु निश्चितं । विष्णुभट्टैस्त्विदं प्रोक्तं**

छंदोमंजरिमादिता ॥१॥ छंदोमंजरी कथ्यते ॥ प्रथमं छन्दः ॥ गायत्री ॥ उदाहरणानि॰ अग्निमीळे ८।८।८ पदपंक्ति, &c.

It ends: इति श्री विष्णुभट्टविरचिता छंदोमंजरी समाप्ता ।

S 4.—This manuscript contains five works. The first four consist of the *Śikṣā Catuṣṭaya*, of which the first three works are probably written by the same scribe. The first part gives the *Śikṣā* in 6 leaves, the second the *Jyotiṣa* in 4, the third the *Chandas* in 7 leaves, the fourth the *Nighaṇṭu*.[1] The first and third were copied in *Śaka* 1665, and the fourth in *Śaka* 1660. All these four parts are complete in themselves individually, each being separately numbered. The name of their former owner is Bhaṭṭa Jayanārāyaṇa of Themṭi.

The *Nighaṇṭu* consists of 9 leaves. The text is bounded on each side by a pair of double red lines. It is a neatly-written manuscript, The accent is marked with red ink. The size of the paper is $9\frac{1}{2}'' \times 3\frac{3}{4}''$. For further details see *Catalogus Codd. MSS. Bib. Bodl.*, by Winternitz and Keith, vol. ii, p. 105.

The manuscript belongs to the longer recension, and does not seem to have been used by Roth.

W 1.—This contains two different manuscripts. The first is *Vedārthadīpikā*, a commentary on the *Sarvānukramaṇī* by Ṣaḍguruśiṣya.

The second is the *Nighaṇṭu*. It begins on f. 1 v., and ends on f. 10 r. It is without accent, quite modern, and full of mistakes. It is Roth's F. It belongs to the shorter recension.

For further details, see *Catalogus Codd. MSS, Bib. Bodl.*, by Winternitz and Keith, vol. ii, p. 104.

W 2.—This manuscript contains three different works.

I. The first work is the *Śikṣā Catuṣṭaya*. It is a continuously-written manuscript, the four parts ending on f. 3 v., f. 6 v., f. 11 v., and f. 23 respectively. The *Nighaṇṭu* is given without accent. It is Roth's C, and belongs to the shorter recension. For further details see *Catalogus Codd. MSS. Bib. Bodl.*, vol. ii, p. 104.

W 3. II. This is the second manuscript bound in the volume just mentioned. It gives the *Nighaṇṭu* in 24 leaves. It is without accent. The name of the scribe, partially obliterated by yellow pigment, is the following: भट्टनारायणसुतविश्रामेण लिखितं ॥ रामेश्वरपठनार्थम् ॥ परोपकारार्थम् ॥

It is Roth's D, and belongs to the shorter recension.

III. The third manuscript is the *Anuvākānukramaṇī*.

W 4.—This manuscript contains two different works. The first is the *Śikṣā Catuṣṭaya*. Its first three parts are written continuously. The

[1] The fifth is the *Uttaraṣaṭkam* of the *Nirukta*.

Nighaṇṭu is separated from the rest. It ends on f. 16, which gives a list of the total number of words and *Khaṇḍas* for each *adhyāya* as follows:—

	Khaṇḍa	words			
1st	17	412	4th	3	279
2nd	22	516	5th	6	151
3rd	30	410			

It is Roth's E, and belongs to the longer recension.

To these manuscripts, which I have directly collated myself, may be added the A and B which were used by Roth (not directly collated by me), besides C.D.E.F = W 1, W 2, W 3, W 4, and क, ख, ग, घ, ङ, and च used by Sāmaśrami, in his edition, published in the Bib. Ind.

b. **Two recensions.**

The manuscripts fall into two distinct groups: M 2, M 3, W 1, W 2, W 3 and ग form one family group, and M 1, M 4, C 1, C 2, C 3, C 4, S, W 4; A, B, E; क, ख, घ, ङ, and च the other. The former may be called the shorter recension, the latter the longer. The chief reason for calling the former group the shorter recension is that at the end of every section the explanation is more concise than in the other. The latter not only gives an extended explanation at the end of every section, but also adds the number of the words enumerated in the section. Besides, at the end of every chapter, it gives a summary of the sections by quoting the first word of every section, and adds the number of the sections in the chapter. In many sections the shorter recension gives fewer words. It is difficult to decide which of these two represents the original. But as far as the longer explanation at the end of every section is concerned, it is quite obvious that it is a later addition. The evidence of the manuscripts shows that this addition was gradual. For instance, let us take the first section of the first chapter. All the manuscripts of the shorter recension agree in giving the text as follows: गोचेति पृथिव्याः. Manuscript W 2 gives the number of the section only, i.e. ॥ १ ॥, and throughout it follows this method, which seems to have been the original one. Gradually a change was introduced: along with the number of the section, the number of the words in the section was added, and a numerical figure placed immediately before the number of the section, as the evidence of manuscripts M 2 and W 3 indicates, in the first section of the first chapter, ॥ २१ ॥ is placed before ॥ १ ॥ i.e. गोचेति पृथिव्याः ॥ २१ ॥ १ ॥ In this connexion it is interesting to note that manuscripts W 1 and M 3 at first agree with W 2, but gradually come round to the side of M 2 and W 3. The next stage of development is marked by the incorporation of the numerical word in substitution for the figure in the body of the explanation, as ॥ गोचेत्येकविंशतिः पृथिव्याः ॥. This is most clearly seen in the sections containing verbs, for instance, in sec. 16 of the first chapter, all the stages appear very clearly:

a. घुमदिति ज्वलतिकर्माणः ॥ १६ ॥ W 1, W 2.

b. „ „ ॥ ११ ॥ १६ ॥ M 2, M 3, W 3.

c. घुमदित्येकादश ज्वलतिकर्माणः ॥ १६ ॥ Manuscripts of longer recension.

From the verbs the process was extended by analogy to nouns, perhaps in imitation of Yāska's own words or for the sake of parallelism, नामधेयानि was also introduced. Last of all came the summary and the statement of the sections in every chapter.

Yāska's description of the *Nighaṇṭu* । *Samāmnāyaḥ Samāmnātaḥ* । *Sa vyākhyātavyaḥ* । N. I. 1.—and taking into consideration the fact that in some cases, like that of *Nighaṇṭu* II. 6, 8, 11, &c., his only explanation is that a particular word has so many synonyms—suits the shorter recension better, for in the case of the longer recension such an explanation is superfluous. *Nighaṇṭu* II. 11, the shorter recension reads शक्वरीति गवां, while the longer has: शक्वरीति नव गोनामानि, and Yāska's only explanation (N. 3. 9) is: गोनामान्युत्तराणि नव. To call this the explanation of the longer recension is absurd, while in the case of the shorter recension it may be accepted as an explanation to a certain extent.

c. Devarāja and his commentary.

Devarājayajvan explains every single word of the *Nighaṇṭu*; his commentary therefore is valuable, for it shows the state of the *Nighaṇṭu* in his day. Moreover, in the introduction to his Commentary, he gives a general description of the many manuscripts of the *Nighaṇṭu* known to him. He says: तेषु च केषुचिदर्थेषु लेखकप्रमादादिभिः कानिचित्पदान्यधिकान्यासन्। अन्येषु च कानिचिन्न्यूनानि। अपरेषु च कानिचिदपहाय कानिचित् विन्यस्तानि। अक्षराणि च विपर्यस्तानि। एवं व्याकीर्णेषु कोशेषु नियमैकभूतस्य प्रतिपदनिर्वचननिगमप्रदर्शनपरस्य कस्यचिद् व्याख्यानस्याभावात् नैघण्टुकं काण्डमुत्सन्नप्रायमासीत्।

He has attempted to supply a critical edition, for he says that Yāska explained 150 words of the *Naighaṇṭuka Kāṇḍa*, and Skandasvāmi, in his commentary on Yāska, added some more, bringing the total to 200, so the evidence of Yāska and Skandasvāmi was very valuable for these 200 words. About the rest he says: अन्येषां च पदानामस्मत् कुले समाम्नायाध्ययनस्याविच्छेदात्-श्रीवेङ्कटाचार्यतनयस्य माधवस्य भाष्यकृतौ नामानुक्रमण्या आख्यातानुक्रमण्याः स्वरानुक्रमण्या निपातानुक्रमण्या निर्बन्धानुक्रमण्यास्तदीयस्य भाष्यस्य च बहुशः पर्यालोचनात् बहुदेशसमानीतात् बहुकोशनिरीक्षणाच्च पाठः संशोधितः।

Devarāja has frequently given the readings of former commentators like Skandasvāmi, Bhaṭṭa Bhāskaramiśra, and Mādhava, when he differed from them. His commentary has therefore the value of a collation of a number of manuscripts, brought as he says from various parts of the country, and also of the collation of former commentaries. I have carefully examined it and noted all the differences, as the foot-notes to the text will show.

d. Roth's edition of the Nighaṇṭu.

Roth examined the commentary of Devarāja, but the manuscripts which he used were probably defective, so that his results are unsatisfactory. Often he attributes readings to Devarāja which are not to be found in the published text of that commentator; for instance (I. 11) the reading **मा** is attributed to Devarāja, who actually reads **माः**; he also passes over variants given by Devarạja. Devarāja gives **नना** as a variant for **नमा**, which Roth does not mention. Similarly Devarāja gives **सुरा** (I. 12) as a different reading, which Roth again does not notice. Devarāja gives **प्रयः** for **पयः**, which Roth ignores. Other cases are:

I. 14. Roth attributes **यह्व्वः** to Dev., who reads **यठ्ह्यः**, and gives **यव्वाः** as a variant.

I. 13. Dev. gives **ऋतावर्यः** for **वर्यः** as the reading of Mādhava, unnoticed by Roth.

I. 13. Dev. gives **रेवत्यः** for **स्रवन्त्यः** as another reading, unnoticed by Roth.

I. 14. Roth attributes **उच्चैश्रवसः** to Dev., whose actual reading is **श्रौच्चैश्रवसः**

I. 15. Dev. reads **उषसः** for **उषसां** and gives **उषसः** as the reading of Skandasvāmi, unnoticed by Roth.

I. 16. Dev. gives **भ्लाश्यति** as another reading for **भ्राश्यति** unnoticed by Roth.

II. 1. Dev. gives **चर्षत्वम्** as the reading of Mādhava for **चक्रत्**, Roth does not notice it.

II. 5. Dev. gives **अथर्यवः** as a different reading for **अथर्यः**, Roth does not notice it.

II. 7. Dev. gives **प्रयः** as the reading of Skandasvāmi also, but he further gives **श्रवः** as a variant. Roth does not notice it.

II. 7. Dev. gi es **सुतः** as a variant for **वयः**, Roth does not notice it.

It is unnecessary to multiply instances, for all such cases can be easily found in my foot-notes to the text of the *Nighaṇṭu*.

Roth does not give any various readings for the fourth chapter of the *Nighaṇṭu*, although the evidence of the manuscripts as shown in this edition proves that there are several such variants.

There are a few inaccuracies of accent, for instance in III. 13. अभि नै ये is accented in manuscripts, but not so in Roth's edition.

There is, however, a serious omission in IV. 2. हरयाणः has been omitted between अहयाणः and आरितः. That the omission is an oversight appears from the fact that though this section is stated to contain 84 words, Roth's edition has only 83. Yāska explains every word of the fourth and fifth chapters of the *Nighaṇṭu*. His evidence is therefore particularly valuable for a critical edition of the fourth and fifth chapters. He gives हरयाणः in its proper place and explains it. Both the recensions agree in reading हरयाणः between अहयाणः and आरितः, and the testimony of Devarāja and Yāska supports this reading The omission[1] in Roth's edition is thus evidently due to an oversight.

The evidence of Yāska on the fourth and fifth chapters of the *Nighaṇṭu* indicates that he follows the longer recension. Thus in IV. 1 the shorter recension gives इषिरः, but Yāska reads इषिरेण, which is also the reading of the longer recension. Again नु च, which is omitted by the shorter recension, is explained by Yāska. In IV. 2 दूतः is omitted by the shorter recension, but not by Yāska. Devarāja has also followed the longer recension, and this choice seems to be followed by a long line of commentators, and is also, as Devarāja says, supported by an unbroken tradition in his own family. The shorter recension has undoubtedly preserved the original form of the text, at least towards the end of the sections, but the weighty testimony of Yāska is against it. I have therefore given the text and the order in which the words occur in accordance with the longer recension, though at the end of every section I have placed side by side the text of both recensions.

e. Bib. Ind. edition of the Nighaṇṭu.

Sāmaśrami's edition of the *Nighaṇṭu* is useful, for besides publishing the commentary of Devarāja Yajvan it supplies a much larger number of various readings than Roth. But it suffers from the one defect of presenting only Devarāja's reading of the text of the *Nighaṇṭu*. The commentary of Devarāja, however valuable as giving the various readings of the manuscripts of his time, cannot be made the sole basis of an edition of the *Nighaṇṭu*. Moreover, occasionally the text in this edition contains words which are not justified either by the evidence of the manuscripts of

[1] This was admitted, and later on rectified by Roth himself.

both recensions, or even by that of Devarāja himself. For instance, on p. 236, appears the word संसति, which does not exist anywhere; again, on p. 257, we find साचिवित् instead of the correct form साचीवित्. Sāmaśrami seems to have used six manuscripts, from which he gives a number of various readings in foot-notes, but in the constitution of the text he has consistently followed Devarāja. Hence it is not a critical edition, from the point of view of constituting an independent text of the *Nighaṇṭu* based on manuscript evidence.

f. The title of the work.

Sāyaṇācārya in the *Ṛgvedabhāṣyabhūmikā* has given the title of *Niruktam* to this list of words. He says: अर्थावबोधे निरपेक्षतया पदजातं यत्रोक्तं तन्निरुक्तम्। गौः। ग्मा। ज्मा। क्ष्मा। क्षा। क्षमा इत्यारभ्य वसवः। वाजिनः। देवपत्न्यो देवपत्न्य इत्यन्तो यः पदानां समाम्नायः समाम्नातस्तस्मिन् ग्रन्थे पदार्थावबोधाय परापेक्षा न विद्यते.....। तदेतन्निरुक्तं त्रिकाण्डम्.... पञ्चाध्यायरूपे काण्डत्रयात्मक एतस्मिन् ग्रन्थे परनिरपेक्षितया पदार्थस्योक्तत्वात् तस्य ग्रन्थस्य निरुक्तत्वमिति।

Madhusūdanasvāmi, the author of the *Prasthānabheda* has also given the title of *Niruktam* to this list of words. Similarly Sāmaśrami follows Sāyaṇa in calling the work *Niruktam*, although he adds in brackets (*Nighaṇṭu*). Sāyaṇa is evidently wrong in giving the title of *Niruktam* to the *Samāmnāya*, for Yāska distinctly states that it is called *Nighaṇṭu*. *Samāmnāyaḥ samāmnātaḥ . . . . tam imam Samāmnāyaṃ Nighaṇṭava ityācakṣate* । (N. I. 1). The list of words can only be called *Nighaṇṭu*, and it is wrong to call it *Niruktam*; the term *Nirukta* can be applied only when some etymological explanations are given. Moreover, all the manuscripts call it *Nighaṇṭu*.

g. The division of the Nighaṇṭu.

The *Nighaṇṭu* contains five chapters, the first three are called the *Naighaṇṭuka Kāṇḍa*, the fourth the *Naigama Kāṇḍa*, and the fifth the *Daivata Kāṇḍa*. In other words it may be said that

the *Naighaṇṭuka Kāṇḍa* deals with synonyms;
the *Naigama Kāṇḍa* deals with homonyms;
the *Daivata Kāṇḍa* deals with deities.

There is some sort of a principle discernible in the arrangement of the synonyms in the first three chapters. The first chapter deals with physical things like earth, air, water, and objects of nature like cloud, dawn, day and night, &c. The second chapter deals with man, his limbs, like arm, finger, objects and qualities associated with man, such as wealth, prosperity, anger, battle, &c.

The third chapter deals with abstract qualities such as heaviness, lightness, &c. The arrangement, of course, is not scientific, nor, in many cases, even systematic, but it shows at least an attempt to group the words methodically. The compilation of the *Nighaṇṭu* is the earliest known attempt in lexicography. In India it marks the beginning of the *Kośa* literature, and later *Kośās* have sometimes been called *Nighaṇṭavas*. The *Nighaṇṭu* contains only a small number of the words of the *Ṛgveda*, and as it does not contain any explanations of the words collected, in Sanskrit or any other language, the modern term 'dictionary' cannot be applied to it, although the *Kośās* can be so called. It should rather be called a vocabulary, which is a book 'containing a collection of words of a language, dialect, or subject'—when 'the words are few in number, being only a small part of those belonging to the subject, or when they are given without explanation, or some only are explained, or explanations are partial'.

h. The author of the Nighaṇṭu.

Nothing definite is known of the author of the *Nighaṇṭu*. There is a vague reference to the time of its compilation in the *Nirukta* I. 20, which attributes the compilation of the *Nighaṇṭu* along with other *Vedāñgas* to a later generation of the sages who had no direct perception of *dharma* (truth).

The following two verses occur in the *Mokṣa parvan* of the *Mahābhārata*, chapter 342. 86, 87:

वृषो हि भगवान् धर्मः ख्यातो लोकेषु भारत ।
निघण्टुकपदाख्याने विद्धि मां वृषमुत्तमम् ॥
कपिर्वराहः श्रेष्ठश्च धर्मश्च वृष उच्यते ।
तस्माद् वृषाकपिं प्राह कश्यपो मां प्रजापतिः ॥

Some conclude from the second verse that Kaśyapa,[1] the Prajāpati, is the author of the *Nighaṇṭu*, for the word *vṛṣākapi* occurs in the *Nighaṇṭu*. It is not safe to build any argument upon such evidence, for supposing that Kaśyapa did invent the word *vṛṣākapi* he would be the last person to put his own word in a list of difficult words like those of the *Nighaṇṭu*. The *Nighaṇṭu* is probably not the production of a single individual, but the result of the united efforts of a whole generation, or perhaps of several generations.

[1] The theory of Kaśyapa's authorship is indeed absurd, and hardly deserves any mention, but as many people in India believe in it, and seriously put it forward, I thought it necessary to make a passing reference to it.

THE NIRUKTA

a. Earlier editions of the Nirukta.

The *editio princeps* of the *Nirukta* was brought out by Rudolph Roth, and published at Göttingen in 1852. Sanskrit scholarship in Europe was then in its infancy. The bulk of the Vedic literature was as yet accessible in manuscripts only. Even the text of the *Ṛgveda* in print was not available, Max Müller having given to the world the first two volumes only of his edition of the *Ṛgveda* with Sāyaṇa's commentary.[1] Guides to Vedic studies which are now indispensable, such as Prof. Macdonell's *Vedic Grammar,* and books of reference like Bloomfield's *Vedic Concordance,* did not exist at that time. There was not even a good *Vedic* dictionary. Taking these facts into consideration, Roth's achievement was remarkable. He was the first to observe that the text of the *Nirukta* has been handed down in two recensions, a shorter and a longer one, and to prepare a critical edition of the same based on the manuscript material to which he then had access. It must be admitted that as far as the text of the *Nirukta* is concerned Roth's work has not been superseded so far, and this fact alone is very creditable to the author of a work published nearly 70 years ago, and speaks highly of the critical judgement exercised by him in the constitution of the text.

But it is obvious that a work produced under such circumstances and about three-quarters of a century ago shows certain defects and limitations. First of all, the materials at his disposal were scanty. For instance, he seems to have consulted only one manuscript of Durga's commentary, i.e. MS. Mill 142,[2] by no means an accurate manuscript, and Roth's incorrect quotations from Durga's commentary, which I have pointed out in my notes, are perhaps due to the errors of this manuscript. Hence he could not have found it a very reliable guide. Secondly, many of the then prevailing methods of indicating references are now obsolete, as, for instance, Roth's division of the *Ṛgveda* into *Maṇḍala, anuvāka,* &c., which has curtailed, to some extent, the usefulness of his *Nachweisung*, pp. 217–28. He gives a list of various readings at the end of the first and the second part of the *Nirukta,* but does not specify that such and such a variant is to be found in such and such a manuscript, a very unsatisfactory method of procedure, which no modern editor would follow. Further, Roth has adopted the text of the longer recension in his edition, but he does not

[1] Professor J. Wackernagel has been kind enough to write to me from Bâle that as Roth's *Nirukta* first began to be printed in 1847, he could not therefore have made use of Max Müller's edition of the *Ṛgveda,* the preface to the first volume of which is dated Oct. 1849.

[2] Described by Keith in the *Catalogue of Sanskrit Manuscripts in the Bodleian Library,* vol. ii, p. 108.

show any reason for this preference. As proved by me elsewhere, the longer recension does not represent the original text of the *Nirukta*. Again, he divided the *pariśiṣṭa* into two chapters, the 13th and the 14th, a division not supported by the evidence of older manuscripts, which makes the whole of the *pariśiṣṭa* to consist of one chapter (the 13th) only. Roth is also wrong in using the term *Naigama Kāṇḍam* as applicable to the first three chapters of the *Nirukta*, the right term being *Naighaṇṭuka Kāṇḍam*. Further, there are some inaccuracies in the text of the *Nirukta* itself, which I have pointed out in my notes. Again, there is the inexplicable inconsistency in using large type for printing some Vedic quotations, and small type for others, even when they are of the same length, and are cited from the same Veda. For instance, the passage **आपित्वे नः प्रपित्वे तूयमा गहि** [1] is printed in large type and is accented, whilst the immediately following passage **अभीके चिदुलोककृत्** [2] is printed in small type, and is not accented, although both quotations are from the *Ṛgveda*. Other examples are: **उपोप मे परा मृश मा मे दभ्राणि मन्यथाः** [3] is in large type and accented, but **नमो महद्भ्यो नमो अर्भकेभ्यः** [4] is in small type [5] and unaccented. Again, **तिरश्चिदर्यया परि वर्ति . . . .** [6] is in large type and accented; while **पात्रेव भिन्दन्त्सत एति . . . .** [7] is in small type and unaccented; and **अमी य ऋक्षा निहितास उच्चा** [8] is in large type and accented; while **पश्यन्तो द्यामिव स्तृभिः** [9] is in small type and unaccented. Again, **यस्यामुशन्तः प्रहराम शेपम्** [10] is in large type [11] and accented; while **त्रिः स्म माह्नः श्नथयो वैतसेन** [12] is in small type and unaccented. And **यस्य शुष्माद्रोदसी अभ्यसेताम्** [13] is in large type and accented; while **रेजते अग्ने पृथिवी मखेभ्यः** [14] is in small type and unaccented.

In one case, Roth treats both quotations in the same manner: **वम्रीभिः पुत्रमग्रुवो अदानम्** [15] is in large type [16] and accented. **यदत्त्युपजिह्विका यद्वम्रो अति सर्पति** [17] is also in large type and accented.

1 RV. viii. 4. 3; N. iii. 20, Roth's ed., p. 62.
2 RV. x. 133. 1.
3 RV. i. 126. 7.
4 RV. i. 27. 13.
5 Roth's ed., p. 63.
6 RV. v. 75. 7.
7 RV. vii. 104. 21.
8 RV. i. 24. 10.
9 RV. iv. 7. 3.
10 RV. x. 85. 37.
11 Roth's ed., p. 64.
12 RV. x. 95. 5.
13 RV. ii. 12. 1.
14 RV. vi. 66. 9.
15 RV. iv. 19. 9.
16 Roth's ed., p. 63.
17 RV. viii. 102. 21.

This practice of Roth is misleading, and is perhaps responsible for the fact that several Vedic passages printed in small type are omitted as occurring in the *Nirukta* by Bloomfield in his *Vedic Concordance*; a few such examples are the following: स्वसुर्जारः शृणोतु नः,[1] printed in small type and without accents in Roth's edition,[2] is not mentioned in VC. as being quoted by Yāska, and similarly—

अभीके चिदुलोककृत्[3]
गातुं कृण्वन्नुषसो जनाय[4]
कुत्साय मन्मन्नह्यश्च[5]
वया इव रुरुहुः सप्त विस्रुहः[6]

and also षळर आहुरर्पितम्, a fragment of RV. I. 164. 12, and quoted in the *Nirukta* 4. 27, and गभस्तिपूतः, a fragment of VS. 7. 1, quoted in N. 5. 6, are ignored. (Besides the reference of परं मृत्यो अनुपरेहि पन्थां[7] is wrong in VC.[8] It is quoted in N. 11. 7, and not in N. 10. 7, as stated there. Also the reference to वीहि शूर पुरोडाशम्[9] is wrong in VC.,[10] where it is RV. III. 46. 3, while the correct reference is RV. III. 41. 3. Other cases are: ऊर्व इव पप्रथे कामो अस्मे, RV. III. 30. 19c, is wrongly given as IV. 30. 19c in VC, cf. p. 285a; the reference of श्येनो न दीयन्नन्वेति पाथः is wrongly given as IX. 63. 5b in VC., p. 936b, while the correct reference is VII. 63. 5b.)

The Bib. Ind. Edition of the Nirukta.

This was published at Calcutta under the editorship of *Sāmaśrami* from 1882–91. Its chief merit is that it, for the first time, supplies us with the commentary of *Devarāja Yajvan* on the *Nighaṇṭu* and of *Durga* on the *Nirukta*. It also adds an index to the words of the *Nighaṇṭu* as well as to the words of the *Nirukta*. The practical utility of this index, however, suffers much from its being separated into three indexes, one for each volume and not consisting of one single whole. Besides many misprints and errors of *Sandhi*, the text constituted is not very valuable from the critical point of view, and is thus not a trustworthy basis for further research. The editor, although his text generally agrees with the shorter

[1] RV. vi. 55. 5; N. iii. 16; VC., p. 1052 b.
[2] Roth's ed., p. 60.
[3] RV. x. 133. 1; N. iii. 20; Roth's ed., p. 62; VC., p. 95 b.
[4] RV. iv. 51. 1: N. iv. 25; Roth's ed., p. 74; VC., p. 346 b.
[5] RV. iv. 138. 1; N. iv. 25; *loc. cit.*, VC., p. 328 b.
[6] RV. vi. 7. 6; N. vi. 3; Roth's ed., p. 91; VC., p. 839 b.
[7] RV. x. 81. 1; N. xi. 7.
[8] Cf. Bloomfield, *Vedic Concordance*, p. 566 b.
[9] RV. iii. 41. 3; N. iv. 19.
[10] Cf. p. 897 b.

recension, does not seem to realize that there are two recensions of the text of the *Nirukta*, and has thus unconsciously introduced an element of eclecticism in his edition. For instance, he omits the phrase: आचार्यः कस्मात् (vol. ii, p. 49), probably on account of its being not found in the manuscripts of the shorter recension, but he puts the line सुवासाः कल्याणवासाः कामयमाना ऋतुकालेषु (vol. ii, p. 132) within brackets in his constituted text, although it is omitted by manuscripts of the shorter recension. Further, he omits the passage: वृत्वा चां तिष्ठतीति वा चा चीयते निवासकर्मणः from his text, adding it in a foot-note with the remark: इत्यधिकः पाठः (vol. ii, p. 181). This shows that he does not follow any general plan with regard to the additional passages of the longer recension, as he sometimes puts them within brackets in the text itself, and sometimes adds them in foot-notes. This would also imply that he does not regard the passage, which he puts within brackets, as interpolations, but only those which he adds in foot-notes; this, to say the least of it, is altogether an arbitrary distinction, made with reference to the additional passages of the longer recension. Further, he is not consistent even in this, for occasionally he puts passages of the shorter recension within brackets as well (see vol. iii, pp. 121–22). Examples might be multiplied. Both these editions (i.e. Roth and Bib. Ind.) are very meagrely punctuated, and many sentences, being not properly divided, are misleading or tend to be obscure.

The Bombay Edition.

Another excellent edition of the *Nirukta*, together with Durga's commentary, is that of Mahāmahopādhyāya, P. Śivadatta, published at Bombay in 1912. In type, in paper, and in general get-up it marks a distinct improvement on its predecessors. The sentences are intelligently divided, and, to a great extent, the obscurities due to defective punctuation in previous editions have been removed. The text followed is that of the longer recension, and the criticism to which Roth's text is subject, except his inconsistency with regard to the use of large and small type, is applicable to the Bombay edition as well. The editor does not state whether he uses any manuscripts or not in the constitution of his text. As a matter of fact, as expressly mentioned in his introductory remarks, he has taken the two previous editions as the basis of his own work. A critical edition of the *Nirukta* professing to represent the archetype as closely as possible, and based on the manuscript material hitherto not utilized is therefore still a *desideratum*. I have, on these grounds, undertaken to edit the *Nirukta* afresh.

Detailed Description of Manuscripts.[1]

MS. *Max Müller Memorial, e. 8.* M 1.

PART I. A.D. 1749.

Contents: The *Nirukta* of Yāska in the longer recension, the text of which consists of two manuscripts, containing the two parts (the *pūrvārdha* and the *uttarārdha*) respectively. The work is divided into chapters (*adhyāyas*) and sections (*khaṇḍas*) thus: Chapter I, which contains 20 sections, begins on f. 1 v. and ends on f. 10 r. Chapter II, 28 sections, ends on f. 21 r. Chapter III, 22 sections, ends on f. 32 v. Chapter IV has 27 sections, and ends on f. 42 v. Chapter V, 28, sections, ends on f. 53 v. Chapter VI, 36 sections, ends on f. 68 r. The chapters are written consecutively, and at the end of each chapter there is added a short summary, quoting the first word or words of every section—thus indicating and also expressly stating the number of sections in the chapter. The text is bounded on both sides by double red lines, sometimes carelessly drawn, regularly up to f. 25 r., after which similar red lines only occasionally appear. A short red vertical stroke is placed above the letter where it indicates the application of the rules of euphonic combination, and is also used to mark the termination of a sentence, being thus a sign of punctuation. The *daṇḍa* appears at the end of a section only, but also points out the beginning and ending of a quotation. The red vertical stroke is often confusing as the accent in Vedic quotations is also marked with red ink.

There are two figures drawn vertically in red ink on f. 1 r. One looks like a goddess, probably *Durgā*, seated in a chariot with a flying banner, the other is the god *Gaṇeśa*, seated on an ornamented lotus, to which is added in black ink the representation of a small bird, probably a peacock. The two figures contain between them the words: (*sic*) ॥ **निरुक्ते पूर्वषट्‌ प्रारंभः** ॥ An attempt has been made to colour ff. 14, 29, 42, 49, 64 with yellow pigment, which is frequently used also to obliterate, though only with partial success, individual words, syllables, and letters. Black pigment is also employed to obliterate, for instance on f. 24 v., where half a line is completely covered. The manuscript is neat, well preserved, and accurate. It is the best among those belonging to the longer recension.

[1] From the point of view of the general reader, the detailed description of the manuscripts can be much curtailed. But as the manuscripts of the Max Müller Memorial and Chandra Shum Shere collections have not been so far catalogued, this description, in addition to supplying information with regard to the manuscripts material available for a critical edition, is also intended to serve the purpose of a descriptive catalogue. And as Professor A. A. Macdonell is in favour of it, I have retained the whole of it, without any curtailment.

Size: $8\frac{3}{4}'' \times 3\frac{3}{4}''$.
Material: Paper.
Number of leaves: ii. + 68.
Number of lines per folio: 9; ff. 3 v.–13 v. have 10 lines each.
Character: Devanāgarī.
Date: On fol. 68 r.: (*sic*) सके १६७१ (= A. D. 1749 प्रमाथीनामसंवत्सरे आश्वीनवद्यतृतीयाह्नि लिखितं (i.e. finished on the third day in the first fortnight of the month of Āśvan).

Scribe: On f. 68 r.: (*sic*) कासीनाथ अनंत पुस्तकं लिख्यते श्री सदाशिवार्पणमस्तु ॥ ॥ श्री ॥ छ ॥. He seems to be a faithful copyist, for he remarks (*sic*):

यादृशं पुस्तकं दृष्ट्वा तादृशं लिखितं मया ।
यदि शुद्धमशुद्धं वा मम दोष न विद्यते ॥

Peculiarity of spelling: *t* is doubled in conjunction, e.g. *tya* = *ttya*.

PART II. A. D. 1775.

Contents: The *Nirukta* of Yāska, Chapters VII–XIII, in the longer recension. The text is divided into chapters (*adhyāyas* and *khaṇḍas*), and sections thus: Chapter VII has 31 sections, begins on f. 1 v. and ends on f. 11 r. Chapter VIII has 22 sections, and ends on f. 16 r. Chapter IX has 43 sections, and ends on f. 24 r. Chapter X has 47 sections, and ends on f. 33 r. Chapter XI has 50 sections, and ends on f. 43 v. Chapter XII has 46 sections, and ends on f. 54 v. Chapter XIII has 50 sections, and ends on f. 70 r. The so-called two chapters of the *pariśiṣṭa* are treated as one. All the chapters are written consecutively without a break. Chapter VII begins with श्री गणेशाय नमः ॥ श्री वेदपुरुषाय नमः ॥ Chapters VIII and X begin with ॥ हरिः ओ३म् ॥ Chapter IX with ॥ श्री हरिः ओ३म् ॥ Chapter XI with छ ॥ श्री विठलप्रसन्न ॥ छ ॥ Chapter XII with ॥ ॐ ॥, and Chapter XIII with ॥ श्री ॥ ॐ ॥. Sect. 14 of the thirteenth chapter also begins with ॥ ॐ ॥ The last word of the 13th section of the same chapter is repeated. At the end of each chapter a short summary, which quotes the first word or words of each section and states the number of sections in the chapter, is subjoined. The text is bounded on both sides by double red lines from f. 11 r. to f. 33 v. Punctuation is similar to that of Part I. Ff. 6 r.–10 v. do not give the Vedic stanza in full in the text itself, where the first few words only of the stanza are written, while the remaining part of the stanza is added in the margin. Black pigment is used to obliterate a part of the line on ff. 60 v. and 63 r. F. 66 is coloured light blue. This is also a neat, well-preserved, and accurately written manuscript.

Size: $8\frac{3}{4}'' \times 3\frac{3}{4}''$, and after f. 32, $8\frac{1}{2}'' \times 3\frac{3}{4}''$.

Material: Paper.
Number of leaves: 70 + ii blank.
Number of lines per folio: 9.
Character: Devanāgarī.
Date: On f. 70 r. (*sic*) संवत् १८॥३१ (= A.D. 1775) विश्वावसु संवत्सरे चैत्र ०शु १३ (i.e. finished on the thirteenth day of the bright fortnight of the month of *Caitra*).
Scribe: On f. 70 r.: भृगुविश्वनाथभट्ट.

Although these two parts are brought together in the same volume in order to make up the text of the *Nirukta* they are not related to each other except in so far as they both belong to the longer recension. They were copied at different times as their respective dates show. And the fact that the first part uses the Śaka era, while the second, the Vikrama era, indicates that the former comes from the south, while the latter from the north. For the sake of convenience I have used the sign M 1 for both these parts.

MS. *Max Müller Memorial, d. 23.* M 2.

Contents: The first half (Chapters I–VI) of the *Nirukta* in the longer recension. The text is divided into chapters and sections thus: Chapter I begins with श्री गणेशाय नमः॥ on f. 1 v., has 20 sections, and ends on f. 10 r. Chapter II has 28 sections, and ends on f. 19 r. Chapter III has 22 sections, and ends on f. 27 v. Chapter IV has 27 sections, and ends on f. 35 v. Chapter V has 28 sections, and ends on f. 44 r. Chapter VI has 36 sections, and ends on f. 55 v. The text is bounded on both sides by double red lines. Punctuation is similar to M 1. The Vedic stanzas are not given in full, but the word ऋक् is added after the first two or three words of the quotation thus: f. 5 r. अक्षण्वंतः कर्णवन्तः॥ ऋक्॥ In *Saṁdhi* the sign of the elision of short *a* is retained, but not always, e.g. f. 2 r. वर्धतेऽपचीयते and जायतेऽस्ति, *loc. cit.* Ff. 5, 10, 15, 20, 25, 30, 35, 40, 45, 50, i.e. every fifth except the last is coloured with yellow pigment.

It is a very neat and beautifully written and modern manuscript.
Size 10¾″ × 4½″.
Material: Paper.
Number of leaves: ii + 55 + ii blank.
Number of lines: 9.
Character: Devanāgarī.
Date: Not given, but looks modern.
Scribe: Not known.
The colophon runs: इति निरुक्ते षष्ठोऽध्यायः॥ शुभं भवतु॥

MS. *Max Müller Memorial, d. 24.* M 3.

Contents: The *Nirukta* of Yāska in the shorter recension. The *pariśiṣṭa* is treated as one chapter, and all the 13 chapters are written consecutively, the *pūrvārdha* being separated from the *uttarārdha* only by the words: (*sic*) ॥ इति अर्द्धः ॥ The text is divided into *adhyāyas*, *pādas*, and *khaṇḍas* thus: Chapter I begins on f. 1 v. with the words ॥ श्री गणेशाय नमः ॥ has 4 *pādas*, which end on ff. 3 r., 7 r., 9 v., and 11 v. respectively.

The sections are numbered continuously—the numbering of sections in each *pāda* being not afresh, but the continuation from the previous section—thus Chapter I has 27 sections; the 1st *pāda* comes to an end after the 5th section; 2nd *pāda* after the 15th section; the 3rd *pāda* after the 21st section; and the 4th *pāda* after the 27th section. Chapter II has 7 *pādas*: 1st *pāda* has 7 sections, and end on f. 14 r.; 2nd *pāda* has 5 sections, and ends on f. 16 r.; 3rd *pāda* has 3 sections, and ends on f. 17 r. (where it is wrongly stated । तृतीयस्यार्द्धः ।); 4th *pāda* has 7 sections, and ends on f. 18 v.; 5th *pāda* has 3 sections, and ends on f. 19 v.; 6th *pāda* has 5 sections, and ends on f. 21 r.; 7th *pāda* has 6 sections, and ends on f. 23 v. Sections in this chapter are not numbered continuously, but at the end of the chapter; the total number of the sections is stated thus: (*sic*) सप्तमः पादः । खांडकां ३६ । द्वितीयोध्यायः. Chapter III has 4 *pādas*; the 1st *pāda* has 7 sections, and ends on f. 26 r.; the 2nd *pāda* has 6 sections, and ends on f. 29 v.; the 3rd *pāda* has 6 sections, and ends on f. 32 r.; the 4th *pāda* has 6 sections, and ends on f. 35 r. As in Chapter II, the total number of sections is stated to be 25. Chapter IV has 4 *pādas*; the 1st *pāda* has 8 sections, and ends on f. 37 v.; the 2nd *pāda* has 8 sections, and ends on f. 40 r; the 3rd *pāda* has 6 sections, and ends on f. 43 r; the 4th *pāda* has 7 sections, and ends on f. 45 v. As before, the total number of sections is given in the colophon on f. 45 v. as 29. Chapter V has 4 *pādas*; the 1st *pāda* has 6 sections, and ends on f. 48 v.; the 2nd *pāda* has 8 sections, and ends on f. 51 v.; the 3rd *pāda* has 7 sections, and ends on f. 54 r.; the 4th *pāda* has 10 sections, and ends on f. 57 v.; the total number of sections being given as 31. Chapter VI has 5 *pādas*; the 1st *pāda* has 5 sections, and ends on f. 60 r.; the 2nd *pāda* has 13 sections, and ends on f. 65 v.; the 3rd *pāda* has 8 sections, and ends on f. 68 v.; the 4th *pāda* has 5 sections, and ends on f. 70 v.; the 5th *pāda* has 8 sections, and ends on f. 73 v.; the total number of sections, i. e. 39, being added in the colophon, which runs as follows: (*sic*) पंचमः पादः ॥ षष्ठोध्यायः । षांड्यकां ३९ ॥ क्ष ॥ ६ ॥ इति अर्द्धः ॥ Chapter VII has 7 *pādas*; the 1st *pāda* has 5 sections, and ends on f. 75 v.: the 2nd *pāda* has 3 sections, and ends on f. 76 v. (wrongly numbered as 75 on the restored part); the 3rd *pāda* has 10 sections, and ends on f. 79 r.; the 4th *pāda* has 5 sections, and ends on f. 80 v.; the 5th *pāda* has 3 sections, and ends on f. 81 v.; the 6th *pāda* has 9 sections, and ends on f. 83 v.; the 7th *pāda* has 9 sections, and ends on f. 86 v.; the total number of sections, i.e. 44, is added in the colophon. Chapter VIII has 3 *pādas*; the 1st *pāda* has 4 sections, and ends on f. 88 r.; the 2nd *pāda* has 12 sections, and ends on f. 91 v.; the 3rd *pāda* has 7 sections, and ends on f. 93 v.; the total number of sections, 23, is stated in the colophon as before. Chapter IX has 4 *pādas*; the 1st *pāda* has 10 sections, and ends on f. 96 r.; the 2nd *pāda* has 11 sections, and ends on f. 98 v.; the 3rd *pāda* has 13 sections, and ends on f. 102 r.; the 4th *pāda* has 9 sections, and ends on f. 104 r.; the total number of sections being 43. Chapter X has 4 *pādas*; the 1st *pāda* has 13 sections, and ends on f. 108 r.; the 2nd *pāda* has 11 sections, and ends on f. 110 v.; the 3rd *pāda* has 13 sections, and ends on f. 114 r.; the 4th *pāda* has 10 sections, and ends on f. 116 v.; the total number of sections being 47. Chapter XI has 4 *pādas*; the 1st *pāda* has 12 sections, and ends on f. 119 r.; the 2nd *pāda* has 9 sections, and ends on f. 121 v.; the 3rd *pāda* has 13 sections, and ends on f. 125 r. (the colophon is completely obliterated with black pigment); the 4th *pāda* has 16 sections, and ends on f. 128 v.; the total number of sections being 50. Chapter XII has 4 *pādas*; the 1st *pāda* has 11 sections, and ends on f. 131 v.; the 2nd *pāda* has 8 sections, and ends on f. 133 v.; the 3rd *pāda* has 15 sections, and ends on f. 136 v.; the 4th *pāda* has 12 sections, and ends on f. 140 r.; the total number of sections, as stated in the colophon, is 46. Chapter XIII, written consecutively, has 4 *pādas*; the 1st *pāda* has 13 sections—the last word of the 13th section is repeated, a sign of the termination of the chapter—and ends on f. 144 r.; the 2nd *pāda* has 19 sections, and ends on f. 152 v.; the 3rd *pāda* has 9 sections, and ends on f. 155 r.; the 4th *pāda* has 7 sections, and ends on f. 157 v.

It marks the accent not only on Vedic stanzas, but on fragments of Vedic quotations also, several words preceding the quotation are similarly marked. The *daṇḍa* appears at the end of a section, or the beginning and end of a quotation.

Size: $9\frac{1}{2}'' \times 3\frac{1}{2}''$.
Material: Paper.
Number of leaves: ii + 157 + ii blank.
Number of lines: 8; f. 157 has 9 lines.
Character: Devanāgarī.
Date: Not given, but rather old.
Scribe: Not known.

Injuries: It is a very much injured manuscript; f. 12 is torn on the left-hand side, and the text is restored on a patched-up piece of paper; a part of ff. 23 and 52 is injured and the text is similarly restored; on f. 153 v. and 154 v. the right half is restored; f. 157 is restored in a different hand-writing. Besides, the leaves are torn in innumerable marginal spaces, but without injuring the text.

Peculiarity of spelling: It has preserved the old calligraphy. Some of the chief peculiarities are: ध् with आ is sometimes written as धन; e.g. f. 1 v., line 5, प्रधान is written प्रधनन. Cf. also f. 1 v., line 6.

ऐ is written as ाए; e.g. f. 1 v., line 5, तत्रै = तात्रे; f. 2 v., line 1, तेनैव = °तेानेव; f. 63 r., line 2, नैरुक्ताः = ानेरुक्ताः, and so on.

ए is occasionally written as ।/, e.g. f. 2 r, line 5, वेदे = वेाद and जायते = जायात, line 6, वर्धते = वर्धात; f. 2 v., line 8, व्यपेत्येतस्य = व्यपेात्यतस्य.

But in the case of ए this method is not always adhered to; occasionally ए is written in the ordinary way, e.g., f. 2 v., line 5, अर्वागर्थे and not अर्वागार्थ; f. 2 v., line 7, पूजितार्थे and not पूजितार्थ; f. 63 r., line 2, यदन्ये and not यदान्य, व्ययेयुः and not व्याययुः.

औ is written as ाओ, e.g., f. 2 r., line 1, गौः = ागोः, line 2, वचनमौदुंबरायणः = वचनामोदुंबरायणः, line 8, सांयौगिकानां = संायोगिकानां.

Occasionally प is written like य, and the sign of उ in conjunction is added, not at the bottom, but on the side of a letter; e.g., f. 1 v., line 3, इत्यौपमन्यवो = इत्यौयमन्यवो; but f. 2 r, line 1. पुरुषो is written in the ordinary way; f. 1 v., line 3, स्युः = स्यः.

त् is written as a short horizontal stroke in conjunction with other letters; e.g., f. 1 v., line 4, चत्वारि = चत्वारि, line 6, सत्व = सत्व; f. 2 r, line 5, अनित्यत्वात्कर्म° = अनित्यत्वात्कर्म°; f. 1 v., line 7, मूर्त्तं = मूर्त्तं.

त् is occasionally written as a short horizontal stroke even when it is not a conjunct consonant; e.g., f. 2 r., line 2, चतुष्टं = चतुष्टं, but in conjunction with य it is written in the ordinary way; e.g., cf. अनित्य above, and प्रभृत्य°, f. 1 v., line 6. There is dittography also, e.g., f. 2 r., line 3, युगपदुत्पन्नान्नां.

The manuscript belongs to a period when calligraphy was still in a process of transition, consequently it preserves the old and new forms of letters side by side; it cannot therefore be later than the fifteenth century. I think that among the manuscripts of the *Nirukta* in the Bodleian this is the oldest and best manuscript belonging to the shorter recension.

MS. *Max Müller Memorial, e. 9.* M 4.

Contents: The *Nirukta* (7–14 chapters; the *pariśiṣṭa* is treated as two chapters) in the longer recension. The text is punctuated with a short and vertical stroke, indicating *Saṁdhi* and the termination of a sentence, while the *daṇḍa* appears at the end of a section, or the commencement and end of a quotation. Accent is marked with red ink in Vedic quotations. The work is divided into chapters and sections, thus: Chapter VII begins with ॥ श्री गणेशाय नमः ॥ हरिः ॐम् ॥ on f. 1 v., has 31 sections, and ends on f. 15 v. Chapter VIII has 22 sections, and ends on f. 23 v.; Chapter IX has 43 sections, and ends on f. 35 r. Chapter X has 47 sections, and ends on f. 49 r. Chapter XI has 50 sections, and ends on f. 61 v. Chapter XII has 46 sections, and ends on f. 75 r. Chapter XIII has 13 sections, and ends on f. 79 v. Chapter XIV has 37 sections, and ends on f. 96 r. All the 14 chapters are written consecutively, and at the end of each chapter a summary similar to that described on p. 1 is added.

Size: 11″ × 5″.
Material: paper.
Number of leaves: ii + 96 + ii blank.
Number of lines: 7.
Character: Devanāgarī.
Date: Not given.
Scribe: Not known.

The colophon on f. 96 r. runs as follows: ॥ इति निरुक्ते परिशिष्ठश्चतुर्दशोध्यायः ॥ १४ ॥ श्री रामजयंराम्जयजयराम श्री ॥

It is a neat, well-written, fairly accurate, and-modern manuscript.

MS. *Chandra Shum Shere, d. 178.* C 1.

The text of the *Nirukta* is made up of two different manuscripts, which contain Chapters I–VI and VII–XII respectively, but both are incomplete, and both belong to the longer recension. The two parts are separated by a fragment of a third manuscript (ff. 38–43), which gives a part of Chapters XI and XII. The fragment has no value for the purpose of collation, and is therefore ignored.

PART I.

Contents: The *Nirukta* (Chapters I–VI) in the longer recension. The text is divided into chapters and sections thus: Chapter I begins on f. 1 v., has 20 sections, and ends on f. 7 v; Chapter II has 28 sections, and ends on f. 12 r.; Chapter III has 22 sections, and ends on f. 18 v.;

Chapter IV has 27 sections, and ends on f. 25 r.; Chapter V has 28 sections, and ends on f. 30 r.; Chapter VI has 35 sections only, the remaining sections are missing. The text is bounded on both sides by double red lines ff. 1–21; by double black lines ff. 11 r, 17 v, and 22–36; f. 12 is written in a different handwriting. The accent is marked in red ink in Vedic stanzas only. Double short vertical red strokes are used to indicate *sandhi* and the end of a sentence, which are replaced by similar black strokes from f. 7 v.–f. 12 r., which are again replaced by a similar single red stroke ff. 19–30. The *daṇḍa*, as usual, appears at the end of a section only, or at the commencement and the termination of a quotation. The chapters are written consecutively. Numerous notes are added on the margin, and sometimes between the lines of the text also, e.g. ff. 2, 3, 12, 18 v., 19. At the end of each chapter a short summary, as described on page 1, is subjoined:

Size 13″ × 5″.

Material: paper.

Number of leaves: 1 + 36 + i blank.

Number of lines: 10 ff. 1–25; 11 ff. 26–36.

Character: Devanāgarī.

Date: The last leaves of the manuscript are missing; neither the date nor the name of the scribe is known. From its appearance the manuscript looks old, f. 8 is numbered as f. 9, and f. 9 as f. 11, and the mistake continues up to the end; the reference to folios are therefore to the number added in pencil.

Injuries: It is injured in many places, e.g. ff. 7–12 on the top (left).

PART II.

Contents: The *uttarārdha* of the *Nirukta* (Chapters VII–XII) in the longer recension. The text is divided into chapters and sections thus: Chapter VII begins on f. 1 v. with the words ॥ श्री गणेशाय नमः ॥ ॐ ॥ has 31 sections, and ends on f. 11 r (= f. 54 r.); Chapter VIII has 22 sections, and ends on f. 15 v. (= f. 58 v.); Chapter IX has 43 sections, and ends on f. 23 v. (= f. 66 v.); Chapter X has 47 sections, and ends on f. 32 r. (= f. 75 r.); Chapter XI has 30 sections, and ends on f. 40 v. (= f. 83 v.); Chapter XII has 43 sections only, and ends on f. 48 v. (= f. 91 v.); the remaining portion of the manuscript is missing. All the chapters are written consecutively, and at the end of each chapter a summary similar to that of Part I is added. The text is bounded on both sides by two sets on double black lines, ff. 1–34 (ff. 44–77) and ff. 41–48 (ff. 84–91); and by similar red lines ff. 35–40 (ff. 78–83). The accent is marked in red ink in Vedic stanzas only, and a short vertical red stroke is occasionally used for punctuation; the use of the *daṇḍa* is similar to that of Part I. F. 9 (= f. 52) is written in a different handwriting.

Size: $11\frac{9}{10}'' \times 4\frac{1}{2}''$.
Material: paper.
Number of leaves: 48 + i blank.
Number of lines: 9–10.
Character: Devanāgarī.
Date: The last part of the manuscript is missing; consequently the date and the name of the scribe are not known.

Injuries: ff. 18 (= 61), 34–40 (= 77–83) are slightly injured in the top margin; f. 22 (= 65) is practically defaced by black and yellow ink, and f. 28 (= 71) by water.

MS. *Chandra Shum Shere, d. 181.* C 2.

The text is made up of two different manuscripts.

PART I.

Contents: The *pūrvārdha* of the *Nirukta* in the longer recension. The manuscript is fragmentary and incomplete, containing Chapters I, IV, V, and a part of the first section of the VI. The text is divided into chapters and sections. Chapter I has 20 sections, and ends on f. 13 v. Chapter IV has 27 sections, and ends on f. 26 r. Chapter V has 28 sections, and ends on f. 40 r. The accent is marked in red ink in Vedic stanzas only, while a short vertical red stroke is used for punctuation. The words (*sic*) **इति नीरुक्ते पुर्वषट्के प्रथमोध्यायः ॥** are wrongly added at the bottom of f. 1 v. in a different handwriting. F. 1 r. has a figure of Gaṇeṣa drawn rather crudely in red with two female attendants.

Size: $13\frac{1}{5}''' \times 5\frac{1}{2}''$.
Material: paper.
Number of leaves: i + 40.
Number of lines: 7–8.
Character: Devanāgarī.
Date and scribe: Not known.

Injuries: ff. 13–14 are slightly injured by worms. It looks modern. The numbering in the original is wrong; the reference is to the number added in pencil. It is full of mistakes.

Peculiarity of spelling: f. 2, l. 1 **व्रज्या** is written as **व्रर्ज्य**, f. 2, l. 1 **गौ** is written as **गैं**.

PART II.

Contents: The *uttarārdha* of the *Nirukta* (Chapters VII–XIII) in the longer recension. The text is divided into chapters and sections thus: Chapter VII has 31 sections, and ends on f. 6 v. (= 46 v.); the colophon adds: श्री रामो जयतितरां ॥ छ ॥ Chapter VIII has 22 sections, and ends on f. 10 r. (= 50 r.); Chapter IX has 43 sections, and ends on f. 15 r. (= 55 r.); Chapter X has 47 sections, and ends on f. 20 v (= 60 v.); Chapter XI has 50 sections, and ends on f. 26 v. (= 66 v.); Chapter XII has 46 sections, and ends on f. 32 r. (= 72 r.); Chapter XIII begins on f. 32 v. (= 72 v.), has 13 sections, and ends on f. 34 v. (= 74 v.): the colophon runs (*sic*) ॥ इति निरुक्ते उत्तरषट्के सप्तमोध्यायः ॥ छ ॥ शुभं भवतु ॥ छ ॥ श्री महागणपतये नमः ॥ the last chapter, which is also named XIII, has 37 sections, which are not numbered anew, but continuously from the previous section, and ends on f. 42 r. (= 82 r.). Chapters VIII–XII are written consecutively, and a summary, similar to the one described on p. 1, is added at the end of each chapter, but the summary on f. 42 r. (= 82 r.) also includes that of the first 13 sections, although the summary of these sections is already subjoined on f. 34 v. (= 74 v.).

The colophon on f. 42 r (= 82 r) runs thus: ॥ इति निरुक्ते त्रयोदशोध्यायः ॥ The text is bounded on both sides by double black lines, ff. 1–23 (= 41–63) and ff. 38–42 (=78–82) by similar red lines, ff. 24–36 (=64–76), f. 37 (=77) is coloured yellow. A short vertical red stroke is employed for punctuation, the dropping of *visarga* is indicated by adding them on the top of the letter just before the red stroke, e.g. f. 1 v. (= 41 v.), l. 3: प्रत्यचकृताँ आध्यात्मि° ; *op. cit.* l. 4: पृथिव्याँ इंद्रम° ; *op. cit.* l. 8: °पुरुषयोगाँ अहमिति , and so on.

Occasionally the short red stroke is written ।ऽ, but the sign ऽ is not meant to point out the elision of short *a*, e.g. *op. cit.* l. 5: प्रवोचँमिंद्रे. Sometimes ऽ is replaced by ×. The *daṇḍa* appears at the end of a section, or at the beginning and end of a quotation. The accent is marked in red ink on Vedic stanzas.

Size: $13\frac{1}{5}'' \times 5\frac{3}{5}''$.
Material: paper.
Number of leaves: 42 + i blank.
Number of lines: 12–17.
Character: Devanāgarī.
Date and scribe: Not known.
Injuries: f. 1 (= 41), ff. 21–22 (= 61–22), f. 23 (= 63) are slightly injured.
It is a neat, but closely written manuscript.

MS. *Chandra Shum Shere, d. 182.* C 3.

The text of the *Nirukta* is made up of two manuscripts.

Part I.

Contents: The *pūrvārdha* of the *Nirukta* in the longer recension. The work is divided into chapters and sections thus: Chapter I begins on f. 1 v. with the words: (*sic*) **श्री गणेश । श्री रामाय नमः**, has 20 sections, and ends on f. 7 r. Chapter II has 28 sections, and ends on f. 12 r. (ff. 8–9, containing sections 3–11 of the second chapter, are missing in the original). Chapter III has 22 sections, and ends on f. 18 r. (ff. 19 and 21–23, containing sections 11–12 and 14–19, are missing in the original). Chapter IV has 27 sections, and ends on f. 23 v. Chapter V has 28 sections, and ends on f. 29 v. Chapter VI has 36 sections, and ends on f. 38 r. The chapters are written consecutively, the summary is added as usual, punctuation and accents in Vedic stanzas are marked in red ink. The text is bounded on both sides by double black lines, f. 1 r. has a few laudatory verses written on it and the words: (*sic*) **अथ परिशीष्टं ॥ हंस शुचिषदिति । ऋक्**.

A part of line 9 on f. 5 r., and of line 4 on f. 7 r., of line 5 on f. 7 v., is obliterated with black pigment. Two lines are added to the top of f. 13 v., f. 19 v. is partially defaced by light red ink, and half a line on f. 20 r. is similarly obliterated with red pigment. Colophon on f. 38 r. runs thus: **॥ इति निरुक्ते पूर्वषट्के षष्ठो ध्यायः ॥ श्री रामचन्द्राय नमः ॥ श्री विश्वेश्वराय नमः ॥ शुभमस्तु ॥ श्री वक्रतुंडाय नमः ॥** A female figure is drawn on f. 38 v., and a list of several articles is added. The prominent difference of ink, characters, carelessness, occasionally disproportionate red vertical strokes, frequent use of red ink for marginal notes, smudging of the black ink, give a very untidy appearance to the manuscript.

Size: $12\frac{1}{2}'' \times 5\frac{3}{10}''$.
Material: Paper.
Number of leaves: i + 38 + i blank.
Number of lines: 10–11.
Character: Devanāgarī.
Date and scribe: Not known.

The name of the owner is given on f. 1 r. as Goḍabole Lakṣmaṇa Bhaṭṭa.

Peculiarity of spelling: It occasionally writes **र** as **न**, e.g., f. 1 v., line 1, **श्री रामाय = श्री नामाय**. Like M 1, it frequently doubles *t* in conjunction with other letters, e.g. f. 1 v., line 2, **समाहृत्य = समाहृत्त्य**; line 3, **इत्यौपमन्यवः = इत्त्यौपमन्यवः**; line 4, **चत्वारि = चत्त्वारि**; line 8, **नित्यं = नित्त्यं**.

Part II.

Contents: The *uttarārdha* of the *Nirukta* (Chapters X–XIII) in the longer recension. The text is divided into chapters and sections thus: Chapter X begins on f. 1 r. (=40 r.), has 47 sections, and ends on f. 16 v. (= 55 v.). Chapter XI has 50 sections, and ends on f. 31 v. (= 70 v.). These two chapters are written consecutively. Chapter XII begins with ॥ श्री गणेशाय नमः ॥ has 46 sections, and ends on f. 13 v. (= 83 v.). This seems to be a different manuscript from the previous one containing Chapters X–XI; the pagination begins anew, the handwriting is different, and unlike the former the text is bounded on both sides by double red lines. The *pariśiṣṭa* is separated from Chapter XII, and is treated as one chapter. The numbering of leaves starts anew from the first. It begins with ॥ श्री ॥, on f. 1 r. (= 84 r.), has 50 sections, and ends on 14 v. (= 97 v.). The last word of the 13th section is repeated, but the summary is added at the end of the 50th section. The summary, as usual, is added at the end of every chapter. The accent is marked in red ink in Vedic quotations, while a short vertical red stroke is used for punctuation. A line in different handwriting is added at the bottom of f. 1 v. (= 40 v.). A line and a half in red ink is added on the right-hand margin of f. 22 r. (= 61 r.); part of the 50th section of the eleventh chapter is finished off on the top and right-hand margin on f. 31 v. (= 70 v.). A line is added on the top of f. 11 v. (= 81 v.). Section 43 of Chapter XIII is left out in the text, but added on the top and the margin on the right on f. 13 r. (= 96 r.).

Size: 9″ × 4″.

Material: Paper.

Number of leaves: 31 + 13 + 12 (= 58) + i blank.

Number of lines: 7 to 9.

Character: Devanāgarī.

Date and scribe: Not known; the colophon runs thus: ॥ श्री निरुक्त उत्तरषट्के सप्तमोध्यायः ॥

Injuries: It is slightly injured by worms in several places, e.g. ff. 7–4 (= 47–54) and ff. 1–3 (= 84–86).

It has a modern look.

MS. *Chandra Shum Shere, d. 179.* C 4.

The text is made up of two manuscripts, containing the *pūrvārdha* and the *uttarārdha*, with the *pariśiṣṭa* respectively, each being copied by a different scribe, at a different place and period. They will therefore be separately described.

MS. 1. A.D. *1629 Copied at Benares.*

Contents: The *pūrvārdha* of the *Nirukta* in the shorter recension; the text is divided into chapters, *pādas*, and sections, thus: Chapter I has 6 *pādas*; the 1st *pāda* contains 5 sections, and ends on f. 2 v.; it is not stated where the 2nd *pāda* comes to an end, probably it should be ended after the 4th section, as the number of the following section begins anew; the 3rd *pāda* has six sections, and ends on f. 6 v.; the 4th *pāda* has 4 sections, and ends on f. 8 r.; the 5th *pāda* has 2 sections, and ends on f. 9 v.; the 6th *pāda* has 6 sections, and ends on f. 11 v.; 27 being the total number of sections given in the colophon, which runs thus: (*sic*) ॥ ६ ॥ २१ ॥ इति नैरुक्ते प्रथमोध्यायस्य षष्ठमः पादः ॥ प्रथमोध्यायः समाप्तः ॥

Chapter II has 7 *pādas*: the 1st *pāda* contains 7 sections, and ends on f. 13 v.; 2nd *pāda* contains 5 sections, and ends on f. 16 r.; 3rd *pāda* contains 3 sections, and ends on f. 17 r.; 4th *pāda* contains 7 sections, and ends on f. 18 v.; 5th *pāda* contains 3 sections, and ends on f. 19 v.; 6th *pāda* contains 5 sections, and ends on f. 21 r.; 7th *pāda* contains 6 sections, and ends on f. 23 r.; the total number of sections being 36. Chapter III has 4 *pādas*: 1st *pāda* contains 7 sections, and ends on f. 25 v.; 2nd *pāda* contains 6 sections, and ends on f. 28 v.; 3rd *pāda* contains 6 sections, f. 30 containing sections 5–6 is missing; 4th *pāda* contains 6 sections, and ends on f. 33 v.; the total number of the sections being 25. Chapter IV has 4 *pādas*: 1st *pāda* has 8 sections, and ends on f. 35 v.; 2nd *pāda* has 8 sections, f. 38 containing a part of the 8th section of the 2nd *pāda*, and the 1–2 sections of the 3rd *pāda* is missing; 3rd *pāda* has 6 sections, and ends on f. 40 v.; 4th *pāda* has 7 sections, and ends on f. 43 v. Chapter V has 4 *pādas*: 1st *pāda* contains 6 sections, and ends on f. 46 r.; 2nd *pāda* contains 8 sections; f. 48 containing sections 6–8 is missing; 3rd *pāda* contains 7 sections, and ends on f. 51 r.; 4th *pāda* contains 10 sections, and ends on f. 54 r.; the total number of sections being 31. Chapter VI has 6 *pādas*: 1st *pāda* contains 5 sections, ending on f. 56 r.; 2nd *pāda* contains 6 sections, and ends on f. 58 r.; 3rd *pāda* contains 7 sections, and ends on f. 61 r.; 4th *pāda* has 8 sections, and ends on f. 64 r.; 5th *pāda* has 5 sections, and ends on f. 66 r.; 6th *pāda* has 8 sections, and ends on f. 68 v.; f. 1 is missing. The text is bounded on both sides by double black lines. Punctuation is similar to that of C 3. Occasionally marginal notes are added in red ink.

Size: $8\frac{3}{10}'' \times 3\frac{4}{5}''$.
Material: paper.
Number of leaves: i + 64.

Number of lines: 10.

Character: Devanāgarī.

Date: on f. 68 v. (= 64 v.): (*sic*) **इति संवत् १६८३ वर्षे वैशाखवद्य ४ बुधे** (i.e. completed on Wednesday in the former half of the month Vaiśākha A.D. 1627).

Scribe: on f. 68 v. (= 64 v.): (*sic*) **च· हाउसुत् च· शिवासुत् च· उंरसुत् च· फफीपुत्र शामेन ल्यखीतं पठनार्थं ॥**

Place: on f. 68 v. (= 64 v.): (*sic*) **॥ अविमुक्तवाराणशीमध्ये ल्यषीतं वृद्धनगरवास्तव्यं ॥ गंगायै नमः ॥**

Injuries: ff. 1, 30, 38, 48 are missing; f. 22 is injured, and slightly defaced, and f. 33 is defaced by marginal notes.

Peculiarity of spelling: **ए** is occasionally written as ।/, e.g. f. 2 r. line 2: **इतरेतरोपदेशः = इतरेतरोपादशः** f. 2 r., line 8: **वर्द्धते = वर्द्धात** f. 2 v., line 4: **प्र परे° = प्र पार°** **श्री** is occasionally written as ।/। e.g. f. 2 v., line 2: **नामाख्यातयोः = नामाख्यातायाः** but cf. line 3, f. 2 v., line 8: **सर्वतो = सर्वाता** **र** is occasionally written in conjunction thus: f. 3 r., line 2: **प्रतिषेधार्थीयो = प्रतिषेधाथरयो**, line 4: **उपमाथरयः**

Manuscript containing the *uttarārdha*. A.D. *1691.*
Copied at Dacca.

Contents The second part (Chapters VII–XII) of the *Nirukta* in the shorter recension; the text is divided into chapter, *pāda*, and section. In this division, and the number of *pādas* in a chapter, and that of sections in a *pāda*, it agrees with M 3. The 7 *pādas* of Chapter VII end on ff. 3 r. (= 67 r.), 4 v. (= 68 v.), 7 v. (= 71 v.), 9 r. (= 73 r.), 10 v. (= 74 v.), 13 r. (= 77 r.), 16 v. (= 80 v.) respectively; the 3 *pādas* of Chapter VIII end on ff. 18 r. (= 82 r.), 21 v. (=85 v.) 24 r. (= 88 r.) respectively; the 4 *pādas* of Chapter IX end on ff. 27 v. (= 91 v.); 30 r. (= 94 r.), 33 v. (= 97 v.), 35 v. (= 99 v.) respectively; the 4 *pādas* of Chapter X end on ff. 39 v. (= 103 v.), 42 v. (106 v.), 46 r. (110 r.), 48 v. (= 112 v.) respectively; the 4 *pādas* of Chapter XI end on ff. 51 v. (= 115 v.), 54 r. (= 118 r.), 58 v. (= 122 v.), 62 v. (126 v.) respectively; the 4 *pādas* of Chapter XII end on ff. 65 v. (=129 v.), 68 r. (= 132 r.), 71 v. (= 135 v.), 75 v. (= 139 v.) respectively. f. 56 r. (= 120 r.) is left blank. The text is bounded on both sides by treble black lines. The accent in Vedic quotations is marked in red ink. The short vertical stroke is replaced by a similar black stroke for punctuation. The use of the *daṇḍa* is similar to M 3.

The *pariśiṣṭa* is separated from Chapter XII, and is contained in ff. 76–94 (= 140–158). The division of the text into *pādas* and *Khaṇḍas* is identical with M 3. The 4 *pādas* of Chapter XIII end on ff. 80 v. (= 144 v.), 89 r. (= 153 r.), 91 v. (= 155 v.), 94 r. (= 158 r.) respectively.

Pagination is continued from the end of Chapter XII. The date given on f. 94 r. (= 158 r.): (*sic*) **संव १७४५ वर्षे ज्येठमासे शुक्लपचे १५ गुरुवासरे ॥** cannot be genuine, for it is clear from the numbering of folios that it must have been written after Chapter XII, which was finished in **संवत् १७४७**; hence, it could not be earlier than **१७४७**. The name of the scribe is Harīrāma, a resident of Muphalīpura. The colophon runs thus: (*sic*) **अद्येह धोलकामध्ये मुफलीपुरवास्तव्यं वृद्धनगरज्ञातीय पंचोलीढुसासुतक्षण सु० हरीहर सु० हरीरामेन स्वयं लिषितं.**

Size: 9″ × 4″.
Material: Paper.
Number of leaves: 94 + i blank.
Number of lines: 8.
Character: Devanāgarī.
Date: on f. 75 v. (= 139 v.): **स्वस्ति श्री संवत् १७४७** (= A. D. 1691) **ना वरषे भादुवा वदि ५ बुधे.**

Scribe: on f. 75 v. (= 139 v.): **दीचत् सोमेश्वर**: he seems to have taken great pains in copying the manuscript, for he remarks:

(*sic.*) **भग्नपृष्ठिकटिग्रीवाबधमुष्टिरधोमुखं ॥**
कष्टेन लिखितं ग्रन्थं यत्नेन परिपालयेत् ॥

Place: on f. 75 v. (= 139 v.) (*sic*) **॥ श्री ढाकामध्ये ल्षषितंमिदं ॥**
Injuries: ff. 1–11 (= 65–75) are slightly defaced.
Peculiarity of spelling: it occasionally writes **ऐ** as in Part I, e. g.

f. 1 v. (= 65 v.), line 1 **दैवतं** = **ादेवतं**
" " " **प्राधान्य०** = **प्राधन्य०**
" " 3 **०आर्थपत्यम्** = **आर्थपत्यम्**

Some of the figures for numbers are occasionally slightly different: **४** = **ડ।**, **५** = **च्**, **७** = **ک** f. 73 r. (= 137 r.), **श्री** is written as **ॐ**; f. 73 r. (= 137 r.), line 8: **श्रीमासः** = **ॐमासः**.

MS. *Chandra Shum Shere, d. 180.* C 5.

The text is made up of two manuscripts which are described separately.

MS. containing the pūrvārdha, A. D. *1758.*

Contents: Chapters I–VI of the *Nirukta* in the shorter recension. The text is divided into *pādas* and sections. It agrees with C[4] in having six *pādas* in Chapter I. It is carelessly written, and full of mistakes. The text is bounded by double red lines up to f. 24, and by similar black lines, ff. 25–67. Ff. 55 v., 56 are defaced by disproportionate marginal notes. F. 57 is wrongly numbered 56 in the original. The first four lines on the top of f. 58 r. are to be crossed. Two geometrical figures are drawn on f. 1 r.

Size: $8\frac{1}{4}'' \times 4\frac{1}{4}''$.
Material: Paper.
Number of leaves: i + 67.
Number of lines: 7–14.
Character: Devanāgarī.
Date: on f. 67 v. (*sic*) **संवत् १८१४ गुर्जरे मीती चै ३त्र वदि ८ शुक्रे** (= A. D. 1758).
Scribe: The name of the owner is added in a different handwriting on f. 67 v.: **आ पोथि भामंगलरामसुत् नाथुराम नि छे शुभं भवति** (i.e. this book belongs to Nāthurāma, son of Bhāmaṅgabarāma).

MS. containing the uttārardha with the pariśiṣṭa, dated A.D. *1479.*

Contents: Chapters VII–XIII of the *Nirukta* in the shorter recension, written consecutively. The text is divided into *pādas* and *Khaṇḍas*, agreeing with C 4 in the number of *pādas* and *Khaṇḍas*, distributed in each chapter and *pāda* respectively. The seven *pādas* end on ff. 2 v. (= 69 v.), 3 v. (= 70 v.), 5 v. (= 72 v.), 7 r. (= 74 r.), 8 r. (= 75 r.), 9 v. (= 76 v.), 12 r. (= 79 r.); the three *pādas* of Chapter VIII on ff. 13 r. (= 80 r.), 16 r. (= 83 r.), 17 v. (= 84 v.); the four *pādas* of Chapter IX on ff. 20 r. (= 87 r.), 22 r. (= 89 r.), 24 v. (= 91 v.), 26 r. (= 93 r.); the four *pādas* of Chapter X on ff. 29 v. (= 96 v.), 31 v. (= 98 v.), 34 v. (= 101 v.), 36 v. (= 103 v.); the four *pādas* of Chapter XI on ff. 39 r. (= 106 r.), 41 r. (= 108 r.), 43 v. (= 110 v.), 46 v. (= 113 v.); the four *pādas* of Chapter XII on ff. 49 r. (= 116 r.), 51 r. (= 118 r.), 54 r. (= 121 r.), 56 v. (= 123 v.); the four *pādas* of Chapter XIII on ff. 60 r. (= 127 r.), 67 r. (= 134 r.), 69 v. (= 136 v.), 71 v. (= 138 v.). The text is bounded on both sides by double black lines. The accent in Vedic stanzas is marked in red ink. Punctuation is similar to M 3. It is a very good manuscript, neat and accurate.

Size: $8\frac{3}{4}'' \times 3\frac{1}{2}''$.
Material: Paper.
Number of leaves: 72 + i blank.
Number of lines: 9.
Character: Devanāgarī.

Date: on f. 71 v. (= 138 v.): ॥ स्वस्ति संवत् १५३५ (= A. D. 1479) वर्षे भाद्रुवा शुदि ११ ऽवोह.

Scribe: on f. 71 v. (= 138 v.): पीतांबरेण निरुक्तं संपूर्णं लिखितमस्ति ॥ शुभं ॥ The Colophon runs thus: (*sic*) श्री अलिप्राकारे महाराजाधिराय श्री भाणविजयराज्ये आभ्यंतरनागरज्ञातीय संम्राटूस्त्रपति महायाज्ञक श्री श्री शंकरसुत याज्ञक श्री प्रयागदाससुतः या० लङ्क आमध्ययनार्थं पीतांबरेण &c. The name of the owner is given on f. 72 r. (= 139 r): याज्ञिक श्री प्रयागदाससुतज्ञ याज्ञिक श्री लङ्क आनि पोथि ॥ Rites and sacrifices performed by the owner at various places of pilgrimages like Kurukṣetra, Benares, &c., are enumerated on f. 72 r. (= 139 r.).

Peculiarity of spelling: ष is always written as ख, ए is written as ।/, g. वर्षे = वार्ष on f. 71 v., line 6.

f. 54 r. (= 121 r.), line 3: देवगणाः = ादवगणाः

„ „ „ 4: तेषां = ातषां and so on.

ऐ is written as ।/ए, e. g.

f. 53 v. (= 120 v.), line 9: भवत्येंद्ग्राम् = भवात्येंद्ग्राम्

„ „ „ 2: पितेषां = पितेषां and so on.

ओ is written as ।/।, e. g.

f. 53 v. (= 120 v.), line 1: पवित्रवंतो = पवित्रवांता

„ „ „ 2: पुराणो = पुराणा

„ „ „ 6: शृणोत्वजा० = शृणात्वजा०.

औ is written as ।/औ, e. g.

f. 5 r. (= 72 r.), line 6: वेत्वोपमिकम् = ।वात्वोपमिकम्

त् in conjunction with य् is written as a short vertical stroke, and with स् or व् as a horizontal stroke, e. g.

प्रेत्य = प्रेय; इत्यपि = इयपि

उत्साह = उसाह; त्व = व and so on.

च is written variously as द्द or द्द or द्द.

Injuries: ff. 9 (= 76), 10 (= 77), 19 (= 86), 29 (= 96) are slightly injured.

MS. *Chandra Shum Shere, e. 61.* C 6.

Contents: The *Nirukta* of Yāska in the longer recension. It consists of three manuscripts; the first contains Chapters I–V in 86 leaves (86 v. gives a part of the first section of Chapter VI); the second, Chapter VI in

27 leaves (numbered in the original as 47–73 = 87–113); the third, Chapters VII–XIV, in 78 leaves (= 114–191). The division of the text into Chapters (*adhyāya*) and sections (*Khaṇḍas*), the punctuation, and the method of marking the accent in Vedic stanzas are identical with M 4. The text is bounded by double red lines only occasionally. F. 3 is replaced by a leaf in a later handwriting. Ff. 87–92 are written on blue paper. A summary similar to M 4 is added at the end of each chapter.

Size: $8\frac{1}{4}'' \times 4''$ (ff. 1–86) and $7\frac{3}{4}'' \times 3\frac{3}{4}$ (ff. 87–113), $7\frac{1}{2}'' \times 3\frac{1}{4}''$ (ff. 114–191).
Material: Paper.
Character: Devanāgarī.
Number of leaves: i + 191 + i blank.
Number of lines: 7 (ff. 1–113), 7–10 (ff. 114–191).
Date and Scribe: Not known.

The name of the owner is added on f. 114 r.: ॥ इदं पुस्तकं वटवृक्षवीरेश्वर-भट्टस्येदं पुस्तकं योगीश्वर्यैं नमः ॥

MS. *Chandra Shum Shere, d. 183.* C 7.

Contents: The *uttarārdha* of the *Nirukta*, Chapters VII–XI, and sections 1–27 of Chapter XII in the shorter recension. The text is bounded by treble black lines on both sides, and is divided into *pādas* and *Khaṇḍas*. The numbering of sections does not begin anew in each *pāda*, but is consecutive for the whole chapter, and agrees with the manuscripts of the longer recension. It looks old; the ink is totally effaced in several parts, which makes it difficult to read; but it is not really old, for it does not display any characteristics of old writing. It is full of mistakes. Three lines are added at the bottom on f. 13 v., 52 v. Marginal notes are occasionally written.

Size: $9\frac{3}{4}'' \times 3\frac{1}{2}''$.
Material: Paper.
Number of leaves: i + 58 + i blank.
Number of lines per folio: 7.
Character: Devanāgarī.
Date and Scribe: Not known, for the last leaves are missing.

Peculiarity of spelling: त् is occasionally written as a short horizontal stroke in conjunction. F. 1 v., line 1; ॰स्तुतीनां = ॰स्तुतीनां, f. 1 v., line 2: स्तुतिं = स्तुतिं. म् is doubled in conjunction with र्, e.g. कर्म = कर्म्म. F. 58 v. is torn in two.

MS. *Wilson 488.* W 1.

Yāska's Nirukta, A.D. *1768.*

This is described in detail by Keith in the *Catalogue of Sanskrit Manuscripts,* vol. ii, p. 107. His description may be supplemented by the following: the Colophon on f. 79 v. runs thus: (*sic*) ॥ श्री ॥

मंगलं लेखकानां च पाठकानां च मंगलं ।
मंगलं सर्वजंतुनां मंगलं सर्वमंगलं ॥
यादृशं पुस्तकं दृष्टा तादृशं लिखितं मया
यदि शुद्धमशुद्धं वा मम दोषो न दीयतां ॥२॥

Two more verses are added in a different hand, one being a slight modification of a verse from the *Pañcatantra.* The *pūrvārdha* and the *uttarārdha* are written in different hands.

Peculiarity of spelling: ल् and त् are occasionally doubled in conjunction with र्, e. g.

f. 1 v., line 7: °तयोर्लक्षणं = तयोर्ल्लक्षणं
f. 2 r., „ 2: मूर्तं = मूर्त्तं

Number of lines per folio: 7 (ff. 1–21), 9 (ff. 22–79), 7 (ff. 80–162), 8 (ff. 163–183).

Injuries: Ff. 53–63 are slightly injured by worms on the left marginal top.

MS. *Wilson 491.* W 2.

This manuscript is described in detail by Keith in the *Catalogue of Sanskrit Manuscripts in the Bodleian Library,* vol. ii, p. 106. His description may be supplemented as follows:

Peculiarity of spelling: It writes धा as धम

ए is occasionally written as ।/, e. g. वर्धते = वर्धात
ऐ „ „ „ „ ।/ए, „ तचैतं = ताचेतं
ओ „ „ „ „ ।/।, „ मंचो = मांचा
औ „ „ „ „ ।/ओ, „ सांयौगिक = सांयोगिक

Number of lines per folio: 8 (ff. 1–61), 9 (ff. 62–78), 8 (ff. 79–91), 9 (ff. 92–101), it varies from 10–11 (ff. 102–130).

F. 104 is upside down. The size of leaves (ff. 79–86) is: $8\frac{3}{4}'' \times 3\frac{1}{2}''$. Ff. 79–130 are written in a handwriting different from that of the previous folios.

MS. *Wilson 474.* W 3.

This is described in detail by Keith in the *Catalogue of Sanskrit Manuscripts in the Bodleian Library*, vol. ii, p. 107. His description may be supplemented by the following:

Peculiarity of spelling: **ए** is occasionally written as ।/, e.g. f. 2 r. line 2: **ईशे** = **ईाश**; **च्यवते** = **च्यवात**; **पवते** = **पवात**; f. 2 r., line 3; **इंद्रेण°** = **इंाद्रण**; **वेविषाणा** = **ावविषाणा**.

ऐ is written as ।/ए, e.g. **इंद्रेणैते** = **इंाद्राणेते**.

ओ „ „ „ ।/।, „ **इंद्रो** = **इंाद्रा**; **तृत्सवो** = **तृत्सावा**.

But its chief peculiarity is that it frequently doubles consonants in conjunction, e.g. f. 2 r., line 2: **पृथिव्व्या**, **व्** is doubled, **इन्न्द्रम्**, **न्** is doubled; **तृत्त्सावा**, **त्** is doubled; line 4: **किञ्ञ्न**, **ञ्** is doubled; line 5: **वीर्य्याणि**, **य्** is doubled; **प्प्रवोचम्**, **प्** is doubled; line 6: **प्प्रत्त्यच्च°** for **प्रत्यच°**; line 7: **सर्व्व**, **व** is doubled; f. 2 v., line 2: **चिदन्न्यद्व्विशंसत** for **चिदन्यद्विशंसत**, f. 3 r., line 1: **अल्लपश**, **ल** is doubled; line 6: **बहुलम्**, **ह्** is doubled, **याह्म्मेषु**, **ह्म** is doubled; f. 4 r., line 1: **ाभाजास्यदम्मपुष्करिणीवावश्श्मेति** for **भोजस्येदम्पुष्करिणीव वेश्मेति**, and so on.

MS. *Mill 144.* Mi.

Copied at Ahmedabad, A. D. *1730.*

This is described in detail by Keith in the *Catalogue of Sanskrit Manuscripts in the Bodleian Library*, vol. ii, p. 106. It occasionally doubles **त्** in conjunction with other consonants, e.g. f. 2 r., line 8: **प्रतिषेधत्त्यस्तीत्त्युत्त्पन्नस्य** &c.

The numbering of sections does not begin anew in each *pāda*, but is continuous, and agrees with the longer recension as to the total number of sections in Chapters IX–XII. It belongs to the shorter recension.

MS. *Sanskrit, e. 17.* S.

A. D. *1781.*

This is described in detail by Keith in the *Catalogue of Sanskrit Manuscripts in the Bodleian Library*, vol. ii, p. 105. The text is punctuated as usual, and divided into chapters and sections. A summary similar to the one described on p. 1 is added at the end of each chapter. It belongs to the longer recension. The text is bounded on both sides by two sets of double red lines. It is a neat and accurate manuscript.

The Relationship of the MSS.: two recensions.

The manuscripts fall into two groups, and for the sake of convenience and brevity, may be called A and B—A representing the longer and B the shorter recension None of the manuscripts grouped in these two families is earlier than A.D. 1479. Although they have been copied from earlier manuscripts—often with great labour and trouble as some of the scribes remark—neither of them transmits the text of the *Nirukta* in an uninterpolated state. Both recensions add the *pariśiṣṭa*—which can be proved to be an interpolation by independent testimony—as an integral part of the text, and cannot, therefore, be the faithful representatives of the archetype. Moreover, both have besides the *pariśiṣṭa*, an entire section or the equivalent of a section added on to them. These additions are meaningless. The commentary on the Vedic stanzas quoted therein is very poor, and written in a style quite different from that of Yāska. For instance, there can hardly be any doubt as to the interpolated character of ix. 2, which is given as a constituent part of the text by the manuscripts of both recensions. Further, the commentary on the Vedic stanza in xi. 7 is meaningless and written in a different style. The Vedic stanza, being quite easy, requires no explanation. Yāska generally does not comment on easy Vedic stanzas, simply remarking: *iti sā nigada-vyākhyātā*[1], i.e. 'this stanza is explained by the mere reading'. In all such cases, this note of Yāska comes after easy Vedic stanzas only. It would thus be intelligible, if it had followed immediately the Vedic stanzas in xi. 7. But as the text now stands, it is placed just after a very difficult Vedic stanza in xi. 8. This is contrary to Yāska's method. It is clear that the words: *iti sā nigada-vyākhyātā* were originally placed immediately after the Vedic stanzas in xi. 7. The intervening passage is an interpolation, and rather a clumsy one, for it can be easily detected. This is further proved by the fact that Durga, who repeats every word of Yāska in his commentary, ignores them. How these additions gradually find their way into the text is illustrated by the following example. There is an easy quotation in xii. 2, and Yāska, as usual, simply adds: *iti sā nigada-vyākhyātā*. Some interpolators have endeavoured to add after these words a short comment. Thus some manuscripts here subjoin the following remark: **वसातिषु स्म चरथो वसातयो रातयो वसन्ते ..... सुरातयोः ॥**

Further, each recension contains passages, which, being superfluous, are omitted by the other, or are amplified versions of those in the other. For example, B adds, between vii. 19 and 20, one entire section, which is omitted by A. It is clearly an interpolation as the commentary on the Vedic stanzas is identical with that of xiv. 33 with slight alterations.

[1] Cf. N. x. 18, 24; xi. 3, 45; xii. 31.

Again, in B the commentary on the Vedic stanza quoted in v. 27, reads as follows: सुदेवस्त्वं कल्याणदानो यस्य तव देव सप्त सिंधवः प्राणायानुचरन्ति काकुदं सूर्म्यं सुषिरामिवेत्यपि निगमो भवति ॥ २७ ॥

A's version of this is greatly amplified:

सुदेवस्त्वं कल्याणदेवः कमनीयदेवो वा भवसि वरुण यस्य ते सप्त सिंधवः सिन्धुस्रवणाद्यस्य ते सप्त स्रोतांसि तानि ते काकुदमनुचरन्ति । सूर्मिः कल्याणोर्मिः स्रोतः सुषिरमनु यथा । बीरिटं तैटीकिरन्तरिक्षमेवमाह पूर्वं वयतेरुत्तरमिरतेर्वयांसीरन्त्यस्मिन्भांसि वा । तदेतस्यामृच्युदाहरन्त्यपि निगमो भवति ॥ २७ ॥

Further, A contains a long passage in 6.5: इन्द्र ऋषीन्पप्रच्छ .... व्याख्याताः omitted by B.

d. 'Omissio ex homoeoteleuto' in Sanskrit Manuscripts.

It is clear, therefore, that both the recensions cannot faithfully represent the archetype. Hence the question arises which of them adheres more closely to the original? Roth adopted the text as given by the longer recension in his edition, without, however, assigning adequate reasons for his preference. The same text is also adopted by most of the editors of the *Nirukta*. This text, as has been shown above, does not represent the original. It is true that often the longer recension preserves the better text, for sometimes passages are omitted by accident. The eye of the scribe wanders from a particular word to the same or to a similar word, occurring further on in the text, with the result that the intervening words are omitted. This phenomenon known as *omissio ex homoeoteleuto* is universal and of very frequent occurrence. The following example illustrates this kind of omission. In copying the lines: 'The book, which is rather scarce, was till very lately of absolute necessity for the Student of the Christian hymnology, above all for the Student of Adam of St. Victor's hymns',[1] the eye of the copyist wandered from the student of the first to the same word in the second line and the words 'of the Christian .... for the' were left out. The same thing happened to the scribe of MS. C 3. In copying the sentence: सोऽदेवानसृजत तत्सुराणां सुरत्वम् । असोरसुरानसृजत तदसुराणामसुरत्वमिति विज्ञायते his eye wandered from the word असृजत in the first line to the same word in the second line, with the result that the words तत्सुराणां सुरत्वम् । असोरसुरान् were left out.

Again, in copying N. vi. 22: स्थूरं राधः शताश्वं कुरुङ्गस्य दिविष्टिषु । RV. VIII. 4. 19. स्थूरः समाश्रितमात्रो महान्भवति । the eye of the scribe wandered from the स्थूरं of the first line to the similar word स्थूरः in the second line,

[1] Clark, *Descent of Manuscripts*, p. 1.

consequently the intervening words राधः शताश्वं . . . . दिविष्टिषु were omitted in MS. C 3.

Further in N. ii. 26: देवोऽनयत्सविता सुपाणिः कल्याणपाणिः। पाणिः पणायतेः पूजाकर्मणः प्रगृह्य पाणी देवान्पूजयन्ति। तस्य वयं प्रसवे याम उर्वीः। देवोऽनयत्सविता सुपाणिः is the first *pāda* of the second hemistich of the stanza of RV. III. 33. 6. Unconsciously the scribe remembered the second *pāda* तस्य वयं प्रसवे याम उर्वीः and wrote it down immediately after finishing the first *pāda* with the result that the intervening words कल्याणपाणिः। पाणिः पणायते . . . . पूजयन्ति are missing in MS. C 4. It cannot therefore be concluded that the shorter recension is always the best, for sometimes omissions are accidental.

e. **Dittography in Sanskrit Manuscripts.**

On the other hand, there is also the phenomenon called dittography, i.e. the repetition or addition of a few words or sentences. An excellent example of dittography is furnished by *The Globe* on July 9, 1915.

'The *Echo de Paris* publishes a message from Cettinje announcing the message from Cettinje announcing the appointment as Governor of Scutari of Bojo Petrovitch.'[1] The part of the second line is a verbatim repetition of a part of the first line.

In N. ii. 28, उत स्य वाजी क्षिपणिं तुरण्यति ग्रीवायां बद्धो अपि . . . . क्रतुं दधिक्राः . . . .

अपिकक्ष आसनीति व्याख्यातम्। क्रतुं वाजी क्षिपणिं तुरण्यति ग्रीवायां बद्धो दधिक्राः . . . . the eye of the scribe wandered by chance after क्रतुं to the Vedic stanza, and he mechanically copies the whole of the first line except उत स्य in MS. C 5.

Again, in N. vi. 8, the scribe of the MS. Mi. repeats गृह्णातिकर्मा वा.

Further there are some passages whose omission by B is absolutely unjustifiable. Yāska explains every word occurring in the fourth chapter of the *Nighaṇṭu*. The omission of the passages containing the explanation of any of these words is therefore inconsistent with Yāska's plan. Examples of such omissions are the following. Yāska explains निमृंभाः (*Ngh.* 4. 3. 12) in N. vi. 3, but the passage: निमृंभा निम्रध्यहारिणः is omitted by B. Again, Yāska explains चोष्कस्य (*Ngh.* 4. 3. 28) in N. vi. 6 as चोष्कस्य चयणस्य, which is omitted by B. This omission makes the following Vedic quotation meaningless.

Further, in commenting upon a Vedic stanza, Yāska always starts from the very beginning of the stanza. To leave out the first few words and to

[1] Clark, *op. cit.*, p. 6.

begin from somewhere in the middle of the stanza is altogether foreign to his practice, yet if the text of B be followed, the omission of the passage: **यवमिव वृकेणाश्विनौ निवन्तौ** (N. vi. 26) would involve Yāska in an inconsistency. All this shows that B is not absolutely reliable.

Now let us examine A. The majority of the manuscripts of A belong to a period later than those of B. Thus, not one of them has preserved the old spelling, while most of the B MSS. retain this peculiarity, i.e.

of writing	ए	as	।/	as	वार्ष	for	वर्षें
,,	ऐ	,,	।/ए	,,	।वेश्य	,,	वैश्य
,,	ओ	,,	।/।	,,	चाया	,,	चयो
,,	ह्ल	for	ढ	,,	वोह्लारः	,,	वोढारः

Again, some of the A MSS. divide the *pariśiṣṭa* into the so-called thirteenth and the fourteenth chapters, while those of B put the whole of the *pariśiṣṭa* into one chapter only, which is numbered the thirteenth.

It has already been pointed out that A contains an obvious interpolation in N. vi. 5, and an amplified version of B's comment in N. v. 27. Besides these there are shorter passages scattered throughout the book which are omitted by B and are suspected to be interpolations. One very fertile and insidious source of interpolations is supplied by Yāska's own method of giving etymological explanations. He does not content himself with one derivation, but goes on adding derivation after derivation of a single word till the whole list of probable, possible, and even fanciful etymologies is exhausted. In many cases, interpolators found it quite easy to add new derivations and attribute them to Yāska. A contains a considerable number of such additions, while B has only two.

The following are a few samples:

N. ii. 6. A reads: **वृक्षो व्रश्चनात्। वृत्वा क्षां तिष्ठतीति वा। क्षा क्षियतेर्निवासकर्मणः। नियतामीमयत्....**

B reads: **वृक्षो व्रश्चनात्। नियतामीमयत्....**

The two derivations are omitted.

N. ii. 10. A reads: **हिरण्यं कस्मात्.... हितरमणं भवतीति वा हृदयरमणं भवतीति वा।**

B reads: **हिरण्यं कस्मात्..... हितरमणं भवतीति वा।**

N. ii. 13. A reads: **सूर्यमादितेयमदितेः पुत्रमेवम्।**

B reads: **सूर्यमादितेयमेवम्।**

N. ii. 20. A reads: **आमिनाने आमिन्वाने अन्योन्यस्याध्यात्मं कुर्वाणे।**

B reads: **आमिनाने अन्योन्यस्याध्यात्मं कुर्वाणे।**

N. ii. 22. A reads: प्रथम इति मुख्यनाम प्रतमो भवति । छन्तचमन्तरिक्षम् । विकर्तनं मेघानां विकर्तनेन मेघानामुदकं जायते ।

B reads: प्रथम इति मुख्यनाम प्रतमो भवति । विकर्तनेन मेघानामुदकं जायते ।

N. iii. 8. A reads: अग्रगामिन्यो भवन्तीति वाग्रगालिन्यो भवन्तीति वाग्रकारिण्यो भवन्तीति वाग्रसारिण्यो भवन्तीति वाङ्कना भवन्ति ....

B reads: अग्रगामिन्यो भवन्तीति वाग्रगालिन्यो भवन्तीति वाग्रकारिण्यो भवन्तीति वाङ्कना भवन्ति ....

N. iii. 10. A reads: आखण्डयितः । खण्डं खण्डयतेः तडिदित्यन्तिकवधयोः....

B reads: आखण्डयितः । तडिदित्यन्तिकवधयोः ....

N. iii. 15. A reads: को वां शयने विधवेव देवरम् । देवरं कस्माद् द्वितीयो वर उच्यते । विधवा विधातृका भवति ।

B reads: को वां शयने विधवेव देवरम् । विधवा विधातृका भवति । In this particular case it is obvious that the passage देवरं कस्मात्, &c., is an interpolation, for as the words stand in the first line, Yāska would naturally give the etymological explanation of विधवा first and then of देवर, not vice versā. As a matter of fact he does so; after explaining विधवा he says: देवरो दीव्यतिकर्मा. This would have been absurd if the reading of A represents the original.

N. iii. 16. A reads: ब्राह्मणा इव वृषला इवेति । वृषलो वृषशीलो भवति वृषाशीलो वा ॥ १६ ॥

B reads: ब्राह्मणा इव वृषला इवेति ॥ १६ ॥

N. iii. 19. A reads: निर्णीतान्तर्हित .... षट् । निर्णीतं कस्मात् । निर्णिक्तं भवति ।

B reads: निर्णीतान्तर्हित .... षट् ।

N. iv. 2. A reads: मर्यादा .... स्यात् । मर्यादा मर्यैरादीयते । मर्यादा मर्यादिनो विभागः ।

B reads: मर्यादा .... स्यात् । मर्यादा मर्यादिनो विभागः ।

N. iv. 10. A reads: लक्ष्मी र्लाभाद्वा लक्षणाद्वा लप्स्यनाद्वा लाञ्छनाद्वा ...

B reads: लक्ष्मी र्लाभाद्वा लक्षणाद्वा लाञ्छनाद्वा ...

N. iv. 13. A reads: ईर्मान्ताः समीरितान्ताः सुसमीरितान्ताः पृथ्वन्ता वा ।

B reads: ईर्मान्ताः समीरितान्ताः पृथ्वन्ता वा ।

N. iv. 15. A reads: कन्या कमनीया भवति । क्वेयं नेतव्येति वा । कमनेनानीयत इति वा । कनते र्वा ।

B reads: कन्या कमनीया भवति । क्वेयं नेतव्येति वा । कनतेर्वा ।

N. iv. 19. A reads: उदकं हर उच्यते। लोका हरांस्युच्यन्ते। असृग्गहनी हरसी उच्येते।

B reads: उदकं हर उच्यते। लोका हरांस्युच्यन्ते।

N. v. 3. A reads: पानैरिति वा स्नाशनैरिति वा स्पर्शनैरिति वा।

B reads: पानैरिति वा स्नाशनैरिति वा।

N. v. 12. A reads: तृप्रप्रहारी क्षिप्रप्रहारी सृप्रप्रहारी।

B reads: तृप्रप्रहारी।

N. v. 26. A reads: जिह्वा कोकुवा। कोकूयमाना वर्णान्नुदतीति वा। कोकूयते र्वा स्याच्छब्दकर्मणः।

B reads: जिह्वा कोकुवा। कोकूयमाना वर्णान्नुदतीति वा।

N. vi. 8. A reads: जिगर्ति गिरतिकर्मा वा गृणातिकर्मा वा गृह्णातिकर्मा वा।

B reads: जिगर्ति गिरतिकर्मा वा गृह्णातिकर्मा वा

N. vi. 16. A reads: अभवत सर्वेऽग्रगमनेनेति वाग्रगरणेनेति वाग्रसंपादिन इति वा।

B reads: अभवत सर्वेऽग्रगमनेनेति वाग्रसंपादिन इति वा।

N. vi. 33. A reads: शीर्यते बिठे। बिठमन्तरिक्षम्। बिठं बीरिटेन व्याख्यातम्।

B reads: शीर्यते बिठे। बिठं बीरिटेन व्याख्यातम्।

N. vi. 32. A reads: बुन्द इषुर्भवति बिन्दो वा भिन्दो वा भयदो वा . . .

B reads: बुन्द इषुर्भवति भिन्दो वा भयदो वा . . .

N. vi. 33. A reads: ऋदूपे अर्दनपातिनौ गमनपातिनौ शब्दपातिनौ दूरपातिनौ वा मर्मण्यर्दनवेधिनौ गमनवेधिनौ शब्दवेधिनौ दूरवेधिनौ वा।

B reads: ऋदूपे अर्दनपातिनौ गमनपातिनौ वा मर्मण्यर्दनवेधिनौ गमनवेधिनौ वा।

Instances might be multiplied, but the above examples suffice to show that A has been much more tampered with than B.

Fortunately, as has been said above, Durga repeats every word of the *Nirukta* in his commentary, so that the text of the *Nirukta* 'in toto' can be reproduced from his commentary alone. This commentary therefore serves the purpose of a manuscript of the *Nirukta* and supplies valuable information about the condition of the text in its author's time. Durga does not recognize the *pariśiṣṭa* as an integral part of the *Nirukta*, as in fact he is even unaware of its existence. Thus his commentary preserves the text of the *Nirukta* as current before the addition of the *pariśiṣṭa*. Further, it derives great value from the fact that Durga displays critical judgement in the adoption of readings in the text, while giving variants and adding critical notes on them. For example, in N. i. 2, he reads अयुगपत् but gives युगपत् as a variant, adding: युगपदुत्पन्नानामयुगपदुत्पन्नानामित्युभावपि पाठौ व्याहारं प्राप्नुतः ।

Again, in N. i. 12, he reads संविज्ञातानि but gives संविज्ञानानि as a variant, adding अथवा संविज्ञानानि तानि संविज्ञातानि तानि चेत्युभावप्येतौ पाठौ ।

Again, in N. iii. 15, he remarks: अपि नं य इत्यस्य निघण्टुसूचस्य दुर्मदासो न सुरायामित्यनेनैव गतार्थतेति मन्यमानाः केचिदच निगमं नाधीयते । अपरे पुनः समाम्नायानुक्रमोऽयमिति मन्यमाना एवमेवं निगममधीयते ।

Again, in N. iii. 21, he reads अविनाशि but gives अविनाश as a variant, adding: अन्ये त्वधीयते अविनाश नामेति । तेषामविनाशस्यैव नाम ।

Again, in N. iv. 19, he reads स्युः but gives असन् as a variant, adding: भाष्येऽपि स्युरित्येषः पाठः । (*sic*) असनित्येषः प्रमादपाठः ।

Again, in N. vi. 2, he remarks: निरजे गा इत्यच केचित्पशुगव्य एता इति व्याचक्षते ।

Again, in N. vi. 4, he reads अवनायान्नम् but gives अवनेनान्नम् and अनेनान्नम् as variants.

Again, in N. vi. 6, he reads चयणस्य but gives चीणस्य as a variant, adding: चीणस्येत्येवमेके मन्यन्ते । तत्पुनरनुपपन्नम् । चयणस्येति हि भाष्यकारो निराह ।

Again, on N. vi. 21, he remarks: ऋज्ञतिः प्रसाधनकर्मा । भाऋजीक इत्यनेन गतार्थतामस्य मन्यमानो भाष्यकारो निगमं नाधीते । केचित्त्वचैतं शेषमधीयते । दूतं वो विश्ववेदसं . . . . 3. 5. 8. 1.

Again, on N. vi. 33, he remarks: भाष्यमच न सम्यगिव लक्ष्यते । तस्य सम्यक् पाठोऽन्वेष्यः । ततो योज्यम् ।

This shows that Durga took pains to ascertain the correct readings and has handed down a sort of critical edition of the *Nirukta*, as it existed in his time.

f. 1. Three stages of interpolations.

We have thus manuscript materials which belong to three distinct periods.

(1) D, i.e. the commentary of Durga, written before the edition of the *pariśiṣtas* and embodying the whole text of the *Nirukta*, represents the earliest period, i.e. about the thirteenth century A.D.

(2) B, i.e. the manuscripts of the shorter recension represent a period later than D,—when the *pariśiṣtas* were added, but not divided as yet into different chapters, and when the old orthography was still prevalent.

(3) A, i.e. the manuscript of the longer recension, represents a still later period when the *pariśiṣṭas* had been divided into chapters and the old orthography had gone out of use.

A collation of these three different recensions indicates that three distinct stages of interpolations in the *Nirukta* can be clearly traced. For example, let us take a passage in N. i. 4. On collating D, B, and A, we find that the reading of D has been expanded in B, and that of B in A.

N. i. 4. D reads: आचार्यश्चिदिदं ब्रूयादिति पूजायाम्। दधिचिदित्युपमार्थे। कुल्माषांश्चिदाहरेत्यवकुत्सिते। नु इत्येषो ....

B reads: आचार्यश्चिदिदं ब्रूयादिति पूजायाम्। आचार्य आचारं ग्राहयत्याचिनोत्यर्थानाचिनोति बुद्धिमिति वा। दधिचिदित्युपमार्थे। कुल्माषांश्चिदाहरेत्यवकुत्सिते। कुल्माषाः कुलेषु सीदन्ति। नु इत्येषो ....

A reads: आचार्यश्चिदिदं ब्रूयादिति पूजायाम्। आचार्य कस्मात्। आचार्य आचारं ग्राहयत्याचिनोत्यर्थानाचिनोति बुद्धिमिति वा। दधिचिदित्युपमार्थे। कुल्माषांश्चिदाहरेत्यवकुत्सिते। कुल्माषाः कुलेषु सीदन्ति। नु इत्येषो ....

Another example for these three stages is suppled by N. ix. 2, as follows:

D reads:

अश्वो व्याख्यातः। तस्यैषा भवति॥१॥

मा नो मित्रो वरुणो अर्यमायुरिन्द्र ....

B reads:

अश्वो व्याख्यातः। तस्यैषा भवति॥१॥

अश्वो वोळ्हा सुखं ..... इन्द्रायेन्दो परि स्रव॥

अश्वो वोळ्हा सुखं वोळ्हा। सुखमिति कल्याणनाम। कल्याणं पुण्यं सुहितं भवति। मानो व्याख्यातः। तस्यैषा भवति॥२॥

मा नो मित्रो वरुणो अर्यमायुरिन्द्र ....

A reads:

अश्वो व्याख्यातः। तस्यैषा भवति॥१॥

अश्वो वोळ्हा सुखं .... इन्द्रायेन्दो परि स्रव॥

अश्वो वोळ्हा सुखं वोळ्हा रथं वोळ्हा। सुखमिति कल्याणनाम। कल्याणं पुण्यं सुहितं भवति। सुहितं गम्यतीति वा। हसैता वा पाता वा पालयिता वा। शेपमृच्छतीति। वारि वारयति। मानो व्याख्यातः। तस्यैषा भवति॥२॥

मा नो मित्रो वरुण अर्यमायुरिन्द्र ....

It has been shown above that the list of etymologies increases as one passes from the text of B to that of A. In the same manner the list of etymologies increases in B as compared with D. The following are some examples.

N. i. 4. D reads: कुल्माषांश्चिदाहरेत्यवकुत्सिते। नु इत्येषोः . . . .

B reads: कुल्माषांश्चिदाहरेत्यवकुत्सिते। कुल्माषाः कुलेषु सीदन्ति। नु इत्येषो . . . .

D reads: वयाः शाखा वेतेः। शाखाः खशयाः।

B reads: वयाः शाखा वेते र्वातायना भवन्ति। शाखाः खशयाः शक्नोते र्वा।

N. i. 7. D reads: बृहद्वदेम स्वे वेदने। बृहदिति महतो नामधेयम्।

B reads: बृहद्वदेम स्वे वेदने। भगो भजतेः। बृहदिति महतोनामधेयम्।

N. ii. 22. D reads: बृबूकमित्युदकनाम . . . शब्दकर्मणो भ्रंशते र्वा॥२२॥

B reads: बृबूकमित्युदकनाम . . . . शब्दकर्मणो भ्रंशते र्वा। पुरीषं पृणातेः पूरयते र्वा॥२२॥

N. ii. 26. D reads:

तस्य वयं प्रसवे याम उर्वीः।
प्रत्याख्यायान्तत आशुस्रुवः॥२६॥

B reads:

तस्य वयं प्रसवे याम उर्वीः।
उर्व्य ऊर्णोते र्वृणोतेरित्यौर्णवाभः।
प्रत्याख्यायान्तत आशुस्रुवः॥२६॥

N. iii. 18. D reads: सिंहः सहनात्। संपूर्वस्य वा हन्तेः संहाय हन्तीति वा।

B reads: सिंहः सहनात्। हिंसे र्वा स्याद् विपरीतस्यः। संपूर्वस्य वा हन्तेः संहाय हन्तीति वा।

N. v. 4. D reads: शर्या अङ्गुलयो भवन्ति। शर्या इषवः शरमय्यः।

B reads: शर्या अङ्गुलयो भवन्ति। सृजन्ति कर्माणि। शर्या इषवः शरमय्यः।

N. v. 23. D reads:

उदष्याणो अघायतः समस्मात्।
इति पंचम्याम्॥२३॥

B reads:

उदष्याणो अधायतः समस्मात्।
इति पंचम्याम्। उदष्यतिरकर्मकः।
अथापि प्रथमाबहुवचने।
नभन्तामन्यके समे॥२३॥

MS. C 1 agrees with B except that the last line **नभन्तामन्यके समे** is omitted.

N. vi. 3. D reads:

उद्धर रचः सहमूलमिन्द्र ।
वृश्चमध्यम् । प्रतिशृणीह्यग्रम् ।

B reads:

उद्धर रचः सहमूलमिन्द्र ।
मूलं मोचनाद्वा मोषणाद्वा मोहनाद्वा ।
वृश्चमध्यम् । प्रतिशृणीह्यग्रम् ।

N. vi. 8. D reads: **देवो देवान्प्रत्यक्तया कृपा कल्पितया ॥ ८॥**

B reads: **देवो देवान्प्रत्यक्तया कृपा । कृपा कृप्नुतेर्वा कल्पतेर्वा ॥ ८॥**

N. vi. 24. D reads: **गल्दा धमनयो भवन्ति ।**

A reads: **गल्दा धमनयो भवन्ति । गलनमासु धीयते ।**

B omits it altogether.

N. vi. 28. D reads: **अन्या किल . . . . कच्येव युक्तं लिबुजेव वृक्षम् ।**

B reads: **अन्या किल . . . . कच्येव युक्तं लिबुजेव वृक्षम् । लिबुजा व्रततिर्भवति लीयते विभजन्तीति । व्रततिर्वरणाच्च सयनाच्च ततनाच्च ।**

f. 2. **Parallel instance of Servius, commentator of Virgil.**

Thus the stages of interpolation at different periods can be traced. The principle of the 'best MSS.' is obviously inapplicable in this case, for none of the manuscripts can be called the best. All that is available is the best manuscript of each family, and the best plan, under the circumstances, would be to place all the three families side by side. Fortunately it is possible to do so, for the successive interpolations from one family to another are invariably the amplifications of the text of a shorter recension, and are thrust between sentences wherever the text could be so enlarged with impunity, as, for instance, in multiplying the number of etymologies and attributing them all to Yāska. I have, however, distinguished the evidence of Durga's commentary from that of the manuscripts of the *Nirukta*, although Durga's commentary is very important for suppiying such valuable evidence for the history of the text of the *Nirukta*, it cannot, strictly speaking, be called a manuscript of the *Nirukta*. The relation of the shorter to the longer recension is shown by the use of square brackets, which contain the additional passages of the longer recension, while the relation of the shorter recension to the text preserved by Durga is indicated by foot-notes. An analogous example is furnished by Latin literature. The text of Servius, commentator of Virgil, shows a similar threefold amplification, the three stages of interpolation being pointed out by Thilo in his edition. I think the text of the *Nirukta* reproduced from Durga represents the archetype as closely as it is possible to restore it with the help of the present materials. I have collated[1] sixteen manuscripts myself, besides taking into account fourteen manuscripts collated by Roth, and eight by the editor of the *Nirukta* in Bib. Ind. Thus, directly and indirectly, the evidence of about forty manuscripts has been available for this edition, and the text may therefore be regarded as more or less settled.

g. Commentators of Yāska.

Although, from an early period, Yāska's work has been recognized as one of the most important *vedāṅgas* by the orthodox tradition of literary India, he, unlike Pāṇini, has not had many commentators. This does not mean that he had few followers or that his speculations did not dominate the thought of succeeding generations. On the contrary, he has been acknowledged to be the pre-eminent authority on etymology. Hence (at first sight) it seems rather inexplicable that his work should have been commented upon by so few people. One reason of this paucity is that Yāska's work itself is a commentary and not an independent treatise, hence it did not stand in need of much elucidation. Secondly, it is written in classical Sanskrit prose, and, notwithstanding its somewhat archaic and terse style, is easily intelligible to the reader as compared, for instance, with the aphorisms of Pāṇini; consequently there was not much demand for further comment. Yet three commentators, at least, are known to have elucidated Yāska's work.

(1) Ugra is mentioned as a commentator on the *Nirukta* by Aufrecht in his *Catalogus Catalogorum.*[2] But no other information, about his personality, the character of his work, and the time when he lived, is available. No reference is made to him by any of the other writers in the same field.

(2) The second commentator is Skandasvāmi, mentioned by Devarājayajvan.[3] A manuscript of his work exists in the Bibliothèque Nationale, Paris,[4] and a friend of mine from Lahore has recently informed me that he has obtained a complete manuscript of his commentary.

[1] Since then, on my visit to Paris, I have been able, through the courtesy of Professor Sylvain Lévi, to examine the *Nirukta* manuscripts in the Bibliothèque Nationale, Nos. 257–64, described by Cabaton in the *Catalogue sommaire des Manuscrits Sanskrits et Pāli*, pp. 39–40. All of them, except the first collated by Roth, belong to the nineteenth century. They all represent the text of the longer recension, and do not afford any other variants. The contents of Nos. 263 and 264 is Durga's commentary, which comes to an end with the twelfth chapter.

[2] Vol. i, p. 297.

[3] See Bib. Ind. ed., vol. i, pp. 2–4.

[4] *Loc. cit.* (Aufrecht).

(3) But the most important of all these commentators is Durga. He seems to be later than Devarājayajvan who is familiar with the then extant commentaries on the Vedas, the *Nighaṇṭu*, and the *Nirukta*, and who does not mention Durga in the long list of the authorities used by him for the purpose of his own work. Although a conclusion based on the argument of silence is not cogent, yet in this particular case, it is justified to assume that Durga is not referred to because he was posterior to Devarāja, hence Durga would also be later than Skandasvāmī. Durga's commentary is published, and has superseded the works of his predecessors. His work is important for two reasons: (1) he is the last of the commentators, and therefore represents the fullest development of the traditional interpretation of the *Nirukta*; (2) the very fact that it has survived at the cost of earlier commentaries indicates its importance. We shall therefore examine his work somewhat in detail.

Date of Durga.

It has already been pointed out that in all probability he is later than Devarājayajvan, though this assumption hardly helps us, for the date of Devarāja himself is not known. However, Durga's lower limit can be determined almost with certainty. A manuscript [1] of his commentary in the Bodleian Library is dated 1387 A.D. The date is genuine and is accepted as such by Professor A. B. Keith.[2] The manuscript was copied at Bhṛgu Kṣetra in the reign of Mahārāṇā—Durgasiṁhavijaya. Thus he could not be later than 1387 A.D. It is difficult to identify any particular site with Bhṛgu Kṣetra, but probably it was situated somewhere between the Sarasvatī and the Jamnā. As Durga wrote his commentary in a hermitage near Jammu, a place not easily accessible in the absence of modern means of communication, the migration of the MS. of his commentary to Bhṛgu Kṣetra presupposes the lapse of sufficient time in order to account for the spreading of his fame as a commentator from the isolated heights of Jammu to the plains of Bhṛgu Kṣetra. It will not be far from the truth, therefore, to place Durga about the thirteenth century A. D.

Durga does not speak of any predecessors by name nor does he leave any clue as to the sources of his own commentary. Unlike Devarājayajvan, he does not give the slightest information about himself or the general state of the *Nirukta* during his time. That he wrote his commentary in a hermitage near Jammu is proved by the colophon[3] on f. 132 v. at the end of the eleventh chapter of the *Nirukta*, which runs as follows:

[1] MS. Wilson 475.

[2] See *Catalogue of Sanskrit Manuscripts in the Bodleian Library*, vol. ii, p. 108.

[3] MS. Wilson 475.

ऋज्वर्थायां निरुक्तवृत्तौ जम्बूमार्गाश्रमनिवासिन आचार्यभगवद्दुर्गसिंहकृतौ षोडशस्याध्यायस्य चतुर्थः पादः समाप्तः। This shows that the full name of the commentator was Durgasiṁha. The fact that he lived in a hermitage and was addressed as *bhagavat* indicates that he was an ascetic and belonged to some particular order of Sannyāsa. Further, he is a descendant of the family of the Vasiṣṭhas. He does not explain the stanza RV. III. 53. 23, quoted[1] by Yāska to illustrate the meaning of the word *lodham*, because the stanza implies hostility to Vasiṣṭha. He says: यस्मिन्निगम एष शब्दः सा वसिष्ठद्वेषिणी ऋक्। अहं च कापिष्ठलो वासिष्ठः। अतस्तां न निर्ब्रवीमि। 'The stanza, in which this word (*lodham*) occurs is hostile to Vasiṣṭha. And I am a descendant of Vasiṣṭha, belonging to the Kapiṣṭhala branch, hence I do not explain the stanza.'[2]

Sāyaṇa has the following note on it: पुरा खलु विश्वामित्रशिष्यः सुदानाम राजर्षिरासीत्। स च केनचित् कारणेन वसिष्ठद्वेष्योऽभूत्। विश्वामित्रस्तु शिष्यस्य रक्षार्थमाभिर्ऋग्भिर्वसिष्ठमशपत्। इम अभिशापरूपाः। ता ऋचो वसिष्ठा न शृण्वन्ति।
'There was formerly a royal sage named Sudās, a disciple of Viśvāmitra. Somehow, he became an object of Vasiṣṭha's hatred. Then, Viśvāmitra, in order to protect his disciple, reviled Vasiṣṭha with these stanzas. These are the imprecatory stanzas. The Vasiṣṭhas do not pay any attention (lit. listen) to them.'[3] This corroborates Yāska's statement that there are stanzas which contain asseveration and imprecation only.[4]

Durga's commentary is important for it repeats every word of Yāska, thus the text of the *Nirukta* 'in toto' could be reproduced from Durga's work alone. As none of the manuscripts collated by me is older than the fifteenth century, Durga supplies therefore evidence of a very valuable character for the textual criticism of the *Nirukta*. The number of variants attributed by Durga to his predecessors and his frequent remarks that the text is corrupt and that the right reading is to be discovered,—all such cases I have pointed out in my notes,—indicate that there has been no unbroken tradition with regard to the handing down of the text of the *Nirukta*.

Further there seems to have been some sort of revival of the study of the *Nirukta* in the neighbourhood of Jammu in Durga's time, for it seems difficult to imagine that in an isolated place like Jammu, Durga sat down to write his commentary simply for the love of writing a commentary. It is more reasonable to suppose that Durga accomplished this task in order

[1] The *Nirukta*, iv. 14.

[2] Durga's Commentary on the N. iv. 14.

[3] Sāyaṇa on RV. III. 53. Cf. Bib. Ind. edition of the *Nirukta*, vol. ii, p. 416. Cf. Muir, *Sanskrit Texts*.

[4] N. vii. 3.

to meet the demand for a good text, elucidation of obscure passages, and amplification of Yāska's arguments, a demand which a revival of the study of the *Nirukta* had called forth. The examination of the manuscript of Durga's commentary, mentioned above, leads one to the conclusion that Durga did not live to complete his work and that he himself wrote his commentary up to the end of the 11th chapter only. This is indicated by a comparison of colophons in the manuscript which, at the end of the 7th–12th chapters, numbered as 12–17 by Durga consecutively from the five chapters of the *Nighaṇṭu*, are as follows:

(1) At the end of the 7th chap. on f. 50 r. ॥ द्वादशोध्यायः ॥

(2) „ „ 8th chap. on f. 70 v. ॥ इति निरुक्तवृत्तौ त्रयो . . . ध्यायः ॥

(3) „ „ 9th chap. on f. 86 v. ॥ ऋज्वर्थायां निरु . . . समाप्तः ॥

(4) „ „ 10th chap. on f. 112 r. ॥ ऋज्व . . . पंचदशोध्यायः समाप्तः ॥

(5) „ „ 11th chap. on f. 132 v. ॥ ऋज्वर्थायां निरुक्तवृत्तौ जंबूमागाश्रमनिवासिन आचार्यभगवद्दुर्गसिंहकृतौ षोडशस्याध्यायस्य चतुर्थः पादः समाप्तः ॥

A comparison of these five colophons shows that the first four do not contain any reference to Durga by name nor to his honorific titles, which fact implies that they were written by Durga himself, while that at the end of the 11th chapter was added by some disciple, who speaks of Durga as an *ācārya* and addresses him as *bhagavat*. Durga could not have appropriated these titles himself unless he was very vain. Another point in favour of the fifth colophon being written by a person other than Durga is that while the first four colophons say that such and such a chapter has come to an end, the fifth remarks that such a *pāda* of that chapter has come to an end. The colophon at the end of the 11th chapter is the final inscription and as such should have been placed at the end of the 12th chapter, where no such description is found; the colophon there, on f. 150 r., being ॥ सप्तदशस्य चतुर्थः पादः ॥ This leads one to the conclusion that Durga himself wrote his commentary up to the end of the 11th chapter, whose colophon was added by a disciple who also wrote the commentary on the 12th chapter, and faithfully refrained himself from adding the name of Durga in the colophon at the end of the 12th chapter. MS. Mill 142, dated A.D. 1839, and described in the *Catalogues of Sanskrit Manuscripts in the Bodleian Library* by Keith,[1] also preserves the final inscription at the end of the 11th chapter, while on f. 123 v., at the end of the 12th chapter it simply says ॥ सप्तदशस्य चतुर्थः पादः ॥ It is also to be noticed that in this manuscript

[1] Vol. ii, p. 108.

as well, the word *adhyāya* only is used in the earlier colophons while *pāda* makes its appearance in those at the end of the 11th and the 12th chapters. Another point of minor importance may also be adduced in this connexion, i.e. the manuscripts have the following *śloka* at the end of the 12th chapter.

स्त्र्यभिलाषि यथा कामी करोत्यंगविचेष्टितम् ।
स्त्रीसमत्वं तथा कुर्यादयं शृंगारणक्रियाम् ॥

As Durga is shown to be a hermit, to ascribe these verses to him will be highly inappropriate.

Durga and the Pariśiṣṭa.

Both the published editions of Durga's commentary regard the commentary on the portions of the 13th chapter as an integral part of Durga's work. But the MS. Wilson 475,[1] dated 1387 A.D., and MS. Mill 142[1], dated 1839 A.D., do not contain the commentary on the 13th chapter. In both these manuscripts the commentary is completed at the end of the 12th chapter and the MS. Mill 142, expressly say that the work is finished.

॥ समाप्तो ग्रन्थः ॥

Moreover, the 13th chapter was not added to the *Nirukta* by Durga's time, as is proved by his remark in the introductory part of his commentary:

अयं च तस्या द्वादशाध्यायी भाष्यविस्तरः ।
तस्येदमादिवाक्यम् । समाम्नायः समाम्नातः ॥

'And this (the *Nirukta*) is its (the *Nighaṇṭu's*) amplified commentary consisting of twelve chapters whose first sentence is "a list has been handed down by tradition".' Hence the commentary on the 13th chapter was written at a later period and attributed to Durga by some disciple or follower of his.

Yāska's contributions to Etymology, Philology, and Semantics.

1. *Date of Yāska.*

History is the one weak point of Sanskrit literature, being practically non-existent. Not a single systematic chronological record has survived, and so complete is the lack of any data to guide us in this matter that the dates of even the most famous Indian authors like Pāṇini and Kālidāsa are still subject to controversy. Yāska's date cannot therefore be determined with absolute certainty. One can arrive at a relative date

[1] This evidence is, however, inadequate. To make the case plausible, it must be corroborated by the internal evidence, i.e. the difference of style, treatment, &c. With this view I am now systematically examining and comparing the commentary on the twelfth with that of the preceding chapters. Later on I shall add the result of my examination.

only by bringing together the isolated pieces of information supplied by archaeological finds, literary references, and accidental mention of known historical or political events. This evidence, however, is not conclusive, and is differently interpreted by various oriental scholars. There is a great difference of opinion among them about the precise date of Yāska, but at the same time there is also the unanimity which sets down his lower limit as not later than 500 B.C.. As this limit has not been questioned so far (while his upper limit is carried as far as 700 B.C.), it may therefore be safely assumed that Yāska lived at least about a century earlier than Plato. Both Yāska and Plato sum up as it were the results of their predecessors in philological and etymological investigations in the *Nirukta* and the *Cratylus* respectively. Both stand pre-eminent with regard to their age, and have dominated the thought of succeeding generations in their respective countries. Yāska's work is important for the history of philology and etymology. And as the representative record of the researches of ancient Indians, it is of considerable interest for a comparative study of the Indian and Greek achievements in these two branches of knowledge in the earliest period of their history.

2. *Phonetic equipment of Yāska.*

Before we proceed to examine, in detail, the principles laid down by Yāska for etymology, or his speculations in philology, it will be worth while to inquire whether Yāska was a properly qualified person to undertake the task, i.e. whether he possessed any knowledge of sound-laws, or, in other words, whether he received any phonetic training, and of what sort? As has already been pointed out, historical and biographical records about ancient India do not exist, or at least, if they existed, have not survived. Nothing definite is, therefore, known about the life of Yāska, nor about the period in which he lived, nor about the educational system which then prevailed. In the absence of such records it is therefore extremely difficult to ascertain the worth of his qualifications, or the extent of, and his familiarity with, sound-laws. Yet some indirect information can be pieced together by collecting a few isolated data capable of throwing some light on the subject. In the first place, Yāska is acquainted with a vast amount of Sanskrit literature. The numerous exemplary quotations occurring in the *Nirukta* conclusively show that he knew the Ṛg-veda, the Sāma-veda, the Atharva-veda, the Yajur-veda, and their *pada-pāṭhas*, the *Taittirīya Saṁhitā*, the *Maitrāyaṇī Saṁhitā*, the *Kāṭhaka Saṁhitā*, the *Aitareya Brāhmaṇa*, the *Gopatha Brāhmaṇa*, the *Kauṣīṭaki Brāhmaṇa*, the *Śatapatha Brāhmaṇa*, the *Prātiśākhyas*, and some of the *Upaniṣads*. The full list of all the works known to him is given in the Appendix. This shows that Yāska was a man of comprehensive knowledge and vast reading. Secondly, he refers to and quotes the opinions of the various schools of thought which existed in his time, i. e. the school of etymologists, the school of grammarians, the school of ritualists, the school of legendists, the school of *Naidānas* (i. e. specialists, in primary causes). Further, he discusses and criticizes the views of many authorities—his predecessors and contemporaries. The full list of these is also given in the Appendix. The mention of eminent scholars and schools of thought presupposes specialization in their respective departments of knowledge which implies some uniform system of training and a sufficiently high order of education extending over a long period. Otherwise it is difficult to conceive how these various schools could have come into existence at all. Thus it can be assumed without much doubt that Yāska had received some kind of training in one, or more than one, of these schools. He discusses the doctrines of the schools other than his own, and thus seems to have acquired a general familiarity with them to be able to do so. Thirdly, he distinctly mentions the *prātiśākhyas*, i. e. phonetic treatises which record the researches made by ancient Indians in the physiological and the acoustic aspects of Phonetics. These treatises themselves presuppose the existence of the *pada-pāṭhas*, i. e. 'the word texts', which give every word of the *saṁhitā* in its isolated state, i. e. free from the euphonic combinations, and analyse compounds into their component elements. Gradually by the time of Yāska, a strong phonetic feeling had come into existence, as is evident from the scientific arrangement and classification of the Sanskrit alphabet. This shows that Yāska was furnished with some phonetic equipment, such as the state of the scholarship of the time permitted him to acquire. This view is supported by the fact that Yāska is familiar with and recognizes the following phonetic phenomena: (1) Syncope as in जग्मुः (they went) from the root गम् (to go); (2) Metathesis as in स्तोका 'a drop' from श्चुत् (to drop), रज्जुः (rope) from सृज् (to emit), and तर्कु 'knife' from कृत् (to cut), and so on; (3) Anaptyxis, as in आस्थत् from the root अस् (to throw), द्वारः (door) from the root वृ (to cover), भरूजाः from the root भ्रस्ज् (to fry), &c.; (4) haplology as in तृच = *tri* + *ṛca*, i.e. 'three stanzas'.[1] He is also acquainted with assimilation, and has noticed an example of prākṛtization in the Ṛg-veda while explaining कुटस्य by कृतस्य (N. v. 24). For the detailed account of his observations on phonetic phenomena see Chapter II, sections

[1] All these words are found in the *Nirukta*, ii. 1–2. I have cited examples furnished by Yāska himself.

1–2. From what has gone before, it may be concluded that Yāska was a man of extensive reading, that he had pursued a systematic course of study, and that he was furnished with some phonetic equipment. This conclusion is further supported by the fact that his explanations are pervaded with a rationalistic spirit and devoid of the mystifying or supernatural element, a characteristic of the ritualist and the *parivrājaka* school, cf. e.g. Yāska's explanation of *Vṛtra*. He is altogether free from fanaticism, bigotry, and intolerance when he meets Kautsa's adverse criticism of what he believes to be the revealed hymns, but gives rational answers to the various points of objection. He is actuated by a scientific spirit even when he is dealing with gods. Thus, for instance, he classifies gods into various groups, i.e. the terrestrial, the atmospheric, and the celestial according to the sphere of their activity, and assigns definite functions to each. Yāska's classification of gods has nothing corresponding to it in the mythologies of other nations. Further, his treatment of synonyms and homonyms is also scientific. At first he attributes a particular meaning to a particular word, and then supports his assertion by quoting a passage, generally from the Vedic literature, in which that word is used in that particular sense. Whether or not one agrees with him in attributing particular meanings to particular words, it cannot be denied that his method is scientific and; notwithstanding his remote antiquity, surprisingly modern. This scientific spirit, so evident in the *Nirukta*, could be developed by a scientific training only. In the absence of any definite information, the preceding statement will, I think, give some indication as to Yāska's qualifications to undertake the task which he set before himself.

3. *Importance of Etymology.*

Taking both the East and the West together, Yāska is the first writer on etymology. He is also the first to treat it as a science by itself. According to the orthodox Indian tradition, the *Nirukta* has, for a long time, been recognized as a treatise which deals specially with etymology. But the claim of Yāska is not based on this recognition. He has enunciated his doctrines in the *Nirukta*. His remarks on the importance of etymology may sound very commonplace to us, but probably appeared to have the same profoundness of wisdom when they were first uttered about 2,500 years ago, as President Wilson's fourteen points for the modern political world. His arguments for etymology are summarized as follows:

(1) Etymology is essential for the proper understanding of the Vedic texts.

(2) Etymology is the complement of grammar.[1]

(3) Etymology is necessary for the analysis of the *saṁhitā* into the *pada-pāṭha*, and of words into their component elements.

(4) Etymology has practical utility, for it enables one to discover the primary deity of a stanza which bears the characteristic marks of more than one deity, and thus helps to perform the sacrifice with perfection.

(5) Etymology is a science, and should be studied for its own sake, for knowledge is commended, and ignorance is condemned. (Chapter I, sec. 15–17.)

4. *Principles of Etymology.*

Yāska's fundamental notion about language is, that all words can be reduced to their primordial elements which he calls roots. With this idea he lays great emphasis on the point that as every word can be traced to an original root, one should never give up a word as underivable. His first general principle is, 'One should give the etymological explanation of words whose accent and grammatical form are regular, and are accompanied with a radical modification in the usual manner', i. e. in accordance with the laws of phonology. One would hardly question the derivation of पाचक from पच् 'to cook', or of पाठक from पठ् 'to read', or of बोध from बुध् 'to know', or of भेद from भिद् 'to break', and so on. It should be observed that Yāska recognized the importance of accent, and accords it a due place in his principle. It is obvious that the above-mentioned rule is limited in its scope, for only a comparatively small number of words can fulfil the conditions therein laid down. Yāska therefore strikes a note of warning and says that a disproportionate importance should not be attached to grammatical form, for the rules of grammar are not universal like laws of nature, and have many exceptions, adding that one has also to take into consideration phonetic phenomena such as syncope, metathesis, haplology, anaptyxis, assimilation, &c. His second principle is that in case the accent and grammatical form are not regular, and are not accompanied with a radical modification, one should always take his stand on the meaning of the word and endeavour to derive it from some similarity of form, or if there is no such similarity of form, even from the similarity of a single letter or syllable. Thus, according to Yāska, one should not be afraid to derive, *dois, dû, doive, dusse,* &c. from *devoir*, 'to owe', or *iṣṭi* (sacrifice) from the root *yaj* (to sacrifice), on account of the apparent dissimilarity of their form. Comparative philology furnishes the best examples to illustrate Yāska's remark that often there is hardly any resemblance between a word and its original source, i. e. its primitive

[1] *Tad idaṃ vidyā-sthānaṃ vyākaraṇasya kārtsnyam.* N. i. 15.

and derivative forms. Cf. IE. *penque; Skt. *pañca*; Zend. *pañca*; Gk. πέντε; Lat. *quinque*; Lith. *penkè*; Goth. *fimf*; Germ. *fünf*; OE. *fif*; Eng. *five*. Again. French *larme* and English *tear* have only *r* in common, both being otherwise quite different from their original source **dakru*, which assumed an Anglo-Saxon form *tear*, and a primitive Lat. *dacru*. The Eng. *ewe* and Lat. *ovis* have nothing in common, and each has exclusively preserved some parts of their original **owis*. Eng. *four*, Germ. *vier*, have only *r* in common with Gk. τέτταρες. Eng. *quick* (orig. 'alive') has only *i* in common with Gk. βίος (life). Eng. *sit*, and Gk. *hed* (ἕδρα, 'seat') have nothing in common, and each has preserved one exclusive part of the original **sed*. Again, cf. IE. **ghans*; Skt. *haṁsa*; Gk. χήν; Lat. *anser* (for *hanser*); Germ. *Gans*; OE. *gôs*; Eng. *goose*.

But the application of this rule by an incompetent person gives rise to grotesque results; many such cases are supplied by the *Nirukta*, e.g. Śākaṭāyana's derivation of *Sat-ya*, the *ya* of which he formed from the causal of *i*, and *Sat* from *as*, 'to be'. Yāska foresaw the danger of the misuse of his principle. So after laying down his rule, he adds a note of warning. He urges that single words isolated from their context should not be thus derived, for without a knowledge of the context, it is often difficult to know the precise meaning of a word. He recommends that derivations should not be explained for a person not acquainted, or not well acquainted, with grammar, and not for one who has not studied etymology as a pupil. He says, 'One should indeed explain derivations for one's own pupil who has been in residence studying etymology or for one who is capable of understanding; for the intelligent and for the diligent.' N. ii. 3.

The third principle of etymology laid down by Yāska is that one should derive words in accordance with their meanings. 'If their meanings are the same, their etymologies should be the same, if the meanings are different, the etymologies should also be different.' (N. ii. 7.)

This principle is on the whole sound, for in every language there occurs the phenomenon that words of different origin often assume the same form. For instance:

Skt. *Akta* derived from the root *aj* means 'driven'.
" " " " " *añj* " 'besmeared'.
Aja " " " " *aj* " 'driver'.
" = *a-ja* " " " " *jan* " 'not born'.
Aniṣṭa = *an-iṣṭa* from √*iṣ* means 'unwished'.
" = *an-iṣṭa* " √*yaj* " 'not sacrificed'.
Anudāra = *an-udāra* means 'a niggardly man'.

Skt. *Anudāra* = *anu-dāra* means 'followed by a wife'.
 „ = *a-pavana* „ 'without air'.
Apavana = *apa-vana* „ 'a grove'.
 „ = *a-vasāna* „ 'not dressed'.
Avasāna = *ava-sāna* „ 'resting-place'.

English *Abode*. From *abide*, meaning 'delay' or 'dwelling-place'.

Abode. OE. *abeód-an*, connected with the primitive verb *beódan*, meaning 'prognostication'; cf. *fore-bode*.

Abound. OFr. *abunder, abonder, habonder*; Lat. *abundāre*, meaning 'to be plentiful'.

„ = *a-bound*, meaning 'to get limits to'.

Admiral. OFr. *amiral*, derived from the Arabic *amīr-al*, latinized in various ways and assimilated according to popular forms, meaning 'a naval officer'.

„ A by-form of *admirable*. OFr. *amirable*, Lat. *admīrābil-em*, meaning 'exciting admiration'.

Adust. Lat. *adūst-us*, Fr. *aduste*, meaning 'scorched'.

„ = *a-dust*, meaning 'in a dusty condition'.

Aught. OE. *áht*; OHG. *éht*; Goth. *aiht-s*, meaning 'possession'.

„ OE. *á*, *ó* + *whit*; OHG. *eowiht, iowiht*, &c.; ME. *ōht, ōght*, meaning 'anything whatever'.

Bay. OFr. *baie*; Lat. *bāca*, meaning 'a small fruit, a berry'.

„ Fr. *baie*; Lat. *baia*, meaning 'an indentation of sea into land, or of land into the sea'.

„ OFr. *baée*; Lat. type *badāta*, meaning 'the division of a barn'.

„ OFr. *bay*; It. *bada*; Lat. *badare*, 'to open the mouth', meaning 'barking or baying'.

„ Cf. ON. *bágr, bægja*, 'to push back', meaning 'an embankment or dam'.

„ Short form of *bay-antler*, meaning 'the second branch of a stag's horn'.

„ Fr. *bai*; Lat. *badius*, meaning 'a reddish-brown colour'.

Beak. Fr. *bec*; It. *becco*; Sp. *bico*; Late Lat. *beccus*, meaning 'a bird's bill'.

„ 'A justice of the peace'.

„ A variant of *beek*, 'to warm'.

Bear. OE. *bera*; OHG. *bero*; Mod. G. *bär*; cf. ON. *björn*; Lat. *ferus*, meaning 'an animal'.

„ OE. *bęre*; cf. Goth. *barizeins*, meaning 'barley'.

„ OE. and OHG. *ber-an*; ON. *ber-a*; Goth. *bair-an*; Lat. *fer*; Gk. φερ; Skt. *bhar*, meaning 'to carry'.

English *Dole* derived from French *deuil* means 'grief'.
„ related to Teut. *deal*; Ger. *Teil* means 'portion'.
Fame. Fr. *fame*; Lat. *fāma* (report); Gk. *φήμη*, meaning 'public report'.
„ Fr. *faim*; Lat. *fames*; cf. OFr. *afamer*, meaning 'want of food, hunger'.
„ Obsolete form of *foam*.
Fast. OE. *fæstan*; OHG. *fastēn*; ON. *fasta*; Goth. *fastan*, meaning 'to abstain from food'.
„ ME. *fest*; ON. *fest-r*, meaning 'a rope'.
„ Fr. *faste*; Lat. *fastus*, meaning 'arrogance'.
Fold. OE. *folde*; OLG. *folda*; ON. *fold*, related to **felþu*, 'field', meaning 'ground'.
„ OE. *feuldon*; OHG. *faldan*; ON. *falda*; Goth. *falþan*; OTeut. **falþan*; cf. Lith. *pleta*; Gk. *δί-παλτος*, meaning 'to arrange one thing over another'.
„ OE. *falœd*; Mod. LG. *falt*, meaning 'an enclosure for domestic animals'.
„ ME. *fald*; OHG. *fait*; ON. *fald-r*, meaning 'a bend or ply'.
Hound. OE. *hund*; OHG. *hunt* (d-); Goth. *hunds*; ON. *hundr*; Gk. *κύων, κυν*; Skt. *śvan*, meaning 'dog'.
„ ME. *hūn*; ON. *húnn*, meaning 'a projection'.
Seal. OE. *sīol*; OHG. *selah*; ON. *sel-r*, meaning 'an animal'.
„ OFr. *seel*; It. *suggello*; Lat. *sigillum*, meaning 'a device'.
Sound. Derived from Fr. *son*; Lat. *sonus*, means 'noise'.
„ OE. *sund*, means 'strong'.
„ Fr. *sonder*; Lat. *subundare*, means 'testing depths'.

French *Air.* Gk. *ἀήρ*; Lat. *āer-em*; Sp. *aire*, meaning 'the gaseous substance which envelopes the earth'.
„ OFr. *aire*, meaning 'disposition'.
„ It. *aria*, meaning 'melody'.
Champs. Lat. *campus*; It. *campo*; Sp. *campo*, meaning 'field'.
„ OFr. *cant*, meaning 'side'.
Chère. Feminine of *cher*, 'dear'.
„ Gk. *χαρά*, 'face'.
Cousin, -e. Lat. *consobrinus*; It. *cugino, -a*; Sp. *sobrino, -a*; Ptg. *sobrinho, -a*, meaning 'a relative'.
„ Lat. *culicinus*, meaning 'an insect'.
Devant. Preposition meaning 'before'.
„ Pr. participle of *devoir*, 'to owe'.
Feu. Lat. *focus*; It. *fuoco*; Sp. *fuego*; Ptg. *fogo*; OFr. *fou*, meaning 'fire'.

French *Feu*. Derived by Estienne and Scheler from Lat. *fuit* > *feut* > *feu*; by Ménage from Lat. *felix* > *felicis* > *felce* > *feu*; by Littré from OFr. *fahu* > *feü*, connecting with Lat. *fatutus*, meaning 'dead'.

Fier. Lat. *fidare* for (*fidere*); It. *fidare*; Sp. and Ptg. *fiar*, meaning 'to put confidence'.

„ Lat. *ferus*; It. and Sp. *fiero*; Ptg. *fero*, meaning 'proud'.

Firme. Lat. *firmus*; ME. *ferme*, meaning 'firm'; cf. Skt. √*dhṛ*.

„ Med. Lat. *firma*, meaning, a farm'.

Franc. Lat. *francus*; It. *franco*; Sp. and Ptg. *franco*, meaning 'free'.

„ Meaning 'a French coin'.

Geste. Lat. *gestus*, meaning, 'gesture'.

„ Lat. *gesta*; It. *gesta*, meaning 'heroic deed, poetry'; cf. *chanson de geste*.

Louer derived from Lat. *locare* means 'to let'.

„ „ „ „ *laudare* means 'to praise'.

German *acht*. OHG. *ahto*; MHG. *ahte*; Goth. *ahtau*; OE. *eahta*, derived from an IE. root; cf. Skt. *aṣṭau*; Gk. ὀκτώ; Lat. *octo*; Lith. *asztûni*, meaning 'eight'.

„ OHG. *âhta*; MHG. *âhte*; OE. *óht*, meaning 'proscription'.

Ball. From *bellen*, meaning 'barking'.

„ MHG. *bal*, *balles*; cognate with OHG. *ballo*; MHG. *balle*; ME. *bal*, *balle*; OTeut. *ballôn, *ballôn; cf. Lat. *foll-is*, 'something inflated'; Fr. *balle*, meaning 'a ball to play with'.

„ Fr. *bal*; It. *ballo*; Fr. *baler* or *baller*; Lat. *ballare*; Gk. βαλλίζω, meaning 'a dance'.

Bauer. OHG. *bûr*; MHG. *bûr*; LG. *buur*; ON. *búr*; OE. *búr*, 'dwelling'; cf. *neighbour*; OE. *néah-gebúr* and *nach-bar*; E. *bower*; OTeut. **búro(m)*, from Teut. √*bŭ*; IE. √*bhu*; cf. Skt. *bhū* (*bhūmi*, 'earth'); Gk. φύω; Lat. *fui* (*futurus*); meaning 'bird-cage'.

„ OHG. *bûâri*; MHG. *bûwære*; cf. *Erbauer*, *Ackerbauer*, from the √*bauen*, 'to cultivate'; Du. *bouwen*; MHG., MDu. *bûwen*; meaning 'a peasant'.

Bulle. MLG. *bulle*; MDu. *bulle*; Du. *bul*, *bol*; ON. *bole*, *boli*; ME. *bole* (*boole*); cf. ME. *bule*, *bulle* and E. *bull*, *bullock*; meaning 'a buffalo'.

„ MHG. *bulle*; OE. *bulle*; E. *bull*; Fr. *bulle*, derived from Lat. *bulla*, meaning 'a papal mandate'.

German *Geiseln*. Pl. of *geisel*, OHG. *gīsal*; MHG. *gīsel*; OE. *gísel*, meaning 'hostages'.

„ A form of *geiszeln*, MHG. *geiseln*, meaning 'to whip'.

Kehren. OHG. *kēran*; MHG. *kēren*, meaning 'to sweep'.

„ OHG. *kęrian*; MHG. *kęrn*, meaning 'to turn'.

Kiefer. OHG. *kienforha*; MHG. *kienboum* and the corresponding word to OHG. **kienforhe*; cf. *Kien* and *Föhre*, meaning 'Scotch fir, pine tree'.

„ MHG. *kiver, kivel, kivele*; OSaxon. *kâflos*; OE. *ceáfl*, meaning 'jaw'.

Kiel. OHG. *kiol, chiol*; MLG. *kêl, kîl*; MHG. *kiel*; OE. *céol*; OS. *kiol*, meaning 'keel'.

„ MHG. *kîl*; LG. *quiele*; E. *quill*, meaning 'a piece of reed or feather of a bird'.

Laden. OHG. *hladan*; MHG. *laden*; OS. *hladan*; OE. *hladan*; Goth. *(af)halþan*; E. *lade*, meaning 'to load'.

„ OHG. *ladōn*; MHG. *laden*; Goth. *laþon*; OE. *laðian*, meaning 'shop'.

Mandel. MLG. MDu. *mande*; OE. *mand, mǫnd*; E. *maund*, meaning 'to count by fifteen'.

„ OHG. *mandala*; MHG. *mandel*; OFr. *almande*, also *amande, amandre*; cf. Sp. *almendra*; It. *mandorla, mandola*, meaning 'almond'.

Mark. OHG. *marka*; MHG. *marke*; OS. *marka*; OE. *mearc*, meaning 'boundary'.

„ MHG. *mark*; MDu. *marc*; ON. *mǫrk*; OE. *marc*; Med. Lat. *marca, marcus*; Fr. *marc*; It. *marco, marca*, meaning 'a coin'.

„ OHG. *marg, marag*; MHG. *marc, marg*; OS. *marg*; OE. *mearz, mearh*; MDu. *march, marg*; Mod. Du. *merg*; OTeut. **mazgo*; cf. AV. *mazga*; Skt. *majjan*, meaning 'the soft fatty substance of bones'.

Reis. OHG. *hriis*; MHG. *rîs*; ON. *hrís*; MDu. Du. *rijs*; OF. *hrís*, meaning 'twigs or small branches'.

„ MHG. *rîs*; MLG. *riis*; ME. *rys*; OFr. *ris*; It. *riso*; Lat. **orizum*; Gk. *ὄρυζα*; cf. Skt. *vrīhi*, meaning 'rice'.

Hindi *kāma* derived from Skt. *kṛ* means 'work'.

„ „ „ „ *kam* „ 'love'.

Examples might be multiplied. It is clear that such words can be satisfactorily derived only with reference to their meaning, for being derivable from more than one original source, they are liable to be connected with the wrong root unless the derivation is based on the meaning. Yāska's rule is therefore sound. But in criticism of Yāska's rule, it may be remarked that words, having the same origin, come to acquire different meanings. For instance, Lat. *cup(cupido)*, 'to desire', and Skt. *kup*, 'to be angry', have the same common origin. Again, cf. IE *klutós*; Skt. *śrutás*; Gk. *κλυτός*; Lat. *(in)clutus*; OE. *hlūd*; Eng. *loud*. Yāska did not know any other language besides Sanskrit,. his horizon was therefore necessarily limited, yet his familiarity with the two phases of the Sanskrit language, i.e. the Vedic and the classical, which is historically the development of the former, and which in their relation to each other bear a close correspondence to that of the Ionic and the Attic tongues, placed him on a better working ground than those who were not fully conscious of such historical development. There is no passage in the *Cratylus*, for instance, showing that Plato realized that the Attic was historically the outgrowth of the Ionic language. On the contrary, the following passage indicates that he was not aware of any such development.

5. *Plato on Etymology.*

Soc. 'Yes, my dear friend; but then you know that the original names have been long ago buried and disguised by people sticking on and stripping off letters for the sake of euphony, and twisting and bedizening them in all sorts of ways. . . . And the additions are often such that at last no human being can possibly make out the original meaning of the word.'[1] Again, Plato does not recognize that etymology has any scientific or even systematic basis. He does not seem to realize that derivation of words should be governed by some general rules. In addition to the above, I quote the following passage in support of my statement:

Soc. . . . 'Now attend to me; and first, remember that we often put in and pull out letters in words and give names as we please and change the accents.'[2] Evidently he did not attach much importance to accent. The only principle, which can hardly be so called, is contained in the following passage:

Soc. . . . . 'And whether the syllables of the name are the same or not the same, makes no difference, providing the meaning is retained; nor does the addition or subtraction of a letter make any difference so long

[1] Jowett, *Dialogues of Plato* (3rd ed.), vol i, p. 358.

[2] *Ibid.* p. 341.

as the essence of the thing remains in possession of the name and appears in it.'[1]

These three passages from the *Cratylus* indicate that Plato looked upon etymology as a compendium of individual conjecture which would justify Voltaire's famous satire that, 'Etymology is a science in which vowels count for nothing and consonants for very little', and Max Müller's well-known epigram that, 'a sound etymology has nothing to do with sound'. The fundamental difference between Yāska and Plato is that the former distinguished roots from affixes and suffixes, i.e. the radical from the formative element, and hence was able to formulate general principles for analysing words into their constituent parts; the latter did not realize this distinction and consequently made conjecture the basis of etymology. It may be remarked, however, that Sanskrit is generally acknowledged to be more perspicuous than Greek; it was easier therefore to see this distinction in Sanskrit than it was in Greek, and besides Yāska had the advantage of inheriting this knowledge from a long line of predecessors who had made this discovery at a very early period. But Yāska's greatness, even if every one of his etymological explanations is proved to be wrong—as many are manifestly so,—lies in the fact that he is the first to claim a scientific foundation, and also the first to formulate general principles for etymology.

6. *Philological speculations of Yāska.*

In two aphoristic rules, Yāska enunciates his view as to why articulate speech is given preference to other modes of expression, such as gestures, movements of hands and body, &c. He says, 'words are used to designate objects with regard to everyday affairs in the world, on account of their comprehensiveness and minuteness'.[2] Durga, the commentator of Yāska, explains the term 'comprehensiveness', with regard to the psychological process involved in the apprehension of meaning through the instrumentality of the spoken word. He says that there are two phases of consciousness in the human mind, i.e. (1) the manifest, and (2) the unmanifest. When a person desires to express the manifest consciousness, his effort results in the exhalation of breath which modified in the various speech-organs produces the word. The word again pervades the unmanifest consciousness of the hearer, makes it manifest, and thus the meaning is apprehended.[3] Using philological terminology, we may express the same thing by saying that there are permanent word-records in the sub-conscious strata of the human

[1] Jowett, *Dialogues of Plato* (3rd ed.), vol. i, p. 335.

[2] The *Nirukta*, i. 2.

[3] Durga on N. i. 2.

mind. These word-records are brought from the sub-conscious to the conscious state by articulated speech. It may be objected that whatever the psychological process may be, the most important use of the word is to express and convey the meaning to somebody else, and this purpose can equally be accomplished by other methods, such as gestures, movements of hands, face, and eyes. As if Yāska had anticipated this objection, he adds the term 'minuteness' in his aphorism. Durga has the following comment: The movements of hands and the winking of the eyes, &c., are also comprehensive, they will express the meaning and in this manner we will be saved the trouble of studying grammar and the bulky Vedic literature. True, gestures, &c., are comprehensive, but they are not minute, i. e. they involve greater effort in production and are always indefinite. Even discarding Durga's elaborate explanation of 'comprehensiveness', Yāska's aphorism can mean only that words are used in the everyday affairs of the world because they are capable of giving expression to every kind of meaning with their numerous shades of difference, and are produced with comparatively less exertion. There seems to be no doubt that at the time of writing the above-mentioned aphorism, Yāska had in his mind the alternative method of expression by means of gestures, &c. And his argument that words are preferred to gestures, on account of the economy of effort, has a strikingly modern note.

7. *Origin of Language.*

Yāska is a follower of the school of etymologists, whose fundamental doctrines is that all words are derived from original roots.[1] Gārgya and the followers of the school of grammarians do not agree with him.[2] There is also a short discussion about onomatopoeia.[3] Aupamanyava maintains that there is no such thing as onomatopoeia, but Yāska holds that there are some words which are formed by the mere imitation of sounds of nature, mostly the names of birds, such as crow, partridge, &c., but which can be derived otherwise also. It is surprising that in this connexion he does not mention the word cuckoo. Besides the names of birds, he thinks that the following words are similarly formed. *Kituva*[4], 'a gambler'; *dundubhi*[5], 'a drum'; *ciścā kṛṇoti*[6], 'it makes a *ciścā* sound'; *kṛka*[7], the *former* part of *kṛkavāku*, 'a cock'. According to Yāska, onomatopoeia does not play any important part in the foundation of language. He discards

[1] *Nirukta*, i. 12.
[2] *Loc. cit.*
[3] *Op. cit.* iii. 18.
[4] *Ibid.* v. 22
[5] *Ibid.* ix. 12.
[6] *Ibid.* ix. 14.
[7] *Ibid.* xii. 13.

therefore the so-called Bow-wow theory.[1] As Yāska reduces all words to primordial roots, he may therefore be regarded as an adherent of the root-theory.

This again affords a point of difference from the *Cratylus*, where Plato, in attempting to trace the origin of the sounds of the alphabet to the sounds of nature, considers onomatopoeia to be the most important factor in the formation of language. As an objection to his theory, it may be remarked that the objects with which men in primitive society are most familiar would be things like 'cave', 'pit', 'tree', &c., and the naming of these objects precludes all imitation of natural sounds. Words like 'digger', 'weaver', &c., would represent a higher stage of civilization.[2]

8. *Parts of Speech.*

Yāska says that there are four parts of speech: noun and verb, preposition and particle.[3] At first sight, it seems inexplicable that an ancient author like Yāska should mention preposition as a part of speech and should ignore adverbs which historically can be shown to have been evolved at an earlier stage of the linguistic development than the former. The difficulty, however, disappears when it is remembered that prepositions in Sanskrit are seldom used to express case relations, but mostly serve as adverbial prepositions. With Yāska's division of speech into four parts may be compared the remarks of Dionysius of Halicarnassus, who attributes a similar classification to Aristotle.

'Composition is . . . . a certain arrangement of the parts of speech. . . . These were reckoned as three only by Theodectes and Aristotle and the philosophers of those times, who regarded nouns, verbs, and connectives as the primary parts of speech. Their successors, particularly the leaders of the Stoic school, raised the number to four, separating the article from the connectives.'[4] According to Aristotle, 'Diction viewed as a whole is made up of the following parts: the letter (or the ultimate element), the syllable, the conjunction, the article, the noun, the verb, the case, and the speech.'[5]

9. *Aristotle's definition of Noun and Verb.*

Yāska defines the noun and the verb as follows: 'A verb has *becoming* as its fundamental notion, a noun has *being* as its fundamental notion. But where both (i.e. *becoming* and *being*) are dominated by *becoming* as in a verbal noun), a *becoming* arising from a former

[1] Max Muller, *Science of Language*, vol. i, pp. 407–17.

[2] See also Max Muller, *loc. cit.*

[3] *Nirukta*, i. 1.

[4] *Literary Composition*, ch. iii, Roberts's ed., p. 71.

[5] *Poetics*, 20. 1456 b, Bywater's ed., p. 57.

to a later state is denoted by a verb, as 'he goes', 'he cooks', &c.; while the embodiment of the whole process beginning with the original and ending with the final conception, which has assumed the character of *being*, is denoted by a noun, as 'going', 'cooking', &c.[1] Further, *becoming* has six modifications: (1) genesis, (2) existence, (3) alteration, (4) growth, (5) decay, and (6) destruction.[2] With these may be compared Aristotle's definitions of noun and verb. 'A noun or name is a composite significant sound not involving the idea of time, with parts which have no significance by themselves in it. . . . A verb is a composite significant sound involving the idea of time, with parts which have no significance by themselves in it. Whereas the word 'man' or 'white' does not imply when, 'walks' and 'has walked' involve in addition to the idea of walking that of time present or time past.'[3]

In his definition of a verb, Aristotle lays great emphasis on the idea of time, but ignores the idea of action involved in it; his definition is therefore incomplete and states the element of lesser importance only, for of the two ideas of action, and time, the former is of primary and the latter of secondary significance. Yāska has hit on the right word, i.e. *becoming* which expresses both, the notion of action and time as well. Aristotle's definition of a noun is a negative one. He explains what it does not involve, but not what it positively does involve. Yāska, on the other hand, gives a positive definition, setting forth *being* to be the fundamental notion of a noun. Further, he also defines a verbal noun, which is ignored by Aristotle.

Yāska explains prepositions as words which bring into prominence the subordinate meaning of nouns and verbs. He then subjoins a list of twenty prepositions assigning to each its appropriate meaning. Proceeding further, he divides particles into three groups, (1) comparatives, (2) conjunctives, and (3) expletives. He defines these terms, giving a list of the particles of each group, explaining their meanings and illustrating their uses by suitable quotations from Vedic literature. They are treated in detail in the first chapter of the *Nirukta* (sec. 3–9).

Yāska observes the dialectical differences in the spoken language of his time. Thus he points out certain characteristics of the speech of the Aryans and the Kāmbojas, the people of the East, and the people of the North.[4] He acknowledges the relation of the classical to the Vedic Sanskrit. Thus he remarks that their vocabulary is identical,[5] that their use of prepositions and particles with occasional exceptions is similar.[6]

[1] *Nirukta*, i. 1.
[2] *Op. cit.* i. 2.
[3] *Poetics*, 20. 1456 b. 10, Bywater's ed., p. 58.
[4] *Nirukta*, ii. 2.
[5] *Op. cit.* i. 16.
[6] *Op. cit.* i. 3–9.

He seems to be conscious of the historical connexion of the two languages when he says that the words of the one are derived from the roots of the other.[1] He knows that it is not nouns only, but also verbs, which have synonyms. 'So many verbs have the same meaning. So many are the synonym of a noun (lit. being).'[2] He explains homonym as a word which has more than one meaning.[3] He also notices certain idiomatic expressions, whose order is immutably fixed as 'Indra and Agni', 'father and son', but not 'Agni and Indra', 'son and father'.[4]

Semantics.

How names are given.

The epoch of Yāska was an age of remarkable literary activity. There seems to be a general striving after the search of truth in all the departments of human knowledge. On the philosophic side, it marks the beginning of the Upaniṣadic period which preached monotheism of an exalted type, and gave expression to some of the sublimest thoughts ever recorded in the history of mankind. On the religious side, it was the harbinger of the Buddha who was soon to carry out a campaign of vigorous protestantism against the then prevailing ritualistic practices. Even in the matter of style, it is the period of transition which ushered in the era of the aphorism (*sūtra*). As shown above, the age was busy with grammatical and philological speculations, nor was semantics ignored. In the first chapter of the *Nirukta* (see 12–14), Yāska discusses the question, how names are given. The most important arguments are set forth in the form of questions and answers. A critic is introduced who raises the various points of objection, each of which is duly answered by the author. It is a dialogue consisting of two monologues which are put in the mouths of the critic and the author in succession. The arguments are as follows: (1) Every being who performs a particular action should be called by the same name, e. g. every one who runs on the road should be called *aśva* (runner), and not the horse alone; everything that pricks, as a needle or spear for instance, should be called *tṛṇa* (pricker) and not a blade of grass alone. (2) Every being should be given as many names as the actions with which that particular being is associated, e. g. a pillar should be called not *sthūṇā* (i. e. which stands upright) only, but also *darā śayā* (i. e. which rests in a hole), and also *sañjanī* (i. e. which is joined with the beams). (3) Only such words should be used in giving names as are regularly derived from roots according to the rules of grammar, so that

[1] *Nirukta*, ii. 2. [2] *Op. cit.* i. 20. [3] *Op. cit.* iv. 1. [4] *Op. cit.* i. 16.

the meaning of the object which they denote, should be quite clear and free from doubt, e.g. *puruṣa* (man) should be *puri-śaya* (i.e. city-dweller); *aśva* (horse) = *aṣṭa* (i. e. runner); *tṛṇa* (grass) = *tardana* (pricker) and so on. (4) If the name of an object is to be determined by its actions, the being precedes the action (e.g. the horse comes into existence before it actually runs), the designation of a being, which is earlier, from an action, which is subsequent to it, is not tenable (perhaps for the reason that it will leave the being nameless during the interval). (5) People indulge in sophistry in explaining names, as for instance, when it is said that earth (*pṛthivī*) is so called on account of its being broad (*prath*), they do not consider as to who made it broad and on what basis.

Rejoinder.

(1) We find that of the beings who perform a particular action, all do not get the same name but only a few, e.g. every one who cuts wood is not called *takṣaka*, but the carpenter alone is so called; it is the ascetic only who is called *pari-vrājaka* (i. e. a wanderer) and not every one who wanders; it is only the sap of the sugar-cane that is called *jīvana* (i. e. enlivening) and not everything that enlivens; it is only the planet Mars that is called *bhūmi-ja* (i. e. earth-born), and not everything that is born from the earth and so on. He seems to imply that there is a law of specialization by which a particular name comes to be exclusively associated with a particular object.

(2) He means to say that in spite of their manifold activities, objects take their name from one particular action, which is the most important and the most special to them, e.g. a carpenter performs many actions, yet he is called *takṣaka* (i. e. a cutter of wood), because the shaping of things by cutting wood is his most important function and can be specially associated with him. Durga has the following comment on it:

त्वमपि पश्यसि वयमपि पश्याम . . . तच्चन् कश्चित्तच्चेत्युच्यते । अन्यस्तच्चन्नपि न तच्चेत्युच्यते । आह कोऽत्र हेतुरिति । शृणु लोकमेव पृच्छ तमेवोपालभस्व न मयैष नियमः क्रत इति । अथ च तद्यथा समानमीहमानानां कश्चिदेवार्थेन संयुज्यते कश्चिन्न . . . । स्वभावतो हि शब्दानां क्रियाजत्वेऽपि सति काञ्चिदेव क्रियामङ्गीकृत्यावस्थिति र्भवतीति । अथवा क्रियातिशयकृतो नियमः स्यात् । यो हि यदतिशयेन करोति तस्यानेकक्रियावत्त्वेऽपि सति तद्धेतुक एव नामधेयप्रतिलम्भो भवतीत्ययं समाधिः । अथवा न ब्रूमो यो यत्र यदा च तच्चति स एव तच्चेति । किं तर्हि यो यदा यत्र तच्चा भवति स एव तच्चेति . . . पश्यामोऽनेकक्रियायुक्तानामप्येकक्रियाकारितो नामधेयप्रतिलम्भो भवति

. . . तत्र यदुक्तमेकस्यानेकक्रियायोगादनेकनामता प्रसज्येतेति । एतदयुक्तम् । यदि चोक्तमनेकेषामेकनामतैकस्य चानेकनामता प्राप्नोति ततश्च व्यवहाराप्रसिद्धिरिति । नहि तदुभयमस्ति । अनेकेषामेकक्रियायोगेऽपि हि सत्येकस्य चानेकक्रियायोगेऽपि हि सति व्यवस्थित एव शब्दनियमः स्वभावत एव लोके ।

'Thou seest, my friend, and we also see, that one man who cuts wood is called 'carpenter', while another who does the same is not so called. You may well ask the reason. Listen; go and ask the world, quarrel with the world if you like, for it is not I who made this law. But this is what we find: of those who do the same work, some are named in accordance with that activity, others not. You may say that because one object is named in accordance with that activity, therefore others doing the same thing should be similarly named . . . Although all nouns are derived from verbs, the choice of names with reference to a particular action is made by nature (*svabhāvataḥ*); or it may be that the choice is made by the law of special action. A man who performs one particular action more specially, whatever other actions he may perform, will obtain his name from that particular action. This is a settled rule. For we do not call the man, who cuts wood now and then, by the name of carpenter, but him we call carpenter who cuts wood at any time, or in any place and always. This is an instance of a name, the choice of which is made by special action and this name may be freely given to others who perform the same action specially. And if sometimes, or somewhere, some other action is still more special to them, they will obtain their names in accordance with that action only. . . .

We see that persons who perform many actions, obtain their names from one particular action. A carpenter performs many other actions, but he is not called after those activities. . . . If it be said, that many persons who perform the same action, should have a common name, and one person who performs many actions, should have as many names, all that we can say is, that it is contrary to the practice of the world. *Neither is the case.* Whether many persons perform a particular action, or a single person many actions, the law about the names is that the choice is made by natural selection.'[1]

With this may be compared the remarks of Bréal.

'One conclusion is to be drawn from all that has gone before: it is an undoubted fact that Language designates things in an incomplete and

[1] Cf. Max Müller's translation of some parts of the above-quoted passage (*ibid.*, p. 167).

inaccurate manner. *Incomplete*: since we have not exhausted all that can be said of the sun when we have declared it to be shining, or of the horse when we say that it trots. *Inaccurate*: since we cannot say of the sun that it shines when it has set, or of the horse that it trots when it is at rest, or when wounded or dead.

Substantives are signs attached to things: they contain exactly that amount of truth which can be contained by a name, an amount which is of necessity small in proportion to the reality of the object. . . . It will be impossible for language to introduce into the word all the ideas which this entity or object awakens in the mind. Language is therefore compelled to choose.'[1]

(3) Many words whose grammatical form is quite regular are used to denote names of objects, such as *vratati* (creeper), *jāgarūka* (wakeful), *darvi-homī* (one who sacrifices with a ladle), &c.

(4) We find that many objects get names which are based on subsequent actions, e. g. the wood-pecker.

(5) If *pṛthivī* (earth) is derived from √*prath* (to be broad) there is no sophistry at all. It is not necessary to consider as to who made it broad and on what basis, for it is broad to the eye.

Thus the question is discussed in the *Nirukta*. The same question is discussed at length in the *Cratylus* also, wherein Plato propounds three theories and makes the three characters in the dialogue their exponents. Hermogenes holds that names are conventional, arbitrarily given, and altered at will. Its antithesis is represented by Cratylus who maintains that they are natural. Socrates takes an intermediate position and admits that names are natural and at the same time have an element of convention as well.[2]

i. Early anti-Vedic Scepticism.

In the fifteenth section of the first chapter of the *Nirukta*, a critic is introduced in the person of Kautsa, who not only questions the authority of the Vedas, but actually maintains that the Vedic stanzas are meaningless, adducing several arguments in support of his assertion. From the twentieth section of the same chapter it is evident that Yāska believes the Vedic hymns to be revealed, having been handed down from generation to generation by oral tradition, and requiring to be studied with great care; the purpose of his own work being to facilitate this study. As the

[1] *Semantics*, ch. xviii, Eng. trans. by Cust, pp. 171, 172.

[2] Cf. Jowett, *Dialogues of Plato* (3rd ed.), vol. i, pp. 327-8, 358, 366, 378.

Nirukta is one of the six auxiliary treatises of the Veda, it is rather difficult to say with what object Yāska presented and tried to controvert the view of his opponents, for it is inconceivable that the learned theologians would reproduce, in their orthodox books, a controversy which challenges the most fundamental beliefs of their religion. The reproduction of the Kautsa controversy indicates on the one hand, that not only Yāska was endowed with a rationalistic spirit, and was free from bigoted fanaticism, but also that it was possible to carry on such discussions with tolerance at that period of remote antiquity; and implies on the other, that Kautsa was an eminent scholar, or some great personality, or the exponent of some philosophic system, whose thought could not be ignored. Some, however, think that Yāska has invented Kautsa as a convenient method of giving expression to Vedic Scepticism. This view is conjectural, and is not supported by any evidence. Yāska uses the terms *eke,* and *ekam, aparam,* &c. when he wants to refer to something in general, and he could have very well employed the same terms with regard to the above-mentioned controversy, had it not been associated with a particular individual, i. e. Kautsa. There is no ground to doubt the historical existence of the authorities whose opinions are quoted, or referred to, or to whom particular statements are attributed, by Yāska. And unless the contrary can be proved, it may be assumed that Kautsa was an historical entity. It may also be taken for granted that he was the leader of a movement, which may be described as something akin to materialistic rationalism, and which was the result of a remarkable literary activity, a characteristic of the epoch of Yāska, as pointed out elsewhere. But Kautsa was by no means the originator of such a movement, the beginning of which can be traced to an earlier period. Its origin is probably to be sought in sectarianism. For a considerable time, the *Atharva-veda* was not recognized as divine revelation. For the followers of the *Atharva-veda,* it was therefore necessary to demonstrate the superiority of their own Veda to the RV., the SV., and the VS. Perhaps the most effective means, employed for the achievement of this object, was to invent legends and allegorical stories, in which all the four Vedas are introduced, and in which a certain task is proposed for them. The RV., the SV., and the VS. are invariably shown to be incompetent in its performance, and it is given up as too difficult by the three Vedas in succession, being finally accomplished by the AV., whose superiority over the other three Vedas is thus implicitly expressed. I quote the following two stories from the Gopatha Brāhmaṇa in support of my statement:

तान्वागभ्युवाच । अश्वः शम्येतेति । तथेति । तमृग्वेद एत्योवाचाहमश्वं शमेयमिति ।

तस्मा अविसृष्टाय महद्भयं ससृजे । स एतां प्राचीं दिशं भेजे । स होवाचाशान्तो न्वयमश्व इति । तं यजुर्वेद एत्योवाचाहमश्वं शमेयमिति । तस्मा अविसृष्टाय महद्भयं ससृजे । सा एतां प्रतीचीं दिशं भेजे । स होवाचाशान्तो न्वयमश्व इति । तं सामवेद एत्योवाचाहमश्वं शमेयमिति । केन नु त्वं शमिष्यसीति । रथन्तरं नाम मे सामाघोरं चाक्रूरं च तेनाश्वमभिष्टूयते । तस्मा अथ विसृष्टाय तदेव महद्भयं ससृजे । स एतामुदीचीं दिशं भेजे । स होवाचाशान्तो न्वयमश्व इति ।

'Speech said to them, "tame the horse". "Be it so", replied they. Having approached him, the RV. said, "I shall tame the horse". When he set about (accomplishing it), a great terror seized him. He turned her in the eastern direction. He declared, "this horse is wild indeed". The VS. approached him and said, "I shall tame the horse". When he set about (accomplishing it), a great terror seized him. He turned her in the western direction. He declared, "this horse is wild indeed". The SV. approached him and said, "I shall tame the horse". "How indeed wilt thou tame the horse?" "*Rathantaram* is the name of my song of praise which is neither terrific, nor harsh. With that the horse is praised". But when he set about (accomplishing it), the same great terror seized him. He turned her in the northern direction. He declared, "the horse is indeed still wild".'[1]

After these futile attempts, they are advised to seek *Ātharvana* the tamer. They approach him and request him to tame the horse. He prepares the water of tranquillity, which he sprinkles over the horse. From every limb of the horse flames fall down on the ground, and the horse, perfectly tame, salutes the sage.

The object of the following story is to show the incompetency of the three Vedas to afford protection:

ते देवा इन्द्रमब्रुवन् । इमन्नस्तावद्यज्ञं गोपाय . . . . स वै नस्तेन रूपेण गोपाय येन नो रूपेण भूयिष्ठं छादयसि येन शच्यसि गोप्तुमिति । स ऋग्वेदो भूत्वा पुरस्तात्परीत्योपातिष्ठत् । तं देवा अब्रुवन् । अन्यत्तद्रूपं कुरुष्व नैतेन नो रूपेण भूयिष्ठं छादयसि नैतेन शच्यसि गोप्तुमिति । स यजुर्वेदो भूत्वा पश्चात्परीत्योपातिष्ठत् । तं देवा अब्रुवन् । अन्यत्तद्रूपं कुरुष्व । नैतेन नो रूपेण भूयिष्ठं छादयसि नैतेन शच्यसि गोप्तुमिति । स सामवेदो भूत्वा उत्तरतः परीत्योपातिष्ठत् । तं देवा अब्रुवन् । अन्यत्तद्रूपं कुरुष्व । नैतेन नो रूपेण भूयिष्ठं छादयसि नैतेन शच्यसि गोप्तुमिति ।

'The gods said to Indra, "Do now protect this sacrifice of ours. Verily protect us with that form of thine, with which thou affordest us the greatest shelter, with which thou canst best protect us'. He assumed the

[1] GB. i. 2. 18; Bib. Ind. ed., p. 35.

form of the RV., and having approached, stood before them. The gods said to him, "assume some other form; with this form thou canst not afford us the greatest shelter, with this form thou canst not best protect us". He assumed the form of the VS., and having approached stood behind them. The gods said to him, "assume some other form; with this form thou canst not afford us the greatest shelter, with this form thou canst not best protect us". He assumed the form of the SV., and, having approached stood to their north. The gods said to him, "assume some other form; with this form thou canst not afford us the greatest shelter, with this form thou canst not best protect us".'[1]

Indra then assumes the form of the *Brahma-veda*, i. e. the *Atharva-veda*, which is approved by the gods as competent to give them the greatest protection.

It need hardly be said that the efforts of the followers of the *Atharva-veda* were crowned with success, for, in course of time, the AV. was recognized as one of the revealed scriptures. But their method of discrediting the other Vedas gave rise to a movement of inquiry and scepticism—a movement, the traces of which can still be discovered in isolated passages of the *Araṇyakas* and the *Upaniṣads*. Besides the fact that the anti-Vedic ideas have been preserved in the *Āraṇyakas* and the *Upaniṣads*, which, according to the orthodox tradition, are a part of the scriptures, indicates that the movement must have been important and wide-spread, so much so that even some of the Vedic Scholars came under its influence, and freely gave expression to their heterodox views, some of which have survived. I quote the following passages in support of the foregoing conclusion:

एतद्ध स्म वै तद्विद्वांस आहुर्ऋषयः कावषेयाः किमर्था वयमध्येष्यामहे किमर्था वयं यक्ष्यामहे। वाचि हि प्राणं जुहुमः प्राणे वा वाचं यो ह्येव प्रभवः स एवाप्ययः।

'Verily it was so, then the Kāvaṣeyas, the learned seers, said, "to what purpose shall we study the Vedas, to what purpose shall we sacrifice? We sacrifice breath in speech, and speech in breath; whosoever is born is indeed the authoritative person."'[2]

उक्थमुक्थमिति वै प्रजा वदन्ति तदिदमेवोक्थमियमेव पृथिवीतो हीदं सर्वमुत्तिष्ठति यदिदं किञ्च।

'People say, "Hymn, Hymn". This earth indeed, is the hymn, for all, whatever exists springs from it.'[3]

The study of the Vedas is regarded as *avidyā* (non-knowledge) in MU.

[1] GB. i. 2. 19; Bib. Ind. ed., p. 36.
[2] A. A. iii. 2. 6; Keith's ed., p. 139.
[3] A. A. ii. 1. 2; Keith's ed., p. 101.

I. 1. 4–5; as lower knowledge in MU. III. 2. 3; KU. I. 2. 23. The full force of this condemnation will be realized, if it is borne in mind that the *Upaniṣads* are also regarded as revealed books (*śruti*). The case would be analogous if, for instance, St. Paul had declared in one of his epistles that the study of the Bible is non-knowledge, or lower knowledge. The following are the other anti-Vedic passages: *Bṛh. U.*, I. 5. 23; *Kau. U.*, II. 5; *Ch. U.*, V. 11–24; *TU.*, II. 5; *Vivekacūḍāmaṇi* 2; the Jain *Uttarādhyāyana sūtras*, IV. 12; XIV. 12; *Gītā*, II, 42, 45; IX. 21: XI. 48, 53. In order to reconcile them with the pro-Vedic doctrines, the commentators have offered ingenious explanations of these passages.

It is possible that the Buddha came under the influence of this anti-Vedic movement at an early period, which may be responsible for his vehement denunciation not only of Vedic rites and practices, injunctions, and invocations, &c., but of Vedic lore. He held them up to ridicule, and discarded them as an obstacle to final emancipation. His views about Vedic knowledge have been preserved in the form of a dialogue in the *Tevijja sutta* in the *Dīgha Nikāya*. Two Brāhmaṇās, Vāsettha and Bhāradvāja quarrel as to which is the true path. Unable to settle their dispute, they go to the Buddha for a decision. The Buddha holds a conversation with them, and after perplexing and confounding them with analogies and arguments in a Socratic manner, gradually leads them to his own way of thinking, and finally converts them to Buddhism. The important parts of the dialogue with regard to the Vedas are the following:

13. 'Well then, Vāsettha, those ancient *Ṛṣis* of the Brāhmaṇās versed in the three Vedas, the authors of the verses . . . to wit, . . . Vāmadeva, Vessāmitta, Jamadaggi, Āṅgirasa, Bhāradvāja, Vāsettha, Kassapa, and Bhagu—did even they speak thus, saying: "We know it, we have seen it, where Brahmā is, whence Brahmā is, whither Brahmā is?"

"Not so, Gautama!"

15. . . . "Just, Vāsettha, as when a string of blind men are clinging to one another, neither can the foremost see, nor can the middle one see, nor can the hindmost see—just even so, methinks, Vāsettha, is the talk of the Brāhmaṇās versed in the three Vedas but blind talk . . . the talk . . . of the Brāhmaṇās versed in the three Vedas turns out to be ridiculous, mere words, a vain and empty thing."

24. "Again, Vāsettha, if this river Aciravati were full of water even to the brim, and overflowing, and a man with business on the other side, bound for the other side, should come up, and want to cross over, and he, standing on this bank, should invoke the farther bank, and say, 'Come hither, O Farther Bank! Come over to this side!'"

"Now what think you, Vāsettha? Would the farther bank of the river Aciravati, by reason of that man's invoking and praying and hoping and praising, come over to this side?"

"Certainly not, Gautama!"

25. "In just the same way, Vāsettha, do the Brāhmaṇās versed in the three Vedas . . . say thus: 'Indra we call upon, Soma we call upon, Varuṇa we call upon, Īsāna we call upon, Pajāpati we call upon, Brahmā we call upon . . .' Verily, Vāsettha, . . that they, by reason of their invoking and praying and hoping and praising, should after death . . . become united with Brahmā—verily such a condition of things can in no wise be."

35. ". . . Therefore is it that the threefold wisdom of the Brāhmaṇās, wise in their three Vedas, is called a waterless desert, their threefold wisdom is called a pathless jungle, their threefold wisdom is called perdition."'[1]

In criticism of this, it may be remarked that the views of the Buddha concerning Vedic prayer are erroneous. His arguments, and especially his analogy of the bank of the Aciravati, are applicable to any other prayer as well, and thus prayer itself will become an absurdity. Not only is prayer a very important act of worship in every religion, but in the form of the wheel of prayer is the most distinguishing characteristic of Tibetan Buddhism. Moreover, prayer is a psychical phenomenon, it exerts a powerful influence on the mind through the medium of subconscious suggestion, and as such its efficacy is beyond doubt. Further, the analogy of the Buddha is fallacious. To compare not only sentient but omniscient and omnipotent God with an inanimate piece of matter like the bank of a river, and then to deduce a conclusion from this comparison that because the latter does not respond to prayer hence the former also does not do so, is altogether unjustifiable. Nevertheless the Buddha's denunciation of the Vedas developed a strong contempt for them in his followers who often trampled them under foot.[2] It is also probable that these teachings of the Buddha inspired other non-Vedic schools as well. The criticisms of some of these schools are equally vehement, and one seems to hear the reverberated echo of the voice of the Buddha even in some of their expressions. The following passage gives the views of the Cārvāka system:

इति चेत् तदपि न प्रमाणकोटिं प्रवेष्टुमीष्टे । अनृतव्याघातपुनरुक्तदोषैर्दूषिततया वैदिकमन्यैरेव धूर्तवकैः परस्परं कर्मकाण्डप्रामाण्यवादिभि ज्ञानकाण्डस्य ज्ञानकाण्डप्रामाण्यवादिभिः कर्मकाण्डस्य च प्रतिक्षिप्तत्वेन त्रय्या धूर्तप्रलापमात्रत्वेनाग्निहोत्रादेर्जीविकामात्रप्रयोजनत्वात् । तथा चाह भाणकः ।

[1] The *Dialogues of the Buddha*, translated into English by Rhys-Davids, *S.B.B.*, vol. ii, pp. 304–14: cf. also *S.B.E.*, vol. xi, pp. 159–203.

[2] See *Śaṅkaradigvijaya*, the episode of Kumārila Bhaṭṭa's life in a Buddhist monastery.

अग्निहोत्रं त्रयोवेदास्त्रिदण्डं भस्मगुण्ठनम्।
बुद्धिपौरुषहीनानां जीविकेति बृहस्पतिः॥
पशुश्चेन्निहितः स्वर्गं ज्योतिष्टोमे गमिष्यति।
स्वपिता यजमानेन तत्र कस्मान्न हिंस्यते॥

. . . .

त्रयो वेदस्य कर्तारो भण्डधूर्तनिशाचराः।
जर्फरीतुर्फरीत्यादि पण्डितानां वचः स्मृतम्॥

'If you object . . . "how should men of experienced wisdom engage in the Agnihotra and other sacrifices", . . . your objection cannot be accepted as any proof to the contrary, since the Agnihotra, &c. are only useful as means of livelihood, for the Veda is tainted by the three faults of untruth, self-contradiction, and tautology; then again the impostors who call themselves Vedic Paṇḍits are mutually destructive, as the authority of the Jñānakāṇḍa is overthrown by those who maintain that of the Karmakāṇḍa, and vice versā; and lastly, the three Vedas themselves are only the incoherent rhapsodies of knaves, and to this effect runs the popular saying: Bṛihaspati says that the (performance of) Agnihotra, the three Vedas, the three staves, and smearing oneself with ashes, are but means of livelihood for those who have neither sense, nor manliness.'[1]

'If a beast, slain in the *jyotiṣṭoma* sacrifice goes to heaven, why then, does not the sacrificer kill his own father?'[2]

'The three authors of the Veda were buffoons, knaves, and spirits of darkness. *Jarpharī, turpharī*, &c., these are the well-known rhapsodies of the Paṇḍits.'[3]

The *Ārhata* system has the following criticism with regard to the Vedas:

अनादेरागमस्यार्थो न च सर्वज्ञ आदिमान्।
कृत्रिमेण त्वसत्येन स कथं प्रतिपाद्यते॥

'And a non-eternal omniscient being cannot be the subject of an eternal Veda; then how can he be expounded by a spurious and a false Veda?'[4]

Cf. also: 'There was neither the Sāma-veda, nor the Yajur-veda, nor the Ṛg-veda, nor was any work done by man.'[5]

The earlier anti-Vedic scepticism, together with the doctrines of the Buddhist, the Cārvāka, and the Ārhata systems must have created, in

[1] *Sarva-darśana-saṃgrahaḥ*, Bib. Ind. ed., p. 3. For this passage I have adopted Cowell's translation with some modifications.

[2] *Op. cit.*, p. 6.

[3] *Loc. cit.*

[4] *Op. cit.*, p. 28.

[5] *Mahābhārata Vanaparvan*, 11234.

course of time, a considerable amount of opposition to the teachings of the Vedas. It was therefore necessary for the followers of the Vedas to answer the objections of their opponents and to re-establish their position. Hence Jaimini was compelled to devote almost the whole of the first *adhyāya* of the *Pūrva-Mīmāṁsā* to the examination and refutation of such objections. The substance of Kautsa's criticism, together with the subject-matter of Yāska's rejoinder is amplified with numerous additions in the first chapter of the PM. The controversy, however, is too long to be quoted here. Kumārila Bhaṭṭa, the commentator on the PM. was another expounder of Vedic doctrines, and after him the task devolved on the great Śaṅkarācārya, who by his eloquence, vast learning, profound philosophy, and great powers of debate rebuilt the shattered supremacy of the Vedic religion, and extirpated Buddhism [1] and other non-Vedic systems from the land of their birth. But adverse critics of the Veda, even after the great Śaṅkarācārya, have not been altogether unknown in India. For instance, Nānaka, the founder of the Sikh religion, may be mentioned as a notable teacher who laid great emphasis on saintliness, and discarded the Vedas as mere mythical records. He said:

Santa kī mahimā veda na jāṇe
Cāron veda kahāni.

'The greatness of a saint is not known to the Veda; all the four Vedas are merely (books of) stories.'

Hence we find that Sāyaṇācārya again reverts to the same discussion in the introduction of his commentary on the Ṛg-veda. The number of arguments for and against is still further increased. A brief summary of the controversy is subjoined:

Criticism.

'The *primâ facie* view is that there is no such thing as the Veda; how can there be a part of it, as the Ṛg-veda? . . . . It is not possible to admit the existence of the Veda, for it is not capable of definition or proof.' [2]

(1) If the Veda is defined as being the last of three kinds of proofs, perception, inference, and evidence, the definition will be too wide, for it will include the Smṛtis as well.

(2) If the Veda is defined as an instrument of apprehending transcendental things, the definition will again suffer from the same defect.

[1] However, the final blow was dealt by the Mohammedan invaders, who destroyed the Buddhist monasteries in the Northern part of India.

[2] See Max Müller's edition[2] of the RV. with the commentary of Sāyaṇācārya, vol. i, pp. 2-3. The Sanskrit text of the introductory part of Sāyaṇa's commentary, together with an English translation, is given by Peterson in his *Handbook to the Study of the Ṛgveda*, Part I.

(3) The qualifying expression, 'being not the product of human authors', will not improve the definition, for the Vedas are the works of human authors, though they may be super-men.

(4) If you say that by 'human authors' you mean 'men having a corporeal frame', we will draw your attention to the *puruṣa-sūkta*.

(5) If you say that by 'corporeal frame' you mean 'a body which is the result of the actions of a previous life', we will point out that Agni, Vāyu, and Āditya, the authors of the Vedas, were endowed with bodies which were the result of actions of a previous life.

(6) If the Veda is defined as a collection of words (*śabda-rāśiḥ*) consisting of the *mantra* and the *Brāhmaṇa*, it does not hold good, for up till now it has not been settled what is *mantra*, and what is *Brāhmaṇa*.

(7) Nor is there any proof of the existence of the Veda. The scriptural quotations in support of your contention are useless, as they are cited from the Vedas themselves, and nothing can be proved by its own evidence. No man, however clever, can mount his own shoulders.

(8) If you say that the consensus of public opinion is in favour of the Vedas, we will reply that the whole world can be deluded; for instance, the people believe in a blue sky, yet there is no such thing as sky, nor has its blue colour any reality.

Sāyaṇa's rejoinder.

(1) The definition of the Veda as a collection of words, consisting of the *mantra* and the *Brāhmaṇa* is faultless; therefore Āpastamba has said, 'The Veda is the name given to the *mantra* and the *Brāhmaṇa*.'

(2) It is true that things like a jar, or a piece of cloth, &c., are not self-luminous, but it does not follow from this that the sun, and the stars, &c., too have no such character. Granting that it is impossible for a man to mount his own shoulders, nevertheless, the Vedas have the power to illuminate themselves as well as other things.

(3) You have to recognize the various kinds of proofs, including evidence. And the evidence of the Smṛtis, and of tradition cannot but be admitted as proof of the existence of the Veda. Hence, the Vedas cannot be overthrown by any of the infidels like the followers of Cārvāka.

Further criticism.

(1) Admitting that there exists a thing called the Veda, it is not worth a commentary, for the Veda is of no authority (*na hi Vedaḥ pramānam*).

(2) Some define authority as 'an instrument of sound experience', others as 'a means of acquiring knowledge, not known before'. Neither of these is to be found in the Veda.

Then follows an amplified statement of Kautsa's criticism. Sāyaṇa's reply gives the substance of Yāska's rejoinder with additions and modifications, to which is added a long quotation from the first chapter of the *pūrva-Mīmāṃsā,* reference to which has already been made.

It would be superfluous to collect the pro-Vedic passages. The Vedas are the foundation of the whole of Sanskrit literature. But the triumph of the Vedic school is apparent from this fact alone that all the anti-Vedic systems have either perished, or been driven into exile, or been reduced to insignificance. Thus the pre-Buddhistic anti-Vedic scepticism can now be traced in a few isolated passages only. Buddhism, once the state religion of the Mauryan Empire at its zenith under Aśoka,—the then greatest Empire in the world—has been banished from its native land. The Cārvāka and the Ārhata systems have been reduced to insignificance. Their followers are few and far between, and their influence on Indian thought and religion is so small that for all practical purposes it can be safely ignored.

PART II

ENGLISH TRANSLATION

PREFACE

It is my most pleasant duty to thank Professor A. A. Macdonell for looking through the proofs of this volume, but for any errors that remain I am entirely responsible. I have also to thank the University of the Punjab, Lahore, for a generous subvention, without which it would not have been possible to publish the present volume so early.

L. S.

LIST OF ABBREVIATIONS

AA. = Aitareya Āraṇyaka.
AB. = Aitareya Brāhmaṇa.
AP. = Atharva Veda Prātiśākhya.
Ap. Dh. = Āpastamba Dharma Sūtra.
AV. = Atharva Veda.
Bau. = Baudhāyana Dharma Sūtra.
Bhāg.Pu. = Bhāgavata Purāṇa.
Bib. Ind. = Bibliotheca Indica.
Bṛh. D. = Bṛhad-devatā.
Bṛh. U. = Bṛhadāraṇyakopaniṣad.
Ga. = Gautama.
Ga. Dh. = Gautama Dharma Sūtra.
GB. = Gopatha Brāhmaṇa.
IA. = Indian Antiquary.
Īśā U. = Īśāvāsyopaniṣad.
KB. = Kauṣītaki Brāhmaṇa.
KS. = Kāṭhaka Saṃhitā.
Mahān.U. = Mahānārāyaṇa Upaniṣad.
MB. = Mahābhāṣya.
Mbh. = Mahābhārata.
MS. = Maitrāyaṇī Saṃhitā.
MW. = Monier Williams' Dictionary.
N. = Nirukta.
Ngh. = Nighaṇṭu.
N. Su. = Nyāya Sūtra.
Pā. = Pāṇini.
Pu. = Purāṇa.
PM. = Pūrva Mīmāṃsā.
R. Kh. = Ṛgvidhāna Khaṇḍa.
RP. or RPr. = Ṛgveda Prātiśākhya.
RV. = Ṛgveda.
R. Vidh. = Ṛgvidhāna Khaṇḍa.
RVKh. = Ṛgvidhāna Khaṇḍa.
Ṣaḍ. B. = Ṣaḍviṃśa Brāhmaṇa.
ŚB. = Śatapatha Brāhmaṇa.
S. Su. = Sāṃkhya Sūtra.
SV. = Sāma Veda.
SV. B. = Sāmavidhāna Brāhmaṇa.
Śveta. U. = Śvetāśvataropaniṣad.
TA. = Taittirīya Āraṇyaka.
Taṇḍ. B. = Tāṇḍya Brāhmaṇa.
TB. = Taittirīya Brāhmaṇa.
TPr. = Taittirīya Prātiśākhya.
TS. = Taittirīya Saṃhitā.
U. Su. = Uṇādi Sūtra.
Va. = Vasiṣṭha Dharma Śāstra.
Vai. Su. = Vaiśeṣika Sūtra.
VP.,VPr. = Vājasaneyi Prātiśākhya.
VS. = Vājasaneyi Saṃhitā.
VSu. = Vedānta Sūtra.
Ya. or Yājña. = Yājñavalkya Smṛti.

THE NIRUKTA

CHAPTER I

A TRADITIONAL list (of words) has been handed down (to us). It is to be (here) explained. This same list is called *Ni-ghaṇṭavas*.[1] From what (root) is (the word) *Ni-ghaṇṭavas* derived? They are words quoted from the Vedas (*ni-gamāḥ*).[2] Having been repeatedly gathered together [3] from Vedic hymns, they have been handed down by tradition. Aupamanyava holds that, as these are the quoted words of the Vedas, they are called *Ni-ghaṇṭavas* on account of their being quoted (*ni-gamanāt*). Or else (the word *Ni-ghaṇṭavas*) may be (so called) from being fixed only (√*han*), i.e. (a list, in which) they (the words) are fixed together, or collected together (√*hṛ*).

Now, what (are) the four classes [4] of words? They are the following: noun and verb; prepositions and particles. With reference to this, they [5] thus prescribe the definition of noun and verb: the verb has *becoming* as its fundamental notion,[6] nouns have *being* as their fundamental notion.[7] But where both are dominated by *becoming*, a *becoming* arising from a former to a later state is denoted by a verb, as 'he goes', 'he cooks',[8] &c. The embodiment of the whole process from the beginning to the end, which

[1] Cf. Muir, *Sanskrit Texts*, vol. ii, p. 165.

[2] Durga explains *ni-gamāḥ* as: *niś-cayenā-dhikaṁ vā ni-gūḍhārthā ete parijñāthāḥ santo mantrārthān gamayanti jñāpayanti.*

[3] Roth adopted the variant *samāhatya* on the principle, *lectio difficilior potior est*, but this reading is not supported by the evidence of MSS., and, later on, was admitted to be unjustified by Roth himself; see *Erläuterungen*, i. 1, p. 4.

[4] Cf. RP. xii. 5. 699; VP. viii. 52; AP. i. 1; Kauṭilya, *Arthaśāstra*, ii. 10. 28, p. 72; Patañjali, *Mahābhāṣya*, i. 1. 1, Kielhorn's edition, p. 3; Dionysius of Halicarnassus on *Literary Composition*, ch. ii, Roberts's edition, p. 71; Aristotle, *Poetics*, 20, 1456^b 1, Bywater's edition, p. 57; Wackernagel, *Altindische Grammatik*, vol. i, p. lxviii; cf. also *Dharma Saṁgrahaḥ*, xxxv, *Anecdota Oxoniensia*, vol. i, part V, p. 7.

[5] i. e. Preceptors. Durga.

[6] Identical with Bṛh. D. ii. 121, see Professor Macdonell, *Bṛhaddevatā*, vol. ii, p. 65; cf. Kauṭilya, *Arthaśāstra*, *loc. cit.*; RP. xii. 5, 701, 707; VP. viii. 54; the commentator on AP., *J.A.O.S.*, vol. vii, p. 591; PM. ii. 1. 1; Patañjali, *Mahābhāṣya* i. 3. 1, Kielhorn's edition, vol. i, pp. 254, 256; Aristotle, *Poetics*, 20, 1456^b 10, Bywater's edition, p. 58; Gune's trans. IA., vol. xlv, 158.

[7] The same as note 6 except Bṛh. D.; cf. Jowett, *Dialogues of Plato*, vol. i, pp. 368-9: 'Name is not a musical or pictorial imitation . . . but it is expression of the essence of each thing in letters and syllables.'

[8] Cf. Professor Macdonell, *Bṛhaddevatā*, vol. ii, p. 10; cf. Durga's Comm. Cf. PM. ii. 1. 3-4.

has assumed the character of *being*, is denoted by a noun, as 'going', 'cooking', &c. The demonstrative pronoun[1] is a reference to *beings*, as 'cow', 'horse', 'man', 'elephant', &c.;[2] 'to be', to *becoming*, as 'he sits', 'he sleeps', 'he goes', 'he stands', &c.

According to Audumbarāyaṇa speech is permanent in the organs only.[3]

(*Here ends the first section.*[4])

In that case the fourfold division (of words) will not hold good, nor the grammatical connexion, nor the mutual reference of sounds which are not produced simultaneously.[5] Words are used to designate objects, with regard to everyday affairs in the world, on account of their comprehensiveness and minuteness.[6] They, too, are the names of gods as well as of human beings.[7] On account of the impermanence of human knowledge, the stanza, (directing) the accomplishment of action, is (to be found) in the Veda.[8]

According to Vārṣyāyaṇi, there are six modifications of *becoming*: genesis, existence, alteration, growth, decay, and destruction.[9] Genesis denotes only the commencement of the first state, but neither affirms nor denies the later. Existence affirms a being that has been produced. Alteration connotes the modification of elements of a non-decaying being.[10] Growth denotes the increase of one's own limbs or of objects which are associated (with one's self), as he grows by means of victory, or he grows with his

[1] Cf. Patañjali, *Mahābhāṣya: sarvanāma ca sāmānyavāci*: 'And the pronoun is the general exponent.'

[2] Patañjali, *op. cit.* i. 1. 1, vol. i, pp. 1 and 5.

[3] Cf. Patañjali, *op. cit.* i. 1. 1, vol. i, p. 6; i. 1, 6, vol. i, p. 104; i. 1. 8, vol. i, p. 136; i. 4. 4, vol. i, p. 356; Bhandarkar, *Wilson Philological Lectures*, p. 291; Jowett, *Dialogues of Plato*, vol. i, pp. 327, 387, 388; Jaimini; PM. i. 1. 6–23; the *Vedānta sūtras*, i. 3. 28; 4. 28; ii. 1. 4; Kaṇāda, *Vaiśeṣika sūtras*, ii. 2. 21–37; the *Sāṁkhya-pravacana sūtras*, v. 58–60; the *Nyāya sūtras*, i. 1. 7, 54–7; ii. 2. 13–17; iii. 2. 49; the origin and nature of *Śabda* is a subject for discussion in the Buddhist literature also: *Sadda* is an action, *Kathāvatthu*, xii. 3; *Sadda* is physical vibrations, *op. cit.* ix. 9–10; Eng. trans. entitled, 'Points of Controversy', is by S. Z. Aung and C. A. F. Rhys Davids.

[4] Cf. Gune, I. A., *loc. cit.*

[5] Cf. Gune, I. A, *loc. cit.*

[6] Cf. Durga's Comm.; Jowett, *Dialogues of Plato*, vol. i, p. 368.

[7] Cf. Jowett, *op. cit.*, vol. i, p. 333: Soc. 'He often speaks of them; notably and nobly in the places where he distinguishes the different names which gods and men give to the same things', i.e. words are used in giving names to things both by gods and men.

[8] This is tantamount to the statement that the Veda is the repository of eternal and perfect knowledge.

[9] Cf. Bṛh. D. ii. 121; see Professor Macdonell, *Bṛhaddevatā*, vol. ii, p. 65; the passage is quoted verbatim by Patañjali, *op. cit.* i. 3. 1, vol. i, p. 258, except that he calls Vārṣyāyaṇi, *bhagavān*, and uses the past tense.

[10] The word *a-pracyavamānasya* is used by Yāska in order to show that alteration—which may be for better or for worse—is to be interpreted as denoting the former only and not the latter.

body. The term decay denotes its antithesis. Destruction denotes the commencement of the later state, but neither affirms nor denies the former.

(*Here ends the second section.*)

Hence, other modifications of *becoming* are only further developments of those (enumerated above), and should be inferred according to the occasion.

'Unconnected prepositions', says Śākaṭayana, 'have no meaning, but only express a subordinate sense of nouns and verbs.'[1] 'They have various meanings,' says Gārgya; 'hence, whatever their meaning may be, they express that meaning (which brings about) modification in the sense of the noun and the verb.'[2] The word *ā* is used in the sense of 'hitherward';[3] *pra* and *parā* are its antitheses: *abhi*,[4] 'towards'; *prati* is its antithesis: *ati* and *su*, 'approval'; *nir* and *dur* are their antitheses: *ni* and *ava*, 'downwards'; *ud* is their antithesis: *sam*, 'combination'; *vi* and *apa* are its antitheses: *anu*, 'similarity' and 'succession': *api*, 'contact': *upa*, 'accession': *pari*, 'being all around': *adhi*, 'being above', or 'supremacy'.[5] Thus they express various meanings to which attention should be paid.[6]

(*Here ends the third section.*)

Now the particles occur in various senses,[7] both in a comparative sense, in a conjunctive sense,[8] and as expletives. Of them, the following four are used in the sense of comparison.[9] *Iva* (has this sense) both in the classical and in the Vedic Sanskrit: thus 'like Agni', 'like Indra', &c. The word *na* has the sense of negation in classical, and both (i.e. the sense of negation and comparison) in Vedic Sanskrit: thus in the passage, 'They did not recognize

[1] Cf. RP. xii. 5. 707; *upasargo viśeṣa-kṛt*: 'The preposition is the specializer (of meaning)'; VP. viii. 54-5; AP. iv. 3; see Whitney, *J.A.O.S.*, vol. vii, p. 515; Pāṇini, *Aṣṭādhyāyī* i. 4. 58: *prādaya(ḥ) upasargāḥ kriyā-yoge*; Patañjali, *op. cit.* i. 3. 1, vol. i, p. 256: 'A preposition is the distinguishing mark of an action'; cf. also ii. 1. 1, vol. i, p. 365.

[2] Cf. RP. xii. 6. 702-3: 'Prepositions are twenty and they express a meaning together with the other two (i.e. noun and verb)'; Patañjali, *op. cit.* i. 3. 1, vol. i, p. 356: 'But again individual prepositions express the distinction of actions, whenever a word which denotes the same action is used.'

[3] Cf. Pāṇini, *op. cit.* i. 4. 89.

[4] *Op. cit.* i. 4. 91.

[5] Cf. RP. xii. 6. 702-3; VP. vi. 24; Pāṇini, *op. cit.* i. 4. 53; the list of prepositions in RP. and VP. is identical with that of the *Nirukta*, but enumerated in a different order; it is also identical with the list in the *gaṇa-pāṭha*, if the double forms of *niḥ* and *duḥ* are not taken into consideration; cf. also AP. i. 15; the list is incomplete and only half of that given in RP., VP., N., and Pā; prepositions are explained by Pāṇini, *op. cit.* i. 4. 83-97; Patañjali, *op. cit.* i. 4. 4, vol. i, pp. 341, 345-9; Professor Macdonell, *Vedic Grammar*, pp. 414-21; cf. also *A Vedic Grammar for Students*, pp. 208, 211-53, 265-6.

[6] The sentence is omitted by Durga.

[7] Cf. RP. xii. 9. 708: *nipātānām arthavaśān nipātanād ... itare ca sārthakāḥ*.

[8] Cf. Bṛh. D. ii. 89, Professor Macdonell's edition, vol. i, p. 19.

[9] *Op. cit.* ii. 91.

Indra as a god',[1] it has the sense of negation.[2] The established use is (to place it immediately) before that which it makes negative. In the passage 'Like hard drinkers of wine',[3] it has the sense of comparison. The established use is (to place it immediately) after that with which it compares. The word *cid* has many meanings. In the sentence 'Will the teacher kindly explain it?' it is used in the (sense of) respect. [From what root is (the word) *ācārya* derived?] [4] *Ā-cārya* (teacher) is so called because he imparts traditional precepts (*ā-cāra*); [5] or because he systematically arranges (*ā*+√*ci*+*artha*) the various objects (of knowledge), or because he systematically develops the intellectual faculty.[6] In the expression 'like curd', it is used in the sense of comparison; in 'bring even the sour gruel', it is used in the sense of contempt. *Kul-māṣāḥ* (sour gruels) are so called because they are wasted away (*sīdanti*) in families (*kuleṣu*).[7] The word *nu* has many meanings. In the sentence 'therefore he will do it', it is used in assigning a reason; in 'how pray will he do it?' in asking a question, as well as in 'has he really done it?' It is also used in the sense of comparison (as follows):

Of thee like the branches of a tree, O widely invoked one! [8]

Of thee like the branches of a tree, O widely invoked one!

Vayāḥ means branches, (and) is derived from (the root) *vī* (to move): they move in the wind.[9] *Śā-khāḥ* (branches) are so called because they rest in the sky (*kha-śayāḥ*), or (the word) may be derived from (the root) *śak* (to be able).[9]

Now a conjunctive particle is that by whose addition separateness of notions is indeed recognized, but not like an enumerative one, i.e. because of a separation by isolation.[10] The word *ca* is used in the sense of 'aggregation', and is joined together with both, as 'I and you, O slayer of Vṛtra!' [11] *ā* is used in the same sense, as 'for gods and for manes'.[12] The word *vā* is used in the sense of deliberation, as 'Ah, shall I put this earth here or there?' [13] Moreover, it is used in the sense of 'aggregation' (as follows).

(*Here ends the fourth section.*)

[1] x. 86. 1; N. 13. 4.

[2] The passage beginning from, 'Of them ... negation', is translated by Muir; see *Sanskrit Texts*, vol. ii, p. 151.

[3] viii. 2. 12.

[4] The passage within square brackets is omitted by MSS. of the shorter recension.

[5] Cf. Patañjali, *op. cit.* i. 1. 3, p. 38.

[6] The passage beginning, 'From what root ... intellectual faculty', is omitted by Durga.

[7] The sentence is omitted by Durga.

[8] vi. 24. 3.

[9] The sentence is omitted by Durga.

[10] Cf. Gune, IA., vol. xlv, pp. 159-60; see note; cf. Aristotle's definition of a conjunction; *Poetics*, 20, 1457[a] (ed. Bywater), p. 59.

[11] viii. 62. 11.

[12] x. 16. 11.

[13] x. 119. 9.

'Vāyu and thee, Manu and thee.'[1] The words *aha* and *ha* have the sense of 'mutual opposition', and are combined with the former (member), as 'let this man do this, the other that', and 'this man will do this, not that', &c. The letter *u* is also used in the same sense, (being joined) with the later (member), as 'these people tell a lie, those the truth'; it is further used as an expletive, as 'this', 'that'. The word *hi* has many meanings: in (the sentence) 'therefore he will do it', it (is used) to point out the reason; in (the sentence) 'how pray will he do it?' to ask a question; in (the sentence) 'how *can* he analyse it?' to (indicate) displeasure. The word *kila* (is used to express) superiority of knowledge, as 'thus truly it happened'.

Moreover, it is combined with the two (particles) *na* and *nanu* in asking a question, as 'was it not so?' and 'was it so, pray?' The word *mā* denotes prohibition, as 'do not do it', and 'do not take'. The word *khalu* also (denotes prohibition), as 'enough of doing this', and 'have done with it'; further, it is used as an expletive, as 'thus it happened'. The word *śaśvat* has the sense of uncertainty in classical Sanskrit: (in the sentence) 'was it ever so?' it (is used) in an interrogation; (in the sentence) 'was it ever so pray?' in an interrogation but not to oneself. The word *nūnam* has the sense of uncertainty in the classical language, both, i.e. the sense of uncertainty and that of an expletive, in Vedic Sanskrit.[2]

Agastya, having assigned an oblation to Indra, desired to offer it to the Maruts. Indra, having presented himself, lamented (as follows).[3]

(*Here ends the fifth section.*)

There, it seems, it does not exist; there is no to-morrow; who knows that which is not past? The mind of another is apt to waver; lo! the expected is lost.[4]

There, it seems, it does not exist, i.e. there is no to-day nor[5] indeed to-morrow. To-day, on this day. *Dyuḥ* is a synonym of day (so called) because it is bright (√*dyut*). To-morrow, the time that is still expected. Yesterday, the time that has expired. 'Who knows that which is not past?' i.e. who knows that which is yet to come (i.e. the future)? This

[1] TS. i. 7. 7. 2.

[2] Cf. Muir's translation of the sentence, *Sanskrit Texts*, vol. ii, p. 151: 'The particle "nūnam" is used in the *bhāṣā* to signify uncertainty; in the Veda, too, it has that signification, and is also a mere expletive.'

[3] Cf. the story related in Bṛh. D. iv. 46–51; Professor Macdonell's ed., vol. ii, pp. 138–9; see also the different versions of the story, Sieg, *Sagenstoffe des Ṛgveda*, pp. 108–20.

[4] i. 70. 1.

[5] Durga paraphrases *no* by *asmad-artham*. He is wrong, for *no* is accented and could not therefore mean 'for us', i.e. it is not = *nas*, but a compound of the negative particle *na* + *u*. Cf. N. 1. 7.

other word *adbhutam* (' wonderful ') = *abhūtam*, i. e. something which, as it were, is unprecedented. ' The mind of another is apt to waver ', i. e. fickle. Another,[1] a person not to be introduced (to good people). *Cittam* (mind) is derived from (the root) *cit* (to know), ' Lo! the expected is lost ', [even the assigned thing is lost],[2] assigned, i. e. a thing intended (for offering).

Moreover, it (*nūnam*) is used as an expletive.

(*Here ends the sixth section.*)

May that rich reward of thine, O Indra! milk every boon for the singer. Be helpful to the worshippers, do not put us aside, let good fortune (come) to us; may we speak loudly in the assembly with heroes.[3]

May that (reward) of thine milk every boon for the singer. Boon, what is to be chosen. Singer, praiser. Rich reward, i. e. abounding in wealth. The word *magham* is a synonym of wealth, it is derived from (the root) *maṃh*, meaning to give.[4] *Dakṣiṇā* (reward) is derived from (the root) *dakṣ*, meaning to cause to accomplish: it causes the imperfect to be accomplished. Or else, it may be (so called) from circumambulating. With reference to the quarter, (it means) the quarter natural to the hand, i. e. the right hand.[5] *Dakṣiṇaḥ* (right) is derived from (the root) *dakṣ*, meaning to work strenuously, or from *dāś*, meaning to give. *Hastaḥ* (hand) is derived from (the root) *han* (to strike): it is quick to strike. Fulfil the desires of the worshippers. Do not pass us over, do not give, leaving us aside. Let good fortune be for us. May we speak loudly in our own assembly. *Bhaga* (good fortune) is derived from (the root) *bhaj* (to distribute).[6] The word *bṛhat* is a synonym of ' great ': it is grown all round. Having heroes, or having blessed heroes. A hero, he disperses (*vi-īrayati*) the enemies, or it (*vī-ra*) may be derived from (the root) *vī*, meaning to go, or from *vīr* (to be powerful).[7]

[1] Explained by Durga as an offspring of a low-class man who lives in various ways, or who is not to be brought to the assembly of the good.

[2] The passage within square brackets is omitted by the MSS. of the shorter recension and Durga.

[3] ii. 11. 21.

[4] Cf. Patañjali, *op. cit.* vi. 1. 1, vol. iii, p. 16.

[5] This is tantamount to the statement that the word *dakṣiṇā* also means ' the southern quarter '. Durga remarks: *prāṅmukhasya prajāpater yato dakṣiṇo hasto babhūva sā dakṣiṇā dig abhavat*, i. e. the quarter to the right hand of *Prajāpati*, while he stood facing the east, became the southern quarter. The expression, ' natural to the hand ', is to be understood as being pointed out by the right hand while one faces the eastern direction.

[6] The sentence is omitted by Durga.

[7] Durga paraphrases *Vīrayati* by *nānāprakāram mārayati*, i. e. ' he kills in various ways '. He seems to take *vīr* as a non-compound root, and is supported in this interpretation by *Dhātupātha*, xxxv. 49, where *vīr* is enumerated as a verb of the tenth class. But Yāska appears to take it as a compound of *vi* + *īr* (to disperse), for he distinguishes it from the denominative verb, cf. his third derivation.

The word *sīm* has the sense of totality, or is (used) as an expletive:[1]

Āditya sent them forth.[2]

Sent them forth, i. e. sent them forth on all sides. And also:

From all sides the wise one has manifested bright rays.[3]

i. e. The sun has uncovered (them) on all sides. *Su-rucaḥ* means the rays of the sun, (so called) on account of their brilliant light (*su-rocana*). Or else the word *sīma* takes the ablative suffix (*-tas*) without any meaning, i. e. *sīmnaḥ* = *sīmataḥ* = *sīmā-taḥ*, (which means) 'from the boundary'. *Sīmā* means boundary: it forms the seam between two countries. The word *tva*, being a pronoun with the sense of 'opposition', is unaccented. Some hold it to be a synonym of 'half'.

(*Here ends the seventh section.*)

One sits increasing the store of stanzas; a second chants the *gāyatra* hymn in *śakvarī* measures. One, i. e. Brahmā, expounds the science of being; whilst another metes the measure of the sacrifice.[4]

With these words, (the stanza) declares the application of the duties of the priests. One sits increasing the store of stanzas, i. e. the invoker. A stanza (*ṛc*) is a means of worshipping (*arcana*). A second chants the *gāyatra* hymn in *śakvarī* measures, i. e. the chanter. *Gāyatram* is derived from (the root) *gai*, meaning to praise. *Śakvaryaḥ* are stanzas; it is derived from (the root) *śak* (to be able). It is known: because with these he was able to slay Vṛtra, that is the characteristic of the *śakvarī* stanzas.[5] One, i. e. the Brahmā, expounds the science of every being. Brahmā is omniscient: he knows everything; Brahmā is supereminent from knowledge, Brahmā is supereminent all around. One metes the measure of the sacrifice, i. e. the (performing) priest. *Adhvar-yuḥ* (priest) = *adhvara-yuḥ*, i. e. he directs the sacrifice, he is the leader of the sacrifice, or else, he loves the sacrifice. Or (the word is formed) by the addition of (the suffix) *yuḥ* (to √*adhī*) in the sense of studying. *A-dhvara* is a synonym of 'sacrifice': the verb *dhvṛ* means to kill, (*a-dhvara* denotes) the negation of it (killing). According to some, the word (*tva*) is a particle, then how could it be a noun of unaccented character? It is clearly inflected. 'Lo! they call thee,

[1] Cf. Professor Macdonell, *A Vedic Grammar for Students*, p. 249.

[2] ii. 28. 4.

[3] AV. 4. 1. 1; 5. 6. 1; SV. 1. 321; VS. 13. 3.

[4] x. 72. 11.

[5] Cf. KB. xxiii. 2: 'Because with these, he was able to slay *Vṛtra*, hence they (are called) *śakvaryaḥ*.' See Gune, *Bhandarkar Comm. Vol.*, p. 44.

steadfast in friendship ',[1] (here it is) in the accusative; ' for one she yielded her body ',[2] in the dative. Further, it is (inflected) in the nominative plural.

(Here ends the eighth section.)

Friends, having (similar) eyes and ears, were unequal in the speed of their minds. Some are like tanks, which reach up to the mouth, and are suitable for a bath; others indeed are like those which reach up to the breast, and (are meant) to be seen only.[3]

[Friends], having (similar) eyes and ears. *Akṣiḥ* (eye) is derived from (the root) *cakṣ* (to see); ' it is from *añj* (to be beautiful),' says Āgrāyaṇa. It is well known: Therefore, they are, as it were, more beautiful.[4] *Karṇaḥ* (ear) is derived from (the root) *kṛt* (to cut): it has its entrance torn asunder; ' it is from *ṛ* (to go),' says Āgrāyaṇa. It is well known: Going upwards, as it were, they have protruded in space.[4] They were unequal in the speed of their minds. Some reach up to the mouth, others up to the breast.[5] *Āsyam* [6] (mouth) is derived from (the root) *as* (to throw), or else (from *ā-syand*, ' to flow '): food flows towards it. *Daghnam* is derived from (the root) *dagh*, meaning to flow, or from *das* (to be wasted) it is very much wasted. Some are like tanks, suitable for bathing. Suitable for bathing, i. e. fit for bathing; (others are) to be seen only.[7] *Hradaḥ* (tank) is derived from (the root) *hrād*, meaning to make a sound, or from *hlād*, meaning to make cool. Further, it (*tva*) is used in the sense of ' aggregation ', as ' recurrences and possession of Aśvins ';[8] i. e. possession of Aśvins, and recurrences.

Now the words which are used—the sense being complete—to fill up a sentence in prose, and a verse in poetic compositions, are expletives such as *kam*, *īm*, *id*, and *u*.[9]

(Here ends the ninth section.)

Men without garments, and having many children, being afraid of a wolf, as it were, longed for the dewy season [10] to live.[11]

[1] x. 71. 5; cf. N. 1. 20.

[2] x. 71. 4; cf. N. 1. 19.

[3] x. 71. 7.

[4] The quotation is untraced.

[5] ' Some reach up to the mouth ' is explained by Durga as ' unfathomable ', i. e. minds whose depths cannot be reached; ' up to the breast ' as shallow, whose bottom is within sight.

[6] Durga derives *āysam* in two ways: (1) from √*as* (to throw), i. e. food is thrown in the mouth; (2) from √*ā-syand* (to stream), i. e. the mouth begins to water when food is thrown into it, however dry it might have been before.

[7] The sentence is omitted by Durga.

[8] KB. xvii. 4.

[9] Cf. RP. xii. 8. 707; xii. 9. 708; Bṛh. D. ii. 90-1, Professor Macdonell's ed., vol. i, p. 19.

[10] It comprises the period from the middle of January to the middle of March.

[11] The quotation is untraced.

Dewy season to live. *śiśiram* is derived from (the root) *śṛ* (to crush), or *śam* (to put an end to).

He emitted it for pressing;[1] i. e. he created it for pressing (the soma-juice).

May our hymns make him grow.[2] May our hymns, i. e. songs of praise, make him grow. *Giras* (songs) is derived from (the root) *gṛ* (to speak).

This person, whom thou approachest, is for thee.[3] Thine is this man whom thou approachest. *Iva* is also used (as an expletive), as 'they all knew it well', and 'they both knew it well'. Moreover the word *na* is combined with *id*, in (the sense of) 'apprehension'.

(*Here ends the tenth section.*)

With oblations some seek heaven from this world; others press soma-juices in sacrifices. The pure rejoice indeed with their rewards; pursuing crooked ways, lest we should fall into hell.[4]

Hell is going downwards, i. e. falling lower and lower; or it does not contain even slight room for happiness. Moreover the words *na ca* are joined with the word *id*, in interrogation, as 'do they not drink wine?' *Surā* (wine) is derived from (the root) *su* (to press). Thus they are used in various meanings, to which attention should be paid.[5]

(*Here ends the eleventh section.*)

With these words, the four word-classes, i. e. the noun and the verb, prepositions and particles, are explained in their (respective) order. With reference to this, Śākaṭāyana holds that nouns are derived from verbs. This, too, is the doctrine of the etymologists.[6] 'Not all,' say Gargya and

[1] i. 9. 2; AV. 20. 71. 8.

[2] viii. 13. 18.

[3] i. 30. 4; AV. 20. 45. 1; SV. 1. 183; 2. 949.

[4] RV. Khila x. 106. 1.

[5] Pāṇini uses the term *nipāta* to denote not only particles, but also prepositions, see *Aṣṭādhyāyī*, i. 4. 56. The technical word employed by him for particles alone is *avyaya* (*op. cit.* i. 1. 37). Particles are enumerated in the *gaṇa* called *cādayaḥ* (*op. cit.* i. 4. 57). The total number of particles collected in the list is 195. This, however, does not include *cid* and *hi* mentioned by Yāska. Of the 195 particles, 22 only are explained in the *Nirukta*: (1) comparatives, *iva*, *na*, *cid*, and *nu*; (2) conjunctives, *ca*, *ā*, *vā*, *aha*, *ha*, *kila*, &c.; (3) expletives, *kam*, *īm*, *id*, *u*, &c. Cf. Patañjali, *op. cit.* i. 1. 6.; i. 4. 4, vol. i, pp. 94, 340–1; Professor Macdonell, *Vedic Grammar*, p. 429.

[6] Cf. Patañjali, *op. cit.* iii. 3. 1, vol. ii, p. 138: 'And the noun is derived from the verb' says the author in the *Nirukta*. 'The noun indeed is derived from the verb', so say the etymologists, and the son of Śakaṭa in grammar. Among the grammarians, Śākaṭāyana says, 'The noun is derived from the verb'; cf. also Breal, *Semantics*, p. 107: 'It comes from the fact that the verb is the essential and the capital part of our languages, which serves to form substantives and adjectives'; see Moncalm, *The Origin of Thought and Speech*, p. 74:

some of the grammarians, 'but only those, the accent and grammatical form of which are regular and which are accompanied by an explanatory radical modification. Those (nouns), such as cow, horse, man, elephant, &c., are conventional[1] (terms, and hence are underivable).'

Now, if all nouns are derived from verbs, every person who performs a particular action should be called by the same name, i. e. whosoever runs on the road should be called 'runner' (*aśva*, 'horse'); whatever pricks (like needle, &c.), 'pricker' (*tṛṇam*, 'grass'). Further, if all nouns are derived from verbs, a substantive should obtain as many names as the actions with which it is connected; thus a column should also be called 'beam-supporter', and 'that which rests in a hole'.

(*Here ends the twelfth section.*)

Moreover, substantives should be named according to the regular and correct grammatical form of a verb, so that their meanings may be indubitable, e.g. *puruṣa* (man) should take the form of *puri-śaya* (city-dweller); *aśva* (horse), of *aṣṭā* (runner); *tṛṇam* (grass), of *tardanam* (pricker). Further, people indulge in sophistry with regard to current expressions, e.g. they declare that earth (*pṛthivī*) is (so called) on account of being spread (√*prath*); but who spread it, and what was the base? Again, Śākaṭāyana derived parts of one word from different verbs, in spite of the meaning being irrelevant, and of the explanatory radical modification being non-existent, e.g. (explaining *sat-ya*) he derived the later syllable *ya* from the causal form of (the root) *i* (to go), and the former syllable *sat* from the regular form of (the root) *as* (to be). Further, it is said that a *becoming* is preceded by a *being*, (hence) the designation of a prior (*being*) from a posterior (*becoming*) is not tenable; consequently this (theory of the derivation of nouns from verbs) is not tenable.

(*Here ends the thirteenth section.*)

'... there remain in the end certain simple elements of human speech—the primordial roots—which have sufficed to provide the innumerable multitude of words used by the human race'; Max Müller, *Lectures on the science of language*, 6th ed., vol. ii, pp. 70, 80, 86; cf. also AA. ii. 1. 3; ii. 1. 6.

[1] Plato introduces, in the *Cratylus*, a character in the person of Hermogenes who maintains that names are conventional, that they are given arbitrarily and can be altered at will. The diametrically opposite view, that names are natural, is put in the mouth of Cratylus while Socrates takes an intermediate position, admitting that names are natural, while at the same time they have an element of convention also. Some passages of the dialogue relevant to the controversy are given in the additional notes; see Jowett, *Dialogues of Plato*, 3rd ed., vol. i, pp. 324, 327-8, 358, 366, 378.

As to (the statement) that all those (nouns), the accent and grammatical form of which are regular, and which are accompanied by an explanatory radical modification, are derived, (we reply that) in that case it is quite evident. As to (the point) that every person whoever performs a particular action should be called by the same name, we see that in some cases the performers of the action do obtain a common name, while in others they do not, e. g. a carpenter or ascetic, enlivener, earth-born, &c.[1] With this, the following objection is answered as well. As to (the point) that substantives should be named in such a way that their meanings may be indubitable, (we reply that) there are words (of that character), words of rare occurrence, i. e. single words formed by primary suffixes, as creeper, guest, one having matted locks, a wanderer, wakeful, one who sacrifices with a ladle, &c. As to (the objection) that people indulge in sophistry with regard to current expressions, (we reply that) it is with regard to current expressions alone that (etymological) examination is most desirable. With regard to 'they declare that earth (*pṛthivī*) is (so called) on account of being spread (√*prath*); but who spread it, and what was the base?' (we reply that) it is indeed broad to look at, even if it is not spread by others. Moreover, in this way all known words, without any exception, can be found fault with. As to (the point) that a certain individual derived parts of one word from different verbs, (we reply that) the person who made such a derivation in spite of the meaning being irrelevant should be blamed; it is the fault of an individual, not of the science (of etymology).

As to (the argument) that the designation of a prior (*being*) from a posterior *becoming* is not tenable, we see that in some cases prior *beings* do obtain their names from posterior *becomings*, but not in others, as 'a woodpecker', 'one having long locks', &c. *Bilva* is (so called) from being supported or from sprouting.

(*Here ends the fourteenth section.*)[2]

Moreover, without it (etymology) the precise meaning of Vedic stanzas cannot be understood. For one who does not understand the meaning, a thorough investigation of accent and grammatical form is not possible,

[1] The former two, i.e. a carpenter and an ascetic, are examples of cases where people who perform the same action get a common name; the latter two are examples of cases where they do not get a common name, as enlivener means the juice of sugar-cane, and earth-born means the planet Mars.

[2] Cf. Patañjali, *op. cit.* i. 1. 9, vol. i, pp. 175–6. See Introduction, Yāska's contributions to Etymology, Philology, and Semantics; sects. 12–14 are translated rather freely by Max Müller, *History of Ancient Sanskrit Literature*, 2nd ed., pp. 164–8.

hence this science (etymology) is the complement of grammar and a means of accomplishing one's own object.

'If (the object of the science) is to ascertain the meaning of Vedic stanzas, it is useless,' says Kautsa, 'for the Vedic stanzas have no meaning';[1] this is to be established by the following arguments: propositions have their words fixed, their order, too, is immutably fixed.[2] Further, the accomplishment of the ritual form is enjoined by the Brāhmaṇa,[3] as 'Spread it wide',[4] and so he spreads; 'Let me pour out',[5] and so he pours out. Further, their meaning is impossible,[6] as 'Save him, O plant!'[7] and while striking, one declares, 'Do not injure him, O Axe!'[8] Moreover, their meaning is contradictory,[9] as 'There was but one Rudra and no second',[10] and 'Rudras, who on earth are thousands without number';[11] 'O Indra! thou art born without a foe',[12] and 'Indra vanquished hundred armies together'.[13] Further, one enjoins a person who is already acquainted, as 'Address the hymn to Agni which is being kindled'.[14] Besides, it is said, 'Aditi is everything'. 'Aditi is heaven, Aditi is atmosphere,[15] &c.' will be explained later on.[16] Further, their meaning is obscure,[17] as *amyak*,[18] *yādṛśmin*,[19] *jārayāyi*,[20] *kāṇukā*,[21] &c.

(*Here ends the fifteenth section.*)

Vedic stanzas are significant, because (their) words are identical (with those of the spoken language). There is the Brāhmaṇa passage: This indeed is the perfection of the sacrifice, that the prescription of the form, that is to say, the action which is to be performed, is declared by a stanza of the Ṛg or the Yajurveda.[22] 'Playing with their sons and grandsons,

1 Cf. PM. i. 2. 1.

2 *Op. cit.* i. 2. 32.

3 Cf. PM. i. 2. 33.

4 TS. i. 1. 8. 1; vi. 2. 7. 3; cf. MS. i. 1. 9; KS. i. 8; xxxi. 7; TB. iii. 2. 8. 4.

5 Cf. VS. 2. 15.

6 Cf. PM. i. 2. 34–5.

7 TS. i. 2. 1. 1.

8 VS. 4. 1; 5. 42; 6. 15.

9 Cf. PM. i. 2. 36.

10 Cf. TS. i. 8. 6. 1.

11 VS. 16. 54.

12 x. 133. 2; AV. 20. 95. 3; SV. 2. 1152.

13 x. 103. 1; AV. 19. 13. 2; SV. 2. 1199; VS. 17. 33.

14 TS. vi. 3. 7. 1; MS. i. 4. 11; TB. iii. 3. 7. 1; ŚB. i. 3. 5. 2, 3. See Gune, *Bhandarkar Comm. Vol., loc. cit.*

15 i. 89. 10.

16 See N. 4. 23.

17 Cf. Patañjali, *op. cit.* ii. 1. 1, vol. i, p. 363; PM. i. 2. 38.

18 The word occurs once only in RV. i. 169. 3.

19 The word occurs once only in RV. v. 44. 8.

20 The word occurs once only in RV. vi. 12. 2.

21 The word occurs once only in RV. viii. 77. 4.

22 GB. ii. 2. 6; ii. 4. 2; the passage without the words 'or the Yajurveda' is found in AB. i. 4, 13, 15, 17, &c. Cf. Haug's translation: 'What is appropriate in its form, is successful in the sacrifice; that is to say, when the verse (ṛc or yajus) which is recited refers to the ceremony which is being performed.'

&c.'[1] As to (the objection) that propositions have their words fixed, their order too is immutably fixed, (we reply) that it is the same with regard to the everyday speech of the world, as 'Indra and Agni', 'father and son'.[2] As to (the objection) that the accomplishment of the ritual form is enjoined by the Brāhmaṇa, (we reply) that this is a mere reiteration of what has been said already. As to (the objection) that their meaning is impossible, (we reply) that no injury is to be inflicted, so it must be understood by the authority of the Vedic passage. As to (the objection) that their meaning is contradictory, (we reply) that the same (objection) is applicable to the everyday speech of the world, as 'this Brāhmaṇa has no rival', 'this king has no enemies', &c. As to (the objection) that one enjoins a person who is already acquainted, (we reply) that in salutation a person announces his name to one who is already acquainted with it; the mixture of honey and milk is declared (to the guest) who is already acquainted with it. As to (the objection) that Aditi is everything, (we reply) that it is the same in the everyday speech of the world, as 'all fluids reside in water'.[3] As to (the objection) that their meaning is obscure, (we reply) that it is not the fault of the post if the blind man does not see it; it is the fault of the man himself. Just as among the country-folk a man becomes distinguished with (a little) knowledge, so among the scholars of the traditional Vedic lore a man of profound knowledge alone is worthy of praise.[4]

(Here ends the sixteenth section.)

Moreover, without this (etymology) the word-division is not possible.

Be merciful, O Rudra, to the footed wanderer.[5]

The footed wanderer, i. e. cows, provision for the journey: *(avasāya)* is derived from (the root) *av*, meaning to go, with the suffix *asa*; it is therefore not analysed (in the *Padapāṭha*).

Having released the horses.[6]

Here (*ava-sāya* is derived from the root) *so* preceded by the preposition (*ava*); in the sense of releasing it is therefore analysed.

[1] x. 85. 42; AV. 14. 1. 22; this is an example of the identity of words of Vedic stanzas with those of classical Sanskrit.

[2] i. e. The order of words in these idiomatic phrases cannot be reversed, e. g. it will be wrong to say, 'Agni and Indra'; 'son and father'.

[3] Durga's explanation of the example is that water is the source of all fluids, hence all fluids are contained within water.

[4] See Introduction, Early anti-Vedic Scepticism; a summary of the controversy is given by Muir, *op. cit.* vol. ii, pp. 169–72.

[5] x. 169. 1.

[6] i. 104. 1.

Here has come this messenger of death.[1]

(*Nirṛtyā*) is either in the ablative or in the genitive case, (so it is written in the *Padapāṭha*) as ending in the visarjanīya (=*nirṛtyāḥ*).

Far, far away call for death.[2]

Here (*nirṛtyā*) is in the dative case, (so it is written in the *Padapāṭha*) as ending in *ai* (=*nirṛtyai*).

Saṃhitā is the closest conjunction by means of euphonic combination.[3] *Saṃhitā* is based on the original form of words.[4] The phonetic treatises of all schools are based on the original form of words.

Moreover, in the sacrificial act, there are many injunctions with regard to the characteristics of deities. This is to be established by the following. Should some people say, 'We here know the characteristic marks[5] (of deities, we need not therefore study etymology,' set before them the following stanza).

Like Indra, like Vāyu, the gods fill thee with strength.[6]

Here is the characteristic mark of Indra and Vāyu in a stanza addressed to Agni.

Shining like Agni, O Manyu! be strong.[7]

Similarly (the characteristic mark of) Agni (is found) in a stanza addressed to Manyu.[8] *Tviṣitaḥ* means shining. Of this word (the part) *tviṣiḥ* is a synonym of light.

Moreover, there is praise of knowledge and censure of ignorance.

(*Here ends the seventeenth section.*)

He is the bearer of a burden only,—the blockhead who, having studied, does not understand the meaning of the Veda. But he who knows the meaning obtains all good fortune and, with his sins purged off by knowledge, attains heaven.[9]

Whatever is learnt without its being understood is called mere cramming; like dry logs of wood on an extinguished fire, it can never illuminate.[10]

[1] x. 165. 1; AV. 6. 27. 1.

[2] x. 164. 1; AV. 20. 96. 23.

[3] Quoted by Pāṇini, *op. cit.* i. 4. 109; cf. Patañjali, *op. cit.* i. 4. 4, vol. i, p. 354.

[4] Identical with RP. ii. 1. 105, except that the order of words is reversed.

[5] The sentence is incomplete, abrupt, and obscure, very unlike the style of Yāska. The meaning has to be completed by an additional clause put within brackets.

[6] vi. 4. 7; VS. 33. 13.

[7] x. 84. 2; AV. 4. 31. 2.

[8] The meaning is that etymology helps to discover the principal deity to whom a stanza is addressed. This cannot be found out by the knowledge of the characteristic mark only as in the cases adduced by Yāska.

[9] *Saṃhitopaniṣad* B. 3.

[10] *Loc. cit.* quoted with the variant *adhītam* by Patañjali, *op. cit.* i. 1. 1, vol. i, p. 2.

Sthāṇuḥ (post) is derived from (the root) *sthā* (to stand). *Artha* (meaning) is derived from (the root) *ar* (to go), or it is (so called because) it stops from going.[1]

(*Here ends the eighteenth section.*)

Seeing one does not see speech, hearing one does not hear it. And to another she yielded her body like a well-dressed and loving wife to her husband.[2]

Even seeing, one does not see speech; even hearing, one does not hear it. With these words, the hemistich describes the ignorant man. 'And to another she yielded her body', she reveals herself, i.e. knowledge; the manifestation of meaning (is described) by this speech, i.e. the third verse. Like a well-dressed and loving wife to her husband [well dressed at proper seasons, dressed in an auspicious manner, and loving],[3] i.e. just as he (the husband) sees her and hears her at proper seasons: this is the praise of one who understands the meaning.[4] The stanza following this explains it still more (explicitly).

(*Here ends the nineteenth section.*)

They certainly declare one to be steadfast in friendship, him no one can overpower in conflicts (of debates). But that man wanders with a barren delusion; he listened to speech that is without fruit or flower.[5]

Indeed, they declare one to be steadfast in friendship with speech, i.e. taking delight in it, and having thoroughly understood the meaning, or in friendship with gods in a delightful place; they do not overpower him, who knows the meaning well, even in powerful debates. But that man wanders with a barren delusion, i.e. with a symbol of speech. To him (speech) does not grant desires, which are to be granted by speech. Who heard speech without fruit or flower in the abodes of gods and men, for that man speech has no fruit nor flower, or has very little fruit or flower. The meaning of speech is called its fruit and flower. Or the sacrificial stanzas, and stanzas addressed to deities, or the deity and the soul are its fruit and flower.[6]

[1] Durga takes *artha* in the sense of wealth, and explains the two derivations as (1) wealth is approached by greedy people, (2) wealth stops from going with the deceased person to the next world. Durga's explanation of *artha* does not suit the context, which here denotes 'meaning' or 'knowledge'. By *sthūṇā* Durga understands an ass. A person who commits Vedic texts to memory without understanding is compared to an ass bearing a load of sandal-wood, who perceives its weight but not its fragrance.

[2] x. 71. 4; cf. N. 1. 8.

[3] The passage within square brackets is omitted by MSS. of the shorter recension and Durga.

[4] The whole section is quoted by Patañjali, *op. cit.* i. 1. 1, vol. i, p. 4.

[5] x. 71. 5; cf. N. 1. 8.

[6] Cf. Muir, *op. cit.* vol. i, p. 255.

Seers had direct intuitive insight into duty. They by oral instruction handed down the hymns to later generations who were destitute of the direct intuitive insight. The later generations, declining in (power of) oral communication, compiled this work, the Veda, and the auxiliary Vedic treatises, in order to comprehend their meaning. *Bilma* = *bhilma* (division) or illustration.[1]

So many roots have the same meaning. *Dhātuḥ* (root) is derived from (the root) *dhā* (to put). So many are the synonyms of this substantive. This is the homonym of so many meanings. This name of a deity is incidental, the other is primary. With reference to this, the (name) which occurs in a stanza addressed to another deity is called incidental.[2]

(We adore) thee like a horse with long hair.[3]

(We adore) thee like a horse that has long hair. Long hair is for warding off the gad-flies. *Daṃśa* (gad-fly) is derived from (the root) *daṃś* (to bite).

Like a fierce animal, roaming everywhere, haunting the mountains.[4]

As a fierce animal roaming everywhere, haunting the mountains. *Mṛgaḥ* (animal) is derived from (the root) *mṛj*, meaning to go. Fierce, of whom all are afraid. 'Dreadful' is derived from the same root also. *Ku-caraḥ* means 'one who moves in a crooked manner'. If it be an epithet of a deity (it means) 'where does he not go?' Haunting the mountains, living in mountains. *Giriḥ* means a mountain: it is raised up. *Parvata* (mountain) is (so called) because it has joints (*parva*). But *parva* is derived from (the root) *pṛ* (to fill), or from *prī* (to propitiate). Here, during a period of a fortnight, they propitiate the gods. It (mountain) is (so called) on account of the similarity of the joints of the nature of the other (period).[5] Seated on a cloud. A cloud is called mountain from the same reason (i.e. from its being raised). The section which deals with the appellations of deities to whom panegyrics are primarily addressed is called the *daivata*; this we shall explain later on, but the synonyms and homonyms now.

(*Here ends the twentieth section.*)

[1] Cf. Muir, *op. cit.* vol. ii, p. 165; vol. iii, p. 118.

[2] Cf. Bṛh. D. i, 18.

[3] i. 27. 1; SV. 1. 17; 2. 984.

[4] i. 154. 2; x. 182. 2.

[5] According to Durga, a mountain has joints in the form of stone slabs, and a period has joints in the form of time with its various divisions. Cf. Muir, *op. cit.* vol. iv, p. 69.

CHAPTER II

Now (we shall deal with) etymology. With reference to this, the words, the accent and the grammatical form of which are regular and are accompanied by an explanatory radical modification, should be derived in the ordinary manner. But the meaning being irrelevant, and the explanatory radical modification being non-existent, one should always examine them with regard to their meaning, by the analogy of some (common) course of action. If there be no (such) analogy, one should explain them even by the community of a (single) syllable or letter;[1] but one should never (give up the attempt at) derivation. One should not attach (too much) importance to the grammatical form, for these complex formations (*vṛttayaḥ*) are (often) subject to exceptions. One should interpret inflected cases according to the meaning. In *prattam* (= *pra-dattam*, 'given away') and *avattam* (= *ava-dattam* from *ava* √*do*, 'divided') only the initial parts of the root survive. Further, there is aphaeresis of the initial part of the verb *as* (to be) in weak forms, as *staḥ* ('they two are'), *santi* ('they all are'), &c. Further, there is elision of the final part, as in *gatvā* (from √*gam*, 'having gone'), *gatam* (√*gam*, 'gone'), &c. Further, there is elision of the penultimate, as in *jagmatuḥ* (red. form of *gam*, 'they two went'), and *jagmuḥ* (red. form of *gam*, 'they all went').[2] Moreover, there is the modification of the penultimate, as in *rājā* (*rājan*, 'king'), *daṇḍī* (*daṇḍin*, a 'staff-bearer'), &c. Further, there is elision of a letter, as in *tatvā yāmi* (= *tatvā yācāmi*), &c.

Moreover, there is elision of two letters, as in *tṛca* (= *tri* + *ṛca*, 'three stanzas'). Further, there is alteration in the initial part (of the root), as in *jyotiḥ* (√*dyut*, 'light'), *ghanaḥ* (√*han*, 'killer'), *binduḥ* (√*bhid*, 'a drop'), *bāṭyaḥ* (√*bhaṭ*, 'to be hired or nourished'), &c. Further, there is metathesis, as in *stokāḥ* (from √*ścut*, 'a drop'), *rajjuḥ*[3] ('rope'), *sikatāḥ*[4]

[1] Cf. Jowett, *Dialogues of Plato* (3rd ed.), vol. i, p. 335; the *Cratylus*, 393: 'And whether the syllables of the name are the same or not the same makes no difference provided the meaning is retained; nor does the addition or subtraction of a letter make any difference so long as the essence of the thing remains in possession of the name and appears in it.' Also p. 341, Soc. 'Now attend ... and just remember that we often put in and pull out letters in words and give names as we please and change the accents.' And p. 358, Soc. ... 'but then you know that the original names have been long ago buried and disguised by people sticking on and stripping off letters for the sake of euphony, and twisting and bedizening them in all sorts of ways ...' Durga paraphrases *akṣara* (syllable) by *svara* (accent).

[2] Cf. Patañjali, *op. cit.* vi. 1. 1, vol. iii, p. 17.

[3] Durga derives *rajjuḥ* from √*sṛj*, but it is more likely to be derived from √*rasj*.

[4] Durga derives *sikatā* from √*kas*, 'to shine', but it is more probably derived from √*sik* or √*sic*; cf. Patañjali, *op. cit.* i. 1. 2, vol. i, p. 31.

('sand'), *tarku* (√*kṛt*, 'a knife'). Further, there is change in the final part (of the root).[1]

(*Here ends the first section.*)

Oghaḥ (√*vah*, 'flood'), *meghaḥ* (√*mih*, 'cloud'), *nādhaḥ*[2] ('refuge'), *gādhaḥ* (√*gāh*, 'fordable'), *Vadhūḥ* (√*vah*, 'bride'), *madhu* (√*mad*, 'mead'). Further, there is anaptyxis, as in *āsthat* (√*as*, 'to throw'), *dvāraḥ* (√*vṛ*, 'door'), *bharūjā* (√*bhrajj*, 'ripe'. D.), &c. With reference to this, it is pointed out that when a root contains a semi-vowel contiguous to a vowel it becomes the origin of two primary bases. There, if an accomplished form is not derivable from one base, one should try to derive it from the other. Even there, some are of rare occurrence, as *ūtiḥ* (√*av*, 'protection'), *mṛduḥ* (√*mrad*, 'soft'), *pṛthuḥ* (√*prath*, 'broad'), *pṛṣataḥ* (√*pruṣ*, 'a drop'), *kuṇārum* (√*kvaṇ*, 'sounding'). Further, Vedic primary nouns are derived from roots of classical Sanskrit, as *damūnāḥ* (devoted to the house), *kṣetrasādhāḥ* (one who divides the fields), &c.; and also nouns of classical Sanskrit from Vedic roots, as *uṣṇam* (warm), *ghṛtam* (clarified butter).[3] Further, primary forms alone are employed (in speech) among some people; secondary forms among others. The verb *śavati*, meaning to go, is used by the Kambojas only. Kambojas (are so called because) they enjoy blankets (*kambala*), or beautiful things.[4] A blanket (*kambala*) is a desirable object (*kamanīya*). Its modified form *śava* is used by the Aryans: *dāti*, in the sense to cut, is employed by the people of the east, while the people of the north use *dātra* (sickle).[5] In this manner, one should explain single words.

Now with regard to derivatives and compounds, whether of one or more than one member, one should explain their component parts in their respective order, having first divided (the words) into them.[6] Punishable, i.e. a person [a person of punishment] deserving punishment, or something to be accomplished by punishment. *Daṇḍa* (punishment) is derived from

[1] For the detailed examination of this section, see Introduction, Yāska's Contributions, &c.

[2] Durga derives *nādhaḥ* from √*nah* (to bind), but it is probably from √*nādh*; cf. *nādhamānāḥ*.

[3] Cf. Muir, *Sanskrit Texts*, vol. ii, p. 152.

[4] The sentence is omitted by Muir in his translation as if it did not exist. As it is given by MSS. of both recensions and explained by Durga, it cannot be regarded as an interpolation, hence its omission by Muir is unjustified; see *Sanskrit Texts*, vol. ii, p. 356.

[5] Roth denies the correctness of Yāska's statement that the Aryans use *śava* (see *Erläuterungen*, p. 17). His denial is, however, groundless, because Yāska is corroborated by a grammarian of such eminence as Patañjali (see the *Mahābhāṣya*, i. 1. 1, vol. i, p. 9). The passage in the MB. is almost identical with the *Nirukta*.

[6] Cf. Jowett, *Dialogues of Plato* (3rd ed.), vol. i, pp. 368, 370, Soc. 'But the secondary,

(the root) *dad*, meaning to hold. People say, 'Akrūra holds the jewel'.[1] 'The word (*daṇḍa*) is derived from (the root) *dam*,' says Aupamanyava. 'Inflict punishment on him' is (used) in censure. *Kakṣyā* means girth of a horse: it is carried round the region of girth. *Kakṣaḥ* (armpit) is derived from (the root) *gāh* (to plunge into) with the suffix *kṣa*, or from *khyā* (to make known) with redundant reduplication: what is there worth seeing? Or it (may be derived) from *kaṣ*[2] (to rub against). On account of this[3] analogy (i. e. of being rubbed) it means 'human armpit', and on account of the analogy of the arms and their root, the word (signifies armpit) of a horse.

(*Here ends the second section.*)

Royal servant, a servant of the king. *Rājā* (king) is derived from (the root) *rāj* (to shine). *Puruṣaḥ* (person) = *puri-ṣādaḥ* (one who sits in a city), or = *puri-śayaḥ* (one who sleeps in a city), or is derived from (the root) *pṛ* (to fill), i. e. he fills the interior, with reference to the inner soul.

This entire (universe) is filled by that inner soul, to whom there is nothing anterior, nothing subsequent, than whom there is nothing more minute, nor more great, and immovable like a tree, who alone lives in heaven.[4]

This, too, is a quotation. *Viścakadrākarṣa*, 'one who drags about like a despicable dog'. The words *vi* and *cakadra* are used (to denote) 'gait of a dog'; *drāti* means a despicable gait; *kadrāti* means a despicable *drāti*; *cakadrāti* is the same as *kadrāti* with redundant reduplication: he who possesses that (*kadrāti*) is called *viścakadraḥ*. A beauty of auspicious colours, i. e. one whose beauty is like that of auspicious colours. Auspicious, it is desirable. *Varṇaḥ* (colour) is derived from (the root) *vṛ* (to cover). *Rūpam* (beauty) is derived from (the root) *ruc* (to shine). In this manner one should explain derivatives and compounds. One should not explain

as I conceive, derive their significance from the primary.'

Soc. . . . 'Ought we not, therefore, first to separate the letters, just as those who are beginning rhythm first distinguish the powers of elementary, and then of compound sounds?'

Soc. . . . 'Must we not begin in the same way with letters, first separating the vowels, and then the consonants and mutes into classes, according to the received distinctions of the learned?' Cf. Bṛh. D. ii. 106.

[1] The story of Akrūra, a king, and a jewel called *syamantaka* is related in the *Mahābhārata*, the *Bhāgavata* and the *Brahma Purāṇas*, and *Hemacandra*; see the *Nirukta* in Bib. Ind. ed., vol. ii, p. 164, foot-note.

[2] Durga remarks that an armpit always itches, because it is full of perspiration, hence it is constantly rubbed and may be appropriately derived from the root *kaṣ* 'to rub'.

[3] By *tat* Durga understands the armpit of a woman. His explanation that from the analogy of the armpit of a woman the word *kakṣa* means the armpit of a man is arbitrary.

[4] TA. 10. 10. 3; Mahān. U. 10. 4; Śveta U. iii. 9; cf. Muir, *op. cit.* vol. v, p. 374.

isolated syllables, either to a non-grammarian, or to a non-residential pupil, or to one who is (incapable of) understanding it.[1] Eternal indeed is the scorn of the ignorant for knowledge. But one should explain to a residential pupil, or one who is capable of knowing them, the intelligent and the diligent.

(*Here ends the third section.*)

Verily knowledge approached Brāhmaṇa, 'Protect me, I am thy treasure. Do not expound me to the scornful, nor to the unstraightforward, nor to one who has no self-control; thus shall I grow powerful.'[2]

One should honour him as a father and mother, and should never bear enmity towards him who pierces ears with truth, without causing pain, and bestowing ambrosia.[3]

Just as religious students, who, having received instruction, do not honour their teachers with word, thought, and deed, are not to be fed by the teacher, similarly that knowledge does not feed them.

In order to protect thy treasure, O Brahman! expound me to him alone whom thou knowest to be pure, diligent, intelligent, observing the rules of a celibate life, and who never bears enmity towards thee.[4]

Śevadhi means treasure.

(*Here ends the fourth section.*)[5]

Now, therefore, we shall proceed in order. The word *gauḥ* is a synonym of 'earth', (so called) because it goes very far, or because people go over it ($\sqrt{}$*gam*). Or it may be derived from (the root) *gā* with the suffix *au* (*gā* + *au* = *gau*). Moreover, it is a synonym of 'an animal', from the same root also. Further, in the latter meaning, there are Vedic passages where primary forms (of *gauḥ*) are used in a derivative sense: 'Mix soma with milk',[6] i. e. (*gauḥ* is used in the sense) of milk. *Matsaraḥ* means soma; it is derived from (the root) *mand* meaning to satisfy. *Matsaraḥ* is a synonym of greed also: it makes man mad after wealth. *Payas* (milk) is derived from (the root) *pā* (to drink), or from *pyāy* (to swell). *Kṣīram* (milk) is derived from (the root) *kṣar* (to flow), or it is derived from *ghas* (to consume) with the suffix *īra*, like *uśīra* (root of

[1] Cf. AA. iii. 2. 6.

[2] Cf. Manu, ii. 114; Vasiṣṭha, ii. 8; Viṣṇu, xxix. 9.

[3] Cf. Manu, ii. 144; Vasiṣṭha, ii. 10; Viṣṇu, xxx. 47; Āpastamba, i. 1. 14.

[4] Cf. Manu, ii. 115; Vasiṣṭha, ii. 9; Viṣṇu, xxix. 10; all the four stanzas are quoted from *Saṃhitopaniṣad* B. 3, Burnell's ed., pp. 29-32.

[5] According to Roth, the section *in toto* is an interpolation. The evidence of the MSS. and of Durga goes against him, but from the nature of its contents the section seems to be of a spurious character.

[6] ix. 46. 4.

a plant). 'Milking soma, they sit on a cow-skin,'[1] i. e. (*gauḥ* is used in the sense) of cow-skin used for sitting on. *Aṃśuḥ* (soma is so called because) no sooner than it goes in, it is agreeable, or it is agreeable for life. *Carma* (skin) is derived from (the root) *car* (to move) or (it is so called because) it is cut off (from the body). Moreover (*gauḥ*) means skin and phlegm: 'Thou art girded round with skin and phlegm, be strong';[2] this (is said) in praise of a chariot. Moreover, it means tendon and phlegm: 'Girt with tendon and phlegm, it flies when discharged';[3] this is in praise of an arrow. Bow-string is called *gauḥ* also: if it be *gavyā*, it is the derivative form; if not (it is causal), i. e. it sets arrows in motion.

(*Here ends the fifth section.*)

On every strip of wood twanged the well-strung string: thence the men-eating birds flew.[4]

On every strip of wood, i. e. on every bone. *Vṛkṣa* (tree) is (so called) from being cut down (√*vraśc*). [Or it stands having covered (√*vṛ*) the earth *kṣā* (earth); *kṣā* is derived from (the root) *kṣi* meaning to dwell].[5] Twanged the well-strung string, i. e. it makes a sharp ringing sound. The (verb) *mīm* means 'to make a low sound'. From thence birds fly in order to eat men. The word *viḥ* is a synonym of bird, and is derived from (the root) *vī*, meaning to go. Moreover, it is a synonym of arrow also from the same root. The sun is called *gauḥ* also. 'Lo that (charioteer) in the sun who has joints.'[6]

'Having joints means having brilliance,' says Aupamanyava.[7] Moreover, a ray of the sun illuminates the moon.[8] That the illumination of the moon is caused by the sun is to be established by the following: Suṣumṇa is the ray of the sun, the moon is the holder.[9] This, too, is a Vedic passage. That (ray) is called *gauḥ* also. Here indeed they thought of the ray:[10] this we shall explain later on. All the rays are called *gāvaḥ* also.

(*Here ends the sixth section.*)

[1] x. 94. 9.

[2] vi. 47. 26; AV. 6. 125. 1; cf. N. 9. 12.

[3] vi. 75. 11; VS. 29. 48; cf. N. 9. 12.

[4] x. 27. 22.

[5] The passage within square brackets is omitted by the MSS. of the shorter recension and Durga.

[6] vi. 56. 3.

[7] According to Durga, days and nights are joints, hence the sun is called one who has joints.

[8] This shows that Yāska was acquainted with the non-self-luminous character of the moon.

[9] VS. 18. 40; ŚB. ix. 4. 1. 9. Durga explains *suṣumṇa* as 'one who gladdens all beings'.

[10] i. 84. 15; AV. 20. 41. 3; SV. 1. 147; 2. 265; cf. N. 4. 25.

We desire to go to those regions of you two, where are nimble and many-horned rays. There, indeed, shines forth brightly that highest step of the wide-striding Viṣṇu.[1]

We long to go to those regions of you two, where are rays [many-horned], having a large number of horns.[2] The word *bhūri* is a synonym of 'many'; (so called) because it produces much. *Śṛṅga* (horn) is derived from (the root) *śri* (to rest on), or from *śṛ* (to slay), or from *śam* (to destroy); or (it is so called because) it grows up to protect, or it comes out of the head. *Ayāsuḥ* means nimble. There shines forth brightly the highest step, i. e. the loftiest step, of the wide-striding, i. e. of the great-paced, Viṣṇu. *Pādaḥ* (foot) is derived from (the root) *pad* (to go); when it is placed down, (the same word in the neuter gender) means a footstep. The word (also signifies) a quarter of division from the analogy of a quadruped; and other quarters from the analogy of the *pāda* of division.

In like manner, doubts are entertained with regard to other nouns as well; (the rule is that) they should be explained according to their meaning: if their meanings are uniform, their etymologies are uniform; if their meanings are multiform, their etymologies are multiform.[3] With these words, the twenty-one synonyms of earth are dealt with. With reference to them, *nirṛtiḥ* (earth) is (so called) from giving enjoyment; the other word (*nirṛtiḥ*), which signifies calamity, is derived from (the root) *ṛ* (to befall); the latter is confused with the former; their difference (should be noted). The following stanza is addressed to her.

(Here ends the seventh section.)

He, who made it, did not know of it; it was hidden from him who saw it. Encompassed within the womb of the mother, and multiplying greatly, he entered the earth.[4]

'People having many children fall into calamity,' say the ascetics. 'It refers to the phenomenon of rain,' say the etymologists. 'He who made it'; the verbs 'to make' and 'to scatter' are used in connexion with the phenomenon of rain. He did not know of it, i. e. the middle one.[5] He, the middle one, who saw it concealed by the sun, alone knew of it.[6] In the womb of the mother: mother (*mātā*) means atmosphere; in it, the beings are measured out (*nir* √*mā*). Womb means atmosphere: this is a vast

[1] i. 154. 6; cf. Professor Macdonell, *Vedic Reader*, p. 35.

[2] Cf. Muir, *op. cit.*, vol. iv, pp. 73, 74.

[3] In criticism of this rule, it may be remarked that words of different origin often come to acquire the same meaning, and words of the same origin different meanings; see Introduction, Yāska's Contributions, &c.

[4] i. 164. 32; AV. 9. 10. 10.

[5] According to Durga, it refers to cloud.

[6] i.e. Indra alone knew of it. Durga.

region encompassed by air. This other (meaning, i. e.) a woman's womb, is derived from the same root also: it is surrounded.[1] Multiplying greatly, he reaches earth through the phenomenon of rain.[2]

Śākapūṇi[3] made the determination that he would know all the deities. A deity having the two characteristics[4] appeared before him. He did not know her; he said to her, 'I would like to know thee'. She referred him to the following stanza, with the words that it was addressed to her.

(*Here ends the eighth section.*)

Here he snorts, covered by whom the speech, resting on a spluttering (cloud), utters a lowing sound. She indeed frightened the mortal with her (thundering) actions; becoming lightning, she concealed her form.[5]

Here he thunders, surrounded by whom the speech utters a lowing sound, i.e. makes a noise, or (utters a lowing sound) like *māyu*, i.e. the sun.[6] This is the atmospheric speech. Resting on a spluttering[7] cloud, she frightens the mortal with her (thundering) actions,[8] deeds, and, becoming lightning, conceals her form.[9] The word *vavriḥ* is a synonym of form: because it covers (√*vṛ*, to cover). Having overspread the earth with rain, it draws it back again.

(*Here ends the ninth section.*)

The following fifteen (words) are synonyms of gold.[10] From what (root) is *hiraṇyam* derived? It is circulated (*hriyate*) in a stretched form,[11] or it

[1] According to Durga it is surrounded by sinews and flesh.

[2] Two different interpretations of the word *nirṛtiḥ*, (1) as signifying calamity, according to the ascetics; (2) as meaning earth, according to the etymologists, are here presented. Durga remarks that similar differences of interpretation exist with regard to other Vedic passages as well. He cites *dadhi-krāvṇo akāriṣam* as to be recited at the time of eating curds according to AP. vi. 13; the same is also chanted by women, in a horse-sacrifice, in the vicinity of the horse, when the queen has risen. He thinks this difference of application of the same stanza is to be based on different interpretations of the stanza, and points out the importance of etymology for the correct understanding of the Vedic texts and hence for their correct application at sacrifices.

[3] *Śāka-pūṇi* is explained by Durga as a gatherer of herbs.

[4] i. e. Male and female, or the atmospheric or the celestial characteristics. Durga.

[5] i. 164, 29; AV. 9, 10, 7.

[6] The sun is called *māyu*, because he is the measurer of all beings (√*mā*). Durga thinks that the first hemistich describes the internal thunder of a cloud which is yet unmanifested.

[7] Cloud is called spluttering, because it splutters water. *Dhvaṃsani* is translated as '*Wucht*' by Roth.

[8] Durga thinks this refers to the manifested thunder, which produces a most dreadful sound; everybody is frightened and seeks shelter. Roth translates *citibhiḥ* by '*mit Zischen*'.

[9] According to Durga, having manifested herself as lightning and producing rain, she disappears.

[10] According to Durga, synonyms of gold follow those of the earth, because gold, being found in earth, is intimately associated with it.

[11] i. e. In the form of ornaments, being extended in the form of beautiful bracelets, necklaces, &c. Durga.

is circulated from man to man,[1] or it is useful and delightful,[2] [or it is the delight of the heart], or it may be derived from (the root) *hary*, meaning to yearn after.

The following sixteen (words) are synonyms of atmosphere. From what (root) is *antarikṣam* derived? It is intermediate (*antarā*, i.e. between heaven and earth); it is the end of the earth; or it lies between these two (i.e. heaven and earth), or it is imperishable in the bodies. With reference to this, the word *samudra* (atmosphere) is confused with *samudra* (which means terrestrial ocean). From what (root) is *samudra* derived? From it waters flow up (*sam* + *ud* + √*dru*), or waters flow towards it (*sam* + *abhi* + √*dru*), beings take delight in it, or it is a great reservoir of water, or it moistens thoroughly (*sam* √*ud*). Their difference (should be noted). With reference to this, they relate (the following) legend:[3] Devapī and Śantanu, sons of Ṛṣṭiṣeṇa, were two brothers, who belonged to the clan of the Kurus. Śantanu, the younger brother, caused himself to be installed as king. Devāpi retired to practise austerities. From that time the god did not rain for twelve years in the kingdom of Śantanu. The Brāhmaṇas said to him, 'Thou hast committed (an act of) unrighteousness. Because thou hast caused thyself to be installed as king, having put thy elder brother aside, therefore the god does not rain in thy kingdom.' Then he, i.e. Śantanu, sought to invest Devāpi with sovereignty. To him said Devāpi, 'Let me be thy priest and sacrifice for thee'.[4] Here is his hymn expressing a desire for rain.[5] The following is a stanza of this hymn.

(*Here ends the tenth section.*)

The seer Devāpi, son of Ṛṣṭiṣeṇa, acting as the performing priest, knew (how to obtain) the goodwill of the gods. He caused the divine waters to flow from the upper to the lower ocean by means of rain.[6]

Ārṣṭiṣeṇaḥ means the son of Ṛṣṭiṣeṇa (i.e. one whose army is well supplied with spears), or of Iṣita-sena (i.e. one whose army is mobilized). Army is (so called because) it has a commander, or a uniform mode of marching.

[1] i.e. In the form of coins. Durga remarks: *tena hi vyavahāraḥ kriyate*; this shows that there was gold currency in Yāska's time.

[2] 'Even a mouse', says Durga, 'enjoys itself, if it possesses gold, how much more a human being!'

[3] The story is also related in Bṛh. D. vii. 155-7; viii. 1-7; see Professor Macdonell's note in his edition, vol. ii, p. 292; cf. Sieg, *Sagenstoffe des Ṛgveda*, pp. 129-142. The story is also found in different versions in the *Mahābhārata* and many Purāṇas; see Muir, *op. cit.* vol. i, pp. 271-8.

[4] This shows that the different castes were not divided into water-tight compartments by a rigid barrier of mutual exclusiveness. Here we find a *Kṣatriya* acting as a priest, so the promotion from one to the other was not infrequent.

[5] Cf. Muir, *op. cit.* vol. i, pp. 269, 270.

[6] x. 98. 5.

Putra (son): either he very much protects by offering (sacrificial cakes, &c.); or *put* being (the name of) a hell, he (the son) saves one from that.[1] The seer,[2] acting as the performing priest. A seer is (so called) from his having vision. 'He saw the hymns,' says Aupamanyava. It is known: because the self-born Brahma manifested himself to them while practising austerities, they became seers; that is the characteristic of the seers.[3] Devāpi, one who knew, i.e. was aware of (how to obtain) the goodwill of the gods, i.e. the blessed will of the gods, by songs, praise, and gifts to the gods. From the upper to the lower ocean: upper, raised much higher; lower, moving below (the ground). *Adhaḥ* (below), i.e. it does not run; with this word its upward motion is denied. The stanza following this explains this much more.

(Here ends the eleventh section.)

When Devāpi, domestic chaplain to Śantanu, and selected to be the performing priest, imploring kindled fire, the generous Bṛhaspati granted him speech, which was heard by the gods, and which was the winner of rain.[4]

Śan-tanu means, peace to thee, O body, or peace to him in his body. Domestic chaplain is (so called because) they place him in front.[5] Selected to be the performing priest, (he) imploring kindled fire. Which was heard by the gods, i.e. which the gods hear. [Which was the winner of rain], i.e requesting rain. *Rarāṇa* (generous) is a reduplicated form of *rā* (to give). Bṛhaspati was Brahmā; he granted him speech. *Bṛhat* has been fully explained (i. 7; cp. x. 11).

(Here ends the twelfth section.)

The following six (words) are common (synonyms) of sky and sun. Those which primarily belong to the sun will be explained by us later on.[6] From what (root) is *āditya* derived? He takes the fluids, he takes (i.e. eclipses) the light of the luminaries,[7] or he blazes with lustre, or he is the son of Aditi; this last (epithet) however is rarely applied to him in the text of the Ṛgveda, and he has only one hymn addressed[8] (under this epithet).

The sun, son of Aditi,[9] [i.e. the son of Aditi]. In like manner, there

[1] Cf. Manu, ix. 138; Viṣṇu, xv. 44.

[2] Cf. the Rāmāyaṇa, i. 3. 3-7, quoted by Muir, *op. cit.* vol. iv, p. 441.

[3] TA. ii. 9; see Gune, *Bhandarkar Comm. Vol.*

[4] x. 98. 7.

[5] Cf. Bṛh. D. viii. 6.

[6] See N. 12. 8-22.

[7] The word *āditya* is derived from the same root *ā*-√*dā*, in SB. xi. 6. 3. 8; TB. iii. 9. 21. 1; TA. i. 14. 1; Bṛh. U. iii. 9. 5; all the passages bearing on the etymology are cited by Muir, *op. cit.* vol. iv, p. 117.

[8] Aufrecht proposes the variant *a-sūkta-bhāk*, as it has no hymn addressed to it, but one stanza only. See Muir, *loc. cit.* The author, however, means to say that although hymns are addressed, oblations are not offered under this epithet; cf. Durga's remarks.

[9] x. 88. 11; cf. N. 7. 29.

are panegyrics of other deities addressed to them as Ādityas, as in the case of Mitra, Varuṇa, Aryaman, Dakṣa, Bhaga, Aṃśa. Also of Mitra and Varuṇa:

Ādityas, lords of the act of bestowing.[1] Lords of gift. Also of Mitra alone:

May that mortal, O Mitra, be rich in food, who, O Āditya. abides by thy ordinance.[2]

This too is a Vedic quotation. Also of Varuṇa alone:

Now let us be in thy ordinance, O Āditya![3]

The word *vrata*[4] is a synonym of action, having the sense of abstaining: because it enjoins. This other meaning of *vrata* (i.e. a vow) is derived from the same root also: because it chooses. Food is called *vrata* also, because it covers the body.

(*Here ends the thirteenth section.*)

Svar means the sun; it is very distant, it has well dispersed (the darkness), it has well penetrated the fluids, it has well penetrated the light of the luminaries, or it is pierced through with light. *Dyauḥ* (sky) is explained by the same. *Pṛśni* means the sun. 'It is thoroughly pervaded by the bright colour,' say the etymologists. It closely unites the fluids, it closely unites the light of the luminaries, or it is closely united with light. Now sky is (so called because) it is closely united with luminaries and the virtuous. *Nāka* means the sun, [the bearer of fluids], bearer of lights, leader of luminaries. Now the sky: the word *kam* is a synonym of happiness, the opposite of its negative form (i.e. *nākam*).

There is no misery for the man who has departed to the other world.[5]

There is no wretchedness for the man who has departed to the other world; it is the virtuous only who go there. *Gauḥ* means the sun: it causes the fluids to move, it moves in the sky ($\sqrt{}$*gam*). Now the sky is (called *gauḥ*) because it is gone very far from the earth, or because the luminaries move in it. *Viṣṭap* means the sun: it has pervaded the fluids, it has pervaded the light of the luminaries, or it is pervaded with light. Now the sky is (called *viṣṭap*) because it is pervaded by the luminaries and the virtuous. *Nabhas* means the sun: [bearer of fluids], bearer of lights, leader of luminaries. Or else it may be the word *bhanas* itself, in reversed order: it is not that it does not shine. The sky is explained by the same.

(*Here ends the fourteenth section.*)

The following fifteen (words) are synonyms of ray. Ray is (so called)

[1] i. 136. 3; ii. 41. 6; SV. 2. 262.
[2] iii. 59. 2.
[3] i. 24. 15; VS. 12. 12.
[4] Cf. Roth, *Erläuterungen*, p. 21.
[5] See Roth, *op. cit.* p. 21; the quotation is untraced.

on account of restraining. Of these the first five are common (synonyms) of horse and rays.

The following eight (words) are synonyms of quarter. From what (root) is *diśaḥ* derived?[1] It is derived from (the root) *diś* (to point out), or they are (so called) from being within easy reach, or from pervading. With reference to these, the word *kāṣṭhā* is a synonym of many objects. *Kāṣṭhā* means quarters: they are situated having gone across. *Kāṣṭhā* means intermediate quarters: they are situated having crossed each other. The sun is called *kāṣṭhā* also: it is situated having gone across. Destination is called *kāṣṭhā* also: it is situated having gone across. Waters are called *kāṣṭhā* also: they are situated having gone across, i.e. stationary waters.

(*Here ends the fifteenth section.*)

The deposited body was in the midst of waters which neither stay nor rest. Waters march against the secret (outlet) of *Vṛtra*; in deep darkness lay he whose enemy is Indra.[2]

The deposited body, i.e. the cloud, was in the midst of waters which neither stay nor rest, i.e. waters which are non-stationary.[3] *Śarīra* (body) is derived from (the root) *śṛ* (to kill), or from *śam* (to destroy). Waters march against, i.e. know, [the secret] outlet[4] of Vṛtra. *Dīrgha* (long) is derived from *drāgh* (to lengthen). *Tamas* (darkness) is derived from *tan* (to spread). *Ā-śayad* is formed from (the root) *ā-śī* (to lie). Whose enemy is Indra, i.e. Indra is his slayer, or destroyer, therefore he (is called) having Indra as his enemy. But who is Vṛtra? 'It is a cloud,' say the etymologists. ['It is a demon, son of Tvaṣṭā,' say the legendarians.] The phenomenon of rain is produced by the commingling of water (vapours) and lightning (*jyotiṣ*). With reference to this, there are figurative descriptions of battle. Indeed, the descriptions of Vedic stanzas and the narratives of the Brāhmaṇas (depict him), no doubt, as a serpent. By expanding his body, he blocked the channels (of the rivers).[5] When he was killed, waters flowed forth. The following is the stanza which explains this.

(*Here ends the sixteenth section.*)

Having the demon as their master, and the cloud as their guardian, the obstructed waters stood (behind) as kine (held back) by a merchant.

[1] Cf. Roth, *loc. cit.*

[2] i. 32. 10.

[3] According to Durga, these waters are in the interior of the cloud, so as long as the cloud does not rain they move with the moving cloud, and finally rest in the ocean.

[4] Durga explains *niṇyam* as the outlet in the cloud through which the waters flow down. Roth translates *Vṛtrasya niṇyam* as '*von Vṛtra unbemerkt*', i.e. without being noticed by Vṛtra; see *op. cit.* p. 21.

[5] Cf. Muir, *op. cit.* vol. ii, pp. 174-5.

He slew Vṛtra, and reopened that outlet of water which had been closed.[1]

Having the demon as their master,[2] as their overlord. *Dāsa* (slave) is derived from (the root) *das* (to exhaust): he causes the works to be exhausted. Having the cloud as their guardian, i. e. guarded by the cloud, they stood (behind). The cloud (*ahi*) is (so called) on account of its motion:[3] it moves in the atmosphere. This other (meaning of) *ahi*, i. e. a serpent, is derived from the same root also, or from *ā* √*han* (to attack) with its preposition shortened: it attacks. The waters held back as cows by a merchant. *Paṇi* means a merchant; a merchant is (so called) from trading (√*paṇ*). A trader is (so called because) he cleanses his articles of trade. The outlet of waters which had been closed. *Bilam*,[4] the opening through which anything is conveyed, is derived from (the root) *bhṛ* (to convey). He slew Vṛtra and reopened that outlet. Vṛtra is derived from (the root) *vṛ* (to cover), or from *vṛt* (to roll) or from *vṛdh* (to grow). It is known: because he covered, that is the characteristic of Vṛtra.[5] It is known: because he rolled,[6] that is the characteristic of Vṛtra. It is known: because he grew, that is the characteristic of Vṛtra.

(*Here ends the seventeenth section.*)

The following twenty-three (words) are synonyms of night. From what (root) is *rātriḥ* (night) derived? It exhilarates the nocturnal creatures and causes the others to cease work, and makes them strong, or it may be derived from (the root) *rā* meaning to give: the dew is given away during this (period).

The following sixteen (words) are synonyms of dawn. From what (root) is *uṣāḥ* (dawn) derived? (It is so called) because it shines (√*vas*).[7] It is the time subsequent to night. The following stanza is addressed to her.

(*Here ends the eighteenth section.*)

This light, the best of all lights, has come, and has generated a variegated and extensive illumination. Just as being born it gives birth to the sun, so the night has left its seat for the dawn.[8]

[1] i. 32. 11.

[2] Durga explains the compound as a *tatpuruṣa*, but the accent shows that it is a possessive compound. His explanation is: Lords of servants, i. e. a servant, exhausted by the performance of various works entrusted to him, drinks water, and becomes fresh again.

[3] Cf. Bṛh. D. v. 166.

[4] Durga paraphrases *bilam* by *nirgamadvāram*, i. e. an outlet.

[5] TS. ii. 4. 12. 2; i. e. he covered the waters of the atmosphere. Durga.

[6] According to Durga, he was instrumental in setting the waters in motion.

[7] Durga derives *uṣāḥ* from *ucch*, 'to disperse': it disperses darkness. Cf. Bṛh. D. iii. 9.

[8] i. 113. 1; SV. 2. 1099.

This light, the best[1] of all lights, has approached. It has generated a variegated, well-known, and very extensive illumination. Just as being born it gives birth to the sun, i. e. the night[2] to the sun, so the light has left its seat, i. e. place for the dawn. A woman's womb is (so called because) the foetus is joined with it.[3] The following, another stanza, is addressed to her.

(*Here ends the nineteenth section.*)

Resplendent, having a resplendent calf, the white one has come; the black one has left places for her. Having a common relation, immortal, succeeding each other, the two bright ones wander about fashioning the colour.[4]

Having a resplendent calf, i. e. the sun. The word *ruśat* is a synonym of colour; it is derived from (the root) *ruc*, meaning to shine. The sun is called her calf on account of companionship, or of drawing up the juices.[5] Resplendent, the white one has come. *Śvetyā* (the white one) is derived from (the root) *śvit* (to be bright). The black one has left places for her: the one of black colour, i. e. the night. *Kṛṣṇam* (black) is derived from (the root) *kṛṣ* (to drag away): it is the despised colour. Now (the seer) praises them together:[6] having a common relation, having a common tie;[7] immortal, having the characteristic of immortality; succeeding each other [coming after one another], i. e. with reference to each other; the two bright[8] ones wander about, they themselves are bright, (so called) on account of shining. Or else they wander about with heaven, i. e. they wander about along heaven. Fashioning [creating], making each other's inner self.

The following twelve (words) are synonyms of day. From what (root) is *ahaḥ* (day) derived? (It is so called because) people accomplish works during (this period). The following is its incidental occurrence in a stanza addressed to Vaiśvānara.

(*Here ends the twentieth section.*)

[1] Durga remarks that the sun is too hot, the moon is too cool, but the dawn is neither cold nor hot, hence it is the best of all other lights.

[2] The text seems to be corrupt: it should read 'dawn' instead of 'night'; the present reading makes the sentence meaningless. There is a confusion in the sequence of birth.

[3] Cf. 2. 8.

[4] i. 113. 2; SV. 2. 1100.

[5] The dawn is represented as being followed by the sun. She is compared to a cow followed by her calf: this is companionship. As the calf drinks milk from the udder of the cow, so the sun draws up the dew, which is particularly associated with dawn, hence the sun is called her calf. Durga.

[6] The first hemistich describes the points of contrast, i. e. the one is white, the other black, one comes, the other leaves; the second hemistich, the points of resemblance.

[7] The sun is the common tie. Durga.

[8] The night is called bright also, on account of the multitude of shining stars.

The black day and the white day, the two regions roll on with (activities) worthy of knowledge. As soon as born, Vaiśvānara Agni, like a king, has overcome darkness with his light.[1]

The black day, i. e. night. The white day, i. e. bright day. The two regions[2] roll on with activities worthy of knowledge, i. e. which should be known. As soon as born, Vaiśvānara Agni has dispelled darkness with his light like the rising sun, who is the king of all luminaries.

The following thirty (words) are synonyms of cloud. From what (root) is *megha* (cloud) derived? (It is so called) because it sheds water (√*mih*). They are common with the synonyms of mountain up to the two words *upara* and *upala*, which mean cloud: clouds cease to move in it, or the waters are made inactive.[3] The following stanza is addressed to them.

(*Here ends the twenty-first section.*)

In the measurement of gods they stood first; from their division, waters flowed down. The three working in succession warm the earth; the two carry the fertilizing moisture.[4]

In the creation of gods they, i. e. groups of atmospheric gods, stood first.[5] First is a synonym of 'chief': it is foremost. [*Kṛntatram*[6] means atmosphere, i. e. where the clouds are cut into pieces.] By cutting clouds into pieces water[7] is produced. The three working in succession warm the earth, i. e. cloud, wind, and sun cause the herbs to become ripe with heat, cold, and rain. Working in succession, i. e. with their respective functions, they sow the worlds one after another. This other (meaning of) *anūpa*, i. e. a bank of a river, is derived from the same (root) also: it is sown with water. Or else it may (really) be *anvāp*, just like *prāc*; from that form (*anvāp*) *anūpa* may be derived as *prācīna* (from *prāc*). The two carry the fertilizing moisture, i. e. wind and sun (carry) the water (vapours). *Bṛbūkam* (moisture) is a synonym of water; it is derived

[1] vi. 9. 1; AB. v. 15. 5.

[2] Durga paraphrases *rajasī* by *rañjake*, i.e. dyers; and remarks that the day colours the world with light, night with darkness.

[3] The word *upara* (cloud) is derived from *upa* √*ram* (to cease to move). Yāska's explanation, 'the clouds cease to move', is obscure, and is passed over by Durga.

[4] x. 27. 23.

[5] According to Durga, this refers to the creation of clouds, i. e. Prajāpati, while creating gods, created clouds first on account of their importance; for had there been no clouds, the entire universe would have perished for want of rain.

[6] Roth translates *kṛntatram* as 'seed' or 'seedland'; see *op. cit.*, p. 22.

[7] According to Durga, the word *upara* here denotes water. Originally it means 'cloud', then 'the water of the cloud', and lastly 'water in general'. He cites an analogous case of the extension of meaning: 'crying mounds of earth', i. e. mounds of earth here signify people seated on them.

from (the root) *brū*, meaning to make a sound, or from *bhraṃś* (to fall down). *Purīṣam* (fertilizing) is derived from (the root) *pṝ* (to fill), or from the causal of *pṝ*.

(*Here ends the twenty-second section.*)

The following fifty-seven (words) are synonyms of speech. From what (root) is *vāc* (speech) derived? It is derived from (the root) *vac* (to speak). With reference to these, the word *Sarasvatī* is used both in the sense of 'a river' and of 'a deity' in Vedic passages;[1] we shall explain the (Vedic passages) where it is used in the sense of a deity later, and just now those where it is used in the sense of a river.

(*Here ends the twenty-third section.*)

Like one who digs the lotus-stem, she has shattered the peaks of mountains with her might and strong waves. Let us worship Sarasvatī, who sweeps what is far and what is near alike, with well-composed hymns, for our protection.[2]

She (has shattered) with her might, i.e. with crushing powers. The word *śuṣma* is a synonym of strength, (so called) because it crushes (everything). *Bisam* (lotus-stem) is derived from (the root) *bis*, meaning to split, or grow. Peak is (so called because) it is very much raised up, or it is very lofty. With mighty waves. Who sweeps what is far and what is near alike, i.e. who destroys what is on the other, as well as what is on this, bank. *Pāram* means something afar; *avāram*, something near at hand. Let us attend upon the river Sarasvatī with well-composed sublime songs of praise, and acts (of worship), for our protection.[3]

The following hundred and one (words) are synonyms of water. From what (root) is *udakam* (water) derived? (It is so called) because it moistens (√*ud*).

The following thirty-seven (words) are synonyms of river. From what (root) is *nadyaḥ* (rivers) derived? (They are so called because) they produce a sound (√*nad*), i.e. they are roaring. Their character is mostly secondary, and very rarely primary. With reference to this, they relate (the following) legend.[4] The seer Viśvāmitra was the domestic priest of Sudās, the son of Pijavana. *Viśvā-mitra*, friend of all. All, moving

1 Cf. Bṛh.D. ii. 135.

2 vi. 61. 2; TB. ii. 8. 2. 8.

3 Durga also interprets the stanza as addressed to Sarasvatī, the deity; Sarasvatī is the atmospheric speech, the peaks of mountains are the tops of clouds shattered by her strong waves, i.e. mighty thunders. She sweeps what is far and near, i.e. heaven and earth.

4 The story is found in AB. viii. 13-18, Viṣṇu Purāṇa, &c. See Muir, *op. cit.*, vol. i, pp. 337-64; cf. Bṛh.D. iv. 105-6, see Professor Macdonell's edition, vol. ii, pp. 154-5; Sāyaṇa gives an amplified version in his commentary on iii. 33. 1.

together. *Su-dās*, a bountiful giver. *Paijavana*, son of Pijavana. Again *Pi-javana*, one whose speed is enviable, or whose gait is inimitable.[1] Having gathered his wealth, the priest came to the confluence of the Sutlej and the Bias. Others[2] followed him. He, i. e. Viśvāmitra, implored the rivers to become fordable. (He addressed them) in the dual as well as in the plural number. With reference to this we shall explain (the stanza in which he addresses them) in the dual number later, and just now (the stanza in which he addresses them) in the plural number.

(*Here ends the twenty-fourth section.*)

Stop your courses for a moment, ye great floods, at my friendly bidding. I, the son of Kuśika, and desirous of protection, invoke the river with a sublime hymn.[3]

Stop from flowing at my friendly bidding, I who prepare soma (for you). Great flood, rich in water. The word *ṛtam* is a synonym of water, (so called because) it pervades everything. For a moment (stop) your courses,[4] your journeys, or your protections. A moment, a recurring (unit of) time. *Ṛtu* is derived from (the root) *ṛ*, meaning to go. *Muhuḥ* (again) as if the time was indolent (*mūḷhaḥ*) as long as a moment. *Abhī-kṣṇam* = *abhi-kṣaṇam* (a moment). *Kṣaṇa* (an instant) is derived from (the root) *kṣaṇ* (to injure): it is the injured time.[5] *Kālaḥ* (time) is derived from (the root) *kal*, meaning to go. I call upon the river with a great, mighty, sublime, profound panegyric, full of wisdom, for protection. Son of Kuśika. Kuśika was (the name of) a king. The word *kuśika*[6] is derived from (the root) *kruś*, meaning to cry, or *kraṃś*, meaning to cause to shine; or he is a good expounder of meaning. The rivers answered (as follows).

(*Here ends the twenty-fifth section.*)

Indra, the wielder of the thunderbolt, dug our (channels); he smote down Vṛtra, the enclosure of rivers. Savitṛ, the god of beautiful hands, led us (hither), at his stimulation we flow expanded.[7]

Indra, the wielder of the thunderbolt, dug our (channels); the verb *rad* means to dig. He smote down Vṛtra, the enclosure of rivers, has been explained. Savitṛ, the god of beautiful hands, i. e. of auspicious hands, led us (hither). *Pāṇiḥ* (hand) is derived from (the root) *paṇ*, meaning to

[1] According to Durga, it means a person who walks so quickly that others cannot keep pace with him.

[2] i. e. Servants or robbers. Durga.

[3] iii. 33. 5

[4] Durga paraphases *evaiḥ* by *udakaiḥ*, 'with waters', and takes *avanaiḥ* to mean 'prayers', i. e. stop (your course) at our prayers.

[5] Durga remarks that an instant is called 'injured time', because it is so short.

[6] Cf. Roth, *op. cit.*, p. 23.

[7] iii. 33. 6.

worship: they worship gods, having folded their hands. At his stimulation, we flow expanded.[1] *Urvyaḥ* (expanded) is derived from (the root) *ūrṇu* (to cover). 'It is derived from (the root *vṛ* (to cover),' says Aurṇavābha. Having (thus) answered, the rivers consented in the end.

(Here ends the twenty-sixth section.)

We shall listen to thy words, O bard; thou camest from afar with this chariot. I bend myself down for thee, as a nursing mother (for her son), as a maiden to embrace her lover.[2]

We listen to thy words, O bard! Go[3] afar with this chariot. We bend down for thy sake, as a nursing mother for her son, or as a maiden bends herself to embrace her lover.

The following twenty-six (words) are synonyms of horse. Of these, the last eight are (always used) in the plural number. From what (root) is *aśvaḥ* derived? (It is so called because) it trots on the road, or it eats too much. With reference to these, the word *dadhikrā* (horse) is (so called because) it runs while bearing a rider on its back, or it neighs while bearing a rider on its back, or it looks beautiful while bearing a rider on its back. There are Vedic passages where the word is used (both in the sense of) a horse and of a deity. We shall explain those (passages where the word is used in the sense of) a deity later, and in this place those (where it is used in the sense of) a horse.

(Here ends the twenty-seventh section.)

That courser hastens with speed, although it is bound by neck, flank, and mouth. Putting forth its (best) power, *dadhikrā* sprang along the bends of roads.[4]

That courser, i.e. swift runner,[5] trots on the road with speed, i.e. quickly, although it is bound by the neck. *Grīvā* (neck) is derived from (the root) *gṝ* (to swallow), or from *gṝ* (to call out), or from *grah* (to seize). Bound by flank and mouth has been explained. Putting forth its (best) power, i.e. action or intelligence. *Anusaṃtavītvat* is a word (derived) from the simple original form of (the root) *tan* (to spread). Bends of roads, curves of roads.

[1] i.e. He is our lord; he alone has the right to issue orders to us, and not you. Durga.

[2] iii. 33. 10.

[3] Yāska explains *yayātha* (perfect) by *yāhi* (imperative); this gives better sense but cannot be grammatically justified. If it is construed as perfect, the meaning would be equally relevant, i.e. we shall listen to thy words, for thou camest (*ā yayātha*), i.e. thou hast come, from a long distance, and hence deservest some compassion, and so on. Durga follows Yāska; cf. Roth, *op. cit.*, p. 28.

[4] iv. 40. 4; the stanza is translated by Professor Macdonell, *J.R.A.S.*, vol. xxv, p. 439.

[5] Dreadful, i.e. it inspires terror in the heart of those who look at him. Durga.

Panthāḥ (path) is derived from (the root) *pat* (to fall), or from *pad* (to go), or from *panth* (to move). *Aṅkaḥ* (curve) is derived from (the root) *añc* (to bend). *Āpanīphaṇat* is a reduplicated form (intensive) of (the root) *phaṇ* (to bound).

The following ten (words) describe the specified teams of gods for the knowledge of association.

The following eleven verbs mean to shine. That very number of the following (words) is the synonym of flame.

(*Here ends the twenty-eighth section.*)

CHAPTER III

THE following twenty-six (words) are synonyms of action.[1] From what (root) is *karma* (action) derived ? (It is so called) because it is done (√*kṛ*).

The following fifteen (words) are synonyms of offspring.[2] From what (root) is *apatya* (offspring) derived ? (It is so called because) it spreads farther, or with offspring one does not fall [3] (into hell). With reference to this, we shall quote (the following) two stanzas, in order to show that the offspring belongs to the begetter only.[4]

(*Here ends the first section.*)

The treasure of the stranger is indeed to be avoided : may we be masters of eternal wealth. (The child) begotten by another is no son ; he is so for the fool (only) ; O Agni, do not corrupt our paths.[5]

The treasure of the stranger is indeed to be avoided, i.e. it is not to be approached. Stranger, one who is distant. *Rekṇa* is a synonym of wealth : it is left by the deceased (√*ric*). May we be masters of eternal wealth, as of the parental property (The child) begotten by another is no son. The word *śeṣas* is a synonym of offspring : this is what remains of the

[1] According to Durga, synonyms of action follow those of flame, because it is in the flame of the burning fire that actions like the performance of sacrifice, &c., are accomplished.

[2] Synonyms of offspring follow those of action, because procreation is the most important of all actions. Durga.

[3] Cf. Manu, ix. 138 ; Viṣṇu, xv. 44.

[4] Cf. Manu, ix. 31-3 ; the opposite view is expressed in Manu, ix. 43, 49-51, 54 ; Ga. Dh. xviii. 9-14 ; Āp. Dh. ii. 13. 6-7 ; Vasiṣṭha, xvii. 6-9, 63-4.

[5] vii. 4. 7. Durga remarks that the stanza forms a part of a dialogue between Agni and Vasiṣṭha. The latter implored the former to grant him a son, as all his sons had been killed. The former asked him to get a son by adoption or purchase, &c. ; whereupon he denounced all but the legitimate son.

deceased. That is a child for the fool, i.e. insane, only. Do not corrupt our paths. The stanza following this explains it much more.

(*Here ends the second section.*)

The stranger, however delightful, should not be adopted, begotten in another's womb; he should not be regarded (as one's own) even in thought. To his own abode he certainly goes back. Let the new (hero), impetuous and irresistible, come to us.[1]

The stranger should never be adopted, although he may be the most delightful man. The child begotten in another's[2] womb should not be regarded as 'this is my son', even in thought. Now he goes back to the same abode from whence he came. *Okaḥ* (abode) is used as a synonym of dwelling-place. Let the newly-born (hero), impetuous, i.e. swift and overpowering his rivals, come to us; he alone is (the real) son.

Now (some lawgivers) cite the following stanza in support of a daughter's right to inheritance,[3] others hold (that it is to be cited) in support of a son's right to inheritance.

(*Here ends the third section.*)

The husband admits that he (the father) shall obtain a grandson from the daughter,[4] the wise man, honouring the process of the sacred rite. When a father arranges a husband for his daughter, he bears himself with a tranquil mind.[5]

The husband admits the daughter's right to be appointed as a son, with regard to (the discharge of) the duties of offspring. A daughter is (so called because) it is difficult (to arrange) for her welfare,[6] or she fares well at a distance; or (the word *duhitā*) is derived from (the root) *duh*[7] (to milk). He has obtained a grandson, i.e. the son of the daughter is the grandson.[8] The wise man, honouring the process of the procreative sacrifice, i.e. (of the diffusion) of the seminal fluid, which is produced from each and every limb, which is engendered from the heart, and which is inserted in the

[1] vii. 4. 8.

[2] Durga offers two interpretations, (1) i.e. a child begotten on one's own wife from the seed of another man; (2) a child begotten on a woman other than one's own wife. An illegitimate son is already denounced in the preceding stanza, quoted in section 2; I think, therefore, that the adopted child is the object of denunciation in this stanza, hence Durga's second interpretation is more appropriate.

[3] Offspring has been explained as that which spreads farther than the progenitor. Both the son and the daughter continue the line, so both are offspring, and should have equal rights to inheritance. Durga.

[4] The translation of the 1st and 3rd *pāda* is approximate only.

[5] iii. 31. 1; AB. vi. 18. 2.

[6] She is difficult to please, wherever she may be given away in marriage. Durga.

[7] She is always milking wealth, &c., in the form of presents from her father, and she is always demanding something or other. Durga.

[8] Cf. Manu, ix. 133, 136, 139.

mother, (holds) that both children (i.e. the son and the daughter) have the right to inheritance without any distinction (whatsoever).[1] The selfsame view is expressed in the following stanza and *śloka*.

Thou art produced from each and every limb; thou art engendered from the heart itself. Verily, thou art the very soul named son, as such live a hundred autumns.[2]

In the beginning of the creation, Manu, the self-existent, declared himself that according to law the right of inheritance belongs to both children (the son and the daughter) without any distinction (whatsoever).[3]

'Not the daughters,' say some (of the lawgivers). It is known: therefore the man has the right to inheritance, but not the woman. And also: therefore they abandon a woman as soon as she is born, but not the man.[4] Women are given away, sold, and abandoned, but not the man. 'The man also,' retort others, 'as is seen in the case of Śunaḥśepa.' According to another view, this refers to a maiden who has no brother.

[Women, all clad in red garments, move like veins.][5] They stand with their path obstructed like women who have no brother.[6]

They stand like women who have no brother, and whose path is obstructed with regard to procreation and the offering of the sacrificial cake. With these words the simile implies the prohibition of marrying a brotherless maiden.[7] The stanza following this explains it much more.

(Here ends the fourth section.)

Like a brotherless maiden who goes back to men, like one who ascends the pillar of the assembly-room for the acquisition of wealth, like a well-dressed wife longing for her husband, dawn displays her beauty like a smiling damsel.[8]

Like a brotherless maiden who goes towards men, i.e. parental ancestors,[9] (to render) the duties of offspring and to offer the funeral cake, but not to her husband. Like one who ascends the pillar of the

[1] Durga remarks that an identical *garbhādhāna* ceremony is performed, and the same Vedic texts are recited, both for a son and a daughter. The process of birth is the same in both cases, so there is no difference between them.

[2] SB. xiv. 9. 4. 8; Bṛh.U. vi. 4. 8; SV.B. i. 5. 17; Baudhāyana, ii. 2. 14.

[3] The *śloka* is not found in the extant code of Manu. A similar view is expressed: Manu, ix. 130, 133, 139.

[4] MS. iv. 6. 4; iv. 7. 9; cf. also TS. vi. 5. 8. 2; vi. 5. 10. 3.

[5] The passage within square brackets is omitted by the MSS. of the shorter recension and Durga. As Yāska himself does not explain the first hemistich, it is clear that he quoted the second hemistich only. Hence, according to the evidence of Yāska himself, the shorter recension has a better claim to represent the archetype.

[6] AV. 1. 17. 1.

[7] Cf. Manu, iii. 11; Yājña, i. 53.

[8] i. 124. 7.

[9] Cf. Roth, *op. cit.*, p. 25.

assembly-room[1] in order to obtain wealth, i.e. a woman from the south. *Garta* signifies the pillar of the assembly-room; it is derived from (the root) *gṝ* (to invoke): transactions made under it are true. There she who has neither son nor husband ascends. There they strike her with dies. She obtains wealth. The cemetery heap is called *garta* also, being derived from (the root) *gur* (to raise): it is raised up. A cemetery is (a place where) repose is tranquil, or the body becomes tranquil. *Śarīra* (body) is derived from (the root) *śṛ* (to burn), or from *śam* (to destroy). *Śmaśru* (beard) is hair, (so called because) it stands (√*śri*) on the body (*śmani*). *Loma* (hair) is derived from (the root) *lū* (to cut), or from *lī* (to cling to). One should not expose the lower part of the sacrificial post; the negligent sacrificer who exposes the lower part of the sacrificial post shall soon rest in the cemetery.[2] This too is a Vedic quotation. Chariot is called *garta* also, being derived from (the root) *gṝ*, meaning to praise: it is the most praised vehicle.

Ascend the chariot, O Mitra and Varuṇa.[3]

This too is a Vedic quotation. Like a well-dressed wife, eager for the husband at the proper seasons, dawn displays her beauty as a smiling damsel her teeth. There are four similes. One should not marry a brotherless maiden, for his (the husband's) son belongs to him (to the father of the girl).[4] From this, the prohibition of marrying a brotherless maiden[5] and the father's right to appoint his daughter as a son are evident. When a father selects a husband for his unmarried daughter, he unites himself with a tranquil mind.[6] Now (some lawgivers) cite the following stanza (in support) of their denial of a daughter's right to inheritance. Some are of opinion that the major share belongs to the (appointed) daughter.[7]

(Here ends the fifth section.)

The legitimate son did not leave wealth for his sister. He made her the place of depositing the seed of her husband. If the mothers have engendered offspring, one is the performer, and the other is the director, of good deeds.[8]

Na jāmaye means not for the sister. *Jāmiḥ* (sister) is (so called because) others beget *jā*, i.e. offspring, on her, or the word may be derived from (the root) *jam*, meaning to go: she has mostly to go (to the husband's

[1] Durga remarks that the custom of the people of the south is that a woman who has lost her son and husband approaches the dice-board, and the gamblers make a collection for her.

[2] The quotation is untraced.

[3] v. 62. 8.

[4] The quotation is untraced.

[5] Cf. Manu, iii. 11; Yājñavalkya, i. 53.

[6] i.e. He is free from the tormenting anxiety of childlessness. Durga.

[7] Cf. Manu, ix. 134.

[8] iii. 31. 2.

family). The legitimate, i.e. one's own son, left, i.e. gave, wealth. He made her the place of depositing the seed of her husband, i.e. the man who accepts her hand. If the mothers have engendered *vahni*, i.e. a son, and *avahni*, i.e. a daughter, one of them, i.e. the son and the heir, becomes the procreator of children, and the other, i.e. the daughter, is brought up and given away (in marriage) to another person.

(*Here ends the sixth section.*)

The following twenty-five (words) are synonyms of man. From what (root) is *manuṣyāḥ* (men) derived? (They are so called because) they connect their works after having thought about them (√*man*) or because they were created by a wise creator. Again, the verb *manasyati* is used in the sense of being wise. Or they are the offspring of Manu, or of Manus. With reference to this, there are Vedic passages (in which) the word 'five-tribes' is used.

(*Here ends the seventh section.*)

To-day, then, let me first think out the speech with which we, the gods, shall overcome the demons. Ye partakers of sacrificial food, ye holy five-tribes, enjoy my sacrifice.[1]

To-day, then, I will think out the best speech with which we gods may overpower the demons. Demons (*a-su-rāḥ*) are (so called because) they delight in evil places, or they are expelled from places (√*as*, to throw). Or else the word *asuḥ* is a synonym of breath; inhaled, it rests in the body, i.e. endowed with it (*asu-rāḥ*). It is known: he created gods (*surān*) from good (*su*), that is the characteristic of gods; he created demons (*asurān*) from evil (*a-su*), that is the characteristic of demons.[2] Partakers of sacrificial food and holy, i.e. eaters of the sacred food and holy. The word *ūrj* is a synonym of food, (so called) because it gives strength, or it is easy to divide when cooked. Ye five-tribes, enjoy my sacrifice. According to some, (the five-tribes) are the gandharvās, the manes, gods, demons, and evil spirits. 'They are the four castes with niṣāda as the fifth,' says Aupamanyava.[3] From what (root) is *niṣāda* (hunter) derived? (He is so called because) he lives by killing animals. 'Sin is embodied (*ni-* √*sad*) in him,' say the etymologists.

When with the tribe of five peoples.[4]

With the tribe consisting of five peoples. Five, united number, i.e. (remains) uninflected in the masculine, feminine, and neuter genders.

[1] x. 53. 4.
[2] Cf. TB. ii. 3. 8. 2.
[3] Cf. Muir, *op. cit.*, vol. ii, p. 175; see also his note vol. i, p. 177.
[4] viii. 63. 7; AB. v. 6. 8.

The following twelve (words) are synonyms of arm. From what (root) is *bāhu* (arm) derived? (It is so called because) they perform various actions with them.

The following twenty-two (words) are synonyms of finger. From what (root) is *aṅgulayaḥ* (fingers) derived? (They are so called because) they go foremost, or they drip foremost, or they act foremost, [or they move foremost], or they mark, or they bend, or may be (so called) from decorating. The following stanza is addressed to them.

(*Here ends the eighth section.*)

Worship them who have ten protectors, ten girdling circles, ten yoke-straps, ten binding thongs, ten reins; who are immortal, who bear ten car-poles, and who when yoked are ten.[1]

Avanayaḥ means fingers: they promote actions. Girdling circles illumine actions. 'Yoke-straps' is explained by 'binding thong'. Reins penetrate actions. Who bear ten car-poles, and who when yoked are ten. *Dhūḥ* (pole) is derived from (the root) *dhūrv*, meaning to hurt. This other (meaning of) *dhūḥ* is derived from the same (root) also: it hurts (the team), or it supports them.

The following eighteen roots have the meaning 'to desire'.

The following twenty-eight (words) are synonyms of food. From what (root) is *annam* (food) derived? It is brought near (*ā* √*nam*) created beings, or it is derived from (the root) *ad* (to eat).

The following ten roots have the meaning 'to eat'.

The following twenty-eight (words) are the synonyms of power. From what (root) is *balam* (power) derived? Power is (so called because) it sustains; it is derived from (the root) *bhṛ* (to sustain).

The following twenty-eight (words) only are the synonyms of wealth. From what (root) is *dhanam* (wealth) derived? (It is so called) because it gives delight (√*dhi* cl. 5).

The following nine (words) are synonyms of cow.

The following ten roots have the meaning 'to be angry'.

The following eleven (words) are synonyms of anger.

The following hundred and twenty roots have the meaning 'to go'.

The following twenty-six (words) are synonyms of quick. From what (root) is *kṣipram* (quick) derived? (It is so called because) the interval is short.

The following eleven (words) are synonyms of near. From what (root)

[1] x. 94. 7.

is *antikam* (near) derived? (It is so called because) it is brought near (*ā* √*nī*).

The following forty-six (words) are synonyms of battle. From what (root) is *saṃgrāma* (battle) derived? (It is so called) from going together (*sam* √*gam*) or from shouting together (*sam* √*gṝ*), or (because) the two villages have come together. With reference to this, there are Vedic passages (in which) the word *khala* (is used).

(*Here ends the ninth section.*)

Single-handed I overcome this one (opponent); irresistible I overcome two. What can even three do (against me)? In battle I thrash them well, as if they were sheaves. How dare my enemies, who are without Indra, revile me?[1]

Single-handed I overpower this[2] one (opponent); resisting all rivals, I overpower two. What can three do against me? One is the number gone a little (√*i*, to go). Two is the number running farther (√*dru*, 'to run'). Three is the number gone across farthest (*tṛ*, 'to cross'). Four is the number moved most (√*cal*). *Aṣṭa* (eight) is derived from (the root) *aś* (to pervade). Nine, not to be won (√*van*), or not obtained[3] (*na* + *ava* √*āp*). Ten, exhausted[4] (*das*), or whose meaning is seen (√*dṛś*). Twenty, two times ten. A hundred, ten times ten. A thousand, a powerful (number). *Ayutam* (ten thousand), *prayutam* (hundred thousand), *niyutam* (million), of these each latter the former multiplied by ten. *Arbuda* means a cloud: *araṇam* means water;[5] giver of water [cloud], it shines like water, or it seems to be like water. Just as that cloud when raining becomes a large mass, so like that is the number *arbudam* (ten millions). 'In battle I thrash them well, as if they were sheaves', i.e. like sheaves I thrash them well in battle. The word *khala* is a synonym of battle; it is derived from (the root) *khal* (to fall), or *skhal* (to kill).[6] This other (meaning of) *khala*, i.e. threshold, is derived from the same root also: it is scattered over with grain. 'How dare my enemies, who are without Indra, revile me?' i.e. who do not know that I am Indra, or who have no Indra.

[1] x. 48. 7; cf. Bṛh.D. i. 49.

[2] Durga thinks 'this' refers to the universe as a whole and not to any single opponent.

[3] No work is done on the ninth day, and to begin anything on that day is regarded as inauspicious. Durga.

[4] The word *daśa* (ten) recurs in *ekādaśa*, &c. Durga.

[5] Durga explains *araṇam* as *araṇa-śīlam gamaṇa-śīlam ambu*, i.e. from the root *ṛ*, to go. In Monier-Williams's dictionary the meaning 'water' is not attributed to *araṇam*.

[6] i.e. Heroes fall, or kill each other. Durga.

The following ten verbs have the meaning pervade. With reference to these, two synonyms, i. e. *ākṣāṇa* and *āpāna*, are participles, and mean 'pervading', 'obtaining' respectively.

The following thirty-three roots have the meaning 'to kill'. With reference to these, the form *viyātaḥ* is either the present indicative, 'he crushes', or imperative, 'crush'.

Thou art invoked, O shatterer.[1]

O breaker in pieces. [*Khaṇḍa* (fragment) is derived from (th root) *khaṇḍ* (to break).] The word *taḍit* has the joint sense of 'near' and 'killing', (so called) because it kills.[2]

(Here ends the tenth section.)

Through thee, O Lord of prayer, bringer of prosperity, may we obtain wealth which men covet. Chew those niggards, who prevail against us far and near, into a shapeless form.[3]

Through thee, O Lord of prayer, good promoter of prosperity, may we obtain enviable treasures from men. Chew them into shapeless form, i. e. the enemies who are far from us and who are near to us, the niggards,[4] who are not liberal, or who are stingy. The word *apnas* is a synonym of form because it obtains (√*āp*) (something to rest upon). '*Taḍit* means lightning,' says Śākapūṇi, 'for it smites and is seen from afar.' Or else it may be meant to be the synonym of 'near' alone.

Though afar, thou shinest brightly as if near.[5] Although at a distance, thou lookest bright as if near at hand.

The following eighteen (words) are synonyms of thunderbolt. From what (root) is *vajraḥ* (thunderbolt) derived? (It is so called) because it separates.[6] With reference to these, the word *kutsa* is derived from (the root) *kṛt* (to cut). It is also the name of a seer.[7] 'A seer is a composer of hymns,' says Aupamanyava. Further, it has the meaning 'to kill' only; his friend Indra[8] slew drought.[9]

[1] viii. 17. 12; AV. 20. 5. 6; SV. 2. 76.

[2] Durga explains, 'because it kills', as referring to lightning, which, according to him, is called *taḍit* also, because it kills. This is anticipating Śākapūṇi in the next section.

[3] ii. 23. 9.

[4] According to Durga, there are two kinds of enemies, (1) who are difficult to be destroyed, (2) who are easy to be destroyed. The former are the liberal ones; the latter, the niggards.

[5] i. 94. 7.

[6] It separates living beings from life. Durga.

[7] Cf. Roth, *op. cit.*, p. 30; Durga remarks that the word *kutsa*, meaning 'thunderbolt', should be derived from the root *kṛt* (to cut), and meaning 'a seer', from the root *kṛ* (to compose).

[8] i. e. Invigorated by the panegyrics of Kutsa. Durga.

[9] i. e. Something which dries up the juices, a demon, or a cloud. Durga.

The following four roots have the meaning to be prosperous.

The following four (words) are synonyms of lord. With reference to these, the word *ina* means either (1) one who is endowed with prosperity, or (2) who endows others with prosperity.

(*Here ends the eleventh section.*)

Where (birds) of beautiful wings vigilantly invoke the portion of immortality with knowledge. The lord, the guardian of the entire universe, he, the wise one, here approached me, the immature.[1]

Where (birds) [of beautiful wings], i. e. rays of the sun falling in a beautiful manner,[2] invoke, i. e. move towards[3] the portion of immortality, i. e. of water, with consciousness.[4] The lord, the guardian of all created beings, i. e. the sun: he, the wise one, here approached me, the immature one. Wise, having intelligence. Immature, i. e. one who is to be matured. The sun is called as of mature wisdom in the description of the Upaniṣad. This is with regard to the deity.

Now about the self. Where (the birds) of beautiful wings, i. e. senses, easily going astray, vigilantly invoke, i. e. move towards, the portion of immortality, i.e. of knowledge, with consciousness. The lord, the guardian of all senses, i. e. the soul; he, the wise one, here approached me, the immature. Wise, having intelligence. Immature, i. e. one who is to be matured. 'The soul is of mature wisdom' describes the characteristic of the soul.

(*Here ends the twelfth section.*)

The following twelve (words) are synonyms of much. From what (root) is *bahu* (much) derived? (It is so called) because it is produced on a large scale.

The following eleven (words) are synonyms of small. *Hrasva* (small) is derived from (the root) *hras* (to become small).

The following twenty-five (words) are synonyms of great. From what (root) is *mahān* derived? 'He repudiates others through pride,' says Śākapūṇi (*māna* + √*hā*).

Or he is to be respected (√*maṃh*). With reference to these, the two words *vavakṣitha*[5] and *vivakṣase* are the reduplicated forms either of (the root) *vac* (to speak) or of *vah* (to carry).

[1] i. 164. 21; cf. AV. 9. 9. 22.

[2] i. e. They fall on a bright object which is quite free from darkness, or they shine when they fall. Durga.

[3] i.e. They make the water warm, or having seized fluids in the form of vapours go back to the sun. Durga.

[4] i. e. They have full knowledge of what they are required to do. Durga.

[5] Yāska derives *vavakṣitha*, perfect of √*vakṣ* (to wax), from √*vac* or √*vah*.

The following twenty-two (words) are synonyms of home.[1] From what (root) is *gṛhāḥ* (homes) derived? (They are so called) because they seize everything[2] (√*grah*).

The following ten roots have the meaning 'to attend'.[3]

The following twenty (words) are synonyms of happiness.[4] From what (root) is *sukham* (happiness) derived? (It is so called because) it is useful for the senses (*kham*). *Kham* (sense) again is derived from (the root) *khan* (to dig).

The following sixteen (words) are synonyms of beauty. *Rūpa* (beauty) is derived from (the root) *ruc* (to shine).

The following ten (words) are synonyms of praiseworthy.

The following eleven (words) are synonyms of wisdom.

The following six (words) are synonyms of truth. From what (root) is *satya* (truth) derived? (It is so called because) it is spread among the good, or it originates with the good.[5]

The following eight words have the meaning 'to see'. And [the following] roots, *cāyati*, &c., are mixed with nouns.[6]

The following nine words (are enumerated) in order to make the list (complete, i. e. including) all words (classes).[7]

Now, therefore, the similes. When an object bears (some) resemblance to another which is otherwise dissimilar, (it is denoted by a simile), says Gārgya. With reference to this, their function is to compare an inferior quality, or an unknown object, with a higher quality, or a very well known object. Further, (there is also the comparison of) the higher with the inferior.[8]

(*Here ends the thirteenth section.*)

As two thieves, who risk their lives and haunt the forest, have secured (their victim) with ten fingers.[9]

Who risk their lives, who give up their lives.[10] Who haunt the forest, i. e. who frequent the forest: the author compares the two arms, which

[1] It is the great alone who have homes of their own, so synonyms of home follow those of great. Durga.

[2] A house can never be made full. Durga.

[3] Synonyms of the verb 'to attend' follow those of homes, because it is in homes that people attend or are attended. Durga.

[4] Synonyms of happiness come next, because thus attended one feels happy. The happy are the beautiful. Durga.

[5] Cf. Śākaṭāyana's derivation, 1. 13.

[6] Cf. Roth, *op. cit.*, p. 31; Durga remarks that there are three nouns, i. e. *cikyat*, *vicarṣaṇiḥ*, and *viśvacarṣaṇiḥ*, in the list, the rest are verbs.

[7] i. e. prepositions and particles are included also. Durga.

[8] According to Durga, the statement is applicable to the Veda only.

[9] x. 4. 6; cf. Roth, *op. cit.*, pp. 31–2.

[10] i. e. Highwaymen who are determined to rob or to die. Durga.

produce fire by (the process of) friction, with two thieves.[1] 'A thief is (so called because) he does that, i.e. [becomes the doer of that], which is sinful,' say the etymologists. Or the word may be derived from (the root) *tan* (to spread): his activities are manifold,[2] or he is active both during the day as well as night.[3] Have secured (their victim) with ten fingers, have well secured, i.e. have put (in a place of safety). Thus the higher quality (of the arms) is intended (to be compared).

(*Here ends the fourteenth section.*)

Where are you at night, where during the day? O Aśvins, where do you get your necessary things, where do you dwell? Who puts you to bed in a dwelling-place as a widow a husband's brother; and a bride a bride-groom?[4]

Where do you remain at night, and where during the day? Where do you obtain the necessities of life, and where do you dwell? Who puts you to bed as a widow her husband's brother? From what (root) is *devara* derived? (He is) so called (because) he is the second husband.[5] Widow is (so called because) she is without a supporter, or from trembling, or, according to Carmaśiras, from running about.[6] Or else the word *dhava*[7] is a synonym of man; *vi-dhavā* ('widow', is so called because) she is separated from man (*dhava*). The word *devara* means a player (√*div*, 'to play'). *Maryaḥ* means 'a man', i.e. one who has the characteristic of

[1] This is an example where something higher, i.e. the two arms employed in producing fire by friction, is compared with something inferior, i.e. two thieves, who rob people in a forest. The point of comparison is, just as thieves secure their victim, so we tightly fasten the two sticks to produce fire. Durga.

[2] Durga attributes this explanation to the school of grammarians, although there is no evidence to do so.

[3] i.e. He commits thefts in the village during the night and robs people in the forest during the day. Durga.

[4] x. 40. 2.

[5] The passage within square brackets is evidently an interpolation, as shown by the following: (1) the four words *vidhavā*, *devara*, *marya*, and *yoṣā* are explained by Yāska in the same order in which they occur in the second hemistich of x. 40. 2, but this passage disturbs the regular order; (2) the first derivation of *devara* is separated from the second by the intervening explanation of *vidhavā*; this is against the method of Yāska, who places all the etymologies of one word at the same place, connecting them with 'or . . . or'; (3) the passage is omitted by the MSS. of the shorter recension and Durga.

It refers to the Indo-European practice of the *niyoga*, cf. Xenophon, *Rep. lac.* i. 9; Plutarch, *Lives*, part I, ch. iii, sec. 3 and sec. 5; Caesar, *Commentaries*, bk. iv, ch. xiv; Deut. xxv. 5; St. Matthew xxii. 24; Manu, ix. 57–68; Gau. xviii. 4–5; Bau. ii. 4, 9–10; Va. xvii. 56. 61; Yā. i. 68, 69; see Hastings, *Encyclopaedia of Ethics and Religion*, article on *Niyoga*.

[6] i.e. The word is derived from the root *dhū* with *vi*: at the death of her husband, a woman trembles at the dark prospect of the future, or she runs about without being protected by anybody (*vi* √*dhāv*).

[7] Roth thinks *dhava* to be a coined word; see *op. cit.*, p. 32.

being mortal. *Yoṣā* (a woman) is derived from (the root) *yu* (to join).[1] *Kṛṇute . . . ā* = *ā kurute*, i. e. who makes you rest in the dwelling-place.

Now the particles have already been explained. The word 'as' (denotes) a simile of action:

As the wind, as the forest, as the ocean stirs.[2]

As the brilliant fires.[3]

The soul of consumption perishes beforehand as that of a captive bird.[4]

Ātmā (soul) is derived from (the root) *at* (to go), or *āp* (to obtain); i. e. it may be (called) 'obtained' (in the sense) that it is omnipresent.

They of golden breasts, who are like Agni on account of their brilliance.[5]

They who are like Agni, [i. e. the brilliant Maruts of resplendent breasts], brilliant and having golden breasts.[6]

(*Here ends the fifteenth section.*)

Just as one should be afraid of him who takes the four (dice) until they are deposited, so he should not be eager for harsh speech.[7]

Just as one is afraid of a gambler who holds the four [dice],[8] in the same manner one should be afraid of (using) harsh speech. One should never be eager for (using) harsh speech.

The letter *ā* is a preposition, and has already been explained. It is also used in the sense of a simile:

As a consumer to his enjoyment.[9]

Like a consumer to his enjoyment. The sun is here called the consumer: he is the consumer of night; he is the consumer of lights also.[10] Further, there is the Vedic quotation:

May the sister's consumer hear our call.[11]

The author calls dawn his sister, from companionship, or drawing the juices. Or else this human lover may have been meant; the enjoyment

[1] Durga explains that a woman unites herself with a man.

[2] v. 78. 8; according to Durga, it is recited at the time of delivery: O child! ten months old; just as the wind, the forest, and the ocean move freely without any difficulty, so come forth from the womb of the mother without injuring her.

[3] i. 50. 3; AV. 13. 2. 18; 20. 47. 15; VS. 8. 40; ŚB. 4. 5. 4. 11.

[4] x. 97. 11; VS. 12. 85.

[5] x. 78. 2.

[6] According to Durga, some, thinking that the passage, *agnir na ye*, &c., is explained by *durmadāso na surāyām* (N. 1. 4), do not cite the quotation x. 78. 2.

[7] i. 41. 9.

[8] i. e. Before the dice are deposited on the gambling board, or remains in suspense as to whether he will win or lose. Durga.

[9] Frag. of x. 11. 6ᵃ; AV. 18. 1. 23.

[10] Night disappears at the rising of the sun, and the light of the moon and the stars is eclipsed by that of the sun. Durga.

[11] vi. 55. 5.

in that case will refer to the woman, derived from (the root) *bhaj* (to enjoy).

In *meṣaḥ*, &c., the simile is (denoted) by the word *bhūta*, i.e. having disguised as:

Being disguised as a ram, thou hast approached us.[1]

Meṣaḥ (ram) is derived from (the root) *miṣ* (to blink), just as *paśuḥ* (animal) is derived from *paś* [2] (to see).

In Agni, &c., the simile is (denoted) by the word *rūpa*, i.e. having the form of:

Golden in form and glittering like gold sat the offspring of waters golden in colour.[3]

i.e. One whose form is like the colour of gold. And the word *thā* also (is used to denote a simile).

Him (thou milkest) like the ancient, like the former, like all, like the present (sacrificers).[4]

i.e. Just as the ancient, as the former, as all, as these (sacrificers milk). This, it is nearer than that. That, it is farther than this.[5] The word *amuthā* is explained by 'like that'.

The word *vat* (denotes) a simile in accomplishment: Like a Brāhmaṇa, like a contemptible man.[6] As a Brāhmaṇa, as a contemptible man.[7] Contemptible, one who has the nature of an ox, or that of a beast.

(Here ends the sixteenth section.)

Hear Praskaṇva's call, O (Lord of) great ordinances, and having all created beings as thy property, like that of Priyamedha, Atri, Virūpa, and Aṅgiras.[8]

Priyamedhaḥ, i.e. one to whom sacrifices are dear. Just as (thou hast heard the call) of these seers, so hear the call of Praskaṇva. *Praskaṇvaḥ*,[9] a son of Kaṇva, or one born of Kaṇva; it is formed on the analogy of *prāgram* (in front). Bhṛgu [10] was produced in flames, i.e. one who, although being roasted, was not burnt. Aṅgiras (was born) in

[1] viii. 2. 40.

[2] It seems as if Yāska recognized *paś* as an independent root, and not the ordinary form of *dṛś*.

[3] ii. 35. 10.

[4] v. 44. 1.

[5] Cf. Roth, *op. cit.*, p. 32.

[6] The quotation, if it is a quotation and not an invented example on Yāska's part, is untraced.

[7] i.e. He studies like a Brāhmaṇa, or croaks like a contemptible man. The simile refers to some particular accomplishment. Durga.

[8] i. 45. 3.

[9] Cf. Roth, *loc. cit.*

[10] Cf. TB. i. 8. 2. 5; *indrasya . . . tredhā aindryam vīryam parāpatat. Bhṛgus tṛtīyam abhavat*; the seminal fluid of Indra, having his characteristic power, was discharged threefold. The third (person) born was Bhṛgu; cf. Manu, i. 35, 59, which mention Bhṛgu as sprung from fire; MBh. Ādi. 2605 and Vāyū Pu. i.

live coals. Live coals (are so called because) they leave a mark, or they are bright. They said, 'Seek the third in this very place'; therefore *A-tri*[1] is so called, i. e. not three. *Vaikhānasa* is (so called) from being dug out (√*khan*, 'to dig'). *Bhāradvāja* is (so called) from being brought up (√*bhṛ*). *Virūpa*, multiform. Lord of great ordinances, i. e. whose ordinances are great.

(*Here ends the seventeenth section.*)

Now (the rhetoricians) describe metaphors as similes in which the object of comparison is stated without the particles of comparison. 'Lion', 'tiger', &c., denote excellence; 'dog', 'cow', &c., are used in contempt.

The word *kāka* (crow) is an onomatopoetic word. This onomatopoeia is mostly found in the names of birds. 'Onomatopoeia does not exist,' says Aupamanyava. *Kāka* (crow) is (so called because) it is to be driven away (i. e. from √*kal*). *Tittiri* (partridge) is (so called) from hopping (√*tṛ*), or because it has variegated spots of the size of a sesamum seed. A Francolin partridge is (so called) because it is withered like a monkey, or it is swift like a monkey, or it is slightly brown, or it warbles a melodious note. Dog, swift runner, or (the word *śvā*) is derived from (the root) *śav*, meaning to go, or *śvas* (to breathe). Lion (*siṃha*) is (so called) from its power of resistance, or it is derived from (the root) *hiṃs* (to injure) by metathesis, or from *han* (to kill), preceded by the (preposition) *sam*: it kills having collected. Tiger is (so called) from smelling, or it kills having separated.

(*Here ends the eighteenth section.*)

The following forty-four roots have the meaning to worship.

The following twenty-four (words) are synonyms of wise. From what (root) is *medhāvī* (wise) derived? (He is so called because) he is endowed with that, i. e. wisdom. *Me-dhā* (wisdom) is (so called because) it is stored (√*dhā*) in the mind.

The following thirteen (words) are synonyms of praiser. A praiser is (so called) from praising.

The following fifteen (words) are synonyms of sacrifice. From what (root) is *yajña* derived? 'It is a well-known act of worship,' say the

9. 100 describe Bhṛgu as born from the heart of the creator, and Bhāg. Pu. iii. 12. 23 speaks of him as born from the skin of the creator.

[1] Durga relates the following story. Prajāpati took his own seminal fluid, and sacrificed. From the blazing fire Bhṛgu was born; Aṅgiras rose from the ashes. Then the two just born said, 'Seek the third also here', hence the seer who sprang up was called A-tri. Not satisfied as yet, they began to dig, and the seer thus produced was called Vaikhānasa. A similar story is related in Bṛh. D. v. 97-103; see Professor Macdonell's edition, pp. 190–1.

etymologists. Or it is (an act of) supplication (to gods), or it is sprinkled with the yajus formulas. 'It has a large number of the skins of black antelopes,' says Aupamanyava. Or it is directed by the yajus formulas.

The following eight (words) are synonyms of priest. From what (root) is *ṛtvik* (priest) derived? (He is so called because) he is the furtherer of sacrifice. 'He sacrifices with the stanzas of the Ṛgveda,' says Śākapūṇi. Or he sacrifices at proper seasons.

The following seventeen roots have the meaning 'to beg'.

The following ten roots have the meaning 'to give'. The following four roots have the meaning 'to solicit'. The two verbs *svapiti* and *sasti* have the meaning 'to sleep'.

The following fourteen (words) are synonyms of well. From what (root) is *kūpa* (well) derived? (It is so called because) drinking (water) from a well is difficult, or from (the root) *kup* (to be angry).

The following fourteen (words) are the synonyms of thief. From what (root) is *stena* (thief) derived? '(He is so called because) he is the receptacle of sin,' say the etymologists.

The following six (words) are synonyms of what is ascertained, and what is obscure. [From what (root) is *nirṇītam* (ascertained) derived? (It is so called because) it is cleansed (of doubts).]

The following five (words) are synonyms of distant. From what (root) is *dūram* (distant) derived? (It is so called because) it is drawn out (√*dru*), or it is difficult to be reached (*dur* √*i*).

The following six (words) are synonyms of ancient. From what (root) is *purāṇam* (ancient) derived? (It is so called because) it was new in the days of yore.

Also the following six (words) are synonyms of new. From what (root) is *navam* (new) derived? (It is so called because) it is brought just now.

(*Here ends the nineteenth section.*)

The following twenty-six synonyms are in pairs. The words *prapitve* and *abhīke*[1] are (synonyms) of near. *Prapitve*, i. e. arrived at; *abhīke*, i. e. approached.

Come quickly to us, when the drought is arrived.[2]

Lo![3] the maker of room has approached.[4]

These two are the Vedic quotations.

Dabhram and *arbhakam* are (synonyms) of small; *dabhram* is derived

[1] According to Roth (*op. cit.*, p. 34), *prapitvam* refers to morning, and *abhipitvam* to evening. Grassmann attributes to it the meaning 'advance', 'forward course', &c. See *Wörterbuch zum Ṛgveda*, p. 876.

[2] viii. 4. 3; SV. 1. 252; 2. 1071.

[3] Cf. Roth, *loc. cit.*

[4] x. 133. 1; AV. 20. 95. 2; SV. 2. 1151.

from (the root) *dabh* (to destroy): it is easily destroyed. *Arbhakam*, it is extracted (*ava* √*hṛ*).

Come, approach, embrace, do not think (my hair) to be small.[1]
Salutations to the great, salutations to the small.[2]

These two are the Vedic quotations.

Tiras and *satas* are (synonyms) of attained. *Tiras*, i.e. it has crossed over (√*tṛ*). *Satas*, it is moved together (√*sṛ*).

O undeceived ones, come round quickly across the turn.[3]
Smashing like an earthen jar, he attacks the demons who move together.[4]

These two are the Vedic quotations.

Tvaḥ and *nemaḥ* are (synonyms) of half. *Tvaḥ*, not fully spread (i.e. half). *Nemaḥ*, not brought in full (i.e. half). *Ardha* (half) is derived (1) from (the root) *hṛ* (to take away) by metathesis, or (2) it may be derived from (the root) *dhṛ* (to hold), i.e. it is held out (= extracted), or (3) from (the root) *ṛdh* (to increase): a most abundant division.

One half reviles, one half praises.[5]
Half are gods, half are demons.[6]

These two are Vedic quotations.

Ṛkṣāḥ and *stṛbhiḥ* are (synonyms) of stars. *Nakṣatra* (stars) is derived from (the root) *nakṣ*, meaning to go. There is also a Brāhmaṇa passage: These are not gold (*na-kṣatrāṇi*).[7] *Ṛkṣāḥ*[8] (stars) appear to be raised up. *Stṛbhiḥ* (stars) appear to be scattered (in the sky).

These stars which are placed on high.[9]
Looking at the sky with stars, as it were.[10]

These are two Vedic quotations.

Vamrībhiḥ and *upajihvikāḥ* are (synonyms) of emmet. *Vamryaḥ* (emmets) are (so called) from vomiting. *Sīmikā* (emmet) is (so called) from crawling. *Upajihvikāḥ*, smellers.[11]

[Unmarried maidens (have taken) the undivided son from the emmets.][12]
When the emmet eats, when the pismire crawls.[13]

This is the Vedic quotation. [These are two Vedic quotations.]

[1] i. 126. 7.
[2] i. 27. 13; cf. VS. 16. 26.
[3] v. 75. 7.
[4] vii. 104. 21; AV. 8. 4. 21.
[5] i. 147. 2; VS. 12. 42. One half reviles, i.e. demons; one half praises, i.e. gods. Durga.
[6] Cf. MS. ii. 9.
[7] According to Durga, *kṣatra* is a synonym of wealth. The stars glitter like gold.
[8] Cf. Roth, *op. cit.*, p. 35.
[9] i. 24. 10; TA. i. 11. 2.
[10] iv. 7. 3.
[11] Their smelling power is very acute. Durga. i.e. An insect provided with proboscis; cf. Roth, *loc. cit.*; BI. ii. 354.
[12] iv. 19. 9.
[13] viii. 102. 21; VS. 11. 24.

Ūrdaram and *kṛdaram* are (synonyms) of granary.[1] *Ūrdaram*, i.e. pierced upwards (*ud-dīrṇam*), or pierced for food (*ūrje dīrṇam*).

Fills him like a granary with barley.[2]

This is a Vedic quotation. He fills him like a granary with barley. *Kṛdaram*, i.e. something into which a hole is bored (*kṛta-daram*).

Being kindled, anointing the granary[3] of intellects.[4]

This is a Vedic quotation.

(*Here ends the twentieth section.*)

Rambhaḥ and *pinākam* are (synonyms) of staff. *Rambhaḥ*, i.e. people grasp it.[5]

(We) grasped thee as decrepit people their staff.[6]

This is a Vedic quotation. (The sense is that) we lean on thee as decrepit men on their staff. *Pinākam* (bone), i.e. with this one destroys (*pinaṣṭi*).

Clad in skin, trident in hand, whose bow is unbent.[7]

This is a Vedic quotation.

Menāḥ and *gnāḥ* are (synonyms) of women. '*Striyaḥ*' (women) is derived from (the root) *styai*, meaning to be bashful. *Menāḥ* (women) are (so called because) men honour them (*mānayanti*). *Gnāḥ* (women) are (so called because) men go to them (*gacchanti*).

Thou didst make even the wifeless to be possessed of a consort.[8]

Women cut thee, the active spread thee.[9]

These are two Vedic quotations.

Śepaḥ and *vaitasaḥ* are (synonyms) of penis. *Śepaḥ* is derived from (the root) *śap*, meaning to touch.[10] *Vaitasaḥ*, it is faded.[11]

Loving whom we embrace.[12]

Thrice during the day hast thou embraced me.[13]

These are two Vedic quotations.

Ayā and *enā* are (synonyms) of reference.

With this faggot we worship thee, O Agni![14]

Here it is in the feminine gender.

[1] Cf. Durga's explanation, quoted by Roth, *op. cit.*, p. 36.

[2] ii. 14. 11.

[3] Butter is the granary of intellects. Durga.

[4] VS. 29. 1.

[5] According to Roth (*loc. cit.*) *ā-rabh* means to catch hold, to keep hold, or to lean upon.

[6] viii. 45. 20.

[7] KS. 9. 7; cf. VS. 3. 61; ŚB. ii. 6. 2. 7; TS. i. 8. 6. 2.

[8] v. 31. 2.

[9] MS. i. 9. 4; 134. 8; KS. 9. 9.

[10] *Spṛśyate hi tena strī.* Durga.

[11] Cf. Durga's explanation, quoted by Roth, *op. cit.*, p. 37.

[12] x. 85. 37; AV. 14. 2. 38. The translation is not literal.

[13] x. 95. 5. This was addressed by Urvaśī to Purūravas, when the latter implored her to stay.

[14] iv. 4. 15.

With this, to us, O Agni.[1]

Here it is in the neuter gender.

With this husband commingle thy body.[2]

Here it is in the masculine gender.

Siṣaktu and *sacate* are (synonyms) of service.

Let him who is smart attend upon us.[3]

i.e. Let him who is smart serve us.

Attend upon us for thy welfare.[4]

i.e. Serve us for thy welfare.

The word *svasti* is (a synonym) of non-destruction, i.e. honoured existence: it exists well. *Bhyasate* and *rejate* are (synonyms) of fear and trembling.

At whose breath heaven and earth trembled.[5]

The world is afraid of the great ones,[6] O Agni![7]

These are two Vedic quotations.

The following twenty-four (words) are synonyms of heaven and earth. The following stanza is addressed to them.

(Here ends the twenty-first section.)

Of these two, which is prior, which posterior? How were they born, O sages! who knows? All that exists, they themselves support. The two days roll on like chariot-wheels.[8]

Of these two, which is prior, which posterior? How were they born,[9] O sages! who knows them thoroughly? They themselves support all their functions, whatever they are. And their two days, i.e. day and night, roll on as if placed on chariot-wheels.[10] With these words, the seer describes the greatness of heaven and earth.

(Here ends the twenty-second section.)

[1] vii. 16. 1; SV. 1. 45; 2. 99; VS. 15. 32.

[2] x. 85. 27; cf. AV. 14. 1. 21.

[3] i. 18. 2; VS. 3. 29.

[4] i. 1. 9; VS. 3. 24.

[5] ii. 12. 1; AV. 20. 34. 1.

[6] i. e. The Maruts. Durga.

[7] vi. 66. 9.

[8] i. 185. 1; AB. v. 13. 10; KB. 23. 8.

[9] The question is whether they were born simultaneously like twins, or one after another. Durga.

[10] Cf. Roth, *op. cit.*, p. 37.

CHAPTER IV

HOMONYMS

SYNONYMS[1] have been explained. Now therefore we shall take homonyms[2] in their respective order and (such) Vedic words whose grammatical forms are obscure. They call this (i.e. the list of homonyms) *aikapadikam*,[3] (i.e. composed of single words).

Jahā means 'I have killed'.

(*Here ends the first section.*)

O men, what friend has said, Unprovoked I have killed my friend? who flies from us?[4]

The word *maryā* is a synonym of man, or it may be a synonym of boundary. [Boundary, it is settled by men.] Boundary is the (line of) division between two bounded places. *Methati* means to provoke. What innocent man have I ever killed?[5] Who runs away from us because he is afraid of us?

Nidhā means 'a net', (so called) because it is laid (on the ground). *Pāśyā* means a collection of snares. *Pāśaḥ* (snare) is derived from (the root) *paś* (to fasten), on account of being fastened.

(*Here ends the second section.*)

Imploring seers, fond of sacrifices, approached Indra like birds of beautiful wings. Uncover the encompassed, fill our vision, release us as if we were bound by a net.[6]

Vayaḥ is the plural of *vi* (bird). [Of beautiful wings, i.e.] the beautifully falling rays of the sun approached Indra imploring. Uncover our encompassed vision.[7] *Cakṣuḥ* (eye) is derived from (the root) *khyā* (to know), or *cakṣ* (to see). Fill, i.e. enlarge or give. Release us who are bound with snares as it were.

By the region of ribs, hips, and arms.[8]

[1] Lit., many words which have one meaning.

[2] Lit., single words which have many meanings.

[3] According to Durga, *aikapadikam* is a conventional term. Or it may be significant and is rightly applied to the list of homonyms, in which list each word stands by itself, while in the list of synonyms the words are arranged in groups. However, there are a few exceptions in the list of homonyms, as *somoakṣāḥ*, &c.

[4] viii. 45. 37; cf. Roth, *op. cit.*, p. 38.

[5] Durga gives a second interpretation of the sentence as follows: Who will say, 'I am innocent, kill me'.

[6] x. 73. 11; SV. 1. 319.

[7] Cf. Roth, *op. cit.*, p. 38.

[8] Frag. of VS. 21. 43; TB. iii. 6. 11. 1. Durga quotes and explains the stanza in full.

The region of the ribs, i.e. a part (of the body) consisting of joints.[1] *Parśuḥ* (joint) is derived from (the root) *spṛś* (to touch): it touches the back part. *Pṛṣṭham* (back) is derived from (the root) *spṛṣ* (to touch): it is touched by limbs (of the body). A limb is (so called) from being marked, or from being bent.[2] *Śroṇiḥ* (hip) is derived from (the root) *śroṇ*, meaning to go forward, i.e. a hip appears to go forward when a person walks. *Śitāma* means fore-foot (*dos*). *Dos* (fore-foot) is derived from (the root) *dru* (to run). '*Śitāma* means *uterus*,' says Śākapūṇi, 'it is open.' 'It means liver on account of its dark-red colour,' says Taiṭīki. *Śyāmam* (dark-red) is derived from (the root) *śyai* (to cause to congeal). Liver is (so called because) it is cut out with great difficulty.[3] '(*Śitāma*) means fat, because it is white (*śiti*) meat (*māṃsam*)', says Gālava. *Śiti* (white) is derived from (the root) *śo* (to whet). *Māṃsam* (meat), it is honoured;[4] it is thought[5] (delicious); or else, the mind perishes in it. *Medas* (fat) is derived from (the root) *mid* (to grow fat).

(*Here ends the third section.*)

O Indra, wielder of the thunderbolt, give us whatever excellent treasure there is. With both hands bring that wealth to us, O treasure-knower.[6]

Whatever [excellent], glorious, and abundant wealth there is, O Indra; or that which I do not here possess, (i. e. taking *me-ha-nā*)[7] as consisting of three words, that wealth should be given to us, O wielder of the thunderbolt. *Adriḥ* (thunderbolt) is (so called because) with it he splits (mountains), or it may be derived from (the root) *ad* (to eat).

It is well known: they are eaters of soma.[8] The word *rādhas* is a synonym of wealth: with it, they conciliate. Bring that wealth to us, O Lord to whom treasures are known, with both thy hands. Let both thy hands be full.

Damūnās,[9] one who is inclined towards kindness, or one who is inclined to charity, or one who is inclined to self-control. Or else the word *dama* is a synonym of home; (*damūnās*, therefore) may mean, 'one who is devoted to home'. *Manas* (mind) is derived from (the root) *man* (to think).

(*Here ends the fourth section.*)

[1] Joints are called ribs, because they consist of ribs. Durga.

[2] Every limb becomes bent in course of time. Durga.

[3] According to Durga it is cut out with great ease, because it is so soft.

[4] i. e. It is prepared for a person who is to honoured. Durga.

[5] i. e. It is enjoyed by a person with hearty pleasure, or by those who are intelligent. Durga.

[6] v. 39. 1; SV. 1. 345; 2. 522.

[7] Śākalya, the author of the *Ṛgveda padapāṭha*, does not analyse the word *mehanā*, while Gārgya, the author of the *Sāmaveda padapāṭha*, analyses it into *me-iha-na*. Yāska explains it in both ways.

[8] x. 94. 9.

[9] Cf. Roth, *op. cit.*, p. 39.

Devoted to the house, welcome guest in dwelling-places, approach this sacrifice of ours, O wise one! Having destroyed all assailants, bring to us the treasures of our enemies, O Agni.[1]

Atithiḥ (guest), one who goes (√*at*) to the houses, or one who goes to the families or houses of other persons on certain dates[2] (√*i*+*tithiḥ*). The word *duroṇa* is a synonym of house: they (homes) are difficult to be satisfied (*dur*+ √*av*, 'to satisfy'), i.e. difficult to be provided for.[3] Approach this sacrifice of ours, O wise one! Having destroyed all assailants, bring to us the treasures of our enemies, i.e. having destroyed the forces of our adversaries, bring to us the treasures or the food from the homes of our enemies.

Mūṣaḥ means a mouse. *Mūṣikā* (mouse) again is derived from (the root) *muṣ* (to steal). *Mūṣaḥ* is derived from the same root also.

(*Here ends the fifth section.*)

Bricks torment me on every side, like rival wives. O (Indra) of a hundred powers, oppressing cares devour me, thy praiser, as mice the threads. Know, O heaven and earth, of this (state) of mine.[4]

Bricks, i.e. bricks of the well, torment me on every side, like rival wives. As mice devour the greasy threads. Or (*śiśnā*) may mean one's own limbs, i.e. they devour their own limbs;[5] so oppressing cares, desires torment me, the singer of thy praises, O Lord of a hundred powers. [Know, O heaven and earth, of this (state) of mine.] Realize, O heaven and earth, this (state) of mine. This hymn was revealed to Trita fallen into a well.[6] With reference to this, there is an invocation, accompanied with a legend, a stanza, and a *gāthā*.[7] *Trita* was one most eminent in wisdom. Or else the word may have been intended as a synonym of number, i.e. *ekataḥ*, *dvitaḥ*, *tritaḥ*, thus the three were produced.[8]

(*Here ends the sixth section.*)

May we, with an active mind, partake of thy pressed soma, as if it were paternal property. O king soma, prolong our lives, as the sun prolongs the summer days.[9]

May we, with (an active), i.e. quick, or vigorous, or enlightened mind, partake of thy pressed soma-juice, as if it were paternal property.

[1] v. 4. 5; AV. 7. 73. 9.

[2] i.e. He comes to the houses of sacrificers on the full-moon day and other days of sacrifice. Durga.

[3] Durga quotes the following passage: It is difficult indeed to provide for one's family.

[4] i. 105. 8; x. 32. 2: cf. Bṛh.D. 7. 34.

[5] It is the habit of some birds to devour their own tails, and the habit of the mouse is to first besmear its tail with grease and to lick it afterwards. Durga.

[6] Cf. Roth, *op. cit.*, p. 39.

[7] Cf. Sieg, *Sagenstoffe des Ṛgveda*, p. 27.

[8] Cf. Professor Macdonell, *J.R.A.S.* xxv.

[9] viii. 48. 7; KS. 17. 19.

O king soma, make our lives long, as the sun does the days in summer. Days are (so called because) they are of different courses,[1] or they are bright,[2] or they pass away.[3]

The word *kurutana* (do), as well as the words *kartana* (do), *hantana* (kill), and *yātana* (go), have (*na*) as a redundant addition.[4]

Jaṭharam means belly; (all that is) eaten is held in it, or is deposited in it.

(*Here ends the seventh section.*)

Indra, the bull, accompanied by the Maruts, is for battle. Drink soma for rapture after food. Pour down the flood of mead into thy belly. From days of yore thou art the king of soma-draughts.[5]

Indra, accompanied by the Maruts, i.e. having the Maruts as his companions. Bull, i. e. one who brings down rain. For battle, for a delightful battle. Drink soma for rapture, i. e. for a maddening victory, after food, i. e. after meals.[6] Pour down the flood of mead into thy belly. *Madhu* means soma, is derived from (the root) *mad* (to exhilarate), and is compared with soma (on account of the analogy of exhilaration). This other (meaning of) *madhu* (wine) is derived from the same (root) also. Thou art the king of soma-draughts (now, as thou wert) in the former days.

(*Here ends the eighth section.*)

Titaü[7] means a sieve: it is covered with a hide, or it has holes, or its holes are (small) like sesamum seeds.

(*Here ends the ninth section.*)

Where the wise have sifted speech in their minds, as if winnowing grain in a sieve, there friends recognize friendships; the blessed mark is impressed on their speech.[8]

As if winnowing grain in a sieve. *Saktuḥ* (grain) is derived from (the root) *sac* (to cling): it is difficult to wash; or it may be derived from the (root) *kas* (to shine) by metathesis: it is fully blown. Where the wise have sifted speech, i. e. knowledge, in their minds. Wise, very learned, or great thinkers. There friends will recognize friendships. The blessed mark is impressed on their speech. Blessed is explained by fortunate: it is to be

[1] i. e. They are cold during the night and warm during the day. Durga.

[2] i. e. They destroy cold. Durga.

[3] i. e. They are extended, they roll on one after another *ad infinitum*. Durga.

[4] Durga quotes VS. 12. 69; RV. v. 4. 30. 2; and RV. 2. 3. 26. 3 to illustrate *kartana*, *hantana*, and *yātana* respectively.

[5] iii. 47. 1.

[6] Cf. Roth, *op. cit.*, pp. 40–1.

[7] Cf. Patañjali, *op. cit.*, i. 1. 1, vol. i, p. 4.

[8] x. 71. 2.

enjoyed, or acquired by created beings, or its existence is the cause of enjoyment, or it goes to the deserving person. *Lakṣmī* (mark) is (so called) from obtaining, or from indicating, [or from a desire to obtain], or from marking; or it may be derived from (the root) *laṣ*, meaning to desire, or from *lag*, meaning to cling, or from *lajj*, meaning not to praise.[1]

We shall explain *śipre* later on.[2]

(*Here ends the tenth section.*)

That is the divinity of the sun, that is his greatness, that in the midst of actions he rolled up what was spread out. When he has yoked the bay steeds from the stable, night still spreads around her garment for him.[3]

That is the divinity of the sun, that is his greatness, that in the midst of actions, i. e. works which were being done, he gathers together what was spread out. When he has yoked the bay steeds, i. e. the rays of the sun, or the horses. Night still spreads around her garment for him, i. e. it disconnects the bright day from all. Or else it may have been used in the sense of comparison, i. e. like night he spreads his garment. There is also the Vedic quotation:

Weaving what was spread, she wove again.[4]

i. e. She gathered together.

(*Here ends the eleventh section.*)

Verily, thou art seen together with Indra, going with the dauntless (group). Both joyous and of equal valour.[5]

Verily thou art seen together with Indra, going in the company of the dauntless group.[6] Both of you are joyous, happy. Or else the meaning may be 'with that happy group'. 'Of equal valour' is to be similarly explained.

(*Here ends the twelfth section.*)

With well-formed haunches, symmetrical flanks, together the spirited, divine coursers make efforts like swans in rows, when they, the steeds, have reached the celestial path.[7]

With well-formed haunches, with protruding, [well-protruding], or broad haunches. With symmetrical flanks, i. e. whose flanks are compact, or whose head is in the middle. Or else *śiras* refers to the sun, i. e. it follows all created things to rest, and stands in their midst. This other (meaning of)

[1] i. e. Men who have *lakṣmī* do not praise themselves. Durga. The whole section is quoted by Patañjali, *loc. cit.*

[2] See 6. 17.

[3] i. 115. 4; AV. 20. 123. 1; VS. 33. 37.

[4] ii. 38. 4.

[5] i. 6. 7; AV. 20. 40. 1; 70. 3; SV. 2. 200.

[6] i. e. The Maruts. Durga.

[7] i. 163. 10; VS. 29. 21.

śiras (i. e. the human head) is derived from the same root also: the senses depend upon it. Together the spirited [divine coursers]. *Śūraḥ* (spirited) is derived from (the root) *śu*, meaning to go. Divine, born in heaven. Coursers, racers. They make efforts like swans in rows. *Haṃsāḥ* (swans) is derived from (the root) *han* (to smite): they tread the way in lines.

Śreṇi (row) is derived from (the root) *śri* (to combine), they are combined.

When the steeds have reached, i. e. arrived at, the celestial path, track, course. The panegyric of the sun is the panegyric of the horse, for the horse was fashioned from the sun:[1]

O Vasus, ye fashioned forth the horse from the sun.[2]

(*Here ends the thirteenth section.*)

Observing the forests, when thou hast gone to the mothers, the waters. That return of thine, O Agni, is not to be forgotten, when being afar, thou wert here in an instant.

Kāyamāna[3] means observing, or desiring[4] the forests, when thou hast gone to the mothers, the waters, i. e. hast become extinguished. O Agni, that return of thine cannot be forgotten, when being afar and being produced, thou wert here in an instant.

Thinking him a beast, they drive the greedy one away.[5]

Thinking him a beast, they drive the greedy seer away.[6]

(Praise) Agni of purifying flames.[7]

i. e Of pure light:[8] it rests through all, or pervades all.

(*Here ends the fourteenth section.*)

Like two small dolls on their newly-wrought, perforated, wooden seats the bay steeds shine on their courses.[9]

Two dolls, two young maidens.[10] *Kanyā* (maiden) is (so called because) she is an object of love (*kamanīyā*), or (because it is said) to whom should her hand be given, [or because she is brought by the lover], or it may be

[1] According to Durga this gives Yāska's answer to an anticipated objection. The objection is that the stanza is to be interpreted as addressed to the sun, and as such its application to the horse-sacrifice is highly inappropriate. To this Yāska rejoins, that the panegyric of the one is the panegyric of the other, &c.

[2] iii. 9. 2; SV. 1. 53.

[3] 'Avoiding, or being afraid, or respectful.' Grassmann, *op. cit.*, p. 443.

[4] i. e. Desiring the wood, which is the source of thy birth, as well as waters. He quotes: Waters verily are the source of Agni. Return, i. e. lightning, if it is born from waters, or the terrestrial fire, if generated from the friction of the two sticks. Durga.

[5] iii. 53. 23.

[6] Durga ignores the stanza, because it implies hostility to Vasiṣṭha, he himself being a descendant of Vasiṣṭha.

[7] iii. 9. 8; viii. 43. 31; 102. 11.

[8] Cf. Roth, *op. cit.*, p. 42.

[9] iv. 32. 23.

[10] Cf. Roth, *loc. cit.*

derived from (the root) *kan*, meaning to shine. 'The words relating to the seats of the maidens are in the locative singular,' says Śākapūṇi,[1] i. e. on the ornamental wooden seats. *Dāru* (wood) is derived from (the root) *dṝ* (to split), or from *dru* (to injure). *Dru* (wood) is derived from the same (root) also. New, newly made. Small, not large. As they shine on their seats, so the bay steeds shine on their courses. This is a joint panegyric of two bay steeds.

'He has given me this, he has given me that'; having thus enumerated, the seer said:

On the bank of the Suvāstu.[2]

Suvāstu[3] is the name of a river. *Tugva*[4] means a ford, (so called because) people hasten towards it.

Will the Maruts again bend down for us.[5]

Once again, the Maruts bend down for us.

We shall explain the word *nasatah* later on.[6]

Incite Indra, in order to give us wealth, with those gladdening, foaming and exhilarating draughts, which thou hast.[7]

Incite Indra, so that he may give us wealth, with those draughts of thine, which are gladdening, which foam, and which are accompanied with songs of praise.

(*Here ends the fifteenth section.*)

She has appeared like the breast of the pure one, she has displayed lovely traits like a singer. Waking up the sleepers like a mother, this most constant one has come of them that are coming again.[8]

She has appeared like the breast, i. e. light that is exalted, of the pure one. The pure one is the sun, (so called) from purifying. This other (meaning of) *vakṣas* (breast) is derived from the same (root) also: it is exalted in the body. A bird, too, is called the pure one, from the same purifying: it roams over waters. Waters, too, are called the pure one, from the same purifying. *Nodhās* (singer) means a seer: he composes a new hymn. As he makes his desires apparent in his songs of praise, so dawn manifests her beauteous forms. *Adma-sad*[9] (mother)—*adma* means food—i.e. one who sits at a meal, or one who obtains food. Waking up the sleepers, the most constant one has come of them that are coming again.

[1] The author of the *Padapāṭha* agrees with Śākapūṇi.

[2] viii. 19. 37.

[3] Cf. Roth, *op. cit.*, p. 43; Muir, *op. cit.*, vol. ii, p. 344.

[4] 'A sweeping flood, waterfall, and then a secret place,' Roth, *loc. cit.*

[5] vii. 58. 5.

[6] See 7. 17.

[7] ix. 75. 5.

[8] i. 124. 4.

[9] Cf. Roth, *op. cit.*, p. 44.

[Waking up the sleepers], the most constant one has come of them that are coming again.

They, possessors of speech and impetuous.[1]

Impetuous, or ambitious, or having a direct perception. *Vāśī* is a synonym of speech, (so called) because it is spoken.

Let us two praise (him), O priest! sing in answer to me, let us compose an agreeable hymn to Indra.[2]

Some think it to be a panegyric on invocation; others, a recitation on pressing the soma. It is, however, addressed to Indra.

We shall explain the word *paritakmyā* later on.[3]

(Here ends the sixteenth section.)

Suvite = *su* + *ite*, or = *sūte*, i. e. in (the sense of) going well, or to give birth to.

Place me in good position.[4]

This, too, is a Vedic quotation.

Dayatiḥ [5] has many meanings.

Let us protect the old with the new.[6] (In this passage *dayatiḥ*) means to protect.

Who alone here distributes wealth.[7] (In this it) means to give, or to divide.

Irresistible, dreadful, he burns the forests.[8] (In this it) means to burn. Irresistible, one who is difficult to be resisted.

The treasure-knower, slaying his foes.[9] (In this it) means to slay.

These soma-juices are pressed, let the Aśvins, who come at dawn and are of equal valour, drink them. I am (here), indeed, to refresh and to salute you. The crow flying at daybreak has waked me up.[10]

dayamānaḥ,[11] i. e. flying.

The word *nū cit* is a particle, and is used in the sense of ancient and modern; *nū ca* also (is similarly used).

Even to-day as in the days of yore, the same is the work of the rivers.[12]

And to-day the function of the rivers is the same as it was in ancient times.

[1] i. 87. 6.

[2] iii. 53. 3.

[3] See 11. 25.

[4] TS. i. 2. 10. 2; KS. 2. 8.

[5] Cf. Roth, *op. cit.*, pp. 44–5. Durga remarks that Yāska is not conjecturing now as in the case of *suvite*.

[6] KS. 19. 3; TB. iii. 6. 13. 1; cf. VS. 28. 16; N. 9. 43.

[7] i. 84. 7; AV. 20. 63. 4; SV. 1. 389; 2. 691.

[8] vi. 6. 5.

[9] iii. 34. 1; AV. 20. 11. 1.

[10] The quotation is untraced. Durga explains the fourth quarter only and remarks that the rest of the passage is to be discovered.

[11] *Atra dayatir gatyarthaḥ.* Durga.

[12] vi. 30. 3.

The present and the past place of treasures.[1]

The modern and the ancient place of treasures. The word *rayiḥ* is a synonym of wealth; it is derived from (the root) *rā*, meaning to give.

(*Here ends the seventeenth section.*)

May we obtain (lit. know) that unlimited gift of thine.[2]

May we obtain that illimitable gift of thine. The sun is called *akūpāra* also, i. e. unlimited, because it is immeasurable. The ocean, too, is called *akūpāra*, i. e. unlimited, because it is boundless. A tortoise is also called *a-kūpa-ara*, because it does not move in a well.[3] *Kacchapa* (tortoise) is (so called because) it protects (*pāti*) its mouth (*kaccham*),[4] or it protects itself by means of its shell (*kacchena*), or it drinks (√*pā*) by the mouth. *Kaccha* (mouth or shell of a tortoise) = *kha-ccha*, i. e. something which covers (*chādayati*) space (*kham*). This other (meaning of) *kaccha*, 'a bank of a river', is derived from the same (root) also, i. e. water (*kam*) is covered (*chādyate*) by it.

To destroy the demons, he sharpens his horns.[5]

i. e. For the destruction of the demons, he sharpens his horns. *Rakṣas* (demon) is (so called because) life has to be protected (√*rakṣ*) from him, or he attacks (√*kṣaṇ*) in solitary places (*rahasi*), or he approaches (√*nakṣ*) at night (*rātrau*).[6]

Impetuous, Agni with impetuous steeds.[7]

i. e. Swift with swift horses, or nobly-born Agni with horses of noble breed.

Let the agile rest in this sacrifice.[8]

i. e. They who move swiftly.

(*Here ends the eighteenth section.*)

So that the gods be ever for our prosperity, our watchful guardians day by day.[9]

So that the gods may always be the promoters of our prosperity. Watchful, vigilant. Our guardians on every day.

Cyavana[10] is (the name of) a seer: he is the collector of hymns. There are Vedic passages in which it occurs as *cyavāna*:

[1] i. 96. 7.

[2] v. 39. 2; SV. 2. 523.

[3] i. e. On account of its shallowness. Durga.

[4] i. e. As soon as it smells any danger, it draws its mouth within the shell and assumes the characteristic shape of the tortoise.

[5] v. 2. 9.

[6] Roth derives *rakṣas* from √*ṛś*, 'to kill', *op. cit.*, p. 46.

[7] x. 3. 9.

[8] VS. 28. 5.

[9] i. 89. 1; VS. 25. 14; KS. 26. 11.

[10] Cf. Roth, *op. cit.*, p. 46.

You two made the decrepit Cyavāna young again, to move anew like a car.[1]

You two made the decrepit Cyavāna, i. e. who was very old, young again, in order to move about like a car. *Yuvā* (a youth), he stirs (*prayauti*) actions. The verb *takṣati* means to make.

Rajas [2] is derived from (the root) *rañj* (to glow). The two lights are called *rajas*, water is called *rajas*, worlds are called *rajas*, blood and day are called *rajas*.

[Variegated and thundering worlds move in different directions.[3] This is a Vedic quotation.]

Haras is derived from (the root) *hṛ* (to take away). Light is called *haras*, water [4] is called *haras*, worlds [5] are called *haras*, [blood and day are called *haras*. Mix this light with thy light, O Agni.[6] This is a Vedic quotation.]

The wise sacrificed.[7]

People, having a precise knowledge of the various acts of worship, sacrificed.

The word *vyantaḥ* has many meanings.

Looking at the foot of the god with obeisance.[8]

(In this passage it) means 'to see'.

O hero, partake of the oblation.[9]

(In this it) means 'to eat'.

Eat and drink the milk of the cow.[10]

Do you eat and drink the milk of the cow. *Usriyā* [and *usrā*] is a synonym of cow, (so called) because enjoyable things flow from it.

The soma being pressed by the intelligent,[11] the well-conducted lovers of wealth have willingly praised thee, O Indra.[12]

i. e. Having presented the soma, they have praised thee.

Pour down the golden juice in the lap of the wood, prepare it with chisels made of stone.[13]

Pour down the golden juice in the lap of the wood, i. e. of a wooden

[1] x. 39. 4.

[2] Cf. Muir, *op. cit.*, vol. iv, p. 71. Yāska does not illustrate the various meanings of *rajas* by suitable examples. Durga supplies them and explains Yāska's omission by the remark that the word is frequently used in these senses.

[3] v. 63. 3 ; TB. ii. 4. 5. 4.

[4] i. e. It is taken away from a well, &c., by people for living. Durga.

[5] i. e. People, the merit of whose deeds being exhausted, are taken away from them.

[6] x. 87. 25 ; SV. 1. 95.

[7] v. 19. 2.

[8] vi. 1. 4.

[9] iii. 41. 3 ; AV. 20. 23. 3.

[10] i. 153. 4 ; AV. 7. 73. 5.

[11] It is the intelligent alone who are capable of pressing the soma, and not others who do not possess intelligence. Durga.

[12] The quotation is untraced.

[13] x. 101. 10.

cup. The golden juice is the soma, (so called from) its golden colour. This other (meaning of) *hariḥ* (i. e. a monkey) is derived from the same (root) also.[1] Prepare it with chisels made of stone, i. e. with stone-made chisels, or with songs of praise.[2]

May he, the noble one, defy the manifold creatures, let phallus-worshippers not penetrate our sanctuary.[3]

May he overpower them, i. e. the manifold creatures who are hostile[4] to us. Let the phallus-worshippers, i. e. the unchaste—*śiśna*[5] (phallus) is derived from (the root) *śnath* (to pierce)—not approach our sanctuary, i. e. our truth, or sacrifice.

(*Here ends the nineteenth section.*)

Surely there will come those future ages, when kinsmen will behave like strangers. Seek, O fair one, a husband other than me; for him, thy consort, make thy arm a pillow.[6]

There will come those future ages, when kinsmen will act in the manner of strangers. *Jāmi*[7] is a synonym of tautology, fool, and one born in the same caste. Make thy arm a pillow for thy consort; seek, O fair one, a husband other than me is explained (easily).

(*Here ends the twentieth section.*)

Heaven is my father, progenitor; here is my uterine relative; the great earth is my mother. The womb is within the two widespread world-halves; the father here bestowed a life-germ on the daughter.[8]

Heaven is my father, protector, benefactor, progenitor; here is my uterine relative; the great earth is my mother. Relative is (so called) from being connected together. Uterine is (so called) from being fastened together. It is said: children are born fastened to the umbilicus.[9] Hence the near relatives are called as having a common umbilicus, or a common tie. A near relative is (so called) from being well known. The womb is within the two widespread world-halves. Widespread, i. e. spread very wide, or spread very high. There the father bestows the life-germ on the daughter, i. e. the rain-cloud on the earth.

[1] Durga quotes a verse from the *Rāmāyaṇa*, according to which the monkeys are described as 'soft like the *śirīṣa* flower, and glittering like gold'.

[2] In the second case, the meaning would be: prepare, i. e. season or purify the soma-juice with songs of praise, which are comprehensive and sublime. Durga.

[3] vii. 21. 5.

[4] i. e. Who destroy our sacrifices. Durga.

[5] Cf. Roth, *op. cit.*, p. 47.

[6] x. 10. 10; AV. 18. 1. 11.

[7] Cf. Roth, *loc. cit.* Durga remarks that Yāska does not cite passages to illustrate the meaning of *jāmi*; he himself follows suit.

[8] i. 164. 33; cf. AV. 9. 10. 12.

[9] Cf. TS. vi. 1. 7. 2.

[Desirous of peace, desirous of happiness.][1]

Now bestow sinless peace and tranquillity upon us.[2] The words *rapas* and *ripram* are synonyms of sin; i.e. freedom[3] from diseases, and the warding off of dangers. Moreover, a descendant of Bṛhaspati is called *śaṃyu* also:

This we beg of Śaṃyu: to go to the sacrifice; to go to the lord of sacrifice.[4]

This too is a Vedic quotation. (The meaning is) in order to go to the sacrifice, and to the lord of the sacrifice.

(Here ends the twenty-first section.)

Aditi, unimpaired, mother of gods.[5]

(Here ends the twenty-second section.)

Aditi is heaven, Aditi is atmosphere, Aditi is mother, father, and son. Aditi is all the gods, and the five tribes; Aditi, what is born and what shall be born.[6]

With these words, the seers describe the greatness of Aditi. Or else, all these things are unimpaired.

Whom the Bhṛgus raised.[7]

Erire is a reduplicated form of *īr* (to raise), preceded by the preposition *ā*.

(Here ends the twenty-third section.)

People shout after him in battles, as they do after a clothes-stealing thief, or a falcon let loose and swooping downwards, and a glorious herd of cattle.[8]

(People shout) after him as they do after a clothes-stealing thief, i.e. one who steals clothes. *Vastram* (clothes) is derived from (the root) *vas* (to wear). The word *tāyu* is a synonym of thief: 'he is a store-house of sin,' say the etymologists, or it may be derived from (the root) *tas* (to perish).[9] People shout after him in battles. The word *bhara* is a synonym of battle; it is derived (from the root) *bhṛ* (to bear), or *hṛ* (to carry away).[10] Swooping

[1] The explanation within square brackets is contradictory to Yāska's comment and is thus an indirect argument in support of its spurious character.

[2] x. 15. 4; VS. 19. 55; cf. AV. 18. 1. 5.

[3] Cf. Roth, *op. cit.*, p. 48.

[4] TS. ii. 6. 10. 2; ŚB. i. 9. 1. 26.

[5] Durga attributes the two explanations to the school of etymologists and to the school of legendarians respectively.

[6] i. 89. 10; AV. 7. 6. 1; VS. 25. 23.

[7] i. 143. 4.

[8] iv. 38. 5.

[9] i.e. He perishes on account of his unrighteous conduct. Durga.

[10] i.e. The heroes, or the treasures of the enemy are carried away.

downwards, pouncing downwards. Downwards is going down; upwards is going up. Like a falcon let loose.[1] Falcon is (so called because) it swoops in an admirable manner. And a glorious herd of cattle, i. e. a famous herd of cattle: glory and the herd, or wealth and the herd.

Yūtham (herd is derived from (the root) *yu* (to connect): it is compact.

While kindling, the man of noble wisdom extols him,[2] i. e. he praises him.

Mandī (praiseworthy) is derived from (the root) *mand*, meaning to praise.

Worship the praiseworthy (Indra) with hymns and oblations.[3]

Bring worship to the praiseworthy (Indra) in (the form of) panegyrics with offerings of food.

Gauḥ has been explained.[4]

(*Here ends the twenty-fourth section.*)

Indeed, in this place, it is said, they thought of the ray separated from the sun; here in the house of the moon.[5]

In this place, indeed, the rays of the sun, together of their own accord, thought of the separated, i. e. disunited, removed, disconnected, or concealed (ray); there, in the house of the moon.[6]

Gātu has been explained.[7]

[Dawns made a move for man.[8] This too is a Vedic quotation.]

Daṃsayaḥ means works, (so called because) they finish them.

Thinking (to make) the works (fruitful) for the peasant, (you let) the waters (flow).[9]

This too is a Vedic quotation.

He became prosperous, distress does not approach him.[10]

He became prosperous, distress does not come near him. The words *aṃhatiḥ*, *aṃhaḥ*, and *aṃhuḥ* are derived from (the root) *han* (to injure) by metathesis, after making its penultimate the initial part (*han* > *ahn* > *anh* = *aṃh*).

O Bṛhaspati, thou dost destroy the derider.[11]

[1] According to Durga, *jastam* means 'bound', i. e. a falcon in this state cannot fly up, but comes down and kills its prey, being applauded by people. This explanation seems to be far-fetched and illogical, for a bound falcon cannot kill its prey.

[2] x. 45. 1; VS. 12. 18.

[3] i. 101. 1; SV. 1. 380.

[4] See 2. 5.

[5] i. 84. 15; AV. 20. 41. 3; SV. 1. 147; 2. 265.

[6] Cf. Roth, *op. cit.*, p. 49.

[7] See 4. 21.

[8] iv. 51. 1.

[9] x. 138. 1. Cf. Roth, *op. cit.*, p. 49.

[10] i. 94. 2.

[11] i. 90. 5.

O Bṛhaspati, when thou destroyest the derider.[1] *Pīy* means to deride.

Viyute means heaven and earth, (so called) from their remaining apart from each other.

Alike, heaven and earth terminating at a distance.[2] Alike, of equal measure. Measure is (so called) from being measured. *Dūram* has been explained.[3] *Antaḥ* (end) is derived from (the root) *at* (to go).

The word *ṛdhak*[4] is a term (used to denote) the idea of separation.[5] It is also used in the sense of prosperity.

Being prosperous, thou hast sacrificed; being prosperous, thou hast toiled.[6]

In a state of prosperity, thou hast sacrificed; in a state of prosperity, thou hast exerted thyself.

The words *asyāḥ* and *asya* have the acute accent when referring to a primary, and grave when referring to a secondary, object. The more emphatic meaning has the acute accent, the less, the grave.

For the obtainment of this, be near us, O goat-teamed one, gracious and bounteous.[7] [Be glorious, O goat-teamed one.]

For the obtainment of this, be near us.

Gracious, without being angry. *Rarivān* (bounteous) is a reduplicated form of (the root) *rā* (to give). The seer addresses Pūṣan as goat-teamed. Goat-teamed, goats are his coursers. Now the grave accent:

Let her husband, who has a long life, live for hundred autumns.[8]

May her husband, who has a long life, live for hundred autumns. Autumn is (so called because) the herbs become ripe during this period, or the rivers are in flood.

The word *asya* (his) is explained by the word *asyāḥ* (her).

(*Here ends the twenty-fifth section.*)

Lightning is the middlemost brother of this sacrificer who is noble and benevolent. His third brother is butter-backed. Here I saw the lord of the universe with seven sons.[9]

Lightning is the middlemost brother of this sacrificer, i.e. who is worthy of being invoked; who is noble, i.e. who is to be honoured; who is benevolent, benefactor. *Bhrātā* (brother) is derived from (the root) *bhṛ*, meaning to take: he takes a share (of patrimony), or he is to be brought

[1] i.e. One who does not sacrifice and the object of whose life is self-enjoyment.

[2] iii. 54. 7. Cf. Roth, *op. cit.*, p. 50.

[3] See 3. 19.

[4] Cf. Roth, *loc. cit.*

[5] Durga quotes RV. iv. 40. 5 to illustrate the meaning of separation.

[6] VS. 8. 20.

[7] i. 138. 4.

[8] x. 85. 39; AV. 14. 2. 2.

[9] i. 164. 1; AV. 9. 9. 1. Cf. Roth, *op. cit.*, p. 51.

up. His third brother[1] is butter-backed, i.e. this Agni. There I saw the lord of the universe, i.e. the protector of everything, or supporter of everything, or with seven sons; i.e. with the seventh son,[2] or whose sons have gone everywhere.[3] Seven is an extended number. There are seven rays of the sun, they say.

(Here ends the twenty-sixth section.)

Seven yoke the one-wheeled car. One horse having seven names draws it. Three-navelled is the wheel, imperishable and irresistible, on which all these worlds rest.[4]

Seven yoke the one-wheeled car, i.e. the car which moves on a single wheel. *Cakram* (wheel) is derived from (the root) *cak* (to repel), or *car* (to move), or *kram* (to go). One horse having seven names draws it, i.e. the sun: seven rays draw up the juices for him, or the seven seers praise him. The other word *nāma* (name) is derived from the same (root, *nam*) also; (so called) from being drawn up. The second hemistich chiefly describes the year: the three-navelled wheel, i.e. the year with its three seasons, summer, rainy season, and winter. Year is (so called because) people live together by them. Summer, juices are swallowed during this period. Rainy season, during this time it rains. Winter, full of snow. Again, *himam*[5] (snow) is derived from (the root) *han* (to injure), or from *hi* (to hasten). Imperishable, having the characteristic of non-decay. Irresistible, not dependent on anything else. The seer praises the year, on which all created beings rest together, with all measures.

When the five-spoked wheel began to roll.[6]

This is with reference to the five seasons. There is the Brāhmaṇa passage: There are five seasons in the year,[7] taking the winter and the dewy season together.

Six are said to have been inserted.[8]

This is with reference to the six seasons, which are inserted in the navel as spokes. Again, *ṣaṭ* (six) is derived from (the root) *sah* (to bear).

[1] In a stanza addressed to Vāyu, the order of the three gods is as follows: (1) Vāyu, (2) Āditya, (3) Agni; hence Agni is the third. Durga.

[2] Durga attributes to the legendarians the saying: that the sun verily is the seventh son. He also quotes a Brāhmaṇa passage which says that the sun is the seventh and Indra is the eighth.

[3] This refers to the sun, i.e. whose rays go everywhere. Durga.

[4] i. 164. 2.

[5] Cf. Durga's explanation, quoted by Roth, *op. cit.*, p. 51.

[6] i. 164. 13; AV. 9. 9. 11.

[7] Cf. AB. i. 1; ŚB. i. 3. 5. 1; i. 7. 2. 8.

[8] i. 164. 12; AV. 9. 9. 12.

That twelve-spoked one does never decay.[1]

One wheel and twelve fellies.[2]

These are with reference to months. A month is (so called) from measuring.[3] Felly, it is well secured.

In it are placed together three hundred spokes, as it were,[4] and sixty moving one after another.[2]

There is the Brāhmaṇa passage: Verily, there are three hundred and sixty days and nights in a year.[5] This is taking the day and the night together (i. e. as one).

There stood seven hundred and twenty.[6]

There is the Brāhmaṇa passage: Verily, there are seven hundred and twenty days and nights in a year.[7] This is taking the day and the night separately (i. e. as two).

(*Here ends the twenty-seventh section*).

CHAPTER V

HE found the cloud in the course of the rivers.[8]

Susnim means a cloud, (so called because) it is washed.[9]

O men! invoke the best carrier of invocations, the hymn, who is the messenger.[10]

O men, invoke the messenger, i. e. the hymn, who is the best carrier of invocations. *Narā* means men: they repeatedly move (√*nṛtyanti*) in actions.[11] *Dūtaḥ* (messenger) is derived from (the root) *jū* (to be quick), or from *dru* (to run), or from the causal of *vṛ* (to keep back).

[Thou art the messenger of gods and mortals.[12] This too is a Vedic quotation.]

Vāvaśānaḥ is a participle (formed) from (the root) *vaś* (to desire), or from *vāś* (to roar).

1 i. 164. 11; AV. 9. 9. 13.

2 i. 164. 48; AV. 10. 8. 4.

3 i. e. The year is measured, as it were, by months. Durga.

4 According to Durga, the second *na* in the passage has the sense of aggregation.

5 Cf. GB. i. 5. 5; AB. ii. 17; ŚB. i. 3. 5. 9; xii. 3. 2. 3.

6 i. 164. 11; AV. 9. 9. 13.

7 AB. ii. 17; ŚB. xii. 3. 2. 4; cf. GB. i. 5. 5; AA. iii. 2. 1.

8 x. 139. 6.

9 Cf. Roth, *op. cit.*, p. 52. Surrounded on all sides by water-vapours, or flowing on all sides. The course, i. e. the atmosphere. Durga.

10 viii. 26. 16. 4.

11 *Nṛtyanti gātrāṇi punaḥ prakṣipanti.* Durga.

12 x. 4. 2.

Desiring the seven shining sisters.[1] This, too, is a Vedic quotation.

Vāryam (boon) is derived from (the root) *vṛ* (to choose). Or else (it is so called because) it is the best.

We choose that boon, the best protection.[2]

We choose that boon, which is the best (protection), i. e. it is to be protected, or you are its protectors, or it belongs to you.

The word *andhas* is a synonym of food,[3] (so called because) it is to be sought.

With drinking vessels pour down the exhilarating food.[4]

Pour down the exhilarating food [5] with drinking vessels. *Amatram* means a vessel, (so called because) the householders eat from it. The householders (are so called because) they are innumerable.[6] A drinking vessel (is so called because) people drink from it. Darkness is called *andhas* also, because no attention can be fixed in it or because nothing is visible. People also use the expression *andhaṃ tamas*, i. e. 'blinding darkness'. This other (meaning of) *andhas* (blind) is derived from the same root also.

He who has eyes sees, but the blind man cannot know.[7] This, too, is a Vedic quotation.

(*Here ends the first section.*)

Attached to each other, having many streams, rich in water.[8]

Devoted to each other, or without abandoning each other, having many streams and rich in water.[9]

Vanuṣyati means to slay, its grammatical form is not known.

May we slay those who seek to injure us.[10]

This too is a Vedic quotation.

May we, in battle, conquer the perverse, and him who seeks to injure the long-spread (sacrifice).[11]

May we, in battle, conquer the perverse, i. e. the pernicious, the sinful person, who desires to spoil our long-spread sacrifice. *Pāpaḥ* (sinful person) is (so called because) he drinks what is not to be drunk, or having

[1] x. 5. 5.

[2] viii. 25. 13.

[3] *Evam atra dāna-sambandhād andhaḥ śabdo 'nnārtha upapadyate.* Durga.

[4] ii. 14. 1.

[5] i. e. Soma. Durga.

[6] According to Durga, the word *a-mā* denotes something which cannot be measured, i. e. countle s. Householders are therefore called *a-mā* for the same reason.

[7] i. 164. 16 ; AV. 9. 9. 15.

[8] vi. 70. 2 ; cf. Roth, *op. cit.*, p. 52.

[9] i. e. Heaven and earth, who cause much rain to fall, or who support the manifold c reation, and who are rich in clarified butter. Durga.

[10] i. 132. 1 ; viii. 40. 7.

[11] i. e. A person addicted to the gratification of sensual pleasures. Durga.

committed sin, he falls lower and lower;[1] or the word may be (formed) from the intensive of the root *pat* (to fall).

Taruṣyati has the same meaning also.

Accompanied by Indra, may we slay Vṛtra.[2]

This too is a Vedic quotation.

Bhandanā (applause) is derived from (the root) *bhand*,[3] meaning to praise.

The widely-loved bard praises him with many names.[4]

This too is a Vedic quotation.

He utters forth praises which are rich in offspring.[5]

This also (is a Vedic quotation).

Go quickly, O wanton, with some one other than me.[6]

Go at once, O wanton, with some person different from me. Speaking in this manner, thou hurtest me as it were. *Āhanā*[7] (a wanton) is (so called from) her lascivious speech. *Āhanaḥ* (i. e. the vocative) is derived from the same.

Nadaḥ[8] means a seer; it is derived from (the root) *nad*, meaning to praise.

The love of the self-controlled seer has come to me.[9]

The love of the self-controlled seer, i. e. of one who is celibate and who has controlled himself with regard to procreation, has come to me. It is said that with these words a seer's daughter wailed.[10]

(*Here ends the second section.*)

Soma, whose (greatness) neither heaven, nor earth, nor waters, nor atmosphere, nor mountains (fathomed), has flowed.[11]

According to some, *akṣāḥ* is formed from (the root) *aś* (to go).

When the cowherd dwells with kine in a watery place, soma flows from the milked cows.[12]

The fox stalked the approaching lion.[13]

[1] He falls very low in hell. Durga.

[2] vii. 48. 2; KS. 23. 11.

[3] Cf. Roth, *op. cit.*, p. 53.

[4] iii. 3. 4; Durga paraphrases *kavi* (bard) by *krānta-darśana* (of comprehensive vision).

[5] ix. 86. 41.

[6] x. 10. 8; AV. 18. 1. 9. This is a part of a dialogue between Yama and Yamī; cf. Roth, *loc. cit.*

[7] Durga quotes a Brāhmaṇa passage in support of the meaning attributed by him to the word *āhanaḥ*.

[8] Cf. Roth, *loc. cit.*

[9] i. 179. 4; cf. Bṛh. D. i. 53.

[10] Durga identifies the seer's daughter with Lopāmudrā, wife of Agastya. Being love-sick, she addressed this strophe to her celibate husband. The story is related at greater length in Bṛh. D. iv. 57–60; Professor Macdonell's edition, vol. ii, pp. 140–2; cf. Sieg, *op. cit.*, pp. 120–6; Roth, *loc. cit.*

[11] x. 89. 6.

[12] ix. 107. 9; SV. 2. 348.

[13] x. 28. 4. The quotation is irrelevant, and is omitted by Durga.

Some think that (the word *akṣāḥ*) means to dwell in the former, and to flow in the latter quotation.[1] When the cowherd dwells with kine in a watery place, then soma flows from the milked kine. 'In all quotations (the word *akṣāḥ*) means to dwell,' says Śākapūṇi.

The word *śvātram*[1] is a synonym of quick: it is of swift motion.

He, the winged one, Agni, who has all created beings as his property, made quickly whatever moves, the immovable and the movable.[2]

And he, the winged one, Agni, who has all created beings as his property, made in a moment all that moves, the stationary and the non-stationary.[3]

Ūtiḥ (protection) is derived from (the root) *av* (to protect).

To thee (we turn round) for protection, as to a chariot.[4]

This too is a Vedic quotation.

We shall explain *hāsamāne* later.[5]

Vamraka has approached Indra with a soma draught.[6]

i.e. With drinks, or with beautiful hymns, [or with rousing panegyrics].

He found it glowing like a fully-manifest dream.[7]

'Dream' refers to the atmospheric light (i.e. lightning) which is visible occasionally only; he found it flashing like that (lightning).

Twofold existence, and the source of happiness on account of food.[8]

Double existence, i.e. in the middle and the highest sphere. Source of happiness, source of comfort.

As hunters seek game.[9]

As hunters seek game, so panegyrics seek thee.

(*Here ends the third section.*)

Varāhaḥ means a cloud: it brings (√*hṛ*) the best means of livelihood. There is a Brāhmaṇa passage: Thou hast brought the best means of livelihood.[10]

From afar he pierced the cloud by hurling his thunderbolt.[11]

This too is a Vedic quotation. This other (meaning of) *varāhaḥ* (boar)

1 Cf. Roth, *op. cit.*, p. 54.

2 x. 88. 4.

3 Durga takes it to mean that Agni consumes all the movable and immovable things at the time of final dissolution.

4 viii. 68. 1; SV. 1. 354; 2. 1121.

5 See 9. 39.

6 x. 99. 12. Cf. Roth, *loc. cit.*

7 x. 79. 3; cf. Roth, *op. cit.*, p. 55.

8 iii. 17. 5.

9 viii. 2. 6. Durga explains *praiṣāḥ* as panegyrics addressed to thee, and *vrāḥ* as greedy persons; cf. Roth, *loc. cit.*

10 MSS. of the longer recension place the quotation between 'roots also' and 'he tears up', in 1. 9.

11 i. 61. 7; AV. 20. 35. 7.

is derived from the same root also: he tears up the roots, or he tears up all the good roots.

Indra (slew) the ravening boar.[1]

This too is a Vedic quotation. The Aṅgirases are called *varāhās* also:

The Lord of prayer, with the powerful Aṅgirases.[2]

Moreover, these groups of atmospheric gods[3] are called *varāhavaḥ* also:

Seeing the groups of atmospheric gods, of golden chariot-wheels, of iron tusks, running.[4]

Svasarāṇi[5] means days: they move of their own accord. Or else, *svar* means the sun, he causes them to move.

As rays to the days.[6] This too is a Vedic quotation.

Śaryāḥ means fingers: [they create works]. *Śaryāḥ* means arrows: they are made of *Saccharum sara* (*śara*). *Śara* (arrow) is derived from (the root) *śṛ* (to rend).

As with arrows one (pierces), supporting (a bow) with two arms.[7]

This too is a Vedic quotation.

Arkaḥ means a god, (so called) because they worship him. *Arkaḥ* means a stanza, (so called) because it is by means of a stanza that they worship (gods). *Arkam* means food: it causes created beings to shine. *Arkaḥ* means a tree (*Calotropis gigantea*): it is compressed with bitterness.[8]

(Here ends the fourth section.)

Chanters chant thy praises, singers sing the song. Brāhmaṇas raised thee up like a pole, O god of a hundred powers.[9]

Chanters chant thy praises. Singers sing forth the song of thy praise. The Brāhmaṇas raised thee up like a pole, O god of a hundred powers! A pole (*vaṃśa*)[10] is (so called because) it grows in a forest (*vana-śaya*), or is so called from being divided into different parts.

Pavī[10] means the rim of a wheel, (so called) because it brushes away the earth.

Lo! with the rim of their chariots they rend the mountain with their might.[11]

The Maruts destroyed him with the edge of their sword.[12]

These two are Vedic quotations.

1 viii. 66. 10.

2 x. 67. 7; AV. 20. 91. 7.

From the plural number of the word group, Durga concludes that this refers to the Maruts.

4 i. 88. 5; cf. Roth, *op. cit.*, p. 56.

5 Cf. Roth, *loc. cit.*

6 i. 3. 8.

7 ix. 110. 5; SV. 2. 857.

8 It is bitter through and through. Durga.

9 i. 10. 1; SV. i. 342; 2. 694.

10 Cf. Roth, *op. cit.*, p. 57.

11 v. 52. 9.

12 Cf. Durga's remarks quoted by Roth, *loc. cit.*

Vakṣas (breast) has been explained.[1]

Dhanvan means atmosphere: waters flow from it.

It shines brightly from across the atmosphere.[2]

This too is a Vedic quotation.

Sinam means food: it binds created beings together.[3]

With which you bring food to friends.[4]

This too is a Vedic quotation.

Itthā is explained by the word *amuthā*.[5]

Sacā means 'together'.

Being together with the Vasus.[6]

i. e. Being with the Vasus.

Cid is an enclitic particle; it has already been explained.[7] Further, if accented, it is a synonym of animal in the following passage: Thou art animal, thou art mind.[8]

All the enjoyments are stored in thee, or thou stimulatest knowledge.

The letter *ā* is a preposition; it has already been explained.[9] Further, it is used in the sense of 'on'.

Waters in the cloud.[10]

Waters in the cloud, i. e. waters on the cloud. [Waters in the cloud, i. e. waters resting on the cloud.]

Dyumnam is derived from (the root) *dyut* (to shine), and means glory or food.

Bestow upon us glory and treasure.[11]

Bestow upon us glory and treasure.

(*Here ends the fifth section.*)

Pavitram is derived from (the root) *pū* (to purify). A stanza is called *pavitra* (pure):

The stanza with which the gods always purify themselves.[12]

This too is a Vedic quotation. Rays are called *pavitram*:

Purified by rays [pressed by men with stones].[13]

[1] See 4. 16.

[2] x. 187. 2; AV. vi. 34. 3.

[3] Community of meals was a characteristic feature of the Aryan household in ancient times, and even now implies kinship, or community of caste in India. In Hindu Law relationship with a deceased person is determined by one's right to offer the funeral cakes of food; cf. Durga, quoted by Roth, *op. cit.*, p. 58.

[4] iii. 62. 1.

[5] See 3. 16.

[6] Frag. of ii. 31. 1.

[7] See 1. 4.

[8] VS. 4. 19; 12. 53.

[9] See 1. 4.

[10] Frag. of v. 48. 1.

[11] vii. 25. 3.

[12] SV. 2. 652. Cf. Roth, *loc. cit.*

[13] Frag. of VS. 7. 1; read together with what follows within square brackets, it is ix. 86. 34.

This too is a Vedic quotation. Water is called *pavitram*. Having a hundred waters (i. e. streams), rejoicing with food.[1]

i. e. Having much water. Fire is called *pavitram*. Air is called *pavitram*. Soma is called *pavitram*. The sun is called *pavitram*. Indra is called *pavitram*.

Agni is pure, may he purify me. Vāyu, Soma, the Sun, Indra, are pure, may they purify me.[2]

This too is a Vedic quotation.

Todaḥ is derived from (the root) *tud* (to push).

(*Here ends the sixth section.*)

I, the liberal giver, call upon thee, O Agni, in many ways. I am indeed the master (of thy panegyrics). As in the cavity of some great well.[3]

I, who am a liberal giver, invoke thee alone. *Ariḥ* means an unfriendly person; it is derived from (the root) *ṛ* (to injure). The master is called *ariḥ* also, from the same root. Having seen that oblations offered to other deities are sacrificed in fire, the seer declared, 'as in the cavity of some great well'; i. e. as in the opening of some great chasm.[4]

Having a good gait, i. e. one whose manner of walking is good.

Sacrificed to from all sides, the butter-backed having a good gait.[5]

This too is a Vedic quotation.

Śipiviṣṭa and *Viṣṇu* are two synonyms of Viṣṇu.[6] 'The former has a contemptuous meaning', says Aupamanyava.

(*Here ends the seventh section.*)

What was blameable in thee, O Viṣṇu! that thou didst declare, 'I am *Śipiviṣṭa*'. Do not hide this shape from us, for, in battle, thou wert of a different form.[7]

O Viṣṇu, what is there obscure about thyself, i. e. not worthy of being known, that thou sayest to us,[8] 'I am denuded like a phallus', i. e. whose

[1] vii. 47. 3.

[2] The quotation is untraced.

[3] i. 150. 1; SV. 1. 97.

[4] Durga amplifies Yāska's explanation as follows: I invoke thee alone because I am master, i. e. competent to praise thee well, and am capable of offering many oblations. Another reason for invoking Agni alone is his inexhaustible power of consumption, which is compared with that of some deep well or great chasm. *Śaraṇe* is derived from *śṛ* (to injure) and means 'an opening'. The *uterus* is also called *toda*.

[5] v. 37. 1.

[6] Muir attributes the sentence to Aupamanyava. There is no evidence, however, to support this view. Durga does not put it in the mouth of Aupamanyava; cf. *Sanskrit Texts*, vol. iv, p. 505.

[7] vii. 100. 6.

[8] Muir reads the negative particle *na* instead of *naḥ*, 'to us'. This is evidently a

rays are not displayed?[1] Or else, it may be that (the word is used as) a synonym of praise: O Viṣṇu, what is this well-known (shape) of thine, i. e. worthy of being fully known, that thou sayest to us, 'I am enveloped with rays (*śipi-viṣṭa*)',[2] i. e. whose rays are displayed? Rays are here called *śipayaḥ*,[3] i. e. he is enveloped by them. Do not hide this shape from us. The word *varpas* is a synonym of form, (so called) because it covers things. For in the battle, i. e. in the combat, thou wert of a different form;[4] i. e. whose rays are gathered together. The following stanza explains it much more.

(Here ends the eighth section.)

I, a master of hymns, and knowing the sacred customs, to-day praise that name of thine, *Śipiviṣṭa*. I, who am weak, glorify thee, who art mighty, and dwellest beyond this world.[5]

I, a master of hymns, to-day will sing forth that name of thine, *Śipiviṣṭa*. I am master, i. e. lord, of hymns. Or else it is thou who art a master, I, who am weak, praise thee who art mighty. The word *tavasa* is a synonym of mighty: he is risen high. Who dwellest beyond, i. e. very far from this world.

Glowing with heat, i. e. one whose glow has reached us.
May we two together serve the god of glowing heat.[6]
Let us both attend upon the god, whose glow[7] has reached us.
Agile, i. e. one whose speed is great.
The agile has shortened the life of the demon.[8]
He caused the life of the demon to be shortened.

(Here ends the ninth section.)

From two sticks, men with fingers have produced fire by the motion of their hands; a fire, glorious, seen at a distance, lord of the house and active.[9]

mistake, for Roth's edition, which Muir seems to have used, has the right reading *naḥ*. This reading is also supported by the evidence of the MSS. of both recensions and Durga. Cf. *Sanskrit Texts*, vol. iv, p. 88.

[1] i. e. The rising sun at daybreak, when its rays are not displayed. Durga.

[2] *Śipiviṣṭa* is a name of Viṣṇu; this is also shown by the following passage: TS. ii. 5. 5. 2: *Viṣṇave Śipiviṣṭāya*. It means 'a bald person', and according to TS. ii. 2. 12. 5, 'a diseased person whose private parts are exposed'; cf. Muir, *op. cit.*, vol. iv, pp. 88, 504-6.

[3] *Śipi* means 'animal' also, cf. TS. ii. 5. 5. 2: *yajño vai viṣṇuḥ paśavaḥ śipiḥ*.

[4] Cf. Roth, *op. cit.*, p. 59.

[5] vii. 100. 5.

[6] vi. 55. 1.

[7] Whose glow, or whose anger, has reached us. Durga.

[8] iii. 49. 2.

[9] vii. 1. 1; SV. 1. 72; 2. 723.

Dūdhitayaḥ[1] mean fingers: they are employed in (the performance of) actions. Fire-sticks are (so called because) fire rests in them, or because fire is produced from them by attrition. By the motion of their hands, by the circular movement of their hands. They produced fire, glorious, visible at a distance, the lord of the house, and swift.

(*Here ends the tenth section.*)

At one single draught Indra drank thirty lakes full of soma.[2]

At one draught alone Indra drank them together, i. e. along with one another; this is the meaning. (Lakes) full of soma, i. e. dear to his heart, or full to the brim, or consecrated to Indra. Or else Indra is a lover of soma, or he drinks till his desire, his appetite, is completely satisfied.[3] With reference to this, the interpretation of the ritualists is the following: There are thirty libation-vessels consecrated to one deity at the meridional pressing of the soma-juice. These (libation-vessels) they drink at a single draught. They are here called lakes. 'There are thirty days and nights in the second, and thirty in the first half of a month,' say the etymologists. Then the rays drink those same lunar waters which fall on certain days in the second fortnight.[4] There is also a Vedic quotation:

The imperishable one whom the imperishable drink.[5]

They fill him again in the first fortnight. There is also a Vedic quotation:

As the gods cause the moon to grow.[6]

Adhriguḥ (lit. irresistible) means a stanza, (so called) from being at the head of a cow (i. e. = *adhi-guḥ*). Or else it is intended to refer to an injunction, for there is a repetition of words: Toil, O irresistible one, toil well, toil, O irresistible one.[7] Fire also is called irresistible.

(The drops) flow for thee, O irresistible and mighty one.[8]

i. e. One whose motion is unrestrained and who is active. Indra is called irresistible also:

(I send) a gift to the irresistible Indra.[9]

This too is a Vedic quotation.

[1] Cf. Roth, *op. cit.*, p. 60.

[2] viii. 66. 4.

[3] *Kaṇe* ind. is used to denote complete satisfaction, see Pa. i. 4. 66; cf. Roth, *loc. cit.*

[4] Durga remarks that the stanza is addressed to Indra; the explanation of the etymologists presupposes it to be addressed to Āditya, and it is therefore irrelevant. He meets this self-raised objection by citing a Brāhmaṇa passage, 'That Āditya is verily Indra', and gets over the difficulty by identifying the one with the other.

[5] VS. 5. 7; cf. AV. 7. 81. 6.

[6] VS. 5. 7; cf. Roth, *loc. cit.*

[7] AB. ii. 7.

[8] iii. 21. 4.

[9] i. 61. 1; AV. 20. 35. 1.

Āṅgūṣaḥ means a hymn: it is to be chanted aloud.

With this hymn we possess Indra.[1]

With this hymn we have Indra with us.

(*Here ends the eleventh section.*)

With infused energy, rushing to the attack, shaker, impetuous, great hero and foaming, soma surpasses all plants and trees. All the counter-measures did not deceive Indra.[2]

One whose anger is roused, and who rushes to attack, [i. e. who is quick to attack, or who attacks while moving,] i. e. soma, or Indra. *Dhuniḥ* (shaker) is derived from (the root) *dhū* (to shake). The word *śimi* is a synonym of action, or it may be derived from (the root) *śam* (to exert oneself), or from *śak* (to be able). The foaming soma: that which remains as residue after soma is strained is called *ṛjīṣam*, i. e. something which is thrown away, hence soma is called *ṛjīṣī*, i. e. containing the residue. Further, this is used as an epithet of Indra also: *ṛjīṣī*, the wielder of thunderbolt.[3] That portion (i. e. the residue) and the grains belong to his (i. e. Indra's) steeds.[4] Grains are (so called because) they are parched in a kiln, or dried on a board.

Let thy steeds devour grain and sniff at the residue.[5]

This too is a Vedic quotation. (*Babdhām*)[6] is formed by reduplicating the first syllable and removing the penultimate of (the root) *bhas*, which means to devour. Soma surpasses all plants and trees. All the counter-measures do not deceive Indra; i. e. the counter-measures which they adopt against him are of no avail before Indra: they perish before they reach him, i. e. without reaching him at all. Some are of opinion that the stanza is primarily addressed to Indra, while the reference to soma is of secondary character. Others hold that it is primarily addressed to both.

Śmaśā,[7] i. e. something which runs quickly, or runs in the body.

The ridge has held back the water.[8]

The ridge has held back the water.

(*Here ends the twelfth section.*)

[1] i. 105. 19.

[2] x. 89. 5; cf. Roth, *op. cit.*, p. 62.

[3] v. 40. 4; AV. 20. 12. 7.

[4] This is the reason why Indra is called *ṛjīṣī*, i. e. one whose steeds feed on the residue of soma (*ṛjīṣam*).

[5] Cp. Roth, *op. cit.*, p. 63.

[6] Durga refers to the sūtra Pa. vi. 4. 100.

[7] Yāska does not attribute any definite meaning to the word. Durga translates it as 'a river' or 'a vein'. The word occurs in the RV. once only. It is probably connected with *aśman* and means 'an elevated edge', or 'bank'; cf. Roth, *op. cit.*, p. 63.

[8] x. 105. 1; SV. 1. 228.

Urvaśī[1] is (the name of) a naiad, (so called because) she pervades wide regions (*uru* + √*aś* 'to pervade'), or she pervades by means of thighs[2] (*ūru* + √*aś* 'to pervade'), or her desire is great (*uru* + √*vaś* 'to desire'). *Apsarāḥ* (a naiad) is one who moves on water. Or else the word *apsas* is a synonym of beauty; it is derived from the negative of (the root) *psā* (to devour): it is not to be devoured, but to be gazed at, or to be made pervasive.[3] 'It is for clear perception,' says Śākapūṇi. In 'Whatever forbidden food',[4] (*apsas* signifies) something which is not to be eaten. In 'Pervading indeed',[5] (the word signifies) pervasive. (*Apsarāḥ*) is (therefore) one who possesses that (*apsas*), i. e. a beautiful person: the beauty is either acquired by her or given to her.[6] On seeing her, the seminal fluid of Mitra and Varuṇa fell down.[7] It is to this that the following stanza refers.

(*Here ends the thirteenth section.*)

O Vasiṣṭha, thou art a son of Mitra and Varuṇa. O Brahman, thou wert born from the mind of Urvaśī. (Thou art) the drop that fell in divine fervour. All the gods received thee in the atmosphere.[8]

O Vasiṣṭha, thou art certainly the son of Mitra and Varuṇa. O Brahman, thou wert born from the mind of Urvaśī. (Thou art) the drop that fell in divine fervour. Drop,[9] it is well nourished, it is to be absorbed. All the gods supported thee in the atmosphere.[10] *Puṣkaram* means atmosphere: it nourishes (*poṣati*) created beings. Water is called *puṣkaram*, because it is a means of worship (*pūjā-karam*), or to be worshipped (√*pūj*). This other (meaning of) *puṣkaram* (lotus) is derived from the same root also: it is a means of decorating the body (*vapuṣ-karam*). *Puṣyam* (flower) is derived from (the root) *puṣ* (to blossom).

Vayunam is derived from (the root) *vī* (to string): it signifies desire or intelligence.

(*Here ends the fourteenth section.*)

He here spread the unintelligible darkness; he made it intelligible with the sun.[11]

[1] Cf. Roth, *op. cit.*, p. 63.

[2] i.e. In sexual intercourse. Durga.

[3] This is the second derivation of the word *apsas*, i.e. it is derived from the root *āp*, 'to pervade'.

[4] VS. 20. 17. The passage is cited by Yāska to support his first derivation of *apsas* from the negative of *psā*.

[5] VS. 14. 4. The passage is quoted by Yāska to support his second derivation of *apsas* from *āp*, i. e. to show that *apsas* means pervasive.

[6] Roth suspects the genuineness of the passage from 'In whatever . . . given to her'. He was probably misled by the assumption that the passage contains Yāska's remarks. He does not seem to realize that Yāska here cites two short quotations from the VS. in support of the two etymologies of *apsas* given by him.

[7] Cf. Bṛh. D. v. 155.

[8] vii. 33. 11.

[9] Cf. Durga quoted by Roth, *op. cit.*, p. 64.

[10] Cf. Bṛh. D. v. 155.

[11] vi. 21. 3.

He spread unknowable darkness; he made it knowable with the sun.

Vājapastyam means soma.

May we obtain the soma.[1] This too is a Vedic quotation.

Vājagandhyam[2] (has the same meaning) with *gandhya* as the second member of the compound.

May we eat the soma.[3] This too is a Vedic quotation.

Gadhyam is derived from (the root) *grah* (to seize).

Like food which is to be seized, they desire to unite themselves with the straightforward.[4]

This too is a Vedic quotation.

The verb *gadh* means to mix. Mixed on all sides, mixed all around.[5] This too is a Vedic quotation.

Kaura-yāṇa means one whose car is made, whose wisdom is ripe, whose chariot is made.[6] This too is a Vedic quotation.

Taura-yāṇa means one whose car is very quick.

Approach our sacrifice with the Maruts, thy friends of equal power, O Indra whose car is swift.[7]

This too is a Vedic quotation.

Ahra-yāṇa means one whose car does not bring shame on him.

Make it presently, O (Agni) whose car does not bring shame.[8]

This too is a Vedic quotation.

Hara-yāṇa means one whose car is moving constantly.

(We found) silver on him whose car moves constantly.[9] This too is a Vedic quotation.

Who, steady in every action, belongs to all.[10]

i. e. Pervading all hymns.

Vrandī is derived from (the root) *vrand*, meaning to become soft.

(*Here ends the fifteenth section.*)

When thou uprootest forests, roaring at the head of wind, and the draught which makes them soft.[11]

When thou causest the forests to fall with thy deadly weapon, or roaring at the head of the howling wind, and the draught, i. e. the sun who is the drying agent.

The hard became soft.[12]

[1] ix. 98. 12; SV. 2. 1030. Durga derives *vājapastyam* from *vāja* and √*pat* (to fall).

[2] Cf. Roth, *op. cit.*, pp. 64–5.

[3] ix. 98. 12; SV. 2. 1030.

[4] iv. 16. 11.

[5] i. 126. 6.

[6] viii. 23. 11. Cf. Roth, *op. cit.*, p. 65.

[7] Cf. Roth, *ibid.*

[8] iv. 4. 14.

[9] viii. 25. 23.

[10] i. 101. 4.

[11] i. 54. 5.

[12] Fragment of ii. 24. 3.

This too is a Vedic quotation. The verbs *vīḷ* and *vrīḷ*, meaning to be hard, are joined together with the former.

Niṣṣapī means a libidinous person, i. e. devoid of virility. *Pasas* (virility) is derived from (the root) *sap*, meaning to touch.

O, do not hand us over to others, as a libidinous person his wealth.[1]

Just as the libidinous man wastes his wealth on others, so do not ye hand us over to others.

Tūrṇāśam means water, (so called) because it flows quickly.

Like water on a mountain.[2]

This too is a Vedic quotation.

Kṣumpam means a mushroom, (so called because) it is easily shaken.

(*Here ends the sixteenth section.*)

When, with his foot, will he trample the infidel man like a mushroom? When indeed will Indra hear our prayers?[3]

When, with his foot, will he trample the unworshipping man like a mushroom? When indeed will he listen to our hymns? The word *aṅga* is a synonym of quick: it is gone as soon as it is calculated.[4]

Nicumpuṇa means soma, the exhilarating food, i. e. it exhilarates (when mixed) with water.

(*Here ends the seventeenth section.*)

These pressed soma juices accompanied by their consorts flow lovingly to be partaken. Soma spreads to waters.[5]

These pressed soma juices accompanied by their consorts, i. e. waters, flow lovingly to be partaken, i. e. to be drunk. Soma goes to waters. Ocean is called *nicumpuṇa* also: it is filled with water. The last sacrificial ablution is called *nicumpuṇa* also: on this occasion, they recite in a low tone, or they put the sacrificial utensils down.[6]

O last sacrificial ablution.[7]

This too is a Vedic quotation. *Nicumpuṇa* occurs as *nicuṅkuṇa* also.

Padiḥ means a goer, (so called) because he goes.

(*Here ends the eighteenth section.*)

He who catches hold of thee, O morning guest coming with wealth, like a bird with a net, shall be rich in kine, gold, and horses; great is the life which Indra will bestow upon him.[8]

[1] i. 104. 5.

[2] viii. 32. 4.

[3] i. 84. 8.

[4] The sentence is omitted by Durga. The word *aṅga* is here by Yāska derived from √*aṅk*, 'to calculate', and √*añc*, 'to go'.

[5] viii. 93. 22.

[6] i.e. For the purpose of cleansing. Durga.

[7] VS. 3. 48; 8. 27; 20. 18. Cf. Roth, *op. cit.*, p. 67.

[8] i. 125. 2.

He who catches hold of thee, O guest who goest at daybreak, coming with food, as a boy catches a bird in a net, becomes rich in kine, gold, and horses; great indeed is the life which Indra bestows upon him. A net is (so called) from being let loose on the ground, or from lying on the ground, or from being spread on the ground.

Pāduḥ[1] (foot) is derived from (the root) *pad* (to walk).

That bright foot of his manifests light, conceals water, and is never relinquished.[2]

The sun manifests light and conceals water. The word *busam* is a synonym of water. It is derived from (the root) *brū*, meaning to sound, or from *bhraṁś* (to fall). Whatever water he causes to fall by raining, the same he draws back again by means of his rays.

(*Here ends the nineteenth section.*)

Vṛkaḥ[3] means the moon, (so called) because her light is disclosed, or because her light is not sufficient, or because her light is strong (compared with stars).

(*Here ends the twentieth section.*)

The red moon, maker of the month, indeed, saw (the stars) going along the route. Having observed she rises up like a carpenter with a bent back: be witness of this, O heaven and earth.[4]

The red, i. e. bright. Maker of the month, i. e. the moon is the maker of months and fortnights.[5] The moon indeed saw the multitude of stars going along the heavenly route. And having observed every star with which she will come in conjunction, she rises up like a carpenter suffering from a bent back; be witness of this, O heaven and earth. The sun is called *vṛka* also, because he dispels (darkness).

The constant one invoked you, O Aśvins, when you released her from the mouth of the wolf.[6]

There is a legend that dawn was seized by the sun. She called upon the Aśvins, who released her. A dog is called *vṛka* also, on account of biting.

The wolf, the killer of sheep, is indeed his warder.[7]

i. e. Killer of young sheep. A young sheep is (so called because) it is

[1] Cf. Roth, *op. cit.*, p. 67.

[2] x. 27. 24.

[3] Cf. Roth, *op. cit.*, p. 68.

[4] i. 105. 18; cf. Bṛh. D. 2. 112.

[5] The Indian calendar, according to which daily business is transacted, is lunar and not solar. In order to bring it into harmony with the solar calendar, an extra month of about thirty days is added every fourth year.

[6] i. 117. 16.

[7] viii. 66. 8; AV. 20. 97. 2; SV. 2. 1042.

covered with wool. *Ūrṇā* (wool) again, is derived from (the root) *vṛ* (to cover), or from *ūrṇu* (to cover oneself). A she-jackal is called *vṛkī* also.

The father made Ṛjrāśva, who made a gift of a hundred rams to the she-wolf, blind.[1]

This too is a Vedic quotation.

Joṣavākam [2] is a synonym of unknown, i. e. what is to be made known.[3]

(Here ends the twenty-first section.)

O Indra and Agni, promoters of sacrifice, the gods to whom fat oblations are offered! you partake of (the food of that man) who praises you when the soma-juices are pressed, but not of his who speaks what is unknown (to him).[4]

O Indra and Agni, you partake of the food of that man who praises you two when the soma juices are pressed. But the two gods, to whom fat oblations are offered, do not partake of the food of that man who speaks what is unknown to him, i. e. who is a mere reciter.[5]

Kṛttiḥ [6] is derived from the root *kṛt* (to cut): it signifies fame or food.

Great like fame is thy protection, O Indra.[7]

O Indra, thy protection in the atmosphere is very great indeed, like fame. This other (meaning of) *kṛttiḥ* (garment) [8] is derived from the same root also: it is made of cotton threads. Or else it is used for the sake of comparison.[9]

Clad in skin, trident in hand, and with bow outstretched.[10]

[Wander about wearing the skin garment, and come to us bearing the trident.[11]]

This too is a Vedic quotation.

Śva-ghnī [12] means a gambler: he destroys (*hanti*) himself (*svam*). Oneself is (so called because) it is dependent.

As a gambler picks up the die marked with four dots in play.[13]

[1] i. 116. 16.

[2] 'Magniloquence, or challenging speech', cf. Roth, *op. cit.*, p. 68; 'agreeable speech', Grassmann, *Wörterbuch zum Ṛgveda*, p. 500.

[3] i.e. On account of being not understood. Durga.

[4] vi. 59. 4.

[5] i.e. One who recites stanzas on the bank of some river and does not perform any practical work. Durga. He quotes a Brāhmaṇa passage: Because among the gods Indra and Agni have the major share, &c.

[6] 'Hide, skin', &c. Grassmann, *op. cit.*, p. 347.

[7] viii. 90. 6; SV. 2. 762.

[8] According to Durga, the other meaning of the word is 'a girl', so called because she is wrapped in cotton clothes.

[9] This is explained by Durga as giving the third meaning of the word, i. e. 'a skin', from the analogy of a cotton garment.

[10] KS. 9. 7; cf. VS. 3. 61.

[11] VS. 16. 51.

[12] Cf. Grassmann, *op. cit.*, p. 1432.

[13] x. 43. 5; AV. 20. 17. 5.

As a gambler picks up the die marked with four dots in play. *Kitava* is an onomatopoetic word = *kim* + *tava*, i.e. what have you got?[1] Or else it is a benedictory exclamation, 'good luck'.[2]

The word *samam*[3] is an unaccented pronoun and has the sense of comprehensive.

(*Here ends the twenty-second section.*)

Let the weapon of our numerous evil-minded vindictive foes not smite us as a wave does a boat.[4]

Let the weapon of all our evil-minded, i.e. whose minds are sinful, and always vindictive enemies not smite us as a wave does a boat. *Ūrmi* (wave) is derived from (the root) *ūrṇu* (to cover). A boat (*nau*) is (so called because) it is to be pulled through (√*nī*), or the word may be derived from (the root) *nam* (to bend). With reference to this, how can a noun be an enclitic?[5] (It is a noun) for the reason that it is inflected.[6]

Lo! give us wealth on all occasions.[7]

In (the above quotation) the word occurs in the locative case. The verb *śiśīti* means to give.

Protecting from all attacks.[8]

In (the above quotation) it occurs in the ablative case. The verb *uruṣyati* means to protect. It occurs in the nominative plural also:

Let all others be destroyed.[9]

(*Here ends the twenty-third section.*)

O Men, the consumer of waters, who is also the bountiful, fills you with oblation: the father, the observer of the deed.[10]

He causes the waters to be consumed with oblations. The words *piparti* and *papuri* mean either to fill, or to please. The father who observes the deed, the action,[11] i.e. the sun.

[1] i.e. His friends the other gamblers ask him questions like the following: did you win? how much did you win? or, what have you got to stake? &c. Durga; cf. Roth, *op. cit.*, p. 68.

[2] i.e. His friends wish him good luck, as he begins to play.

[3] Cf. Grassmann, *op. cit.*, p. 1478.

[4] viii. 75. 9.

[5] The particles alone are accentless; as nouns always have an accent, it cannot be a noun. This is the objection. Durga.

[6] Yāska's rejoinder to the objection is, that it is accentless is quite obvious, and that it is a noun is shown by the fact that it is inflected and three quotations illustrating its inflexion in the nominative, ablative, and locative are cited. Towards the end of the twenty-second section Yāska says that *samam* is a pronoun; he here uses the word *nāma* in the same sense. Cf. Professor Macdonell, *Vedic Grammar for Students*, p. 495.

[7] viii. 21. 8.

[8] v. 24. 3.

[9] viii. 39. 1–10.

[10] i. 46. 4. Cf. Bṛh.D. 3. 11. 2.

[11] Cf. Roth, *op. cit.*, p. 69. According to Durga, the two words *jāra* and *papuri* are in contrast

The word *śamba*[1] is a synonym of thunderbolt; it is derived from (the root) *śam* (to kill), or from the causal of *śad* (to knock off).

The thunderbolt that is terrible; with that, O widely-invoked one.[2]

This too is a Vedic quotation.

Kepayaḥ[3] = *kapūyāḥ*, i.e. having a stinking smell. The word *kapūyam* is (so called because) it is difficult to be purified, (even) when one tries to expiate a vile deed.

(Here ends the twenty-fourth section.)

The first invokers of gods went forth their several ways, their glorious deeds are hard to surpass. Many, who were not able to ascend the ship of sacrifice, remained in this very world, stinking.[4]

They went forth severally. *Pṛthak* (severally) is derived from (the root) *prath* (to spread). First invokers of gods: i.e. who invoked the gods, and performed glorious and heroic exploits, which are hard to be surpassed by others, i.e. those who were not able to ascend the ship of sacrifice. Now those, who were not able to ascend the ship of sacrifice, remained here, i.e. in this very place, or in debt, or in this world. The word *īrma*[5] is a synonym of arm, (so called because) it is very much moved (*sam* √*īr*).[6]

O son of strength, thou soon drawest all these pressed soma juices which thou supportest thyself.[7]

O son of strength, thou soon favourest all these places which thou supportest thyself.

Aṃsatram,[8] a means of protection from calamity, i.e. a bow, or coat of mail. A coat of mail (*kavacam*) is (so called because) it is bent in a crooked manner (*ku* + *ancitam*), or it is slightly bent (*ka* + *ancitam*), or it is fitted on the body (*kāye* + *ancitam*).

(Here ends the twenty-fifth section.)

Refresh the horses, win fortune, here make a chariot that brings prosperity. Pour down, in the cavity, the drink for men, having wooden troughs, furnished with a stone wheel and pails and armour.[9]

Refresh the horses; win good fortune: let victory be your fortune; make a chariot that brings prosperity. Having wooden troughs: wooden,

to each other, i.e. the sun first consumes the waters by means of evaporation, &c., and then gives them back through rain.

1 Cf. Grassmann, *op. cit.*, p. 1380.

2 x. 42. 7; AV. 20. 89. 7.

3 'Shivering'; cf. Grassmann, *op. cit.*, p. 351.

4 x. 44. 6; AV. 20. 94. 6.

5 Cf. Roth, *op. cit.*, pp. 69–70.

6 i.e. As compared with other limbs of the body. Durga.

7 x. 50. 6.

8 Cf. Grassmann, *op. cit.*, p. 2.

9 x. 101. 7. Cf. Roth, *op. cit.*, p. 70.

made of wood; trough (*ā-hāva*) is (so called) from being invoked. Conveyance (*āvaha*) is (so called) from driving (*ā-√vah*).

Cavity (*avata*) is (so called because) it goes down very deep (*ava-atita*). A stone wheel, i. e. a pervading wheel, or a wheel that frightens away. Having pails of armour: let your armours be the substitutes for pails. *Kośa* (pail) is derived from (the root) *kuṣ* (to draw out): it is drawn out. This other (meaning of) *kośa* (treasure) is derived from the same root also: it is accumulation, a great collection. Pour down the drink for men, water for men. The seer compares a battle with the characteristic of a well.

Palate[1] is called *kākudam*: *kokuvā* signifies tongue, that (tongue) is placed under it. Tongue is (called) *kokuvā* because, being noisy (*kokūyamānā*), it utters sounds. [Or it may be derived from (the root) *kokūy*, meaning to make a sound.] Tongue (*jihvā*) is (so called because) it calls out again and again (*johuvā*). *Tālu* (palate) is derived from (the root) *tṛ* (to cross): it is the highest part (in the mouth), or from *lat* (meaning to be long) by metathesis like *talam* (surface); the word *latā* (creeper) is (derived from the same root) without metathesis.

(*Here ends the twenty-sixth section.*)

O Varuṇa, thou art a benevolent god, into whose palate flow the seven rivers as into a hollow channel.[2]

Thou art a benevolent god, i. e. a bountiful god, into whose palate flow the seven rivers for their course as into a hollow channel. This too is a Vedic quotation.[3]

[Thou art a benevolent god, i. e. a bountiful god, or a munificent god, O Varuṇa, to thee belong the seven rivers. A river (*sindhu*) is (so called) from flowing (*sru*). Into thy palate flow the seven streams. *Su-ūrmi*[4] (channel), i. e. having beautiful waves. Just as a stream (flows) into a hollow channel.

According to Taiṭīki, *bīriṭam*[5] means atmosphere, and is derived in the following manner: the former part from (the root) *ve* and the latter from (the root) *īr*: the birds or luminaries move in it. The following Vedic stanza illustrates this.][6]

(*Here ends the twenty-seventh section*).[7]

[1] Cf. Patañjali, *op. cit.*, i. 1. 1., vol. i, p. 4.

[2] viii. 69. 12; AV. 20. 92. 9.

[3] This is the version of the MSS. of the shorter recension and Durga.

[4] Cf. Grassmann, *op. cit.*, p. 1567; he derived it from √*sṛ* (to move).

[5] 'Troop', cf. Grassmann, *op. cit.*, p. 907; see § 28.

[6] The comment placed within square brackets is the version of the MSS. of the longer recension.

[7] The section is quoted *in toto* by Patañjali, *op. cit.*, i. 1. 1, vol. 1, p. 4.

For them he twisted the grass soft to tread, in the atmosphere they appear like lords of all creation. At night, at dawn, at men's earliest call, (may) Vāyu and Pūṣan (come) with their teams for our welfare.[1]

For them, the grass soft to tread is twisted. They come as protectors or benefactors of all. *Bīriṭam* means atmosphere: it is full of fear or light. Or else it is used for the sake of comparison, i. e. they appear like kings, lords of all, in a great multitude of men. At the termination of night, at the earliest call of men (may) Vāyu and Pūṣan (come) with their teams for our welfare, i. e. protection. With his team, i. e. one whose steeds are yoked. 'Yoked' is (so called) from being restrained or yoked.

Accha[2] is used in the sense of *abhi*. 'It means to obtain', says Śākapūṇi.

Pari, īm, and *sīm* have been explained.[3]

Enam and *enām* are explained by the words *asya* and *asyāḥ*.[4]

Sṛṇi[5] means a hook, (so called) from urging (√*sṛ*). *Aṅkuśa* (hook) is derived from (the root) *anc* (to bend): it is bent.

From the vicinity of the hook, let him here come to ripe grain.[6]

This too is a Vedic quotation.

From the nearest place of the hook, let him come to the ripe herbs, let him come to the ripe herbs.

(*Here ends the twenty-eighth section.*)

CHAPTER VI

O Agni, O Sovereign lord of men, burning quickly with thy flames, thou art born, glowing with bright (days), from the waters, from within the flintstone, from the forest-trees, and from the herbs.[7]

O Agni, burning quickly with thy flames, thou (art born) with bright days. The words *āśu* and *śu* are two synonyms of quick. *Kṣaṇi,* the latter part (of *āśu-śu-kṣaṇi*), is derived from (the root) *kṣaṇ* (to injure): it quickly injures, or procures (*sanoti*) with its flames.[8] *Śuk* is derived from (the root) *śuc* (to shine). Or the nominative has been used for the ablative; this is shown by the context.[9] The former part (of *ā-śuśukṣaṇi*),

[1] vii. 39. 2; VS. 33. 44.

[2] Cf. Grassmann, *op. cit.*, p. 15; cf. Professor Macdonell, *op. cit.*, p. 472.

[3] See 1. 7; cf. Professor Macdonell, *op. cit.*, pp. 476, 486, 496.

[4] See 4. 25.

[5] 'Sickle'; cf. Grassmann, *op. cit.*, p. 1576.

[6] x. 101. 3; VS. 12. 68.

[7] ii. 1. 1; VS. 11. 27.

[8] The division of the word, in the latter case, is the following: *āśu-śuk-ṣaṇi.*

[9] i. e. All the other words, like 'from the waters, from within the stone', &c., are in the ablative.

i. e. the letter *ā*, is a preposition; the latter is formed from the desiderative of the causative of (the root) *śuc*, i. e. desirous of kindling quickly. *Śuci* (glowing) is derived from (the root) *śuc*, meaning to glow. This other (meaning of) *śuci* (pure) is derived from the same root also: 'Sin is removed from him,' say the etymologists.

May Indra make us fearless from all quarters.[1]

Āśāḥ[2] means quarters, (so called) from being situated (*ā-sad*). *Aśāḥ* means intermediate quarters, (so called) from pervading (√*aś*).

Kāśi means fist, (so called) from shining (*pra-kāś*). Fist (*muṣṭiḥ*) is (so called) from releasing (√*muc*), or from stealing (√*muṣ*), or from stupefying (√*muh*).[3]

These boundless regions, which thou hast seized, O Indra, are thy fist, O Lord of wealth.[4]

These two regions, i. e. heaven and earth, having a boundary, are (so called) from being bounded. *Rodhas* means a bank: it restrains the stream. *Kūla* (bank) is derived from (the root) *ruj* (to break) by metathesis; and *loṣṭa* (lumps) without metathesis.[5] Boundless, very extensive. These which thou hast seized are thy great fist, O Lord of wealth!

O Indra, crush the handless, thundering (cloud).[6]

O Indra, having made him handless, crush the cloud that thunders all around.

(*Here ends the first section.*)

The cover easy to pierce, the enclosure of speech, being afraid, yielded before slaughter. He made the paths easy to tread for driving the cattle. The following speech well protected the widely-invoked one.[7]

Alātṛṇa[8] means easy to pierce, i. e. a cloud. *Vala* (cover) is derived from (the root) *vṛ* (to cover). *Vraja* (enclosure) is (so called) because it moves in the atmosphere. Of *go*, i. e. of the atmospheric speech. Being afraid, he yielded before slaughter. He made the paths easy to tread for driving the cattle: he made the paths easy to traverse in order to drive forth the cattle. The flowing speeches well protected the widely-invoked one, i. e. waters on account of their flowing, or speeches on account

[1] ii. 41. 12; AV. 20. 20. 7; 57. 10.

[2] 'Room, cardinal point', cf. Grassmann, *op. cit.*, p. 187.

[3] Fist is called stupefying, because one becomes perplexed as to what its contents are.

[4] iii. 30. 5. 4; Roth, *op. cit.*, p. 72.

[5] *Ruj* 〉 *rūj* 〉 *rūka* 〉 *kūra* by metathesis, and *kūla* by the interchange of *r* and *l*; *ruj* 〉 *roṣṭa* 〉 *loṣṭa* by interchange of *r* and *l*.

[6] iii. 30. 8; VS. 18. 69.

[7] iii. 30. 10.

[8] 'Niggard', cf. Grassmann, *op. cit.*, p. 121.

of being uttered. The rain-water is invoked by a large number of people. The verb *dham* means to go.

(*Here ends the second section.*)

O Indra, tear up the Rakṣas with their root, rend them in the middle, shatter them in the front. How far did you entice him? Throw the burning weapon upon the foe of prayer.[1]

O Indra, tear up the Rakṣas with their root. *Mūlam* (root) is (so called) from releasing (√*muc*), or from stealing (√*muṣ*), or from stupefying (√*muh*).[2] Rend them in the middle, shatter them in the front.

Agram (front) is (so called because) it comes nearest (*ā-gatam*). How far, i. e. up to what country.

Salalūkam[3] means one who is perplexed; it means 'one who is sinful', say the etymologists. Or it may be *sararūkam*, i. e. moving everywhere, formed by reduplicating (the root) *sṛ* (to move). *Tapuṣi* (burning) is derived from (the root) *tap* (to heat). *Heti* (weapon) is derived from (the root) *han* (to kill).

(Indra) indeed (slew) even him who was lying and swelling[4] (with waters), i. e. having auspicious waters, whose waters are auspicious.[5]

Visruhaḥ means streams, (so called) from flowing (*vi* √*sru*).

The seven streams grew like branches.[6] This too is a Vedic quotation.

Vīrudhaḥ means herbs, (so called) from growing (*vi* √*ruh*).

Herbs are our means of salvation.[7] This too is a Vedic quotation.

Nakṣad-dābham[8] means one who strikes down any man who approaches, or who strikes down by means of a weapon which can reach all.

Who strikes the approaching opponent, who is swift and who dwells on mountains.[9] This too is a Vedic quotation.

A-skṛdhoyu[10] means one whose life is not short. The word *kṛdhu* is a synonym of short: it is mutilated.

He whose life is not short, who is undecaying, and who is brilliant.[11]

[1] iii. 30. 17.

[2] Durga omits the sentence *mūlam* to (√*muh*).

[3] 'Melting'; cf. Grassmann, *op. cit.*, p. 1491.

[4] v. 32. 6.

[5] Yāska paraphrases *kaṭ-payam* by *sukha-payasam*; Durga by *kapayam*, i.e. a cloud whose water is sweet; Sāyaṇa by *sukhakaram payo yasya*; 'swelling', Grassmann, *op. cit.*, p. 311; cf. Roth, *op. cit.*, p. 72.

[6] vi. 7. 6.

[7] x. 97. 3; VS. 12. 77.

[8] Durga explains it as *na-kṣad-dābham*, i.e. one who annihilates by his mere presence without killing; annihilating, Grassmann, *op. cit.*, p. 157.

[9] vi. 22. 2; AV. 20. 36. 2.

[10] i. e. Having a long life. Durga. Grassmann, *op. cit.*, p. 157, 'not scanty.'

[11] vi. 22. 3; AV. 20. 36. 3.

This too is a Vedic quotation. [*Niśṛmbhāḥ*[1] means drawing with a firm step.]

(*Here ends the third section.*)

May those goats, who draw with a firm step, bring *Pūṣan*, the refuge of men, in a chariot, may they (come) bearing the good.[2]

May those goats, who draw with a firm step, bring *Pūṣan*, the refuge of men, i. e. the refuge of all the born beings,[3] in a chariot.

Bṛbad-ukthaḥ[4] means a sublime hymn, or one to whom a hymn, or a sublime hymn, is to be addressed.

We invoke him to whom sublime hymns are to be addressed.[5]

This too is a Vedic quotation.

Rdu-udara means soma: its inside (*udara*) is soft, or it is soft in the inside of men.

May I be together with my friend, the soma.[6]

This too is a Vedic quotation.

We shall explain the word *ṛdūpe* later on.[7]

Pulukāma means a man of many desires. Man is indeed of many desires.[8] This too is a Vedic quotation.

Asinvatī means eating insatiably.

Eating insatiably and devouring too much.[9]

This too is a Vedic quotation.

Kapanāḥ means creeping, i. e. worms.

O wise ones, as worms consume[10] a tree.[11]

This too is a Vedic quotation.

Bhā-ṛjīka[12] means one whose light is well known.

With a banner of smoke, (kindled) with fuel, of well-known light.[13] This too is a Vedic quotation.

Rujānāḥ[14] means rivers: they break (*rujanti*) their banks.

He, whose enemy is Indra,[15] crushed down the rivers.[16]

[1] Durga explains the word as 'drawing quickly'; and Grassman as 'stepping firmly', *op. cit.*, p. 735.

[2] vi. 55. 6.

[3] Durga explains *janaśriyam* as 'one whose glory has become manifest', i.e. as a possessive compound, which is impossible from the accent.

[4] Roth doubts the accuracy of Yāska's etymology, which is supported both by M. W. and Grassmann, *op. cit.*, p. 910.

[5] viii. 32. 10. [6] viii. 48. 10.

[7] See 6. 33.

[8] i. 178. 5. Cf. Kālidāsa, *Kumāra-sambhava*, iv.

[9] x. 79. 1.

[10] Lit. steal.

[11] v. 54. 6. Durga also takes *vedhasaḥ* as an epithet of worms, i. e. who penetrate into the inside of a tree and consume its sap.

[12] Durga explains the word as 'of straight or steady light', and Grassmann, *op. cit.*, p. 891, 'of radiating light'.

[13] x. 12. 2; AV. 18. 1. 30.

[14] Cf. Grassmann, *op. cit.*, p. 1173.

[15] Durga takes *indra-śatruḥ* as a *tatpuruṣa* compound, but from the accent it is clearly a possessive compound.

[16] i. 32. 6; TB. 11. 5. 4. 4.

This too is a Vedic quotation.

Jūrṇiḥ[1] (power, or army) is derived from (the root) *jū* (to speed), or *dru* (to run), or *du* (to hurt).

The army dispatched (against us) will not be strong.[2]

The oblation has reached you every day with protection.[3]

The food has reached you from all sides with protection. *Ghraṃsa* means day.

(*Here ends the fourth section.*)

Upalaprakṣaṇī[4] means a woman who grinds grain on stones, or who throws grain down on stones. [Indra asked the seers, 'How does one live in famine?' One of them answered, 'Nine are the means of livelihood in famine, i. e. cart, pot-herbs, kine, net, restraining the flow of water, forest, ocean, mountain, and the king.' This stanza is explained by the mere reading of it.][5]

(*Here ends the fifth section.*)

I am a bard, my father is a physician, my mother a stone-grinder. Planning in various ways, desirous of wealth, we live, following (others) like cattle; flow, Soma, flow for Indra's sake.[6]

I am a bard, i. e. a composer of hymns. My father is a physician. The word *tataḥ* is a synonym of offspring, it means father or son. Stone-grinder, i. e. she who prepares barley meal. *Nanā*, derived from (the root) *nam*, means either mother or daughter. Planning in various ways, i. e. working in various ways. Desirous of wealth, lovers of wealth. We follow the world like kine. 'Flow, Soma, flow for Indra's sake,' this is the solicitation.

Seated, he slays the higher one, in his lap.[7] In the bosom.

Prakalavid[8] means a trader, i. e. one who knows the small, even the minutest parts of a thing.

Bad friends, measuring like a trader.[9]

This too is a Vedic quotation.

[1] Cf. Roth, *op. cit.*, p. 74; Grassmann, *op. cit.*, 493. According to Durga, √*jū* means to injure.

[2] i. 129. 8.

[3] vii. 69. 4; cf. Roth, *loc. cit.*

[4] Durga explains it to mean a maid-servant who prepares the necessary things used for pressing the soma; cf. also his remarks quoted by Roth, *op. cit.*, p. 74. 'Mill-woman'; cf. Grassmann, *op. cit.*, p. 257. Cf. Bṛh. D. vi. 138.

[5] The passage within square brackets is omitted by MSS. of the shorter version and Durga, and is evidently irrelevant. Cp. Bṛh. D., *loc. cit.*

[6] ix. 112. 3. Cf. Roth, *loc. cit.*

[7] x. 27. 13. Indra lets the higher one, i. e. the cone in the form of rain-water, flow in the atmosphere. Durga.

[8] Cf. Roth, *op. cit.*, p. 75; 'reckoning the smallest part', Grassmann, *op. cit.*, p. 864.

[9] vii. 18. 15.

Abhyardhayajvā[1] means one who offers sacrifices having made them into separate parts.

Pūṣā, who sacrifices in separate parts, pours down.[2]

This too is a Vedic quotation.

Īkṣe means thou rulest.

Thou rulest, O King, over the treasures of both (the worlds) indeed.[3] This too is a Vedic quotation.

[*Kṣoṇasya* means of abode.][4]

O Aśvins, ye gave a spacious abode to Kaṇva.[5] This too is a Vedic quotation.

(*Here ends the sixth section.*)

We are thy kinsmen.[6] i. e. We in the nominative. Come to us, O Aśvins of equal power.[7] i. e. To us, in the accusative.

With us who are equally strong, O Bull.[8] i. e. With us, in the instrumental case.

Extend this to us, O Lord of wealth, and wielder of the thunderbolt.[9] i. e. To us, in the dative case.

May he secretly separate the enemy even when far from us.[10] i. e. From us, in the ablative.

Our desire spreads like the submarine fire.[11] i. e. Our, in the genitive case.

Bestow treasures on us, O Vasus.[12] i. e. On us, in the locative case.[13]

Pāthas means atmosphere: it is explained by the word *pathā*.[14]

Like a flying falcon, he sweeps down the atmosphere.[15]

This too is a Vedic quotation.

Water is also called *pāthas*, from drinking (√*pā*, 'to drink'). He observes the water of these rivers.[16]

This too is a Vedic quotation.

Food is also called *pāthas*, from swallowing (√*pā*, to swallow). O wise one, carry up the food of the gods.[17]

[1] 'Most munificent', Durga; 'distributing', Grassmann, *op. cit.*, p. 88.

[2] vi. 50. 5.

[3] vi. 19. 10.

[4] The passage within the square brackets is omitted by MSS. of the shorter recension only, and not by Durga.

[5] i. 117. 8.

[6] VS. 4. 22.

[7] i. 118. 11.

[8] i. 165. 7.

[9] iii. 36. 10.

[10] vi. 47. 13.

[11] iv. 30. 19; TB. ii. 5. 4.

[12] VS. 8. 18.

[13] All these quotations, i.e. seven in all, have been cited to show that the word *asme* is used in all the seven cases.

[14] 'Region, heavenly path, abode', Grassmann, *op. cit.*, p. 805; cf. Roth, *op. cit.*, p. 76.

[15] ix. 63. 5.

[16] vii. 34. 10.

[17] x. 70. 10.

This too is a Vedic quotation.

Savīmani [1] means at the stimulation. We (go) at the stimulation of the divine Savitṛ.[2] This too is a Vedic quotation.

Saprathās means broad all round. O Agni, thou art broad all round.[3] This, too, is a Vedic quotation.

Vidathāni means knowledge. Urging forth knowledge.[4] This too is a Vedic quotation.

(*Here ends the seventh section.*)

Dependent on the sun as it were, all will indeed divide the wealth of Indra among the born and the yet to be born, with vigour; we did not think of every share.[5]

Absolutely dependent they approach the sun. Or else it may have been used for the sake of comparison, i. e. they approach Indra as if he were the sun. Distributing all the treasures of Indra: as he distributes treasures among those who are born and who are yet to be born. Let us think of that portion with vigour, with strength.

Ojas (vigour) is derived from (the root) *oj* (to be strong) or from *ubj* (to subdue).

Āśīḥ [6] (a mixture of milk and soma) is (so called) from being mixed (*ā* √*śṝ*, to mix) or from being slightly cooked (*ā* √*śrā*, to cook). Now the other meaning of *āśīḥ* (benediction) is derived from the root *ā-śās* (to pray for).

For Indra, kine (yield) mixture.[7] This too is a Vedic quotation. And also: That true benediction of mine to the gods.[8]

When the mortal has brought thy share, thou that swallowest most hast consumed the herbs.[9]

When the mortal has obtained thy share for thee, thou that swallowest most hast consumed the herbs. *Jigarti* means to consume, or to invoke, or to seize.

(We are) ignorant, (thou art) wise, we do not perceive thy greatness, thou indeed knowest, O Agni.[11]

We are confused, but thou art not confused; we do not know, but thou, O Agni, surely knowest thy greatness.

[1] Cf. Roth, *op. cit.*, p. 76; Grassmann, *op. cit.*, p. 1493.

[2] vi. 71. 2.

[3] v. 13. 4; SV. 2. 757.

[4] iii. 27. 7; SV. 827.

[5] viii. 99. 3; AV. 20. 58. 1; SV. 1. 267; 2. 669; VS. 33. 41.

[6] Cf. Roth, *op. cit.*, p. 76; 'mixture of hot things, an epithet of milk mixed with soma', Grassmann, *op. cit.*, p. 187.

[7] viii. 69. 6; AV. 20. 22. 6.

[8] TS. iii. 2. 7. 2.

[9] i. 163. 7; x. 72; VS. 29. 18.

[10] Although very tired, the horse swallows grass. This is his greatness, for others in a similar state cannot even move. Durga.

[11] x. 4. 4.

Śāśamānaḥ means praising. (He) who praising verily offers your oblations with sacrifices.[1] This too is a Vedic quotation.

The god with favour turned towards the gods.[2] The god whose favour is directed towards the gods. [*Kṛp* is derived from the root *kṛp* (to pity), or from *kḷp* (to manage).]

(*Here ends the eighth section.*)

For I have heard that you are more liberal than a son-in-law, nay even more than a brother-in-law. Now with this oblation of soma, O Indra and Agni, I will compose a new hymn for you.[3]

I have heard that you are more liberal indeed than a would-be son-in-law,[4] i. e. one whose son-in-lawship is not quite complete.[5] It is well known that the people in the south apply the term *vijāmātā* to the husband of a purchased maiden. By this is meant a bridegroom, whose relationship is not quite complete as it were. *Jāmātā* (son-in-law) is (so called because) he is the progenitor of *jā*, which means offspring. Nay even more than a brother-in-law, i. e. more liberal than a brother-in-law.[6] They, who are well versed in primary causes, remark that a brother-in-law is (so called because) he comes very near on account of his relationship. Or else he is (so called because) he sows parched grain [7] from a winnowing basket. *Lājāḥ* (parched grain) is derived from (the root) *lāj* (to parch). *Syam*, a winnowing basket, is derived from the root *so* (to finish). *Śūrpam* means a sieve for winnowing grain, it is derived from (the root) *śṝ* (to fall off). Now, O Indra and Agni, I shall compose [a new] altogether new hymn for you, along with this oblation of Soma.

We shall explain *omāsaḥ* later on.[8]

(*Here ends the ninth section.*)

O Lord of prayer, make the soma-presser glorious like Kakṣīvat, the son of Uśij.[9]

O Lord of prayer, make the man who presses soma, i. e. who prepares soma, resplendent like Kakṣīvat, the son of Uśij.

Kakṣīvān, who possesses secluded apartments. *Auśija*, son of *Uśij*. *Uśij* is derived from (the root) *vaś*, meaning to desire. Or else the armpit

[1] i. 151. 7.

[2] i. 127. 1 ; AV. 20. 67. 3 ; VS. 15. 47 ; SV. 1. 465 ; 2. 1163.

[3] i. 109. 2.

[4] Cf. Roth, *op. cit.*, p. 79.

[5] i.e. One who lacks the qualities of a worthy son-in-law, but who pleases the girl's father by making many costly presents. Durga.

[6] A brother-in-law, i. e. brother of the wife, is very liberal in his gifts, because he is very desirous of pleasing his sister.

[7] It is a part of the marriage ceremony. The brother-in-law takes grain from a winnowing basket and throws it on the head of the bride and bridegroom.

[8] See 12. 40.

[9] i. 18. 1 ; VS. 3. 28 ; cf. SV. 1. 189 ; 2. 813.

of a man may have been intended: make me, i.e. him (who has fine shoulders), O Lord of prayer, resplendent, me who press, prepare the soma.

(Here ends the tenth section.)

O Indra and Soma, let the wicked man, the vaunter of his evildeeds, be heated like a pot on the fire, being tormented by you. Bear unyielding enmity to the foe of prayer, the eater of raw meat, the malignant man of fierce eyes.[1]

O Indra and Soma, (torment) the vaunter of evil deeds. *Agha* (evil deed) is derived from (the root) *han* with the preposition *ā* shortened, i.e. it kills. *Tapus* is derived from (the root) *tap* (to heat). Pot (*caru*) is (so called because) it is a heap of clay (*mṛc-caya*), or it may be derived from (the root) *car* (to walk), from it waters go up. (Bear enmity) to the foe of prayer, [i.e. one who hates a Brāhmaṇa, and who eats raw meat], to the eater of raw meat, [and to the man whose eyes are fierce], and to the man of dreadful eyes. 'Raw meat is (so called because) it is procured by carving,' say the etymologists. Bear enmity. Unyielding, not ceasing;[2] or else which may not be reconciled even by those who are free from malevolence. Malignant,[3] i.e. a vagabond who goes about (saying) 'What now', or 'What is this, what is this?' for the sake of back-biting. *Piśunaḥ* (back-biter) is derived from (the root) *piś* (to adorn): he adorns (his yarns) in various ways.

(Here ends the eleventh section.)

Make thy powerful throng extensive like a net, go like a king accompanied by his minister, on an elephant. Hastening after the net with speed, thou shootest: transfix the fiends with darts that burn most fiercely.[4]

Make thy powerful throng. Powerful throng (*pājaḥ*)[5] is (so called) from being maintained (√*pāl*). *Prasitiḥ* is (so called) from being fastened (*pra*√*si*): 'noose or net'. Go like a king who is accompanied by his minister, or who is the terror[6] of his enemies, or who is followed by his own attendants, i.e. retinue well-nourished with food,[7] or (riding) a fearless

[1] vii. 104. 2; AV. 8. 4. 2; cf. Roth, *op. cit.*, p. 78.

[2] 'Irreconcilable', Durga; cf. Grassmann, *op. cit.*, p. 53.

[3] 'Fiend', Grassmann, *op. cit.*, p. 325.

[4] iv. 4. 1; VS. 13. 9.

[5] 'Strength or power', Durga; cf. Roth, *op. cit.*, pp. 78–9.

[6] Lit., who acts like a disease for his enemies.

[7] i.e. His body-guard. Durga.

elephant. Hastening after the net with speed: the word *tṛṣvī* is a synonym of quick; it is derived from (the root) *tṛ* (to pass over), or from *tvar* (to hurry). Thou shootest, transfix the fiends with darts that burn, or enflame, or crush down most fiercely.

The disease of evil name, which attacks thy womb.[1]

Amīvā[2] is explained by *abhyamana*, i.e. disease. 'Of evil name' signifies a worm (germ of disease) whose name is sinful. A worm (*kṛmiḥ*) is (so called because) it grows fat (*√mid*) on raw flesh (*kravye*), or it may be derived from (the root) *kram*, meaning to creep, or from *krām* (to crawl).

Transcending all the evil deeds.[3]

Transcending all the crooked and wicked ways. *Apvā*,[4] (something) transfixed with which (a man) is separated (from life or happiness), i.e. disease or fear.

Away, O disease.[5]

This too is a Vedic quotation.

Amatiḥ[6] means 'made at home', or one's own intellect.

Whose intellect is of a high order, whose lustre shone [at stimulation].[7]

This too is a Vedic quotation.

The word *śruṣṭī* is a synonym of quick: it pervades quickly.[8]

(Here ends the twelfth section.)

O Agni, sacrifice quickly for them, i.e. wise Bhaga and Nāsatyas, who are longing for it, in this sacrifice.

O Agni, offer oblations quickly to them who long for, i.e. desire, (their portions) in this sacrifice, i.e. Bhaga and Nāsatyas, i.e. Aśvins. 'They are ever true and never false,' says Aurṇavābha. 'They are promoters of truth,' says Āgrāyaṇa. Or else they are (so called because) they are nose-born.[9] *Purandhi*[10] means very wise. With reference to this, who is very wise? Some think it to be an epithet of Bhaga, who is placed prior to it (in the stanza); according to others, it refers to Indra: he is of manifold

[1] x. 162. 2; AV. 20. 96. 12.

[2] Cf. Roth, *op. cit.*, p. 80; Grassmann, *op. cit.*, p. 93.

[3] AV. 12. 2. 28. The word *duritam* does not occur in the RV. So Yāska was obliged to seek his illustration from AV.

[4] Cf. Grassmann, *op. cit.*, p. 80.

[5] Frag. of x. 103. 12; AV. 3. 2. 5; VS. 7. 44; see 9. 33; cf. SV. 2. 121.

[6] Cf. Roth, *op. cit.*, p. 80; Grassmann, *op. cit.*, p. 90, 'weight, sunshine', &c.

[7] AV. 7. 14. 2.; SV. 1. 464. The word occurs twice in RV. i. 64. 9: 73. 2; but Yāska quotes neither of them.

[8] 'Immediately', Grassmann, *op. cit.*, p. 1439.

[9] Cf. 12. 1.

[10] 'Bountiful', Grassmann, *op. cit.*, p. 824.

activities,[1] and the most dreadful shatterer of cities. Others take it to mean Varuṇa, i. e. who is praised with regard to his intelligence.

This supernatural power of the most wise one.[2] This too is a Vedic quotation.

The word *ruśat*[3] is a synonym of colour; it is derived from (the root) *ruc*, meaning to shine.

The brilliant strength of the kindled one has been seen.[4] This too is a Vedic quotation.

(*Here ends the thirteenth section.*)

There is indeed kinship, O gods destroyers of malignant persons, and there is friendship among you.[5]

O gods destroyers of those who seek to injure others,[6] of you there is indeed kinship, and there is friendship among you. *Apyam* (friendship) is derived from (the root) *āp* (to obtain).

Sudatraḥ[7] means bountiful giver. May Tvaṣṭā the bountiful giver distribute wealth among us.[8] This too is a Vedic quotation.

Suvidatraḥ[9] means benevolent. O Agni, come towards us with benevolent gods.[10] This too is a Vedic quotation. *Ānuṣak*[11] is the name of a series of succession, it clings one to the other.

They spread the grass successively.[12] This too is a Vedic quotation.

Turvaṇiḥ[13] means overpowering.

He, the overpowering, the great, the dustless, (shines) in the atmosphere.[14] This too is a Vedic quotation.

Girvaṇāḥ means a god: they win him over with hymns.

The agreeable; the sublime hymn to the god.[15] This too is a Vedic quotation.

(*Here ends the fourteenth section.*)

[1] According to Durga, *dhi* is a synonym of work, hence *purandhi* means one of manifold activities.

[2] v. 85. 6.

[3] Cf. Grassmann, *op. cit.*, p. 1177.

[4] v. 1. 2; SV. 2. 1097.

[5] viii. 27. 10.

[6] Cf. Roth, *op. cit.*, p. 80; 'who eat violently', Grassmann, *op. cit.*, p. 1167.

[7] 'Liberal, lending out'. Grassmann, *op. cit.*, p. 1534.

[8] vii. 34. 22; VS. 2. 24; 8. 14.

[9] 'Of good knowledge', Grassmann, *op. cit.*, p. 1552.

[10] x. 15. 9; AV. 18. 3. 48.

[11] 'In succession', Grassmann. *op. cit.*. p. 178.

[12] viii. 45. 1; SV. 1. 133: 2. 688; VS. 7. 32.

[13] 'Victorious, triumphant', Grassmann, *op. cit.*, p. 543; cf. Roth, *op. cit.*, p. 81.

[14] i. 56. 3. Durga takes *areṇu pauṃsye* as one compound, but they are two different words, as is indicated by the accent.

[15] viii. 89. 7; SV. 2. 781.

The wind-tossed gods, who seated in a well-tossed region, created all these beings together.[1]

In a well-stirred region, the group of atmospheric gods who are stirred by breath,[2] i.e. wind, and who, while satisfying the earth with fluids, created living beings. The principal clause 'they sacrificed' has been passed over.

Straight is that spear of thine, O Indra.[3]

(The spear) which is hurled towards the enemy or which has reached the enemy.[4]

By his skill, he won everything on which the stake was laid.[5]

By his skill, he won all that on which the stake was laid.

Like a procreating bull, (Agni) has been generated with sacrifices.[6]

(Here ends the fifteenth section.)

Enjoying they have stood forth to you, all of you have become the chiefs, O Ṛbhus.[7]

Enjoying[8] they have stood[9] forth to you. All of you have become the chiefs by going in front, [or by swallowing first of all], or by accomplishing first of all. Or else, the word *agriyā* is *agram* itself with meaningless case-termination.

O Indra, none eat these prescribed oblations, bestow upon us cooked food and soma.[10]

O Indra, eat these prescribed oblations and bestow food. The word *canas*[11] is a synonym of food. *Pacati* is used as a noun.

Accept it cooked from the fatty portion.[12]

This too is a Vedic quotation. Or else it may be in the dual number. It is well known when it is in the singular.

Just as: The cooked oblation of rice, O Agni![13]

Śurudhaḥ[14] means waters: they restrain heat well. They are indeed the first waters of the sacred rite.[15]

[1] x. 82. 4: VS. 17. 28.

[2] '*A-sūrta*, non-bright, dusky', Grassmann, *op. cit.*, p. 157; Roth, *loc. cit.*

[3] i. 169. 3.

[4] In battle, on account of heated imagination, enemies exclaim, 'Oh it is hurled towards me, it is hurled towards me'. Durga.

[5] v. 44. 8: see 1. 15.

[6] vi. 12. 4.

[7] iv. 34. 3.

[8] 'Being attended upon by the gods.' Durga.

[9] Durga paraphrases *pra asthuḥ* by *prasthitāni*, i.e. prescribed. It is quite wrong, for *asthuḥ* is root ao. 3rd pl. of *sthā*.

[10] x. 116. 8.

[11] 'Pleasure, satisfaction, grace', Grassmann, *op. cit.*, p. 435.

[12] Cf. VS. 21. 60.

[13] iii. 28. 2.

[14] 'Hero, strength, invigorating draughts', Grassmann, *op. cit.*, p. 1407.

[15] iv. 23. 8; cf. 10. 41.

Aminaḥ[1] means immeasurable, great, or invulnerable.

Immeasurable with forces.[2] This too is a Vedic quotation.

Jajjhatīḥ means waters (so called because) they produce a sound.

The Maruts like the waters.[3] This too is a Vedic quotation.

A-pratiṣkutaḥ[4] means unopposable, or unrestrainable.

For us who are unrestrainable.[5] This too is a Vedic quotation.

Śāśadānaḥ[6] means eminent.

Eminent he has surpassed even his own intellect.[7] This too is a Vedic quotation.

(*Here ends the sixteenth section.*)

Sṛpraḥ[8] (supple) is (so called) from slipping (√*sṛp*).

This other (meaning of) *sṛpraḥ* is derived from the same root also, i.e. clarified butter, or oil.

(We invoke) the supple-armed for our protection.[9]

This too is a Vedic quotation. *Karasnau* means two arms: they are the promoters[10] of actions (√*kṛ* √*snā*).

Su-śipram[11] is explained by the same also. O thou having very supple limbs, in the food rich in kine.[12] This too is a Vedic quotation.

Śipre[13] means the two jaws or the two nostrils. *Hanu* (jaw) is derived from (the root) *han* (to kill). *Nāsikā* (nose) is derived from (the root) √*nas* (to join).

Open the jaws and pour forth the milk beverage.[14]

This too is a Vedic quotation.

Dhenā[15] (milk beverage) is derived from (the root) *dhā* (to put).

Raṃsu[16] (delightful) is (so called) from giving delight (√*ram*).

He the delightful one perceived with his variegated light.[17]

This too is a Vedic quotation.

Dvi-barhāḥ[18] means one who is great in two, i.e. the atmospheric and the celestial regions.

1 From √*am* (to go): 'impetuous', MW.; 'mighty', &c., Grassmann, *op. cit.*, p. 93.

2 Frag. of vi. 19.1; VS. 7. 39.

3 v. 52. 6.

4 'Irresistible', Grassmann, *op. cit.*, p. 79.

5 i. 7. 6; AV. 20. 17. 12.

6 'Presumptuous, self-confident, splendid, victorious', Grassmann, *op. cit.*, p. 1377.

7 i. 33. 13.

8 'Spreading, extending, oily', &c., Grassmann, *op. cit.*, p. 1577.

9 viii. 32. 10; SV. 1. 217.

10 Lit., bathers (*pra-snātārau*).

11 'Having beautiful lips', Grassmann, *op. cit.*, p. 1554.

12 viii. 21. 8.

13 'Lips', Grassmann, *op. cit.*, p. 1394.

14 i. 101. 10.

15 'Milch cow, mare', &c., Grassmann, *op. cit.*, p. 695.

16 Cf. Grassmann, *op. cit.*, p. 1129.

17 ii. 4. 5.

18 Having 'twofold strength or greatness', &c., Grassmann, *op. cit.*, p. 652.

And the doubly great, immeasurable with his strength.[1]

This too is a Vedic quotation.

Akraḥ[2] (fort) is (so called) from being attacked. Like a fort, the supporter of enemies in battle.[3] This too is a Vedic quotation.

Urāṇaḥ means making abundant.

From days of yore, thou art employed as a messenger, making (the small) abundant.[4] This too is a Vedic quotation.

Stiyāḥ[5] means waters, (so called) from being collected together.

The sprinkler of rivers and the rainer of waters.[6] This too is a Vedic quotation.

Stipāḥ[7] means guardian of waters, or one who guards them who approach him (for protection).

May he be our guardian, aye the protector of our bodies.[8] This too is a Vedic quotation.

Jabāru[9] means one who grows with speed, or who grows causing others to decay, or who grows swallowing (darkness or juice).

The sun was placed on high in the beginning of creation.[10] This too is a Vedic quotation.

Jarūtham[11] means a hymn; it is derived from (the root) *gṛ* (to invoke).

Addressing the hymn, sacrifice to the wise one for wealth.[12] This too is a Vedic quotation.

The word *kuliśa*[13] is a synonym of thunderbolt; it is the shatterer of banks.

Like the branches (of a tree) cut down by the thunderbolt, the cloud rests being in close contact with the earth.[14]

A branch of a tree, (so called because) it is attached to it. This other (meaning of) *skandha*,[15] i.e. shoulder, is derived from the same root also: it is attached to the body. The cloud lies on earth, being in close contact with it.

[1] vi. 19. 1; VS. 7. 39.

[2] 'Standard of an army, banner', Grassmann, *op. cit.*, p. 5.

[3] iii. 1. 12.

[4] iv. 7. 8.

[5] 'Snow-field, glacier', Grassmann, *op. cit.*, p. 1590.

[6] vi. 44. 21.

[7] 'Protector of the household', Grassmann, *loc. cit.*; 'well', Durga.

[8] x. 69. 4.

[9] 'Hastening', Grassmann, *op. cit.*, p. 477; 'the disk of the sun', Durga.

[10] iv. 5. 7.

[11] 'Making old, demon', MW.; 'an epithet of Agni as a consuming agent', Grassmann, *op. cit.*, p. 481.

[12] vii. 9. 6.

[13] 'Axe, hatchet', Grassmann, *op. cit.*, p. 330.

[14] i. 32. 5.

[15] i. e. From √*skandh* 'to be attached'.

Tuñjaḥ[1] (gift) is derived from (the root) *tuj*, meaning to give.

(*Here ends the seventeenth section.*)

I do not lack excellent praise of Indra, the wielder of the thunderbolt, in these subsequent hymns which are addressed to him at every gift.[2]

I find there is no end to the praise of Indra, the wielder of the thunderbolt, in these subsequent hymns which are addressed to him at every gift.

Barhaṇā[3] means strongly.

The far-famed demon was strongly made.[4] This too is a Vedic quotation.

(*Here ends the eighteenth section.*)

Illustrious indeed becomes that man who presses the soma-juice for him during day and during night. The mighty Indra, lord of wealth, strips him bare, who amasses wealth, who is fond of decorating his body, and who is a companion of selfish men.[5]

The word *ghraṃsa* is a synonym of day, (so called because) juices are evaporated during this period. *Ūdhas*[6] means the udder of a cow, (so called) because it is more raised than the other parts, or because it is fastened near the abdomen. From the analogy of giving fatty fluids,[7] night is called *ūdhas* also. The man who presses soma for him during the day and even during the night becomes indeed illustrious.

He strips him bare, i.e. the mighty lord of wealth strips him bare—the man who amasses wealth, who is averse to the spread of righteousness, who is fond of ornaments, who does not sacrifice, who is a fop, who decorates his body gaudily; who is selfish, who is the friend of selfish men.[8]

He cleft the strongholds of him who lay in the bowels of earth, Indra shattered the lofty draught.[9]

Indra cleft the strongholds of him who lay in the holes of earth[10] and shattered the lofty cloud.

(*Here ends the nineteenth section.*)

1 'Shock, assault', MW.; 'start, run, pressing or pushing forward', Grassmann, *op. cit.*, p. 540.

2 i. 7. 7; AV. 20. 70. 30.

3 'Great growth, or slaughter', Durga; 'strength, might', &c., Grassmann, *op. cit.*, p. 900; 'tearing, pulling', MW.

4 i. 54. 3.

5 v. 34. 3.

6 Yāska derives *ūdhas* from *ud√han* or from *upa√nah*; cf. Lat. *ūber*, Gk. οὖθαρ, AS. *ūder*, Irish *uth*, Ger. *euter*.

7 i.e. Dew, Durga.

8 'A companion of the parsimonious', Grassmann, *op. cit.*, p. 318, and *tatanuṣṭi*, 'bragging, ostentatious', p. 512.

9 i. 33. 12.

10 Durga explains *ilībiśa* as cloud, i.e. who rests having closed the outlets (*bila*) of water, which causes the food (*iḷā*) to grow.

Hastening forth for this Vṛtra, O lord who can hold much, hurl the thunderbolt on him. Desiring channels, for the waters to flow, rend him across like the joint of a cow.[1]

Hastening forth, O Lord, hurl the thunderbolt quickly on this Vṛtra. *Kiyedhā*[2] means one holds so much (= *kiyad-dhā*), or one who surrounds many attackers. Desiring channels for the waters to flow, rend the joints of the clouds like those of a cow.

Bhṛmi (whirlwind)[3] is derived from (the root) *bhram* (to move).

Causing enlightenment, thou art the whirlwind of men.[4] This too is a Vedic quotation.

Viṣpitaḥ[5] means great expanse.

Conducting us across this great expanse.[6] This too is a Vedic quotation.

(*Here ends the twentieth section.*)

Let that fluid of ours be wonderful, a cover for many and a self for others. May the brilliant Tvaṣṭā, who loves us, release it for our prosperity and wealth.[7]

May Tvaṣṭā, who loves, i. e. longs for us, release that quickly-flowing, great and self-amassed water[8] for the prosperity of our wealth.

Rāspinaḥ means noisy ; it is derived from (the root) *rap* (to chatter), or *ras* (to make a sound).

Of the life of the noisy.[9] This too is a Vedic quotation.

Ṛñjati means to decorate.

[Thou decoratest thy strength at day-breaks.[10] This too is a Vedic quotation.][11]

The word *ṛju* is derived from the same also.

(Let) Varuṇa (lead us) with right guidance.[12] This too is a Vedic quotation.

[1] i 61. 12 ; AV. 20. 35. 12.

[2] Durga construes *kiyedhā* with Vṛtra, i. e. the cloud who holds unmeasured quantities of water. He overlooks the fact that Vṛtra is in the dative, while *kiyedhā* is in the nominative case. Grassmann (*op. cit.*, p. 326) explains it as 'distributing much'.

[3] i. e. Thou bringest men into the wheel of transmigration.

[4] i. 31. 16.

[5] Something which spreads far and wide on every side, i. e. the wheel of transmigration, Durga. 'Danger, affliction', Grassmann, *op. cit.*, p. 1310.

[6] vii. 60. 7.

[7] i. 142. 2 ; AV. 5. 27. 10.

[8] Durga explains *turīpa* as water, i. e. rain-water, and Grassmann as 'fluid, seminal fluid', *op. cit.*, p. 542. Durga explains *nābhāna* = *na* + *a* + *bhāna*, i. e. brilliant.

[9] Frag. of i. 22. 4.

[10] x. 76. 1 ; cf. Bṛh. D. 7. 116.

[11] Durga remarks that Yāska does not cite any Vedic passage to illustrate *ṛñjati*, for it is explained by *bhārjika*. However, some MSS. give RV. iv. 8. 1.

[12] i. 90. 1 ; SV. 1. 218.

Pratadvasū[1] means they two who have obtained wealth.

O Indra, urge the two bay steeds that have obtained wealth towards us.[2] This too is a Vedic quotation.

(*Here ends the twenty-first section.*)

Send our sacrifice for the worship of the gods, send our prayer for the obtainment of wealth; release the udder at the performance of the sacred rites, let waters be obedient to our call.[3]

Send forth our sacrifice for worshipping the gods, send forth our prayer for the obtainment of wealth. At the performance of sacred rites, at the performance of sacrifice or the yoking of sacrificial car. A car (is so called because) it is covered with the excrement of the animal, or because it moves slowly, or because it produces a creaking sound when it moves. Let waters be obedient to our call full of comfort. Let waters be full of comfort for us.

O Indra, offering much that is good.[4]

O Indra, giving much that has to be won.

Hating the impious, king of both, Indra offers to tribes and men.[5]

He scatters the impious, and always hates them who do not press the soma-juice. He distributes wealth among the soma-pressers. King of both, i.e. king of celestial and terrestrial wealth. The two words *coṣkūyamāṇa* and *coṣkūyate* are reduplicated forms.

Sumat means of one's own accord. That on which my heart is set has approached me of its own accord.[6]

Let that on which my heart is set approach me of its own accord, i.e. by (means of) the sacrifice. This stanza is used in the horse-sacrifice.

Diviṣṭiṣu means sacred rites which lead to heaven. Abundance of wealth consisting of hundred horses in the sacred rites of Kuruṅga.[7]

Sthūra (abundant) is (so called because) it becomes great having been collected in all measures. *Aṇu* (minute) means something which is not abundant. It is the preposition *anu* (used as a noun) with its suffix dropped like *samprati*. *Kuruṅga* was the name of a king, (so called) because he attacked (the tribe of) the Kurus, or because he attacked the dynasties (of his enemies). *Kuru* is derived from (the root) *kṛt* (to cut).

[1] 'Increasing riches', Grassmann, *op. cit.*, p. 867.

[2] viii. 13. 27.

[3] x. 30. 11.

[4] i. 33. 3.

[5] vi. 47. 16.

[6] i. 162. 7; VS. 35. 30.

[7] viii. 4. 19; 24. 29; cf. Bṛh. D. 6. 44.

The word *krūra* (cruel) belongs to the same root also. *Kula* (family) is derived from (the root) *kuṣ* (to knead), it is kneaded.

Dūtaḥ (messenger) has been explained.[1]

Jinvatiḥ means to animate.

Clouds animate the earth, fires the sky.[2] This too is a Vedic quotation.

(*Here ends the twenty-second section.*)

Amatraḥ means 'without measure', 'great', or 'one who is invulnerable'.

Great without measure, mighty in a fortified place.[3] This too is a Vedic quotation.

The wielder of thunderbolts is praised as identical with the hymn.[4]

The wielder of thunderbolts is praised as equal to the hymn.

Anarśarātim[5] means one whose gifts are not vulgar. Vulgar, sinful, unpleasant, crooked.

Praise well the giver of wealth, whose gifts are not vulgar.[6] This too is a Vedic quotation.

Anarvā[7] means one who is not dependent on others.

Increase the independent, mighty, sweet-tongued, and praiseworthy lord of prayer with hymns.[8]

Increase the lord of prayer, who is independent, who does not depend on others, the mighty, the sweet-tongued (whose speech is delightful), or whose tongue is fascinating, the praiseworthy, with hymns, i.e. stanzas of praise, which are the means of worship.

Asāmi[9] is the opposite of *sāmi* (incomplete). *Sāmi* is derived from the root *so* (to kill).

Liberal givers, bear this complete strength.[10]

O ye whose gifts are delightful, bear this strength which is complete.

(*Here ends the twenty-third section.*)

Let me not make thee angry like a wild beast at the time of soma-pressing by straining the soma, or by my always beseeching hymns; for who has not besought the Lord?

[1] See 5. 1.

[2] i. 164. 51.

[3] iii. 36. 4.

[4] x. 22. 2.

[5] 'Whose gifts injure not'. Grassmann, *op. cit.*, p. 53.

[6] viii. 4; AV. 20. 58. 2.

[7] Cf. Grassmann, *op. cit.*, p. 52.

[8] i. 190. 1.

[9] 'Not half, quite complete', Grassmann, *op. cit.*, p. 154.

[10] i. 39. 10.

May we, always beseeching with our hymns, songs, praises, and the straining of the soma,[1] not make thee angry like a wild beast at the time when soma is pressed; for who has not besought the Lord? *Galdā*[2] means vessels, (so called) because the extracted juice is stored in them.

Let the soma-draughts flow into thee, aye! and the extracted juices of vessels.[3] These two words are inflected in various cases. Here it (*galdā*) means the juices which have been extracted in the vessels.

(*Here ends the twenty-fourth section.*)

We do not think ourselves guilty, or poor, or devoid of lustre.[4]

We do not think ourselves to be sinful, or destitute, or devoid of lustre. We are celibate, devoted to study, austerities, generosity, and activity, said the seer.

Bakura[5] means one who gives light, or who inspires awe, or who runs effulgent.

(*Here ends the twenty-fifth section.*)

O Aśvins, working wonders; sowing the grain with the plough, milking food for man, blasting the impious foe with lightning, you made far-spreading light for the Ārya.[6]

[O Aśvins, sowing grain, as it were, with a plough.] *Vṛka* means a plough, (so called) from cutting. *Lāṅgala* (plough) is derived from the root *lag* (to cling), or it is (so called) because it has a tail. *Lāṅgūla* (tail) is derived from (the root) *lag* (to cling), or from *laṅg* (to wave), or from *lamb* (to hang down). Milking food for man. O fair ones![7] Blasting the impious foe with lightning or with (a flood of) water. *Ārya* means the son of the lord.

Bekanāṭāḥ are, indeed, the usurers, (so called) because they make (their principal sum) double, or because they advance on (security) of double (value), or because they demand double (price).

Indra overcomes all the usurers who behold the daylight and the dishonest merchants.[8]

Indra subdues all usurers who behold the daylight, who behold the sun,

[1] viii. 1. 20; SV. 1. 307.

[2] 'Straining of soma', Grassmann, *op. cit.*, p. 388.

[3] i. 15. 1; vii. 92. 22; SV. 1. 197. 2; 1010; VS. 8. 42.

[4] viii. 61. 11.

[5] 'A wind-instrument used in war', Grassmann, *op. cit.*, p. 897.

[6] i. 117. 21.

[7] Durga explains *dasrau* as 'enslavers of enemies', or 'the promoters of works like agriculture, &c., by means of rain'. The passage consisting of the etymological explanations, from *Vṛka* . . . up to (hang down), is omitted by Durga.

[8] viii. 66. 10.

whose vision is limited to the present only, who do not see the (future) days by their action. Merchants are traders.

(*Here ends the twenty-sixth section.*)

O Ādityas, run to us the living ones before the slaughter; where are you, the hearers of our call?[1]

O Ādityas, run[2] to us while we are still alive, i.e. before we are slain; where are you, the hearers of our invocations? It is known to be the composition of the fish caught in a net. The fish[3] are (so called because) they float in water, or they revel in eating each other. Net is (so called) because it moves in water, or it is set in water, or it lies in water.

Aṃhuraḥ means distressed. The word *aṃhūraṇam* is derived from the same root also.

Taking away from the distressed.[4] This too is a Vedic quotation.

The wise established seven boundaries, transgressing even one of them a man falls into distress.[5]

The wise made seven boundaries, a man going beyond even one of them becomes distressed. They are theft, adultery, killing of a learned man, abortion, drinking, habitual addiction to wickedness, and false accusation of heinous crime.[6]

Bata is a particle, it is (used) to denote distress and compassion.

(*Here ends the twenty-seventh section.*)

Alas! thou art a weakling, O Yama, we have not found any heart or spirit in thee. Another, indeed, will embrace thee, resting on thy breast like a woodbine on a tree.[7]

A weakling, i.e. devoid of all strength. O Yama, thou art a weakling, i.e. of little strength. I do not know[8] thy heart, thy mind. Another woman, indeed, will embrace thee, joined with thy breast like a woodbine with a tree. *Libujā* (woodbine) means a creeper: it clings (√*lī*), distributing (*vi-bhaj-antī*). *Vratati* (creeper) is (so called) from selecting (√*vṛ*), or from entwining (√*si*), or from spreading (√*tan*).

[1] viii. 67. 5.

[2] Yāska paraphrases *abhi-dhetana* by *abhi-dhāvata*. The former is imp. of √*dhā* with *abhi*.

[3] *Matsyāḥ* (fish) is derived from √*syand* (to float) and *madhu* (water).

[4] i. 105. 17.

[5] x. 5. 6; AV. 5. 1. 6.

[6] The sentence is quoted by Sāyaṇa in his commentary on x. 5. 6. In Max Müller's second edition of the RV. with Sāyaṇa, the word *bhrūṇahatyām* is omitted, consequently the number of boundaries is six instead of seven.

[7] x. 10. 13; AV. 18. 1. 15.

[8] Yāska paraphrases *avidāma* by *vijānāmi*. The former is the 1st per. plur. aor. of √*vid*; the latter 1st per. sing. pres. of √*jñā*.

Vātāpyam means water: wind (*vātā*) causes it to swell (√*ā pyai*).

Purifying the water, the delight of all.[1] This too is a Vedic quotation.

As a trembling young bird has been placed on a tree.[2]

As a trembling, or anxiously longing, young bird, i. e. the young offspring of a bird. Śākalya has analysed *vāyaḥ* into *vā* and *yaḥ*: then the finite verb would have had the acute accent, and the sense have been incomplete.

The word *ratharyati*[3] means one desirous of something accomplished, or one who desires a chariot.

This god desires a chariot.[4] This too is a Vedic quotation.

(*Here ends the twenty-eighth section.*)

Fatten the perennial cow like food.[5] i. e. which never runs dry.[6]

Ādhavaḥ[7] (agitator) is so called from agitating.

Thou art the perfection of intellects and agitator of priests.[8] This too is a Vedic quotation.

Anavabravaḥ[9] means one whose speech is irreproachable.

Like Indra, thou bringest victory, and thy speech is irreproachable.[10] This too is a Vedic quotation.

(*Here ends the twenty-ninth section.*)

Go to the hill, O barren, one-eyed, hideous, ever-screaming (famine). We frighten thee away with those heroes (lit. beings) of the cloud.[11]

O barren, one-eyed, hideous (famine). 'One-eyed (is so called because) his sight is crooked,' says Aupamanyava. Or it may be derived from the root *kaṇ*, meaning to be small.

The verb *kaṇ* is used to denote the smallness of sound, as 'it sounds inaudible'. A (person) is called *kaṇa* on account of the smallness of his size, and *kāṇa* on account of his short vision, i. e. one-eyed. 'Hideous, i. e. whose manner of walking is crooked,' says Aupamanyava. Or the word (*vi-kaṭa*) may be derived from (the root) *kuṭ* (to be crooked) by metathesis: he is very crooked. Ever-screaming, always screeching, go to the hills. With the heroes of the cloud. *Śirimbiṭha*[12] means a cloud: it is

[1] ix. 35. 5.

[2] x. 29. 1; AV. 20. 76. 1.

[3] 'One who drives in a chariot', Grassmann, *op. cit.*, p. 1139; 'one who desires speed (*raṃhaṇam*)', Durga.

[4] ix. 3. 5; SV. 2. 609.

[5] vi. 63. 8.

[6] Cf. Grassmann, *op. cit.*, p. 152.

[7] 'Shaker, exciter, mixture, combination', Grassmann, *op. cit.*, p. 177.

[8] x. 26. 4.

[9] Cf. Grassmann, *op. cit.*, p. 53.

[10] x. 84. 5; AV. 4. 31. 5.

[11] x. 155. 1; cf. Bṛh. D. viii. 60.

[12] 'Appellation of a man', Grassmann, *op. cit.*, p. 1395.

shattered in the atmosphere. *Biṭham* means atmosphere. *Biṭham* is explained by *bīriṭa*.[1] We frighten thee away with its heroes, i. e. waters. Or else, *śirimbiṭha* is (a name of the seer) Bhāradvāga, who endowed with black ears, destroyed evil fortune (with this stanza). We frighten thee away with his heroes, i. e. actions. The verb *cātay* means to frighten.

Parāśaraḥ[2] means a seer, born from the old and exhausted Vasiṣṭha.

The seer Vasiṣṭha (surrounded by) a hundred demons.[3] This too is a Vedic quotation.

Indra is called *parāśara* also, he is the destroyer of [other] demons.

Indra was the destroyer of the demons.[4] This too is a Vedic quotation.

Krivirdatī[5] means having sharp teeth.

Where your bright weapon, having sharp teeth, rends.[6] This too is a Vedic quotation.

Karūḷatī[7] means having gaps in the teeth. [Or else, having seen some god with gaps in his teeth, the seer made this remark.]

(*Here ends the thirtieth section.*)

May god Aryaman give you all fair and beautiful things. O destroyer (of enemies), may Pūṣā, Bhaga, and the god having gaps in his teeth give you all fair and beautiful things.[8]

Fair (is so called because) it is to be won. Destroyer (is so called) from destroying. But who is the god who has gaps in his teeth? According to some, it is an epithet of Bhaga who comes before it. According to others, this god is Pūṣā, because he has no teeth.[9] Pūṣā is without teeth, says a Brāhmaṇa passage.

O Indra, (make) the tribes liberal and sweet in speech.[10]

O Indra, make us men charitable and soft in speech.[11] This noxious creature thinks me to be without a hero.[12]

This imp desirous of making mischief takes me to be of little strength as it were.

Idaṃyuḥ means desiring this. Moreover, it is used in the sense of 'like that'. The expression 'Indra desirous of wealth' here means 'having wealth'.

[1] See 5. 27.

[2] 'Destroyer, annihilator', Grassmann, *op. cit.*, p. 783.

[3] vii. 18. 21.

[4] vii. 104. 21; AV. 8. 4. 21.

[5] 'Having bloody, formidable teeth', Grassmann, *op. cit.*, p. 359.

[6] i. 166. 6.

[7] 'Having decaying, shattered teeth', Grassmann, *op. cit.*, p. 315.

[8] iv. 30. 24; cf. Bṛh. D. iv. 138.

[9] Cf. Bṛh. D. iv. 139.

[10] i. 174. 2.

[11] Cf. Muir, *op. cit.*, vol. ii, p. 377.

[12] x. 86. 9; AV. 20. 126. 9; cf. Bṛh. D. 1. 53.

Rich in horses, kine, chariots, and wealth.[1] This too is a Vedic quotation.

(Here ends the thirty-first section.)

What are the cows doing in the country of the barbarians? They neither get the milk (to mix) with soma, nor kindle fire. Bring to us the wealth of the usurer. Subdue the low-born to us, O lord of wealth.[2]

What are the cows doing in *Kīkaṭa*? *Kīkaṭa*[3] is the name of a country where the non-Aryans dwell.

Non-Aryan tribes are (so called because it is said), 'What have they done?' or their assumption is that religious rites are useless. They neither get the milk to mix with the soma, nor kindle fire. Bring to us the wealth of the usurer. *Maganda*[4] means a usurer: he advances with the thought that it will come back to him; his son, i. e. born in the family of great usurers, is called *pramaganda*. Or it means an epicurean who assumes that this is the only world and there is no other. Or it may mean impotent,[5] fond of sexual intercourse; or one who paralyses himself, i. e. his testicles. He makes his testicles firm as two pins. Low-born, born in a low family, or whose family is low.[6]

Śākhā (branch) is derived from (the root) *śak* (to be able).

Āṇi (testicles) are (so called) from being fitted (*araṇāt*).

O lord of wealth, subdue him to us. The verb *radhyati* means to subdue.

Bunduḥ[7] means an arrow. [Arrow] it pierces, it inspires awe, or it shines when it flies.

(Here ends the thirty-second section.)

Thy bow is most powerful, strongly made, and well shaped. Thy arrow is golden and swift. Both thy arms which knock down enemies and increase sweetness (for us) are well equipped and fit for war.[8]

Powerful, having a great capacity of discharging arrows, or having an enormous capacity of discharging arrows. Thy bow is well made, well shaped, delightful. Thy golden arrow is the accomplisher. Both thy arms are [fit for battle] beautiful, well equipped for battle. *Ṛdūpe* means

[1] i. 51. 14.

[2] iii. 53. 14.

[3] Cf. Muir, *op. cit.*, vol. ii, p. 350. Sāyaṇa explains *Kīkaṭa* as *atheists* who have no faith and say: 'What is the use of sacrifice, sacred rites, gifts, and oblations? Eat and drink, for there is no world other than this.' 'A name of non-Aryan tribes', Grassmann, *op. cit.*, p. 327.

[4] Sāyaṇa explains it as the name of a king also.

[5] The wealth of such a person, like that of a usurer, is not spent in religious works. Durga.

[6] According to Sāyaṇa, *naicāśākham* is the name of a city.

[7] 'Bow, arrow', Grassmann, *op. cit.*, p. 910.

[8] viii. 77. 11.

knocking down by movement, knocking down by motion, [knocking down by sound, knocking down at great distance], or piercing the vital parts by movement, by motion, [piercing from the sound, or piercing from a distance].

(*Here ends the thirty-third section.*)

From the mountains, Indra transfixed the mellow cloud and held his well-aimed arrow.[1]

From the mountains Indra held the well-aimed arrow and transfixed the well-ripe cloud, the giver of rain-water.

Vṛndam and *vṛndāraka* are explained by *bunda* (arrow).

(*Here ends the thirty-fourth section.*)

This same sacrificer, who is the maker of Yama, carried oblations which the gods enjoy. He is generated every month, day by day; the gods appointed him their oblation-bearer.[2]

This same sacrificer, who is the maker of Yama, carries food which the gods eat. He is generated every month, every fortnight, day after day. And the gods appointed him their oblation-bearer.

Ulbam[3] is derived from the root *ūrṇu* (to cover), or from *vṛ* (to cover). Great was that cover and compact also.[4] This too is a Vedic quotation.

Ṛbīsam[5] means one whose lustre is gone, or taken away, or concealed, or lost.

(*Here ends the thirty-fifth section.*)

You covered the fire with snow during the day. You have bestowed on him strength rich in food. You have brought fire on earth, and you have raised the whole group for their welfare, O Aśvins.[6]

You have covered fire with snow, i. e. water, during the day, i. e. at the end of the summer season. You have bestowed on us and Agni strength rich in food. You have raised that fire which is inside *ṛbīsa*, i. e. earth, herbs, trees of forests and waters. The whole group, i. e. a group consisting of all classes of every kind.

Gaṇa (group) and *guṇa* (quality) are (so called because) they count. All the herbs and living beings who spring to life on earth during the rainy season are but forms of the Aśvins. With these words, the seer praises them, the seer praises them.

(*Here ends the thirty-sixth section.*)

[1] viii. 77. 6.

[2] x. 52. 3.

[3] *Eihaut*, membrane round the embryo, Grassmann, *op. cit.*, p. 266.

[4] x. 51. 1.

[5] According to Durga, it means earth, on account of its non-luminous character.

[6] i. 116. 8; cf. Bṛh. D. ii. 110.

CHAPTER VII

Now, therefore, (we shall explain) the section (of the *Nighaṇṭu*) relating to deities. The section, which enumerates appellations of deities, to whom panegyrics are primarily addressed, is called *daivatam*, i.e. relating to deities. The following is the detailed examination of the same. A particular stanza is said to belong to a deity, to whom a seer addresses his panegyrics[1] with a particular desire, and from whom he wishes to obtain his object.[2] The stanzas, to which reference has just been made,[3] are of three kinds: (1) indirectly addressed, (2) directly addressed, (3) and self-invocations. Of these, the indirectly addressed stanzas are composed (lit. joined) in all the cases of nouns but the verb of the third person (only).

(*Here ends the first section.*)

Indra rules heaven, Indra the earth.[4]
The chanters (praise) very much Indra alone.[5]
These Tṛtsus being active with Indra.[6]
Chant the sāma-stanzas for the sake of Indra.[7]
Without Indra, no place whatsoever is pure.[8]
I will indeed proclaim the heroic exploits of Indra.[9]
Our desires rest on Indra.[10] And so on.

Now the directly addressed stanzas are compositions in the second person and are joined with the word 'thou' as the pronoun.

Thou, O Indra, (art born) from strength.[11]
O Indra, slay our enemies.[12] And so on.

Moreover, the praises are directly, while the objects of praise are indirectly, addressed.

Do not praise any other.[13]
Sing forth, O Kaṇvas.[14]

[1] The praise is of four kinds, according to its reference to (1) one's own name, (2) one's relatives and friends, (3) one's accomplishments, (4) one's beauty. Durga.

[2] Cf. Bṛh. D. 1. 6; Muir, *op. cit.*, vol. ii, p. 195.

[3] The clause 'to which . . . been made' is not the literal translation, but rather gives expression to the contextual meaning of the word *tāḥ* used by Yāska.

[4] x. 89. 10.

[5] i. 7. 1; AV. 20. 38. 4; 20. 47. 4; 20. 70. 7; SV. 1. 198; 2. 146.

[6] vii. 18. 15.

[7] viii. 98. 1; AV. 20. 62. 5; SV. 1. 388; 2. 375.

[8] x. 69. 6; SV. 2. 720.

[9] i. 32. 1; cf. AV. 2. 5. 5.

[10] Cf. Roth, *op. cit.*, p. 100.

[11] x. 153. 2; AV. 20. 93. 5; SV. 1. 120.

[12] x. 152. 4; AV. 1. 21. 2; SV. 2. 1218; VS. 8. 44; 18. 70.

[13] viii. 1. 1; AV. 20. 85. 1; SV. 1. 242; 2. 710.

[14] i. 37. 1.

Approach, O Kuśikas, be careful.[1]

Now self-invocations are compositions in the first person and are joined with the word 'I' as the pronoun, e.g. the hymn of Indra Vaikuṇṭha;[2] the hymn of Lava;[3] or the hymn of Vāk,[4] daughter of Ambhṛṇa, and so on.

(Here ends the second section.)

Indirectly addressed and directly addressed stanzas are by far the most numerous. Self-invocations are few and far between. Moreover, (in some stanzas) there is only praise (of the deity) without any benediction (being invoked), as in the hymn: I will indeed proclaim the heroic exploits of Indra.[5] Further, (in some stanzas) there is only benediction without any praise (being offered), as: May I see well with my eyes, may I be radiant in my face, may I hear well with my ears.[6] This is mostly found in the Yajurveda (*ādhvaryave*) and sacrificial formulae.[7] Further, (in some stanzas) there are asseverations and imprecations:

May I die to-day, if I be a juggling demon.[8]

Now may he be deprived of ten heroes.[9]

Further, (in some stanzas) there is an intention of describing a particular state:

Then was no death, nor indeed immortality.[10]

In the beginning (of creation) there was darkness, hidden in darkness.[11]

Further, (in some stanzas) there is apprehension arising from a particular state:

The benevolent god may fly forth to-day and never return.[12]

I do not know whether I am this or (that).[13] And so on.

Further, (in some stanzas) there are censure and praise:

He alone is guilty who eats alone.[14]

This dwelling-place of a liberal person is (beautiful) like a lotus-bed.[15]

Similarly, there is censure of gambling and praise of agriculture in the dice-hymn.[16] In this manner and with various intentions, seers have visions of their poetic compositions (*mantras*).[17]

(Here ends the third section.)

[1] iii. 53. 11; cf. Bṛh. D. iv. 115.
[2] x. 48; 49.
[3] x. 119.
[4] x. 125.
[5] i. 32. 1; cf. AV. 2. 5. 5.
[6] The quotation has not been traced.
[7] Cf. Muir, *op. cit.*, vol. iii, pp. 211–12.
[8] vii. 104. 15ᵃ; AV. 8. 4. 15ᵃ.
[9] vii. 104. 15ˣ; AV. 8. 4. 15ᶜ.
[10] x. 129. 2.
[11] x. 129. 3; TB. ii. 8. 9. 4.
[12] x. 95. 15.
[13] i. 164. 37; AV. 9. 10. 15; cf. Bṛh. D. i. 56; N. 14. 22.
[14] x. 117. 6; TB. ii. 8. 8. 3.
[15] x. 107. 10.
[16] x. 34.
[17] Cf. Bṛh. D. i. 3.

With reference to this, the following is the ascertainment of the deity of those stanzas whose deity is not specified. Such stanzas belong to the same deity to whom that particular sacrifice, or a part of the sacrifice, is offered. Now, elsewhere than the sacrifice, they belong to Prajāpati according to the ritualists; and to Narāśaṃsa according to the etymologists.[1]

Or else the deity may be an optional one, or even a group of deities.[2] It is, indeed, a very prevalent practice, (in everyday life) in the world, (to dedicate things in common) including what is sacred to gods, to guests, and to the manes.[3] As to the view that a stanza belongs to the deity to whom the sacrifice is offered, (it may be objected) that non-deities are also praised like deities, e.g. the objects beginning with horse and ending with herbs,[4] together with the eight pairs.[5] But he (the student) should not think that matters relating to gods are adventitious as it were. This is to be clearly seen (by the following): On account of the supereminence of the deity, a single soul is praised in various ways. Other gods are the individual limbs of a single soul.[6] Or else, as people say, seers praise objects according to the multiplicities of their original nature, as well as from its universality. They are produced from each other.[7] They are the original forms of each other.[8] They are produced from (action (*karma*)),[9] they are produced from the soul. Soul is even their chariot, their horse, their weapon, their arrows; soul is indeed the all-in-all of gods.[10]

(Here ends the fourth section.)

'There are three deities only,'[11] say the etymologists: (1) Agni, whose sphere is earth; (2) Vāyu or Indra, whose sphere is atmosphere; (3) the sun, whose sphere is heaven.[12] Of these, each receives many appellations on account of his supereminence, or the diversity of his function, just as a priest, although he is one, is called the sacrificer (*hotṛ*), the director of the sacrifice (*adhvaryu*), the possessor of the sacred lore (*brahmā*), and the chanter (*udgātṛ*). Or else they may be distinct, for their panegyrics as

[1] Cf. Roth, *op. cit.*, p. 101.

[2] Cf. Durga, quoted by Roth, *op. cit.*, p. 112.

[3] Cf. AB. i. 14. ii. 6; KB. x. 4; and also AB. i. 15.

[4] Ngh. v. 3. 1–22.

[5] Ngh. v. 3. 29–36.

[6] Cf. Bṛh. D. iv. 143.

[7] As, for instance, Dakṣa is born from Aditi, and Aditi from Dakṣa. Durga.

[8] As for instance, fire, lightning, and the sun are the original forms of each other. Durga.

[9] i.e. To make existence possible by bringing the human works to accomplishment. There will be no crops without the sun and there can be no life without food. Durga.

[10] This is Yāska's rejoinder to the objection that non-deities are praised like deities. The so-called non-deities, says Yāska, are but different manifestations of the same single soul. In other words, Yāska here propounds the doctrine of pantheism. Cf. Bṛh. D. i. 73–74.

[11] AB. ii. 17; KB. viii. 8.

[12] AB. v. 32; SB. xi. 2. 3 1; Sarva. Pari. 2. 8; Bṛh.D. i. 69; cf. RV. x. 158. 1; Muir, *op. cit.*

well as their appellations are distinct.[1] As to the view that (one receives many appellations) on account of the diversity of functions, (it may be remarked) that many men also can do the actions, having divided them among themselves. With regard to it, the community of jurisdiction and enjoyment should be noted, as for instance, the community of men and gods with regard to earth. Community of enjoyment is seen in the following, i. e. the enjoyment of earth by the cloud, together with air and the sun, and of the other world together with Agni. There everything is like the kingdom of man also.

(Here ends the fifth section.)

Now (we shall discuss) the appearance of the gods. Some say that they are anthropomorphic, for their panegyrics as well as their appellations are like those of sentient beings. Moreover they are praised with reference to anthropomorphic limbs:

O Indra, the two arms of the mighty one are noble.[2]

That (heaven and earth), which thou hast seized, is thy fist, O lord of wealth.[3]

Moreover (they are praised) as associated with anthropomorphic objects:

O Indra, come with thy team of two bay steeds.[4]

A beautiful wife and delightful things are in thy house.[5]

Moreover (they are praised) with regard to anthropomorphic actions:

O Indra, eat and drink the (soma) placed before (thee).[6]

Hear our call, O God that hast listening ears.[7]

(Here ends the sixth section.)

Others say that they are not anthropomorphic, because whatever is seen of them is unanthropomorphic, as for instance, fire, air, the sun, earth, the moon, &c. As to the view that their panegyrics are like those of sentient beings, (we reply) that inanimate objects, beginning from dice and ending with herbs,[8] are likewise praised. As to the view that they are praised with reference to anthropomorphic limbs, (we reply) that this (treatment) is accorded to inanimate objects also:

They shout with their green mouths.[9] This is a panegyric of stones.

As to the view that (they are praised) as associated with anthropo-

[1] Sarva. Pari. 2. 13.
[2] vi. 47. 8; AV. 19. 15. 4.
[3] iii. 30. 5.
[4] ii. 18. 4.
[5] iii. 53. 6.
[6] x. 116. 7.
[7] i. 10. 9.
[8] Ngh. v. 3. 4–22.
[9] x. 94. 2.

morphic objects, (we reply) that it is just the same (in the case of inanimate objects):

Sindhu yoked the comfortable car, drawn by a horse.[1]

This is a panegyric of a river. As to the view that (they are praised) with regard to anthropomorphic actions, (we reply) that it is exactly the same (in the case of inanimate objects):

Even before the sacrificer, they taste the delicious oblations.[2] This too is a panegyric of stones. Or else they may be both anthropomorphic and unanthropomorphic. Or else (the unanthropomorphic appearance) of the gods, who are really anthropomorphic,[3] is their counterself in the form of action. (*Karma*) as sacrifice is that of a sacrificer. This is the well-considered opinion of those who are well versed in legendary lore.

(*Here ends the seventh section.*)

It has been said before that there are three deities only. Now we shall explain their shares and companions. Now the following are the shares of Agni: this world, the morning libation, spring, the *Gāyatrī* metre, the triple hymn, the *rathantaram* chant, and the group of gods who are enumerated in the first place.[4]

Agnāyī (wife of Agni), *Pṛthivī* (earth), and *Ilā* (praise) are the women. Now its function is to carry oblations and to invoke the gods. And all that which relates to vision is the function of Agni also. Now the gods with whom Agni is jointly praised are (1) Indra, (2) Soma, (3) Varuṇa, (4) Parjanya, and (5) the Ṛtavas. There is a joint oblation offered to, but no joint panegyric addressed to, Agni and Viṣṇu in the ten books (of the *Ṛgveda*).[5] Moreover there is a joint oblation offered to, but no joint panegyric addressed to, Agni and Pūṣan. With regard to this, the following stanza is cited (in order to show their) separate praise.

(*Here ends the eighth section.*)

May Pūṣan, the wise, the guardian of the universe, whose cattle are never lost, cause thee to move forthwith from this world. May he hand thee over to these manes, and (may) Agni (entrust) thee to the benevolent gods.[6]

May Pūṣan, the wise, whose cattle are never lost, who is the guardian

[1] x. 75. 9.

[2] x. 94. 2.

[3] According to Durga, the visible form of gods, like air, the sun, &c., are the working selves, but the presiding deities of fire, &c., are the real gods and they are anthropomorphic. Cf. Professor Macdonell, *Vedic Mythology*, pp. 15–20.

[4] Ngh. v. 1–3.

[5] Cf. AB. ii. 32; iii. 13; iv. 29; viii. 12, 17; KB. viii. 8. 9; xii. 4; xiv. 1. 3. 5; xxii. 1; GB. i. 1. 17. 21. 29; 2. 24; ii. 3. 10; 12. 16; Bṛh. D. i. 115–18.

[6] x. 17. 3; AV. 18. 2. 54.

of the universe, i.e. he, the sun, is indeed the guardian of all created beings, forthwith cause thee to move from this world. The third verse, 'May he hand thee over to the manes', is doubtful. According to some, it refers to Pūṣan, (mentioned) in the preceding hemistich; according to others this extols Agni, (mentioned) subsequently. (May) Agni (entrust) thee to the benevolent gods.

Suvidatram means wealth: it may be derived from (the root) *vid* (to find) with one preposition (*su*) or from *dā* (to give) with two prepositions (*su* and *vi*).

(*Here ends the ninth section.*)

Now the following are the shares of Indra: the atmosphere, the midday libation, the summer, the *triṣṭubh* metre, the fifteenfold hymn, the great chant,[1] and the gods who are enumerated in the middle place as well as the women.[2] Now his function is to release the waters and to slay Vṛtra. And all action that relates to strength is Indra's function also.[3] Now the gods with whom Indra is jointly praised are Agni, Soma, Varuṇa, Pūṣan, Bṛhaspati, Brahmaṇaspati, Parvata, Kutsa, Viṣṇu, Vāyu. Moreover, Mitra is jointly praised with Varuṇa; Soma with Pūṣan and Rudra; Pūṣan with Vāyu; and Parjanya with Vāta.

(*Here ends the tenth section.*)

Now the following are the shares of Āditya: that world (i.e. heaven), the third libation, the rainy season, the *jagatī* metre, the seventeenfold hymn, the *Vairūpa* chant, and the gods enumerated in the highest place as well as the women.[4] Now his function is to draw out and hold the juices with his rays. All that relates to greatness[5] is Āditya's function also. He is jointly praised with Candramas, Vāyu, and Saṃvatsara.[6] One should frame the remaining portions of seasons, metres, hymns, &c. in accordance with the distribution of the places (already mentioned). Autumn, the *anuṣṭubh* metre, the twenty-fold hymn, the *Vairāja* chant are terrestrial. Winter, the *paṅkti* metre, the twenty-sevenfold hymn, the *Śākvara*[7] chant are atmospheric. The dewy season, the *aticchandas* metres, the thirty-threefold hymn, the *Raivata* chant are celestial.[8]

(*Here ends the eleventh section.*)

[1] Cf. KB. iii. 5; *Yad dīrgham bṛhat*, 'what is long is great'.

[2] Ngh. v. 4.

[3] Cf. AB. ii. 32; iii. 13; iv. 31; viii. 12. 17; KB. viii. 9; xiv. 1. 3. 5; xxii. 2; GB. i. 1-17, 18, 24, 29; ii. 3. 10. 12; 4. 4; Bṛh. D. i. 130-1; ii. 2-5

[4] Cf. Ngh. v. 5.

[5] 'Enigmatical', MW; 'mysterious', Roth.

[6] Cf. AB. ii. 32; iii. 13; v. 1; viii. 12. 17; KB. viii. 9; xiv. 1. 3; xvi. 1; xxii. 3. 5; GB. i. 1. 19. 24. 29; ii. 3. 10; 4. 18; Bṛh. D. ii. 13-16.

[7] Cf. KB: 'These are Śakvarī verses. With these verily Indra was able to slay Vṛtra: that Indra was able to slay Vṛtra with them is the characteristic of Śakvarī verses.'

[8] Cf. AB. v. 4. 6; 12. 19; viii. 7. 12. 17; KB. xxii. 9; xxiii. 3; Bṛh. D. i. 116. 131.

Stanzas are (so called) from thinking, metres from covering, [hymn from praising]. *Yajus* is derived from (the root) *yaj* (to sacrifice). *Sāma* is (so called because) it is measured out by the stanza, or it may be derived from (the root) *as* (to throw). 'He thought it equal to the stanza,' say they who are well versed in Vedic metres.

Gāyatrī[1] is derived from (the root) *gai*, meaning to praise, or from *gam* with *tri* by metathesis, i. e. three-coursed.

There is a Brāhmaṇa passage: 'It fell out of (Brahmā's) mouth while he was singing'. *Uṣṇih* is (so called because) it has stepped out, or it may be derived from (the root) *snih*, meaning to shine. Or comparatively speaking, (it is so called) as if furnished with a head-dress. *Uṣṇīṣa* (head-dress) is derived from (the root) *snai* (to wrap round). *Kakubh* is (so called because) it has an elevation. *Kakubh* and *kubja* (crooked) are derived from (the root) *kuj* (to be crooked) or *ubj* (to press down). *Anuṣṭubh* is (so called) from praising after. There is a Brāhmaṇa passage: It follows the *Gāyatrī*, which consists of three verses only, (with its fourth verse of praise). *Bṛhatī*[2] is (so called) from its great growth.

Paṅkti[3] is a stanza of five verses. The second member of the word *Triṣṭubh*[4] is derived from (the root) *stubh* (to praise). But what does the *tri* mean? (It means swiftest), i. e. it is the swiftest metre. Or (it is so called because) it praises the threefold thunderbolt. It is known: that it praised thrice, that is the characteristic of the *Triṣṭubh*.[5]

(*Here ends the twelfth section.*)

Jagatī[6] is a metre gone farthest, or it has the gait of an aquatic animal. There is a Brāhmaṇa passage: 'The creator emitted it when he was dis inclined to do anything'.[7] *Virāṭ*[8] is (so called) from excelling, or from being at variance with others, or from extension; from excelling, because the syllables are complete; from being at variance, because the (number of) syllables varies; from extension, because the (number of) syllables is very

[1] Cf. GB. ii. 3. 10; Bib. Ind. ed. p. 128: '*Gāyatrī*, verily, consists of eight syllables'. Cf. also AB. iv. 28: '*Gāyatrī* conceived, she gave birth to *Anuṣṭubh*. *Anuṣṭubh* conceived, she gave birth to *Paṅkti*. *Jagatī* conceived, she gave birth to *Aticchandas*.'

[2] Cf. KB. iii. 5: 'What is long is *bṛhat*'.

[3] Cf. AB. v. 19: '*Paṅkti* consists of five verses': KB. xi. 2.

[4] Cf. GB. ii. 3. 10: Bib. Ind. ed. p. 128: *ekādaśākṣarā vai triṣṭup*; cf. also AB. viii. 2.

[5] The third *Khaṇḍa* of the *Daivata Brāhmaṇa*.

[6] 'It spreads like the waves of water.' Durga. Cf. KB. xxx. 11: 'They recite the five metres, *Anuṣṭubh*, *Gāyatrī*, *Uṣṇih*, *Triṣṭubh*, and *Jagatī* during the night, they are verily night metres'.

[7] i.e. When he had lost all pleasure in his work. Durga.

[8] Cf. AB. vi. 20: '*Virāṭ* consists of ten syllables'.

large. Figuratively it is called the ant-waisted.[1] *Pipīlikā* (ant) is derived from (the root) *pel*, meaning to go.[2]

With these words, these deities are dealt with. Those to whom the hymns are addressed, oblations are offered, and stanzas are addressed are by far the most numerous. Some are incidentally mentioned.[3] Moreover, one offers oblations to gods, having announced (lit. joined together) them with their characteristic appellations, as to Indra, the destroyer of Vṛtra, [to Indra, who excels Vṛtra], to Indra, the deliverer from distress, and so on. Some make a list of these also, but they are too numerous to be collected together in a list. I enlist that appellation only which has become a conventional epithet and with reference to which chief praise is addressed (to the deity). Moreover, a seer praises deities with regard to their activities, as (Indra), the Vṛtra-slayer, or the city-destroyer, and so on. Some make a list of these also, but they are too numerous to be collected together in a list. These (epithets) are mere indications of (a particular aspect of the proper) appellations, just as 'give food to a Brāhmaṇa who is hungry, or unguents to one who has taken a bath, or water to one who is thirsty'.[4]

(Here ends the thirteenth section.)

Now, therefore, we shall take up the deities in their respective order. We shall first explain Agni,[5] whose sphere is the earth. From what root is Agni derived? He is the foremost leader,[6] he is led foremost in sacrifices, he makes everything, to which it inclines, a part of himself. 'He is a drying agent', says Sthaulāṣṭhīvi, 'it does not make wet, it does not moisten.' 'It is derived from three verbs', says Śākapūṇi, 'from going, from shining or burning, and from leading.' He, indeed, takes the letter *a* from the root *i* (to go), the letter *g* from the root *añj* (to shine), or *dah* (to burn), with the root *nī* (to lead) as the last member. The following stanza is addressed to him.

(Here ends the fourteenth section.)

[1] This metre has only a few syllables in the middle. Durga.

[2] The whole of the twelfth section and this part of the thirteenth section are almost identical with the third *Khaṇḍa* of the *Daivata Brāhmaṇa*.

[3] Cf. Bṛh. D. i. 17.

[4] The words 'hungry', 'thirsty', &c., merely describe a particular state of a person, but do not represent the individual himself or independent entities; similarly epithets like 'Vṛtra-slayer', &c., indicate a particular activity of a deity, but do not represent the deity itself.

[5] Cf. Professor Macdonell, *Vedic Mythology*, pp. 88–100.

[6] Cf. AB. v. 16: *Agnir netā*, 'Agni is the leader': also the etymology given by Professor Macdonell, *op. cit.*, p. 99: Bṛh. D. ii. 24.

I praise Agni, placed foremost, the god, the priest
Of the sacrifice; the sacrificer and the best bestower of gifts.[1]

I praise Agni, I beseech Agni. The root *īḍ* means to solicit, or to worship. *Purohita* (placed foremost) and *yajña* (sacrifice) have been explained. *Deva* (god) is (so called) from making gifts (√*dā*) or from being brilliant (√*dīp*), from being radiant (√*dyut*), or because his sphere is heaven. He who is called god (*deva*) is also called deity (*devatā*). Sacrificer, invoker. (*Hotā*) (sacrificer) is derived from (the root) *hu* (to sacrifice), says Aurnavābha. 'The best bestower of gifts', the most liberal giver of delightful riches. The following additional stanza is addressed to him also.

(*Here ends the fifteenth section.*)

Agni should be solicited by seers, old as well as new; he shall bring the gods here.[2]

May Agni, who should be solicited, [should be worshipped], by older seers as well as by us, who are the younger ones, bring the gods to this place. He (the student) should not think that Agni refers to this (terrestrial fire) only. The two higher luminaries (lightning and the sun) are called Agni also. With reference to this (the following stanza refers to) the Agni of the middle region.

(*Here ends the sixteenth section.*)

Let them procure Agni like beautiful and smiling maidens of the same mind. Let the streams of clarified butter be united with fuel; enjoying them the god, who has all created beings as his property, is gratified.[3]

Let them[4] bend down towards it like maidens who have the same minds.[5] *Samanam* (of the same mind) is (so called) from breathing together or from thinking together. (Let them bend towards) Agni[6] like beautiful smiling maidens, is a simile. Streams of clarified butter, i. e. of water. Let them be united with fuel. The root *nas* means to obtain or to bend. Enjoying them, the god who has all created beings as his property is gratified. The root *har* means to desire to obtain, i. e. he desires to obtain them again and again.

[1] i. 1. 1; cf. Professor Macdonell, *Vedic Reader*, p. 3.

[2] i. 1. 2.

[3] iv. 58. 8: VS. 17. 96.

[4] i.e. Streams of water bend towards the atmospheric fire. Durga.

[5] i. e. Maidens who possess qualities such as youth, beauty, &c., have the same mind, i. e. of devoting themselves to their common husband. Durga, who thus indirectly supports polygamy.

[6] i. e. The atmospheric fire. Durga.

The wave, rich in honey, has arisen from the ocean.[1] This is regarded as referring to the sun.

He rises, indeed, from the ocean and from the waters.[2] This is a Brāhmaṇa quotation. Moreover, there is a Brāhmaṇa passage: Agni is all the deities.[3] The stanza following the present one explains it more clearly.

(*Here ends the seventeenth section.*)

They call Agni Indra, Mitra, and Varuṇa; (they) also (say) that he is the divine Garutmān of beautiful wings. The sages speak of him who is one in various ways; they call him Agni, Yama, Mātariśvan.[4]

The wise speak of this very Agni, [and] the great self, in various ways, as Indra, Mitra, Varuṇa, Agni, and the divine Garutmān. Divine, born in heaven. Garutmān is (so called because) he is praised, or whose soul is mighty, or whose soul is great. He to whom the hymn is addressed and the oblation is offered, is this very (terrestrial) Agni. These two higher luminaries receive (praise and oblations) under this appellation incidentally only.[5]

(*Here ends the eighteenth section.*)

From what root is *Jātavedāḥ* derived?[6]

He knows all created beings, or he is known to all created beings, or else he pervades every created being, or he has all created beings as his property or wealth, or he has all created beings as his knowledge, i. e. discernment. There is a Brāhmaṇa passage: that because, as soon as he was born, he found the cattle, that is the characteristic of Jātavedas. And also: Therefore, in all seasons, the cattle move towards Agni.[7] The following stanza is addressed to him.

(*Here ends the nineteenth section.*)

(We will press soma for Jātavedas. He shall consume the property belonging to the niggard. He takes us, i. e. the assembly, across all obstacles; Agni carries us across troubles like a river by means of a boat.)[8]

(We will press soma for Jātavedas, i. e. unto Jātavedas, or Jātavedas

[1] iv. 58. 1; VS. 17. 89; cf. AB. i. 22.

[2] KB. xxv. 1. 9; AB. v. 16.

[3] Cf. AB. i. 1; ii. 3; TB. ii. 1. 12; GB. ii. 1. 12; Ṣaḍ. B. 3. 7; ŚB. i. 6. 2. 8; MS. 1. 4. 14.

[4] i. 164. 46; AV. 9. 10. 28.

[5] Cf. Bṛh. D. i. 78.

[6] Cf. Bṛh. D. i. 92; ii. 30–1.

[7] The quotation is untraced. Cf. AB. i. 15: *Agnir hi devānām paśuḥ*, 'Agni indeed is the (sacrificial) animal of the gods'.

[8] i. 99. 1. The stanza is omitted by the MSS. of the longer recension, Roth, and Durga. Cf. 14. 33.

worthy of being worshipped. For the pressing and straining of the immortal king, i.e. the soma, he shall consume, i.e. he will burn with determination, or reduce the property of the niggard to ashes, for the sake of sacrifice. The meaning is that he will cause soma to be offered. He takes us, i.e. the assembly, across all obstacles, all difficult places. Agni carries us across troubles like a river, a very deep and broad stream, by a boat, i.e. he helps us to overcome difficulties as if he were to take us across a river by means of a boat. The following additional stanza is addressed to him also.)[1]

Do ye impel Jātavedas, the strong horse, to sit on this our grass.[2]

With your actions impel Jātavedas, who pervades everywhere. Or else it may be a simile, i.e. Jātavedas, who is like a horse, may he sit on this our grass. In the ten books (of the *Ṛgveda*) there is but a single hymn, containing three stanzas in the Gāyatrī metre, addressed to Jātavedas. But whatever is addressed to Agni, is associated with Jātavedas too. He (the student) should not think that this refers to (terrestrial) Agni alone; even these two upper lights are called Jātavedas also.

With reference to this, (the following stanza refers to) the Agni of the middle region.

Let them procure like maidens of the same mind.[3]

This we have already explained.[4] Now (the following stanza refers to) the sun.

They uplift him, Jātavedas.[5]

We shall explain this later on.[6] He, to whom the hymn is addressed and the oblation is offered, is this very (terrestrial) Agni Jātavedas. These two upper luminaries receive (praise and oblations) under this appellation incidentally only.[7]

(Here ends the twentieth section.)

From what root is *Vaiśvānara* derived?

He leads all men, or all men lead him. Or else, *Vaiśvānara* may be

[1] The whole comment is omitted by MSS. of the longer recension, Roth, and Durga. The stanza, together with its explanation, is spurious. The style in which this passage is written is quite different from that of Yāska and similar to that of the author of the fourteenth chapter. It is, as a matter of fact, almost identical with the commentary of 14. 33. The few minor differences seem to be made with a deliberate intention to give it a different appearance, but without success.

[2] x. 188. 1.

[3] iv. 58. 8; VS. 17. 96.

[4] See § 17.

[5] i. 50. 1; AV. 13. 2. 16; 20. 47. 13; SV. 1. 31; VS. 7. 41; 8. 41.

[6] See 12. 15.

[7] See § 18. Cf. Professor Macdonell, *Vedic Mythology*, pp. 93–4.

a (modified form) of *viśvān-ara*, i. e. who pervades all created beings. The following stanza is addressed to him.

(*Here ends the twenty-first section.*)

May we be in the goodwill of Vaiśvānara, for he indeed is the king, the refuge of all the worlds. Born from this world, he beholds this entire universe. Vaiśvānara stretches with the sun.[1]

Born from this world, he surveys the entire universe. Vaiśvānara stretches together with the sun. May we be in the benevolent will of Vaiśvānara, i. e. of him who is the king and the place of refuge of all created beings. But who is Vaiśvānara? The preceptors say, 'This is the atmospheric fire, for the seer praises him with regard to the phenomenon of rain'.

(*Here ends the twenty-second section.*)

I will proclaim the greatness of the bull. Supplicating men attend upon him who is the slayer of Vṛtra. The Vaiśvānara Agni killed the demon, shook the waters, and shattered Śambara.[2]

I will speak forth the greatness, i. e. the pre-eminence of the bull, i. e. the sprinkler of the waters. Supplicating men, i. e. whose request is to be granted, and who are desirous of rain, attend upon, i. e. serve him, who is the slayer of Vṛtra, i. e. the cloud. *Dasyu* (demon) is derived from (the root) *das*, meaning to lay waste: in him the juices are wasted, or he causes works to be laid waste.[3] The Vaiśvānara Agni slew him, shook the waters, and shattered Śambara, i. e. the cloud.

'Now (the reference is) to that sun,' say the older ritualists. The tradition handed down in the sacred texts is that the increase of libations is in accordance with the ascending order of these worlds. After the ascension, the series of descending is designed. The sacrificer accomplishes this series of descending with the Vaiśvānara hymn,[4] recited on (the occasion of) the invocation addressed to Agni and the Maruts. But he should not lay too much emphasis on the hymn, for it is addressed to Agni. From thence he comes to Rudra and the Maruts, the deities whose sphere is the atmosphere; from thence to Agni, whose sphere is this very world, and it is precisely on this spot that he recites the hymn.[5]

Moreover, the oblation assigned to Vaiśvānara is distributed in twelve potsherds,[6] for his function is twelvefold. Moreover, there is a Brāhmaṇa

[1] i. 98. 1; Vs. 26. 7.

[2] i. 59. 6.

[3] i.e. Works like agriculture, &c., are laid waste if the rain is withheld. Durga.

[4] vi. 8–9.

[5] Cf. Bṛh. D. i. 102–3.

[6] Cf. AB. vii. 9; KB. iv. 3; Bṛh. D. ii. 16–17.

passage: That Āditya verily is Agni Vaiśvānara.[1] Further, the invocations in the liturgy are addressed to Vaiśvānara, the sun, as: 'Who illumines heaven and earth'.[2]

He indeed illuminates both heaven and earth. Further, the *chāndomika* hymn[3] is addressed to Vaiśvānara, the sun:

He shone present in heaven.

He, indeed, shone present in heaven. Further, the *haviṣpāntīya*[4] (i.e. libation to be drunk) hymn is addressed to Vaiśvānara, the sun.

'This very (i.e. terrestrial) fire is Vaiśvānara,' says Śākapūṇi.[5] These two upper lights are called Vaiśvānara also. This (terrestrial) fire is called Vaiśvānara, because it is engendered from them (i.e. the upper lights). But how is it engendered from them? Where the lightning fire strikes a place of shelter,[6] it retains the characteristics of the atmospheric fire, i.e. flashing in waters and becoming extinguished in solid bodies, as long as (that object) is not seized upon. But as soon as it is seized upon, this very (terrestrial) fire is produced, which becomes extinguished in water, and blazes in solid bodies.

Now (the following is the process of its production) from the sun. The sun having first revolved towards the northern hemisphere, a person holds a polished (piece of) white copper, or crystal, focusing the sun-rays in a place where there is some dry cow-dung, without touching it: it blazes forth, and this very (terrestrial) fire is produced.[7] Moreover, the seer has said:

Vaiśvānara stretches with the sun.[8]

But the sun itself cannot stretch together with his own self. A particular thing stretches together with something different only. One kindles this fire from this world, the rays of that one become manifest from the other world. Having seen the conjunction of their light with the flames of this terrestrial fire, the seer made (the above-mentioned) remark.

Now (had Vaiśvānara been the sun), there would have occurred expressions relating to Vaiśvānara in those same hymns and shares which are assigned to celestial deities, i.e. Savitṛ, [Sūrya], Pūṣan, Viṣṇu, and [the Viśvedevās.] And they would have praised him by (attributing to him) the functions of the sun, as thou risest, thou settest, thou revolvest, &c. It is only in the hymns addressed to Agni that there are found expressions

[1] The quotation is untraced.

[2] The quotation is untraced.

[3] VS. 33. 92; cf. KB. xxx. 10, 'cattle verily are chandomas'; cf. also AB. v. 16.

[4] x. 88. 4; cf. GB. i. 2. 20.

[5] Cf. Roth, *op. cit.*, p. 109.

[6] i.e. Wood or water. Durga.

[7] This shows that Yāska was familiar with the scientific law of the refraction of heat and light.

[8] i. 98. 1.

relating to Vaiśvānara. And the seer praises him (by attributing to him) the functions of Agni, as thou carriest, thou cookest, thou burnest, and so on.

As to (the view) that the seer praises him (by attributing) the phenomenon of rain, (we reply) that it is possible with regard to this (terrestrial) fire also.

Uniform with days, this water goes up and falls down again. Clouds bring new life to earth, fires animate heaven.[1]

This stanza is explained by the mere reading of it.

(*Here ends the twenty-third section.*)

The bay steeds having beautiful wings clad in waters fly up their dark course to heaven. They turned round from the seat of waters, and lo! the earth is made wet with clarified butter.[2]

The dark egression, i.e. the night of the sun. Bay steeds having beautiful wings are the draught-animals, i.e. the rays of the sun.[3] When from heaven, from the common dwelling-place of waters, i.e. the sun, they turn down towards the earth, the latter is made wet with clarified butter, i.e. water. The word *ghṛta* is a synonym of water; it is derived from (the root) *ghṛ*, meaning to besprinkle. Moreover, there is a Brāhmaṇa passage: Agni verily sends forth rain from this world. Having become [indeed] the space-coverer (i.e cloud) in the atmosphere, it rains; the Maruts conduct the emitted rain. When, indeed, the sun turns round fire with his rays, then it rains.[4] As to (the view) that after ascension the series of descending is designed, (we reply) that this takes place by the injunction of the sacred texts. As to (the view) that the oblation assigned to Vaiśvānara is distributed in twelve potsherds, (we reply) that the number of potsherds has no (reference to) the explanation (of the function), for the oblation[5] assigned to the sun is distributed in one, as well as in five potsherds. As to the Brāhmaṇa quotation, (we reply) that the Brāhmaṇas, indeed, speak of many divisions, as: the earth is Vaiśvānara, the year is Vaiśvānara, Brāhmaṇa is Vaiśvānara,[6] and so on.

As to (the view) that invocations in the liturgy are addressed to Vaiśvānara, the sun, (we reply) that the liturgy is addressed to this very (terrestrial) fire. 'Who shone for the tribes of men.'[7] As to (the view) that

[1] i. 164. 51; TA. i. 9. 5.

[2] i. 164. 47; AV. 6. 22. 1.

[3] Cf Bṛh. D. ii. 8–9.

[4] TS. ii. 4. 1. 2; KS. xi. 10.

[5] Cf. KB. v. 8: *Atha yat saurya ekakapālaḥ.*

[6] The quotation is untraced.

[7] The quotation is untraced. It is the terrestrial fire which shines for men alone. Durga.

the *chāndomika*[1] hymn is addressed to Vaiśvānara, the sun, (we reply) that it is addressed to this very (i. e. the terrestrial) fire.

Sacrificed with blazing fires.[2] Blazing fires, profusely generated fires, or burning fires; it is with them that the sacrifice is made. As to (the view) that the hymn,[3] 'Libation to be drunk', is addressed to Vaiśvānara, the sun, (we reply) that it is addressed to this very (terrestrial) fire.

(*Here ends the twenty-fourth section.*)

The undecaying and pleasant libation to be drunk is sacrificed in fire which touches heaven and knows the sun. For its maintenance, existence, and support, the gods spread it with food.[4]

The oblation which is to be drunk, which is pleasant and undecaying, is sacrificed in fire which touches heaven and knows the sun. For all the various actions, i. e. maintenance, existence, and support, the gods spread this fire with food. Moreover, the seer said:

(*Here ends the twenty-fifth section.*)

The mighty seized him in the lap of the waters; the tribes attended on the king worthy of honour The messenger brought Agni from the sun, Mātariśvan (brought) Vaiśvānara from afar.[5]

Seated in the lap, in the bosom, of the waters, i. e. in the mighty world of the atmosphere, the groups of mighty atmospheric gods seized him like tribes who wait upon the king. Worthy of honour, having panegyrics addressed to him, or worthy of respect [or worthy of worship]. Whom the messenger of the gods brought from the shining one, the sun who drives away darkness, who impels all things and who is very far. [Or else] the seer called Mātariśvan, the bringer of this Vaiśvānara fire. Mātariśvan is air: it breathes in the atmosphere, or moves quickly in the atmosphere. Now the seer praises him with the following two stanzas in order to enter into all places.

(*Here ends the twenty-sixth section.*)

At night Agni becomes the head of the world. Then in the morning he is born as the rising sun. This is the supernatural power of the holy ones that with full knowledge he accomplishes the work so quickly.[6]

The head is (so called because) the body depends on it. He who is the head[7] of all beings at night is Agni, thence he himself is born as the sun rising

[1] VS. 33. 92.
[2] Śāṅkh. Śr. S. x. 10. 8[c].
[3] x. 88.
[4] x. 88. 1.
[5] vi. 8. 4.
[6] x. 88. 6.
[7] Just as it is impossible to live without a head, so life is not possible without fire. Durga.

in the morning.[1] They know this profound wisdom of the holy gods who accomplish sacrifices: the work that he performs with full knowledge, i. e. hastening he goes through all places. The stanza following this explains it still more.

(*Here ends the twenty-seventh section.*)

With a hymn, in heaven, the gods generated Agni, who fills both heaven and earth, with powers. They made him for a threefold existence indeed. He ripens herbs of every kind.[2]

The gods made that Agni, whom they generated in heaven and earth with a hymn and who fills both heaven and earth, with [powers], i. e. actions, for threefold existence. 'For the terrestrial, atmospheric, and celestial (existence),' says Śākapūṇi. There is a Brāhmaṇa passage: Its third part, which is in heaven, is the sun.[3] With these words, the seer praises him with reference to fire. Now, in the following stanza, the seer praises him with reference to the sun.

(*Here ends the twenty-eighth section.*)

When the holy gods set him, the sun, the son of Aditi, in heaven. When the ever-wandering pair come to life, then they behold all the worlds.[4]

When all the holy gods set him, the sun, [Aditi's son], son of Aditi, in heaven, when the wandering couple, i. e. the couple that always wanders together, i. e. the sun and the dawn, were created. How is the word *mithuna*[5] (couple) derived? It is derived from (the root) *mi*, meaning to depend, with the suffix *thu* or *tha*, having the root *nī* or *van* as the last member. Depending on each other, they lead each other, or win each other.

Its (meaning), i. e. 'human couple', is derived from the same root also; or else they win each other, when they are united. Now in the following stanza, the seer praises him with reference to Agni.[6]

(*Here ends the twenty-ninth section.*)

Where the lower and the higher dispute as to which of us, the two leaders of sacrifice, knows more. The friends who enjoy together, and accomplish the sacrifice, were competent. Now who will decide this?[7]

Where the divine sacrificers, i. e. this (terrestrial) and that atmospheric

[1] Cf. AB. viii: 'The sun verily enters into fire when setting. He then disappears. Agni verily is born as the sun'.

[2] x. 88. 10.

[3] The quotation is untraced.

[4] x. 88. 11.

[5] Cf. AB. v. 16: *mithunaṃ vai paśavaḥ*. 'cattle verily are the couple'.

[6] Cf. Muir, *op. cit.*, vol. v, p. 207.

[7] x. 88. 17.

Agni, dispute, as to which of us two knows more about the sacrifice. Which of the priests, who tell the same tale, and who enjoy together, and who are the accomplishers of sacrifice, will decide this for us? The stanza following this explains it still more clearly.

(Here ends the thirtieth section.)

O Mātariśvan, as long as the birds of beautiful wings wear directly the illumination of dawn, so long the Brāhmaṇa sitting lower than the sacrifice, and approaching the sacrifice, bears it.[1]

As long as there is the illumination or the manifestation of dawn. The particle of comparison is here used in the sense of 'directly', as 'place it directly here'. (As long as) birds of beautiful wings, which fly in a beautiful manner, i.e. these nights, O Mātariśvan, wear the light of the bright colour, so long the Brāhmaṇa sacrificer, who approaches the sacrificer and sits lower than this sacrificer, i.e. this Agni, bears it.

But the recitation of the sacrificer is addressed to Vaiśvānara, who is not Agni: O divine Savitṛ, he chooses thee, i.e. this fire, for the sacrifice, along with thy father, Vaiśvānara. The seer calls this very fire 'Savitṛ' (stimulator), and the atmospheric or the celestial fire, who is the progenitor of all, 'father'. He to whom the hymn is addressed and the oblation is offered is this same (terrestrial) Agni Vaiśvānara. These two upper luminaries receive (praise and oblations) under this appellation incidentally only.

(Here ends the thirty-first section.)

CHAPTER VIII

FROM what root is *draviṇodāḥ* (giver of wealth) derived? *Draviṇam* means wealth (so called) because people run (√*dru*) towards it, or strength (so called) because people run by means of it; *draviṇodāḥ* (therefore) means the giver of wealth or strength.[2] The following stanza is addressed to him.

(Here ends the first section.)

Thou art the giver of wealth. In worship, the priests with stones in their hands adore the god in sacrifices.[3]

It is thou who art the giver of wealth.[4] The word *draviṇasaḥ* means

[1] x. 88. 19.

[2] 'Distributor of blessings'; cf. Roth, *op. cit.*, p. 116; cf. also Grassmann, *op. cit.*, p. 645; cf. Bṛh. D. ii 25.

[3] i. 15. 7.

[4] Roth construes *draviṇodāḥ* with priests, taking it as nom. pl. Yāska, however, explains it as nom. sing.

people who sit down (to distribute) wealth, or who prepare (offerings of) wealth. Or else it means a cup of soma: 'let him drink from this.' They adore, i. e. implore, praise, increase, or worship the god in sacrifices.

But who is this giver of wealth? 'It is Indra', says Krauṣṭuki; 'he is the most liberal giver of strength and wealth,[1] and all deeds relating to strength belong to him.' The seer also says:

I think he is indeed born of energetic strength.[2]

Moreover a seer calls Agni a descendant of the giver of wealth, because he is born from him.[3]

Who generated fire between two stones.[4] This too is a Vedic quotation.

Further, there are expressions relating to the 'giver of wealth' in (stanzas used in) sacrifices and offered to the seasons. 'Indra's drink', again, is the (name) of their vessel. Further, he is praised with reference to the drinking of soma. Further, a seer says: May the giver of wealth and his descendant drink.[5]

'This very (i. e. terrestrial) Agni is called "giver of wealth",' says Śākapūṇi. The expressions referring to 'the giver of wealth' are found in hymns addressed to Agni only.[6]

Gods supported Agni, giver of wealth.[7] This too is a Vedic quotation. As to (the view) that Indra is the most liberal giver of strength and wealth, (we reply) that all gods possess supernatural power. As to (the quotation) 'I think he is indeed born of energetic strength',[8] (we reply) that this very (i. e. terrestrial) fire is produced when churned with energetic strength; he is therefore called 'son of strength', 'offspring of strength', 'child of strength', and so on.[9] As to (the view) that a seer calls Agni 'a descendant of the giver of wealth', (we reply) that he is so called as he is generated by the priests, who are here called 'givers of wealth', because they offer oblations.[10]

This son of seers is the overlord.[11] This too is a Vedic quotation. As to (the view) that 'Indra's drink' is the name of their drinking-cup, (we reply) that it is a mere apportionment,[12] as all the cups used in drinking soma are called 'belonging to Vāyu'. As to (the view) that he is

[1] Cf. Bṛh. D. iii. 61.
[2] x. 73. 10.
[3] i. e. Agni is born from Indra. Durga.
[4] ii. 12. 3; AV. 20. 34. 3.
[5] The quotation is untraced.
[6] Cf. Bṛh. D. iii. 65.
[7] i. 96. 1.
[8] x. 73. 10.
[9] Cf. Professor Macdonell, *Vedic Mythology*, p. 91; cf. Bṛh. D. iii. 62, 64.
[10] Cf. Bṛh. D. iii. 63-4.
[11] AV. 4. 39. 9; VS. 5. 4.
[12] Roth translates *bhaktimātram* as *ehrende* (*Einladung*), i. e. 'honouring invitation'. See *op. cit.*, p. 116: the etymological meaning of *bhakti* (√*bhaj*) is distribution, cf. Grassmann, *op. cit.*, p. 921. Durga's explanation of the same word is not quite clear.

praised with reference to the drinking of soma, (we reply) that this happens in his (Agni's) case also.

Accompanied by associating troops, and rejoicing, drink soma.[1] This too is a Vedic quotation. As to (the quotation) 'May the giver of wealth and his descendants drink', (we reply) that it refers to this very (i. e. terrestrial) fire.

(*Here ends the second section.*)

May thy draught animals, with which thou drivest without being injured, become fat. O lord of the forest, O courageous one, drink thou soma, O giver of wealth, from (the cup called) *neṣṭra*, together with the seasons.[2]

May thy draught animals, i. e. the team which draws (the chariot), with which thou drivest, without suffering any injury, become fat. Be firm. Having stirred[3] and having approved,[4] O courageous one, (drink) thou from the *neṣṭra* (cup), placed on the subordinate altar. *Dhiṣṇya* = *dhiṣaṇya*, i. e. the subordinate altar, (so called) because it is the place of recitation. *Dhiṣaṇā* [means speech] is derived from (the root) *dhiṣ* used in the sense 'to hold'.[5] Or else it distributes or procures intelligence. He is called 'the lord of forests', because he is the protector or benefactor[6] of forests. *Vanam* (forest) is derived from (the root) *van* (to win). Drink with the seasons, i. e. with periods of time.

(*Here ends the third section.*)

Now therefore the *Āprī* deities. From what root is *Āprī* derived? From (the root) *āp* (to obtain) or from *prī* (to please). There is also a Brāhmaṇa passage: One pleases them with *Āprī* hymns.[7] Of these, *Idhma* (fuel) comes foremost. Fuel is (so called) from being kindled (*sam* √*idh*). The following stanza is addressed to him.

(*Here ends the fourth section.*)

[1] v. 60. 8.

[2] ii. 37. 3.

[3] 'Having mixed, i. e. mixed together with the finger. It is the habit of the people who drink, to shake the liquid with their finger.' Durga.

[4] Durga paraphrases *abhi-gūrya* by *abhyudyamya*, i. e. 'having lifted up'; Roth (*op. cit.*) translates *aufnehmend*, i. e. 'taking up', cf. Grassmann, *op. cit.*, p. 402.

[5] 'Speech holds the meaning, for eternal indeed is the connexion between speech and meaning.' Durga.

[6] According to Durga, Agni is the protector of forests, or trees of forests, because he does not burn them, although he is capable of doing so, as he exists in their interior. Roth has misunderstood Durga, as the following remark of his shows: 'Agni is so called because, according to Durga, he can burn wood'. See *op. cit.*, p. 116; cf. Bṛh. D. iii. 26.

[7] AB. ii. 4; KB. x. 3. 2.

Kindled to-day in the abode of man, O god, having all created beings as thy property, thou offerest sacrifice to the gods. And, O wise one, having plenty of friends, bring (them); thou art the messenger, thou art the learned bard.[1]

Kindled to-day in the house of every man, O god, having all created beings as thy property, thou offerest sacrifice to the gods. And O wise one, i. e. one who possesses knowledge, having plenty of friends,[2] bring them. Thou art the messenger, thou art the [learned], i. e. having profound knowledge, bard. '*Idhma* is sacrifice,' says Kātthakya. 'It is Agni,' says Śākapūṇi.

Tanūnapāt,[3] 'one's own son'. ['It is clarified butter,' says Kātthakya.] The word *napāt* is a synonym of offspring which does not immediately succeed a person (i. e. a grandson):[4] it is very much propagated downwards. In this case, the cow is called *tanū* (because) delicious things are prepared (*tatāḥ*) from her. Milk is produced from the cow, and the clarified butter is produced from milk. 'It is Agni,' says Śākapūṇi. Waters are here called *tanū* (because) they are spread in the atmosphere. Herbs and trees are produced from waters and this (fire) is produced from herbs and trees. The following stanza is addressed to him.

(*Here ends the fifth section.*)

O bright-tongued Tanūnapāt, having anointed the leading paths of the sacred rite with honey, be sweet. Directing the act of worship and our thoughts together with our prayers, carry our sacrifice to the gods.[5]

'*Narā-śaṃsa* is sacrifice', says Kātthakya; 'seated men (*narāḥ*) praise (√*śaṃs*) gods in sacrifice.'[6] 'It is Agni', says Śākapūṇi; 'he is to be praised by men.' The following stanza is addressed to him.

(*Here ends the sixth section.*)

Of these, the gods, who are skilful, pure, meditative, and who enjoy both kinds of oblations, we will praise the greatness of the adorable Narāśaṃsa with sacrifices.[7]

[1] x. 110. 1; AV. 5. 12. 1; VS. 29. 25.

[2] Durga explains the word *mitrá-mahaḥ* as 'one who is honoured by his friends'; according to Roth, *op. cit.*, p. 117, it means *huldreich*, i. e. 'gracious'. The accent shows it to be a possessive compound, and it may be translated as 'one whose might is his friends'; cf. Grassmann, *op. cit.*, p. 1040.

[3] According to Durga, it means a 'grandson', and signifies (1) clarified butter, i. e. the offspring of milk, which is itself produced from the cow: thus clarified butter is the grandson of the cow; (2) Agni, the grandson of waters, i. e. the offspring of trees and herbs which are produced from waters. According to Roth, *loc. cit.*, it does not necessarily mean 'a grandson', but 'a descendant in general'; cf. Grassmann, *op. cit.*, p. 520, 'a son of one's own self'.

[4] Cf. Bṛh. D. ii. 27.

[5] x. 110. 2; AV. 5. 12. 2; VS. 29. 26.

[6] Cf. Bṛh. D. ii. 28; iii. 2–3.

[7] vii. 2. 2; VS. 29. 27.

Of these,[1] the gods, who are of noble deeds, pure, promoters of meditation, and who enjoy oblations of both kinds, i.e. the soma and other oblations, or the mystical and the supplementary ones, we will highly praise the greatness of the holy Narāśaṃsa.

Īlaḥ[2] is derived from (the root) *īḍ*, meaning to praise, or from *indh* (to kindle). The following stanza is addressed to him.

(*Here ends the seventh section.*)

Being invoked thou art to be praised and worshipped. O Agni, come united with the Vasus. O great one, thou art the sacrificer of the gods. As such, O excellent sacrificer, do thou sacrifice to them, incited (by us).[3]

Being invoked thou shouldest be praised and worshipped. O Agni, come associated together with the Vasus. O great one, thou art the sacrificer of the gods. The word *yahva* is a synonym of great, i.e. gone (√*ya*), and invoked (√*hu*). As such, O excellent sacrificer, do thou sacrifice to them, incited (by us). Incited, impelled, or implored. Excellent sacrificer, the best sacrificer.

Barhiḥ[4] (grass) is (so called) from growing rapidly. The following stanza is addressed to him.

(*Here ends the eighth section.*)

The grass in the eastern direction is twisted at daybreak with injunctions for the covering of this earth. He spreads it farther and farther to make the best and most comfortable seat for the gods and Aditi.[5]

The grass in the eastern direction is strewn at daybreak, in the first period of the day, with injunctions in order to cover[6] this earth. He spreads it [farther and farther]: it is scattered to a great extent, or spread to a great extent. Best, excellent, or very wide. A most comfortable seat for the gods and Aditi. The word *syonam* is a synonym of comfort; it is derived from (the root) *so* (to rest): they rest in it, or it is to be resorted to.

[1] Roth (*op. cit.*, p. 118) construes *eṣām* with *Narāśaṃsasya*, i.e. the plural with the singular, which is grammatically impossible. He defends himself by saying that *Narāśaṃsasya* = *Narāṇām*, but without any support or justification. He explains this as *virorum imperium tenens*, i.e. 'holding power over men'. Cf. Grassmann, *op. cit.*, p. 713.

[2] Cf. AB. ii. 1, i.e. the food of oblation. According to Roth, *loc. cit.*, it means one to whom prayer is addressed, i.e. Agni.

[3] x. 110. 3; AV. 5. 12. 3; VS. 29. 28.

[4] Cf. Professor Macdonell, *Vedic Mythology*, p. 154.

[5] x. 110. 4; AV. 5. 12. 4; VS. 29. 29.

[6] Roth, *op. cit.*, p. 119, translates *vastoḥ* by *diluculo*, i.e. 'at dawn', and Durga explains it as 'for covering'. Cf. Grassmann, *op. cit.*, p. 1238.

Dvārāḥ (door) is derived from (the root) *jū* (to press forward), or from *dru* (to move), or from the causal of *vṛ* (to exclude). The following stanza is addressed to them.

(*Here ends the ninth section.*)

Spacious doors remain wide open like beautiful wives for their husbands. O divine doors, great and all-impellers, be easy of access to the gods.[1]

Having spaciousness, make yourself wide open as exceedingly beautiful wives do their thighs for their husbands in sexual intercourse. The thighs are the most beautiful parts (of the body). O divine doors, mighty, i. e. great. All-impellers, i. e. all come to the sacrifice through them. 'It is the door of the house,' says Kātthakya. 'It is Agni,' says Śākapūṇi.

Uṣāsānaktā = dawn and night. Dawn has been explained. The word *naktā* is a synonym of night: it anoints beings with dew; or else it is (called) night (because) its colour is indistinct.[2] The following stanza is addressed to them.

(*Here ends the tenth section.*)

Pressing forward, adorable, brought near each other, dawn and night the divine women, mighty, shining beautifully and putting forth beauty adorned in a radiant manner, may sit down on the seat[3] (*yoni*).

Smiling or causing good sleep,[4] may (they) take their seat or sit down, i. e. the holy ones, neighbours of each other, divine women, mighty, shining beautifully, i. e. resplendent, and putting forth beauty adorned in a radiant manner. *Śukra* (radiant) is derived from (the root) *śuc*, meaning to shine. The word *peśas* is a synonym of beauty; it is derived from (the root) *piś* (to adorn): it is well adorned.

Daivyā hotārā means the two divine sacrificers, i. e. this (terrestrial) and that (atmospheric) Agni. The following stanza is addressed to them.

(*Here ends the eleventh section.*)

The two divine sacrificers are foremost, sweet-voiced, and the measurers of sacrifice for the man to worship. They are inciters, active in the sacrifices, and with injunctions point out the light in the eastern direction.[5]

[1] x. 110. 5; AV. 5. 12. 5; VS. 29. 30.

[2] Cf. Bṛh. D. iii. 9.

[3] x. 110. 6; AV. 5. 12. 6; 27. 8; VS. 29. 31.

[4] Yāska explains *suṣrayantī* as 'smiling, or causing sleep'. Durga follows Yāska. According to Roth, *op. cit.*, p. 119, it is a denominative form of *suṣvi*, 'to distribute'; cf. Sāyaṇa's derivation quoted by Roth, *loc. cit.* It is, however, a participle of *suṣvi* which is derived from *su* (to press), and means 'pressing'; cf. Grassmann, *op. cit.*, p. 1558.

[5] x. 110. 7; AV. 5. 12. 7; VS. 29. 32.

The two divine sacrificers are foremost, endowed with sweet speech, and the creators of sacrifice for the man [for every man] to worship. They are inciters, workers in sacrifices, who enjoin that one should offer sacrifice in the eastern direction.

Tisro devīḥ means the three goddesses. The following stanza is addressed to them.

(*Here ends the twelfth section.*)

May the light of the sun come to our sacrifice quickly, and speech, here instructing like man: May Sarasvatī and the three goddesses of noble deeds sit on this most comfortable seat of grass.[1]

May the light of the sun come soon to our sacrifice. The sun is (called) *bharata*: its light (therefore) is (called) *bhāratī*.[2] And (may) speech, instructing here like a man, (come to us). May Sarasvatī and the three goddesses of noble actions sit on this comfortable seat of grass.

'*Tvaṣṭṛ*'[3] (is so called because) it pervades quickly,' say the etymologists. Or it may be derived from (the root) *tviṣ*, meaning to shine, or from *tvakṣ*, meaning to do. The following stanza is addressed to him.

(*Here ends the thirteenth section.*)

O wise and excellent sacrificer, incited (by us) sacrifice here to-day to the god Tvaṣṭṛ, who adorned these two progenitors, i.e. heaven and earth, and all the worlds with beauty.[4]

O wise and excellent sacrificer, incited (by us) sacrifice here to-day to god Tvaṣṭṛ, who made these two progenitors, i.e. heaven and earth, and all created beings beautiful. According to some, Tvaṣṭṛ is an atmospheric deity, because he is enlisted among the atmospheric gods.[5] 'He is Agni,' says Śākapūṇi. The following, another stanza, is addressed to him.

(*Here ends the fourteenth section.*)

Spreader of light, the beautiful one grows among them, elevated by his own glory in the lap of the oblique. Both were afraid of Tvaṣṭṛ, who was being born, turning back, they both serve the lion.[6]

Light is (so called) from making (things) well known. The diffuser of light, the beautiful one grows among them. *Cāru* (beautiful) is derived from the root *car* (to be diffused). *Jihmam* (oblique) is derived from the

[1] x. 110. 8; AV. 5. 12. 8; VS. 29. 33.

[2] According to Yāska, *bhāratī* means 'the light of the sun'. But *bhāratī* and *iḷā* evidently stand in opposition to each other: i. e. as goddesses of speech; cf. Grassmann, *op. cit.*, p. 933.

[3] Cf. Professor Macdonell, *Vedic Mythology*, pp. 116, 117; cf. Bṛh. D. iii. 16.

[4] x. 110. 9; AV. 5. 12. 9; VS. 29. 34.

[5] Cf. Bṛh. D. iii. 25.

[6] i. 95. 5.

root *hā* (to bound). Elevated, held up. By his own glory, by the glory of his own self. In the lap, i. e. bosom. Both were afraid of Tvaṣṭṛ, who was being born. [Turning back, they both serve the lion.] Heaven and earth, or day and night, or the two sticks of wood: turned towards the lion, i. e. the vanquisher, they both [1] attend upon him.

(*Here ends the fifteenth section.*)

Vanaspatiḥ [2] (lord of herbs) has been explained. The following stanza is addressed to him.

(*Here ends the sixteenth section.*)

Preparing the food and the season by oblations to the gods, bestow them thyself. May the lord of herbs, the god pacifier, and Agni enjoy the oblations with honey and clarified butter.[3]

Having prepared [4] the food and oblations at the proper time of performing the sacrifice, bestow thyself on thyself. May these three, i. e. the lord of herbs, the god pacifier, and Agni, enjoy the oblation with honey and clarified butter.[5]

But who is the lord of herbs? 'It is the sacrificial post,' says Kātthakya. 'It is Agni,' says Śākapūṇi. The following, another stanza, is addressed to him.

(*Here ends the seventeenth section.*)

O lord of herbs, lovers of the gods anoint thee with divine honey in sacrifice. Whether thou standest uplifted or whether thy abode is in the lap of this mother, here bestow wealth on us.[6]

Lovers of the gods anoint thee, O lord of herbs, with divine honey and clarified butter in sacrifice. Whether thou standest uplifted, or whether thy dwelling-place is made in the lap, i. e. bosom, of this mother, thou shalt give us riches.

'It is Agni,' says Śākapūṇi. The following, another stanza, is addressed to him.

(*Here ends the eighteenth section.*)

[1] The word both refers to the two arms of the priest who produces fire by attrition. Cf. Roth, p. 120.

[2] See above, § 3.

[3] x. 110. 10; AV. 5. 12. 10; VS. 29. 35.

[4] Roth, *op. cit.*, p. 120, translates *samanjan* as *schlingend*, i. e. swallowing.

[5] Yāska, followed by Durga, explains *madhunā* as a noun, i. e. 'with honey'. Roth, *loc. cit.*, makes it an attribute of *ghṛtena*, i. e. 'with sweet butter', a very far-fetched explanation. The same word occurs in iii. 8. 1, quoted in the next section, coupled with *daivyena*, i. e. 'divine'. From the comparison of this passage it is clear that *madhunā* cannot be taken as an attribute.

[6] iii. 8. 1.

O lord of herbs, having golden wings, circumambulating and having fastened oblations with a cord, carry them to the gods along the most straight paths of sacrifice; this is thy object from the days of yore.[1]

O lord of herbs, (carry) oblations to the gods; having golden wings, i. e. wings of the sacred law. Or else it may have been used for the sake of comparison, i. e. whose wings glitter like gold. This is thy object from the days of yore, it is an ancient object of thine, hence we address thee. Carry (oblations) along the paths of sacrifice, which are the most straight, i. e. whose course is most straight, which abound in water, and which are free from darkness. The following, another stanza, is addressed to him.

(*Here ends the nineteenth section.*)

O lord of herbs, learned in all the ways, having fastened the oblations with the most beautiful cord, carry them to the gods, O thou desirous of bestowing, and among the immortals proclaim the giver.[2]

O lord of herbs, having fastened with the most beautiful cord,[3] carry the oblations of the giver[4] to the gods [in sacrifice]: learned in all ways, i. e. well versed in all branches of knowledge. And proclaim the giver among the immortals, i. e. gods.

Consecrations by saying 'hail!' (they are so called because) the word *svāhā* (hail!) is uttered in them; or speech herself said, 'well, ho!' or one addresses himself, or one offers oblation consecrated with (*svāhā*) 'hail'. The following stanza is addressed to them.

(*Here ends the twentieth section.*)

As soon as he was born, he measured the sacrifice, Agni became the leader of the gods. May the gods eat the oblations consecrated by the utterance of 'hail' in the speech of this sacrificer, set up in the eastern direction.[5]

As soon as he was born, he created the sacrifice. Agni became the chief of the gods. May the gods eat the oblation consecrated with the utterance of 'hail' in the speech, i. e. mouth, of this sacrificer, set up in the eastern direction. [With these words they sacrifice.]

With these words the *Āprī* deities are dealt with. Now who is the

[1] MS. 4. 3. 7; 208. 10; KS. 18. 21; TB. iii. 6. 11. 2.

[2] x. 70. 10; MS. 4. 13. 7; 209. 1; KS. 18. 21. Cf. TB. iii. 6. 12. 1.

[3] 'With a well-twisted, strong cord', Roth, *op. cit.*, p. 121.

[4] Yāska explains *didhiṣoḥ* as gen. sing., i. e. 'of the giver'. Durga amplifies it by the remark: 'of the giver, i. e. of the sacrificer'. The word has no accent and can therefore be vocative only and refer to Agni, i. e. 'desirous of bestowing'. Roth, *loc. cit.*, attributes the following meanings to it: 'wooer, bridegroom, husband', Grassmann, *op. cit.*, p. 600.

[5] x. 110. 11; AV. 5. 12. 11; VS. 29. 36.

god to whom the introductory and the concluding oblations are offered?[1] According to some, they are offered to Agni.

(Here ends the twenty-first section.)

The introductory and the concluding oblations are exclusively mine. Give me, O gods, the juicy portion of the offering: butter of waters and the fragrant exhalations of herbs. May the life of Agni be long.[2]

The introductory and the concluding oblations are exclusively thine, and so will be the juicy portions of the offerings; nay, this whole sacrifice will be thine, O Agni; to thee will bow down the four quarters.[3]

Further, there is a Brāhmaṇa passage: Verily, to Agni belong the introductory, and to Agni the concluding oblations.[4] According to others, they have the metres as their deities. There is a Brāhmaṇa passage: Verily, to the metres belong the introductory, and to metres the concluding oblations.[5] According to others, they have the seasons as their deities. There is a Brāhmaṇa passage: Verily, to the seasons belong the introductory, to the seasons the concluding oblations.[6] [According to others, they have sacrificial animals as their deities. There is a Brāhmaṇa passage: Verily, to sacrificial animals belong the introductory, to sacrificial animals the concluding oblations.[7]] According to others, they have breath as their deity. There is a Brāhmaṇa passage: Verily, to breath belong the introductory, to breath the concluding oblations.[8] According to others, they have soul as their deity. There is a Brāhmaṇa passage: Verily, to soul belong the introductory, to soul the concluding oblations.[9]

But the well-considered view is that they are addressed to Agni. The rest is mere apportionment. Then why are these views put forward? It is well known: A person, about to utter the sound *vaṣaṭ*, should meditate on the particular deity to whom the oblation is offered.[10]

With these words, these eleven *Āpri* hymns are dealt with. Of these, the hymns of Vasiṣṭha, Atri, Vadhryaśva, and Gṛtsamada are addressed to Narāśaṃsa; the hymns of Medhātithi, Dīrghatamas, and that of invitation (*praiṣas*) to both (i.e. Narāśaṃsa and Tanūnapāt). The hymns other than those (mentioned above) are therefore addressed to Tanūnapāt, to Tanūnapāt.[11]

(Here ends the twenty-second section.)

[1] Cf. Muir, *op. cit.*, vol. ii, pp. 175–6.
[2] x. 51. 8.
[3] x. 51. 9.
[4] Cf. Muir, *loc. cit.*
[5] Cf. SB. i. 3. 2. 9.
[6] Cf. ŚB. i. 3. 2. 8; KB. iii. 4; MS. 1. 4. 12.
[7] Cf. KB. iii. 4.
[8] Cf. KB. vii. 1: x. 3; AB. i. 11. 17; ŚB. xi. 2. 7. 27.
[9] Cf. TS. vi. 1. 5. 4.
[10] Cf. GB. ii. 3. 4; AB. iii. 8.
[11] Cf. Roth, *op. cit.*, p. 122; cf. Bṛh. D. ii. 154–7.

CHAPTER IX

Now therefore we shall take up in order the terrestrial beings to which panegyrics are addressed. Of these, the horse is the foremost. *Aśva* (horse) has been explained.[1] The following stanza is addressed to him.

(*Here ends the first section.*)

The horse as draught animal desires a comfortable chariot and the encouraging shout of the inciter; the male organ (desires) the two hairy rims; the frog (desires) the pond; flow, Indu, flow for Indra's sake.[2]

The horse as a draught animal; the draught animal (desires) a comfortable (chariot) [the draught animal a chariot]. The word *sukham* (comfortable) is a synonym of 'good'.

Good is auspicious, very suitable [or it proceeds in a very suitable manner. Laughter; goer, or protector, or benefactor; the male organ goes towards. Water causes to conceal.] *Māna* has been explained. The following stanza is addressed to him.

(*Here ends the second section.*)[3]

Let not Mitra, Varuṇa, Aryaman, Āyu, Indra, Ṛbhukṣan, and the Maruts overlook us, because we will proclaim the heroic deeds of the horse, the courser, born of the gods, in the assembly.[4]

On account of our proclaiming the heroic deeds of the horse, the courser, the racer, born of the gods, in the assembly, i.e. at sacrifice, may not Mitra, Varuṇa, Aryaman, Āyu, Vāyu, the swift one, Indra, the wide dweller or the king of the Ṛbhus, and the Maruts overlook us.

A bird (is so called because) it is able to lift itself up, or to make a sound, or to rush along, or else they wish him to be always auspicious, or the word (*śakuni*, bird) may be derived from (the root) *śak* (to be able).[5] The following stanza is addressed to him.

(*Here ends the third section.*)

Crying violently and proclaiming its nativity, it impels speech as a rower a boat. O bird, be highly auspicious. May no apparition whatsoever find thee anywhere.[6]

[1] See 2. 27; cf. also 1. 12.

[2] ix. 112. 4.

[3] The section *in toto* must be spurious; cf. Roth, *op. cit.*, p. 125. *Mānaḥ* as a masc. is senseless, for it refers to *mā naḥ*, 'not us', of the following quotation, nor has it been explained.

[4] i. 162. 1; VS. 25. 24.

[5] The etymological explanations of *śakuni* given by Yāska are the following: (1) √*śak* and √*nī*, (2) √*śak* and √*nad*, (3) √*śam* and √*kṛ*.

[6] ii. 42. 1; cf. Bṛh. D. iv. 94.

It cries violently, proclaiming its birth, i.e. its name is onomatopoetic. It propels speech as a rower does a boat. O bird, be highly auspicious i.e. exceedingly auspicious. *Maṅgalam* (auspicious) is derived from (the root) *gṝ*, meaning to praise.[1] Or else (from *gṝ*, to swallow), i.e. it swallows evil things.[2] Or else (the word) is *aṅga-lam*, i.e. having limbs.[3] According to the etymologists (it is derived from √*masj*), i.e. it submerges sin. Or else (people say) 'let it come to me'.[4] May no overpowering force find thee on any side.

A bird uttered a lowing sound to Gṛtsamada, as he was about to proceed (to acquire) a particular object.[5] This is indicated by the following stanza.

(*Here ends the fourth section.*)

O bird, speak out what is auspicious in the south, and that which is auspicious in the north. Say what is auspicious in front of us and also what is auspicious behind us.[6]

The stanza is explained by the mere reading of it.

Gṛtsamada = *Gṛtsa-madana*, i.e. wise and joyful. The word *gṛtsa* is a synonym of wise; it is derived from (the root) *gṝ*, meaning to praise.

Maṇḍūkāḥ (frogs) = *majjūkāḥ*, i.e. divers, (so called) from diving. Or the word may be derived from (the root) *mad*, meaning to rejoice, or from *mand*, meaning to be satisfied. 'It is derived from (the root) *maṇḍ* (to decorate),' say the grammarians.[7] Or else, their abode (*okas*) is in water (*maṇḍe*). *Maṇḍa* (water) is derived from (the root) *mad* (to rejoice) or from *mud* (to be merry).[8] The following stanza is addressed to them.

(*Here ends the fifth section.*)

Sleeping for a year, the frogs have uttered forth speech, impelled by the cloud, like Brāhmaṇas engaged in religious rites.[9]

Sleeping for a year, the Brāhmaṇas, who are engaged in religious rites, i.e. who have taken the vow of silence. Or else a simile may have been intended, i.e. (uttered speech) like Brāhmaṇas, who are engaged in religious rites. The frogs have uttered forth speech which has been impelled by the cloud.[10]

[1] The bird is an object of praise. Durga.

[2] Auspiciousness destroys misfortunes as soon as they arise. Durga.

[3] According to Durga, *lam* = *ram*, the possessive suffix: the letter *m* is added without any meaning, and *anga* signifies the various ingredients, as honey, milk, &c., of the mixture.

[4] i.e. *Mangala* is derived from the root *gam* with *mām*, i.e. 'going to me'.

[5] 'Signifying success.' Durga.

[6] RVKH. 2. 43. 1; cf. Professor Macdonell, *Vedic Mythology*, p. 152.

[7] 'The frogs are adorned with variegated lines on their skin by nature.' Durga.

[8] The sentence is omitted by Durga.

[9] vii. 103. 1; AV. 4. 15. 13; cf. Bṛh. D. vi. 27.

[10] Cf. Professor Macdonell, *Vedic Mythology*, p. 151.

Vasiṣṭha, desirous of rain, praised the cloud. Frogs applauded him. On seeing the applauding frogs, he praised them. This is indicated by the following stanza.

(*Here ends the sixth section.*)

O frog, join me. O swimmer, invoke rain. Float in the middle of the pond, having spread your four feet.[1]

The stanza is explained by the mere reading of it.

Dice (*akṣāḥ*) are (so called because) they are obtained (√*aś*) by gamblers, or (wealth) is obtained through them. The following stanza is addressed to them.

(*Here ends the seventh section.*)

The waving ones of the great (tree), growing in windy places, rolling on the gambling board, intoxicate me. The ever-wakeful berry of the *vibhīdaka* tree appears to me like a draught of soma that grows on the Mūjavat mountain.[2]

The waving berries of the mighty[3] *vibhīdaka* tree intoxicate me. Growing in windy places, i.e. growing on mountain slopes. Rolling on the gambling board. Board (*iriṇam*) is free from debt[4] (*nir-ṛṇam*). It is derived from (the root) *ṛṇ* (to go), i.e. it is distant. Or else, herbs have been removed from it. Like a draught of soma growing on the Mūjavat mountain. *Maujavataḥ*, i.e. grown on Mūjavat. Mūjavat is the name of a mountain, (so called because) it abounds in *Saccharum sara* (*muñja*). *Muñja* is (so called because) it is thrown out (√*muc*) by a kind of rush. *Iṣīkā* (a kind of rush) is derived from (the root) *iṣ*, meaning to go. This other (meaning of) *iṣīkā* (i. e. arrow) is derived from the same root also. *Vibhīdaka* (name of a tree) is (so called) from piercing. Wakeful is (so called) from keeping awake.[5] The poet praises them (i. e. dice) in the first and condemns them in the succeeding stanzas.[6] This is known to be the composition of a seer made miserable by dice.

Grāvāṇaḥ (stones) is derived from (the root) *han* (to kill), or from *gṛ* (to praise), or from *grah* (to seize). The following stanza is addressed to them.[7]

(*Here ends the eighth section.*)

[1] RVKH. 7. 103.

[2] x. 34. 1; R. Vidh. 3. 10. 1; cf. Bṛh. D. vii. 36.

[3] Yāska takes *bṛhato* as an adjective, agreeing with *vibhīdakasya* to be supplied, as in the text of the RV. *vibhīdakaḥ* in the nom. sing. is the subject of the second line.

[4] Debts incurred on the gambling board, unlike others, are not payable by the descendants of the debtors. Durga.

[5] According to Durga, dice are called wakeful, because they keep the winner awake through the joy of winning, and the loser on account of the misery of his loss.

[6] See x. 34. 2–14.

[7] x. 94. 1.

Let them proclaim. Let us proclaim. Address the stones who speak in return, when ye, O unsplit mountains, quick and rich in soma, together bear the sound, i. e. invocation for Indra.[1]

Let them proclaim. Let us proclaim. Address the stones who speak in return. When unsplit mountains, i. e. who are not to be split up. Quick, making haste. Together (producing) soma. *Śloka* (call) is derived from (the root) *śṝ* (to break open). *Ghoṣa* (sound) is derived from (the root) *ghuṣ* (to sound). You are rich in soma, or you are in the abodes of one who is rich in soma.

A *nārāśaṃsa* stanza is that with which men are praised. The following stanza is addressed to it.

(*Here ends the ninth section.*)

I present, with wisdom, the sublime hymns of Bhāvya, who dwells on the Sindhu—the unsurpassed king who, desirous of glory, measured out a thousand libations for me.[2]

Sublime hymns, i. e. not childish, or not few. A child—turning round for strength—is to be brought up. Or else his mother is sufficient for him, or his mother is (a source of) strength for him. Or the word *bāla* (child) is derived from *bala* (strength), with the negative particle placed in the middle.[3] I present with wisdom, i. e. with ingenuity of mind, or praise, or intelligence. Of the King Bhāvya, who dwells on the Sindhu, and who prepared a thousand libations for me—the king who is unsurpassed, or who is not hasty, or who does not hurry, and who is desirous of praise.

(*Here ends the tenth section.*)

A king obtains praise on account of being associated with sacrifice, and the paraphernalia of war from their association with the king. Of these, the chariot comes first. *Rathaḥ* (chariot) is derived from (the root) *raṁh*, meaning to speed, or from *sthira* by metathesis:[4] one sits in a chariot with joy, or from *rap* (to chatter) [or from *ras* (to make a sound)].[5] The following stanza is addressed to it.[6]

(*Here ends the eleventh section.*)

[1] Cf. Professor Macdonell, *op. cit.*, pp. 154–5.

[2] i. 126. 1; cf. Bṛh. D. iii. 155.

[3] The passage, 'A child . . . in the middle', is omitted by Durga. It gives the etymological explanation of a word which neither occurs in the text of the RV., nor in that of Yāska, hence I agree with Durga in thinking that the passage is spurious.

[4] i e. *sthira* > *thara*, and by metathesis *ratha*.

[5] The last two etymologies are omitted by Durga.

[6] Cf. Professor Macdonell, *op. cit.*, p. 155.

O lord of forests, our friend, promoter, and a noble hero, indeed be firm in body. Thou art girt with cowhide, be strong. May thy rider win what is to be won.[1]

O lord of forests, indeed be firm in thy limbs. Thou art our friend, promoter, and a noble hero, i. e. a blessed hero. Thou art girt with cow-hide, hence be strong, i. e. be very firm. May thy rider win what is worthy of winning.

The word *dundubhi*[2] (drum) is onomatopoetic. Or else it is (so called) being made of a split tree.[3] Or it may be derived from (the verb) *dundubhya*, meaning to make a sound. The following stanza is addressed to it.

(*Here ends the twelfth section.*)

Fill earth and heaven also with thy roar. Let the immovable and the movable think of thee everywhere. Besides, O drum, together with Indra and the gods, keep off the enemy farther than afar.[4]

Fill earth and heaven with thy roar. Let them all that are immovable, i. e. stationary, and that are non-stationary, think highly of thy loud call. O drum, associated together with Indra and the gods, disperse the enemy farther than what is very far.

Quiver is the receptacle of arrows. The following stanza is addressed to it.[5]

(*Here ends the thirteenth section.*)

The father of many (daughters), and whose sons are many, clangs and clashes, having reached the field of battle. Slung on the back, the quiver, when hurled forth, conquers strifes and all the hostile armies.[6]

The father of many (daughters) and whose sons are many is with reference to arrows. When exposed, it smiles as it were. Or it is an onomatopoetic word. *Saṅkāḥ* (strife) is derived from (the root) *sac* (to suffer), or from *kṝ* (to scatter), preceded by the preposition *sam*. Slung on the back it conquers when hurled forth, is explained.

Handguard is (so called because) it is held firmly on the hand. The following stanza is addressed to it.

(*Here ends the fourteenth section.*)

[1] vi. 47. 26; AV. 6. 125. 1; VS. 29. 52.

[2] Cf. Professor Macdonell, *op. cit.*, p. 155.

[3] This gives the first derivation of the word *dundubhi*, i.e. the former part from *druma* (tree), and the latter from the root *bhid*.

[4] vi. 47. 29; AV. 6. 126. 1; VS. 29. 55.

[5] Cf. Professor Macdonell, *loc. cit.*

[6] vi. 75. 5; VS. 29. 42.

Like a serpent, it encompasses the arm with its coils, protecting it from the impact of the bowstring. May the manly handguard, learned in all expedients, well protect the man from all sides.[1]

Like a serpent, it encircles the arm with its coils, shielding it from the strokes of the bowstring. The handguard well versed in all the sciences. A man is (so called because) he possesses abundance of manly spirit,[2] or the word *pumān* (man) is derived from (the root) *puṃs* (to crush).

Bridles have been explained.[3] The following stanza is addressed to them.

(*Here ends the fifteenth section.*)

Seated on the car, a skilful charioteer guides his steeds in front of him, to whatever place he likes. Admire the greatness of the bridles. From behind, the reins give direction to the mind.[4]

Seated on the car, a skilful charioteer, i. e. a noble charioteer, guides his steeds, which are in front of him, to whatever place he likes. I worship the greatness of bridles. The reins, although they are behind, give direction to the mind.

Dhanus[5] (bow) is derived from the root *dhanv*, meaning to go, or to kill: the arrows are discharged from it. The following stanza is addressed to it.

(*Here ends the sixteenth section.*)

May we win kine with the bow, and with the bow the combat. May we win dreadful battles with the bow. The bow brings the desires of the enemy to naught. May we conquer all quarters with bow.[6]

The stanza is explained by the mere reading of it.

Samadaḥ (battle) = *sam-adaḥ* (i. e. eating together) from (the root) *ad* (to eat),[7] or = *sam-madaḥ* (i. e. raging together) from (the root) *mad* (to rage).

Jyā (bowstring) is derived from (the root) *ji* (to conquer), or from *ji* (to conquer, cl. ix), or it is (so called because) it causes arrows to fly quickly. The following stanza is addressed to it.

(*Here ends the seventeenth section.*)

Coming close to the ear as if desirous of whispering a secret, and embracing its dear friend, this string, stretched on the bow, and leading us to salvation in battle, utters a low shrill sound like a woman.[8]

[1] vi. 75. 14 ; VS. 29. 51.

[2] Compared to a woman, who is poor in spirit, a man has more manly strength. Durga.

[3] See 3. 9.

[4] vi. 75. 6 ; VS. 29. 43.

[5] Cf. Professor Macdonell, *loc. cit.*

[6] vi. 75. 2 ; VS. 29. 39.

[7] People devour each other, as it were, in battle. Durga.

[8] vi. 75. 3 ; VS. 29. 40.

It comes close to the ear as if desirous of speaking. Embracing, as it were, its dear friend, i. e. the arrow. It utters a [shrill] sound like a woman. This string stretched on the bow. In battle, in strife. Leading us to salvation, [leading us across].

Iṣu[1] (arrow) is derived from (the root) *iṣ*, meaning to go [or to kill]. The following stanza is addressed to it.

(Here ends the eighteenth section.)

She wears a beautiful wing. Deer is her tooth. When hurled, she flies girt with cow-phlegm. May the arrows grant us protection there where men run to and fro.[2]

She wears a beautiful wing is with reference to the swift feathers of arrows. Her tooth is made of the horn of deer.[3] Or else it is derived from (the root) *mṛg* (to pursue).[4] 'When hurled, she flies girt with cow-phlegm', has been explained.[5] May the arrows grant us protection there where men run in the same direction and in the opposite direction, i. e. protection in battles.

Lashing rod is called whip. Whip (*kaśā*) is (so called because) it reveals (*pra-kāśayati*) danger to the horse. Or else it is derived from (the root) *kṛṣ* (to drag) on account of being small. Further, speech is called (*kaśā* because) it reveals meaning, or it rests in space; or it is derived from (the root) *kruś* (to make a noise). The following stanza is addressed to the horsewhip.

(Here ends the nineteenth section.)

They strike their thighs and deal blows on their buttocks. O lashing rod, impel sagacious horses in battles.[6]

They strike their thighs, i. e. their moving thigh-bones. *Sakthi* (thigh-bone) is derived from (the root) *sac* (to be united), the body is fixed in it. And they deal blows on their buttocks.[7] *Jaghanam* (buttock) is derived from (the verb) *jaṅghanya* (to strike repeatedly). O lashing rod, impel horses that are [sagacious,] of highly-developed intelligence, in battles, i. e. contests, or conflicts.

[1] Cf. Professor Macdonell, *loc. cit.*

[2] vi. 75. 11; VS. 29. 48.

[3] This gives the detailed description of an arrow. The pointed end is made of the horn of a deer, which is very sharp, and the rest is covered with beautiful wings. Cf. Durga's remarks.

[4] According to Durga, certain arrows possess the power of pursuing even an invisible enemy and of discrimination in attack.

[5] See 2. 5.

[6] vi. 75. 13.

[7] Durga takes *jaṅghanti* as a particle in the vocative case, agreeing with *aśvājanī*. This explanation is wrong. Not only is it opposed to that of Yāska, but *jaṅghanti*, as the accent indicates, cannot be in the vocative case.

Mortar (*ulūkhalam*) is (so called because) it causes to spread out (*uru-karam*), or it has a hole at the top, or it prepares food (*ūrj-karam*). There is a Brāhmaṇa passage:[1] 'Make me large,' said he. Then indeed he became a mortar. Verily, they call it *uru-karam* (causing to spread out), indirectly *ulūkhalam*, i.e. mortar. The following stanza is addressed to it.

(*Here ends the twentieth section.*)

Whenever, O Mortar, thou art set to work from house to house. Then utter thy brightest sound like the trumpet of the conquerors.[2]

The stanza is explained by the mere reading of it.

(*Here ends the twenty-first section.*)

Vṛṣabhaḥ means one who rains down offspring,[3] or who increases the seed very much. *Vṛṣabhaḥ* is therefore so called from raining, i.e. whose characteristic is to rain. The following stanza is addressed to him.

(*Here ends the twenty-second section.*)

Thundering they approached him. In the midst of the strife, they made the bull shed water. Through him Mudgala won a hundred thousand well-nourished kine in battle.[4]

Thundering they approached him is explained. They made the bull shed water in the midst [of battle], i.e. the place of conquest or swiftness. Through him (he conquered) the king of beautiful possessions.[5] The verb *bharv* means to eat. Or else, Mudgala won a thousand well-nourished kine in battle. The word *pradhana* is a synonym of battle: treasures are scattered forth in it.

Wooden mace, i.e. mace made of wood. With reference to it they relate a legend. A seer Mudgala, a descendant of Bhṛmyaśva, having yoked his bull and a wooden mace, and having fought in battle, won the contest. This is indicated by the following stanza.

(*Here ends the twenty-third section.*)

Look at this yoke of the bull and the wooden mace lying in the middle of battle, with which Mudgala won a hundred thousand kine in battles.[6]

Look at this yoking together of the bull, and the wooden mace lying in the middle of battle, with which Mudgala won a hundred thousand kine in battles. The word *pṛtanājyam*[7] is a synonym of battle, (so called) from dispersing or conquering hostile armies. *Mudgala* means one who possesses

[1] Cf. ŚB. vii. 5. 1. 12.

[2] i. 28. 5; AB. vii. 17; cf. Bṛh. D. iii. 101.

[3] *Prajotpatti-kāraṇaṃ retaḥ sincati yonau.* Durga.

[4] x. 102. 5.

[5] According to Durga, *sūbharvan* means a prosperous country, especially rich in barley.

[6] x. 102. 9.

[7] Cf. Roth, *op. cit.*, p. 130.

beans, or who swallows beans, or passion, or pride, or joy.[1] *Bhārmyaśva*, a son of Bhṛmyaśva. *Bhṛmyaśva* means one whose horses are always wandering, or he is (so called) from horse-breeding.

The word *pituḥ* is a synonym of food. It is derived from (the root) *pā* (to protect), or from *pā* (to drink), or from *pyāy* (to swell). The following stanza is addressed to it.

(*Here ends the twenty-fourth section.*)

Verily I will praise the food, the holder of great invigorating strength; with whose vigour Trita rent Vṛtra limb by limb.[2]

I praise the food which contains great invigorating strength. The word *taviṣī*[3] is a synonym of strength. It is derived from (the root) *tu*, meaning to increase. With whose vigour, i. e. power, Trita, i. e. Indra who abides in three places, rends Vṛtra limb by limb.

Rivers have been explained.[4] The following stanza is addressed to them.

(*Here ends the twenty-fifth section.*)

Hear this my hymn of praise, O Gaṅgā, Yamunā, Sarasvatī, Śutudrī together with Paruṣṇi, Marudvṛdhā with Asiknī, and Ārjīkīyā with Vitastā and Susomā.[5]

Attend[6] to this my hymn of praise, O Gaṅgā, Yamunā, Sarasvatī, Śutudrī, Paruṣṇī, Marudvṛdhā with Asiknī; hear, O Ārjīkīyā with Vitastā and Susomā.[7] This is the general sense. Now (follows) the etymological explanation of every word. Gaṅgā is (so called) from going (√*gam*).[8] Yamunā, she flows, joining herself (with other rivers), or she flows gently.[9] Sarasvatī—the word *saras* is a synonym of water, it is derived from (the root) *sṛ* (to flow)—rich in water. Śutudrī, quick runner, rapid runner,[10] or it runs swiftly like one who is goaded. Irāvatī is called Paruṣṇī, i. e. having joints, [shining,] winding. Asiknī, non-bright, non-white. The word *sitam* is a synonym of white colour, its antithesis is (denoted by) *a-sitam*. Marudvṛdhā, i. e. swollen by all other rivers and winds. Vitastā, not burnt,[11] mighty, having high banks. Ārjīkīyā is called Vipāś, so called

[1] Cf. Roth, *op. cit.*, p. 129.

[2] i. 187. 1.

[3] Cf. Roth, *op. cit.*, p. 130.

[4] See 2. 24.

[5] x. 75. 3.

[6] Cf. Muir, *op. cit.*, vol. ii, p. 342.

[7] Cf. M. A. Stein, *Bhandarkar Comm. Vol.*, pp. 21–9.

[8] i. e. She goes to the best place, or sends created beings to the best place. Durga.

[9] There are no waves in it. Durga.

[10] Cf. Mbh. Ādi-par., verse 6752, *Śatadhā vidrutā yasmāc chatadrur iti viśrutā* 1.

[11] Durga says, on the authority of the *Sāmidheni Brāhmaṇa*, that there was fire called *Vaidehaka* which consumed all rivers except this one.

because) it rises in *ṛjūka*, or it flows in a straight line. The Vipāś is (so called) from bursting forth, or from loosening fetters, or from being extended. It is called fetterless because the fetters of the moribund Vasiṣṭha were loosened in it.[1] Formerly it was called Uruñjirā. Suṣomā is the Sindhu, (so called because) rivers flow towards it. Sindhu is (so called) from flowing.

Apaḥ (waters) is derived from (the root) *āp* (to obtain). The following stanza is addressed to them.

(*Here ends the twenty-sixth section.*)

Ye waters are indeed beneficent. As such bestow strength on us, so that we may look upon great happiness.[2]

Ye waters are indeed a source of comfort. As such bestow food on us, so that we may look upon great happiness, i. e. delight.

Herbs (*oṣa-dhayaḥ*) are (so called because) they suck (*dhayanti*) the burning element [3] (*oṣat*), or (because) people suck them when something is burning (in the body). Or else they suck the morbid element (*doṣa*). The following stanza is addressed to them.

(*Here ends the twenty-seventh section.*)

I think there are indeed one hundred and seven abodes of the tawny ones, the herbs, that were produced three ages before the gods, in days of yore.[4]

I think there are indeed one hundred and seven abodes of the tawny ones, i. e. tawny-coloured ones, the herbs, which carry off (disease) produced three ages before the gods, in days of yore. There are three kinds of abodes, i. e. places, names, and species. Here species are meant.[5] Or else there are seven hundred [6] vital parts of man, the herbs are applied on them.

Night has been explained.[7] The following stanza is addressed to it.

(*Here ends the twenty-eighth section.*)

O night, the terrestrial region of the father together with (atmospheric) places has been well filled. Thou art great, and encompassest the abodes of heaven; the dreadful darkness draws all around.[8]

[1] Cf. Mbh. Ādi-par., verses 6745 and 6750.

[2] x. 9. 1.

[3] There are two etymologies given, (1) from √*uṣ* (to burn) and √*dhe* to suck, (2) from √*duṣ* and √*dhe*.

[4] x. 97. 1. Cf. Professor Macdonell, *op. cit.*, p. 154.

[5] i. e. There are 107 kinds of herbs.

[6] Yāska explains *śatám* . . *saptá ca* as *sapta-śatam*, i. e. 700. According to the ordinary meaning of the words used, as indicated by the accent and *ca*, the phrase can only mean 'a hundred and seven'.

[7] See 2. 18.

[8] RVKH. x. 127. 1.

O night, thou hast well filled the terrestrial region along with the places of the middle (region). Great, mighty, thou encompassest the abodes of heaven; the dreadful darkness draws all round the region.

Wilderness[1] is the wife of desert. Desert (*araṇya*) is (so called because) it is far (*apa-arṇa*) from the village, or because it is dull (*a-ramaṇa*). The following stanza is addressed to her.

(*Here ends the twenty-ninth section.*)

O wilderness, how is it that thou who disappearest in deserts ever onwards dost not seek the village? it appears that fear does not find thee.[2]

The seer[3] addresses her with the words, 'O wilderness, how is it that thou who disappearest in deserts, i. e. forests, like one directed to some place onwards, dost not seek the village? It appears as if fear does not find thee.' Or the word *iva* is used in the sense of slight apprehension (i. e. the slightest fear).

Faith (*śrad-dhā*) is (so called) on account of being based on truth (*śrad*).[4] The following stanza is addressed to it.

(*Here ends the thirtieth section.*)

Through faith is fire kindled, through faith is oblation offered. With our speech we announce faith at the head of fortune.[5]

Through faith is fire well kindled, through faith is oblation well offered.[6] With our speech we announce faith to be at the head, i. e. the chief limb of fortune, i. e. prosperity.

Earth has been explained.[7] The following stanza is addressed to it.

(*Here ends the thirty-first section.*)

O Earth, be pleasant, thornless providing a resting-place; grant us extensive protection.[8]

O Earth, be comfortable, thornless providing a resting-place. *Ṛkṣaraḥ* means 'thorn', it is derived from (the verb) *ṛch* (to be stiff). *Kaṇṭakaḥ* (thorn) is (so called) (because it says to itself), Whom (*kam*) should I hurt

[1] Cf. Professor Macdonell, *op. cit.*, p. 154.

[2] x. 146. 1.

[3] Durga remarks that the poet lost his way in the forest, and being puzzled as to what direction it was, and being afraid, addresses the goddess of the forest, 'How is it that I am afraid and thou art not?'

[4] Durga remarks that *śrad-dhā* means that intuitive attitude which one assumes towards religion and secular and spiritual matters and which does not undergo any change. The tutelary deity of this intuition is called *śraddhā*. Cf. Professor Macdonell, *op. cit.*, p. 119–20.

[5] x. 151. 1.

[6] Durga quotes a passage which says that the gods do not accept the oblations of the faithless.

[7] See 1. 13–14.

[8] i. 22. 15.

(*tāpayāmi*)? or it may be derived from (the verb) *kṛt* (to pierce), or from *kaṇṭ*, meaning to go, i. e. it is very prominent on the tree. Grant us (let them grant)[1] protection from all sides, i. e. extensive protection.

Apvā (disease) has been explained.[2] The following stanza is addressed to it.

(*Here ends the thirty-second section.*)

Infatuating the heart of these (our enemies), seize their limbs; depart, O Apvā, approach (them), burn with flames in their hearts. Let our enemies abide in blinding darkness.[3]

Infatuating the heart [the intellect] of these (our enemies), seize their limbs; depart, O Apvā, approach them, burn their hearts with flames. Let our enemies grope in blinding darkness.

Agnāyī[4] is the wife of Agni. The following stanza is addressed to her.

(*Here ends the thirty-third section.*)

I call upon the wife of Indra, the wife of Varuṇa, and the wife of Agni for welfare and for drinking soma.[5]

The stanza is explained by the mere reading of it.

(*Here ends the thirty-fourth section.*)

Now, therefore, the eight pairs, mortar and pestle. Mortar[6] has been explained. Pestle (*musalam*) is (so called because) it moves again and again (*muhuḥ-saram*). The following stanza is addressed to them.

(*Here ends the thirty-fifth section.*)

Adorable, best winners of food, they are held aloft, devouring food like steeds.[7]

Worthy of being worshipped with sacrifices, best distributors of food, they are held aloft,[8] devouring food like steeds.

Two receptacles of oblations, i. e. depositories of oblations. The following stanza is addressed to them.

(*Here ends the thirty-sixth section.*)

[1] The passage within brackets is omitted by the manuscripts of the longer recension and Durga.

[2] See 6. 12.

[3] x. 103. 12.

[4] Cf. Professor Macdonell, *op. cit.*, pp. 124–5. Yāska's explanation that Agnāyī is the wife of Agni is liable to criticism, for in the following stanza she is associated with drinking soma—a function not very appropriate for the wife of Agni.

[5] i. 22. 12.

[6] See 9. 20.

[7] i. 28. 7.

[8] The mortar is mounted or made to stand upright; the pestle is lifted up for pounding. Durga.

O ye free from treachery, let the holy gods sit in your lap; here, to-day, to drink the soma.[1]

Let them (gods) sit in your lap, in your bosom, [or else, O ye not to be injured]. Holy gods, accomplishers of sacrifice; here, to-day, for the drinking of soma. Heaven and earth have been explained.[2] The following stanza is addressed to them.

(Here ends the thirty-seventh section.)

To-day may heaven and earth extend our accomplishment, this sky-touching sacrifice, to the gods.[3]

To-day may heaven and earth extend farther our performance, i.e. this sky-touching sacrifice, to the gods.

Vipāś and Śutudrī have been explained.[4] The following stanza is addressed to them.

(Here ends the thirty-eighth section.)

Like two bright cows, like two licking mothers, Vipāś and Śutudrī hasten forth eagerly with their waters from the lap of the mountains, contending like two mares let loose.[5]

From the lap of the mountains, i.e. from their mountainous abode. Eagerly, i.e. longingly.[6] Like two mares who are released, or who are out of temper. Contending—the verb *hās* is used in (the sense of) emulation—or who are excited. Like two [bright] beautiful cows, two mothers licking together,[7] Vipāś and Śutudrī hasten forth with their waters.

The ends of the bow are (so called because) they send forth arrows, or they are made of wood, or they never fail. The following stanza is addressed to them.

(Here ends the thirty-ninth section.)

Approaching each other like women of the same mind, they bear (arrows) in their lap as a mother does a son. May these quivering ends of the bow, having a mutual understanding, drive away the enemy, the unfriendly people.[8]

Approaching each other like two women who have the same thought, they bear arrows in their lap, i.e. bosom, as a mother does a child. May these destructive ends of the bow, having a mutual understanding, drive away the enemy, the unfriendly people.

[1] ii. 41. 21.
[2] See 1. 13. 14; 3. 22.
[3] ii. 41. 20.
[4] See 2. 24; 9. 26.
[5] iii. 33. 1.
[6] i.e. Longing for their mutual confluence or the sea. Durga.
[7] i.e. Two mothers who want to lick the same calf.
[8] vi. 75. 4.

Wind and sun.[1] *Śunaḥ* means wind, (so called) because it moves quickly in the atmosphere. *Sīraḥ* means the sun, (so called) from moving (√*sṛ*). The following stanza is addressed to them.

(*Here ends the fortieth section.*)

O wind and sun, enjoy this praise. Sprinkle ye both this (earth) with whatever water you make in heaven.[2]

The stanza is explained by the mere reading of it.

The two approving goddesses, the two goddesses who approve without reflection, i. e. heaven and earth, or day and night. According to Kātthakya, they are crop and season. The following invitation is addressed to them.

(*Here ends the forty-first section.*)

The two approving goddesses who bestow treasures: of these two, one shall remove the ills and hostilities, and the other shall bring noble treasures for the sacrificer. Do ye both eat in order to win and to bestow treasures. Sacrifice.[3]

The two approving goddesses, i. e. the two goddesses who approve without reflection. [Who bestow treasures,] who distribute treasures. Of these two, one causes ills and hostilities to be removed, and the other brings excellent treasures for the sacrificer, in order to win or bestow treasures. Do ye both eat, drink, or desire the sacrifice. With these words, the invitation is expressed.

Two goddesses worshipped with food-oblations, two goddesses who are to be worshipped with food-oblations, i.e. heaven and earth, or day and night. According to Kātthakya, they are crop and season. The following invitation is addressed to them.

(*Here ends the forty-second section.*)

The two goddesses worshipped with food-oblations: one shall bring the strengthening food, and the other a common meal and drink. May we partake of the old with the new and of the new with the old. The two goddesses worshipped with food-oblations, and causing strength, have bestowed that strengthening food. Do ye both eat in order to win and to bestow treasures. Sacrifice.[4]

The two goddesses worshipped with food-oblations, i. e. who are to be worshipped with food-oblations. One brings food and juice, and the other common meal and drink. May we partake of the old with the new and of the new with the old. The two goddesses worshipped with food-oblations,

[1] Cf. Professor Macdonell, *op. cit.*, pp. 126–30.
[2] iv. 57. 5.
[3] KS. 19. 13; MS. 4. 13. 8; 210. 1.
[4] KS. 19. 13; MS. 4. 13; 210. 4.

and causing strength, have bestowed that strengthening food. Do ye both eat and drink or enjoy desire, in order to win and to bestow treasures. Sacrifice. With these words, the invitation is expressed.

(Here ends the forty-third section.)

CHAPTER X

Now, therefore, (we shall take up) the deities of the middle region. Of these, Vāyu[1] (wind) is the foremost. *Vāyu* (wind) is derived from (the verb) *vā* (to blow), or it may be derived from the verb *vī* (meaning to move). 'It is derived from the verb *i* (to go),' says Sthaulāṣṭhīvi, 'the letter *v* being meaningless.' The following stanza is addressed to him.

(Here ends the first section.)

Come, O beautiful Vāyu, these soma-juices are made ready. Drink them, hear (our) call.[2]

Come, O Vāyu, worthy of being seen. These soma-juices are made ready [i. e. prepared]; drink them and hear our call. What deity other than the atmospheric will the seer thus address?[3]

The following, another stanza, is addressed to him.

(Here ends the second section.)

May the ever-running steeds, the chariot-horses, who move in a straight line, bring the vigorous Indra, in a car of beautiful wheels, towards the old and the new food: lest the nectar of Vāyu be wasted.[4]

The constantly-running steeds, the chariot-horses, i. e. the horses which draw the chariot. Who move in a straight line, i. e. whose course is straight. May (they) bring Indra, who is becoming very powerful, in a car of blessed wheels, in order to join the old and the new[5] food. The word *śravas* is a synonym of food, (so called) because it is heard (√*śru*). So that the

[1] Cf. Professor Macdonell, *op. cit.*, pp. 81–3.

[2] i. 2. 1.

[3] The commentator here criticizes Yāska's view that Vāyu is foremost among the atmospheric deities. He claims that place for Indra. He then endeavours to justify Yāska by trying to identify Vāyu with Indra. He says: 'It is indeed well known that Indra, whose sphere is the atmosphere, drinks soma. The preparation of soma-juice is meant for him only. It is not to be pressed for any other deity. Vāyu is therefore Indra himself.'

[4] vi. 37. 3; cf. Bṛh. D. v. 107.

[5] Cf. 4. 17. Durga explains new as the soma which is gathered and offered at the same time; old, as the soma which is gathered at the morning libation and offered at the midday or the evening libation.

soma-draught of this Vāyu may not[1] be wasted. According to some, the stanza is primarily addressed to Indra, the function of Vāyu being subordinate; according to others, it is primarily addressed to both.

Varuṇa is (so called) because he covers (√*vṛ*). The following stanza is addressed to him.

(*Here ends the third section.*)

Varuṇa sent forth the cloud, opening downwards, and created heaven, earth, and the intermediate space. With it, the king of the entire universe moistens earth as rain the barley.[2]

Varuṇa (sent forth) the cloud, whose door opens downwards. (A cloud, *kabandham,* is so called because) *kavanam*, which means water, is deposited into it. Water is called *kabandham* also—the verb *bandh*[3] is used to denote an unfixed state—it is comfortable and unrestrained. He creates heaven, earth, and the intermediate space. With that greatness, the king of the entire universe moistens earth as rain does barley.[4] The following, another stanza, is addressed to him.

(*Here ends the fourth section.*)

I praise him, who possesses seven sisters at the birth of rivers, and who belongs to the middle region, with noble speech, hymns of the manes, and panegyrics of Nābhāka at the same time. Let all others be killed.[5]

I praise him well with speech, i. e. song or eulogy, equal to the respectable hymns of the manes and the panegyrics of Nābhāka at the same time. Nābhāka was a seer who, in his speech, called him one having seven sisters at the birth of these flowing (rivers). He (Varuṇa)[6] is called one belonging to the middle region. Now this is he himself. Let all others be killed.[7] All others, who bear enmity to us, who are evil-minded, i. e. whose minds or whose thoughts are sinful, shall not be suffered to live.

[1] There is no negative particle in the text of the RV. Yāska uses the verb *das* in 1. 9, which is explained by Durga as *kṣayārthasya*. It may be that Yāska derives the negative meaning from the preposition *vi*. However, this explanation does not hold good, for Yāska uses the words: *na vi dasyet*, paraphrased by Durga as *avidaste 'nupakṣiṇe*.

[2] v. 85. 3.

[3] According to Durga, the word *kavanam* is derived from √*kav*, 'to go'. He says: *bandhir anibhṛtatve. nibhṛtas tāvad acapalaḥ. Tadviparītavācī bandhiḥ. Kaṃ ca tac capalaṃ ceti kabandham.*

[4] This stanza does not bring out with sufficient clearness the characteristic of the atmospheric Varuṇa, rain being mentioned as a function of the celestial sun. The stanza therefore leaves one in doubt as to whether Varuṇa is an atmospheric or a celestial deity. The ambiguity, however, is cleared by the next stanza.

[5] vii. 41. 2.

[6] Cf. Professor Macdonell, *op. cit.*, pp. 22–9.

[7] The root *nabh* means 'to kill' according to Ngh. ii. 19.

Rudra[1] is (so called) because he bellows (*rauti*), or because he runs (*druvati*) vociferating (int. of *ru*), or it is derived from the causal of the verb *rud* (to roar). There is a Kaṭhaka passage: Because he has roared, that is the characteristic of Rudra. There is a Hāridravika passage. Because he roared, that is the characteristic of Rudra. The following stanza is addressed to him.

(*Here ends the fifth section.*)

Bear these songs to Rudra of strong bow and swift arrows, the god rich in food, irresistible, the assailant, the disposer, armed with sharp weapons. May he hear us![2]

Bear these songs to Rudra of massive bow and swift arrows, the god who abounds in food,[3] unassailable by his opponents, the assailant, the disposer, and armed with sharp weapons. May he hear us. The word *tigma* is derived from (the root) *tij*, meaning to sharpen. *Āyudham* (weapon) is (so called) from killing. The following, another stanza, is addressed to him.

(*Here ends the sixth section.*)

May that bright weapon of thine, which, hurled down from heaven, flies on earth, avoid us. O god of authoritative speech, thou hast a thousand medicines; do thou not hurt our sons and descendants.[4]

May that bright weapon of thine, which is hurled down from heaven, i.e. from beyond heaven, (avoid us). *Didyut* (bright weapon) is derived from (the root) *do* (to cut), or from *dyu* (to assail), [or from *dyut* (to shine)].[5] It flies on earth. *Kṣmā* means earth, it flies on it or along it. Or else it flies bringing destruction. May it pass us over. O god of authoritative speech, a thousand medicines belong to thee; do thou not injure our sons and grandsons. *Tokam* (offspring) is derived from the verb *tud*[6] (to push). *Tanayam* (son) is derived from the verb *tan* (to spread). Agni is called Rudra also.[7] The following stanza is addressed to him.

(*Here ends the seventh section.*)

O thou who art skilled in praise, be active for the worship of every man; a beautiful hymn for Rudra.[8]

[1] Cf. Professor Macdonell, *op. cit.*, pp. 74–7.

[2] vii. 46. 1.

[3] Yāska explains *svadhāvne* as *annavate.* Roth, *op. cit.*, p. 185, attributes to it the meaning 'independent', *selbständig*, or 'magnificent by nature', *selbstherrlich*; cf. also Muir, *op. cit.*, vol. iv, p. 314.

[4] vii. 46. 3.

[5] Two other derivations suggested are the following: (1) √*dī* 3 cl. 'to shine', √*div* 4 cl. 'to cast'.

[6] He is pushed, as it were, by his father, who urges him to do this or who prohibits him from doing that.

[7] Agni is identified with Rudra; cf. AV. 7. 87. 1: *yo agnau rudra yo apsv antar . . . tasmai rudrāya namo astv agnaye.*

[8] i. 27. 10; SV. 1. 15; 2. 1013.

Jarā[1] means praise; it is derived from (the verb) *jṛ*, meaning to praise. He who receives praise, or awakens another by praise, (is called *jarā-bodha*). Be active, i. e. do that, so that every man may be able to sacrifice; a beautiful hymn for Rudra.

Indra[2] is (so called because) he divides food (*irā* + *dṛ*), or he gives food (*irā* + *dā*), or he bestows food (*irā* + *dhā*), or he sends food (*irā* + *dāraya*), or he holds food (*irā* + *dhāraya*), or he runs for the sake of soma (*indu* + *dru*), or he takes delight in soma (*indu* + *ram*), or he sets beings on fire (√*indh*). It is known: that because they animated him with vital breaths, that is the characteristic of Indra.[3] 'He is (so called) from doing everything (lit. this),' says Āgrāyaṇa. 'He is (so called) from seeing everything (*idam* + *dṛś*),' says Aupamanyava. Or the word is derived from (the verb) *ind*, meaning to be powerful, i. e. being powerful he tears the enemies asunder, or puts them to flight. Or he honours the sacrificers. The following stanza is addressed to him.

(*Here ends the eighth section.*)

Thou didst pierce the spring, create channels, and rich in water send them forth knocking against each other. O Indra, thou didst uncover the great cloud, emit the streams, and smite down the giver (of water).[4]

Thou didst pierce the spring. *Ut-sa* (spring) is (so called) [from moving upwards (*ut*-√*sṛ*)], or from rising upwards (*ut*-√*sad*), or from flowing upwards (*ut*-√*syand*), or it is derived from the verb *ud* (to issue out). Thou didst create its channels. Thou, rich in water, didst send forth these atmospheric multitudes (of clouds) having water, and pressing each other hard. The verb *ram* means to stop or to emit. O Indra, thou didst uncover the great mountain, i. e. the cloud emitted its streams and smote him down, i. e. the giver whose function is to give (rain). The following other stanza is addressed to him.

(*Here ends the ninth section.*)

The wise god, who immediately on his birth became foremost and who surpassed (other) gods in strength, at whose breath heaven and earth tremble on account of the greatness of his might, he, O men, is Indra.[5]

Who as soon as he was born became foremost, the wise god, who, with his strength, i. e. strong action, subdued, i. e. seized all around, protected all around, or surpassed (other) gods; at whose power even heaven and earth trembled on account of the greatness of his might, i. e. on account

[1] Cf. Roth, *op. cit.*, p. 136; Muir, *op. cit.*, vol. iv, pp. 299, 300.

[2] Cf. Professor Macdonell, *op. cit.*, pp. 54–67.

[3] The quotation is untraced.

[4] v. 32. 1; SV. 1. 315.

[5] ii. 12. 1; AV. 20. 34. 1.

of the mightiness of his power. He, O men, is Indra. Thus the gratification of the seer who had an intuitive insight into reality expresses itself conjoined with a narrative.[1]

Parjanyaḥ[2] (cloud) is derived from (the verb) *tṛp* (to be satisfied) by reversing the first and the last (letter): one who gives satisfaction and is favourable to men (*tṛp+janyaḥ = pṛt+janyaḥ = parj+janyaḥ = par+janyaḥ*), or he is (so called because) he is the best conqueror (*paraḥ+ √jin*), or he is the best progenitor (*paraḥ+ √jan*), or he is the bestower of juices (*pra + √ṛj*). The following stanza is addressed to him.

(*Here ends the tenth section.*)

He strikes down trees and he strikes down demons, the entire universe was afraid of the great slaughter. Even the guileless fly from the rainer, when Parjanya thundering strikes the evil-doers.[3]

He strikes down the trees and he strikes down the demons. All beings are afraid of this great slaughter. Great, indeed, is his slaughter. Even the innocent, being afraid, run away from him whose function is to rain, when Parjanya thundering strikes the evil-doers, i. e. men who commit sinful acts.

Bṛhas-patiḥ[4] is the protector or supporter of the great. The following stanza is addressed to him.

(*Here ends the eleventh section.*)

On all sides he saw water bound up by the cloud like fish dwelling in shallow water. Having rent (the cloud) with a dreadful roar, Bṛhaspati drew it out like a cup from a tree.[5]

On all sides he saw water bound up by the all-pervading cloud like fish living in shallow water. He took it out like a cup from the tree. From what verb is *camasaḥ* (cup) derived? (from √*cam*) i. e. they drink in it. Bṛhaspati having rent it with a dreadful roar, i. e. sound.

Brahmaṇas-patiḥ is the protector or supporter of *brahma*. The following stanza is addressed to him.

(*Here ends the twelfth section.*)

All the rays of the sun drank that very stream of water, pervading and flowing downwards, which Brahmaṇaspati pierced with his might, and together they poured an abundant spring rich in water.[6]

[1] According to Durga, the seer Gṛtsamada, a friend of Indra, who had enjoyed his companionship, expresses his gratification in the stanza. He remarks that the stanzas of the RV. often refer to historical events also. He offers an alternative explanation for 'conjoined with a narrative', i.e. which is worthy of being related to posterity.

[2] Cf. Professor Macdonell, *op. cit.*, pp. 83-5.

[3] v. 83. 2.

[4] Cf. Professor Macdonell, *op. cit.*, 101-4. Cf. above, 2. 12; Bṛh. D. ii. 1.

[5] x. 68. 8; AV. 20. 16. 8.

[6] ii. 24. 4.

All the rays of the sun, which appear like the sun, drink that very stream of water, pervading, flowing, and spreading downward, which Brahmaṇaspati pierced with his might, i. e. with power. And together they pour out the abundant springs, rich in water, i. e. abounding in water.

(*Here ends the thirteenth section.*)

Lord of the abode [1]—*kṣetram* (abode) is derived from (the verb) *kṣi*, meaning to dwell—the protector or supporter of the dwelling-place. The following stanza is addressed to him.

(*Here ends the fourteenth section.*)

We will win with the lord of the abode as with a friend; bring to us a horse or cow, O nourisher. He shall be gracious to us for such (gift).[2]

We will win with the lord of the abode as with a very friendly person. Bring, O nourisher, a well-nourished cow and horse. He shall be gracious to us for such (gift).

With strength or wealth. The verb *mṛl* means to give. The following stanza is addressed to him.

(*Here ends the fifteenth section.*)

O lord of the abode, bestow upon us the wave, rich in honey, distilling honey, and well purified like clarified butter, as a cow does its milk. May the lords of the sacred law be gracious to us.[3]

Bestow upon us, O lord of the abode, as a cow her milk, the honeyed wave, distilling honey, i. e. water, well purified like clarified butter. May the lords or protectors of law be gracious to us. The verb *mṛlay* means to protect, or to worship. With reference to this some think that the recurrence of the same expression in the same stanza means tautology, as for instance, 'the wave rich in honey', and 'distilling honey'; others think that the recurrence of the same expression in the same verse (*pāda*) is tautology, as for instance, 'Golden in form, he is golden in appearance'.[4] Another school of thought does not admit tautology, if there is some difference, even if it is very slight, as for instance, 'as from water the frogs', and 'as frogs from water'.[5]

Vāstoṣ-patiḥ [6] (house-lord)—*vāstuḥ* (house) is derived from (the verb)

[1] Cf. Professor Macdonell, *op. cit.*, p. 138.

[2] iv. 57. 1.

[3] iv. 57. 2.

[4] ii. 35. 10.

[5] x. 166. 5.

[6] Cf. Professor Macdonell, *op. cit.*, p. 138.

vas, meaning to dwell—is the lord or protector of the house. The following stanza is addressed to him.

(*Here ends the sixteenth section.*)

O lord of the house, thou art the killer of disease, wearing all forms; be our very kind friend.[1]

O lord of the house, thou art the killer of disease, wearing all forms; be our very happy friend. The word *śeva* is a synonym of happiness (*sukha*). The verb *śiṣ* takes the suffix *va*, which replaces the letter next to the penultimate (i. e. ṣ) and optionally takes *guṇa*.[2]

The word *śiva* is derived from the same root also. He becomes the deity of all those forms that he longs for.

Maghavā assumes every form.[3] This too is a Vedic quotation.

Vācas-pati is the lord or protector of speech. The following stanza is addressed to him.

(*Here ends the seventeenth section.*)

Come again, O lord of speech, together with the divine mind. O lord of wealth, make me happy, let my body (depend) on me alone.[4]

The stanza is explained by the mere reading of it.

Apāṃ napāt[5] is explained by the offspring of the self (*tanū-napāt*).[6] The following stanza is addressed to him.

(*Here ends the eighteenth section.*)

Offspring of waters, who shines within the waters without fuel, whom priests implore in sacrifices; thou hast given us honeyed waters with which Indra grew in vigour.[7]

Who [will shine, i. e.] shines in the interior of waters without fuel, whom wise men praise in sacrifices; O offspring of waters, give us honeyed waters for pressing the soma with which Indra grows in vigour, i. e. in vigorous action.

Yama[8] is (so called) because he governs (√*yam*). The following stanza is addressed to him.

(*Here ends the nineteenth section.*)

With oblation, worship the king, Yama, son of Vivasvat (the sun), who has departed along the great heavenly heights, who has made the path clear for many, and who is the rendezvous of men.[9]

[1] vii. 55. 1.
[2] *Śiṣ* + *va* > *śiva* and, with *guṇa*, *śeva*.
[3] iii. 53. 8.
[4] AV. 1. 1. 2.
[5] Cf. Professor Macdonell, *op. cit.*, pp. 69-71.
[6] See 8. 5.
[7] x. 30. 4; AV. 14. 1. 37.
[8] Cf. Professor Macdonell, *op. cit.*, p. 171.
[9] x. 14. 1; cf. AV. 18. 1. 49.

Who has departed: who has gone round the heavenly heights, i.e. elevations and depressions. The verb *av* means to go.[1] The sense is: and with oblation, worship the king, Yama, the son of Vivasvat (the sun), who has shown the path to many and who is the rendezvous of men. The verb *duvasyati* means to worship. Agni is called Yama also. The following stanzas proclaim him.

(*Here ends the twentieth section.*)

Like a spear hurled, it inspires awe as the archer's arrow of bright appearance.[2]

Yama, indeed, is what is born, Yama, what shall be born; he is the maidens' lover, the matrons' lord.[3]

With the moving and the non-moving oblation we obtain him, the kindled god, as cows do their abode in the evening.[4]

These are hemistichs. Like a spear hurled, it inspires terror (among enemies) or courage (among friends), as does the archer's arrow of bright appearance, of dreadful appearance, [of strong appearance, of glorious appearance], of great appearance, or of shining appearance.

Yama indeed was born, associated with Indra.

Ye are twin brothers, whose mother is here and there.[5]

This too is a Vedic quotation. Yama is, as it were, what is born and what shall be born. Maidens' lover, i.e. one who causes maidens to be loved.[6] Matrons' lord, i.e. one who causes matrons to be protected. Matrons have Agni as their chief deity, on account of their association with sacrifice.

Agni was thy third husband.[7] This too is a Vedic quotation.

As cows obtain their home in the evening so may we obtain the kindled god, who is well kindled with pleasant things, with our non-stationary, moving, i.e. oblation in the form of an animal, and non-moving, stationary, i.e. oblation in the form of herbs.

Mi-tra[8] is (so called) because he preserves (*trāyate*) from destruction (*pra-mī-ti*) or because he runs (*dravati*) measuring things together (√*mi*), or

[1] It is not clear why Yāska introduces the verb *av*, 'to go'. Durga does not throw any light on it.

[2] i. 66. 7.

[3] i. 66. 8.

[4] i. 66. 9. According to Durga, the word *vaḥ* in the text of the RV. is an expletive.

[5] vi. 59. 2.

[6] Indian marriage is accomplished by taking seven steps round the fire-altar. Fire is here called maidens' lover, because fire causes the marriage to be accomplished, with which the period of maidenhood comes to an end.

[7] x. 85. 40; AV. 14. 2. 3.

[8] Cf. Professor Macdonell, *op. cit.*, pp. 29–30.

the word is derived from the causal of (the verb) *mid* (to be fat). The following stanza is addressed to him.

(*Here ends the twenty-first section.*)

Proclaiming, Mitra leads men forth, Mitra supported earth and heaven. Ever watchful, Mitra beheld the tribes. To Mitra sacrifice the fat oblations.[1]

Proclaiming, i. e. speaking encouraging words, Mitra leads men ; Mitra alone supports earth and heaven. Without winking Mitra beholds the tribes. The word *kṛṣṭayaḥ* is a synonym of men, (so called) because they are active, or because their bodies are long (*vi-kṛṣṭa*). 'To Mitra sacrifice the fat oblations' has been explained. The verb *hu* means to give.[2]

Kaḥ is (so called because) he is loving, or surpassing, or happy. The following stanza is addressed to him.

(*Here ends the twenty-second section.*)

In the beginning, the golden foetus took shape ; he was the sole existing lord of the universe. He supported this earth and heaven. Let us, with oblations, worship the god Ka.[3]

The golden foetus ; the foetus made of gold, or he whose foetus is made of gold. The word *garbhaḥ* (foetus) is derived from the verb *gṛbh* (used) in the sense of praising, or (so called because) it swallows useless things. Now when a woman receives the life-germs (*guṇān*) and her own life-germs are brought into contact with them, fertilization takes place.[4] He came into existence in the beginning. He was the sole existing lord of the universe. He supports earth and heaven. 'Let us, with oblations, worship the god Ka' is explained. The verb *vidh* means to give.

Sarasvat has been explained.[5] The following stanza is addressed to him.

(*Here ends the twenty-third section.*)

Be our protector with those waves of thine, O Sarasvat, which are rich in honey and distil clarified butter.[6]

The stanza is explained by the mere reading of it.

(*Here ends the twenty-fourth section.*)

[1] iii. 59. 1.

[2] The sentence is omitted by Durga.

[3] x. 121. 1 ; AV. 4. 2. 7 ; Vs. 13. 4 ; 23. 1 ; 25. 10.

[4] Durga describes the process of fertilization as follows : 'When a woman receives from a man the life-germs, i. e. the essence of the marrow of his bones, &c., in the form of seminal fluid and brings them (i. e. spermatozoa) in contact with her own life-germs, i. e. the essence of her flesh and blood in the form of her germinating fluid, then by the mutual contact of the male and female fluid in the interior of the uterus which is capable of receiving them, fertilization of a woman takes place. Or when a woman admires the qualities of a man, on account of her love for him, and a man a woman, the result of their mutual admiration is passion, and passionate intercourse produces fertilization.'

[5] i. e. By *Sarasvatī*.

[6] vii. 96. 5.

Viśvakarman is the maker of all. The following stanza is addressed to him.

(Here ends the twenty-fifth section.)

Viśvakarman is sagacious, mighty, creator, disposer, and supreme beholder. The objects of their desire rejoice together with food, where beyond the seven seers, they declare (only) one to exist.[1]

Viśvakarman is of a penetrating mind, pervading, creator, disposer, and the most supreme beholder of beings. The objects of their desire, i.e. objects which are loved or sought after, or approached, or thought about, or aimed at. They rejoice with waters. Where these seven seers, i.e. luminaries. Beyond them is the sun. In him (the sun) they (the luminaries) become one. This is with reference to the deity.

Now with reference to the soul.

Viśvakarman is of a penetrating mind, pervading, creator, and disposer, and the most supreme manifester of the senses. The objects of worship of these (senses), i.e. objects desired, or sought after, or approached, or thought about, or aimed at. They rejoice together with food. Where these seven seers, i.e. the senses. Beyond them is the soul. In him (the soul) they (senses) become one. This expounds the course of the life of the soul.[2] With reference to it they relate a legend. Viśvakarman, the son of Bhuvana, sacrificed all beings in a universal sacrifice.[3] He sacrificed even himself in the end. This is indicated by the following stanza.

Who sacrificed all these created beings.[4] The following stanza explains it still more explicitly.

(Here ends the twenty-sixth section.)

O Viśvakarman, growing with oblations, thyself sacrifice earth and heaven. On both sides let other men be stupified. Here may Indra be our inciter.[5]

[1] x. 82. 2.

[2] The manuscripts of the longer recension read *etasmin*, while those of the shorter read *asmin*. I prefer the latter to the former, because a comparison of the *adhi-daivata* and *adhy-ātma* explanation of the stanza shows that Yāska intends to bring about a contrast between his two interpretations. For this reason he uses *teṣam*, *etāni*, *tebhyaḥ*, and *etasmin* in the former, and *eṣām*, *imāni*, *ebhyaḥ* in the latter. The corresponding word for *etasmin* is therefore *asmin*, hence I conclude that the reading of the shorter recension is the correct one.

[3] Universal sacrifice is regarded as very efficacious. Cf. ŚB. xiii. 7. 1. 1: 'Ah, I will sacrifice myself in created beings, and created beings in myself. Then, having sacrificed himself in all created beings and created beings in himself, he acquired superiority, sovereignty, and overlordship over all created beings. Likewise, a man having sacrificed all oblations and all created beings in a universal sacrifice, acquires superiority, sovereignty, and overlordship.' Cf. also Manu, xii. 91; Iśa. U. 6; AP. i. 23. 1; Muir, *op. cit.*, vol. v, p. 372.

[4] x. 81. 1; VS. 17. 17.

[5] x. 81. 6; SV. 2. 939; VS. 17. 22.

O Viśvakarman, growing with oblations, thyself sacrifice earth and heaven. On both sides let other men, i.e. rivals, be stupified. Let Indra, who is pre-eminent in knowledge, here be our inciter.

Tārkṣya [1] is explained by Tvaṣṭṛ: (1) he dwells (*kṣayati*) in the crossed-over place (√*tṝ*), i.e. atmosphere; (2) he protects (*rakṣati*) objects quickly (*tūrṇam*); or (3) it is derived from (the verb) *aś* (to pervade). The following stanza is addressed to him.

(*Here ends the twenty-seventh section.*)

Let us, here, invoke Tārkṣya, who is rich in food, incited by gods, mighty, impeller of chariots, the felly of whose wheel is unhurt and who is a hero in battle, quickly for our welfare.[2]

(Let us invoke) him who is exceedingly rich in food. *Jūti* signifies motion or pleasure; *deva-jūtam* therefore means one who is incited by the gods, or pleased by them. Endowed with might, transporter of chariots, the felly of whose wheel is uninjured and who is victorious in battles. Let us be quick and here invoke Tārkṣya for our welfare. What god other than the atmospheric would the seer have thus addressed?[3] The following stanza is addressed to him.

(*Here ends the twenty-eighth section.*)

Who even spread, with his might, the five tribes in a moment, as the sun, with his light, does the waters. A hundredfold, a thousandfold in his speed. Like a hurled javelin, they cannot keep him back.[4]

Who also spreads five human tribes, in a moment, with his might, i.e. strength, as the sun does the waters with his light. His motion gains a hundredfold, a thousandfold speed. Like a discharged arrow made of reeds, they cannot keep him back.

Manyu [5] (anger) is derived from (the verb) *man*, meaning to shine, or to be angry, [or to slay]: arrows shine through anger. The following stanza is addressed to him.

(*Here ends the twenty-ninth section.*)

Accompanied by thee on the same chariot, O Manyu, let our heroes, demolishing, making hairs stand on their end, unassailable, swift like Maruts, having pointed arrows, sharpening their weapons, fire-incarnate rush forth towards the (enemy).[6]

[1] Cf. Professor Macdonell, *op. cit.*, p. 148.

[2] x. 178. 1; AV. 8. 85. 1; SV. 1. 382.

[3] The characteristic of the atmospheric gods is strength. They perform deeds of valour, and all that requires power. The author thinks that this trait is clearly attributed to Tārkṣya in the stanza, and according to him, therefore, Tārkṣya can be no other than an atmospheric deity.

[4] x. 178. 3; AB. iv. 20.

[5] Cf. Professor Macdonell, *op. cit.*, p. 119.

[6] x. 84. 1; AV. 4. 31. 1.

Having mounted the same chariot with thee, O Manyu, let our heroes, demolishing, causing the hair to stand on end, unassailable, swift like the Maruts, having pointed arrows, sharpening their weapons, rush forward towards the enemy. Fire-incarnate, i.e. destroying like fire, or armed, or wearing a coat of mail.

Dadhikrā has been explained.[1] The following stanza is addressed to him.

(Here ends the thirtieth section.)

Dadhikrā spread out the five tribes with might as the sun the waters with his light. Thousand-gaining, hundred-gaining is the swift courser. May he commingle these speeches with honey.[2]

Dadhikrā spreads out water [with might] with strength as the sun the five human tribes with light. Thousand-gaining, hundred-gaining is the swift, i.e. having speed, courser, i.e. having motion. May he commingle these speeches of ours with honey, i.e. water. *Madhu* (honey) is derived from the verb *dham* (to blow) reversed.

Savitṛ[3] (is so called because) he is the stimulator of all. The following stanza is addressed to him.

(Here ends the thirty-first section.)

Savitṛ has fixed the earth with supports; Savitṛ has fastened heaven in unsupported space; Savitṛ has milked the atmosphere, shaking itself like a horse, and the ocean bound in illimitable space.[4]

Savitṛ caused the earth to be fastened with supports. In the supportless atmosphere Savitṛ has made the heaven firm. Savitṛ has milked the cloud fastened in the atmosphere, i.e. fastened in the illimitable space, or fastened in space which does not move quickly, or hasten, i.e. (the cloud) which moistens, shaking[5] itself like a horse. What other god than the atmospheric one would the seer have thus described? The sun is called Savitṛ also. He is so praised in the *Hiraṇyastūpa* hymn.[6] The seer *Hiraṇyastūpa* proclaimed this hymn in the act of worship. This is indicated by the following stanza.

(Here ends the thirty-second section.)

[1] See 2. 27. Cf. Professor Macdonell, *op. cit.*, p. 148.

[2] iv. 38. 10.

[3] Cf. Professor Macdonell, *op. cit.*, p. 32.

[4] x. 179. 1.

[5] The word *dhuni* is explained by Durga as 'shaking', and also by Roth, *op. cit.*, p. 143. But in his famous lexicon he attributes to it the meaning 'sounding', which is adopted both by Muir, *op. cit.*, vol. iv, pp. 110–11, and Max Müller.

[6] x. 149.

Like Āngirasa Hiraṇyastūpa, I invite thee, O Savitṛ, to this sacrificial food. Thus worshipping and bowing before thee for protection, I kept watch as for a stalk of soma.[1]

Golden tuft of hair: a tuft of hair made of gold or one having a golden tuft of hair. *Stūpa* (tuft of hair) is derived from the verb *styai* (to be collected into a heap), i. e. a collection. O Savitṛ, like Āngirasa, I invite thee to this sacrifice, i. e. sacrificial food. Thus worshipping, bowing before thee for protection, I keep watch as for a stalk of soma.

Tvaṣṭṛ has been explained.[2] The following stanza is addressed to him.

(*Here ends the thirty-third section.*)

The divine stimulator, multiform Tvaṣṭṛ, generated and nourished manifold mankind. All these created beings and the great divinity of the gods are solely his.[3]

The divine stimulator, omniform Tvaṣṭā, nourished mankind by the gift of juice. And he generated them in various ways. All these beings, i. e. waters, are his. And for him is the one great divinity of the gods, i. e. the state of being endowed with wisdom or with the bread of life. The word *as-u* is a synonym of wisdom: (1) it throws out the senseless; and sense is thrown into it (√*as*, to throw); (2) or the word *asu-ratva* has its first letter (*v*) elided.

Vāta[4] (wind) is (so called) because he blows (*vāti*). The following stanza is addressed to him.

(*Here ends the thirty-fourth section.*)

May Vāta blow towards us what is healing, full of happiness and comfort for our heart. He shall prolong our lives.[5]

May Vāta blow towards us the healing medicines and what is full of happiness and comfort for our heart. And may he prolong our life.

Agni has been[6] explained. The following stanza is addressed to him.

(*Here ends the thirty-fifth section.*)

Thou art invited to this beautiful sacrifice for the drinking of soma. Come, O Agni, with the Maruts.[7]

Thou art invited to this beautiful sacrifice for the drinking of soma.

[1] x. 149. 5.

[2] See 8. 13; cf. Professor Macdonell, *op. cit.*, p. 116.

[3] iii. 55. 19; AV. 18. 1. 5.

[4] Cf. Professor Macdonell, *op. cit.*, pp. 81-3.

[5] x. 186. 1; SV. 1. 184; 2. 1190.

[6] See 7. 4.

[7] i. 19. 1; SV. 1. 16.

As such, O Agni, come together with the Maruts. What god other than the atmospheric one would the seer thus address? The following stanza is addressed to him.

(*Here ends the thirty-sixth section.*)

I prepare the sweet mead for thee to drink first. Come, O Agni, with the Maruts.[1]

I prepare the sweet mead, i. e. made of soma, for thee to drink first, i. e. to partake of first. As such, O Agni, come together with the Maruts.

(*Here ends the thirty-seventh section.*)

Vena is derived from (the root) *ven*, meaning to long for. The following stanza is addressed to him.

(*Here ends the thirty-eighth section.*)

This Vena impels them who are in the womb of the variegated one. Light is the chorion in measuring the region of vapours. At the contact of waters and the sun, the wise kiss him with thoughts like an infant.[2]

This Vena impels (them who are) in the womb of the variegated one, i. e. in the womb of one who is endowed with variegated colours, i. e. waters. Light is the chorion, his light serves the purpose of chorion. The chorion develops with the external membrane of the foetus, or it is joined with the external membrane. At the coming together of waters and the sun, wise men kiss, lap, praise, cause to grow, or worship, with hymns as they do an infant. Infant (*śiśu*) is (so called because) he is worthy of praise (*śaṃsanīya*), or it is from (the root) *śi*, meaning to give.[3] Foetus is obtained after a long time.

Asu-nīti is (so called because) it carries breath away (*asūn nayati*). The following stanza is addressed to it.

(*Here ends the thirty-ninth section.*)

O Asunīti, support the mind with us for the continuation of life, prolong well our age. Make us happy in the sight of the sun, do thou increase our body with clarified butter.[4]

O Asunīti, support the mind within us for a longer life. And prolong our age, and make us complete for beholding the sun. The verb *radh* is used in the sense 'to be subdued'.

We will not be subjected to the foe, O King Soma![5] This too is

[1] i. 19. 9; viii. 3. 7; AV. 20. 99. 1; SV. 1. 256; 2. 923.
[2] x. 123. 1; VS. 7. 16.
[3] It is given by man to woman. Durga.
[4] x. 59. 5.
[5] x. 128. 5; AV. 5. 3. 7.

a Vedic quotation. Do thou increase the self, i. e. the body, with clarified butter.

Ṛtaḥ has been explained.[1] The following stanza is addressed to him.

(*Here ends the fortieth section.*)

Of Ṛta, indeed, are the earlier invigorating draughts. Contemplation of Ṛta kills vices. The call of Ṛta awakening and illuminating, pierced even the deaf ears of the living being.[2]

Of Ṛta, indeed, are the earlier invigorating draughts. Consciousness of Ṛta kills all that should be avoided. The call of Ṛta pierces the ears even of the deaf. Deaf, whose ears are closed. Causing to wake and making bright the ears of the living being, of the moving being, of man, of light, or of water.

Indu is derived from (the verb) *indh* (to kindle) or from *ud* (to moisten). The following stanza is addressed to him.

(*Here ends the forty-first section.*)

May I proclaim that to the auspicious Indu who, like one to be invoked, is vigorous. He stirs prayer; the slayer of demons stirs prayer. May he himself drive away from us the mockery of the scoffer with slaughter. May the wicked drop down, lower and lower, like some insignificant thing, may he drop down.[3]

I proclaim that to the auspicious Indu, like one who is worthy of being invoked, who is vigorous, rich in food, or full of desire, he causes our prayers to stir; and the slayer of demons causes them to stir with strength. May he himself drive away the man who scoffs and his mockery from us with slaughter. May the wicked drop down. Even lower than that may he drop down, like an insignificant thing. Some think that repetition (of the same words) adds a greater force to a (particular) sentiment, as for instance: Oh, she is beautiful, oh, she is beautiful. This (repetition) is characteristic (of the style) of Parucchepa.[4] He was a seer. He whose organ is (large) like a joint, he whose organ is in every joint.

With these words, the twenty-seven appellations of deities are dealt with. Hymns are addressed and oblations are offered to them. Of these,

[1] See 2. 25; 3. 4; 4. 9; 6. 22.

[2] iv. 23. 8; cf. 6. 16.

[3] i. 129. 6; cf. Bṛh. D. iv. 4.

[4] Cf. Muir, *op. cit.*, vol. i, p. 195; vol. iii, p. 212. Parucchepa is mentioned in TS. ii. 5. 8. 3. Nṛmedha and Parucchepa dispute as to whose knowledge is of a superior kind. They try to kindle fire in moist wood. The former produces smoke only, the latter a flame, and thus establishes his superiority.

the following, i. e. Vena, Asunitī, Ṛta, and Indu, do not have oblations offered to them.

Prajā-pati [1] is the protector or supporter of creatures. The following stanza is addressed to him.

(*Here ends the forty-second section.*)

O Prajāpati, no one except thyself did encompass all these created things. With whatever desire we sacrifice to thee, let that be ours. May we be lords of treasures.[2]

O Prajāpati, no one, indeed, other than thyself encompassed all those created things. With whatever desire we sacrifice to thee, let that be ours. May we be lords of treasures: (this) is a benediction.

Ahi has been explained.[3] The following stanza is addressed to him.

(*Here ends the forty-third section.*)

With hymns thou singest (the praise) of Ahi, born in the waters, sitting in the lowest part of the rivers, in vapours.[4]

With hymns thou singest (the praise) of Ahi, born in waters, sitting in the lowest part of the rivers, in vapours, [in waters]. *Budhnam* means atmosphere: waters are held bound in it; the other word *budhnam* (body) is derived from the same root also, i. e. breath is held bound in it. He, who is Ahi, is *budhnya*, i. e. a dweller in atmosphere, *budhnam* meaning atmosphere. The following stanza is addressed to him.

(*Here ends the forty-fourth section.*)

May Ahi who dwells in the atmosphere not put us to hurt. May the sacrifice of this man, the lover of sacred rites, never fail.[5]

May Ahi who dwells in the atmosphere not put us to injury. May his sacrifice never fail, i. e. of the lover of sacrifice.

Su-parṇa (having beautiful wings) has been explained.[6] The following stanza is addressed to him.

(*Here ends the forty-fifth section.*)

One had beautiful wings, he has entered the ocean, he beholds this entire universe. With a pure mind I saw him from near, him the mother kisses and he kisses the mother.[7]

One has beautiful wings; he enters into ocean; he beholds all these

[1] Cf. Professor Macdonell, *op. cit.*, p. 118.
[2] x. 121. 10; AV. 7. 80. 3; VS. 10. 20; 23. 65.
[3] See 2. 17.
[4] vii. 34. 16.
[5] vii. 34. 17; cf. Bṛh. D. v. 165.
[6] See 4. 3; 7. 24.
[7] x. 144. 4; AA. iii. 1. 6. 15.

created beings. With a pure mind I saw him. Here the seer, who had intuitive insight into reality, (expresses) his pleasure in a narration.[1]

The mother, i. e. atmospheric speech, kisses him and he kisses the mother. *Purū-ravas* is (so called) because he cries too much. The following stanza is addressed to him.

(Here ends the forty-sixth section.)

On his being born, the goers (*gnāḥ*) sat together and the rivers flowing by themselves strengthened him, when, O Purūravas, the gods strengthened thee for the great battle, for slaying the barbarian.[2]

On his being born the goers, i. e. waters, (so called) from going, or else the divine women, sat together, and the rivers, [flowing by themselves,] moving by themselves, strengthened him, when the gods strengthened thee, O Purūravas, for the great battle, for the delightful combat, for slaying the barbarian, the gods (strengthened thee), the gods.

(Here ends the forty-seventh section.)

CHAPTER XI

Śyena (falcon) has been explained.[3] The following stanza is addressed to him.

(Here ends the first section.)

Having seized soma, the falcon bore a thousand, ten thousand libations together. Here, in the enjoyment of soma, the bountiful left the illiberal behind, and the wise the dull-witted man.[4]

Having seized soma, the falcon carried a thousand, ten thousand libations at the same time. (The word) thousand is used with reference to the sacrifice, in which soma is pressed a thousand times. In the sacrifice there are ten thousand soma-draughts, or there are ten thousand gifts in connexion with the pressing of soma. There the bountiful left the unfriendly, i. e. the non-liberal, behind in the enjoyment of soma, and the wise the dull-witted man.

He is praised with reference to the drinking of soma, and in a hymn addressed to Indra; he is therefore identified with Indra.

[1] Cf. Muir, *op. cit.*, vol. ii, p. 196.
[2] x. 95. 7.
[3] See 4. 24.
[4] iv. 26. 7.

Soma is a plant: the word is derived from (the root) *su* (to press): it is pressed again and again. Its character (as a deity) is mostly secondary and only rarely primary. In order to point out its (primary use) in the hymns relating to soma-juice while it is being purified, we shall quote (the following stanza).

(*Here ends the second section.*)

Be pure with thy sweetest and most gladdening stream. O soma, thou art pressed for Indra to drink.[1]

The stanza is explained by the mere reading of it.

Now here is another stanza addressed to him or to the moon, as follows.

(*Here ends the third section.*)

Because they grind the herbs together, one thinks that he has drunk the soma. Of the soma which the Brāhmaṇas know, none whatsoever partakes.[2]

The hemistich, 'Because they grind the herbs together, one thinks that he has drunk the soma', refers to the uselessly-pressed soma, which is not soma at all. Of the soma which the Brāhmaṇas know, none whatsoever, i. e. no one who does not offer sacrifice, can partake. This is with reference to sacrifice.

Now with reference to the deity. The hemistich, 'Because they grind the herbs together, one thinks that he has drunk the soma', refers to the soma pressed with the Yajus formula, which is not soma at all. Of the soma which the Brāhmaṇas know, i. e. the moon, none whatsoever, i. e. no one who is not a god, can partake.

The following, another stanza, is addressed to him, or to the moon.

(*Here ends the fourth section.*)

O god, when they drink thee, forth thenceforward thou thrivest again. Wind is the protector of soma; the month is the maker of years.

O god, when they begin to drink thee, forth thenceforward thou again thrivest; this refers to some particular libations, or to the first and second fortnights of the lunar month. Wind is the protector of soma. The seer calls wind its protector on account of companionship or extracting the juice.[4] The month is the maker of years, of annual periods, i. e. the plant soma on account of its (assuming) particular shapes, or the moon.

Can-dramās[5] (the moon) is (so called because) it roams about noticing (√*cay* + √*dram*) or is bright and measures (*candra-mā*), or its measure is bright. *Candra* (bright) is derived from (the verb) *cand*, meaning to

[1] ix. 1. 1; SV. 1. 468; 2. 39; VS. 26. 25.
[2] x. 85. 3; AV. 14. 1. 3.
[3] x. 85. 5; cf. AV. 14. 1. 14.
[4] Cp. 2. 20.
[5] Cp. Bṛh. D. vii. 129.

shine. The word *candanam* (sandalwood) is derived from the same root also.

It roams about beautifully, or it roams about for a long time. Or the former part of the word (*candramās*) is derived from (the verb) *cam* (to drink). *Cāru* (bright) is derived from (the verb) *ruc* (to shine) reversed. The following stanza is addressed to him.

(*Here ends the fifth section.*)

When he is born, he is ever new, the banner of day he goes before dawns. Approaching he distributes their share among the gods; the moon extends farther long life.[1]

When he is born he is ever new to the beginning of the first fortnight. 'The banner of days he goes before dawns' refers to the end of the second fortnight.

According to some the second verse has the sun as its deity. 'Approaching he distributes their share to the gods' refers to the half-monthly oblation of clarified butter. The moon farther extends long life.

Mṛtyu (death) is (so called) because he makes people die. 'He is (so called because) he causes the dead to be removed,' says Śatabalākṣa, the son of Mudgala. The following stanza is addressed to him.

(*Here ends the sixth section.*)

Away, O Death, depart along the path that is thine own, but different from the road of the gods. I speak to thee, who hast eyes and possessest the power of hearing. Do not injure our children, nor our heroes.[2]

Away, O Death, certainly, O Death, certainly depart, O Death, with this it is declared, O Death, the dead is for him who causes him to be removed, O Death. It is derived from (the verb) *mad* or from *mud*. The following stanza is addressed to them.

(*Here ends the seventh section.*)

Here is the impetuous meeting of the two mighty ones. O Indra and Viṣṇu, the drinker of the pressed soma-juice avoids you. You two turn aside that which is directed towards mortal man, aye, the dart of the archer Kṛśānu.[3]

The stanza is explained by the mere reading of it.

Viśvānara has been explained.[4] The following stanza is addressed to him.

(*Here ends the eighth section.*)

[1] x. 85. 19; cf. AV. 7. 81. 2.

[2] x. 18. 1; AV. 12. 2. 21; VS. 35. 7.

[3] i. 155. 2. The stanza together with the commentary on x. 18. 1 in the 7th section is omitted by Durga; cf. Roth, *op. cit.*, p. 147.

[4] See 7. 21.

Bring your worship to the great (god) who is being exhilarated, and (who is giver of) food, who is dear to all men, who is all-powerful; to Indra, whose great strength is very overpowering, whose great glory and power heaven and earth honour.[1]

Honour [you], with praise, the great god, giver of sacrificial food, who is being exhilarated, i.e. who is rejoicing, who is being praised, or who is being implored; who is dear to all men, and who is all-powerful; and to Indra, in whose pleasure there is exceedingly great strength and most praiseworthy glory and power bestowed on men. Heaven and earth worship you. What god other than the atmospheric would the seer have thus addressed?

The following, another stanza, is addressed to him.

(Here ends the ninth section.)

Viśvānara the divine stimulator has lifted up the all-impelling immortal light.[2]

The meaning is that Viśvānara, the god who stimulates, has lifted up the all-impelling immortal light.

Dhātṛ[3] is the creator of all. The following stanza is addressed to him.

(Here ends the tenth section.)

May Dhātṛ give uninjured life extending to the sacrificer. We meditate on the goodwill of the god whose laws are true.[4]

May Dhātṛ give prolonged and undecaying livelihood to the liberal worshipper.

We meditate on the goodwill, the blessed will, of the god whose laws are true.

Vidhātṛ is explained by dhātṛ. The following is his incidental mention in a stanza addressed to many deities.

(Here ends the eleventh section.)

In the law of King Soma and Varuṇa, in the protection of Bṛhaspati and Anumati, to-day in thy invocation, O Maghavan, and of Dhātṛ and Vidhātṛ, I partook of the jars.[5]

The meaning is: induced by these deities I partook of the jars full of soma-juice. *Kalaśa* (jar) [from what verb is it derived?] is (so called because) *kalāḥ*, particular measures of soma, are deposited in it (*kalā-* + √*śī*).

[1] x. 50. 1.
[2] vii. 76. 1; cf. Bṛh. D. vi. 11.
[3] Cf. Professor Macdonell, *op. cit.*, p. 115.
[4] AV. 7. 17. 2.
[5] x. 167. 3.

Kaliḥ and *kalāḥ* are both derived from (the root) *kṝ* (to scatter): their measures are scattered.

(*Here ends the twelfth section.*)

Now therefore (we shall deal with) the groups of atmospheric deities. Of these, the Maruts[1] come first. *Ma-rutaḥ*, of measured sound (√*mi* + √*ru*), or of measured brilliancy (√*mi* + √*ruc*), or they run very much (*mahad* + *dru*). The following stanza is addressed to them.

(*Here ends the thirteenth section.*)

Come, O Maruts, with chariots charged with lightning, of good speed, furnished with spears and having horses as their wings. Fly to us like birds, O ye that have wise counsel, with the most wholesome food.[2]

O Maruts, with (chariots) charged with lightning. Of good speed, i.e. that turn well, or praise well, or shine well. Come with chariots furnished with spears. Having horses as their wings, as the means of flying. Fly to us like birds with the most wholesome food. Having wise counsel: whose works are blessed or whose wisdom is blessed.

Rudras have been explained.[3] The following stanza is addressed to them.

(*Here ends the fourteenth section.*)

Come, O Rudras, accompanied by Indra, of one accord, riding in golden chariots for prosperity. This thought from us longs for you, (come) like springs from heaven for one who seeks water in the hot season.[4]

Come, O Rudras, with Indra, accordant for the action of bringing prosperity. This thought from us yearns strongly for you as the thirsty for the divine springs of water. *Tṛṣṇaj* is derived from (the verb) *tṛṣ* (to be thirsty). *Udanyuḥ*[5] (one who seeks water) is derived from the verb *udanya* (to moisten).

Ṛ-bhavaḥ are (so called because) they shine widely (*uru* + √*bhā*), or they shine with sacred rite (*ṛta* + √*bhā*), or they live with sacred rite (*ṛta* + √*bhū*).[6] The following stanza is addressed to them.

(*Here ends the fifteenth section.*)

Having performed laborious works with zeal, institutors of sacrifice, being mortals, they attained immortality. The Ṛbhus, sons of Sudhanvan,

[1] Cf. Professor Macdonell, *op. cit.*, p. 77.

[2] i. 88. 1.

[3] See 10. 5; cf. Professor Macdonell, *op. cit.*, p. 74.

[4] v. 57. 1.

[5] Durga remarks that some commentators explain *udanyu* as a bird called *cātaka*, at whose prayer divine springs of water come down from heaven.

[6] Cf. Professor Macdonell, *op. cit.*, pp. 131–4.

radiant like the sun, mixed things together with their works during the year.[1]

Having finished the works with utmost quickness, the bearers, or the wise Ṛbhus, attained immortality although they were mortals. The Ṛbhus, sons of Sudhanvan, looking like the sun, or wise like the sun. They mixed things together with their works, i. e. actions during the year.

Ṛbhu, Vibhvau, and Vāja were the three sons of Sudhanvan, a descendant of Aṅgiras.[2] With reference to them there are Vedic passages which mention the first and the last (Ṛbhu and Vāja) in the plural number, but not the middle one. With regard to this, i. e. the use of plural number of Ṛbhu and the praising together of the cup, there are many hymns in the ten books (of the Ṛgveda). The rays of the sun are called Ṛbhus also.

When you slept in the house of the unconcealable one, because (you were) there, hence, O Ṛbhus, you did not come here to-day.[3]

The unconcealable one is the sun, (so called because) he cannot be concealed. Because you slept in his house; as long as you remain there, so long you cannot be here.

Aṅgirasas have been explained.[4] The following stanza is addressed to them.

(Here ends the sixteenth section.)

These seers are indeed multiform, moreover they are inscrutable. They are sons of Aṅgiras; they were born of Agni.[5]

These seers have many forms. Their actions are inscrutable, or their wisdom is profound. They are sons of Aṅgiras. 'They were born of Agni': with these words their birth from Agni is described.

The Manes have been explained.[6] The following stanza is addressed to them.

(Here ends the seventeenth section.)

Let the lower manes who press soma, go upwards, up the higher ones, and up the middle ones. May the manes who followed breath, who are harmless, and who know the sacred rites, come to us at our invocations.[7]

Let the lower manes go upwards, let the higher manes go upwards, let the middle manes go upwards. Who press soma, i. e. who prepare the soma-juice. Who went in pursuit of breath, i. e. life. Who are harmless, i. e. who are not hostile. And who know what is truth and what is sacrifice. May the manes come at our call. Yama is said to be an

[1] i. 110. 4.
[2] Cp. Bṛh. D. iii. 83.
[3] i. 161. 11.
[4] See 3. 17; cf. Professor Macdonell, *op. cit.*, p. 142.
[5] x. 62. 5.
[6] See 4 21.
[7] x. 15. 1; AV. 18. 1. 44; VS. 19. 49.

atmospheric deity,[1] the manes are therefore regarded as atmospheric deities also. Aṅgirasas have been explained.[2] Manes have been explained.[3] Bhṛgus have been explained.[4] *Atharvāṇas*,[5] i. e. motionless—the verb *tharv* means 'to move', its negation—i. e. who are without motion. The following stanza is addressed to them in common.

(*Here ends the eighteenth section.*)

Aṅgirasas and our manes of ninefold gaits, Atharvāṇas and Bhṛgus, the soma-pressers: may we be in the goodwill of those holy ones, in the blessed favour of their minds.[6]

Aṅgirasas and our manes of nine gaits, i.e. whose ways of going lead in nine directions. Atharvāṇas and Bhṛgus, the soma-pressers, i.e. who prepare the soma-juice. May we be in the goodwill, in the blessed will of the holy ones, in the auspicious, excellent, generous, or blessed favour of their minds. 'This refers to a group of atmospheric deities,' say the etymologists. 'They are manes,' says the tradition. Moreover, seers are praised.

(*Here ends the nineteenth section.*)

Their splendour is dazzling like that of the sun, their greatness is unfathomed like that of the ocean, their speed is like that of the wind. Your hymn, O Vasiṣṭhas, cannot be imitated by any other.[7] This is the (panegyric).

Āptyāḥ[8] is derived from (the verb) *āp* (to obtain). The following is their incidental occurrence in a stanza addressed to Indra.

(*Here ends the twentieth section.*)

Praiseworthy, multiform, great, most supreme lord, worthy of being obtained among those to be obtained, he crushed seven demons with his strength; and he overpowers many adversaries.[9]

Worthy of praise, of many forms, very wide, most supreme master, worthy of being obtained of those who should be obtained, who tears to pieces the seven givers or the seven gift-makers with his strength; who overpowers many adversaries. The verb *sākṣ* means to obtain.

(*Here ends the twenty-first section.*)

[1] Cf. Professor Macdonell, *op. cit.*, p. 171.

[2] See 3. 17; cf. Professor Macdonell, *op. cit.*, p. 142.

[3] See 4. 21.

[4] See 3. 17; cf. Professor Macdonell, *op. cit.*, p. 140.

[5] Professor Macdonell, *op. cit.*, p. 141.

[6] x. 14. 6; AV. 18. 1. 58.

[7] vii. 33. 8.

[8] Cf. Professor Macdonell, *op. cit.*, p. 67.

[9] x. 120. 6; AV. 20. 107. 9.

Now, therefore, (we shall deal with) the groups of atmospheric goddesses. Of these Aditi [2] comes first. Aditi has been explained.[1] The following stanza is addressed to her.

(*Here ends the twenty-second section.*)

At the birth and ordinance of Dakṣa, thou attendest, O Aditi, on the two kings Mitra and Varuṇa. In births of diverse forms, Aryaman of the seven priests and rich in chariots has his path unobstructed.[2]

O Aditi, thou attendest on two kings, Mitra and Varuṇa, at the birth and the ordinance, i. e. action, of Dakṣa. The verb *vivāsti* is used in the sense of attending. *Rich in obligations, he attends upon* (*gods*).[3] Or it is used in the sense of 'praying for'.[4] Aryaman, i. e. the sun, having many chariots,[5] and whose path is unobstructed, i. e. unimpeded, chastises the enemy.[6] Seven priests: seven rays extract juices for him, or seven seers praise him. In births of diverse forms, i. e. activities, sunrises.[7]

They say that Dakṣa is a son of Aditi and is praised among the sons of Aditi. But Aditi is the daughter of Dakṣa.

Dakṣa was born from Aditi, and Aditi sprang into life from Dakṣa.[8] This (is the text) also.[9]

How can this be possible? (We reply) they may have had the same origin, or, in accordance with the nature of gods, they may have been born from each other, or they may have derived their characteristics from each other.[10] Agni is called Aditi also. The following stanza is addressed to him.

(*Here ends the twenty-third section.*)

May we be those to whom, O Aditi, mistress of noble wealth, thou wilt grant perfect innocence, and whom thou wilt impel with blessed strength, and food rich in offspring.[11]

O Aditi, mistress of noble wealth, (may we be they) to whom thou givest innocence, i. e. faultlessness, in the entire sphere of action. *Āgas* is derived from (the root) *gam*, preceded by the preposition *ā*. *Enas* (sin) is derived from (the root) *i* (to go). *Kil-bīṣam*: destroyer of glory, i. e. averseness to the performance of noble deeds: it destroys the reputation of a person.

[1] Cf. Professor Macdonell, *op. cit.*, p. 120.

[2] x. 64. 5; cf. Bṛh. D. vii. 104.

[3] i. 12. 9; SV. 2. 196; VS. 6. 23.

[4] i. e. She prays that 'may these two sons of mine work for the good of the world'. Durga.

[5] According to Durga it means 'very swift'.

[6] By the enemy Durga understands darkness, i. e. the sun dispels darkness.

[7] i. e. The rising of the sun in different parts of the sky at different periods. Durga.

[8] x. 72. 4.

[9] According to Durga, 'also' here denotes cause.

[10] Cf. 7. 4; ŚB. iii. 1. 3. 3. See Roth, *op. cit.*, pp. 150-1; Muir, *op. cit.*, vol. iv, p. 13.

[11] i. 94. 15.

And whom thou impellest with blessed strength, i. e. vigour, and goods, [wealth] rich in offspring. May we be those persons.

Saramā is (so called) from moving (√*sṛ*). The following stanza is addressed to her.

(*Here ends the twenty-fourth section.*)

With what desire has Saramā attained this place? The road leads far off to distant regions. What is the errand for us? what was the night? and how hast thou crossed the waters of the Rasā?[1]

With what desire has Saramā come here? The road is distant. *Jaguriḥ* (leading) is derived from the intensive form of the verb *gam* (to go). (Far off), i. e. winding with curves. What was the errand with regard to us? what night? *Paritakmyā* means night, (so called) because *takma* surrounds it on both sides. *Takma* is a synonym of heat, (so called) because it goes away (√*tak*). How hast thou crossed the waters of the Rasā? Rasā, a river, is derived from (the verb) *ras*, meaning to make a sound. Or else how (hast thou crossed) those roaring waters? There is a legend that the bitch of the gods, sent forth by Indra, conversed with the demons called Paṇis.

Sarasvatī has been explained.[2] The following stanza is addressed to her.

(*Here ends the twenty-fifth section.*)

May Sarasvatī, who purifies, who possesses large stores of food, and who is rich in devotion, like our sacrifice.[3]

May Sarasvatī, our purifier, having abundant stores of food, and rich in devotion, i. e. in acts of worship, like the sacrifice.[4] The following, another stanza, is addressed to her.

(*Here ends the twenty-sixth section.*)

With her banner Sarasvatī makes the great ocean manifest. She presides over all devotions.[5]

With her banner, i. e. with her activity or wisdom, Sarasvatī makes the great ocean manifest, i. e. causes it to be known. She presides over all these sacrifices. This is applied to the objects of speech; speech is therefore regarded as belonging to the sphere of the atmosphere.

Speech has been explained.[6] The following stanza is addressed to her.

(*Here ends the twenty-seventh section.*)

[1] x. 108. 1; cf. Bṛh. D. viii. 26.
[2] See 2. 23.
[3] i. 3. 10; SV. 1. 189; VS. 20. 84.
[4] Durga explains it as 'may she carry the sacrifice to the gods'.
[5] i. 3. 12; VS. 20 86.
[6] See 2. 23.

When Vāc, speaking unknown words, sat down as the charming queen of the gods, the four milked food and milk, but where did her best portion go?[1]

When Vāc, speaking unknown, i.e. unintelligible, words,[2] sat down as the [charming] pleasant[3] queen of the gods, all the four quarters milked food and waters. But where did her best portion go?[4] It may be that which goes to the earth or that which is taken away by the rays of the sun. The following, another stanza, is addressed to her.

(*Here ends the twenty-eighth section.*)

The gods generated divine speech. Animals of all shapes speak it. May that charming milch cow, in the form of speech bestowing on us strength-giving food, easily approach us.[5]

The gods generated the goddess Vāc.[6] Animals of all shapes speak it, i.e. animals whose sounds are articulate, and those whose sounds are inarticulate. May that pleasant milch cow, in the form of Vāc bestowing food and juice on us, easily approach us.

'Anumatī and Rākā are two wives of gods,' say the etymologists. 'They are the days of full moon,' say the ritualists. It is known: that which is the earlier day of full moon is Anumatī, that which is later is Rākā.[7]

Anumati (approbation) is (so called) on account of approving (*anu* + √*man*). The following stanza is addressed to her.

(*Here ends the twenty-ninth section.*)

O Anumati, do thou approve of it and bring peace to us. Impel us for expert judgement, prolong our lives.[8]

Do thou approve, O Anumati, and bring happiness to us. Bestow food on our offspring and prolong our lives.

Rākā is derived from (the verb) *rā*, meaning to give. The following stanza is addressed to her.

(*Here ends the thirtieth section.*)

With noble praise I call upon Rākā of noble invocations. Let the blessed one hear us and wake up herself. With unbreakable needle let her sew the work. May she give us a hero worthy of a hundredfold praise.[9]

[1] viii. 100. 10.

[2] i.e. In the form of thunder. Durga.

[3] i.e. Giving satisfaction or delight to the whole world on account of producing rain. 'Sat down,' i.e. when she begins to produce rain. Durga.

[4] i.e. Having caused the herbs to grow, where do these showers go; where do they come from every year? Durga.

[5] viii. 100. 11.

[6] Durga explains *devī* as 'giver of waters'.

[7] AB. vii. 11; Ṣaḍ. B. iv. 6; GB. 2. 1. 10.

[8] AV. 7. 20. 2; VS. 34. 8; cf. Bṛh. D iv. 88.

[9] ii. 32. 4; AV. 7. 48. 1.

With excellent praise, I invoke Rākā, to whom excellent invocations are addressed. May the blessed one hear us. May she wake up herself. With an unbreakable needle may she sew the work together, i. e. function of procreation. *Sūcī* (needle) is derived from (the verb) *siv* (to sew). May she give us a hero of a hundred gifts, worthy of praise, i. e. whose praises should be proclaimed.

'Sinīvālī and Kuhū are two wives of gods,' say the etymologists. 'They are the days on which the moon is invisible,' say the ritualists. It is known: that which is the earlier day on which the moon is invisible is Sinīvālī, that which is later is Kuhū.[1]

Sinī-vālī: *sinam* means food: it makes created beings strong (*sināti*); *vālam* means a particular period, and is derived from (the verb) *vṛ* (to cover)—i. e. rich in food in that period, or hairy. Or it is (so called) because the moon being very minute during this period is to be attended, as it were, with a hair. The following stanza is addressed to her.

(*Here ends the thirty-first section.*)

O broad-hipped Sinīvālī, thou who art the sister of the gods, enjoy this oblation which is offered to thee, and grant, O goddess, offspring to us.[2]

O Sinīvālī, having broad thighs. *Stuka*, (thigh or tuft of hair), derived from (the verb) *styai* (to be heaped together), means a heap, i. e. having a large tuft of hair, or praise. Thou art the sister of the gods. *Svaṣā* (sister) = *su* + *asā*, i. e. she who sits (*sīdati*) among her own people (*sveṣu*). Enjoy this oblation, i. e. food. O goddess, grant us offspring.

Kuhū is derived from the verb *guh* (to conceal). Or (it is said) where has she been? Or at what place is she invoked? Or where does she sacrifice the offered oblation? The following stanza is addressed to her.

(*Here ends the thirty-second section.*)

I invoke again and again Kuhū of noble actions and invocations, who knows her work, in this sacrifice. May she give us the glory of our manes: as such, O goddess, we worship thee with oblation.[3]

I invoke Kuhū of noble deeds, to whom the actions are known, and of noble invocations, in this sacrifice. May she give us the glory of our manes, i. e. ancestral property or ancestral fame. 'As such, O goddess, we worship thee with oblations' is explained.

Yamī has been explained.[4] The following stanza is addressed to her.

(*Here ends the thirty-third section.*)

[1] AB. viii. 1; Ṣaḍ. B. iv. 6; GB. 2. 1. 10.
[2] ii. 32. 6; AV. 7. 46. 1; VS. 34. 10.
[3] AV. 7. 47. 1.
[4] Cf. 10. 19; Professor Macdonell, *op. cit.*, p. 171.

(Embrace) another, O Yamī, another shall embrace thee as a creeper a tree. Do thou seek his heart and he thine, with him make the blessed contract.[1]

Indeed, Yamī, thou wilt embrace some one else and he thee, as a creeper does a tree. Do thou seek his heart and let him seek thine. With him make the blessed contract, i. e. blessed and auspicious. Yamī loved Yama who repulsed her, such is the legend.

(*Here ends the thirty-fourth section.*)

Urvaśī has been explained.[2] The following stanza is addressed to her.

(*Here ends the thirty-fifth section.*

Who shone like a flash of lightning bearing to me the desired watery (gifts). From the waters has been born a noble and strong hero. Urvaśī extends long life.[3]

Who shone like a flash of lightning bringing to me the desired watery (gifts), i. e. waters of the world of the atmosphere. When (this takes place) then certainly is born from the waters this lord, strong hero, i. e. man, or who is favourable to men, or the offspring of men. Well born, very nobly born. Now Urvaśī increases long life.

Pṛthivī (earth) has been explained.[4] The following stanza is addressed to her.

(*Here ends the thirty-sixth section.*)

There indeed, O earth, thou bearest the instrument of splitting the mountains, O great one, and abounding in heights, thou quickenest the earth with thy might.[5]

Truly thou holdest, O earth, the instrument of splitting, of rending, [of tearing asunder] mountains, i. e. clouds, in that region, O great one, thou, abounding in declivities, or in water, quickenest the earth with thy greatness.

Indrāṇi is the wife of Indra. The following stanza is addressed to her.

(*Here ends the thirty-seventh section.*)

I have heard the wife of Indra to be the most fortunate among these women. Like others, her husband never dies from old age. Indra is supreme over all.[6]

1 x. 10. 14; cf. AV. 18. 1. 16.
2 See 5. 13; cf. Professor Macdonell, *op. cit.*, p. 134.
3 x. 95. 10.
4 See 1. 13. 14.
5 v. 84. 1.
6 x. 86. 11; AV. 20. 126. 11. For the refrain cf. *Deutschland über alles.*

I have heard the wife of Indra to be the most fortunate among these women. Never, indeed, does her husband die from old age even in extreme years. We say this to Indra, who is supreme over all. The following, another stanza, is addressed to her.

(Here ends the thirty-eighth section.)

I never rejoice, O Indrāṇi, without my friend Vṛṣākapi, whose watery and dear oblation here goes to the gods. Indra is supreme over all.[1]

O Indrāṇī, I never enjoy myself without my friend Vṛṣākapi, whose watery oblation, i.e. cooked in water, or seasoned with water, which is pleasant, now goes to the gods. We say this to Indra, who is supreme over all.

Gaurī is derived from (the verb) *ruc*, meaning to shine. This other word *gaura*, which means white colour, is derived from the same root also: it is praiseworthy. The following stanza is addressed to her.

(Here ends the thirty-ninth section.)

Fashioning waters Gaurī lowed, one-footed, two-footed, aye, four-footed, eight-footed, nine-footed, and having become thousand-syllabled in the highest heaven.[2]

Fashioning, creating waters Gaurī lowed. One-footed with the middle (air). Two-footed, with the middle (air) and the sun. Four-footed, with the quarters. Eight-footed, with the quarters and intermediate quarters. Nine-footed, with the quarters, intermediate quarters, and the sun. Thousand-syllabled, i.e. having much water in the highest heaven. The following, another stanza, is addressed to her.

(Here ends the fortieth section.)

Oceans flow down from her, thereby the four quarters subsist. Thence flows the imperishable; on that the entire universe lives.[3]

Oceans flow down from her, i.e. the clouds pour rain, and all the created beings, dependent on the quarters, live thereby. Thence flows the imperishable water; on that all created beings live.

Gauḥ has been explained.[4] The following stanza is addressed to her.

(Here ends the forty-first section.)

The cow lowed after the blinking calf. On its forehead she made the sound *hiṅ* for recognition. Longing for the flow of the warm milk-stream, she utters a lowing sound and swells with milk.[5]

[1] x. 86. 12; AV. 20. 126. 12.
[2] i. 164. 41; cf. AV. 9. 10. 21.
[3] i. 164. 42; AV. 9. 10. 22; 13. 1. 42.
[4] See 2. 5.
[5] i. 164. 28; cf. AV. 9. 10. 6.

The cow lowed after the calf, who blinks, or who does not blink, i. e. the sun. On its forehead she made the *hiṅ* sound for recognition. Longing for the flow, i. e. oozing, of the warm, i. e. fresh milk,[1] she utters a lowing sound and swells with milk. Or else she lows like *māyu*, i. e. the sun. This is the atmospheric speech. 'This is the giver of warm milk,' say the ritualists.

Dhenu (milch cow) is derived from (the root) *dhe* (to suck), or from *dhi* (to nourish). The following stanza is addressed to her.

(*Here ends the forty-second section.*)

I call upon this milch cow which is easy to milk. The deft-handed cow-herd shall milk her. Savitṛ shall generate the best stimulation. I will well proclaim the heat kindled around us.[2]

I call upon this milch cow which is milked easily, and the cow-milker of blessed hand milks her. May Savitṛ produce the best stimulation for us. This, indeed, is the best of all stimulations, the water or milk which is prepared with a yajus formula.

Fire is kindled all around, I will proclaim it well. This is the atmospheric speech. 'This is the giver of warm milk,' say the ritualists.

Aghnyā (cow) is (so called because) she is not to be killed, ($a+\sqrt{han}$), or she is the destroyer of sin. The following stanza is addressed to her.

(*Here ends the forty-third section.*)

Be indeed fortunate with good pasture, hence may we also be fortunate. Eat grass, O cow, and always drink limpid water while wandering.[3]

Be fortunate indeed as eating good pasture. Hence may we now be fortunate. Eat grass, O cow! Always drink limpid water while wandering. The following, another stanza, is addressed to her.

(*Here ends the forty-fourth section.*)

Making the *hiṅ* sound, the treasure queen, desiring the calf of treasures with her mind, has approached. Let this cow yield milk for the two Aśvins, and may she grow for greater prosperity.[4]

The stanza is explained by the mere reading of it.

Pathyā means fortune, (so called because) it dwells in the atmosphere the word *panthās* denoting atmosphere.

The following stanza is addressed to it.

(*Here ends the forty-fifth section.*)

[1] According to Durga, 'the oozing', &c., is the flow of rain and the evaporation of water.

[2] i. 164. 26; AV. 7. 73. 7; 9. 10. 4.

[3] i. 164. 40; AV. 7. 73. 11; 9. 10. 20.

[4] 164. 27; AV. 7. 73. 8; 9. 10. 5.

The fortune which comes abounding in wealth to riches is best indeed in the distant atmosphere. May she preserve us at home and abroad. May she, whose guardians are the gods, be easy of access.[1]

Fortune is indeed best in the distant atmosphere. She comes abounding in wealth to riches, i. e. treasures which are worthy of being sought after. May she protect us at home, i. e. in our own dwelling-place, and abroad, i. e. in travelling to distant places. May she be easy of access. The guardian goddess, i. e. who protects the gods, or whom the gods protect.

Uṣas (dawn) has been explained.[2] The following stanza is addressed to her.

(*Here ends the forty-sixth section.*)

Being afraid, Uṣas has fled from the shattered car, because the strong bull has struck it down.[3]

Being afraid, Uṣas has fled from the shattered car, i. e. the cloud. *Anas* means wind, derived from (the verb) *an* (to breathe). Or else it may be for the sake of comparison, i. e. as if from the car. *Anas* means a car, (so called) because rags are tied to (*ā-nah*) it, or it may be derived from (the verb) *an*, meaning to live: it is a means of livelihood for people.[4]

Cloud is called *anas* from the same verb also. Because the strong bull, the rainer, i. e. the atmospheric god, has struck it down. The following, another stanza, is addressed to her.

(*Here ends the forty-seventh section.*)

Here lies her car, shattered and all broken into pieces. She has fled afar.[5]

Here lies her car, shattered in such a manner as if it were a different car altogether. Broken into pieces, i. e. without a single connected piece. Dawn has fled afar, being pushed out, or being pursued.

Iḷā has been explained.[6] The following stanza is addressed to her.

(*Here ends the forty-eighth section.*)

May Iḷā, the mother of the herd, or Urvaśī praise us with the rivers. May Urvaśī, praising with the mighty heaven, and concealing the prepared thing of the living man, accompany us for the increase of the strength-giving portion.[7]

[1] x. 63. 16.

[2] See 2. 18.

[3] iv. 30. 10.

[4] This shows that some sort of hackney carriages, or carriages which plied for hire, were obtainable in the time of Yāska.

[5] iv. 30. 11.

[6] See 8. 7.

[7] v. 41. 19; cf. Bṛh. D. v. 37.

May Iḷā, the mother of the herd [the mother of all], or Urvaśī with rivers praise us. Or may Urvaśī, praising with the mighty heaven, i. e. the great heaven, and concealing the prepared thing, i. e. the ready-made thing of the living being, [of the man,] of light, or of water, attend to the increase of our food.

Rodasī is the wife of Rudra.[1] The following stanza is addressed to her.

(*Here ends the forty-ninth section.*)

We invoke indeed the glorious chariot of the Maruts, wherein has stood Rodasī, bearing delightful things, in the company of the Maruts.[2]

We invoke the swift, the famous chariot of the Maruts, i. e. the cloud, wherein has stood Rodasī bearing the delightful waters, in the company of, i. e. together with, the Maruts.

(*Here ends the fiftieth section.*)

CHAPTER XII

Now, therefore, (we shall deal with) the celestial deities. Of these, the Aśvins come first. The Aśvins[3] are (so called) because they two pervade (√*as*) everything, one with moisture, the other with light. 'They are called Aśvins on account of their having horses (*aśva*),' says Aurṇavābha.[4] Who then are the Aśvins? According to some they are heaven and earth;[5] day and night, according to others. Some take them to be the sun and the moon, (while) the historians regard them as two virtuous kings. Their time is after midnight, which, in consequence, is an impediment to the appearance of light. The part in the dark is the atmosphere, and the part in the light is the sun. The following stanza is addressed to them.

(*Here ends the first section.*)

[1] Cf. Sāyaṇa on i. 167. 4: 'Some say that the wife of *Rudra* is called *Rodasī*, others think that this is the name given to the wives of the Maruts. The latter view is the right one.' Cf. *op. cit.*, i. 167. 5; Rodasī is the wife of Marut, or lightning. Cf. Muir, *op. cit.*, vol. iv, p. 420.

[2] v. 56. 8.

[3] Cf. Professor Macdonell, *op. cit.*, p. 49.

[4] Cf. Muir, *op. cit.*, vol. ii, p. 176.

[5] Cf. ŚB. iv. 1. 5. 16:
अथ यदश्विनावितीमे ह वै द्यावापृथिवी प्रत्यक्षमश्विनाविमे हीदं सर्वमश्नुवाताम् ।

You wandered like two black clouds during the nights. O Aśvins, when was it that you came to the gods?[1]

The stanza is explained by the mere reading of it.[2] It is with reference to their separate individual praise that the hemistich is addressed to the two Aśvins, who are mostly praised conjointly, and whose time and functions are identical. One is called the son of night, the other son of dawn. The following, another stanza, is addressed to them.

(*Here ends the second section.*)

Born here and there, they are conjointly praised with reference to their own names and a spotless body. One of you is the victor, the promoter of noble sacrifice; the other is regarded as the blessed son of heaven.[3]

Born here and there they two are praised together with reference to a body unstained by sin and to their own names. One of you two is the victor, the furtherer of very great strength, i.e. belonging to the middle region; the other is considered the blessed son of heaven, i.e. the sun. The following, another stanza, is addressed to them.

(*Here ends the third section.*)

Awaken the two early-yoking Aśvins. May they come here to drink of this soma.[4]

Awaken the Aśvins, who yoke early in the morning. May they two come here to drink of this soma. The following, another stanza, is addressed to them.

(*Here ends the fourth section.*)

Offer sacrifice and impel the two Aśvins in the morning; there is no divine worship: that in the evening is unaccepted; also another than us sacrifices and gives satisfaction. The earlier a sacrificer worships, the more he gains.[5]

Sacrifice and impel the Aśvins early in the morning; there is not an oblation offered to the gods in the evening: that is not enjoyed, another than us should sacrifice and give satisfaction. The earlier one sacrifices, the more he wins, i.e. he is the best winner. Their time is up to the rising of the sun; during this period[6] other deities are invoked.

Uṣas is derived from (the verb) *vaś*, meaning to desire. The other *uṣas*

[1] The quotation is untraced.

[2] Cf. Roth, *op. cit.*, p. 159.

[3] i. 181. 4.

[4] i. 22. 1.

[5] v. 77. 2.

[6] According to Durga, the time immediately following that of the Aśvins is the time for sacrifice, during which many deities are invoked.

(dawn) is derived from (the verb) *vas* (to shine), and belongs to the middle region. The following stanza is addressed to her.

(*Here ends the fifth section.*)

O Uṣas, abounding in food, bring to us variegated (wealth), with which we may support son and grandson.[1]

O Uṣas, rich in food, bring that [variegated,] noteworthy, [respectable] wealth to us, so that we may support our sons and grandsons thereby. The following, another stanza, is addressed to her.

(*Here ends the sixth section.*)

These same dawns have raised their banners, they anoint the sun in the eastern half of the region. Like bold heroes making their weapons ready, the red mother cows proceed.[2]

These same dawns have lifted up their banner, i. e. light. The plural number may have been used for one deity only, in order to show respect. Together they anoint the eastern half of the intermediate world with the light. Like bold heroes making their weapons bright.[3] The preposition *nir* has been used in place of the preposition *sam*.

I go to their meeting-place as a woman to her lover.[4] This too is a Vedic quotation.

They go forth; the rays (*gāvaḥ*) are (so called) on account of going (√*gam*). They are called red (*a-ruṣīḥ*), on account of shining (*ā*-√*ruc*). Mothers (*mā-taraḥ*): the measurers (√*mā*) of light.

Sūryā[5] is the wife of the sun. This very dawn (*uṣas*) after the expiry of a good deal of time (becomes *sūryā*). The following stanza is addressed to her.

(*Here ends the seventh section.*)

O Sūryā, ascend this world of nectar, which is very bright, free from impurities, multiform, golden in colour, easy to turn and with beautiful wheels, in order to bring comfort to thy husband.[6]

Shining beautifully, whose impurity has been destroyed, omniform. Or the terms may have been used for the sake of comparison, i. e. bright like a beautiful Kiṃśuka flower, soft like the silk-cotton tree. *Kiṃśuka* is derived from (the verb) *kraṃś*, meaning to illumine. *Śalmaliḥ* (silk-cotton tree) is (so called) because it is easy to pierce, or because it abounds in pricking

[1] i. 92. 13; SV. 2. 1081; VS. 34. 33.

[2] i. 92. 1; SV. 2. 1105; cf. Bṛh. D. iii. 124.

[3] i.e. They make the world bright as soldiers do their weapons. Durga.

[4] x. 34. 5. The passage is cited to illustrate the interchange of the prepositions *nir* and *sam*.

[5] x. 85. 20; cf. AV. 14. 1. 61.

[6] Cf. Professor Macdonell, *op. cit.*, p. 30.

thorns. O Sūryā, ascend the world of nectar, i.e. of water. Do so, in order to bring happiness to thy husband. There is a Brāhmaṇa passage: Savitṛ gave Sūryā in marriage to King Soma, or to Prajāpati.[1]

Vṛṣākapāyī is the wife of Vṛṣākapi. This very (*Sūryā*) after the expiry of a good deal of time (becomes *Vṛṣākapāyī*). The following stanza is addressed to her.

(*Here ends the eighth section.*)

O Vṛṣākapāyī, abounding in wealth, having noble sons and fair daughters-in-law, Indra shall eat thy bulls and the agreeable oblation, which can do everything. Indra is supreme over all.[2]

O Vṛṣākapāyī, abounding in wealth. Having a noble son, i.e. the atmospheric Indra. Having a fair daughter-in-law, i.e. the atmospheric speech. A daughter-in-law is (so called because) she sits well, or procures well. Or else she procures *su*, which means offspring. May Indra devour thy sprinkling bulls, i.e. these atmospheric heaps of clouds. *Ukṣan* (sprinkling bull) is derived from the verb *ukṣ*, meaning to grow, i.e. they grow with water. Make thy oblation agreeable, which brings infinite happiness [the oblation which brings happiness]. We say this to Indra, i.e. the sun, who is supreme over all.

Saraṇyū is (so called) on account of moving. The following stanza is addressed to her.

(*Here ends the ninth section.*)

They concealed the immortal lady from the mortals; having made one of like appearance, they gave her to the sun. And Saraṇyū bore the Aśvins when that took place, and deserted the two twins.[3]

They concealed the immortal lady from the mortals. Having made one of similar appearance, they gave her to the sun. Saraṇyū supported the Aśvins when that took place, and deserted the two twins. 'The atmospheric (Indra) and the atmospheric speech (are meant),' say the etymologists; 'Yama and Yamī,' say the historians. With reference to this, they relate a legend.[4]

Saraṇyū daughter of Tvaṣṭṛ bore twins, Yama and Yamī, to Vivasvat the sun. She having substituted another lady of similar appearance, and having assumed the shape of a mare, ran away. He, Vivasvat, the sun, having also assumed the shape of a horse, pursued her, and joined her.

[1] AB. iv. 7; cf. KB. xviii. 1; cf. Gune, *Bhand. Comm. Vol.*, p. 49

[2] x. 86. 13; AV. 20. 126. 13.

[3] and [4] The legend is related in greater detail in Bṛh. D. vi. 162–3; vii. 1–7; see Professor Macdonell's edition, vol. i, pp. 78–9; vol. ii, pp. 251–3. Cf. Roth, *op. cit.*, p. 161; Muir, *op. cit.*, vol. v, pp. 227–8.

Thence the Aśvins were born. Manu was born from the lady of similar appearance. This is indicated by the following stanza.

(*Here ends the tenth section.*)

Tvaṣṭṛ celebrates the marriage of his daughter: hence this entire universe comes together. Being married, the wife of the great Vivasvat, and the mother of Yama, disappeared.[1]

Tvaṣṭṛ celebrates the marriage of his daughter.

[This entire universe comes together.] All these created beings come together. Being married, the wife of the mighty Vivasvat, and the mother of Yama, disappeared, i. e. the night, who is the wife of the sun, disappears at sunrise.

(*Here ends the eleventh section.*)

Savitṛ has been explained.[2] His time is that when the sky, with its darkness dispelled, is overspread by the rays of the sun. The following stanza is addressed to him.

(*Here ends the twelfth section.*)

The wise one puts on all forms. He has generated bliss for the biped and the quadruped. Noble Savitṛ has looked on heaven. He shines bright after the departure of dawn.[3]

The discreet one puts on all the brilliant lights. Wise (*kavi*) is (so called) because his presence is desired (√*kam*), or the word is derived from (the root) *kav* (to praise). He generates bliss for bipeds and quadrupeds. Noble Savitṛ has seen heaven. He shines brightly after the departure of dawn. It is known from the list where animals are enumerated[4] that a goat, having characteristic black marks on the lower parts, is sacred to the sun.[5]

From what analogy is this so? From the analogy that at his time it is dark below on earth. Having characteristic black marks on the lower parts, i. e. dark in the lower parts. From what analogy is this so?[6] Having kindled the sacred fire, one should not approach a lovely dark maiden. It is only for the enjoyment and not for any sacred purpose that a lovely dark maiden is approached. From the analogy that she belongs to the dark race.[7] It is known in the list that enumerates

[1] x. 17. 1; AV. 3. 31. 5; 18. 1. 53; cf. Bṛh. D. vii. 7.

[2] See 10. 31.

[3] v. 81. 2; VS. 12. 3.

[4] VS. 29. 48.

[5] TS. v. 5. 22. 1; VS. 22. 58.

[6] and [7] The question is: 'how does the word *rāmā* come to signify "dark"?' The answer is this. The word *rāmā* literally means a lovely maiden, but it has acquired the significance 'dark' because the maiden belongs to the dark race.

animals:[1] the cock is sacred to the sun.[2] From what analogy is this so? (The cock is sacred to the sun), because he announces the time (of the sun). The former part of the word *kṛka-vāku* is onomatopoetic, the latter is derived from (the root) *vac* (to speak).

Bhaga has been explained.[3] His time is previous to the sunrise. The following stanza is addressed to him.

(*Here ends the thirteenth section.*)

May we invoke the early-conquering Bhaga, the fierce son of Aditi, him who is the supporter. Thinking of whom the destitute, even the rich, aye even the king says, 'Bestow on me'.[4]

May we invoke the early-conquering Bhaga, the fierce son of Aditi, him who is the supporter of all. Thinking of whom the destitute, i. e. the poor desirous of becoming rich. Even the rich—the word *tura* (rich) is a synonym of Yama, being derived from the verb *tṝ* (to cross), or from *tvar* (to hasten), i. e. on account of hastening, Yama is (called) of 'quick-gait'—even the king says to him, i. e. Bhaga, 'Bestow'. They say that Bhaga is blind: it is not visible, while it has not risen. There is a Brāhmaṇa passage: Prāśitra destroyed both his eyes.[5] It is known: Bhaga (fortune) goes to man,[6] i. e. the sun after rising goes to men.

Sūrya[7] is derived from *sṛ* (to move), or from *sū* (to stimulate), or from *svīr* (to promote well). The following stanza is addressed to him.

(*Here ends the fourteenth section.*)

Rays uplift him, the god who has all created things as his property, i. e. Sūrya, for all to see.[8]

The meaning is that the rays lift up Sūrya, who has all created things as his property, for all beings to see.

[What god other than the sun would the seer have thus addressed?] The following, another stanza, is addressed to him.

(*Here ends the fifteenth section.*)

The variegated splendour of the gods, the eye of Mitra, Varuṇa, and Agni, has gone up. He has filled heaven, earth, and the intermediate space. Sūrya is the soul of the moving and the stationary.[9]

[1] VS. 29. 48.
[2] VS. 24. 35; TS. v. 5. 18. 1; MS. 3. 14. 15: 175. 9.
[3] See 3. 16.
[4] vii. 41. 2.
[5] KB. vi. 3; cf. ŚB. i. 7. 4. 6; GB. 11. 1. 2; cf. Gune, *op. cit.*
[6] The quotation is untraced.
[7] Cf. Professor Macdonell, *op. cit.*, p. 30.
[8] i. 50. 1; AV. 13. 2. 16; 20. 47. 13.
[9] i. 115. 1; AV. 13. 2. 35; 20. 107. 14.

The noteworthy splendour of the gods, the perception of Mitra, Varuṇa, and Agni, has gone up. He has filled heaven, earth, and the intermediate space by his greatness [that greatness]. Sūrya is the soul of the movable and the immovable (universe).

Now when he goes on account of the increase of rays, he is called Pūṣan.[1] The following stanza is addressed to him.

(Here ends the sixteenth section.)

Thy one form is bright, thy other is holy. Day and night are dissimilar in form. Like heaven art thou. Thou protectest all arts, indeed. Here let thy gifts be blessed, O Pūṣan, rich in food.[2]

Thy one form is bright, bright-red. Thy other is holy, i. e. to which the sacrifice is offered. Thy function is to make the day and the night of different forms. And thou art like heaven. Thou protectest all sciences. Here let thy gift be full of fortune, O Pūṣan, abounding in food. The following, another stanza, is addressed to him.

(Here ends the seventeenth section.)

Made ready with desire, he has reached the worshipful overlord of every path with speech. He shall give us invigorating draughts of sparkling surface. Pūṣan shall accomplish our every thought.[3]

Made ready with desire, he has reached, or come in contact with, the worshipful supreme overlord of every path. May he give us treasures of noteworthy surface, and may Pūṣan accomplish our every action.

Now that which is set free becomes Viṣṇu. *Viṣṇu*[4] is derived from (the root) *viś* (to pervade), or from *vy-aś* (to interpenetrate). The following stanza is addressed to him.

(Here ends the eighteenth section.)

Viṣṇu strode over this (universe). Thrice he planted his foot, enveloped in dust.[5]

Viṣṇu strides over this and all that exists. Thrice he plants his foot, [for threefold existence]. 'On earth, in the intermediate space, and in heaven,'[6] says Śākapūṇi. 'On the mountain of sunrise, on the meridian, and on the mountain of sunset,' says Aurṇavābha.

Enveloped in his [dust], i. e. the foot-print is not visible in the stormy

[1] Cf. Professor Macdonell, *op. cit.*, p. 35.

[2] vi. 58. 1; SV. 1. 75.

[3] vi. 49. 8; VS. 34. 42.

[4] See 5. 8-9; cf. Professor Macdonell, *op. cit.*, p. 37.

[5] i. 22. 17; AV. 7. 26. 4.

[6] Cf. Muir, *op. cit.*, vol. ii, p. 177. According to Durga this refers to the terrestrial, the atmospheric, and the celestial Agni.

atmosphere. Or it is used in a metaphorical sense, i.e. his footstep is not visible, as if enveloped in a dusty place. *Pāṃsavaḥ* (dust) is (so called) because it is produced (√*sū*) by feet (*pādaiḥ*) or else it lies scattered on the ground, or it is trodden down.

(*Here ends the nineteenth section.*)

Viśvānara has been explained.[1] The following is his incidental mention in a stanza addressed to Indra.

(*Here ends the twentieth section.*)

I invoke for you the lord of Viśvānara, whose prowess is unhumbled, with the desires of human beings, and with the protection of chariots.[2]

In this sacrifice I invoke Indra, (lord) of Viśvānara, i.e. the sun, of unhumbled prowess, or of mighty strength, with desires, courses, or protection of men, i.e. of mortals along with the protection, i.e. path, of chariots.

Varuṇa has been explained.[3] The following stanza is addressed to him.

(*Here ends the twenty-first section.*)

The eye with which, O pure Varuṇa, thou seest the active sacrificer among men.[4]

The word *bhuraṇyu* is a synonym of 'quick'. *Bhuraṇyu* means a bird: it flies to a long distance; it carries one to the heavenly world also. Flying together with (bird), the sacrificer is called *bhuraṇyu* also.

With this perception, O purifier, thou seest the actively striving sacrificer among men. The words 'we praise that eye of thine' must be supplied. Or else the context (should be sought) in the following stanza.

(*Here ends the twenty-second section.*)

The eye with which, O pure Varuṇa, thou seest the active sacrificer among) men:[5]

with that thou reachest heaven in various ways, measuring the wide region and days with nights, and seeing many generations, O sun![6]

Thou reachest heaven in different directions, measuring the broad region, the mighty world, and days with *aktus*, i.e. nights, and seeing, O Sūrya, many generations, i.e. creatures. Or else (the context is to be sought) in its preceding stanza.

(*Here ends the twenty-third section.*)

[1] See 7. 21.
[2] viii. 68. 4; SV. 1. 364.
[3] See 10. 3.
[4] i. 50. 6; AV. 13. 2. 21.
[5] i. 50. 6.
[6] i. 50. 7.

The eye with which, O pure Varuṇa, thou seest the active sacrificer among men:[1]

(with that eye) thou risest before the tribes of gods, before men, before all (to enable them) to behold the light.[2]

Before all this [thou risest. Light is called 'facing this' because it faces everything]. Thou beholdest (this).[3] Or else (the context is to be sought) in the stanza itself.

(Here ends the twenty-fourth section.)

The eye with which, O pure Varuṇa, thou seest the active sacrificer among men,[4] with the same eye thou beholdest us men also.

Keśī, having long hair—by hair, rays are meant, i. e. endowed with rays, (so called) on account of shining (*kāś*), [or on account of being very bright (*pra-√kāś*)]. The following stanza is addressed to him.

(Here ends the twenty-fifth section.)

Keśin bears fire, Keśin water, Keśin heaven and earth, Keśin this entire universe for beholding the light, Keśin is called this light.[5]

Keśin (bears) fire and water. The word *viṣam* is a synonym of water, derived from the verb *vi-snā* from *snā* preceded by *vi*, meaning to purify, or from *sac* (to accompany) preceded by *vi*. He supports heaven and earth. Keśin beholds this, i. e. all this. Keśin is called this light. With these words the seer describes the sun.

Moreover, these other two lights are called Keśin (having long hair) also: (terrestrial) fire on account of the smoke, and (the atmospheric) fire on account of mist. The following stanza is addressed to them in common.

(Here ends the twenty-sixth section.)

Three lights (having long hair) perceive at the proper season. One of them strews in the year. One beholds the entire universe with its powers. Of one the sweep is seen, but not its shape.[6]

Three lights (having long hair) perceive at the proper season, i. e. they behold at the right time. One of them strews in the year, i. e. the fire burns the earth. One beholds everything with its actions, i. e. the sun. Of one the motion is seen, but not its shape, i. e. the middle one.

Now he who, with his rays, causes everything to quiver is called

[1] i. 50. 6.
[2] i. 50. 5; AV. 13. 2. 20; 20. 47. 17.
[3] Cf. Roth, *op. cit.*, p. 176.
[4] i. 50. 6.
[5] x. 136. 1; cf. Bṛh. D. viii. 49.
[6] i. 164. 44; AV. 9. 10. 26; cf. Bṛh. D. i. 95.

Vṛṣākapi, i.e. the shaker with his rays. The following stanza is addressed to him.

(*Here ends the twenty-seventh section.*)

O Vṛṣākapi, thou who art the destroyer of dreams, who art about to set along the path once more; come again, we two will regulate the prosperous course. Indra is supreme over all.[1]

O Vṛṣākapi, thou who art the destroyer of dreams, i. e. the sun, by rising (in the morning), causes dreams to be destroyed. As such thou art about to set along the path once more. Come again, we two will regulate the well-stimulated actions. We say this to Indra, i. e. the sun, who is supreme over all.

Yama has been explained.[2] The following stanza is addressed to him.

(*Here ends the twenty-eighth section.*)

Here, where under a tree of beautiful leaves Yama drinks together with the gods, our father, lord of the house, longs for the old ones.[3]

Where under a tree of beautiful leaves or in the chosen dwelling-place (of the virtuous). Or else it may have been used for the sake of comparison, i. e. as if under a tree of beautiful leaves.

Vṛkṣaḥ (tree) is (so called because) it is felled.

Palāśam (leaf) is (so called) from falling.

Yama goes together with the gods, i. e. the sun with rays. There may the protector or supporter of us all long for the old ones.

Aja ekapād:[4] the one-footed driver, or he protects with one foot, or he drinks with one foot, or he has only one foot. He does not draw one foot out.[5] This too is a Vedic quotation.

(*Here ends the twenty-ninth section.*)

The daughter of lightning, thunder, the one-footed driver, supporter of heaven, the Sindhu, the waters of the ocean, the all-gods, and Sarasvatī, together with prayers and praise, shall hear my words.[6]

Pavi means a javelin, because it tears the body open; *pavī-ram* means a pointed weapon, i. e. furnished with javelins; *pavī-ra-vān*, one who possesses this weapon, i. e. Indra.

Indra stood at the head.[7] This too is a Vedic quotation. Its deity is speech, *Pāvīravī*, and *pāvīravī* is divine speech. Thundering, i. e. reverberation of the speech of another. And the one-footed driver, supporter of

[1] x. 86. 21; AV. 20. 126. 21.
[2] See 10. 19.
[3] x. 135. 1.
[4] Cf. Professor Macdonell, *op. cit.*, p. 73.
[5] AV. 11 4. 21.
[6] x. 65. 13.
[7] x. 60. 3.

heaven, and the river, and waters of the ocean (atmosphere), all the gods, and Sarasvatī, may hear these words of mine, joined with *purandhi*, i. e. praise, and joined with prayers, i. e. rites.

Pṛthivī (earth) has been explained.[1] The following is her incidental mention in a stanza addressed to Indra and Agni.

(*Here ends the thirtieth section.*)

Whether, O Indra and Agni, you two dwell on the highest, on the middlemost, or even on the lowest earth. From thence come, both of you. O mighty lords! Now drink of the pressed soma.[2]

The stanza is explained by the mere reading of it.

Samudraḥ has been explained.[3] The following is its incidental mention in a stanza addressed to Pavamāna.

(*Here ends the thirty-first section.*)

Having a purifying instrument they sit round speech, their ancient father preserves the ordinance. Varuṇa placed the mighty ocean across, the wise were able to begin in the waters.[4]

Having a purifying instrument, having a ray, the groups of atmospheric gods sit round [atmospheric speech]. Their ancient, i. e. old and atmospheric, father preserves the ordinance, i. e. the course of action. Varuṇa places the mighty ocean across, i. e. within. Now the wise are able to begin, i. e. to commence the work in the *dharuṇa*, i. e. in the waters. The one-footed driver has been explained.[5]

Pṛthivī (earth) has been explained.[6] Ocean has been explained.[7] The following is their incidental mention in another stanza addressed to many deities.

(*Here ends the thirty-second section.*)

May the serpent of the depth hear us. May the one-footed driver, the earth, the ocean, the all-gods, the promoters of truth, who are invoked and praised, and the stanzas uttered by wise men, protect us.[8]

Also may the serpent of the depth hear us. And may the one-footed driver, the earth, the ocean, the all-gods, the promoting truth or promoting sacrifice, and who are invoked and praised with stanzas, and the stanzas uttered by wise men, i. e. uttered by intelligent men, protect us.

Dadhyaṅ, i. e. driver (*akta*) towards meditation (*dhyānam*), or medita-

1 See i. 13. 14; 9. 31; 11. 36.
2 i. 108. 10.
3 See 2. 10.
4 ix. 73. 3.
5 12. 29. 33.
6 i. 13. 14; 12. 30.
7 iv. 2. 10; 12. 30.
8 vi. 50. 14; VS. 34. 53.

tion is driven into him. *Atharvan* has been explained.[1] *Manu* is (so called) from thinking (√*man*). The following is their incidental mention in a stanza addressed to Indra.

(*Here ends the thirty-third section.*)

Whatever devotion Atharvan, father Manu, and Dadhyaṅ have spread, as before the prayers and hymns have come together in Indra, who respects self-rule.[2]

May the devotion which Atharvan, Manu, the father of the Mānavas, and Dadhyaṅ have spread, prayers, i. e. pious works, and hymns come together as before in that Indra, who respecting self-rule, pays homage according to law.

(*Here ends the thirty-fourth section.*)

Now, therefore, (we shall proceed with the) groups of celestial gods. Of these, the Ādityas come first. The Adityas have been explained.[3] The following stanza is addressed to them.

(*Here ends the thirty-fifth section.*)

I sacrifice these hymns, whose surface is brilliant with clarified butter, with a ladle to the Ādityas, who are eternal sovereigns. May Mitra, Aryaman, Bhaga, mighty Varuṇa, Dakṣa, and Aṃśa hear us.[4]

Whose surface is brilliant with clarified butter, i. e. emitting clarified butter, or distilling clarified butter, [or distributing clarified butter, or dripping clarified butter]. I sacrifice oblations with ladle to the Ādityas for a long time [in order to live long] or who are kings for a long time. May Mitra and Aryaman, and Bhaga, and the creator of many births, Dakṣa, Varuṇa, and Aṃśa hear these hymns of ours. Aṃśa is explained by Aṃśu.

Seven seers have been explained.[5] The following stanza is addressed to them.

(*Here ends the thirty-sixth section.*)

Seven seers are placed in the body, seven protect the seat without neglect. Seven works went to the world of setting where two gods who never sleep and sit on the sacrifice keep watch.[6]

Seven seers are placed in the body, i. e. rays in the sun. Seven protect the seat, i. e. the year without neglect, i. e. without being negligent. Seven pervading ones: they alone go to the world of the sleeping one, i. e. the setting sun. There wake two gods who never sleep and sit at sacrifice, i. e.

[1] See 11. 18.
[2] i. 80. 16; cf. Bṛh. D. iii. 121.
[3] 2. 13.
[4] ii. 27. 1; VS. 34. 54.
[5] See 10. 26.
[6] VS. 34. 55.

the air and the sun. This is with reference to the deity. Now with reference to the self. Seven seers are placed in the body, i. e. six senses and the seventh knowledge in the soul. Seven protect the seat without neglect, i. e. they do not neglect the body. Seven works : these same go to the world of the sleepy one, i. e. the setting soul. There two gods who never sleep and sit at the sacrifice keep watch, i. e. the self of wisdom and lustre. Thus he describes the course of the self. The following, another stanza, is addressed to them.

(Here ends the thirty-seventh section.)

The ladle having side holes and its bottom turned upwards—wherein is placed the omniform glory. Here sit together the seven seers who became the guardians of this great one.[1]

The ladle having side holes and a top-knot, or which expands at the top, wherein is placed the omniform glory. Here sit together the seven seers, i. e. rays who became guardians of this mighty one. This is with reference to the deity. Now with reference to the self. The ladle having holes on the sides and held fast at the top, or arousing at the top, wherein is placed the omniform glory. Here sit together the seven seers, i. e. the senses which became the guardians of this mighty one. Thus he describes the course of the self.

The gods have been explained.[2] The following stanza is addressed to them.

(Here ends the thirty-eighth section.)

May the blessed goodwill of the righteous gods, may the gift of the gods, turn down towards us. We honoured the friendship of the gods, may the gods prolong our age so that we may live.[3]

May we (live) [in the goodwill], in the blessed will of gods, who go straight, or who go at the proper season. May the gift of the gods turn down towards us. We honoured the friendship of the gods. May the gods prolong our age so that we may live long.

Viśve devāḥ, all the gods. The following stanza is addressed to them.

(Here ends the thirty-ninth section.)

Come, O All-gods, protectors and supporters of men, and gracious to the pressed soma of the worshipper.[4]

Protectors or to be protected; supporters of men, all-gods, come here, liberal to the sacrificer of the pressed soma. With reference to this, there is found in the ten books (of the Ṛgveda) only one hymn, composed in the

[1] AV. 10. 8. 9.
[2] See 7. 15.
[3] i. 89. 2 ; VS. 25. 15.
[4] i. 3. 7 ; VS. 7. 33 ; 33. 47.

Gāyatrī metre and containing three stanzas, which is addressed to the *Viśve devāḥ* (all-gods). But anything which is addressed to many deities is used in the place of those (hymns) addressed to the all-gods. 'Only that hymn which has the characteristic word "all" should be used for them,' says Śākapūṇi. This principle, however, cannot be of very wide application. The hymn,[1] '*One tawny*', contains ten stanzas of two verses each, without any characteristic mark. The hymn [2] of Bhūtāṃśa, son of Kaśyapa, addressed to the Aśvins, has the characteristic mark in one stanza only (out of eleven). The *Abhitaṣṭīya* hymn [3] has the characteristic mark in one stanza only.

The gods who are to be propitiated are (so called) because they lead straight to the goal. The following stanza is addressed to them.

(*Here ends the fortieth section.*)

The gods worshipped sacrifice with sacred rites. Those were the first ordinances. Becoming great they verily obtained heaven, where dwell the earlier gods who are to be propitiated.[4]

The gods worshipped sacrifice with sacred rites, i. e. gods worshipped Agni by performing sacrifices (lit by kindling fire). There is a Brāhmaṇa passage: Agni was the victim. They immolated him, with him they made sacrifice.[5] Those were the first ordinances. Having become great they verily enjoyed heaven together, where dwell the earlier gods who are to be propitiated, i. e. who lead straight to the goal. 'They are a group of gods whose sphere is heaven,' say the etymologists. The tradition is that that was the first epoch of the gods.

Vasus are (so called) because they put on everything. On account of the Vasuṣ Agni is called Vāsava, this is the explanation; hence they are terrestrial. On account of the Vasus Indra is called Vāsava, this is the explanation; hence they are atmospheric. Vasus are the rays of the sun, (so called) on account of shining forth; hence they are celestial. The following stanza is addressed to them.

(*Here ends the forty-first section.*)

We have made your seat easy to approach, O gods, you who were pleased to come to this libation. Having eaten and drunk, may all the Vasus bestow treasures on us.[6] We have made your paths easy to traverse. O gods, you were pleased to come to this libation. Having eaten and

[1] viii. 29. [2] x. 106. [3] iii. 38.
[4] i. 164. 50; x. 90. 16; AV. 7. 5. 1; VS. 31. 16.
[5] AB. i. 16; cf. Muir, *op. cit.*, vol. ii, p. 177.
[6] TS. i. 4. 44. 2; cf. AV. 7. 97. 4; VS. 8. 18.

drunk, may all the Vasus bestow treasures on us. The following, another stanza, is addressed to them.

(*Here ends the forty-second section.*)

The divine Vasus have here enjoyed themselves with the earth. The bright ones have embellished themselves in the wide atmosphere. O you, moving in extensive space, make your paths hitherward. Listen to this our messenger, who has started on his journey.[1]

The divine Vasus enjoyed themselves here with the earth. *Jmā* means earth. The dwellers on earth and the bright ones, i. e. shining ones, embellished, i. e. cause to reach or to enjoy in the wide atmosphere. Make these paths lead towards us, O swift ones, and listen to this our messenger, i. e. Agni, who has started on his journey.

Vājinaḥ (impetuous) has been explained.[2] The following stanza is addressed to them.

(*Here ends the forty-third section.*)

May the impetuous ones of measured speed and shining brightly be favourable to us in invocations at divine service. Chewing the serpent, the wolf, and the demons, they shall quickly move diseases from us.[3]

May the impetuous ones be a source of happiness for us in invocations at divine service, i. e. sacrifice. Of measured speed, of well-measured speed. Shining brightly, moving beautifully, or praising beautifully, or shining beautifully. Chewing the serpent, the wolf, and the demons, may the divine coursers soon remove diseases from us.

Divine wives, wives of the gods. The following stanza is addressed to them.

(*Here ends the forty-fourth section.*)

May the willing wives of the gods protect us. May they befriend us for offspring and winning of booty. Grant us protection, O goddesses whose sphere is earth, and who abide in the ordinance of waters, and who are easy to invoke.[4]

May the willing wives of the gods protect us. May they befriend us [for offspring, i. e.] for begetting children, and for winning food. May those goddesses who are on earth, and who are also in the ordinance, i. e. pious work, of waters, and who have noble invocations addressed to them, grant us protection, i. e. shelter. The following, another stanza, is addressed to them.

(*Here ends the forty-fifth section.*)

[1] vii. 39. 3.
[2] See 2. 28.
[3] vii. 38. 7; VS. 9. 16; 21. 10.
[4] v. 46. 7; AV. 7. 49. 1.

May the divine women, wives of gods: Indrāṇī, Agnāyī, Aśvinī, and Rāṭ, enjoy themselves. May Rodasī and Varuṇānī hear us. May the goddesses enjoy that which is the proper season of consorts.[1]

Moreover may the divine women, wives of the gods, enjoy themselves: Indrāṇī, the wife of Indra; Agnāyī, wife of Agni; Aśvinī, wife of the Aśvins; Rāṭ, she who shines; Rodasī, wife of Rudra; Varuṇānī, wife of Varuṇa. May the goddesses enjoy, i. e. long for that, the proper season of consorts.

(Here ends the forty sixth section.)

[1] v. 46. 8.

EXEGETICAL AND CRITICAL NOTES

CHAPTER I

1. 1.*] Muir translates the passage as follows: 'A sacred record (*samāmnāya*) has been compiled, which is to be expounded. This is called the Nighaṇṭus.'[1] His rendering of *samāmnāya* by 'a sacred record' is not quite correct. It may be that he has been led to this conclusion on account of misunderstanding the following explanatory note of Durgācārya: 'The meaning is, that this compilation has been put together by seers, as being an illustration for understanding the meaning of the Vedic stanzas, in a single list, divided into five chapters.' He explains the word *samāmnāya* as follows: 'The list of words beginning with *gaus* and ending with *devapatnī* is called *samāmnāya*. . . . It is called *samāmnāya* because it is handed down by tradition.' That the word *samāmnāya* means 'a list' or 'a traditional list' is further shown by the following passages:

Athāto varṇasamāmnāyaṃ vyākhyāsyāmaḥ.[2]

'Now we shall explain the list of letters.'

Atha varṇasamāmnāyaḥ.[3]

'Now the list of letters.'

The *Tri-bhāṣya-ratna* has the following comment:

'*sam* denotes aggregation; *ā* tradition; and *mnāya* signifies the instruction handed down from generation to generation in succession.' Cf. also: *padākṣara-samāmnāyaṃ chandasy eva pratiṣṭhitam.*[4]

Muir also leaves out the words *imaṃ samāmnāyam* in his translation of the third sentence, which may be translated as 'this same list'.

1. 3.] Yāska gives three derivations of the word *Nighaṇṭu*: (1) from √*gam* with the preposition *ni*, (2) from √*han* with *ni*, (3) from √*hṛ* with *ni*. None of them is satisfactory as they do not account for the cerebral *ṭ*. Durga, fully conscious of the unsatisfactory character of Yāska's etymologies, tries to get over the difficulty by the following ingenious theory of his own. He says: 'The arrangement of words is indeed threefold, i. e. those whose grammatical form is (1) direct, (2) indirect, and (3) obscure. With reference to them, the root is explicitly stated in words of direct grammatical forms; it is inherent in those of indirect forms. As regards words of obscure forms, the process of

* The bracketed figure does not represent the chapter and the sections, but the sections and the line.

[1] Muir, *op. cit.*, vol. ii, p. 165.

[2] Vpr. viii. 1.

[3] Tpr. i. 1.

[4] *Anuvākānukramaṇī*, 1. 6.

explanation is the following: having been reduced from the state of obscurity to that of the words of indirect forms, they should be explained by those of direct forms, e. g. *ni-ghaṇṭavaḥ* is a word whose grammatical form is obscure. The same (being reduced to) *ni-gantavaḥ* attains to the state of a word of indirect form, and as *ni-gamayitāraḥ* to that of a word of direct form.'

This theory acquires some plausibility from the explanation of Aupamanyava, but there is no evidence to show that Yāska agreed with Durga's threefold classification. On the contrary, Yāska does not follow the process laid down by Durga, that words of obscure forms should be explained by those of direct forms through the intermediation of those of indirect forms. This fact alone is sufficient to indicate that Yāska did not subscribe to the view of the commentator.

Another more or less fanciful derivation of the word *nighaṇṭu* is suggested from the root *granth* or *grath* by transposition, which, however, has the merit of accounting for the cerebralization through *r*, i. e. 'a list of words which have been strung together', or from √*ghaṭ* or √*ghaṇṭ* with *ni*, 'to join together', i. e. 'a list of words which have been joined together'.

1. 6.] Gune translates the passage as follows: 'Nouns are where being predominates and a verb is where becoming predominates respectively.'[1] The translator has changed the order of the original without any justification.

1. 7.] Owing to the want of precise punctuation the commentator has not clearly understood the passage. He ends the sentence with *bhavataḥ* and gets over the difficulty of grammar by construing *bhavataḥ* twice as follows: **अथ पुनर्यत्रैते उभे भवतः . . . . . भावप्रधाने भवतः ।**

Roth[2] seems to agree with the commentator in the punctuation and interpretation of the passage. Both interpret **तद्यत्र** as referring to a sentence, but there is hardly any justification for attributing this sense to **तद्यत्र**. It immediately follows Yāska's definition of nouns, which definition is not comprehensive, for it excludes all verbal nouns whose fundamental notion is more a *becoming* than a *being*. In order, therefore, to reconcile his definition with this class of nouns and to draw a clear line of demarcation between verbs and verbal nouns, Yāska expresses his meaning more definitely at greater length in this sentence. There should be no full stop after *bharataḥ*. The sentence should be read thus: **तद्यत्रोभे भावप्रधाने भवतः पूर्वापरीभूतं भावमाख्यातेनाचष्टे व्रजति पचतीति । उपक्रमप्रभृत्यपवर्गपर्यन्तं मूर्तं सत्त्वभूतं सत्त्वनामभिर्व्रज्या पक्तिरिति ।** 'Where both are dominated by a *becoming*, a *becoming* arising from a former to a latter state is denoted by a verb, as "he goes", "he cooks", &c.; the embodiment (of the whole process) from the beginning to the end, which has assumed the character of *being*, by a noun, as "going", cooking", &c.' The difference is this: a *becoming* in the course of a process or state of flux is denoted by a verb, but the embodiment of the complete process is denoted by a noun.[3]

[1] IA., vol. xlv, p. 158. [2] Cf. *op. cit.*, p. 4. [3] Cf. Gune, *loc. cit.*

The commentator cites the following two stanzas to show clearly the difference between nouns and verbs:

'They call that notion by the term verb, which is connected with many actions, which proceeding from a former to a later state is yet one, and which is accomplished through the termination of the actions.

A *becoming*, produced by the completion of action, capable of being expressed by a word ending in a primary affix, and joined with number, case, inflexion, and gender, should then be regarded as a noun.'

1. 8.] With a view to further distinguish nouns from verbs, Yāska says in this sentence, that there is a specific difference in the use of terminology applicable to nouns and verbs, e. g. *beings* can only be pointed out by a demonstrative pronoun, as 'this cow', 'that elephant', &c. Verbs, on the other hand, cannot be so pointed out. In order to indicate them, one is obliged to use the verb 'to be'. The use of different technical terms, which are non-interchangeable, shows that there is some fundamental difference of notions between them, the characteristics of which have already been mentioned.

1. 10.] In the original text, the sentence forms a part of the first section, and is immediately followed by the second. It introduces a controversy, i. e. whether words are permanent or impermanent,—a controversy which in its character differs altogether from the subject-matter of the first section. To begin the second section with this sentence would have been therefore a more logical division of the sections, and more in harmony with the modern conception of what constitutes a paragraph. That a section of the *Nirukta* more or less corresponds to a paragraph is indicated by the evidence of older MSS. which place the full stop, i. e. *daṇḍa*, at the end of, and very seldom within the section itself, excepting the commencement and the conclusion of a quotation. This is further supported by the fact that, in most cases, one section is devoted to the explanation of one Vedic stanza only. Hence it is argued that the division of the text of the *Nirukta* into sections, as constituted at present, is illogical and arbitrary. It is therefore proposed [1] to discard in this respect the authority of the MSS., which has been hitherto strictly followed, and 'to make sections according to the most natural division'.[2] 'Faithfulness', says Gune, 'is indeed a merit, but it should not be overdone, at least not where reason says otherwise.'[3] The suggestion is rather a bold one and, I think, contrary to the canons of modern editorship. The suggested improvements can very well be shown in foot-notes, but the wisdom of rearranging the text itself in opposition to the evidence of the MSS. is doubtful. However, there are practical difficulties in accepting this suggestion. Redivision of sections would involve the transference of a considerable number of passages to new sections, and would thereby reduce the utility of various books of reference, as far as these passages are concerned. Further, if the sections of the *Nirukta* do not harmonize with the modern con-

[1] Cf. Gune, *op. cit.*, p. 157. [2] *loc. cit.* [3] *loc. cit.*

ception of what constitutes a paragraph, does it necessarily follow that they are illogical? Is this, by itself, a conclusive proof of their arbitrary character? To my mind, the answer is in the negative, for the ancients may have had a different conception of the constitution of a paragraph. As far as Yāska is concerned, a careful examination of all the sections of the *Nirukta* indicates that Yāska proceeds methodically in his division of the text into sections, which division is based on a general principle. By the time of Yāska very great weight was attached to the Vedas, especially by that scholar himself, as is evident from Chapter I. particularly from his rejoinder to the adverse criticism of Kautsa. To him, a Vedic stanza was of the utmost importance, and accordingly formed a very suitable beginning for a new section. There are 400 sections altogether in the first twelve chapters of the *Nirukta*, distributed among those chapters as follows:

Chapter.	Sections.	Chapter.	Sections.	Chapter.	Sections.
I	20	V	28	IX	43
II	28	VI	36	X	47
III	22	VII	31	XI	50
IV	27	VIII	22	XII	46

329 sections out of the total of 400 begin with a Vedic stanza. The sections which do not so begin, and which in many cases could not so begin, as for instance those in the introductory remarks and discussions of the first and the seventh chapters, are shown in the following list:

Chapter I. 1, 2*, 3*, 4, 5*, 12, 13, 14, 15, 16, 17.
,, II. 1, 2*, 3*, 4, 5, 10, 13, 14, 15, 18. 23.
,, III. 1, 7, 13. 18, 19, 20, 21.
,, IV. 1, 17, 22.
,, V. 4, 6, 13, 20.
,, VI. 5, 17, 23.
,, VII. 1, 3, 4, 5, 6, 7*, 8. 10, 11, 12, 13*, 14, 19, 21.
,, VIII. 1, 4, 16.
,, IX. 1, 11*, 22, 35.
,, X. 1, 14, 25, 38.
,, XI. 1, 13, 22, 35.
,, XII. 1, 12, 20, 35.

The total number of these sections is 72, of which eight only, marked with an asterisk, can be regarded as arbitrarily divided when judged by the modern conception. One explanation is the following. In beginning a section with a Vedic stanza or verse, it became necessary to place its short introductory note at the end of the previous section, e. g. *Athāpi prathamā bahuvacane.*[1] It appears that this method of putting a short sentence of a section at the end of a previous section—which was a necessity in the case of sections beginning with Vedic stanzas—has been mechanically extended to the eight sections mentioned above. From what has gone before, it will be clear that the sections in the *Nirukta* are not illogically nor arbitrarily divided, but are based on a general principle adopted by Yāska. Gune's suggestion to rearrange the sections and to discard the authority of the MSS. is therefore unacceptable.

'Speech is permanent in the organs only' means that the character of speech is evanescent. Sounds disappear as soon as they are uttered. They have no existence beyond articulation by the vocal organs and their corresponding cognition by the sense of hearing. With this may be compared the remarks of Patañjali:

'BECAUSE SPEECH IS SET IN MOTION BY INDIVIDUAL LETTERS AND BECAUSE THE LETTERS ARE ANNIHILATED AS SOON AS THEY ARE UTTERED.'

'Speech is set in motion by individual sounds. One cannot produce two sounds simultaneously. Take the word *gauḥ*, for instance: when the sound *g* is being produced, neither *au* nor the *visarjanīya* can be uttered; when *au* is being produced, neither *g* nor the *visarjanīya* can be given utterance; and when the *visarjanīya* is being produced, one can neither pronounce *g* nor *au*, because they are annihilated as soon as they are uttered. The sounds indeed are perishable after being uttered, i. e. as soon as they are uttered they have perished.'[2]

Durga has the following comment: 'As soon as the speech of the speaker is an act of utterance in the organ, so long only it is possible to say that it exists, but fallen from lips it no longer exists. . . . And the sounds that have perished and that have not perished cannot be conjoined.' The question whether words are eternal or non-eternal was a very important subject of discussion among the ancient Indians. For instance, cf. Patañjali:[3]

'But again, is the word eternal or non-eternal (lit. created)? Whether it is eternal or non-eternal is thoroughly discussed in the *Saṃgraha*.[4] There the

[1] N. 1. 15. The reference in IA., *loc. cit.*, of this passage to p. 43 in Roth's edition is wrong, 43 being a misprint for 34.

[2] *Mahābhāṣya*, i. 4. 4; Kielhorn's edition, vol. i, p. 356.

[3] *op. cit.*, i. 1. 1, vol. i, p. 6.

[4] According to Nāgoji, *Saṃgraha* is a grammatical treatise by Vyāḍi. Cf. *Catalogus catalogorum*, vol. i, p. 686. The name of Vyāḍi is well known in Sanskrit Literature. He seems to have been a man of versatile genius, being famous as a grammarian, lexicographer, writer of authoritative books on medicine and poetics. As a grammarian, he is mentioned in Ṛpr. iii. 14. 17; vi. 12. 13; xii. 15; Kātyāyana's Vārttika 45 on Pāṇini's Sūtra, i. 2. 64. As a lexicographer and medical author, he is quoted by numerous writers on those subjects, see *Catalogus catalogorum*, vol. i, p. 618. Aufrecht attributes the *Saṃgraha* to Patañjali himself although it is quoted by him. Tradition mentions Patañjali as the curer of the three evils, (1) the evils of body, (2) evils of speech, and (3) evils of mind, and represents him as having written three masterpieces, i. e. (1) the *Caraka Saṃhitā*, (2) the *Mahābhāṣya*, and (3) the *Yogasūtras*, in order to remove the three evils respectively. But nowhere is he credited with the authorship of another grammatical treatise.

arguments against (the proposition) are stated, as well as the arguments in favour thereof. The conclusion (arrived at) in that work is this, that although the word is eternal, it is also non-eternal; the definition being applicable in both ways.' Patañjali, however, does not seem to agree with the conclusion arrived at in the *Saṃgraha*. He remarks:[1]

'*The twofold character of words is not proved.*

'Twofoldness of (the character of) words is not proved. If it be said that twofoldness has been proved, this cannot be maintained.' He says further:[2]

'Words are eternal. In the eternal words there must be sounds which are perpetual, unchangeable, and free from elision, addition, and modification.

'This is proved by the eternity of sounds . . . words are eternal.'

The character of words is discussed by him at greater length in his comment on the *vārttikā*: **सिद्धे शब्दार्थसंबन्धे**.[3] The argument may be summarized as follows:

The relation of words to the objects they denote is eternal. This power of denotation of objects is natural and uncreated,[4] and so are the objects. It may be objected that although matter is uncreated, yet the various forms into which it is moulded are non-eternal; e.g. the earth is not created by man, but the various pots and jars, into which it is shaped, are the creations of a potter, hence the words denoting these forms cannot be eternal. To this the answer is given that the form is eternal also, for it is not something radically different from the matter, but only a particular state which the matter assumes at a particular time. 'But how is it known that word, object, and their mutual relation are eternal?' From the ordinary usage of the world. In daily life, people perceive objects and use words to denote them. They do not make any effort in creating them, because effort is necessary in producing what is non-eternal only; e.g. a man desirous of using a pot goes to the house of a potter and says, 'Please make me a pot, I want to use it', but a man desirous of employing a word does not go to the house of a grammarian and say, 'Please, sir, make me a word, I want to use it'. People perceive objects and use words to denote them without any effort.[5]

The way in which Patañjali refers to the *Saṃgraha* shows that it was a work of some eminent scholar and was very well known in his time. Further Patañjali does not agree with the conclusion arrived at in the *Saṃgraha*; he is therefore not likely to be its author. Nāgoji seems to be right in ascribing its authorship to Vyāḍi, who, besides being quoted several times, is mentioned as an *ācārya* along with *Śākalya* and *Gārgya* in Rpr. xiii. 12.

No MS. of the *Saṃgraha*, nor of any other work by Vyāḍi, has been so far discovered, except a solitary MS. of *Vyāḍi paribhāṣā Vṛtti*, in the temple library of the Mahārājā of Jammu and Cashmere. The MS. is described in Stein's *Catalogue of Skt. MSS.* on p. 47. The description of the MS. is very meagre, so it is impossible to judge whether or not it is a genuine work by Vyāḍi.

[1] *op. cit.* i. 1. 1. 6, vol. i, p. 104.

[2] *op. cit.* i. 1. 1. 8, vol. i, p. 136.

[3] *op. cit.* i. 1. 1. 1, vol. i, p. 6.

[4] Cf. Jaimini, PM. i. 1. 5.

[5] Cf. Bhandarkar, *Wilson, Philological Lectures*, p. 291.

With this may be compared the remarks of Plato in the *Cratylus*:[1]

Soc. 'And speech is a kind of action?'

Her. 'True.'

Soc. 'And will a man speak correctly who speaks as he pleases? Will not the successful speaker rather be he who speaks in the natural way of speaking . . .?'

Soc. 'And we saw that actions were not relative to ourselves, but had a special nature of their own.'

The question of the eternity of words was important not only to the grammarians and philologists, but also to the followers of the orthodox systems of philosophy. To their mind authoritativeness of the divine relation, i. e. the Veda, seemed to be involved and to depend on the solution of this principle. Hence the question forms a topic of discussion in almost every school of thought. It has been very fully treated by Jaimini in the first of his *Pūrvamīmāṃsā*. The arguments against the eternity of words are set forth in i. 1. 6–11; their refutation is contained in i. 1. 12–17; further arguments in support of the eternity of words are given in i. 1. 18–23. Some of the arguments are as follows:

Words are Eternal.

(1) Words are eternal because they are not uttered for the sake of utterance alone, but to express some meaning, and no meaning could ever be comprehended, had the words been transient.

(2) Because everywhere there is a universal cognition of words.

(3) Because the number is not used. When one word has been used several times, it is usually spoken of as having been used so many *times* and not that *so many* words have been used. This shows that the sameness or the unchangeable character of the word is recognized even when it is uttered or used after intervals; hence words are eternal.

Audumbarāyaṇa's view as to the nature of words may be regarded as based on a doctrine akin to that of flux. With this may be compared the following remarks of Plato in the *Cratylus*:[2]

Soc. 'I myself do not deny that the givers of names did really give them the idea that all things were in motion and flux; which was their sincere but, I think, mistaken opinion. . . . Tell me, whether there is or is not any absolute beauty or good, or any other absolute existence?'

Crat. 'Certainly, Socrates, I think so.'

Soc. '. . . But let me ask whether the true beauty is not always beautiful.'

Crat. 'Certainly.'

Soc. 'And can we rightly speak of a beauty which is always passing away? . . . Must not the same thing be born and retire and vanish *while the word is in our mouth*?'

[1] Jowett, *Dialogues of Plato*, vol. i, p. 327 (3rd ed.).

[2] Jowett, *Dialogues of Plato*, vol. i, pp. 387–8.

Soc. 'Nor can we reasonably say, Cratylus, that there is knowledge at all, if everything is in a state of transition and there is nothing abiding.'

2. 1.] As most of the MSS. do not mark the *avagraha*, the sign of *a*, it is not clear whether the reading represents *yugapat* or *ayugapat*. The few MSS. that do mark the *avagraha* are inconsistent, as they use it only occasionally. Their evidence is therefore not cogent. However, none of the MSS. mark the *avagraha* in this particular instance. Nevertheless I think the reading represents *ayugapat*. My reasons are as follows: (1) From the physical point of view, to produce simultaneously more than one sound is an impossibility; *yugapat* would therefore convey no sense.

(2) The context points to *ayugapat*, for the sentence is intended to show the absurdity of Audumbarāyaṇa's view that speech is permanent only in the organ. But if we read *yugapat* the whole sentence becomes meaningless, for then the grammatical relation of the sounds which are produced simultaneously is possible, even if it is held that speech is permanent in the organ only.

(3) This is in agreement with the view taken by Durga, who reads *ayugapat* and gives *yugapat* as a variant.

(4) Another objection to the reading *yugapat* is that it would make grammar superfluous. When words are produced simultaneously their mutual connexion is simultaneous also. Durga remarks, 'The unconnected alone is connected (with something). In this case (i. e. reading *yugapat*) the roots are for ever connected with prepositions and affixes; and affixes with elision, addition, and modification of letters.'

Durga attributes the statement तच्च चतुष्ट्वं . . . योगश्च to the *Pūrvapakṣa* and thinks the rejoinder to begin with the words व्याप्तिमत्त्वात्तु शब्दस्य, a view which cannot be maintained. The sentence तच्च चतुष्ट्वं, &c., is a negative sentence; it refutes the view of Audumbarāyaṇa. According to Durga's interpretation, the controversy would be divided into three parts as follows:

(1) Audumbarāyaṇa. Words are permanent in the organs only.

(2) Pūrvapakṣa. In that case the fourfold classification, &c., of words cannot be maintained.

(3) Yāska's rejoinder. On account of the pervasiveness and minuteness of words, the fourfold classification can be maintained. Durga thus introduces a third party into the discussion and tends to make out Yāska as supporting the view of Audumbarāyaṇa, by refuting his critic.

I think there are only two parties, i. e. Audumbarāyaṇa and Yāska; No. 1 gives the view of the former, No. 2 the rejoinder of the latter; while No. 3 does not relate to this controversy at all, but deals with an altogether new topic, i. e. the superiority of speech over gestures, &c. Yāska's rejoinder begins, therefore, with तच्च चतुष्ट्वं, &c.

2. 2.] It may be objected that there is no necessity for using words, for the meaning can very well be conveyed by means of gestures. To this Yāska replies that gestures, facial expressions, movements of hands and eyes, require comparatively greater effort in their production, and are always indefinite. Their meaning can never be absolutely clear, it always involves some doubt. The word 'minute' implies comparatively less effort and greater accuracy. Patañjali refers to the same subject as follows: 'The meaning is clearly understood when the word is uttered. "Bring the cow", "Eat the curd": these words having been uttered, the cow is brought, and the curd is eaten.' With this may also be compared the remarks of Plato in the *Cratylus*:[1]

Soc. 'And here I will ask you a question: suppose that we had no voice or tongue, and wanted to communicate with one another, should we not, like the deaf and dumb, make signs with the hands and head and the rest of the body?'

Her. 'There would be no choice, Socrates.'

Soc. 'We should imitate the nature of the thing; the elevation of our hands to heaven would mean lightness and upwardness; heaviness and downwardness would be expressed by letting them drop to the ground; if we were describing the running of a horse, or any other animal, we should make our bodies and their gestures as like as we could to them.'

2. 3.] Words are used to designate objects not only by men, but by gods also. Like Yāska, Plato also thinks that gods use words in giving names to things, and it follows therefore that the names given by gods would be the right names:[2]

Soc. 'He often speaks of them; notably and nobly in the places where he distinguishes the *different names which Gods and men give to different things*. . . . For the Gods must clearly be supposed to call things by their right and natural names; do you not think so?'

Her. 'Why, of course they call them rightly, if they call them at all. But to what are you referring?'

Soc. 'Do you not know what he says about the river in Troy . . . "Whom", as he says, "the Gods call Xanthus, and men call Scamander".'

Her. 'I remember.'

Soc. '. . . Or about the bird which, as he says, "The Gods call Chalcis, and men Cymindis": . . . Or about Batieia and Myrina:

"The hill which men call Batieia and the Immortals the tomb of the Sportive Myrina".'

If words are used with reference to gods—human knowledge being neither perfect nor permanent—mistakes are likely to be made in addressing and invoking gods, which will make them angry and render various acts of worship, like sacrifice, &c., fruitless. In order to do away with such mistakes, injunctions, invocations, and hymns, &c., which are meant to complete and make worship fruitful, are laid down in the Vedas. A part of this paragraph is written in the *sūtra* style, which style may therefore be regarded to have commenced about the time of Yāska. This is probably the earliest specimen of the *sūtra* style.

[1] Jowett, *op. cit.* vol. i, p. 368. [2] Jowett, *op. cit.*, vol. i, p. 333.

Like Yāska, Jaimini also lays emphasis on the Veda as being the source of *dharma*: '*Dharma* is the object, the source of which is the Vedic injunction.'[1] And also: 'On account of the prescription of action being the object of the Veda.'[2]

3. 3.] Cf. *Vājasaneyiprātiśākhya*:[3] 'A verb denotes an action, and a preposition makes that action specific.' The *Ṛgvedaprātiśākhya*:[4]

'The prepositions are twenty; with the other two (i. e. noun and verb) they express a meaning. They are: *pra, abhi, ā, parā, niḥ, duḥ, anu, vi, upa, apa. sam, pari, prati, ni, ati, adhi, su, ud, ava,* and *api*.' This list is identical with that of the *Nirukta*, except that they are enumerated in a different order.

Cf. the *Taittirīyaprātiśākhya*[5]: '*ā, pra, ava, upa, abhi, adhi, prati, vi, ni,* are prepositions.' It contains only half the number of prepositions. Cf. Pāṇini:[6] '*Pra*, &c., are called prepositions when joined with verbs.' The list of the prepositions is given in the *gaṇa* called *prādayaḥ*, which is identical with that of the *Nirukta*, if the double forms of *niḥ* and *duḥ*, in the former, are not taken into consideration. The technical term used by Pāṇini for preposition is *karmapravacanīya*. He uses the word *upasarga* in a wider sense, i. e. covering both prepositions and adverbs. The various meanings of the prepositions are explained by Pāṇini, i. 4. 83–97.[7] Cf. also the *Atharvavedaprātiśākhya*:[8] 'Disjoined from the verb, however, are such as are used without significance . . .'[9]

4. 1.] Particles are classified by Yāska under three groups:

(1) Particles of comparison, which are only four in number, and whose meanings and uses are illustrated by suitable examples. Yāska does not define the term *upamā* (comparison) in this connexion, but discusses its meaning later on.[10]

(2) Particles which denote *karmopasaṃgraha*, Yāska's explanation of which term is not clearly expressed, nor does Roth[11] make it more lucid. The obscurity has led Durga to misinterpret the sentence. He takes *karmopasaṃgraha* as equivalent to *samuccaya*, i. e. 'aggregation'; this is only one of the meanings expressed by the said term, which is very comprehensive. It is quite obvious that the term is designed to cover all the meanings expressed by the particles enumerated in the second group, i. e. those beginning with *ca* and ending with

[1] PM. i. 1. 2.

[2] *Op.cit.*, i. 2. 1. Questions like the eternity of *śabda*, the impermanence of human knowledge, the infallibility of the Veda, form topics of discussion in almost every system of philosophy; cf. VSu. i. 3. 28; i. 4. 28; ii. 1. 4; ii. 4. 20; NSu. i. 1. 7; ii. 1. 54–7; ii. 2. 13–17; iii. 2. 49; VaiSu. ii. 2. 21–37; vi. 1. 1; x. 2. 9; SpSu. v. 45–51; v. 37–40; v. 58–61.

[3] viii. 54. The list of the prepositions is given in vi. 24, which is identical with that of the *Nirukta*.

[4] xii. 6: 702.

[5] i. 15.

[6] i. 4. 58.

[7] Cf. Patañjali, i. 4. 4: vol. i, pp. 341, 345–9; see foot-note (in the text).

[8] iv. 3.

[9] Translated by Whitney, *J.A.O.S.*, vol. vii, p. 515.

[10] N. 3. 13.

[11] *Erläuterungen*, p. 6.

tva. Gune translates the sentence *yasyāgamāt*, &c., as follows :[1] 'Owing to whose advent (i. e. use) separateness of the अर्थ (senses or ideas) is indeed known, but not as in simple enumeration owing to separate position or independent mention, that is कर्मोपसंग्रह, i. e. adding or putting together of the senses or ideas.'

One must admit that the meaning of the term is not quite clear. One does not know what is the precise difference between 'simple enumeration' and 'putting together'. My translation of the sentence is the following: 'That by whose addition separateness of notions is indeed recognized, but not as an enumerative one, i. e. on account of a separateness by isolation, is a conjunction.' I think 'conjunction' is the nearest corresponding word in English which will cover all the meanings expressed by the particles of the second group, and which is therefore equivalent to *karmopasamgraha*. For example, in the sentence, हन्ताहं पृथिवीमिमां निदधानीह वेह वा । 'Ha! I will put this earth here or there',[2] separateness of place is recognized by the use of the particle *vā*; the repetition of *iha* by itself would have failed to convey the idea of different places. This notion of separateness is expressed, not by a categorical enumeration as horse, cow, man, elephant, &c., but by the use of the particle. Again, in the sentence, अयमहेदं करोत्वयमिदम्, 'Let one man do this, the other that',[3] two distinct actions are mentioned, the notion of whose distinctness is conveyed by the particle *aha*. The particles of the second group are explained with appropriate examples in the *Nirukta*, i. 4–9. With this definition of a conjunction may be compared the following remarks of Aristotle :[4]

'A conjunction is (*a*) a non-significant sound which, when one significant sound is formable out of several, neither hinders nor aids the union, and which, if the speech thus formed stands by itself (apart from other speeches), must not be inserted at the beginning of it, e. g. *μέν, δή. τοί. δέ*; or (*b*) a non-significant sound capable of combining two or more significant sounds into one; e. g. *ἀμφί, περί*, &c.

(3) Particles which do not express any meaning, but are merely used to fill up a sentence in prose or verse, are expletives. They are enumerated towards the end of the ninth section; they are four in number: *kam*, *īm*, *id*, and *u*; but later (in the tenth) *iva* is added to this list. Quotations showing their uses are cited and explained in the tenth section. The meaning of *id*, when combined with *na* and *na ca*, is discussed and illustrated by suitable examples in the eleventh section. Thus *id* combined with *na* is used to denote apprehension: 'lest we should', &c.; *id* combined with *na ca* is used in asking questions: 'don't they drink?' The above-mentioned list of the particles of the third class is by no means complete. Some particles of the second group, i. e. *u*,

[1] IA., vol. xlv, p. 159.
[2] N. 1. 4.
[3] N. 1. 5.
[4] *Poetics*, 20. 1457ᵃ (ed. Bywater), p. 59.

khalu, *nūnam*, are occasionally used as expletives, and *sīm* in Vedic Sanskrit. *Sīm* was originally the accusative singular of a pronoun, related to *sā*, as *kīm* to *ka*. It appears in the Ṛgveda as an enclitic particle.[1]

7. 3.] Roth thinks that Yāska explains *nūnam* by *adyatanam*, 'to-day', and remarks, 'J. hat darin Unrecht'.[2] This view is erroneous. According to Yāska, the particle *nūnam* is used (1) to signify 'uncertainty', and (2) as an expletive. These two uses are exemplified by two respective quotations, the former illustrating its meaning of 'uncertainty', the latter showing its use as an expletive. Hence it is that, in the latter case, Yāska neither repeats nor paraphrases *nūnam* by any other word in his commentary, indicating thereby that it is an expletive, while in the former quotation *nūnam* is repeated by Yāska in his explanation, showing thereby that it has the sense of 'uncertainty'. The word *adyatanam* is not intended to paraphrase *nūnam*, but is added for the sake of amplifying Indra's brief statement.

12. 2.] Cf. the following passages: AA. ii. 1. 3: **अथातो रेतसः सृष्टिः । . . . . . प्रजानां रेतो हृदयं हृदयस्य रेतो मनो मनसो रेतो वाग्वाचोः रेतः कर्म** 'Now, therefore, the origin of seed. . . . Heart is the seed of people, mind is the seed of heart, speech is the seed of mind, and *action is the seed of speech*.' AA. ii. 1. 6: **तस्य वाक्तन्तिर्नामानि दामानि तदस्येदं वाचा तन्त्या नामभिर्दामभिः सर्वं सितं सर्वं हीदं नामनी"३ सर्वं वाचाभिवदति ।** 'Speech is his thread, names the chords. All this is woven by this speech of his, in the form of thread and names as chords. For all this is names, and by his speech he names everything.' Cf. also Ch. U. vi. 5. 1–4; 6. 1–5; vii. 2. 1; vii. 12. 2. See Keith, A.A. Translation.

Śākaṭāyana: a famous ancient grammarian, quoted in RV. Prā. i. 13, 17; xiii. 16, 747 (Max Müller's ed., pp. 13 and 271); in Vāj. Prā. iii. 8, 11, 86; iv. 1, 126, 188; in A. Prā. ii. 24; in *Aṣṭādhyāyī* iii. 4, 111; viii. 3, 18; 4, 50; and in N. 1. 3, 12. No work of his has been preserved The *Śabdānuśāsana* quoted by Vopadeva and various other writers is the work of a modern Jain grammarian called Śākaṭāyana.[3] Aufrecht regards him as the author of the *Uṇādisūtras*. They, however, cannot be the work of the ancient Śākaṭāyana, for they clearly bear a modern stamp. Belvalkar[4] attributes the *Uṇādisūtras* to Pāṇini. His argument is that 'they use *saṁjñās* such as *hrasva*, *dīrgha*, *pluta*, *udātta*, *lopa*, *samprasāraṇa*, and *abhyāsa* in the same sense in which Pāṇini uses them'. This argument is inconclusive because, the works of Pāṇini's predecessors being lost, we have no means of judging whether or not he is indebted to them for those terms. Some at least of these *saṁjñās* or technical terms were derived from a common stock; Yāska himself, for instance, makes use of a few of them, as

[1] See Professor Macdonell, *A Vedic Grammar for Students*, pp. 249, 452.

[2] *op. cit.*, p. 6.

[3] On the authenticity and date of the modern Śākaṭāyana, see IA., vol. xliii, pp. 205–12.

[4] *Systems of Sanskrit Grammar*, p. 25.

lopa, *abhyāsa*, &c. Again, in some cases Pāṇini's teaching, as pointed out by Belvalkar himself, runs counter to the *Uṇādisūtras*.[1] Thus to ascribe the authorship of the *U. Sūtras* to Pāṇini does not rest on firm ground. Moreover, Patañjali's defence of Pāṇini against the adverse criticism of Kātyāyana[2] is that 'the *Uṇādi* words are crude forms of nouns which are not derived'.[3] This statement implies that Patañjali did not regard all nouns as derivable from verbs. He also attributes the same doctrine to Pāṇini, and Patañjali, I think, cannot be accused of not knowing well, or misunderstanding Pāṇini. So, according to this testimony, both Pāṇini and Patañjali were the followers of the school of Gārgya. The *Uṇādisūtras*, on the contrary, are the product of the school of Śākaṭāyana, whose fundamental doctrine was that all nouns are derived from verbs; they cannot therefore be attributed to Pāṇini. It is probable that, in their original form, they were written by Śākaṭāyana, but were extended and modified by subsequent writers, and in spite of their modernness still bear traces of their ancient origin.

Gārgya: an ancient grammarian, quoted by Yāska i. 3, 12; iii. 13, and Pāṇini. iv. 1. 105; vii. 3. 99; viii. 3. 20; 4. 67, and mentioned by Durga as the author of the *padapāṭha* of the *Sāmaveda*. No work of his has survived. Both Pāṇini and Patañjali seem to be his followers, for they regard the *Uṇādis* as underivable. It is therefore no wonder that his work, after the appearance of the *Aṣṭādhyāyī*, has not survived.

12. 3.] The sentence तद्यत्र स्वरसंस्कारौ .... पुरुषो हस्तीति which is somewhat difficult, is differently interpreted by various writers. The crux lies in the word *saṃ-vijñātāni*. Durga paraphrases this word as follows: *samaṃ vijñātāni aikamatyena vijñātāni*, 'discriminated unanimously; i. e. discriminated with absolute agreement'. Max Müller[4] translates it by 'intelligible', Roth by 'arbitrarily named'.[5] Roth's translation seems to be based on Durga's second explanation of the same term, which is as follows: *saṃ-vijñāna-padam itīha śāstre rūḍhi-śabdasyeyaṃ saṃjñā*: 'in this (branch of) knowledge, the term *saṃ-vijñāna* is a technical expression used for a conventional word.' Durga resorts to the Comparative Method and quotes: *tāny apy eke samāmananti* ... *saṃ-vijñāna-bhūtaṃ syāt*,[6] in support of his explanation. He is further corroborated by a comparison of all the passages of the *Nirukta* in which the word *saṃ-vijñāna* or (with the omission of the prep. *vi*) *saṃ-jñāna* occurs.[7] We may therefore take the word to signify 'a conventional term'.

The next problem in the sentence is the punctuation. Max Müller[8] takes *saṃ-vijñatāni*, &c., as the principal clause to complete the relative clause *tad yatra*

[1] Pāṇini's sūtra vi. 2. 139 is opposed to USu. iv. 226.

[2] On the relation of the three grammarians, see Kielhorn, *Pāṇini, Kātyāyana, and Patañjali*.

[3] The *Mahābhāṣya*, viii. 1. 1, vol. iii, p. 241.

[4] *History of Ancient Skt. Lit.*, p. 165.

[5] *op. cit.*, p. 9, 'willkürlich benannt'.

[6] N. 7. 13.

[7] Cf. Gune's note, IA., vol. xlv, p. 173.

[8] *op. cit.*, p. 165.

. . . *syātām*, and translates as follows: 'For first, if the accent and formation were regular in all nouns and agreed entirely with the appellative power (of the root), nouns such as *go* (cow), *aśva* (horse), *puruṣa* (man) would be in themselves intelligible.' He succeeds in thus construing the sentence by translating *yatra* by 'if'; leaving out *tāni*; and by attributing to *saṃ-vijñātāni* a meaning not borne out by the comparison of passages. Roth divides the sentence by placing a semicolon after *syātām* and takes *saṃ-vijñātāni*, &c., as a co-ordinate clause; but in order to connect the two clauses, he supplies the word *dagegen*. Durga offers two interpretations. Firstly, he places a full stop after *tāni* and takes the words *yathā gaur aśva*, &c., as a co-ordinate clause, supplying, however, the words *na punaḥ*; the translation of the sentence according to this interpretation would be the following: 'The words whose accent and grammatical formation are regular and which are accompanied with an explanatory radical element are unanimously recognized to have been derived from roots; but not words like "cow", "horse", "man", "elephant", &c.'

Secondly, he places a full stop after *syātām* and takes *saṃ-vijñātāni*, &c., as an independent sentence. According to this division, the first sentence would consist of one single relative clause, without any principal clause. To meet this difficulty he remarks: '*Tad ākhyātajaṃ guṇakṛtam iti pratīma iti vākya śeṣaḥ.*' 'We think that the words, "that is derived from a verb", must be supplied as a supplementary clause.' The translation according to this interpretation is the following: 'Those words whose accent and grammatical formation are regular, and which are accompanied with an explanatory radical element, are derived from roots. Words like "cow", "horse", "man", "elephant", are conventional terms.'

Gune does not seem to be aware of this second interpretation of Durga and independently arrives at a conclusion [1] identical with that of Durga, and suggests the adoption of the supplementary words: *sarvaṃ tat prādeśikam.*[2] These words occur in Yāska's rejoinder in section 14. His argument is that, in his rejoinder, Yāska always first repeats the words of his opponent and then answers the objection. According to Gune, the sentence placed within the words *yatho etad* and *iti* exactly represents the original statement of the critic. The sentence placed within these words in Yāska's rejoinder in section 14 contains the supplementary clause *sarvaṃ tat prādeśikam*, which, being thus assigned to the critic by Yāska himself, must have formed a part of the sentence under discussion. He remarks, 'And we are also sure, comparing the initial passage [i. e. in the *pūrvapakṣa*] with its counterpart in Yāska's reply at R. 36. 10. that सर्वं तत् प्रादेशिकम् must have been there. Its omission is strange and unaccountable. Perhaps it is the scribe's mistake. . . .'[3] In other words, Gune thinks that the passage in Yāska's rejoinder could be used as a MS. (archetype). furnishing evidence which cannot be challenged, for the critical edition of the

[1] IA., *loc. cit.* [2] N. 1. 14. [3] IA., *loc. cit.* and p. 174.

original passage of the critic in section 12. A closer examination, however, does not support this theory, for a comparison of the statements of the critic with those assigned to him by Yāska, in his rejoinder, shows that Yāska repeats, and puts between *yatho etad* and *iti*, only so many words of his opponent as are necessary for the controversy. He does not repeat them *in toto*. It is evident, if one compares section 13 and section 14:

Pūrvapakṣa.	*Yāska's rejoinder.*
1. 13: अथापि य एषां न्यायवान्कार्मनामिकः संस्कारो यथा चापि प्रतीतार्थानि स्युस्तथैनान्याचक्षीरन्	1. 14: यथो एतद्यथा चापि प्रतीतार्थानि स्युस्तथैनान्याचक्षीरन्निति ...
अथानन्वितेऽर्थेऽप्रादेशिके विकारे पदेभ्यः पदेतरार्धान्संचस्कार शाकटायनः।	यथो एतत्पदेभ्यः पदेतरार्धान्त्संचस्कारेति ...

In both these cases, Yāska repeats only a part of his opponent's statements. Gune's assertion is therefore unfounded; hence his suggestion as regards the adoption of a supplementary clause cannot be accepted.

The sentence can, however, be explained without having recourse to an assumed interpolation. The difficulty will disappear if a full stop be placed after *syātām* and the passage *na sarvāṇīti . . . syātām* be construed as one sentence. I would then translate: 'Not all the words,' say Gārgya and some other grammarians, 'but only those, the accent and grammatical form of which are regular and which are accompanied by an explanatory radical element. Those such as "cow", "horse", "man", "elephant", &c., are conventional terms.'

Durga has the following theory about nouns: 'There is a threefold order of nouns; i. e. (1) those whose roots are apparent; (2) those whose roots can be inferred; (3) and those whose roots are non-existent. With reference to this, the nouns whose roots are apparent are such as "doer", "bringer", &c. Nouns whose roots can be inferred are such as "cow", "horse", &c. Nouns whose roots are non-existent are such as *ḍittha*, *ḍavittha aravinda*, and *vārviṇḍa*, &c.'

It is quite evident that Yāska, a follower of the school of etymologists—whose fundamental doctrine is that all nouns are derived from roots—could not have recognized the third category of his commentator, who thus appears to be a follower of the school of Gārgya.

14.] With the *Nirukta* controversy about the origin and nature of names may be compared a somewhat similar discussion in the *Cratylus*, where Plato propounds three theories, represented by the three characters of the dialogue. He puts in the mouth of Hermogenes the doctrine that names are conventional. The opinion of Cratylus that names are natural is diametrically opposed to this. Socrates takes an intermediate view. He refutes the view of Hermogenes that names are given arbitrarily and altered at will:

Soc. 'Well, now, let me take an instance. Suppose that I call a man a horse or a horse a man, you mean to say that a man will be rightly called a horse by me individually, and rightly called a man by the rest of the world; and a horse again would be rightly called a man by me and a horse by the world: That is your meaning?'[1]

He then expounds the principle of the natural correctness of names.

Soc. 'Then the actions also are done according to their proper nature, and not according to our opinion of them? In cutting, for example, we do not cut as we please . . . but we cut . . . according to the natural process of cutting;' . . .

Her. 'I should say that the natural way is the right way.' . . .

Soc. 'And this holds good of all actions?'

Her. 'Yes.'

Soc. 'And speech is a kind of action?'

Her. 'True.' . . .

Soc. 'And is not naming a part of speaking? for in giving names men speak.

Her. 'That is true.'

Soc. '. . . Is not naming also a sort of action?'

Her. 'True.'

Soc. 'And we saw that actions were not relative to ourselves, but had a special nature of their own?'

Her. 'Precisely.'

Soc. 'Then the argument would lead us to infer that names ought to be given according to a natural process, and with a proper instrument, and not at our pleasure: in this and no other way shall we name with success.'[2]

Socrates also admits the element of convention in names:

Soc. 'Yes, my dear friend; but then you know that the original names have been long ago buried and disguised by people sticking on and stripping off letters for the sake of euphony, and twisting and bedizening them in all sorts of ways: and time too may have had a share in the change.' . . .[3]

Also:

Soc. 'To say that names which we do not understand are of foreign origin; and this is very likely the right answer, and something of this kind may be true of them; but also the original forms of words may have been lost in the lapse of ages; names have been so twisted in all manner of ways, that I should not be surprised if the old language when compared with that now in use would appear to us to be a barbarous tongue.'[4]

Cratylus maintains that names are either true or not names at all:

Crat. 'Very true, Socrates; but the case of language, you see, is different; for when by the help of grammar we assign the letters *a* or *b*, or any other letters, to a certain name, then, if we add, or subtract, or misplace a letter, the

[1] Jowett, *Dialogues of Plato, Cratylus*, p. 385.
[2] *Ibid.*, p. 387.
[3] *Ibid.*, p. 414.
[4] *Ibid.*, p. 421.

name which is written is not only written wrongly, but not written at all; and in any of these cases becomes other than a name.' . . .

Soc. 'I believe that what you say may be true about numbers, which must be just what they are, or not be at all; for example, the number ten at once becomes other than ten if a unit be added or subtracted, and so of any other number: but this does not apply to that which is qualitative or to anything which is represented under an image.'[1]

As regards the derivation of names:

Soc. 'All the names that we have been explaining were intended to indicate the nature of things.'

Her. 'Of course.'

Soc. 'And that this is true of the primary quite as much as of the secondary names.' . . .

Soc. 'But the secondary, as I conceive, derive their significance from the primary.'

Her. 'That is evident.'

Soc. 'Very good, but then how do the primary names which precede analysis show the nature of things?' . . .

Soc. 'But how shall we further analyse them? . . . Ought we not, therefore, first to separate the letters, just as those who are beginning rhythm first distinguish the powers of elementary, and then of compound sounds?' . . .[2]

Plato's doctrine, 'that names rightly given are the likenesses and images of the things which they name',[3] does not hold good, for in a large number of cases names are not the images of things themselves, but of our concept of them. It was Locke who first pointed this out, and Max Müller amplified his argument as follows: 'Each time that we use a general name, if we say dog, tree, chair, we have not these objects before our eyes, only our concepts of them; there can be nothing in the world of sense corresponding even to such simple words as dog, tree, chair. We can never expect to see a dog, a tree, a chair. Dog means every kind of dog from the greyhound to the spaniel; tree, every kind of tree from the oak to the cherry; chair, every kind of chair from the royal throne to the artisan's stool. . . . People often imagine that they can form a general image of a dog by leaving out what is peculiar to every individual dog.'[4]

In an elaborate discussion, Mādhava brings together the views of various grammarians as to the meaning of words and its cognition: Vājapyāyana maintains that all words express a *generic* meaning and a particular substance is apprehended after the apprehension of the *genus* which has an intimate relation with them. Vyāḍi maintains that words mean individual things, that they explicitly express the individual substance, while the *genus* is implied.

[1] Jowett, *Dialogues of Plato, Cratylus*, p. 378.
[2] *Ibid.*, pp. 367-70.
[3] See *ibid.*, p. 387.
[4] *Science of Thought*, pp. 77, 78, cited by Moncalm.

Pāṇini, he says, accepts both views. He attributes to words a *generic* meaning, for he says the singular is used to denote the class, while the plural may be optionally used (Pā. i. 2. 58); on the other hand, by i. 2. 64, his acceptance of the individualistic theory is quite apparent (*Sarvadarśana-saṃgraha*, p. 145). But the next question is, how does the cognition of the meaning, whether *generic* or individualistic, take place? For instance, when the word 'cow' is pronounced, there is a simultaneous cognition of dewlap, tail, hump, hoofs, and horns. Is this cognition produced by the single letters composing the word 'cow', or by their aggregation? The first alternative is not tenable, for the cognition of the object cannot be the result of a string of separate and individual letters without some unifying cause, as a garland cannot be made from a collection of separate flowers without the unifying string. The second alternative is impossible, for there can be no aggregation of sounds, each of which ceases to exist as soon as it is pronounced. If you attribute a 'manifesting' power to the letters, this power can be exercised only in succession and not simultaneously. Moreover, if each letter has a separate manifesting power, then the pairs of words *rasa, sara*; *vana, nava*; *nadī, dīna*; *rāma, māra*; *rājā, jārā*, &c., since the pairs have the same number of the same letters, should each have had the same meaning. Moreover, the baseless assumption of aggregation would involve mutual dependence. Since it is impossible that letters should convey the meaning by themselves, we have to accept the hypothesis of a unifying factor which is all-pervading and whose existence is independent of letters, and which is technically called *sphoṭa* (*Sarvadarśana-saṃ.*, *Bib. Ind.*, pp. 140–4).

16. 1.] This is a very important statement made by Yāska. He is fully aware of the close relationship of the Vedic language with the *bhāṣā* of his own times, which could be no other than the classical Sanskrit. Further, he seems to be conscious of the historical growth of the latter from the former, when he says that the nouns of the *bhāṣā* are derived from Vedic roots. It is needless to point out that it completely answers Kautsa's criticism that the Vedas are meaningless; for many words which they daily use in the *bhāṣā* are identical with those used in the Vedas, and if in the *bhāṣā* they do express any meaning, they must do so in the Veda. It would be absurd for Kautsa to deny that the words in the spoken language express a meaning. Thus he is constrained to admit that the Vedas have a meaning. A similar objection appears in Sāyaṇa's preface to the Ṛgveda: **तदेवमेतैस्तदर्थशास्त्रादिभिर्हेतुभिर्मंत्राणामर्थप्रत्यायनार्थत्वं नास्ति** 'From all these reasons, (it is clear) that there is no intelligible significance in the Vedas.' One of the examples here given is as follows: 'Suppose a woman named Pūrṇikā is plying the pestle. A Brāhmaṇa boy called Māṇavaka is committing to memory a pestle-stanza, just close to her. The recitation of the stanza does not keep time with the fall of the pestle at every stroke. No meaning is conveyed to the woman, nor is there any intention to convey any meaning to her. Similarly, at the performance of sacrifices, the recitation of Vedic stanzas does not convey any meaning.' In answering this, Sāyaṇa quotes अविशिष्टस्तु वाक्यार्थः (Pū. Mī. i. 1. 31): 'But the meaning of (Vedic) expressions is not different,' his comment being वाक्यार्थो लोकवेदयोरविशिष्टः 'The meaning of expressions of the Vedic Sanskrit and of the popular speech is not different.' As to the example, the Brāhmaṇa boy does not intend to convey any meaning at the time of learning his lesson, and the woman therefore does not understand, a woman, moreover, being incapable of understanding the Veda: at sacrifices the priest does intend to convey a meaning, and others *do* understand it. And if at any particular time there is no intention of conveying a meaning, it would be altogether unjustifiable to conclude that there is no meaning at all.

16. 4.] The objection is that because the Brāhmaṇa text prescribes the complete form of the sacrificial acts, the Vedic stanzas are superfluous, the only use being their mere recitation. Yāska's reply is that the Brāhmaṇa text merely reiterates what is enjoined by the Veda. Sāyaṇa here quotes: मंत्राभिधानात् 'because it is mentioned in the Vedic stanzas', and his comment is: यथा लोके यः कुर्विति ब्रूते स कारयत्येव तथात्रापि यः प्रथस्वेति ब्रूते स प्रथयत्येव। 'just as in popular speech, he who says "do this" is the causer of the performance of the action, so in this case too, he who says "spread" is the prescriber of the act of spreading'. And to suppose that the use of the Vedic stanzas consists solely in recitation would be attributing a transcendent importance to them. We need not go so far; 'for', says Sāyaṇa, 'their non-transcendent use is the expression of meaning': अर्थाभिधायकत्वे तु दृष्टं लभ्यते।

16. 5.] Cf. Sāyaṇa's preface (p. 3): ओषधे त्रायस्वैनमिति मंत्रो दर्भविषयः। स्वधिते मैनं हिंसीरिति क्षुरविषयः। . . . . . एतेष्वचेतनानां दर्भक्षुरपाषाणानां चेतनवत्संबोधनं श्रूयते। ततो . . . विपरीतार्थबोधकत्वाद्प्रामाण्यम्। 'The stanza, "O herb, save him", is about grass. The stanza, "O axe, do not injure him", refers to an axe. . . . In these stanzas, inanimate objects, grass, axe, and stones, are addressed like sentient beings. Therefore the Veda, on account of such absurd invocations which are contrary to common sense, is of no authority.' He further quotes the Sūtra (Pū. Mī. i. 2. 35), अचेतनार्थसंबन्धात् 'because a meaning is attributed to lifeless things', and his comment is that lifeless things such as grass, stones, and axe are described as if they were living beings and had the powers of saving, injuring, hearing, &c. The answer is as follows: The inanimate things themselves are not addressed in these Vedic stanzas, but their immanent deities, which have been treated at length by Bādarāyaṇa. He further quotes, अभिधानेऽर्थवादः 'There is a figurative description in such expressions.' His comment is: 'This is very frequently employed in poetical compositions. For instance, a river is described as having a pair of *cakravāka* birds for her breasts, a row of swans for her teeth, a *kāsa* plant for her garment, and moss for her hair. Similarly, the Vedic texts invoking inanimate objects should be construed as implying praise. If by cultivation the plant will protect, much more so will the cultivator; if even the stones listen to the morning recitation of the Vedic texts, how much more will the learned Brāhmaṇas.

16. 6.] Cf. Sāyaṇa's preface (p. 3):

एक एव रुद्रो . . . यावज्जीवमहं मौनीति वाक्यवद्व्याघातबोधकत्वादप्रामाण्यम् . . . . . .

एकस्यापि रुद्रस्य स्वमहिम्ना सहस्रमूर्ति . . . नास्ति . . . . व्याघातः ।

'The Veda is not authoritative, because statements like "One Rudra alone, &c." are contradictory, as if one were to say that he is observing the vow of silence for life. . . .'

'There is no such contradiction, because even one Rudra by his greatness can take on a thousand forms.' He further quotes the fifth Sūtra: गुणाद्विप्रतिषेधः स्यात् । 'On account of the figurative description, there will be no contradiction' (*ibid.* i. 2. 47).

16. 8.] Cf. Sāyaṇa's preface:

तत्र मंत्राः केचिदबोधकाः । अम्यक्सा . . . । यादृश्मिन् . . . जर्भरी तुर्फरीतू . . . नह्येतैर्मंत्रैः कश्चिदप्यर्थोऽवबुध्यते । . . . .

'Now some of the stanzas convey no meaning . . . *amyaksā* . . . *yādṛśmin*, . . . &c. These stanzas express no meaning at all.' To this Sāyaṇa replies by repeating Yāska's sentence that it is not the fault of the post if the blind man does not see it. He further quotes: सतः परमविज्ञानम् 'The meaning exists, but it is obscure' (*ibid.* i. 2. 49). His comment is: विद्यमान एवार्थः प्रमादालस्यादिभिर्न ज्ञायते । तेषां निगमनिरुक्तव्याकरणवशेन धातुतोऽर्थः परिकल्पयितव्यः । 'The meaning does exist, but it is not recognized by people on account of their neglect, laziness, &c. Their meaning should be inferred from the root in accordance with etymology and grammar and parallel passages.' Then he explains *jarbhari* and *turpharītū* as names of the Aśvins.

17. 1.] After pointing out the great importance of etymology for an accurate analysis of words into their constituent elements, Yāska incidentally defines *saṃhitā* as 'the closest conjunction (of original words) by means of euphonic combination' or as 'based on original words'. By means of using certain words, Yāska always gives a general indication of the source of his quotations. If the quotation is from the Vedas or Saṃhitās like the MS. KS., &c., he regularly uses the phrase *athāpi nigamo bhavati*; if it is from the Brāhmaṇas, he uses the words *iti vijñāyate, iti ca*, &c. Quotations from other sources are similarly indicated; thus two quotations—one from some metrical law-treatise—are introduced with the words: *tad etad ṛkchalokābhyām abhyuktam* (see 3. 4), but he nowhere cites without acknowledgement; as his definitions of Saṃhitā are not qualified with any such phrase, I take them to be Yāska's own. The first is adopted by Pāṇini (i. 4. 109), the second by the RV. Prā. (ii. 1): Yāska is consequently earlier than Pāṇini and the extant *R. Prātiśākhya*.

It is, however, very likely that the Prātiśākhyas were known to Yāska in an earlier form. Probably the sentence, 'that the grammatical treatises (*pārṣadāni*) of all the different schools are based on the original forms of words', alludes to the Prātiśākhyas, these being the oldest grammatical treatises. Sometimes the words *pārṣada* and *prātiśākhya* are interchanged, as is shown by the evidence of a MS. in the Bodleian, which uses the word *pārṣada* in the place of *prātiśākhya*. This leads to the conclusion that Yāska knew some *prātiśākhyas*, although he is earlier than the modern *R. Prātiśākhya*.

17. 6.] Yāska here intends to point out the practical utility of etymology for the performance of sacrificial rites. For the success of sacrifice, it is of the highest importance to know the deity of a stanza. Sometimes the general principle that a stanza belongs to a deity whose characteristic mark it bears is not applicable, for instance, to a stanza which bears the characteristic marks of more than one deity. In such cases, one has to find out which deity is primarily and which is incidentally mentioned, and this, Yāska implies, can only be done with the help of etymology; hence the importance of etymology for practical purposes like the performance of sacrifices.

17. 17.] The last point adduced by Yāska in favour of the science of etymology is that knowledge should be acquired for its own sake. He quotes two stanzas from the Ṛgveda to show that it is through knowledge that one is purged of his defects, attains an unassailable position, and all the joys and blessings of this world and the next. His arguments in favour of etymology may be summarized as follows:

(1) Etymology is the complement of grammar and is therefore essential for understanding the meaning of the Vedic texts.

(2) It is essential for an accurate analysis of words into their constituent elements.

(3) It is of great importance for the performance of sacrifice, for it enables one to find out precisely the deity of a particular stanza, and to recite the appropriate texts while offering oblations to various gods.

(4) Lastly, knowledge for its own sake is commended and ignorance condemned.

18.] Roth thinks the whole of the eighteenth section is an interpolation. The second stanza is quoted by Patañjali in the *Mahābhāṣya*.[1] If Roth is right, the interpolation is an old one.

20. 10.] The paragraph traces the origin and the necessity of compiling the list of words called the Nighaṇṭu. The hymns were revealed by direct intuition to the primeval bards. They handed them down to their successors by oral instruction. Later generations being devoid of direct intuition, and being weary of oral instruction, compiled with a desire to facilitate the study of the Vedas,

[1] See foot-note in the text.

the Nighaṇṭu, the Veda, and the Vedāṅgas. The last sentence attributes the compilation of the Nighaṇṭu, the Veda, and the Vedāṅga to the same period. Yāska, however, makes it clear that by compilation of the Veda he does not mean the composition of the Vedic hymns, which, he says, were revealed by direct intuition. Yet what he intended to convey by the 'compilation' of the Veda is not clear. According to Durga it refers to the growth of the branches (*śākhā*) of the Veda. But it more probably refers to the constitution of the Saṃhitā text and the arrangement of the hymns of the Ṛgveda into ten books. Yāska several times refers to the ten books of the Ṛgveda with the term *dāśatayīṣu*; and he expressly states that it was the hymns and not the Saṃhitā text that was revealed to the primeval seers. This definition of Saṃhitā, moreover, indicates that he regarded it as a later production. Thus it is likely that by 'compilation of the Veda' Yāska means the constitution of the Saṃhitā text. The use of the singular number here is significant.

It would be equally interesting to ascertain what Yāska meant by the Vedāṅgas. He could not possibly mean the six traditional Vedāṅgas for the simple reason that some of the Vedāṅgas, like Pāṇini's *Aṣṭadhyāyi*, are much later than Yāska and therefore could not have been known to him. Secondly, though Yāska's *Nirukta* itself is a Vedāṅga now, he himself could not have been so presumptuous as to regard his own commentary as a Vedāṅga. Nor did he regard the Nighaṇṭu as a Vedāṅga, for he refers to it as 'the list', and its separate mention in the sentence, 'later generations . . . compiled the Nighaṇṭu, the Veda, and the Vedāṅga'. suffices to show that to Yāska the Nighaṇṭu meant something different from the Vedāṅgas. Yāska quotes from many Brāhmaṇas, and he was obviously familiar with most of them. The large number of Brāhmaṇa quotations in the *Nirukta* indicates that in Yāska's time the Brāhmaṇas were popular treatises, not only for the performance of sacrifices, but as handbooks of the common stock of wisdom. From their auxiliary character in the study of the Veda, it might be argued that in Yāska's time the Brāhmaṇas were included in the Vedāṅgas. This argument acquires some plausibility from the fact that in the above sentence Yāska says nothing about the compilation of the Brāhmaṇas, thus implying that they are Vedāṅgas. This inference is, however, invalidated by Yāska's practice of regularly mentioning these works by their proper name, i. e. Brāhmaṇa. Nor does he anywhere give any hint whatsoever that their study is essential for the proper understanding of the Vedas. But on the other hand he does say that without etymology it is not possible to understand the meaning of the Veda. Etymology, therefore, is an auxiliary science for the study of the Veda. In Yāska's time there was an established school of etymologists, whose opinions he quotes on more than twenty occasions. The standard treatise of this school would therefore constitute one of the Vedāṅgas. Yāska further says that etymology is the complement of grammar. In his view grammar is therefore equally important for understanding the Vedas. Besides individual grammarians,

Yāska on several occasions also refers to the school of grammarians. Their standard work would thus be another Vedāṅga. In his discussions Yāska moreover quotes the opinions of the two schools of ritualists, the older and the younger. Their most authoritative work or works would form another Vedāṅga. Two other schools, those well versed in legendary lore and in Vedic metres, are also quoted. Their standard works would form additional Vedāṅgas. These would give rise to the later Vedāṅgas and subsequently, after the time of Pāṇini, become stereotyped in the most authoritative surviving work of each school. Astronomy would, as less essential, have been added later, and the number of Vedāṅgas finally accepted as six.

20. 12.] This gives a general description of the contents and the main divisions of the Nighaṇṭu. The first part deals with the synonyms both of nouns and verbs; the second with homonyms; the third with deities, whether primarily or incidentally mentioned. Then comes the explanation of the primary and incidental mention and the definition of the *daivata*.

CHAPTER II

1.] The MSS. of the longer recension and the commentator read *guṇena*, while those of the shorter one *vikāreṇa*. Both are consistent in their reading, for they have their respective reading in N. 1. 14, the greater part of the first sentence in which—and also its counterpart in section 12—is identical with the passage under discussion. The authority of the commentator no doubt throws greater weight on the side of *guṇena*, which, on that ground, was adopted by Sāmaśrami, who, finding that four of his MSS. read *vikāreṇa*, remarks in the foot-note,[1] *paraṃ vṛtti-viruddhaḥ*, and ignores it without any further comment, as if that fact alone were sufficient for its condemnation. Roth does not seem to have any knowledge of the variant *vikāreṇa*, for he does not mention it in his list of *Abweichende Lesungen der kürzeren Recension.*[2] The variant *vikāreṇa*, however, gives a better meaning. If we adopt the reading *guṇena*, the translation of the sentence would be the following: 'With regard to those words, the accent and grammatical formation of which are regular, and *which are accompanied by an explanatory radical element*, (we say that) they should be explained in the ordinary manner.' To a follower of the school of etymologists the phrase underlined would be meaningless, for, according to their fundamental doctrine, every word is accompanied by its radical element. Yāska, in this case, would be placed on the horns of a dilemma: either he must give up the fundamental doctrine of his school, or recognize the absurdity of his sentence. The meaning is considerably improved by adopting the reading

[1] *Bib. Ind.*, vol. ii, p. 147. [2] pp. 105-12.

vikāreṇa; the translation of the sentence in this case is the following: 'With regard to those words, the accent and grammatical formation of which are regular, and *which are accompanied by an explanatory radical modification*, (we say that) they should be explained in the ordinary manner.' Yāska in this case is saved from the above dilemma. Further, in the immediately following sentence *vikāra* actually makes its appearance and is coupled with *prādeśika* also. In my opinion *vikāreṇa* is therefore the original reading.

2.] The meaning of Yāska, when he says that some Vedic nouns are derived from the roots of the classical Sanskrit and vice versa, is not quite clear. At first sight he would here seem to regard the Vedic and the classical Sanskrit as two distinct languages with two different sets of roots, which in some cases have mutually influenced each other. But from his remarks in the first chapter it is evident that he is conscious of the close relationship between the Vedic and the classical languages. To Kautsa's criticism that the Vedic hymns are meaningless, Yāska replies[1] that they are significant because their words are identical with those of the spoken language. He notices[2] the uses of prepositions and particles common to the two languages. He seems to realize as well that the one is historically the outgrowth of the other when he points out that the meaning of a particular word in the classical Sanskrit is only an extension from that of the Vedic language. In fact, as expounder of the Nighaṇṭu and the commentator of about 600 Vedic stanzas, he could not have failed to observe the close affinity of the Vedic and classical Sanskrit. Considering these facts, the distinction made by Yāska between the roots of the Vedic and the classical Sanskrit would seem inexplicable. With a view to reconcile these apparently contradictory views, I propose to interpret the passage as follows: the statement that Vedic nouns are derived from classical roots means that the roots from which those particular words are derived do not occur in verbal forms in the Veda, but survive in the classical language only. Agni is called *damūnas* in the Vedic hymns. Yāska would no doubt have derived the word *damūnas* from the root *dam*, 'to become tame'. He would say that although the root *dam* is still used in the sense of 'becoming tame' in classical Sanskrit, it does not occur in this sense in the Vedic language. Similarly, when he says that classical words like *uṣṇam*, *ghṛtam*, &c., are derived from Vedic roots, all that he means is that the roots *uṣ* and *ghṛ* are used in their respective meanings 'to burn' and 'to drip' in the Vedic language only, and that they have lost these meanings in the classical language.

2. 10.] Yāska here notices the dialectical difference of the spoken Sanskrit, or what otherwise may be called provincialisms. He divides people into those who employ primary forms and those who employ secondary forms. According to this distinction the Kambojas and the Easterners use primary and the Āryas and the Northerners derivative secondary forms. Yāska differentiates the Āryas from the Easterners and the Northerners. This shows that the Easterners

[1] See 1. 14. [2] See 1. 3–4.

and the Northerners were not Āryas - at least, were not regarded as such by Yāska—although they must have been brought under the influence of the Āryas to such an extent as even to adopt their language. The same distinction in almost identical words is made by Patañjali in the *Mahābhāṣya*.[1] Roth's[2] denial of the correctness of Yāska's statement that the Āryas use *śava* in the sense of motion is groundless, because Yāska is corroborated by a grammarian of such eminence as Patañjali. Moreover, Roth seems to forget that Yāska's statement is made with regard to the spoken language only as distinguished from the written. At the same time Roth's suggestion that the whole passage: शवतिर्गति . . . . . शव इति is spurious and added by a more learned grammarian than Yāska cannot be accepted, because Patañjali quotes the sentence: शवतिर्गतिकर्मा कम्बोजेष्वेव भाषितो भवति विकार एनमार्या भाषन्ते शव इति । although the etymological explanation of the words *kambojās* and *kambala* looks suspicious in itself, besides being very clumsily thrust between शवतिर्गतिकर्मा कंबोजेष्वेव भाष्यते and विकारमस्यार्येषु &c., which are in fact the two component parts of a complete sentence. Moreover, the passage in the *Mahābhāṣya* does not contain these etymological explanations. It is thus very likely that they were added later on.

2. 18.] Yāska derives the word *daṇḍa* from the root *dad*, 'to hold'. In order to show that the root *dad* is not pure invention on his part, Yāska gives an example illustrating the use of the root *dad* in the sense of 'holding'. The commentator remarks that *dad* is used in this sense even in Vedic Sanskrit also, and cites विश्वेदेवाः पुष्करे त्वा ददन्त in support of his statement. He further adds that Akrūra was the king of *Vṛṣṇyandhaka* and held a jewel called *syamantaka*. This story (of the *syamantaka* jewel and King Akrūra) is related in the *Bhāgavata* and *Brahma purāṇas*. the *Mahābhārata*, and Hemacandra.[3]

2. 21.] Yāska gives three derivations for the word *kakṣa*. Durga interprets the word *kakṣa* in three different ways, probably in order to match the etymological explanation. Durga's interpretations can be deduced from the etymologies of *kakṣa*: it is possible that Yāska himself intended to express the different meanings of the word. If so, it would be an illustration of his principle that the derivations should be different when meanings are different. *Kakṣa* means (1) the region of the girth, hence *kakṣyā* means girth, i. e. the belt carried round the region of the girth; (2) cords used in churning milk. In this sense it is derived from the root *gāh*, 'to churn', with the suffix *kṣ*. Durga remarks: कक्षो गाहतेर्विलोडनार्थस्य । कक्ष्योरेव हि बलेन विलोडयति स्त्री दध्यादि द्रव्यम् । (3) Armpit, as the most concealed part of the human body, and not therefore to be made known. In this sense it is derived from the root *khyā*, 'to make known', in two ways: (*a*) from the reduplicated form of the root

[1] Patañjali, *Mahābhāṣya* I. 1. 1, p. 9. [2] Roth, *Nirukta*: *Erläuterungen*, p. 17.
[3] See *Bib. Ind.* ii. 164, foot-note.

khyā, i. e. *kakhyaḥ > kakṣaḥ*, the reduplication being useless; (*b*) from the root *khyā* with *kiṃ*, i. e. *kiṃ*, *khyaḥ > kakṣaḥ*. The meaning would be: What is there to be made known in the armpit? Nothing. Being hidden, it should not be exposed. Durga's comment is: **एवं किमस्मिन् ख्यापनीयमस्ति न किञ्चिदप्यदर्शनीयत्वात्गूहनीयोऽयमित्यर्थः ।** (4) Armpit, as the most rubbed part of the human body, either (*a*) on account of the motion of the arms, or (*b*) in order to allay the itching sensation caused by perspiration. In this sense, it is derived from the root *kaṣ* 'to rub'. Durga remarks: **नित्यकालं ह्यसौ स्वेदशीलत्वात्कण्डूं ददाति ततो नखैः कष्यते यतस्तस्मात्कषणक्रियायोगात्कक्ष इत्युच्यते ।**

Yāska's attempt to derive *kakṣa* from *gāh* and *khyā* is futile. It is impossible to derive *kakṣa* from *gāh* or *khyā*. The nearest approach to a phonetically accurate etymology is the derivation of *kakṣa* from the root *kaṣ*.[1] It is, however, doubtful whether all the etymologies given above are genuine. As shown elsewhere, many are interpolated.

2. 24.] Durga explains **तत्सामान्यात्** by **स्त्रीकचस्य सामान्यात्**. There is nothing in the text to justify Durga's explanation of **तत्**. Further, it confuses the sense of the text, Durga's comment being: **स्त्रीकचस्य सामान्याद् मनुष्यकचो ऽपि कच इत्युच्यते ।**, 'on account of its similarity with the female armpit the male armpit is also called *kakṣa* (armpit).' The words **तत्सामान्यात्** come immediately after **कषतेर्वा**. Yāska's meaning seems to be the following: The word *kakṣa* is derived from the root *kaṣ* (to rub). From this similarity (of being rubbed) the human armpit is so called (i. e. *kakṣa*).

3. 13.] Roth[2] translates the passage as follows: 'But even simple (*einfache*) words one should explain neither to a non-grammarian, nor to a stranger, nor to any one else (*sonst einem*) who is unfit (*untauglich*) for this science.' The literal rendering of Yāska's words would be: 'He should not explain simple words (*ekapadāni*), not to a non-grammarian, nor to a stranger, or to one who does not know (anything about) this (science).' Yāska goes on to say: 'But one should explain (the *ekapadāni*) to one whom he knows, or to one who is capable of understanding, or to a wise and pious man.' By *ekapadāni* Yāska evidently means primary (nominal) derivatives, the explanation of which in *Nirukta* 2. 2 he contrasts with that of secondary derivatives (*taddhitas*) and compounds (*samāsas*), while in this passage he states to what kind of people (secondary derivatives and compounds, as well as) even simple words (i.e. primary derivatives), should not be explained. Durga has the following comment: **प्रकरणोपपदरहितानि यानि सन्ति तानि केवलान्येव . . . . . . न निर्ब्रूयान्न निर्वक्तव्यानि । किं कारणम् । तेषां प्रकरणादुपपदाद्वार्थः शक्यतेऽवधारयितुम् । सोऽसौ प्रकरणानभिज्ञोऽन्यथैव निर्ब्रूयात् ततश्च प्रत्यवायेन योगादपहारश्च स्यात् ।**

The commentator quotes **जहा** in support of his remarks and indicates that on

[1] Cf. Zend *kaṣa*, Lat. *coxa*, O.H.G. *hahsa*.

[2] See *Erläuterungen*, p. 18, note on ii. 3. 10.

examining the word **जहा** in its isolated state, it cannot be said whether it is derived from the root *han*, 'to kill', or *hā*, 'to abandon'. He also quotes a stanza from the Ṛgveda and shows that the character of *mā*, whether it is a pronoun or a particle, can be ascertained by context only. The argument is that in order to give the etymological explanation of a word, one should know its meaning, which can be fully realized with the help of the context only, hence the warning against explaining isolated words.

4.] Roth[1] thinks that the verses quoted in the section are interpolated. It is remarkable that they are accented. The accent, however, is not marked with strict grammatical accuracy. Roth[1] thinks that this is an example of unskilful admixture of the grammatical and the musical accentuation. The verses are quoted from the *Saṃhitopaniṣad.*[2] With the exception of the third verse, they are identical in subject-matter with Manu ii. 114, 115, 144 ; Vasiṣṭha ii. 8, 9, 10 ; Viṣṇu xxix. 9, 10, xxx. 47 ; Āpastamba i. 1, 14. The fourth section has no connexion whatsoever with the preceding or the following section and interrupts the otherwise logically harmonious order of the text.

5.] From here begins the explanation of the words of the *Nighaṇṭu* in the order in which they occur in that list. All the synonyms enumerated in the first three chapters of the *Nighaṇṭu* are disposed of in the remaining part of the second and the third chapters. Every synonym is not explained. Only a few are selected for this purpose, others are passed over. Yāska contents himself with indicating the general method of explanation. The commentator characterizes the work of Yāska on the three sections of synonyms as follows: **किंलक्षणा पुनरसौ व्याख्येति । उच्यते । तत्त्वपर्यायभेदसंख्यासंदिग्धसंदिग्धोदाहरणतन्निर्वचनविभागेन यदाख्यानं सा व्याख्या नैघण्टुके प्रकरणे ।** What, then, is the characteristic of this commentary? We reply that this commentary on the three sections of synonyms is that which explains a state, synonym, analysis, number, doubtful derivations and quotations, as well as their different interpretations. Examples are as follows: (1) State—the word *gauḥ* is a synonym of earth ; (2) Synonym—the declaration of an obscure by a well-known substantive, as the word *gauḥ* means the sun ; (3) Analysis—the word *gauḥ* means the sun because it moves (*gacchati*) in the atmosphere ; (4) Number—there are twenty-one synonyms of earth ; (5) Doubtful derivation—the word *nirṛtiḥ* is derived from the root *ram* with *ni*, or from the root *ṛ*. In the former case it means the goddess of death, in the latter distress ; (6) Doubtful quotation—'He who made it', &c. ; (7) Different interpretations—the ascetics hold that a man of large progeny comes to grief, &c.

6. 7.] According to Yāska, the sun is called *gauḥ* also. In order to illustrate this meaning of the word *gauḥ*, he quotes RV. vi. 56. 3. The word *gauḥ* occurs in the locative singular in the stanza, which, according to Yāska, means 'in the sun'. But Durga explains **गवि** by **गमनशीले मुहूर्तमप्यनवस्थायिनि**. Roth trans-

[1] See *Erläuterungen*, p. 18.

[2] Burnell's edition, pp. 29-32.

lates गवि by 'through the course of clouds' (*durch den . . . Wolkenzug*). In his explanation Durga remarks: उताप्यथेति छन्दसि समानार्थाः । The joints (*paruṣe*) are the days and nights according to Aupamanyava. He explains चक्रं as (1) the wheel-shaped brilliant disk that is constantly revolving; (2) as the cycle of time with its divisions and subdivisions into year, seasons, month, fortnight, day, night, hour, minute, second, and the twinkling of the eye.

6. 11.] Roth thinks that in the sentence: सोऽपि गौरुच्यते refers to the moon. His argument is that if the sun is called *gauḥ*, the moon, to which a ray of the sun brings light, can also be so called. And he attributes the same meaning to the word *goḥ* in the stanza RV. i. 84. 15 quoted by Yāska. This explanation is misleading and does not suit the context. The word in the sentence does not refer to the moon, but to that particular ray of the sun which illumines the moon. This is a case of extension of meaning. The sun is called *gauḥ*, then each of its rays is called *gauḥ*. This meaning becomes clear from the sentence which follows the one under discussion, wherein Yāska says: सर्वेऽपि रश्मयो गाव उच्यन्ते, 'all the rays are called *gāvaḥ* also.' This shows that स in the previous sentence refers to one ray and not to the moon. Durga interprets the passage rightly. He remarks: सोऽपि सुषुम्णो रश्मिरेक एव गौरित्युच्यते.

7. 1.] Durga explains गावः by रश्मयः in accordance with the meaning given to it by Yāska. Roth translates it by cattle (*Rinder*). As to Durga's explanation of the dual वां see Roth's note on ii. 7, *Erläuterungen*, p. 19.

8. 1.] The stanza RV. i. 164. 32 is quoted to explain the meaning of *Nirṛtiḥ*.

According to the interpretation of the ascetics, *nirṛtiḥ* means distress. The stanza in that case would mean: The man, who causes impregnation (गर्भं करोति), does not know the reality, for he acts either in a moment of passion or with a desire to get a son. When he comes to know of it, he still does not realize his responsibility, for the foetus is hidden from him. But the child nourished in the mother's womb is born in course of time. Thus multiplying, the poor man, unable to make adequate provision for the bringing up of his children, comes to grief. Durga's words are: कश्चिद् बहुप्रजा बह्वपत्यो दरिद्रः पुरुषः दुष्पोषत्वादपत्यानां व्यापन्नत्वात् कृच्छ्रं दुःखमापद्यते ।

This passage foreshadows the Malthusian doctrine. Another different interpretation of the followers of the school of ascetics is that the man who causes impregnation becomes himself involved in transmigration, and being born again and again, comes to grief. This is an admonition to lead a celibate life.

According to the interpretation of the etymologists, the word *nirṛtiḥ* means earth. The meaning of the stanza then would be: The cloud which discharges the rain-water does not know anything about it, as to where it comes from. It is hidden from the atmospheric cloud which sees it falling, because in the atmosphere it exists in the form of vapours, while the rain-water, swelling in the atmosphere and increasing in various ways, falls to the ground.

Roth thinks it refers to lightning which quickly disappears in the clouds and leaves an abundant progeny in the form of showers of rain (*Regengüsse*) which fall on the earth. See *Erläuterungen*, p. 20, note on ii. 8. 1.

8. 11.] The legend of Śākapūṇi, together with the whole of the ninth section, has no bearing on the subject-matter of the chapter and is altogether out of place. It certainly produces the impression of an interpolation. See Roth, *loc. cit.*

9. 2.] The second half of the second hemistich is interpreted by Durga as referring to the re-evaporation of the rain-water. As atmospheric deity in the form of lightning, it brings rain down. As celestial deity in the form of the sun, it takes the water up by evaporation. Thus the deity has the double characteristic. This explanation seems to fit in with Yāska's sentence तस्मै देवतोभयलिङ्गा प्रादुर्बभूव ।

13. 4.] The sentence is a little puzzling with regard to its context. According to the normal construction, the word एतत् in the sentence should refer to the word आदित्यः; but this does not suit the meaning of the passage, for in the Ṛgveda it is neither applied rarely to the sun, nor precluded from being the receptacle of offerings. Durga explains the passage satisfactorily by construing एतत् with the last derivation in the preceding sentence; the meaning then would be that the epithet आदितेय is rarely used in the Ṛgveda with reference to the sun and has only one hymn addressed to him, while oblations are not offered to him under this appellation.

Durga also refers to disagreement among the commentators with regard to the interpretation of this sentence. See Roth, *Erläuterungen*, p. 21, note on ii. 13.

19. 5.] Dawn is explained by Yāska as the time subsequent to night and antecedent to sunrise. So figuratively it may be said that the night gives birth to the dawn, and the dawn to the sun. The passage: यथा प्रसूता सवितुः प्रसवाय रात्रिरादित्यस्यैवं . . . . . योनिमरिचत् । is not clear. The sequence of the genesis of the dawn and the sun does not proceed in any order. The words underlined disturb the regular succession of the birth of the dawn and the sun. The text in this particular place seems to be corrupted. The meaning will be relevant if the word उषा . . . . . be substituted for रात्रिः । The translation in that case would be: 'just as being born she gives birth to the sun, i.e. the dawn to the sun, so the night has left place for dawn.' Durga's comment is the following: यथोषा आदित्यस्य जन्मनो हेतुस्तदनन्तरजन्मत्वादेवं रात्रिरुषसो जन्मनो हेतुरिति ।

20. 4.] The sun is called the calf of the dawn from two analogies: (1) The calf always goes with the mother. The sun and dawn also appear simultaneously. On account of this companionship the sun is described as the calf. (2) The calf enjoys the privilege of taking milk from the udder of the mother cow; the sun also drinks the dew which falls at early dawn and is looked upon as the calf sucking the milk. See Roth, *op. cit.*, p. 22.

21. Roth thinks that Yāska has wrongly introduced the sun in his explanation of the second hemistich of the stanza RV. vi. 9. 1. At first sight it may appear far-fetched, but the simile is apt and justifiable. The text of the Veda is the following: 'Being born the Vaiśvānara fire has overcome darkness with its light like the king.' Yāska's explanation of the same is the following: 'Being born, i. e. being kindled, the Vaiśvānara fire has dispelled darkness with its light like the sun who is the king of all luminaries.' The dispelling of darkness by Agni could aptly be compared with that of the sun alone, hence Yāska's explanation is far from being unduly far-fetched.

24.] See Roth's note on **बिसखा**, *op. cit.* It may be pointed out that the meaning 'digger of a lotus stalk' is more appropriate for the force of comparison. Durga also explains the stanza by interpreting *sarasvatī* as atmospheric speech, and by paraphrasing 'peaks of mountains' by 'tops of clouds', 'waves' by 'thunders', 'sweeping what is far and near' by 'sweeping heaven and earth'.

28.] The stanza is translated by Professor Macdonell in *J.R.A.S.* See vol. xxx, pp. 439, 471–2.

Durga has the following comment: 'The horse hastens forth in spite of being bound in several places. Anything else bound in a single place would not have been able to move, much less to hasten forth.' See Roth, *op. cit.*, p. 23.

CHAPTER III

4. 4.] Durga's argument for looking upon the daughter as equal to the son is that the daughter's son is a grandson. A sonless man can have no grandson; hence if a man had a grandson, he has a son *ipso facto*. Consequently the daughter would be equal to a son. This argument is not very sound. For it will be applicable in case a man has both a son and a daughter, will give to the daughter a status equal to that of the son, and will entitle her to all the rights and privileges of a son. Historically this is not true of the Aryan family. The daughter never enjoyed equality with a son as far as succession and inheritance were concerned, for on marriage she passed out of the *patria potestas* of the paterfamilias.

Durga's second argument for the equality of a son and a daughter is that the sacrificial rites performed on the birth of a son are identical with those performed on the birth of a daughter; the sacred texts used in the celebration of the *garbhādhāna* ceremony are the same; and finally the physical and physiological processes involved in procreation are without any distinction whatsoever in begetting a male or a female child. It will be superfluous to add that Durga's comment gives the argument employed in the text in an amplified

[1] 14. 9. 4. 8. [2] Cf. ix. 130.

state. Metrical passages from the *Śatapatha Brāhmaṇa*[1] and Manu[2] are cited in support of the view stated above, while the *Maitrāyaṇī Saṃhitā*[1] is quoted to corroborate the ideas of the opposite school. Both pros and cons are thus placed side by side.

4. 15.] The passage shows that women were sold and abandoned. Durga explains sale and abandonment as marriages by purchase and capture. It may also refer to slavery. Abandonment in fact survived among some Indian communities, noticeably the Rajputs, who exposed female children. This led to infanticide, to which the British Government has put a stop only in modern times.

Roth[2] thinks that the passage beginning with अङ्गादङ्गात् and ending with पितुश्च पुत्रभावः is an interpolation for the following reasons: (1) the explanation of the two hemistichs of the stanza (RV. iii. 31. 1) quoted in the fourth section is separated in a forced manner, (2) the length of the intervening passage; (3) the looseness of its connexion; (4) the designation of the metrical passage अङ्गादङ्गात् &c. as a stanza of the Ṛgveda (*ṛk*)—a term which Yāska never uses and which is evidently a mistake in the present case, as the verses do not belong to the Ṛgveda, nor possibly could belong to any other of its recensions, on account of their form and contents; (5) finally, the deviation from the purpose of the chapter is remarkable. Roth, however, is unable to say whether the whole or a part of the intervening passage is an interpolation. The only justification which he finds for this irrelevancy is that scholars were particularly busy with the controversy concerning the laws of inheritance.

All external evidence—i. e. of the MSS. of both recensions and of Durga, who has preserved a critical text of the *Nirukta* in his commentary—is against Roth's conclusion. As to the internal evidence, the argument of violent separation of the explanation of the two hemistichs and of the looseness of connexion is exaggerated, for the passage up to न दुहितर इत्येके is an amplified exposition of the second pāda of the first hemistich. As to Roth's fourth argument, the very fact that the word *ṛk* is not used to denote a stanza of the Ṛgveda in the *Nirukta*—as Roth himself says—shows that it did not then express the meaning attributed to it by Roth. On the contrary, the word *nigama* is always employed by Yāska to indicate a Vedic passage. The author using a different word for a metrical Brāhmaṇa passage shows that he was fully conscious of the difference between the Vedic and non-Vedic passages. Hence it is not a mistake. As to the deviation from the subject proper of the chapter, it may be said that ancient authors had nothing which could correspond to the modern system of foot-notes; they were obliged therefore to put any discussion arising out of cognate or allied subjects within the text itself.

No doubt the intervening passage is a long one and has no other parallel in

[1] 4. 6. 4; 4. 7. 9.

[2] See *op. cit.*, iii. 4, p. 24.

the *Nirukta,* yet to regard it as an interpolation without some positive proof would be going too far. The assumption would be more or less conjectural.

4. 16.] The followers of a third school, representing a compromise between the two other schools which champion the rights of the daughter and the son respectively, hold that it is the brotherless daughter who has a right to inherit the patrimony. Durga states the case for a brotherless daughter as follows: The brotherless girl alone inherits the patrimony and not one who has a brother. The male agnates, who have the right to offer the funeral cake to the deceased, and are alive, preclude a woman from inheritance, because she contributes to the growth not of her father's but of a different family, i. e. of her husband, hence she has no right to claim a share in her father's property. But a brotherless daughter is different. In that case there is no one to perform the funeral rites for the deceased, and because the daughter's son discharges these duties through the relationship of his mother, his mother, i. e. the brotherless daughter, is entitled to inherit the property of her late father. A stanza is quoted from AV. (i. 17. 1). The MSS. of the shorter recension and the *Bib. Ind.* edition of the *Nirukta* cite the second hemistich only. The MSS. of the longer recension and Durga according to the Bombay edition of the *Nirukta* give the stanza in full. From the fact that in the text of the *Nirukta* the second hemistich is alone explained, one may conclude that originally the quotation was limited to the second half of the AV. stanza only. Durga remarks that the stanza is used in the preparation of medicines for a woman suffering from excessive menstruation. The charm signifies: Let all the blood-vessels come to a standstill, like brotherless daughters who find their path obstructed.

See Roth, *op. cit.*, pp. 25-6.

5.] Roth seems to have misunderstood the significance of the first pāda of the stanza RV. i. 124. 7, quoted in the fifth section. He thinks that a brotherless maiden becomes homeless after the death of her father. Being homeless and destitute she approaches men boldly. This is not what is meant. The meaning is that a daughter, although given away in marriage and therefore usually lost to the parental family, comes back to discharge the duties of a son because she is brotherless. Both dawn and the brotherless daughter are conceived as going away from their natal home, and the point of comparison lies in their return; the one comes back next morning in accordance with the law of nature, the other by the law of society. The simile is rather crude.

There are four similes in the stanza. Roth seems to have noticed three only. *Na*, the particle of comparison, is used four times, and Yāska also says that there are four similes. They are as follows: (1) dawn comes back to men like a daughter who has no brother; (2) she goes to obtain wealth like one who mounts the platform in the gambling-hall; (3) like a well-dressed wife desiring her husband; and (4) like a smiling maiden, she discloses her beauty.

गर्तारुक् is explained in the *Nirukta* and by Durga as meaning a southern woman who goes to the gambling hall to obtain wealth. **गर्तः** is interpreted as सभास्थाणुः, which, according to Durga, means अक्षनिर्वपणपीठं, i. e. the seat or place where the die is thrown. The word गर्तः is derived from the root *gṛ* (to invoke) and acquires this sense because it is सत्यसंगरः, which is explained by Durga as follows: संगीर्यते हि तत्र सत्यमिदमत्र पतितमिदमत्र न पतितमित्येवम् । प्रायेण कितवास्तत्रानृतं ब्रुवते ।

Durga does not seem to have a very clear idea of the peculiar custom to which he refers. At one place, he says: 'If a sonless woman goes there, she obtains wealth. The gamblers give her wealth. This is the custom of the southern people.' At another place, he says: 'The woman who has lost her son and husband mounts it, i. e. takes her seat on it in the midst of the gamblers. Then she obtains wealth from the relatives of her husband, i. e. her share of the property, settled upon her by her husband.' Whether the wealth was given by the gamblers or by the relatives of the deceased husband is not made clear; the precise nature of the custom remains therefore doubtful. In this connexion it may be mentioned that among the orthodox Hindus of Northern India, there still prevails a custom called *jholibharaṇā*, i. e. 'filling the lap', according to which the members of a woman's paternal family fill her lap with money on her becoming a widow. This attempt to explain a passage of the Ṛgveda with regard to the customs of Southern India indicates that the expounder himself belonged to the south. It will be going too far to read the peculiar customs of the south in the Ṛgveda. This confused and altogether far-fetched explanation of the stanza, together with a number of irrelevant derivations which follow the explanation, and the use of the epithet *nigama* with regard to a passage which is apparently a Brāhmaṇa quotation, make the authenticity of the passage doubtful.

गर्तारुक् should be interpreted to mean, 'one who fights in a chariot'; the simile then would be natural. 'Like a chariot-fighter, the dawn comes to obtain wealth.'

5. 10.] Roth paraphrases उपरस्य *von dem oberen unbehauenen Theil*, i. e. unhewn upper part. It is more likely that the lower part is meant, which, according to Durga, should be covered with earth and grass. The meaning seems to be that the lower part of the sacrificial post should be buried in the ground and not exposed to sight. Durga says that the unhewn part of a sacrificial post is called *upara*. I think the part meant is lower and not upper, for the upper part remaining above the surface of the earth will still be exposed even if it be smeared over with mud and grass. Further, the part to be buried under ground is likely to be left unhewn.

5. 19.] This is the explanation of the second hemistich of RV. iii. 31. 1, quoted in the fourth section. According to Durga the daughter here means the brotherless daughter. He remarks: This is the second half of the stanza left over. This is explained to support the theory of 'the brotherless daughter'. The first hemistich should be similarly interpreted. The sonless man has the daughter's son as his grandson only when the daughter is brotherless and the rite of 'appointment' is performed. But he has no such claim on the sons of those daughters who have brothers. Otherwise all the husbands will be deprived of their sons and marriage itself will be useless and a burden. Or every male child will have a double pedigree. Moreover, every wife being the daughter of somebody may be called upon by her father to remain in her paternal home. This will throw society in confusion. Therefore the son of that daughter only who is duly appointed in accordance with law belongs to her father, but not the son of a daughter who has a brother.

According to Durga the texts which advocate equality between a son and a daughter refer to a brotherless daughter. **रेत:सेकं** is explained as **रेतस: सेक्तारं यो दुहितरि रेत: सिञ्चति तं जामातारम्**, i. e. husband.

Durga explains **प्रार्जयति** 'he arranges, or selects, or makes him approach', **संगमेन मनसा**, i. e. free from the anguish of sonlessness.

6.] The meaning of the word **वह्नि:** is obscure. Yāska followed by Durga explains it by **वोढा** in the fourth section and by **पुत्रम्** in the sixth. Moreover, he seems to take **वह्नि:** as a copulative compound standing for both man and woman.

8.] Durga makes the following remarks on the stanza RV. x. 53. 4: The ṛsiship is that of *Śaucīka Agni*, and this is his dialogue with the *Viśvedevās*.[1] Roth's criticism of it is, that although a mythological element is found in the two preceding hymns, it is entirely lacking in this hymn.

Durga takes **देवा:** as a vocative, which is not only against Yāska's explanation, but is impossible on account of the accent. The translation of the stanza according to Durga would be as follows: 'I know that most excellent strength of speech with which we shall overcome the evil spirits. O gods, partakers of food and accomplishers of sacrifice, and ye five-tribes, favour my sacrifice.'

8. 9.] Two explanations are given of 'the five-tribes', in the *Nirukta*. According to one view, 'the five-tribes' are the gandharvas, manes, gods, evil spirits, and demons; according to Aupamanyava, they are the four castes and the *Niṣādas*. The former is highly improbable, because the five-tribes are called upon to participate in the sacrifice and an invitation to demons and to evil spirits to share the sacrifice is inconceivable on the part of any sacrificer. The evidence of the stanza itself is against this view. The first hemistich mentions the overthrow of the evil spirits in clear and unmistakable terms. Further, on account of the eternal hostility between the gods, the guardians and promoters of the sacrifice, on one hand, and the evil spirits and demons, the disturbers and destroyers of the sacrifice, on the other, it does not seem possible that both gods and demons could be thus asked to enjoy the sacrifice. A gathering of this kind could never be harmonious. The latter explanation

[1] See Roth, *op. cit.*, pp. 27-8.

is undoubtedly the better one. Yāska quotes RV. viii. 63. 7 to show that the five-tribes[1] of the stanza under discussion are meant to be human, and thus supports this view by implication. Durga, of course, agrees with Yāska. This means that the four castes and the *Niṣādas* shared the sacrifice in common. This would imply some sort of inter-dining among the various castes, and would show that the water-tight compartments into which the various castes are divided, and separated by rigid barriers of mutual exclusiveness, did not exist in Yāska's time. Further, the epithet 'holy' (*yajñiyāsaḥ*) is applied to 'five-tribes'. If we accept Aupamanyava's view, all the four tribes and the *Niṣādas* would be holy. This would mean, even if the *Niṣādas*, who according to the etymologists are sinful beings, are excluded, that the lower castes were not despised by the upper ones, especially the Brāhmaṇas, which would again imply greater equality for the former and less tyranny on the part of the latter. This shows that, unlike the moderns, the ancient Brāhmaṇas could not have regarded themselves as polluted by the mere sight or the touch of the lower castes, otherwise the latter would neither have been invited to partake of the sacrifice, nor called holy; i. e. the problem of the pariah and the 'untouchables' had not then arisen, or rather the pariah and the 'untouchables' themselves did not exist.

10. 9.] The etymological explanation अम्बुसञ्ज्ञातीति वाम्बुमञ्ज्ञवतीति वा । is not found in Durga's commentary. As shown in the introduction, the passage therefore is an interpolation. The spurious character of the passage is indicated by the internal evidence also: Yāska has already explained the word *ambu-da* (cloud) as the giver (from the √*da* to give) of water (*ambu*). The passage in question is, therefore, superfluous. Moreover, it does not explain the etymology of the word *ambu-da*. Besides, here the derivation of *ambu-da* is of secondary importance; it is the word *arbu-da* that Yāska wants to explain. For this purpose he finds it necessary to explain *arṇam* first, and explains *ambu-da* incidentally. It is reasonable to expect that in such a case he would not attach too much importance to *ambu-da*. This evidence, together with Durga's omission of the passage, leads me to the conclusion stated above.

12.] According to Durga, the meaning of the stanza i. 163. 21 is as follows: 'The rays of the sun—which fall on a bright object whose darkness is removed, or which are bright when they fall—having obtained a share of the immortal water from the earth, and being accompanied by it, join all creatures in invocation; or, having seized the fluids, respectfully go back to the sun. They have the knowledge of their duties. The lord, wise guardian of the entire universe, i.e. the sun, approached me, whose intellect is immature.'

With regard to the soul, the meaning is as follows: the senses, well placed in their several organs, having obtained a share of the immortal knowledge, stimulate the consciousness of the inner person with regard to external

[1] See Macdonell and Keith, *Vedic Index*, under *pañca janāḥ*.

objects, or approach the faculty of discrimination, bearing the knowledge of external objects in order to bring about their cognition. The senses themselves have no power of apprehension. They are but the unconscious instruments of the conscious *puruṣa*, who is the doer, and whose nature is knowledge. The lord, guardian of all senses, i.e. the soul, the wise one, has entered me, the immature one.

15. 4.] '*Devaraḥ* is so called because he is the second husband.' This refers to the custom called *niyoga*. It prevailed among the Jews[1] and was also an Indo-European[2] practice. It is also found among the Purans, a Borneo jungle people of very primitive type, among the Bayaka in Africa, among the Aleuts, and Thlinkeats, and Koloshes.[3]

15. 13.] Roth translates पुरा जीवगृभो यथा as *noch ehe sie gleichsam ans Leben greift*, i.e. 'before it, so to say, attacks life'. Durga explains the same words as: यथा जीवग्राहस्य पुरा एव हननादहतस्यैव जीवो नश्येत् । The passage is quoted in order to illustrate the use of *yathā* as a particle of comparison.

20. 9.] Roth says that, according to Durga, the inaccurate diction of Yāska has given rise to the divergent reading अप्राप्तस्येत्येकेऽधीयते । (*op. cit.*, iii. 20. 7, pp. 34–5). Roth probably has misunderstood Durga. At any rate, Durga does not say anything about the 'inaccurate manner of expression of Yaska'. It is also not clear to me in what Yāska's inaccuracy consists. Moreover, Roth's quotation from Durga's commentary is defective; Durga's sentence runs thus:

अप्राप्तस्यैकेऽधीयते तथापि योज्यम् । . . . . सतः संस्तृतं भवति । एकीभूय स्तृतं भवति ।

The words underlined are mutilated and भवति is omitted in Roth's quotation. Durga only wants to say that some MSS. of the *Nirukta* have the variant अप्राप्तस्य. And in his paraphrase of the two Vedic quotations, RV. v. 75. 7 and vii. 104. 21, he explains both तिरः and सतः not by the meaning attributed to them by the reading प्राप्तस्य but by that of the variant. His remark is as follows:

तिरश्चिदर्यया तिरोऽप्यप्राप्तेऽपि दूर एव स्थाने . . . . सतः प्रदेशाद् दूरादित्यर्थः ।

[1] See Deuteronomy xxv. 5; St. Matthew xxii. 24.

[2] See Xenophon, *Rep. Lac.* i. 9, cited by Grote, ii. 6, p. 520, and note at the end of vol. ii.

[3] See Hobhouse, *Evolution of Morals*, pp. 34–5.

CHAPTER IV

Durga, after the usual benedictory stanza, quotes two verses without indicating their source, to the effect that a seer, after greatly expanding knowledge, should expound it briefly, for in the world an adherence to prolixity and conciseness is desired of learned men (according to the exigencies of the occasion). He takes this dictum as a test of sound scholarship and applies it to the commentary of Yāska. He shows that it is followed by Yāska, who is concise and also prolix as the occasion demands. According to him, brevity is the characteristic of the second and the third chapters of the *Nirukta*, commenting on the synonyms which should be and are explained briefly, i.e. by giving the necessary information about a particular word, its synonyms, their number, quotations to obviate ambiguity of meaning, and explanation of the same. All this exposition is brief. He then notices omissions on the part of Yāska in the explanation of synonyms in the *Nirukta*. 'In this part of his commentary of the *Nirukta*', he remarks, 'one single meaning indicates many words and many words denote one single meaning.' He adds that the different shades of the meanings of these words are not explained. In order to make his meaning clear he gives the following example: 102 words beginning with वर्तते and ending with अयधुः are explained to have the general meaning of motion. But a particular word expresses a particular kind of motion only to the exclusion of others; e.g. the verb *kasati* denotes hopping only and not flying; लोठते is used in the sense of rolling only —in connexion with a ball, for instance; श्चोतते expresses 'trickling' and is used in connexion with liquids only. Thus the specific forms of the general meaning should be investigated. Further, the usage of different provinces is not explained. In some places the common words are used to denote technical expressions and vice versa. These arguments of Durga may be supplemented by drawing attention to the fact that only a few of the synonyms are explained—the rest are passed over. With this section of Yāska's commentary Durga contrasts his commentary on homonyms. He points out that the whole list of the homonyms is explained word by word. Different meanings of one word are fully explained and illustrated with Vedic quotations. The characteristic of Yāska's commentary on homonyms is therefore prolixity.

2. 11.] Many meanings are attributed to the word शिताम. On account of its different interpretations by Yāska and his contemporaries, and the several theories put forward by Durga, the word seems to have lost its precise meaning at an early period. It is evident that the word means a particular part of the sacrificial animal. Durga's one theory is that the body of an animal can be divided into: (1) external parts, as shoulders, hips, &c.; (2) internal parts, as tongue, heart, &c. He thinks that the two words preceding शिताम in the passage quoted by Yāska refer to the external parts of the body, i.e. flanks and hips, hence शिताम would naturally also refer to some external part. This is the argument adduced by him while explaining Yāska's sentence that the word शिताम means 'forearm' (*dos*). The word *dos* is derived by Yāska from the root *dru* (to run), 'because', says Durga, 'it is with the strength of the forearm that animals run'. Durga's second theory is that the two words preceding शिताम in the passage referred to above describe successive parts of the body; शिताम therefore would mean a part which comes next to hips, i.e. arms. It is for this reason that he paraphrases योनिः by गुदः and derives विषितः from the root विष् 3 cl. 'to pervade', and explains विषितो भवति as व्याप्तः स पुरीषेण भवति . . . अथवा . . विस्रस्तमांसः स भवति, i.e. it is full of ordure, . . . or its flesh is loose. I myself derive विषितः from सो with वि and translate it as 'it is open'. The various meanings attributed to शिताम are the following: (1) 'forearm', by Yāska; (2) *yoniḥ* (*uterus*) explained as equivalent to *anus*, according to Durga, by Śākapūṇi; (3) 'liver' on account of its dark colour (*śyāman*), by Taiṭīki; (4) fat, lit. white meat (*śiti-māṃsa*), by Gālava.[1] Durga remarks, 'Thus it is clear that the grammatical form and the meaning of the word शिताम are not (precisely) known'.

11.] Durga explains RV. i. 115. 4 as follows: 'The divinity and the greatness of the sun is that, ignoring all workers in the midst of their work, he rolls up the net of light which is difficult to be gathered by others, but which the sun rolls up in an instant, without much trouble and without any other help. He has yoked the bay steeds—i. e. rays which draw up fluids—from the stable, i. e. the earth. The earth is the *sadhastham*, for it is hence that rays extract fluids.' The meaning is that when the rays are withdrawn from the earth, night spreads her garment over all.

15.] Roth translates the word कनीनका as 'image', and Langlois as 'marionette'. According to Yāska, however, it means a 'maiden'. Durga explains it by शालभञ्जिका, i.e. an image made of the *śāla* tree.

17.] The quotation इमे सुता इन्द्वः &c., has not yet been traced. In both the *Bib. Ind.* and the Bombay editions of Durga's commentary the stanza is given in full. But Durga explains the fourth verse only. His remark, that the rest is to be discovered (मृग्योऽन्य शेषः), indicates that he did not know the other verses of the stanza. To include the first three verses in the above-mentioned editions of Durga's commentary is therefore a mistake.

18.] Yāska quotes one Vedic passage only to illustrate his meanings of the two words अकूपारस्य and दावने. The order in which these two words occur in the *Nighaṇṭu* is reversed in Yāska's quotation. According to Yāska, the word अकूपारस्य means 'sun, ocean, and the tortoise'. Durga paraphrases the word by अकुत्सितपूरणस्य, i. e. 'complete without any flaw', and further explains the

[1] See Roth, *op. cit.*, iv. 3. 6, pp. 38-9.

term as that which may be sufficient in this, and glorious in the next world. Durga's derivation of अकूपारस्य is the following: अकूपारस्य < अकुपरणस्य < अकुत्सितपूरणस्य। He says: अत्र कुरिति कुत्सार्थः परणं पूरणमुच्यते कुत्सितं परणं कुपरणं न कुत्सितं परणमकुपरणम्।

Durga notices the difference of the order of the two words in the *Nighaṇṭu* and the *Nirukta*, and concludes that the *Nighaṇṭu* and the *Nirukta* are the works of different authors. See Roth, *op. cit.*, iv. 18, p. 45.

The word सुतुकः is explained as 'moving swiftly', i. e. derived from the root √*tuj*, or as 'having good offspring'. On the latter Durga remarks. 'The word *tuk* is a synonym of offspring. The offspring of Agni is intended to be golden. And Agni himself is called of golden seed, and so on.' Durga paraphrases सुप्रजोभिः by कुलजैः, i. e. 'of noble breed', or the horses who have noble foals, for it is the noble horses only who can breed noble foals. i. e. the fact of breeding noble foals implies praise of the horses. and the possession of such horses implies praise of Agni.

19.] Durga's explanation of शिश्नदेवाः does not indicate any reference to phallism. There is no evidence to show that Durga or Yāska was even aware of its existence. According to them the phrase denotes profligate persons whose sole or chief end in life is to gratify their sensual desires. But the phrase is a possessive (*Bahuvrīhi*) compound, and can be translated accurately only as 'they whose god is the phallus'. It may be that the cult of the phallus, inasmuch as it originated from the aborigines, was not known to Yāska or Durga. In ancient times it was a widespread cult, and in one form or another survived in many Roman Catholic countries, like Belgium, France, and Italy, down to the middle of the eighteenth century. Phallic remains are discovered all over the world, notably in Ireland. According to some, the maypole and the cross are also phallic survivals—a very doubtful conclusion. The worship of Śiva as the *lingam* may remotely be connected with it. See Hastings, *Encyclopaedia of Religion and Ethics*, 'Phallism'. Cf. also phallic objects, monuments, and remains.

21.] Durga explains the stanza RV. i. 164. 33 as follows: 'Heaven is my father, the progenitor, and the great earth is my mother, because the rain descends from heaven to earth, helps the various herbs and plants to grow. which nourish the body and endow it with the seed of future generations: heaven and earth are therefore the primaeval cause of life. The intermediate space is the womb, i.e. the source of rain-water. The father has bestowed the life-germ on the daughter, i.e. the cloud has bestowed the rain-water on the earth. The earth is here called the daughter (*du-hitā*) because it is placed at a great distance from the cloud (*dūre-hitā*).'

21. 10.] Yāska takes शंयोः as a compound and explains शमनं and यावनं. This analysis is in agreement with that of the author of the *Padapatha*. Durga remarks that Yāska has divided one word having the ablative or genitive ending into two words of the accusative case, and in order to connect the sense of the passage has supplied the words 'diseases' and 'dangers' in the *Nirukta*. Roth agrees with Yāska's explanation. Cf. *op. cit.*, p. 48.

23.] Durga explains माता (mother) by सर्वभूतनिर्माची, i.e. fashioner of all beings; पुत्रः as पुरुणो बहुनः पापात्त्रायते।, i.e. one who saves from a great sin. According to the interpretation of the etymologists the meaning of the stanza would be as follows: 'Heaven is unimpaired, the intermediate space is unimpaired. He is the mother, the father, and the son. The *Viśvedevās* are unimpaired. the five-tribes are unimpaired, and all that is born, or is yet to be born.'

24.] Roth's translation of the second hemistich is not clear. The word जसुरिम् is explained as जस्तम् by Yāska, which is paraphrased by Dūrga as बद्धम् 'bound'. He says: . . . . . बद्धं स्नायुतन्तुना य एष याजिक इति प्रसिद्धो राज्ञां स हि बद्धत्वादुत्पतितुमत्यर्थं न शक्नोति नीचैरेव गच्छति गत्वा च शशकादीनि हिनस्ति सत्त्वानि। . . . न ह्यबद्धः श्येनो नीचैरयते। There is a contradiction in Durga's explanation: a falcon that is bound cannot pursue its prey; जस्तम् derived from the √जस् means 'liberate', 'free', 'let loose'. Cf. Roth, *op. cit.*, iv. 24, p. 48.

25. 12.] Durga explains देवपीयुम् as one who is addicted to self-enjoyment and who does not sacrifice to the gods.

25. 19.] Yāska does not cite any passage to illustrate ऋधक् in the sense of 'separate', &c. Durga supplies the quotation RV. vi. 40. 5 for this purpose. He says that some commentators interpret the passage (VS. 8. 20) quoted by Yāska in two ways, i.e. taking alternately the two meanings of ऋधक् 'separate', and 'prosperity'.

Cf. Roth, *op. cit.*, 14, p. 50.

25. 25.] Roth thinks that the text is corrupt and the word अजाश्व is superfluous. I do not agree with Roth, for with a proper punctuation the sentence is quite clear. It is to be read thus: अजाश्वेति पूषणमाह। अजाश्व। अजा अजनाः। 'The author calls Pūṣan goat-teamed. Goat-teamed, i.e. goats are the coursers.' Cf. Roth, *op. cit.*, 18. p. 51.

CHAPTER V

Durga explains सस्निम् as 'wrapped up in waters, flowing on all sides, or well-washed, i. e. a cloud'. He explains चरणे as 'in the atmosphere', and नदीनाम् as 'of waters'. According to Durga, the sense is as follows: Indra found the cloud in the atmosphere and noticed its strength, so he bored holes into it for the waters to flow down. The waters then proclaimed Indra to be *Gandharva*. Durga adds, 'it is heard that Indra is *Gandharva* and the Maruts are his nymphs'.

3.] Durga explains पक्वम् by अभिव्यक्तम्, i. e. manifest, and paraphrases ससम् by स्वप्नम् after Yāska. According to him, lightning remains invisible during eight months, appearing in the rainy season only, hence the epithet अनित्यदर्शनं is used with regard to it. Cf. Roth, *op. cit.*, 15, p. 55.

4.] According to Durga, the groups of atmospheric gods here refer to the Maruts, for the word group has been used in the plural number and it is the Maruts only who have several groups, each consisting of seven members. He then quotes the Brāhmaṇa passage: ते सप्तसप्त मरुतां गणाः। He further says that Rudra is called *varāha* also, and quotes RV. i. 114. 5, in support of his statement. Cf. Roth, *op. cit.*, 5. p. 56.

7.] Yāska's explanation of RV. i. 150. 1 is confused. He explains अरिः by अमित्रः But a worshipper cannot be unfriendly to the god whom he worships. Roth connects अरिः with अरणः and deduces the meaning, 'strange, stranger, guest, and a hostile person'. The other meaning, 'lord', attributed to अरिः by Yāska is equally unsatisfactory as far as the present passage is concerned. Durga makes an attempt to explain अरिः as 'competent to offer oblations and sing praises'. But by so doing he ignores the interrogative particle स्वित्. Yāska's explanation of the third pāda is obscure. Durga derives शरणे from the root शृ to injure, and paraphrases it by बिले. According to him the sense is that just as many streams flow into some wide cave, and notwithstanding the large number of streams the holding capacity of the cave is not affected thereby, so many oblations are poured into fire, without affecting the latter's capacity to consume them. Having seen this phenomenon, the seer proclaimed, तोदस्येव शरण आ महस्य, i. e. (oblations flow into fire as waters) into the cavity of a great well. Cf. Roth, *op. cit.*, p. 59.

7.] Muir[1] attributes the sentence, 'the words *Śipiviṣṭa* and *Viṣṇu* are two names of Viṣṇu', to Aupamanyava. This, however, is not correct. The first

[1] Cf. *Sanskrit Texts*, vol. iv, p. 505.

sentence contains Yāska's own remark, while the second gives the view of Aupamanyava. Durga puts the second sentence only in the mouth of Aupamanyava, and his interpretation is supported by internal evidence also. Durga remarks that of the two names of *Viṣṇu*, the first alone is illustrated, because the second belongs to the *daivata kāṇḍa*. Cf. Roth, *op. cit.*, v. 8, p. 59.

12.] Durga remarks that some think the stanza x. 89. 5 to be chiefly addressed to Indra, and explains the third pāda as follows: i. e. Indra pervades everything as Soma does all plants and trees. Following Yāska, Durga suggests two alternative interpretations: he ascribes (1) the first hemistich and the fourth pāda to Indra, and the third pāda to Soma. (2) the first three pādas to Soma and the last to Indra. The meaning would be, (1) Indra, who is infused with energy, who rushes to the attack, the shaker of enemies, the impetuous, the great hero armed with the thunderbolt—him all counter-measures do not deceive; they perish even before they reach him; may he and Soma which surpasses all plants and trees favour us; (2) may Soma which infuses energy, which flows quickly, the shaker of vessels, active, exhilarating, foaming, and surpassing all plants and trees, and Indra whom all counter-measures do not deceive; they perish even before him; favour us. In both cases, Durga thinks this to be a joint panegyric to Indra and Soma. Cf. Roth, *op. cit.*, v. 12, p. 62.

24.] Yāska explains **कुटस्य** by **कृतस्य**. This shows that he noticed this example of Prākṛtization in the Ṛgveda. Whether he deduced any general principle of Prākṛtization, or whether he was even aware of the existence of this phenomenon, is doubtful. Durga mechanically repeats Yāska's words. Apparently the paraphrase of **कुटस्य** by **कृतस्य** did not strike him as unusual.

25.] Durga explains the second hemistich of the stanza x. 44. 6 as follows: 'Men, who were unable to obtain thy favour and who could not ascend the ship of sacrifice, being chiefly addicted to sensual pleasures, committed vile deeds and consequently obtained bodies appropriate to their deeds in accordance with the law of *Karma*.' He then quotes a passage without indicating its source: **अथ य इह कपूयचरणा अभ्याशो ह यत्ते कपूयां योनिमापद्येरन् श्वयोनिं वा सूकरयोनिं वा चण्डालयोनिं वा ।** Now there is a prospect that they, whose deeds are vile, will obtain a vile form of existence, i. e. that of a dog, or of a pig, or of a low-born man' (Chānd. Up. v. 10. 7).

25.] Durga remarks that some commentators explain the stanza x. 50. 6 with reference to Agni, i. e. Agni is called the son of strength (*sūno sahasaḥ*) as he is produced by strongly twirling one stick on another. This explanation, according to him, is inaccurate, for it is contrary to the context, as the hymn (x. 50) is addressed to Indra. He thinks that the epithet, 'son of strength', here refers to Indra, who is so called because he is the son of *prāṇa*. Cf. Roth, *op. cit.* 7, p. 70.

26.] Durga explains the stanza x. 101. 7 as follows: 'Refresh these horses with water and fodder as the battle is near at hand. Win a good victory with the refreshed horses. A victory, when one's dear friend, brothers, sons, &c., are killed, is not good. Having a noble car, pour down men into this well of battle as if they were water,' &c. He explains **अवतः** as **कूपः स हि खन्यमानो महानवातितोऽवाङतितो भवति गत इत्यर्थः ।**

CHAPTER VI

Yāska divides the word *āśu-śu-kṣaṇiḥ* into three parts and says, '*āśu*- and *śu* are synonyms of quick'. The latter part, *kṣaṇiḥ*, is derived from the root *kṣaṇ* (to injure). According to him the word therefore means, 'injuring very quickly.' Durga has not rightly understood Yāska and consequently misconstrues the sentence. He thinks that the word *śu* occurring in Yāska's statement does not refer to the second part of the word *āśu-śu-kṣaṇiḥ*, but to an altogether different word which means 'space', and which has been used by Yāska incidentally only: **शु- इत्येतदत्र प्रासङ्गिकम्** . . . . He says that of the three parts *āśu-śu-kṣaṇiḥ*, Yāska explains the first (*āśu*) and the third (*kṣaṇiḥ*) but passes over the second (*śu*), adding that *śu* is derived from the root *śuc*, 'to shine'. Durga's explanation of Yāska's division and derivation of *āśu-śu-kṣaṇiḥ* is quite wrong, and it is surprising to note that he could thus misunderstand Yāska's very clear statement. After deriving each individual part of *āśu-śu-kṣaṇiḥ*, Yāska explains the meaning as **आशु शुचा क्षणोति**. It appears that Durga has connected these three words with each part of *āśu-śu-kṣaṇiḥ* respectively and hence his mistake. It may be again pointed out that Yāska very clearly says that the words *āśu* and *śu* are synonyms of 'quick', and he nowhere derives *śu* from *śuc*. Yāska offers another etymological explanation of *ā-śuśu-kṣaṇiḥ*. The first part *ā* is the preposition and the second part is formed from the desiderative form of the root *śuc*. Grassmann agrees with Yāska's second derivation. Cf. *op. cit.*, p. 188. Roth probably was not aware of the contradiction in Durga's explanations of Yāska.

2.] Durga explains **गवान्** by waters stored up in the interior of the cloud. When the cloud is pierced, waters flow down without any other obstruction. Running by downward channels they protect reservoirs like lakes, tanks, &c. He paraphrases **पुरुहूतम्** by **उदकम्**. He gives a second interpretation of the same as follows: The rain-water coming down from a pierced cloud is invoked by the people. They shout with joy, 'Oh! how fine'. Words like these coming out of people's mouths protect the rain-water. He takes **वाणीः** in the sense of 'waters' in the first case, and in the sense of 'shouts of people' in the second, and derives **वाणी:** from the root **वह** (to flow) in the former and from **वच्** in the latter sense.

3.] Durga explains **आ कीवत:** as 'from every side'. The meaning, according to him, is, 'Uproot them from every side so that the enemy, even if they try their best, may not be able to know from which side they are being uprooted. Or uproot them without a trace.' Durga's last sentence is strikingly modern. His words are: **यथा न किञ्चिदप्यवशिष्यते ।**

4.] In his paraphrase of the stanza v. 54. 6 Durga explains **वेधस:** in two ways: (1) as an epithet of worms, i. e. the worms which penetrate a tree and consume its sap; (2) as an epithet of the Maruts, i. e. O wise Maruts, you steal the waters of a cloud as worms the sap of a tree. Durga's second interpretation is the correct one; **वेधस:** is in the vocative case as the accent indicates, and can only be connected with the Maruts.

6.] According to Durga, a mother is called *nanā* (from √*nam*) because she stoops in her various acts of kindness, such as giving suck to the baby. A daughter is called *nanā* also, because she stoops down while she attends on her father. He remarks that if the word *tatas* is taken in the sense of 'a father', then *nanā* would mean 'a mother'; but if the former signifies 'a son', then the latter would mean 'a daughter'. He paraphrases *bhiṣak* by *brahmā* and remarks that *brahmā* is called *bhiṣak* because it is he who prepares remedy (*bheṣaja*) for sacrifice when the disease of expiation becomes manifest. He then cites a passage which looks like a Brāhmaṇa quotation: 'Verily is this sacrifice cured where there is a *Brahmā* who knows so much.' He adds that *bhiṣak* means a physician also.

6.] The passage containing the explanation and illustration of the word *kṣoṇasya*, and placed within square brackets, is omitted by the MSS. of the shorter recension. The omission however is not justified. The genuineness of the passage is beyond doubt, for the word *kṣoṇasya* occurs in the list of homonyms enumerated in the fourth section of the *Nighaṇṭu*, and must therefore be explained and illustrated, as every word in the above-mentioned list is so treated according to Yāska's plan. If the passage in question is omitted, *kṣoṇasya* would be left unexplained. Thus a gap would be created which would make the otherwise complete commentary of Yāska on homonyms incomplete. The unjustifiable character of the omission is further proved by the evidence of Durga, who does not question the authenticity of the passage.

8.] Yāska's explanation of the stanza viii. 99. 3 is very unsatisfactory. He suggests two alternative interpretations. He ignores the particle *iva* in his first, and *id* and *na* in both his interpretations. Durga has not rightly followed his second interpretation, wherein the meaning of the particle *iva* is explained. Durga mistakes the explanation of *iva* for that of *id*, passed over by Yāska in both cases. Durga justifies Yāska by saying that *iva, id,* and *na* are expletives. This is I think the only instance where *na* has been taken as an expletive.

Both Yāska and Durga paraphrase *bhakṣata* by a participle. For the form *bhakṣata*, see Professor Macdonell's *Vedic Grammar for Students*, p. 401.

14.] Yāska explains **रिशादसः** by **रेशयदारिणः** Durga reads **रेशयदासिनः** and gives **रेशयदारिणः** as a variant. None of the MSS. which have been collated so far, except one utilized by the editor of the *Nirukta* in the *Bib. Ind.* and specified by him as **ङ**, have the reading **रेशयदासिनः**, although Durga's reading acquires a certain amount of plausibility as to its correctness on account of the similarity of sound, for **रिशादसः** and **रेशयदासिनः** are more similar to each other than **रिशादसः** and **रेशयदारिणः** Durga's explanation of the word **यो हि रेशयति हिंसावान्भवति तस्मै त आयुधान्यस्यन्ति।** is far-fetched. He divides *riśād-asaḥ* contrary to Yāska, who seems to take it as *riśa-dasaḥ*, i. e. destroyers of the enemy. A more natural way of explaining the word would be *riśa-adaḥ*, i. e. devourers of the enemy. Grassmann explains it as 'destroyers of violent acts'. Roth's quotation of Durga's comment is inaccurate. He makes the sibilant in *dāsinaḥ* palatal, while it is dental. Cf. Roth, *op. cit.*, vi. 14, p. 80.

15. Yāska construes **असूर्ते** as the nom. pl. and explains it by **असुसमीरिताः** or **वातसमीरिताः** as an epithet of the atmospheric gods. Evidently he derives **असूर्ते** from **असु** and **ईर्** — a poor etymology. In the text of the Ṛgvedic stanza (x. 82. 4) **असूर्ते** is immediately followed by **सूर्ते**. The former is the opposite of the latter, and both are in the same case, yet according to Yāska the former is the nom. pl. while the latter is the loc. sing.; the former is an epithet of the gods, the latter of the region. This interpretation is very unsatisfactory and destroys the contrast intended to be brought about by the use of two opposite terms. Durga mechanically follows Yāska. The natural way would be to take **असूर्ते** and **सूर्ते** both as loc. sing. and to connect them with **रजसि**. This will bring out the contrast. **सूर्ते** is derived from **सृ** (to move), i. e. trodden, and **असूर्ते** as its opposite would mean 'untrodden'. I translate the Vedic passage as follows: 'seated in the region which is trodden and which is not trodden,' &c. Grassman translates **असूर्त** as 'not illumined', 'dusky'; see *Wörterbuch*, p. 157.

15.] Yāska paraphrases **जारयायि** by **अजायि**, i. e. he derives it from the root *jan* (to be born). But grammatically it is ao. pass. of the root **जॄ** (to grow old), and the sense will suit the Vedic quotation better than that expressed by *jan*, i. e. Agni has been made old by sacrifices as a father of cows by his many children. It occurs only once in the RV.

Durga remarks: **यथा साण्डः पुत्रपौत्रादिभिरनेकधा प्रजायत एवं यज्ञेषु विह्रियमाणोऽनेकधा जायतेऽग्निः।**

16.] Yāska remarks that *pacatā* is used as a noun in x. 116. 8, that it occurs in the singular and dual numbers, and quotes VS. 21. 60 and RV. iii. 28. 2 to support his statement. Durga goes still farther and says that *pacatā* is used in the plural also: **एतद्ध्येकवचनं द्विवचनं बहुवचनं वा भवति प्रकरणविशेषात्।** As if to illustrate his remark, he construes *pacatā* in the above-mentioned stanza with *havīṃṣi*: पचता पक्वानीमानि हवींषि. In the hemistich verb precedes object, as अद्धि before हवींषि and दधिष्व before पचता उत सोमम्. The translation should therefore be: 'accept graciously the cooked viands and the soma'.

19.] Durga gives three explanations of the word *ūdhas*: (1) The hand-press full of soma-juice, taking it as a noun; (2) below, taking it as an adverb. The meaning then would be: release the soma-juice in various vessels and cups below the skin used for straining purposes. ऊध इव सोमपूर्णमधिषवणचर्म ..... ऊधसोऽधस्तात् ....; (3) below or above; the meaning is: release the straining-skin which is below or above the sacrificial car: यदेतय[illegible]शकटस्याधस्तादुपरि वाधिषवणचर्म।

22.] Durga takes व्युदस्यति to be Yāska's explanation of चोष्कूयते. He is evidently wrong, for Yāska clearly says that both चोष्कूयमाण and चोष्कूयते are intensive forms, paraphrasing the former by ददत् and the latter by अभ्यादधाति.

28.] The author of the *Ṛgvedapadapāṭha* analyses *vāyaḥ* into *vā* and *yaḥ*. Yāska rightly objects to this analysis, for the relative pronoun would introduce a dependent clause whose finite verb, according to the rules of accentuation, should have the acute accent. And because the finite verb has the grave accent, it shows that the clause is not dependent and therefore Śākalya's analysis is not correct. Yāska's other objection to the analysis is that the meaning will be incomplete. Yāska takes *vāyaḥ* as one word, meaning the young of a bird. For the accent of the verb in a dependent clause, see Pā. viii. 1. 66; Professor Macdonell's *A Vedic Grammar for Students*, p. 467.

30.] Durga reads नामभिः instead of कर्मभिः and explains: तेन यानि दृष्टानि नामानि संभवनसमर्थानि स्तुतिसंयुक्तानि तैर्वयं त्वं नाशयामः। Famine is personified. On account of starvation, the sight of famine-stricken people becomes dim, therefore famine is called one-eyed. On account of insufficient nourishment, people totter on their legs, therefore famine is spoken of as having a crooked gait. Famishing people scream, and so famine is called screaming. It is called barren because there are no crops, or because people are no longer liberal in their gifts.

33.] The entire section, including the stanza together with the commentary, seems to be spurious. Yāska never cites more than one Vedic quotation to illustrate the same meaning of a word. The commentary on this stanza bears the stamp of a different commentator. As the style has affinities with comments of the *pariśiṣṭas*, it is likely that it has been added by the author of these. The explanation of *ṛdūpe* and *ṛdūvṛdhā* is not satisfactory. Durga has also noticed this doubtful explanation and remarks: भाष्यमत्र न सम्यगिव लक्ष्यते तस्य सम्यक् पाठोऽन्वेष्यस्ततो योज्यम्।

Cf. Roth, *op. cit.*, p. 98.

APPENDIX

AN ALPHABETICAL LIST OF STORIES RELATED IN THE *NIRUKTA*

Akrūra and the Jewel	2. 1
Agastya and Indra	1. 5–6
Aṅgiras' birth	3. 17
Atri's birth	3. 17
Aśvins (birth of Aśvins)	12. 10
Aśvins, Uṣas, and Āditya	5. 21
Āditya, Uṣas, and Aśvins	5. 21
Āditya, Saraṇyū, and Aśvins	12. 10
Indra and Agastya	1. 5–6
Indra and the Seers (means of livelihood in a famine)	6. 5
Urvaśī and Mitrāvaruṇā (birth of Vasiṣṭha)	5. 13
Uṣas, Āditya, and Aśvins	5. 21
Trita cast into a well	4. 6
Devāpi and Śantanu	2. 10-12
Paṇis and Saramā	11. 25
Brāhmaṇa and Vidyā	2. 4
Bhāradvāja's birth	3. 17
Bhṛgu's birth	3. 17
Mitrāvaruṇā and Urvaśi (birth of Vasiṣṭha)	5. 13
Mudgala and his victory	9. 23–24
Yama and Yamī	11. 34
Lopāmudrā's love	5. 2
Vasiṣṭha and the frogs	9. 6
Vasiṣṭha and his fetters	9. 26
Vidyā and Brāhmaṇa	2. 4
Viśvakarman and the Universal Sacrifice	10. 26
Viśvāmitra and the rivers	2. 24–27
Vaikhānasa's birth	3. 17
Śantanu and Devāpi	2. 10–12
Śākapūṇi and a deity	2. 8
Śunaḥśepa	3. 4
Saraṇyū, Āditya, and Aśvins	12. 10
Saramā and Paṇis	11. 25
Savitṛ, Sūryā, and Soma (marriage of Sūryā)	12. 8
Sūryā, Savitṛ, and Soma	12. 8
Soma, Savitṛ, and Sūryā	12. 8

INDEX OF AUTHORITIES CITED IN THE *NIRUKTA*

A LIST OF QUOTATIONS OCCURRING IN THE *NIRUKTA*, ARRANGED IN THE ORDER OF THE *SAMHITĀS*.

Ṛgveda.

Book I.

	RV.	N.
I.	1. 1	7. 15
	1. 2	7. 16
	1. 9	3. 21
	2. 1	10. 2
	3. 7	12. 40
	3. 8	5. 4
	3. 10	11. 26
	3. 12	11. 27
	6. 7	4. 12
	7. 1	7. 2
	7. 6	6. 16
	7. 7	6. 18
	9. 2	1. 10
	10. 9	7. 6
	12. 9	11. 23
	15. 1	6. 24
	15. 7	8. 2
	18. 1	6. 10
	18. 2	3. 21
	19. 1	10. 36
	19. 9	10. 37
	22. 1	12. 4
	22. 12	9. 34
	22. 15	9. 32
	22. 17	12. 19
	24. 10	3. 20
	24. 15	2. 13
	27. 1	1. 20
	27. 10	10. 8
	27. 13	3. 20
	28. 5	9. 21
	28. 7	9. 36
	30. 4	1. 10
	31. 16	6. 20

	RV.	N.
I.	32. 1	7. 2
	32. 5	6. 17
	32. 6	6. 4
	32. 10	2. 10
	32. 11	2. 17
	33. 3	6. 22
	33. 12	6. 19
	33. 13	6. 16
	37. 1	7. 2
	39. 10	6. 23
	41. 9	3. 16
	45. 3	3. 17
	46. 4	5. 24
	50. 1	7. 20; 12. 15
	50. 3	3. 15
	50. 5	12. 24
	50. 6	12. 22–25
	50. 7	12. 23
	51. 14	6. 31
	54. 3	6. 18
	54. 5	5. 16
	56. 3	6. 14
	59. 6	7. 23
	61. 1	5. 11
	61. 7	5. 4
	61. 12	6. 20
	66. 7	10. 21
	66. 8	10. 21
	66. 9	10. 21
	80. 16	12. 34
	84. 7	4. 17
	84. 8	5. 17
	84. 15	4. 25
	87. 6	4. 16
	88. 1	11. 14
	88. 5	5. 4
	89. 1	4. 19

	RV.	N.
I.	89. 2	12. 39
	89. 10	1. 15
	90. 1	6. 21
	92. 1	12. 7
	92. 13	12. 6
	94. 2	4. 25
	94. 7	3. 11
	94. 15	11. 24
	95. 5	8. 15
	96. 1	8. 2
	96. 7	4. 17
	98. 1	7. 22, 23
	99. 1	7. 20
	101. 1	4. 24
	101. 4	5. 15
	101. 10	6. 17
	104. 1	1. 17
	104. 5	5. 16
	105. 8	4. 16
	105. 17	6. 27
	105. 18	5. 21
	105 19	5. 11
	108. 10	12. 31
	109. 2	6. 9
	110. 4	11. 16
	113. 1	2. 19
	113. 2	2. 20
	115. 1	12. 16
	115. 4	4. 11
	116. 8	6. 36
	116. 16	5. 21
	117. 8	6. 6
	117. 16	5. 21
	117. 21	6. 26
	118. 11	6. 7
	122. 4	6. 21
	124. 4	4. 16
	124. 7	3. 5
	125. 2	5. 19
	126. 1	9. 10
	126. 6	5. 13
	126. 7	3. 20
	127. 1	6. 8
	129. 6	10. 42
	129. 8	6. 4
	132. 1	5. 2
	134. 2	4. 19
	*136. 3	2. 13
	138. 4	4. 25
	142. 10	6. 21
I.	143. 4	4. 23
	147. 2	3. 20
	150. 1	5. 7
	151. 7	6. 8
	153. 4	4. 19
	154. 2	1. 20
	154. 6	2. 17
	155. 2	11. 8
	161. 11	11. 6
	162. 1	9. 3
	162. 2	9. 2
	162. 7	6. 22
	163. 2	4. 13
	163. 7	6. 8
	163. 10	4. 13
	164. 1	4. 26
	164. 2	4. 27
	164. 11	4. 27
	164. 12	4. 27
	164. 13	4. 27
	164. 16	5. 1
	164. 21	3. 12
	164. 26	11. 43
	164. 27	11. 45
	164. 28	11. 42
	164. 29	2. 9
	164. 32	2. 8
	164. 33	4. 21
	164. 37	7. 3
	164. 40	11. 44
	164. 41	11. 40
	164. 42	11. 41
	164. 44	12. 27
	164. 46	7. 18
	164. 47	7. 24
	164. 48	4. 27
	164. 50	12. 41
	164. 51	7. 23
	165. 7	6. 7
	166. 6	6. 30
	169. 3	6. 15
	170. 1	1. 6
	174. 2	6. 31
	179. 4	5. 2
	179. 5	6. 4
	181. 4	12. 3
	185. 1	3. 22
	187. 1	9. 25
	190. 1	6. 23
	190. 5	4. 25

Book II.

	RV.	N.
II.	1. 1	6. 1
	4. 5	6. 17
	11. 21	1. 7
	12. 1	10. 10
	12. 3	8. 2
	14. 1	5. 1
	14. 11	3. 20
	15. 10	1. 7
	16. 9	1. 7
	17. 9	1. 7
	18. 4	7. 6
	18. 9	1. 7
	19. 9	1. 7
	20. 9	1. 7
	23. 9	3. 11
	24. 3	5. 16
	24. 4	10. 13
	27. 1	12. 36
	28. 4	1. 7
	31. 1	5. 5
	32. 4	11. 31
	32. 6	11. 32
	35. 10	3. 16; 10. 16
	37. 3	8. 3
	38. 4	4. 11
	41. 6	2. 13
	41. 12	6. 1
	41. 20	9. 38
	41. 21	9. 37
	42. 1	9. 4

Book III.

	RV.	N.
III.	1. 12	6. 17
	3. 4	5. 2
	8. 1	8. 18
	9. 2	4. 14
	9. 8	4. 14
	17. 5	5. 3
	21. 4	5. 11
	27. 7	6. 7
	28. 2	6. 16
	30. 5	6. 1; 7. 6
	30. 8	6. 1
	30. 10	6. 2
	30. 17	6. 3
	30. 19	6. 7
	31. 1	6. 4
III.	31. 2	3. 6
	33. 1	9. 39
	33. 5	2. 25
	33. 6	2. 26
	33. 10	2. 27
	34. 1	4. 17
	36. 4	6. 25
	36. 10	6. 7
	41. 3	4. 19
	47. 1	4. 8
	49. 2	5. 9
	53. 3	4. 16
	53. 6	7. 6
	53. 8	10. 17
	53. 11	7. 2
	53. 14	6. 32
	53. 23	4. 14
	54. 7	4. 25
	55. 19	10. 34
	59. 1	10. 22
	59. 2	2. 13
	62. 1	5. 5

Book IV.

	RV.	N.
IV.	4. 1	6. 12
	4. 14	5. 15
	4. 15	3. 21
	5. 7	6. 18
	7. 3	3. 20
	7. 8	6. 17
	16. 11	5. 15
	19. 9	3. 20
	23. 8	10. 41
	26. 7	11. 2
	30. 10	11. 47
	30. 11	11. 48
	30. 24	6. 31
	32. 23	4. 15
	34. 3	6. 16
	38. 5	4. 24
	38. 10	10. 31
	40. 4	2. 28
	51. 1	1. 5
	57. 1	10. 16
	57. 2	10. 16
	57. 5	9. 41
	58. 1	7. 17
	58. 8	7. 17, 20

Book V.

	RV.	N.
V.	1. 2	6. 13
	2. 9	4. 18
	13. 4	6. 7
	24. 3	5. 23
	31. 2	3. 21
	32. 1	10. 9
	32. 6	6. 3
	34. 3	6. 19
	37. 1	5. 7
	39. 1	4. 4
	39. 2	4. 18
	40. 4	5. 11
	44. 1	3. 16
	44. 8	6. 15
	46. 7	12. 45
	46. 8	12. 46
	48. 1	5. 5
	52. 6	6. 16
	52. 9	5. 6
	54. 6	6. 4
	56. 8	11. 50
	57. 1	11. 15
	60. 8	8. 2
	62. 8	3. 5
	63. 5	4. 19
	75. 7	3. 20
	77. 2	12. 5
	78. 8	3. 15
	81. 2	12. 13
	83. 2	10. 11
	85. 3	10. 4
	85. 6	6. 13

Book VI.

	RV.	N.
VI.	1. 4	4. 19
	4. 7	1. 17
	6. 5	4. 17
	7. 6	6. 3
	8. 4	7. 26
	9. 1	2. 21
	12. 4	6. 15
	19. 1	6. 16, 17
	19. 10	6. 6
	21. 3	5. 15
	22. 2	6. 3
	22. 3	6. 3
	24. 3	1. 4
VI.	30. 3	4. 17
	37. 3	10. 3
	44. 21	6. 17
	47. 8	7. 6
	47. 13	6. 7
	47. 16	6. 22
	47. 26	9. 12
	47. 29	9. 13
	49. 8	12. 18
	50. 5	6. 6
	50. 14	12. 33
	55. 1	5. 9
	56. 3	2. 6
	58. 1	12. 17
	59. 2	10. 21
	59. 4	5. 22
	61. 2	2. 24
	63. 8	6. 29
	66. 9	3. 2
	70. 2	5. 2
	71. 2	6. 7
	75. 2	9. 17
	75. 3	9. 18
	75. 4	9. 40
	75. 5	9. 14
	75. 6	9. 16
	75. 11	9. 19
	75. 13	9. 19
	75. 14	9. 15

Book VII.

	RV.	N.
VII.	1. 1	5. 10
	2. 2	8. 17
	4. 7	3. 2
	4. 8	3. 3
	9. 6	6. 17
	16. 1	3. 21
	18. 5	6. 6; 7. 2
	18. 15	7. 2
	18. 21	6. 30
	21. 5	4. 19
	25. 3	5. 3
	33. 8	11. 20
	33. 10	6. 7
	33. 11	5. 14
	34. 16	10. 44
	34. 17	10. 45
	34. 22	6. 14
	38. 7	12. 44

	RV.	N.
VII.	39. 2	5. 28
	39. 3	12. 43
	39. 4	6. 3
	41. 2	12. 14
	46. 1	10. 6
	46. 3	10. 7
	47. 3	5. 6
	48. 2	5. 2
	55. 1	10. 7
	58. 5	4. 15
	60. 7	6. 20
	63. 5	6. 7
	69. 4	6. 4
	76. 1	11. 10
	82. 1	5. 2
	86. 5	10. 24
	100. 5	5. 9
	103. 11	9. 6
	104. 15	7. 3
	104. 21	6. 30

Book VIII.

VIII.	1. 1	7. 2
	1. 20	6. 24
	2. 6	5. 3
	2. 12	1. 14
	2. 40	3. 16
	3. 17	10. 37
	3. 21	5. 15
	4. 3	3. 30
	4. 19	6. 22
	13. 18	1. 10
	13. 27	6. 21
	17. 12	3. 10
	19. 37	4. 15
	21. 8	5. 23
	24. 29	6. 22
	25. 13	5. 1
	25. 22	5. 15
	26. 16	5. 1
	27. 10	6. 14
	32. 4	5. 16
	32. 10	6. 4
	35. 1	5. 5
	39. 1	5. 23 ; 10. 5
	41. 2	10. 5
	43. 31	4. 14
	45. 1	6. 14
	45. 20	3. 21

	RV.	N.
VIII.	45. 37	4. 2
	48. 7	4. 7
	48. 10	6. 4
	61. 11	6. 25
	62. 11	1. 4
	63. 7	3. 8
	66. 8	5. 21
	66. 10	6. 26
	67. 5	6. 27
	68. 1	5. 3
	68. 4	12. 21
	69. 6	4. 8
	69. 12	5. 27
	75. 9	5. 23
	77. 4	5. 11
	77. 6	6. 34
	77. 10	5. 4
	77. 11	6. 33
	89. 7	6. 14
	90. 6	5. 22
	92. 22	6. 24
	93. 23	5. 18
	98. 1	7. 2
	99. 3	6. 8
	99. 4	6. 23
	100. 10	11. 28
	100. 11	11. 29
	102. 11	4. 14
	102. 21	3. 20

Book IX.

IX.	1. 1	11. 3
	3. 5	6. 29
	46. 4	2. 5
	69. 6	77. 2
	73. 3	12. 32
	75. 5	4. 15
	86. 34	5. 5
	86. 41	5. 2
	93. 5	6. 27
	98. 12	5. 12
	107. 9	5. 3
	110. 5	5. 4
	112. 3	6. 6

Book X.

X.	3. 7	4. 18
	4. 2	5. 1
	4. 4	6. 8

	RV.	N.
X.	4. 6	3. 14
	5. 5	5. 1
	5. 6	6. 27
	7. 2	6. 8
	9. 1	9. 27
	10. 8	5. 2
	10. 10	4. 20
	10. 13	6. 28
	10. 14	11. 34
	11. 6	3. 16
	12. 2	6. 4
	14. 1	10. 20
	14. 6	11. 19
	15. 1	11. 18
	15. 4	4. 21
	15. 9	6. 14
	16. 11	1. 4
	17. 1	12. 11
	17. 2	12. 10
	17. 3	7. 9
	18. 1	11. 7
	22. 2	6. 23
	26. 4	6. 29
	27. 13	6. 6
	27. 22	2. 6
	27. 23	2. 22
	27 24	5. 19
	28. 4	5. 3
	29. 1	6. 28
	30. 4	10. 19
	30. 11	6. 22
	34. 1	9. 8
	34. 5	12. 7
	39. 4	4. 19
	40. 2	3. 15
	42. 7	5. 24
	43. 5	5. 22
	44. 6	5. 25
	45. 1	4. 24
	48. 7	3. 10
	50. 1	11. 9
	50. 6	5. 25
	51. 1	6. 35
	51. 8	8. 22
	51. 9	8. 22
	52. 3	6. 35
	53. 4	3. 8
	59, 5	10. 40
	60. 3	12. 30
	62. 5	11. 17

	RV.	N.
X.	63. 16	11. 46
	64. 5	11. 23
	65. 13	12. 30
	67. 7	5. 4
	68. 8	10. 12
	69. 4	6. 17
	70. 10	6. 7; 8. 20
	71. 2	4. 10
	71. 4	1. 8, 19
	71. 5	1. 8, 20
	71. 7	1. 9
	72. 4	11. 23
	72. 11	1. 8
	73. 10	8. 2
	73. 11	4. 3
	75. 5	9. 26
	75. 9	7. 7
	*76. 1	6. 21
	78. 2	3. 15
	79. 1	6. 4
	79. 3	5. 3
	81. 1	10. 26
	81. 6	10. 27
	82. 2	6. 15; 10. 26
	82. 4	6. 15
	84. 1	10. 30; 11. 37
	84. 2	1. 17
	84. 5	6. 29
	85. 3	11. 4
	85. 5	11. 5
	85. 19	11. 6
	85. 20	12. 8
	85. 27	3. 21
	85. 37	3. 21
	85. 39	4. 25
	85. 40	10. 21
	85. 42	1. 16
	86. 1	1. 4; 13. 4
	86. 9	8. 31
	86. 11	11. 38
	86. 12	11. 39
	86. 13	12. 9
	86. 21	12. 28
	88. 1	7. 25
	88. 4	5. 3
	88. 6	7. 27
	88. 10	7. 28
	88. 11	2. 13; 7. 29
	88. 17	7. 30
	88. 19	7. 31

	RV.	N.
X.	89. 5	5. 12
	89. 6	5. 3
	89. 10	7. 2
	90. 16	12. 41
	94. 1	9. 9
	94. 2	7. 7
	94. 7	3. 9
	94. 9	2. 9
	95. 5	3. 21
	95. 7	10. 47
	95. 10	11. 36
	95. 14	7. 3
	97. 1	9. 28
	97. 3	6. 3
	97. 11	3. 15
	98. 5	2. 11
	98. 7	2. 12
	99. 12	5. 3
	101. 3	5. 28
	101. 7	5. 26
	101. 10	4. 19
	102. 5	9. 23
	102. 9	9. 24
	103. 1	1. 15
	103. 12	9. 33
	105. 1	5. 12
	107. 10	7. 3
	108. 1	11. 25
	110. 1	8. 5
	110. 2	8. 6
	110. 3	8. 8
	110. 4	8. 9
	110. 5	8. 10
	110. 6	8. 11
	110. 7	8. 12
	110. 8	8. 13
	110. 9	8. 14
	110. 10	8. 17

	RV.	N.
X.	110. 11	8. 21
	114. 4	10. 46
	116. 7	7. 6
	116. 8	6. 16
	117. 6	7. 3
	119. 9	1. 4
	120. 6	11. 21
	121. 1	10. 23
	121. 10	10. 43
	123. 1	10. 39
	128. 5	10. 40
	129. 2	7. 3
	129. 3	7. 3
	133. 1	3. 20
	133. 2	1. 15
	135. 1	12. 29
	136. 1	12. 26
	138. 1	4. 25
	139. 6	5. 1
	146. 1	9. 30
	149. 1	10. 32
	149. 5	10. 33
	151. 1	9. 31
	152. 4	7. 2
	153. 2	7. 2
	155. 1	6. 30
	162. 2	6. 12
	164. 1	1. 17
	165. 1	1. 17
	166. 5	10. 16
	167. 3	11. 12
	169. 1	1. 17
	178. 1	10. 28
	178. 3	10. 28
	180. 20	1. 20
	186. 1	10. 35
	187. 2	5. 5
	188. 1	7. 20

Atharva Veda.

Stanzas occurring in the Ṛigveda are indicated by an asterisk.

AV.	N.	AV.	N.
1. 1. 2	10. 18	7. 20. 2	11. 30
*1. 5. 1	9. 27	*7. 26. 2	1. 20
1. 17. 1	3. 4	*7. 26. 4	12. 10
*1. 21. 2	7. 2	*7. 46. 1	11. 22
*2. 5. 5	7. 2	*7. 48. 1	11. 31
*3. 2. 5	6. 12 ; 9. 33	7. 49. 1	12. 45
*3. 16. 2	12. 14	*7. 73. 5	4. 19
*3. 17. 2	5. 28	*7. 73. 7	11. 43
*3. 31. 5	12. 11	*7. 73. 8	11. 45
4. 1. 1	1. 7	*7. 73. 9	4. 5
*4. 2. 7	10. 23	*7. 73. 11	11. 44
*4. 15. 13	9. 6	*7. 80. 3	10. 43
*4. 31. 1	10. 30	*7. 81. 2	11. 6
*4. 31. 2	1. 17	7. 81. 6	5. 11
*4. 31. 5	6. 29	7. 83. 3	2. 13
4. 39. 9	8. 2	*7. 84. 3	1. 20
*5. 1. 6	6. 27	*7. 85. 1	10. 28
*5. 3. 7	10. 40	7. 97. 3	6. 7 ; 12. 42
5. 6. 1	1. 7	7. 97. 4	12. 42
*5. 12. 1	8. 5	*8. 3. 24	4. 18
*5. 12. 2	8. 6	*8. 4. 2	6. 11
*5. 12. 3	8. 8	*8. 4. 15	7. 3
*5. 12. 4	7. 9	*8. 4. 21	6. 30
*5. 12. 5	8. 10	*9. 9. 1	4. 26
*5. 12. 6	8. 11	*9. 9. 2	4. 27
*5. 12. 7	8. 12	*9. 9. 11	4. 27
*5. 12. 8	8. 13	*9. 9. 12	4. 27
*5. 12. 9	8. 12	*9. 9. 13	4. 27
*5. 12. 10	8. 17	*9. 9. 15	5. 1 ; 14. 20
*5. 12. 11	8. 21	*9. 9. 22	3. 12
*5. 27. 1	6. 21	*9. 10. 4	11. 43
*5. 27. 8	8. 11	*9. 10. 5	11. 45
*6. 22. 1	7. 24	*9. 10. 6	11. 42
*6. 27. 1	1. 17	*9. 10. 7	2. 9
*6. 34. 3	5. 5	*9. 10. 10	2. 8
*6. 125. 1	2. 5 ; 9. 12	*9. 10. 12	4. 21
*6. 126. 1	9. 13	*9. 10. 15	7. 3
*7. 5. 1	12. 41	*9. 10. 20	11. 44
*7. 6. 1	1. 15 ; 4. 23	*9. 10. 21	11. 40
7. 10. 5	11. 33	*9. 10. 22	11. 41
7. 14. 2	6. 12	*9. 10. 26	12. 27
7. 17. 2	11. 11	*9. 10. 28	7. 18

AV.	N.
*10. 8. 4	4. 27
*10. 8. 9	12. 38
11. 4. 21	11. 29
*12. 2. 21	11. 7
12. 2. 28	6. 12
*13. 1. 42	11. 41
*13. 2. 16	7. 20 ; 12. 15
*13. 2. 18	3. 15
*13. 2. 20	12. 24
*13. 2. 21	12. 22–25
*13. 2. 22	12. 23
*13. 2. 35	12. 16
*13. 3. 9	7. 24
*14. 1. 3	11. 4
*14. 1. 4	11. 5
*14. 1. 21	3. 21
*14. 1. 22	1. 16
*14. 1. 37	10. 19
*14. 1. 61	12. 8
*14. 2. 2	4. 25
*14. 2. 3	10. 21
*14. 2. 38	3. 21
*18. 1. 5	10. 34
*18. 1. 9	5. 2
*18. 1. 11	4. 20
*18. 1. 15	6. 29
*18. 1. 16	11. 34
*18. 1. 23	3. 16
*18. 1. 30	6. 4
*18. 1. 44	11. 18
*18. 1. 49	10. 20
*18. 1. 51	4. 21
*18. 1. 53	12. 11
*18. 1. 58	11. 19
*18. 2. 19	9. 32
*18. 2. 33	12. 10
*18. 2. 54	7. 9
18. 3. 48	6. 14
18. 4. 69	2. 13
*19. 13. 2	1. 15
*19. 15. 4	7. 6
*20. 5. 6	3. 10
*20. 11. 1	4. 17
*20. 12. 17	5. 12
*20. 16. 8	10. 12
*20. 17. 5	5. 22
*20. 20. 7	6. 1
*20. 22. 6	6. 8
*20. 23. 3	4. 19
*20. 34. 1	3. 21 ; 10. 10

AV.	N.
*20. 34. 3	8. 2
*20. 35. 1	5. 11
*20. 35. 7	5. 4
*20. 35. 12	6. 20
*20. 36. 2	6. 3
*20. 36. 3	6. 3
*20. 38. 4	7. 2
*20. 40. 1	4. 12
*20. 41. 3	2. 6 ; 4. 25
*20. 45. 1	1. 10
*20. 47. 4	7. 2
*20. 47. 13	7. 20 ; 12. 15
*20. 47. 15	3. 15
*20. 47. 17	12. 24
*20. 47. 18	12. 22–25
*20. 47. 19	12. 23
*20. 57. 10	6. 1
*20. 58. 1	6. 8
*20. 58. 2	6. 23
*20. 62. 5	7. 2
*20. 63. 4	4. 17
*20. 63. 5	5. 17
*20. 67. 3	6. 8
*20. 70. 3	4. 12
*20. 70. 12	6. 16
*20. 70. 13	6. 18
*29. 71. 8	1. 10
*20. 76. 1	6. 28
*20. 85. 1	7. 2
*20. 89. 7	5. 24
*20. 91. 7	5. 4
*20. 92. 3	6. 8
*20. 93. 5	7. 2
*20. 94. 6	5. 25
*20. 95. 2	3. 20
*20. 95. 3	1. 15
*20. 96. 12	6. 12
*20. 96. 23	1. 17
*20. 97. 2	5. 21
*20. 99. 1	10. 37
*20. 107. 9	11. 21
*20. 107. 14	12. 16
*20. 123. 1	4. 11
*20. 126. 1	1. 4
*20. 126. 9	6. 31
*20. 126. 11	11. 38
*20. 126. 12	11. 39
*20. 126. 13	12. 9
*20. 126. 21	12. 28

Sāma Veda.

SV.	N.	SV.	N.
*1. 15	10. 8	*1. 468	11. 3
*1. 16	10. 36	*2. 39	11. 3
*1. 17	1. 20	*2. 76	3. 10
*1. 31	12. 15	*2. 99	3. 21
*1. 45	3. 21	*2. 146	7. 2
*1. 53	4. 14	*2. 196	11. 23
*1. 72	5. 10	*2. 200	4. 12
*1. 75	12. 17	*2. 262	2. 13
*1. 95	4. 19	*2. 265	2. 6 ; 4. 25
*1. 97	5. 7	*2. 293	10. 37
*1. 120	7. 2	*2. 348	5. 3
*1. 133	6. 14	*2. 375	7. 2
*1. 139	6. 10	*2. 522	4. 4
*1. 147	2. 6 ; 4. 25	*2. 523	4. 18
*1. 183	1. 10	*2. 609	6. 28
*1. 184	10. 35	*2. 652	5. 6
*1. 189	11. 26	*2. 669	6. 8
*1. 197	6. 24	*2. 670	6. 23
*1. 198	7. 2	*2. 688	6. 14
*1. 217	6. 17	*2. 691	4. 17
*1. 218	6. 21	*2. 693	5. 17
*1. 228	5. 12	*2. 694	5. 5
*1. 242	7. 2	*2. 710	7. 2
*1. 252	3. 20	*2. 720	7. 2
*1. 256	10. 37	*2. 723	5. 10
*1. 267	6. 8	*2. 757	6. 7
*1. 315	10. 9	*2. 762	5. 22
*1. 319	4. 3	*2. 781	6. 14
*1. 321	1. 7	*2. 813	6. 10
*1. 332	10. 28	*2. 827	6. 7
*1. 342	5. 5	*2. 841	6. 8
*1. 345	4. 4	*2. 857	5. 4
*1. 354	5. 3	*2. 939	10. 27
*1. 364	12. 21	*2. 949	1. 10
*1. 380	4. 24	*2. 971	6. 16
*1. 388	7. 2	*2. 975	5. 8
*1. 389	4. 17	*2. 976	5. 9
*1. 464	6. 12	*2. 984	1. 20
*1. 465	6. 8	*2. 1010	6. 24

Vājaneyi Saṃhitā.

VS.	N.	VS.	N.
*2. 24	6. 14	*3. 28	6. 10
*3. 24	3. 21	*3. 29	3. 21
*3. 26	5. 23	3. 48	5. 18

VS.	N.
3. 61	3. 21 ; 5. 22
4. 1	1. 15
4. 19	5. 5
4. 22	6. 7
*4. 25	6. 12
5. 4	8. 2
5. 5	4. 17
*5. 20	1. 20
5. 42	1. 15
*6. 3	2. 7
6. 15	1. 15
*6. 23	11. 23
7. 1	5. 6
*7. 12	3. 16
*7. 16	10. 39
*7. 32	6. 14
*7. 33	12. 40
*7. 38	4. 8
*7. 39	6. 16, 17
*7. 41	7. 20 ; 12. 15
*8. 14	6. 14
8. 18	6. 7 ; 12. 42
8. 20	4. 25
8. 27	5. 18
*8. 40	3. 15
*8. 41	7. 21 ; 12. 15
*8. 42	6. 24
*8. 44	7. 2
*9. 14	2. 28
*9. 16	12. 44
*10. 16	3. 5
*10. 20	10. 43
*11. 24	3. 20
*11. 27	6. 1 ; 13. 1
*11. 50	9. 27
*12. 3	12. 13
*12. 12	2. 13
*12. 18	4. 24
*12. 42	3. 20
12. 53	5. 5
*12. 68	5. 28
*12. 75	9. 28
*12. 77	6. 3
*12. 85	3. 15
*13. 3	1. 7
*13. 4	10. 23
*13. 9	6. 12
*15. 32	3. 2[illegible]
*15. 47	6. 8
16. 51	5. 22

VS.	N.
16. 54	1. 15
*17. 17	10. 26
*17. 22	10. 27
*17. 26	10. 26
*17. 28	6. 15
*17. 33	1. 15
*17. 44	6. 12 ; 9. 33
*17. 89	7. 17
18. 40	2. 6
*18. 69	6. 1
*18. 70	7. 2
*18. 71	1. 20
*19. 49	11. 18
*19. 50	11. 19
*19. 55	4. 21
*19. 65	1. 4
20. 18	5. 18
*20. 84	11. 26
*20. 86	11. 27
*21. 10	12. 44
21. 43	4. 3
*23. 1	10. 23
*23. 65	10. 43
*25. 10	10. 23
*25. 14	4. 19
*25. 15	12. 39
*25. 23	1. 15 ; 4. 23
*25. 24	9. 3
*25. 30	6. 22
*26. 7	7. 22, 23
*26. 25	11. 3
*27. 20	6. 21
28. 5	4. 18
28. 16	4. 17 ; 9. 43
29. 1	3. 20
*29. 13	4. 13
*29. 18	6. 8
*29. 21	4. 13
*29. 25	8. 5
*29. 26	8. 6
*29. 27	8. 7
*29. 28	8. 8
*29. 29	8. 9
*29. 30	8. 10
*29. 31	8. 11
*29. 32	8. 12
*29. 33	8. 13
*29. 34	8. 14
*29. 35	8. 17
*29. 36	8. 21

VS.	N.
*29. 39	9. 17
*29. 40	9. 18
*29. 41	9. 40
*29. 42	9. 14
*29. 43	9. 16
*29. 48	2. 5 ; 9. 19
*29. 51	9. 15
29. 52	2. 5 ; 9. 12
*29. 55	9. 13
*31. 16	12. 41
*33. 13	1. 17
*33. 23	11. 9
*33. 31	12. 15
*33. 32	12. 22–25
*33. 37	4. 11
*33. 41	6. 8
*33. 44	5. 28
*33. 47	12. 40
*33. 92	7. 23
*34. 7	9. 25
*34. 8	11. 30
*34. 10	11. 32
*34. 33	12. 6
*34. 35	12. 14
34. 42	12. 18
*34. 53	12. 33
*34. 54	12. 30
*34. 55	12. 37
*35. 7	11. 7
*35. 21	9. 32
36. 14	9. 27

PART III

SANSKRIT TEXT

PREFACE.

On my return home to India, a systematic and exhaustive search for the hitherto unutilised mss. of the *Nirukta* was made. I myself undertook an extensive tour in Rajputana, Baroda, Tihri-Garhwal and Cashmere and examined the state collections of sanskrit mss. I also visited Benares, Patna, Madras, Madura, and Tanjore. I wrote to scholars, and librarians in charge of sanskrit mss. throughout the country. I was therefore able to secure the use of several mss. hitherto not utilised for the constitution of the text. These mss. are as follows:—

Bk.[1] This ms. belongs to the state Library, Bikaner. The loan was secured for the University of the Panjab through the courtesy of Mahārāja S'rī Sir Bhairon Singhji, K. C. I. E., Vice-President, Council, Bikaner.

Contents. The *Nirukta* of Yāska in the shorter recension containing the two parts i. e. the *pūrvārdha* and the *uttarārdha* in III leaves. It is a badly preserved ms. and full of mistakes.

Size: $9\frac{3}{8}'' \times 4\frac{2}{5}''$ Material: Paper. No. of leaves: III

No. of lines per folio: 8. Characters: Devanāgarī.

Date: on f. IIIr. (sic.) श्री सारदाप्रसंनोस्तु ॥ संवत् बाणाग्निसंसेन्दुमार्गे । असितपक्षके । अष्टम्यां विधुवारे हि लिखिता पत्तने पुरे i. e. 1735 Vik.=1679 A. D.

The colophon ends thus: (sic.) महाराजाधिराजस्य धर्मभारधुरंधर । अमूपसिंहप्रतापो यावच्चंद्रो दिवाकरः प्रत्यक्षरं गणनया ग्रंथमानमयोदितं । अनुष्टुभां सहस्रे द्वे शतैः पंचभिरन्वितैः ग्रं० २५००.

BK.[2] Contents: the *S'ikṣā Catuṣṭaya* written without a break. The ms. is injured in many places. *Nighanṭu* is given from f. 9 r. to f. 18r.

Size: $9\frac{3}{5}'' \times 4\frac{2}{5}''$. Material: Paper. No. of leaves: 18.

No. of lines: 8. Characters: Devanāgarī. Date: on f. 18 r:

sic: शुभं भवतुः ॥ ग्रं० ३७५ संवत् १७३५ वर्षे मार्गशीर्षं वदि १० गुरुदिने श्री पत्तमनगरे लिखितं । महाराजाधिराज श्री अनूपसिंहजी विजयराज्ये ॥ शिवमस्तु ॥

R.[1] A ms. written on paper in Devanāgarī characters,

obtained through the courtesy of the Curator, Central Library, Baroda. The contents are the 1st half of the *Nirukta*. It is full of mistakes and belongs to the longer recension.

Size: $8\frac{1}{5}'' \times 3\frac{3}{5}''$. Number of leaves: 69.

Number of lines: 9.

Date: sic. **शके ॥ १६ ॥ ९९ ॥ हेमलंब्रीनामसंवत्सरे श्रावणमासे शुद्धपक्षे षष्ठम्यां तिथौ ॥ मंदवासरे सिद्धेश्वरसंनिधौ कृष्णतीरे समाप्तः ॥ लेखकपाठयोः शुभमस्तु ॥**

Scribe: sic. **थत्थेइत्युपमामकृदाक्षंध × रात्रौ ४ च्चेमसिगिपं ॥ ॥ यादृशं पुस्तकं दृष्ट्वा तादृशं लिखितं मया ॥ यदि शुद्धमशुद्धं वा मम दोषो न विद्यते ॥ गजाननार्पणमस्तु ॥ कृष्णपबाई प्रसन् ॥ राम् ॥**

Peculiarities: The colophon at the end of the 1st chapter runs thus: **॥ इति नैरुक्ते प्रथमोध्यायः ॥**; at the end of the 3rd chapter thus: sic. **॥ इति नैरुक्ते ॥ पूर्वषट्रके ॥ तृतीयोध्यायः समाप्ता नि ॥ ७ ॥ ॐ ॥ शके ॥ १६ ॥ ९९ ॥ हेमलंबीनामसंवत्सरे ॥ आपाढशुद्धअष्टम्यां तिथौ संक्रांतपर्वणि समाप्तः ॥**; at the end of the 4th chapter thus: **॥ इति नैरुक्ते पूर्वपट्के चतुर्थोध्यायः समाप्तोयं भवति वा ॥** Evidently *ayam* refers to the 4th chapter and not to the *Nirukta* as the 5th chapter is immediately continued. But the use of *vā* does not seem to be correct in this case.

Sandhi and spelling: The *visarga* is retained but at the same time euphonically combined i. e. a double process is introduced, e. g. f. 1v: **व्याख्यातव्यःस्तमिमं......समाम्नाताःस्ते** etc. The *avagraha* is not marked, e. g. f. 2r. **जायतेस्ति** f. 1v. **औपमन्यवोपि** etc. The dental nasal is avoided in conjunction, being reduced to *anusvāra*, e. g. f. 1v. **निगमनांनिघंटव उच्यंते =०नान्नि०**

F. 2r. **अर्थांनिराहुः** f. 6v. **निष्पंनेभिः**

=०र्थान्नि० **=०पन्ने०**

R.[2] A neat, well-written, well-preserved and complete ms. of the *Nirukta* in Devanāgarī characters.

Size: $8\frac{1}{2}'' \times 4\frac{1}{5}''$. Number of leaves: 69 + 77 + i blank=147. Three leaves 75–77 are wrongly numbered as 85–87.

Number of lines: 9.

No date is given. The name of the scribe is not known. The ms. looks about 200 years old. It belongs to the longer recension and does not give any new variants.

R.[3] It contains the 2nd half of the *Nirukta*, written on paper in Devanāgarī characters.

Size: $8\frac{1}{5}'' \times 3\frac{4}{5}''$. Number of leaves: 83+i blank. Number of lines: 9.

Date: sic. । ॐ। शके । १७०५। शोमंकृभामसंवत्सरे माघवद्यषष्ठी इदं पुस्तकं समाप्तं.

The owner seems to be one Rāmakṛṣṇa. He is saluted like a god which is rather unusual: श्री। रामकृष्णमालिकाय नमः। Or the word *Mālika* does not refer to the owner of the ms. but to God, who is *the master* of all.

The ms. belongs to the longer recension. It represents a very late stage of textual expansion. The colophon at the end runs thus: इति नैरुक्ते उत्तरषट्के अष्टमोध्यायः ।

R[4]. A fragment of the 1st half of the *Nirukta*, written in Devanāgarī characters on paper. It looks old. It is illegible in many places. Ink is bleached by age. It belongs to the shorter recension.

Size: $9\frac{1}{2}'' \times 3\frac{1}{2}''$. Number of lines: 7. Number of leaves: 61· Eight leaves are supplied in a different handwriting.

Kn. A palm leaf ms. written in old Canarese characters, presented to the Panjab University Library, Lahore. It belongs to the shorter recension and sometimes gives important readings.

Size: $11\frac{1}{2}'' \times 1\frac{1}{2}''$. Number of leaves: 94+i blank. Number of lines: 7.

No date is given, but as it is written in old Canarese characters, it must be at least 300 years old, and might be older.

R[5]. The text of the *Nirukta* is made up by 2 different mss. The 1st half is given in 60+i blank leaves.

Size: $9\frac{1}{2}'' \times 3\frac{1}{2}''$. Number of lines: 9. Date is not given. The name of the scribe is also unknown. The colophon ends thus:— sic. इति निरुक्ते पूर्वषट्के षष्ठोध्यायः। शुभं भवतु। भग्नपृष्टिकटिग्रीवा बद्धदृष्टिरधोमुखः। कष्टेन लिखितं ग्रंथं यत्नेन प्रतिपालयेत् ॥ गणपति ॥ प्रसन् ॥ विश्वेश्वरार्पणमस्तु। The ms. belongs to the longer recension.

The 2nd half is given in i + 65 leaves.

Size: $9'' \times 3\frac{1}{2}''$. Number of lines: 9.

Date: ॥ शके १६८१ प्रमाथीनामसंवत्सरे कार्तिकशुद्धदशम्यायां तिथौ सौम्यवासरे तद्दिने पुस्तकं समाप्तं ।

Colophon ends thus: (sic.) भग्नपृष्टिकटिग्रीवास्तब्धदृष्टिरधोमुखः। यत्नेन लिखितं ग्रन्थं कष्टेन परिपालयेत् ॥ तैलाद्रक्षेजलाद्रक्षेद्रक्षेच्छिथिलबंधनात्। मूर्खहस्ते न दातव्यं एवं वदति पुस्तकं ॥ यादृशं पुस्तकं दृष्ट्वा तादृशं लिखितं मया। यदि शुद्धमशुद्धं वा मम दोषो न विद्यते ॥ ७ ॥ ७ ॥ ७ ॥ ७ ॥ ७ ॥ श्री कृष्णपरमात्मने नमः ॥ श्री गोविन्दपरमात्मने नमः ॥

The text belongs to the longer recension, both the pariśiṣṭas being given in full.

R.[6] An incomplete ms. of the 1st half of the *Nirukta*. The 1st leaf is missing. It looks old and has preserved the old spelling. The text belongs to the shorter recension. In many parts it is illegible.

Size: 9″ × 4″. Number of leaves: 78.

Number of lines: 8. Characters: Devanāgarī. Material: paper.

The text is given up to the 34th section of the 6th chapter. The last leaf is missing.

R.[7] A fragment of an old ms. gives the text of the *Nirukta* in the shorter recension from the words अथाप्येते माध्यमका देवगणा......of the 4th section of the 5th chapter up to: प्राचीनं बर्हिः प्रदिशा पृथिव्या of the 9th section of the 8th chapter. The 7th ch. begins thus: (sic.) नुं नामा यास्काचार्याय = ॐ नमो०

Size: 9″ × 4½″. Number of leaves:...54-97...missing. Number of lines: 9. Characters: Devanāgarī. Material: paper. Spelling: old. Date etc: unknown.

R[8]. A ms., the contents of which are the 2nd half of the *Nirukta*.

Size: 9″ × 4″. Number of leaves: 62.

Number of lines per page: 9. Characters: Devanāgarī. Material: paper.

Date: sic. नुं स्वस्ति संवत् १५४८ वर्षे पौषवदि १४ गुरोवृद्धनागरज्ञातीय ज्ञाचीचासुत नागापठनार्थं अन्येषां श्रात्रीणां पठनार्थं लिषितमिदं ॥ ७ ॥ शुभं भवतु ॥

The Paris'iṣṭas are given together as one chapter, being bodily separated from the 12th ch. of the *Nirukta*.

Spelling is old. The paper is very much worn. There is no ground to suspect the date. The external appearance, the state of the paper, which unmistakably bears the stamp of old age, and the internal evidence of old spelling support the above mentioned date. It belongs to the shorter recension. The following case of accidental omission is to be noted.

F. 29r. l. 6 from top:

आ दधिक्राः शवसा पंचकृष्टीः सूर्य इव ज्योतिषापस्ततान ।
सहस्त्रसाः शतसा वाज्यर्वा पृणक्तु मध्वा समिमा वचांसि ॥

आतनोति दधिक्राः शवसा बलेनापः सूर्य इव ज्योतिषा पंच मनुष्यजातानि...सूर्य इति ज्योतिषा.

The eye of the scribe wandered from the 1st line to the similar words in the 3rd line with the result that the intervening passage अपस्ततान...बलेनापः was omitted.

D. A ms. brought for me by my friend P. Bhagavaddatta. B. A. It is a neatly written, well preserved ms., and belongs to the longer recension.

Size: $6\frac{1}{4}'' \times 2\frac{1}{2}''$. Number of leaves: 112+128+i+21=261. There are 3 parts. The 1st two parts contain the 1st and the 2nd half of the *Nirukta* respectively. The contents of the last 21 leaves are the Nighaṇṭu. Number of lines: 7. Characters: Devanāgarī. Material: paper.

Date on f. 112r. (sic.) शके १६४६ । क्रोधीसंवत्सरे भाद्रपदशुद्ध १३ तद्दिने समाप्तं ।

Scribe:—(sic.) जामखेडकर इत्युपनाम्ना यज्ञेश्वरेण लिखितं ॥ गजानन
Date on f. 128r. (= 240): (sic.) ॥ शके १६४६ क्रोधीनामसंवत्सरे मार्गशीर्ष कृष्ण ८ भृगौ तद्दिने इदं पुस्तकं संपूर्णम् ।

Scribe: जामखेडकर इत्युपनाम्ना कृष्णभट्टात्मजयज्ञेश्वरेणेदं लिखितं । Colophon ends with the usual statement: यादृशं पुस्तकं दृष्ट्वा etc.

Date on f. 21r (=261r): sic. ॥ शके १६८५ सुभोनुनामसंवत्सरे आश्विन-कृष्णद्दमिदं समाप्तं ॥

Scribe: जामखेडकर धुंडिराजभट्टात्मजगोविंदभट्टेन लिखितं ॥

There is a good ms. of the *Nirukta* in the library of H. H. the Mahārājā of Alwar. All my efforts to secure a loan of this ms. were fruitless, as the authorities refused to lend the ms. to the Panjab University on any terms. Even a copy of the ms. could not be obtained. But H. H. the Mahārājā was kind enough to let me see the ms. On examining a few test passages, I found that no new variants were forthcoming. Its collation was therefore unnecessary.

Besides, six mss. of the Raghunātha Temple Library, Jammu were collated by Principal Raghubar Dayal M. A; M. O. L. of the S. D. College, as far as the 12th section of the 1st chapter of the *Nirukta*. He was good enough to place the result of this collation at my disposal. On carefully examining the critical notes supplied by Principal Raghubar Dayal, I did not find any new variants. I did not therefore feel justified in collating the mss. afresh.

The evidence supplied by the Indian mss. further supports the conclusion, deduced from the collation of European mss.

The evidence of the European mss. was discussed at length in my *Introduction to the Nirukta*, published by the Oxford University Press in 1920. *The Introduction* was sold out within a few years of its publication and is now out of print. New readers of the *Nirukta* will require information with regard to the principles of the constitution of the text. For their benefit, the relevant part of the *Introduction* is reproduced.

The Relationship of the MSS.: two recensions.

The manuscripts fall into two groups, and for the sake of convenience and brevity, may be called A and B—A representing the longer and B the shorter recension. None of the manuscripts grouped in these two families is earlier than A. D. 1479. Although they have been copied form earlier manuscripts—often with great labour and trouble as some of the scribes remark—neither of them transmits the text of the *Nirukta* in an uninterpolated state. Both recensions add the *paris'iṣṭa*—which can be proved to be an interpolation by independent testimony—as an integral part of the text, and cannot, therefore, be the faithful representatives of the archetype. Moreover, both have besides the *paris'iṣṭa*, an entire section or the equivalent of a section added on to them. These additions are meaningless. The commentary on the Vedic stanzas quoted therein is very poor, and written in a style quite different from that of Yāska. For instance, there can hardly be any doubt as to the interpolated character of ix. 2, which is given as a constituent part of the text by the manuscripts of both recensions. Further, the commentary on the Vedic stanza in xi. 7 is meaningless and written in a different style. The Vedic stanza, being quite easy, requires no explanation.

Yāska generally does not comment on easy Vedic stanzas, simply remarking: *iti sā nigada-vyākhyātā*[1], i. e. 'this stanza is explained by the mere reading'. In all such cases, this note of Yāska comes after easy Vedic stanzas only. It would thus be intelligible, if it had followed immediately the Vedic stanzas in xi. 7. But as the text now stands, it is placed just after a very difficult Vedic stanza in xi. 8. This is contrary to Yāska's method. It is clear that the words: *iti sā nigada-vyākhyātā* were originally placed immediately after the Vedic stanzas in xi. 7. The intervening passage is an interpolation, and rather a clumsy one, for it can be easily detected. This is further proved by the fact that Durga, who repeats every word of Yāska in his commentary, ignores them. How these additions gradually found their way into the text is illustrated by the following example. There is an easy quotation in xii. 2, and Yāska, as usual, simply adds: *iti sā nigada-vyākhyātā*. Some interpolators have endeavoured to add after these words a short comment. Thus some manuscripts here subjoin the following remark: **वसातिषु स्म चरथो वसातयो रातयो वसन्ते......सुरातयोः ॥**

Further, each recension contains passages, which, being superfluous, are omitted by the other, or are amplified versions of those in the other. For example, B adds, between vii. 19 and 20, one entire section, which is omitted by A. It is clearly an interpolation as the commentary on the Vedic stanzas is identical with that of xiv. 33 with slight alterations.

Again, in B the commentary on the Vedic stanza quoted in v. 27, reads as follows: **सुदेवस्त्वं कल्याणदानो यस्य तव देव सप्त सिंधवः प्राणायानुक्षरन्ति काकुदं सूर्म्यं सुषिरामिवेत्यपि निगमो भवति ॥ २७ ॥**

A's version of this is greatly amplified:

सुदेवस्त्वं कल्याणदेवः कमनीयदेवो वा भवसि वरुण यस्य ते सप्त सिंधवः सिन्धु स्रवणाद्यस्य ते सप्त स्रोतांसि तानि ते काकुदमनुक्षरन्ति । सूर्मिः कल्याणोर्मिः स्रोतः सुषिरमनु यथा । बीरिटं तैटीकिरन्तरिक्षमेवमाह पूर्वं वयतेरुत्तरमिरतेर्वयांसीरन्त्यस्मिन्भांसि वा । तदेतस्यामृच्युदाहरन्त्यपि निगमो भवति ॥ २७ ॥

Further, A contains a long passage in 6. 5: **इन्द्र ऋषीन्पप्रच्छ... व्याख्याताः** omitted by B.

'Omissio ex homoeoteleuto' in Sanskrit Manuscripts.

It is clear, therefore, that both the recensions cannot faithfully

---

1 Cf. N. x. 18. 24; xi. 3, 45; xii. 31.

represent the archetype. Hence the question arises which of them adheres more closely to the original? Roth adopted the text as given by the longer recension in his edition, without, however, assigning adequate reasons for his preference. The same text is also adopted by most of the editors of the *Nirukta*. This text, as has been shown above, does not represent the original. It is true that often the longer recension preserves the better text, for sometimes passages are omitted by accident. The eye of the scribe wanders from a particular word to the same or to a similar word, occurring further on in the text, with the result that the intervening words are omitted. This phenomenon known as *omissio ex homoeoteleuto* is universal and of very frequent occurrence. The following example illustrates this kind of omission. In copying the lines: 'The book, which is rather scarce, was till very lately of absolute necessity for the Student of the Christian Hymnology, above all for the Student of Adam of St. Victor's hymns',[1] the eye of the copyist wandered from the student of the first to the same word in the second line and the words 'of the Christian...for the' were left out. The same thing happened to the scribe of ms. C 3. In copying the sentence: सोऽर्देवानसृजत तत्सुराणां सुरत्वम् । असोरसुरानसृजत तदसुराणामसुरत्वमिति विज्ञायते his eye wandered from the word असृजत in the first line to the same word in the second line, with the result that the words तत्सुराणां सुरत्वम् । असोरसुरान् were left out.

Again, in copying N. vi. 22: स्थूरं राधः शताश्वं कुरुङ्गस्य दिविष्टिषु । RV. VIII. 4. 19. स्थूरः समाश्रितमात्रो महान्भवति । the eye of the scribe wandered from the स्थूरं of the first line to the similar word स्थूरः in the second line, consequently the intervening words राधः शताश्वं... दिविष्टिषु were omitted in ms. C 3.

Further in N. ii. 26: देवोऽनयत्सविता सुपाणिः कल्याणपाणिः । पाणिः पणायतेः पूजाकर्मणः प्रगृह्य पाणी देवान्पूजयन्ति । तस्य वयं प्रसवे याम उर्वीः । देवोऽनयत्सविता सुपाणिः is the first *pāda* of the second hemistich of the stanza of RV. III. 33. 6. Unconsciously the scribe remembered the second *pāda* तस्य वयं प्रसवे याम उर्वीः and wrote it down immediately after finishing the first *pāda* with the result that the intervening words कल्याणपाणिः । पाणिः पणायते...पूजयन्ति are missing in ms. C 4. It cannot therefore be concluded that the shorter recension is always the best, for sometimes omissions are accidental.

---

1. Clark, *Descent of Manuscripts*, p. 1.

Dittography in Sanskrit Manuscripts.

On the other hand, there is also the phenomenon called dittography, i. e. the repetition or addition of a few words or sentences. An excellent example of dittography is furnished by *The Globe* on July 9, 1915.

The *Echo de paris* publishes a message from Cettinje announcing the message form Cettinje announcing the appointment as Governor of Scutari of Bojo Petrovitch."[1] The part of the second line is a verbatim repetition of a part of the first line.

In N. ii. 28, उत स्य वाजी क्षिपणिं तुरण्यति ग्रीवायां बद्धो अपि......क्रतुं दधिक्राः..............

अपिकक्ष आसनीति व्याख्यातम् । क्रतुं वाजी क्षिपणिं तुरण्यति ग्रीवायां बद्धो दधिक्राः... the eye of the scribe wandered by chance after क्रतुं to the Vedic stanza, and he mechanically copies the whole of the first line except उत स्य in ms. C 5.

Again, in N. vi. 8, the scribe of the ms. Mi. repeats गृह्णातिकर्मा वा.

Further there are some passages whose omission by B is absolutely unjustifiable. Yāska explains every word occurring in the fourth chapter of the *Nighaṇṭu*. The omission of the passages containing the explanation of any of these words is therefore inconsistent with Yāska's plan. Examples of such omissions are the following. Yāska explains निशृंभाः (*Ngh*. 4. 3. 12.) in N. vi. 3, but the passage: निशृंभा निश्रथ्यहारिणः is omitted by B. Again, Yāska explains क्षोणस्य (*Ngh*. 4. 3. 28) in N. vi. 6 as क्षोणस्य क्षयणस्य, which is omitted by B. This omission makes the following Vedic quotation meaningless.

Further, in commenting upon a Vedic stanza, Yāska always starts from the very beginning of the stanza. To leave out the first few words and to begin from somewhere in the middle of the stanza is altogether foreign to his practice, yet if the text of B be followed, the omission of the passage: यवमिव वृकेणाश्विनौ निवन्तौ (N. vi. 26) would involve Yāska in an inconsistency. All this shows that B is not absolutely reliable.

---

1 Clark, *op. cit.*, p. 6.

Now let us examine A. The majority of the manuscripts of A belong to a period later than those of B. Thus not one of them has preserved the old spelleing, while most of the B mss. retain this peculiarity, i. e.

of writing	ए	as	।/	as	वार्ष	for	वर्षे
,,	ऐ	,,	।/ए	,,	।वेश्य	,,	वैश्य
,,	ओ	,,	।/।	,,	-ाया	,,	त्रयो
,,	ह्ल	for	ढ	,,	वोह्लारः	,,	वोढारः

Again, some of the A. MSS. divide the *paris'iṣṭa* into the so-called thirteenth and the fourteenth chapters, while those of B put the whole of the *paris'iṣṭa* into one chapter only, which is numbered the thirteenth.

It has already been pointed out that A contains an obvious interpolation in N. vi. 5, and an amplified version of B's comment in N. v. 27. Besides these there are shorter passages scattered throughout the book which are omitted by B and are suspected to be interpolations. One very fertile and insidious source of interpolations is supplied by Yāska's own method of giving etymological explanation. He does not content himself with one derivation, but goes on adding derivation after derivation of a single word till the whole list of probable, possible, and even fanciful etymologies is exhausted. In many cases, interpolators found it quite easy to add new derivations and attribute them to Yāska. A contains a considerable number of such additions, while B has only two.

The following are a few samples:

N. ii. 6. A reads: वृक्षो व्रश्चनात् । वृत्वा क्षां तिष्ठतीति वा । क्षा क्षियतेर्निवासकर्मणः । नियतामीमयत्......

B reads: वृक्षो व्रश्चनात् । नियतामीमयत्......

The two derivations are omitted.

N. ii. 10. A reads: हिरण्यं कस्मात्......हितरमणं भवतीति वा हृदयरमणं भवतीति वा ।

B reads: हिरण्यं कस्मात्......हितरमणं भवतीति वा ।

N. ii. 13. A reads: सूर्यमादितेयमदितेः पुत्रमेवम् ।

B reads: सूर्यमादितेयमेवम् ।

N. ii. 20. A reads: आमिनाने आमिन्वाने अन्योन्यस्याध्यात्मं कुर्वाणे ।
B reads: आमिनाने अन्योन्यस्याध्यात्मं कुर्वाणे ।

N. ii. 22. A reads: प्रथम इति मुख्यनाम प्रतमो भवति । कृन्तत्रमन्तरिक्षम् । विकर्तनं मेघानां विकर्तनेन मेघानामुदकं जायते ।
B reads: प्रथम इति मुख्यनाम प्रतमो भवति । विकर्तनेन मेघानामुदकं जायते ।

N. iii. 8. A reads: अग्रगामिन्यो भवन्तीति वाग्रगालिन्यो भवन्तीति वाग्रकारिण्यो भवन्तीति वाग्रसारिण्यो भवन्तीति वाङ्क्ना भवन्ति...
B reads: अग्रगामिन्यो भवन्तीति वाग्रगालिन्यो भवन्तीति वाग्रकारिण्यो भवन्तीति वाङ्क्ना भवन्ति...

N. iii. 10. A reads: आखण्डयितः । खण्डं खण्डयतेः तडिदित्यन्तिकवधयोः...
B reads: आखण्डयितः । तडिदित्यन्तिकवधयोः...

N. iii. 15. A reads: को वां शयने विधवेव देवरम् । देवरः कस्माद् द्वितीयो वर उच्यते । विधवा विधातृका भवति ।
B reads: को वां शयने विधवेव देवरम् । विधवा विधातृका भवति ।
In this particular case it is obvious that the passage देवरः कस्मात्, &c., is an interpolation, for as the words stand in the first line, Yāska would naturally give the etymological explanation of विधवा first and then of देवर, not vice versa. As a matter of fact he does so; after explaining विधवा he says: देवरो दीव्यतिकर्मा. This would have been absurd if the reading of A represents the original.

N. iii. 16. A reads: ब्राह्मणा इव वृपला इवेति । वृपलो वृषशीलो भवति वृषाशीलो वा ॥ १६ ॥
B reads: ब्राह्मणा इव वृपला इवेति ॥ १६ ॥

N. iii. 19. A reads: निर्णीतान्तर्हित...पदं । निर्णीतं कस्मात् । निर्णिक्तं भवति ।
B reads: निर्णीतान्तर्हित...पदं ।

N. iv. 2. A reads: मर्यादा...स्यात् । मर्यादा मर्यैरादीयते । मर्यादामर्यादिनो-र्विभागः ।
B reads: मर्यादा...स्यात् । मर्यादामर्यादिनोर्विभागः ।

N. iv. 10. A reads: लक्ष्मीर्लाभाद्वा लक्षणाद्वा लप्स्यनाद्वा लाञ्छनाद्वा...
B reads: लक्ष्मीर्लाभाद्वा लक्षणाद्वा लाञ्छनाद्वा...

N. iv. 13. A reads: ईर्मान्ताः समीरितान्ताः सुसमीरितान्ताः पृथ्वन्ता वा ।
B reads: ईर्मान्ताः समीरितान्ताः पृथ्वन्ता वा ।

N. iv. 15. A reads: कन्या कमनीया भवति । क्वेयं नेतव्येति वा कमनेनानीयत इति वा । कनतेर्वा ।

B reads: कन्या कमनीया भवति । क्वेयं नेतव्येति वा । कनतेर्वा ।

N. iv. 19. A reads: उदकं हर उच्यते । लोका हरांस्युच्यन्ते । असृगहनी हरसी उच्येते ।

B reads: उदकं हर उच्यते । लोका हरांस्युच्यन्ते ।

N. v. 3. A reads: पानैरिति वा स्पाशनैरिति वा स्पर्शनैरिति वा ।

B reads: पानैरिति वा स्पाशनैरिति वा ।

N. v. 12. A reads: तृप्रप्रहारी क्षिप्रप्रहारी सृप्रप्रहारी ।

B reads: तृप्रप्रहारी ।

N. v. 26. A reads: जिह्वा कोकुवा । कोकूयमाना वर्णान्नुदतीति वा । कोकूयतेर्वा स्याच्छब्दकर्मणः ।

B reads: जिह्वा कोकुवा । कोकूयमाना वर्णान्नुदतीति वा ।

N. vi. 8. A reads: जिगर्तिर्गिरतिकर्मा वा गृणातिकर्मा वा गृह्णातिकर्मा वा ।

B reads: जिगर्तिर्गिरतिकर्मा वा गृह्णातिकर्मा वा ।

N. vi. 16. A reads: अभवत सर्वेऽग्रगमनेनेति वाग्रगरणेनेति वाग्रसंपादिन इति वा ।

B reads: अभवत सर्वेऽग्रगमनेनेति वाग्रसंपादिन इति वा ।

N. vi. 33. A reads: शीर्यते बिठे । बिठमन्तरिक्षम् । बिठं बीरिटेन व्याख्यातम् ।

B reads: शीर्यते बिठे । बिटं बीरिटेन व्याख्यातम् ।

N. vi. 32. A reads: बुन्द इषुर्भवति बिन्दो वा भिन्दो वा भयदो वा...

B reads: बुन्द इषुर्भवति भिन्दो वा भयदो वा...

N. vi. 33. A reads: ऋदूपे अर्दनपातिनौ गमनपातिनौ शब्दपातिनौ दूरपातिनौ वा मर्मण्यर्दनवेधिनौ गमनवेधिनौ शब्दवेधिनौ दूरवेधिनौ वा ।

B reads: ऋदूपे अर्दनपातिनौ गमनपातिनौ वा मर्मण्यर्दनवेधिनौ गमनवेधिनौ वा ।

Instances might be multiplied, but the above examples suffice to show that A has been much more tampered with than B.

Fortunately, as has been said above, Durga repeats every word of the *Nirukta* in his commentary, so that the text of the *Nirukta in toto* can be reproduced from his commentary alone. This commentary therefore serves the purpose of a manuscript of the *Nirukta* and supplies valuable information about the condition of the text in its author's time. Durga does not recognize the *paris'iṣṭa* as an integral part of the *Nirukta*, as in fact he is even unaware of its existence. Thus his commentary preserves the text of the *Nirukta* as current before the addition of the *paris'iṣṭa*.

Further, it derives great value from the fact that Durga displays critical judgment in the adoption of readings in the text, while giving variants and adding critical notes on them. For example, in N. i. 2, he reads अयुगपत् but gives युगपत् as a variant, adding: युगपदुत्पन्नानामयुगपदुत्पन्नानामित्युभावपि पाठौ व्याहारं प्राप्तुतः ।

Again, in N. i. 12, he reads संविज्ञातानि but gives संविज्ञानानि as a variant, adding अथवा संविज्ञानानि तानि संविज्ञातानि तानि चेत्युभावप्येतौ पाठौ ।

Again, in N. iii. 15, he remarks: अग्निर्न य भ्रात्रा निघण्टुसूत्रस्य दुर्मदासो न सुरायामित्यनेनैव गतार्थतेति मन्यमानाः केचिदत्र निगमं नाधीयते । अपरे पुनः समाम्नायानुक्रमोऽयमिति मन्यमाना एवमेव निगममधीयते ।

Again, in N. iii. 21, he reads अविनाशि but gives अविनाश as a variant, adding: अन्ये त्वधीयते अविनाशनामेति । तेषामविनाशस्यैव नाम ।

Again, in N. iv. 19, he reads स्युः but gives असन् as a variant, adding: भाष्येऽपि स्युरित्येष पाठः । असन्नित्येप प्रमादपाठः ।

Again, in N. vi. 2, he remarks: निरजे गा इत्यत्र केचित्पशुगव्य एता इति व्याचक्षते ।

Again, in N. vi. 4, he reads अवनायान्नम् but gives अवनेनान्नम् and अनेनान्नम् as variants.

Again, in N. vi. 6, he reads क्षयणस्य but gives क्षीणस्य as a variant, adding: क्षीणस्येत्येवमेके मन्यन्ते । तत्पुनरनुपपन्नम् । क्षयणस्येति हि भाष्यकारो निराह ।

Again, in N. vi. 21, he remarks: ऋञ्जतिः प्रसाधनकर्मा । भाऋजीक इत्यनेन गतार्थतामस्य मन्यमानो भाष्यकारो निगमं नाधीते । केचित्त्वत्रैतं शेषमधीयते । दूतं वो विश्ववेदसं......

Again, on N. vi. 33, he remarks: भाष्यमत्र न सम्यगिव लक्ष्यते । तस्य सम्यक् पाठोऽन्वेष्यः । ततो योज्यम् ।

This shows that Durga took pains to ascertain the correct readings and has handed down a sort of critical edition of the *Nirukta*, as it existed in his time.

Three stages of interpolations.

We have thus manuscript materials which belong to three distinct periods.

(1) D, i. e. the commentary of Durga, written before the addition of the *paris'iṣṭas* and embodying the whole text of the *Nirukta*, represents the earliest period, i. e. about the thirteenth century A. D.

(2) B, i. e. the manuscripts of the shorter recension, represents a period later than D,—when the *paris'iṣṭas* were added, but not divided as yet into different chapters, and when the old orthography was still prevalent.

(3) A, i. e. the manuscripts of the longer recension, represents a still later period when the *paris'iṣṭas* had been divided into chapters and the old orthography had gone out of use.

A collation of these three different recensions indicates that three distinct stages of interpolations in the *Nirukta* can be clearly traced. For example, let us take a passage in N. i. 4. On collating D, B, and A, we find that the reading of D has been expanded in B, and that of B in A.

N. i. 4. D reads: आचार्यश्चिदिदं ब्रूयादिति पूजायाम् । दधिचिदित्युपमार्थे । कुल्मापांश्चिदाहरेत्यवकुत्सिते । नु इत्येषो......

B reads: आचार्यश्चिदिदं ब्रूयादिति पूजायाम् । आचार्य आचारं ग्राहयत्याचिनोत्यर्थानाचिनोति बुद्धिमिति वा । दधिचिदित्युपमार्थे । कुल्मापांश्चिदाहरेत्यवकुत्सिते । कुल्मापाः कुलेषु सीदन्ति । नु इत्येषो......

A reads: आचार्यश्चिदिदं ब्रूयादिति पूजायाम् । आचार्यः कस्मात् । आचार्य आचारं ग्राहयत्याचिनोत्यर्थानाचिनोति बुद्धिमिति वा । दधिचिदित्युपमार्थे । कुल्मापांश्चिदाहरेत्यवकुत्सिते । कुल्माषाः कुलेषु सीदन्ति । नु इत्येषो......

Another example for these three stages is supplied by N. ix. 2, as follows:

D reads: अश्वो व्याख्यातः । तस्यैषा भवति ॥ १ ॥
मा नो मित्रो वरुणो अर्यमायुरिन्द्र......

B reads: अश्वो व्याख्यातः । तस्यैषा भवति ॥ १ ॥
अश्वो वोळ्हा सुखं......इन्द्रायेन्दो परि स्रव ॥

अश्वो वोळ्हा सुखं वोळ्हा । सुखमिति कल्याणनाम । कल्याणं पुण्यं सुहितं भवति । मानो व्याख्यातः । तस्यैषा भवति ॥ २ ॥

मा नो मित्रो वरुणो अर्यमायुरिन्द्र......

A reads: अश्वो व्याख्यातः । तस्यैषा भवति ॥ १ ॥
अश्वो वोळ्हा सुखं......इन्द्रायेन्दो परि स्रव ॥

अश्वो वोळ्हा सुखं वोळ्हा रथं वोळ्हा । सुखमिति कल्याणनाम । कल्याणं पुण्यं सुहितं भवति । सुहितं गम्यतीति वा । हसैता वा पाता वा पालयिता वा । शेपमृच्छतीति । वारि वारयति । मानो व्याख्यातः । तस्यैषा भवति ॥ २ ॥

मा नो मित्रो वरुणो अर्यमायुरिन्द्र......

It has been shown above that the list of etymologies increases as one passes from the text of B to that of A. In the same manner the list of etymologies increases in B as compared with D. The following are some examples.

N. i. 4. D reads: कुल्माषांश्चिदाहरेत्यवकुत्सिते । नु इत्येषो...

B reads: कुल्माषांश्चिदाहरेत्यवकुत्सिते । कुल्माषाः कुलेषु सीदन्ति । नु इत्येषो...

D reads: वयाः शाखा वेतेः । शाखाः खशयाः ।

B reads: वयाः शाखा वेतेर्वातायना भवन्ति । शाखाः खशयाः शक्नोतेर्वा ।

N. i. 7. D reads: बृहद्वदेम स्वे वेदने । बृहदिति महतो नामधेयम् ।

B reads: बृहद्वदेम स्वे वेदने । भगो भजतेः । बृहदिति महतो नामधेयम् ।

N. ii. 22. D reads: बृबूकमित्युदकनाम शब्दकर्मणो भ्रंशतेर्वा ॥ २२ ॥

B reads: बृबूकमित्युदकनाम...शब्दकर्मणो भ्रंशतेर्वा । पुरीषं पृणातेः पूरयतेर्वा ॥ २२ ॥

N. ii. 26. D reads: तस्य वयं प्रसवे याम उर्वीः ।
प्रत्याख्यायान्तत आशुश्रुवुः ॥ २६ ॥

B reads: तस्य वयं प्रसवे याम उर्वीः ।
उर्व्य ऊर्णोतेर्वृणोतेरित्यौर्णवाभः ।
प्रत्याख्यायान्तत आशुश्रुवुः ॥ २६ ॥

N. iii. 18. D reads: सिंहः सहनात् । संपूर्वस्य वा हन्तेः संहाय हन्तीति वा ।

B reads: सिंहः सहनात् । हिंसेर्वा स्याद् विपरीतस्य । संपूर्वस्य वा हन्तेः संहाय हन्तीति वा ।

N. v. 4. D reads: शर्या अङ्गुलयो भवन्ति । शर्या इषवः शरमय्यः ।

B reads: शर्या अङ्गुलयो भवन्ति । सृजन्ति कर्माणि । शर्या इषवः शरमय्यः ।

N. v. 23. D reads: उरुष्या णो अघायतः समस्मात् ।
इति पञ्चम्याम् ॥ २३ ॥

B reads: उरुष्या णो अघायतः समस्मात् ।
इति पञ्चम्याम् । उरुष्यतिरकर्मकः ।
अथापि प्रथमाबहुवचने ।
नभन्तामन्यके समे ॥ २३ ॥

MS. C 1 agrees with B except that the last line नभन्तामन्यके समे is omitted.

N. vi. 3. D reads: उद्धर रक्षः सहमूलमिन्द्र ।
वृश्च मध्यम् । प्रति श्टणीह्यग्रम् ।

B reads: उद्धर रक्षः सहमूलमिन्द्र ।
मूलं मोचनाद्वा मोषणाद्वा मोहनाद्वा ।
वृश्च मध्यम् । प्रति श्र्णीह्यग्रम् ।

N. vi. 8. D reads: देवो देवान्प्रत्यक्तया कृपा कल्पितया ॥ ८ ॥
B reads: देवो देवान्प्रत्यक्तया कृपा । कृपा कृमुतेर्वा कल्पतेर्वा ॥ ८ ॥

N. vi. 24. D reads: गल्दा धमनयो भवन्ति ।
A reads: गल्दा धमनयो भवन्ति । गलनमासु धीयते ।
B omits it altogether.

N. vi. 28. D reads: अन्या किल...कक्ष्येव युक्तं लिबुजेव वृक्षम् ।
B reads: अन्या किल......कक्ष्येव युक्तं लिबुजेव वृक्षम् । लिबुजा व्रततिर्भवति लीयते विभजन्तीति । व्रततिर्वरणाच्च सयनाच्च ततनाच्च ।

Parallel instance of Servius, commentator of Virgil.

Thus the stages of interpolation at different periods can be traced. The principle of the 'best mauuscript' is obviously inapplicable in this case, for none of the manuscripts can be called the best. All that is available is the best manuscript of each family, and the best plan, under the circumstances, would be to place all the three families side by side. Fortunately it is possible to do so, for the successive interpolations from one family to another are invariably the amplifications of the text of a shorter recension, and are thrust between sentences wherever the text could be so enlarged with impunity, as, for instance, in multiplying the number of etymologies and attributing them all to Yāska. I have, however, distinguished the evidence of Durga's commentary from that of the manuscripts of the *Nirukta*, although Durga's commentary is very important for supplying such valuable evidence for the history of the text of the *Nirukta*, it cannot, strictly speaking, be called a manuscript of the *Nirukta*. The relation of the shorter to the longer recension is shown by the use of square brackets, which contain the additional passages of the longer recension, while the relation of the shorter recension to the text preserved by Durga is indicated by foot-notes. An analogous example is furnished by Latin literature. The text of Servius, commentator of Virgil, shows a similar threefold amplification; the three stages of interpolations being pointed out by Thilo in his edition. I think the text of the *Nirukta* reproduced from Durga represents the archetype as closely as it is possible to restore it with the help of the present materials. I have collated thirty-seven manuscripts myself, and in addition have taken into account the evidence of fourteen manuscripts collated by Roth, eight by the editor of the *Nirukta* in Bib. Ind., and six by Principal Raghubar Dayal as stated above. Thus, directly and indirectly, the evidence of sixty five manuscripts is available for this edition. I doubt if any useful, hitherto unutilised ms. of the *Nirukta* will now be forthcoming. The text may, therefore, be regarded as more or less settled.

The present text is in the main identical with the text, which I constituted at Oxford, and which served as the basis of my English translation. But as a result of the collation of Indian mss., this text is somewhat further developed than that used for the translation. There are certain variations in detail, see for example, line 3 on page 35. Thus the present text differs from the basis of my translation although the difference is not considerable. This may serve to show the existence of the differnce until such time as I may be able to publish a revised edition of the translation based on the final text.

The text is followed by Appendix I. Parallel passages from the *Saṁhitās*, the *Brāhmaṇas*, the *Prātis'ākhyas*, the *Bṛhaddevatā*, the *Aṣṭādhyāyī*, the *Mahābhāṣya*, the *Arthas'āstra* of Kauṭalya and other works of Vedic and Classical Sanskrit are compared with the text of the *Nirukta*. The Appendix I will be useful for the history of the *Nirukta*. One could see at a glance the extent to which Yāska is indebted to his predecessors and the influence, exercised by him, on his successors. It will also be useful in enabling one to estimate the originality of Yāska's contribution.

It was formerly proposed to add Appendix II, containing the hitherto unknown and unpublished commentary of Mahes'vara on the *Nirukta*. But as the text of the *Nirukta* is already very much delayed and the addition of Appendix II would require considerable time, the publication of the commentary is being withheld for the present.

Commentators of Yāska.

Although, from an early period, Yāska's work has been recognized as one of the most important *vedāṅgas* by the orthodox tradition of literary India, he, unlike Pāṇini, has not had many commentators. This does not mean that he had few followers or that his speculations did not dominate the thought of succeeding generations. On the contrary, he has been acknowledged to be the pre-eminent authority on etymology. Hence, at first sight, it seems rather inexplicable that his work should have been commented upon by so few people. One reason of this paucity is that Yāska's work itself is a commentary and not an independent treatise, hence it did not stand in need of much elucidation. Secondly, it is written in classical Sanskrit prose, and, notwithstanding its somewhat archaic and terse style, is easily intelligible to the reader as compared, for instance, with the aphorisms of Pāṇini; consequently there was not much demand for further comment. Yet four commentators, at least, are known to have elucidated Yāska's work.

(1) Ugra is mentioned as a commentator on the *Nirukta* by Aufrecht in his *Catalogus Catalogorum*.[1] But no other information, about his personality, the character of his work, and the time when he lived, is available. No reference is made to him by any of the other writers in the same field.

A ms. in the Library of the Asiatic Society of Bengal is entitled 'Ugra's commentary on the *Nirukta*'. It is, however, not Ugra's but Durga's commentary. In writing the name of Durga, the letter D was accidentally omitted by the scribe, i. e. Bhagvad-durga was written Bhagvad-urga. This Urga became Ugra by metathesis. The cataloguer never looked at the commentary. He did not even read other colophons, otherwise he would not have committed such a blunder. This misspelt name of Durga appears as Ugra. I suppose it was this ms., which served as the source of Aufrechts' information.

(2) Another commentator is Skandasvāmin, mentioned by Devarājayajvan in his commentary on the *Nighaṇṭu*:—**भगवता यास्केन समाम्नायं...निर्ब्रुवता नैगमदेवताकाण्डपठितानि पदानि प्रत्येकमुपादाय निरुक्तानि दर्शितनिगमानि च।...अन्यानि तु ग्रन्थविस्तरभीत्या सामान्येन निर्वचनलक्षणस्योक्तत्वात्...उपेक्षितानि। स्कन्दस्वामी** च तत एव निरुक्तमनुजगाम। तत्र तु...अभीकं इत्यादीनि च **षड्विंशतिश्च भाष्यकारेण बहुवक्तव्यत्वात् प्रकरणश एव निरुक्तानि। स्कन्दस्वामिना च व्याख्यातानि।... नैगम-**

1 Vol. i, p. 297.

देवताकाण्डगतानां च पदानां भाष्यकारेण निरुक्तानां स्कन्दस्वामिना च तद्व्याख्यातानां... भाष्यकारेणैव तत्र तत्र निगमेषु प्रसङ्गान्निरुक्तानि स्कन्दस्वामिना च निगमव्याख्यानेषु अन्यानि च पदानि शतद्वयमात्राण्युपात्तानि । तेन च समाम्नायपठितानां पदानामन्येभ्यो व्यावृत्त्यर्थं किञ्चिच्चिह्नं कृतम् । अतस्तेषां पाठशुद्धिस्तत्रैव शुद्धा ।...निर्वचनं च निरुक्तं स्कन्दस्वामिकृतां निरुक्तटीकां...निरीक्ष्य क्रियते[1] ।

It is clear that Devarāja was well acquainted with the commentary of Skandasvāmin on the *Nirukta*, and utilised the same in writing his own commentary on the *Nighaṇṭu*. No ms. of Skanda's commentary on the *Nirukta* has yet come to light. He is anterior to Devarāja.

Date of Devarāja.

(*a*) Devarāja quotes Bhoja frequently, see pp. 20, 21, 29, 35, 37, 43, 55, 69, 77, 93, 117, 130, 145, 166, 173, 175, 181, 182, 183, 184, 187, 193, 197, 198 etc. of the first volume of the Bib.Ind. edition of the *Nirukta*. Devarāja is therefore later than Bhoja.

(*b*) Devarāja quotes the *Daiva*, a work on grammar by Deva:—(sic.) क्षपेः क्षपयन्ति क्षान्त्यां प्रेरणे क्षपयेत् इति दैवम्[2] । This occurs in the *Daiva*[3] as follows:—क्षम्पेः क्षम्पयति क्षान्त्यां प्रेरणे क्षपयेदिति । 136. The quotation is almost identical. The difference may be attributed to the faulty reading of the mss. But even accepting the identity of the passage, the quotation does not lead to any definite result for the date of Deva is still subject to controversy.

(*c*) Devarāja twice quotes a passage from a *Dhātuvṛtti*. The passage is the following:—(sic.) क्षप् प्रेरणे । क्षपि क्षान्त्याम् इति कथादिषु पठितोऽपि बहुलमेतन्निदर्शनमित्यस्योदाहरणत्वेन धातुवृत्तौ पठ्यते[4] । The same quotation occurs a second time as follows:—(sic.) क्षप प्रेरणे । कथादिष्वपठितोऽपि बहुलमेतन्निदर्शनम् इत्यस्योदाहरणत्वेन धातुवृत्तौ पठ्यते[5] ।

The only extant *Dhātuvṛtti* is that of Sāyaṇācārya and the passage is not found therein. Nor is it likely to occur in Sāyaṇa's *Dhātuvṛtti* because Devarāja is anterior to Sāyaṇa as the latter quotes the former, the quotation being the following:—उस्राशब्दात्स्वार्थे पृषोदरा-

1. See Bib. Ind. ed., vol. i, pp. 2–4.
2. See, *op. cit.* p. 43. commentary on क्षपा Ngh. I. 7.
3. Trivandrum Sanskrit Series No. 1. p. 95.
4. *The Nirukta*, Bib. Ind. ed. vol. I. p. 43.
5. Op. cit. vol. I. p. 109.

दित्वेन घप्रत्यय इति निघण्टुभाष्यम्[1] । Devarāja's comment on the word उस्रिया Ngh. II. 11. is the following:—उस्रशब्दात् पृषोदरादित्वेन स्वार्थे घः । अर्थः पूर्ववत्[2] । Sāmas'ramī's edition of the commentary of Devarāja is capable of improvements. Max Muller's ms. of Devarāja's commentary reads उस्रा for उस्र of Sāmas'ramī. It is clear however that Sāyaṇācārya is posterior to Devarāja, who therefore could not have quoted from the *Dhātuvṛtti* of the former.

The above mentioned quotation of the *Dhātuvṛtti* also occurs in the *Puruṣakāra*, a commentary on the *Daiva* by *Kṛṣṇalīlās'uka-muni*, as follows:—क्षपि क्षान्त्याम् । क्षप प्रेरणे । भीमसेनेन कथादिष्वपठितोऽप्ययं बहुलमेतन्निदर्शनमित्युदाहरणत्वेन धातुवृत्तौ पठ्यते[3] । This comment is written on verse 136 of the *Daiva*, quoted by Devarāja. It is therefore very probable that Devarāja's quotation of the *Dhātuvṛtti* is borrowed from the *Puruṣakāra*. Devarāja will therefore be later than the author of the *Puruṣakāra*. The lower limit of the *Puruṣakāra* can be easily fixed for Hemacandra is quoted three times:—

(1) हेमचन्द्रस्तु वातणिति पठित्वा सुखसेवनयोरित्येक इति चोक्त्वा वेत्येक इत्यप्याह[4] ।

(2) क्षीणातीति हेमचन्द्रः[5] ।

(3) चुरादेराकृतिगणत्वाद् धारयतीति हेमचन्द्रः[6] ।

The upper limit of the *Puruṣakāra* can also be fixed with certainty for it is quoted by Sāyaṇācārya in his *Dhātuvṛtti*:—

(1) "कुर्द खुर्द गुर्द गुद क्रीडायामेवात्र कैयटपुरुषकारमैत्रेयादिषु तृतीयो न पठ्यते ।

(2) लाज लजि भर्त्सने च...इति पुरुषकारः ।

(3) इट किट कटी गतौ...अयं पक्षः समर्थितः पुरुषकारे[7] ।"

The second quotation is found in the published text as follows:—लज लाजि भर्त्सने । लाज लजि भर्त्सने च[8] ।...

---

1. Sāyaṇa's commentary on RV. I. 62. 3. Also, see, Max Muller's 2nd edition, IV. CXXXIII.

2. *The Nirukta*, Bib. Ind. ed. I. 230.

3, Trivandrum Sanskrit Series No. I. p. 95.

4. Trivandrum Sanskrit Series No. I. p. 22.

5. Op. cit. I. 24.

6. Op. cit. I. 37.

7. Quoted by Gaṇapatis'āstrī in op. cit. p. III.

8. Op. cit. p. 61.

(*d*) Devarāja quotes the *Padamañjarī* in his commentary on the word एतग्वा[1]—(sic). एतग्वा शब्दोऽश्वे वर्तते । तथा च । विशाखाषाढौ मन्थदण्डयोरित्यत्र पदमञ्जरी । "विशाखाषाढशब्दौ रूढिरूपेण मन्थदण्डयोर्वर्तेते । तेन यथा कथञ्चित्साधुत्वानुशासनार्थं व्युत्पत्तिः क्रियत इति[2] ।

Haradatta, the author of the *Padamañjarī* is also mentioned[3]. Haradatta was the son of Padmakumāra, a younger brother of Agnikumāra, and a pupil of Aparājita. The *Padamañjarī* is a commentary on the well-known *Kāśikā* and later than the *Mahābhāṣyapradīpa* of kaiyyaṭa, who is mentioned by the author of the *Sarvadars'anasaṁgraha*. The *Padamañjarī* is assigned to c. 1100 A. D. by Prof. Belvalkar in his *Systems of Sanskrit Grammar*. Devarāja therefore must be later than the 11th century A. D.

(*e*) Devarāja also quotes Bharatasvāmin:—छन्दोगानां सामकल्पे पठितोऽयं मन्त्रः । व्यचेर्व्याप्तिकर्मणः वेकुरा इति भरतस्वामिभाष्यम्[4] ।

In his introductory remarks, Devarāja mentions a Bharatasvāmin as a commentator of the Veda. The quotation shows that Bharatasvāmin belonged to the Sāmaveda and must have therefore written a commentary on that Veda. A ms. of the commentary of Bharatasvāmin on the Sāmaveda is mentioned by Burnell in his *Sanskrit mss. in the Palace at Tanjore*[5]. The commentary of Bharata was written in the reign of king Rāma of the Hosala dynasty. King Rāma reigned at Devagiri from 1272,3—1310 A. D. The commentary is therefore to be assigned to the end of the 13th century. Devarāja is therefore later than the 13th century. But as he is quoted by Sāyaṇācārya, he is earlier than the middle of the 14th century A. D. He may therefore be assigned to the beginning of the 14th century.

Devarāja also quotes one Durga[6]. This Durga however is not the commentator of Yāska but a commentator of the *Kātantrasūtrapāṭha*, the standard work of the Kātantra School of grammar. This Durga is quoted by Hemacandra and is assigned to the 8th century A. D[7].

---

1. Ngh. I. 14.
2. *The Nirukta*, Bib. Ind. ed. I. 147.
3. Op. cit. pp. i. 174, 240, 245, 246 etc.
4. *The Nirukta*, Bib. Ind. ed. I. 95.
5. *Vedic and Technical Literature*, Part I. p. 11, ed. 1879.
6. *The Nirukta*, Bib. Ind. ed. p. i. 112.
7. Belvalkar, *Systems of Sanskrit Grammar*, p. 87.

(3) But the most important of all these commentators is Durga. He seems to be later than Devarājayajvan who is familiar with the then extant commentaries on the Vedas, the *Nighaṇṭu*, and the *Nirukta*, and who does not mention Durga in the long list of the authorities used by him for the purpose of his own work. Although a conclusion based on the argument of silence is not cogent, yet in this particular case, it is justified to assume that Durga is not referred to because he was posterior to, or a contemporary of, Devarāja. The latter made an exhaustive study of the commentaries on the *Nighaṇṭu* aud the *Nirukta* and could not have ignored the very important work of the former. Durga would also be later than Skandasvāmin. Durga's commentary is published, and has superseded the works of his predecessors. His work is important for two reasons: (1) he is a later commentator, and therefore represents a fuller development of the traditional interpretation of the *Nirukta*; (2) the very fact that it has survived at the cost of earlier commentaries indicates its importance. We shall therefore examine his work somewhat in detail.

Date of Durga.

It has already been pointed out that in all probability Durga is posterior to, or a contemporary of, Devarājayajvan, and therefore later than the beginning of the 14th century A. D. However, Durga's upper limit can be determined almost with certainty. A manuscript[1] of his commentary in the Bodleian Library is dated 1387 A. D. The date is genuine and is accepted as such by Professor A. B. Keith.[2] The manuscript was copied at Bhṛgukṣetra in the reign of Mahārāṇā—Durgasiṁhavijaya. Thus he could not be later than 1387 A. D. It is not definitely known as to which particular site was represented by Bhṛgukṣetra but probably it is to be identified with the present Broach.[3] As Durga wrote his commentary in a hermitage near Jammu, a place not easily accessible in the absence of modern means of communications, the migration of the ms. of his commentary to Bhṛgukṣetra

1. MS. Wilson 475.

2. See *Catalogue of Sanskrit Manuscripts in the Bodleian Library*, vol. ii, p. 108.

3. See, The Imperial Gazatteer of India Vol., IX. p. 18.

presupposes the lapse of half a century at least in order to account for the spreading of his fame as a commentator from the isolated heights of Jammu to the plains of Bhṛgukṣetra. It will not be far from the truth, therefore, to place Durga about the beginning of the fourteenth century A. D.

Durga does not speak of any predecessors by name nor does he leave any clue as to the sources of his own commentary. Unlike Devarājayajvan, he does not give the slightest information about himself or the general state of the *Nirukta* during his time. That he wrote his commentary in a hermitage near Jammu is proved by the colophon[1] on f. 132 v. at the end of the eleventh chapter of the *Nirukta*, which runs as follows: ऋज्वर्थायां निरुक्तवृत्तौ जम्बूमार्गाश्रमनिवासिन आचार्यभगवद्दुर्गसिंहस्य कृतौ षोडशस्याध्यायस्य चतुर्थः पादः समाप्तः। This shows that the full name of the commentator was Durgasiṁha. The fact that he lived in a hermitage and was addressed as *bhagavat* indicates that he was an ascetic and belonged to some particular order of Sannyāsa. Further, he was a descendant of the family of the Vasiṣṭhas. He does not explain the stanza RV. III. 53. 23, quoted[2] by Yāska to illustrate the meaning of the word *lodham*, because the stanza implies hostility to Vasiṣṭha. He says: यस्मिन्निगम एष शब्दः सा वसिष्ठद्वेषिणी ऋक्। अहं च कापिष्ठलो वासिष्ठः। अतस्तां न निर्ब्रवीमि। 'The stanza, in which this word (*lodham*) occurs is hostile to Vasiṣṭha. And I am a descendant of Vasiṣṭha, belonging to the Kapiṣṭhala branch, hence I do not explain the stanza.'[3]

Sāyaṇa has the following note on it: पुरा खलु विश्वामित्रशिष्यः सुदा नाम राजर्षिरासीत्। स च केनचित् कारणेन वसिष्ठद्वेष्योऽभूत्। विश्वामित्रस्तु शिष्यस्य रक्षार्थमाभिर्ऋग्भिर्वसिष्ठमशपत्। इमा अभिशापरूपाः। ता ऋचो वसिष्ठा न शृण्वन्ति।

'There was formerly a royal sage named Sudās, a disciple of Viśvāmitra. Somehow, he became an object of Vasiṣṭha's hatred. Then, Viśvāmitra, in order to protect his disciple, reviled Vasiṣṭha with these stanzas. These are the imprecatory stanzas. The Vasiṣṭhas do not pay any attention (lit. listen) to them.'[4] This corroborates Yāska's statement that there are stanzas which contain asseveration and imprecation only.[5]

---

1. MS. Wilson 475.
2. The *Nirukta*, iv. 14.
3. Durga's Commentary on the N. iv. 14.
4. Sāyaṇa on RV. III. 53. Cf. Bib. Ind. edition of the *Nirukta*, vol. ii, p. 416.
5. N. vii. 3.

Durga's commentary is important for it repeats every word of Yāska, thus the text of the *Nirukta in toto* could be reproduced from Durga's work alone. As none of the manuscripts collated by me is older than the fifteenth century, Durga supplies therefore evidence of a very valuable character for the textual criticism of the *Nirukta*. The number of variants attributed by Durga to his predecessors and his frequent remarks that the text is corrupt and that the right reading is to be discovered,—all such cases I have pointed out in my notes,—indicate that there has been no unbroken tradition with regard to the handing down of the text of the *Nirukta*.

Further there seems to have been some sort of a revival of the study of the *Nirukta* in the neighbourhood of Jammu in Durga's time, for it seems difficult to imagine that in an isolated place like Jammu, Durga sat down to write his commentary simply for the love of writing a commentary. It is more reasonable to suppose that Durga accomplished this task in order to meet the demand for a good text, elucidation of obscure passages, and amplification of Yāska's arguments, a demand which a revival of the study of the *Nirukta* had called forth. The examination of the manuscript of Durga's commentary, mentioned above, leads one to the conclusion that Durga did not live to complete his work and that he himself wrote his commentary up to the end of the 11th chapter only. This is indicated by a comparison of colophons in the manuscript which, at the end of the 7th–12th chapters, numbered as 12–17 by Durga consecutively from the five chapters of the *Nighaṇṭu*, are as follows:

(1) At the end of the 7th chap. on f. 50 r. ॥ द्वादशोध्यायः ॥

(2) „ „ 8th chap. on f. 70 v. ॥ इति निरुक्तवृत्तौ त्रयो…ध्यायः॥

(3) „ „ 9th chap. on f. 86 v. ॥ ऋज्वर्थायां निरु…समाप्तः ॥

(4) „ „ 10th chap. on f. 112r. ॥ऋज्व…पंचदशोध्यायः समाप्तः॥

(5) „ „ 11th chap. on f. 132v. ॥ ऋज्वर्थायां निरुक्तवृत्तौ जम्बूमार्गाश्रमनिवासिन आचार्यभगवद्दुर्गसिंहस्य कृतौ षोडशस्याध्यायस्य चतुर्थः पादः समाप्तः ॥

A comparison of these five colophons shows that the first four do not contain any reference to Durga by name nor to his honorific titles, which fact implies that they were written by Durga himself, while that at the end of the 11th chapter was added by some disciple, who speaks of Durga as an *ācārya* and addresses him as *bhagavat.* Durga could not have appropriated these titles himself unless he was very vain. Another point in favour of the fifth colophon being written by a person other than Durga is that while the first four colophons say that such and such a chapter has come to an end, the fifth remarks that such a *pāda* of that chapter has come to an end. The colophon at the end of the 11th chapter is the final inscription and as such should have been placed at the end of the 12th chapter, where no such description is found; the colophon there, on f. 150 r., being ॥ सप्तदशस्य चतुर्थः पादः ॥ This leads one to the conclusion that Durga himself wrote his commentary up to the end of the 11th chapter, whose colophon was added by a disciple who also wrote the commentary on the 12th chapter, and faithfully refrained himself from adding the name of Durga in the colophon at the end of the 12th chapter. MS. Mill 142, dated A. D. 1839, and described in the *Catalogues of Sanskrit Manuscripts in the Bodleian Library* by Keith,[1] also preserves the final inscription at the end of the 11th chapter, while on f. 123 v., at the end of the 12th chapter it simply says ॥ सप्तदशस्य चतुर्थः पादः ॥ It is also to be noticed that in this manuscript as well, the word *adhyāya* only is used in the earlier colophons while *pāda* makes its appearance in those at the end of the 11th and the 12th chapters. Another point of minor importance may also be adduced in this connection, *i. e.* the manuscripts have the following *s'loka* at the end of the 12th chapter.

स्त्र्यभिलाषे यथा कामी करोत्यंगविचेष्टितम् ।
स्त्रीसमक्षं तथा कुर्यादयं श्रृंगारणक्रियाम् ॥

As Durga is shown to be a hermit, to ascribe these verses to him will be highly inappropriate.

Durga and the paris'iṣṭa.

Both the published editions of Durga's commentary regard the commentary on the portions of the 13th chapter as an integral part of Durga's work. But the ms. Wilson 475, dated 1387 A. D., and ms. Mill 142, dated 1839 A. D., do not contain the commentary on the 13th chapter. In both these manuscripts the commentary

1. Vol. ii, p. 108.

is completed at the end of the 12th chapter and the ms. Mill 142, expressly says that the work is finished. ॥ समाप्तो ग्रन्थः ॥ Moreover, the 13th chapter was not added to the *Nirukta* by Durga's time, as is proved by his remark in the introductory part of his commentary:

अयं च तस्या द्वादशाध्यायी भाष्यविस्तरः ।
तस्येदमादिवाक्यम् । समाम्नायः समाम्नातः ॥

'And this (the *Nirukta*) is its (the *Nighaṇṭu's*) amplified commentary consisting of twelve chapters whose first sentence is "a list has been handed down by tradition".' Hence the commentary on the 13th chapter was written at a later period and attributed to Durga by some disciple or follower of his.

(4) Barbarasvāmin is mentioned as an old commentator of the *Nirukta* by Mahes'vara. Aufrecht is not aware of his existence. All the mss. of Mahes'vara's commentary, discovered up till now, have the reading Barbara, but I doubt the genuineness of this reading. I think Barbarasvāmin stands for Skandasvāmin. There is however a Varavara mentioned as a commentator of *Gītā*. This information is contained in the following passage:— श्रीमद्यतिवरापरावतारभूतश्रीवरवरमुनिवर्यविरचिता भगवद्गीताव्याख्या । This commentary was entitled *Bālabodhinī* as well as *Gītārthasaṃgrahadīpikā*. The author Varavara was a pupil of S'ailanātha, a follower of Rāmānuja, and lived in A. D. 1370. See the *S'āstramuktāvalī* series, no. 25., Kanchi edition, 1906.

(5) Another commentator is Mahes'vara, a ms. of whose commentary I discovered at the Government Library of Sanskrit MSS. at Madras. A complete Palm leaf ms. of Mahes'vara's commentary, written in Malyalam characters exists in the Lalchand Library, attached to the D. A. V. College, Lahore. The Baroda Central Library too contains a fragment of the commentary. This fragment comes up to the end of the 1st chapter of the *Nirukta* only. I have collated all the three mss. for my forthcoming edition of the commentary.

Mahes'vara is unknown to Aufrecht, as his name is not mentioned as a commentator of the *Nirukta* in the *Catalogus Catalogorum*. He, however, appears to be later than Durga. An examination of Mahes'vara's commentary shows that the explanation is much more amplified than that of Durga. It represents a still later stage of development in the traditional interpretation of the text. The internal evidence indicates a date posterior to that of Durga. Besides, Durga is mentioned by name. The passage is the following:—तस्य निरुक्तस्य पञ्चाध्याया गौर्ग्मा इत्यादयो निघण्टवः । तेषां व्याख्यानार्थं षष्ठप्रभृति समाम्नायः समाम्नातः इत्यादि यास्कस्य भाष्यम् । तस्य पूर्वटीकाकारैर्बर्बरस्वामि-भगवद्दुर्गप्रभृतिभिर्विस्तरेण व्याख्यातस्य...अभ्याससिद्ध्यर्थं...ग्रन्थावृत्तिः क्रियते ।

Mahes'vara is certainly later than the 13th century A. D. The following two stanzas occur in the Baroda ms: —

विश्वेशं माधवं दुण्ढिं दण्डपाणिं च भैरवम् ।
वन्दे काशीं गुहां गङ्गां भवानीं मणिकर्णिकाम् ॥ १ ॥
माधवीयास्त्रयीधर्मशास्त्रोपनिषदात्मकाः ।
ग्रन्था मद्भ्रातरो ये च तत्सुखार्थं यतामहे ॥ २ ॥

These two stanzas are not found in the Madras and the Lahore mss. They seem to be spurious. Had they been genuine, Mahes'vara could not be assigned to a period earlier than the 15th century A. D. On other grounds too, Mahes'vara could hardly have lived before the 15th or the 16th century. He calls Durga a *Pūrvaṭīkākāra*, *i. e.* 'an ancient commentator'. He could hardly have called Durga 'an ancient', had he not been separated from the latter by several centuries. To call Tennyson an ancient poet, at present, would be atrocious although Shakespeare may be so described. The idea that a person is ancient, is generally associated with the lapse of a few centuries. It will not, in my opinion, be far from truth to assign Mahes'vara to the 16th century A. D.

Acknowledgment of help.

It is my most pleasant duty to thank my former teacher, Mr. A. C. Woolner M. A. (Oxon.); C. I. E., Principal of the Oriental College, Lahore; University Professor of Sanskrit; Dean of University Instruction etc. etc. for many valuable suggestions. He has been kind enough to include the present volume in the Panjab University Oriental Series. I have also to thank my friend P. Bhagavad Datta B. A. Superintendent of the Research Department of the D. A. V. College, Lahore, for drawing my attention to the *Bālakrīḍā*, the commentary of Vis'varūpācārya, who attributes a hitherto untraced quotation of the *Nirukta*

(p. 61. line 18.) to the *S'ruti* of the Bhāllavis and for partly correcting the proofs of several chapters. My thanks are also due to the Manager of the Nirṇaya-sāgara Press, Bombay.

When I undertook the present task, I had no idea of the labour involved in it. Nor will the general reader have any adequate notion of the time and labour spent in producing the present volume. The word to word collation of thirty seven mss. can be appreciated by such persons only as have done some critical editing themselves. Apart from mechanical labour, it will not be generally realised how much hard thinking is often necessary for the proper punctuation of the text. Several sentences are unintelligible simply for want of proper punctuation. A judicious employment of a comma or a full stop removes the difficulty and makes the sense quite clear. To put a comma or full stop may look like a trivial matter in itself. But it is not so. It often means very hard thinking. Division of several knotty sentences, *e. g.* lines 1-2 on p. 28 has cost me hours of concentrated thought. But I do not grudge the time and labour. I would do it over again, if necessary. And my ample reward will be to know that the present edition has made the study of the *Nirukta* easier even to a small extent.

The result of ten year's constant work is embodied in this edition. It is yet far from perfect. No one is more conscious of its defects than myself. It is capable of further improvements. All genuine criticism will, therefore, be most welcome. But there are undoubtedly critics, whose vocation is to find faults only. They must live and be true to their nature, as the poet says:—

अतिरमणीये काव्ये पिशुनोऽन्वेषयति दूषणान्येव ।
अतिसुन्दरेऽपि वपुषि व्रणमेव हि मक्षिकानिकरः ॥

ORIENTAL COLLEGE,
LAHORE.
12-11-1926.

Lakshman Sarup.

अथ निघण्टुः ।

अथ प्रथमोऽध्यायः ।

गौः । ग्मा । ज्मा[1] । क्ष्मा । क्षा । क्षमा[2] । क्षोणी[3] । क्षितिः । अवनिः । उर्वी । पृथ्वी । मही । रिपः । अदितिः । इळा[4] । निर्ऋतिः । भूः । भूमिः । पूषा[5] । गातुः[6] । गोत्रेति[7] पृथिव्याः [गोत्रेत्येकविंशतिः पृथिवीनामधेयानि] ॥ १ ॥

हेम । चन्द्रम् । रुक्मम् । अयः । हिरण्यम् । पेशः । कृशनम् । लोहम् । कनकम् । काञ्चनम् । भर्म । अमृतम् । मरुत् । दत्रम्[9] । जातरूपमिति हिरण्यस्य[10] [जातरूपमिति पञ्चदश हिरण्यनामानि] ॥ २ ॥

अम्बरम् । वियत् । व्योम । बर्हिः । धन्व[11] । अन्तरिक्षम् । आकाशम् । आपः । पृथिवी । भूः । स्वयम्भूः[12] । अध्वा । पुष्करम् । सगरः[13] । समुद्रः । अध्वरमित्यन्तरिक्षस्य[14] । [अध्वरमिति षोडशान्तरिक्षनामानि] ॥३॥

---

१. ग्मा. BK 2.

२. क्षामा. M 2, M 3, W 1, W 2, W 3; BK 2, ग; क्षमः ख.

३. क्षोणि. S; क्षोणिः Dev. क्षोणी is also given as a different reading by Deva: क्षोणीति ईकारान्तं केचित् पठन्तीति.

४. इला M 2, M 3, W 1, W 2, W 3; BK 2.

५. पृथि BK 2.

६. गातुः Comes immediately after निर्ऋतिः in M 2, M 3, W 1, W 2, W 3; BK 2.

७. गात्रेति०. Roth, हृ. गोत्रेति पृथिव्याः is the text of M 2, M 3, W 1, W 2, W 3, ग, BK 2. The text within [ ] is given by M 4, C 1, C 2, C 3, C 4, S, W 4; क. ख. घ; A.

८. हेमा. ख.

९. दत्तम्. M 2, M 3, W 1, W 2, W 3; BK 2.

१०. जातरूपमितिहिरण्यस्य. X; [जात०... नामानि]. Y.

११. धन्वा. ख.

१२. स्वयम्भुः is given as a different reading by Dev; स्वयम्भवत्युकारान्तं केषुचित् ।......। निगमस्यादर्शनादुभयमपि लिखितं निगमदर्शनान्निर्णयः कार्यः ॥

१३. सगरम्. M 2, M 3, W 1, W 2, W 3; ग. BK2.

१४. अध्वर०...०क्षस्य. X; [अध्वर...नामानि]. Y.

स्वः । पृश्निः । नाकः[1] । गौः । विष्टप् । नभ[2] इति साधारणानि [नभ इति षट् साधारणानि] ॥ ४ ॥

खेदयः[3] । किरणाः[4] । गावः । रश्मयः । अभीशवः । दीधितयः[5] । गभस्तयः । वनम् । उस्राः । वसवः । मरीचिपाः[6] । मयूखाः[7] । सप्त ऋषयः[8] । साध्याः । सुपर्णा[9] इति रश्मीनाम् [सुपर्णा इति पञ्चदश रश्मिनामानि] ॥ ५ ॥

आताः । आशाः । उपराः । आष्ठाः । काष्ठाः । व्योम । ककुभः[10] । हरित[11] इति दिशाम् [हरित इत्यष्टौ दिङ्नामानि] ॥ ६ ॥

श्यावी । क्षपा[12] । शर्वरी । अक्तुः[13] । ऊर्म्या । रम्या[14] । यम्या । नम्या । दोषा । नक्ता । तमः । रजः । असिक्नी[15] । पयस्वती[16] । तमस्वती । घृताची । शिरिणा[17] । मोकी[18] । शोकी । ऊधः । पयः । हिमा । वस्वेति[19] रात्रेः [वस्वीति[20] त्रयोविंशती रात्रिनामानि] ॥ ७ ॥

विभावरी । सूनरी । भास्वती । ओदती । चित्रामघा । अर्जुनी[21] । वाजिनी । वाजिनीवती । सुम्नावरी । अहना । द्योतना । श्वेत्या । अरुषी । सूनृता । सूनृतावती । सूनृतावरीत्युषसः[22] [सूनृतावरीति षोडशोषोनामानि] ॥ ८ ॥

---

१. नाकाः ख.
२. नभ...साधारणानि, X; [नभ......साधारणानि]. Y.
३. स्वेदयः BK 2.
४. किंरणाः W 1.
५. दिधीतयः च.
६. मरीचिपा. W. 3.
७. मयुखाः ख. मयूष्टाः BK. 2.
८. सप्तर्षयः च.
९. सुपर्ण. C 2. सुपर्णा......रश्मीणाम्. X; [सुपर्णा...नामानि]. Y.
१०. व्योमाककुभः । BK. 2.
११. हरित...दिशाम्. X [हरित...०नामानि]. Y.
१२. क्षपपा. W 3.
१३. अक्नुः । BK 2.
१४. रम्या. X; See (Roth's edition. p. 6) note under (7. 1), and also under (7. 2).
१५. अशिक्नी. ख.
१६. तमस्वती । पयस्वती M 2, M 3, W 1, W 2, W 3; ख, BK 2.
१७. श्रीणा. X, BK 2.
१८. Long vowels i. e. ई, ऊ and आ are shortened in मोकी । शोकी । ऊधः । and हिमा in the Ms. ख.
१९. वस्वेती रात्रेः X; [वस्वीति...०नामानि] Y.
२०. बस्विति etc. ख. Roth attributes वसी to Devarāja; it is not found in his commentary, published in Bib. Ind. The editor says in a note, that he found this reading in two of his Mss.
२१. अर्ज्जुनी. M 2.
२२. सूनृतावरीत्युपसः X; [सूनृता........नामानि] Y.

वस्तोः[1] । द्युः[2] । भानुः । वासरम् । स्वसराणि । घ्रंसः । घर्मः । घृणः[3] । दिनम् । दिवा[4] । दिवेदिवे । द्यविद्यवीत्यह्नः[5] । [द्यविद्यवीति द्वादशाहर्नामानि] ॥ ९ ॥

अद्रिः । ग्रावा । गोत्रः । बलः[6] । अश्नः । पुरुभोजाः । बलिशानः[7] । अश्मा[8] । पर्वतः । गिरिः । व्रजः । चरुः । वराहः । शंबरः । रौहिणः[9] । रैवतः । फलिगः । उपरः । उपलः । चमसः । अहिः । अभ्रम्[10] । बलाहकः[11] । मेघः । दृतिः[12] । ओदनः[13] । वृषन्धिः[14] । वृत्रः । असुरः । कोश इति मेघानाम्[15] [कोश इति त्रिंशन्मेघनामानि] ॥ १० ॥

श्लोकः । धारा । इळा[16] । गौः । गौरी । गान्धर्वी । गभीरा । गम्भीरा । मन्द्रा । मन्द्राजनी । वाशी । वाणी । वाणीची । वाणः । पविः । भारती । धमनिः । नाळीः[17] । मेना[18] । मेळिः[19] । सूर्या । सरस्वती । निवित् । स्वाहा । वग्नुः[20] । उपब्दिः । मायुः । काकुत्[21] । जिह्वा । घोषः । स्वरः । शब्दः । स्वनः । ऋक् । होत्रा । गीः । गाथा । गणः । धेना ।

१. वास्ता: BK 2.

२. द्यौ: क, Dev. द्यु: is also given by Devarāja as a different reading केचित् द्युरिति पठन्ति.

३. घृणि: X, BK. 2.

४. धिवा BK 2.

५. द्यविद्यवीव्यह्न: X; [द्यवि......नामानि] Y.

६. बल: M. 3; लव: BK 2.

७. बलिशान: क; पर्शान: M 2, BK 2, M 3, W 2, W 3; पर्णन: W 1.

८. अनुमा च.

९. रोहिण: M. 2.

१०. अभ्वम् X; BK 2.

११. बलाहक: M 3, M 4, C 1, C 2, C 3, C 4, S, W 1, W 2.

१२. दत्तिः च.; इतिः BK 2.

१३. ओदनम् X.

१४. गृषन्धि: M 2; विषन्धि: is also given by Devarāja, as another reading; नुदनं BK 2.

१५. कोश:...मेघानाम्. X; [कोश...नामानि] Y.

१६. इला. BK 2.

१७. नीलि: M 2, M 3, W 1, W 2, W 3; नालि: ग. च; BK 2; नाली. 'क'. ख. घ.

१८. मेलि: M 2, M 3, W 1, W 2, W 3; ग; BK 2.

१९. मेनि: M 2, M 3, W 1, W 2, W 3; ग; BK 2.

२०. गम्नु: M 2, M 3, W 1, W 2, W 3; ग; BK 2.

२१. काकुप् M 2, M 3, W 1, W 2, W 3 ग; BK 2.

ग्नाः[१] । विपा । नना[२] । कशा । धिषणा । नौः । अक्षरम् । मही । अदितिः । शची । वाक् । अनुष्टुप् । धेनुः । वल्गुः[३] । गल्दा[४] । सरः[५] । सुपर्णी । बेकुरेति[६] वाचः [बेकुरेति सप्तपंचाशद्वाङ्नामानि] ॥ ११ ॥

अर्णः । क्षोदः । क्षद्म[७] । नभः । अम्भः । कबन्धम्[८] । सलिलम् । वाः । वनम् । घृतम् । मधु[९] । पुरीषम् । पिप्पलम् । क्षीरम् । विषम् । रेतः । कशः[१०] । जन्म[११] । बृबूकम् । बुसम् । तुग्र्या । बुर्बुरम्[१२] । सुक्षेम[१३] । धरुणम् । सुरा[१४] । अररिन्दानि[१५] । ध्वस्मन्वत् । जामि[१६] । आयुधानि । क्षपः । अहिः । अक्षरम्[१७] । स्रोतः । तृप्तिः । रसः । उदकम् । पयः[१८] । सरः । भेषजम् । सहः । शवः[१९] । यहः[२०] । ओजः[२१] । सुखम् । क्षत्रम् । आवयाः । शुभम् । यादुः[२२] । भूतम् । भुवनम् । भविष्यत् । आपः[२३] । महत् । व्योम ।

---

१. Roth gives ग्ना as the reading of Devarāja, but it is not found in the published text of his commentary in Bib. Ind.

२. नम्ना. Dev. नना is also given by Devarāja as a different reading.

३. वग्नुः M 2, M 3, W 1, W 2, W 3; ग.

४. गल्दा ख. W 4; गल्दः W 1, W 2, BK 2, M 2, M 3; ग.; गलदः W 3.

५. रसः M 2, M 3, W 1, W 2; ग; BK 2, रासः W 3.

६. बेकुरेतिवाचः X; [बेकुरेति......नामानि] Y.

७. क्षद्मः BK 2, M 2, M 3, W 1, W 2, W 3; ग; क्षन्न. च; क्षद्मा. ख.

८. कवन्धम् M 2, M 3, W 1, W 2, W 3; ख. ग. घ. च, BK 2.

९. मधू M 2.

१०. शकम् M 2, M 3, W 1, W 3; BK 2, शकं W 2.

११. जह्म M 2, M 3, W 1, W 3, ग; BK 2; ब्रह्म W 2.

१२. बुबुरः M 2, M 3, W 1, W 2, W 3, ग; बर्बुरम् क. ख. घ. ङ. च.; बुबूरः BK 2.

१३. सुक्षेमः BK 2, सुक्षेमा ख; सुक्षोम. is given by Devarāja as another reading.

१४. सिरा. Dev.; he also gives सुरा as another reading.

१५. अरविन्दानि BK 2.

१६. जामिः M 2, M 3, W 1, W 2, W 3; ख; ग; BK 2, Devarāja gives जामिवत् as another reading.

१७. अक्षरा. M 2, M 3, W 1, W 2, W 3, ग, BK 2.

१८. प्रयः Dev. क.

१९. शिवः BK 2.

२०. यहः is omitted by M 2, M 3, W 1, W 2, W 3; BK 2.

२१. तुजः BK 2.

२२. यादः M 2, M 3, W 1, W 2, W 3; ग, BK 2.

२३. महत् । आपः । Dev. and ग.

यशः । महः । स्वर्णीकम्[1] । स्वृतीकम्[2] । सतीनम् । गहनम्[3] । गभीरम् । गम्भरम् । ईर्म[4] । अन्नम् । हविः । सद्म । सदनम् । ऋतम् । योनिः । ऋतस्य योनिः । सत्यम् । नीरम्[5] । रयिः । सत् । पूर्णम् । सर्वम् । अक्षितम् । बर्हिः । नाम । सर्पिः । अपः । पवित्रम् । अमृतम् । इन्दुः । हेम[6] । स्वः । सर्गाः[7] । शम्बरम् । अभ्वम्[8] । वपुः । अम्बु । तोयम् । तूयम्[9] । कृपीटम्[10] । शुक्रम्[11] । तेजः । स्वधा । वारि[12] । जलम् । जलाषम् । इदमित्युदकस्य[13] [इदमित्येकशतमुदकनामानि] ॥ १२ ॥

अवनयः । यव्याः[14] । खाः । सीराः । स्रोत्याः । एन्यः । धुनयः । रुजानाः । वक्षणाः । खादोअर्णाः । रोधचक्राः । हरितः । सरितः । अग्रुवः । नभन्वः[15] । वध्वः । हिरण्यवर्णाः । रोहितः । सस्रुतः । अर्णाः । सिन्धवः । कुल्याः । वर्यः[16] । उर्व्यः[17] । इरावत्यः । पार्वत्यः[18] । स्रवन्त्यः[19] । ऊर्जस्वत्यः । पयस्वत्यः । तरस्वत्यः । सरस्वत्यः । हरस्वत्यः । रोधस्वत्यः ।

---

१. स्वर्णीकम् M 1, M 2, M 3, W 1, W 2, W 3; ख. ग. घ. ङ; BK 2.

२. स्मृतीकं । स्वृतीकम् । सतीकं । सतीनं BK 2, M 2, M 3, W 1, W 2, W 3, ग. सतीकम् is given by Devarāja as another reading for स्वृतीकम्.

३. गह्वरम् M 2, M 3, W 1, W 2, W 3, BK 2.

४. कं M 2, M 3, W 1, W 2, W 3, BK 2.

५. निरम् M 2.

६. हेमा. ख.

७. स्वर्गाः, M 3, W 1; सर्ग्राः BK 2.

८. अभ्यम् BK 2.

९. तूयम् is omitted by M 2, M 3, W 1, W 2, W 3, ग.

१०. तृपीटम् M 2, M 3, W 1, W 2, W 3; त्रिपीटम् BK 2.

११. शुक्तम्. च.

१२. अक्षरं is added after वारि by BK 2, M 2, M 3, W 1, W 2, W 3, ग.

१३. इदमि...कस्य. X; [इदमि॰...नामानि] Y.

१४. यह्व्यः क and Dev. यह्व्याः is also given by Devarāja as another reading.

१५. नभन्वाः M 2, M 3, W 1, W 2, W 3, BK 2.

१६. वय्यः M 2, M 3, W 1, W 2, W 3, ऋतावर्यः is given by Devarāja, as another reading of वर्यः on the authority of माधव, 'इदं नाम माधवः ऋतावर्य इत्यपठत्'। He says that Skanda Svāmī does not state the words नदीनाम "अत्र स्कन्दस्वामिना नदीनामेति नोक्तम् । वाप्यः BK 2.

१७. ऊर्व्य. W 2.

१८. वार्बत्यः M 2, M 3, W 1, W 2, W 3, ग. BK 2.

१९. अवत्यः M 2, M 3, W 1, W 3, BK 2; अर्वत्यः W 2; रेवत्यः is given by Devarāja, as another reading of स्रवन्त्यः

भास्वत्यः । अजिगः । मातरः । [१]नद्य इति [२]नदीनाम् [नद्य इति सप्तत्रिंशन्नदीनामानि] ॥ १३ ॥

अत्यः । [३]हयः । अर्वा । वाजी । सप्तिः । वह्निः । दधिक्राः । दधिक्रावा । [४]एतग्वः । एतशः । पैद्वः । दौर्गहः । औच्चैश्रवसः । तार्क्ष्यः । आशुः । ब्रध्नः । अरुषः । [५]मांश्चत्वः । [६]अव्यथयः । [७]श्येनासः । सुपर्णाः । पतङ्गाः । नरः । [८]ह्रार्याणाम् । हंसासः । [९]अश्वा इत्यश्वानाम् [अश्वा इति षड्विंशतिरश्वनामानि] ॥ १४ ॥

हरी इन्द्रस्य । रोहितोऽग्नेः । हरित आदित्यस्य । रासभावश्विनोः । अजाः पूष्णः । पृषत्यो मरुताम् । अरुण्यो गाव [१०]उपसाम् । श्यावाः सवितुः । विश्वरूपा बृहस्पतेः । नियुतो वायोरिति [[११]दश] आदिष्टोपयोजनानि ॥ १५ ॥

भ्राजते । भ्राशते । [१२]भ्राश्यति । दीदयति । शोचति । मन्दते । भन्दते । रोचते । [१३]ज्योतते । द्योतते । द्युमदिति [[१४]एकादश] ज्वलतिकर्माणः ॥ १६ ॥

---

१. नद्य इति नदीनां X ; [नद्य...नामानि] Y.

२. नदीनाम BK 2.

३. हेत्यः BK 2.

४. एतग्वा Dev.

५. माःश्चत्वः ग; Devarāja gives मंश्चत्वः as a different reading; and मंश्चतु as a reading of Mādhava. मांश्चत्वः M 2, M 3, BK 2; मांश्चत्वः Roth.

६. व्यथयः M 2, M 3, W 1, W 2, W 3, BK 2.

७. स्येनासः ख.

८. वार्याणां M 2, M 3, W 1, W 2, W 3, BK 2.

९. अश्वा...अश्वानाम् X ; [अश्वा...नामानि] Y.

१०. उपसः Dev. and Skanda Svāmī and क.

११. Omitted by X.

१२. भ्लाशयते M 2, M 3, W 1, W 2, W 3, BK 2 ; भ्लाशते 'ग'; भ्लाशयति is given by Devarāja as a different reading.

१३. द्योतते । ज्योतते । Deva. and क. छन्दयते is given as a variant for ज्योतते by Devarāja.

१४. एकादश is omitted by X.

जमत् । कल्मलीकिनम् । जञ्जणाभवन् । मल्मलाभवन् । अर्चिः । शोचिः । तपः । तेजः । हरः । [2]हृणिः । [3]शृङ्गाणि शृङ्गाणीति ज्वलतः [शृङ्गाणीत्येकादश ज्वलतो नामधेयानि] ॥ १७ ॥

इति निघण्टौ प्रथमोऽध्यायः ।

[गौर्हेमाम्बरं स्वः खेदय आताः श्यावी विभावरी वस्तोरद्रिः श्लोकोर्णो वनयोत्यो हरी इन्द्रस्य भ्राजते जमदिति सप्तदश] M 1, M 4, C 1, C 2, C 3, C 4, S, W 4,

---

अथ द्वितीयोऽध्यायः ।

अपः । अप्नः । दंसः । [5]वेपः । वेपः । [6]विष्ट्वी । व्रतम् । कर्वरम् । [7]कुरुणम् । [8]शक्म । क्रतुः । करणानि । करांसि । करिक्रत् । [9]करन्ती । [10]चक्रत् । [11]कर्त्वम् । कर्तोः । कर्तवे । कृत्वी । धीः । शची । शमी । शिमी । शक्तिः । [12]शिल्पमिति कर्मणः [शिल्पमिति षड्विंशतिः कर्मनामानि] ॥ १ ॥

तुक् । तोकम् । [13]तनयः । तोक्म । तक्म । शेपः । अप्नः । गयः । जाः । अपत्यम् । [14]यहुः । सूनुः । नपात् । प्रजा । [15]बीजमित्यपत्यस्य [[16]बीजमिति पञ्चदशापत्यनामानि] ॥ २ ॥

---

१. पयः च.

२. घृणिः Dev. and कः हृणिः ग; हृणिः is also given by Devarāja as a different reading, on the authority of Skanda Svāmī.

३. शृङ्गाणि......ज्वलतः X; [शृङ्गाणि...... नामधेयानि] Y.

४. भृङ्गाणि. च.

५. वेशः M 2, M 3, W 1, W 2, W 3; ग, च, BK 2.

६. विष्टी. च.

७. करणम् M 2, M 3, W 1, W 2, W 3, BK 2; it is placed after क्रतुः by Devarāja.

८. शग्म M 2, M 3, W 1, W 2, W 3, BK 2; शक्मं च.

९. करन्ति M 2, M 3, W 1, W 2, W 3; ग.

१०. चक्रतुः is given by Devarāja, as a different reading. He attributes the reading चर्कृत्यम् to Mādhava अस्य स्थाने चर्कृत्यमिति माधवीये दृष्टमिति.

११. कर्तुम्. M 2, M 3, W 1, W 2, W 3, BK 2.

१२. शिल्पमिति कर्मणः X; [शिल्पम... नामानि] Y.

१३. तनयं BK 2, M 2, M 3, W 1, W 2, W 3.

१४. जहुः BK 2.

१५. बीजम् M 2, M 3, W 1, W 2, W 3; ख.

१६. बीजमित्यपत्यस्य X; [बीजमि°...... नामानि] Y.

[1]मनुष्याः । नरः । [2]धवाः । जन्तवः । विशः । क्षितयः । कृष्टयः । चर्षणयः । [3]नहुषः । हरयः । मर्याः । मर्त्याः । मर्ताः । व्राताः । तुर्वशाः । द्रुह्यवः । [4]आयवः । यदवः । अनवः । पूरवः । जगतः । तस्थुषः । पञ्च-जनाः । विवस्वन्तः । [5]पृतना इति मनुष्याणाम् [पृतना इति पञ्चविंशतिर्मनु-ष्यनामानि] ॥ ३ ॥

आयती । च्यवाना । अभीशू । अप्नवाना । विनङ्गृसौ । गभस्ती । करस्नौ । [6]बाहू । [7]भुरिजौ । [8]क्षिपस्ती । शक्वरी । [9]भरित्रे इति बाह्वोः [भरित्रे इति द्वादश बाहुनामानि] ॥ ४ ॥

अग्रुवः । [10]अण्व्यः । [11]क्षिपः । [12]विशः । शर्याः । रशनाः । धीतयः । [13]अथर्यः । विपः । कक्ष्याः । अवनयः । [14]हरितः । स्वसारः । जामयः । सनाभयः । योक्त्राणि । योजनानि । धुरः । शाखाः । अभीशवः । [15]दीधि-तय इत्यङ्गुलीनाम् [[16]गभस्तय इति द्वाविंशतिरङ्गुलिनामानि] ॥ ५ ॥

वश्मि । उ[17]श्मसि । वेति । वेनति । [18]वेसति । वाञ्छति । [19]वष्टि ।

---

१. मनुष्याः । नराः । नरः । M 2, M 3, W 1, W 2, W 3, BK 2.

२. धवाः is omitted by M 2, M 3, W 1, W 2 and W 3.

३. नहुषाः M 2, M 3, W 1, W 2, W 3; BK 2.

४. आयुवः M 1; अयवः ग.

५. पृतना…मनुष्याणाम्. X, [पृतना…… नामानि] Y.

६. बाहू M 2, M 3, W 1; M 1, W 4.

७. भूरिजौ. M 3.

८. क्षिपती is given by Devarāja, as another reading–क्षिपतीति पाठान्तर-मिति.

९. भरित्रे…बाह्वोः X; [भरित्रे…नामानि] Y.

१०. विभ्राः is added after अण्व्यः by 'ग'.

११. विशः । क्षिपः । Dev.

१२. विशः BK 2, M 2, M 3, W 1, W 2, W 3; वृशः ख.

१३. अथर्याः M 2, M 3, W 1, W 2, W 3, ग. अथर्यवः is given by Devarāja, as another reading–अथर्यव इति पाठो बहुषु दृष्ट इति.

१४. रोहितः is added after हरितः by M 2, M 3, W 1, W 2, W 3, BK 2.

१५. दीधितय…नाम् X; [गभस्तयः… नामानि] Y.

१६. गभस्तयः is omitted by M 2, M 3, W 1, W 2, W 3.

सुहस्त्याः and स्वसुतः are given by Devarāja, as different readings.

१७. अववेति is added after उश्मसि by M 2, M 3, W 1, W 2, W 3, BK 2.

१८. वेशति is given by Devarāja as another reading.

१९. वेष्टि. R and ङ.

वनोति । जुषते । [1]हर्यति । आ [2]चके । [3]उशिक् । मन्यते । [4]छन्त्सत् । चाकनत् । चकमानः । कनति । कानिषदिति [[5]अष्टादश] कान्तिकर्माणः ॥ ६ ॥

अन्धः । [6]वाजः । पयः । [7]श्रवः । पृक्षः । पितुः । [8]सुतः । [9]सिनम् । अवः । [10]क्षु । [11]धासिः । इरा । इळा । इषम् । ऊर्क् । रसः । स्वधा । [12]अर्कः । [13]क्षद्म । [14]नेमः । ससम् । नमः । आयुः । सूनृता । [15]ब्रह्म । वर्चः । [16]कीलालमित्यन्नस्य । [कीलालम् । [17]यश इत्यष्टाविंशतिरन्ननामानि] ॥ ७ ॥

आ वयति । भवति । [18]बभस्ति । वेति । वेवेष्टि । अविष्यन् । [19]बप्सति । भसथः । बब्धाम् । [20]ह्वयतीत्यत्तिकर्माणः । [ह्वरतीति दशात्तिकर्माणः] ॥ ८ ॥

ओजः । [21]पाजः । शवः । तवः । तरः । [22]त्वक्षः । [23]शर्धः । बाधः । नृम्णम् । तविषी । शुष्मम् । शुष्णम् । दक्षः । [24]वीळु । च्यौत्नम् । शूषम् । सहः । यहः ।

---

१. ईर्यर्त्ति is added after हर्यति by ख.

२. अचके. ख; is omitted by M 2, M 3, W 1, W 2, W 3.

३. उशत् M 2, M 3, W 1, W 2, W 3, BK 2.

४. शंसनत् M 2, M 3, W 1, W 2, W 3, BK 2.

५. Omitted by M 2, M 3, W 1, W 2, W 3.

६. पाजः is added after वाजः by M 2, M 3, W 1, W 2, W 3, BK 2.

७. प्रयः is given by Devarāja, as another reading, on the authority of Skanda Svāmī; श्रवः is omitted by M 2, M 3, W 1, W 2, W 3, BK 2.

८. Devarāja reads वयः and gives सुतः as another reading; सुतं M 2, M 3, W 1, W 2, W 3; BK 2.

९. सीनम् ग.

१०. क्षुत् M 2, M 3, W 1, W 2, W 3; BK 2; क्षुमत् ग.

११. धासि M 2, M 3, BK 2.

१२. अर्कः is omitted by Devarāja and क. वयः is added after अर्कः in BK 2.

१३. क्षद्मः ख.

१४. नेम M 2, M 3, BK 2.

१५. ब्रह्मः M 2.

१६. कीलाल०......०स्य. X; [यश...... नामानि] Y.

१७. यशः is omitted by M 2, M 3, W 1, W 2, W 3.

१८. बिभर्ति BK 2.

१९. बपति । बभसि । भसथः । BK 2.

२०. ह्वयतीत्यत्तिकर्माणः X; [ह्वरती...कर्माणः] Y.

२१. वाजः Devarāja. पाजः is given by him as another reading on the authority of Skanda Swāmī.

२२. तृक्षः X, BK 2.

२३. शर्द्धः BK 2.

२४. वीलु W 1, W 2, W 3.

वधः । वर्गः । वृजनम् । वृक्[1] । मज्मना[2] । पौंस्यानि । धर्णसिः[3] । द्रविणम् । स्यन्द्रासः । शम्बरमिति[4] बलस्य [शम्बरमित्यष्टाविंशतिर्बलनामानि] ॥ ९ ॥

मघम् । रेक्णः । रिक्थम् । वेदः । वरिवः । श्वात्रम् । रत्नम् । रयिः । क्षत्रम् । भगः । मीळ्हुम्[5] । गयः[6] । द्युम्नम्[7] । इन्द्रियम् । वसु । रायः । राधः । भोजनम् । तना । नृम्णम्[8] । बन्धुः[9] । मेधा । यशः । ब्रह्म । द्रविणम् । श्रवः[10] । वृत्रम्[11] । ऋतमिति[12] धनस्य [वृतमित्यष्टाविंशतिरेव धननामानि] ॥ १० ॥

अघ्न्या । उस्रा । उस्रिया । अही । मही । अदितिः[13] । इळा । जगती । शक्करीति[14] गवाम् [शक्करीति नव गोनामानि] ॥ ११ ॥

रेळते । हेळते । भामते । हृणीयते[15] । श्रीणाति । श्रेषति[16] । दोधति । वनुष्यति । कम्पते । भोजत इति [दंश[17]] क्रुध्यतिकर्माणः ॥ १२ ॥

हेळः । हरः । घृणिः[18] । त्यजः । भामः । एहः । ह्वरः[19] । तपुषी । जूर्णिः । मन्युः । व्यथिरिति[20] क्रोधस्य [व्यथिरित्येकादश क्रोधनामानि] ॥ १३ ॥

---

१. विट् X, BK 2.
२. मयमना BK 2.
३. धर्णसि घ. ङ. and Devarāja.
४. शम्बरमिति बलस्य X: [शम्बर...... नामानि] Y.
५. मीळहम् क.
६. नृम्णं is added after गय: by M 2, M 3, W 1, W 2, W 3: ग.
७. नृम्णम् । द्युम्नम् । इंद्रियम् । BK 2.
८. It is placed after गय: by X, BK2.
९. बन्धु M 2, M 3, W 1, W 2, W 3, BK 2.
१०. शव: W 1, W 2, BK 2, W 3, M 2, M 3.
११. वित्तम् M 2, M 3, W 1, W 2, W 3, BK 2 ; Devarāja does not accept it:—अत्र स्कन्दस्वामिना वृत्रं धननामेति व्याख्यातत्वात् केपुचित् कोशेपु दृश्यमानमपि वित्तमिति न पठनीयमिति.
१२. ऋतमिति धनस्य X [वृतमि०...नामानि] Y.
१३. अढिति: ङ.
१४. शक्करीति गवां X, [शक्करीति...नामानि] Y.
१५. हृणीयते. Dev.
१६. is omitted by M 3.
१७. is omitted by X.
१८. घृणि: Dev. Skanda Svāmī reads हृणि:, which is doubted by Devarāja.
१९. वर: M 2, M 3, W 1, W 2, W 3. BK 2.
२०. व्यथि:...०स्य X. [व्यथि०...नामानि] Y.

वर्तते । अयते[१] । लोटते[१] । लोठते[१] । स्यन्दते । कसति । सर्पति । स्यमति[१] । स्रवति । स्रंसते । अवति । श्चोतति । ध्वंसति[१] । वेनति । मार्ष्टि । भुरण्यति । शवति । कालयति । पेलयति । कण्टति । पिस्यति । विस्यति । मिस्यति । प्रवते । प्लवते[२] । च्यवते । कवते । गवते[१] । नवते । क्षोदति । नक्षति । सक्षति । म्यक्षति । सचति । ऋच्छति । तुरीयति । चतति । अतति । गाति । इयक्षति । सश्चति । त्सरति । रंहति । यतते । भ्रमति । ध्रजति । रंजति[१] । लंजति[१] । क्षियति[१] । धमति । मिनाति[३] । ऋण्वति । ऋणोति । स्वरति । सिसर्ति । विषिष्टि[४] । योषिष्टि[५] । रिणाति[६] । रीयते । रेजति[७] । दध्यति । दभ्नोति[८] । युध्यति[९] । धन्वति । अरुषति[१०] । आयति । डीयते[११] । तकति । दीयति । ईषति । फणति । हनति । अर्दति । मर्दति । सस्रते । नसते । हर्यति । इयर्ति । ईर्ते । ईङ्खते[१२] । त्रयति । श्वात्रति । गन्ति । आ गनीगन्ति । जङ्गन्ति । जिन्वति[१३] । जसति । गमति । ध्रति । ध्राति । ध्रयति । वहते । रथर्यति । जेहते[१४] । ष्वःकति[१] । क्षुम्पति[१] । प्साति[१] । वाति[१] । याति[१] । इषति[१५] । द्राति । द्रूळति । एजति । जमति । जवति । वश्चति । अनिति । पवते । हन्ति । सेधति । अगन् । अजगन् । जिगाति[१६] । पतति । इन्वति । द्रमति । द्रवति । वेति । हयन्तात्[१७] । एति । जगायात्[१८] । अयुथुः[१९] इति द्वाविंशशतं गतिकर्माणः ॥ १४ ॥

१. Not explained by Devarāja.
२. प्लवते is repeated by M 1.
३. मिनोति is given by Dev., as another reading.
४. वेशिष्टि ख. ग. च, W 2; वेपिष्टि Roth. & Bh.
५. योशिष्टि ख.
६. ऋणाति W 2.
७. नेदति ग.
८. दभ्नोति ग. C. D. F.
९. युध्यते ग.
१०. अरुष्यति is give by Devaraja, as another reading: द्वित्रयोः प्रदेशयोः अरुष्यतिर्गतिकर्मेत्यपि । उभयथा दृष्टमपि बहुषु प्रदेशेषु दर्शनात अरुषतीति पाठो युक्तः ।
११. सीयते. क and Devarāja. डीयते is given as a variant by Dev.
१२. ईङ्खयति M 1.
१३. जगाति. ग. C. D F.
१४. रथर्यति is placed after as well as before जेहते by M 1.
१५. जायति. ग. C. D. F.
१६. Devarāja gives जगति as another reading, on the authority of Skanda Svāmi.
१७. हन्तात् Dev. हयन्तात् is also given by Devarāja as another reading.
१८. जगायात् Roth.
१९. अयथुः Dev.

इरज्यति । पत्यते । क्षयति[१] । राजतीति [चत्वार[२]] ऐश्वर्यकर्माणः ॥२१॥

राष्ट्री । अर्यः । नियुत्वान्[३] । इन[४] इन इतीश्वरस्य [इन इन इति चत्वारीश्वरनामानि] ॥ २२ ॥

इति निघण्टौ द्वितीयोऽध्यायः ।

Y adds the following :—

अपस्तुङ्मनुष्या आयत्यग्रुवो वश्म्यन्ध आवयत्योजो मघमघ्या रेळते हेळो वर्तते नु तळिद्रण इन्वति दभ्नोति दिद्युदिरज्यति राष्ट्रीति द्वाविंशतिः ॥

इति निघण्टौ द्वितीयोऽध्यायः समासः ।

— ——————

अथ तृतीयोऽध्यायः ।

उरु । तुवि । पुरु । भूरि । शश्वत् । विश्वम्[५] । परीणसा[६] । व्यानशिः । शतम्[७] । सहस्रम् । सलिलम्[८] । कुविदिति[९] बहोः [कुविदिति द्वादश बहुनामानि] ॥ १ ॥

ऋहन्[१०] । ह्रस्वः । निघृष्वः[११] । मायुकः । प्रतिष्ठा । कृधु[१२] । वम्रकः । दभ्रम्[१३] । अर्भकः । क्षुल्लकः[१४] । अल्पकमिति[१५] ह्रस्वस्य [अल्प इत्येकादश ह्रस्वनामानि] ॥ २ ॥

१. क्षियति. ग, BK 2.
२. omitted by X.
३. पतिः is given as a Variant by Dev.
४. इन इन…वरस्य X; [इन इन…नामानि] y.
५. विश्वम् and परीणसा are not explained by Devarāja.
६. परोणसा Roth.
७. व्यानशिशतम् । BK 2.
८. सरिरं X, BK 2.
९. कुविदिति बहोः X, [कुविदि…नामानि] y.
१०. रिहं BK 2; ऋहन्. च.
११. तृपमः is added after निघृष्वः by BK 2, M 2; M 3, W 3 ग; and त्रिपमः by W 1, W 2.
१२. कृधुकः M 2, M 3, W 1, W 2, W 3; कृधुकः BK 2.
१३. दहरकः M 2, M 3, W 1, W 2, W 3, BK 2.
१४. omitted by BK 2. M 2. M 3, W 1, W 2, W 3.
१५. अल्पकमिति ह्रस्वस्य X; [अल्प…नामानि] y.

Sec. 14 according to the shorter recension is as follows:—

वर्तते[१] । अयते । लोटते । लोठते । स्यन्दति । कसति । सर्पति । स्यमति । स्रवति । स्रंसति । श्चोतति । ध्वंसति । वेनति । मार्ष्टि । भुरण्यति । शवति । कालयति । पेलयति । कण्टति । पिस्यति । विस्यति । मिस्यति । प्रवते । प्लवते । च्यवते । कवते । गवते । अवते । क्षोदति । सक्षति । इयक्षति । मियक्षति । सचति । अचति । ऋच्छति । तुरीयति । त्सरति । अतति । पतति । चेतति । सश्चति । रंहति । भ्रमति । ध्रजति । रजति । लजति । क्षियति । क्षिणोति । ऋण्वति[२] । सिसर्ति । वेषिष्टि । योषिष्टि[३] । रिणाति[५] । ऋणर्ति[४] । इयर्ति । रीयते । नेदति । नख्यति । दध्यति । दभ्नोति । युध्यते[६] । धन्वति । अरर्षति[७] । अलर्षति[८] । डीयते । तकति । दीयते । ईषति । कणन्वि । संस्रति[९] । सिस्रति । धवति । धावति । हम्मति[१०] । हयति । ईर्ते । जयति[११] । श्वात्रति । गन्ति । गनीगन्ति । जगन्ति । जगाति । जगति । गमति । मिनति । ध्रति । ध्राति । ध्रयति । ध्रुवति । वल्गूयति । अथर्यति । ईहते । जेहति[१२] । वदति । राति । रूल्हति । एजति । वञ्चति । पःकति[१३] । ष्वःकति[१४] । क्षुम्पति । प्साति । वाति । याति । जायति । पतयति । पवते । हन्ति । सेधति । अगन् । अजगन् । आगनीगन्ति[१५] । गाति । जिगाति । इन्वति । व्रजति । द्रवति[१६] । द्रुम्मति । वेति । हयन्ता[१७] । जगायात्[१८] । अयुधुरिति गतिकर्माणः ॥ १४ ॥

१. वतति W 2; सचति W 1.
२. रिण्वति W 1.
३. वेशिष्टि । योशिष्टि । Roth & Bhad.
४. ऋणाति W 1, W 3, M 2, M, 3, BK 2, Roth & Bhad.
५. रिणाति BK 2.
६. युध्यते is omitted by M 2.
७. अर्षति M 2; अरिरिर्षति BK 2.
८. अलर्षति W 2.
९. सस्रति । Bhad.
१०. हम्पति । Bhad.
११. जयति BK 2.
१२. जेहते । Roth & Bhad.
१३. पप्कति BK 2.
१४. ष्वप्कति BK 2.
१५. आग्नीगन्ति W 2.
१६. दृवति । Roth & Bhad.
१७. हंयन्ता W 3. हयन्तात् । Roth & Bhad.
१८. जगयात् M 2.

नु । मक्षु । द्रवत् । ओषम् । जी[1]राः । जूर्णिः । शूर्ताः । शू[2]घनासः । शीभम् । तृषु[3] । तू[4]यम् । तू[5]र्णिः । अजिरम् । भुरण्युः । शु[6] । आ[7]शु । प्रा[8]शुः । तू[9]तुजिः । तू[10]तुजानः । तुज्यमानासः । अज्राः । सा[11]चीवित् । द्यु[12]गत् । ताजत् । तरणिः । वा[13]तरंहा इति क्षिप्रस्य [वातरंहा इति षड्विंशतिः क्षिप्रनामानि] ॥ १५ ॥

त[14]ळित् । आ[15]सात् । अम्बरम् । तु[16]र्वशे । अस्तमीके । आके । उपाके । अ[17]र्वाके । अन्तमानाम् । अवमे । उ[18]पम इत्यन्तिकस्य [उपम इत्येकादशान्तिकनामानि] ॥ १६ ॥

रणः । विवाक् । वि[19]खादः । नदनुः । भरे । आक्रन्दे । आहवे । आजौ । पृतनाज्यम् । अभीके । समीके । ममसत्यम् । नेमधि[20]ता । सङ्काः । समितिः । समनम् । मीळ्हे । पृतनाः । स्पृधः । मृधः । पृ[21]त्सु । समत्सु । [22]संमर्ये । समरणे । स[23]मोहे । समिथे । सं[24]ख्ये । सङ्गे । संयुगे । स[25]ङ्गथे । [26]सङ्क्रमे । वृत्रतूर्ये । पृक्षे । आणौ । शू[27]रसातौ । वाजसातौ । समनीके । खले ।

१. जिराः ख.
२. शूघनाः M 2, M 3, W 1, W 2, W 3, ग; BK 2; शुघनसाः ख; शूघनाशः च.
३. तृष्पु BK 2.
४. तोयम् M 2, M 3, W 1, W 2, W 3, ग, BK 2.
५. तूर्णि ख. ग.
६. शूः ग; शुः BK 2.
७. आशुः M 2, M 3, W 1, W 2, W 3, ग. ख. च.
८. प्राशुवित् M 2, प्राशुजित् M 3, BK 2, प्राशुचित् W 1, W 2; प्राशुवित् W 3.
९. तूतुजानासः M 2, M 3 W 1, W 2, W 3, BK 2.
१० तूतुजित्. M 2, M 3, W 1, W 2, W 3, BK 2. तूतुजानः S'iva.
११. साचीवत् M 2, M 3, W 1, W 2, W 3.
१२. युगत् M 2, M 3, W 1, W 2, W 3, BK 2.
१३. वात…क्षिप्रस्य X; [वात…नामानि] Y.
१४. तलित् ख. ग. च.
१५. आसा X, BK 2.
१६. तुर्वशः च.
१७. अर्वाकः च.
१८. उपम…कस्य X; [उपम…नामानि] Y.
१९. विखादः is omitted by M 2, M 3, नदन्वः । विषादत । BK 2.
२०. नेमधितिः X; BK 2.
२१. पृत्सुधः X.
२२. is omitted by M 2, M 3, W 1, W 2, W 3, B K 2.
२३. संमोहे M 1, Roth.
२४. संखे क and Devarāja.
२५. समर्थे, M 2, M 3, W 1, W 2, W 3. BK 2.
२६. is omitted by M 2, M 3, W 1, W 2, W 3, BK 2.
२७. प्रधने is added before शूरसातौ by M 2, M 3, W 1, W 2, W 3, BK 2.

खजे । पौंस्ये । महाधने । वाजे । अ[1]ज्म । सद्म । संयत् । संव[2]त इति स
[संवत इति षट्चत्वारिंशत्सङ्ग्रामनामानि] ॥ १७ ॥

इन्वति । न[3]क्षति । आक्षाणः । आनट् । आ[4]ष्टे । आपानः । उ
नशत् । आ[5]नशे । अश्नुत इति [दश[6]] व्याप्तिकर्माणः ॥ १८ ॥

वभ्नोति । श्न[7]थति । ध्नरति । धूर्वति । तृणक्ति । वृश्चति । कृ[8]ण्व
कृन्तति । श्व[9]सिति । न[10]भते । अ[11]र्दयति । स्तृणाति । स्नेहयति । यातया
स्फुरति । स्फुलति । निर्वपन्तु । अवतिरति । वियातः । आतिरत् । तळित
आखण्डल । द्रूणाति । र[12]म्णाति । शृणाति । शम्नाति । तृ[13]णेळ्हि । ताळ्हि
नितोशते । निर्बर्हयति । मि[14]नाति । [15]मिनोति । ध[16]मतीति वधकर्माणः [धमती
त्रयस्त्रिंशद्वधकर्माणः] ॥ १९ ॥

दिद्यु[17]त् । नेमिः । हेतिः । नमः । पविः । सृ[18]कः । वधः । वज्रः ।
अर्कः । कुत्सः । कुलिशः । तु[19]ञ्जः । ति[20]ग्मः । मे[21]निः । स्वधितिः । सायकः ।
[22]परशुरिति वज्रस्य [परशुरित्यष्टादश वज्रनामानि] ॥ २० ॥

१. अग्मन् । सग्मन् । समीथे । सङ्गथे । संयतः M 2, M 3, W 1, W 2, W 3, BK 2.
२. संवत…ग्रामस्य X; [संवत…नामानि] y.
३. ननक्षे M 2, M 3, W 1, W 2, W 3, ग, BK 2.
४. आष्टः M 2, M 3, W 1, W 2, W 3, BK 2.
५. आनशे comes before अशत् in M 2, M 3, W 1, W 2, W 3, BK 2.
६. is omitted by X.
७. श्रथति is added after श्नथति by M 2, M 3, W 1, W 2, W 3, BK 2.
८. कृणत्ति X, BK 2.
९. श्वसति. X.
१०. नभति. M 3, W 1, W 2, W 3, ग; BK 2; नक्षति M 2.
११. अर्दति । मर्दति । स्नेहति । याचति । M 2, M 3, W 1, W 2, W 3, BK 2
१२. शम्नाति । मिनाति । M 2, M 3, W 1, W 2, W 3, BK 2.
१३. त्रिणेह्लि (तृणेह्लि M 2) ताह्लि । नितोशयति । M 2, M 3, W 2, W 3, BK 2.
१४. omitted by M 2, M 3, W 1, W 2, W 3, BK 2.
१५. जूर्वति is added after मिनोति by M 2, M 3 W 1, W 2, W 3, BK 2.
१६. धमतीति…कर्माणः X; [धमतीति…कर्माणः] y.
१७. विद्युत् BK 2.
१८. वज्रः । सृकः । वृकः । वधः । अर्कः । कुत्सः । मेनिः । कुलिशः । तुञ्जः । तिग्मः । स्वधितिः । M 2, M 3, W 1, W 2, W 3, BK 2.
१९. तुजः Devarāja.
२०. तिग्मम् Dev.
२१. नेभिः BK 2.
२२. परशु…वज्रस्य X; [परशु…नामानि] y.

[1]म॒हत् । ब्र॒ध्नः । [2]ऋ॒ष्वः । बृ॒हत् । [3]उ॒क्षि॒तः । त॒वसः॑ । त॒वि॒षः । [4]म॒हि॒षः अभ्वः॑ । ऋ॒भु॒क्षाः । उ॒क्षा । वि॒हा॑याः । य॒ह्वः । [5]व॒व॒क्षि॑थ । वि॒व॒क्षसे । अ॒म्भृ॒णः । [6]मा॒हि॒नः । ग॒भी॒रः । [7]क॒कु॒हः । [8]र॒भ॒सः । [9]व्रा॒धन् । [10]वि॒र॒प्शी । [11]अ॒द्भु॒तम् । [12]बंहि॑ष्ठः । [13]ब॒र्हि॒षीति म॒हतः [बर्हिषदिति पञ्चविंशतिर्महन्नामानि] ॥ ३ ॥

गयः॑ । कृ॒द॒रः । [14]गर्तः॑ । ह॒र्म्यम् । [15]अस्त॑म् । [16]प॒स्त्य॑म् । दु॒रो॒णे । [17]नी॒ळम् । दु॒र्याः । स्व॒स॑राणि । अ॒मा । दमे॑ । कृत्तिः॑ । [18]योनिः॑ । [19]सद्म॑ । श॒र॒णम् । व॒रू॑थम् । छ॒र्दिः । छ॒दिः । छा॒या । [20]शर्म॑ । [21]अ॒ज्मेति गृहाणाम् [अज्मेति द्वाविंशतिर्गृहनामानि] ॥ ४ ॥

[22]इ॒र॒ज्यति॑ । वि॒धेम॑ । स॒प॒र्यति॑ । न॒म॒स्यति॑ । दु॒व॒स्यति॑ । ऋ॒ध्नोति॑ । ऋ॒णद्धि॑ । ऋ॒च्छति॑ । [23]सप॑ति । विवासतीति [[24]दश] परिचरणकर्माणः ॥ ५ ॥

---

१. महः X, BK 2.

२. ऋथः BK 2.

३. उक्षः X; BK 2.

४. महिषः । अभ्वः come after उक्षितः in M 2, M 3, W 1, W 2, W 3, BK 2.

५. ववक्षथा. BK 2.

६. गभीरः । माहिनः । M 2, M 3, W 1, W 2, W 3, BK 2.

७. ककुहस्तिना X; BK 2.

८. भरसः BK 2.

९. व्राधम् BK 2, X.

१०. विरप्सी. BK 2.

११. अद्भुतः BK 2; X.

१२. बर्हिष्ठः BK 2; X.

१३. बर्हिषीति महतः X; [बर्हिषद्...॰मानि] y.

१४. गर्भः M 1.

१५. नीरं M 2, M 3, W 1, W 2, W 3, BK 2.

१६. अस्त्यम् M 2, M 3, W 1, W 2, W 3; is added after अस्तम् in BK 2.

१७. नीळम् is omitted by M 2, M 3, BK 2, W 1, W 2, W 3.

१८. योनि S, W 4.

१९. शर्म X, BK 2.

२०. वर्म. X; BK 2.

२१. अज्मेति गृहाणाम् X; [अज्मेति...नामानि] y.

२२. इरध्यति M 2, M 3, W 1, W 2, W 3, BK 2.

२३. शवति M 2, M 3, W 1, W 2, W 3, BK 2.

२४. दश is omitted by X.

शिम्बाता । शतरा । शातपन्ता । शिल्गुः[1] । स्यूमकम्[2] । शेवृधम्[3] । मयः । सुग्म्यम् । सुदिनम्[4] । शूषम् । शुनम् । शंगमम्[5] । भेषजम् । जलाषम् । स्योनम् । सुम्नम्[6] । शेवम् । शिवम् । शम्[7] । कदिति[8] सुखस्य [कमिति विंशतिः सुखनामानि] ॥ ६ ॥

निर्णिक् । वव्रिः । वर्पः । वपुः[9] । अमतिः । अप्सः । प्सुः[10] । अम्बः[11] पिष्टम् । पेशः । कृशनम् । मरुत्[12] । अर्जुनम् । ताम्रम् । अरुषम् । शंष्यमिति[13] रूपस्य [शिल्पमिति षोडश रूपनामानि] ॥ ७ ॥

अस्रेमा[14] । अनेमा[15] । अनेद्यः[16] । अनवद्यः । अनभिशस्त्यः[17] । उक्थ्यः[18] । सुनीथः । पाकः । वामः । वयुनमिति[19] प्रशस्यस्य [वयुनमिति दश प्रशस्यनामानि] ॥ ८ ॥

केतुः[20] । केतः । चेतः । चित्तम् । क्रतुः । असुः । धीः । शची । माया । वयुनम् । अभिख्येति[21] प्रज्ञायाः [अभिख्येत्येकादश प्रज्ञानामानि] ॥ ९ ॥

---

१. शिल्गु M 2, M 3, W 1, W 2, W 3; शर्म क. and Devarāja.

२. शेवृधम् X, BK 2.

३. स्यूम । कम् । X, BK 2.

४. सुद्दिनम् BK 2.

५. शं BK 2, X.

६. सुम्नम् is omitted by M 2, M 3, W 1, W 2, W 3; BK 2.

७. शग्म्यम् M 2, M 3, W 1, W 2, W 3, BK 2.

८. कद्रिति सुखस्य X; [कमिति...नामानि] Y.

९. अपुः is added after वपुः by M 2, M 3, W 1, W 2, W 3, BK 2.

१०. प्सु M 1, M 4, C 1, C 2, C 3, C 4, S, W 4; बप्सः M 2, M 3, W 1, W 2, W 3; BK 2.

११. omitted by X; BK 2.

१२. प्सरः क. and Dev.

१३. शष्यमितिरूपस्य X; [शिल्पमिति...... नामानि] Y.

१४. अस्रेमाः M 2, M 3, W 1, W 2, W 3; BK 2, and S'iva, Sāma.

१५. अनेमा is omitted by M 2, M 3, W 1, W 2, W 3, BK 2; अनेमाः S'iva, Sāma.

१६. अनिंद्यः M 2, M 3, W 1, W 2, W 3, BK 2.

१७. अनभिशस्तिः । अनवद्यः । M 2, M 3, W 1, W 2, W 3, BK 2.

१८. उत्छ्यः M 3, W 2, W 3; उत्छयाः M 2, उक्ष्य W 1.

१९. वयुन०...०स्य X; [वयुन०...नामानि] Y.

२०. केतः । केतुः । X; BK 2,

२१. अभि०...प्रज्ञायाः X; [अभि०...नामानि] Y.

बट् । श्रत् । सत्रा । [1]अद्धा । इत्था । [2]ऋतमिति सत्यस्य [ऋतमिति षट् सत्यनामानि] ॥ १० ॥

[3]चिक्यत् । चाकनत् । अचक्ष्म । चष्टे । वि चष्टे । विचर्षणिः । विश्वचर्षणिः । अवचाकशदिति [[4]अष्टौ] पश्यतिकर्माणः ॥ ११ ॥

हिकम् । [5]नुकम् । सुकम् । [6]आहिकम् । [7]आकीम् । नकिः । माकिः । नकीम् । [8]आकृतमित्यामिश्राणि [आकृतमिति नवोत्तराणि पदानि सर्वपदसमाम्नानाय] ॥ १२ ॥

इदमिव । इदं यथा । अग्निर्न ये । चतुरश्चिद्ददमानात् । ब्राह्मणा व्रतचारिणः । वृक्षस्य नु ते पुरुहूत वयाः । जार आ भगम् । मेषो भूतो३ऽभि यन्नयः । [9]तद्रूपः । तद्वर्णः । तद्वत् । तथेत्युपमाः ॥ १३ ॥

अर्चति । गायति । रेभति । स्तोभति । गूर्धयति । [10]गृणाति । [11]जरते । [12]ह्वयते । [13]नदति । पृच्छति । रिहति । धमति । कृपायति । कृपण्यति । [14]पनस्यति । [15]पनायते । [16]वल्गूयति । मन्दते । [17]भन्दते । छन्दति । [18]छदयते । शशमानः । [19]रञ्जयति । [20]रंजयति । शंसति । स्तौति । यौति । रौति । नौति । भनति । पणायति । पणते । सपति । [21]पपृक्षाः । महयति । वाजयति । पूजयति । मन्यते । [22]मदति । रसति । स्वरति । वेनति । मन्द्रयते । जल्पतीति चतुश्चत्वारिंशदर्चतिकर्माणः ॥ १४ ॥ According to the other recension the list of words from भन्दते onward is the following:—

---

१. इत्था । अद्धा । X; BK 2.
२. ऋतमि…सत्यस्य X; [ऋतमि०……नामानि] Y.
३. चिक्यम् । चन । चाक्ष्म । M 2, M 3, W 1, W 2, W 3; BK 2.
४. is omitted by X.
५. सुकम् । नुकम् । X; BK 2.
६. आहिकम् is omitted by M 2, M 3, W 1, W 2, W 3, BK 2.
७. आकीम् । नकीम् । नकिः । माकीम् । माकिः । M 2, M 3, W 1, W 2, W 3, BK 2.
८. आकृतमित्यामिश्राणि X; [आकृतमिति……समाम्नाय] Y.
९. तद्रुपः M 3.
१०. सृणति BK 2.
११. जरति X, BK 2.
१२. ह्वयति X, BK 2.
१३. रिहति । धमति । नदति । पृछति । कृपा । X; BK 2.
१४. पणस्यति. X; BK 2.
१५. पणायते M 2, M 3, W 1, W 2, W 3, Roth.
१६. कृपणयति । पणस्यति । पणायते । वल्गूयन्ति । BK 2.
१७. भन्दते is omitted by W 1, W 2, W 3, BK 2.
१८. छदयति. X; छद्येति. BK 2.
१९. रजयति । रज्ञयति । M 2, M 3, W 1, W 2, W 3, BK 2.
२०. जरयति Deva.
२१. पिप्रक्षाः ग. C. D. F.
२२. मंदति M 1, C 4, S, W 1.

(भन्दते । भणति । भणायते[1] । स्वपिति । पिपृक्षाः[2] । महयति । वाजयति । पूजयति । स्वदति । मदति । रसति । वेनति । कल्पते । जल्पति । मन्त्रयते । वन्दत इत्यर्चतिकर्माणः ॥ १४ ॥) M 2, M 3 W 1, W 2, W 3.

विप्रः । विग्रः । गृत्सः । धीरः । वेनः । वेधाः[3] । कण्वः । ऋभुः[4] । नवेदाः । कविः[5] । मनीषी[6] । मन्धाता । विधाता । विपः[7] । मनश्चित् । विपश्चित् । विपन्यवः[8] । आकेनिपः[9] । उशिजः । कीस्तासः । अद्धातयः[10] । मतयः । मतुथाः[11] । मेधाविन[12] इति मेधाविनाम् [वाघत[13] इति चतुर्विंशतिर्मेधाविनामानि] ॥ १५ ॥

रेभः । जरिता । कारुः । नदः[14] । स्तामुः[15] । कीरिः । गौः । सूरिः । नादः । छन्दः । स्तुप् । रुद्रः । कृपण्युरिति त्रयोदश स्तोतृनामानि (रेभः । जरिता । कारुः । कीरिः । तामुः । सूरिः । रुद्रः । नदः । नादः । छन्दः । स्तुत् । गौः । कृपण्युरिति स्तोतृणाम्[16]) ॥ १६ ॥

यज्ञः । वेनः । अध्वरः[17] । मेधः । विदथः । नार्यः[18] । सवनम् । होत्रा । इष्टिः । देवताता । मखः । विष्णुः । इन्दुः । प्रजापतिः । घर्म इति यज्ञस्य । [घर्म[19] इति पञ्चदश यज्ञनामानि] ॥ १७ ॥

---

१. पणायते Roth.

२. पियुक्षाः BK 2.

३. मेधः X; BK 2.

४. ऋपुः BK 2.

५. कवि M 2, M 3, W 1, W 2, W 3, BK 2.

६. मनीषिः Bib. Ind.

७. विपः is omitted by M 2, M 3, W 1, W 2, W 3, विधाता and विपः omitted by BK 2.

८. विपन्युः X, BK 2.

९. आकेनिपः । केनिपः । X, BK 2.

१०. अध्धातयः M 1; श्रद्धातयः BK 2.

११. मनुष्याः ग.

१२. मेधाविन......०नाम् X.

१३. [वाघत......नामानि] Y.

१४. नादः M 1.

१५. तामुः ग. C. D. F.

१६. Words within brackets are the text of the shorter recension.

१७. मेधः । नायी । अध्वरः । विदथः । M 2, M 3, W 1, W 2, W 3, BK 2.

१८. नायी M 2, M 3, W 1, W 2, W 3; नारी ग.

१९. घर्म...यज्ञस्य X; [घर्म.....नामानि] Y.

भरताः[1] । कुरवः । वाघतः । वृक्तबर्हिषः । यतस्रुचः । मरुतः । सबाधः[2] । देवयव[3] इत्यष्टावृत्विजाम् [देवयव इत्यष्टावृत्विङ्नामानि] ॥ १८ ॥

ईमहे । यामि । मन्महे । दद्धि[4] । शग्धि । पूर्धि[5] । मिमिड्ढि[6] । मिमीहि । रिरिड्ढि । रिरीहि । पीपरत् । यन्तारः । यन्धि[7] । इषुध्यति । मदेमहि । मनामहे । मायत इति [सप्तदश[8]] याच्ञाकर्माणः ॥ १९ ॥

दाति । दाशति । दासति । राति । रासति । पृणक्षि[9] । पृणाति[10] । शिक्षति । तुञ्जति[11] । मंहत इति [दश[12]] दानकर्माणः ॥ २० ॥

परि स्रव[13] । पवस्व । अभ्यर्ष । आशिष इति [चत्वारः[14]] अध्येषणाकर्माणः ॥ २१ ॥

स्वपिति सस्तीति द्वौ स्वपितिकर्माणौ ॥ २२ ॥

कूपः[15] । कातुः[16] । कर्तः[15,17] । वव्रः । काटः । खातः । अवतः । [18]क्रिविः । सूदः । उत्सः । ऋश्यदात्[19] । कारोतरात्[20] । कुशयः । केवट[21] इति कूपस्य [केवट इति चतुर्दश कूपनामानि] ॥ २३ ॥

---

१. भारताः क. and Devarāja.

२. सबाधः is placed after वृक्तबर्हिषः by M 2, M 3, W 1, W 2, W 3, BK 2.

३. देवयव...०जाम् X; [देवयव......नामानि] Y.

४. दद्धि. M 1; दृधि M 2, M 3, W 1, W 3; दृन्धि W 2.

५. पूर्धि M 1.

६. रिरीहि । भिमीहि । रिरिड्ढि । मिमिड्ढि । BK 2.

७. यन्ति M 2, M 3, W 1, W 2, W 3; BK 2.

८. सप्तदश omitted by X.

९. पृणक्ति M 2, M 3, W 1, W 2, W 3, BK 2.

१०. वृश्चति is added after पृणाति by M 2, M 3, W 1, W 2, W 3, BK 2. प्रीणाति BK 2.

११. तुञ्जति is omitted by M 2, M 3, W 1, W 2, BK 2, W 3.

१२. दश is omitted by X.

१३. परिश्रव. ख.

१४. चत्वारः omitted by X.

१५. वव्रः M 2, M 3, W 2, W 3; वव्रः W 1; वप्रः BK 2. काटः is placed after वव्रः by M 2, M 3, W 1, W 2, W 3, BK 2.

१६. कारुः M 2; कानुः W 3.

१७. खातः । अवटः । अवतः । M 2, M 3, W 1, W 2, W 3, BK 2.

१८. क्रिवि M 2; कृवि M 3, W 1, W 2, W 3; कूपः is placed after क्रिवि in M 3, W 1, W 2, W 3, after कृवि. BK 2.

१९. ऋशदात् W 1; रिश्यदात् M 3.

२०. कारोतरः M 2, M 3, W 1, W 2, W 3.

२१. केवट...कूपस्य X; [केवट......नामानि] Y.

तृपुः[1] । तक्वा[2] । रिभ्वा । रिपुः । रिक्वा । रिहायाः । तायुः । तस्करः । वनर्गुः । हुरश्चित् । मुषीवान् । मलिम्लुचः । अघशंसः । वृक[3] इति स्तेनस्य [वृक इति चतुर्दशैव स्तेननामानि] ॥ २४ ॥

निण्यम् । संस्वः[4] । सनुतः । हिरुक् । प्रतीच्यम् । अपीच्यमिति [पद्[5]] निर्णीतान्तर्हितनामधेयानि ॥ २५ ॥

आके । पराके । पराचैः । आरे । परावत[6] इति दूरस्य [परावत इति पञ्च दूरनामानि] ॥ २६ ॥

प्रत्नम् । प्रदिवः । प्रवयाः । सनेमि । पूर्व्यम् । अह्नायेति[7] पुराणस्य [अह्नायेति पट् पुराणनामानि] ॥ २७ ॥

नवम् । नूत्नम् । नूतनम् । नव्यम् । इदा । इदानीमिति[8] नवस्य [इदानीमिति षळेव नवनामानि] ॥ २८ ॥

प्रपित्वे । अभीके । दभ्रम् । अर्भकम् । तिरः । सतः । त्वः । नेमः । ऋक्षाः[9] । स्तृभिः । वम्रीभिः[10] । उपजिह्विका । ऊर्दरम् । कृदरम् । रम्भः । पिनाकम् । मेना । ग्नाः । शेपः । वैतसः । अया । एना । सिपक्तु[11] । सचते । भ्यसते[12] । रेजते[13] इति द्विशः [रेजते इति षड्विंशतिर्द्विश उत्तराणि नामानि] ॥ २९ ॥

---

१. त्रिपुः M 2, M 3, W 1, W 2, W 3, BK 2.

२. रिपुः । तक्वा । तृक्वा । रिक्वा । रिह्वा । M 2, M 3, W 1, W 2, W 3, BK 2.

३. वृक,......स्तेनस्य X; [वृक......नामानि] Y.

४. सम्तः BK 2.

५. पट् is omitted by X.

६. परावत......दूरस्य X; [परावत...... नामानि] Y.

७. अह्नायेति......पुराणस्य X; [अह्नायेति... नामानि] Y.

८. इदानीमिति नवस्य X; [इदानी...... नामानि] Y.

९. ऋक्षा BK 2.

१०. स्त्रीभिः BK 2.

११. सिपक्ति M 2, M 3, W 1, W 2, W 3, BK 2.

१२. नंसते ग.

१३. रेजते...द्विशः X; [रेजते ...नामानि] Y.

स्वधे[1] । पुरंन्धी । धिषणे । रोदसी[2] । क्षोणी । अम्भसी । नभसी[3] । रजसी । सदसी । सद्मनी । घृतवती । बहुले । गभीरे । गम्भीरे । ओण्यौ[4] । चम्वौ । पार्श्वौ । मही । उर्वी । पृथ्वी[5] । अदिती । अही । दूरे[6] अन्ते । अपारे[7] अपारे इति द्यावापृथिव्योः [अपारे अपारे इति चतुर्विंशतिर्द्यावापृथिवीनामधेयानि[8] नामधेयानि] ॥ ३० ॥

इति निघण्टौ तृतीयोऽध्यायः ।

M 1, M 4, C 1, C 2, C 3, C 3, S, W 4 added the following summary :—

उर्वी हन्महद्गय इरज्यति शिम्बाता निर्णिगस्नेमा केतुर्वेद् चिक्यद्धिकमिदमिवार्चति विप्रो रेभो यज्ञो भरता ईमहे दाति परि स्तव स्वर्पति कूपस्तृपुर्निण्यमाके प्रत्नन्नवम् प्रपित्वे स्वधे त्रिंशत् ॥

इति निघण्टौ तृतीयोऽध्यायः समाप्तः ।

अथ चतुर्थोऽध्यायः ।

जहा । निधा । शितामं[9] । मेहना[10] । दमूनाः[11] । मूषः[12] । इषिरेण[13] । कुरुतनं । जठरे[14] । तितउ । शिप्रे । मध्या । मन्दू । ईर्मान्तासः । कायमानः । लोधम् । शीरम् । विद्रधे । द्रुपदे । तुग्वनि । नसन्ते[15] । नसन्त । आहनसः ।

---

१. सधे. M 2, M 3, W 1, W 2, W 3.

२. रोधसी is added after रोदसी by M 2, M 3, W 1, W 2, W 3, BK 2.

३. नभसी is omitted by M 2, M 3, W 1, W 2, W 3, BK 2.

४. ओण्यौ । नप्त्र्यौ । चम्व्यौ । पार्श्व्यौ । M 2, M 3, W 1, W 2, W 3; BK 2. Ms. ग has नप्त्रौ.

५. पृथ्वी । बृहती । दूरे अन्ते । अपारे etc. M 2, M 3, W 1, W 2, W 3.

६. दूरे । अन्ते । M 3; दूरे ध्वी. BK 2, अन्ते । क. ग.

७. अपारे......०पृथिव्योः X [अपारे...... नामधेयानि] Y.

८. ०द्यावापृथिव्यो र्नाम: M 1.

९. शिताम । निधा । BK 2.

१०. मेहना: BK 2.

११. दमुना: ग.

१२. मूशः च.

१३. इषिर: M 2, M 3, W 1, W 2, W 3, BK 2.

१४. जठरम् ख. ग.

१५. नसत: X & Y, BK 2, Roth. नसन्त S'iva and Sāma. The authority of the Mss. of both recensions has been discarded for this particular word because Yāska, a much older authority than all the Mss. put together, reads नसन्त.

अब्रसत् । इष्मिणः । वाहः । परितक्म्या[1] । सुविते । दयते । नूचित् । नूच[2] । दावने । अकूपारस्य । शिशीते । सुतुकः[3] । सुप्रायणाः । अप्रायुवः । च्यवनः[4] । रजः । हरः । जुहुरे । व्यन्तः । क्राणाः[5] । वाशी । विषुणः । जामिः[6] । पिता । शंयोः । अदितिः । एरिरे[7] । जसुरिः । जरते । मन्दिने । गौः । गातुः । दंसयः । तूताव । चयसे । वियुते । ऋधक् । अस्याः[8] । अस [अस्येति[9] द्विषष्टिः पदानि] ॥ १ ॥

सस्निम् । वाहिष्ठः । दूतः[10] । वावशानः । वार्यम् । अन्धः[11] । असश्चन्ती । वनुष्यति । तरुष्यति[12] । भन्दनाः । आहनः । नदः । सोमो अक्षाः । श्वात्रम् । ऊतिः । हासमाने । पड्भिः । ससम् । द्विता । व्राः । वराहः । स्वसराणि । शर्याः । अर्कः । पविः । वक्षः[13] । धन्व । सिनम्[14] । इत्था । सचा । चित् । आ[15] । द्युम्नम् । पवित्रम् । तोदः । स्वञ्चाः । शिपिविष्टः । विष्णुः । आघृणिः । पृथुज्रयाः । अथर्युम्[16] । काणुका । अध्रिगुः । आङ्गूषः[17] । आपान्तमन्युः[18] । श्मशा[19] । उर्वशी । वयुनम् । वाजपस्त्यम् । वाजगन्ध्यम् । गध्यम्[20] । गधिता[21] । कौरयाणः । तौरयाणः । अह्रयाणः । हरयाणः[22] । आरितः । व्रन्दी[23] । निष्षपी[24] । तूर्णाशम् । क्षुम्पम् । निचुम्पुणः । पदिम् । पादुः । वृकः । जोषवाकम् । कृत्तिः । श्वघ्नी । समस्य । कुटस्य । चर्षणिः । शम्बः । केपयः । तूतुमाकृषे । अंसत्रम् । काकुदम्[25] । वीरिटे । अच्छ । परि । ईम्[26] । सीम्[27] । एनम् । एनाम् सृणिः[28] [सृणिरिति चतुरुत्तरमशीतिः पदानि] ॥ २ ॥

---

१. परितक्या ग.
२. नूच is omitted by M 2, M 3, W 1, W 2, W 3, BK 2.
३. सुलुकः BK 2.
४. च्यवानः a variant given by yāska.
५. क्राणां BK 2.
६. जामि W 1.
७. एरिति BK 2.
८. आंस्या W 3.
९. अस्य X ; [अस्येति…पदानि] Y.
१०. दूतः is omitted by M 2, M 3, W 1, W 2, W 3, BK 2.
११. अह्नः ख.
१२. सरुष्यते. क.
१३. वक्ष. M 3.
१४. सितम् क.
१५. आद्युम्नम् । M 3.
१६. अथयुम् M 3.
१७. आंगूष्टः । BK 2.
१८. अपान्तमन्युः M 1.
१९. श्यसा च.
२०. गन्ध्यम्. ग.
२१. गध्यति M 2, W 1, W 2, BK 2. गध्यतिः M 3, W 3.
२२. हरयाणः is omitted by Roth.
२३. व्रन्दिनः M 2, M 3, W 1, W 2, W 3, BK 2.
२४. निःपपी M 1, W 1 ; निष्पपी BK 2.
२५. काकुटम् M 3.
२६. ई W 1.
२७. सी. W 1.
२८. सृणिः M 2, M 3, W 1, W 2, W 3 ; [सृणि……पदानि] Y.

आशुशुक्षणिः[१] । आशाभ्यः । काशिः । कृणारुम् । अलातृणः । सल-
लूकम् । कृत्पयम् । विस्रुहः[२] । वीरुधः । नक्षद्दाभम् । अस्कृधोयुः ।
निशृम्भाः । बृबदुक्थम् । ऋदूदरः । ऋदूपे । पुलुकामः । असिन्वती ।
कपना । भाऋजीकः[३] । रुजानाः । जूर्णिः । ओमना । उपलप्रक्षिणी ।
उपसि । प्रकलवित्[४] । अभ्यर्धयज्वा । ईक्षे । क्षोणस्य । अस्मे । पाथः ।
सवीमनि । सप्रथाः । विदथानि । श्रायन्तः । आशीः । आजीगः[५] । अमूरः ।
शशमानः । देवो[६] देवाच्या कृपा । विजामातुः । ओमासः । सोमानम् ।
अनवायम् । किमीदिने । अमवान्[७] । अमीवा । दुरितम् । अप्वा[८] । अमतिः ।
श्रुष्टी । पुरन्धिः । रुशत् । रिशादसः । सुदत्रः । सुविदत्रः । आनुषक् ।
तुर्वणिः । गिर्वणसे[९] । अमूर्त्ते मूर्त्ते । अभ्यक् । याद्दृश्मिन् । जारयायि ।
अग्रिया । चनः । पचता । शुरुधः । अमिनः । जञ्झतीः[१०] । अप्र-
तिष्कुतः[११] । शाशदानः[१२] । सृप्रः । सुशिप्रः[१३] । शिप्रे[१४] । रंसु । द्विबर्हाः । अक्रः ।
उराणः । स्तियानाम् । स्तिपाः[१५] । जबारु । जरूथम् । कुलिशः । तुञ्जः ।
बर्हणा[१६] । ततनुष्टिम् । इलीबिशः । क्रियेधाः । भृमिः । विष्पितः । तुरीपम् ।
रास्पिनः । ऋञ्जतिः[१७] । ऋजुनीती[१८] । प्रतद्वसू । हिनोत । चोष्कूयमाणः ।
चोष्कूयते । सुमत् । दिविष्टिषु । दूतः । जिन्वति । अमत्रः । ऋचीषमः ।
अनर्शरातिम् । अनर्वा । असामि । गल्दया । जल्हवः । बकुरः । बेकनाटान् ।

---

१. आशुशूक्षणिः W 1.

२. विस्रुधः W 1.

३. भाऋजीकः W 1.

४. प्रकलवीत् W 1.

५. आजीगः W 1.

६. देवो देवाच्या । कृपा । ख. ग. च.

७. अमः BK 2, M 2, M 3, W 2, W 3; अयः W 1.

८. अप्वे Dev; अघा BK 2.

९. गिर्वणा: Y & Sāma.

१०. जझ्झतीः M 2, W 2; जञ्झतीः M 3.

११. अप्रतिष्कृतः BK 2.

१२. The third section comes to an end after शाशदानः in M 2, M 3, W 1, W 2, W 3.

१३. सशिगः W 1.

१४. omitted by C 3 & S.

१५. स्निपं BK 2. जबारुं । BK 2.

१६. बर्हणाः BK 2.

१७. ऋंजाता BK 2.

१८. ऋजुनीता is omitted by M 2, M 3, W 1, W 2, W 3, BK 2.

अभिधेतन । अंहुरः । बतः । वाताप्यंम् । चाकन् । रथर्यति । असंक्राम्[1] ।
आधवः । अनवब्रवः । सदान्वे । शिरिम्बिठः[2] । पराशरः । क्रिविर्दती[3] ।
करूलती । दनः । शरारुः । इदंयुः । कीकंटेषु । बुन्दः । बृन्दम् । किः ।
उल्बम् । ऋबीसम्बीसम्[4] [ऋबीसमृबीसमिति त्रैयस्त्रिंशच्छतं[5] पदानि] ॥ ३[6] ॥

इति निघण्टौ चतुर्थोऽध्यायः ।

M 1, M 4, C 1, C 2, C 3, C 4, S, W 4 add the following summary'.

जहा सस्निमाशुशुक्षणिस्त्रीणि ।

इति निघण्टौ चतुर्थोऽध्यायः समाप्तः ।

अथ पञ्चमोऽध्यायः ।

अग्निः । जातवेदाः । वैश्वानर[7] [इति त्रीणि पदानि] ॥ १ ॥

द्रविणोदाः । इध्मः । तनूनपात् । नराशंसः । ईळः[8] । बर्हिः । द्वारः ।
उषासानक्ता । दैव्या होतारा । तिस्रो देवीः । त्वष्टा । वनस्पतिः । स्वाहा[9]-
कृतय [इति त्रयोदशपदानि] ॥ २ ॥

अश्वः । शकुनिः । मण्डूकाः । अक्षाः । ग्रावाणः । नाराशंसः[10] ।
रथः । दुन्दुभिः । इषुधिः । हस्तघ्नः । अभीशवः । धनुः । ज्या । इषुः ।
अश्वाजनी[11] । उलूखलम् । वृषभः । द्रुघणः । पितुः । नद्यः । आपः । ओषधयः ।
रात्रिः । अरण्यानी[12] । श्रद्धा[13] । पृथिवी । अप्वा । अग्नायी । उलूखलमुसले ।

---

१. असरथर्यति is added before असक्राम् by M 2; असक्रात् BK 2.

२. शिरिम्बिठः is omitted by M 2, M 3, W 1, W 2, W 3, BK 2.

३. कृविर्दति BK 2.

४. ऋबीसमृबीसम् X; [ऋबीस...पदानि] Y. कबीसमृबीसम् BK 2.

५. द्वात्रिंशच्छतं C 3, S. Roth. Bhad; Säma.

६. M 2, M 3, W 1, W 2, W 3 have ॥ ४ ॥ instead of ॥ ३ ॥

७. वैश्वानरः । द्रविणोदाः etc, M 2, M 3, W 1, W 2, W 3, BK 2.

८. इलः क. ख. ग. BK 2.

९. स्वाहाकृतयः ॥ १ ॥ M 2, M 3, W 1, W 2, W 3; ०कृतय...॥ २ ॥ y.

१०. नराशंसः M 1, M 4, C 1, C 2, C 4, S, W 4.

११. अश्वाजनि । उलूखलं मुशलं । BK 2.

१२. अरण्यानि ग. च. अरंण्यानी M 2, M 3.

१३. श्रद्धा । पृथिवी । M 3.

हविर्धाने । द्यावापृथिवी[1] । विपाट्छुतुद्री[2] । आर्त्नी । शुनासीरौ । देवी जोष्ट्री । देवी ऊर्जाहुती [इति[3] षट्त्रिंशत् पदानि] ॥ ३ ॥

वायुः । वरुणः । रुद्रः । इन्द्रः । पर्जन्यः । बृहस्पतिः । ब्रह्मणस्पतिः । क्षेत्रस्य पतिः । वास्तोष्पतिः । वाचस्पतिः । अपां नपात् । यमः । मित्रः । कः । सरस्वान् । विश्वकर्मा । तार्क्ष्यः । मन्युः । दधिक्राः । सविता । त्वष्टा । वातः । अग्निः । वेनः । असुनीतिः । ऋतः । इन्दुः । प्रजापतिः । अहिः । अहिर्बुध्न्यः । सुपर्णः । पुरूरवा[4] [इति द्वात्रिंशत् पदानि] ॥ ४ ॥

श्येनः । सोमः । चन्द्रमाः । मृत्युः । विश्वानरः । धाता । विधाता । मरुतः । रुद्राः । ऋभवः । अङ्गिरसः । पितरः । अथर्वाणः । भृगवः[5] । आप्त्याः[6] । अदितिः । सरमा । सरस्वती । वाक् । अनुमतिः । राका । सिनीवाली । कुहूः[7] । यमी । उर्वशी । पृथिवी । इन्द्राणी । गौरी । गौः । धेनुः । अघ्न्या । पथ्या । स्वस्तिः । उषाः[8] । इळा । रोदसी[9] [इति षट्त्रिंशत् पदानि] ॥ ५ ॥

अश्विनौ । उषाः । सूर्या । वृषाकपायी । सरण्यूः । त्वष्टा । सविता । भगः[10] । सूर्यः । पूषा । विष्णुः । विश्वानरः । वरुणः । केशी । केशिनः । वृषाकपिः । यमः । अज एकपात् । पृथिवी । समुद्रः । अथर्वा[11] । मनुः । दध्यङ् । आदित्याः । सप्तऋषयः । देवाः । विश्वेदेवाः । साध्याः । वसवः । वाजिनः । देवपत्न्यो[12] देवपत्न्य [इत्येकत्रिंशत् पदानि] ॥ ६ ॥

इति निघण्टौ पञ्चमोऽध्यायः ।

M 1, M 4, C 1, C 2, C 3, C 4, S, W 4 add the following summary'.

अग्निर्द्रविणोदा अश्वो वायुः श्येनोऽश्विनौ षट् ।

इति निघण्टौ पञ्चमोऽध्यायः समाप्तः ।

---

१. द्यावापृथिव्यौ M 2, M 3, W 1, W 2, W 3, BK 2.

२. विपाट्छुतुद्र्यौ M 2, M 3, W 1, W 2, W 3, BK 2.

३. [–] is omitted by X, BK 2; ॥ २ ॥ X. ॥ ३ ॥ Y.

४. पुरूरवा ॥ ३ ॥ X; BK 2. पुरूरवा...... ॥ ४ ॥ Y.

५. ऋषयः is added after भृगवः by X, BK 2.

६. आप्त्या BK 2.

७. कुल्हः C 3, कुह्व W 2, W 3, ग.

८. ग adds इषा after उषाः; उषा BK 2.

९. रोदसी ॥ ४ ॥ X; रोदसी......॥ ५ ॥ Y.

१०. सगः BK 2.

११. दध्यङ् । अथर्वा । मनुः । Dev.

१२. देवपत्न्यः ॥ ५ ॥ X; ०देवपत्न्य......॥ ६ ॥ Y.

ॐ

श्रीयास्कमुनिविरचितं निरुक्तं प्रारभ्यते ।

अथ प्रथमोऽध्यायः ।

समाम्नायः[1] समाम्नातः[2] । स व्याख्यातव्यः । तमिमं समाम्नायं निघण्टव इत्याचक्षते । निघण्टवः कस्मात् । निगमा[3] इमे भवन्ति । छन्दोभ्यः समाहृत्य समाहृत्य[4] समाम्नाताः । ते निगन्तव एव सन्तो निगमनान्निघण्टव[5] उच्यन्त इत्यौपमन्यवः । अपि वा हननादेव स्युः । समाहता भवन्ति । यद्वा समाहृता भवन्ति ।

तद् यानि चत्वारि पदजातानि नामाख्याते[6] चोपसर्गनिपाताश्च तानीमानि भवन्ति[7] । तत्रैतन्नामाख्यातयोर्लक्षणं प्रदिशन्ति । भावप्रधानमाख्यातम् । सत्त्वप्रधानानि

---

१. The word समाम्नायः means 'a list,' or 'a traditional list'; cf. VPR. viii. i:

अथातो वर्णसमाम्नायं व्याख्यास्यामः । TPR. i. 1. अथ वर्णसमाम्नायः ।

अनुवाकानुक्रमणी 1. 6:

पदाक्षरसमाम्नायं छन्दस्येव प्रतिष्ठितम् ।

Durga: समाङ्पूर्वस्य म्नातेरभ्यासार्थस्य कर्मणि कारके समाम्नायः । समभ्यस्यते मर्यादयायमिति समाम्नायः ।

cf. also त्रिभाष्यरत्न on TPR. i. 1.

२. cf. Sāyaṇa, *Int. to RV. p. 31*:

तत् व्याख्यानं च समाम्नायः समाम्नात इत्यारभ्य तस्यास्तस्यास्ताद्भाव्यमनुभवत्यनुभवतीत्यंतैर्द्वादशभिरध्यायैर्यास्को निर्ममे । तदपि निरुक्तमित्युच्यते ।

३. Durga explains the term in the following way:

निश्चयेनाधिकं वा निगूढार्था एते परिज्ञाताः सन्तो मन्त्रार्थान् गमयन्ति ज्ञापयन्ति ततो निगमसंज्ञा···इमे भवन्ति ।

४. Roth adopted the variant समाहत्य on the principle *lectio difficilior potior est*. This reading was adopted on the evidence of a single Ms. unsupported by any other. Roth was rather hasty in doing so and later on he rectified this mistake. All the Mss. that I have collated and Durga read समाहृत्य.

५. निगमनां निघ॰ BK 1.

६. ॰ख्यातो BK 1.

७. cf. RPR. 12. 5: 699:

नामाख्यातमुपसर्गो निपातश्चत्वार्याहुः पदजातानि शब्दाः ।

APR. i. 1: चतुर्णां पदजातानां नामाख्यातोपसर्गनिपातानां संध्यपद्यौ गुणौ प्रातिज्ञम् ।

VPR. 8. 52: तच्चतुर्धा नामाख्यातोपसर्गनिपाताः ।

KAS.' II. 10: 28. p. 72: वर्णसंघातः पदम् । तच्चतुर्विधम् । नामाख्यातोपसर्गनिपाताश्चेति ।

PMbh. i. 1. 1: p. 3: चत्वारि पदजातानि । नामाख्यातोपसर्गनिपाताश्च ।

SDS. p. 140: ननु नामाख्यातभेदेन पदद्वैविध्यप्रतीतेः कथं चातुर्विध्यमुक्तमिति चेन्मैवं प्रकारान्तरस्य प्रसिद्धत्वात् । तदुक्तं प्रकीर्णके । द्विधा कैश्चित् पदं भिन्नं चतुर्धा पंचधापि वा । अपोद्धृत्यैव वाक्येभ्यः प्रकृतिप्रत्ययादिवादति ॥

नामानि[१] । तद् यत्रोभे भावप्रधाने भवतः पूर्वापरीभूतं भावमाख्यातेनाचष्टे[२] । व्रजति पचतीति । उपक्रमप्रभृत्यपवर्गपर्यन्तं[३] मूर्तं सत्त्वभूतं सत्त्वनामभिः । व्रज्या पक्तिरिति[४] । अद इति सत्त्वानामुपदेशः[५] । गौरश्वः पुरुषो हस्तीति । भवतीति भावस्य । आस्ते शेते व्रजति तिष्ठतीति[६] ।

कर्मप्रवचनीयेन वै पंचमेन सह पदस्य पंचविधत्वमिति हेलराजो व्याख्यातवान्। कर्मप्रवचनीयास्तु.....उपसर्गेष्वेवान्तर्भवन्तीत्यभिसन्धाय पदचातुर्विधं भाष्यकारेणोक्तं युक्तमिति विवेक्तव्यम् ।

Sāyaṇa, *Int. to RV. p.* 21: तत्र हि चत्वारि पदजातानि नामाख्याते चोपसर्गनिपाताश्च ।

cf. Dionysius of Halicarnassus: *Literary Composition. Ch. iii, Robert's ed. p.* 71. "Composition is......a certain arrangement of the parts of speech...These were reckoned as three only by Theodects and Aristotle and the philosophers of those times, who regarded nouns, verbs, connectives as the primary parts of speech. Their successors, particularly the leaders of the stoic school, raised the number to four, separating the article from the connectives".

cf. Aristotle, *Poetics* 20. 1456 *b Bywater's ed. p.* 57: 'Diction viewed as a whole is made up of the following parts: the letter (or the ultimate element) the syllable, the conjunction, the article, the noun, the verb, the case, and the speech.

८. तत्रैतं नाम०. BK 1.

१. cf. RPR. 12. 5: 700-1, 707:

तन्नाम येनाभिदधाति सत्त्वं तदाख्यातं येन भावं स धातुः । क्रियावाचकमाख्यातं ......सत्त्वाभिधायकं नाम ।

The following stanza is cited by the commentator on the APR. in the beginning of the 4th ch. *J. A. O. S. Vol.* 7. *p.* 591:

आख्यातं यत्क्रियावाचि नाम सत्त्वाख्यमुच्यते ।
निपाताश्चादय सर्वे उपसर्गास्तु प्रादयः॥

VPR. 8. 54-55:

क्रियावाचकमाख्यातमुपसर्गो विशेषकृत् । सत्त्वाभिधायकं नाम निपाताः पादपूरणाः ॥

BD. ii. 121: भावप्रधानमाख्यातम् ।

KAS'. II. 10: 28. p. 72:

अविशिष्टलिङ्गमाख्यातं क्रियावाचि । तत्र नाम सत्त्वाभिधायि ।

JPM: 2. 1. 1: भावार्थाः कर्मशब्दास्तेभ्यः क्रिया प्रतीयते । एष ह्यर्थो विधीयते ।

SDS. p. 144: भाववचनो धातुरिति। ......क्रियावचनो धातुरिति ।

cf. Plato, *the Cratylus*; Jowett: *Dialogues of Plato p. i.* 368-9:

'Name is not a musical or pictorial imitation......but it is expression of the essence of each thing in letters and syllables'.

cf. Aristotle, *Poetics* 20. 1456 *b* 10 *Bywater', ed. p.* 58: 'A noun or name is a composite significant sound not involving the idea of time, with parts which have no significance by themselves in it.... A verb is a composite significant sound involving the idea of time, with parts which have no significance by themselves in it. Whereas the word 'man' or 'white' does not imply when, 'walks' and 'has walked' involve in addition to the idea of walking that of time present or time past'.

२. आचष्ट BK 1.

३. ०पवर्गपर्यन्तमूहूर्त्तं BK 1.

४. पंक्तिरिति BK 1.

५. The 1st section comes to an end in Mss. of the shorter recension.

६. इति is omitted by G.

इन्द्रियनित्यं[1] वचनमौदुम्बरायणः ॥ १ ॥

तत्र चतुष्ट्वं नोपपद्यते । अ[2]युगपदुत्पन्नानां[3] वा शब्दानामितरेतरो[4]पदेशः । शास्त्रकृतो योगश्च[5] । व्याप्तिमत्त्वात्तु शब्दस्या[6]णीयस्त्वाच्च शब्देन संज्ञाकरणं व्यवहारार्थं लोके । तेषां मनुष्यवद् देवताभिधानम् । पुरुषविद्यानित्यत्वात्[7] कर्मसंपत्तिर्मन्त्रो वेदे[8] ।

षड्भावविकारा भवन्तीति[9] वार्ष्यायणिः । जायतेऽस्ति विपरिणमते वर्धतेऽपक्षीयते विनश्यतीति[10] । जायत इति पूर्वभावस्यादिमाचष्टे[11] । नापरभावमाचष्टे न प्रतिषेधति । अस्तीत्युत्पन्नस्य सत्त्वस्यावधारणम् । विपरिणमत इत्य[12]प्रच्यवमानस्य तत्त्वाद् विकारम् । वर्धत इति स्वाङ्गाभ्युच्चयम् । सांयौगिकानां वार्थानाम् । वर्धते विजयेनेति वा । वर्धते शरीरेणेति वा । अपक्षीयत इत्येतेनैव व्याख्यातः प्रतिलोमम् । विनश्यतीत्य[13]परभावस्यादिमाचष्टे । न पूर्वभावमाचष्टे न प्रतिषेधति ॥ २ ॥

अतोऽन्ये भावविकारा एतेषामेव विकारा भवन्तीति ह स्माह[14] । ते यथावचनमभ्यूहितव्याः[15] ।

न निर्बद्धा उपसर्गा अर्थान्निराहुरिति शाकटायनः । नामाख्यातयोस्तु कर्मोपसंयोगद्योतका भवन्ति[16] । उच्चावचाः पदार्था भवन्तीति गार्ग्यः[17] । तद् य एषु पदार्थः प्राहुरिमे तं नामाख्यातयोरर्थविकरणम्[18] ।

आ[19] इत्यर्वागर्थे । प्र परा इत्येतस्य प्रातिलोम्यम् । अभि इत्याभिमुख्यम् । प्रति इत्येतस्य प्रातिलोम्यम् । अति सु इत्यभिपूजितार्थे । निर् दुर् इत्येतयोः प्रातिलोम्यम् । नि अव इति विनिग्रहार्थीयौ[20] । उद् इत्येतयोः प्रातिलोम्यम् । सम् इत्येकीभावम् । वि अप इत्येतस्य प्रातिलोम्यम्[21] । अनु इति सादृश्यापरभावम् । अपि इति

---

१. नित्यं is omitted in BK.
२. Durga gives युगपत् as a variant.
३. ०त्पंन्नानां BK.
४. ०मितरोतरो BK.
५. ०कृतोपयोगश्च A.
६. शब्दायणीमत्वाच्च BK.
७. ०नित्यात् W. 2.
८. Here ends the second section in BK.
९. इति is omitted in BK.
१०. cf. BD. ii. 121; PMbh. i. 3. 1. p. i. 258.
११. आयष्टे BK.
१२. द्व्याप्र० BK.
१३. ०तीत्यपभाव० BK.
१४. स्याह BK.
१५. cf. BD. ii. 122.
१६. भवन्तीति G. cf. RP. 12. 6: 702; VP. 8. 54–55; KAS'. II. 10: 28. p. 72; PMbh. i. 3. 1. p. 256; ii. 1. 1. p. 365.
१७. cf. RP. 12. 5: 707.
१८. cf. BD. ii. 94. Here ends the 4th section in BK.
१९. आ आ BK.
२०. विनिग्रहार्थीयौ M 1, C 2, C 3, C 6. cf. SRV. I. 124. 11. p. i. 566:
अत्रावशब्दो विनिग्रहार्थीयो न्यवेति विनिग्रहार्थीयौ । इति यास्केनोक्तत्वात् ।
२१. cf. SRV. I. 123. 7. p. i. 559:
अपेत्येतस्य प्रातिलोम्यं......अभीत्याभिमुख्यमिति यास्कः ।

संसर्गम् । उप इत्युपजनम् । परि इति सर्वतोभावम् । अधि इत्युपरिभावमैश्वर्यं वा । एवमुच्चावचानर्थान्प्राहुः । त उपेक्षितव्याः[1] ॥ ३ ॥[2]

अथ निपाता उच्चावचेष्वर्थेषु निपतन्ति[3] । अप्युपमार्थे । अपि कर्मोपसंग्रहार्थे । अपि पदपूरणाः[4] । तेषामेते चत्वार उपमार्थे भवन्ति[5] ।

इवेति भाषायां च । अन्वध्यायं च ।

अग्निरिव[6] । इन्द्र इव[7] । इति ।

नेति प्रतिषेधार्थीयो भाषायाम्[8] । उभयमन्वध्यायम् ।

नेन्द्रं देवममंसत[9] ।

इति प्रतिषेधार्थीयः । पुरस्तादुपाचारस्तस्य यत्प्रतिषेधति ।

दुर्मदासो न सुरायाम्[10] ।

इत्युपमार्थीयः । उपरिष्टादुपाचारस्तस्य येनोपमिमीते[11] ।

चिदित्येषोऽनेककर्मा । आचार्यश्चिदिदं ब्रूयात् । इति पूजायाम् । [आचार्यः कस्मात्[12]] आचार्य आचारं ग्राहयति । आचिनोत्यर्थान् । आचिनोति बुद्धिमिति[13] वा[14] । दधिचित् । इत्युपमार्थे[15] । कुल्माषांश्चिदाहर[16] । इत्यवकुत्सिते[17] । कुल्माषाः[18] कुलेषु सीदन्ति[19] ।

---

१. The sentence एवमु...उपेक्षितव्याः is omitted by Durga.

२. Here ends the 5th sec. of the 1st pāda in BK.

३. cf. SRV. I. 124. 12. p. i. 566:
उच्चावचेष्वर्थेषु निपतन्तीति यास्केनोक्तत्वात् ।

४. cf. BD. ii. 89; RP. 12. 8: 707; VP. 8. 55.

५. भवन्तीति R. भवन्ति is omitted by C 2, G, S. cf. BD. ii. 91:
इव न चिन्नु चत्वार उपमार्था भवन्ति ते ।

६. RV. X. 84. 2; 106. 3.

७. RV. X. 84. 5; 166. 2; 173. 2.

८. cf. BD. ii. 92.

९. RV. X. 86. 1.

१०. RV. VIII. 2. 12.

११. cf. SRV. I. 8. 5; 124. 4. pp. i. 61, 563. Here ends the 1st sec. of the 2nd pāda in BK.

१२. Omitted in BK. C 4, C 5, Kn, M 3, M i, R 4, R 6, W 1, W 2, W 3. and Durga.

१३. cf. PMbh. i. 1. 3. p. 38:
आचार्याचारात् संज्ञासिद्धिः ।

१४. The whole sentence from आचार्य... वा is omitted by Durga.

१५. cf. SRV. I. 169. 3. p. i. 737:
चिदित्युपमार्थे । इति यास्केनोपमार्थस्योक्तत्वात् ।

१६. कुलमासांश्चिद् BK.

१७. Quoted by SRV. I. 129. 10. p i. 588.

१८. कुलमासाः BK.

१९. The sentence कुल्माषाः कुलेषु सीदन्ति is omitted by Durga.

नु इत्येषोऽनेककर्मा। इदं नु करिष्यति। इति हेत्वपदेशे। कथं नु करिष्यति। इत्यनुपृष्टे। नन्वेतदकार्षीत्[1]। इति च। अथाप्युपमार्थे भवति[2]।

वृक्षस्य नु ते पुरुहूत वयाः[3]।

वृक्षस्येव ते पुरुहूत शाखाः। वयाः[4] शाखा वेतेः। वातायना भवन्ति[5]। शाखाः खशयाः। शक्नोतेर्वा[6]।

अथ यस्यागमादर्थपृथक्त्वमह[7] विज्ञायते न त्वौद्देशिकमिव[8] विग्रहेण पृथक्त्वात् स कर्मोपसंग्रहः[9]।

चेति समुच्चयार्थ उभाभ्यां संप्रयुज्यते।

अहं च त्वं च वृत्रहन्[10]। इति।

एतस्मिन्नेवार्थे[11]।

देवेभ्यश्च पितृभ्य आ[12]। इत्याकारः।

वेति विचारणार्थे।

हन्ताहं[13] पृथिवीमिमां नि दधानीह वेह वा[14]। इति।

अथापि समुच्चयार्थे भवति॥ ४॥

वायुर्वा त्वा मनुर्वा त्वा। इति[15]।

अह इति च ह इति च विनिग्रहार्थीयौ[16]। पूर्वेण संप्रयुज्येते। अयमहेदं करोत्वयमिदम्[17]। इदं ह करिष्यतीदं न[18] करिष्यतीति।

---

१. ०कार्षीः M i, M 3, BK.

२. Quoted by SRV. I. 91. 3. p. i. 403: तदुक्तं यास्केन। अथाप्युपमार्थे भवति। वृक्षस्य...वयाः। Here ends the 2nd section of the 2nd pāda in BK.

३. RV. VI. 24. 3.

४. The passage वयाः...भवन्ति is quoted by SRV. I. 59. 1. p. i. 291.

५. वातायना भवन्ति is omitted by Durga.

६. शक्नोतेर्वा is omitted by Durga.

७. ०पृथक्त्वमहमिति BK; ०पृथक्त्वमिति ह A, G.

८. चौद्देशिकम् BK.

९. च. W 1, W 2, M i, BK.

१०. RV. VIII. 62. 11. The अ of अहं is elided after संप्रयुज्यते by the Mss. of the longer recension. The first *i* of *iti* is accented in the Mss. but as I have separated it from the Vedic quotation, I leave it unaccented.

११. Quoted by SRV. I. 48. 16. p. i. 246.

१२. RV. X. 16. 11.

१३. cf. BD. i. 56: प्रमादस्थेप हन्ताहं etc.

१४. RV. X. 119. 9.

१५. TS. 1. 7. 7. 2; KS. 13. 14. Here ends the 3rd Section of the 2nd pāda in BK.

१६. त्रिनिग्रहार्थीयौ M 1, C 2, C 3, C 6, BK.

१७. इदम् is omitted by Roth.

१८. नु M 2, M 3, W 1, W 2, C 4, C 5, BK.

अथाप्युकार एतस्मिन्नेवार्थ उत्तरेण। मृषेमे वदन्ति सत्यमु ते वदन्तीति। अथापि पदपूरणः।

इदमु[१]। तदु[२]।

हीत्येषोऽनेककर्मा। इदं हि करिष्यति। इति हेत्वपदेशे। कथं हि करिष्यति। इत्यनुपृष्टे। कथं हि व्याकरिष्यति। इत्यसूयायाम्।

किलेति विद्याप्रकर्षे। एवं किलेति। अथापि न ननु इत्येताभ्यां संप्रयुज्यतेऽनुपृष्टे। न किलैवम्। ननु किलैवम्।

मेति प्रतिषेधे। मा कार्षीः। मा हार्षीरिति च।

खल्विति च। खलु कृत्वा। खलु कृतम्। अथापि पदपूरणः। एवं खलु तद् बभूवेति।

शश्वदिति विचिकित्सार्थीयो भाषायाम्। शश्वदेवम्। इत्यनुपृष्टे। एवं शश्वत्। इत्यस्वयं पृष्टे।

नूनमिति विचिकित्सार्थीयो भाषायाम्। उभयमन्वध्यायं विचिकित्सार्थीयश्च पदपूरणश्च।

अगस्त्य[३] इन्द्राय हविर्निरूप्य मरुद्भ्यः संप्रदित्सांचकार। स इन्द्र एत्य परिदेवयांचक्रे[४] ॥ ५ ॥

न नूनमस्ति नो श्वः कस्तद्वेद यदद्भुतम्।
अन्यस्य चित्तमभि संचरेण्यमुताधीतं विनश्यति[५] ॥

न नूनमस्त्यद्यतनम्। नो एव श्वस्तनम्। अद्यास्मिन् द्यवि। द्युरित्यह्नो नामधेयम्। द्योतत इति सतः। श्व उपाशंसनीयः[६] कालः। ह्यो हीनः कालः। कस्तद्वेद यदद्भुतम्। कस्तद्वेद यदभूतम्। इदमपीतरदद्भुतमभूतमिव[७]। अन्यस्य चित्तम्। अभिसंचरेण्यमभिसंचारि। अन्यो नानेयः। चित्तं चेततेः। उताधीतं विनश्यतीति। [अप्याध्यातं विनश्यति[८]] आध्यातमभिप्रेतम्।

अथापि पदपूरणः[९] ॥ ६ ॥

---

१. RV. IV. 51. 1.

२. RV. I. 62. 6.

३. The passage अगस्त्य···चक्रे is quoted by SRV. I. 170. 1. p. i. 739; cf. BD. iv. 48–50.

४. Here ends the 4th sec. of the 2nd pāda. BK. cf. BD. IV. 50-51.

५. RV. I. 170. 1.

६. उपासंसनीयः BK.

७. ०भूतमिति वा. BK.

८. अप्याध्यातं विनश्यति is omitted by BK, C 4, C 5, Kn, M 3, M i, R 4, R 6, W 1, W 2, W 3, and Durga.

९. Here ends the 5th sec. of the 2nd pāda. BK.

नूनं सा ते प्रति वरं जरित्रे दुहीयदिन्द्र दक्षिणा मघोनी ।
शिक्षा स्तोतृभ्यो माति धग्भगो नो बृहद्वदेम विदथे सुवीराः ॥[1]

सा ते प्रतिदुग्धां[2] वरं जरित्रे । वरो वरयितव्यो भवति । जरिता गरिता । दक्षिणा मघोनी मघवती । मघमिति धननामधेयम् । मंहतेर्दानकर्मणः[3] । दक्षिणा दक्षतेः समर्धयतिकर्मणः । व्यृद्धं समर्धयतीति । अपि वा प्रदक्षिणागमनात्[4] । दिशमभिप्रेत्य । दिग्घस्तप्रकृतिर्दक्षिणो हस्तः । दक्षतेरुत्साहकर्मणः । दाशतेर्वा स्याद् दानकर्मणः । हस्तो हन्तेः । प्राशुर्हनने[5] । देहि स्तोतृभ्यः कामान् । मास्मानतिदंहीः । मास्मानतिहाय दाः । भगो नोऽस्तु । बृहद्वदेम स्वे वेदने । भगो भजतेः[6] । बृहदिति महतो नामधेयम् । परिवृहळं[7] भवति । वीरवन्तः कल्याणवीरा वा[8] । वीरो वीरयत्यमित्रान् । वेतेर्वा स्याद्गतिकर्मणः वीरयतेर्वा[9] ।

सीमिति परिग्रहार्थीयो वा पदपूरणो वा ।

प्र सीमादित्यो असृजत्[10] ।

प्रासृजदिति वा । प्रासृजत् सर्वत इति वा ।

वि सीमतः सुरुचो वेन आवः[11] । इति च ।

व्यवृणोत् सर्वत आदित्यः । सुरुच आदित्यरश्मयः । सुरोचनात्[12] ।

अपि वा सीमेत्येतदनर्थकमुपबन्धमाददीत पंचमीकर्माणम् । सीम्नः सीमतः सीमातो[13] मर्यादातः । सीमा मर्यादा । विषीव्यति[14] देशाविति ।

त्व इति विनिग्रहार्थीयम् । सर्वनामानुदात्तम्[15] । अर्धनामेत्येके[16] ॥ ७ ॥

---

१. RV. II. 11. 21
cf. SRV. VIII. 10. 21. p. iii. 290 :
उक्तं च यास्केन । अथापि पदपूरणः । नूनं सा ते प्रति वरं जरित्रे etc.

२. प्रतिदग्धं C 5.

३. cf. PMbh. VI. 1. 1. p. 16 : मंहतिर्दानकर्मा । cf. SRV. I. 57. 1. p. i. 284 : मंहति र्दानकर्मा ।

४. ०प्रति BK.

५. cf. SRV. VI. 30. 2. p. ii : 770 :
उक्तं यास्केन । हस्तो हन्तेः प्राशुर्हनने । cf. also SRV IX. 79. 4. p. iii. 729 :
हस्तो हन्तेरिति निरुक्तम् ।

६. भगो भजतेः is omitted by Durga.

७. परिवृढं C 2, C 6, M 1, M 4, R 1, R 2, R 5, S 6, M 3, W 3.

८. ०वीरो वा BK.

९. The passage वीरो…वा is quoted by SRV. X. 10. 2. p. IV. 21. cf. also II. 11. 21. p. ii. 32 :
वीरो… वेत्यंतं निरुक्तमनुसंधेयम् ।

१०. RV. II. 28. 4.

११. AV. 4. 1. 1; 5. 6. 1; SV. 1. 321; VS. 13. 3.

१२. सुरोचनाः G.

१३. सीमामतो BK.

१४. विसीव्यति W 1, Mi, C 4, BK.

१५. cf. SRV. I. 113. 5. p. i. 498:
यदाह त्व इति…सर्वनामानुदात्तम् ।

१६. Here ends the 6th sec. of the 2nd pāda in BK.

ऋचां त्वः पोषमास्ते पुपुष्वान्गायत्रं त्वो गायति शक्वरीषु ।
ब्रह्मा त्वो वदति जातविद्यां यज्ञस्य मात्रां वि मिमीत उ त्वः ॥[1]

इत्यृत्विक्कर्मणां विनियोगमाचष्टे । ऋचामेकः पोषमास्ते पुपुष्वान् । होता । ऋगर्चनी[2] । गायत्रमेको गायति शक्वरीषु । उद्गाता । गायत्रं गायतेः स्तुतिकर्मणः । शक्वर्य ऋचः । शक्नोतेः ।

तद् यदाभिर्वृत्रमशकद्धन्तुं तच्छक्वरीणां शक्वरीत्वम्[3] ।

इति विज्ञायते । ब्रह्मैको जाते जाते विद्यां वदति । ब्रह्मा । सर्वविद्यः । सर्वं वेदितुमर्हति[4] । ब्रह्मा परिवृढः[5] श्रुततः । ब्रह्म परिवृढं[6] सर्वतः । यज्ञस्य मात्रां विमिमीत एकः । अध्वर्युः । अध्वर्युरध्वरयुः । अध्वरं युनक्ति । अध्वरस्य नेता । अध्वरं कामयत इति वा[7] । अपि वाधीयाने युरुपबन्धः । अध्वर इति यज्ञनाम । ध्वरतिर्हिंसाकर्मा । तत्प्रतिषेधः ।

निपात इत्येके । तत्कथमनुदात्तप्रकृति नाम स्यात् । दृष्टव्ययं तु भवति[8] ।

उत त्वं सख्ये स्थिरपीतमाहुः[9] । इति द्वितीयायाम् ।

उतो त्वस्मै तन्वं वि सस्रे[10] । इति चतुर्थ्याम् ।

अथापि प्रथमा[11]बहुवचने ॥ ८ ॥

अक्षण्वन्तः कर्णवन्तः सखायो मनोजवेष्वसमा बभूवुः ।
आदघ्नास उपकक्षास उ त्वे ह्रदा इव स्नात्वा उ त्वे ददृश्रे ॥[12]

अक्षिमन्तः कर्णवन्तः [सखायः[13]] । अक्षि चष्टेः[14] । अनक्तेरित्याग्रायणः ।

तस्मादेते व्यक्ततरे इव भवतः[15] ।

इति ह विज्ञायते । कर्णः कृन्ततेः । निकृत्तद्वारो भवति । ऋच्छतेरित्याग्रायणः ।

ऋच्छन्तीव खे उदगन्ताम्[15] ।

---

१. RV. X. 71. 11.

२. cf. SRV. X. 71. 11. p. IV. 223: ऋचामेकः पोषमास्ते…ऋगर्चनी । इत्यादि-निरुक्तानुसारेण ।

३. cf. KB. 23. 2; cf. AB. 5. 7. 3.

४. The passage ब्रह्मैको…मर्हति is quoted by SRV. I. 162. 5. p. i. 685.

५. परिवृढः C 2, C 6, M 1, M 4, R 1, R 2, R 5, S, M 3, W 3.

६. परिवृढं C 2, C 6, M 1, M 4, R 1, R 2, R 5, S, M 3, W 3.

७. Quoted by SRV. II. 14. 1. p. ii. 41; cf. also II. 1. 2. p. ii. 2.

८. cf. BD. ii. 114.

९. RV. X. 71. 5; cf. N. 1. 20.

१०. RV. X. 71. 4; cf. N. 1. 19.

११. प्रथमा० Kn.

१२. RV. X. 71. 7.

१३. Omitted by BK, C 4, C 5, Kn, M 3, Mi, R 4, R 6, W 1, W 2, W 3 and S.

१४. cf. SRV. X. 71. 7. p. IV. 222: चष्टेरित्यादिकं निरुक्तमत्र द्रष्टव्यम् ।

१५. The quotation is untraced.

इति ह विज्ञायते। मनसां प्रजवेष्वसमा बभूवुः। आस्यदघ्ना अपरे। उपकक्षदघ्ना अपरे। आस्यमस्यतेः। आस्यन्दत[1] एनं[2] दन्नमिति वा। दघ्नं दघ्यतेः स्रवतिकर्मणः। दस्यतेर्वा स्यात्। विदस्ततरं भवति। प्रस्नेया ह्रदा इवैके ददशिरे[3]। प्रस्नेया स्नानार्हाः[4]। ह्रदो ह्रादतेः[5] शब्दकर्मणः। ह्लादतेर्वा स्याच्छीतीभावकर्मणः।

अथापि समुच्चयार्थे भवति।

पर्याया इव त्वदाश्विनम्[6]।

आश्विनं च पर्यायाश्चेति।

अथ ये प्रवृत्तेऽर्थेऽमिताक्षरेषु[7] ग्रन्थेषु वाक्यपूरणा आगच्छन्ति पदपूरणास्ते[8] मिताक्षरेष्वनर्थकाः। कमीमिद्विति[9] ॥ ९ ॥

निष्ट्वक्रासश्चिदिन्नरो भूरितोका वृकादिव।

बिभ्यस्यन्तो ववाशिरे शिशिरं जीवनाय कम्[10] ॥

शिशिरं जीवनाय। शिशिरं शृणातेः शम्नातेर्वा।

एमेनं सृजता सुते[11]।

आसृजतैनं सुते।

तमिद्वर्धन्तु नो गिरः[12]।

तं वर्धयन्तु नो गिरः स्तुतयः। गिरो गृणातेः।

अयमु ते समतसि[13]।

अयं ते समतसि।

इवोऽपि दृश्यते। सु विदुरिव। सु विज्ञायेते इव[14]।

---

१. आस्यन्दन्त Kn.

२. एतद०. S'ivadatta's edition. cf. PMbh. i. 1. 4. p. i. 61: अस्यन्त्यनेन वर्णानित्यास्यम्। अन्नमेतदास्यन्दत इति वास्यम्।

३. ददर्शिरे C 4.

४. The Mss. of the longer and the shorter recension except Kn. read the passage as follows: प्रस्नेया ह्रदा इवैके प्रस्नेया ददशिरे स्नानार्हाः। I have adopted the variant on the authority of a single Ms. because it makes the text intelligible.

५. The printed editions read ह्रदतेः।

६. KB. 17. 4.

७. मिताक्षरेषु M 1, M 3

८. पदपूरणार्थे BK, C 4, M 3, R 4, R 6, W 3.

९. Quoted by SRV. I. 9. 2. p. i. 64; cf. also I. 50. 1; 123. 11; pp. i. 248, 561; cf. RP. 12. 9: 708; BD. ii. 90–91.

१०. The quotation is untraced. cf. SRV. V. 83. 10. p. ii. 678: कमित्ययं शिशिरं जीवनाय कम्। Ms. Kn. cites the pratīkas only but gives this quotation in full.

११. RV. I. 9. 2; AV. 20. 71. 8. see. SRV. loc. cit.

१२. RV. VIII. 92. 21; IX. 61. 14.

१३. RV. I. 30. 4; AV. 20. 45. 1; SV. 1. 183; 2. 949.

१४. इति वा Kn.

अथापि नेत्येष इदित्[१]येतेन संप्रयुज्यते परिभये ॥ १० ॥

हविर्भिरेके स्वरितः सचन्ते सुन्वन्त एके सवनेषु सोमान् ।
शचीर्मदन्त उत दक्षिणाभिर्नेज्जिह्मायन्त्यो नरकं पताम[२] ॥ इति

नरकं न्यरकं नीचैर्गमनम् । नास्मिन् रमणं स्थानमल्पमप्यस्तीति वा ।

अथापि न चेत्येष इदित्येतेन संप्रयुज्यतेऽनु[३]पृष्टे । न चेत् सुरां पिबन्तीति । सुरा सुनोतेः । एवमुच्चावचेष्वर्थेषु निपतन्ति । त उपेक्षितव्याः ॥ ११ ॥

इतीमानि चत्वारि पदजातान्यनुक्रान्तानि । नामाख्याते चोपसर्गनिपाताश्च ।

तत्र नामान्याख्यातजानीति शाकटायनो नैरुक्तसमय[४]श्च । न सर्वाणीति गार्ग्यो वैयाकरणानां चैके तद्[५] यत्र स्वरसंस्कारौ समर्थौ प्रादेशिकेन विकारेणा[६]न्वितौ स्याताम्[७] । संविज्ञा[८]तानि तानि यथा गौरश्वः पुरुषो हस्तीति ।

अथ चेत् सर्वाण्याख्यातजानि नामानि स्युर्यः कश्च तत्कर्म कुर्यात् सर्वं तत् सत्त्वं तथाचक्षीरन् । यः कश्चाध्वानमश्नुवीताश्वः स वचनीयः स्यात् । यत् किञ्चित्तृन्द्यात् तृणं तत् ।

अथापि चेत् सर्वाण्याख्यातजानि नामानि स्युर्यावद्भिर्भावै[९]: संप्रयुज्येत तावद्भ्यो नामधेयप्रतिलम्भः स्यात् । तत्रैवं स्थूणा दरशया वा संजनी च स्यात् ॥१२॥

अथापि य एषां न्यायवान् कार्मनामिकः संस्कारो यथा चापि प्रतीतार्थानि स्युस्तथैनान्याचक्षीरन् । पुरुषं पुरिशय इत्याचक्षीरन् । अष्टेत्यश्वम् । तर्दनमिति तृणम् ।

अथापि निष्पन्नेऽभिव्याहारेऽभिविचारय[१०]न्ति । प्रथनात्पृथिवीत्याहुः । क एनामप्रथयिष्यत् । किमाधारश्चेति ।

---

१. इदित्येन Kn.

२. RVKH. 10. 106. 1.

३. परिभयेऽनुपृष्टे Kn.

४. cf. BD. i. 23-24, 26-27, 30-31:

तत्खल्वाहुः कतिभ्यस्तु नाम जायते ।
सत्त्वानां वैदिकानां वा यद्वान्यदिह किंचन ॥
नवभ्य इति नैरुक्ताः पुराणाः कवयश्च ये ।
मधुकः श्वेतकेतुश्च गालवश्चैव मन्वते ॥
चतुर्भ्य इति तत्राहुर्यास्कगार्ग्यरथीतराः ।
....
सर्वाण्येतानि नामानि कर्मतस्त्वाह शौनकः ।
....
नाकर्मकोऽस्ति भावो हि न नामास्ति निरर्थकम् ।
नान्यत्र भावान्नामानि तस्मात्सर्वाणि कर्मतः ॥

cf. PMbh. iii. 3. 1. p. 138.

नाम च धातुजमाह निरुक्ते । नाम खल्वपि धातुजम् । एवमाहुर्नैरुक्ताः । व्याकरणे शकटस्य च तोकम् । वैयाकरणानां च शाकटायन आह धातुजं नामेति ।

५. cf. SRV. I. 1. 1. p. i. 25. With regard to the punctuation at this place see my *English Translation of the Nirukta* note on pp. 212, 213.

६. गुणेन C 1, C 2, C 3, C 6, M 1, M 2, R 1, R 2, R 5, S; Kn.

७. Gune proposes to add a clause सर्वं प्रादेशिकम् after स्याताम्. But see my note *Translation of the Nirukta* pp. 212, 213.

८. Durga gives संविज्ञानानि as a variant.

९. च Kn.

१०. ०विचारयन्तीति Kn.

अथानन्वितेऽर्थेऽप्रादेशिके विकारे पदेभ्यः पदेतरार्धान्त्संचस्कार शाकटायनः। एतेः कारितं च यकारादिं चान्तकरणमस्तेः शुद्धं च सकारादिं च।

अथापि सत्त्वपूर्वो भाव इत्याहुः। अपरस्माद्भावात् पूर्वस्य प्रदेशो नोपपद्यत इति। तदेतन्नोपपद्यते ॥ १३ ॥

यथो हि नु वा एतत् तद् यत्र स्वरसंस्कारौ समर्थौ प्रादेशिकेन विकारेणा[1]न्वितौ स्यातां[2] सर्वं प्रादेशिकमित्येवं सत्य[3]नुपालम्भ एष भवति।

यथो एतद् यः सर्व तत्कर्म कुर्यात् सर्वं तत् सत्त्वं तथाचक्षीरन्निति पश्यामः समानकर्मणां नामधेयप्रतिलम्भमेकेषां नैकेषां यथा तक्षा परिव्राजको जीवनो भूमिज इति।

एतेनैवोत्तरः प्रत्युक्तः।

यथो एतद् यथा चापि प्रतीतार्थानि स्युस्तथैनान्याचक्षीरन्निति सन्त्यल्पप्रयोगाः कृतोऽप्यैकपदिका यथा व्रततिर्दमूना जाट्य[4] आट्णारो[5] जागरूको दर्विहोमीति।

यथो एतन्निष्पन्नेऽभिव्याहारेऽभिविचारयन्तीति भवति हि निष्पन्नेऽभिव्याहारे योगपरीष्टिः। प्रथ[6]नात्पृथिवीत्याहुः। क एनामप्रथयिष्यत् किमाधारश्चेति। अथ वै दर्शनेन पृथुः। अप्रथिता चेदप्य[7]न्यैः। अथाप्येवं सर्व एव दृष्टप्रवादा उपालभ्यन्ते।

यथो एतत्पदेभ्यः पदेतरार्धान्त्संचस्कारेति योऽनन्वितेऽर्थे संचस्कार स तेन गर्ह्यः[8]। सैषा पुरुषगर्हा न शास्त्रगर्हा[9] [इति[10]]।

यथो एतदपरस्माद् भावात्पूर्वस्य प्रदेशो नोपपद्यत इति पश्यामः पूर्वोत्पन्नानां सत्त्वानामपरस्माद्भावान्नामधेयप्रतिलम्भमेकेषां नैकेषां यथा विल्वादो लम्ब[11]चूडक इति। विल्वं भरणाद्वा भेदनाद्वा ॥ १४ ॥

अथापीदमन्तरेण मन्त्रेष्वर्थप्रत्ययो न विद्यते। अर्थमप्रतिय[12]तो नात्यन्तं स्वरसंस्कारोद्देशः। तदिदं विद्यास्था[13]नं व्याकरणस्य कार्त्स्न्यम्। स्वार्थसाधकं च[14]।

यदि मन्त्रार्थप्रत्ययायानर्थकं भवतीति कौत्सः। अनर्थका हि मन्त्राः। तदेतेनोपेक्षितव्यम्।

---

१. गुणेन C 1, C 2, C 3, C 6, M 1, M 2, R 1, R 2, R 5, S; Kn.

२. स्यातामिति Kn.

३. सत्यमुपालम्भ Mi, C 5, Kn.

४. जाठ्य M 1, M 3, Mi, W 1, W 2, C 2, C 3, C 4, C 6; जाथ्य M 2.

५. आट्नारो C 2, C 3, C 6, M 1, M 2, W 2.

६. प्रथमनात् W 2.

७. चेदथान्यैः M 3.

८. गर्हः C 4, C 5, M 3, Mi, W 2.

९. न शास्त्रगर्हा is omitted by C 2, Kn.

१०. Omitted by BK, C 4, C 5, Kn, M 3, Mi, R 4, R 6, W 1, W 2, W 3.

११. लम्बचूलुक C 5; लम्बचुलक C 4, Mi.

१२. ०प्रतीयतो C 4.

१३. विद्यास्थानं Kn.

१४. Quoted by SRV. p. i. 21.

नियतवाचो युक्तयो नियतानुपूर्व्या भवन्ति।
अथापि ब्राह्मणेन रूपसंपन्ना विधीयन्ते।

उरु प्रथस्व[1] । इति प्रथयति।

प्रोहाणि[2] । इति प्रोहति।

अथाप्यनुपपन्नार्था भवन्ति।

ओषधे त्रायस्वैनम्[3] ।

स्वधिते मैनं हिंसीः[4] । इत्याह हिंसन्।

अथापि विप्रतिषिद्धार्था भवन्ति।

एक एव रुद्रोऽवतस्थे न द्वितीयः[5] ।

असंख्याता सहस्राणि ये रुद्रा अधि भूम्याम्[6] ।

अशत्रुरिन्द्र जज्ञिषे[7] ।

शतं सेना अजयत् साकमिन्द्रः[8] । इति।

अथापि जानन्तं संप्रेष्यति।

अग्नये समिध्यमानायानुब्रूहि[9] । इति।

अथाप्याहादितिः सर्वमिति।

अदितिर्द्यौरदितिरन्तरिक्षम्[10] । इति।

तदुपरिष्टाद्[11] व्याख्यास्यामः।
अथाप्यविस्पष्टार्था भवन्ति।

अम्यक्[12] । यादृश्मिन्[13] । जारयायि[14] । काणुका[15] । इति ॥ १५ ॥

---

१. VS. 1. 22; TS. i. 1. 8. 1; VI. 2. 7. 3; KS. 1. 8; 31. 7; Ms. i. 1. 9.

२. cf. VS. 2. 15: प्रोहामि.

३. TS. i. 2. 1. 1; 3. 5. 1; VI. 3. 3. 2; KS. ii. 1; Ms. i. 2. 1; iii. 9. 3; cf. VS. 4. 1; 5. 42; 6. 15: ओषधे त्रायस्व; cf. S'B. iii. 1. 2. 7.

४. VS. 4. 1; 5. 42; 6. 15; TS. i. 2. 1. 1; 3. 5. 1; VI. 3. 3. 2; KS. ii. 1; Ms. i. 2. 1; iii. 9. 3; cf. S'B. iii. 1. 2. 7; 6. 4. 10; 8. 2. 12.

५. cf. TS. i. 8. 6. 1.

६. VS. 16. 54; Ms. ii. 9. 9.

७. RV. X. 133. 2; AV. 20. 95. 3; SV. 2. 1152.

८. RV. X. 103. 1; AV. 19. 13. 2; SV. 2. 1199; VS. 17. 33.

९. TS. VI. 3. 7. 1; Ms. 1. 4. 11; TB. III. 3. 7. 1; S'B. ii. 5. 2. 9.

१०. RV. I. 89. 10.

११. See N. 4. 23.

१२. Occurs once only in RV. I. 169. 3.

१३. Occurs once only in RV. V. 44. 8.

१४. Occurs once only in RV. VI. 12. 4.

१५. Occurs once only in RV. VIII. 77. 4.

All the 4 words are written, in the Mss. I have collated, without the accent. But as they are the words of the Ṛgveda, I have restored the accent.

अर्थवन्तः शब्दसामान्यात् ।

एतद् वै यज्ञस्य समृद्धं यद् रूपसमृद्धं यत्कर्म क्रियमाणमृग्यजुर्वाभिवदति ।

इति च ब्राह्मणम् ।[1]

क्रीळन्तौ पुत्रैर्नप्तृभिः ।[2] इति ।

यथो एतन्नियतवाचो युक्तयो नियतानुपूर्व्या भवन्तीति लौकिकेष्वप्येतत् । यथा । इन्द्राग्नी । पितापुत्रौ । इति ।

यथो एतद् ब्राह्मणेन रूपसंपन्ना विधीयन्त इत्युदितानुवादः स भवति ।

यथो एतदनुपपन्नार्था भवन्तीत्याम्नायवचनादहिंसा[3] प्रतीयेत ।

यथो एतद् विप्रतिषिद्धार्था भवन्तीति लौकिकेष्वप्येतत् । यथा । असपत्नो[4]ऽयं ब्राह्मणः । अनमित्रो राजा । इति ।

यथो एतज्जानन्तं संप्रेष्यतीति जानन्तमभिवादयते[5] । जानते मधुपर्कं प्राह [इति] ।

यथो एतददितिः सर्वमिति लौकिकेष्वप्येतत् । यथा । सर्वरसा अनुप्राप्ताः पानीयम् । इति ।

यथो एतदविस्पष्टार्था भवन्तीति नैष स्थाणोरपराधो यदेनमन्धो न पश्यति । पुरुषापराधः स भवति । यथा जानपदीषु विद्यातः पुरुषविशेषो भवति पारोवर्य-वित्सु[7] तु खलु वेदितृषु भूयोविद्यः प्रशस्यो भवति ॥ १६ ॥[6]

अथापीदमन्तरेण पदविभागो न विद्यते ।

अवसाय पद्वते रुद्र मृळ ।[8] इति ।

पद्वदवसं गावः पथ्यदनम् । अवतेर्गत्यर्थस्यासो नामकरणः । तस्मान्नावगृह्णन्ति ।

---

१. GB. II. 2. 6; cf. AB. 1. 4. 9; 1. 13; 16; 17 etc. The quotation in AB. is found without ऋग्यजुर्वा.

२. RV. X. 85. 42; AV. 14. 1. 22.

३. cf. Manu V. 39; 44:

यज्ञार्थं पशवः सृष्टाः स्वयमेव स्वयंभुवा ।
यज्ञस्य भूत्यै सर्वस्य तस्माद् यज्ञे वधोऽवधः ॥

या वेदविहिता हिंसा नियतास्मिंश्चराचरे ।
अहिंसामेव तां विद्यात् वेदाद् धर्मो हि निर्बभौ ॥

४. संपत्नो C 5; सपत्नो Mi.

५. cf. Manu II. 130, 122:

मातुलांश्च पितृव्यांश्च श्वशुरानृत्विजो गुरून् ।
असावहमिति ब्रूयात् प्रत्युत्थाय यवीयसः ॥

अभिवादात्परं विप्रो ज्यायांसमभिवादयन् ।
असौनामाहमस्मीति स्वं नाम परिकीर्तयेत् ॥

cf. also II. 123–125.

६. Omitted by BK, C 4, C 5, Kn, M 3, Mi, R 4, R 6, W 1, W 2, W 3.

७. परोवर्यविग्सु C 5.

८. RV. X. 169. 1.

अव सायाश्वान्[1] । इति ।

स्यतिरुपसृष्टो[2] विमोचने । तस्मादवगृह्णन्ति[3] ।

दूतो निर्ऋत्या इदमा जगाम[4] । इति ।

पंचम्यर्थप्रेक्षा वा । षष्ठ्यर्थप्रेक्षा वा । आःकारान्तम् ।

परो निर्ऋत्या आ चक्ष्व[5] । इति ।

चतुर्थ्यर्थप्रेक्षा । ऐकारान्तम् ।

परः सन्निकर्षः संहिता[6] । पदप्रकृतिः संहिता[7] । पदप्रकृतीनि सर्वचरणानां पार्षदानि ।

अथापि याज्ञे[8] दैवतेन बहवः प्रदेशा भवन्ति । तदेतेनोपेक्षितव्यम् । ते चेद् ब्रूयुर्लिङ्गज्ञा अत्र स्म[9] इति ।

इन्द्रं न त्वा शवसा देवता वायुं पृणन्ति[10] । इति ।

वायुलिङ्गं चेन्द्रलिङ्गं चाग्नेये मन्त्रे ।

अग्निरिव मन्यो त्विषितः सहस्व[11] । इति ।

तथाग्निर्[12]मान्यवे मन्त्रे । त्विषितो ज्वलितः । त्विषिरित्यप्यस्य दीप्तिर्नाम[13] भवति ।

अथापि ज्ञानप्रशंसा भवति । अज्ञाननिन्दा च ॥ १७ ॥

स्थाणुरयं भारहारः किलाभूदधीत्य वेदं न विजानाति योऽर्थम् ।
योऽर्थज्ञ इत्सकलं भद्रमश्नुते नाकमेति ज्ञानविधूतपाप्मा ॥
यद् गृहीतमविज्ञातं निगदेनैव शब्द्यते ।
अनग्नाविव शुष्कैधो न तज्ज्वलति कर्हिचित् ॥

---

१. RV. I. 104. 1. See Sāyaṇa's commentary on the same.

२. ०रुपस्पृष्टो C 5.

३. cf. SRV. VII. 28. 4. p. iii. 62.

४. RV. X. 165. 1; AV. 6. 27. 1.

५. RV. X. 164. 1; AV. 20. 96. 23.

६. cf. Paṇini. i. 4. 109; cf. PMbh. i. 4. 4. p. i. 354.

७. RP. 2. 1: 105.

८. यज्ञे C 5.

९. cf. BD. ii. 39, 109 B, 110 B.

१०. RV. VI. 4. 7; VS. 33. 13.

११. RV. X. 84. 2; AV. 4. 31. 2; cf. N. 1. 4.

१२. अथाग्नि Kn.

१३. दीप्तिर्नाम C 1, M 3, Mi.

१४. cf. BD. ii, 119.

१५. cf. S. U. B. 3. Comm. and S'āṅkh. B. XIV.

१६. cf. PMbh. i. 1. 1. p. i. 2:

यदधीतमविज्ञातं निगदेनैव शब्द्यते ।
अनग्नाविव शुष्कैधो न तज्ज्वलति कर्हिचित् ॥

cf. Sāyaṇa's comm. on the *Mantra Brāhmaṇa*:

यदधीतमविज्ञातं......कर्हिचित् ॥

The whole passage: अथापि ज्ञानप्रशंसा......कर्हिचित् is quoted by SRV. p. i. 15.

स्थाणुस्तिष्ठतेः । अर्थोऽर्तेः । अरणस्थो वा ॥ १८ ॥

उत त्वः पश्यन्न ददर्श वाचमुत त्वः शृण्वन्न शृणोत्येनाम् ।
उतो त्वस्मै तन्वं वि सस्रे जायेव पत्य उशती सुवासाः ॥

अप्येकः पश्यन्न पश्यति वाचम् । अपि च शृण्वन्न शृणोत्येनाम् । इत्यविद्वांसमाहार्धम् । अप्येकस्मै तन्वं विसस्र इति स्वमात्मानं विवृणुते । ज्ञानं प्रकाशनमर्थस्याह । अनया वाचा । उपमोत्तमया वाचा । जायेव पत्ये कामयमाना सुवासाः [ऋतुकालेषु सुवासाः कल्याणवासाः कामयमानाः] । ऋतुकालेषु यथा स एनां पश्यति स शृणोति । इत्यर्थज्ञप्रशंसा । तस्योत्तरा भूयसे निर्वचनाय ॥ १९ ॥

उत त्वं सख्ये स्थिरपीतमाहुर्नैनं हिन्वन्त्यपि वाजिनेषु ।
अधेन्वा चरति माययैष वाचं शुश्रुवाँ अफलामपुष्पाम् ॥

अप्येकं वाक्सख्ये । स्थिरपीतमाहुः रममाणं विपीतार्थम् । देवसख्ये । रमणीये स्थान इति वा । विज्ञातार्थम् । यं नाप्नुवन्ति वाग्ज्ञेयेषु बलवत्स्वपि । अधेन्वा ह्येष चरति मायया । वाक्प्रतिरूपया । नास्मै कामान्दुग्धे वाग्दोह्यान् देवमनुष्यस्थानेषु यो वाचं श्रुतवान् भवत्यफलामपुष्पामिति । अफलास्मा अपुष्पा वाग्भवतीति वा । किंचित्पुष्पफलेति वा । अर्थं वाचः पुष्पफलमाह । याज्ञदैवते पुष्पफले । देवताध्यात्मे वा ।

साक्षात्कृतधर्माण ऋषयो बभूवुः । तेऽवरेभ्योऽसाक्षात्कृतधर्मभ्य उपदेशेन [12]

---

१. cf. SRV. II. 39. 1; V. 43. 1; pp. ii. 117, 587: अर्थोऽर्तेरिति यास्कः ।

२. RV. X. 71. 4; cf. N. 1. 8.

३. cf. SRV. X. 71. 4. p. IV. 221: अप्येकः......वाचमित्यादि निरुक्तमत्र द्रष्टव्यम् ।

४. ०र्थम् C 4, C 5.

५. cf. PM bh. i. 1. 1. p. i. 4.

६. Omitted by BK, C 4, C 5, Kn, M 3, Mi, R 4, R 6, W 1, W 2, W 3 and Durga.

७. Sāyaṇa reads अर्थज्ञस्य प्रशंसा See SRV. p. i. 16.

८. Quoted by SRV. p. i. 17.

९. RV. X. 71. 5; cf. N. 1. 8.

१०. cf. SRV. X. 71. 5. p. IV. 221: अप्येकं........पीतमित्यादि निरुक्तमनुसंधेयम् ।

११. याज्ञदेवते C 1, C 2, C 3, C 6, M 1, M 2, R 1, R 2, R 5, S.

१२. The whole passage साक्षात्कृत... वेदाङ्गानि च is quoted by Helārāja in his commentary on the *Vākyapadīya* of Bhartṛhari; Ben. S. S. Vol. II. I. p. 39. (1905).

मन्त्रान्संप्रादुः । उपदेशाय ग्लायन्तोऽवरे बिल्मग्रहणायेमं ग्रन्थं समाम्नासिषुः । वेदं च वेदाङ्गानि च[2] । विल्मं[3] भिल्मं भासनमिति वा ।

एतावन्तः समानकर्माणो धातवः । धातुर्दधातेः । एतावन्त्यस्य सत्त्वस्य नामधेयानि । एतावतामर्थानामिदमभिधानम् । नैघंटुकमिदं देवतानाम । प्राधान्येनेदमिति । तद् यदन्यदैवते[4] मन्त्रे निपतति नैघंटुकं तत्[5] ।

अश्वं न त्वा वारवन्तम्[6] ।

अश्वमिव त्वा वालवन्तम् । वाला दंशवारणार्था भवन्ति । दंशो दशतेः ।

मृगो न भीमः कुचरो गिरिष्ठाः[7] ।

मृग इव भीमः कुचरो गिरिष्ठाः । मृगो मार्ष्टेर्गतिकर्मणः[8] । भीमो बिभ्यत्यस्मात्[9] । भीष्मोऽप्येतस्मादेव । कुचर इति चरति कर्म कुत्सितम्[10] । अथ चेद् देवताभिधानम् । क्वायं न चरतीति । गिरिष्ठा गिरिस्थायी । गिरिः पर्वतः । समुद्गीर्णो भवति । पर्ववान् पर्वतः । पर्व पुनः पृणातेः प्रीणातेर्वा । अर्धमासपर्व । देवानस्मिन्प्रीणन्तीति । तत् प्रकृतीतरत्सन्धिसामान्यात् । मेघस्थायी । मेघोऽपि गिरिः[11] एतस्मादेव ।

तद् यानि नामानि प्राधान्यस्तुतीनां देवतानां तद् दैवतमित्याचक्षते । तदुपरिष्टाद् व्याख्यास्यामः[12] । नैघण्टुकानि नैगमानीहेह ॥ २० ॥

इति प्रथमोऽध्यायः ।

---

१. संप्राहुरुपदेशात् Helārāja. *op. cit.*

२. चेत्यागमप्रामाण्यात् । Helārāja. *op. cit.*

३. Harivṛṣabha in his commentary on the *Vākyapadīya* of Bhartṛhari Ben. S. S. Nos. 11, 19, 24. (1887) p. 3. remarks: ऋषयः साक्षात्कृतधर्माणो...बिल्मं समामनन्ति...वेदवेदाङ्गानि बिल्मः ।

४. ०देवते C 1, C 2, C 3, C 6, M 1, M 2, R 1, R 2, R 5, S.

५. cf. BD. i. 18, 19:

मन्त्रेऽन्यदैवतेऽन्यानि निगद्यन्तेऽत्र कानिचित् ।
सालोक्यात्साहचर्याद्वा तानि नैपातिकानि तु ॥

६. RV. I. 27. 1; SV. 1. 17; 2. 984.

७. RV. I. 154. 2; X. 180. 2.

८. Quoted by SRV. I. 145. 5. p. i. 645.

९. Quoted by SRV. I. 55. 1. p. i. 278.

१०. cf. BD. i. 33: अपि कुत्सितनामायम् ।

११. Quoted by SRV. I. 145. 2. p. i. 662. cf. also I. 51. 5; V. 56. 4; VIII. 63. 12.

१२. See N. 7-12.

[समाम्नायस्तत्रचतुष्ट्वमतोऽन्येऽथ निपाता वायुर्वान्वा न नूनं नूनं सा त ऋचां-न्त्वोऽक्षण्वन्तो निष्ट्वक्रासो हविर्भिरितीमान्यथापि यो यथो हि न्वथापीदमर्थवन्तो-ऽथापीदं स्थाणुरयमुत त्वः पश्यन्नुत त्वं सख्ये विंशतिः ॥]

॥ इति निरुक्ते पूर्वषट्के प्रथमोऽध्यायः समाप्तः ॥

Small figure on this page represents the corresponding section of the first chapter of the *Nirukta*.

ॐ

अथ द्वितीयोऽध्यायः ।

अथ निर्वचनम् । तद् येषु पदेषु स्वरसंस्कारौ समर्थौ प्रादेशिकेन विकारेणान्वितौ[1] स्यातां[2] तथा तानि निर्ब्रूयात् । अथानन्वितेऽर्थेऽप्रादेशिके विकारेऽर्थनित्यः परीक्षेत । केनचिद् वृत्तिसामान्येन । अविद्यमाने सामान्येऽप्यक्षरवर्णसामान्यान्निर्ब्रूयात् । न त्वेव न निर्ब्रूयात्[3] । न संस्कारमाद्रियेत[4] । विशयवत्यो[5] हि वृत्तयो भवन्ति । यथार्थं विभक्तीः सन्नमयेत् ।

प्रत्तमवत्तमिति धात्वादी एव शिष्येते । अथाप्यस्तेर्निवृत्तिस्थानेष्वादिलोपो भवति । स्तः । सन्तीति । अथाप्यन्तलोपो भवति । गत्वा । गतमिति । अथाप्युपधालोपो भवति । जग्मतुः । जग्मुरिति[6] । अथाप्युपधाविकारो भवति । राजा[7] । दण्डीति । अथापि वर्णलोपो भवति । तत्त्वा यामि । इति । अथापि द्विवर्णलोपः[8] । तृच इति । अथाप्यादिविपर्ययो भवति । ज्योतिः । घनः । बिन्दुः । वाट्य इति । अथाप्याद्यन्तविपर्ययो भवति । स्तोकाः । रज्जुः । सिकताः । तर्क्विति[9] ।

अथाप्यन्तव्यापत्तिर्भवति ॥ १ ॥

ओघः । मेघः । नाधः । गाधः । वधूः । मध्विति । अथापि वर्णोपजनः । आस्थत् । द्वारः । भरूजेति ।

तद् यत्र स्वरादनन्तरान्तस्थान्तर्धातुर्भवति तद् द्विप्रकृतीनां स्थानमिति प्रदिशन्ति । तत्र सिद्धायामनुपपद्यमानायामितरयोपपिपादयिषेत् । तत्राप्येकेऽल्पनिष्पत्तयो भवन्ति । तद् यथैतत् । ऊतिः । मृदुः । पृथुः । पृषतः । कुणारुमिति ।

---

१. गुणेन. C 1, C 2, C 3, C 6, M 1, M 2, R 1, R 2, R 5, S; Durga; Roth's and S'ivadatta's edition.

२. cf. N. I. 14.

३. cf. SRV. I. 1. 1. p. i. 25.

४. Quoted in the *Māṭhara Vṛtti* on the *Sāṅkhyakārikā* XXII. ed. by Sāhityācārya. Benares 1922, p. 37 :

अप्यक्षरवर्णसामान्यान्निर्ब्रूयात् । न संस्कारमाद्रियेत् । इति नैरुक्तश्रुतिप्रामाण्यात् ।. It should be noted that the intervening sentence न त्वेव न निर्ब्रूयात् is omitted and the *Nirukta* is raised to the dignity of a *S'ruti.*

५. विषयवत्यो C 1, C 2, C 3, C 6, M 1, M 2, R 1, R 2, R 5, S; M 3, Mi.

६. cf. PMbh. VI. 1. 1. p. iii. 17; उपधालोपस्यावकाशः ...जग्मतुः । जग्मुः । जघ्नतुः । जघ्नुः ।

७. राला. C 5.

८. cf. BD. ii. 116.

९. cf. PMbh. i. 1. 2. p. i. 31। कृतेस्तर्कुः । कसेः सिकताः । हिंसेः सिंहः । cf. also Vol. ii. p. 87. कृतेराद्यन्तविपर्ययश्च ॥ uṇā. Sū. 1. 17. Aufrecht's edition p. 7.

अथापि भाषिकेभ्यो धातुभ्यो नैगमाः कृतो भाष्यन्ते । दमूनाः । क्षेत्रसाधा इति । अथापि नैगमेभ्यो भाषिकाः । उष्णम् । घृतमिति ।

अथापि प्रकृतय एवैकेषु भाष्यन्ते । विकृतय एकेषु । शवतिर्गतिकर्मा कंबोजेष्वेव भाष्यते । कंबोजाः कंबलभोजाः । कमनीयभोजा वा । कंबलः कमनीयो भवति । विकारमस्यार्येषु भाषन्ते । शव इति । दातिर्लवनार्थे प्राच्येषु । दात्रमुदीच्येषु । एवमेकपदानि निर्ब्रूयात् ।

अथ तद्धितसमासेष्वेकपर्वसु वानेकपर्वसु च पूर्वं पूर्वमपरमपरं प्रविभज्य निर्ब्रूयात् । दण्ड्यः पुरुषः [दण्डपुरुषः] । दण्डमर्हतीति वा । दण्डेन संपद्यत इति वा । दण्डो ददातेर्धारयतिकर्मणः । अक्रूरो ददते मणिमित्यभिभाषन्ते । दमनादित्यौपमन्यवः । दण्डमस्याकर्षतीति गर्हायाम् ।

कक्ष्यारज्जुरश्वस्य । कक्षं सेवते । कक्षो गाहतेः । क्स इति नामकरणः । ख्यातेर्वानर्थकोऽभ्यासः । किमस्मिन् ख्यानमिति । कषतेर्वा । तत्सामान्यान्मनुष्यकक्षः । बाहुमूलसामान्यादश्वस्य ॥ २ ॥

राज्ञः पुरुषो राजपुरुषः । राजा राजतेः । पुरुषः पुरि षादः । पुरि शयः । पूरयतेर्वा । पूरयत्यन्तरित्यन्तरपुरुषमभिप्रेत्य ।

यस्मात्परं नापरमस्ति किंचिद् यस्मान्नाणीयो न ज्यायोऽस्ति कश्चित् ।
वृक्ष इव स्तब्धो दिवि तिष्ठत्येकस्तेनेदं पूर्णं पुरुषेण सर्वम् ॥ ३ ॥

इत्यपि निगमो भवति ।

विश्वकद्राकर्षः । वीति चकद्र इति श्वगतौ भाष्यते । द्रातीति गतिकुत्सना । कद्रातीति द्रातिकुत्सना । चकद्राति कद्रातीति सतोऽनर्थकोऽभ्यासः । तदस्मिन्नस्तीति विश्वकद्रः ।

कल्याणवर्णरूपः । कल्याणवर्णस्येवास्य रूपम् । कल्याणं कमनीयं भवति । वर्णो वृणोतेः । रूपं रोचतेः । एवं तद्धितसमासान्निर्ब्रूयात् ।

---

१. cf. PMbh. i. 1. 1. p. i. 9; शवतिर्गतिकर्मा कम्बोजेष्वेव भाषितो भवति ।

२. कंबल...भवति is quoted by Kṣīrasvāmin in his commentary on the *Amarakoṣa* II. 9. 107. Poona ed. (1913) p. 157.

३. cf. PMbh. i. 1. 1. p. i. 9; विकार एनमार्या भाषन्ते शव इति...दातिर्लवनार्थे प्राच्येषु दात्रमुदीच्येषु ।

४. चानेक०. C 1, C 2, C 3, C 6, M 1, M 2, R 1, R 2, R 5, S; C 4, C 5, Mi, W 1, W 2; Roth's edition.

५. Omitted by BK, C 4, C 5, Kn, M 3, Mi, R 4, R 6, W 1, W 2, W 3; and Durga.

६. cf. BD. ii. 106.

७. ददते०. C 1, C 2, C 3, C 6, M 1, M 2, R 1, R 2, R 5, S.

८. ०कर्षतेति C 1, C 2, C 3, C 6, M 1, M 2, R 1, R 2, R 5, S.

९. cf. SRV. I. 126. 4. p. i. 571: कक्ष्यारज्जुरश्वस्येति यास्केनोक्तत्वात् ।

१०. पुरुषादः W 2.

११. किंचित् C 2, C 3, C 4, C 5, C 6, M 3, Mi, W 1, W 2.

१२. TA. 10. 10. 3; Mu. 10. 4.

नैकपदानि निर्ब्रूयात् । नावैयाकरणाय । नानुपसन्नाय । अनिदंविदे वा । नित्यं ह्यविज्ञातुर्विज्ञानेऽसूया । उपसन्नाय तु निर्ब्रूयात् । यो वालं विज्ञातुं स्यात् । मेधाविने । तपस्विने वा ॥ ३ ॥

विद्या ह वै ब्राह्मणमाजगाम गोपाय मा शेवधिष्टेऽहमस्मि ।
असूयकायानृजवेऽयताय न मा ब्रूया वीर्यवती तथा स्याम् ॥
य आतृणत्त्यवितथेन कर्णावदुःखं कुर्वन्नमृतं संप्रयच्छन् ।
तं मन्येत पितरं मातरं च तस्मै न द्रुह्येत् कतमच्चनाह ॥
अध्यापिता ये गुरुं नाद्रियन्ते विप्रा वाचा मनसा कर्मणा वा ।
यथैव ते न गुरोर्भोजनीयास्तथैव तान्न भुनक्ति श्रुतं तत् ॥
यमेव विद्याः शुचिमप्रमत्तं मेधाविनं ब्रह्मचर्योपपन्नम् ।
यस्ते न द्रुह्येत् कतमच्चनाह तस्मै मा ब्रूया निधिपाय ब्रह्मन् ॥

इति । निधिः शेवधिरिति ॥ ४ ॥

अथातोऽनुक्रमिष्यामः । गौरिति पृथिव्या नामधेयम् । यद् दूरं गता भवति । यच्चास्यां भूतानि गच्छन्ति । गातेर्वौकारो नामकरणः ।

अथापि पशुनामेह भवत्येतस्मादेव । अथाप्यस्यां ताद्धितेन कृत्स्नवन्निगमा भवन्ति ।

गोभिः श्रीणीत मत्सरम् ।

इति पयसः । मत्सरः सोमः । मन्दतेस्तृप्तिकर्मणः । मत्सर इति लोभनाम । अभिमत्त एनेन धनं भवति । पयः पिबतेर्वा प्यायतेर्वा । क्षीरं क्षरतेः । घसेर्वेरो नामकरणः । उशीरमिति यथा ।

अंशुं दुहन्तो अध्यासते गवि ।

इत्यधिषवणचर्मणः । अंशुः शमष्टमात्रो भवति । अननाय शं भवतीति वा । चर्म चरतेर्वा । उच्चृतं भवतीति वा ।

अथापि चर्म च श्लेष्मा च ।

१. cf. Manu II. 114; Su. III.; Vas. II. 8; Viṣṇu XXIX. 9.

२. आतृणत्त्ववि०. C 5.

३. cf. Manu II. 144; Vas. II. 10; Viṣṇu. XXX. 47; Āp. 1. 1. 14.

४. cf. Manu II. 115; Vas. II. 9; Viṣṇu XXIX. 10.

५. All the 4 verses are found in SU. B. 3. (Burnell. pp. 29–32). Quoted by SRV. p. i. 22.

६. cf. SRV. I. 158. 2. p. i. 672: तथा च निरुक्तं गौरिति…नामकरणः । cf. S'B. VI. 1. 2. 34. Weber's ed. p. 505: इमे वै लोका गौर्यद्धि किं च गच्छतीमांस्तल्लोकान् गच्छति ।

७. RV. IX. 46. 4.

८. RV. X. 94. 9.

९. Quoted by SRV. IX. 89. 6; 97. 14; pp. iii. 759, 780.

गोभि॑ः सन्न॑द्धो असि वी॒ळय॑स्व॑[1] ।

इति रथस्तुतौ । अथापि स्नाव च श्लेष्मा च ।

गोभि॑ः सन्न॑द्धा पतति॒ प्रसू॑तां[2] ।

इतीषुस्तुतौ ।

ज्यापि गौरुच्यते । गव्या चेत् ताद्धितम् । अथ चेन्न । गव्या गमयतीषू-निति ॥ ५ ॥

वृक्षेवृ॑क्षे॒ निय॑ता मीमय॒द् गौस्ततो॒ वय॒ः प्र प॑तान्पूरु॒षादः॑[3] ।

वृक्षेवृक्षे धनुषिधनुषि । वृक्षो व्रश्चनात् [वृत्वा क्षां तिष्ठतीति वा । क्षा क्षियतेः । निवासकर्मणः[4]] नियता मीमयद् गौः शब्दं करोति । मीमयतिः शब्दकर्मा । ततो वयः प्रपतन्ति । पुरुषानदनाय[5] । विरिति शकुनिनाम । वेतेर्गतिकर्मणः । अथापीषुनामेह भवत्येतस्मादेव ।

आदित्योऽपि गौरुच्यते ।

उ॒तादः॑ प॑रु॒षे गँवि॒[7] ।

पर्ववति भास्वतीत्यौपमन्यवः । अथाप्यस्यैको रश्मिश्चंद्रमसं प्रति दीप्यते तदेतेनोपेक्षितव्यम् । आदित्यतोऽस्य दीप्तिर्भवति ।

सु॒षु॒म्णः सूर्य॑रश्मिश्च॒न्द्रमा॑ गन्ध॒र्वः[8] ।

इत्यपि निगमो भवति । सोऽपि गौरुच्यते ।

अत्राह॒ गोर॑मन्वत॑[9] ।

इति । तदुपरिष्टाद्[10] व्याख्यास्यामः । सर्वेऽपि रश्मयो गाव उच्यन्ते ॥ ६ ॥

---

१. RV. VI. 47. 26; AV. 6. 125. 1; cf. N. 9. 12.

२. RV. VI. 75. 11; VS. 29. 48; cf. N. 9. 12

३. RV. X. 27. 22.

४. Omitted by BK, C 4, C 5, Kn, M3, Mi, R 4, R 6, W 1, W 2, W 3.

५. Quoted by SRV. VI. 75. 11. p. ii. 890.

६. cf. BD. ii. 111.

७. RV. VI. 56. 3.

८. VS. 18. 40; S'B. IX. 4. 1. 9; cf. सुपुम्नः etc. TS. 111. 4. 7. 1.

९. RV. I. 84. 15; AV. 20. 41. 3; SV. 1. 147; 2. 265; cf. N. 4. 25. The passage: अथाप्यस्यैको...गोरमन्वतेति is quoted by SRV. I. 84. 15; p. i. 379.

१०. N. 4. 25.

ता वां वास्तून्युश्मसि गमध्यै यत्र गावो भूरिशृङ्गा अयासः ।
अत्राह तदुरुगायस्य वृष्णः परमं पदमव भाति भूरि ॥

तानि वां वास्तूनि कामयामहे गमनाय यत्र गावो [भूरिशृंगा] बहुशृंगाः । भूरीति बहुनो नामधेयम् । प्रभवतीति सतः । शृंगं श्रयतेर्वा । शृणातेर्वा । शम्नातेर्वा । शरणायोद्गतमिति वा । शिरसो निर्गतमिति वा । अयासोऽयनाः । तत्र तदुरुगायस्य विष्णोर्महागतेः परमं पदं परार्ध्यस्थमवभाति भूरि । पादः पद्यतेः । तन्निधानात् पदम् । पशुपादप्रकृतिः प्रभागपादः । प्रभागपादसामान्यादितराणि पदानि ।

एवमन्येषामपि सत्त्वानां संदेहा विद्यन्ते । तानि चेत् समानकर्माणि समाननिर्वचनानि । नानाकर्माणि चेन्नानानिर्वचनानि । यथार्थं निर्वक्तव्यानि । इतीमान्येकविंशतिः पृथिवीनामधेयान्यनुक्रान्तानि ।

तत्र निर्ऋतिर्निरमणात् । ऋच्छतेः कृच्छ्रापत्तिरितरा । सा पृथिव्या संदिह्यते । तयोर्विभागः । तस्या एषा भवति ॥ ७ ॥

य ईं चकार न सो अस्य वेद य ईं ददर्श हिरुगिन्नु तस्मात् ।
स मातुर्योना परिवीतो अन्तर्बहुप्रजा निर्ऋतिमा विवेश ॥

बहुप्रजाः कृच्छ्रमापद्यत इति परिव्राजकाः । वर्षकर्मेति नैरुक्ताः । य ईं चकारेति करोतिकिरती संदिग्धौ वर्षकर्मणा । न सो अस्य वेद मध्यमः । स एवास्य वेद मध्यमो यो ददर्शादित्योपहितम् । स मातुर्योनौ । मातान्तरिक्षम् । निर्मीयन्तेऽस्मिन् भूतानि । योनिरन्तरिक्षम् । महानवयवः । परिवीतो वायुना । अयमपीतरो योनिरेतस्मादेव । परियुतो भवति । बहुप्रजा भूमिमापद्यते वर्षकर्मणा ।

शाकपूणिः संकल्पयाञ्चक्रे । सर्वा देवता जानानीति । तस्मै देवतोभयलिङ्गा प्रादुर्बभूव । तां न जज्ञे । तां पप्रच्छ । विविदिषाणि त्वेति । सास्मा एतामृचमादिदेश । एषा मद् देवतेति ॥ ८ ॥

अयं स शिङ्क्ते येन गौरभीवृता मिमाति मायुं ध्वसनावधि श्रिता ।
सा चित्तिभिर्नि हि चकार मर्त्यं विद्युद्भवन्ती प्रति वव्रिमौहत ॥

---

१. RV. I. 154. 6.

२. Omitted by BK, C 4, C 5, Kn, M 3, Mi, R 4, R 6, W 1, W 2, W 3.

३. बहुलो BK, C 4, C 5, Kn, M 3, Mi, R 4, R 6, W 1, W 2, W 3.

४. अयनात् C 4, M 3, Mi, W 1.

५. cf. SRV. I. 154. 6. p. i. 664. अयं मन्त्रो यास्केन...व्याख्यातः । तानि वां... पादः पद्यतेः । cf. PMbh. i. 2. 3. p. I. 247: पद्यतेः पादः ।

६. RV. I. 164. 32; AV. 9. 10. 10.

७. Quoted by SRV. I. 160. 2. p. i. 674.

८. जानामीति C 1, C 2, C 3, C 6, M 1, M 2, R 1, R 2, R 5, S.

९. SRV. I. 164. 29. p. i. 709; साचायं स शिंक्त इत्येषा मद् देवता तत्र प्रतीयमानं मन्त्रस्वरूपमित्युपदिदेश ।

१०. RV. I. 164. 29; AV. 9. 10. 7.

अयं स शब्दायते येन गौरभिप्रवृत्ता मिमाति। मायुं शब्दं करोति। मायुमिवादित्यमिति वा। वागेषा माध्यमिका। ध्वंसने मेघेऽधिश्रिता। सा चित्तिभिः [कर्मभिर्नीचैः[१]] निकरोति मर्त्यम्। विद्युद्भवन्ती प्रत्यूहते वव्रिम्। वव्रिरिति रूपनाम। वृणोतीति सतः। वर्षेण प्रच्छाद्य पृथिवीं तत्पुनरादत्ते॥ ९॥

हिरण्यनामान्युत्तराणि पंचदश। हिरण्यं कस्मात्। ह्रियत आयम्यमानमिति वा। ह्रियते जनाज्जनमिति[२] वा। हितरमणं भवतीति वा [हृदयरमणं भवतीति वा[३]]। हर्यतेर्वा स्यात् प्रेप्साकर्मणः[४]।

अन्तरिक्षनामान्युत्तराणि षोडश[५]। अन्तरिक्षं कस्मात्। अन्तरा क्षान्तं भवति। अन्तरेमे इति वा। शरीरेष्वन्तरक्षयमिति[६] वा।

तत्र समुद्र इत्येतत् पार्थिवेन समुद्रेण संदिह्यते। समुद्रः कस्मात्। समुद्द्रवन्त्यस्मादापः। समभिद्रवन्त्येनमापः। संमोदन्तेऽस्मिन्भूतानि। समुदको भवति। समुनत्तीति[७] वा। तयोर्विभागः।

तत्रेतिहासमाचक्षते। देवापिश्चार्ष्टिषेणः शंतनुश्च कौरव्यौ भ्रातरौ बभूवतुः[८]। स शंतनुः कनीयान्[९]अभिषेचयांचक्रे[१०]। देवापिस्तपः प्रतिपेदे। ततः शंतनो राज्ये द्वादश वर्षाणि देवो न ववर्ष[११]। तमूचुर्ब्राह्मणाः। अधर्मस्त्वया चरितः। ज्येष्ठं भ्रातरमन्तरित्याभिषेचितम्। तस्मात्ते देवो न वर्षतीति। स शंतनुर्देवापिं शिशिक्ष राज्येन। तमुवाच देवापिः। पुरोहितस्तेऽसानि। याजयानि च त्वेति[१२]। तस्यैतद् वर्षकामसूक्तम्[१३]। तस्यैषा भवति॥ १०॥

आर्ष्टिषेणो होत्रमृषिर्निषीदन्देवापिर्देवसुमतिं चिकित्वान्।
स उत्तरस्मादधरं समुद्रमपो दिव्या असृजद्वर्ष्या अभि[१४]॥

आर्ष्टिषेण ऋष्टिषेणस्य पुत्रः[१५]। इषितसेनस्येति वा। सेना सेश्वरा। समानग-

---

१. Omitted by BK, C 4, C 5, Kn, M 3, Mi, R 4, R 6, W 1, W 2, W 3.

२. Quoted by SRV. III. 54. 11. p. ii. 309; cf. also VI. 72. 3. p. ii. 882.

३. Omitted by BK, C 4, C 5, Kn, M 3, Mi, R 4, R 6, W 1, W 2, W 3; and Durga

४. The whole passage हिरण्यं कस्मात्... प्रेप्साकर्मणः is quoted by SRV. I. 22. 5. p. i. 115.

५. पोलश C 5, Mi.

६. ०न्तरिक्षयमिति BK, C 4, C 5, Kn, M 3, Mi, R 4, R 6, W 1, W 2; W 3.

७. The passage समुद्रः कस्मात्...समुनत्तीति वा। is quoted by SRV I. 30. 18. p. i. 156; cf. also I. 160. 4, VI. 72. 3; pp. i. 675; ii. 884.

८. cf. BD. VII. 155.

९. कलीयान् C 5.

१०. cf. BD. VII. 156; VIII. 1.

११. cf. BD. VIII. 2.

१२. cf. BD. VIII. 4-5.

१३. cf. SRV. X. 98. 1. p. IV. 324.

१४. RV. X. 98. 5.

१५. cf. SRV. X. 98. 5. p. IV. 325.

तिर्वा[१] । पुत्रः पुरु त्रायते । निपरणाद्वा । पुन्नरकं ततस्त्रायत इति वा । होत्रस्तृषिर्निषीदन् । ऋषिर्दर्शनात्[२] । स्तोमान्ददर्शेत्यौपमन्यवः ।

तद्यदेनांस्तपस्यमानान् ब्रह्म स्वयंभ्वभ्यानर्षत् [त ऋषयोऽभवन्[३]] तदृषीणामृषित्वम्[४] ।

इति विज्ञायते । देवापिर्देवानामाप्त्या स्तुत्या च प्रदानेन च देवसुमतिं देवानां कल्याणीं मतिं चिकित्वांश्चेतनावान्[५] । स उत्तरस्मादधरं समुद्रम् । उत्तर उद्धततरो भवति । अधरोऽधोरः । अधो न धावतीत्यूर्ध्वगतिः प्रतिषिद्धा । तस्योत्तरा भूयसे निर्वचनाय ॥ ११ ॥

यद्देवापिः शन्तनवे पुरोहितो होत्राय वृतः कृपयन्नदीधेत् ।
देवश्रुतं वृष्टिवनिं रराणो बृहस्पतिर्वाचमस्मा अयच्छत्[६] ॥

शन्तनुः शं तनोऽस्त्विति वा । शमस्मै तन्वा अस्त्विति वा । पुरोहितः पुर एनं दधति[७] । होत्राय वृतः कृपायमाणोऽन्वध्यायत् । देवश्रुतं देवा एनं शृण्वन्ति [वृष्टिवनिं] वृष्टियाचिनम् । रराणो रातिरभ्यस्तः । बृहस्पतिर्ब्रह्मासीत् । सोऽस्मै वाचमयच्छत्[८] । बृहदुपव्याख्यातम् ॥ १२ ॥

साधारणान्युत्तराणि षड् दिवश्चादित्यस्य च । यानि त्वस्य प्राधान्येनोपरिष्टा[९]त्तानि व्याख्यास्यामः । आदित्यः कस्मात् । आदत्ते रसान् । आदत्ते भासं ज्योतिषाम् । आदीप्तो भासेति वा । अदितेः पुत्र इति वा । अल्पप्रयोगं त्वस्यैतदार्चाभ्याम्नाये सूक्तभाक् ।

सूर्यमादितेयम्[११] ।

[अदितेः पुत्रम्[१२]] । एवमन्यासामपि देवतानामादित्यप्रवादाः स्तुतयो भवन्ति । तद् यथैतन्मित्रस्य वरुणस्यार्यम्णो दक्षस्य भगस्यांशस्येति ।

अथापि मित्रावरुणयोः ।

---

१. cf. SRV. I. 68. 10; 40. 2; 125. 3; pp. i. 329, 212, 568. cf. Manu. IX. 138.

२. Quoted by SRV. IX. 96. 6. p. iii. 770.

३. Omitted by BK, C 4, C 5, Kn, M 3, Mi, R 4, R 6, W 1, W 2, W 3.

४. TA. ii. 9. The words within the brackets are not omitted in TA.

५. Quoted by SRV. I. 70. 6. p. i. 333.

६. RV. X. 98. 7.

७. Quoted by SRV. I. 1. 1. p. i. 24. cf. BD. VIII. 6.

८. Omitted by BK, C 4, C 5, Kn, M 3, Mi, R 4, R 6, W 1, W 2, W 3.

९. cf. BD. VIII. 8 B.

१०. See N. 12. 8-22.

११. RV. X. 88. 11; cf. N. 7. 29.

१२. Omitted by BK, C 4, C 5, Kn, M 3, Mi, R 4, R 6, W 1, W 2, W 3.

आ॒दि॒त्या दानु॑न॒स्पती॑[१] ।

दानपती । अथापि मित्रस्यैकस्य ।

प्र स मि॑त्र॒ मर्तो॑ अस्तु॒ प्रय॑स्वा॒न्यस्त॑ आदित्य॒ शिक्ष॑ति व्र॒तेन॑[२] ।

इत्यपि निगमो भवति । अथापि वरुणस्यैकस्य

अथा॑ व॒यमा॑दित्य व्र॒ते तव॑[३] ।

व्रतमिति कर्मनाम । निवृत्तिकर्म वारयतीति सतः[५] । इदमपीतरद्व्रतमेतस्मादेव वृणोतीति सतः[४] । अन्नमपि व्रतमुच्यते । यदावृणोति शरीरम् ॥ १३ ॥

स्वरादित्यो भवति । सु अरणः । सु ईरणः । स्वृतो रसान् । स्वृतो भासं ज्योतिषाम् । स्वृतो भासेति वा[६] । एतेन द्यौर्व्याख्याता । पृश्निरादित्यो भवति । प्राश्नुत एनं वर्ण इति नैरुक्ताः[७] । संस्प्रष्टो रसान् । संस्प्रष्टा भासं ज्योतिषाम् । संस्प्रष्टो भासेति वा । अथ द्यौः । संस्पृष्टा ज्योतिर्भिः पुण्यकृद्भिश्च ।

नाक आदित्यो भवति [नेता रसानाम्[८]] नेता भासाम् । ज्योतिषां प्रणयः । अथ द्यौः । कमिति सुखनाम । प्रतिषिद्धं प्रतिषिध्येत ।

न॒ वा अ॒मुं लो॒कं ज॒ग्मुषे॒ किं च॒ नाक॑म्[९] ।

न वा अमुं लोकं जग्मुषे[१०] किं च नासुखम् । पुण्यकृतो ह्येव तत्र गच्छन्ति ।

गौरादित्यो भवति । गमयति रसान् । गच्छत्यन्तरिक्षे । अथ द्यौः । यत्पृथिव्या अधिदूरं गता भवति । यच्चास्यां ज्योतींषि गच्छन्ति । विष्टवादित्यो[११] भवति । आविष्टो रसान् । आविष्टो भासं ज्योतिषाम् । आविष्टो भासेति वा । अथ द्यौः । आविष्टा ज्योतिर्भिः पुण्यकृद्भिश्च ।

नभ आदित्यो भवति । [नेता रसानां[१२]] । नेता भासाम् । ज्योतिषां प्रणयः[१३] । अपि वा भन एव स्याद्विपरीतः ।

---

१. RV. I. 136. 3; II. 41. 6; SV. 2, 262.

२. RV. III. 59. 2.

३. RV. I. 24. 15; VS. 12. 12.

४. वृणोतीति सतः Durga and Bib. Ind.

५. निवृत्तिकर्म वारयतीति सतः Durga and Bib. Ind.

६. Cf. SRV. I. 112. 5; 148. 1; VII. 10. 2. pp. i. 488; 650; iii. 25.

७. Cf. SRV. IX. 83. 3. p. iii. 734

८. Omitted by BK, C 4, C 5, Kn, M 3, Mi, R 4, R 6, W 1, W 2, W 3; and Durga.

९. The quotation is untraced. Cf. SRV. I. 125. 5. p. i. 569.

१०. गतवते C 1, C 2, C 3, C 6, M 1, M 2, R 1, R 2, R 5, S; and Roth, edition.

११. विष्टपा० C 3; विष्टवा०. W 1.

१२. Omitted by BK, C 4, C 5, Kn, M 3, Mi, R 4, R 6, W 1, W 2, W 3, and Durga.

१३. प्रभव: BK, C 4, C 5, Kn, M 3, Mi, R 4, R 6, W 1, W 2, W 3.

न न भातीति वा । एतेन द्यौर्व्याख्याता ॥ १४ ॥

रश्मिनामान्युत्तराणि पंचदश । रश्मिर्यमनात् । तेषामादितः साधारणानि पञ्चाश्वरश्मिभिः ।

दिङ्नामान्युत्तराण्यष्टौ । दिशः कस्मात् । दिशतेः । आसदनात् । अपि वाभ्यशनात् ।

तत्र काष्ठा इत्येतदनेकस्यापि सत्त्वस्य [नाम[1]] भवति । काष्ठा दिशो भवन्ति । क्रान्त्वा स्थिता भवन्ति । काष्ठा उपदिशो भवन्ति । इतरेतरं क्रान्त्वा स्थिता भवन्ति । आदित्योऽपि काष्ठोच्यते । क्रान्त्वा स्थितो भवति । आज्यन्तोऽपि[2] काष्ठोच्यते । क्रान्त्वा स्थितो भवति[3] । आपोऽपि काष्ठा उच्यन्ते । क्रान्त्वा स्थिता भवन्तीति[4] स्थावराणाम् ॥ १५ ॥

अतिष्ठन्तीनामनिवेशनानां काष्ठानां मध्ये निहितं शरीरम् ।
वृत्रस्य निण्यं वि चरन्त्यापो दीर्घं तम आशयदिन्द्रशत्रुः ।[5]

अतिष्ठन्तीनामनिविशमानानामित्यस्थावराणां काष्ठानां मध्ये निहितं शरीरं मेघः । शरीरं शृणातेः । शम्नातेर्वा । वृत्रस्य [निण्यं[6]] निर्णामं विचरन्ति विजानन्त्याप इति । दीर्घं द्राघतेः । तमस्तनोतेः । आशयदाशेतेः[8] । इन्द्रशत्रुरिन्द्रोऽस्य शमयिता वा शातयिता वा । तस्मादिन्द्रशत्रुः । तत्को वृत्रः । मेघ इति नैरुक्ताः । [त्वाष्ट्रोऽसुर इत्यैतिहासिकाः ।][9] अपां च ज्योतिषश्च मिश्रीभावकर्मणो वर्षकर्म जायते[7] । तत्रोपमार्थेन युद्धवर्णा भवन्ति । अहिवत्तु खलु मन्त्रवर्णा ब्राह्मणवादाश्च । विवृद्ध्या शरीरस्य स्रोतांसि निवारयाञ्चकार । तस्मिन् हते प्रसस्यन्दिर[10] आपः । तदभिवादिन्येषर्ग्भवति ॥ १६ ॥

---

1. Omitted by BK, C 4, C 5, Kn, M 3, Mi, R 4, R 6, W 1, W 2, W 3.
2. आज्यन्त्वो W 1; अज्यत्यंतो C 5.
3. Cf. SRV. VIII. 80. 8; X. 103. 9. pp. iii. 529; IV. 340.
4. Cf. SRV. I. 37. 10. p. i. 202.
5. RV. I. 32. 10.
6. Omitted by BK, C 4, C 5, Kn, M 3, Mi, R 4, R 6, W 1, W 2, W 3.
7. जाघते: C 5.
8. ०दाशयते: BK, C 4, C 5, Kn, M 3, Mi, R 4, R 6, W 1, W 2, W 3.
9. त्वाष्ट्रो…इत्यैतिहासिका: is omitted by BK, C 4, C 5, Kn, M 3, Mi, R 4, R 6, W 1, W 2, W 3, and Durga. The passage अतिष्ठन्तीनाम…इत्यैतिहासिका: is quoted by SRV. I. 32. 10. p. i. 170.
10. प्रशस्यन्दिर BK, C 4, C 5, Kn, M 3, Mi, R 4, R 6, W 1, W 2, W 3.

दासपत्नीरहिंगोपा अतिष्ठन्निरुद्धा आपः पणिनेव गावः ।
अपां बिलमपिहितं यदासीद्वृत्रं जघन्वाँ अप तद्ववार ॥

दासपत्नीर्दासाधिपत्न्यः । दासो दस्यतेः । उपदासयति कर्माणि । अहिगोपा अतिष्ठन् । अहिना गुप्ताः । अहिरयनात् । एत्यन्तरिक्षे ।

अयमपीतरोऽहिरेतस्मादेव । निर्ह्रसितोपसर्गः । आहन्तीति । निरुद्धा आपः पणिनेव गावः । पणिर्वणिग्भवति । पणिः पणनात् । वणिक् पण्यं नेनेक्ति । अपां बिलमपिहितं यदासीत् । बिलं भरं भवति बिभर्तेः । वृत्रं जघ्निवान् । अपववार तत् । वृत्रो वृणोतेर्वा । वर्ततेर्वा । वर्धतेर्वा ।

यदवृणोत्तद्वृत्रस्य वृत्रत्वम् । इति विज्ञायते । यदवर्तत तद्वृत्रस्य वृत्रत्वम् । इति विज्ञायते । यदवर्धत तद्वृत्रस्य वृत्रत्वम् । इति विज्ञायते ॥ १७ ॥

रात्रिनामान्युत्तराणि त्रयोविंशतिः । रात्रिः कस्मात् । प्ररमयति भूतानि नक्तञ्चारीणि । उपरमयतीतराणि ध्रुवीकरोति । रातेर्वा स्याद्दानकर्मणः । प्रदीयन्तेऽस्यामवश्यायाः ।

उषोनामान्युत्तराणि षोडश । उषाः कस्मात् । उच्छतीति सत्याः । रात्रेरपरः कालः । तस्या एषा भवति ॥ १८ ॥

इदं श्रेष्ठं ज्योतिषां ज्योतिरागाच्चित्रः प्रकेतो अजनिष्ट विभ्वा ।
यथा प्रसूता सवितुः सवायँ एवा रात्र्युषसे योनिमारैक् ॥

इदं श्रेष्ठं ज्योतिषां ज्योतिरागमत् । चित्रं प्रकेतनं प्रज्ञाततममजनिष्ट विभूततमम् । यथा प्रसूता सवितुः प्रसवाय रात्रिरादित्यस्यैवं रात्र्युषसे योनिमरिचत् स्थानम् । स्त्रीयोनिरभियुत एनां गर्भः ।

तस्या एषापरा भवति ॥ १९ ॥

---

१. RV. I. 32. 11.
२. Cf. BD. V. 166.
३. तद् C 4, Mi, W 1, W 2.
४. Cf. TS. II. 4. 12. 2. स इमाँल्लोकानवृणोत् । यदिमाँल्लोकानवृणोत् तद् वृत्रस्य वृत्रत्वम् ।
५. All the three quotations are untraced. The passage: दासपत्नी... विज्ञायते in quoted by SRV. I. 32. 11. p. i. 170; Cf. also I. 124. 10. p. i. 566.
६. ०विंशती BK, C 4, C 5, Kn, M 3, Mi, R 4, R 6, W 1, W 2, W 3
७. प्ररमयति......इतराणि is quoted by SRV. III. 34. 4. p. ii. 219.
८. Cf. BD. iii. 9.
९. षोलश C 3, C 5.
१०. Cf. BD. III. 9.
११. Cf. BD. iii. 8. Dawn is a *kalā* i. e. 16th portion of night.
१२. RV. I. 113. 1; SV. 2. 1099.
१३. The text seems to be corrupt. I propose to read उषाः for रात्रिः, this will make the line intelligible.
१४. इदं श्रेष्ठं...स्थानम् is quoted by SRV. I. 113. 1. p. i. 496.

रुशद्वत्सा रुशती श्वेत्यागादारैगु कृष्णा सदनान्यस्याः ।
समानबन्धू अमृते अनूची द्यावा वर्णं चरत आमिनाने ॥

रुशद्वत्सा सूर्यवत्सा । रुशदिति वर्णनाम[१] । रोचतेर्ज्वलतिकर्मणः[२] । सूर्यमस्या वत्समाह । साहचर्यात् । रसहरणाद्वा । रुशती श्वेत्यागात् । श्वेत्या श्वेततेः । अरिचत् कृष्णा सदनान्यस्याः कृष्णवर्णा रात्रिः । कृष्णं कृष्यतेः । निकृष्टो वर्णः । अथैने संस्तौति । समानबन्धू समानबन्धने । अमृते अमरणधर्माणौ । अनूची [अनूच्या-विति[५]] । इतीतरेतरमभिप्रेत्य । द्यावा वर्णं चरतः । ते एव द्यावौ । द्योतनात् । अपि वा द्यावा चरतस्तया [सह[६]] चरत इति स्यात् । आमिनाने [आमिन्वाने] । अन्योन्यस्याध्यात्मं कुर्वाणे[७] ।

अहर्नामान्युत्तराणि द्वादश । अहः कस्मात् । उपाहरन्त्यस्मिन् कर्माणि । तस्यैष निपातो भवति वैश्वानरीयायामृचि ॥ २० ॥

अहश्च कृष्णमहरर्जुनं च वि वर्तेते रजसी वेद्याभिः ।
वैश्वानरो जायमानो न राजावातिरज्ज्योतिषाग्निस्तमांसि[८] ॥

अहश्च कृष्णं रात्रिः शुक्लं चाहरर्जुनम् । विवर्तेते रजसी वेद्याभिर्वेदितव्याभिः[९] प्रवृत्तिभिः । वैश्वानरो जायमान इव । उद्यन्नादित्यः । सर्वेषां ज्योतिषां राजा । अवाहन्नग्निर्ज्योतिषा तमांसि ।

मेघनामान्युत्तराणि त्रिंशत् । मेघः कस्मात् । मेहतीति[१०] सतः । आ उपर उपल इत्येताभ्यां साधारणानि पर्वतनामभिः । उपर उपलो मेघो भवति । उपरमन्तेऽस्मिन्नभ्राणि । उपरता आप इति वा । तेषामेषा भवति ॥ २१ ॥

देवानां माने प्रथमा अतिष्ठन्कृन्तत्रादेषामुपरा उदायन् ।
त्रयस्तपन्ति पृथिवीमनूपा द्वा बृबूकं वहतः पुरीषम्[११] ॥

---

१. RV. I. 113. 2.

२. Cf. SRV. VI. 64. 1. p. ii. 865.

३. Cf. SRV. I. 92. 2. p. i. 410.

४. Cf. SRV. I. 35. 2; 123. 2. pp. i. 186, 557.

५. Omitted by BK, C 4, C 5, Kn, M 3, Mi, R 4, R 6, W 1, W 2, W 3.

६. Omitted by BK, C 4, C 5, Kn, M 3, Mi, R 4, R 6, W 1, W 2, W 3, and Durga.

७. The passage रुशद्वत्सा...कुर्वाणे is quoted by SRV. I. 113. 2. p. i. 497.

८. RV. VI. 9. 1.

९. विद्याभि० C 6.

१०. मेहयतीति C 4, W 1.

११. RV. X. 27. 23.

देवानां निर्माणे प्रथमा अतिष्ठन्माध्यमिका देवगणाः[1] । प्रथम इति मुख्यनाम । प्रतमो[2] भवति[3] । [कृन्तत्रमन्तरिक्षम् । विकर्तनं मेघानाम[4] ।] विकर्तनेन मेघानामुदकं जायते । त्रयस्तपन्ति पृथिवीमनूपाः । पर्जन्यो वायुरादित्यः शीतोष्णवर्षैरोषधीः पाचयन्ति । अनूपा अनुवपन्ति लोकान्त्स्वेन स्वेन कर्मणा । अयमपीतरोऽनूप एतस्मादेव । अनूप्यत उदकेन । अपि वान्वाविति स्यात् । यथा प्रागिति । तस्यानूप इति स्यात् । यथा प्राचीनमिति । द्वा बृबूकं वहतः पुरीषं । वाय्वादित्या उदकम् । बृबूकमित्युदकनाम । ब्रवीतेः [वा[4]] शब्दकर्मणः । भ्रंशतेर्वा । पुरीषं पृणातेः । पूरयतेर्वा[5] ॥ २२ ॥

वाङ्नामान्युत्तराणि सप्तपञ्चाशत् । वाक् कस्मात् । वचेः । तत्र सरस्वतीत्येतस्य नदीवद्देवतावच्च निगमा भवन्ति[6] । तद् यद्देवतावदुपरिष्टात्तद्व्याख्यास्यामः । अथैतन्नदीवत्[7] ॥ २३ ॥

इयं शुष्मेभिर्बिसखा इवारुजत्सानु गिरीणां तविषेभिरूर्मिभिः ।
पारावतघ्नीम[8]वसे सुवृक्तिभिः सरस्वतीमा विवासेम धीतिभिः[9] ।

इयं शुष्मैः शोषणैः । शुष्ममिति बलनाम । शोषयतीति सतः । बिसं बिस्यतेर्भेदनकर्मणः । वृद्धिकर्मणो वा । सानु संमुच्छ्रितं[10] भवति[11] । समुन्नुन्नमिति[12] वा । महद्भिरूर्मिभिः । पारावतघ्नीं पारावारघातिनीम्[13] । पारं परं भवति । अवारमवरम् । अवनाय सुप्रवृत्ताभिः[14] [शोभनाभिः[15]] स्तुतिभिः सरस्वतीं [नदीं[15]] कर्मभिः परिचरेम ।

उदकनामान्युत्तराण्येकशतम् । उदकं कस्मात् । उनत्तीति सतः ।

नदीनामान्युत्तराणि सप्तत्रिंशत् । नद्यः कस्मात् । नदना [इमा[15]] भवन्ति । शब्दवत्यः । बहुलमासां नैघण्टुकं[16] वृत्तम् । आश्चर्यमिव प्राधान्येन ।

तत्रेतिहासमाचक्षते[17] । विश्वामित्र ऋषिः सुदासः पैजवनस्य पुरोहितो बभूव ।

---

१. Cf. SRV. X. 27. 23. p. IV. 80.
२. प्रथमो C 5, M 3, Mi, W 1, W 2.
३. Cf. SRV. I. 123. 2. p. i. 557; VI. 72. 1. p. ii. 883.
४. Omitted by BK, C 4, C 5, Kn, M 3, Mi, R 4, R 6, W 1, W 2, W 3.
५. Cf. SRV. III. 22. 4. p. ii. 194; omitted along with पूरयतेर्वा by Durga.
६. Cf. SRV. I. 3. 12. p. i. 40; Cf. BD. ii. 135-136.
७. See N. 11. 25-27.
८. परावतघ्नीम॰ M 1.
९. RV. VI. 61. 2.
१०. समुद्धृतं C.
११. Quoted by SRV. I. 128. 3. p. i. 580; Cf. also II. 23. 7. p. ii. 65.
१२. समुन्ननमिति M 1, M 2, W 3; is omitted along with वा by C 3; समुन्नं नयतीति वा Durga.
१३. Quoted by SRV. VI. 61. 2. p. ii. 855.
१४. सुप्रवृक्ताभिः BK, C 4, C 5, Kn, M 3, Mi, R 4, R 6, W 1, W 2, W 3.
१५. Omitted by BK, C 4, C 5, Kn, M 3, Mi, R 4, R 6, W 1, W 2, W 3.
१६. नैकण्टुकं M 3.
१७. तत्रेदिहास॰ C 3.

विश्वामित्रः सर्वमित्रः । सर्वं संसृतम् । सुदाः कल्याणदानः । पैजवनः पिजवनस्य पुत्रः । पिजवनः पुनः स्पर्धनीयजवो वा । [1]अमिश्रीभावगतिर्वा । स वित्तं गृहीत्वा विपाट्छुतुद्र्योः सम्भेदमाययौ । अनुययुरितरे । स विश्वामित्रो नदीस्तुष्टाव । गाधा भवतेति । अपि द्विवत् । अपि बहुवत्[2] । तद् यद् द्विवदुपरिष्टात्[3]तद् व्याख्यास्यामः । अथैतद्बहुवत् ॥ २४ ॥

रमध्वं मे वचसे सोम्याय ऋतावरीरुप मुहूर्तमेवैः[4] ।
प्र सिन्धुमच्छा बृहती मनीषावस्युरह्वे कुशिकस्य सूनुः[5] ।

उपरमध्वं मे वचसे सोम्याय सोमसम्पादिने । ऋतावरीर्ऋतवत्यः । ऋतमित्युदकनाम । [6]प्रत्यृतं भवति । मुहूर्तमेवैरयनैरवनैर्वा । मुहूर्तो मुहुर्ऋतुः । [7]ऋतुरर्त्तेर्गतिकर्मणः । मुहुर्मूढ[8] इव कालः । यावदभीक्ष्णं चेति । अभीक्ष्णमभिक्षणं भवति । क्षणः क्षणोतेः । प्रक्ष्णुतः कालः । कालः कालयतेर्गतिकर्मणः । प्राभिह्वयामि सिन्धुं बृहत्या महत्या मनीषया मनस ईषया स्तुत्या प्रज्ञया वावनाय । कुशिकस्य सूनुः । कुशिको राजा बभूव[9] । क्रोशतेः शब्दकर्मणः । क्रंशतेर्वा स्यात्प्रकाशयति कर्मणः । साधु विक्रोशयिताऽर्थानामिति वा । नद्यः प्रत्यूचुः ॥ २५ ॥

इन्द्रो अस्माँ अरदद्वज्रबाहुरपाहन्वृत्रं परिधिं नदीनाम् ।
देवोऽनयत्सविता सुपाणिस्तस्य वयं प्रसवे याम उर्वीः[10] ॥

इन्द्रोऽस्मानरदद्वज्रबाहुः[11] । रदतिः खनतिकर्मा । अपाहन् वृत्रं परिधिं नदीनामिति व्याख्यातम् । देवोऽनयत्सविता । सुपाणिः कल्याणपाणिः । पाणिः पणायतेः[12] पूजाकर्मणः[13] । प्रगृह्य पाणी देवान् पूजयन्ति[14] । तस्य वयं प्रसवे याम उर्वीः[15] । उर्व्य[16] ऊर्णोतेः । वृणोतेरित्यौर्णवाभः[17] । प्रत्याख्यायान्तत आशुश्रुवुः ॥ २६ ॥

---

१. Cf. SRV. I. 63. 8. p. i. 313.

२. Cf. BD. IV. 106, 107.

३. N. 9. 39.

४. RV. III. 33. 5.

५. Cf. SRV. I. 2. 8. p. i. 3.

६. प्रसृतं C 3.

७. ऋतुः is omitted by C 5.

८. मूढ C 6, M 1, M 2.

९. Cf. SRV. III. 33. 5. p. ii. 243.

१०. RV. III. 33. 6.

११. बाहू BK, C 4, C 5, Kn, M 3, Mi, R 4, R 6, W 1, W 2, W 3.

१२. पणयते C 4, M 3.

१३. cf. SRV. I. 22. 5; III. 54. 11. pp. i. 115; ii. 309.

१४. The passage कल्याणपाणि…पूजयन्ति is omitted by C 4.

१५. cf. SRV. III. 33. 6. p. ii. 244.

१६. ऊर्व्यं BK, C 4, C 5, Kn, M 3, Mi, R 4, R 6, W 1, W 2, W 3.

१७. उर्व्य…त्यौर्णवाभः is omitted by Durga.

आ ते कारो शृणवामा वचांसि ययाथ दूरादनसा रथेन ।
नि ते नंसै पीप्यानेव योषा मर्यायेव कन्या शश्वचै ते ॥

आशृणवाम ते कारो वचनानि । याहि दूरादनसा च रथेन च निनमाम ते पाययमानेव योषा पुत्रम् । मर्यायेव कन्या परिष्वजनाय । निनमा इति वा ।

अश्वनामान्युत्तराणि षड्विंशतिः । तेषामष्टा उत्तराणि बहुवत् । अश्वः कस्मात् । अश्नुतेऽध्वानम् । महाशनो भवतीति वा । तत्र दधिक्रा इत्येतद् दधत् क्रामतीति वा । दधत् क्रन्दतीति वा । दधदाकारी भवतीति वा । तस्याश्ववद्देवतावच्च निगमा भवन्ति । तद् यद् देवतावदुपरिष्टात्तद् व्याख्यास्यामः । अथैतदश्ववत् ॥ २७॥

उत स्य वाजी क्षिपणिं तुरण्यति ग्रीवायां बद्धो अपि कक्ष आसनि ।
क्रतुं दधिक्रा अनु संतवीत्वत्पथामङ्कांस्यन्वापनीफणत् ॥

अपि स वाजी वेजनवान् । क्षेपणमनु तूर्णमश्नुतेऽध्वानम् । ग्रीवायां बद्धः । ग्रीवा गिरतेर्वा । गृणातेर्वा । गृह्णातेर्वा । अपि कक्ष आसनीति व्याख्यातम् । क्रतुं दधिक्राः कर्म वा प्रज्ञां वा । अनुसंतवीत्वत् । तनोतेः पूर्वया प्रकृत्या निगमः । पथामङ्कांसि पथां कुटिलानि । पन्थाः पततेर्वा । पद्यतेर्वा । पन्थतेर्वा । अङ्कोऽञ्चतेः । आपनीफणदिति फणतेश्चर्करीतवृत्तम् ॥

दशोत्तराण्यादिष्टोपयोजनानीत्याचक्षते साहचर्यज्ञानाय ।

ज्वलतिकर्माण उत्तरे धातव एकादश ।

तावन्त्येवोत्तराणि ज्वलतो नामधेयानि नामधेयानि ॥ २८ ॥

इति द्वितीयोऽध्यायः ।

---

१. RV. III. 33. 10.

२. cf. SRV. III. 33. 10. p. ii. 246.

३. cf. BD. ii. 56.

४.

५. RV. IV. 40. 4.

६. cf. SRV. IV. 40. 4. p. ii. 458.

७. The following passage is added after क्रतुं by C 5: वाजी क्षिपणिं तुरण्यति ग्रीवायां बद्धः ।

८. cf. SRV. I. 123. 8. p. i. 560.

[[1]अथ निर्वचनमो[2]घो रा[3]ज्ञो वि[4]द्या ह व अथातोऽनुक्रमिष्यामो वृक्षेर्वृक्षे तावां घास्तूनि र्य ई चकारायं सं शिङ्क्ते हिरण्यनामान्यार्ष्टिषेणो य[12]द्देवापिः [13]साधारणानि [14]स्वरादित्यो र[15]श्मिनामान्यति[16]ष्ठन्तीनां [17]द्वासपत्नी [18]रात्रिनामानीदं[19] श्रेष्ठं रु[20]शद्वत्साह[21]श्वं कृष्णं दे[22]वानां माने वा[23]ङ्नामानीयं[24] शुष्मेभि र[25]मध्वं म इन्द्रो[26] अस्मानाते[27] कारावुर्तस्य वाज्यष्टाविंशतिः ॥]

॥ इति निरुक्ते पूर्वषट्के द्वितीयोऽध्यायः समाप्तः ॥

Small figure on this page represents the corresponding section of the second chapter of the *Nirukta*.

॥ अथ तृतीयोऽध्यायः ॥

कर्मनामान्युत्तराणि षड्विंशतिः । कर्म कस्मात् । क्रियत इति सतः ।

अपत्यनामान्युत्तराणि पञ्चदश । अपत्यं कस्मात् । अपततं भवति । नानेन पततीति वा[1] । तद् यथा जनयितुः प्रजा[2] । एवमर्थीये ऋचा उदाहरिष्यामः ॥ १ ॥

परिषद्यं ह्यरणस्य रेक्णो नित्यस्य रायः पतयः स्याम ।
न शेषो अग्ने अन्यजातमस्त्यचेतानस्य मा पथो वि दुक्षः[3] ॥

परिहर्तव्यं हि नोपसर्तव्यम् । अरणस्य रेक्णः । अरणोऽपार्णो भवति । रेक्ण इति धननाम । रिच्यते प्रयतः । नित्यस्य रायः पतयः स्याम । पित्र्यस्येव धनस्य[4] । न शेषोऽग्ने अन्यजातमस्ति । शेष इत्यपत्यनाम । शिष्यते प्रयतः[5] । अचेतयमानस्य तत्प्रमत्तस्य भवति । मा नः पथो विदूदुष[6] इति ।

तस्योत्तरा भूयसे निर्वचनाय ॥ २ ॥

न हि ग्रभायारणः सुशेवोऽन्योदर्यो मनसा मन्तवा उ ।
अधा चिदोकः पुनरित्स एत्या नो वाज्यभीषाळेतु नव्यः[7] ॥

न हि ग्रहीतव्यो अरणः सुसुखतमोऽपि । अन्योदर्यो मनसापि न मन्तव्यः । ममायं [पुत्रः[8]] इति । अथ स ओकः पुनरेव तदेति यत[9] आगतो भवति । ओक इति निवासनामोच्यते । ऐतु नो वाजी वेजनवान् । अभिषहमाणः[10] सपत्नान् । नवजातः स एव पुत्र इति ।

अथैतां[11] दुहितृदायाद्य उदाहरन्ति । पुत्रदायाद्य इत्येके ॥ ३ ॥

---

१. cf. Manu. IX. 138; Viṣṇu. XV. 44.

२. cf. Manu. IX. 32, 35-41. The diametrically opposite view is given IX. 48-54. cf. also Vas. XVII. 6-9; 63-64; Ap. Dh. II. 13. 6-7; Ga. Dh. XVIII. 9-14.

३. RV. VII. 4. 7.

४. cf. SRV. VII. 4. 7. p. iii. 14.

५. cf. SRV. I. 93. 4; p. i. 418.

६. cf. SRV. VII. 4. 7. p. iii. 14.

७. RV. VII. 4. 8.

८. Omitted by BK, C 4, C 5, Kn, M 3, Mi, R 4, R 6, W 1, W 2, W 3.

९. यते BK, C 4, C 5, Kn, M 3, Mi, R 4, R 6, W 1, W 2, W 3.

१०. अभिषह्यमाण: C 4, C 5.

११. अथैनां Durga and S'ivadatta's edition. cf. BD. IV. 110-111.

शासद्वह्निर्दुहितुर्नप्त्यंगाद्विद्वाँ ऋतस्य दीधितिं सपर्यन्।
पिता यत्र दुहितुः सेकमृञ्जन्त्सं शग्म्येन मनसा दधन्वे[1] ॥

प्रशास्ति वोळ्हा[2] सन्तानकर्मणे दुहितुः पुत्रभावम्[3]। दुहिता[4] दुर्हिता। दूरे हितो[5]। दोग्धेर्वा। नप्तारमुपागमत्। दौहित्रं पौत्रमिति। विद्वान् प्रजननयज्ञस्य। रेतसो वा। अङ्गादङ्गात्संभूतस्य हृदयादधिजातस्य मातरि प्रत्यृतस्य। विधानं पूजयन्[6]। अविशेषेण मिथुनाः पुत्रा दायादा[7] इति। तदेतदृक्छ्लोकाभ्यामभ्युक्तम्।

अङ्गादङ्गात्संभवसि हृदयादधिजायसे।
आत्मा वै पुत्रनामासि स जीव शरदः शतम्[8] ॥ इति।

अविशेषेण पुत्राणां दायो भवति धर्मतः।
मिथुनानां विसर्गादौ मनुः स्वायंभुवोऽब्रवीत्[9] ॥

न दुहितर इत्येके।

तस्मात्पुमान् दायादोऽदायादा स्त्री[10]।

इति विज्ञायते।

तस्मात्स्त्रियं जातां परास्यन्ति न पुमांसम्[11]।

इति च।

स्त्रीणां दानविक्रयातिसर्गा विद्यन्ते न पुंसः। पुंसोऽपीत्येके। शौनःशेपे दर्शनात्। अभ्रातृमतीवाद इत्यपरम्।

[अमूर्या यन्ति जामयः सर्वा लोहितवाससः[12]]
अभ्रातर इव योषास्तिष्ठन्ति हतवर्त्मनः[13] ॥

---

१. RV. III. 31. 1. The Second hemistich is paraphrased by yāska in the last part of the fifth Section.

२. वोढा, C 1, C, 2, C 3, C, 6, M 1, M 2, R 1, R 2, R 5, S.

३. cf. BD. IV. 112.

४. Omitted by C 5.

५. cf. SRV. I. 34. 5. p. i. 182.

६. cf. SRV. III. 31. 1. p. ii. 226.

७. दायदा C 5.

८. S'B. XIV. 9. 4. 8, BU. VI. 4. 8; SVB. 1. 5. 17.

९. cf. Manu. IX. 130, 133, 139; Ba. II. 3. 14.

१०. The quotation is untraced. cf. Ms. 4. 6. 4; 4. 7. 9: यत्स्थालीं रिंचन्ति न दारुमयं तस्मात्पुमान् दायादः स्यदायादा। यत्स्थालीं परास्यन्ति न दारुमयं तस्मात् स्त्रियं जातां परास्यन्ति न पुमांसम्।

११. Durga gives the quotation in the following manner: अथ यत् स्थालीं परास्यन्ति हवनकर्मणो न तथा जुह्वति न दारुमयं परास्यन्ति हवनकर्मणः दारुमयेणैव जुह्वति तस्मात् स्त्रियं जातां परास्यन्ति परस्मै प्रयच्छन्ति न पुमांसम्।

१२. Omitted by BK, C 4, C 5, Kn, M 3, Mi, R 4, R 6, W 1, W 2, W 3; and Durga.

१३. cf. AV. 1. 17. 1.

अभ्रातृका इव योपास्तिष्ठन्ति सन्तानकर्मणे पिण्डदानाय हतवर्मानः[1]। इत्यभ्रातृकाया अनिर्वाह औपमिकः। तस्योत्तरा भूयसे निर्वचनाय ॥ ४ ॥

अभ्रातेव पुंस एति प्रतीची गर्तारुगिव सनये धनानाम् ।
जायेव पत्य उशती सुवासा उषा हस्रेव नि रिणीते अप्सः[2] ॥

अभ्रातृकेव पुंसः पितृनेत्यभिमुखी सन्तानकर्मणे पिण्डदानाय न[3] पतिम्। गर्तारोहिणीव धनलाभाय दाक्षिणाजी[4]। गर्तः सभास्थाणुः। गृणातेः। सत्यसङ्गरो[5] भवति। तं तत्र यापुत्रा यापतिका सारोहति । तां तत्राक्षेणाघ्नन्ति[6] । सा रिक्थं लभते[7] । श्मशानसंचयोऽपि गर्त उच्यते। गुरतेः। अपगूर्णो भवति। श्मशानं श्मशयनम्। श्म शरीरम्। शरीरं शृणातेः। शम्नातेर्वा। श्मश्रु लोम। श्मनि[8] श्रितं भवति। लोम लुनातेर्वा। लीयतेर्वा।

नोपरस्याविष्कुर्याद्[9] यदुपरस्याविष्कुर्याद् गर्तेष्ठाः स्यात्प्रमायुको यजमानः[10]।

इत्यपि निगमो भवति।

रथोऽपि गर्त उच्यते[11]। गृणातेः स्तुतिकर्मणः। स्तुततमं यानम्।

आ रोहथो वरुण मित्र गर्तम्[12] ।

इत्यपि निगमो भवति।

जायेव पत्ये कामयमाना सुवासा ऋतुकालेषूषा[13] हसनेव दन्तान्विवृणुते रूपाणीति। चतस्र उपमाः।

नाभ्रात्रीमुपयच्छेत तोकं ह्यस्य तद् भवति[14]।

इत्यभ्रातृकाया उपयमनप्रतिषेधः[15] प्रत्यक्षः । पितुश्च पुत्रभावः । पिता यत्र दुहितुरप्रत्ताया रेतःसेकं प्राजयति। संदधात्यात्मानं संगमेन मनसेति।

अथैतां जाम्या रिक्थप्रतिषेध उदाहरन्ति[16]। ज्येष्ठं पुत्रिकायां[17] इत्येके ॥ ५ ॥

---

१. cf. Manu. III. 11; Ya. I. 53.

२. RV. I. 124. 7.

३. Omitted by C 2, C 5, C 6, M 1, M 2, M 3, W 3.

४. दाक्षिणाय. BK, C 4, C 5, Kn, M 3, Mi, R 4, R 6, W 1, W 2, W 3. दाक्षिणाजा SRV.

५. ०सङ्करो W 2.

६. तत्राक्षैराघ्नन्ति C 1, C 2, C 3, C 6, M 1, M 2, R 1, R 2, R 5, S.

७. cf. SRV. I. 124. 7. p. i. 565.

८. श्मनि C 4.

९. ०विः कुर्या. C 1, C 2, C 3, C 6, M 1, M 2, R 1, R 2, R 5, S.

१०. The quotation in untraced.

११. cf. SRV. V. 62. 5. p. ii. 643.

१२. RV. V. 62. 8.

१३. उषा is omitted by C 5.

१४. The quotation is untraced.

१५. cf. Manu. III. 11; Ya. I. 53.

१६. cf. BD. IV. 111: रिक्थस्य दुहितुर्दानं नेत्यृचि प्रतिपिध्यते।

१७. cf. Manu. IX. 134.

न जामये तान्वो रिक्थमारैक् चकार गर्भं सनितुर्निधानम्।
यदी मातरो जनयन्त वह्निमन्यः कर्ता सुकृतोरन्य ऋन्धन्॥

न जामये भगिन्यै। जामिरन्येऽस्यां जनयन्ति जामपत्यम्। जमतेर्वा स्याद्गतिकर्मणः। निर्गमनप्राया भवति। तान्वं आत्मजः पुत्रः। रिक्थं प्रारिचत् प्रादात्। चकारैनां गर्भनिधानीम्। सनितुर्हस्तग्राहस्य। यदी मातरो जनयन्त। वह्निं पुत्रम्। अवह्निं च स्त्रियम्। अन्यतरः सन्तानकर्ता भवति पुमान्दायादः। अन्यतरोऽर्द्धयित्वा जामिः प्रदीयते परस्मै॥ ६॥

मनुष्यनामान्युत्तराणि पञ्चविंशतिः।

मनुष्याः कस्मात्। मत्वा कर्माणि सीव्यन्ति। मनस्यमानेन सृष्टाः। मनस्यतिः पुनर्मनस्वीभावे। मनोरपत्यम्। मनुषो वा।

तत्र पञ्चजना इत्येतस्य निगमा भवन्ति॥ ७॥

तदद्य वाचः प्रथमं मंसीय येनासुराँ अभि देवा असाम।
ऊर्जाद उत यज्ञियासः पञ्चजना मम होत्रं जुषध्वम्॥

तदद्यवाचः परमं मंसीय येनासुरानभिभवेम देवाः। असुरा असुरताः। स्थानेष्वस्ताः। स्थानेभ्य इति वा। अपि वासुरिति प्राणनाम। अस्तः शरीरे भवति। तेन तद्वन्तः।

सोर्देवानसृजत तत् सुराणां सुरत्वम्। असोरसुरानसृजत तदसुराणामसुरत्वम्।

इति विज्ञायते।

ऊर्जाद उत यज्ञियासः। अन्नादाश्च यज्ञियाश्च। ऊर्गित्यन्ननाम। ऊर्जयतीति

---

१. RV. III. 31. 2. cf. BD. i. 57, where it is quoted as an example of denial.

२. अजनिम्° M 3; अजैनम्° C 4, C 5, Mi, W 1, W 2.

३. °अपचम् C 5. cf. A B. 7. 3. 1.

४. तान्वा M 3, Mi.

५. cf. BD. ii. 113.

६. यदि ह C 1, C 3, M 1, M 2, R. cf. SRV. III. 31. 2. p. ii. 227.

७. अजनयन्त SRV. loc. cit.

८. cf. SRV. III. 31. 2; I. 123. 5; pp. ii. 227; i. 558. cf. अर्थो हि कन्या परकीय एव Sak. IV.

९. असुरा C 5,

१०. होरात्रं C 3, M 3.

११. RV. X. 53. 4.

१२. Cf. SRV. X. 53. 4. p. IV. 158.

१३. Cf. TB. ii. 3. 8. 2, 4. तेनासुनाऽसुरानसृजत तदसुराणामसुरत्वम्।

१४. यज्ञेयासः C 5.

सतः । पक्कं सुप्रवृक्णमिति वा । पञ्चजना मम होत्रं जुषध्वम् । गन्धर्वाः पितरो देवा असुरा रक्षांसीत्येके[1] । चत्वारो वर्णा निषादः पञ्चम इत्यौपमन्यवः । निषादः कस्मात् । निषदनो भवति । निषण्णमस्मिन्पापकमिति नैरुक्ताः ।[2] [3]

यत्पाञ्चजन्यया विशा[4] ।

पञ्चजनीनया[5] विशा । पञ्च पृक्ता संख्या । स्त्रीपुंनपुंसकेष्वविशिष्टा ।

बाहुनामान्युत्तराणि द्वादश । बाहुः कस्मात् । प्रबाधत आभ्यां कर्माणि ।

अङ्गुलिनामान्युत्तराणि द्वाविंशतिः । अङ्गुलयः कस्मात् । अग्रगामिन्यो भवन्तीति वा । अग्रगालिन्यो भवन्तीति वा । अग्रकारिण्यो भवन्तीति वा । [अग्रसारिण्यो भवन्तीति वा[6]] अङ्कना भवन्तीति वा । अञ्जना[7] भवन्तीति वा । अपि वाभ्यञ्जनादेव[8] स्युः । तासामेषा भवति ॥ ८ ॥

दशावनिभ्यो दशकक्ष्येभ्यो दशयोक्त्रेभ्यो दशयोजनेभ्यः ।
दशाभीशुभ्यो अर्चताजरेभ्यो दश धुरो दश युक्ता वहद्भ्यः[9] ॥

अवनयोऽङ्गुलयो भवन्ति । अवन्ति कर्माणि[10] । कक्ष्याः प्रकाशयन्ति कर्माणि । योक्त्राणि योजनानीति व्याख्यानम् । अभीशवोऽभ्यश्नुवते कर्माणि[11] । दश धुरो दश युक्ता वहद्भ्यः । धूर्धूर्वतेर्वधकर्मणः । इयमपीतरा धूरेतस्मादेव ।

विहन्ति[12] वहम्[13] । धारयतेर्वा[14] ।

कान्तिकर्माण उत्तरे धातवोऽष्टादश ।

अन्ननामान्युत्तराण्यष्टाविंशतिः । अन्नं कस्मात् । आनतं भूतेभ्यः । अत्तेर्वा ।

अत्तिकर्माण उत्तरे धातवो दश ।

---

१. Cf. BD. VII. 68; cf. AB. III. 31. 5.

२. Cf. BD. VII. 69—72; SRV. I. 89. 10; VIII. 32. 22; pp. i. 399; iii. 390.

३. Omitted by Durga. निपद्यतीति is added by C 1.

४. RV. VIII. 63. 7.

५. पञ्चजनीयया C 1, M 3.

६. Omitted by BK, C 4, C 5, Kn, M 3, Mi, R 4, R 6, W 1, W 2, W 3, & Durga.

७. अञ्जना BK, C 4, C 5, Kn, M 3, Mi, R 4, R 6, W 1, W 2, W 3.

८. वाभ्यञ्जनादेव॰. C 1, C 2, C 3, C 6, M 1, M 2, R 1, R 2, S, R. 5. Roth.

९. RV. X. 94. 7.

१०. Cf. SRV. I. 62. 10. p. i. 309.

११. Cf. SRV. I. 38. 12. p. i. 206.

१२. विहति C 3.

१३. वहे C 5.

१४. Cf. SRV. X. 94. 7. p. IV. 206.

बलनामान्युत्तराण्यष्टाविंशतिः । बलं कस्मात् । बलं भरं भवति । बिभर्तेः ।

धननामान्युत्तराण्यष्टाविंशतिरेव । धनं कस्मात् । धिनोतीति सतः ।

गोनामान्युत्तराणि नव ।

क्रुध्यतिकर्माण उत्तरे धातवो दश ।

क्रोधनामान्युत्तराण्येकादश ।

गतिकर्माण उत्तरे धातवो द्वाविंशशतम्[१] ।

क्षिप्रनामान्युत्तराणि षड्विंशतिः । क्षिप्रं कस्मात् । संक्षिप्तो विकर्षः ।

अन्तिकनामान्युत्तराण्येकादश । अन्तिकं कस्मात् । आनीतं भवति ।

संग्रामनामान्युत्तराणि षट्चत्वारिंशत् । संग्रामः कस्मात् । संगमनाद्वा । संगरणाद्वा । संगतौ ग्रामाविति वा ।

तत्र खल इत्येतस्य निगमा भवन्ति ॥ ९ ॥

अभी३ दमेकमेको अस्मि निष्षाळ्[२]भी द्वा किमु त्रयः करन्ति ।
खले न पर्षान्प्रति हन्मि भूरि किं मा निन्दन्ति शत्रवोऽनिन्द्राः[३] ॥

अभिभवा[४]मीदमेकमेकः । अस्मि निष्षहमाणः । सपत्नानभिभवामि । द्वौ किं मा त्रयः कुर्वन्ति । एक इता संख्या । द्वौ द्रुततरा संख्या । त्रयस्तीर्णतमा संख्या । चत्वारश्चलिततमा संख्या । अष्टावश्नोतेः । नव न वननीया । नावाप्ता[५] वा । दश दस्ता । दृष्टा[६]र्था वा । विंशतिर्द्विदशं[७]तः । शतं दशदशतः । सहस्रं सहस्वत् । अयुतं प्रयुतं नियुतं[८] तत्तदभ्यस्तम् ।

अर्बुदो मेघो भवति । अरणमम्बु । तद्दः । [अम्बुदो] अम्बुमद्भातीति वा । अम्बुमद्भवतीति वा । स यथा महान्बहुर्भवति वर्षंस्तदिवार्बुदम् । खले[११] न पर्षान्प्रति हन्मि भूरि । खल इव पर्षान् प्रतिहन्मि भूरि । खल इति संग्रामनाम । खलतेर्वा । स्खलतेर्वा । अयमपीतरः खल एतस्मादेव । समास्कन्नो भवति । किं मा निन्दन्ति शत्रवोऽनिन्द्राः । य इन्द्रं न विदुः[१२] । इन्द्रो ह्यहमस्मि । अनिन्द्रा इतर इति वा ।

---

१. द्वाविंशं शतम् C 1, C 2, C 3, C 6, M 1, M 2, R 1, R 2, R 5, S.

२. निःषाळ० C 6, M 1; निःषाट् C 3; निःषालः C 4.

३. RV. X. 48. 7; cf. BD. I. 49.

४. Cf. SRV. X. 48. 7. p. IV. 146.

५. नावाप्ता C 6

६. दिष्टार्था C 3.

७. Omitted by C 5.

८. नियुतं. C 1, C 2, C 3, C 6, M 1, M 2, R 1, R 2, R 5, S.

९. अयुतं C 1, C 2, C 3, C 6, M 1, M 2, R 1, R 2, R 5, S.

१०. Omitted by BK, C 4, C 5, Kn, M 3, Mi. R 4, R 6, W 1, W 2, W 3. अम्बुमद्भातीति is omitted by Durga;

११. खलेन Roth.

१२. विविदुः C 1, C 2, C 3, C 6, M 1, M 2, R 1, R 2, R 6, S.

व्याप्तिकर्माण उत्तरे धातवो दश । तत्र द्वे नामनी आक्षाण आश्नुवानः । आपान आप्नुवानः ।

वधकर्माण उत्तरे धातवस्त्रयस्त्रिंशत् । तत्र वियात इत्येतद् वियातयत इति वा । वियातयेति वा ।

आखण्डल प्र हूयसे[1] ।

आखण्डयितः । [खण्डं खण्डयतेः[2]] ।

तळिदित्यन्तिकवधयोः[3] संसृष्टकर्म । ताळयतीति[4] सतः ॥ १० ॥

त्वया वयं सुवृधा ब्रह्मणस्पते स्पार्हा वसु मनुष्या ददीमहि ।
या नो दूरे तळितो या अरातयोऽभि सन्ति जम्भया ता अनप्नसः[5] ॥

त्वया वयं सुवर्धयित्रा ब्रह्मणस्पते स्पृहणीयानि वसूनि मनुष्येभ्य आददीमहि । याश्च नो दूरे तळितो याश्चान्तिके । अरातयोऽदानकर्माणो वा । अदानप्रज्ञा वा । जम्भय ता अनप्नसः । अप्न इति रूपनाम[6] । आप्नोतीति सतः ।

विद्युत्तळिद्भवतीति शाकपूणिः । सा ह्यवताळयति । दूराच्च दृश्यते । अपि त्विदमन्तिकनामैवाभिप्रेतं स्यात् ।

दूरे चित्सन्तळिदिवाति रोचसे[7] ।

दूरेऽपि सन्नन्तिक इव संदृश्यस[8] इति ।

वज्रनामान्युत्तराण्यष्टादश । वज्रः कस्मात् । वर्जयतीति[9] सतः । तत्र कुत्स इत्येतत् कृन्ततेः । ऋषिः कुत्सो भवति । कर्ता स्तोमानामित्यौपमन्यवः । अथाप्यस्य[10] वधकर्मैव भवति । तत्सख इन्द्रः शुष्णं जघानेति[11] ।

ऐश्वर्यकर्माण उत्तरे धातवश्चत्वारः ॥

ईश्वरनामान्युत्तराणि चत्वारि । तत्रेन इत्येतत् सनित ऐश्वर्येणेति वा । सनितमनेनैश्वर्यमिति वा ॥ ११ ॥

यत्रा सुपर्णा अमृतस्य भागमनिमेषं विदथाभि स्वरन्ति ।
इनो विश्वस्य भुवनस्य गोपाः स मा धीरः पाकमत्रा विवेश[12] ॥

---

१. RV. VIII. 17. 12; AV. 20. 5. 6. SV. 2. 76.

२. Omitted by BK, C 4, C 5, Kn, M 3, Mi, R 4, R 6, W 1, W 2, W 3, Durga.

३. तडिदि॰ C 1, C 2, C 3, C 6, M 1, M 2, R 1, R 2, R 5, S.

४. ताडयतीति. C 1, C 2, C 3, C 6, M 1, M 2, R 1, R 2, R 5, S.

५. RV. II. 23. 9.

६. Cf. SRV. II. 23. 9. p. ii. 66.

७. RV. I. 94. 7.

८. Cf. SRV. I. 94. 7. p. i. 423.

९. वज्रयतीति C 4, C 5, M 3, Mi, W 1.

१०. अत्रा॰ C 1, C 6 M 1, M 2.

११. Cf. SRV. I. 11. 7. p. i. 78.

१२. RV. I. 164. 21; cf. AV. 9. 9. 22.

यत्र [सुपर्णाः] सुपतना आदित्यरश्मयः । अमृतस्य भागमुदकस्य । अनिमिषन्तो वेदनेनाभिस्वरन्तीति वा । अभिप्रयन्तीति वा । ईश्वरः सर्वेषां भूतानां गोपायितादित्यः । स मा धीरः पाकमत्रा विवेशेति । धीरो धीमान् । पाकः पक्तव्यो भवति[3] ।

विपक्वप्रज्ञ आदित्यः ।

इत्युपनिषद्वर्णो भवति । इत्यधिदैवतम् ।

अथाध्यात्मम् । यत्र [सुपर्णाः] सुपतनानीन्द्रियाणि । अमृतस्य भागं ज्ञानस्य । अनिमिषन्तो वेदनेनाभिस्वरन्तीति वा । अभिप्रयन्तीति वा । ईश्वरः सर्वेषामिन्द्रियाणां गोपायितात्मा । स मा धीरः पाकमत्रा विवेशेति । धीरो धीमान् । पाकः पक्तव्यो भवति । विपक्वप्रज्ञ[6] आत्मा । इत्यात्मगतिमाचष्टे ॥ १२ ॥

बहुनामान्युत्तराणि द्वादश । बहुः कस्मात् । प्रभवतीति सतः ॥

ह्रस्वनामान्युत्तराण्येकादश । ह्रस्वो ह्रसतेः ।

महन्नामान्युत्तराणि पञ्चविंशतिः । महान् कस्मात् । मानेनान्याञ्जहातीति शाकपूणिः । मंहनीयो भवतीति वा । बहु ववक्षिथ विवक्षस इत्येते वक्तेर्वा वहतेर्वा साभ्यासात् ।

गृहनामान्युत्तराणि द्वाविंशतिः । गृहाः कस्मात् । गृह्णन्तीति सताम् ।

परिचरणकर्माण उत्तरे धातवो दश ।

सुखनामान्युत्तराणि विंशतिः । सुखं कस्मात् । सुहितं खेभ्यः । खं पुनः खनतेः ।

रूपनामान्युत्तराणि षोडश । रूपं रोचतेः ।

प्रशस्यनामान्युत्तराणि दश ।

प्रज्ञानामान्युत्तराण्येकादश ।

सत्यनामान्युत्तराणि षट् । सत्यं कस्मात् । सत्सु तायते । सत्प्रभवं भवतीति वा ।

अष्टा उत्तराणि पदानि पश्यतिकर्माण [उत्तरे[10]] धातवश्चायतिप्रभृतीनि च । नामान्यामिश्राणि ।

नवोत्तराणि पदानि[11] सर्वपदसमाम्नानाय ।

---

१. Omitted by BK, C 4, C 5, Kn, M 3, Mi, R 4, R 6, W 1, W 2, W 3.

२. Cf. SRV. I. 164. 21. p. i. 705.

३. Cf. SRV. I. 31. 14; 129. 1; pp. i. 163, 583.

४. The quotation is untraced.

५. अनिमिषन्ति BK, C 4, C 5, Kn, M 3, Mi, R 4, R 6, W 1, W 2, W 3.

६. ०प्रज्ञा M 3.

७. मांहनीयो M 3.

८. Cf. SRV. V. 30. 1. p. ii. 551.

९. प्रशंस्य Mi.

१०. Omitted by BK, C 4, C 5, Kn, M 3, Mi, R 4, R 6, W 1, W 2, W 3; and Durga.

११. Cf. SRV. X. 50. 5. p. iv. 152: तथापि हिकं नुकमित्यादीनि नवोत्तराणि पदानीत्युक्तान्यास्काचार्यः ।

अथात उपमाः। यदतत्तत्सदृशमिति गार्ग्यः। तदासां कर्म। ज्यायसा वा गुणेन प्रख्याततमेन वा कनीयांसं वाप्रख्यातं वोपमिमीते। अथापि कनीयसा ज्यायांसम्॥ १३॥

तनूत्यजेव तस्करा वनर्गू रशनाभिर्दशभिरभ्यधीताम्[1]॥

तनूत्यक् तनूत्यक्ता। वनर्गू वनगामिनौ। अग्निमन्थनौ बाहू तस्कराभ्याम्[2]उपमिमीते। तस्करस्तत्करोति [तत्करो भवति[3]] यत्[4]पापकमिति नैरुक्ताः। तनोतेर्वा स्यात्। सन्ततकर्मा भवति। अहोरात्रकर्मा वा। रशनाभिर्दशभिर्[5]अभ्यधीताम्। [अभ्यधीनामिति] अभ्यधाताम्। ज्यायांस्तत्र गुणोऽभिप्रेतः॥ १४॥

कुह स्विद् दोषा कुह वस्तोरश्विना कुहाभिपित्वं करतः कुहोषतुः।
को वां शयुत्रा विधवेव देवरं मर्यं न योषा कृणुते सधस्थ आ[6]॥

क्व स्विद्रात्रौ भवथः क्व दिवा। क्वाभिप्राप्तिं कुरुथः। क्व वसथः। को वां शयने विधवेव देवरम्। [देवरः कस्मात्। द्वितीयो वर उच्यते] । विधवा विधातृका भवति। विधवनाद्वा। विधावनाद्वेति[7] चर्मशिराः[8]। अपि वा धव इति मनुष्यनाम। तद्वियोगाद्विधवा। देवरो दीव्यतिकर्मा। मर्यो मनुष्यो मरणधर्मा। योषा यौतेः। आकुरुते सधस्थाने[9]।

अथ निपाताः पुरस्तादेव व्याख्याताः। यथेति कर्मोपमा।

यथा वातो यथा वनं यथा समुद्र एजति[10, 11]॥

भ्राजन्तो अग्नयो यथा[12]॥

आत्मा यक्ष्मस्य नश्यति पुरा जीवगृभो यथा[13]॥

आत्माततेर्वा। आप्तेर्वा। अपि वाप्त इव स्यात्। यावद् व्याप्तिभूत इति।

अग्निर्न ये भ्राजसा रुक्मवक्षसः[14]।

---

१. RV. X. 4. 6.

२. Cf. SRV. X. 4. 6. p. iv. 9.

३. Omitted by BK, C 4, C 5, Kn, M 3, Mi, R 4, R 6, W 1, W 2, W 3; and Durga.

४. यतः करोति पापकमिति Durga.

५. Omitted by BK, C 4, C 5, Kn, M 3, Mi, R 4, R 6, W 1, W 2, W 3; and Durga.

६. RV. X. 40. 2.

७. विधवनाद्वेति S'ivadatta's ed.

८. प्रचर्मशिराः S'ivadatta's ed.

९. सह०. C 1, C 2, C 3, C 6, M 1, M 2, R 1, R 2, R 5, S. and Roth's edition.

१०. Cf. SRV. X. 40. 2. p. iv. 121.

११. RV. V. 78. 8.

१२. RV. I. 50. 3; AV. 13. 2. 18; 20. 47. 15; VS. 8. 40.

१३. RV. X. 97. 11; VS. 12. 85.

१४. RV. X. 78. 2. According to Durga some Mss. do not read the quotation thinking that *na* is already explained: दुर्मदासो न सुरायाम् see N. 1. 4.

अग्निरिव ये [मरुतो भ्राजमाना रोचिष्णूरस्का[1]] भ्राजस्वन्तो रुक्मवक्षसः ॥ १५ ॥

चतुरश्चिद्ददमानाद्बिभीयादा निधातोः ।
न दुरुक्ताय स्पृहयेत्[2] ॥

चतुरश्चिद्[3] [अक्षान्[4]] धारयत इति । तद्यथा कितवाद्बिभीयादेवमेव दुरुक्ताद्बिभीयात् । न दुरुक्ताय स्पृहयेत् कदाचित् ।

आ इत्याकार उपसर्गः पुरस्तादेव व्याख्यातः । अथाप्युपमार्थे दृश्यते ।

जार आ भगम्[5] ।

जार इव भगम् । आदित्योऽत्र जार उच्यते । रात्रेर्जरयिता[6] । स एव भासाम् । तथापि निगमो भवति ।

स्वसुर्जारः[7] शृणोतु नः[8] । इति

उषसमस्य स्वसारमाह साहचर्यात् । रसहरणाद्वा । अपि त्वयं मनुष्यजार एवाभिप्रेतः[9] स्यात् । स्त्रीभगस्तथा स्यात् । भजतेः ।

मेष इति भूतोपमा ।

मेषो भूतो ३ऽभि यन्नयः[10] ।

मेषो मिषतेः । तथा पशुः पश्यतेः[11] ।

अग्निरिति रूपोपमा ।

हिरण्यरूपः स हिरण्यसंदृगपां नपात्सेदु हिरण्यवर्णः[12] ।

हिरण्यवर्णस्येवास्य रूपम् ।

था इति च ।

तं प्रत्नथा[13] पूर्वथा विश्वथेमथा[14] ।

प्रत्न[15] इव पूर्व इव विश्व इवेम इवेति । अयमेततरोऽमुष्मात् । असावस्ततरोऽस्मात् । अमुथा यथासाविति व्याख्यातम् ।

वदिति सिद्धोपमा ।

---

१. Omitted by BK, C 4, C 5, Kn, M 3, Mi, R 4, R 6, W 1, W 2, W 3.

२. RV. I. 41. 9.

३. चिद् is omitted by Kn. and Sāyana.

४. Cf. SRV. I. 41. 9. p. i. 217: चतुरोऽक्षान्धारयत...स्पृहयेत् ।

५. Fragment of RV. X. 11. 6; AV. 18. 1. 23.

६. Cf. PMbh. जरयन्तीति जाराः । जीर्यन्ति तैर्जाराः । vol. II. p. 147.

७. जार C 4, M 3.

८. RV. VI. 55. 5.

९. एवाभिप्रेतं W 2; ०प्रेत C 4, M 3.

१०. RV. VIII. 2. 40.

११. Cf. SB. VI. 2. 1. 4: यदपश्यत्तस्मादेते पशवस्तं श्वेतमपश्यत्तस्माद्वेवैते पशवः । Weber's edition p. 507.

१२. RV. II. 35. 10.

१३. प्रत्नथा W 1.

१४. RV. V. 44. 1; VS. 7. 12.

१५. प्रत्न W 1.

ब्राह्मणवद्वृषलवत् ।

ब्राह्मणा इव वृषला इवेति । [वृषलो वृषशीलो भवति । वृषाशीलो वा] ॥ १६ ॥

प्रियमेधवदत्रिवज्जातवेदो विरूपवत् ।
अङ्गिरस्वन्महिव्रत प्रस्कण्वस्य श्रुधी हवम् ॥

प्रियमेधः । प्रिया अस्य मेधा । यथैतेषामृषीणामेवं प्रस्कण्वस्य शृणु ह्वानम् । प्रस्कण्वः कण्वस्य पुत्रः । कण्वप्रभवः । यथा प्राग्रम् । अर्चिषि भृगुः संबभूव । भृगुर्भृज्यमानो न देहे । अङ्गारेष्वङ्गिराः । अङ्गारा अङ्कनाः [अञ्चनाः] । अत्रैव तृतीयमृच्छतेत्यूचुः । तस्मादत्रिः । न त्रयं इति । विखननाद्वैखानसः । भरणाद्भारद्वाजः । विरूपो नानारूपः । महिव्रतो महाव्रत इति ॥ १७ ॥

अथ लुप्तोपमान्यर्थोपमानीत्याचक्षते । सिंहो व्याघ्र इति पूजायाम् । श्वा काक इति कुत्सायाम् । काक इति शब्दानुकृतिः । तदिदं शकुनिषु बहुलम् । न शब्दानुकृतिर्विद्यत इत्यौपमन्यवः । काकोऽपकालयितव्यो भवति । तित्तिरिस्तरणात् । तिलमात्रचित्र इति वा । कपिञ्जलः कपिरिव जीर्णः । कपिरिव जवते । ईषत्पिङ्गलो वा । कमनीयं शब्दं पिञ्जयतीति वा । श्वा शुयायी । शवतेर्वा स्याद्गतिकर्मणः । श्वसितेर्वा । सिंहः सहनात् । हिंसेर्वा स्याद् विपरीतस्य । संपूर्वस्य वा हन्तेः । संहाय हन्तीति वा व्याघ्रो व्याघ्राणात् । व्यादाय हन्तीति वा ॥ १८ ॥

अर्चतिकर्माण उत्तरे धातवश्चतुश्चत्वारिंशत् ।

मेधाविनामान्युत्तराणि चतुर्विंशतिः । मेधावी कस्मात् । मेधया तद्वान्भवति । मेधा मतौ धीयते ।

स्तोतृनामान्युत्तराणि त्रयोदश । स्तोता स्तवनात् ।

---

१. The quotation is untraced. Mss. of the longer recension do not accent the passage.

२. Omitted by BK, C 4, C 5, Kn, M 3, Mi, R 4, R 6, W 1, W 2, W 3; and Durga.

३. RV. I. 45. 3.

४. Cf. SRV. I. 139. 9. p. i. 623.

५. Cf. SRV. I. 44. 6. p. i. 225.

६. Cf. SRV. I. 45. 3. p. i. 229; cf. BD. V. 99.

७. Cf. AB. iii. 34: येऽङ्गारा आसंस्तेऽङ्गिरसोऽभवन् । Cf. SRV. I. 1. 6; 127. 2; X. 62. 5; 67. 2. pp. i. 27, 574; IV. 186, 206.

८. Omitted by BK, C 4, C 5, Kn, M 3, Mi, R 4, R 6, W 1, W 2, W 3; and Durga.

९. Cf. SRV. I. 139. 9. p. i. 623.

१०. °द्वैसानसः W 1.

११. Cf. SRV. I. 45. 3. p. i. 229.

१२. हिंसेर्वा...विपरीतस्य is omitted by Durga. Cf. PMbh. हिंसेः सिंहः Vol. II. p. 87.

यज्ञनामान्युत्तराणि पञ्चदश। यज्ञः कस्मात्। प्रख्यातं यजति कर्मेति नैरुक्ताः। याच्ञो भवतीति वा। यजुरुन्नो भवतीति वा। बहुकृष्णाजिन इत्यौपमन्यवः। यजूंष्येनं नयन्तीति वा।

ऋत्विङ्नामान्युत्तराण्यष्टौ। ऋत्विक् कस्मात्। ईरणः। ऋग्यष्टा भवतीति शाकपूणिः। ऋतुयाजी भवतीति वा।

याच्ञाकर्माण उत्तरे धातवः सप्तदश।

दानकर्माण उत्तरे धातवो दश।

अध्येषणाकर्माण उत्तरे धातवश्चत्वारः।

स्वपितिम्रस्तीति द्वौ स्वपितिकर्माणौ।

कूपनामान्युत्तराणि चतुर्दश[1]। कूपः कस्मात्। कु पानं भवति। कुप्यतेर्वा।

स्तेननामान्युत्तराणि चतुर्दश। स्तेनः कस्मात्। संस्त्यानमस्मिन्पापकमिति नैरुक्ताः।

निर्णीतान्तर्हितनामधेयान्युत्तराणि षट्। [निर्णीतं कस्मात्। निर्णिक्तं भवति[2]]

दूरनामान्युत्तराणि पञ्च। दूरं कस्मात्। द्रुतं भवति। दुरयं वा।

पुराणनामान्युत्तराणि षट्। पुराणं कस्मात्। पुरा नवं भवति।

नवनामान्युत्तराणि षळेव। नवं कस्मात्। आनीतं भवति॥ १९॥

द्विश उत्तराणि नामानि षड्विंशतिः। प्रपित्वेऽभीक इत्यासन्नस्य[3]। प्रपित्वे प्राप्ते। अभीकेऽभ्यक्ते[4]।

आपित्वे नः प्रपित्वे तूयमा गहि[5]।
अभीके चिदुलोककृत्[6]।

इत्यपि निगमौ भवतः।

दभ्रमर्भकमित्यल्पस्य[7]। दभ्रं दभ्नोतेः[8]। सुदम्भं भवति। अर्भकमवहृतं भवति।

उपोप मे परा मृश मा मे दभ्राणि मन्यथाः[9]।
नमो महद्भ्यो नमो अर्भकेभ्यः[10]।

1. चतुर्दशैव Roth's and S'ivadatta's edition.
2. Omitted by BK, C 4, C 5, Ku, M 3, Mi, R 4, R 6, W 1, W 2, W 3.
3. Cf. SRV. I. 126. 3. p. i. 571.
4. Cf. SRV. I. 104. 1. p. i. 457.
5. RV. VIII. 4. 3; SV. 1. 252; 2. 1071
6. RV. X. 133. 1; AV. 20. 95. 2; SV. 2. 1151.
7. Cf. SRV. I. 31. 6. p. i. 160.
8. दभ्नोते: C 5, M 3, Mi.
9. RV. I. 126. 7; cf. BD. IV. 3.
10. RV. I. 27. 13; cf. VS. 16. 26.

इत्यपि निगमौ भवतः ।

तिरः सत इति प्राप्तस्य[1] । तिरस्तीर्णं भवति । सतः संसृतं भवति[2] ।

> तिरश्चिदर्यया परि वर्तिर्यातमदाभ्या[3] ।
> पात्रेव भिन्दन्सत एति रक्षसः[4] ॥

इत्यपि निगमौ भवतः ।

त्वो नेम इत्यर्धस्य[5] । त्वोऽपततः । नेमोऽपनीतः । अर्धं हरतेर्विपरीतात् । धारयते र्वा स्यात् । उद्धृतं भवति । ऋध्नोते र्वा स्यात् । ऋद्धतमो[6] विभागः ।

> पीयति त्वो अनु त्वो गृणाति[7] ।

> नेमे देवा नेमेऽसुराः[8] ।

इत्यपि निगमौ भवतः ।

ऋक्षाः स्तृभिरिति[9] नक्षत्राणाम्[10] । नक्षत्राणि नक्षतेर्गतिकर्मणः[11] ।

> नेमानि क्षत्राणि[12]

इति च ब्राह्मणम्[13] । ऋक्षा उदीर्णानीव ख्यायन्ते । स्तृभिस्तीर्णानीव ख्यायन्ते ।

> अमी य ऋक्षा निहितास उच्चा[14] ।
> पश्यन्तो द्यामिव स्तृभिः[15] ।

इत्यपि निगमौ भवतः ।

वम्रीभिरुपजिह्विका इति सीमिकानाम् । वम्र्यो वमनात् । सीमिका स्यमनात् । उपजिह्विका उपजिघ्र्यः ।

---

१. अप्रासस्य is given as a variant by Durga.

२. Cf. SRV. VI. 75. 9; VII. 104. 21.

३. RV. V. 75. 7.

४. RV. VII. 104. 21; AV. 8. 4. 21.

५. Cf. SRV. I. 72. 4; 147. 2; V. 61. 8; VI. 33. 5. pp. i. 340, 648; ii. 639, 777.

६. ऋद्धमो S'ivadatta's edition.

७. RV. I. 147. 2; VS. 12. 42.

८. Cf. MS. I. 11. 9.

देवाश्च वा असुराश्चास्पर्धन्त नेमे देवा आसन्नेमेऽसुराः ।

९. Cf. SRV. I. 24. 10. p. i. 132.

१०. Cf. SRV. I. 166. 11. p. i. 728.

११. Cf. Tait. B. I. 5. 2. 5, 6: अमुं स लोकं नक्षते । तन्नक्षत्राणां नक्षत्रत्वम् । देवगृहा वै नक्षत्राणि ।......यानि वा इमानि पृथिव्याश्चित्राणि तानि नक्षत्राणि ।

१२. Quotation is untraced. Cf. Tait. Br. II. 7. 18. 3. न वा इमानि क्षत्राण्यभूवन्निति । तन्नक्षत्राणां नक्षत्रत्वम् ।

१३. Cf. SRV. I. 50. 2. p. i. 248.

१४. RV. I. 24. 10.

१५. RV. IV. 7. 3.

[वम्रीभिः पुत्रमग्रुवो अदानम्]
यदत्त्युपजिह्विका यद्वम्रो अतिसर्पति[2] ।

इत्यपि निगमो भवति [निगमौ भवतः[3]]
ऊर्दरं कृदरमित्यावपनस्य । ऊर्दरमुद्दीर्णं भवति । ऊर्जं दीर्णं वा ।

तमूर्दरं न पृणता यवेन[4] ।

इत्यपि निगमो भवति । तमूर्दरमिव पूरयति यवेन । कृदरं कृतदरं भवति ।

समिद्धो अञ्जन् कृदरं मतीनाम्[5] ।

इत्यपि निगमो भवति ॥ २० ॥
रम्भः पिनाकमिति दण्डस्य । रम्भ आरभन्त एनम् ।

आ त्वा रम्भं न जिव्रयो ररम्भ[6] ।

इत्यपि निगमो भवति । आरभामहे त्वा जीर्णा इव दण्डम्[7] ।
पिनाकं प्रतिपिनष्ट्यनेन

कृत्तिवासाः पिनाकहस्तोऽवततधन्वा[8] ।

इत्यपि निगमो भवति ।
मेना ग्ना इति स्त्रीणाम्[9] । स्त्रियः स्त्यायतेरपत्रपणकर्मणः[10] । मेना मानयन्त्येनाः[11] । ग्ना गच्छन्त्येनाः[12] ।

अमेनाँश्चिज्जनिवतश्चकर्थ[13] ।

ग्नास्त्वाकृन्तन्नपसोऽतन्वत[14] ।

इत्यपि निगमौ भवतः ।
शेपो वैतस इति पुंस्प्रजननस्य[15] । शेपः शपतेः स्पृशतिकर्मणः । वैतसो वितस्तं भवति ।

---

१. RV. IV. 19. 9. It is omitted by BK, C 4, C 5, Kn, M 3, Mi, R 4, R 6, W 1, W 2, W 3, and Durga.

२. RV. VIII. 102. 21; VS. 11. 24.

३. निगमौ भवतः is read by C 1, C 2, C 3, M 1, M 2, R 1, R 2, R 5, S. and Roth.

४. RV. II. 14. 11.

५. VS. 29. 1.

६. RV. VIII. 45. 20.

७. Cf. SRV. VIII. 45. 20. p. iii. 432.

८. KS. 9. 7; cf. VS. 3. 61.; S'B. 2. 6. 2. 7; TS. 1. 8. 6. 2.

९. Cf. SRV. I. 51. 13; I. 161. 4; IV. 34. 7; V. 43. 6. pp. i. 260, 679; ii. 415, 558.

१०. स्त्रियः...कर्मणः is omitted in the passage quoted by SRV. I. 15, 3. 62. 7. pp. i. 93, 308; cf. also I. I. 51. 13. p. i. 260. Cf. PMbh. स्त्यायतेरेव स्त्री......स्त्यायत्यस्यां गर्भ इति । Vol. I. p. 245, 246.

११. Quoted by SRV. I. 51. 13. p. i. 260.

१२. Quoted by SRV. I. 15. 3. p. i. 93.

१३. RV. V. 31. 2.

१४. MS. 1. 9. 4: 134. 8; KS. 9. 9.

१५. Cf. SRV. IX. 113. 4; X. 95. 4. pp. iii, 829; IV. 310.

यस्यामुशन्तः प्रहराम शेपम्[1] ।
त्रिः स्म माह्नः श्नथयो वैतसेन[2] ।

इत्यपि निगमौ भवतः ।

अयैनेत्युपदेशस्य ।

अया ते अग्ने समिधा विधेम[3] । इति स्त्रियाः ।
एना वो अग्निम्[4] । इति नपुंसकस्य ।
एना पत्या तन्वं संसृजस्व[5] । इति पुंसः ।

सिषक्तु[6] सचत इति सेवमानस्य[7] ।

स नः सिषक्तु यस्तुरः[8] । स नः सेवतां यस्तुरः ।
सचस्वा नः स्वस्तये[9] । सेवस्व नः स्वस्तये[10] ।

स्वस्तीत्यविनाशन[11]नाम । अस्तिरभिपूजितः । सु[12] अस्तीति ।
भ्यसते रेजत इति भयवेपन[13]योः ।

यस्य शुष्माद्रोदसी अभ्यसेताम्[14] ।
रेजते अग्ने पृथिवी मखेभ्यः[15] ।

इत्यपि निग[16]मौ भवतः ।

द्यावापृथिवीनामधेयान्युत्तराणि चतुर्विंशतिः ।

तयोरेषा भवति ॥ २१ ॥

---

१. RV. X. 85. 37; cf. AV. 14. 2. 38.

२. RV. X. 95. 5.

३. RV. IV. 4. 15.

४. RV. VII. 16. 1; SV. 1. 45; 2. 99; VS. 15. 32.

५. RV. X. 85. 27; cf. AV. 14. 1. 21.

६. सिषक्ति BK, C 4, C 5, Kn, M 3, Mi, R 4, R 6, W 1, W 2, W 3.

७. Cf. SRV. I. 18. 2; 38. 8. pp. i 104, 205.

८. RV. I. 18. 2; VS. 3. 29.

९. RV. I. 1, 9; VS. 3. 24.

१०. Cf. SRV. VIII, 5. 2. p. iii. 255.

११. ०विनाशि. Roth's edition. Durga gives विनाश as a Variant.

१२. स्वस्तीति C 1, C 2, C 3, C 6, M 1, M 2, R 1, R 2, R 5, S; & Roth. Cf. SRV. VIII. 1. 1. p. iii. 6; cf. also I. 35. 1; 89. 6.

१३. Cf. SRV. I. 31. 3; 87. 3; II. 12. 1; pp. i. 159, 390; ii. 32.

१४. RV II. 12. 1; AV. 20. 34. 1.

१५. RV. VI. 66. 9.

१६. निगमो Roth's edition.

कतरा पूर्वा कतरापरायोः कथाजाते कवयः को विवेद।
विश्वं त्मना बिभृतो यद्ध नाम वि वर्तेते अहनी चक्रियेव[1]॥

कतरा पूर्वा कतरापरैनयोः। कथं जाते। कवयः क एने विजानाति। सर्वमात्मना बिभृतो यद्ध। एनयोः कर्म। विवर्तेते चैनयोः। अहनी अहोरात्रे। चक्रियेव चक्रयुक्ते इवेति। द्यावापृथिव्योर्महिमानमाचष्ट आचष्टे[2]॥ २२॥

इति तृतीयोऽध्यायः।

[कर्मनामानि परिचयं न हि ग्रभाय शासद्वह्निरभ्रातेवं न जामये मनुष्यनामानि तदद्य दशावनिभ्योऽभीदं त्वया वयं यत्रा सुपर्णा बहुनामानि तनूत्यजेव कुहस्विच्चतुरश्चित्प्रियमेधवदर्थ लुप्तोपमान्यर्चति द्विशो रम्भः कतरा पूर्वा द्वाविंशतिः॥][3]

॥ इति निरुक्ते पूर्वषट्के तृतीयोऽध्यायः समाप्तः॥

---

१. RV. I. 185. 1.
२. Cf. SRV. I, 185. 1. p. i. 772.
३. Small figure within brackets represents the corresponding section of the third chapter of the *Nirukta*.

॥ अथ चतुर्थोऽध्यायः ॥

एकार्थमनेकशब्दमित्येतदुक्तम् । अथ यान्यनेकार्थान्येकशब्दानि[1] तान्यतोऽनुक्रमिष्यामः । अनवगतसंस्काराश्च निगमान् । तदैकपदिकमित्याचक्षते ।

जहा जघानेत्यर्थः ॥ १ ॥

को नु मर्या अमिथितः सखा सखायमब्रवीत् ।
जहा को अस्मदीषते[2] ॥

मर्या इति मनुष्यनाम । मर्यादाभिधानं वा स्यात् । [मर्यादा मर्यैरादीयते[3]] मर्यादा मर्यादिनोर्विभागः । मेथतिराक्रोशकर्मा । अपापकं जघान कमहं जातु । कोऽस्मद्भीतः पलायते[4] ।

निधा पाश्या भवति । यन्निधीयते । पाश्या पाशसमूहः । पाशः पाशयतेः । विपाशनात् ॥ २ ॥

वयः सुपर्णा उप सेदुरिन्द्रं प्रियमेधा ऋषयो नाधमानाः ।
अप ध्वान्तमूर्णुहि पूर्धि चक्षुर्मुमुग्ध्य१स्मान्निधयेव बद्धान्[5] ॥

वयो वेर्बहुवचनम् । [सुपर्णाः] सुपतना आदित्यरश्मय उपसेदुरिन्द्रं याचमानाः[6] । अपोर्णुह्याध्वस्तं चक्षुः । चक्षुः ख्यातेर्वा । चष्टेर्वा । पूर्धि पूरय देहीति वा । मुञ्चास्मान् पाशैरिव बद्धान् ॥

पार्श्वतः श्रोणितः शितामतः[9] ।

पार्श्वं पर्शुमयमङ्गं भवति । पर्शुः स्पृशतेः । संस्पृष्टा पृष्ठदेशम् । पृष्ठं स्पृशतेः[10] । संस्पृष्टमङ्गैः । अङ्गमङ्गनात् । अञ्चनाद्वा । श्रोणिः श्रोणतेर्गतिचलाकर्मणः । श्रोणि-

---

१. यान्यन्येका० M 3.
२. RV. VIII. 45. 37.
३. Omitted by BK, C 4, C 5, Kn, M 3, Mi, R 4, R 6, W 1, W 2, W 3;
४. Quoted by SRV. VIII. 45. 37. p. iii. 435. cf. BD. ii. 109,
५. RV. X. 73. 11; SV. 1. 319.
६. याजमानाः C 3.
७. Cf. SRV. I. 164. 14. p. i. 701,
८. Cf. SRV. 1. 35. 12. p. i. 195.
९. Fragment of VS, 21. 43.
१०. Cf. SRV. I. 164. 1. p. 1. 696.
११. श्रोयते: C 5.

श्चलतीव गच्छतः। दोः शितामं भवति। दोर्द्रवतेः। योनिः शितामेति शाकपूणिः। विषितो भवति। श्यामतो यकृत्त इति तैटीकिः। श्यामं श्यायतेः। यकृद् यथा कथा च कृत्यते। शितिमांसतो मेदस्त इति गालवः। शितिः श्यतेः। मांसं माननं वा। मानसं वा। मनोऽस्मिन्त्सीदतीति वा। मेदो मेद्यतेः॥ ३॥

यदि॑न्द्र चित्र मे॒हनास्ति त्वादा॑तमद्रिवः।
राधस्तन्नो॑ विदद्वस उभयाह॒स्त्या भर॑ ॥

यदिन्द्र [चित्रं] चायनीयं मंहनीयं धनमस्ति। यन्म इह नास्तीति वा। त्रीणि मध्यमानि पदानि। त्वया नस्तद् दातव्यम्। अद्रिवन्। अद्रिरादृणात्येनेन। अपि वात्तेः स्यात्।

ते सो॒मादो॑ इति ह विज्ञायते।

राध इति धननाम। राध्नुवन्त्यनेन। तन्नस्त्वं वित्तधनोभाभ्यां हस्ताभ्यामाहर। उभौ समुब्धौ भवतः।

दमूना दममना वा। दानमना वा। दान्तमना वा। अपि वा दम इति गृहनाम। तन्मनाः स्यात्। मनो मनोतेः॥ ४॥

जुष्टो॒ दमू॑ना॒ अति॑थिर्दुरो॒ण इ॒मं नो॑ य॒ज्ञमुप॑ याहि वि॒द्वान्।
विश्वा॑ अग्ने अभि॒युजो॑ वि॒हत्या॑ शत्रूय॒तामा भ॑रा॒ भोज॑नानि ॥

अतिथिरभ्यतितो गृहान्भवति। अभ्येति तिथिषु परकुलानीति वा। [पर]

१. Cf. BD. ii. 114.

२. शामं M 2.

३. चिद् C 1.

४. कृद्यते C 4, C 5, M 3, Mi.

५. शतेः C 3, C 5, M 3, W 2.

६. RV. V. 39. 1; SV. 1. 345; 2. 522.

७. Omitted by, BK, C 4, C 5, Kn, M 3, Mi, R 4, R 6, W 1, W 2, W 3.

८. Quoted by SRV. V. 39. 1. p. ii. 573.

९. Quoted by SRV. VIII. 4. 21. p. iii. 254.

१०. स्यात् is omitted by C 1. cf. SRV. I. 129. 10. p. i. 588.

११. RV. X. 94. 9. It looks as if Yāska did not think it to be a Vedic quotation otherwise he would have used the words, as he usually does:, इत्यपि निगमो भवति instead of इति ह विज्ञायते which are generally used with Brāhmaṇa quotations.

१२. Omitted by Durga.

१३. समुबद्धौ BK, C 4, C 5, Kn, M 3, Mi, R 4, R 6, W 1, W 2, W 3.

१४. Cf. SRV. I. 123. 3; VI. 71. 4. pp. i. 558, ii. 883.

१५. Cf. SRV. I. 60. 4; IV. 11. 5; pp. i. 295: ii. 381.

१६. RV. V. 4. 5; AV. 7. 73. 9.

१७. परगृहाणीति वा परकुलानीति वा M 1.

१८. Omitted by BK, C 4, C 5, Kn, M 3, Mi, R 4, R 6, W 1, W 2, W 3.

गृहाणीति वा[1]। दुरोण इति गृहनाम। दुरवा भवन्ति दुस्तर्पाः। इमं नो यज्ञमुपयाहि विद्वान्। सर्वा अग्ने अभियुजो विहत्य शत्रूयतामाभर[3] भोजनानि। विहत्या[4]न्येषां बलानि शत्रूणां भव[5]नादाहर भोजनानीति वा। धनानीति वा।

मूषो मूषिका इत्यर्थः। मूषिकाः पुनर्मुष्णातेः। मूषोऽप्येतस्मादेव[6] ॥ ५ ॥

सं मा तपन्त्यभितः सपत्नीरिव पर्शवः ।
मूषो न शिश्ना व्यदन्ति माध्यः स्तोतारं ते शतक्रतो
वित्तं मे अस्य रोदसी[7] ॥

सन्तपन्ति मामभितः सपत्न्य इवेमाः पर्शवः कूपपर्शवः। मूषिका इवास्नातानि सूत्राणि व्यदन्ति[8]। स्वाङ्गाभिधानं वा स्यात्। शिश्नानि व्यदन्तीति वा[9]। सन्तपन्ति माध्यः कामाः[10]। स्तोतारं ते शतक्रतो [वित्तं मे अस्य रोदसी[11]]। जानीतं मेऽस्य द्यावापृथिव्याविति।

त्रितं कूपेऽवहितमेतत्सूक्तं प्रतिबभौ। तत्र ब्रह्मेतिहासमिश्रमृङ्मिश्रं गाथामिश्रं भवति। त्रितस्तीर्णतमो मेधया बभूव। अपि वा संख्यानामैवाभिप्रेतं स्यात्। एकतो द्वितस्त्रित इति त्रयो बभूवुः[12] ॥ ६ ॥

इषिरेण ते मनसा सुतस्य भक्षीमहि पित्र्यस्येव रायः ।
सोम राजन्प्र ण आयूंषि तारीरहानीव सूर्यो वासराणि[13] ॥

ईषणेन वैषणेन[14] वार्षणेन वा। ते मनसा सुतस्य भक्षीमहि पित्र्यस्येव धनस्य। प्रवर्धय च न आयूंषि सोमराजन्। अहानीव सूर्यो वासराणि। वासराणि वेसराणि विवासनानि गमनानीति वा।

कुरुतनेत्यनर्थका उपजना भवन्ति। कर्तनहन्तनयातनेति।

जठरमुदरं भवति। जग्धमस्मिन्ध्रियते[15] धीयते वा ॥ ७ ॥

---

१. अयमपीतरोऽतिथिरेतस्मादेव is added after वा by Durga & S'ivadatta.
२. Cf. SRV. III. 25. 5. p. ii. 200.
३. ०आहर C 1, C 4, C 5, M 3.
४. निहत्य० C 1, C 2, C 3, M 1, M 2, R 1, R 2, R 5, S.
५. भवतामाहर BK, C 4, C 5, Kn, M 3, Mi, R 4, R 6, W 1, W 2, W 3.
६. Cf. SRV. I. 105. 8. p. i. 464.
७. RV. I. 105. 8; X. 32. 2; cf. BD. VII. 34.
८. वदन्ति C 3, C 4, C 5, M 3.
९. Cf. SRV. I. 105. 8. p. i. 464.
१०. Cf. SRV. X. 33. 3; p. IV. 99.
११. Omitted by BK, C 4, C 5, Kn, M. 3, Mi, R 4, R 6, W 1, W 2, W 3.
१२. Cf. SRV. X. 1. 3. p. IV, 2. Durga cites the following passage: भार्यागारेणाभ्युपादयत् तत एकतोऽजायत। द्वितीयं ततो द्वितः। तृतीयं ततस्त्रितः।
१३. RV. VIII. 48. 7.
१४. Cf. SRV. I. 128. 5. p. i. 581.
१५. Cf. SRV. I. 112. 17. p. i. 492.

मरुत्वाँ इन्द्र वृषभो रणाय पिबा सोममनुष्वधं मदाय ।
आ सिञ्चस्व जठरे मध्व ऊर्मिं त्वं राजासि प्रदिवः सुतानाम्[1] ॥

मरुत्वानिन्द्र [मरुद्भिः[2]] तद्वान् । वृषभो वर्षितापाम्[3] । रणाय रमणीयाय संग्रामाय । पिब सोमम् । अनुष्वधमन्वन्नम् । मदाय मदनीयाय जैत्राय । आसिञ्चस्व जठरे मधुन ऊर्मिम् । मधु सोममित्यौपमिकं माद्यतेः । इदमपीतरन्मध्वेतस्मादेव । त्वं राजासि पूर्वेष्वप्यहःसु सुतानाम्[4] ॥ ८ ॥

तितउ परिपवनं भवति । ततवद्वा । तुन्नवद्वा । तिलमात्रतुन्नमिति वा[5] ॥ ९ ॥

सक्तुमिव तितउना पुनन्तो यत्र धीरा मनसा वाचमक्रत ।
अत्रा सखायः सख्यानि जानते भद्रैषां लक्ष्मीर्निहिताधि वाचि[6] ॥

सक्तुमिव परिपवनेन पुनन्तः । सक्तुः सचतेः । दुर्धावो भवति । कसतेर्वा[7] स्याद्विपरीतस्य । विकसितो भवति । यत्र धीरा मनसा वाचमकृषत प्रज्ञानम् । धीराः प्रज्ञानवन्तो ध्यानवन्तः[8] । तत्र सखायः सख्यानि संजानते । भद्रैषां लक्ष्मीर्निहिताधिवाचि [इति[9]] । भद्रं भगेन व्याख्यातम् । भजनीयं[10] भूतानामभिद्रवणीयम् । भवद्रमयतीति वा । भाजनवद्वा । लक्ष्मीर्लाभाद्वा । लक्षणाद्वा । [लप्स्यनाद्वा[11]] । लाञ्छनाद्वा[12] । लषते वा स्यात्प्रेप्साकर्मणः । लग्यते वा स्यादाश्लेषकर्मणः । लज्जते वा स्यादश्लाघाकर्मणः[13] ।

शिप्रे इत्युपरिष्टाद्[14] व्याख्यास्यामः ॥ १० ॥

तत्सूर्यस्य देवत्वं तन्महित्वं मध्या कर्तोर्विततं सं जभार ।
यदेदयुक्त हरितः सधस्थादाद्रात्री वासस्तनुते सिमस्मै[15] ॥

तत्सूर्यस्य देवत्वं तन्महित्वं मध्ये यत्कर्मणां क्रियमाणानां विततं संह्रियते । यदासावयुङ्क्त[16] हरणानादित्यरश्मीन् । हरितोऽश्वानिति[17] वा । अथ रात्री वासस्तनुते सिमस्मै ।

---

१. RV. III. 47. 1; VS. 7. 38.

२. Omitted by BK, C 4, C 5, Kn, M 3, Mi, R 4, R 6, W 1, W 2, W 3.

३. वा is added after अपाम् by C 3.

४. Quoted by SRV. III. 47. 1. p. ii. 284.

५. Quoted by SRV. X. 71. 2. p. iv. 220.

६. RV. X. 71. 2.

७. कपते: C 4, M 3.

८. ज्ञानवन्त: W 2.

९. Omitted by BK, C 4, C 5, Kn, M 3, Mi, R 4, R 6, W 1, W 2, W 3.

१०. भन्दनीयं is added. after भजनीय by C 1.

११. Omitted by BK, C 4, C 5, Kn, M 3, Mi, R 4, R 6, W 1, W 2, W 3.

१२. लञ्छनाद्वा BK, C 4, C 5, Kn, M 3, Mi, R 4, R 6, W 1, W 2, W 3.

१३. Cf. PMbh. i. 1. 1. p. i. 4.

१४. See N. 6. 17.

१५. RV. I. 115. 4; AV. 20. 123. 1; VS. 33. 37.

१६. ०युक्त BK, C 4, C 5, Kn, M 3, Mi, R 4, R 6, W 1, W 2, W 3; cf. SRV. I. 115. 4.

१७. अश्वानीति W 2.

वेसरमहरवयुवती सर्वस्मात्[1] । अपि वोपमार्थे स्यात् । रात्रीव वासस्तनुत इति । तथापि निगमो भवति ।

पुनः समव्यद्वितंतं वयन्ती[2] । समनात्सीत् ॥ ११ ॥

इन्द्रेण सं हि दृक्षसे सञ्जग्मानो अबिभ्युषा ।
मन्दू समानवर्चसा[3] ॥

इन्द्रेण हि संदृश्यसे संगच्छमानोऽबिभ्युषा गणेन । मन्दू मदिष्णू । युवां स्थः । अपि वा मन्दुना तेनेति स्यात् । समानवर्चसेत्येतेन व्याख्यातम्[4] ॥ १२ ॥

ईर्मान्तासः सिलिकमध्यमासः संशूरणासो दिव्यासो अत्याः ।
हंसा इव श्रेणिशो यतन्ते यदाक्षिषुर्दिव्यमज्ममश्वाः[5] ॥

ईर्मान्ताः समीरितान्ताः । [सुसमीरितान्ताः[6]] पृथ्वन्ता वा । सिलिकमध्यमाः संसृतमध्यमाः शीर्षमध्यमा वा । अपि वा शिर आदित्यो भवति । यदनुशेते सर्वाणि भूतानि । मध्ये चैषां तिष्ठति । इदमपीतरच्छिर एतस्मादेव । समाश्रितान्येतदिन्द्रियाणि भवन्ति । संशूरणासः [दिव्यासो अत्याः] शूरः शवतेर्गतिकर्मणः । दिव्या दिविजाः । अत्या अतनाः[7] । हंसा इव श्रेणिशो यतन्ते । हंसा हन्तेर्घ्नन्त्यध्वानम्[8] । [श्रेणिश इति[9]] श्रेणिः श्रयतेः । समाश्रिता भवन्ति । यदाक्षिषुर्यदापन्[10] । दिव्यमज्ममजनिमाजिमश्वाः[11] ।

अस्त्यादित्यस्तुतिरश्वस्य । आदित्यादश्वो निस्तष्ट इति ।

सूरादश्वं वसवो निरतष्ट[12] । इत्यपि निगमो भवति ॥ १३ ॥

कायमानो वना त्वं यन्मातृरजगन्नपः ।
न तत्ते अग्ने प्रमृषे निवर्तनं यद्दूरे सन्निहाभवः[13] ॥

कायमानश्चायमानः कामयमान इति वा । वनानि । त्वं यन्मातृरपोऽगम उपशाम्यन् । न तत्ते अग्ने प्रमृष्यते निवर्तनम् । दूरे यत् सन्निह भवसि जायमानः[14] ।

---

१. वासरम् SRV. I. 115. 4. p. i. 511.
२. RV. II. 38. 4.
३. RV, I. 6. 7; AV. 20. 40. 1; 70. 3; SV. 2. 200.
४. Cf. SRV. I. 6. 7. p. i. 52; cf. BD. ii. 141.
५. RV. I. 163. 10; VS. 29. 21.
६. Omitted by BK, C 4, C 5, Kn, M 3, Mi, R 4, R 6, W 1, W 2, W 3.
७. अथानुदात्तं is added often अतनाः by C 1.
८. P.Mbh. Vol. III. p. 21, हम्मतेर्हंसः । हन्तेर्हंसः । हन्त्यध्वानमिति ।
९. Omitted by BK, C 4, C 5, Kn, M 3, Mi, R 4, R 6, W 1, W 2, W 3.
१०. यदापुः SRV. I. 163. 10. p. i. 694.
११. Cf. SRV. loc. cit.
१२. RV. I. 163. 2; VS. 29. 13.
१३. RV. III. 9. 2, SV. 1. 53.
१४. Cf. SRV. III. 9. 2. p. ii. 160.

लोधं नयन्ति पशु मन्यमानाः[1] ।

लुब्धमृषिं नयन्ति पशुं मन्यमानाः ।

शीरं पावकशोचिषम्[2] । पावकदीप्तिम् । अनुशायिनमिति वा । आशिनमिति वा[3] ॥ १४ ॥

कनीनकेव विद्रधे नवे द्रुपदे अर्भके[4] ।
बभ्रू यामेषु शोभेते[5] ॥

कनीनके कन्यके । कन्या कमनीया भवति । क्वेयं नेतव्येति[7] वा [कमनेनानीयत इति वा[6]] कनतेर्वा स्यात्कान्तिकर्मणः । कन्ययोरधिष्ठानप्रवचनानि । सप्तम्या एकवचनानीति शाकपूणिः । व्यृद्धयोर्दारुपाद्वोः[8] । दारु दृणातेर्वा । द्रूणातेर्वा[9] । तस्मादेव द्रु । नवे नवजाते । अर्भके अवृद्धे[10] । ते यथा तदधिष्ठानेषु शोभेते एवं बभ्रू यामेषु शोभेते । बभ्रुवोरश्वयोः[11] संस्तवः[12]

इदं च मेऽदात्[13] इदं च मेऽदादित्यृषिः प्रसंख्यायाह ।

सुवास्त्वा अधि तुग्वनि[14] ।

सुवास्तुर्नदी । तुग्व तीर्थं भवति । तूर्णमेतदायन्ति ।

कुविन्नंसन्ते मरुतः पुनर्नः[15] ।

पुनर्नो नमन्ते[16] मरुतः । नसन्त[17] इत्युपरिष्टाद्[18] व्याख्यास्यामः ।

---

१. RV. III. 53. 23; cf. BD. IV. 117–120. Durga Remarks: यस्मिन् निगमे एष शब्दः सा वसिष्ठद्वेषिणी ऋक् । अहं च कापिष्ठलो वासिष्ठः । अतस्तां न निर्ब्रवीमीति ।

२. RV. III. 9. 8; VIII. 43. 31; 102. 11.

३. Cf. SRV. VIII. 102. 11. p. iii. 596.

४. RV. IV. 32. 23.

५. Cf. SRV. I. 123. 10. p. i. 560.

६. Omitted by BK, C 4, C 5, Kn, M 3, Mi, R 4, R 6, W 1, W 2, W 3.

७. Cf. BD. IV. 44.

८. विद्धयोः C 1, M 1,

९. दृणातेः C 4, C 5, C 6, M 3, W 2.

१०. व्यवृद्धे C 5.

११. रश्मयोः C 4, C 5, M 3, Mi, W 2.

१२. Cf. BD. IV. 144.

१३. अदात् is omitted by M 3, W 2.

१४. RV. VIII. 19. 37.

१५. RV. VII. 58. 5.

१६. नवन्ते C 4, C 5, M 3, W 1, W 2.

१७. नसत BK, C 4, C 5, Kn, M 3, R 4, R 6, W 1, W 2, W 3.

१८. See. N. 7. 17.

ये ते मदा॑ आह॒नसो॒ विहा॑यस॒स्तेभि॒रिन्द्रं॑ चोदय॒ दात॑वे म॒घम्[१] ।

ये ते मदाअाहननवन्तोवंचनवन्तस्तैरिन्द्रं[२] चोदय दानाय मघम् ॥ १५ ॥

उपो॑ अदर्शि शु॒न्ध्युवो॒ न वक्षो॒ नो॒धा इ॑वा॒विर॑कृत प्रि॒याणि॑ ।

अ॒द्म॒सन्न स॑स॒तो बो॒धय॑न्ती शश्व॒त्त॒मागा॒त्पुन॑रे॒युषी॑णाम्[३] ॥

उपादर्शि शुन्ध्युवः । शुन्ध्युरादित्यो भवति । शोधनात् । तस्यैव वक्षो भासाध्यूढम्[४] । इदमपीतरद्वक्ष एतस्मादेव । अध्यूढं[५] काये । शकुनिरपि शुन्ध्युरुच्यते । शोधनादेव । उदकचरो भवति । आपोऽपि शुन्ध्युव उच्यन्ते । शोधनादेव । नोधा ऋषिर्भवति । नवनं दधाति[६] । स यथा स्तुत्या कामानाविष्कुरुत एवमुषा रूपाण्याविष्कुरुते । अद्मसत् । अद्मान्नं भवति । अद्मसादिनीति वा । अद्मसानिनीति[८] वा । ससतो बोधयन्ती । शश्वत्तमागात्पुनरेयुषीणाम् । [स्वपतो बोधयन्ती] शाश्वतिकतमागात्पुनरेयुषीणाम्[१०] ।

ते वाशी॑मन्त इ॒ष्मिणः॑[११] ।

ईषणिन इति वेषणिन इति वार्षणिन इति वा । वाशीति वाङ्नाम । वाश्यत इति सत्याः ।

शंसा॑वाध्वर्यो॒ प्रति॑ मे गृणी॒हीन्द्रा॑य॒ वाहः॑ कृणवाव॒ जुष्ट॑म्[१२] ।

अभिवहनस्तुतिमभिषवणप्रवादां[१३][१४][१५] स्तुतिं[१६] मन्यन्ते । ऐन्द्री त्वेव शस्यते ।

परितक्म्येत्युपरिष्टाद् व्याख्यास्यामः[१७] ॥ १६ ॥

---

१. RV. IX. 75. 5.

२. Cf. SRV. IX. 75. 5. p. iii. 723.

३. RV. I. 124. 4.

४. भालोऽध्यूढम् C 1, C 2, C 3, C 6, M 1, M 2, R 1, R 2, R 5, S; भालोध्यूढम् S'ivadatta.

५. अध्यूढं C 1, C 2, C 3, C 6, M 1, M 2, R 1, R 2, R 5, S.

६. Cf. SRV. I. 61. 14. p. i. 302.

७. °मुखा C 5.

८. अन्नसानिनीति C 1, C 2, C 3, C 6, M 1, M 2, R 1, R 2, R 5, S; cf. SRV. I. 124. 4.

९. Omitted by BK, C 4, C 5, Kn, M 3, Mi, R 4, R 6, W 1, W 2, W 3.

१०. आगामिनीनाम् C 1, C 2, C 3, C 6, M 1, M 2, R 1, R 2, R 5, S & Roth. SRV. I. 124. 4-the entire passage being quoted.

११. RV. I. 87. 6.

१२. RV. III. 53. 3.

१३. अभिभवन° C 5.

१४. °अधिषवणा° C 1, C 2, C 3, C 6, M 1, M 2, R 1, R 2, R 5, S & Durga.

१५. °प्रवादा BK, C 4, C 5, Kn, Mi; R 4, R 6, W 1, W 2, W 3.

१६. स्तुति C 4, M 3, W 2.

१७. See N. 11. 25.

सुविते सु इते सूते सुगते । प्रजायामिति वा ।

सुविते मा धाः[1] । इत्यपि निगमो भवति ।

दयतिरनेककर्मा ।

नवेन पूर्वं दयमानाः स्याम[2] । इत्युपदयाकर्मा ।

य एक इद्विदयते वसु[3] । इति दानकर्मा वा विभागकर्मा वा ।

दुर्वर्तुर्भीमो दयते वनानि[4] । इति दहतिकर्मा । दुर्वर्तुर्दुर्वारः ।

विदद्वसुर्दयमानो वि शत्रून्[5] । इति हिंसाकर्मा ॥

इमे सुता इन्दवः प्रातरित्वना सजोषसा पिबतमश्विना तान् ।

अहं[6] हि वामूतये वन्दनाय मां वायसो दोषा दयमानो अबूबुधत्[7] ॥

दयमान[8] इति ।

नू चिदिति निपातः । पुराणनवयोः[9] । नू चेति च ।

अद्या चिन्नू चित्तदपो नदीनाम्[10] ।

अद्य च पुरा च तदेव कर्म नदीनाम् ।

नू च पुरा च सदनं रयीणाम्[11][12] ।

अद्य च पुरा च सदनं रयीणाम् । रयिरिति धननाम । रातेर्दानकर्मणः ॥ १७ ॥

विद्याम तस्य ते वयमकूपारस्य दावने[13] ।

विद्याम तस्य ते वयमकूपरणस्य दानस्य । आदित्योऽप्यकूपार उच्यते । अकूपारो भवति दूरपारः[14] । समुद्रोऽप्यकूपार उच्यते । अकूपारो भवति महापारः । कच्छपोऽप्यकूपार उच्यते । अकूपारो न कूपमृच्छतीति । कच्छपः कच्छं पाति । कच्छेन पातीति वा । कच्छेन पिबतीति वा[15] । कच्छः खच्छः[16] खच्छदः । अयमपीतरो नदीकच्छ एतस्मादेव । कमुदकम् । तेन छाद्यते ।

शिशीते शृङ्गे रक्षसे विनिक्षे[17] ।

---

१. TS. i. 2. 10.2; KS. 2. 8.

२. KS. 19.13; TB. 111. 5. 13. 1; N. 9. 43; cf. VS. 28. 16.

३. RV. I. 84. 7; AV. 20. 63. 4; SV. 1. 389; 2. 691.

४. RV. VI. 6. 5.

५. RV. III. 34. 1; AV. 20. 11. 1.

६. अयं C 1, C 2, C 3, M 1, R 1, R 2, R 5, S.

७. Quotation is untraced Durga explains the 4th pāda only & remarks. मृग्योऽत्रशेषः ।

८. दीयमान C 1.

९. Cf. SRV. I. 136. p. i. 612.

१०. RV. VI. 30. 3.

११. रयीण्यम् C 4, M 3, W 2.

१२. RV. I. 96. 7.

१३. RV. V. 39. 2; SV. 2. 523.

१४. Quoted by SRV. X. 109. 1. p. IV. 364.

१५. cf. PMbh. Vol. II. p. 98. कच्छेन पिबति कच्छपः ।

१६. स्वच्छः C 1.

१७. RV. V. 2. 9.

निश्यति शृङ्गे रक्षसो विनिक्षणाय[1] । रक्षो रक्षितव्यमस्मात्[2] । रहसि क्षणोतीति वा । रात्रौ नक्षत इति वा ।

अ॒ग्निः सु॒तुकः॑ सु॒तुके॑भि॒रश्वैः[3] ।

सुतुकनः सुतुकनैरिति वा । सुप्रजाः सुप्रजोभिरिति वा ।

सु॒प्रा॒य॒णा अ॒स्मिन्य॒ज्ञे वि श्र॑यन्ताम्[4] ।

सुप्रगमना[5] ॥ १८ ॥

दे॒वा नो॒ यथा॒ सद॒मिद्वृ॒धे अस॒न्नप्रा॑युवो रक्षि॒तारो॑ दि॒वेदि॑वे[6] ।

देवा नो यथा सदा वर्धनाय स्युः । अप्रायुवोऽप्रमाद्यन्तः । रक्षितारश्च । अहन्यहनि ।

च्यवन ऋषिर्भवति । च्यावयिता स्तोमानाम् । च्यवानमित्यप्यस्य निगमा भवन्ति ।

यु॒वं च्यवा॑नं स॒न॒यं यथा॒ रथं॒ पुन॒र्युवा॑नं च॒रथा॑य तक्षथुः[8] ।

[9]युवं च्यवनम्[10] । सनयं पुराणम् । यथा रथं पुनर्युवानं चरणाय ततक्षथुः । युवा प्रयौति कर्माणि । तक्षतिः करोतिकर्मा[11] ।

रजो रजतेः । ज्योती रज उच्यते[12] । उदकं रज उच्यते[13] । लोका रजांस्युच्यन्ते[14] । असृगहनी रजसी उच्येते[15] ।

[रजां॑सि चि॒त्रा वि च॑रन्ति त॒न्यवः॑[16] । इत्यपि निगमो भवति ।][17]

१. Cf. SRV. V. 2. 9. p. ii. 502.

२. Cf. SRV. I. 35. 10; 129. 11; pp. i. 190, 588.

३. RV. X. 3. 7.

४. VS. 28. 5.

५. लुप्रगमाना: C 4, C 5, M 3, W 2.

६. RV. I. 89. 1; VS. 25. 14.

७. असन् is given as a variant by Durga who however attributes it to the carelossness of the Scribes' इत्येषः प्रमादपाठः ।

८. RV. X. 39. 4.

९. युवां M 1.

१०. च्यवानं M 2.

११. Quoted by SRV. X. 39. 4. p. IV. 117.

१२. Quoted by SRV. VI. 62. 2. p. ii. 859.

१३. Cf. SRV. I. 161. 1; 164. 14; II. 39. 7. pp. i. 676, 701; ii. 119.

१४. Cf. SRV. I. 33. 7; 35. 2; 50. 7; 90. 7; 110. 6; VI. 70. 5; X. 129. 1; pp. i. 176, 186, 250, 401, 482; ii. 879; IV. 423. cf. 'SB. VI. 3. 1. 18. इमे वै लोका रजाꣳसि ।

१५. Cf. SRV. I. 124. 5. p. i. 564. The entire passage: रजो रजते उच्येते is quoted SRV. I. 19. 3. p. i. 107.

१६. RV. V. 63. 5.

१७. Omitted by BK, C 4, C 5, Kn, M 3, Mi 1, R 4, R 6, W 1, W 2, W 3; and Durga. It is struck out in C 1.

हरो हरतेः । ज्योतिर्हर उच्यते । उदकं हर उच्यते । लोका हरांस्युच्यन्ते[2] । असृगहनी हरसी उच्येते ।

[प्रत्यग्ने हरसा हरः शृणीहि[3] । इत्यपि निगमो भवति ।][4]

जुहुरे वि चितयन्तः[5] । जुह्विरे विचेतयमानाः ।

व्यन्त इत्येषोऽनेककर्मा ।

पदं देवस्य नमसा व्यन्तः[6] । इति पश्यतिकर्मा ।

वीहि शूर पुरोळाशम्[7] । इति खादतिकर्मा ।

वीतं पातं पयस उस्रियायाः[8] । अश्नीतं पिबतं पयस उस्रियायाः । उस्रियेति गोनाम । उस्राविणोऽस्यां भोगाः[9] । [उस्रेति च[10]]

त्वामिन्द्र मतिभिः सुते सुनीथासो वसूयवः[11] ।

गोभिः क्राणा अनूषत[12] ॥

गोभिः कुर्वाणा[13] अस्तोषत ।

आ तू षिञ्च हरिमीं द्रोरुपस्थे वाशीभिस्तक्षताश्मन्मयीभिः[14] ।

आसिञ्च हरिं द्रोरुपस्थे द्रुममयस्य । हरिः सोमो हरितवर्णः । अयमपीतरो हरिरेतस्मादेव । वाशीभिस्तक्षताश्मन्मयीभिः । वाशीभिरश्ममयीभिरिति वा । वाग्भिरिति वा[15] ।

स शर्धदर्यो विषुणस्य जन्तोर्मा शिश्नदेवा अपि गुर्ऋतं नः[16] ।

स उत्सहतां यो विषुणस्य जन्तोर्विषमस्य । मा शिश्नदेवा अब्रह्मचर्याः । शिश्नं श्नथतेः[17] । अपि गुर्ऋतं नः । सत्यं वा यज्ञं वा[18] ॥ १९ ॥

१. Cf. SRV. X. 87. 25. p. IV. 278.

२. हरा उच्यन्ते BK, C 4, C 5, Kn, M 3, Mi, R 4, R 6, W 1, W 2, W 3.

३. RV. X. 87. 25; SV. 1. 95.

४. Omitted by BK, C 4, C 5, Kn, M 3, Mi, R 4, R 6, W 1, W 2, W 3, and Durga. The line प्रत्यग्ने... भवति is struck out in C 1.

५. RV. V. 19. 2.

६. RV. VI. 1. 4.

७. RV. III. 41. 3; AV. 20. 23. 3.

८. RV. I. 153. 4; AV. 7. 73. 5.

९. उत्स्राविणो SRV. III. 31. 11. p. 231.

१०. Omitted by BK, C 4, C 5, Kn, M 3, Mi, R 4, R 6, W 1, W 2, W 3.

११. The quotation is untraced.

१२. Cf. RV. I. 134. 2.

१३. Cf. SRV. I. 134. 2. p. i. 605: क्राणाः कुर्वाण इति यास्कः ।

१४. RV. X. 101. 10

१५. वाग्निरिति C 4, C 5, M 3, Mi, W 2.

१६. RV. VII. 21. 5.

१७. Quoted by SRV. X. 27. 19. p. IV. 79.

१८. Cf. SRV. I. 2. 8; VII. 22. 5. pp. i. 33; iii. 50.

आ घा ता गच्छानुत्तरा युगानि यत्र जामयः कृणवन्नजामि।
उप बर्बृहि वृषभाय बाहुमन्यमिच्छस्व सुभगे पतिं मत्[1]॥

आगमिष्यन्ति तान्युत्तराणि युगानि। यत्र जामयः करिष्यन्त्यजामिकर्माणि। जाम्यतिरेकनाम। बालिशस्य वा। समानजातीयस्य[2] वोपजनः। उपधेहि वृषभाय बाहुम्। अन्यमिच्छस्व सुभगे पतिं मदिति व्याख्यातम्॥ २०॥

द्यौर्मे पिता जनिता नाभिरत्र बन्धुर्मे माता पृथिवी महीयम्।
उत्तानयोश्चम्वो३र्योनिरन्तरत्रा पिता दुहितुर्गर्भमाधात्[3]॥

द्यौर्मे पिता पाता वा पालयिता[4] वा जनयिता। नाभिरत्र बन्धुर्मे माता पृथिवी महतीयम्[5]। बन्धुः संबन्धनात्। नाभिः संनहनात्।

नाभ्या सन्नद्धा गर्भा जायन्ते[6]।

इत्याहुः। एतस्मादेव ज्ञातीन् सनाभय इत्याचक्षते[7]। सबन्धव इति च। ज्ञातिः संज्ञानात्। उत्तानयोश्चम्वो३र्योनिरन्तः। उत्तान उत्ततानः। ऊर्ध्वतानो[8] वा। तत्र पिता दुहितुर्गर्भं दधाति पर्जन्यः पृथिव्याः।

[शंयुः सुखंयुः।][9]

अथा नः शं योररपो[10] दधात[11]।

रपो रिप्रमिति पापनामनी भवतः[12]। शमनं च रोगाणां यावनं[13] च भयानाम्[14]। अथापि शंयुर्बार्हस्पत्य उच्यते[15]।

तच्छंयोरावृणीमहे गातुं यज्ञाय गातुं यज्ञपतये[16]।

इत्यपि निगमो भवति। गमनं यज्ञाय गमनं यज्ञपतये॥ २१॥

---

१. RV. X. 10. 10; AV. 18. 1. 11.
२. असमानजाती०. Durga.
३. RV. I. 164. 33; AV. 9. 10. 12.
४. Omitted by Durga.
५. महीयम् Durga.
६. Cf. TS. VI. 1. 7. 2.
७. ०न्त्सनाभय M 1, M 2.
८. ऊर्ध्वतानो C 1, C 2, C 3, C 6, M 1, M 2, R 1, R 2, R 5, S.
९. Omitted by BK, C 4, C 5, Kn, M 3, Mi, R 4, R 6, W 1, W 2, W 3.
१०. ०ररयो M 3.
११. RV. X. 15. 4; VS. 19. 55; Cf. AV. 18. 1. 15.
१२. Cf. SRV. I. 157. 4; VIII. 67. 21, pp. i. 670; iii. 493; Cf. BD. VII. 95.
१३. पावनं C 3, M 3.
१४. Quoted by SRV. I. 93. 7. p. i. 419; Cf. also I. 106. 5. p. i. 470.
१५. Cf. 'SB. I. 9. 1. 24. शंयुर्ह वै बार्हस्पत्यः
१६. TS. ii. 6. 10. 2; S'B. i. 9. 1. 26.

अदितिरदीना देवमाता ॥ २२ ॥

अदि॑ति॒र्द्यौरदि॑तिर॒न्तरि॑क्ष॒मदि॑तिर्मा॒ता स पि॒ता स पु॒त्रः ।

विश्वे॑ दे॒वा अदि॑तिः॒ पञ्च॒ जना॒ अदि॑तिर्जा॒तमदि॑ति॒र्जनि॑त्वम्[2] ॥

इत्यदितेर्विभूतिमाचष्टे[3] । एनान्यदीनानीति वा ।

यमेरि॒रे भृग॑वः[4] ।

परिर इतीर्तिरुपसृष्टोऽभ्यस्तः ॥ २३ ॥

उ॒त स्मै॑नं वस्त्र॒मथिं॒ न ता॒युमनु॑ क्रोशन्ति क्षि॒तयो॒ भरे॑षु ।

नी॒चाय॑मानं॒ जसु॑रिं॒ न श्येनं श्रव॒श्चाच्छा॑ पशु॒मच्च॑ यू॒थम्[5] ॥

अपि स्मैनं वस्त्रमथिमिव वस्त्रमाथिनम्[6] । वस्त्रं वस्तेः । तायुरिति[7] स्तेननाम । संस्त्यानमस्मिन् पापकमिति नैरुक्ताः । तस्यतेर्वा स्यात् । अनुक्रोशन्ति क्षितयः संग्रामेषु । भर इति संग्रामनाम । भरतेर्वा । हरतेर्वा[8] । नीचायमानं नीचैरयमानम्[9] । नीचैर्निचितं[10] भवति । उच्चैरुच्चितं[11] भवति । जस्तमिव श्येनम् । श्येनः शंसनीयं गच्छति । श्रवश्चाच्छा पशुमच्च । यूथम् श्रवश्चापि पशुमच्च यूथम् । प्रशंसां च यूथं च । धनं च यूथं चेति वा । यूथं यौतेः । समायुतं भवति ।

इन्धा॑न एनं जरते स्वा॒धीः[12] । गृणाति ।

मन्दी मन्दतेः स्तुतिकर्मणः[13] ।

प्र म॒न्दिने॑ पितु॒मद॑र्चता॒ वचः॑[14] । प्रार्चत मन्दिने पितुमद्वचः ।

गौर्व्याख्यातः[15] ॥ २४ ॥

अत्राह॒ गोर॑मन्वत॒ नाम॒ त्वष्टु॑रपी॒च्य॑म् ।

इ॒त्था च॒न्द्रम॑सो गृ॒हे[16] ॥

---

१. Cf. BD. ii. 46.

२. RV. I. 89. 10; AV. 7. 6. 1; VS. 25. 23.

३. Cf. SRV. I. 89. 10. p. i. 399.

४. RV. I. 143. 4.

५. RV. IV. 38. 5.

६. Quoted by SRV. IV. 38 5. p. ii. 454.

७. त्वायुः M 3.

८. भारत C 5.

९. Cf. SRV. I. 132. 1. p. i. 598.

१०. निश्चितं Mi.

११. उचितं M 3; उच्चृतं C 3.

१२. RV. X. 45. 1; VS. 12. 18.

१३. Quoted by SRV. I. 101. 1. p. i. 446.

१४. RV. I. 101. 1; SV. 1. 380.

१५. See N. 2. 5.

१६. RV. I. 84. 15; AV. 20. 41. 3; SV. 1. 147; 2. 265.

अत्र ह गोः सममंसतादित्यरश्मयः स्वं नाम। अपीच्यमपचितम्[1]। अपगतम्[2]। अपिहितम्। अन्तर्हितं[3] वा। अमुत्र चन्द्रमसो गृहे।

गातुर्व्याख्यातः[4]।

[गातुं कृणवन्नुषसो जनाय[5]। इत्यपि निगमो भवति।][6]

दंसयः कर्माणि। दंसयन्त्येनानि।

कुत्साय मन्मन्नह्यश्च दंसयः[7]। इत्यपि निगमो भवति।

स तूताव नैनमश्नोत्यंहतिः[8]।

स तुताव नैनमंहतिरश्नोति। अंहतिश्चांहश्चांहुश्च[9] हन्तेः। निरूढोपधात्। विपरीतात्।

बृहस्पते चयसे इत्पियारुम्[10]।

बृहस्पते यश्चातयसि[11] देवपीयुम्। पीयतिर्हिंसाकर्मा[12]। वियुते द्यावापृथिव्यौ। वियवनात्[13]।

समान्या वियुते दूरेअन्ते[14]।

समानं संमानमात्रं भवति। मात्रा मानात्। दूरं व्याख्यातम्[15]। अन्तोऽततेः। ऋधगिति पृथग्भावस्य प्रवचनं भवति। अथाप्यृध्नोत्यर्थे दृश्यते[16]।

ऋधगया ऋधगुताशमिष्ठाः[17]।

---

१. Omitted by C 3.

२. अपचितम् is Omitted by C 3; is preceded by अपगतम् in C 1, C 6, M 1, M 2.

३. अनन्तर्हितम् BK, C 4, C 5, Kn, M 3, Mi, R 4, R 6, W 1, W 2, W 3.

४. See N. 4. 21.

५. RV. IV. 51. 1.

६. Omitted by BK, C 4, C 5, Kn, M 3, Mi, R 4, R 6, W 1, W 2, W 3.

७. RV. X. 138. 1.

८. RV. I. 94. 2.

९. चांहः is omitted by C 5.

१०. RV. I. 190. 5.

११. Quoted by SRV. I. 190. 5. p. i. 788.

१२. पीयुतिः C 1, C 2, C 3, C 5, C 7, Mi, W 2, W 3.

१३. वियमनात् C 5, M 3, Mi, W 2; वियुमनात् C 4.

१४. RV. III. 54. 7.

१५. See N. 3. 19.

१६. Quoted by SRV. IX. 64. 30. p. iii. 683.

१७. VS. 8. 20.

ऋभुवन्नयाक्षीः । ऋभुवन्नशमिष्ठा इति च । अस्या इति चास्येति[1] चोदात्तं प्रथमादेशे । अनुदात्तमन्वादेशे । तीव्रार्थतरमुदात्तम्[2] । अल्पीयोऽर्थतरमनुदात्तम्[3] ।

अस्या ऊ षु ण उप सातये भुवोऽहेळमानो ररिवाँ अजाश्व[4] ।

[श्रवस्यतामजाश्व ।][5]

अस्यै नः सातय उपभव । अहेळमानोऽक्रुध्यन् । ररिवान् । रातिरभ्यस्तः । अजाश्वेति पूषणमाह[6] । अजाश्व अजा अजनाः[7] ।

अथानुदात्तम् ।

दीर्घायुरस्या यः पतिर्जीवाति शरदः शतम्[8] ।

दीर्घायुरस्या यः पतिर्जीवतु स शरदः शतम् । शरच्छ्रता[9] अस्यामोषधयो[10] भवन्ति । शीर्णा आप इति वा ।

अस्येत्यस्या इत्येतेन व्याख्यातम् ॥ २५ ॥

अस्य वामस्य पलितस्य होतुस्तस्य भ्राता मध्यमो अस्त्यश्नः ।
तृतीयो भ्राता घृतपृष्ठो अस्यात्रापश्यं विश्पतिं सप्तपुत्रम्[11] ॥

अस्य वामस्य वननीयस्य । पलितस्य पालयितुः । होतुर्ह्वातव्यस्य । तस्य भ्राता मध्यमोऽस्त्यशनः । भ्राता भरतेर्हरतिकर्मणः । हरते भागं भर्तव्यो भवतीति वा । तृतीयो भ्राता घृतपृष्ठोऽस्यायमग्निः[12] । तत्रापश्यं सर्वस्य पातारं वा पालयितारं वा[13] । विश्पतिं सप्तपुत्रं सप्तमपुत्रं[14] सर्पणपुत्रमिति वा । सप्त सृप्ता संख्या । सप्तादित्यरश्मय इति वदन्ति ॥ २६ ॥

---

१. चास्या इति BK, C 4, C 5, Kn, M 3, Mi, R 4, R 6, W 1, W 2, W 3.

२. ०मनुद्यत्तम् C 3.

३. Quoted by SRV. VII. 34. 4. p. iii. 78.

४. RV. I. 138. 4.

५. Omitted by BK, C 4, C 5, Kn, M 3, Mi, R 4, R 6, W 1, W 2, W 3.

६. Quoted by SRV. I. 138. 4. p. i. 618.

७. आज्या C 5.

८. RV. X. 85. 39; AV. 14. 2. 2.

९. शरच्छ्रिता M 3.

१०. अस्या ओषधयो M 3.

११. RV. I. 164. 1; AV. 9. 9. 1.

१२. Cf. BD. IV. 33.

१३. Cf. SRV. I. 9. 4. p. i. 65.

१४. Durga remarks: सप्तमो ह्यसावादित्यः पुत्र इत्येवमैतिहासिका मन्यन्ते । ब्राह्मणोऽपि च । ......तस्मिन्नादित्यः सप्तम इन्द्रोऽष्टतम इति ह विज्ञायते । अथवा सप्तसंख्यायुक्ता अस्य रश्मयः पुत्रास्तेनासौ सप्तपुत्रः ।

सप्त युञ्जन्ति रथमेकचक्रमेको अश्वो वहति सप्तनामा ।
त्रिनाभि चक्रमजरमनर्वं यत्रेमा विश्वा भुवनाधि तस्थुः ॥[1]

सप्त युञ्जन्ति रथम् । एकचक्रमेकचारिणम्[2] । चक्रं चकतेर्वा । चरतेर्वा । क्रामतेर्वा[3] । एकोऽश्वो वहति सप्तनामादित्यः । सप्तास्मै रश्मयो रसानभिसन्नामयन्ति । सप्तैनमृषयः स्तुवन्तीति वा । इदमपीतरन्नामैतस्मादेव । अभिसन्नामात् । संवत्सरप्रधान उत्तरोऽर्धर्चः । त्रिनाभि चक्रम् । त्र्यृतुः संवत्सरः[4] । ग्रीष्मो वर्षा हेमन्त इति । संवत्सरः संवसन्तेऽस्मिन्[5]भूतानि । ग्रीष्मो ग्रस्यन्तेऽस्मिन्रसाः । वर्षा वर्षत्यासु पर्जन्यः । हेमन्तो हिमवान् । हिमं पुनर्हन्तेर्वा । हिनोतेर्वा । अजरमजरणधर्माणम् । अनर्वमप्रत्यृतमन्यस्मिन्[6] । यत्रेमानि सर्वाणि भूतान्यभिसन्तिष्ठन्ते । तं संवत्सरं सर्वमात्राभिः स्तौति[7] ।

पञ्चारे चक्रे परिवर्तमाने[8] ।

इति पञ्चर्तुतया[9] ।

पञ्चर्तवः संवत्सरस्य[10] ।

इति च ब्राह्मणम् । हेमन्तशिशिरयोः समासेन[11] ।

षळर आहुरर्पितम्[12] ।

इति षळृतुतया । अराः प्रत्यृता नाभौ । षट् पुनः सहतेः ।

द्वादशारं नहि तज्जराय[13] ।

द्वादश प्रधयश्चक्रमेकम्[14] ।

इति मासानाम् । मासा मानात्[15] । प्रधिः प्रहितो भवति ।

तस्मिन्त्साकं त्रिशता न शङ्कवोऽर्पिताः षष्टिर्न चलाचलासः[16][17] ।

षष्टिश्च ह वै त्रीणि च शतानि संवत्सरस्याहोरात्राः[18] ।

इति च ब्राह्मणं समासेन ।

---

१. RV. 1. 164. 2; AV. 9. 9. 2; 13. 3. 8.
२. Quoted by SRV. I. 164. 2. p. i. 697.
३. Cf. SRV. X. 101. 7. p. IV. 336.
४. Cf. GB. I. 5. 5.
५. संवसन्ति C 3.
६. अन्यस्मिन् is omitted by C 3.
७. ०मात्राभिष्टौति M 3.
८. RV. I. 164. 13; AV. 9. 9. 11.
९. ०र्तुतायाः C 4, M 3, W 2.
१०. Cf. AB. i. 1. 14: द्वादश मासाः पंचर्तवो हेमन्तशिशिरयोः समासेन तावान्संवत्सरः । Cf. S'B. i. 7. 2. 8; XII. 3. 2. 1; Tāṇḍ B. XVIII. 2. 14; 4. 11.
११. ०शिशिरसमासेन BK, C 4, C 5, Kn, M 3, Mi, R 4, R 6, W 1, W 2, W 3.
१२. RV. I. 164. 12; AV. 9. 9. 12.
१३. RV. I. 164. 11; AV. 9. 9. 3.
१४. RV. I. 164. 48; AV. 10. 8. 4.
१५. Quoted by SRV. I. 164. 48. p. i. 718.
१६. चलापः M 3.
१७. RV. I. 164. 48; AV. 10. 8. 4.
१८. Cf. GB. I. 5. 5. त्रीणि च ह वै शतानि षष्टिश्च संवत्सरस्याहोरात्राणि । Cf. AB. II. 17. 2: त्रीणि च वै शतानि षष्टिश्च संवत्सरस्याहानि । Cf. S'B. XII. 3. 2. 3. त्रीणि च वै शतानि षष्टिश्च संवत्सरस्याहानि । Cf. KB. iii. 2.

सप्त शतानि विंशतिश्च तस्थुः ।[1]

सप्त च वै शतानि विंशतिश्च संवत्सरस्याहोरात्राः ।[2]

इति च ब्राह्मणं विभागेन विभागेन ॥ २७ ॥

इति चतुर्थोऽध्यायः ।

[[१]एकार्थं [२]कोनु वयः [३]सुपर्णा [४]यदिन्द्र [५]जुष्टो दमूनाः [६]सं मा तपन्ती[७]षिरेण [८]मरुत्वांस्[९]तितउ [१०]सक्तुमिव [११]तत्सूर्यस्य[१२]इन्द्रेण [१३]समीर्मान्तासः [१४]कायमानः [१५]कानीनके[१६]वोपो अदर्शि [१७]सुविते [१८]विद्याम [१९]देवानो [२०]अघा [२१]द्यौर्मे [२२]ऽदितिर[२३]दिति[२४]रुतस्मा[२५]त्राहास्य [२६]वामस्य [२७]सप्त युञ्जन्ति सप्तविंशतिः ॥][3]

॥ इति निरुक्ते पूर्वषट्के चतुर्थोऽध्यायः समाप्तः ॥

---

१. RV. I. 164 11; AV. 9. 9. 13.

२. Cf. GB. I. 5. 5; AB. II. 17. 4; S'B. XII. 3. 2. 4; AA. III. 2. 1.

३. Small figure within brackets represents the corresponding section of the fourth chapter of the *Nirukta*.

अथ पञ्चमोऽध्यायः ।

सस्निमविन्दच्चरणे नदीनाम्[1] । सस्निं संस्नातं मेघम् ।

वाहिष्ठो वां हवानां स्तोमो दूतो हुवन्नरा[2] ।

वोढृतमो ह्वानानां स्तोमो दूतो हुवन्नरौ । नरा मनुष्या नृत्यन्ति कर्मसु[3] । दूतो जवतेर्वा । द्रवतेर्वा । वारयतेर्वा ।

[दूतो देवानामसि मर्त्यानाम्[4] । इत्यपि निगमो भवति][5]

वावशानो वष्टेर्वा । वाश्यतेर्वा ।

सप्त स्वसृररुषीर्वावशानः[6] । इत्यपि निगमो भवति ।

वार्यं वृणोतेः । अथापि वरतमम् ।

तद्वार्यं वृणीमहे वरिष्ठं गोपयत्यम्[8] ।

तद्वार्यं[7] वृणीमहे । वर्षिष्ठं गोपायितव्यम् । गोपायितारो यूयं स्थ । युष्मभ्यमिति वा ।

अन्ध इत्यन्ननाम । आध्यानीयं भवति ।

आमत्रेभिः सिञ्चता मद्यमन्धः[9] ।

आसिञ्चतामत्रैर्मदनीयमन्धः[10] । अमत्रं पात्रम् । अमा अस्मिन्मदन्ति[11] । अमा पुनरनिर्मितं भवति । पात्रं पानात् ।

तमोऽप्यन्ध उच्यते । नास्मिन्ध्यानं भवति[12] । न दर्शनम् । अन्धन्तम इत्यभिभाषन्ते । अयमपीतरोऽन्ध एतस्मादेव ।

---

१. RV. X. 139. 6.

२. RV. VIII. 26. 16.

३. Quoted by SRV. I. 149. 2. p. i. 652.

४. RV. X. 4. 2.

५. Omitted by BK, C 4, C 5, Kn, M 3, Mi, R 4, R 6, W 1, W 2, W 3.

६. RV. X. 5. 5.

७. तद्वीर्यं C 5.

८. RV. VIII. 25. 13.

९. RV. II. 14. 1.

१०. मद्यमन्धः BK, C 4, C 5, Kn, M 3, Mi, R 4, R 6, W 1, W 2, W 3.

११. नदन्ति C 4, C 5, M 3. Quoted by SRV. II. 14. 1. p. ii. 41.

१२. Quoted by SRV. I. 62. 5. p. i. 307.

पश्यदक्षण्वान्न वि चेतदन्धः[1] । इत्यपि निगमो भवति ॥ १ ॥

असंश्चन्ती भूरिधारे पयस्वती[2] ।

असज्यमाने इति वा । अव्युदस्यन्त्याविति वा । बहुधारे उदकवत्यौ ।[3]

वनुष्यतिर्हन्तिकर्मा । अनवगतसंस्कारो भवति[4] ।

वनुयाम वनुष्यतः[5] । इत्यपि निगमो भवति ।

दीर्घप्रयज्युमति यो वनुष्यति वयं जयेम पृतनासु दूढ्यः[6] ।

दीर्घप्रततयज्ञमभिजिघांसति यो वयं तं जयेम पृतनासु । दूढ्यं दुर्धियं पापधियम् । पापः पाताऽपेयानाम् । पापत्यमानोऽवाङेव पततीति वा । पापत्यतेर्वा स्यात्[7] ।

तरुष्यतिरप्येवंकर्मा ।

इन्द्रेण युजा तरुषेम वृत्रम्[8] । इत्यपि निगमो भवति ।

भन्दना भन्दतेः स्तुतिकर्मणः ।

पुरुप्रियो भन्दते धामभिः कविः[9] । इत्यपि निगमो भवति ।

स भन्दना उदियर्ति प्रजावतीः[10] । इति च ।

अन्येन मदाहनो याहि तूयम्[11] ।

अन्येन मदहनो गच्छ क्षिप्रम् । आहंसीव भाषमाणेत्यसभ्यभाषणादाहना इव भवति[12] । एतस्मादाहनः स्यात्[13] ।

ऋषिर्नदो भवति । नदतेः स्तुतिकर्मणः ।

नदस्य मा रुधतः काम आगन्[14] ।

नदनस्य मा रुधतः काम आगमत् । संरुद्धप्रजननस्य ब्रह्मचारिणः । इत्यृषिपुत्र्या विलपितं वेदयन्ते[15] ॥ २ ॥

१. RV. I. 164. 16; AV. 9. 9. 15.
२. RV. VI. 70. 2.
३. Quoted by SRV. VI. 70. 2. p. ii. 880.
४. Quoted by SRV. I. 73. 9; 121. 10. pp. i. 347, 547.
५. RV. I. 132. 1; VIII. 40. 7.
६. RV. VII. 82. 1.
७. पापत्यतेर्वा स्यात् is omitted by Durga.
८. RV. VII. 48. 2.
९. RV. III. 3. 4.
१०. RV. IX. 86. 41.
११. RV. X. 10. 8; AV. 18. 1. 9.
१२. ०णेत्यभ्य० C 3.
१३. स्या: C 5, M 3.
१४. RV. I. 179. 4; Cf. BD. i. 53: विलापः स्यान्नदस्य मा । Macdonell translates नदस्य 'as of the reed'.
१५. Quoted by SRV. I. 179. 4. p. i. 758.

न यस्य द्यावापृथिवी न धन्व नान्तरिक्षं नाद्रयः सोमो अक्षाः[1]।

अक्ष्णोतेरित्येवमेके।

अनूपे गोमान्गोभिरक्षाः सोमो दुग्धाभिरक्षाः[2]।

लोपाशः सिंहं प्रत्यञ्चमत्साः[3]।

क्षियतिनिगमः पूर्वः क्षरतिनिगम उत्तर इत्येके। अनूपे गोमान् गोभिर्यदा क्षियत्यथ सोमो दुग्धाभ्यः क्षरति। सर्वे क्षियतिनिगमा इति शाकपूणिः।

श्वात्रमिति क्षिप्रनाम। आशु अतनं भवति।

स पतत्रीत्वरं स्था जगद्यच्छ्वात्रमग्निरकृणोज्जातवेदाः[4]।

स पतत्रि चेत्वरं स्थावरं जङ्गमं च यत्तत् क्षिप्रमग्निरकरोज्जातवेदाः[5]।

ऊतिरवनात्।

आ त्वा रथं यथोतये[6]। इत्यपि निगमो भवति।

हासमाने इत्युपरिष्टाद् व्याख्यास्यामः[7]।

वम्रकः पड्भिरुप सर्पदिन्द्रम्[8]।

पानैरिति वा। स्पाशनैरिति वा। [स्पर्शनैरिति वा][9]

ससं न पक्वमविदच्छुचन्तम्[10]।

स्वप्नमेतन्माध्यमिकं[11] ज्योतिरनित्यदर्शनम्[12]। तदिवाविदज्ज्वाज्वल्यमानम्।

द्विता च सत्ता स्वधया च शंभुः[13]।

द्वैधं[14] सत्ता मध्यमे च स्थान उत्तमे च। शंभुः सुखभूः[15]।

---

१. RV. X. 89. 6.

२. RV. IX. 107. 9; SV. 2. 348.

३. RV. X. 28. 4; Omitted by Durga.

४. RV. X. 88. 4.

५. Quoted by SRV. X. 88. 4. p. IV. 279.

६. RV. VIII. 68. 1; SV 1. 354; 2. 1121.

७. See N. 9. 39.

८. RV. X. 99. 12.

९. Omitted by Bk, C 4, C 5, Kn, M 3, Mi, R 4, R 6, W 1, W 2, W 3, and Durga.

१०. RV. X. 79. 3.

११. मध्यमं BK, C 4, C 5, Kn, M 3, Mi, R 4, R 6, W 1, W 2, W 3.

१२. Cf. SRV. VIII. 72. 4. p. iii 509: अत्र यास्कः। स्वप्नमेतन्मध्यमं ज्योतिरनित्यदर्शनम्.

१३. RV. III. 17. 5.

१४. द्विधं C 3, M 3.

१५. Quoted by SRV. III. 17. 5. p. ii. 184.

मृगं न व्रा मृगयन्ते[1] ।

मृगमिव व्रात्याः प्रैषाः ॥ ३ ॥

वराहो मेघो भवति । वराहारः ।

वरमाहारमाहार्षीः[2] । इति च ब्राह्मणम् ।

विध्यद्वराहं तिरो अद्रिमस्ता[3] । इत्यपि निगमो भवति ।

अयमपीतरो वराह एतस्मादेव । वृहति मूलानि । वरं वरं मूलं वृहतीति वा ।

वराहमिन्द्र एमुषम्[4] । इत्यपि निगमो भवति ।

अङ्गिरसोऽपि वराहा उच्यन्ते ।

ब्रह्मणस्पतिर्वृषभिर्वराहैः[5] ।

अथाप्येते माध्यमका देवगणा वराहव उच्यन्ते[6] ।

पश्यन्हिरण्यचक्रानयोदंष्ट्रान्विधावतो वराहून्[7] ।

स्वसराण्यहानि भवन्ति । स्वयं सारीण्यपि वा । स्वरादित्यो भवति । स एनानि सारयति ।

उस्रा इव स्वसराणि[8] । इत्यपि निगमो भवति[9] ।

शर्या अंगुलयो भवन्ति । [सृजन्ति कर्माणि][10] शर्या इषवः शरमय्यः[11] । शरः शृणातेः ।

शर्याभिर्न भरमाणो गभस्त्योः[12] ।

इत्यपि निगमो भवति ।

---

१. RV. VIII. 2.6.

२. The quotation is untraced. It is inserted after एतस्मादेव further-down by C 1, C 2, C 3, C 6, M 1, M 1, M 2, R 1, R 2, R 5, S; Cf. SRV. I. 61. 7. p. i. 299.

३. RV. I. 61. 7; AV. 20. 35. 7.

४. RV. VIII. 77. 10.

५. RV. X. 67. 7. AV. 20. 91. 7.

६. Quoted by SRV. I. 88. 5. p. i. 394.

७. RV. I. 88. 5.

८. RV. I. 3. 8.

९. Cf. SRV. I. 3. 9; VIII. 88. 1; pp. i. 39; iii. 543.

१०. Omitted by BK, C 4. C 5, Kn, M 3, Mi, R 4, R 6, W 1, W 2, W 3, and Durga.

११. Quoted by SRV. I. 148. 4. p. i.651.

१२. RV. IX. 110. 5; SV. 2. 857.

अर्को देवो भवति । यदेनमर्चन्ति[1] । अर्को मन्त्रो भवति । यदनेनार्चन्ति । अर्कमन्नं भवति । अर्चति भूतानि । अर्को वृक्षो भवति । संवृत्तः कटुकिम्ना[2] ॥ ४ ॥

> गायन्ति त्वा गायत्रिणोऽर्चन्त्यर्कमर्किणः ।
> ब्रह्माणस्त्वा शतक्रत उद्वंशमिव येमिरे[3] ॥

गायन्ति त्वा गायत्रिणः । प्रार्चन्ति तेऽर्कमर्किणः । ब्रह्माणस्त्वा[4] शतक्रत उद्येमिरे वंशमिव । वंशो वनशयो भवति । वननाच्छ्रूयत इति वा[5] ।

पवी रथनेमिर्भवति । यद्विपुनाति[6] भूमिम् ।

> उत पव्या रथानामद्रिं भिन्दन्त्योजसा[7] ।

> तं मरुतः क्षुरपविना व्ययुः[8] ।

इत्यपि निगमौ भवतः । वक्षो व्याख्यातम्[10] ।

धन्वान्तरिक्षम् । धन्वन्त्यस्मादापः[11] ।

> तिरो धन्वाति रोचते[12] । इत्यपि निगमो भवति ।

सिनमन्नं भवति । सिनाति भूतानि[13] ।

> येन स्मा सिनं भरथः सखिभ्यः[14] । इत्यपि निगमो भवति ।

इत्थामुथेत्येतेन व्याख्यातम्[15] ।

सचा सहेत्यर्थः[16] ।

> वसुभिः सचा भुवा[17] । वसुभिः सह भुवौ[18] ।

---

१. अर्चयन्ति C 4, C 5, M 3.

२. Quoted by SRV. I. 10. 1. p. i. 68. Sāyana reads सवृतः for संवृत्तः ।

३. RV. I. 10. 1; SV. I. 342; 2. 694.

४. ब्राह्मणाः C 1, C 2, C 3, C 6, M 1, M 2, R 1, R 2, R 5, S, & Roth.

५. Quoted by SRV. I. 10. 1. p. i. 68.

६. Cf. SRV. I. 138. 3; V. 62. 2; also I. 88. 2. pp. i. 620; ii. 642; i. 393.

७. RV. V. 52. 9.

८. व्ययु: C 4, C 5, M 3, Mi, W 1.

९. According to Durga, the quotation is from Some Brāhmaṇa, the passage in full being. देवा वै वृत्रस्य मर्म नाविदन् । तं मरुतः क्षुरपविना व्ययुः । सान्तपनं समतपंस्तस्मात् सान्तपनाः । इत्येतस्मिन्नपि च ब्राह्मणे etc.

१०. See N. 4. 16.

११. Quoted by SRV. I. 95. 10. p. i. 431.

१२. RV. X. 187. 2; AV. 6. 34. 3.

१३. Quoted by SRV. I. 61. 4. p. i.297.

१४. RV. III. 62. 1.

१५. See. N. 3. 16.

१६. Quoted by SRV. I. 7. 2; 34. 11; pp. i. 55, 185.

१७. Fragment of RV. II. 31. 1; VIII. 35. 1.

१८. भूवौ M 3.

चिदिति निपातोऽनुदात्तः पुरस्तादेव व्याख्यातः[1] । अथापि पशुनामेह भवत्युदात्तः ।

चिदसि मनोऽसि[2] । चितास्त्वयि भोगाः । चेतयसे इति वा ।

आ इत्याकार उपसर्गः पुरस्तादेव व्याख्यातः[3] । अथाप्यध्यर्थे दृश्यते ।

अभ्र आँ अपः[4] । अभ्रा आ अपोऽभ्रे ऽध्यय इति । [अभ्रे आ अपोऽपोऽभ्रेऽधीति][5]

द्युम्नं द्योततेः । यशो वान्नं वा[6] ।

अस्मे द्युम्नमधि रत्नं[7] च धेहि । अस्मासु द्युम्नं च रत्नं च धेहि[8] ॥ ५ ॥

पवित्रं पुनातेः । मन्त्रः पवित्रमुच्यते ।

येन देवाः पवित्रेणात्मानं पुनते सदा[9] । इत्यपि निगमो भवति ।

रश्मयः पवित्रमुच्यन्ते ।

गभस्तिपूतः[10] [नृभिरद्रिभिः सुतः ।][11] इत्यपि निगमो भवति ।

आपः पवित्रमुच्यन्ते ।

शतपवित्राः स्वधया मदन्तीः[12] । बहूदकाः[13] ।

अग्निः पवित्रमुच्यते । वायुः पवित्रमुच्यते । सोमः पवित्रमुच्यते । सूर्यः पवित्रमुच्यते[14] । इन्द्रः पवित्रमुच्यते ।

अग्निः पवित्रं स मा पुनातु वायुः सोमः[15] सूर्य इन्द्रः[16] ।

---

१. See N. 1. 4.

२. VS. 4. 19; 12. 53.

३. See N. 1. 4.

४. Fragment of RV. V. 48. 1.

५. This is the text of C 1, C 2, C 3, C 6, M 1, M 2, R 1, R 2, R 5, S, and Roth.

६. Quoted by SRV. I. 37. 4. p. i. 200.

७. RV. VII. 25. 3.

८. Quoted by SRV. VII. 25. 3. p. iii. 57.

९. SV. 2. 652.

१०. Fragment of VS. 7. 1. Read together with what follows in square brackets it is: RV. IX. 86. 34. S'ivadatta gives 2 quotations, one from VS. 7. 1, the other form RV. IX. 86. 34. and reads: इत्यपि निगमौ भवतः ।

११. Omitted by BK, C 4, C 5, Kn, M 3, Mi, R 4, R 6, W 1, W 2, W 3.

१२. RV. VII. 47. 3.

१३. बहुदकाः M 3, W 1.

१४. सूर्यः पवित्रमुच्यते is omitted here but is added in the beginning of the following section in C 1

१५. सोमा C 1, C 2, C 3, C 6, M 1, M 2, R 1, R 2, R. 5; Mi.

१६. The quotation is not traced.

पवित्रं ते मा पुनन्तु । इत्यपि निगमो भवति ।

तोदस्तुद्यतेः[1] ॥ ६ ॥

पुरु त्वा दाश्वान्वोचेऽरिरग्ने तव स्विदा ।

तोदस्येव शरण आ महस्य[2] ॥

बहु दाश्वांस्त्वामेवाभिह्वयामि । अरिरमित्र ऋच्छतेः । ईश्वरोऽप्यरिरेतस्मादेव । यदन्यदेवत्या अग्नावाहुतयो हूयन्त इत्येतद् दृष्ट्वैवमवक्ष्यत्[3] । तोदस्येव शरण आ महस्य । तुदस्येव शरणेऽधिमहतः[4] ।

स्वश्वाः सु अश्वनः ।

आ जुह्वानो घृतपृष्ठः स्वश्वाः[5] । इत्यपि निगमो भवति ।

शिपिविष्टो विष्णुरिति विष्णोर्द्वे नामनी भवतः । कुत्सितार्थीयं पूर्वं भवतीत्यौपमन्यवः ॥ ७ ॥

किमित्ते विष्णो परिचक्ष्यं भूत्प्र यद्ववक्षे शिपिविष्टो अस्मि ।

मा वर्पो अस्मदप गूह एतद् यदन्यरूपः समिथे बभूथ[6] ॥

किं ते विष्णोऽप्रख्यातमेतद्भवत्यप्रख्यापनीयं[7] यन्नः प्रब्रूषे शेप इव निर्वेष्टितोऽस्मीत्यप्रतिपन्नरश्मिः[8] । अपि वा प्रशंसानामैवाभिप्रेतं स्यात् । किं ते विष्णो प्रख्यातमेतद्भवति प्रख्यापनीयं यदुत प्रब्रूषे शिपिविष्टोऽस्मीति प्रतिपन्नरश्मिः । शिपयोऽत्र रश्मय उच्यन्ते । तैराविष्टो भवति । मा वर्पो अस्मदप गूह एतत् । वर्प इति रूपनाम । वृणोतीति सतः[9] । यदन्यरूपः समिथे संग्रामे भवसि संयतरश्मिः[10] ।

तस्योत्तरा भूयसे निर्वचनाय ॥ ८ ॥

---

१. Omitted by C 3.

२. RV. I. 150. 1; SV. 1. 97.

३. ०मवक्षत BK, C 4, C 5, Kn, M 3, Mi, R 4, R 6, W 1, W 2, W 3.

४. Quoted by SRV. I. 150. 1. p. i. 653.

५. RV. V. 37. 1.

६. RV. VII. 100. 6.

७. विष्णोः प्रख्यनाम० SRV. VII. 100. 6. p. iii. 208.

८. अस्मीति प्रतिपन्नरश्मिः S'ivadatta. It is evidently a mistake. The editor seems to have ignored the reading of Durga whose commentary he has edited with the text of the *Nirukta*.

९. वर्प इति...सतः is placed at the beginning of the 2nd pāda of the following stanza by C 3.

१०. The passage: शिपिविष्टो विष्णुरिति... संयतरश्मिः is quoted by SRV. VII. 100. 6. p. iii. 208.

प्र तत्ते[१] अद्य शिपिविष्ट नामार्यः शंसामि वयुनानि विद्वान्।
तं त्वा गृणामि तवसमतव्यान्क्षयन्तमस्य रजसः पराके ॥

तत्तेऽद्य शिपिविष्ट नामार्यः प्रशंसामि। अर्योऽहमस्मीश्वरः[२] स्तोमानाम्। अर्यस्त्वमसीति वा। तं त्वा[३] स्तौमि तवसमतव्यान्। तवस इति महतो नामधेयम्। उदितो भवति। निवसन्तमस्य रजसः। पराके पराक्रान्ते।

आघृणिरागतहृणिः।

आ घृणे सं सचावहै[४]। आगतहृणे संसेवावहै[५]।

पृथुज्रयाः पृथुजवः।

पृथुज्रया अमिना[६]दायुर्दस्योः। प्रामापयदायुर्दस्योः ॥ ९ ॥

अग्निं[७] नरो दीधितिभिररण्योर्हस्तच्युती जनयन्त प्रशस्तम्।
दूरेदृशं गृहपतिमथर्युम्[८] ॥

दीधितयोऽङ्गुलयो भवन्ति। धीयन्ते कर्मसु। अरणी प्रत्यृत एने अग्निः। समरणाज्जायत इति वा। हस्तच्युती हस्तप्रच्युत्या। जनयन्त प्रशस्तं दूरे दर्शनं गृहपतिमतनवन्तम्[९][१०] ॥ १० ॥

एकया प्रतिधा पिबत्साकं सरांसि त्रिंशतम्।
इन्द्रः सोमस्य काणुका[११] ॥

एकेन प्रतिधानेनापिबत्। साकं सहेत्यर्थः। इन्द्रः सोमस्य काणुका। कान्तकानीति वा। क्रान्तकानीति वा[१२]। कृतकानीति वा। इन्द्रः सोमस्य कान्त इति वा। कणेघात इति वा[१२]। कणेहतः। कान्तिहतः।

तत्रैतद् याज्ञिका वेदयन्ते। त्रिंशदुक्थपात्राणि माध्यन्दिने सवन एकदेवतानि। तान्येतस्मिन् काल एकेन प्रतिधानेन पिबन्ति। तान्यत्र सरांस्युच्यन्ते। त्रिंशदपरपक्षस्याहोरात्राः। त्रिंशत्पूर्वपक्षस्येति नैरुक्ताः। तद् या एताश्चान्द्रमस्य आगामिन्य आपो भवन्ति रश्मयस्ता अपरपक्षे पिबन्ति। तथापि निगमो भवति।

---

१. RV. VII. 100. 5.
२. अर्योऽहमीश्वरः is omitted by C 3.
३. तन्वा S'ivadatta.
४. RV. VI. 55. 1.
५. Cf. BD. iii. 95 B, 96 B, घृणि is explained by दीप्ति.
६. अमिनीदा०. M 3, W 1.
७. RV. III. 49. 2.
८. Cf. SRV. III. 49. 2. p. ii. 288.
९. RV. VII. 1. 1; SV. 1. 72; 2. 723.
१०. Cf. SRV. VII. 1. 1; VIII. 77. 4.
११. RV. VIII. 77. 4.
१२. Cf. Kumārila, Tantra Vārtika, Benares ed. p. 66 or I. 2. 49. अथवा कान्तकानीत्यादयो निरुक्तोक्ताः काणुकाशब्दविकल्पा योजनीयाः

यमक्षितिमक्षितयः पिबन्ति[1] । इति ।

तं पूर्वपक्ष[3] आप्याययन्ति । तथापि निगमो भवति ।

यथा देवा अंशुम[4]प्याययन्ति[5] । इति ।

अध्रिगुर्मन्त्रो भवति । गव्यधिकृतत्वात् । अपि वा प्र[6]शासनमेवाभिप्रेतं स्यात् । शब्दवत्त्वात् ।

अध्रिगो शमीध्वं सु[7]शमि शमीध्वं शमीध्वमध्रिग[8]विति ।

अग्निरप्यध्रिगुरुच्यते ।

तुभ्यं श्चोतन्त्यध्रिगो शचीव[9]ः । अधृतगमनकर्मवन् ।

इन्द्रोऽप्यध्रिगुरुच्यते[10] ।

अध्रिगव ओहमिन्द्राय[11] । इत्यपि निगमो भवति ।

आङ्गूषः स्तोम आघोषः[12] ।

एनाङ्गूषेण वयमिन्द्रवन्तः[13] ।

अनेन स्तोमेन वयमिन्द्रवन्तः[14] ॥ ११ ॥

आपान्तमन्युस्तृपलप्रभर्मा धुनिः शिमीवाञ्छरुमाँ ऋजीषी ।

सोमो विश्वान्यतसा वनानि नार्वागिन्द्रं प्रतिमानानि देभुः[15] ॥

आपातितमन्युः । तृप्रप्रहारी । [क्षिप्रप्रहारी सृप्रप्रहारी[16]] सोमो वेन्द्रो वा । धुनिर्धूनोतेः । शिमीति कर्मनाम । शमयतेर्वा । शक्नोतेर्वा । ऋजीषी सोमः । यत्सोमस्य पूयमानस्यातिरिच्यते तदृजीषमपार्जितं भवति । तेनर्जीषी सोमः । अथाप्यैन्द्रो निगमो भवति ।

ऋजीषी वज्री[17] । इति ।

---

१. According to Durga, some read अक्षितम्.
२. VS. 5. 7; of AV. 7. 81. 6; TS. ii. 4. 14. 1.
३. ०पक्षाप्याययन्ति C 1, C 4, M 1, M 2. M 3.
४. आंशुम् C 4, M 3.
५. VS. 5. 7.
६. प्रशंसानामैवा० BK, C 4, C 5, Kn, M 3, Mi, R 4, R 6, W 1, W 2, W 3.
७. सु C 5.
८. AB. ii. 7. 11.
९. RV. III. 21. 4.
१०. Quoted by SRV. I. 61. 1. p. i. 296.
११. RV. I. 61. 1; AV. 20. 35. 1.
१२. Quoted by SRV. I. 61. 2; 62. 1; pp. i. 297, 304.
१३. RV. I. 105. 19.
१४. Quoted by SRV. I. 105. 19. p. i. 468.
१५. RV. X. 89. 5.
१६. Omitted by BK, C 4, C 5, Kn, M 2, Mi, R 4, R 6, W 1, W 2, W 3. क्षिप्रप्रहारी is omitted by C 3. and सृप्रप्रहारी by Durga. It is however quoted by SRV. IX. 97. 8. p. iii. 778.
१७. RV. V. 40 4; AV. 20. 12. 7.

हर्योरस्य स भागो धानाश्चेति । धाना भ्राष्ट्रे हिता भवन्ति । फले हिता भवन्तीति वा ।

बब्धां ते हरी धाना उप ऋजीषं जिघ्रताम्[1] ।

इत्यपि निगमो भवति । आदिनाभ्यासेनोपहितेनोपधामादत्ते । बभस्तिरत्ति-[2]कर्मा । सोमः सर्वाण्यतसानि वनानि । नार्वागिन्द्रं प्रतिमानानि दभ्नुवन्ति[3] । यैरेनं प्रतिमिमते नैनं तानि दभ्नुवन्ति[4] । अर्वागेवैनमप्राप्य[5] विनश्यन्तीति । इन्द्रप्रधानेत्येके । नैघण्टुकं सोमकर्म । उभयप्रधानेत्यपरम् ।

श्मशा शु अश्नुत इति वा । श्माश्नुत इति वा ।

अवं श्मशा रुधद्वाः[6] ।

अवारुधच्छ्मशा वारिति ॥ १२ ॥

उर्वश्यप्सरा[7] । उर्वभ्यश्नुते । ऊरुभ्यामश्नुते[8] । उरुर्वा वशोऽस्याः[9] । अप्सरा अप्सारिणी । अपि वाप्स इति रूपनाम[10] । अप्सातेः । अप्सानीयं भवति । आदर्शनीयम् । व्यापनीयं वा । स्पष्टं दर्शनायेति शाकपूणिः ।

यदप्सः[12] । इत्यभक्षस्य ।

अप्सो नाम[13] ।

इति व्यापिनः । तद्रा भवति रूपवती । तदनयात्तमिति वा । तदस्यै दत्तमिति वा । तस्या दर्शनान्मित्रावरुणयो रेतश्चस्कन्द[14] । तदभिवादिन्येषर्ग्भवति ॥ १३ ॥

---

१. The quotation is untraced.

२. बभत्तिरत्ति०. C 4, M 3, W 2.

३. दभ्नुवन्ति C 3.

४. The passage आपातितमन्यु...दभ्नुवन्ति is quoted by SRV. X. 89. 5. p. IV. 284 where the lines हर्योरस्य... ...बभस्तिरत्तिकर्म do not occur.

५. अर्वाङ्गेवै० C 4, M 3, W 1.

६. RV. X. 105. 1; SV. 1. 228.

७. Cf. BD. VII. 153.

८. उरुभ्याम् S'ivadatta. उरु is evidently a mistake for ऊरु. ऊरु occuring in Durga's commentary is correctly printed in the same edition.

९. Quoted by SRV. IV. 2. 18. p. ii. 353.

१०. Cf. BD. ii. 59.

११. Quoted by SRV. VII. 4. 6. p. iii. 14.

१२. KS. IX. 4. MS. I. 10. 2. Cf. VS. 20. 17. According to Durga, the quotation is the following.

यद् ग्रामे यदरण्ये यत्सभायां यदिन्द्रिये । यदेनश्चकृमा वयं यदप्सश्चकृमा वयं यदेकस्यापि धर्मणि एनस्ततोऽवयजनमसि स्वाहा ॥

VS. 20. 17 is the following:

यद् ग्रामे यदरण्ये यत्सभायां यदिन्द्रिये । यच्छूद्रे यदर्ये यदेनश्चकृमा वयं यदेकस्याधि धर्मणि तस्यावयजनमसि ॥

१३. VS. 14. 4.

१४. Cf. BD. V. 149.

उतासि मैत्रावरुणो वसिष्ठोर्वश्या ब्रह्मन्मनसोऽधिजातः ।
द्रप्सं स्कन्नं ब्रह्मणा दैव्येन विश्वेदेवाः पुष्करे त्वाददन्त [1] ॥

अप्यसि मैत्रावरुणो वसिष्ठ । उर्वश्या ब्रह्मन् मनसोऽधिजातः । द्रप्सं स्कन्नम् । ब्रह्मणा दैव्येन । द्रप्सः संभृतः [2] । प्सानीयो [3] भवति । सर्वे देवाः पुष्करे त्वाधारयन्त [4] । पुष्करमन्तरिक्षम् । पोषति [5] भूतानि । उदकं [6] पुष्करम् । पूजाकरम् । पूजयितव्यम् [7] । इदमपीतरत्पुष्करमेतस्मादेव । पुष्करं वपुष्करं वा । पुष्पं पुष्पतेः ।

वयुनं वेतेः । कान्तिर्वा । प्रज्ञा वा ॥ १४ ॥

स इत्तमोऽवयुनं ततन्वत्सूर्येण वयुनवच्चकार [9] ।

स तमोऽप्रज्ञानं ततन्वत् । सं [10] तं सूर्येण प्रज्ञानवच्चकार ।

वाजपस्त्यं [11] वाजपतनम् ।

सनेम वाजपस्त्यं [12] । इत्यपि निगमो भवति ।

वाजगन्ध्यं गध्यत्युत्तरपदम् [13] ।

अश्याम वाजगन्ध्यम् [14] । इत्यपि निगमो भवति ।

गध्यं गृह्णातेः [15] ।

ऋज्रा वाजं न गध्यं युयूषन् [16] । इत्यपि निगमो भवति [17] ।

गध्यतिर्मिश्रीभावकर्मा [18] ।

आ गधिता परि गधिता [19] । इत्यपि निगमो भवति ।

कौरयाणः कृतयानः ।

---

१. RV. VII. 33. 11.

२. संभृत C 1, C 2. C 3, C 4, C 6, M 1, M 2.

३. प्सानीयो भवति भक्षणीयो भरणीयश्च । Durga.

४. Cf. BD. V. 155.

५. पोषधि C 5, M 3, W 1, W 2.

६. उकम् S'ivadatta.

७. वा is added after पूजयितव्यम् by C 1, C 3, M 1.

८. =पद्मम् Durga.

९. RV. VI. 21. 3.

१०. सूतं S'ivadatta.

११. वाजपस्त्यं is omitted by C 5.

१२. RV. IX. 98. 12; SV. 2. 1030.

१३. गध्यमित्युत्तर० Mi.

१४. RV. IX. 98. 12; SV. 2. 1030.

१५. Quoted by SRV. I. 126. 6. p. i. 572.

१६. RV. IV. 16. 11.

१७. Cf. SRV. IV. 16. 11. p. ii. 391.

१८. Cf. SRV. I. 126. 6; IV. 38. 4; pp. i. 572; ii. 454.

१९. RV. I. 126. 6.

पाकस्थामा कौरयाणः[1] । इत्यपि निगमो भवति ।

तौरयाणस्तूर्णयानः ।

स तौरयाण उप याहि यज्ञं मरुद्भिरिन्द्र सखिभिः सजोषाः[2] ।

इत्यपि निगमो भवति ।

अह्रयाणोऽह्रीतयानः ।

अनुष्टुया कृणुह्यह्रयाणः[3] । इत्यपि निगमो भवति ।

हरयाणो हरमाणयानः ।

रजतं हरयाणे[4] । इत्यपि निगमो भवति ।

य आरितः कर्मणिकर्मणि स्थिरः[5] । प्रत्यृतः स्तोमान्[6] ।

व्रन्दी व्रन्दतेर्मृदूभावकर्मणः ॥ १५ ॥

नि यद्वृणक्षि श्वसनस्य मूर्धनि शुष्णस्य चिद्व्रन्दिनो रोरुवद्वना[7] ।

निवृणक्षि यच्छ्वसनस्य मूर्धनि शब्दकारिणः । शुष्णस्यादित्यस्य [च[8]] शोषयितु । रोरूयमाणो वनानीति वा[9] । वधेनेति वा[10] ।

अव्रन्दन्त वीळिता[11] । इत्यपि निगमो भवति ।

वीळयतिश्च व्रीळयतिश्च संस्तम्भकर्माणौ[12] । पूर्वेण संप्रयुज्येते ।

निष्षपी[13] स्त्रीकामो भवति । विनिर्गतसपः । सपः[14] सपतेः[15] स्पृशतिकर्मणः[16] ।

मा नो मघेव निष्षपी[13] परा दाः[17] ।

१. RV. VIII. 3. 21.

२. The quotation is untraced. See Roth, p. 65.

३. RV. IV. 4. 14.

४. RV. VIII. 25. 23.

५. RV. I. 101. 4.

६. Cf. SRV. VIII. 33. 5. p. iii. 392.

७. RV. I. 54. 5.

८. Omitted by BK, C 4, C 5, Kn, M 3, Mi, R 4, R 6, W 1, W 2, W 3.

९. Omitted by C 3.

१०. Cf. SRV. I. 54. 5. p. i. 275,...वन्तनीति वा धनानीति वा ।

११. Fragment of RV. II. 24. 3.

१२. Cf. SRV. II. 24. 3. p. ii. 70.

१३. निष्पपी C 6, M 3, Mi, W 1, W 2.

१४. स्पशः M 3, Mi; स्पसः C 4, W 1; स्पसं W 2. It is omitted altogether in C 5.

१५. स्पशते: M 3, Mi, स्पसते ल; स्पंसते: W 2.

१६. Cf. SRV. IX. 97. 37. p. iii. 786. सपतिः स्पृशतिकर्मेति नैरुक्ताः ।

१७. RV. I. 104. 5.

स यथा धनानि विनाशयंति[1] मा नस्त्वं तथा परादाः ।

तूर्णाशमुदकं भवति । तूर्णमश्नुते[2] ।

तूर्णाशं न गिरेरधि[3] । इत्यपि निगमो भवति ।

क्षुम्पमहिच्छत्रकं भवति । यत् क्षुभ्यते ॥ १६ ॥

कदा मर्तमराधसं पदा क्षुम्पमिव स्फुरत् ।
कदा नः शुश्रवद्गिर इन्द्रो अङ्ग[4] ॥

कदा मर्तमनाराधयन्तं पादेन क्षुम्पमिवावस्फुरिष्यति[5] । कदा नः श्रोष्यति[6] च गिर इन्द्रो अङ्ग । अङ्गेति क्षिप्रनाम[7] । अङ्कितमेवाञ्चितं[8] भवति[9] ।

निचुम्पुणः सोमः । निचान्तपृणः[10] । निचमनेन प्रीणाति ॥ १७ ॥

पत्नीवन्तः सुता इम उशन्तो यन्ति वीतये ।
अपां जग्मिर्निचुम्पुणः[11] ॥

पत्नीवन्तः सुता इमेऽद्भिः सोमाः कामयमाना यन्ति वीतये पानायापाम् । गन्ता निचुम्पुणः ।

समुद्रोऽपि निचुंपुण उच्यते । निचमनेन पूर्यते । अवंभृथोऽपि[12] निचुंपुण उच्यते । नीचैरस्मिन् क्वणन्ति । नीचैर्दधतीति वा ।

अवभृथ निचुम्पुणः[13] । इत्यपि निगमो भवति ।

निचुंपुण निचुंकुणेति च ।

पदिर्गन्तुर्भवति[14] । यत्पद्यते ॥ १८ ॥

सुगुरसत्सुहिरण्यः स्वश्वो बृहदस्मै वय इन्द्रो दधाति ।
यस्त्वा यन्तं वसुना प्रातरित्वो मुक्षीजयेव पदिमुत्सिनाति[15] ॥

---

१. विभजति SRV. I. 104. 5. p. i, 459.

२. अश्नुते: BK, C 4, C 5, Kn, M 3, Mi, R 4, R 6, W 1, W 2, W 3; Quoted by SRV. VIII. 32. 4. p. iii. 387.

३. RV. VIII. 32. 4.

४. RV. I. 84. 8.

५. अवस्फुरसि BK, C 4, C 5, Kn, M 3, Mi, R 4, R 6, W 1, W 2, W 3, and Durga.

६. शृणेति BK, C 4, C 5, Kn, M 3, Mi, R 4, R 6, W 1, W 2, W 3, and Durga.

७. The passage: क्षुम्पमहिच्छत्रकं...क्षिप्रनाम is quoted by SRV. I. 84. 8. p. i. 376.

८. अंचितमेवांकितम् C 1, C 2, C 3, C 6, M 1, M 2, R 1, R 2, R 5, S.

९. The passage: अङ्गेति...भवति is omitted by Durga.

१०. Cf. SRV. VIII. 93. 22. p. iii. 563.

११. RV. VIII. 93. 22.

१२. निभृथो M 1.

१३. VS. 3. 48; 8. 27; 20. 18.

१४. Cf. SRV. I. 125. 2. p. i. 568.

१५. RV. I. 125. 2.

सुगुर्भवति । सुहिरण्यः । स्वश्वः । महच्चास्मै वय इन्द्रो दधाति यस्त्वा यन्तमन्नेन । प्रातरागामिन्नतिथे । मुक्षीजयेव[1] पदिमुत्सिनाति कुमारः । मुक्षीजा मोचनाच्च । शयनाच्च[2] । ततनाच्च ।

पादुः पद्यतेः ।

आविः स्वः कृणुते गूहते बुसं स पादुरस्य निर्णिजो न मुच्यते[3] ।

आविष्कुरुते भासमादित्यः । गूहते बुसम् । बुसमित्युदकनाम । ब्रवीतेः शब्दकर्मणः । भ्रंशतेर्वा । यद्वर्षन्पातयत्युदकं रश्मिभिस्तत्प्रत्यादत्ते ॥ १९ ॥

वृकश्चन्द्रमा भवति । विवृतज्योतिष्को वा । विकृतज्योतिष्को वा । विक्रान्तज्योतिष्को वा ॥ २० ॥

अरुणो मासकृद्[4] वृकः पथा यन्तं[5] ददर्श हि ।
उज्जिहीते निचाय्या तष्टेव पृष्ठ्यामयी वित्तं मे अस्य रोदसी[8] ॥

अरुण आरोचनः । मासकृन्मासानां चार्धमासानां च कर्ता[6] [भवति[7]] चन्द्रमाः । वृकः पथा यन्तं ददर्श नक्षत्रगणम् । अभिजिहीते निचाय्य येन येन योक्ष्यमाणो भवति चन्द्रमाः । तक्ष्णुवन्निव पृष्ठरोगी । जानीतं मेऽस्य द्यावापृथिव्याविति ।

आदित्योऽपि वृक उच्यते । यदा वृङ्क्ते ।

अजोहवीदश्विना वर्तिका वामास्नो यत्सीममुञ्चतं वृकस्य[9] ।

आह्वयदुषा[10] अश्विनावादित्येनाभिग्रस्ता । तामश्विनौ प्रमुमुचतुः[11] । इत्याख्यानम्[12] ।

श्वापि वृक उच्यते । विकर्तनात् ।

वृकश्चिदस्य वारण उरामथिः[13] । उरणमथिः ।

उरण ऊर्णावान्भवति । ऊर्णा पुनर्वृणोतेः । ऊर्णोतेर्वा ।

वृद्धवाशिन्यपि वृक्युच्यते ।

---

१. मक्षीजयेव C 1, C 2, C 3, C 6, M 1, M 2, R 1, R 2, R 5, S.

२. सयनाच्च C 1, C 3, C 6, M 2, W 2.

३. RV. X. 27. 24.

४. मा सकृत् is attributed to a different recension by Durga who paraphrases as follows: सकृत् मां ददर्श ।

५. RV. I. 105. 18; cf. BD. ii. 112.

६. Cf. BD. ii. 112.

७. Omitted by BK, C 4, C 5, Kn, M 3, Mi, R 4, R 6, W 1, W 2, W 3.

८. Cf. I. SRV. I. 105. 18. p. i. 463.

९. RV. I. 117. 16.

१०. अजह्वयत् BK, C 4, C 5, Kn, M 3, Mi, R 4, R 6, W 1, W 2, W 3.

११. प्रमुमुंचतु: BK, C 4, C 5, Kn, M 3, Mi, R 4, R 6, W 1, W 2, W 3.

१२. Quoted by SRV. I. 117. 16. p. i. 528.

१३. RV. VIII. 66. 8; AV. 20. 97. 2; SV. 2. 1042.

शतं मेषान्वृक्यै चक्षदानमृज्राश्वं तं पितान्धं चकार[1] ।

इत्यपि निगमो भवति ।

जोष[वाकं][2] इत्यविज्ञातनामधेयम् । जोषयितव्यं भवति ॥ २१ ॥

य इन्द्राग्नी सुतेषु वां स्तवत्तेष्वृतावृधा ।

जोषवाकं वदतः पज्रहोषिणा न देवा भसथश्चन[3] ॥

य इन्द्राग्नी सुतेषु वां सोमेषु स्तौति तस्याश्नीथः । अथ योऽयं जोषवाकं वदति विजंजपः प्राजितहोषिणौ न देवौ तस्याश्नीथः[4] ।

कृत्तिः कृन्ततेः । यशो वा । अन्नं वा ।

महीव कृत्तिः शरणा त इन्द्र[5] ।

सुमहत्त इन्द्र शरणमन्तरिक्षे[6] कृत्तिरिवेति[7] । इयमपीतरा कृत्तिरेतस्मादेव । सूत्रमयी । उपमार्थे वा ।

कृत्तिवासाः पिनाकहस्तो अवततधन्वा[8] ।

[कृत्तिं वसान आचर पिनाकं बिभ्रदागहि[9] ।]

इत्यपि निगमो भवति ।

श्वघ्नी कितवो भवति । स्वं हन्ति[10] । स्वं पुनराश्रितं भवति ।

कृतं न श्वघ्नी वि चिनोति देवने[11] ।

कृतमिव श्वघ्नी विचिनोति देवने । कितवः किं तवास्तीति शब्दानुकृतिः । कृतवान्वा[12] । आशीर्नामकः ।

सममिति परिग्रहार्थीयम् । सर्वनामानुदात्तम् ॥ २२ ॥

मा नः समस्य दूढ्यः परिद्वेषसो अंहुतिः ।

ऊर्मिर्न नावमा वधीत्[13] ॥

---

१. RV. I. 116. 16.

२. Omitted by BK, C 4, C 5, Kn, M 3, Mi, R 4, R 6, W 1, W 2, W 3.

३. RV. VI. 59. 4.

४. Cf. SRV. VI. 59. 4. p. ii. 849.

५. RV. VIII. 90. 6; SV. 2. 762.

६. अन्तरिक्षम् BK, C 4, C 5, Kn, M 3, Mi, R 4, R 6, W 1, W 2, W 3.

७. Cf. SRV. VIII. 90. 6. p. iii. 549.

८. KS. 9. 7; Cf. अवततधन्वा पिनाकावसः etc. VS. 3. 61; S'B. ii. 6. 2. 17; अवततधन्वाकृत्तिवासाः पिनाकहस्तः TS. i. 8. 6. 2. Omitted by Durga and C 2, C 3, C 6, M 1, M 2, R 1, R 2, R 5, S.

९. VS. 16. 51. Omitted by BK, C 4, C 5, Kn, M 3, Mi, R 4, R 6, W 1, W 2, W 3; C 1, and Roth.

१०. Cf. SRV. VIII. 45. 38. p. iii. 435.

११. RV. X. 43. 5; AV. 20. 17. 5; Cf. RV. X. 42. 9; AV. 7. 50. 6; 20. 89. 9.

१२. कितवान्वा C 3, C 4, C 5, Mi, W 1, W 2.

१३. RV. VIII. 75. 9.

मा नः सर्वस्य दुर्धियः पापधियः सर्वतो द्वेषसो अंहतिः ।

ऊर्मिरिव नावमावधीत् । ऊर्मिरूर्णोतेः । नौः प्रणोत्तव्या भवति । नमतेर्वा । तत्कथमनुदात्तप्रकृतिनाम स्यात् । दृष्टव्ययं तु भवति ।

उतो समस्मिन्ना शिशीहि नो वसो[२] ।

इति सप्तम्याम् । शिशीतिर्दानकर्मा ।

उरुष्या णो अघायतः समस्मात्[३] ।

इति पञ्चम्याम् । उरुष्यतिरकर्मकः[४] । अथापि प्रथमा बहुवचने ।

नभन्तामन्यके समे[५] ॥ २३ ॥

हविषा जारो अपां पिपर्ति पपुरिर्नरा ।
पिता कुटस्य चर्षणिः[६] ॥

हविषापां जरयिता[७] । पिपर्ति पपुरिरिति पृणातिनिगमौ[८] वा । प्रीणातिनिगमौ वा । पिता कृतस्य कर्मणश्चायितादित्यः[९] ।

शम्ब इति वज्रनाम । शमयतेर्वा । शातयतेर्वा[१०] ।

उग्रो यः शम्बः पुरुहूत तेन[११] । इत्यपि निगमो भवति ।

केपयः कपूया भवन्ति । कपूयमिति । पुनाति कर्म कुत्सितम् । दुष्पूयं भवति ॥ २४ ॥

पृथक्प्रायन्प्रथमा देवहूतयोऽकृण्वत श्रवस्यानि दुष्टरा ।
न ये शेकुर्यज्ञियां नावमारुहमीर्मैव ते न्यविशन्त केपयः[१२] ॥

पृथक्प्रायन् । पृथक् प्रथतेः । प्रथमा देवहूतयः । ये देवानाह्वयन्त । अकुर्वत श्रवणीयानि यशांसि । दुरनुकराण्यन्यैः । येऽशक्नुवन् यज्ञियां नावमारोढुम् ।

अथ ये नाशक्नुवन् यज्ञियां नावमारोढुम् । ईर्मैव ते न्यविशन्त । इहैव ते न्यविशन्त । ऋणे हैव[१३] ते न्यविशन्त ।

---

१. Cf. SRV. VIII. 75. 9. p. iii. 519.

२. RV. VIII. 21. 8.

३. RV. V. 24. 3; VS. 3. 26.

४. उरुष्यती रक्षाकर्मा C 1, C 2, C 3, C 6, M 1, M 2, R 1, R 2, R 5, S and Roth. Cf. SRV. I. 58. 8; 19. 15; 119. 6.

५. RV. VIII. 39. 1—10. The passage उरुष्यति...समे is omitted by Durga; नभन्तामन्यके समे is omitted by C 1.

६. RV. I. 46. 4.

७. जारयिता C 3.

८. ०निगमो C 5.

९. Cf. SRV. I. 46. 4. p. i. 232.

१०. Cf. SRV. X. 42. 7. p. IV. 127.

११. RV. X. 42. 7; AV. 20. 89. 7.

१२. RV. X. 44. 6; AV. 20. 94. 6.

१३. नैव BK, C 4, C 5, Kn, M 3, Mi, R 4, R 6, W 1, W 2, W 3.

अस्मिन्नेव लोक इति वा । ईर्मं इति बाहुनाम । समीरिततरो भवति ।

एता विश्वा सवना तूतुमाकृषे स्वयं सूनो सहसो यानि दधिषे[2] ।

एतानि सर्वाणि स्थानानि तूर्णमुपाकुरुषे । स्वयं बलस्य पुत्र यानि धत्स्व ।

अंसत्रमंहसस्त्राणम् । धनुर्वा । कवचं वा । कवचं कु अंचितं भवति । कांचितं भवति । कायेऽञ्चितं भवतीति वा ॥ २५ ॥

प्रीणीताश्वान्हितं जयाथ स्वस्तिवाहं रथमित्कृणुध्वम् ।
द्रोणाहावमवतमश्मचक्रमंसत्रकोशं सिञ्चता नृपाणम्[3] ॥

प्रीणीताश्वान्त्सुहितं जयथ । जयनं वो हितमस्तु । स्वस्तिवाहनं[4] रथं कुरुध्वम् । द्रोणाहावम् । द्रोणं द्रुममयं भवति । आहाव आह्वानात् । आवह आवहनात् । अवतोऽवातितो महान्भवति । अश्मचक्रमशनचक्रमसनचक्रमिति वा । अंसत्रकोशम् । अंसत्राणि वः[5] कोशस्थानीयानि सन्तु । कोशः कुष्णातेः । विकुषितो भवति । अयमपीतरः कोश एतस्मादेव । सञ्चय आचितमात्रो महान्भवति । सिंचत नृपाणं नरपाणम् । कूपकर्मणा संग्राममुपमिमीते ।

काकुदं तालवित्याचक्षते । जिह्वा कोकुवा । साऽस्मिन्धीयते । जिह्वा कोकुवा । कोकूयमाना वर्णान्नुदतीति[6] वा[7] । [कोकूयतेर्वा स्याच्छब्दकर्मणः ।][8] जिह्वा जोह्वा । तालु तेरतेः । तीर्णतममङ्गम्[10] । लततेर्वा स्याद् [लंबकर्मणः[11]] विपरीतात् । यथा तलम् । लतेत्यविपर्ययः ॥ २६ ॥

सुदेवो असि वरुण यस्य ते सप्त सिन्धवः ।
अनुक्षरन्ति काकुदं सूर्म्यं सुषिरामिव[12] ॥

सुदेवस्त्वं कल्याणदानः । यस्य तव देव सप्त सिन्धवः प्राणायानुक्षरन्ति काकुदम्[13] । सूर्म्यं सुषिरामिवेति । अपि निगमो भवति[14] ॥ २७ ॥

---

१. Cf. SRV. X. 45. 6. p. IV. 132.

२. RV. X. 50. 6.

३. RV. X. 101. 7.

४. स्वस्तिवान् C 3.

५. वा BK, C 4, C 5, Kn, M 3, Mi, R 4, R 6, W 1, W 2, W 3.

६. एनान्नुदतीति BK, C 4, C 5, Kn, M 3, Mi, R 4, R 6, W 1, W 2, W 3.

७. Cf. PMbh. i. 1. 1. p. i. 4.

८. Omitted by BK, C 4, C 5, Kn, M 3, Mi, R 4, R 6, W 1, W 2, W 3.

९. तलतेः C 1, C 3.

१०. अङ्गः C 3.

११. Omitted by C 1, C 2, C 3, C 6, M 1, M 2, R 1, R 2, R 5, S.

१२. RV. VIII. 69. 12; AV. 20. 92. 9.

१३. Cf. PMbh. i. 1. 1. p. i. 4.

१४. This is the text of BK, C 4, C 5, Kn, M 3, R 4, R 6, W 1, W 2, W 3.

[सुदेवस्त्वं कल्याणदेवः । कमनीयदेवो वा भवसि वरुण । यस्य ते सप्त-सिंधवः । सिंधुः स्रवणात् । यस्य ते सप्त स्रोतांसि । तानि ते काकुदमनुक्षरन्ति । सूर्मिः कल्याणोर्मिः । स्रोतः सुषिरमनु यथा । बीरिटं तैटीकिरन्तरिक्षमेवमाह पूर्वं वयतेः । उत्तरमिरतेः । वयांसीरन्त्यस्मिन् । भांसि वा । तदेतस्यामृच्युदाहरन्ति । अपि निगमो भवति ॥ २७ ॥][1]

प्र वां॑वृजे सु॒प्रया ब॒र्हिरे॑षा॒मा वि॒श्पती॑व बीरि॑ट इयाते ।
वि॒शाम॒क्तोरु॒षसः॑ पू॒र्वहू॑तौ वा॒युः पू॒षा स्व॒स्तये॑ नि॒यु॒त्वान्॑[2] ॥

प्रवृज्यते सुप्रायणं बर्हिरेषाम् । एयाते सर्वस्य पातारौ वा पालयितारौ वा । बीरिटमन्तरिक्षम् । भियो वा भासो वा ततिः । अपि वोपमार्थे स्यात् । सर्वपती इव राजानौ । बीरिटे गणे मनुष्याणाम् । रात्र्या विवासे पूर्वस्यामभिहूतौ । वायुश्च नियुत्वान् । पूषा च स्वस्त्ययनाय । नियुत्वान्नियुतोऽस्याश्वाः । नियुतो नियमनाद्वा । नियोजनाद्वा ।

अच्छाभेराप्तुमिति शाकपूणिः ।
परीं सीमिति व्याख्यातम्[3] ।

एनमेनामस्या अस्येत्येतेन व्याख्यातम्[4] ।

सृणिरङ्कुशो भवति सरणात् । अङ्कुशोऽञ्चतेः । आकुंचितो[5] भवतीति वा ।

नेदी॑य इत्सृ॒ण्यः॑ प॒क्वमेया॑त्[6] । इत्यपि निगमो भवति ।

अन्तिकतममंकुशादायात् । पक्वमौषधमागच्छत्विति । आगच्छत्विति ॥ २८ ॥

इति पञ्चमोऽध्यायः ।

[संस्निमसंश्चन्तीन यस्य[3] वराहो गायन्ति त्वां पवित्रं पुरु त्वां किमित्ते प्रतत्तेऽग्निर्नर एकया पान्तमन्युरुर्वश्यप्सरा उतासि सं इन्द्रियत्कदा मर्ते पत्नीवन्तः सुगुरसदृकश्चन्द्रमा अरुणो मा ये इन्द्राग्नी मा नः समस्य हविषा जारः पृथक्प्रायन्प्रीणीताश्वान्सुदेवः प्रवांवृजेऽष्टाविंशतिः ॥][7]

॥ इति निरुक्ते पूर्वषट्के पञ्चमोऽध्यायः समाप्तः ॥

---

१. This is the text of C 1, C 2, C 3, C 6, M 1, M 2, R 1, R 2, R 5, S. The entire passage is added after the shorter version in Mi.

२. RV. VII. 39. 2; VS. 33. 44.

३. व्याख्याताः C 1, C 2, C 3, C 6, M 1, M 2, R 1, R 2, R 5, S. See N. 1. 7.

४. See N. 4. 25.

५. आकुसितो C 1, C 6, M 3.

६. RV. X. 101. 3; VS. 12. 68; S'B. VII. 2. 2. 5.

७. Small figure within brackets represents the corresponding section of the fifth chapter of the *Nirukta*.

अथ षष्ठोऽध्यायः।

त्वमग्ने द्युभिस्त्वमाशुशुक्षणिस्त्वमद्भ्यस्त्वमश्मनस्परि।
त्वं वनेभ्यस्त्वमोषधीभ्यस्त्वं नृणां नृपते जायसे शुचिः॥

त्वमग्ने द्युभिरहोभिः[२]। त्वमाशुशुक्षणिः। आशु इति च शु इति च क्षिप्रनामनी भवतः[३]। क्षणिरुत्तरः[४]। क्षणोतेः। आशु शुचा क्षणोतीति वा। सनोतीति वा। शुक् शोचतेः। पञ्चम्यर्थे वा प्रथमा। तथा हि वाक्यसंयोगः। आ इत्याकार उपसर्गः पुरस्तात्। चिकीर्षितज उत्तरः। आशुशोचयिषुरिति। शुचिः शोचतेः। ज्वलतिकर्मणः। अयमपीतरः शुचिरेतस्मादेव। निःषिक्तमस्मात्पापकमिति नैरुक्ताः।

इन्द्र आशाभ्यस्परि सर्वाभ्यो अभयं करत्।

आशा दिशो भवन्ति। आसदनात्। आशा उपदिशो भवन्ति। अभ्यशनात्।
काशिर्मुष्टिः[६] प्रकाशनात्। मुष्टिर्मोचनाद्वा। मोषणाद्वा। मोहनाद्वा।

इमे चिदिन्द्र रोदसी अपारे यत्संगृभ्णा मघवन्काशिरित्ते।

इमे चिदिन्द्र रोदसी रोधसी द्यावापृथिव्यौ। विरोधनात्। रोधः कूलं निरुणद्धि स्रोतः। कूलं रुजतेः। विपरीतात्। लोष्टोऽविपर्ययेण। अपारे दूरपारे। यत्संगृभ्णासि मघवन्। काशिस्ते महान्[९]।

अहस्तमिन्द्र सं पिणक्कुणारुम्[१०]।

अहस्तमिन्द्र कृत्वा संपिण्ढि[११] परिक्वणनं मेघम्[१२]॥ १॥

अलातृणो वल इन्द्र व्रजो गोः पुरा हन्तोर्भयमानो[१३] व्यार।
सुगान्पथो अकृणोन्निरजे गाः प्रावन्वाणीः पुरुहूतं[१४] धमन्तीः[१५]॥

---

१. RV. II. 1. 1; VS. 11. 27.
२. Cf. SRV. II. 1. 1. p. ii. 1.
३. Cf. SRV. IV. 58. 7. p. ii. 493.
४. उत्तरम् M 3.
५. RV. II. 41. 12; AV. 20. 20. 7; 57. 10.
६. SRV. III. 30. 5. p. ii. 219.
७. RV. III. 30. 5.
८. SRV. I. 38. 11. p. i. 206.
९. Cf. S'abara on Mīmāṃsā sūtra IX. 1. 9.
१०. RV. III. 30. 8; VS. 18. 69.
११. संपिड्ढि BK, C 4, C 5, Kn, M 3, Mi, R 4, R 6, W 1, W 2, W 3; संपिद्धि C 3.
१२. SRV. III. 30. 8. p. ii. 220.
१३. हतो० C 1, C 3, M 2.
१४. पुरुहूत C 3, C 5, M 1, M 2.
१५. RV. III. 30. 10.

अलातृणोऽलमातर्दनो मेघः। वलो वृणोतेः। व्रजो व्रजत्यन्तरिक्षे। गोरेतस्या[1] माध्यमिकाया वाचः। पुरा हननाद्धयमानो व्यार। सुगान्पथो अकृणोन्निरजे गाः। सुगमनान्पथो अकरोत्[2]। निरजनाय[3] गवाम्। प्रावन्वाणीः पुरुहूतं धमन्तीः[4]। आपो वा नहनात्। वाचो वा वदनात्। बहुभिराहूतमुदकं भवति। धमतिर्गतिकर्मा ॥ २ ॥

उद्वृह रक्षः सहमूलमिन्द्र वृश्चा मध्यं प्रत्यग्रं शृणीहि।

आ कीवतः सललूकं चकर्थ ब्रह्मद्विषे तपुषिं[5] हेतिमस्य[6] ॥

उद्धर रक्षः सहमूलमिन्द्र। मूलं मोचनाद्वा। मोषणाद्वा। मोहनाद्वा[7]। वृश्च मध्यम्। प्रति शृणीह्यग्रम्। अग्रमागतं भवति। आ कियतो[8] देशात्। सललूकं संलुब्धं भवति। पापकमिति नैरुक्ताः। सररुकं[9] वा स्यात्। सर्तेरभ्यस्तात्[10]। तपुषिस्तपतेः। हेतिर्हन्तेः[11]।

त्वं चिदित्था कत्पयं शयानम्[12]।

सुखपयसम्। सुखमस्य पयः।

विस्रुह आपो भवन्ति। विस्रवणात्।

वया इव रुरुहुः सप्त विस्रुहः[13]। इत्यपि निगमो भवति।

वीरुध ओषधयो भवन्ति। विरोहणात्।

वीरुधः पारयिष्णवः[14]। इत्यपि निगमो भवति।

नक्षद्दाभम्। अश्नुवानदाभम्। अभ्यशनेन दभ्नोतीति वा।

नक्षद्दाभं ततुरिं पर्वतेष्ठाम्[15]। इत्यपि निगमो भवति।

अस्कृधोयुरकृध्वायुः। कृध्विति ह्रस्वनाम। निकृत्तं भवति[16]।

यो अस्कृधोयुरजरः स्वर्वान्[17]। इत्यपि निगमो भवति।

---

१. घोरेतस्या M 3.

२. ऽकरोत् C 1, C 2, C 3, C 6, M 1, M 2, R 1, R 2, R 5, S; Roth and S'iva.

३. निर्गमनाय C 1, C 2, C 3, C 6, M 1, M 2, R 1, R 2, R 5, S; Roth and S'iva; Cf. SRV. III. 30. 10.

४. SRV. III. 30. 10; Cf. I. 33. 9; 51. 5. pp. i. 177. 255.

५. तपूषिं C 1, C 3, C 5, M 1, M 2, M 3, Mi, W 2.

६. RV. III. 30. 17.

७. मूलं...मोहनाद्वा is omitted by Durga.

८. कीयतो C 5, M 3, Mi, W 1, W 2.

९. सरलूकं C 5; सररूकं C 6.

१०. अभ्यस्तात् BK, C 4, C 5, Kn, M 3, Mi, R 4, R 6, W 1, W 2, W 3.

११. SRV. III. 30. 17. p. ii. 224.

१२. RV. V. 32. 6.

१३. RV. VI. 7. 6.

१४. RV. X. 97. 3; VS. 12. 77.

१५. RV. VI. 22. 2; AV. 20. 36. 2.

१६. SRV. VI. 67. 11. p. ii. 874.

१७. RV. VI. 22. 3; AV. 20. 36. 3.

[निशृंभा निश्रथ्यहारिणः][1][2] ॥ ३ ॥

आजासः पूषणं रथे निशृंभास्ते जनश्रियम् ।
देवं वहन्तु बिभ्रतः[3] ॥

आवहन्त्वजाः पूषणं रथे । निश्रथ्यहारिणस्ते । जनश्रियं जातश्रियम् ।

बृबदुक्थो महदुक्थः । वक्तव्यमस्मा उक्थमिति[4] । बृबदुक्थो वा ।

बृबदुक्थं हवामहे[5] । इत्यपि निगमो भवति ।

ऋदूदरः सोमः । मृदूदरः[6] । मृदूदरेष्विति[7] वा ।

ऋदूदरेण सख्या सचेय[8] । इत्यपि निगमो भवति ।

ऋदूपे इत्युपरिष्टाद्[9] व्याख्यास्यामः ।

पुलुकामः पुरुकामः ।

पुलुकामो हि मर्त्यः[10] । इत्यपि निगमो भवति ।

असिन्वती असंखादन्त्यौ ।

असिन्वती बप्सती भूर्यत्तः[11] । इत्यपि निगमो भवति ।

कपनाः कंपनाः क्रिमयो भवन्ति ।

मोषथा वृक्षं कपनेव वेधसः[12] । इत्यपि निगमो भवति ।

भाऋजीकः प्रसिद्धभाः[13] ।

धूमकेतुः समिधा भाऋजीकः[14] । इत्यपि निगमो भवति ।

रुजाना नद्यो भवन्ति । रुजन्ति कूलानि[15] ।

सं रुजानाः पिपिष इन्द्रशत्रुः[16] । इत्यपि निगमो भवति ।

---

१. निश्रथ्यहारिणः C 6.
२. Omitted by BK, C 4, C 5, Kn, M 3, Mi, R 4, R 6, W 1, W 2, W 3.
३. RV. VI. 55. 6.
४. SRV. VIII. 32. 10. p. iii. 388.
५. RV. VIII. 32. 10; SV. 1. 217.
६. Cf. SRV. II. 33. 5. p. ii. 98.
७. मृदुरुदरेष्विति C 1, C 2, C 3, C 6, M 1, M 2, R 1, R 2, R 5, S; Roth, S'iva°.
८. RV. VIII. 48. 10.
९. See N. 6. 33.
१०. RV. I. 179. 5. Cf. Kālidāsa : मनोरथानामगतिर्न विद्यते । Kumāra-Sambhava. IV.
११. RV. X. 79. 1.
१२. RV. V. 54. 6.
१३. SRV. I. 44. 3. p. i. 224.
१४. RV. X. 12. 2; AV. 18. 1. 30.
१५. कुलानि C 1. Quoted by SRV. I. 32. 6. p. i. 168.
१६. RV. I. 32. 6.

जूर्णिर्जवतेर्वा । द्रवतेर्वा । दू[1]नोतेर्वा[2] ।

क्षिप्ता जूर्णिर्न वक्षति[3] । इत्यपि निगमो भवति ।

परि घ्रंसमोमना वां वयो गात्[4] ।

पर्यगाद्वां[5] घ्रंसमहरर्व[6]नायान्नम् ॥ ४ ॥

उपलप्र[7]क्षिणी । उपलेषु प्रक्षिणाति । उपलप्रक्षेपिणी वा ।

[इन्द्र ऋषीन् पप्रच्छ । दुर्भिक्षे केन जीवतीति । तेषामेकः प्रत्युवाच ।

शकटं शाकिनी गावो जालमस्यन्दनं वनम् ।
उदधिः पर्वतो राजा दुर्भिक्षे नव वृत्तयः[8] ॥

इति सा निगदव्याख्याता][9] ॥ ५ ॥

कारुरहं ततो भिषगुपलप्रक्षिणी नना ।
नानाधियो वसूयवोऽनु गा इव तस्थिमेन्द्रायेन्दो परिस्रव[10] ॥

कारुरहमस्मि । कर्ता स्तोमानाम् । ततो भिषक् । तत इति सन्ताननाम । पितुर्वा । पुत्रस्य वा । उपलप्रक्षिणी सक्तुकारिका । नना[11] नमतेः । माता वा । दुहिता वा । नानाधियो नानाकर्माणः । वसूयवो वसुकामाः । अन्वास्थिताः स्मो गाव इव लोकम्[12] । इन्द्रायेन्दो परिस्रव । इत्यध्येषणा ।

आसीन ऊर्ध्वामुपसि क्षिणाति[13] । उपस्थे ।

प्रकलविद्वणिग्भवति । कलाश्च वेद प्रकलाश्च ।

दुर्मित्रासः प्रकलविन्मिमानाः[14] । इत्यपि निगमो भवति ।

अभ्यर्धयज्वा । अभ्यर्धयन्यजति[15] ।

---

१. जूनोतेः BK, C 4, C 5, Kn, M 3, Mi, R 4, R 6, W 1, W 2, W 3; वारयतेः C 3.

२. Quoted by SRV. I. 129. 8. p. i. 587.

३. RV. I. 129. 8.

४. RV. VII. 69. 4.

५. वा M 3, Mi, W 1, W 2.

६. अवनोन्नम् BK, C 4, C 5, Kn, M 3, Mi, R 4, R 6, W 1, W 2, W 3; Durga gives अवनेनान्नम् and अनेनान्नम् as variants.

७. Sāyaṇa adds इति after ०प्रक्षिणी. See SRV. IX. 113. 3. p. iii. 829.

८. The quotation is not traced. Cf. BD. VI. 137—138.

९. The passage within square brackets is omitted by BK, C 4, C 5, Kn, M 3, Mi, R 4, R 6, W 1, W 2, W 3.

१०. RV. IX. 112. 3.

११. मना C 3.

१२. The passage उपलप्रक्षिणी...लोकं is cited SRV. IX. 113. 3. p. iii. 829. The story of Indra and the seers does not occur in this quotation of Sāyaṇa.

१३. RV. X. 27. 13.

१४. RV. VII. 18. 15.

१५. Quoted by SRV. VI. 30. 5. p. ii. 829.

सिषक्ति पूषा अभ्यर्धयज्वा[1] । इत्यपि निगमो भवति ।

ईक्ष ईशिषे ।

ईक्षे हि वस्व उभयस्य राजन्[2] । इत्यपि निगमो भवति ।

[क्षोणस्य[3] क्षयणस्य[4] ।

महः क्षोणस्याश्विना कण्वाय[5] । इत्यपि निगमो भवति][6] ॥ ६ ॥

अस्मे ते बन्धुः[7] । वयमित्यर्थः ।

अस्मे यातं नासत्या सजोषाः[8] । अस्मानित्यर्थः ।

अस्मे समानेभिर्वृषभ पौंस्येभिः[9] । अस्माभिरित्यर्थः ।

अस्मे प्र यन्धि मघवन्नृजीषिन्[10] । अस्मभ्यमित्यर्थः ।

अस्मे आराच्चिद् द्वेषः सनुतर्युयोतु[11] । अस्मदित्यर्थः ।

ऊर्व इव पप्रथे कामो अस्मे[12] । अस्माकमित्यर्थः ।

अस्मे धत्त वसवो वसूनि[13] । अस्मास्वित्यर्थः ।

पाथोऽन्तरिक्षम् । पथा व्याख्यातम्[14] ।

श्येनो न दीयन्नन्वेति पाथः[15] । इत्यपि निगमो भवति ।

उदकमपि पाथ उच्यते पानात् ।

आ चष्ट आसां पाथो नदीनाम्[16] । इत्यपि निगमो भवति ।

अन्नमपि पाथ उच्यते पानादेव ।

देवानां पाथ उप वक्षि विद्वान्[17] । इत्यपि निगमो भवति ।

---

१. RV. VI. 50 5.

२. RV. VI. 19. 10.

३. क्षीणस्य is given as a variant by Durga.

४. Quoted by SRV. I. 117. 8. p. i. 525.

५. RV. I. 117. 8.

६. Omitted by BK, C 4, C 5, Kn, M 3, Mi, R 4, R 6, W 1, W 2, W 3.

७. VS. 4. 22.

८. RV. I. 118. 11.

९. RV. I. 165. 7.

१०. RV. III. 36. 10.

११. RV. VI. 47. 13.

१२. RV. III. 30. 19. The reference of RV. III. 30. 19. is wrongly given in VC. as IV. 30. 19.

१३. VS. 8. 18.

१४. SRV. I. 113. 8; 154. 5. pp. i, 499, 663.

१५. RV. VII. 63. 5; its reference in VC. is wrongly given as IX. 63. 5.

१६. RV. VII. 34. 10.

१७. RV. X. 70. 10.

सवीमनि प्रसवे ।

देवस्य वयं सवितुः सवीमनि[1] । इत्यपि निगमो भवति ।

सप्रथाः सर्वतः पृथुः[2] ।

त्वमग्ने सप्रथा असि[3] । इत्यपि निगमो भवति ।

विदथानि वेदनानि ।

विदथानि प्र चोदयन्[5] । इत्यपि निगमो भवति ॥ ७ ॥

श्रायन्त इव सूर्यं विश्वेदिन्द्रस्य भक्षत ।

वसूनि जाते जनमान ओजसा प्रति भागं न दीधिम[6] ॥

समाश्रिताः सूर्यमुपतिष्ठन्ते । अपि वोपमार्थे स्यात् । सूर्यमिवेन्द्रमुपतिष्ठन्त इति । सर्वाणीन्द्रस्य धनानि विभक्षमाणाः । स यथा धनानि विभजति जाते च जनिष्यमाणे च । तं वयं भागमनुध्यायाम । ओजसा बलेन[7] । ओज ओजतेर्वा । उब्जतेर्वा ।

आशीराश्रयणाद्वा । आश्रपणाद्वा । अथेयमितराशीराशास्तेः ।

इन्द्राय गाव आशिरम्[8] । इत्यपि निगमो भवति ।

सा मे सत्याशीर्देवेषु[9] । इति च ।

यदा ते मर्तो अनु भोगमानळादिद्ग्रसिष्ठ ओषधीरजीगः[10] ।

यदा ते मर्तो भोग[11]मन्वापदथ ग्रसितृतम ओषधीरगारीः । जिगर्ति[12]र्गिरतिकर्मा वा[13] । [गृणातिकर्मा वा[14] ।] गृह्णातिकर्मा वा[15] ।

---

१. Quoted by SRV. VI. 72. 2. p. ii. 882.

२. RV. VI. 71. 2.

३. Quoted by SRV. V. 13. 4; VI. 68. 9. pp. ii. 529, 876.

४. RV. V. 13. 4; SV. 2. 757.

५. RV. III. 27. 7; SV. 2. 827.

६. RV. VIII. 99. 3; AV. 20. 58. 1; SV. 1. 267; 2 669; VS. 33. 41.

७. Quoted by SRV. VIII. 99. 3. p. iii. 585.

८. RV. VIII. 69. 6; AV. 20. 22. 6; 92. 3; SV. 2. 841.

९. TS. iii. 2. 7. 2.

१०. RV. I. 163. 7; X. 7. 2; VS. 29. 18.

११. भागम् C 3.

१२. जीगर्त्ति BK, C 4, C 5, Kn, M 3, Mi, R 4, R 6, W 1, W 2, W 3.

१३. Quoted by SRV. VI. 65. 1. p. ii. 867.

१४. Omitted by BK, C 4, C 5, Kn, M 3, Mi, R 4, R 6, W 1, W 2, W 3, and Durga. It is added however on the marginal space, probably by a later scribe, in C 4.

१५. गृह्णातिकर्मा वा is repeated in Mi. Cf. SRV. X. 29. 1. p. IV. 85.

मूरा अमूर न वयं चिकित्वो महित्वमग्ने त्वमङ्ग वित्से ।[1]

मूढा वयं स्मः । अमूढस्त्वमसि । न वयं विद्मो महित्वमग्ने[3] । त्वं तु वेत्थ ।[2]

शशमानः शंसमानः[4] ।

यो वां यज्ञैः शशमानो ह दाशति[5] । इत्यपि निगमो भवति ।

देवो देवाच्या कृपा[6] ।

देवो देवान्प्रत्यक्तया कृपा[7] । [कृप् कृपतेर्वा । कल्पतेर्वा ।][8] ॥ ८ ॥

अश्रवं हि भूरिदावत्तरा वां विजामातुरुत वा घा स्यालात् ।

अथा सोमस्य प्रयती युवभ्यामिन्द्राग्नी स्तोमं जनयामि नव्यम्[9] ॥

अश्रौषं हि बहुदातृतरौ[10] वाम् । विजामातुः । असुसमाप्ताज्जामातुः[11] । विजामातेति शश्वद्दाक्षिणाजाः[12] क्रीतापतिमाचक्षते । असुसमाप्त इव वरोऽभिप्रेतः । जामाता । जा अपत्यम् । तन्निर्माता । उत वा घा स्यालात् । अपि च स्यालात् । स्याल आसन्नः संयोगेनेति नैदानाः । स्याल्लाजानावपतीति वा । लाजा[13] लाजतेः[14] । स्यं शूर्पं स्यतेः । शूर्पमशनपवनम् । शृणातेर्वा[15] । अथ सोमस्य प्रदानेन युवाभ्यामिन्द्राग्नी स्तोमं जनयामि [नव्यं][16] नवतरम्[17] ।

ओमास इत्युपरिष्टाद्[18] व्याख्यास्यामः ॥ ९ ॥

सोमानं स्वरणं कृणुहि ब्रह्मणस्पते ।

कक्षीवन्तं य औशिजः[19] ॥

---

१. RV. X. 4. 4.

२. Cf. SRV. I. 68. 8. p. i. 329.

३. महत्त्वम् C 1, C 2, C 3, C 6, M 1, M 2, R 1, R 2, R 5, S; Roth and S'iva.

४. Cf. SRV. I. 141. 10. p. i. 633.

५. RV. I. 151. 7.

६. RV. I. 127. 1; AV. 20. 67. 3; SV. 1. 465; 2. 1163; VS. 15. 47.

७. कृपा कृप्तुतेर्वा कल्पतेर्वा is added by C 5, M 3. Durga reads: कृपा कल्पितया । Cf. SRV. I. 127. 1. p. i. 573.

८. Omitted by C 5, M 3, and Durga. C 1 strikes it out.

९. RV. I. 109. 2.

१०. बहुदायितरौ BK, C 4, C 5, Kn, M 3, Mi, R 4, R 6, W 1, W 2, W 3.

११. असमाप्तात् BK, C 4, C 5, Kn, M 3, Mi, R 4, R 6, W 1, W 2, W 3.

१२. दाक्षिणात्याः is the proposed emendation by S'ivadatta.

१३. राजा राजतेः C 5, M 3.

१४. लाजा लाजतेः is omitted by Durga.

१५. शृणातेः शम्नातेर्वा SRV. I. 109. 2.

१६. Omitted by BK, C 4, C 5, Kn, M 3, Mi, R 4, R 6, W 1, W 2, W 3.

१७. Cf. SRV. loc. cit.

१८. See N. 12. 40.

१९. RV. I. 18. 1; VS. 3. 28; Cf. सोमानां SV. 1. 139; 2. 813.

सोमानां[1] सोतारं प्रकाशनवन्तं कुरु ब्रह्मणस्पते कक्षीवन्तमिव य औशिजः। कक्षीवान् कक्ष्यावान्[2]। औशिज उशिजः पुत्रः। उशिग्वष्टेः कान्तिकर्मणः। अपि त्वयं मनुष्यकक्ष एवाभिप्रेतः स्यात्। तं सोमानां सोतारं मां प्रकाशनवन्तं कुरु ब्रह्मणस्पते[3] ॥ १० ॥

इन्द्रा॑सोमा॒ सम॒घशं॑सम॒भ्य१॒॑घं तपु॑र्ययस्तु च॒रुर॑ग्नि॒वाँ इ॑व।

ब्र॒ह्म॒द्विषे॑ क्र॒व्यादे॑ घो॒रच॑क्षसे॒ द्वेषो॑ धत्तमनवा॒यं कि॑मी॒दिने॑[4] ॥

इन्द्रासोमावघस्य शंसितारम्। अघं हन्तेः। निर्ह्रसितोपसर्गः। आहन्तीति। तपुस्तपतेः। चरुर्मृच्चयो भवति। चरतेर्वा। समुच्चरन्त्यस्मादापः। ब्रह्मद्विषे [ब्राह्मणद्वेष्ट्रे। क्रव्यादे][5] क्रव्यमदते। [घोरचक्षसे][5] घोरख्यानाय। क्रव्यं विकृत्ताज्जायत[6] इति नैरुक्ताः। द्वेषो धत्तम्। अनवायमनवयवम्। यदन्ये न व्यवेयुः[7]। अद्वेषस इति वा। किमीदिने। किमिदानीमिति चरते। किमिदं किमिदमिति वा। पिशुनाय चरते। पिशुनः पिंशतेः। विपिंशतीति[8] ॥ ११ ॥

कृ॒णु॒ष्व पाजः॒ प्रसि॑तिं॒ न पृ॒थ्वीं या॒हि राजे॒वाम॑वाँ॒ इभे॑न।

तृ॒ष्वीमनु॒ प्रसि॑तिं द्रूणा॒नोऽस्ता॑सि॒ विध्य॑ र॒क्षस॒स्तपि॑ष्ठैः[9] ॥

कुरुष्व पाजः। पाजः पालनात्[10]। प्रसितिमिव पृथ्वीम्। प्रसितिः प्रसयनात्[11]। तंतुर्वा। जालं वा[12]। याहि राजेव। अमात्यवान्। अभ्यमनवान्। स्ववान्वा। इरा[13]भृता गणेन गतभयेन। हस्तिनेति वा। तृष्व्यानु प्रसित्या द्रूणानः। तृष्वीति क्षिप्रनाम। तरतेर्वा। त्वरतेर्वा। असितासि। विध्य रक्षसः। तपिष्ठैः। तप्ततमैः[14]। तृप्ततमैः[15]। प्रपिष्ठतमैरिति वा।

यस्ते॒ गर्भ॒ममी॑वा दु॒र्णामा॒ योनि॑मा॒शये॑[16]।

अमीवाभ्यमनेन व्याख्यातः। दुर्णामा[17] क्रिमिर्भवति पापनामा। क्रिमिः क्रव्ये मेद्यति। क्रमतेर्वा स्यात्सरणकर्मणः। क्रामतेर्वा।

अ॒ति॒ क्राम॑न्तो दु॒रि॒तानि॒ विश्वा॑[18]।

---

1. सोमानं Roth.
2. Cf. SRV. I. 51. 13. p. i. 260.
3. Cf. SRV. I. 18. 1. p. i. 103. Also Cf. PMbh. Vol. III. p. 33.
4. RV. VII. 104. 2; AV. 8. 4. 2.
5. Omitted by BK, C 4, C 5, Kn, M 3, Mi, R 4, R 6, W 1, W 2, W 3.
6. विकृत्ताज्जायत C 4, C 5, M 3.
7. व्येयुः C 3, C 5, M 3.
8. Quoted by SRV. X. 87. 24. p. IV. 277.
9. RV. IV. 4. 1; VS. 13. 9.
10. पानात् BK, C 4, C 5, Kn, M 3, Mi, R 4, R 6, W 1, W 2, W 3.
11. प्रसहनात् BK, C 4, C 5, Kn, M 3, Mi, R 4, R 6, W 1, W 2, W 3.
12. SRV. X. 87. 15. p. IV. 275.
13. इरावता SRV. IV. 4. 1.
14. तप्ततमैस्तपिष्ठतमैरिति वा SRV. loc. cit.
15. SRV. loc. cit.
16. RV. X. 162. 2; AV. 20. 96. 12.
17. दुर्नामा C 4, C 5, M 3, Mi.
18. Cf. AV. 12. 2. 28.

अतिक्रममाणा दुर्गतिगमनानि सर्वाणि।

अप्वा यदेनया विद्धोऽपवीयते। व्याधिर्वा। भयं वा।

अप्वे परेहि[1]। इत्यपि निगमो भवति।

अमतिरमामयी। मतिरात्ममयी।

ऊर्ध्वा यस्यामतिर्भा अदिद्युतत्[2] [सवीमनि][3]।

इत्यपि निगमो भवति।

श्रुष्टीति क्षिप्रनाम। आशु अष्टीति[4]॥ १२॥

ताँ अध्वर उशतो यक्ष्यग्ने श्रुष्टी भगं नासत्या पुरंन्धिम्[5]।

तानध्वरे यज्ञे। उशतः कामयमानान्। यजाग्ने। श्रुष्टी भगम्। नासत्यौ चाश्विनौ। सत्यावेव नासत्यावित्यौर्णवाभः। सत्यस्य प्रणेतारावित्याग्रायणः। नासिकाप्रभवौ बभूवतुरिति वा[6]।

पुरन्धिर्बहुधीः[7]। तत्कः पुरन्धिः। भगः पुरस्तात्तस्यान्वादेश इत्येकम्। इन्द्र इत्यपरम्। स बहुकर्मतमः। पुरां च दारयितृतमः। वरुण इत्यपरम्। तं प्रज्ञया स्तौति।

इमामू नु कवितमस्य मायाम्[8]। इत्यपि निगमो भवति।

रुशदिति वर्णनाम। रोचतेर्ज्वलतिकर्मणः।

समिद्धस्य रुशददर्शि पाजः[9]। इत्यपि निगमो भवति॥ १३॥

अस्ति हि वः सजात्यं रिशादसो देवासो अस्त्याप्यम्[10]।

अस्ति हि वः। समानजातिता रेशयदारिणो[11] देवाः। अस्त्याप्यम्। आप्यमाप्नोतेः।

सुदत्रः कल्याणदानः[12]।

---

१. Fragment of RV. X. 103. 12; AV. 3. 2. 5; VS. 7. 44; N. 9. 33; Cf. SV. 2. 1211.

२. AV. 7. 14. 2; SV. 1. 464; VS. 4. 25. The word अमतिः occurs in RV. I. 64. 9; 73. 2. but Yāska has not quoted from the RV.

३. Omitted by Bk, C 4, C 5, Kn, M 3, Mi, R 4, R 6, W 1, W 2, W 3.

४. Quoted by SRV. I. 67. 2; VI. 68. 1. pp. i. 326; ii. 874.

५. RV. VII. 39. 4.

६. Cf. SRV. VIII. 5. 23; 42. 4; also I. 3. 3; 34. 7.

७. बहुविः C 5, M 3; बहुभिः Mi, W 1; बहुधिः C 4, W 2. Cf. SRV. I. 5. 3; 116. 7; 134. 3; VII. 9. 6. pp. i. 46, 515, 605; iii. 24.

८. RV. V. 85. 6.

९. RV. V. 1. 2; SV. 2. 1097.

१०. RV. VIII. 27. 10.

११. Durga reads रेशयदासिनः & gives रेशयदारिणः as a variant.

१२. Quoted by SRV. I. 164. 49. p. i, 719.

त्वष्टा सुदत्रो विदधातु रायः[1] । इत्यपि निगमो भवति ।

सुविदत्रः कल्याणविद्यः ।

आग्ने याहि सुविदत्रेभिरर्वाङ्[2] । इत्यपि निगमो भवति ।

आनुषगिति नामानुपूर्वस्य[3] । अनुषक्तं भवति ।

स्तृणन्ति बर्हिरानुषक्[4] । इत्यपि निगमो भवति ।

तुर्वणिस्तूर्णवनिः[5] ।

स तुर्वणिर्महाँ अरेणु[6] पौंस्ये । इत्यपि निगमो भवति ।

गिर्वणा देवो भवति । गीर्भिरेनं वनयन्ति[7] ।

जुष्टं गिर्वणसे बृहत्[8] । इत्यपि निगमो भवति ॥ १४ ॥

असूर्ते सूर्ते रजसि निषत्ते ये भूतानि समकृण्वन्निमानि[9] ।

असुसमीरिताः सुसमीरिते वातसमीरिताः[10] । माध्यमका देवगणाः । ते[11] रसेन पृथिवीं तर्पयन्तः । भूतानि च कुर्वन्ति । त आयजन्त । इत्यतिक्रान्तं प्रतिवचनम् ।

अम्यक्सा त इन्द्र ऋष्टिः[12] । अमाक्तेति वा । अभ्यक्तेति ।

याद्दृश्मिन्धायि तमपस्यया विदत्[13] ।

२ याद्दृशेऽधायि तमपस्ययाविदत् ।

उस्रः पितेव जारयायि यज्ञैः[14] ।

उस्र इव गोपिताजायि यज्ञैः ॥ १५ ॥

प्र वोऽच्छा जुजुषाणासो अस्थुरभूत विश्वे अग्रियोत वाजाः[15] ।

प्रास्थुर्वो[16] जोषयमाणा अभवत सर्वे । अग्रगमनेनेति वा । [अग्रगरणेनेति वा ।][17] अग्रसंपादिन इति वा ।

---

१. RV. VII. 34. 22; VS. 2. 24; 8. 14.

२. RV. X. 15. 9; AV. 18. 3. 48.

३. Quoted by SRV. VIII. 12. 11. p. iii. 297.

४. RV. VIII. 45. 1; SV. 1. 133; 2. 688; VS. 7. 32.

५. Quoted by SRV. I. 56. 3. p. i. 283.

६. RV. I. 56. 3.

७. SRV. I. 62. 1. p. i. 304.

८. RV. VIII. 89. 7; SV. 2. 781.

९. RV. X. 82. 4; VS. 17. 28.

१०. वाजसमीरिताः BK, C 4, C 5. Kn, M 3, Mi, R 4, R 6, W 1, W 2, W 3.

११. ये C 1, C 2, C 3, C 6, M 1, M 2, R 1, R 2, R 5, S.

१२. RV. I. 169. 3.

१३. RV. V. 44. 8; Cf. N. 1. 15.

१४. VI. 12. 4

१५. RV. IV. 34. 3.

१६. प्रणस्थुः M 2.

१७. Omitted by BK, C 4, C 5, Kn, M 3, Mi, R 4, R 6, W 1, W 2, W 3.

अपि वाग्रमित्येतदनर्थकमुपबंधमाददीत।

अद्रीदिन्द्र प्रस्थितेमा हवींषि चनो दधिष्व पचतोत सोमम्[1]।

अद्रीन्द्र प्रस्थितानीमानि हवींषि चनो दधिष्व। चन इत्यन्ननाम। पचतिर्नामीभूतः।

तं मेदुस्तः प्रति पचताग्रभीष्टाम्[2]।

इत्यपि निगमो भवति।

अपि वा मेदसश्च पशोश्च[3]। सात्त्वं द्विवचनं स्यात्। यत्र ह्येकवचनार्थः प्रसिद्धं[4] तद्भवति।

पुरोळा अग्ने पचतः[5]। इति यथा।

शुरुध आपो भवन्ति। शुचं संरुन्धन्ति।

ऋतस्य हि शुरुधः सन्ति पूर्वीः[6]। इत्यपि निगमो भवति।

अमिनो[7]ऽमितमात्रो महान्भवति। अभ्यमितो वा।

अमिनः सहोभिः[8]। इत्यपि निगमो भवति।

जज्झतीरापो भवन्ति। शब्दकारिण्यः[9]।

मरुतो जज्झतीरिव[10]। इत्यपि निगमो भवति।

अप्रतिष्कुतः। अप्रतिस्कृतः। अप्रतिस्खलितो वा[11]।

असमभ्यमप्रतिष्कुतः[12]। इत्यपि निगमो भवति।

शाशदानः शाशाद्यमानः[13]।

प्र स्वां मतिमतिरच्छाशदानः[14]। इत्यपि निगमो भवति॥ १६॥

---

१. RV. X. 116. 8.

२. MS. IV. 13. 9. Cf. मेदस्तः प्रति पचत VS. 21. 60; 28. 23, 46.

३. वशोश्च C 4, C 5, M 3.

४. प्रसिद्धिम् C 4, C 5, M 3.

५. RV. III. 28. 2.

६. RV. IV. 23. 8; Cf. N. 10. 41.

७. अमीनो W 1.

८. Fragment of RV. VI. 19. 1; VS. 7. 39; Cf. N. 6. 17.

९. Quoted SRV. V. 52. 6. p. ii. 613.

१०. RV. V. 52. 6.

११. Quoted SRV. I. 7. 6. p. i. 56.

१२. RV. I. 7. 6; AV. 20. 17. 12; SV. 2. 971.

१३. शाशाद्यदान: C 3. Quoted SRV. I. 123. 10; 124. 6. pp. i. 560, 564.

१४. RV. I. 33. 13.

सृप्रः सर्पणात् । इदमपीतरत् सृप्रमेतस्मादेव । सर्पिर्वा । तैलं वा ।

सृप्रकरस्नमूतये[1] । इत्यपि निगमो भवति ।

करस्नौ बाहू । कर्मणां प्रस्नातारौ[2] ।

सुशिप्रमेतेन व्याख्यातम् ।

वाजे सुशिप्र गोमति[3] । इत्यपि निगमो भवति ।

शिप्रे हनू नासिके वा[4] । हनुर्हन्तेः । नासिका नसतेः ।

विष्यस्व शिप्रे वि सृजस्व धेने[5] । इत्यपि निगमो भवति ।

धेना दधातेः ।

रंसु[6] रमणात् ।

स चित्रेण चिकिते रंसु भासा[7] । इत्यपि निगमो भवति ।

द्विबर्हा द्वयोः स्थानयोः परिवृढः । मध्यमे च स्थान उत्तमे च ।

उत द्विबर्हा अमिनः सहोभिः[8] । इत्यपि निगमो भवति ।

अक्र आक्रमणात् ।

अक्रो न बभ्रिः समिथे महीनाम्[9] । इत्यपि निगमो भवति ।

उराण उरु कुर्वाणः[10] ।

दूत ईयसे प्रदिव उराणः[11] । इत्यपि निगमो भवति ।

स्तिया आपो भवन्ति । स्त्यायनात्[12] ।

वृषा सिन्धूनां वृषभः स्तियानाम्[13] । इत्यपि निगमो भवति ।

स्तिपा स्तियापालनः[14] । उपस्थितान् पालयतीति[15] ।

१. RV. VIII. 32. 10; SV. 1. 217.

२. Quoted SRV. III. 18. 5; VIII. 32. 10. pp. ii. 186; iii. 388.

३. RV. VIII. 21. 8.

४. Quoted SRV. I. 9. 3; 29. 2; III. 30. 3. pp. i. 65, 150; ii. 218.

५. RV. I. 101. 10.

६. रमणीयेषु is added after रंसु by Durga.

७. RV. II. 4. 5.

८. Quoted SRV. VII. 8. 6. p. iii. 23.

९. RV. VI. 19. 1; VS. 7. 39; Cf. N. 6. 16.

१०. RV. III. 1. 12.

११. Quoted SRV. III. 19. 2; IX. 109. 9. pp. ii. 187; iii. 822.

१२. RV. IV. 7. 8.

१३. Quoted SRV. VII. 5. 2. p. iii. 16.

१४ स्तियानम् C 3.

१५. RV. VI. 44. 21.

१६. स्तृपापालनः BK, C 4, C 5, Kn, M 3, Mi, R 4, R 6, W 1, W 2, W 3.

१७. वा is added by Roth.

स नः स्तिपा उत भवा तनूपाः । इत्यपि निगमो भवति ।[1]

जबारु जवमानरोहि । जरमाणरोहि[2] । गरमाणरोहीति वा ।

अग्रे रूप आरुपितं जबारु[3] । इत्यपि निगमो भवति ।

जरूथं गरूथं गृणातेः ।

जरूथं हन्यक्षि राये पुरंधिम्[4] । इत्यपि निगमो भवति ।

कुलिश इति वज्रनाम । कूलशातनो भवति ।

स्कन्धांसीव कुलिशेना विवृक्णाहिः शयत उपपृक्पृथिव्याः[5] ।

स्कन्धो वृक्षस्य समास्कन्नो[6] भवति । अयमपीतरः[7] स्कन्ध एतस्मादेव । आस्कन्नं काये । अहिः शयत उपपर्चनः पृथिव्याः ।[8]

तुंजस्तुंजतेर्दानकर्मणः ॥ १७ ॥

तुञ्जेतुञ्जे य उत्तरे स्तोमा इन्द्रस्य वज्रिणः ।
न विन्धे अस्य सुष्टुतिम्[9] ॥

दाने दाने य उत्तरे स्तोमा इन्द्रस्य वज्रिणो नास्य तैर्विन्दामि समाप्तिं स्तुतेः[10] ।

बर्हणा परिबर्हणा ।

बृहच्छ्रवा असुरो बर्हणा कृतः[11] । इत्यपि निगमो भवति ॥ १८ ॥

यो अस्मै घ्रंस उत वा य ऊधनि सोमं सुनोति भवति द्युमाँ अह ।
अपाप शक्रस्ततनुष्टिमूहति तनूशुभ्रं मघवा यः कवासखः[12] ॥

घ्रंस इत्यहर्नाम । ग्रस्यन्तेऽस्मिन्रसाः ।

गोरूध उद्धततरं भवति । उपोन्नद्धमिति वा । स्नेहानुप्रदानसामान्याद्रात्रिरप्यूध उच्यते । स योऽस्मा[13] अहन्यपि वा रात्रौ सोमं सुनोति भवत्यह[14] द्योतनवान् ।

---

१. RV. X. 69. 4.

२. Cf. SRV. IV. 5. 7. p. ii. 367: जबारु जरमाणरोहीति वा जवमानरोहीति वेति यास्कः ।

३. RV. IV. 5. 7.

४. RV. VII. 9. 6.

५. RV. I. 32. 5.

६. समास्कन्धो M 3.

७. इदम् BK, C 4, C 5, Kn, M 3, Mi, R 4, R 6, W 1, W 2, W 3.

८. स्कन्धो वृक्षस्य...काये is omitted by Durga.

९. RV. I. 7. 7; AV. 20. 70. 13.

१०. स्तुवे C 6. Quoted SRV. I. 7. 7. p. i. 57.

११. RV. I. 54. 3.

१२. RV. V. 34. 3.

१३. ऽस्माहनन्यपि M 3; ऽस्मा अहन्नपि C 5, W 1, W 2.

१४. भवति ह BK, C 4, C 5, Kn, M 3, Mi, R 4, R 6, W 1, W 2, W 3.

अपोहत्यपोहति शक्रः। तितनिषुं[1] धर्मसन्तानादपेतमलंकरिष्णुमयज्वानम्। तनूशुभ्रं तनूशोभयितारम्। मघवा यः। कवासखो यस्य कपूयाः सखायः।

न्यविध्यदिलीबिशस्य दृळ्हा वि शृङ्गिणमभिनच्छुष्णमिन्द्रः[2]।

निरविध्यदिलाबिलशयस्य[3] दृढानि। व्यभिनच्छृङ्गिणं शुष्णमिन्द्रः॥ १९॥

अस्मा इदु प्र भरा तूतुजानो वृत्राय वज्रमीशानः कियेधाः।
गोर्न पर्व वि रदा तिरश्चेष्यन्नर्णांस्यपां चरध्यै[4]॥

अस्मै प्रहर। तूर्णं[5] त्वरमाणः। वृत्राय वज्रमीशानः। कियेधाः कियद्धा इति वा। क्रममाणधा इति वा। गोरिव पर्वाणि विरद मेघस्य। इष्यन्नर्णांसि। अपां चरणाय[6]।

भृमिर्भ्राम्यतेः।

भृमिरस्यृषिकृन्मर्त्यानाम्[7]। इत्यपि निगमो भवति।

विष्पितो[8] विप्राप्तः।

पारं नो अस्य विष्पितस्य पर्षन्[9]। इत्यपि निगमो भवति॥ २०॥

तन्नस्तुरीपमद्भुतं पुरु वारं पुरु त्मना।
त्वष्टा पोषाय वि ष्यतु राये नाभा नो अस्मयुः[10]॥

तन्नः। तूर्णापि। महत्। संभृतम्। आत्मना। त्वष्टा धनस्य पोपाय विष्यतु। इत्यस्मयुः। अस्मान् कामयमानः।

रास्पिनो रास्पी। रपतेर्वा। रसतेर्वा।

रास्पिनस्यायोः[11]। इत्यपि निगमो भवति।

ऋञ्जतिः प्रसाधनकर्मा[12]।

---

१. ततनिषुं BK, C 4, C 5, Kn, M 3, Mi, R 4, R 6, W 1, W 2, W 3.
२. RV. I. 33. 12.
३. Quoted SRV. I. 33. 12. p. i. 178.
४. RV. I. 61. 12; AV. 20. 35. 12.
५. Quoted SRV. I. 61. 6. p. i. 299.
६. Cf. SRV. I. 61. 12. p. i. 302. Sāyaṇa reads: ०र्णांस्यां चरणाय.
७. RV. I. 31. 16.
८. विप्राप्तः BK, C 4, C 5, Kn, M 3, Mi, R 4, R 6, W 1, W 2, W 3.
९. RV. VII. 60. 7.
१०. RV. I. 142. 10; AV. 5. 27. 10; VS. 27. 20.
११. Fragment of RV. I. 22. 4.
१२. Quoted SRV. I. 6. 9; 37. 3; 54. 2; IV. 21. 5; pp. i. 53, 200, 273; ii. 411.

[आ वं ऋञ्जस ऊर्जां व्युष्टिषु । इत्यपि निगमो भवति ।][2]

ऋजुरित्यप्यस्य भवति ।

ऋजुनीती नो वरुणः[3] । इत्यपि निगमो भवति ।

प्रतद्वसू प्रात्तवसू ।

हरी इन्द्र प्रतद्वसू अभि स्वर[4] । इत्यपि निगमो भवति ॥ २१ ॥

हिनोतां नो अध्वरं देवयज्या हिनोत ब्रह्म सनये धनानाम् ।

ऋतस्य योगे वि ष्यध्वमूधः श्रुष्टीवरीर्भूतनास्मभ्यमापः ॥

प्रहिणुत नोऽध्वरं देवयज्यायै । प्रहिणुत ब्रह्म धनस्य सननाय[6] । ऋतस्य योगे । यज्ञस्य योगे । याज्ञे शकट इति वा । शकटं शकृदितं[8] भवति । शनकैस्तकतीति वा । शब्देन तकतीति वा । सुखवतीः [श्रुष्टीवरी]भूतनास्मभ्यमापः । [सुखवत्यो भवतास्मभ्यमापः ।][10]

चोष्कूयमाण इन्द्र भूरि वामम्[11] ।

दददिन्द्र बहुवननीयम्[12][13] ।

एधमानद्विळुभयस्य राजा चोष्कूयते विश इन्द्रो मनुष्यान्[14] ।

व्युदस्यति[15] । एधमानानहर्द्वेष्टि असुन्वतः । सुन्वतोऽभ्यादधाति । उभयस्य राजा । दिव्यस्य च पार्थिवस्य च । चोष्कूयमाण इति चोष्कूयतेश्चर्करीतवृत्तम् ।

सुमत्स्वयमित्यर्थः[16] ।

---

१. RV. X. 76. 1.

२. Omitted by BK, C 4, C 5, Kn, M 3, Mi, R 4, R 6, W 1, W 2, W 3, and Durga. The commentator says Yāska did not cite any quotation to illustrate the meaning of ऋञ्जतिः।

३. RV. I. 90. 1; SV. 1. 218.

४. RV. VIII. 13. 27.

५. RV. X. 30. 11.

६. सननाय C 3, C 4, Mi & Roth; सवनाय S'ivadatta.

७. Cf. SRV. X. 30. 11. p. IV. 90.

८. शकृदतं C 5, M 3, W 1, W 2.

९. Omitted by C 1, C 2, C 3, C 6, M 1, M 2, R 1, R 2, R 5, S.

१०. Omitted by BK, C 4, C 5, Kn, M 3, Mi, R 4, R 6, W 1, W 2, W 3.

११. RV. I. 33. 3.

१२. बहुवदनीयम् C 3.

१३. Quoted SRV. VIII. 7. 41. p. iii. 270.

१४. RV. VI. 47. 16.

१५. विदस्यति W 2.

१६. Quoted SRV. I. 100. 16; 156. 2; 162. 7. pp. i. 444, 667, 685.

उप प्रागात्सुमन्मेंधायि मन्म[1] ।

उपप्रैतु मां [स्वयं[2]] यन्मे मनोऽध्यायि यज्ञेन । इत्याश्वमेधिको मन्त्रः ।

दिविष्टिषु दिव एषणेषु ।

स्थूरं राधः शताश्वं कुरुङ्गस्य[3] दिविष्टिषु[4] ।

स्थूरः । समाश्रितमात्रो महान्भवति । अणुरनु स्थवीयांसम् । उपसर्गो लुप्तनामकरणः[5] । यथा संप्रति । कुरुङ्गो[6] राजा बभूव । कुरुगमनाद्वा । कुलगमनाद्वा । कुरुः कृन्ततेः । क्रूरमित्यप्यस्य भवति । कुलं कुष्णातेः । विकुषितं भवति ।

दूतो व्याख्यातः[7] ।

जिन्वतिः प्रीतिकर्मा ।

भूमिं पर्जन्या जिन्वन्ति दिवं जिन्वन्त्यग्नयः[8] ।

इत्यपि निगमो भवति[9] ॥ २२ ॥

अमत्रोऽमात्रो महान्भवति । अभ्यमितो वा[10] ।

महाँ अमत्रो वृजने विरप्शि[10] । इत्यपि निगमो भवति ।

स्तवै वज्र्यृचीषमः[11] । स्तूयते वज्र्यृचा समः[12] ।

अनर्शरातिमनश्लीलदानम् । अश्लीलं पापकम् ।

अश्रिमत्[13] । विषमम् ।

अनर्शरातिं वसुदामुप स्तुहि[14] । इत्यपि निगमो भवति ।

अनर्वा अप्रत्यृतोऽन्यस्मिन् ।

अनर्वाणं वृषभं मन्द्रजिह्वं बृहस्पतिं वर्धया नव्यमर्कैः[15] ।

---

१. RV. I. 162. 7; VS. 25. 30.

२. Omitted by BK, C 4, C 5, Kn, M 3, Mi, R 4, R 6, W 1, W 2, W 3.

३. कुरङ्गस्य. C 3, M 3, W 1.

४. RV. VIII. 4. 19; cf. VIII. 24. 29; cf. BD. VI. 44.

५. उपसर्गलुप्तः BK, C 4, C 5, Kn, M 3, Mi, R 4, R 6, W 1, W 2, W 3.

६. कुरङ्गो C 5, W 1.

७. See. N. 5. 1.

८. अग्नयः is omitted by C 3. RV. I. 164. 51; cf. N. 7. 23.

९. Quoted SRV. I. 61. 9. p. i. 300.

१०. RV. III. 36. 4.

११. RV. RV. X. 22. 2.

१२. Quoted SRV. I. 61. 1. p. i. 296.

१३. अश्लिमत् BK, C 4, C 5, Kn, M 3, Mi, R 4, R 6, W 1, W 2, W 3. Cf. SRV. VIII. 99. 4. p. iii. 586.

१४. RV. VIII. 99. 4; AV. 20. 58. 2; Cf. SV. 2. 670.

१५. RV. I. 190. 1; Cf. BD. IV. 63.

अनर्वमप्रत्यृतमन्यस्मिन् । वृषभम् । मन्द्रजिह्वं मन्दनजिह्वं । मोदनजिह्वमिति वा । बृहस्पतिं वर्धय नव्यमर्कैः । अर्चनीयैः स्तोमैः ॥

असामि सामिप्रतिषिद्धम् । सामि स्यतेः ।

असाम्योजो बिभृथा सुदानवः ।

असुसमाप्तं बलं बिभृतं कल्याणदानाः ॥ २३ ॥

मा त्वा सोमस्य गल्दया सदा याचन्नहं गिरा ।

भूर्णिं मृगं न सवनेषु चुक्रुधं क ईशानं न याचिषत् ॥

मा चुक्रुधं त्वां सोमस्य गालनेन सदा याचन्नहम् । गिरा गीत्या स्तुत्या । भूर्णिमिव मृगम् । न सवनेषु चुक्रुधम् । क ईशानं न याचिष्यत इति । [गल्दा धमनयो भवन्ति । गलनमासु धीयते ।][8]

आ त्वा विशन्त्विन्दव आ गल्दा धमनीनाम्[9] ।

नानाविभक्तीत्येते भवतः । आगलना धमनीनामित्यत्रार्थः ॥ २४ ॥

न पापासो मनामहे नारायासो न जल्हवः[10] ।

न पापा मन्यामहे[11] । नाधनाः । न ज्वलनेन हीनाः । अस्त्यस्मासु ब्रह्मचर्यमध्ययनं तपो दानकर्मेत्यृषिरवोचत् ।

बकुरो भास्करः । भयंकरः । भासमानो द्रवतीति वा ॥ २५ ॥

यवं वृकेणाश्विना वपन्तेषं दुहन्ता मनुषाय दस्रा ।

अभि दस्युं बकुरेणा धमन्तोरु ज्योतिश्चक्रथुरार्याय[12] ॥

[यवमिव वृकेणाश्विनौ निवपन्तौ ।][13] वृको लाङ्गलं भवति । विकर्तनात्[14] ।

---

१. Cf. SRV. I. 190. 1. p. i. 787.

२. Omitted by M 3, W 2.

३. Quoted by SRV. V. 25. 2. p. ii. 541.

४. RV. I. 39. 10.

५. बिभृथम् Mi; बिभृथ C 4, C 5, M 3, W 1, W 2, and Sāyana on RV. I. 39. 10. p. i. 211.

६. RV. VIII. 1. 20; SV. 1. 307.

७. याचिष्यति BK, C 4, C 5, Kn, M 3, Mi, R 4, R 6, W 1, W 2, W 3.

८. Omitted by BK, C 4, C 5, Kn, M 3, Mi, R 4, R 6, W 1, W 2, W 3. गलनमासु धीयते is omitted by Durga.

९. आ त्वा विशन्त्विन्दवः RV. I. 15. 1[b]; VIII. 92. 22[a].

१०. RV. VIII. 61. 11.

११. Quoted SRV. VIII. 61. 17. p. iii. 474.

१२. RV. I. 117. 21.

१३. Omitted by BK, C 4, C 5, Kn, M 3, Mi, R 4, R 6, W 1, W 2, W 3.

१४. Quoted SRV. VIII. 22. 6. p. iii. 344.

लाङ्गलं लगंतेः[1] । लाङ्गूलवद्वा । लाङ्गूलं लगतेः । लंगतेः । लंवतेर्वा[2] । अन्नं दुहन्तौ[3] मनुष्याय दर्शनीयौ । अभिधमन्तौ । दस्युं वकुरेण ज्योतिषा[4] वोदकेन वा । अयं ईश्वरपुत्रः ।

वेकनाटाः खलु कुसीदिनो भवन्ति । द्विगुणकारिणो वा । द्विगुणदायिनो वा । द्विगुणं कामयन्त इति वा ।

इन्द्रो विश्वान्वेकनाटाँ अहर्दृश उत क्रत्वा पणीँरभि ।[5]

इन्द्रो [यः[6]] सर्वान् बेकनाटान् । अहर्दृशः सूर्यदृशः । य इमान्यहानि पश्यन्ति न पराणीति वा । अभिभवति[7] कर्मणा । पणींश्च वणिजः ॥ २६ ॥

जीवान्नो अभि धेतनादित्यासः पुरा हथात् ।
कद्ध स्थ हवनश्रुतः ॥[8]

जीवतो नोऽभिधावतादित्याः पुरा हननात् । क नु स्थ ह्वानश्रुत इति ।

मत्स्यानां जालमापन्नानामेतदार्षं वेदयन्ते । मत्स्या मधा उदके स्यन्दन्ते । माद्यन्तेऽन्योन्यं भक्षणायेति वा । जालं जलचरं भवति । जलेभवं वा । जलेशयं वा ।

अंहुरोऽंहस्वान्[9] । अंहूरणमित्यप्यस्य भवति ।

कृण्वन्नंहूरणादुरु[10] । इत्यपि निगमो भवति ।

सप्त मर्यादाः कवयस्ततक्षुस्तासामेकामिदभ्यंहुरो गात्[11] ।

सप्त मर्यादाः[12] कवयश्चक्रुः । तासामेकामप्यभिगच्छन्[13] नंहस्वान्भवति । स्तेयं तल्पारोहणं ब्रह्महत्यां भ्रूणहत्यां सुरापानं दुष्कृतस्य[14] कर्मणः पुनः पुनः सेवां पातकेऽनृतोद्यमिति[15] ।

वत इति निपातः । खेदानुकम्पयोः ॥ २७ ॥

---

१. लङ्गते: Roth.
२. The passage वृको लाङ्गलं...लंवते र्वा is omitted by Durga.
३. दुहन्तो C 5, W 1, W 2.
४. ज्योतिषो BK, C 4, C 5, Kn, M 3, Mi, R 4, R 6, W 1, W 2, W 3.
५. RV. VIII. 66. 10.
६. Omitted by BK, C 4, C 5, Kn, M 3, Mi, R 4, R 6, W 1, W 2, W 3.
७. अीभभवन्ति C 5.
८. RV. VIII. 67. 5.
९. अहूस्वाणं BK, C 4, C 5, Kn, M 3, Mi, R 4, R 6, W 1, W 2, W 3; अहस्वानं M 1, M 2.
१०. RV. I. 105. 17.
११. RV. X. 5. 6; AV. 5. 1. 6.
१२. सप्तैव मर्यादा: C 1, C 2, C 3, C 6, M 1, M 2, R 1, R 2, R 5, S; Roth and S'iva.
१३. अधिगच्छन् BK, C 4, C 5, Kn, M 3, Mi, R 4, R 6, W 1, W 2, W 3.
१४. दुष्कृतकर्मण: C 4, C 5, M 3, W 1.
१५. Quoted by SRV. X. 5. 6. p. IV. 11. The word भ्रूणहत्यां is missing in the passage cited by Sāyaṇa, consequently the number of boundaries is only six.

व॒तो ब॑तासि यम॒ नैव ते॒ मनो॒ हृद॑यं चाविदाम ।
अ॒न्या कि॒ल त्वां क॒क्ष्ये॑व यु॒क्तं परि॑ष्वजाते॒ लिबु॑जेव वृ॒क्षम्[1] ॥

वतो बलाद॑तीतो[2] भवति । दुर्बलो बतासि यम । नैव ते मनो हृदयं च विजा-
नामि[3] । अन्या किल त्वां परिष्वंक्ष्यते कक्ष्येव युक्तं लिबुजेव वृक्षम् । लिबुजा व्रतति-
र्भवति । लीयते विभजन्तीति । व्रततिर्वरणाच्च । सयनाच्च[4] । ततनाच्च[5] ।

वाताप्यमुदकं भवति । वात एतदाप्याययति ।

पु॒ना॒नो वा॒ताप्यं॑ वि॒श्वश्च॑न्द्रम्[6] । इत्यपि निगमो भवति ।

वने॒ न वा॒यो न्य॑धायि चा॒कन्[7] ।

वन इव । वायो वेः पुत्रः । चायन्निति वा । कामयमान इति वा । वेति च य
इति च चकार शाकल्यः । उदात्तं त्वेवम्[8]आख्यातमभविष्यत् । असुसमाप्तश्चार्थः ।

र॑थर्यतीति[9] सिद्धस्तत्प्रेप्सुः[10] । रथं कामय॑न्त[11] इति वा ।

ए॒ष दे॒वो र॑थर्यति[12] । इत्यपि निगमो भवति ॥ २८ ॥

धे॒नुं न॒ इषं॑ पिन्वत॒मसं॑क्राम्[13] । असंक्रमणीम्[14] ।

आधव आधवनात् ।

म॒ती॒नां च॒ साध॑नं॒ विप्रा॑णां चाध॒वम्[15] । इत्यपि निगमो भवति ।

अनवब्रवोऽनवक्षि॑प्तवचनः[16] ।

वि॒जे॒ष॒कृदिन्द्र॑ इवानवब्र॒वः[17] । इत्यपि निगमो भवति ॥ २९ ॥

---

१. RV. X. 10 13; AV. 18. 1. 15.

२. बलादतितो BK, C 4, C 5, Kn, M 3, Mi, R 4, R 6, W 1, W 2, W 3.

३. विजानीमः C 1, C 2, C 3, C 6, M 1, M 2, R 1, R 2, R 5, S; Roth and S'iva.

४. शयनाच्च C 4, C 5, M 3, Mi, W 1.

५. The passage लिबुजा व्रतति...ततनाच्च is omitted by Durga.

६. RV. IX. 35. 5.

७. RV. X. 29. 1; AV. 20. 76. 1.

८. Cf. BD. ii. 114.

९. त्वेतत् BK, C 4, C 5, Kn, M 3, Mi, R 4, R 6, W 1, W 2, W 3.

१०. रथं हर्यति is added after रथर्यतीति by Durga.

११. कामयन्त BK, C 4, C 5, Kn, M 3, Mi, R 4, R 6, W 1, W 2, W 3; C 6, M 1, M 2.

१२. RV. IX. 3. 5; SV. 2. 609.

१३. RV. VI. 63. 8.

१४. Quoted by SRV. VI. 63. 8. p. ii. 864.

१५. RV. X. 26. 4.

१६. ऽनवक्षिप्रवचनः BK, C 4, C 5, Kn, M 3, Mi, R 4, R 6, W 1, W 2, W 3. Quoted by SRV. X. 84. 5. p. IV. 252.

१७. RV. X. 84. 5; AV. 4. 31. 5.

अरायि काणे विकटे गिरिं गच्छ सदान्वे ।
शिरिम्बिठस्य सत्त्वभिस्तेभिष्ट्वा चातयामसि ॥[1]

अदायिनि काणे विकटे । काणो[2]ऽविक्रान्तदर्शन इत्यौपमन्यवः । कणतेर्वा स्यादणूभावकर्मणः । कणतिः शब्दाणूभावे भाष्यते । अनुकणतीति । मात्राणूभावात्कणः । दर्शनाणूभावात्काणः । विकटो विक्रान्तगतिरित्यौपमन्यवः । कुटतेर्वा स्यात् [विपरीतस्य[3]] विकुटितो भवति । गिरिं गच्छ । सदानोनुवे शब्दकारिके । शिरिम्बिठस्य सत्त्वभिः । शिरिम्बिठो मेघः । शीर्यते बिठे । [बिठमन्तरिक्षं[4]] बिठं वीरिटेन व्याख्यातम्[5] । तस्य सत्त्वैरुदकैरिति स्यात् । तैष्ट्वा चातयामः । अपि वा शिरिम्बिठो भारद्वाजः कालकर्णोपेतः । अलक्ष्मीर्निर्णाशयाञ्चकार[6] । तस्य सत्त्वैः कर्मभिरिति स्यात् । तैष्ट्वा चातयामः । चातयतिर्नाशने ।

पराशरः पराशीर्णस्य वसिष्ठस्य स्थविरस्य जज्ञे ।

पराशरः शतयातुर्वसिष्ठः[8] । इत्यपि निगमो भवति ।

इन्द्रोऽपि पराशर उच्यते । [परा] शातयिता यातूनाम् ।

इन्द्रो यातूनामभवत्पराशरः[9] । इत्यपि निगमो भवति ।

क्रिविर्दती विकर्तनदन्ती ।

यत्रा वो दिद्युद्रदति क्रिविर्दती[10] । इत्यपि निगमो भवति ।

करूलती कृत्तदती । [अपि वा देवं कश्चित्कृत्तदन्तं दृष्ट्वैवमवक्ष्यत][11] ॥ ३० ॥

वामं वामं त आदुरे देवो ददात्वर्यमा ।
वामं पूषा वामं भगो वामं देवः करूलती[12] ॥

वामं वननीयं भवति[13] । आदुरिरादरणात् । तत्कः करूलती । भगः पुरस्तात्तस्यान्वादेश इत्येकम् । पूषेत्यपरम् । सोऽदन्तकः[14] ।

अदन्तकः पूषा[15] । इति च ब्राह्मणम् ।

---

1. RV. X. 155. 1.
2. काणे Roth.
3. Omitted by BK, C 4, C 5, Kn, M 3, Mi, R 4, R 6, W 1, W 2, W 3.
4. Omitted by BK, C 4, C 5, Kn, M 3, Mi, R 4, R 6, W 1, W 2, W 3.
5. बिठं...व्याख्यातम् is omitted by C 6.
6. निर्नाशयांचकार. C 1, C 2, C 3, C 6, M 1, M 2, R 1, R 2, R 5, S.
7. नामभिः C 1 and Durga.
8. RV. VII. 18. 21.
9. RV. VII. 104. 21; AV. 8. 4. 21.
10. RV. I. 166. 6.
11. Omitted by BK, C 4, C 5, Kn, M 3, Mi, R 4, R 6, W 1, W 2, W 3, and Durga.
12. RV. IV. 30. 24.
13. Quoted by SRV. IV. 30 24; VI. 71. 4; VII. 18. 1. pp. ii. 434, 883; iii. 36.
14. Cf. BD. IV. 139 B.
15. Cf. KB. VI. 13. SB. 1. 7. 4. 7.

दनो॒ विश॑ इन्द्र मृ॒ध्रवा॑चः ।

दानमनसो नो मनुष्यानिन्द्र मृदुवाचः कुरु[2] ।

अ॒वीरा॑मिव॒ माम॒यं श॒रारु॑र॒भि मन्य॑ते[3] ।

अबलामिव मामयं बालोऽभिमन्यते संशिशरिषुः ।

इदंयुरिदं कामयमानः । अथापि तद्धदर्थे भाष्यते[4] । वसूयुरिन्द्रो वसुमानि-त्यर्थः[5] ।

अ॒श्व॒युर्ग॑व्यू रथ॒युर्व॑सू॒युः[6] [इन्द्रः[7] ।] इत्यपि निगमो भवति[8] ॥ ३१ ॥

किं ते॑ कृण्वन्ति॒ कीक॑टेषु॒ गावो॒ नाशिरं॑ दु॒ह्रे न त॑पन्ति घ॒र्मम् ।

आ नो॑ भर॒ प्रम॑गन्दस्य॒ वेदो॑ नैचाशा॒खं म॑घवन्रन्धया नः[9] ॥

किं ते कुर्वन्ति कीकटेषु गावः । कीकटा नाम देशोऽनार्यनिवासः[10] । कीकटाः किंकृताः । किं क्रियाभिरिति प्रेप्सा [वा[11]] । नैव चाशिरं दुहे । न तपन्ति घर्मं हर्म्यम्[12] । आहर नः[13] प्रमगन्दस्य धनानि । मगन्दः कुसीदी । माङ्गदो मामागमिष्य-तीति[14] च ददाति । तदपत्यं प्रमगन्दः । अत्यन्तकुसीदिकुलीनः[15][16] । प्रमदको वा योऽय-मेवास्ति लोको न पर इति प्रेप्सुः । पण्डको वा । पण्डकः पण्डगः प्रार्दको वा प्रार्द-यत्याण्डौ । आण्डावाणी इव व्रीडयति । तत् त्वं[17] नैचाशाखं नीचाशाखो नीचैः[18] शाखः । शाखाः शक्नोतेः । आणिररणात् । तन्नो मघवन्रन्धयेति । रध्यतिर्वश-गमने[19] ।

१. RV. I. 174. 2.

२. Quoted by SRV. I. 174. 2. p. i. 748.

३. RV. X. 86. 9; AV. 20. 126. 9; Cf. BD. i. 53. Macdonell translates अवीरा as 'without a husband'.

४. Quoted by SRV. VIII. 92. 30. p. iii. 557.

५. Cf. SRV. I. 51. 14. p. i. 260. वसुमानित्यर्थः ।

६. RV. I. 51. 14.

७. Omitted by BK, C 4, C 5, Kn, M 3, Mi, R 4, R 6, W 1, W 2, W 3.

८. Cf. SRV. I. 51. 14. p. i. 260.

९. RV. III. 53. 14.

१०. Cf. SRV. III. 53. 14. p. ii. 302, कीकटा etc.

११. Omitted by BK, C 4, C 5, Kn, M 3, Mi, R 4, R 6, W 1, W 2, W 3.

१२. Cf. SRV. III. 53. 14. p. ii. 302 वरणं.

१३. Omitted by C 5, M 3, Mi.

१४. मां गमिष्यतीति BK, C 4, C 5, Kn, M 3, Mi, R 4, R 6, W 1, W 2, W 3.

१५. अत्यन्तः W 1.

१६. ०कुसीदः BK, C 4, C 5, Kn, M 3, Mi, R 4, R 6, W 1, W 2, W 3.

१७. तत् स्वं BK, C 4, C 5, Kn, M 3, Mi, R 4, R 6, W 1, W 2, W 3; तस्तम्भे Roth, S'ivadatta.

१८. नैचैः BK, C 4, C 5, Kn, M 3, Mi, R 4, R 6, W 1, W 2, W 3. Cf. SRV. III. 53. 14. p. ii. 302.

१९. The passage नैचाशाखं...वशगमने is omitted by Durga. Quoted by SRV. loc. cit.

बुन्द इषुर्भवति[1] । [बिन्दो वा[2] ।] भिन्दो वा । भयदो वा । भासमानो द्रवतीति वा ॥ ३२ ॥

तुविक्षं ते सुकृतं सूमयं धनुः साधुर्बुन्दो हिरण्ययः ।
उभा ते बाहू रण्या सुसंस्कृत ऋदूपे चिदृदूवृधा[3] ॥

तुविक्षं बहु[4]विक्षेपं महाविक्षेपं वा ते सुकृतं सूमयं सुसुखं धनुः । साधयिता ते बुन्दो हिरण्मयः[5] । उभौ ते बाहू [रण्यौ[6]] रमणीयौ सांग्राम्यौ [वा[6]] । ऋदूपे[7] अर्दनपातिनौ । गमनपातिनौ [शब्दपातिनौ दूरपातिनौ][8] वा । मर्मण्यर्दनवेधिनौ । गमन[9]वेधिनौ [शब्दवेधिनौ दूरवेधिनौ][10] वा ॥ ३३ ॥

निराविध्यद्गिरिभ्य आ धारयत्पक्वमोदनम् ।
इन्द्रो बुन्दं स्वाततम्[11] ॥

निरविध्यद्गिरिभ्य आधारयत्पक्वम् । ओदनमुदकदानं मेघम् । इन्द्रो बुन्दं स्वाततम् ।

वृन्दं बुन्देन व्याख्यातम् । वृन्दारकश्च ॥ ३४ ॥

अयं यो होता किरु स यमस्य कमप्यूहे यत्समञ्जन्ति देवाः ।
अहरहर्जायते मासि मास्यथा देवा दधिरे हव्यवाहम्[12] ॥

अयं यो होता कर्ता स यमस्य । कमप्यू [ऊहे[13]] अन्नमभिवहति यत्समश्नुवन्ति देवाः । अहरहर्जायते । मासे मासे । अर्धमासेऽर्धमासे वा । अथ देवा निदधिरे हव्यवाहम्[14] ।

---

१. Quoted by SRV. VIII. 45. 4. p. iii. 430.

२. Omitted by BK, C 4, C 5, Kn, M 3, Mi, R 4, R 6, W 1, W 2, W 3; & Durga. C 3 reads बुन्दो वा.

३. RV. VIII. 77. 11.

४. बहुविक्षम् BK, C 4, C 5, Kn, M 3, Mi, R 4, R 6, W 1, W 2, W 3; M 1; बहुविक्षपम् C 3.

५. हिरण्ययः Roth and S'ivadatta.

६. Omitted by BK, C 4, C 5, Kn, M 3, Mi, R 4, R 6, W 1, W 2, W 3.

७. Cf. N. 6. 4.

८. Omitted by BK, C 4, C 5, Kn, M 3, Mi, R 4, R 6, W 1, W 2, W 3, and Durga.

९. Quoted by SRV. VIII. 77. ii. p. iii. 525.

१०. Omitted by BK, C 4, C 5, Kn, M 3, Mi, R 4, R 6, W 1, W 3, and Durga, who remarks : भाष्यमत्र न सम्यगिव लक्ष्यते तस्य सम्यक् पाठोऽन्वेष्यस्ततो योज्यम् । Omitted also by SRV. VIII. 77. 11. p. iii. 525.

११. RV. VIII. 77. 6.

१२. RV. X. 52. 3.

१३. Omitted by BK, C 4, C 5, Kn, M 3, Mi, R 4, R 6, W 1, W 2, W 3.

१४. अथ देवा...हव्यवाहम् is omitted by C 3.

उल्बमूर्णोतेः । वृणोतेर्वा ।

महत्तदुल्बं स्थविरं तदासीत्[1] । इत्यपि निगमो भवति ।

ऋबीसमपगतभासम् । अपहृतभासम् । अन्तर्हितभासम् । गतभासं वा ॥३५॥

हिमेनाग्निं घ्रंसमवारयेथां पितुमतीमूर्जमस्मा अधत्तम् ।
ऋबीसे अत्रिमश्विनावनीतमुन्निन्यथुः सर्वगणं स्वस्ति ॥[2]

हिमेनोदकेन[3] ग्रीष्मान्तेऽग्निं घ्रंसमहरवारयेथाम् । अन्नवतीं चास्मा ऊर्जमधत्तमग्नये । योऽयमृबीसे पृथिव्यामग्निरन्तरौषधिवनस्पतिष्वप्सु तमुन्निन्यथुः । सर्वगणं सर्वनामानं । गणो गणनात् । गुणश्च । यद्वृष्ट ओषधय उद्यन्ति प्राणिनश्च पृथिव्यां तदश्विनो रूपं तेनैनौ स्तौति स्तौति ॥ ३६ ॥

इति षष्ठोऽध्यायः ।

[त्वमग्नेऽलातृण उद्वृहाजास उपलप्रक्षिणीकारुरहमंस्से ते श्रायन्त इवाश्वं हि सोमानं स्वरणमिन्द्रा सोमा कृणुष्वपाजस्तां अध्वरेऽस्ति हिवोऽसूते प्रवोच्छा सृप्रस्तुञ्जे तुञ्जे यो असा अंसा इदु तन्नस्तुरीपं हिनोतानोमित्रो मातवा नं पापासो यवं वृकेण जीवान्नो वंतो वतासि धेनुन्नोऽरायि काणे वामं वामं किं ते तुविक्षं ते निरविध्यदयं यो होता हिमेनाग्नि षट्त्रिंशत् ॥]

॥ इति निरुक्ते पूर्वषट्के षष्ठोऽध्यायः समाप्तः ॥

॥ इति नैगमं काण्डं पूर्वार्धश्च समाप्तम् ॥

---

१. RV. X. 51. 1. Cf. BD. VII. 80.

२. RV. I. 116. 8. Cf. BD. ii. 110.

३. Quoted by SRV. I. 116. 8. p. i. 516.

४. Small figure within brackets represents the corresponding section of the sixth chapter of the *Nirukta*.

अथोत्तरषट्कं प्रारभ्यते।

अथ सप्तमोऽध्यायः ।

ॐ ॥ अथातो दैवतम् । तद्यानि नामानि प्राधान्यस्तुतीनां देवतानां तद् दैवतमित्याचक्षते । सैषा देवतोपपरीक्षा । यत्काम ऋषिर्यस्यां देवतायामार्थपत्य[1]मिच्छ-[2]न्स्तुतिं प्रयुङ्क्ते[3] तद्दैवतः स मन्त्रो[4] भवति[5]। तास्त्रिविधा ऋचः[6] । परोक्षकृताः। प्रत्यक्षकृताः। आध्यात्मिक्यश्च । तत्र परोक्षकृताः सर्वाभिर्नामविभक्तिभिर्युज्यन्ते । प्रथमपुरुषैश्चाख्यातस्य[7] ॥ १ ॥

इन्द्रो दिव इन्द्र ईशे पृथिव्याः[8] ।
इन्द्रमिद् गाथिनो बृहत्[9] ।
इन्द्रेणैते तृत्सवो वेविषाणाः[10] ।
इन्द्राय साम गायत[11] ।
नेन्द्रादृते पवते धाम किं चन[12] ।
इन्द्रस्य नु वीर्याणि प्र वोचम्[13] ।
इन्द्रे कामा अयंसत[14] । इति ।

अथ प्रत्यक्षकृता मध्यमपुरुषयोगाः । त्वमिति चैतेन सर्वनाम्ना[15] ।

---

१. ०मर्थ० 'च', 'छ'.

२. ०मिच्छन्नूस्तुतिं M 1; ०मिछंस्तुतिं C 1, C 2; ०मिछँस्तुतिं C 6.

३. प्रयुंक्ते C 1, C 2, C 6, M 1, M 3.

४. मंत्रो C 1, C 2, C 6, M 1, M 3.

५. Cf. BD. i. 6; *Bṛhatsarvānukramaṇikā*, p. 1. यत्काम ऋषि र्मन्त्रद्रष्टा वा भवति यस्यां देवतायामार्थपत्यमिच्छता- स्तुतिः प्रयुज्यते सा देवता तस्य मन्त्रस्य भवति।

६. Cf. BD. i. 34: मन्त्रा नानाप्रकाराः स्युर्दृष्टा ये मन्त्रदर्शिभिः ।

७. The passage: तास्त्रिविधा...... चाख्यातस्य is quoted by SRV. I. 6. 9. p. i. 53.

८. RV. X. 89. 10.

९. RV. I. 7. 1; AV. 20. 38. 4; 20. 47. 4; 20. 70. 7; SV. 1. 198; 2. 146.

१०. RV. VII. 18. 15.

११. RV. VIII. 98. 1; AV. 20. 62. 5; SV. 1. 388; 2. 375.

१२. RV. IX. 68. 6; SV. 2. 720.

१३. RV. I. 32. 1; Cf. AV. 2. 5. 5.

१४. The quotation is untraced.

१५. Cf. BD. i. 11.

त्वमिन्द्र ब॒ला॒दधि[1] ।

वि नं इन्द्र॒ मृधो जहि[2] । इति

अथापि प्रत्यक्षकृताः स्तोतारो भवन्ति । परोक्षकृतानि स्तोतव्यानि ।

मा चि॒दन्यद्वि[3] शंसत[4] ।

कण्वा अ॒भि प्र गायत[5] ।

उप॒ प्रेत कुशिकाश्चे॒तयध्वम्[6] । इति ।

अथाध्यात्मिक्य उत्तमपुरुषयोगाः । अहमिति चैतेन सर्वनाम्ना । यथैतदिन्द्रो वैकुण्ठः[7] । लवसूक्तम्[8] । वागाम्भृणीयमिति[9] ॥ २ ॥

परोक्षकृताः प्रत्यक्षकृताश्च मन्त्रा भूयिष्ठाः । अल्पश आध्यात्मिकाः ।

अथापि स्तुतिरेव भवति नाशीर्वादः[11] ।

इन्द्र॑स्य॒ नु वी॒र्या॑णि॒ प्र वो॑चम्[12] । इति । यथैतस्मिन्त्सूक्ते ।

अथाप्याशीरेव न स्तुतिः ।

सुचक्षा अहमक्षीभ्यां भूयासम् । सुवर्चा मुखेन । सुश्रुत्कर्णाभ्यां भूयासम्[13] । इति ।

तदेतद्बहुलमाध्वर्यवे याज्ञेषु च मन्त्रेषु ।

अथापि शपथाभिशापौ ।

अ॒द्या मु॑रीय॒ यदि॑ यातु॒धानो॒ अस्मि[14] ।

अधा॒ स वी॒रैर्द॒शभि॒र्वि यू॑याः[15] । इति ।

अथापि कस्यचिद्भावस्याचिख्यासा[16] ।

न मृ॒त्युरा॑सीद॒मृतं॒ न तर्हि[17] ।

तम॑ आसी॒त्तम॑सा गू॒ळ्हमग्रे[18] ।

---

१. RV. X. 153. 2; AV. 20. 93. 5; SV. 1. 120.

२. RV. X. 152. 4; AV. 1. 21. 2; SV. 2. 1218; VS. 8. 44; 18. 70.

३. स्विद्० M 1.

४. RV. VIII. 1. 1; AV. 20. 85. 1; SV. 1. 242; 2. 710.

५. RV. I. 37. 1.

६. RV. III. 53. 11; cf. BD. IV. 115.

७. The second section ends here in BK, C 4, C 5, Kn, M 3, Mi, W 1, W 2, W 3, R 7, R 8.

८. RV. X. 48—49.

९. RV. X. 119.

१०. RV. X. 125.

११. Cf. BD. i. 35.

१२. RV. I. 32. 1; cf. AV. 2. 5. 5.

१३. Cf. Pāraskara gr. sū. II 6. 19; Ās'va. gr. sū. III. 6. 7.

१४. RV. VII. 104. 15; AV. 8. 4. 15.

१५. RV. VII. 104. 15; AV. 8. 4. 15.

१६. Cf. BD. i. 36.

१७. RV. X. 129. 2; cf. BD. i. 58: न मृत्युरासीदित्येतामाचिख्यासां प्रचक्षते ।

१८. RV. X. 129. 3.

अथापि परिदेवना कस्माच्चिद्भावात्[1]।

सुदेवो अद्य प्रपतेदनावृत्[2]।
न वि जानामि यदि वेदमस्मि[3]। इति।

अथापि निन्दाप्रशंसे[4]।

केवलाघो भवति केवलादी[5]।
भोजस्येदं पुष्करिणीव वेश्म[6]।

एवमक्षसूक्ते[7] द्यूतनिन्दा च कृषिप्रशंसा च। एवमुच्चावचैरभिप्रायैर्ऋषीणां[8] मन्त्रदृष्टयो भवन्ति॥ ३॥

तद्येऽनादिष्टदेवता[9] मन्त्रास्तेषु देवतोपपरीक्षा[10]। यद्देवतः स यज्ञो वा यज्ञाङ्गं वा तद्देवता भवन्ति[11]। अथान्यत्र यज्ञात्प्राजापत्या इति याज्ञिकाः[12]। नाराशंसा इति नैरुक्ताः। अपि वा सा कामदेवता स्यात्। प्रायोदेवता वा। अस्ति ह्याचारो बहुलं लोके। देवदेवत्यमतिथिदेवत्यं पितृदेवत्यम्।

याज्ञदैवतो मन्त्र इति। अपि ह्यदेवता देवतावत् स्तूयन्ते। यथाश्वप्रभृतीन्योषधिपर्यन्तानि[13]। अथाप्यष्टौ द्वन्द्वानि[14]। स न मन्येतागन्तूनिवार्थान्[15] देवतानाम्। प्रत्यक्षदृश्यमेतद्भवति। माहाभाग्याद् देवताया एक आत्मा बहुधा स्तूयते[16]। एकस्यात्मनोऽन्ये देवाः प्रत्यङ्गानि भवन्ति। अपि च सत्त्वानां प्रकृतिभूमभिर्ऋषयः स्तुवन्तीत्याहुः। प्रकृतिसार्वनाम्न्याच्च[17]। इतरेतरजन्मानो भवन्ति[18]। इतरेतरप्रकृतयः। कर्मजन्मानः।

---

१. Cf. BD. i. 35.

२. RV. X. 95. 14. Cf. BD. i. 53: सुदेव इति तु स्पृहा। Quoted as an example of desire.

३. RV. I. 164. 37; AV. 9. 10. 15; cf. BD. i. 56: न वि जानामि संज्वरः quoted as an example of agitation. The passage: अथापि परिदेवना......वेदमस्मि is cited by SRV. I. 164. 37. p. i. 713.

४. Cf. BD. i. 35.

५. RV. X. 117. 6; TB. ii. 8. 8. 3; cf. Manu. III. 118.

६. RV. X. 107. 10.

७. RV. X. 34.

८. Cf. BD. i. 3.

९. तद्ये नादिष्ट० C 1, C 2, C 6, M 1.

१०. Cf. BD. i. 20.

११. भवति C 2; cf. BD. VII. 16.

१२. Cf. BD. VII. 17.

१३. The 4th section ends here in BK, C 4, C 5, C 7, Kn, M 3, Mi, R 7, R 8, W 1, W 2, W 3. See Ngh. V. 3. 1—22.

१४. अथाप्यष्टौ द्वन्द्वानि is omitted by Durga. See Ngh. V. 3. 29—36; N. 9. 35—43.

१५. ०वार्थानां क. ख. ग.

१६. Cf. BD. IV. 143.

१७. ०सार्वनाम्याच्च C 1; ०सार्वनाम्र्याच्च. Lahore edition of Rājārāma.

१८. Cf. BD. i. 71.

आत्मजन्मानः। आत्मैवैषां[1] रथो भवति। आत्माश्वः[2]। आत्मायुधम्[3]। आत्मेषवः। आत्मा सर्वं देवस्य[4][5] ॥ ४ ॥

तिस्र एव देवता इति नैरुक्ताः[6]। अग्निः पृथिवीस्थानः। वायुर्वेन्द्रो वान्तरिक्षस्थानः। सूर्यो द्युस्थानः[7]। तासां माहाभाग्यादेकैकस्या अपि बहूनि नामधेयानि भवन्ति। अपि वा कर्मपृथक्त्वात्[8]। यथा होताध्वर्युर्ब्रह्मोद्गातेत्यप्येकस्य सतः। अपि वा पृथगेव स्युः। पृथग्घि स्तुतयो भवन्ति। तथाभिधानानि[10]। यथो एतत्कर्मपृथक्त्वादिति[9] बहवोऽपि विभज्य कर्माणि कुर्युः। तत्र संस्थानैकत्वं[11] संभोगैकत्वं चोपेक्षितव्यम्। यथा पृथिव्यां मनुष्याः पशवो देवा इति स्थानैकत्वम्[12]। संभोगैकत्वं च दृश्यते। यथा पृथिव्याः पर्जन्येन च वाय्वादित्याभ्यां च संभोगः[13]। अग्निना चेतरस्य लोकस्य। तत्रैतन्नरराष्ट्रमिव[14] ॥ ५ ॥

अथाकारचिन्तनं देवतानाम्। पुरुषविधाः स्युरित्येकम्। चेतनावद्धि स्तुतयो भवन्ति। तथाभिधानानि[15]।

अथापि पौरुषविधिकैरङ्गैः संस्तूयन्ते।

ऋष्वा त इन्द्र स्थविरस्य बाहू[16]।

यत्सं गृभ्णा मघवन्काशिरित्ते[17]।

अथापि पौरुषविधिकैर्द्रव्यसंयोगैः।

आ द्वाभ्यां हरिभ्यामिन्द्र याहि[18]।

कल्याणीर्जाया सुरणं गृहे ते[19]।

अथापि पौरुषविधिकैः कर्मभिः।

---

१. Cf. BD. i. 74: तेजस्त्वेवायुधं प्राहुर्वाहनं चैव यस्य तत्। iii. 85: विश्वेषां ते ततश्चक्रुर्वाहनान्यायुधानि तु। IV. 143: आयुधं वाहनं चापि स्तुतौ यस्येह दृश्यते। तमेव तु स्तुतं विद्यात् तस्यात्मा बहुधा हि सः॥

२. आत्माश्वा: C 1, C 6, Roth.

३. अत्मा०. Roth.

४. Cf. BD. i. 73: तेषामात्मैव तत्सर्वम्।

५. देवस्य देवस्य ॥ ५ ॥ प्रथमः पादः BK, C 4, C 5, C 7, M 3, Mi, R 7, R 8, W 1, W 2, W 3.

६. Cf. AB. ii. 17. 17; V. 32. 1; KB. VIII. 8; S'B. XI. 2. 3. 1.

७. Cf. AB. V. 32. 1; S'B XI. 2. 3. 1; BD. i. 69.

८. Cf. BD. i. 70—71.

९. पृथन्कात् C 6, M 1.

१०. तथापिधानानि M 3.

११. सस्थानैकत्वं M 1.

१२. च is added after स्थानैकत्वम् in Bib. Ind. ed. of N. Cf. KB. 1. 1: अस्मिन् वै लोके उभये देवमनुष्याः आसुः।

१३. संभोगो अग्निना क.

१४. तत्रैतं नरराष्ट्रम् क.

१५. तथापिधानानि M 3.

१६. RV. VI. 47. 8; cf. AV. 19. 15. 4.

१७. RV. III. 30. 5.

१८. RV. II. 18. 4.

१९. RV. III. 53. 6.

अद्धीन्द्र पिब च प्रस्थितस्य ।[1]
आश्रुत्कर्ण श्रुधी हवम्[2] ॥ ६ ॥

अपुरुषविधाः स्युरित्यपरम् । अपि तु यद् दृश्यते[3]ऽपुरुषविधं तत् । यथाग्निर्वायुरादित्यः पृथिवी चन्द्रमा इति । यथो एतच्चेतनावद्वद्धि स्तुतयो भवन्तीत्यचेतनान्यप्येवं स्तूयन्ते । यथाक्षप्रभृतीन्योषधिपर्यन्तानि । यथो एतत्पौरुषविधिकैरङ्गैः संस्तूयन्त इत्यचेतनेष्वप्येतद्भवति ।

अभि क्रन्दन्ति हरितेभिरासभिः[4] । इति ग्रावस्तुतिः ।

यथो एतत्पौरुषविधिकैर्द्रव्यसंयोगैरित्येतदपि तादृशमेव ।

सुखं रथं युयुजे सिन्धुरश्विनम्[5] । इति नदीस्तुतिः ।

यथो एतत्पौरुषविधिकैः कर्मभिरित्येतदपि तादृशमेव ।

होतुश्चित्पूर्वे हविरद्यमाशत[6] । इति ग्रावस्तुतिरेव ।

अपि वोभयविधाः[7] स्युः । अपि वा पुरुषविधानामेव सतां कर्मात्मान एते स्युः । यथा यज्ञो यजमानस्य । एष चाख्यानसमयः ॥ ७ ॥

तिस्र एव देवता इत्युक्तं पुरस्तात् । तासां भक्तिसाहचर्यं व्याख्यास्यामः । अथैतान्यग्निभक्तीनि । अयं लोकः । प्रातः सवनं । वसन्तः । गायत्री । त्रिवृत्स्तोमः । रथंतरं साम । ये च देवगणाः समाम्नाताः प्रथमे स्थाने । अग्नायी पृथिवीळेति[8] स्त्रियः । अथास्य कर्म । वहनं[9] च हविषामावाहनं च देवतानाम् । यच्च [किञ्चिद्[10]] दार्ष्टिविषयिकमग्निकर्मैव तत्[11] । अथास्य[12] संस्तविका देवाः । इन्द्रः । सोमः । वरुणः । पर्जन्यः । ऋतवः । आग्नावैष्णवं हविर्न त्वृक्संस्तविकी दशतयीषु विद्यते । अथाप्याग्नापौष्णं हविर्न तु संस्तवः[13] । तत्रैतां विभक्त[14]स्तुतिमृचम्[15]उदाहरन्ति ॥ ८ ॥

---

१. RV. X. 116. 7.
२. RV. I. 10. 9.
३. यद्दृश्यते M 1. The last section ends after दृश्यते in C 1, C 2, C 6, M 1, M 4, S.
४. RV. X. 94. 2.
५. RV. X. 75. 9.
६. RV. X. 94. 2.
७. Cf. AB. ii. 32. 1; iii. 13. 1; IV. 29. 1; VIII. 12. 4; KB. VIII. 9; XII. 4; XIV. 1, 3, 5; XXII. 1; GB. I. 1. 17, 29; 2. 24; II. 3. 10, 12, 16; BD. i. 115.
८. ०वीलेति C 1, C 2, C 6, M 1, M 4, S.
९. हवनं C 2.
१०. Omitted by BK, C 4, C 5, C 7, Kn, M 3, Mi, R 7, R 8, W 1, W 2, W 3.
११. ०कर्मैतत् Roth; cf. BD. i. 119, 120.
१२. यथास्य. Mi.
१३. Cf. BD. i. 117—119.
१४. विभक्ति C 1, C 2, C 6, M 1, M 4.
१५. Cf. BD. iii. 41.

पूषा त्वेतश्च्यावयतु प्र विद्वाननष्टपशुर्भुवनस्य गोपाः ।
स त्वैतेभ्यः परि ददत्पितृभ्योऽग्निर्देवेभ्यः सुविदत्रियेभ्यः[1] ॥

पूषा त्वेतः प्रच्यावयतु । विद्वान् । अनष्टपशुः । भुवनस्य गोपा इत्येष हि सर्वेषां भूतानां गोपायिता [आदित्यः[2]] । स त्वैतेभ्यः परिददत्[3]पितृभ्य इति सांशयिकस्तृतीयः पादः । पूषा पुरस्तात्तस्यान्वादेश इत्येकम् । अग्निरुपरिष्टात्तस्य प्रकीर्तनेत्यपरम् । अग्निर्देवेभ्यः सुविदत्रियेभ्यः । सुविदत्रं धनं भवति । विन्दतेर्वैकोपसर्गात् । ददातेर्वा[4] स्याद् द्व्युपसर्गात् ॥ ९ ॥

अथैतानीन्द्रभक्तीनि । अन्तरिक्षलोकः । माध्यंदिनं सवनम् । ग्रीष्मः । त्रिष्टुप् । पञ्चदशस्तोमः । बृहत्साम[5] । ये च देवगणाः समाम्नाता मध्यमे स्थाने[6] याश्च स्त्रियः । अथास्य कर्म रसानुप्रदानं वृत्रवधः । या च का च[7] बलकृतिरिन्द्रकर्मैव[8] तत् । अथास्य संस्तविका देवाः । अग्निः । सोमः । वरुणः । पूषा । बृहस्पतिः । ब्रह्मणस्पतिः । पर्वतः । कुत्सः । विष्णुः । वायुः[9] । अथापि मित्रो वरुणेन संस्तूयते । पूष्णा रुद्रेण च सोमः । वायुना[10] च पूषा । वातेन च पर्जन्यः[11] ॥ १० ॥

अथैतान्यादित्यभक्तीनि । असौ लोकः । तृतीयसवनम् । वर्षा । जगती । सप्तदशस्तोमः । वैरूपं साम[12] । ये च देवगणाः समाम्नाता उत्तमे स्थाने[13] याश्च स्त्रियः । अथास्य कर्म रसादानं रश्मिभिश्च रस[14]धारणम्[15] । यच्च[16] किञ्चित्प्रवह्लितमादित्यकर्मैव तत् । चन्द्रमसा वायुना संवत्सरेणेति संस्तवः[17] । एतेष्वेव स्थानव्यूहेष्वृतुच्छन्दः-

१. RV. X. 17. 3; AV. 18. 2. 54.

२. Omitted by BK, C 4, C 5, C 7, Kn, M 3, R 7, R 8, W 1, W 2, W 3.

३. परिददात् M 3.

४. दधतिर्वा C 4, C 7, M 3, Mi, W 2, W 3, W 4.

५. Cf. BD. i. 130—131.

६. Cf. AB. ii. 32. 1; iii. 13. 1; IV. 31. 1; VIII. 12. 4; KB. VIII. 9; XIV. 1, 3, 5; XVI. 1; XXII. 2; GB. I. 1. 17, 18, 29; 2. 24; II. 2. 10, 12; II. 4. 4.

७. चित् BK, C 4, C 5, C 7, Kn, M 3, Mi, R 7, R 8, W 1, W 2, W 3.

८. Cf. BD. i. 87; ii. 6.

९. Cf. BD. ii. 2—3.

१०. अग्निना C 1, C 2, C 6, M 1, M 4, S. & Roth. The corresponding passage in BD. reads वायुना ।.

११. Cf. BD. ii. 4, 5, 13, 14.

१२. Cf. BD. ii. 13—14.

१३. Cf. AB. II. 32. 1; III. 13. 1; V. 1. 1; VIII. 12. 4; KB. VIII. 9; XIV. 1, 3; XVI. 1; XXII. 3, 5; GB. I. 1. 19, 29; 2. 24; II. 3. 10; 4. 18.

१४. रसाधारणं C 1, C 2, C 6, M 1, M 4; S; Roth.

१५. रश्मिभिश्च रसधारणं is omitted by Durga.

१६. यत्तु C 4, C 5, C 7, M 3, Mi, R 7, R 8, W 1, W 2, W 3.

१७. Cf. BD. ii. 15—16.

स्तोमपृष्ठस्य भक्तिशेषमनुकल्पयीत । शरदनुष्टुबेकविंशस्तोमो वैराजं सामेति पृथिव्यायतनानि[1] । हेमन्तः पङ्क्तिस्त्रिणवस्तोमः शाक्वरं सामेत्यन्तरिक्षायतनानि[2] । शिशिरोऽतिच्छन्दास्त्रयस्त्रिंशस्तोमो रैवतं सामेति द्युभक्तीनि[3] ॥ ११ ॥

मन्त्रा मननात् । छन्दांसि छादनात्[4] । [स्तोमः स्तवनात् ।][5] यजुर्यजतेः[6] । साम सम्मितमृचा । अस्यतेर्वा । ऋचा समं मेन इति नैदानाः । गायत्री गायतेः स्तुतिकर्मणः[7] । त्रिगमना वा विपरीता । गायतो मुखादुदपतत्[8] । इति च ब्राह्मणम्[9] । उष्णिगुत्स्नाता भवति । स्निह्यतेर्वा स्यात्कान्तिकर्मणः । उष्णीषिणी वेत्यौपमिकम् । उष्णीषं स्नायतेः । ककुप् ककुभिनी भवति । ककुप्[10] च कुब्जश्च कुजतेर्वा । उब्जतेर्वा । अनुष्टबनुष्टोभनात् ।

गायत्रीमेव त्रिपदां सतीं चतुर्थेन पादेनानुष्टोभति[11] । इति च ब्राह्मणम् । बृहती परिवर्हणात् । पङ्क्तिः पञ्चपदा[12] । त्रिष्टुप् स्तोभत्युत्तरपदा । का तु त्रिता स्यात् । तीर्णतमं छन्दः । त्रिवृद्वज्रः । तस्य स्तोभनीति वा ।

यत् त्रिरस्तोभत् तत् त्रिष्टुभस्त्रिष्टुप्त्वम् । इति विज्ञायते ॥ १२ ॥

जगती गततमं छन्दः[13] । जलचर[14]गतिर्वा ।

जल्गल्यमानोऽसृजत्[13] । इति च ब्राह्मणम् । विराड्विराजनाद्वा । विराधनाद्वा । विप्रापणाद्वा । विराजनात्संपूर्णाक्षरा । विराधनादूनाक्षरा । विप्रापणादधिकाक्षरा । पिपीलिकमध्येत्यौपमिकम् । पिपीलिका पेलतेर्गतिकर्मणः ।

इतीमा देवता अनुक्रान्ताः । सूक्तभाजः । हविर्भाजः । ऋग्भाजश्च भूयिष्ठाः । काश्चिन्निपातभाजः[15] । अथोताभिधानैः संयुज्य हविश्चोदयति । इन्द्राय वृत्रघ्ने[16] ।

---

१. Cf. AB. V. 4. 1; VIII. 12. 4; KB. XXII. 9; BD. i. 116.

२. Cf. AB. V. 6. 1; VIII. 12. 8; KB. XXIII. 3; BD. i. 130—131; SRV. p. i. 2.

३. Cf. AB. V. 12. 1; VIII. 12. 4; BD. ii. 13—14.

४. Cf. Chhā. up. I. 4. 2. यदेभिरच्छादयंस्तच्छन्दसां छन्दस्त्वम् ।

५. Omitted by BK, C 4, C 5, C 7, Kn, M 3, Mi, R 7, R 8, W 1, W 2, W 3; and Durga.

६. Quoted by SRV. p. i. 2.

७. Devtadhyāya Br. III. 2.

८. Devtādhyāya Br. III. 3.

९. The passage: त्रिगमना...ब्राह्मणम् is omitted by Durga.

१०. ककुब्कुज° M 3; ककुप् च कुजते Durga who places कुब्जश्च after उब्जतेर्वा ।

११. Daivata Brāhmaṇa III.

१२. Cf. AB. V. 19. 6; KB. I. 3, 4; XI. 2; XII. 2; XIX. 4, 7; GB. I. 3. 8, 10; 4. 24.

१३. Cf. Daivata Brahmaṇa III.

१४. जलचलगतिः Mi, W 1, W 2; Roth attributes the variant चलाचलगतिः to the shorter recension.

१५. Cf. BD. i. 17; VIII. 129.

१६. MS. II. 2. 11.

[इन्द्राय वृत्रतुरे[1] ।] इन्द्रायाँहोमुचे[2] इति । तान्यप्येके समामनन्ति । भूयांसि तु समाम्नानात्[3] । यत्तु संविज्ञानभूतं स्यात्प्राधान्यस्तुति तत्समामने । अथोत कर्मभिर्ऋषिर्देवताः स्तौति । वृत्रहा । पुरन्दरः । इति । तान्यप्येके समामनन्ति । भूयांसि तु समाम्नानात् । व्यञ्जनमात्रं तु तत् तस्याभिधानस्य भवति । यथा ब्राह्मणाय बुभुक्षितायौदनं देहि । स्नातायानुलेपनम् । पिपासते पानीयमिति ॥ १३ ॥

अथातोऽनुक्रमिष्यामः । अग्निः पृथिवीस्थानः । तं प्रथमं व्याख्यास्यामः । अग्निः कस्मात् । अग्रणीर्भवति । अग्रं यज्ञेषु प्रणीयते । अङ्गं नयति सन्नममानः । अक्नोपनो भवतीति स्थौलाष्ठीविः । न क्नोपयति न स्नेहयति । त्रिभ्य आख्यातेभ्यो जायत इति शाकपूणिः । इतात् । अक्ताद्दग्धाद्वा । नीतात् । स खल्वेतेरकारमादत्ते गकारमनक्तेर्वा दहतेर्वा नीः परः । तस्यैषा भवति[6] ॥ १४ ॥

अग्निमीळे पुरोहितं यज्ञस्य देवमृत्विजम् ।
होतारं रत्नधातमम्[7] ॥

अग्निमीळेऽग्निं याचामि । ईळिरध्येषणाकर्मा । पूजाकर्मा वा । पुरोहितो व्याख्यातो यज्ञश्च । देवो दानाद्वा । दीपनाद्वा । द्योतनाद्वा । द्युस्थानो भवतीति वा । यो देवः सा देवता[10] । होतारं ह्वातारम् । जुहोतेर्होतेत्यौर्णवाभः[11] । रत्नधातमं रमणीयानां धनानां दातृतमम्[12] ।

तस्यैषापरा भवति ॥ १५ ॥

अग्निः पूर्वेभिर्ऋषिभिरीड्यो नूतनैरुत ।
स देवाँ एह वक्षति[13] ॥

---

१. Omitted by Bk, C 4, C 5, C 7, Kn, M 3, Mi, R 7, R 8, W 1, W 2, W 3.

२. MS. II. 2. 10.

३. Cf. BD. ii. 71.

४. Cf. BD. ii. 24; Cf. S'aṅkara on Vedāntasūtra i. 2. 7. 28 : अग्निशब्दोऽप्यग्रणीत्वादियोगाश्रयेण परमात्मविषय एव भविष्यति ।
Cf. S'B. II. 2. 4. 2.
तद्वाऽएनमेतदग्रे देवानामजनयत । तस्मादग्निरग्रिर्ह वै नामैतद्यदग्निरिति ।
Cf. also S'B. VI. 1. 1. 11.
स यदस्य सर्वस्याग्रमसृज्यत तस्मादग्निरग्रिर्ह वै तमग्निरित्याचक्षते परोक्षम् ।
Cf. also RV. VI. 16. 48.
अग्निं देवासो अग्रियम् ।

५. Cf. BD. i. 91.

६. Cf. SRV. I. i. 1. p. i. 24.

७. RV. I. 1. 1.

८. N. 2. 12.

९. Cf. N. 3. 19. यज्ञस्य Mi, M 3. Cf. SRV. I. 1. 1. p. i. 24.

१०. यो देवः सा देवता is omitted by Durga.

११. Quoted by SRV. I. 127. 1. p. i. 573.

१२. Quoted by SRV. I. 1. 1. p. i. 24.

१३. RV. I. 1. 2.

अग्निर्यः पूर्वैर्ऋषिभिरीळितव्यो [वन्दितव्यो] ऽस्माभिश्च नवतरैः स देवानिहावहत्विति । स न मन्येतायमेवाग्निरिति । अप्येते उत्तरे ज्योतिषी अग्नी उच्येते ।

ततो नु मध्यमः ॥ १६ ॥

अभि प्रवन्त समनेव योषाः कल्याण्यः स्मयमानासो अग्निम् ।
घृतस्य धाराः समिधो नसन्त ता जुषाणो हर्यति जातवेदाः ॥

अभिनमन्त समनस इव योषाः । समनं समननाद्वा । संमाननाद्वा । कल्याण्यः । स्मयमानासः । अग्निमित्यौपमिकम् । घृतस्य धारा उदकस्य धाराः समिधो नसन्त । नसतिराप्नोतिकर्मा वा । नमतिकर्मा वा । ता जुषाणो हर्यति जातवेदाः । हर्यतिः प्रेप्साकर्मा । विहर्यतीति ।

समुद्रादूर्मिर्मधुमाँ उदारत् । इत्यादित्यमुक्तं मन्यन्ते ।

समुद्राद्ध्येषोऽद्भ्य उदेति । इति च ब्राह्मणम् ।

अथापि ब्राह्मणं भवति ।

अग्निः सर्वा देवताः । इति । तस्योत्तरा भूयसे निर्वचनाय ॥ १७ ॥

इन्द्रं मित्रं वरुणमग्निमाहुरथो दिव्यः स सुपर्णो गरुत्मान् ।
एकं सद्विप्रा बहुधा वदन्त्यग्निं यमं मातरिश्वानमाहुः ॥

इममेवाग्निं महान्तं [च] आत्मानं बहुधा मेधाविनो वदन्ति । इन्द्रं मित्रं वरुणमग्निं दिव्यं च गरुत्मन्तम् । दिव्यो दिविजः । गरुत्मान् गरणवान् । गुर्वात्मा । महात्मेति वा ।

---

१. Omitted by Bk, C 4, C 5, C 7, Kn, M 3, Mi, R 7, R 8, W 1, W 2, W 3.

२. RV. IV. 58. 8; VS. 17. 96.

३. ०कर्माभिहर्यतीति C 4, W 1; ०कर्माभिहर्यतीभिः Mi; कर्माविहर्यतीति C 5, M 3, W 2, W 3. Cf. SRV. I. 57. 2. p. i. 285; I. 62. 2. p. i. 311.

४. विहर्यतीति is omitted by Durga.

५. RV. IV. 58. 1; VS. 17. 89; cf. AB. i. 22; समुद्रादूर्मिमुदियर्ति वेनः ।

६. KB. XXV. 1.

७. AB. II. 3. Taitt. B. I. 4. 4. 10. Cf. AB. I. 1. 4; Tāṇḍ. B. II. 1. 12; GB. II. 1. 12; Ṣaḍ. B. III. 7; S'B. I. 6. 2. 8; MS. I. 4. 14. वै is added after अग्निः in all these passages.

८. RV. I. 164. 46; AV. 9. 10. 28.

९. Omitted by C 1, C 2, C 3, C 6, M 1, M 4, R 2, R 3, R 5, S; cf. SRV. I. 164. 46. p. i. 718; महान्तमात्मानम् ।

१०. गुरुर्वात्मा C 1. गुर्वात्मा महात्मेति वा is omitted by Durga.

११. Cf. SRV. loc. cit.

यस्तु सूक्तं भजते यस्मै हविर्निरुप्यतेऽयमेव सोऽग्निः । निपातमेवैते उत्तरे ज्योतिषी एतेन नामधेयेन भजेते[3] ॥ १८ ॥

जातवेदाः कस्मात् । जातानि वेद । जातानि वैनं विदुः । जाते जाते विद्यत इति वा । जातवित्तो वा । जातधनः । जातविद्यो वा जातप्रज्ञानः ।

यत्तज्जातः पशूनविन्दत [इति] तज्जातवेदसो जातवेदस्त्वम्[6] । इति ब्राह्मणम् ।

तस्मात्सर्वानृतून्पशवोऽग्निमभिसर्पन्ति । इति [illegible] ।

तस्यैषा भवति ॥ १९ ॥

[जातवेदसे सुनवाम सोममरातीयतो नि दहाति वेदः ।
स नः पर्षदति दुर्गाणि विश्वा नावेव सिन्धुं दुरितात्यग्निः ॥

जातवेदस इति जातवेदस्यां वैवं जातवेदसेऽर्चाय सुनवाम सोममिति । प्रसवायाभिषवाय सोमं राजानममृतमरातीयतो यज्ञार्थमिति स्मोः । निदहाति निश्चयेन दहति भस्मीकरोति । सोमो ददादित्यर्थः । स नः पर्षदति दुर्गाणि विश्वानि दुर्गमानि स्थानानि नावेव सिन्धुं नावा सिन्धुं सिन्धुं नावा नदीं जलदुर्गां महाकूलां तारयति । दुरितात्यग्निरिति दुरितानि तारयति । तस्यैषापरा भवति ॥ २ ॥ २५ ॥][10]

प्र नूनं जातवेदसमश्वं हिनोत वाजिनम् ।
इदं नो बर्हिरासदे ॥

प्रहिणुत जातवेदसं कर्मभिः समश्नुवानम् । अपि वोपमार्थे स्यात् । अश्वमिव जातवेदसमिति । इदं नो बर्हिरासीदत्विति । तदेतदेकमेव[12] जातवेदसं गायत्रं तृचं

---

१. Cf. BD. i. 78: निरुप्यते हविर्यस्मै सूक्तं च भजते च या ।

२. Cf. BD. i. 67:
इहाग्निभूतस्त्वृषिभिर्लोके स्तुतिभिरीळितः । जातवेदास्तुतो मध्ये स्तुतो वैश्वानरो दिवि ॥

३. Cf. BD. ii. 30: भूतानि वेद etc. AB. II. 39. प्राणो वै जातवेदाः स हि जातानां वेद ।

४. Cf. BD. i. 92: यद्विद्यते हि जातः etc. Cf. also ii. 31.

५. Omitted by BK, C 4, C 5, C 7, Kn, M 3, Mi, R 7, R 8, W 1, W 2, W 3.

६. MS. I. 8. 2. Cf. AB. III. 36. SB. IX. 5. 1. 68:
तद्यज्जातं जातं विन्दते तस्माज्जातवेदाः ।

७. MS. I. 8. 2.

८. Cf. SRV. I. 44. 1. p. i. 223; I. 127. 1. p. i. 573.

९. RV. I. 99. 1.

१०. The section within brackets is omitted by C 1, C 2, C 3, C 6, M 1, M 4, R 2, R 3, R 5, S; and Durga. Cf. N. 14. 33.

११. RV. X. 188. 1; cf. BD. VIII. 88.

१२. ॰मिव C 4, C 5, C 7, M 3, Mi, W 1, W 3; तदेकमिव R 2; तदेकमेव Roth.

दशतयीषु विद्यते । यत्तु किञ्चिदाग्नेयं तज्जातवेदसानां स्थाने युज्यते । स न मन्ये-तायमेवाग्निरिति । अप्येते उत्तरे ज्योतिषी जातवेदसी उच्येते । ततो नु मध्यमः ।

अभि प्रवन्त समनेव योषाः । इति तत्पुरस्ताद् व्याख्यातम् ।

अथासावादित्यः ।

उदु त्यं जातवेदसम् । इति । तदुपरिष्टाद् व्याख्यास्यामः ।

यस्तु सूक्तं भजते यस्मै हविर्निरुप्यतेऽयमेव सोऽग्निर्जातवेदाः । निपातमेवैते उत्तरे ज्योतिषी एतेन नामधेयेन भजेते ॥ २० ॥

वैश्वानरः कस्मात् । विश्वान्नरान्नयति । विश्व एनं नरा नयन्तीति वा । अपि वा विश्वानर एव स्यात् । प्रत्यृतः सर्वाणि भूतानि तस्य वैश्वानरः ।

तस्यैषा भवति ॥ २१ ॥

वैश्वानरस्य सुमतौ स्याम राजा हि कं भुवनानामभिश्रीः ।
इतो जातो विश्वमिदं वि चष्टे वैश्वानरो यतते सूर्येण ॥

इतो जातः सर्वमिदमभिविपश्यति । वैश्वानरः संयतते सूर्येण । राजा यः सर्वेषां भूतानामभिश्रयणीयस्तस्य वयं वैश्वानरस्य कल्याण्यां मतौ स्यामेति ।

तत्को वैश्वानरः । मध्यम इत्याचार्याः । वर्षकर्मणा ह्येनं स्तौति ॥ २२ ॥

प्र नू महित्वं वृषभस्य वोचं यं पूरवो वृत्रहणं सचन्ते ।
वैश्वानरो दस्युमग्निर्जघन्वाँ अधूनोत्काष्ठा अव शम्बरं भेत् ॥

---

१. RV. X. 188.

२. जातवेदसा C 4, C 5, C 7, M 3, Mi, W 1, W 2, W 3.

३. Cf. BD. i. 90, 97.

४. RV. IV. 58. 8.

५. N. 7. 17.

६. RV. I. 50. 1; AV. 13. 2. 16; 20. 47. 13; SV. 1. 31; VS. 7. 41; 8. 41.

७. N. 12. 15.

८. Cf. BD. i. 67.

९. Cf. BD. ii. 66.

१०. Cf. S'aṅkara on Vedāntasūtra I. 2. 28.

विश्वश्चायं नरश्चेति । विश्वेषां वायं नरः । विश्वे वा नरा अस्येति विश्वानरः परमात्मा सर्वात्मत्वात् विश्वानर एव वैश्वानरः । तद्धितो ऽनन्यार्थः । राक्षसवायसादिवत् ।

११. Cf. SRV. I. 60. 6; III. 2. 1; VII. 5. 4. pp. i. 293; ii. 133; iii. 16.

१२. भूवना० Roth.

१३. RV. I. 98. 1; VS. 26. 7.

१४. Cf. BD. i. 67: स्तुतो वैश्वानरो दिवि ।

१५. RV. I. 59. 6.

प्रब्रवीमि तत् । महत्त्वं[1] माहाभाग्यम् । वृषभस्य वर्षितुरपाम् । यं पूरवः पूरयितव्या मनुष्याः । वृत्रहणं मेघहनम् । सचन्ते सेवन्ते वर्षकामाः[2] । दस्युर्दस्यतेः । क्षयार्थात् । उपदस्यन्त्यस्मिन्रसाः । उपदासयति कर्माणि । तमग्निर्वैश्वानरो घ्नन्[3] । अवाधूनोदपः काष्ठा अभिनत् । शम्बरं मेघम्[4] ।

अथासावादित्य इति पूर्वे याज्ञिकाः[5] । एषां लोकानां रोहेण सवनानां रोह आम्नातः । रोहात्प्रत्यवरोहश्चिकीर्षितः । तामनुकृतिं होताग्निमारुते शस्त्रे वैश्वानरीयेण सूक्तेन[6] प्रतिपद्यते[7] । सोऽपि न स्तोत्रियमाद्रियेत । आग्नेयो[8] हि भवति । तत आगच्छति मध्यमस्थाना देवता । रुद्रं च मरुतश्च । ततोऽग्निमिहस्थानमत्रैव स्तोत्रियं शंसति ।

अथापि वैश्वानरीयो द्वादशकपालो भवति[9] । एतस्य हि द्वादशविधं कर्म ।

अथापि ब्राह्मणं भवति ।

असौ वा आदित्योऽग्निर्वैश्वानरः[10] । इति ।

अथापि निवित्सौर्यवैश्वानरी भवति ।

आ यो द्यां भात्या पृथिवीम्[11] । इति । एष हि द्यावापृथिव्यावाभासयति ।

अथापि छान्दोमिकं[12] सूक्तं सौर्यवैश्वानरं भवति ।

दिवि पृष्टो अरोचत[13] । इति । एष हि दिवि पृष्टो अरोचतेति ।

अथापि हविष्पान्तीयं सूक्तं[14] सौर्यवैश्वानरं भवति[15] ।

अयमेवाग्निर्वैश्वानर इति शाकपूणिः[16] । विश्वानरावित्येते[17] उत्तरे ज्योतिषी । वैश्वानरोऽयं यत् ताभ्यां जायते[18] । कथं त्वयमेताभ्यां[19] जायत इति ।

---

१. महित्वम् C 1, C 2. Cf. SRV. I. 60. 6. p. i. 293.

२. Quoted by SRV. III. 13. 2. p. ii. 171.

३. जघन्वान् Durga.

४. Quoted by SRV. I. 60. 6. p. i. 293.

५. Cf. BD. i. 67. S'B. IX. 3. 1. 25. स यः स वैश्वानरः असौ स आदित्यः ।

६. RV. VI. 8—9.

७. Cf. BD. i. 102: रोहात् प्रत्यवरोहेण etc. Cf. AB. XII. 3. स वैश्वानरीयेणाग्निमारुतं प्रत्यपद्यत ।

८. Cf. BD. i. 103.

९. Cf. AB. VII. 9. 1; KB. IV. 3; cf. BD. ii. 16—17. S'B. VI. 6. 1. 5 वैश्वानरो द्वादशकपालः ।

१०. MS. II. 1. 2. Cf. KB. IV. 3; XIX. 2: असौ वै वैश्वानरो योऽसौ तपति ।

११. S'S'. 8. 22. 1.

१२. छन्दोमिकं M 3.

१३. VS. 33. 92.

१४. RV. X. 88.

१५. Cf. BD. ii. 16—17.

१६. Cf. GB. I. 2. 20.

१७. विश्वानरावेते उत्तरे C 4, C 5, C 7, M 3, Mi, W 1, W 2, W 3.

१८. Cf. BD. i. 101.

१९. स्वयम् BK, C 4, C 5, C 7, M 3, Mi, R 7, R 8, W 1, W 2, W 3.

यत्र वैद्युतः शरणमभिहन्ति यावदनुपात्तो भवति मध्यमधर्मैव तावद् भवत्युदकेन्धनः शरीरोपशमनः । उपादीयमान एवायं सम्पद्यत उदकोपशमनः शरीरदीप्तिः ।

अथादित्यात् । उदीचि प्रथमसमावृत्त आदित्ये कंसं वा मणिं वा परिमृज्य प्रतिस्वरे यत्र शुष्कगोमयमसंस्पर्शयन् धारयति तत्प्रदीप्यते । सोऽयमेव सम्पद्यते ।

अथाप्याह ।

वैश्वानरो यतते सूर्येण । इति । न च पुनरात्मनात्मा संयतते ।

अन्येनैवान्यः संयतते । इत इममादधात्यमुतोऽमुष्य रश्मयः प्रादुर्भवन्ति । इतोऽस्यार्चिषस्तयोर्भासोः संसङ्गं दृष्ट्वैवमवक्ष्यत् ।

अथ यान्येतान्यौत्तमिकानि सूक्तानि भागानि वा सावित्राणि वा [सौर्याणि वा] पौष्णानि वा वैष्णवानि वा [वैश्वदेव्यानि वा] तेषु वैश्वानरीया प्रवादा अभविष्यन् । आदित्यकर्मणा चैनमस्तोष्यन्निति । उदेषीति अस्तमेषीति । विपर्येषीति । आग्नेयेष्वेव हि सूक्तेषु वैश्वानरीयाः प्रवादा भवन्ति । अग्निकर्मणा चैनं स्तौतीति । वहसीति । पचसीति । दहसीति ।

यथो एतद्वर्षकर्मणा ह्येनं स्तौतीत्यस्मिन्नप्येतदुपपद्यते ।

समानमेतदुदकमुच्चैत्यव चाहभिः ।
भूमिं पर्जन्या जिन्वन्ति दिवं जिन्वन्त्यग्नयः ॥

इति सा निगदव्याख्याता ॥ २३ ॥

कृष्णं नियानं हरयः सुपर्णा अपो वसाना दिवमुत्पतन्ति ।
त आ ववृत्रन्त्सदनादृतस्यादिद् घृतेन पृथिवी व्युद्यते ॥

---

१. ०नुपात्तो C 4, C 5, C 7, M 3, Mi, R 7, R 9, W 1, W 2, W 3.

२. ०उदकेन्धनु C 7, M 3, Mi.

३. RV. I. 98. 1; VS. 26. 7. See N. 7. 22.

४. ०रात्मानमात्मा C 1, C 2, C 6, M 1, M 4.

५. Quoted by SRV. I. 98. 1. p. i. 437; cf. also IV. 5. 7. p. ii. 366.

६. Omitted by BK, C 4, C 5, C 7, Kn, M 3, Mi, R 7, R 8, W 1, W 2, W 3, and Durga.

७. Omitted by BK, C 4, C 5, C 7, Kn, M 3, Mi, R 7, R 8, W 1, W 2, W 3.

८. दहसीति is added after स्तौतीति by M 3.

९. RV. I. 164. 51.

१०. RV. I. 164. 47; AV. 6. 22. 1.

कृष्णं निरयणं रात्रिः । आदित्यस्य हरयः सुपर्णा हरणा आदित्यरश्मयः[1] । ते यदामुतोऽर्वाञ्चः पर्यावर्तन्ते[2] । सहस्थानादुदकस्यादित्यात् । अथ घृतेनोदकेन पृथिवी व्युद्यते । घृतमित्युदकनाम । जिघर्तेः सिञ्चतिकर्मणः ।

अथापि ब्राह्मणं भवति ।

अग्निर्वा इतो वृष्टिं समीरयति धामच्छैद्दिवि[3] [खलु वै][4] भूत्वा वर्षति मरुतः सृष्टां वृष्टिं नयन्ति । यदा [खलु वै][4] असावादित्योऽग्निं[5] रश्मिभिः पर्यावर्ततेऽथ वर्षति[6] । **इति ।**

यथो एतद्रोहात् प्रत्यवरोहश्चिकीर्षित इत्याम्नायवचनादेतद् भवति ।

यथो एतद्वैश्वानरीयो द्वादशकपालो भवतीत्यनिर्वचनं कपालानि[7] भवन्ति[8] । अस्ति हि सौर्य एककपालः पञ्चकपालश्च ।

यथो एतद् ब्राह्मणं भवतीति बहुभक्तिवादीनि हि ब्राह्मणानि भवन्ति । पृथिवी वैश्वानरः[9] । संवत्सरो वैश्वानरः[10] । ब्राह्मणो वैश्वानरः[11] । **इति ।**

यथो एतन्निवित्सौर्यवैश्वानरी भवतीत्यस्यैव सा भवति ।

यो विड्भ्यो मानुषीभ्यो दीदेत्[12] । **इत्येष हि विड्भ्यो मानुषीभ्यो दीप्यते[13] ।**

यथो एतच्छान्दोमिकं[14] सूक्तं[15] सौर्यवैश्वानरं भवतीत्यस्यैव तद्भवति ।

---

१. Quoted by SRV. I. 164. 47. p. i. 718.

२. Cf. BD. ii. 8—9.

३. धामछदिव C 1, C 2, C 6, M 1, M 4, S.

४. Omitted by BK, C 4, C 5, C 7, Kn, M 3, Mi, R 7, R 8, W 1, W 2, W 3.

५. न्यङ् C 1, C 2, C 6, M 1, M 4, S; Roth.

६. Cf. KS. XI. 10. अग्निर्वा इतो वृष्टिमुदीरयति धामच्छदिव भूत्वा वर्षति मरुतस्सृष्टां वृष्टिं नयन्ति ॥ यदासा आदित्योऽर्वाङ् रश्मिभिः पर्यावर्ततेऽथ वर्षति । Schroeder's edition vol. i. p. 157.

Cf. TS. II. 4. 10. अग्निर्वा इतो वृष्टिमुदीरयति मरुतः सृष्टां नयन्ति यदा खलु वा असावादित्यो न्यङ् रश्मिभिः पर्यावर्ततेऽथ वर्षति धामच्छदिव खलु वै भूत्वा वर्षति । Ānandās'rama ed. pp. 1722-3. Cf. MS. II. 4. 8: अग्निर्वा इतो वृष्टिमीट्टे मरुतोऽमुतश्च्यावयन्ति तां सूर्यो रश्मिभिर्वर्षति । This last quotation is cited by PMbh. vol. i. p. 256.

७. करालानि M 3.

८. भवति M 1. The passage अनिर्वचनं कपालानि भवन्ति is omitted by Durga.

९. Cf. S'B. XIII. 3. 8. 3.

इयं (पृथिवी) वै वैश्वानरः ।

१०. S'B. V. 2. 5. 15; VI. 6. 1. 5.

संवत्सरो वैश्वानरः ।

११. Cf. Taitt. Br. III. 7. 3. 2.

एष वा अग्निर्वैश्वानरः यद्ब्राह्मणः ।

१२. S'S'. 8. 22. 1. Cf. KB. V. 8.

१३. दीदयति C 4, C 5, C 7, M 3, Mi, W 1, W 2, W 3.

१४. ०छन्दोमिकं M 3.

१५. VS. 33. 92.

जमदग्निभिराहुतः । इति । जमदग्नयः प्रजमिताग्नयो वा । प्रज्वलिताग्नयो वा । तैरभिहुतो[2] भवति ।

यथो एतद्धविष्पान्तीयं सूक्तं[3] सौर्यवैश्वानरं भवतीत्यस्यैव तद्भवति ॥ २४ ॥

हुविष्पान्तमजरं स्वर्विदि दिविस्पृश्याहुतं[4] जुष्टमग्नौ ।
तस्य भर्मणे भुवनाय देवा धर्मणे कं स्वधयापप्रथन्त[3] ॥

हविर्यत्पानीयम् । अजरम् । सूर्यविदि । दिविस्पृशि । अभिहुतं जुष्टमग्नौ । तस्य भरणाय च भावनाय च धारणाय च । एतेभ्यः सर्वेभ्यः[5] कर्मभ्यो देवा इममग्निमन्नेनापप्रथन्त[6] । अथाप्याह ॥ २५ ॥

अपामुपस्थे महिषा अगृभ्णत विशो राजानमुप तस्थुर्ऋग्मियम् ।
आ दूतो अग्निमभरद्विवस्वतो वैश्वानरं मातरिश्वा परावतः ॥[7]

अपामुपस्थ उपस्थाने महत्यन्तरिक्षलोक आसीना महान्त इति वागृह्णत माध्यमिका देवगणाः । विश इव राजानमुपतस्थुः । ऋग्मियमृग्मन्तमिति वा । अर्चनीयमिति वा [पूजनीयमिति वा ।][8] अहरद्यं दूतो देवानां विवस्वत आदित्यात् । विवस्वान्विवासनवान् । प्रेरितवतः परागताद्वा [अपि वा][8] अस्याग्नेर्वैश्वानरस्य मातरिश्वानमाहर्तारमाह । मातरिश्वा वायुः[9] । मातर्यन्तरिक्षे श्वसिति । मातर्याश्वनितीति वा[10] ।

अथैनमेताभ्यां सर्वाणि स्थानान्यभ्यापादं स्तौति ॥ २६ ॥

मूर्धा भुवो भवति नक्तमग्निस्ततः सूर्यो जायते प्रातरुद्यन् ।
मायामू तु यज्ञियानामेतामपो यत्तूर्णिश्चरति प्रजानन्[11] ॥

१. Ās'v. S'raut. VIII. 9.

२. तैराहुतो C 4, Mi, W 1, W 2; तैराहूतो C 5, M 3, W 3.

३. RV. X. 88. 1.

४. आहुतं C 4, C 5, C 7, M 3, Mi, W 1, W 2, W 3.

५. कर्मेभ्यः Mi. सर्वेभ्यः is however added on the margin at bottom, obviously a different and probably some later scribe.

६. ०प्रथन्तेति C 4, C 5, M 3, Mi, W 1, W 2, W 3. Cf. SRV. X. 88. 1. p. IV. 278.

७. RV. VI. 8. 4.

८. Omitted by BK, C 4, C 5, C 7, Kn, M 3, Mi, R 7, R 8, W 1, W 2, W 3.

९. Cf. AB. II. 38: प्राणो मातरिश्वा । Cf. also S'B. VI. 4. 3. 4: अयं वै वायुर्मातरिश्वा योऽयं पवते ।

१०. Quoted SRV. III. 6. 9. p. ii. 145.

११. RV. X. 88. 6.

मूर्धा[1] मूर्तमस्मिं[2]न्धीयते । मूर्धा यः सर्वेषां भूतानां भवति नक्तमग्निः । ततः सूर्यो जायते प्रातरुद्यन्त्स एव । प्रज्ञां त्वेतां मन्यन्ते यज्ञियानां देवानां यज्ञसंपादिनाम् । अपो यत्कर्म चरति प्रजानन्त्सर्वाणि स्थानान्यनुसंचरति[3] त्वरमाणः[4] ।

तस्योत्तरा भूयसे निर्वचनाय ॥ २७ ॥

स्तोमेन हि दिवि देवासो अग्निमजीजनञ्छक्तिभी रोदसिप्राम् ।
तमू अकृण्वंस्त्रेधा भुवे कं स ओषधीः पचति विश्वरूपाः[5] ॥

स्तोमेन हि [6]यं दिवि देवा[7] अग्निमजनयन्[8] [शक्तिभिः] कर्मभिर्द्यावापृथिव्योः [आ] पूरणम् । तमकुर्वंस्त्रेधाभावाय । पृथिव्यामन्तरिक्षे दिवीति शाकपूणिः ।

यदस्य दिवि तृतीयं तदसावादित्यः[10] । इति [हि[9]] ब्राह्मणम्[11] । तदग्नीकृत्य स्तौति ।

अथैनमेतयादित्यीकृत्य स्तौति ॥ २८ ॥

यदेदेनमदधुर्यज्ञियासो दिवि देवाः सूर्यमादितेयम् ।
यदा चरिष्णू[12] मिथुनावभूतामादित्प्रापश्यन्भुवनानि विश्वा[13] ॥

यदैनमदधुर्यज्ञियाः सर्वे दिवि देवाः सूर्यम् [आदितेयम्[14]] अदितेः पुत्रम् । यदा चरिष्णू मिथुनौ प्रादुरभूतां सर्वदा सहचारिणौ । उषाश्चादित्यश्च । मिथुनौ कस्मात् । मिनोतिः श्रयतिकर्मा । थु इति नामकरणः । थकारो वा । नयतिः परः । वनिर्वा । समाश्रितावन्योन्यं नयतः । वनुतो वा । मनुष्यमिथुनावप्येतस्मादेव । मेथन्तावन्योन्यं वनुत इति वा[15] ।

अथैनमेतयाग्नीकृत्य स्तौति ॥ २९ ॥

यत्रा वदेते अवरः परश्च यज्ञन्योः कतरो नौ वि वेद ।
आ शेकुरित्सधमादं सखायो नक्षन्त यज्ञं क इदं वि वोचत्[16] ॥

---

१. मूर्धा M 4.

२. Quoted by SRV. I. 59. 2. p. i. 291.

३. ०संचरते C 4, C 5, C 7, M 3, Mi, R 7, R 8, W 1, W 2, W 3.

४. Quoted by SRV. X. 88. 6. p. IV. 279.

५. RV. X. 88. 10.

६. यं हि C 1, C 2, C 3, C 6, M 1, M 4, R 2, R 3, R 5, S.

७. देवासो C 1, C 2, C 6, M 1, M 4, S. Cf. SRV. X. 88. 10. p. IV. 280.

८. ०अजनयत् Mi.

९. Omitted by BK, C 4, C 5, C 7, Kn, M 3, Mi, R 7, R 8, W 1, W 2, W 3.

१०. The quotation is untraced.

११. Cf. SRV. loc. cit.

१२. चरिष्णु M 3.

१३. RV. X. 88. 11.

१४. Omitted by BK, C 4, C 5, C 7, Kn, M 3, Mi, R 7, R 8, W 1, W 2, W 3.

१५. Quoted by SRV. X. 88. II. p. IV. 281.

१६. RV. X. 88. 17.

यत्र विवदेते दैव्यौ होतारौ। अयं चाग्निरसौ च मध्यमः। कतरो नौ यज्ञे भूयो वेद। इत्याशक्नुवन्ति। तत्सहमर्दनं[1] समानाख्याना ऋत्विजस्तेषां यज्ञं समश्नु[2]-वानानां को न इदं विवक्ष्यतीति[3]।

तस्योत्तरा भूयसे निर्वचनाय॥ ३०॥

> यावन्मात्रमुषसो न प्रतीकं सुपर्ण्यो वसते मातरिश्वः।
> तावद्दधात्युप यज्ञमायन्ब्राह्मणो होतुरवरो नि षीदन्[4]॥

यावन्मात्रमुषसः प्रत्यक्तं भवति प्रतिदर्शनमिति वा। अस्त्युपमानस्य संप्रत्यर्थे प्रयोगः[5]। इहेव निधेहीति यथा। सुपर्ण्यः सुपतनाः। एता रात्रयो वसते मातरिश्वञ्ज्योतिर्वर्णस्य। तावदुपदधाति यज्ञमागच्छन् ब्राह्मणो होतास्याग्नेर्होतुरवरो निषीदन्।

होतृजपस्त्वनग्नि[6]र्वैश्वानरीयो भवति[7]। देव सवितरेतं त्वा वृणतेऽग्निं होत्राय सह पित्रा वैश्वानरेण[8]। इति। इममेवाग्निं सवितारमाह। सर्वस्य प्रसवितारम्। मध्यमं वा। उत्तमं वा पितरम्।

यस्तु[9] सूक्तं भजते यस्मै[10] हविर्निरुप्यतेऽयमेव सोऽग्निर्वैश्वानरः। निपातमेवैते उत्तरे ज्योतिषी एतेन नामधेयेन भजेते भजेते[11]॥ ३१॥

इति सप्तमोऽध्यायः।

---

१. ०मदवनं M 3.

२. समाश्नु० C 4, C 5, C 7, M 3, Mi, W 1, W 2, W 3.

३. Quoted by SRV. X. 88. 17. p. IV. 282.

४. RV. X. 88. 19.

५. Cf. SRV. I. 57. 3; 88. 6; VI. 4. 3; pp. i. 285, 394; ii. 697.

६. ०स्त्वमग्नि० C 4, C 5, M 3, Mi, W 1.

७. The whole passage: यावन्मात्रमुषसः ......भवति is quoted by SRV. X. 88. 19. p. IV. 283.

८. This is the quotation of recitation AS'. 1. 3. 23; S'S'. 1. 6. 2.

९. यस्तु M 3.

१०. Cf. BD. i. 67.

११. MSS. of both the recensions repeat भजेते but not Roth.

[अथा[1]तो दैवतमि[2]न्द्रो दिवः [3]परोक्षकृतास्त[4]द्ये तिस्र एव देवता [6]अथाकारचिन्तन-मंपुरुषविधास्तिस्र एव देवता इत्युक्तं पूर्षात्वेतोऽथैतानीन्द्रभक्तीन्यथैतान्यादित्य-भक्तीनि [12]मंन्त्रा मननाज्ज[13]गती गततमम[14]थातोऽनुक्रमिष्यामोऽग्नि[15]मीलेऽ[16]ग्निः पूर्वेभि-र[17]भिप्रवन्ते[18]न्द्रं मित्रं [19]जातवेदाः कस्मात्[20]प्रनूनं वै जातवेदसं वै[21]श्वानरः कस्माद्वै[22]श्वानरस्य प्रनू महित्वं [24]कृष्णं नियानं हवि[25]ष्पान्तमपामु[26]पस्थे [27]मूर्धा भुवः स्तो[28]मेन यदे[29]देन यत्रा[30]वदेते यावन्[31]मात्रमेकत्रिंशत्।]

॥ इत्युत्तरषट्के प्रथमोऽध्यायः ॥

॥ इति निरुक्ते सप्तमोऽध्यायः ॥

Small figure on this page represents the corresponding section of the seventh chapter of the *Nirukta*.

अथाष्टमोऽध्यायः।

द्रविणोदाः कस्मात्। धनं द्रविणमुच्यते। यदेनमभिद्रवन्ति[1]। बलं वा द्रविणम्। यदेनेनाभिद्रवन्ति। तस्य दाता द्रविणोदाः[2]।

तस्यैषा भवति[3]॥ १॥

द्रविणोदा द्रविणसो ग्रावहस्तासो अध्वरे।
यज्ञेषु देवमीळते[4]॥

द्रविणोदा यस्त्वम्[5]। द्रविणस इति द्रविणसादिन इति वा। द्रविणसानिन इति वा। द्रविणसस्तस्मात्पिबत्विति[6] वा। यज्ञेषु देवमीळते। याचन्ति स्तुवन्ति वर्धयन्ति पूजयन्तीति[7] वा।

तत्को द्रविणोदाः। इन्द्र इति क्रौष्टुकिः। स बलधनयोर्दातृतमः[8]। तस्य च सर्वा बलकृतिः।

ओजसो जातमुत मन्य एनम्[9]। इति चाह।

अथाप्यग्निं द्राविणोदसमाह। एष पुनरेतस्माज्जायते।

यो अश्मनोरन्तरग्निं जजान[10]। इत्यपि निगमो भवति।

अथाप्यृतुयाजेषु द्राविणोदसाः प्रवादा भवन्ति[11]। तेषां पुनः पात्रस्येन्द्रपानमिति भवति।

अथाप्येनं सोमपानेन स्तौति। अथाप्याह।

द्रविणोदाः पिबतु द्राविणोदसः[12]। इति।

---

१. यदेनद्भि° C 1, C 2, C 3, M 1, M 4, W 2, W 3; द्व is crossed and म added on the margin in C 5; द added on the margin is corrected to म in W 1.

२. Cf. BD. ii. 25. Cf. S'B. VI. 3. 3. 13. द्रविणोदा इति द्रविणᳪ ह्येभ्यो ददाति।

३. Quoted by SRV. I. 15. 7. p. i. 94.

४. RV. I. 15. 7.

५. यस्तम् C 1, C 6.

६. पिबतीति C 6.

७. पूजयतीति C 7.

८. Cf. BD. iii. 61.

९. RV. X. 73. 10.

१०. RV. II. 12. 3; AV. 20. 34. 3.

११. Quoted by SRV. I. 15. 7. p. i. 95.

१२. RV. II. 37. 4.

अयमेवाग्निर्द्रविणोदा[1] इति शाकपूणिः । आग्नेयेष्वेव हि सूक्तेषु द्राविणोदसाः प्रवादा भवन्ति[2] ।

देवा अग्निं धारयन्द्रविणोदाम्[3] । इत्यपि निगमो भवति ।

यथो एतत्स बलधनयोर्दातृतम इति सर्वासु देवतास्वैश्वर्यं विद्यते ।

यथो एतदोजसो जातमुत मन्य एनमिति चाहेति । अयमप्यग्निरोजसा बलेन मथ्यमानो जायते । तस्मादेनमाह सहसस्पुत्रं सहसः सूनुं सहसो यहुम्[5] ।

यथो एतदग्निं द्राविणोदसमाहेति । ऋत्विजोऽत्र द्रविणोदस उच्यन्ते । हविषो दातारस्ते चैनं जनयन्ति[6] ।

ऋषीणां पुत्रो अधिराज एषः[7] । इत्यपि निगमो भवति ।

यथो एतत्तेषां पुनः पात्रस्येन्द्रपानमिति भवतीति भक्तिमात्रं तद्भवति[8] । यथा वायव्यानीति सर्वेषां सोमपात्राणाम् ।

यथो एतत्सोमपानेनैनं स्तौतीत्यस्मिन्नप्येतदुपपद्यते ।

सोमं पिब मन्दसानो गणश्रिभिः[9] । इत्यपि निगमो भवति ।

यथो एतद् द्रविणोदाः पिबतु द्राविणोदस इत्यस्यैव[10] तद्भवति ॥ २ ॥

मेद्यन्तु ते वह्नयो येभिरीयसेऽरिषण्यन्वीळयस्वा वनस्पते ।
आयूया धृष्णो अभिगूर्या त्वं नेष्ट्रात्सोमं द्रविणोदः पिब ऋतुभिः ॥

मेद्यन्तु ते । वह्नयो वोळ्हारः[11] । यैर्यासि । अरिष्यन् । दृढीभव । आयूय धृष्णो अभिगूर्य त्वं नेष्ट्रीयात् । धिष्ण्यात्[12] । धिष्णो धिष्ण्यो धिषणाभवः । धिषणा [वाक्[13]] धिषेर्दधात्यर्थे । धीसादिनीति वा धीसानिनीति वा । वनस्पत इत्येनमाह । एष हि वनानां पाता वा पालयिता वा[14] । वनं वनोतेः । पिब । ऋतुभिः[15] कालैः ॥ ३ ॥

---

१. द्रविद्रोदा M 3.

२. Cf. BD. iii. 65.

३. RV. I. 96. 1-7.

४. Cf. BD. iii. 62.

५. Cf. BD. iii. 64.

६. Quoted by SRV. II. 37. 4. p. ii. 113.

७. AV. 4. 39. 9; VS. 5. 4.

८. Cf. BD. iii. 63-64.

९. RV. V. 60. 8.

१०. RV. II. 37. 3.

११. वोढारः C 1, C 3, M 4, S.

१२. धिष्ण्यो धिषण्यो Roth.

१३. Omitted by BK, C 4, C 5, C 7, Kn, M 3, Mi, R 7, R 8, W 1, W 2, W 3.

१४. Cf. BD. iii. 26.

१५. पिपर्तुभिः C 2, M 1, M 3, M 4, W 2.

अथात आप्रियः । आप्रियः कस्मात् । आप्नोतेः[1] । प्रीणातेर्वा ।

आप्रीभिराप्रीणाति[2] । इति च ब्राह्मणम् ।

तासामिध्मः प्रथमागामी भवति । इध्मः समिन्धनात्[3] ।

तस्यैषा भवति ॥ ४ ॥

समिद्धो अद्य मनुषो दुरोणे देवो देवान्यजसि जातवेदः ।
आ च वह मित्रमहश्चिकित्वान्त्वं दूतः कविरसि प्रचेताः[4] ॥

समिद्धोऽद्य मनुष्यस्य मनुष्यस्य गृहे देवो देवान्यजसि जातवेदः । आ च वह मित्रमहः । चिकित्वांश्चेतनावान् । त्वं दूतः कविरसि । [प्रचेताः] प्रवृद्धचेताः । यज्ञेध्म इति कात्थक्यः । अग्निरिति शाकपूणिः ।

तनूनपात् [आज्यमिति कात्थक्यः ।][5] नपादित्यननन्तरायाः प्रजाया नामधेयम् । निर्णततमा भवति । गौरत्र तनूरुच्यते । तता अस्यां भोगाः । तस्याः पयो जायते । पयस आज्यं जायते । अग्निरिति शाकपूणिः । आपोऽत्र तन्व उच्यन्ते । तता अन्तरिक्षे । ताभ्य ओषधिवनस्पतयो जायन्ते । ओषधिवनस्पतिभ्य एष जायते । तस्यैषा भवति ॥ ५ ॥

तनूनपात्पथ ऋतस्य यानान्मध्वा समञ्जन्त्स्वदया सुजिह्व ।
मन्मानि धीभिरुत यज्ञमृन्धन्देवत्रा च कृणुह्यध्वरं नः[10] ॥

तनूनपात्पथ ऋतस्य यानान्यज्ञस्य यानान् । मधुना समञ्जन्त्स्वदय कल्याणजिह्व । मननानि च नो धीभिर्यज्ञं च समर्धय । देवान्नो यज्ञं गमय ।

नराशंसो यज्ञ इति कात्थक्यः[11] । नरा अस्मिन्नासीनाः शंसन्ति । अग्निरिति शाकपूणिः । नरैः प्रशस्यो भवति[12] । तस्यैषा भवति ॥ ६ ॥

नराशंसस्य महिमानमेषामुप स्तोषाम यजतस्य यज्ञैः ।
ये सुक्रतवः शुचयो धियंधाः स्वदन्ति देवा उभयानि हव्या[13] ॥

---

१. Cf. Taitt. B. II. 2. 8. 6:
आप्रीभिराप्नुवन् ।

२. KB. X. 3; AB. ii. 4. 1.

३. Cf. BD. ii. 158.

४. RV. X. 110. 1; AV. 5. 12. 1; VS. 29. 25.

५. Omitted by BK, C 4, C 5, C 7, Kn, M 3, Mi, R 7, R 8, W 1, W 2, W 3.

६. कार्थक्यः C 7, M 3.

७. Cf. BD. ii. 27.

८. तनुरूच्यते C 7.

९. ०मृधन्देवत्रा C 5, M 3, Mi, W 1, W 2.

१०. RV. X. 110. 2; AV. 5. 12. 2; VS. 29. 26.

११. कात्थंक्यः C 7, M 3.
Cf. AB. II. 24:
एष वै यज्ञो नराशंसपङ्क्तिः ।

१२. Cf. BD. ii. 28; iii. 2-3.

१३. RV. VIII. 2. 2; VS. 29. 27.

नराशंसस्य महिमानमेषामुपस्तुमो यज्ञियस्य यज्ञैः । ये सुकर्माणः शुचयो धियं धारयितारः स्वदयन्तु देवा उभयानि हवींषि । सोमं चेतराणि चेति वा । तान्त्राणि चावापिकानि चेति वा ।

ईळ ईट्टेः स्तुतिकर्मणः । इ[2]न्धतेर्वा । तस्यैषा भवति ॥ ७ ॥

आ॒जुह्वा॑न॒ ईळ्यो॒ वन्द्य॒श्चा या॑ह्यग्ने॒ वसु॑भिः स॒जोषा॑ः ।
त्वं दे॒वाना॑मसि यह्व होता॒ स ए॑नान्यक्षीषि॒तो यजी॑यान्[3] ॥

आहूयमान ईळितव्यो वन्दितव्यश्च । आयाह्यग्ने वसुभिः सहजोषणः । त्वं देवानामसि यह्व होता । यह्व इति महतो नामधेयम् । या[4]तश्च हूतश्च भवति । स एनान्यक्षीषितो यजीयान् । इषितः प्रेषित इति वाधीष्ट इति वा । यजीयान्यष्टृतरः ।

बर्हिः परिबर्हणात्[5] । तस्यैषा भवति ॥ ८ ॥

प्रा॒चीनं॑ ब॒र्हिः प्र॒दिशा॑ पृथि॒व्या वस्तो॑र॒स्या वृ॑ज्यते॒ अग्रे॒ अह्ना॑म् ।
व्यु॑ प्रथते वि॒तरं॒ वरी॑यो दे॒वेभ्यो॒ अदि॑तये स्यो॒नम्[6] ॥

प्राचीनं बर्हिः प्रदिशा पृथिव्या वसनाय । अस्याः प्रवृज्यतेऽग्रेऽह्नां[7] बर्हिः पूर्वाह्णे । तद्विप्रथते [वितरं][8] विकीर्णतरमिति वा विस्तीर्णतरमिति वा । वरीयो वरतरम् । उरुतरं वा । देवेभ्यश्चादितये च स्योनम् । स्योनमिति सुखनाम स्यतेः । अवस्यन्त्येतत् । सेवितव्यं भवतीति वा ।

द्वारो जवतेर्वा । द्रवतेर्वा । वार[9]यतेर्वा । तासामेषा भवति ॥ ९ ॥

व्यच॑स्वतीरुर्वि॒या वि श्र॑यन्तां॒ पति॑भ्यो॒ न जन॑यः॒ शुम्भ॑मानाः ।
देवी॑र्द्वारो बृ[10]हतीर्विश्वमिन्वा[11] दे॒वेभ्यो॑ भवत सुप्राय॒णाः[12] ॥

व्यञ्चनवत्य उरुत्वेन विश्रयन्ताम् । पतिभ्य इव जायाः । ऊरू मैथुने धर्मे शुशोभिषमाणाः । वरत[13]ममङ्गमूरू । देव्यो द्वारः । बृहत्यो महत्यः । विश्वमिन्वा विश्वमाभिरेति यज्ञे । गृहद्वार इति कात्थ[14]क्यः । अग्निरिति शाक[15]पूणिः ।

---

१. Quoted by SRV. VII. 2. 1. p. iii. 8.
२. Cf. BD. iii. 4.
३. RV. X. 110. 3; AV. 5. 12. 3; VS. 29. 28.
४. जातश्च C 7, M 3, W 2; a ज is added just above य in Mi.
५. Cf. BD. iii. 5.
६. RV. X. 110. 4; AV. 5. 12. 4; VS. 29. 29.
७. प्रवृज्यते अग्ने अह्नां W 3.
८. Omitted by BK, C 4, C 5, C 7, Kn, M 3, Mi, R 7, R 8, W 1, W 2, W 3.
९. Quoted by SRV. VII. 17. 2. p. iii. 35.
१०. वृहस्पती M 3.
११. ०र्विश्श्वमिन्वा W 3.
१२. RV. X. 110. 5; AV. 5. 12. 5; VS. 29. 30.
१३. वरतरम० C 4, C 5, C 7, M 3, Mi, W 1, W 2, W 3.
१४. कात्थेक्यः C 7, M 3.
१५. Cf. BD. iii. 6.

उषासानक्ता । उषाश्च नक्ता च । उषा व्याख्याता । नक्तेति रात्रिनाम । अनक्ति भूतान्यवश्यायेन । अपि वा नक्ताव्यक्तवर्णा[3] । तयोरेषा भवति ॥ १० ॥

आ सुष्वयन्ती यजते उपाके उषासानक्ता सदतां नि योनौ ।
दिव्ये योषणे बृहती सुरुक्मे अधि श्रियं शुक्रपिशं दधाने[4] ॥

सेष्मीयमाणे इति वा । सुष्वापयन्त्याविति वा । सीदतामिति वा । न्यासीदतामिति वा । यज्ञिये उपक्रान्ते दिव्ये योषणे । बृहत्यौ महत्यौ । सुरुक्मे सुरोचने । अधिदधाने शुक्रपेशसं श्रियम् । शुक्रं शोचतेर्ज्वलतिकर्मणः । पेश इति रूपनाम । पिंशतेः । विपिशितं भवति ।

दैव्या होतारा दैव्यौ होतारौ । अयं चाग्निरसौ च मध्यमः । तयोरेषा भवति ॥ ११ ॥

दैव्या होतारा प्रथमा सुवाचा मिमाना यज्ञं मनुषो यजध्यै ।
प्रचोदयन्ता विदथेषु कारू प्राचीनं ज्योतिः प्रदिशा दिशन्ता[7] ॥

दैव्यौ होतारौ प्रथमौ सुवाचौ निर्मिमानौ यज्ञं मनुष्यस्य [मनुष्यस्य[8]] यजनाय । प्रचोदयमानौ यज्ञेषु कर्तारौ पूर्वस्यां दिशि यष्टव्यमिति प्रदिशन्तौ ।

तिस्रो देवीस्तिस्रो देव्यः । तासामेषा भवति ॥ १२ ॥

आ नो यज्ञं भारती तूयमेत्विळा मनुष्वदिह चेतयन्ती ।
तिस्रो देवीर्बर्हिरेदं स्योनं सरस्वती स्वपसः सदन्तु[9] ॥

एतु नो यज्ञं भारती क्षिप्रम् । भरत आदित्यस्तस्य भाः । इळा च मनुष्यवदिह चेतयमाना । तिस्रो देव्यो बर्हिरिदं सुखं सरस्वती च सुकर्माण आसीदन्तु ।

त्वष्टा तूर्णमश्नुत इति नैरुक्ताः । त्विषेर्वा स्यात् । दीप्तिकर्मणः[11] । त्वक्षतेर्वा[12] स्यात् । करोतिकर्मणः[13] । तस्यैषा भवति ॥ १३ ॥

---

१. Cf. S'B. VI. 7. 2. 3.
अहोरात्रे वै नक्तोषासा ।

२. N. 2. 18.

३. Cf. BD. iii. 9.

४. RV. X. 110. 6; AV. 5. 12. 6; 27. 8; VS. 29. 31.

५. Quoted by SRV. I. 49. 2. p. i. 217.

६. Cf. BD. iii. 11.

७. RV. X. 110. 7; AV. 5. 12. 7; VS. 29. 32.

८. Omitted by BK, C 4, C 5, C 7, Kn, M 3, Mi, R 7, R 8, W 1, W 2, W 3.

९. RV. X. 110. 8; AV. 5. 12. 8; VS. 29. 33.

१०. Quoted by SRV I. 22. 10. p. i. 117.

११. वृद्धिकर्मणः Cf. SRV. I. 142. 11. p. i. 637.

१२. तक्षते C 4, C 5, C 7, M 3, Mi, W 1, W 2, W 3.

१३. Quoted by SRV. loc. cit.; cf. BD. iii. 16.

य इमे द्यावापृथिवी जनित्री रूपैरपिंशद्भुवनानि विश्वा ।
तमद्य होतरिषितो यजीयान्देवं त्वष्टारमिह यक्षि विद्वान् ॥[1]

य इमे द्यावापृथिव्यौ जनयित्र्यौ रूपैरकरोद् भूतानि च सर्वाणि । तमद्य होतरिषितो यजीयान् देवं त्वष्टारमिह यज विद्वान् ।

माध्यमिकस्त्वष्टेत्याहुः । मध्यमे च स्थाने समाम्नातः । अग्निरिति शाकपूणिः । तस्यैषापरा भवति ॥ १७ ॥

आविष्ट्यो वर्धते चारुरासु जिह्मानामूर्ध्वः स्वयशा उपस्थे ।
उभे त्वष्टुर्बिभ्यतुर्जायमानात्प्रतीची सिंहं प्रति जोषयेते[3] ॥

आविरावेदनात् । तस्यो वर्धते चारुरासु । चारु चरतेः । जिह्मं जिहीतेः । ऊर्ध्वमुच्छ्रितं भवति[4] । स्वयशा आत्मयशाः । उपस्थ उपस्थाने । उभे त्वष्टुर्बिभ्यतुर्जायमानात् । [प्रतीची सिंहं प्रति जोषयेते ।][6] द्यावापृथिव्याविति वा । अहोरात्रे इति वा । अरणी इति वा । प्रत्यक्ते सिंहं सहनं प्रत्यासेवेते ॥ १५ ॥

वनस्पतिर्व्याख्यातः । तस्यैषा भवति ॥ १६ ॥

उपावसृज त्मन्या समञ्जन्देवानां पाथ ऋतुथा हवींषि ।
वनस्पतिः शमिता देवो अग्निः स्वदन्तु हव्यं मधुना घृतेन ॥

उपावसृजात्मनात्मानं समञ्जन्देवानामन्नमृतावृतौ हवींषि काले काले । वनस्पतिः शमिता देवो अग्निरित्येते त्रयः स्वदयन्तु हव्यं मधुना च घृतेन च ।

तत्को वनस्पतिः । यूप इति कात्थक्यः । अग्निरिति शाकपूणिः । तस्यैषापरा भवति ॥ १७ ॥

---

१. RV. X. 110. 9; AV. 5. 12. 9; VS. 29. 34.

२. Cf. BD. iii. 15, 25.

३. RV. I. 95. 5.

४. ऊर्ध्वं उच्छ्रितो भवति C 1, C 2, C 6, M 1, M 4, S & Roth; cf. SRV. I. 95. 5. p. i. 429.

५. जिह्मं...भवति is omitted by Durga.

६. Omitted by BK, C 4, C 5, C 7, Kn, M 3, Mi, R 7, R 8, W 1, W 2, W 3.

७. इति वापि चैते प्रत्यक्ते SRV. I. 95. 5. p. i. 429.

८. SRV. loc. cit.

९. N. 8. 3.

१०. RV. X. 110. 10; AV. 5. 12. 10; VS. 29. 35.

त्मन्या C 4, C 5, C 7, M 3, Mi, W 1, W 2, W 3.

११. कात्थक्यः C 7, M 3.

१२. Cf. BD. iii. 28. According to BD. IV. 100. the stanza अञ्जन्ति त्वाम् RV. III. 8. 1. is addressed to यूप, the sacrificial post.

अञ्जन्ति त्वामध्वरे देवयन्तो वनस्पते मधुना दैव्येन ।
यदूर्ध्वस्तिष्ठा द्रविणेह धत्ताद्यद्वा क्षयो मातुरस्या उपस्थे ॥

अञ्जन्ति त्वामध्वरे देवान्कामयमाना वनस्पते मधुना दैव्येन च घृतेन च । यदूर्ध्वः स्थास्यसि । द्रविणानि च नो दास्यसि । यद्वा ते कृतः क्षयो मातुरस्या उपस्थ उपस्थाने ।

अग्निरिति शाकपूणिः । तस्यैषापरा भवति ॥ १८ ॥

देवेभ्यो वनस्पते हवींषि हिरण्यपर्ण प्रदिवस्ते अर्थम् ।
प्रदक्षिणिद्रशनया नियूय ऋतस्य वक्षि पथिभी रजिष्ठैः ॥

देवेभ्यो वनस्पते हवींषि हिरण्यपर्ण ऋतपर्ण । अपि वोपमार्थे स्यात् । हिरण्यवर्णपर्णेति । प्रदिवस्ते अर्थं पुराणस्ते सोऽर्थो यं ते प्रब्रूमः । यज्ञस्य वह पथिभी रजिष्ठैर्ऋजुतमैः । रजस्वलतमैः । तपिष्ठतमैरिति वा । तस्यैषापरा भवति ॥ १९ ॥

वनस्पते रशनया नियूय पिष्टतमया वयुनानि विद्वान् ।
वह देवत्रा दिधिषो हवींषि प्र च दातारममृतेषु वोचः ॥

वनस्पते रशनया नियूय सुरूपतमया । वयुनानि विद्वान् प्रज्ञानानि प्रजानन् । वह देवान् [यज्ञे] दातुर्हवींषि । प्रब्रूहि च दातारममृतेषु देवेषु ।

स्वाहाकृतयः । स्वाहेत्येतत्सु आहेति वा । स्वा वागाहेति वा । स्वं प्राहेति वा । स्वाहुतं हविर्जुहोतीति वा । तासामेषा भवति ॥ २० ॥

सद्यो जातो व्यमिमीत यज्ञमग्निर्देवानामभवत्पुरोगाः ।
अस्य होतुः प्रदिश्यृतस्य वाचि स्वाहाकृतं हविरदन्तु देवाः ॥

---

१. RV. III. 8. 1.

२. धास्यसि C 4, C 5, C 7, M 3, Mi, W 1, W 2, W 3.

३. Quoted by SRV. III. 8. 1. p. ii. 155.

४. KS. XVIII. 21; MS. 4. 13. 7: 208. 10.

५. वहा M 3.

६. KS. XVIII. 21; MS. 4. 13. 7: 209. 1; cf. RV. X. 70. 10. (...नियूया)

७. Omitted by BK, C 4, C 5, Kn, M 3, Mi, R 7, R 8, W 1, W 2, W 3; it is added on the margin by a different probably later scribe in C 7.

८. According to Durga स्वा वागाह is a quotation from some Brāhmaṇa. He remarks: अथवेदमन्यद् ब्राह्मणानुगतं निर्वचनम् ।, adding the quotation: विज्ञायते हि । तं स्वा वागभ्यवदत् । जुहुधीति । तत् स्वाहाकारस्य जन्म । Cf. KS. VI. 1. MS. I. 8. 1.

९. Cf. BD. iii 29.

१०. RV. X. 110. 11; AV. 5. 12. 11; VS. 29. 36.

सद्यो जायमानो निरमिमीत यज्ञम् । अग्निर्देवानामभवत्पुरोगामी । अस्य होतुः प्रदिश्यृतस्य वाच्यास्ये स्वाहाकृतं हविरदन्तु देवाः [इति यजन्ति][1] ।

इतीमा आप्रीदेवता अनुक्रान्ताः ।

अथ किंदेवताः प्रयाजानुयाजाः । आग्नेया इत्येके ॥ २१ ॥

प्रयाजान्मे अनुयाजाँश्च केवलानूर्जस्वन्तं हविषो दत्त भागम् ।
घृतं चापां पुरुषं चौषधीनामग्नेश्च दीर्घमायुरस्तु देवाः[3] ॥

तव प्रयाजा अनुयाजाश्च केवल ऊर्जस्वन्तो हविषः सन्तु भागाः ।
तवाग्ने यज्ञो३ऽयमस्तु सर्वस्तुभ्यं नमन्तां प्रदिशश्चतस्रः[4] ॥

आग्नेया वै प्रयाजा आग्नेया अनुयाजाः । इति च ब्राह्मणम्[6] ।

छन्दोदेवता[7] इत्यपरम् ।

छन्दांसि वै प्रयाजाश्छन्दांस्यनुयाजाः[8] । इति च ब्राह्मणम् ।

ऋतुदेवता इत्यपरम् ।

ऋतवो वै प्रयाजा ऋतवोऽनुयाजाः[10] । इति च ब्राह्मणम् ।

[पशुदेवता इत्यपरम् ।

पशवो[9] वै प्रयाजाः पशवोऽनुयाजाः[11] । इति च ब्राह्मणम् ।][12]

प्राणदेवता इत्यपरम् ।

प्राणा वै प्रयाजाः प्राणा[13] वा अनुयाजाः[14] । इति च ब्राह्मणम् ।

आत्मदेवता इत्यपरम् ।

---

१. Omitted by BK, C 4, C 5, Kn, M 3, Mi, R 7, R 8, W 1, W 2, W 3; is added on the margin in C 7.

२. Cf. SRV. I. 188. 1. p. i. 782.

३. RV. X. 51. 8.

४. RV. X. 51. 9.

५. The quotation is untraced.

६. आग्नेया...ब्राह्मणम् is omitted by Durga.

७. Durga does not comment on the following passages remarking: अथ नानादेवताः प्रवादा इत्युक्तम्...छन्दोदेवता इत्येवमादि ।

८. Cf. S'B. i. 3. 2. 9: छन्दांसि ह्यनुयाजाः ।

९. पशवो C 4, C 5, C 7, M 3, Mi, W 1, W 2, W 3.

१०. Cf. KB. III. 4. S'B. i. 3. 2. 8; MS. i. 4. 12: ऋतवो वै प्रयाजाः ।

११. Cf. KB. III. 4.

१२. Omitted by BK, C 4, C 5, C 7, Kn, M 3, Mi, R 7, R 8, W 1, W 2, W 3.

१३. अपाना अनुयाजाः C 4, C 5, C 7, M 3, Mi, W 1, W 2, W 3.

१४. Cf. AB. i. 11. 3; 17. 14; KB. VII. 1; X. 3; S'B. XI. 2. 7. 27. Cf. KS. XXVI. 9: प्राणा वै प्रयाजाः । Schroeder's ed. vol ii. p. 133.

आत्मा वै प्रयाजा आत्मा[१] वा अनुयाजाः[२] । इति च ब्राह्मणम् ।

आग्नेया इति तु स्थितिः । भक्तिमात्रमितरत्[३] । किमर्थं पुनरिदमुच्यते ।
यस्यै देवतायै हविर्गृहीतं स्यात् तां मनसा ध्यायेद्वषट्करिष्यन्[४] । **इति ह विज्ञायते ।**

इतीमान्येकादशाप्रीसूक्तानि । तेषां वासिष्ठमात्रेयं वाध्र्यश्वं गार्त्समदमिति नाराशंसवन्ति । मैधातिथं दैर्घतमसं प्रैषिकमित्युभयवन्ति । अतोऽन्यानि तनूनपात्वन्ति तनूनपात्वन्ति[५] ॥ २२ ॥

इत्यष्टमोऽध्यायः ।

[द्रविणोदाः[१] कस्माद् द्रविणोदा[२] द्रविणसो मेद्यन्तु[३] तेऽथातः[४] आप्रियः समिद्धो[५] अद्य[६] तनूनपा[७]न्नराशंस[८]स्याजुह्वानः प्राचीनं[९] बर्हिर्व्यच[१०]स्वतीरासुष्वयन्ती[११] दैव्या[१२] होतारा नो यक्षं[१३] य इमे[१४] आविष्ट्यो[१५] वनस्पति[१६]रूपां[१७]वसृजाअन्ति[१८] त्वा देवेभ्यो[१९] वनस्पते[२०] रशनया नियूय सद्योजातः[२१] प्रयाजान्मे[२२] द्वाविंशतिः ॥][६]

॥ इत्युत्तरषट्के द्वितीयोऽध्यायः ॥

॥ इति निरुक्तेऽष्टमोऽध्यायः समाप्तः ॥

---

१. प्रजा अनुयाजाः C 4, C 5, C 7, M 3, Mi, W 1, W 2, W 3.

२. Cf. TS. VI. 1. 5. 4; cf. KS. XXIII. 9. आत्मा वै प्रयाजाः प्रजानुयाजाः । Schroeder's ed. vol. ii. p. 85.

३. Cf. BD. iii. 29.

४. Cf. AB. iii. 8. 1: यस्मै तां ध्यायेद्वषट्करिष्यन् । GB. II. 3. 4: यस्मै...तां मनसा ध्यायन् वषट्कुर्यात् ।

५. Cf. BD. ii. 154—157.

६. Small figure within brackets represents the corresponding section of the eighth chapter of the *Nirukta*.

अथ नवमोऽध्यायः ।

अथ यानि पृथिव्यायतनानि सत्त्वानि स्तुतिं लभन्ते तान्यतोऽनुक्रमिष्यामः । तेषामश्वः प्रथमागामी भवति । अश्वो व्याख्यातः । तस्यैषा भवति ॥ १ ॥

अश्वो॒ वोळ्हा॑ सु॒खं रथं॑ हस॒नामु॑पम॒न्त्रिणः॑ ।

शेपो॒ रोम॑ण्वन्तौ॑ भे॒दौ॑ वारिन्म॒ण्डूक॑ इच्छ॒तीन्द्रा॑येन्दो॒ परि॑ स्रव ॥

अश्वो वोळ्हा । सुखं वोळ्हा [रथं वोळ्हा][3] । सुखमिति कल्याणनाम । कल्याणं पुण्यं सुहितं भवति । [सुहितं गम्यतीति वा । हसेता वा पाता वा पालयिता वा । शेपमृच्छतीति । वारि वारयति ।][3]

मा नो व्याख्यातः । तस्यैषा भवति ॥ २ ॥

मा नो॑ मि॒त्रो वरु॑णो अर्य॒मायुरिन्द्र॑ ऋभु॒क्षा म॒रुतः॒ परि॑ ख्यन् ।

यद्वा॒जिनो॑ दे॒वजा॑तस्य॒ सप्तेः॑ प्रव॒क्ष्यामो॑ वि॒दथे॑ वी॒र्या॑णि ॥

यद्वाजिनो देवैर्जातस्य सप्तेः सरणस्य प्रवक्ष्यामो यज्ञे विदथे वीर्याणि । मा नस्त्वं मित्रश्च वरुणश्चार्यमा चायुश्च वायुरयन इन्द्रश्चोरुक्षयण ऋभूणां राजेति वा मरुतश्च परिख्यन् ।

शकुनिः शक्नोत्युन्नेतुमात्मानम् । शक्नोति नदितुमिति वा । शक्नोति तकितुमिति वा । सर्वतः शङ्करोऽस्त्विवति वा । शक्नोतेर्वा । तस्यैषा भवति ॥ ३ ॥

---

१. See N. 2. 27; cf. 1. 12.

२. RV. I. 162. 2.

३. Omitted by BK, C 4, C 5, C 7, Kn, M 3, Mi, R 7, R 8, W 1, W 2, W 3.

४. The passage: अथ यानि पृथिव्यायतनानि...कल्याणनाम seems to have been written by a different scribe in C[2]. f. 10[r]. The letters are larger, lines crooked, and stand in marked contrast to the rest of the page.

५. The second section is omitted by Durga and given in a foot-note by Roth. But it is found in the MSS. of both recensions and is also enumerated in the summary at the end of the chapter in the MSS. of longer recensions.

६. RV. I. 162. 1; VS. 25. 24.

७. देवजातस्य C 1.

८. विदथे is omitted by M 3; partially obliterated with yellow pigment in W 1; added on the margin in W 2, C 7.

कनिक्रदज्जनुषं प्रब्रुवाण इयर्ति वाचमरितेव नावम् ।
सुमङ्गलश्च शकुने भवासि मा त्वा काचिदभिभा विश्व्या विदत् ॥[1]

न्यक्रन्दीज्जन्म प्रब्रुवाणः[2] । यथास्य शब्दस्तथा नामेरयति वाचम् । ईरयितेव नावम् । सुमङ्गलश्च शकुने भव । कल्याणमङ्गलः । मङ्गलं गिरतेर्गृणात्यर्थे । गिरत्यनर्थानिति वा[3] । अङ्गलमङ्गवत् । मज्जयति पापकमिति[4] नैरुक्ताः । मां गच्छत्विति वा । मा च त्वा काचिदभिभूतिः सर्वतो विदत् ।

गृत्समदमर्थमभ्युत्थितं कपिञ्जलोऽभिववाशे[5] । तदभिवादिन्येषर्ग्भवति[6] ॥ ४ ॥

भद्रं वद दक्षिणतो भद्रमुत्तरतो वद ।
भद्रं पुरस्तान्नो वद भद्रं पश्चात्कपिञ्जल ॥[7]

इति सा निगदव्याख्याता ।

गृत्समदो गृत्समदनः[8] । गृत्स इति मेधाविनाम[9] । गृणातेः स्तुतिकर्मणः[10] ।

मण्डूका मज्जूका मज्जनात् । मदतेर्वा मोदतिकर्मणः । मन्दतेर्वा तृप्तिकर्मणः । मण्डयतेरिति वैयाकरणाः[11] । मण्ड एषामोक इति वा । मण्डो मदेर्वा मुदेर्वा[12] ।

तेषामेषा भवति[13] ॥ ५ ॥

संवत्सरं शशयाना[15] ब्राह्मणा व्रतचारिणः ।
वाचं पर्जन्यजिन्वितां प्र मण्डूका अवादिषुः ॥[14]

संवत्सरं शिश्याना ब्राह्मणा व्रतचारिणोऽब्रुवाणाः[16] । अपि वोपमार्थे स्यात् । ब्राह्मणा इव व्रतचारिण इति । वाचं पर्जन्यप्रीतां प्रावादिषुर्मण्डूकाः ।

---

१. RV. II. 42. 1; cf. BD. IV. 94.

२. प्रक्रवाणः M 3.

३. Quoted by SRV. II. 42. 1. p. ii. 125.

४. पावकम् M 3.

५. Cf. BD. IV. 93.

६. पर्गभवति Roth.

७. RVKH. 2. 43. 1.

८. गृत्सोमदनः C 4, C 5, C 7, Kn, M 3, Mi, R 7, R 8, W 1, W 2, W 3.

९. Quoted by SRV. VII. 4. 2. p. iii. 13.

१०. SRV. II. 20. 8. p. ii. 57; cf. BD. IV. 78.

११. Cf. Uṇādi sūtra IV. 42. शलिमण्डिभ्यामूकण् ।

१२. मण्डो मदेर्वा मुदेर्वा is omitted by Durga.

१३. Cf. SRV. VII. 103. 1. p. iii. 211.

१४. RV. VII. 103. 1; AV. 4. 15. 13; cf. BD. VI. 27.

१५. शयानाः C 4, M 3, Mi, W 1, W 2, W 3.

१६. ब्रुवाणाः C 5, W 1; ब्रुवाणादपि C 4, C 7, Mi, W 3, द is partially obliterated with red ink and an अ added on the margin in W 2; ब्रवणादपि M 3. Cf. Kumārila Bhaṭṭa, Tantra Vārtika, Benares ed. p. 200 or I. 3. 18: ...निरुक्ते... ब्राह्मणो...ब्रवणादिति प्रयुक्तम् ।

वसिष्ठो वर्षकामः पर्जन्यं तुष्टाव । तं मण्डूका अन्वमोदन्त । स मण्डूकाननुमोदमानान्दृष्ट्वा तु[१]ष्टाव । तदभिवादिन्येषर्ग्भवति ॥ ६ ॥

उप प्र[२] वद मण्डू[३]कि वर्षं मा वद तादुरि ।
मध्ये[४] ह्रदस्य प्लवस्व विगृह्य चतुरः पदः ॥

इति सा निगदव्याख्याता ।

अक्षा अश्नुवत एनानिति वा । अभ्यश्नुवत एभिरिति वा । तेषामेषा भवति ॥ ७ ॥

प्रावेपा मा बृहतो मादयन्ति प्रवातेजा इरिणे वर्वृताना: ।
सोमस्येव मौजवतस्य भक्षो विभीदको जागृविर्मह्यमच्छान्[५] ॥

प्रवेपिणो मा महतो विभीदकस्य फलानि मादयन्ति । प्रवातेजाः प्रवते[६]जाः । इरिणे वर्तमानाः । इरिणं निर्ऋणम्[७] । ऋणातेः[८] । अपार्णं भवति । अपरता अस्मादोषधय इति वा । [सोमस्येव मौजवतस्य भक्षः ।][९] मौजवतो मूजवति जातः । मूजवा[१०]न्पर्वतो मुञ्जवान् । मुञ्जो विमुच्यत इषीकया । इषीकेषतेर्गतिकर्मणः । इयमपीतरेषीकैतस्मादेव । विभीदको विभेदनात् । जागृविर्जागरणा[११]त् । मह्यमचच्छदत्[१२] । प्रशंसत्येनान्प्रथमया । निन्दत्युत्तराभिः । ऋषेरक्षपरिद्यूनस्यैतदार्षं वेदय[१३]न्ते ।

ग्रावाणो हन्तेर्वा । गृ[१४]णातेर्वा । गृह्णातेर्वा । तेषामेषा भवति ॥ ८ ॥

प्रैते वदन्तु प्र वयं वदाम ग्रावभ्यो वाचं वदता वदद्भ्यः ।
यदद्रयः पर्वताः साकमाशवः श्लोकं घोषं भरथेन्द्राय सोमिनः[१५] ॥

---

१. Quoted by SRV. VII. 103. 1. p. iii. 211.

२. प्लु C 4, C 5, C 7, M 1, M 4.

३. मण्डूका C 7.

४. AV. 4. 15. 14.

५. RV. X. 34. 1; cf. BD. VII. 36.

६. प्रवणेजा: C 1, C 2, C 6, M 1, M 4, S; & Roth; ते is partially obliterated with red ink and णे added on the margin in W 2; Durga gives both *i. e.* प्रवणेजा: as well as प्रवतेजा: I. Sāyaṇa reads प्रवणेजा: ।

७. निरिणम् C 4, C 5, C 7, M 3, Mi, W 2, W 3; W 1 agrees with the reading of the longer recension.

८. रिणाते: C 4, C 5, C 7, M 3, Mi, W 2, W 3; W 1 agrees with the reading of the longer recension.

९. Omitted by BK, C 4, C 5, C 7, Kn, M 3, Mi, R 7, R 8, W 1, W 2, W 3.

१०. मुजवान् M 3; Sāyaṇa also reads मुजवान्. See SRV. X. 34. 1. p. IV. 101.

११. Quoted by SRV. III. 24. 3. p. ii. 198.

१२. Cf. SRV. X. 34. 1. p. IV. 101.

१३. The passage: प्रशंसत्येनान्……… …वेदयन्ते is omitted by Durga.

१४. गृणातेर्वा is omitted by S'ivadatta although given by Durga.

१५. RV. X. 94. 1.

प्रवदन्त्वेते । प्रवदाम वयम् । ग्रावभ्यो वाचं वदत वदद्भ्यः । यदद्रयः पर्वता अदरणीयाः[1] सह सोममाशवः क्षिप्रकारिणः । श्लोकः[2] शृणोतेः । घोषो घुष्यतेः । सोमिनो यूयं स्थेति वा । सोमिनो गृहेष्विति वा ।

येन नराः प्रशस्यन्ते स नाराशंसो मन्त्रः ।

तस्यैषा भवति ॥ ९ ॥

[3]अमन्दान्स्तोमान्प्र भरे मनीषा सिन्धावधि क्षियतो भाव्यस्य ।
यो मे सहस्रममिमीत सवानतूर्तो राजा श्रव इच्छमानः ॥

अमन्दान्स्तोमानबालिशाननल्पान्वा । बालो बलवर्ती[4] भर्तव्यो भवति । अम्बास्मा अलं भवतीति वा । अम्बास्मै बलं भवतीति वा । बलो वा प्रतिषेधव्यवहितः[5] । प्रभरे मनीषया मनस[6] ईषया स्तुत्या प्रज्ञया वा । सिन्धावधि निवसतो भावयव्यस्य राज्ञः । यो मे सहस्रं निरमिमीत सवानतूर्तो राजातूर्ण इति वा । अत्वरमाण इति वा । प्रशंसामिच्छमानः ॥ १० ॥

यज्ञसंयोगाद्राजा स्तुतिं लभेत । राजसंयोगाद् युद्धोपकरणानि । तेषां रथः प्रथमागामी भवति । रथो रंहतेर्गतिकर्मणः । स्थिरतेर्वा स्याद्विपरीतस्य । रममाणोऽस्मिंस्तिष्ठतीति वा[7] । रपतेर्वा [रसतेर्वा][8] । तस्यैषा भवति ॥ ११ ॥

वनस्पते वीड्वङ्गो[9] हि भूया अस्मत्सखा प्रतरणः सुवीरः ।
गोभिः सन्नद्धो असि वीळयस्वास्थाता ते जयतु जेत्वानि[10] ॥

वनस्पते दृळ्हाङ्गो[11] हि भव । अस्मत्सखा प्रतरणः सुवीरः कल्याणवीरः । गोभिः सन्नद्धो असि । वीळयस्वेति संस्तम्भस्व । आस्थाता ते जयतु जेतव्यानि ।

---

१. आदरणीयाः C 4, C 5, C 7, M 3, Mi, W 1, W 2, W 3; Durga, & S'ivadatta.

२. श्लोकः......घुष्यतेः is omitted by Durga.

३. RV. I. 126. 1; cf. BD. III. 155.

४. बलभर्ता C 4, C 5, C 7, M 3, Mi, W 1, W 2, W 3.

५. The passage बालो......प्रतिषेधव्यवहितः is omitted by Durga. Etymological explanation of a word which occurs neither in the text of the RV. nor in that of Yāska is irrelavont and suspicious.

६. मनसः is omitted by Durga.

७. रममाणो......वा is omitted by Durga.
Cf. PMbh. vol. I. p. 327. line 15. रमन्तेऽस्मिन्रथ इति ।

८. रपतेर्वा रसतेर्वा is omitted by Durga; रसतेर्वा is omitted by BK, C 4, C 5, C 7, Kn, M 3, Mi, R 7, R 8, W 1, W 2, W 3.

९. वीड्वङ्गो M 3.

१०. RV. VI. 47. 26; AV. 6. 125. 1; VS. 29. 52.

११. दृढांगो C 1, C 2, C 6, M 1, S; & Roth & S'ivadatta.

दुन्दुभिरिति शब्दानुकरणम् । द्रुमो भिन्न इति वा । दुन्दुभ्यतेर्वा स्याच्छब्द-कर्मणः[1] । तस्यैषा भवति ॥ १२ ॥

उप श्वासय पृथिवीमुत द्यां पुरुत्रा ते मनुतां विष्ठितं जगत् ।
स दुन्दुभे सजूरिन्द्रेण देवैर्दूराद्दवीयो अप सेध शत्रून्[2] ॥

उपश्वासय पृथिवीं च दिवं च । बहुधा ते घोषं मन्यताम् । विष्ठितं स्थावरं जङ्गमं च यत् । स दुन्दुभे सहजोषण इन्द्रेण च देवैश्च । दूराद्दूरतरमपसेध शत्रून् ।

इषुधिरिषूणां निधानम्[3] । तस्यैषा भवति ॥ १३ ॥

बह्वीनां पिता बहुरस्य पुत्रश्चिश्चा कृणोति समनावगत्य ।
इषुधिः सङ्काः पृतनाश्च सर्वाः पृष्ठे निनद्धो जयति प्रसूतः[4] ॥

बह्वीनां[5] पिता बहुरस्य पुत्र इतीषूनभिप्रेत्य । प्रस्मयत इवापाव्रियमाणः[6] । शब्दानुकरणं वा[7] । सङ्काः सचतेः । संपूर्वाद्वा किरतेः । पृष्ठे निनद्धो जयति प्रसूत इति व्याख्यातम् ।

हस्तघ्नो हस्ते हन्यते । तस्यैषा भवति ॥ १४ ॥

अहिरिव भोगैः पर्येति बाहुं ज्याया हेतिं परिबाधमानः ।
हस्तघ्नो विश्वा वयुनानि विद्वान्पुमान्पुमांसं परि पातु विश्वतः[8] ॥

अहिरिव भोगैः[9] परिवेष्टयति बाहुम् । ज्याया वधात्परित्रायमाणः । हस्तघ्नः सर्वाणि प्रज्ञानानि प्रजानन् । पुमान्पुरुमना भवति । पुंसतेर्वा[10] ।

अभीशवो व्याख्याताः[11] । तेषामेषा भवति ॥ १५ ॥

रथे तिष्ठन्नयति वाजिनः पुरो यत्र यत्र कामयते सुषारथिः ।
अभीशूनां महिमानं पनायत मनः पश्चादनु यच्छन्ति रश्मयः[12] ॥

---

१. स्याद्वधकर्मणः C 4, C 5, C 7, M 3, Mi, W 1, W 2, W 3 and Sāyaṇa; see SRV. VI. 47. 29. p. ii. 815.

२. RV. VI. 47. 29; AV. 6. 126. 1.

३. Quoted SRV. VI. 75. 5. p. ii. 888.

४. RV. VI. 75. 5; VS. 29. 42.

५. बहूनां C 1, C 2, C 6, M 1, M 4, S; Roth & S'ivadatta; ह्वी is crossed and हू added on the margin in C 7.

६. प्रस्मयत इति वा वध्रीयमाणः C 4, C 5, C 7, M 3, W 1, W 2; प्रस्मयतद्गति वा वध्रीयमाणः Mi; प्रस्मयत इति वार्पव्रियमाणः W 3.

७. शब्दानुकरणा वा M 3.

८. RV. VI. 75. 14; VS. 29. 51.

९. Cf. PMbh. vol. II. p. 340. l. 16. अथवा भोगशब्दः शरीरवाच्यपि दृश्यते । तद्यथा । अहिरिव भोगैः पर्येति बाहुम् । अहिरिव शरीरैरिति गम्यते ।

१०. Quoted SRV. VI. 75. 14. p. ii. 891; cf. also VII. 6. 1.

११. N. 3. 9.

१२. RV. VI. 75. 6; VS. 29. 43.

रथे तिष्ठन्नयति वाजिनः पुरस्तात्सतो यत्र यत्र कामयते । सुषारथिः कल्याणसारथिः । अभीशूनां महिमानं पूजयामि[2] । मनः पश्चात्सन्तो[3]ऽनुयच्छन्ति रश्मयः[4] ।

धनुर्धन्वतेर्गतिकर्मणः । वधकर्मणो वा । धन्वन्त्यस्मादिषवः । तस्यैषा भवति ॥ १६ ॥

धन्वना गा धन्वनाजिं जयेम धन्वना तीव्राः समदो जयेम ।
धनुः शत्रोरपकामं कृणोति धन्वना सर्वाः प्रदिशो जयेम[5] ॥

इति सा निगदव्याख्याता । समदः समदो वात्तेः । सम्मदो वा मदतेः[6] ।

ज्या जयतेर्वा । जिनातेर्वा । प्रजावयतीषूनिति वा । तस्या एषा भवति ॥ १७ ॥

वक्ष्यन्तीवेदा गनीगन्ति कर्णं प्रियं सखायं परिषस्वजाना ।
योषेव शिङ्क्ते विततावि धन्वञ्ज्या इयं समने पारयन्ती[7] ॥

वक्ष्यन्तीवागच्छति कर्णं प्रियमिव सखायमिषुं परिष्वजमाना । योषेव [शिङ्क्ते] शब्दं करोति । वितताधि धनुषि ज्येयं समने संग्रामे पारयन्ती [पारं नयन्ती][8] ।

इषुरीषतेर्गतिकर्मणः[10] । [वधकर्मणो वा ।][11] तस्यैषा भवति ॥ १८ ॥

सुपर्णं वस्ते मृगो अस्या दन्तो गोभिः सन्नद्धा पतति प्रसूता ।
यत्रा नरः सं च वि च द्रवन्ति तत्रास्मभ्यमिषवः शर्म यंसन्[12] ॥

सुपर्णं वस्त इति वाजानभिप्रेत्य । मृगमयोऽस्या दन्तः । मृगयतेर्वा । गोभिः सन्नद्धा पतति प्रसूतेति व्याख्यातम्[13] । यत्र नराः संद्रवन्ति च विद्रवन्ति च तत्रास्मभ्यमिषवः शर्म यच्छन्तु[14] शरणं संग्रामेषु ।

अश्वाजनीं कशेत्याहुः । कशा प्रकाशयति भयमश्वाय । कृष्यतेर्वाणूभावात् । वाक्पुनः प्रकाशयत्यर्थान् । खशया[15] । क्रोशतेर्वा । अश्वकशाया एषा भवति ॥ १९ ॥

---

१. नयसि L.

२. पूजयति W 1; पूजयतः C 4; पूजयत C 5, C 7, M 3, Mi, W 2, W 3; and Sāyaṇa, cf. SRV. VI. 75. 6. p. ii. 889.

३. सतो C 4, C 5, M 3, Mi, W 2, W 3; and Sāyaṇa loc. cit. W 1, C 7 agree with the text of the longer recension.

४. Quoted SRV. loc. cit.

५. RV. VI. 75. 2; VS. 29. 39.

६. Quoted SRV. VI. 75. 2. p. ii. 888.

७. RV. VI. 75. 3; VS. 29. 40.

८. Omitted by BK, C 4, C 5, C 7, Kn, M 3, Mi, R 7, R 8, W 1, W 2, W 3.

९. Omitted by BK, C 4, C 5, C 7, Kn, M 3, Mi, R 7, R 8, W 1, W 2, W 3; quoted by SRV. VI. 75. 3. p. ii. 888.

१०. इषुरिषतेः Roth.

११. Omitted by C 4, C 7, M 3, Mi, W 1, W 3; is underlined in C 5; वधकर्मणो वेति भाष्ये पाठः is added on the margin in W 2.

१२. RV. VI. 75. 11; VS. 29. 48.

१३. N. 2. 5.

१४. Cf. SRV. VI. 75. 11. p. ii. 890 सुपर्णं...शर्म शरणं प्रयच्छन्तु ।

१५. न्कशया M 3, but a ख is added just above क on the margin in M 3.

आ जङ्घन्ति सान्वेषां जघनाँ उप जिघ्नते ।
अश्वाजनि प्रचेतसोऽश्वान्त्समत्सु चोदय[1] ॥

आघ्नन्ति[2] सानून्येषां सरणानि सक्थीनि । सक्थि सचतेः । आसक्तोऽस्मिन् कायः । जघनानि चोपघ्नन्ति[3] । जघनं जङ्घन्यतेः[4] । अश्वाजनि [प्रचेतसः[5]] प्रवृद्धचेतसोऽश्वान्त्समत्सु समरणेषु संग्रामेषु[6] चोदय ।

उलूखलमुरुकरं वा । ऊर्ध्वखं वा । ऊर्क्करं[7] वा ।

उरु मे कुरु[8] । इत्यब्रवीत् ।

तदुलूखलमभवत् ।

उरुकरं वैतदुलूखलमित्याचक्षते परोक्षेण । इति च ब्राह्मणम् ।

तस्यैषा भवति ॥ २० ॥

यच्चिद्धि त्वं गृहेगृह उलूखलक युज्यसे ।
इह द्युमत्तमं वद जयतामिव दुन्दुभिः[10] ॥

इति सा निगदव्याख्याता ॥ २१ ॥

वृषभः प्रजां वर्षतीति वा । अतिबृहति रेत इति वा । तद्वर्षकर्मा वर्षणाद्वृषभः । तस्यैषा भवति ॥ २२ ॥

न्यक्रन्दयन्नुपयन्त एनममेहयन्वृषभं मध्य आजेः ।
तेन सूभर्वं शतवत्सहस्रं गवां मुद्गलः प्रधने जिगाय[11] ॥

न्यक्रन्दयन्नुपयन्त इति व्याख्यातम् । अमेहयन्वृषभं मध्ये । [आजेः[12]] आजयनस्याजवनस्येति वा । तेन [तं][12] सूभर्वं राजानम् । भर्वतिरत्तिकर्मा[13] । तद्वा सूभर्वं

---

१. RV. VI. 75. 13.

२. आघ्नति C 4, C 5, C 7, Mi, W 1, W 2, W 3; अघ्नति M 3.

३. चोपघ्नते M 3; चोपघ्नन्ति Sāyaṇa.

४. Cf. SRV. I. 28. 2. p. i. 147.

५. Omitted by BK, C 4, C 5, C 7. Kn, M 3, Mi, R 7, R 8, W 1, W 2, W 3.

६. Quoted SRV. VI. 75. 13. p. ii. 891.

७. उत्करं M 3, W 1, W 2, W 3; उर्करं C 4, C 5, Mi; उर्करं वोर्ध्वखं Rot.

८. Cf. S'B. VII. 5. 1. 22: उरु मे करदिति तदुरुकरम् । उरुकरं ह वै तदुलूखलमित्याचक्षते परोक्षम् । Cf. SRV. I. 28. 5. p. i. 148.

९. The section comes to an end here in S'ivadatta's edition. It is however against the evidence of the MSS. of both recensions,

१०. RV. I. 28. 5; cf. BD. iii. 101.

११. RV. X. 102. 5.

१२. Omitted by BK, C 4, C 5, C 7, Kn, M 3, Mi, R 7, R 8, W 1, W 2, W 3.

१३. भर्वतिरत्तिकर्मा is omitted by Durga, underlined by Roth; Sāyaṇa reads भुर्वतिरत्तिकर्मा SRV. I. 56. 1; 143. 5.

सहस्रं गवां मुद्गलः प्रधने जिगाय। प्रधने इति सङ्ग्रामनाम। प्रकीर्णान्यस्मिन् धनानि भवन्ति।

द्रुघणो द्रुममयो घनः। तत्रेतिहासमाचक्षते। मुद्गलो भार्म्यश्व ऋषिर्वृषभं च द्रुघणं च युक्त्वा सङ्ग्रामे व्यवहृत्याजिं जिगाय। तदभिवादिन्येषर्ग्भवति॥ २३॥

इ॒मं तं प॑श्य वृ॒ष॒भस्य॑ यु॒ञ्जं काष्ठा॑या॒ मध्ये॑ द्रु॒घ॒णं शया॑नम्।
येन॑ जि॒गाय॑ श॒तव॑त्स॒हस्रं॒ गवां॒ मुद्ग॑लः पृत॒नाज्ये॑षु॥

इमं तं पश्य वृषभस्य सहयुजं काष्ठाया मध्ये द्रुघणं शयानम्। येन जिगाय शतवत्सहस्रं गवां मुद्गलः पृतनाज्येषु। पृतनाज्यमिति सङ्ग्रामनाम। पृतनानाम-जनाद्वा। जयनाद्वा। मुद्गलो मुद्गवान्। मुद्गगिलो [वा]। मदनं गिलतीति वा। मदंगिलो वा। मुदंगिलो वा। भार्म्यश्वो भृम्यश्वस्य पुत्रः। भृम्यश्वो भृमयोऽस्याश्वाः। अश्वभरणाद्वा।

पितुरित्यन्ननाम। पातेर्वा। पिबतेर्वा। प्यायतेर्वा। तस्यैषा भवति॥ २४॥

पि॒तुं नु स्तो॑षं म॒हो ध॒र्माणं॒ तवि॑षीम्।
यस्य॑ त्रि॒तो व्योज॑सा वृ॒त्रं विप॑र्वम॒र्दय॑त्॥

तं पितुं स्तौमि महतो धारयितारं बलस्य। तविषीति बलनाम। तवतेः [वा] वृद्धिकर्मणः। यस्य त्रित ओजसा बलेन। त्रितस्त्रिस्थान इन्द्रो वृत्रं विपर्वाणं व्यर्दयति।

नद्यो व्याख्याताः। तासामेषा भवति॥ २५॥

इ॒मं मे॑ गङ्गे यमुने सरस्वति॒ शुतु॑द्रि॒ स्तोमं॑ सचता॒ परु॒ष्ण्या।
अ॒सि॒क्न्या म॑रुद्वृधे वि॒तस्त॒यार्जी॑कीये शृणु॒ह्या सु॒षोम॑या॥

---

१. प्रधनमिति SRV. I. 52. 9. p. i. 265.

२. Quoted SRV. loc. cit.

३. घण: Roth.

४. Cf. BD. viii. 12; SRV. X. 102. 1. p. IV. 338.

५. RV. X. 102. 9; cf. BD. VIII. 11.

६. पृतनाज्य इति C 4, C 5, C 7, M 3, W 2, W 3; पृतनाज्यद्ति Mi.

७. Omitted by BK, C 4, C 5, C 7, Kn, M 3, Mi, R 7, R 8, W 1, W 2, W 3.

८. Cf. SB. I. 9. 2. 20. AB. I. 13. अन्नं वै पितुः।

९. RV. I. 187. 1; VS. 34. 7.

१०. Omitted by BK, C 4, C 5, C 7, Kn, M 3, Mi, R 7, R 8, W 1, W 2, W 3.

११. N. 2. 24.

१२. RV. X. 75. 5.

इमं मे गङ्गे यमुने सरस्वति शुतुद्रि परुष्णि स्तोममासेवध्वम्। असिक्न्या च सह मरुद्वृधे वितस्तया चार्जीकीय आशृणुहि सुषोमया चेति समस्तार्थः। अथैकपदनिरुक्तम्। गङ्गा गमनात्। यमुना प्रयुवती गच्छतीति वा। प्रवियुतं गच्छतीति वा। सरस्वती। सर इत्युदकनाम। सर्तेः। तद्वती। शुतुद्री शुद्राविणी। क्षिप्रद्राविणी। आशु तुन्नेव द्रवतीति वा। इरावतीं परुष्णीत्याहुः। पर्ववती [भास्वती] कुटिलगामिनी[3]। असिक्न्यशुक्लासिता। सितमिति वर्णनाम। तत्प्रतिषेधोऽसितम्। मरुद्वृधाः[4] सर्वा नद्यो मरुत एना वर्धयन्ति। वितस्ताविदग्धा विवृद्धा महाकूला[5]। आर्जीकीयां विपाडित्याहुः[6]। ऋजीकप्रभवा[7] वा। ऋजुगामिनी वा। विपाड् विपाटनाद्वा। विपाशनाद्वा। विप्रापणाद्वा। पाशा अस्यां व्यपाश्यन्त वसिष्ठस्य मुमूर्षतः। तस्माद्विपाडुच्यते[8]। पूर्वमासीदुरुञ्जिरा। सुषोमा सिन्धुः। यदेनामभिप्रसुवन्ति नद्यः। सिन्धुः स्यन्दनात्[9]।

आप आप्नोतेः[10]। तासामेषा भवति ॥ २६ ॥

आपो हि ष्ठा मयोभुवस्ता न ऊर्जे दधातन।
महे रणाय चक्षसे[11] ॥

आपो हि स्थ सुखभुवस्ता नोऽन्नाय धत्त। महते च नो रणाय रमणीयाय [च[12]] दर्शनाय।

ओषधय ओषद्धयन्तीति वा। ओषत्येना धयन्तीति वा। दोषं धयन्तीति वा।

तासामेषा भवति ॥ २७ ॥

या ओषधीः पूर्वा जाता देवेभ्यस्त्रियुगं पुरा।
मनै नु बभ्रूणामहं शतं धामानि सप्त च[13] ॥

---

१. Cf. SRV. X. 75. 5. p. IV. 232.

२. Omitted by C 4, M 3, Mi, W 1, W 3; the reading of C 5, C 7, W 2 is that of the longer recension.

३. कुटिल॰ M 3.

४. मरुद्वृधः C 4, M 3, Mi, W 1, W 3.

५. महाकुला M 3, W 3.

६. विपालित्याहुः C 4, M 1, M 3, Mi, W 1, W 3.

७. ऋजूकप्रभवा C 1, C 2, C 3, C 6, M 1, M 4, R 2, R 3, R 5, S; & Roth. Cf. Durga: ऋर्जीको नाम पर्वतः। तस्मात् प्रभवति।

८. ॰विपालुच्यते M 1, M 3.

९. Cf. SRV. I. 125. 4. p. i. 569.

१०. Cf. S'B. VI. 1. 1. 9.
यदाप्नोत्तस्मादापः।
also Uṇādi sūtra II. 58.
आप्नोतेर्ह्रस्वश्च।

११. RV. X. 9. 1; AV. 1. 5. 1; SV. 2. 1187; VS. 11. 50; 36. 14.

१२. Omitted by BK, C 4, C 5, C 7, Kn, M 3, Mi, R 7, R 8, W 1, W 2, W 3.

१३. RV. X. 97. 1; VS. 12. 75.

या ओषधयः पूर्वा जाता देवेभ्यस्त्रीणि युगानि पुरा मन्ये नु तद्बभ्रूणामहं बभ्रुवर्णानां हरणानां भरणानामिति वा । शतं धामानि सप्त च [इति[2]] । धामानि त्रयाणि भवन्ति । स्थानानि । नामानि । जन्मानीति । जन्मा[3]न्यत्राभिप्रेतानि । सप्तशतं पुरुषस्य मर्मणां तेष्वेना दधतीति वा ।

रात्रिर्व्याख्याता । तस्या एषा भवति ॥ २८ ॥

आ रात्रि पार्थिवं रजः पितुरप्रायि धामभिः ।
दिवः सदांसि बृहती वि तिष्ठस आ त्वेषं वर्तते तमः ॥

आपूपुरस्त्वं रात्रि पार्थिवं रजः । स्थानैर्मध्यमस्य । दिवः सदाँसि । बृहती महती वितिष्ठस आवर्तते त्वेषं तमो रजः ।

अरण्यान्यरण्यस्य पत्नी । अरण्यमपार्णम् । ग्रामादरमणं भवतीति वा । तस्या एषा भवति ॥ २९ ॥

अरण्यान्यरण्यान्यसौ या प्रेव नश्यसि ।
कथा ग्रामं न पृच्छसि न त्वा भीरिव विन्दती३ँ ॥

अरण्यानीत्येनामामन्त्रयते । यासावरण्यानि वनानि पराचीव नश्यसि कथं ग्रामं न पृच्छसि । न त्वा भीर्विन्दतीवेति । इवः परिभयार्थे वा ।

श्रद्धा श्रद्धानात् । तस्या एषा भवति ॥ ३० ॥

श्रद्धयाग्निः समिध्यते श्रद्धया हूयते हविः ।
श्रद्धां भगस्य मूर्धनि वचसा वेदयामसि ॥

श्रद्धयाग्निः साधु समिध्यते । श्रद्धया हविः साधु हूयते । श्रद्धां भगस्य भागधेयस्य मूर्धनि प्रधानाङ्गे वचनेनावेदयामः ।

---

१. भरणानां हरणानामिति वा C 4, C 5, C 7, M 3, Mi, W 1, W 2, W 3; cf. SRV. X. 97. 1. p. IV. 319: या…भरणानां हरणानां…

२. Omitted by BK, C 4, C 5, C 7, Kn, M 3, Mi, R 7, R 8, W 1, W 2, W 3.

३. स्थानानि C 4, M 3, Mi; is corrected to जन्मानि in C 7; जन्मानि is partially obliterated with black ink & स्थानानि added on the margin in W 2; स्थानानि is added on the margin although no attempt is made to obliterate जन्मानि in W 1.

४. Cf. SRV. X. 97. 1. p. IV. 319: …प्रेतानि सप्तशतानि सप्तशतं…दधति । Cf. also S'B. VII. 2. 4. 26.

५. N. 2. 18.

६. AV. 19. 47. 1; VS. 34. 32.

७. RV. X. 146. 1.

८. Cf. SRV. X. 147. 1. p. IV. 462.

९. भरस्य M 3.

१०. RV. X. 151. 1.

पृथिवी व्याख्याता[1] । तस्या एषा भवति ॥ ३१ ॥

स्योना पृथिवि भवानृक्षरा निवेशनी ।
यच्छा नः शर्म सप्रथः[2] ॥

सुखा नः पृथिवि भव । अनृक्षरा निवेशनी । ऋक्षरः कण्टक ऋच्छतेः[3] । कण्टकः कन्तपो वा । कृन्ततेर्वा । कण्टतेर्वा स्याद्गतिकर्मणः । उद्गततमो[4] भवति । यच्छ नः शर्म । [यच्छन्तु[5]] शरणं सर्वतः पृथु[6] ।

अप्वा व्याख्याता[7] । तस्या एषा भवति ॥ ३२ ॥

अमीषां चित्तं प्रतिलोभयन्ती गृहाणाङ्गान्यप्वे परेहि ।
अभि प्रेहि निर्दह हृत्सु[8] शोकैरन्धेनामित्रास्तमसा सचन्ताम्[9] ॥

अमीषां चित्तानि [प्रज्ञानानि[10]] प्रतिलोभयमाना गृहाणाङ्गान्यप्वे परेहि । अभिप्रेहि । निर्दहैषां हृदयानि शोकैः । अन्धेनामित्रास्तमसा संसेव्यन्ताम् ।

अग्नाय्यग्नेः पत्नी । तस्या एषा भवति ॥ ३३ ॥

इहेन्द्राणीमुप ह्वये वरुणानीं स्वस्तये ।
अग्नायीं सोमपीतये[11] ॥

इति सा निगदव्याख्याता ॥ ३४ ॥

अथातोऽष्टौ द्वन्द्वानि । [उलूखलमुसले[12] ।] उलूखलं व्याख्यातम्[13] । मुसलं मुहुः सरम् । तयोरेषा भवति ॥ ३५ ॥

---

१. N. 1. 13, 14.

२. RV. I. 22. 15; cf. AV. 18. 2. 19:
स्योनास्मै भव पृथिव्यनृक्षरा निवेशनी ।
यच्छास्मै शर्म सप्रथाः ॥
Cf. VS. 35. 21:
स्योना पृथिवि नो भवानृक्षरा निवेशनी ।
यच्छा नः शर्म सप्रथाः ॥

३. Cf. SRV. I. 41. 4. p. i. 215.

४. उद्गततरो C 4, C 5, C 7, M 3, Mi, W 1, W 2, W 3.

५. Omitted by C 1, C 2, C 3, C 6, M 1, M 4, R 2, R 3, R 5, S.

६. Cf. SRV. I. 22. 15. p. i. 118.

७. N. 6. 12.

८. Durga reads हृत् सुशोकैः

९. RV. X. 103. 12; SV. 2. 1211; VS. 17. 44; cf. AV. 3. 2. 5; cf. BD. viii. 13 B.

१०. Omitted by BK, C 4, C 5, Kn, M 3, Mi, R 7, R 8, W 1, W 2, W 3.

११. RV. I. 22. 12.

१२. Omitted by BK, C 4, C 5, C 7, Kn, M 3, Mi, R 7, R 8, W 1, W 2, W 3.

१३. N. 9. 20.

आयजी वाजसातमा ता ह्युच्चा विजर्भृतः ।
हरी इवान्धांसि बप्सता[1] ॥

आयष्टव्ये अन्नानां संभक्ततमे ते ह्युच्चैर्विह्रियेते हरी इवान्नानि[2] भुञ्जाने[3] ।

हविर्धाने हविषां निधाने । तयोरेषा भवति ॥ ३६ ॥

आ वामुपस्थमद्रुहा देवाः सीदन्तु यज्ञियाः ।
इहाद्य सोमपीतये[4] ॥

आसीदन्तु वामुपस्थमुपस्थानम् [अद्रोग्धव्ये इति वा][5] यज्ञिया देवा यज्ञसंपादिन इहाद्य सोमपानाय ।

द्यावापृथिव्यौ व्याख्याते[6] । तयोरेषा भवति ॥ ३७ ॥

द्यावा नः पृथिवी इमं सिध्रमद्य दिविस्पृशम् ।
यज्ञं देवेषु यच्छताम्[7] ॥

द्यावापृथिव्यौ न इमं साधनमद्य दिविस्पृशं यज्ञं देवेषु नियच्छताम्[8] ।

विपाट्छुतुद्र्यौ व्याख्याते[9] । तयोरेषा भवति ॥ ३८ ॥

प्र पर्वतानामुशती उपस्थादश्वे इव विषिते हासमाने ।
गावेव शुभ्रे मातरा रिहाणे विपाट्छुतुद्री पयसा जवेते[10] ॥

पर्वतानामुपस्थादुपस्थानात् । उशत्यौ कामयमाने । अश्वे इव विमुक्ते इति वा । विषण्णे इति वा । हासमाने । हासतिः स्पर्धायां । हर्षमाणे वा । गावाविव [शुभ्रे][11] शोभने मातरौ[12] संरिहाणे[13] । विपाट्छुतुद्री[14] पयसा प्रजवेते[15] ।

---

१. RV. I. 28. 7.

२. इवांधानि C 4, C 5, C 7, M 3, Mi; अन्नानि is corrected to अंधानि in W 3.

३. Quoted by SRV. I. 28. 7. p. i. 148.

४. RV. II. 41. 21.

५. Omitted by BK, C 4, C 5, C 7, Kn, M 3, Mi, R 7, R 8, W 1, W 2, W 3.

६. N. 1. 13, 14; 3. 22.

७. RV. II. 41. 20.

८. निगच्छताम् M 3; नियच्छताविपाट् W 3.

९. N. 2. 24; 9. 26.

१०. RV. III. 33. 1.

११. Omitted by BK, C 4, C 5, C 7, Kn, M 3, Mi, R 7, R 8, W 1, W 2, W 3.

१२. संमातरौ C 4, C 5, C 7, M3, Mi, W 2, W 3; मातरौ is corrected to संमातरौ in W1.

१३. रिहाणे C 4, C 5, C 7, M 3, Mi, W 2, W 3; संरिहाणे is corrected to रिहाणे in W 1.

१४. विपाट्छुतुद्र्यौ C 1, C 2, C 3, C 6, M 1, M 4, S; W 2; Roth.

१५. Cf. SRV. III. 33. 1. p. ii. 242.

आर्त्नी अर्त्न्यौ वा। अरण्यौ वा। अरिपण्यौ वा।

तयोरेषा भवति॥ ३९.॥

ते आचरन्ती समनेव योषा मातेव पुत्रं बिभृतामुपस्थे।
अप शत्रून्विध्यतां संविदाने आर्त्नी इमे विष्फुरन्ती अमित्रान्॥

ते आचरन्त्यौ समनसाविव योषे मातेव पुत्रं बिभृतामुपस्थ उपस्थाने। अपविध्येतां शत्रून्संविदाने आर्त्न्याविमे विघ्नत्यावमित्रान्।

शुनासीरौ। शुनो वायुः। शु एत्यन्तरिक्षे। सीर आदित्यः सरणात्। तयोरेषा भवति॥ ४०॥

शुनासीराविमां वाचं जुषेथां यद्दिवि चक्रथुः पयः।
तेनेमामुप सिञ्चतम्॥

इति सा निगदव्याख्याता।

देवी जोष्ट्री देव्यौ जोषयित्र्यौ। द्यावापृथिव्याविति वा। अहोरात्रे इति वा। सस्यं च समा चेति कात्थक्यः। तयोरेष संप्रैषो भवति॥ ४१॥

देवी जोष्ट्री वसुधीती ययोरन्याघा द्वेषांसि यूयवदान्या-
वक्षद्वसु वार्याणि यजमानाय वसुवने वसुधेयस्य वीतां यज॥

देवी जोष्ट्री। देव्यौ जोषयित्र्यौ। [वसुधीती] वसुधान्यौ। ययोरन्याघानि द्वेषांस्यवयावयत्यावहत्यन्या वसूनि वननीयानि यजमानाय। वसुवननाय च। वसुधानाय च। वीतां पिबेतां कामयेतां वा। यजेति संप्रैषः।

देवी ऊर्जाहुती। देव्या ऊर्जाह्वान्यौ। द्यावापृथिव्याविति वा। अहोरात्र इति वा। सस्यं च समा चेति कात्थक्यः। तयोरेष संप्रैषो भवति॥ ४२॥

देवी ऊर्जाहुती इषमूर्जमन्या वक्षत्सग्धिं सपीतिमन्या नवेन पूर्वं दयमानाः स्याम पुराणेन नवं तामूर्जमूर्जाहुती ऊर्जयमाने अधातां वसुवने वसुधेयस्य वीतां यज॥

---

१. RV. VI. 75. 4; VS. 29. 41.

२. अप शत्रून्विध्यतां C 4, C 5, C 7, M 3, Mi, W 2, W 3; the figures of २ and १ are placed respectively on शत्रून् and विध्यतां in W 1.

३. Cf. SRV. VI. 75. 4. p. ii. 888.

४. Cf. SRV. IV. 57. 5. p. ii. 490; cf. BD. V. 8.

५. RV. IV. 57. 5.

६. कात्थक्य: M 3.

७. KS. 19. 13; MS. 4. 13. 8: 210. 1.

८. Omitted by BK, C 4, C 5, C 7, Kn, M 3, Mi, R 7, R8, W 1, W 2, W 3.

९. ययो॰ M 3.

१०. वरणीयानि M 3.

११. कात्थक्य: M 3.

१२. KS. 19. 13; MS. 4. 13. 8: 210. 4, 7.

देवी ऊर्जाहुती । देव्या ऊर्जाह्वान्यौ । अन्नं च रसं चावहति [आवहेति[1]] अन्या । सहर्जग्धिं[2] च सहपीतिं[3] चान्या । नवेन पूर्वं दयमानाः स्याम । पुराणेन नवम् । तामूर्जमूर्जाहुती ऊर्जयमाने अधाताम् । वसुवननाय च । वसुधानाय च । वीतां पिबेतां कामयेतां वा । यजेति संप्रैषो यजेति[4] संप्रैषः ॥ ४३ ॥

॥ इति नवमोऽध्यायः ॥

[अथ[1] यान्यश्वो वोळ्हा[2] मा[3] नो मित्रः कनिक्रदद्[4] भद्रं वद[5] संवत्सरमुप[6] प्र वद प्रावेपा[7] मा प्रैते[8] वदन्त्वमन्द्रा[10]न्यक्ष[11]संयोगाद्वनस्पते[12] उप[13] श्वासय वह्नीनाम[14]हिरिव[15] भोगै रथे[16] तिष्ठन्धन्वना[17] गा वक्ष्यन्तीवेदा[18] सुपर्ण[19] वस्त आ[20] जङ्घन्ति यच्चिद्धि[21] त्वं वृषभो[22] न्यक्र-न्द्यग्निम्[23]इमं[24] तं पितुं[25] न्विमं[26] म आपोहिष्ठा[27] या[28] ओषधीरा[29] रात्र्यरण्यानि[30] श्रद्धया[31] ऽग्निः स्योना[32]मीषां[33] चित्तसिहेन्द्रा[34]ण्यथातो[35]ऽष्टावा[36]यज्यां[37] वां द्यावा[38] नः प्र पर्वतानां[39] ते आचरन्ती[40] शुनासीरौ[41] देवी[42] जोष्ट्री देवी[43] ऊर्जाहुती त्रिचत्वारिंशत् ॥][5]

॥ इत्युत्तरषट्के तृतीयोऽध्यायः ॥

॥ इति निरुक्ते नवमोऽध्यायः ॥

---

१. Omitted by BK, C 4, C 5, C 7, Kn, M 3, Mi, R 7, R 8, W 1, W 2, W 3.

२. सहसर्गिध C 4, C 7, M 3, Mi; सुसंग्धि W 2.

३. सहसपीतिं C 4, C 5, C 7, M 3, Mi, W 1, W 2, W 3.

४. यजेति संप्रैषः is given only once in Roth.

५. Small figure within brackets represents the corresponding section of the ninth chapter of the *Nirukta*.

अथ दशमोऽध्यायः

अथातो मध्यस्थाना देवताः।

तासां वायुः प्रथमागामी भवति। वायुर्वातेः। वेतेर्वा स्याद्गतिकर्मणः। एतेरिति स्थौलाष्ठीविः। अनर्थको वकारः। तस्यैषा भवति ॥ १ ॥

वाय॒वा या॑हि दर्शते॒मे सोमा॒ अरं॑कृताः।
तेषां॑ पाहि श्रु॒धी हव॑म् ॥

वायवायाहि दर्शनीयेमे सोमा अरङ्कृता [अलङ्कृताः]। तेषां पिब शृणु नो ह्वानमिति। कमन्यं मध्यमादेवमवक्ष्यत्।

तस्यैषापरा भवति ॥ २ ॥

आ॒स॒स्रा॒णासः॑ शवसा॒नमच्छेन्द्रं॑ सुच॒क्रे र॒थ्या॑सो॒ अश्वाः॑।
अ॒भि श्रव॒ ऋज्य॑न्तो वहेयु॒र्नू चि॒न्नु वा॒योर॒मृतं॒ वि द॑स्येत् ॥

आसस्रवांसः। अभिबलायमानमिन्द्रम्। कल्याणचक्रे रथे योगाय। रथ्या अश्वा रथस्य वोढारः। ऋज्यन्त ऋजुगामिनोऽन्नमभिवहेयुः। नवं च पुराणं च। श्रव इत्यन्ननाम। श्रूयत इति सतः। वायोश्चास्य भक्षो यथा न विदस्येदिति। इन्द्रप्रधानेत्येके नैघण्टुकं वायुकर्म। उभयप्रधानेत्यपरम्।

वरुणो वृणोतीति सतः। तस्यैषा भवति ॥ ३ ॥

नी॒चीन॑बारं॒ वरु॑णः॒ कव॑न्धं॒ प्र स॑सर्ज॒ रोद॑सी अ॒न्तरि॑क्षम्।
तेन॒ विश्व॑स्य॒ भुव॑नस्य॒ राजा॒ यवं॒ न वृ॒ष्टिर्व्यु॑नत्ति॒ भूम॑ ॥

१. RV. I. 2. 1.

२. Omitted by BK, C 4, C 5, C 7, Kn, M 3, Mi, R 8, W 1, W 2, W 3.

३. Cf. SRV. I. 2. 1. p. i. 30.

४. अवक्षत् C 4, C 5, C 7, M 3, Mi, W 1, W 2, W 3.

५. RV. VI. 37. 3.

६. पुराण M 3.

७. Cf. SRV. I. 11. 7; 49. 2; 91. 17; pp. i. 78, 247, 407; also III. 11. 6. p. ii. 167.

८. Cf. BD. ii. 33.

९. RV. V. 85. 3.

नीचीनद्वारं वरुणः । कवन्धं मेघम्[१] । कवनमुदकं भवति । तदस्मिन्धीयते[२] । उदकमपि कवन्धमुच्यते । बन्धिरनिभृतत्वे । कमनिभृतं च । प्रसृजति । द्यावापृथिव्यौ चान्तरिक्षं[३] च[४] महत्त्वेन । तेन सर्वस्य भुवनस्य राजा यवमिव वृष्टिर्व्युनत्ति भूमिम् ।

तस्यैषापरा भवति ॥ ४ ॥

तमू षु समना गिरा पितॄणां च मन्मभिः ।
नाभाकस्य प्रशस्तिभिर्यः सिन्धूनामुपोदये सप्तस्वसा स मध्यमो
नभन्तामन्यके समे[५] ॥

तं स्वभिष्टौमि समान्या[६] गिरा गीत्या स्तुत्या । पितॄणां च मननीयैः स्तोमैः । नाभाकस्य प्रशस्तिभिः । ऋषिर्नाभाको बभूव । यः स्यन्दमानानाम्[७] आसामुपोदये[८] सप्तस्वसारमेनमाह वाग्भिः स मध्यम इति निरुच्यते । अथैष एव भवति । नभन्तामन्यके समे । मा भूवन्नन्यके सर्वे ये नो द्विषन्ति दुर्धियः पापधियः पापसंकल्पाः[९] ।

रुद्रो रौतीति सतः[१०] । रोरूयमाणो द्रवतीति वा । रोदयतेर्वा ।

यदरुदत्तद्रुद्रस्य रुद्रत्वम्[११] । इति काठकम् ।

यदरोदीत्तद्रुद्रस्य रुद्रत्वम्[१२] । इति हारिद्रविकम् ।

तस्यैषा भवति ॥ ५ ॥

इमा रुद्राय स्थिरधन्वने गिरः क्षिप्रेषवे देवाय स्वधाव्ने ।
अषाळ्हाय सहमानाय वेधसे तिग्मायुधाय भरता शृणोतु नः[१३] ॥

इमा रुद्राय । दृढधन्वने । गिरः । क्षिप्रेषवे । देवाय । अन्नवते । अषाळ्हा-[१४]

---

१. Quoted by SRV. V. 85. 3. p. ii. 680.

२. कमस्मिन्धीयते C 4, C 5, C 7, M 3, Mi, W 1, W 2, W 3.

३. वान्तरिक्षं C 4, C 5, C 7, M 3, Mi, W 1, W 2, W 3.

४. Omitted but added on the margin in M 3.

५. RV. VIII. 41. 2.

६. समान्या C 4, C 5, C 7, M 3, Mi, W 1, W 2, W 3.

७. स्यन्दनानाम् C 4, C 5, C 7, M 3, Mi, W 1, W 2, W 3.

८. आसामपामुपोदये SRV. VIII. 41. 2. p. iii. 416.

९. Quoted by SRV. VIII. 41. 2. p. iii. 416. The passage ये नो द्विषन्ति ...पापसंकल्पाः is omitted by Durga.

१०. Quoted by SRV. I. 158. 1. p. i. 671.

११. Cf. KS. XXV. 1.

१२. TS. i. 5. 1. 1; cf. S'B. IX. 1. 1. 6; BD. ii. 34.

१३. RV. VII. 46. 1.

१४. अषाढाय C 1, C 2, C 6, M 4, S and Roth.

यान्यैः[1] । सहमानाय । विधात्रे । तिग्मायुधाय । भरत । शृणोतु नः । तिग्मं तेजतेः । उत्साहकर्मणः[2] । आयुधमायोधनात्[3] ।

तस्यैषापरा भवति ॥ ६ ॥

या ते दिद्युदवसृष्टा दिवस्परि क्ष्मया चरति परि सा वृणक्तु नः ।
सहस्रं ते स्वपिवात भेषजा मा नस्तोकेषु तनयेषु रीरिषः[4] ॥

या ते दिद्युदवसृष्टा । दिवस्परि दिवोऽधि । दिद्युद् द्युतेर्वा [द्योततेर्वा[5]] । क्ष्मया चरति । क्ष्मा पृथिवी । तस्यां चरति । तया चरति । विक्ष्मापयन्ती[6] चरतीति वा । परिवृणक्तु[7] नः सा । सहस्रं ते स्वाप्तवचन भैषज्यानि । मा नस्त्वं पुत्रेषु [च[5]] पौत्रेषु च रीरिषः । तोकं तुद्यतेः । तनयं तनोतेः ।

अग्निरपि रुद्र उच्यते[8] । तस्यैषा भवति ॥ ७ ॥

जराबोध तद्विविड्ढि विशेविशे यज्ञियाय ।
स्तोमं रुद्राय दृशीकम्[9] ॥

जरा स्तुतिः[10] । जरतेः स्तुतिकर्मणः[11] । तां बोध । तया बोधयितरिति वा । तद्विविड्ढि । तत्कुरु । मनुष्यस्य मनुष्यस्य यजनाय । स्तोमं रुद्राय दर्शनीयम्[12] ।

इन्द्र इरां दृणातीति वा[13] । इरां ददातीति वा । इरां दधातीति वा । इरां दारयत[14] इति वा । इरां धारयत[15] इति वा । इन्दवे द्रवतीति[16] वा । इन्दौ रमत इति वा । इन्धे भूतानीति वा ।

---

१. अन्नैः C 4, C 5, C 7, M 3, Mi, W 1, W 2; अन्यैः is corrected to अन्नैः in W 3.

२. तिग्मं...कर्मण: is quoted by SRV. VII. 18. 18. p. iii. 41; is omitted by Durga.

३. आयुधमायोधनात् is omitted by Durga.

४. RV. VII. 46. 3.

५. Omitted by BK, C 4, C 5, C 7, Kn, M 3, Mi, R 8, W 1, W 2, W 3.

६. विक्ष्मापयति C 4, C 5, C 7, M 3, Mi, W 1, W 2, W 3.

७. परिवृणाक्तु M 3.

८. Cf. S'B. V. 2. 4. 13:
यो वै रुद्रः सोऽग्निः ।
and also S'B. V. 3. 1. 10:
अग्निर्वै रुद्रः ।

९. RV. I. 27. 10; SV. 1. 15; 2. 1013.

१०. Quoted by SRV. X. 59. 2. p. IV. 171.

११. Quoted by SRV. I. 123. 5. p. i. 558; cf. also I. 38. 5.

१२. Quoted by SRV. I. 27. 10. p. i. 145.

१३. Cf. BD. ii. 36; cf. SRV. I. 156. 5. p. i. 668.

१४. दारयतीति वा SRV. I. 3. 5. p. i. 36.

१५. धारयतीति वा SRV. loc. cit. cf. also IX. 5. 7. p. iii. 609.

१६. द्रमते M 3; द्रवत इति C 4, C 5, C 7, Mi, W 1, W 2, W 3.

तद्यदेनं प्राणैः समैन्धं[1]स्तदिन्द्रस्येन्द्रत्वम् । इति विज्ञायते[2] ।

इदं करणादित्याग्रयणः[3] । इदं दर्शनादित्यौपमन्यवः । इन्दतेवैश्वर्यकर्मणः[4] । इन्दञ्छत्रूणां[5] दारयिता[6] वा । द्रावयिता वा । आदरयिता च यज्वनाम्[7] ।

तस्यैषा भवति ॥ ८ ॥

अदर्दरुत्समसृजो वि खानि त्वमर्णवान्बद्बधानाँ अरम्णाः ।
महान्तमिन्द्र पर्वतं वि यद्वः सृजो वि धारा अव दानवं हन्[8] ॥

अदृणा उत्सम् । उत्स [उत्सरणाद्वा[9]] । उत्सदनाद्वा । उत्स्यन्दनाद्वा । उनत्तेर्वा[10] ।[11] व्यसृजोऽस्य खानि । त्वमर्णवानर्णस्वतः । एतान्[12]माध्यमिकान्त्संस्त्यायान् । बाबध्यमानानरम्णाः । रम्णातिः संयमनकर्मा । विसर्जनकर्मा वा । महान्तमिन्द्र पर्वतं मेघं यद्व्यवृणोः । व्यसृजोऽस्य धाराः । अवाहन्[13]नेनं [दानवं[14]] दानकर्माणम् ।

तस्यैषापरा भवति ॥ ९ ॥

यो जात एव प्रथमो मनस्वान्देवो देवान्क्रतुना पर्यभूषत् ।
यस्य शुष्माद्रोदसी अभ्यसेतां नृम्णस्य मह्ना स जनास इन्द्रः[15] ॥

यो जात[16] एव प्रथमो मनस्वी देवो देवान् । क्रतुना कर्मणा । पर्यभवत्पर्यगृह्णा-

---

१. समैन्धत C 4, C 5, C 7, M 3, Mi, W 1, W 2, W 3; cf. SRV. below note 7.

२. The quotation is untraced.
Cf. S'B. VI. 1. 1. 2:

एष एवेन्द्रस्तानेष प्राणान्मध्यत इन्द्रियेणैन्ध यदैन्ध तस्मादिन्ध इन्धो ह वै तमिन्द्र इत्याचक्षते परोऽक्षम् ।

३. Cf. SRV. IX. 5. 7. p. iii. 609:
तथा च यास्कः । इन्द्र इरां दृणातीति वा । इरां दारयत इति वा । इरां धारयतीति वा । इन्धे भूतानीति वा ।

तद्यदेनं प्राणैः समैधत तदिन्द्रस्येन्द्रत्वमिति विज्ञायते ।

४. Cf. SRV. I. 156. 5. p. i. 668.

५. इञ्छत्रूणां Roth; SRV. I. 3. 4. p. i. 36.

६. Cf. SRV. X. 48. 6. p. IV. 146:
इन्द्रः शत्रूणां दारयितेति निरुक्तम् ।

७. The entire passage इन्द्र इरां दृणातीति...यज्वानम् is quoted by SRV. I. 3. 4. p. i. 36.

८. RV. V. 32. 1; SV. 1. 315.

९. Omitted by BK, C 4, C 5, C 7, Kn, M 3, Mi, R 8, W 1, W 2, W 3; also by Sāyaṇa, see, SRV. V. 32. 1. p. ii. 559.

१०. उन्नयनात् C 4, C 5, C 7, M 3, Mi, W 1, W 2, W 3.

११. उनत्तेर्वा स्यात् SRV. loc. cit.

१२. The passage अदृणा उत्सम्...एतान् is quoted by SRV. loc. cit.

१३. अवहन्नेनं C 1, C 2, C 3, C 6, M 1, M 4, R 2, R 3, R 5, S.

१४. Omitted by BK, C 4, C 5, C 7, Kn, M 3, R 8, W 1, W 2, W 3.

१५. RV. II. 12. 1; AV. 20. 34. 1.

१६. जायमानः C 1, C 2, C 3, C 6, M 1, M 4, R 2, R 3, R 5, S.

त्पर्यरक्षदत्यक्रामदिति वा। यस्य बलाद् द्यावापृथिव्यावप्यबिभीतां नृम्णस्य महा बलस्य महत्त्वेन। स जनास इन्द्र इति।

ऋषेर्दृष्टार्थस्य प्रीतिर्भवत्याख्यानसंयुक्ता[1]।

पर्जन्यस्तृपेः। आद्यन्तविपरीतस्य। तर्पयिता जन्यः। परो जेता वा। परो[2] जनयिता वा। प्राजयिता वा रसानाम्[3]।

तस्यैषा भवति॥ १०॥

वि वृक्षान्हन्त्युत हन्ति रक्षसो विश्वं बिभाय भुवनं महावधात्।
उतानागा ईषते वृष्ण्यावतो यत्पर्जन्यः स्तनयन्हन्ति दुष्कृतः[4]॥

विहन्ति[5] वृक्षान्। विहन्ति च रक्षांसि। सर्वाणि चास्माद्[6]भूतानि बिभ्यति महावधात्। महान्ह्यस्य वधः[7]। अप्यनपराधो भीतः पलायते वर्षकर्मवतो यत्पर्जन्यः स्तनयन्हन्ति दुष्कृतः पापकृतः[8]।

बृहस्पतिर्बृहतः पाता वा। पालयिता वा[9]। तस्यैषा भवति॥ ११॥

अश्नापिनद्धं मधु पर्यपश्यन्मत्स्यं न दीन उदनि क्षियन्तम्।
निष्टज्जभार चमसं न वृक्षाद्बृहस्पतिर्विरवेणा विकृत्य[10]॥

अशनवता मेघेनापिनद्धं मधु पर्यपश्यत्। मत्स्यमिव दीन उदके निवसन्तम्। निर्जहार तच्चमसमिव वृक्षात्। चमसः कस्मात्। चमन्त्यस्मिन्निति। बृहस्पतिर्विरवेण शब्देन विकृत्य।

ब्रह्मणस्पतिर्ब्रह्मणः पाता वा[11]। पालयिता वा। तस्यैषा भवति॥ १२॥

अश्मास्यमवतं ब्रह्मणस्पतिर्मधुधारमभि यमोजसातृणत्।
तमेव विश्वे पपिरे स्वर्दृशो बहु साकं सिसिचुरुत्समुद्रिणम्[12]॥

---

1. The entire passage यो जात एव... आख्यानसंयुक्ता। is quoted by SRV. II. 12. 1. p. ii. 32.
2. परो is omitted by SRV. V. 83. 1. p. ii. 676.
3. The passage पर्जन्यस्तृपेः...रसानाम् is quoted by SRV. loc. cit. Cf. BD. ii. 37—38.
4. RV. V. 83. 2.
5. Sāyaṇa adds पर्जन्यो before विहन्ति; see SRV. V. 83. 2. p. ii. 676.
6. चास्मद् S'ivadatta.
7. व्यधः M 3. The passage महान्ह्यस्य वधः is omitted by Durga.
8. The passage विहन्ति वृक्षान्...पापकृतः is quoted by SRV. loc. cit. अयं मन्त्रो निरुक्ते स्पष्टं व्याख्यातः। तदेवात्र लिख्यते। etc.
9. Cf. BD. ii. 39.
10. RV. X. 68. 8; AV. 20. 16. 8.
11. Cf. BD. ii. 40.
12. RV. II. 24. 4.

अशनवन्तमास्यन्दनवन्तम्[1]। अवातितं ब्रह्मणस्पतिर्मधुधारम्। अभि यमोजसा बलेनाभ्यतृणत्तमेव सर्वे पिबन्ति रश्मयः सूर्यदृशः। बह्वेनं सह सिञ्चन्त्युत्समुद्रिणमुदकवन्तम्॥ १३॥

क्षेत्रस्य पतिः। क्षेत्रं क्षियते[2]र्निवासकर्मणः। तस्य पाता वा पालयिता[3] वा। तस्यैषा भवति॥ १४॥

> क्षेत्रस्य पतिना वयं हितेनेव जयामसि।
> गामश्वं पोषयित्वा स नो मृळातीदृशे॥[4]

क्षेत्रस्य पतिना[5] वयं सुहितेनेव जयामः। गामश्वं पुष्टं पोषयितृ चाहरेति। स नो मृळातीदृशे। बलेन वा धनेन वा। मृळतिर्दानकर्मा[6]। तस्यैषापरा भवति॥ १५॥

> क्षेत्रस्य पते मधुमन्तमूर्मिं धेनुरिव पयो अस्मासु धुक्ष्व।
> मधुश्चुतं घृतमिव सुपूतमृतस्य नः पतयो मृळयन्तु[7]॥

क्षेत्रस्य पते मधुमन्तमूर्मिं धेनुरिव पयोऽस्मासु धुक्ष्वेति। मधुश्चुतं घृतमिवोदकं सुपूतम्। ऋतस्य नः पातारो वा पालयितारो वा मृळयन्तु। मृळयतिरुपदया[8]कर्मा। पूजाकर्मा वा[9]।

तद्यत्समान्यामृचि समानाभिव्याहारं भवति तज्जामि भवतीत्येकम्। मधुमन्तं मधुश्चुतमिति यथा। यदेव समाने पादे समानाभिव्याहारं भवति तज्जामि भवतीत्यपरम्।

> हिरण्यरूपः स हिरण्यसंदृग्[10]। इति यथा।

यथा कथा च विशेषोऽजामि भवतीत्यपरम्।

> मण्डूका इवोदकान्मण्डूका उदकादिव[11]। इति यथा।

---

१. Quoted by SRV. II. 24. 4. p. ii. 71.

२. क्षीयतेः C 4, C 5, C 7, M 3, Mi, W 1, W 2, W 3.

३. Cf. BD. ii. 41.

४. RV. IV. 57. 1.

५. Quoted by SRV. IV. 57. 1. p. ii. 489.

६. मृळतिरुपदयाकर्मा पूजाकर्मा वा C 4, C 5, C 7, M 3, Mi, W 1, W 2, W 3; cf. SRV. X. 64. 1. p. iv. 193: मृळतिरुपदयाकर्मेति यास्कः।

७. RV. IV. 57. 2.

८. मृळतिर्दानकर्मा C 4, C 5, C 7, M 3, Mi, R 8, W 1, W 2, W 3.

९. The passage मृळतिरुपदयाकर्मा पूजाकर्मा वा is omitted by Durga.

१०. RV. II. 35. 10.

११. RV. X. 166. 5.

वास्तोष्पतिः । वास्तुर्वसतेर्निवासकर्मणः[1] । तस्य पाता वा पालयिता वा[2] । तस्यैषा भवति ॥ १६ ॥

अमीवहा वास्तोष्पते विश्वा रूपाण्याविशन् ।
सखा सुशेव एधि नः[3] ॥

अभ्यमनहा वास्तोष्पते सर्वाणि रूपाण्याविशन्त्सखा नः सुसुखो भव । शेव इति सुखनाम । शिष्यतेः । वकारो नामकरणः । अन्तस्थान्तरोपलिङ्गी । विभाषितगुणः । शिवमित्यप्यस्य भवति । यद्यद्रूपं कामयते तत्तद्देवता भवति[4] ।

रूपं रूपं मघवा बोभवीति[5] । इत्यपि निगमो भवति ।

वाचस्पतिर्वाचः पाता वा[6] पालयिता वा । तस्यैषा भवति ॥ १७ ॥

पुनरेहि वाचस्पते देवेन मनसा सह ।
वसोष्पते नि रामय मय्येव तन्वं१ मम[7] ॥

इति सा निगदव्याख्याता ।

अपां नपात्तनूनप्त्रा व्याख्यातः[8] । तस्यैषा भवति ॥ १८ ॥

यो अनिध्मो दीदयदप्स्व१न्तर्यं विप्रास ईळते अध्वरेषु ।
अपां नपान्मधुमतीरपो दा याभिरिन्द्रो वावृधे वीर्याय[9] ॥

योऽनिध्मो [दीदयद्[10]] दीप्यते[11]ऽभ्यन्तरमप्सु यं मेधाविनः स्तुवन्ति यज्ञेषु सोऽपांनपान्मधुमतीरपो देह्यभिषवाय । याभिरिन्द्रो वर्धते । वीर्याय वीरकर्मणे ।

यमो यच्छतीति सतः[12] । तस्यैषा भवति ॥ १९ ॥

परेयिवांसं प्रवतो महीरनु बहुभ्यः पन्थामनुपस्पशानम् ।
वैवस्वतं संगमनं जनानां यमं राजानं हविषा दुवस्य[13] ॥

---

१. वास्तु वसतेः C 4, C 5, C 7, M 3, Mi, W 1, W 2, W 3.

२. Cf. BD. ii. 44.

३. RV. VII. 55. 1.

४. Cf. SRV. VII. 56. 1. p. iii. 114: यद्यद्रूपं कामयन्ते तत्तद्देवता विशन्तीति यास्कः ।

५. RV. III. 53. 8.

६. Cf. BD. ii. 45.

७. AV. 1. 1. 2.

८. N. 8. 5.

९. RV. X. 30. 4; AV. 14. 1. 37.

१०. Omitted by BK, C 4, C 5, C 7, Kn, M 3, Mi, R 8, W 1, W 2, W 3.

११. दीप्यते C 1, C 2, C 3, C 6, M 1, M 4, S; Durga & S'ivadatta.

१२. Cf. BD. ii. 48.

१३. RV. X. 14. 1; cf. AV. 18. 1. 49.

परेयिवांसं पर्यागतवन्तम् । प्रवत उद्वतो निवत इति । अवतिर्गतिकर्मा । बहुभ्यः पन्थानमनुपस्पाशयमानम्[१] । वैवस्वतम् । संगमनं जनानाम् । यमं राजानं हविषा दुवस्येति । दुवस्यतिराध्नोतिकर्मा[२] ।

अग्निरपि यम उच्यते । तमेता ऋचोऽनुप्रवदन्ति ॥ २० ॥

सेनेव सृष्टामं दधात्यस्तुर्न दिद्युत्त्वेषप्रतीका[३] ॥

यमो ह जातो यमो जनित्वं जारः कनीनां पतिर्जनीनाम्[४] ॥

तं वश्चराथा वयं वसत्यास्तं न गावो नक्षन्त इद्धम्[५] ॥

इति द्विपदाः । सेनेव सृष्टा भयं वा बलं वा दधाति । अस्तुरिव दिद्युत्त्वेषप्रतीका[६] । भयप्रतीका । [बलप्रतीका यशःप्रतीका[७]][८] महाप्रतीका[९] दीप्तप्रतीका वा ।

यमो ह जात इन्द्रेण सह संगतः ।

यमाविहेह मातरा[१०][११] ॥

इत्यपि निगमो भवति ।

यम इव जातः । यमो जनिष्यमाणः । जारः कनीनाम् । जरयिता कन्यानाम् । पतिर्जनीनाम् । पालयिता जायानाम् । तत्प्रधाना हि यज्ञसंयोगेन भवन्ति ।

तृतीयो अग्निष्टे पतिः[१२] । इत्यपि निगमो भवति[१३] ।

तं वः । चराथा चरन्त्या । पश्वाहुत्या । वसत्या च । निवसन्त्या । औषधाहुत्या । अस्तं यथा गाव आप्नुवन्ति तथाप्नुयाम[१४] । इद्धं समृद्धं भोगैः ।

मित्रः प्रमीतेः[१५] । त्रायते । संमिन्वानो द्रवतीति वा । मेदयतेर्वा[१६] । तस्यैषा भवति ॥ २१ ॥

---

१. पन्थामनुपस्पा० C 4, C 5, C 7, M 3, Mi, W 1, W 2, W 3.

२. दुवस्यती राध्नोतिकर्मा C 1, C 2, C 3, C 6, M 1, M 4, R 2, R 3, R 5, S.

३. RV. I. 66. 7.

४. RV. I. 66. 8.

५. RV. I. 66. 9.

६. Quoted by SRV. I. 66. 8. p. i. 325.

७. यशःप्रतीका is omitted by Roth.

८. बलप्रतीका यशःप्रतीका is omitted by BK, C 4, C 5, C 7, Kn, M 3, Mi, R 8, W 1, W 2, W 3, & Durga.

९. महप्रतीका C 4, C 5, M 3, Mi, W 2, W 3.

१०. The quotation is untraced.

११. RV. VI. 59. 2.

१२. RV. X. 85. 40; AV. 14. 2. 3.

१३. Cf. SRV. I. 66. 8. p. i. 325.

१४. The passage तं वश्चराथा......आप्नुयाम is quoted by SRV. I. 66. 10. p. i. 326.

१५. प्रमीयते: C 4, C 5, C 7, M 3, Mi, W 1, W 3. Cf. SRV. I. 156. 1. p. i. 667.

१६. मेदते: M 3.

मित्रो जनान्यातयति ब्रुवाणो मित्रो दाधार पृथिवीमुत द्याम् ।
मित्रः कृष्टीरनिमिषाभि चष्टे मित्राय हव्यं घृतवज्जुहोत ॥

मित्रो जनानायातयति प्रब्रुवाणः शब्दं कुर्वन् । मित्र एव धारयति पृथिवीं च दिवं च । मित्रः कृष्टीरनिमिषन्नभिविपश्यतीति । कृष्टय इति मनुष्यनाम । कर्मवन्तो भवन्ति । विकृष्टदेहा वा । मित्राय हव्यं घृतवज्जुहोतेति व्याख्यातम् । जुहोतिर्दानकर्मा ।

कः कमनो वा । क्रमणो वा । सुखो वा । तस्यैषा भवति ॥ २२ ॥

हिरण्यगर्भः समवर्तताग्रे भूतस्य जातः पतिरेक आसीत् ।
स दाधार पृथिवीं द्यामुतेमां कस्मै देवाय हविषा विधेम ॥

हिरण्यगर्भो हिरण्यमयो गर्भः । हिरण्यमयो गर्भोऽस्येति वा । गर्भो गृभेः । गृणात्यर्थे । गिरत्यनर्थानिति वा । यदा हि स्त्री गुणान्गृह्णाति गुणाश्चास्या गृह्यन्तेऽथ गर्भो भवति । समभवदग्रे भूतस्य जातः पतिरेको बभूव । स धारयति पृथिवीं च दिवं च । कस्मै देवाय हविषा विधेमेति व्याख्यातम् । विधतिर्दानकर्मा ।

सरस्वान्व्याख्यातः । तस्यैषा भवति ॥ २३ ॥

ये ते सरस्व ऊर्मयो मधुमन्तो घृतश्चुतः ।
तेभिर्नोऽविता भव ॥

इति सा निगदव्याख्याता ॥ २४ ॥

विश्वकर्मा सर्वस्य कर्ता । तस्यैषा भवति ॥ २५ ॥

विश्वकर्मा विमना आद्विहाया धाता विधाता परमोत संदृक् ।
तेषामिष्टानि समिषा मदन्ति यत्रा सप्तऋषीन्पर एकमाहुः ॥

---

१. RV. III. 59. 1.

२. जनान्यातयति SRV. III. 59. 1. p. ii. 328.

३. ब्रुवाणः C 1, C 2, C 3, C 6, M 1, M 4, R 2, R 3, R 5, S.

४. जुहोतिर्दानकर्मा is omitted by Durga. The entire passage मित्रो जनान्......दानकर्मा is quoted by SRV. III. 59. 1. p. ii. 328.

५. Cf. BD. ii. 47.

६. RV. X. 121. 1; AV. 4. 2. 7; VS. 13. 4; 23. 1; 25. 10.

७. N. 2. 23. Cf. BD. ii. 51.

८. सरस्वन् C 1, C 2, C 6, M 1, M 4, S, Durga & S'ivadatta.

९. RV. VII. 96. 5.

१०. Cf. BD. ii. 50.

११. RV. X. 82. 2; VS. 17. 26.

विश्वकर्मा विभूतमना व्याप्ता धाता च । विधाता च । परमश्च संद्रष्टा भूतानाम् । तेषामिष्टानि वा कान्तानि वा क्रान्तानि वा गतानि वा मतानि वा नतानि वा । अद्भिः सह संमोदन्ते यत्रैतानि सप्तऋषीणानि ज्योतींषि । तेभ्यः पर आदित्यः । तान्येतस्मिन्नेकं भवन्तीत्यधिदैवतम् ।

अथाध्यात्मम् । विश्वकर्मा विभूतमना व्याप्ता धाता च । विधाता च । परमश्च संदर्शयितेन्द्रियाणाम् । एषामिष्टानि वा कान्तानि वा क्रान्तानि वा गतानि वा मतानि वा नतानि वा । अन्नेन सह संमोदन्ते यत्रेमानि सप्तऋषीणानीन्द्रियाणि । एभ्यः पर आत्मा । तान्यस्मिन्नेकं भवन्तीत्यात्मगतिमाचष्टे ।

तत्रेतिहासमाचक्षते । विश्वकर्मा भौवनः सर्वमेधे सर्वाणि भूतानि जुहवाञ्चकार । स आत्मानमप्यन्ततो जुहवाञ्चकार । तदभिवादिन्येषर्ग्भवति ।

य इमा विश्वा भुवनानि जुह्वत् । इति ।

तस्योत्तरा भूयसे निर्वचनाय ॥ २६ ॥

विश्वकर्मन्हविषा वावृधानः स्वयं यजस्व पृथिवीमुत द्याम् ।
मुह्यन्त्वन्ये अभितो जनास इहास्माकं मघवा सूरिरस्तु ॥

विश्वकर्मन्हविषा वर्धयमानः स्वयं यजस्व पृथिवीं च दिवं च । मुह्यन्त्वन्ये अभितो जनाः सपत्नाः । इहास्माकं मघवा सूरिरस्तु प्रज्ञाता ।

तार्क्ष्यस्त्वष्ट्रा व्याख्यातः । तीर्णेऽन्तरिक्षे क्षियति । तूर्णमर्थं रक्षति । अश्नोतेर्वा । तस्यैषा भवति ॥ २७ ॥

त्यमू षु वाजिनं देवजूतं सहावानं तरुतारं रथानाम् ।
अरिष्टनेमिं पृतनाजमाशुं स्वस्तये तार्क्ष्यमिहा हुवेम ॥

तं भृशमन्नवन्तम् । जूतिर्गतिः । प्रीतिर्वा । देवजूतं देवगतं देवप्रीतं वा ।

---

१. Cf. SRV. X. 82. 2. p. IV. 247: अत्र विश्वकर्मा विभूतमना व्याप्तेत्यादि निरुक्तमनुसन्धेयम् ।

२. संद्रष्टा C 4, C 5, C 7, M 3, Mi, W 1, W 2, W 3.

३. तान्येतस्मिन् C 1, C 2, C 3, C 6, C 7, M 1, M 4, S.

४. The passage विश्वकर्मा......भवति is quoted by SRV. X. 81. 1. p. IV. 214. Cf. S'B. XIII. 7. 1.

५. RV. X. 81. 1; VS. 17. 17.

६. RV. X. 81. 6; SV. 2. 939; VS. 17. 22.

७. Quoted by SRV. X. 81. 6. p. IV. 246.

८. N. 8. 13.

९. Cf. BD. ii. 58.

१०. RV. X. 178. 1; AV. VII. 85. 1; SV. 1. 332.

११. SRV. X. 178. 1. p. IV. 503: देवगतं is omitted by Sāyaṇa.

सहस्वन्तं तारयितारं रथानामरिष्टनेमिं पृतनाजितम् । आशुं स्वस्तये तार्क्ष्यमिह ह्वयेमेति ।

कमन्यं मध्यमादेवमवक्ष्यत्[1] ।

तस्यैषापरा भवति ॥ २८ ॥

सद्यश्चिद्यः शवसा पञ्च कृष्टीः सूर्य इव ज्योतिषापस्ततान[2] ।
सहस्रसाः शतसा अस्य रंहिर्न स्मा वरन्ते युवतिं न शर्याम् ॥

सद्योऽपि यः शवसा बलेन तनोत्यपः सूर्य इव ज्योतिषा पञ्च मनुष्यजातानि । सहस्रसानिनी शतसानिन्यस्य सा गतिः । न स्मैनां वारयन्ति प्रयुवतीमिव शरमयीमिषुम्[3] ।

मन्युर्मन्यतेः[4] । दीप्तिकर्मणः । क्रोधकर्मणः [वधकर्मणो[5]] वा[6] । मन्यन्त्यस्मादिषवः[7][8] ।

तस्यैषा भवति ॥ २९ ॥

त्वया मन्यो सरथमारुजन्तो हर्षमाणासोऽधृषिता मरुत्वः ।
तिग्मेषव आयुधा संशिशाना अभि प्र यन्तु नरो अग्निरूपाः[9] ॥

त्वया मन्यो सरथमारुह्य रुजन्तो[10] हर्षमाणासोऽधृषिता मरुत्वस्तिग्मेषव आयुधानि संशिश्यमाना अभिप्रयन्तु नरः । अग्निरूपा अग्निकर्माणः । सन्नद्धाः कवचिन इति वा ।

दधिक्रा व्याख्यातः[11] । तस्यैषा भवति ॥ ३० ॥

---

१. अवक्षत् C 4, C 5, C 7, M 3, Mi, W 1, W 3.

२. RV. X. 178. 3.

३. Quoted by SRV. X. 178. 3. p. IV. 504

४. Cf. BD. ii. 53.

५. Omitted by BK, C 4, C 5, C 7, Kn, M 3, Mi, R 8, W 1, W 2, W 3.

६. Quoted by SRV. II. 24. 2; X, 83. 1; 87. 13; pp. ii. 70; IV. 219. 275.

७. मन्युन्त्य० Roth.

८. मन्यन्त्यस्मादिषवः is omitted by Durga.

९. RV. X. 84. 1; AV. 4. 31. 1.

१०. Cf. SRV. X. 84. 1. p. IV. 251.

११. N. 2. 27.

आ द॒धि॒क्राः शव॑सा॒ पञ्च॑ कृ॒ष्टीः सूर्य॑ इ॒व ज्योति॑षा॒पस्त॑तान ।
स॒ह॒स्र॒साः श॑त॒सा वा॒ज्यर्वा॑ पृ॒णक्तु॒ मध्वा॒ समि॒मा वचां॑सि ॥[1]

आतनोति दधिक्राः [शवसा[2]] वलेनापः सूर्य इव ज्योतिषा पञ्च मनुष्यजातानि । सहस्रसाः शतसा । वाजी वेजनवान् । अर्वा ईरणवान् । संपृणक्तु नो मधुनोदकेन वचनानीमानीति । मधु धमतेर्विपरीतस्य ।

सविता सर्वस्य प्रसविता[3] । तस्यैषा भवति ॥ ३१ ॥

स॒वि॒ता य॒न्त्रैः पृ॑थि॒वीम॑रम्णादस्कम्भ॒ने स॑वि॒ता द्याम॑दृंहत् ।
अश्व॑मिवाधुक्ष॒द्धुनि॑म॒न्तरि॑क्षम॒तूर्ते॑ ब॒द्धं स॑वि॒ता स॑मु॒द्रम् ॥[4]

सविता यन्त्रैः पृथिवीमरमयदनारम्भणे[5]ऽन्तरिक्षे । सविता द्यामदृंहत् । अश्वमिवाधुक्षद्धुनिमन्तरिक्षे मेघम् । बद्धमतूर्ते । बद्धमतूर्ण इति वा । अत्वरमाण इति वा । सविता समुदितारमिति[6] ।

कमन्यं मध्यमादेवमवक्ष्यत्[7] । आदित्योऽपि सवितोच्यते[8] । तथा च हैरण्यस्तूपे[9] स्तुतः । अर्चन्हिरण्यस्तूप ऋषिरिदं सूक्तं प्रोवाच । तदभिवादिन्येषर्ग्भवति ॥ ३२ ॥

हिर॑ण्यस्तूपः सवित॒र्यथा॑ त्वाङ्गि॒रसो॑ जु॒ह्वे वाजे॑[10] अ॒स्मिन् ।
ए॒वा त्वार्च॒न्नव॑से॒ वन्द॑मानः॒ सोम॑स्येवां॒शुं प्रति॑ जागरा॒हम् ॥[11]

हिरण्यस्तूपो हिरण्मयः स्तूपः । हिरण्मयः स्तूपोऽस्येति वा । स्तूपः स्त्यायतेः संघातः । सवितर्यथा त्वाङ्गिरसो जुह्वे वाजेऽन्नेऽस्मिन्नेवं त्वार्चन् । अवनाय वन्दमानः सोमस्येवांशुं प्रतिजागर्म्यहम्[12] ।

---

१. RV. IV. 38. 10.

२. Omitted by BK, C 4, C 5, C 7, Kn, M 3, Mi, R 8, W 1, W 2, W 3.

३. Cf. BD. ii. 62.
Cf. S'B. I. 1. 2. 17.
सविता वै देवानां प्रसविता ।

४. RV. X. 149. 1.

५. ०नालम्बने C 4, C 5, C 7, M 3, Mi, W 1, W 2, W 3.

६. Quoted by SRV. X. 149. 1. p. IV. 467.

७. कमन्यमादित्यादेवमवक्ष्यत् W 2; कमन्यमादित्यादेवमवक्षत् C 4, C 5, M 3, Mi, W 1, W 3.

८. Cf KB. VII. 6. असौ वै सविता योऽसौ तपति ।

९. हिरण्यस्तूपे C 4, C 5, M 3, Mi, W 1, W 2, W 3; हि is corrected to है in C 7.

१०. वोजे Roth.

११. RV. X. 149. 5.

१२. Quoted by SRV. X. 150. 5. p. IV. 468.

त्वष्टा व्याख्यातः[1]। तस्यैषा भवति ॥ ३३ ॥

देवस्त्वष्टा सविता विश्वरूपः पुपोष प्रजाः पुरुधा जजान ।
इमा च विश्वा भुवनान्यस्य महद्देवानामसुरत्वमेकम्[2] ॥

देवस्त्वष्टा सविता सर्वरूपः पोषति प्रजा रसानुप्रदानेन। बहुधा चेमा जनयति। इमानि च सर्वाणि भूतान्युदकान्यस्य। महच्चास्मै देवानामसुरत्वमेकम्[3]। प्रज्ञावत्त्वं वा। अनवत्त्वं वा। अपि वासुरिति प्रज्ञानाम। अस्यत्यनर्थान्। अस्ताश्चास्यामर्थाः[4]। असुरत्वमादिलुप्तम्।

वातो वातीति सतः। तस्यैषा भवति ॥ ३४ ॥

वात आ वातु भेषजं शंभु मयोभु नो हृदे ।
प्र ण आयूंषि तारिषत्[5] ॥

वात आवातु भैषज्यानि। शंभु मयोभु च नो हृदयाय। प्रवर्धयतु च[6] न आयुः। अग्निर्व्याख्यातः[7]। तस्यैषा भवति ॥ ३५ ॥

प्रति त्यं चारुमध्वरं गोपीथाय प्र हूयसे ।
मरुद्भिरग्न आ गहि[8] ॥

तं प्रति चारुमध्वरं सोमपानाय प्रहूयसे। सोऽग्ने मरुद्भिः सहागच्छेति[9]। कमन्यं मध्यमादेवमवक्ष्यत्[10]। तस्यैषापरा भवति ॥ ३६ ॥

अभि त्वा पूर्वपीतये सृजामि सोम्यं मधु ।
मरुद्भिरग्न आ गहि[11] ॥

अभिसृजामि त्वा पूर्वपीतये पूर्वपानाय। सोम्यं मधु सोममयम्। सोऽग्ने मरुद्भिः सहागच्छेति ॥ ३७ ॥

वेनो वेनतेः कान्तिकर्मणः[12]। तस्यैषा भवति ॥ ३८ ॥

---

१. N. 8. 13.

२. RV. III. 55. 19; AV. 18. 1. 5.

३. ॰मेकत्वम् C 4, C 5, C 7, M 3, Mi, W 1, W 2, W 3.

४. ॰मनर्थाः C 4, C 5, C 7, M 3, Mi, W 1, W 2, W 3.

५. RV. X. 186. 1; SV. 1. 184; 2. 1190.

६. प्रवर्धय च C 4, C 5, C 7, M 3, Mi, W 1, W 2, W 3.

७. N. 7. 14.

८. RV. I. 19. 1; SV. 1. 16.

९. Quoted by SRV. I. 19. 1. p. i. 107.

१०. अवक्षत् C 4, C 5, C 7, M 3, Mi; W 1, W 2, W 3.
Cf. BD. iii. 76.

११. RV. I. 19. 9; VIII. 3. 7; AV. 20. 99. 1; SV. 1. 256; 2. 923.

१२. Quoted by SRV. IX. 73. 2; 97. 22; X. 64. 2. pp. iii. 717, 782; IV. 193; Cf. BD. ii. 52.

अयं वेनश्चोदयत्पृश्निगर्भा ज्योतिर्जरायू रजसो विमाने।
इममपां संगमे सूर्यस्य शिशुं न विप्रा मतिभी रिहन्ति ॥

अयं वेनश्चोदयत्। पृश्निगर्भाः प्राष्टवर्णगर्भाः। आप इति वा। ज्योतिर्जरायुः। ज्योतिरस्य जरायुस्थानीयं भवति। जरायु जरया गर्भस्य। जरया यूयत इति वा। इममपां च संगमने सूर्यस्य च शिशुमिव विप्रा मतिभी रिहन्ति। लिहन्ति। [स्तुवन्ति।] वर्धयन्ति। पूजयन्तीति वा। शिशुः शंसनीयो भवति। शिशीतेर्वा स्यात् दानकर्मणः। चिरलब्धो गर्भो भवति।

असुनीतिः। असून्नयति[4]। तस्यैषा भवति ॥ ३९ ॥

असुनीते मनो अस्मासु धारय जीवातवे सु प्र तिरा न आयुः।
रारन्धि नः सूर्यस्य संदृशि घृतेन त्वं तन्वं वर्धयस्व[6] ॥

असुनीते मनोऽस्मासु धारय। चिरं जीवनाय। प्रवर्धय च न आयू रन्धय च नः सूर्यस्य संदर्शनाय।

रध्यतिर्वशगमनेऽपि दृश्यते।

मा रधाम द्विषते सोम राजन्[7]। इत्यपि निगमो भवति।

घृतेन त्वमात्मानं तन्वं वर्धयस्व।

ऋतो व्याख्यातः। तस्यैषा भवति ॥ ४० ॥

ऋतस्य हि शुरुधः सन्ति पूर्वीर्ऋतस्य धीतिर्वृजिनानि हन्ति।
ऋतस्य श्लोको बधिरा ततर्द कर्णा बुधानः शुचमान आयोः ॥

ऋतस्य हि शुरुधः सन्ति पूर्वीः। ऋतस्य प्रज्ञा वर्जनीयानि हन्ति। ऋतस्य श्लोको बधिरस्यापि कर्णावातृणत्ति। बधिरो बद्धश्रोत्रः। कर्णौ बोधयन्। दीप्यमानश्च। [आयोः] अयनस्य[12] मनुष्यस्य। ज्योतिषो वोदकस्य वा।

इन्दुरिन्धेः। उनत्तेर्वा। तस्यैषा भवति ॥ ४१ ॥

---

१. RV. X. 123. 1; VS. 7. 16.

२. Omitted by BK, C 4, C 5, C 7, Kn, M 3, Mi, R 8, W 1, W 2, W 3.

३. इति C 4, C 5, C 7. M 3, Mi, W 1, W 2, W 3.

४. Cf. BD. ii. 54.

५. Op. cit. VII. 93.

६. RV. X. 59. 5.

७. RV. X. 128. 5; AV. 5. 3. 7.

८. N. 2. 25; 3. 4; 4. 9; 6. 22.

९. श्लोका Roth.

१०. RV. IV. 23. 8.

११. Omitted by BK, C 4, C 5, C 7, Kn, M 3, Mi, R 8, W 1, W 2, W 3.

१२. अयनश्च W 2.

प्र तद्वोचेयं भव्यायेन्दवे हव्यो न य इषवान्मन्म रेजति रक्षोहा मन्म रेजति ।
स्वयं सो असदा निदो वधैरजेत दुर्मतिम् ।
अव स्रवेदघशंसोऽवतरमव क्षुद्रमिव स्रवेत्[1] ॥

प्रब्रवीमि तद् भव्यायेन्दवे । हवनार्ह इव । य इषवानन्नवान् । कामवान्वा । मननानि च नो रेजयति । रक्षोहा च । बलेन रेजयति । स्वयं सोऽस्मदभिनिन्दितारम् । वधैरजेत दुर्मतिम् । अवस्रवेदघशंसः । ततश्चावतरं क्षुद्रमिवावस्रवेत् । अभ्यासे भूयाँसमर्थं मन्यन्ते । यथा । अहो दर्शनीय । अहो दर्शनीय इति ।

तत्परुच्छेपस्य शीलम् । परुच्छेप ऋषिः । [पर्ववच्छेपः[2] ।] परुषिपरुषि शेपोऽस्येति वा ।

इतीमानि सप्तविंशतिर्देवतानामधेयान्यनुक्रान्तानि । सूक्तभाञ्जि हविर्भाञ्जि[3] । तेषामेतान्यहविर्भाञ्जि । वेनः । असुनीतिः । ऋतः । इन्दुः ।

प्रजापतिः प्रजानां पाता वा पालयिता वा । तस्यैषा भवति ॥ ४२ ॥

प्रजापते न त्वदेतान्यन्यो विश्वा जातानि परि ता बभूव ।
यत्कामास्ते जुहुमस्तन्नो अस्तु वयं स्याम पतयो रयीणाम्[4] ॥

प्रजापते न हि त्वदेतान्यन्यः सर्वाणि जातानि तानि परिबभूव[5] । यत्कामास्ते जुहुमः । तन्नो अस्तु । वयं स्याम पतयो रयीणाम् । इत्याशीः ।

अहिर्व्याख्यातः[6] । तस्यैषा भवति ॥ ४३ ॥

अब्जामुक्थैरहिं[7] गृणीषे बुध्ने नदीनां रजःसु[8] षीदन्[9] ॥

अप्सुजमुक्थैरहिं[10] गृणीषे बुध्ने नदीनां रजस्सु [उदकेषु[11]] सीदन्[12] । बुध्नमन्तरिक्षम् । बद्धा अस्मिन्धृता आप [इति वा][13] । इदमपीतरद् बुध्नमेतस्मादेव । बद्धा अस्मिन्धृताः प्राणा इति ।

---

१. RV. I. 129. 6.
२. Omitted by BK, C 4, C 5, C 7, Kn, M 3, Mi, R 8, W 1, W 2, W 3; added on the margin in C 7; explained by Durga.
३. Cf. BD. i. 17; VIII. 129.
४. RV. X. 121. 10; AV. 7. 80. 3; VS. 10. 20; 23. 65.
५. परि तानि बभूव C 4, C 5, C 7, M 3, Mi, W 1, W 2, W 3.
६. N. 2. 17.
७. ०मुक्कैर० C 7.
८. रजः सुषीदन् M 3, W 2; रजष्सुषीदनु C 7; रजस्सुषीदन् W 3.
९. RV. VII. 34. 16.
१०. अप्सुजामु० C 4, C 5, C 7, M 3, Mi, W 1, W 2, W 3.
११. Omitted by BK, C 4, C 5. C 7, Kn, M 3, Mi, R 8, W 1, W 2, W 3.
१२. षीदन् Roth.
१३. इति वा is omitted by BK, C 4, C 5, C 7, Kn, M 3, Mi, R 8, W 1, W 2, W 3.
Cf. SRV. VII. 34. 16. p. iii. 80: बुध्ने नदीनां रजःसूदकेषु सीदन् बुध्नमन्तरिक्षम् । बद्धा अस्मिन्धृता आप इति !; cf. also VII. 6. 7. p. iii. 19. तथा च यास्कः । बुध्नमन्तरिक्षम् । बद्धा अस्मिन्धृता आप इति वा ।

योऽहिः स बुध्न्यः । बुध्नमन्तरिक्षम् । तन्निवासात् । तस्यैषा भवति ॥ ४४ ॥

मा नोऽहिर्बुध्न्यो रिषे धान्मा यज्ञो अस्य स्रिधदृतायोः ।

मा च नोऽहिर्बुध्न्यो रेषणाय धात् । मास्य यज्ञोखा च स्रिधत् । यज्ञकामस्य ।

सुपर्णो व्याख्यातः । तस्यैषा भवति ॥ ४५ ॥

एकः सुपर्णः स समुद्रमा विवेश स इदं विश्वं भुवनं वि चष्टे ।
तं पाकेन मनसापश्यमन्तितस्तं माता रेळ्हि स उ रेळ्हि मातरम् ॥

एकः सुपर्णः स समुद्रमाविशति । स इमानि सर्वाणि भूतान्यभिविपश्यति । तं पाकेन मनसापश्यमन्तितः । इत्यृषेर्दृष्टार्थस्य प्रीतिर्भवति । आख्यानसंयुक्ता । तं माता रेळ्हि । वागेषा माध्यमिका । स उ मातरं रेळ्हि ।

पुरूरवा बहुधा रोरूयते । तस्यैषा भवति ॥ ४६ ॥

समस्मिञ्जायमान आसत ग्ना उतेमवर्धन्नद्यः स्वगूर्ताः ।
महे यत्त्वा पुरूरवो रणायावर्धयन्दस्युहत्याय देवाः ॥

समासतास्मिञ्जायमाने । ग्ना गमनादापः । देवपत्न्यो वा । अपि चैनमवर्धयन् । नद्यः [स्वगूर्ताः] स्वयंगामिन्यः । महते च यत् त्वा पुरूरवः । रणाय रमणीयाय संग्रामायावर्धयन् दस्युहत्याय च देवा देवाः ॥ ४७ ॥

॥ इति दशमोऽध्यायः ॥

---

१. बुध्नो M 3.

२. Cf. BD. V. 166.

३. RV. VII. 34. 17; cf. V. 41. 16.

४. N. 4. 3; 7. 24.

५. RV. X. 114. 4.

६. रेढि C 1, C 2, C 6, M 4, R 2, R 3, S; Roth & S'ivadatta.

७. Cf. BD. ii. 59.

८. RV. X. 95. 7.

९. Omitted by BK, C 4, C 5, C 7, Kn, M 3, Mi, R 8, W 1, W 2, W 3.

[अथातो मध्यस्थाना वाय[2]वा याह्यासस्त्रो[3]णासो नी[4]चीनबारन्तमू[5]ष्विर्मा[6] रुद्राय या[7] ते दिद्युज्जरा[8]बोधाद[9]र्दरुघ्यो[10] जात एव वि वृ[11]क्षानश्चा[12]पिनद्धमश्मा[13]स्यमवतं क्षेत्रस्य[14] पतिः क्षेत्रस्य[15] पतिना क्षेत्रस्य[16]पतेऽमीव[17]हा पुन[18]रेहि यो [19]अनिध्मः परेयि[20]वांसं सेनेव[21] सृष्टा मित्रो[22] जनान्हिरण्य[23]गर्भो ये[24] ते सरस्व विश्व[25]कर्मा सर्वस्य विश्व[26]कर्मा विमना विश्व[27]कर्मन्हविषा त्य[28]मू षु से[29]द्यश्चिद्यस्त्व[30]या मन्यवा द[31]धिक्राः सवि[32]ता यन्त्रैर्हि[33]रण्यस्तूपो दे[34]वस्त्वष्टा वा[35]त आ वातु प्र[36]ति त्यमभि[37] त्वा वे[38]नो वेनतेरयं वे[39]नोऽसु[40]नीत ऋतस्य[41] हि प्र त[42]द्वोचेयं प्रजा[43]पतेऽब्जा[44]मुक्थैर्मा [45]नोऽहिरे[46]कः सुपर्णः स[47]मस्मिन्सप्तचत्वारिंशत् ॥]

॥ इत्युत्तरषट्के चतुर्थोऽध्यायः ॥

॥ इति निरुक्ते दशमोऽध्यायः समाप्तः ॥

Small figure on this page represents the corresponding section of the tenth chapter of the *Nirukta*.

अथैकादशोऽध्यायः।

श्येनो व्याख्यातः। तस्यैषा भवति ॥ १ ॥

आदाय श्येनो अभरत्सोमं सहस्रं सवाँ अयुतं च साकम्।
अत्रा पुरंन्धिरजहादरांतीर्मदे सोमस्य मूरा अमूरः ॥

आदाय श्येनोऽहरत्सोमम्। सहस्रं सवान्। अयुतं च सह। सहस्रं सहस्रसाव्यमभिप्रेत्य। तत्रायुतं सोमभक्षाः। तत्संबन्धेनायुतं दक्षिणा इति वा। तत्र पुरन्धिरजहादमित्रानदानानिति वा। मदे सोमस्य मूरा अमूरः [इति]। ऐन्द्रे च सूक्ते सोमपानेन च स्तुतः। तस्मादिन्द्रं मन्यन्ते।

ओषधिः सोमः सुनोतेः। यदेनमभिषुण्वन्ति। बहुलमस्य नैघण्टुकं वृत्तम्। आश्चर्यमिव प्राधान्येन।

तस्य पावमानीषु निदर्शनायोदाहरिष्यामः॥ २॥

स्वादिष्ठया मदिष्ठया पवस्व सोम धारया।
इन्द्राय पातवे सुतः ॥

इति सा निगदव्याख्याता।

अथैषापरा भवति। चन्द्रमसो वा। एतस्य वा ॥ ३ ॥

सोमं मन्यते पपिवान्यत्संपिंषन्त्योषधिम्।
सोमं यं ब्रह्माणो विदुर्न तस्याश्नाति कश्चन ॥

सोमं मन्यते पपिवान्यत्संपिंषन्त्योषधिमिति वृथासुतमसोममाह। सोमं यं ब्रह्माणो विदुरिति। न तस्याश्नाति कश्चनायज्वेत्यधियज्ञम्।

---

१. N. 4. 24.

२. RV. IV. 26. 7. अमूर: Roth.

३. सहस्रं W 2.

४. ०भक्ष्या: M 3.

५. ०मित्रान्नदाना० M 3, W 2.

६. Omitted by BK, C 4, C 5, C 7, Kn, M 3, Mi, R 8, W 1, W 2, W 3.

७. Omitted by C 2.

८. RV. IX. 1. 1; SV. 1. 468; 2. 39; VS. 26. 25.

९. RV. X. 85. 3; AV. 14. 1. 3.

अथाधिदैवतम् । सोमं मन्यते पपिवान्यत्संपिंषन्त्योषधिमिति यजुःसुतमसोममाह । सोमं यं ब्रह्माणो विदुश्चन्द्रमसम् । न तस्याश्नाति कश्चनादेव इति ।

अथैषापरा भवति । चन्द्रमसो वा । एतस्य वा ॥ ४ ॥

यत्त्वा देव प्र पिबन्ति तत आ प्यायसे पुनः ।
वायुः सोमस्य रक्षिता समानां मास आकृतिः[1] ॥

यत् त्वा देव प्रपिबन्ति तत आप्यायसे पुनरिति नाराशंसानभिप्रेत्य । पूर्वपक्षापरपक्षाविति वा । वायुः सोमस्य रक्षिता । वायुमस्य रक्षितारमाह । साहचर्यात् । रसहरणाद्वा[2] । समानां संवत्सराणां मास आकृतिः सोमः । रूपविशेषैरोषधिः । चन्द्रमा वा ।

चन्द्रमाश्चायन्[3]द्रमति । चन्द्रो माता । चान्द्रं मानमस्येति वा[4] । चन्द्र[5]श्चन्दतेः । कान्तिकर्मणः[6] । चन्दनमित्यप्यस्य भवति । चारु[7] द्रमति[8] । चिरं द्रमति । चमेर्वा पूर्वम्[9] । चारु रुचेर्विपरीतस्य ।

तस्यैषा भवति ॥ ५ ॥

नवोनवो भवति जायमानोऽह्नां केतुरुषसामेत्यग्रम् ।
भागं देवेभ्यो वि दधात्यायन्प्र चन्द्रमास्तिरते दीर्घमायुः[10] ॥

नवोनवो भवति जायमानः । इति पूर्वपक्षादिमभिप्रेत्य । अह्नां केतुरुषसामेत्यग्रम् । इत्यपरपक्षान्तमभिप्रेत्य । आदित्यदैवतो द्वितीयः पाद इत्येके । भागं देवेभ्यो विदधात्यायन् । इत्यर्धमासेज्यामभिप्रेत्य । प्रवर्धयते चन्द्रमा दीर्घमायुः ।

मृत्युर्मारयतीति सतः । मृतं च्यावयतीति[11] [वा[12]] शतबलाक्षो मौद्गल्यः । तस्यैषा भवति ॥ ६ ॥

परं मृत्यो अनु परेहि पन्थां यस्ते स्व इतरो देवयानात् ।
चक्षुष्मते शृण्वते ते ब्रवीमि मा नः प्रजां रीरिषो मोत वीरान्[13] ॥

---

१. RV. X. 85. 5; cf. AV. 14. 1. 14.

२. Cf. BD. VII. 144.

३. चान्द्रमिति M 3; चान्द्रमति W 2; चायन्द्रवति C 4, C, 5 C 7, Mi, W 1, W 3.

४. Cf. BD. VII. 129 B.

५. चन्द्रं चन्दतेः C 4, C 5, C 7, M 3, Mi, W 1, W 2, W 3.

६. Quoted by SRV. VI. 65. 2. p. ii. 86.

७. वारु M 3.

८. द्रवति C 4, C 5, C 7, M 3, Mi, W 1, W 3; द्रवति is corrected to द्रमति on the margin in M 3.

९. Cf. BD. VII. 129 (B).

१०. RV. X. 85. 19; cf. AV. 7. 81. 2.

११. Cf. BD. ii. 60.

१२. Omitted by BK, C 4, C 5, C 7, Kn, M 3, Mi, R 8, W 1, W 2, W 3.

१३. RV. X. 18. 1; AV. 12. 2. 21; VS. 35. 7.

परं मृत्यो । ध्रुवं मृत्यो । ध्रुवं परेहि मृत्यो । कथितं तेन मृत्यो । मृतं च्यावयते भवति मृत्यो । मदेर्वा मुदेर्वा । तेषामेषा भवति ॥ ७ ॥

त्वेषमित्था समरणं शिमीवतोरिन्द्राविष्णू सुतपा वामुरुष्यति[1] ।
या मर्त्याय प्रतिधीयमानमित्कृशानोरस्तुरसनामुरुष्यथः[2] ॥[3]

इति सा निगदव्याख्याता ।

विश्वानरो व्याख्यातः[4] । तस्यैषा भवति ॥ ८ ॥

प्र वो महे मन्दमानायान्धसोऽर्चा विश्वानराय विश्वाभुवे ।
इन्द्रस्य यस्य सुमखं सहो महि श्रवो नृम्णं च रोदसी सपर्यतः ॥[5]

प्रार्चत [यूयं][6] स्तुतिं महतेऽन्धसोऽन्नस्य दात्रे । मन्दमानाय मोदमानाय स्तूयमानाय[7] शब्दायमानायेति वा । विश्वानराय सर्वं विभूताय । इन्द्रस्य यस्य प्रीतौ सुमहद्बलम् । महच्च श्रवणीयं यशः । नृम्णं च बलं नृन्नतम्[8] । द्यावापृथिव्यौ वः परिचरत इति ।

कमन्यं मध्यमादेवमवक्ष्यत्[9] ।

तस्यैषापरा भवति ॥ ९ ॥

उदु ज्योतिरमृतं विश्वजन्यं विश्वानरः सविता देवो अश्रेत् ॥[10]

उदशिश्रियत्[11] । ज्योतिः । अमृतम् । सर्वजन्यम् । विश्वानरः सविता देव इति ।

धाता सर्वस्य विधाता[12] । तस्यैषा भवति ॥ १० ॥

१. वामरुष्यति M 3.

२. प्रतिधायमान° C 2.

३. RV. I. 155. 2. The text परं मृत्यो... रसनामुरुष्यथ! is regarded as spurious by Roth. It is given however by MSS. of both the recensions but is ignored by the commentator Durga.

४. N. 7. 21.

५. RV. X. 50. 1; VS. 33. 23.

६. Omitted by BK, C 4, C 5, C 7, Kn, M 3, Mi, R 8, W 1, W 2, W 3.

७. मोदमानाय स्तूयमानाय is omitted by Durga.

८. नन्नतं S'ivadatta.

९. °प्रवक्षत् M 3.

१०. RV. VII. 76. 1.

११. उदशिश्रयत् C 4, C 5, M 3, Mi, W 1, W 2, W 3.

१२. Cf. BD. ii. 57.

धा॒ता द॑दातु दा॒शुषे॒ प्राचीं॑ जी॒वातु॒मक्षि॑ताम्[1] ।
व॒यं दे॒वस्य॑ धीमहि सु॒म॒तिं स॒त्यध॑र्मणः[2] ॥

धाता ददातु दत्तवते प्रवृद्धां जीविकौमनुपक्षीणाम्[3]। वयं देवस्य धीमहि सुमतिं कल्याणीं मतिं[4] सत्यधर्मणः ।

विधाता धात्रा व्याख्यातः। तस्यैष निपातो भवति बहुदेवतायामृचि[5] ॥ ११ ॥

सोम॑स्य॒ राज्ञो॒ वरु॑णस्य॒ धर्म॑णि॒ बृह॒स्पते॒रनु॑मत्या[6] उ॒ शर्म॑णि ।
तवा॒हम॒द्य म॑घव॒न्नुप॑स्तुतौ॒ धात॒र्विधा॑तः क॒लशाँ॑ अभक्षयम्[7] ॥

इत्येताभिर्देवताभिरभिप्रसूतः सोमकलशानभक्षयमिति । कलशः [कस्मात्[8]]। कला अस्मिञ्छेरते मात्राः । कलिश्च कलाश्च किरतेः । विकीर्णमात्राः ॥ १२ ॥

अथातो मध्यस्थाना देवगणाः । तेषां मरुतः प्रथमागामिनो भवन्ति । मरुतो मितराविणो[9] वा । मितरोचिनो[10] वा । महद्[11] द्रवन्तीति वा । तेषामेषा[12] भवति ॥ १३ ॥

आ वि॒द्युन्म॑द्भिर्मरुतः स्व॒र्कै रथे॑भिर्यात ऋष्टि॒मद्भि॒रश्व॑पर्णैः ।
आ वर्षि॑ष्ठया न इ॒षा वयो॒ न प॑प्तता सुमायाः[13] ॥

विद्युन्मद्भिर्मरुतः। स्वर्कैः स्वञ्चनैरिति वा। स्वर्चनैरिति वा। स्वर्चिभिरिति वा । रथैरायात। ऋष्टिमद्भिः । अश्वपर्णैरश्वपतनैः । वर्षिष्ठेन च नोऽन्नेन वय इवापतत। सुमायाः कल्याणकर्माणो वा। कल्याणप्रज्ञा वा[14]।

रुद्रा व्याख्याताः[15]। तेषामेषा भवति ॥ १४ ॥

---

१. ०मक्षितिम् C 4, C 5, C 7, M 3, Mi, W 1, W 2, W 3.

२. Cf. AV. 7. 17. 2:

धा॒ता द॑धातु दा॒शुषे॒ प्राचीं॑ जी॒वातु॑मक्षि॑ताम् ।

व॒यं दे॒वस्य॑ धीमहि सु॒म॒तिं वि॒श्वरा॑धसः ॥

३. जीविताम० C 4, C 5, M 3, Mi, W 1, W 3.

४. मतिं सुमतिं सत्यधर्मणः C 4, C 5, C 7, M 3, Mi, W 1, W 2, W 3.

५. बहुदेवतामृचि C 4, C 5, M 3, Mi, W 1, W 3.

६. अनुमत्या is omitted by W 2.

७. RV. X. 167. 3. अभक्षम् C 4, C 5, C 7, Mi, W 1, W 2, W 3; अक्षभक्षं यं M 3.

८. Omitted by BK, C 4, C 5, C 7, Kn, M 3, Mi, R 8, W 1, W 2, W 3.

९. अमितराविणो is given as a variant by Durga.

१०. अमितरोचिनः is given as a variant by Durga.

११. महद्द्रवन्तीति वा Roth.

१२. तेषामेषामेषा C 4, C 5.

१३. RV. I. 88. 1.

१४. Quoted by SRV. I. 88. 1. p. i. 392.

१५. N. 10. 5.

आ रुद्रास इन्द्रवन्तः सजोषसो हिरण्यरथाः सुविताय गन्तन ।
इयं वो अस्मत्प्रति हर्यते मतिस्तृष्णजे न दिव उत्सा उदन्यवे[१] ॥

आगच्छत रुद्रा इन्द्रेण । सहजोषणाः । सुविताय कर्मणे । इयं वोऽस्मदपि प्रतिकामयते मतिः । तृष्णज इव दिव उत्सा उदन्यवे । तृष्णक् तृष्यतेः[२] । उदन्युरुदन्यतेः[३] ।

ऋभव उरु भान्तीति वा । ऋतेन भान्तीति वा । ऋतेन भवन्तीति वा[४] । तेषामेषा भवति ॥ १५ ॥

विष्ट्वी शमी तरणित्वेन वाघतो मर्तासः सन्तो अमृतत्वमानशुः ।
सौधन्वना ऋभवः सूरचक्षसः संवत्सरे समपृच्यन्त धीतिभिः[५] ॥

कृत्वा कर्माणि क्षिप्रत्वेन । वोळ्हारो[६] मेधाविनो वा[७] । मर्तासः सन्तोऽमृतत्वमानशिरे । सौधन्वना ऋभवः सूरख्याना वा । सूरप्रज्ञा वा । संवत्सरे समपृच्यन्त [धीतिभिः[८]] कर्मभिः ।

ऋभुर्विभ्वा वाज इति सुधन्वन आङ्गिरसस्य त्रयः पुत्रा बभूवुः[९] । तेषां प्रथमोत्तमाभ्यां बहुवन्निगमा भवन्ति न मध्यमेन[१०] । तदेतदृभोश्च बहुवचनेन चमसस्य च संस्तवेन बहूनि दशतयीषु सूक्तानि भवन्ति ।

आदित्यरश्मयोऽप्यृभव उच्यन्ते[११] ।

अगोह्यस्य यदसस्तना गृहे तदद्येदमृभवो नानु गच्छथ[१२] ।

अगोह्य आदित्योऽगूहनीयः । तस्य यदस्वपथ गृहे । यावत्तत्र भवथ न तावदिह भवथेति ।

अङ्गिरसो व्याख्याताः[१३] । तेषामेषा भवति ॥ १६ ॥

विरूपास इदृषयस्त इद्गम्भीरवेपसः ।
ते अङ्गिरसः सूनवस्ते अग्नेः परि जज्ञिरे[१४] ॥

---

१. RV. V. 57. 1.

२. तृप्यते C 1.

३. तृष्णक् तृष्यतेः । उदन्युरुदन्यतेः । is omitted by Durga.

४. Quoted by SRV. I. 20. 4. p. i. 110.

५. RV. I. 110. 4.

६. वोढारो C 1, C 2, C 3, C 6, M 4, S; Roth & S'ivadatta.

७. Quoted by SRV. III. 60. 4. p. ii. 332.

८. Omitted by BK, C 4, C 5, Kn, M 3, Mi, R 8, W 1, W 2, W 3.

९. Cf. BD. iii. 83; cf. SRV. I. 110. 2, 4. pp. i. 480-1.

१०. Cf. BD. iii. 89 B; cf. SRV. I. 111. 4. p. i. 485.

११. Quoted by SRV. I. 161. 11. p. i. 682.

१२. RV. I. 161. 11.

१३. N. 3. 17.

१४. RV. X. 62. 5.

बहुरूपा ऋषयः । ते गम्भीरकर्माणो वा । गम्भीरप्रज्ञा वा । तेऽङ्गिरसः पुत्राः । तेऽग्नेरधिजज्ञिरे । इत्यग्निजन्म ।

पितरो व्याख्याताः[१] । तेषामेषा भवति ॥ १७ ॥

उदीरतामवर उत्परास उन्मध्यमाः पितरः सोम्यासः ।
असुं य ईयुरवृका ऋतज्ञास्ते नोऽवन्तु पितरो हवेषु[२] ॥

उदीरतामवरे । उदीरतां परे । उदीरतां मध्यमाः पितरः । सोम्याः सोमसंपादिनस्[३]तेऽसुं ये प्राणमन्वीयुः[४] । अवृका अनमित्राः । सत्यज्ञा वा यज्ञज्ञा वा । ते न आगच्छन्तु पितरो ह्वानेषु ।

माध्य[५]मिको यम इत्याहुः[६] । तस्मान्माध्यमिकान्पितॄन्मन्यन्ते ।

अङ्गिरसो व्याख्याताः[७] । पितरो व्याख्याताः[८] । भृगवो व्याख्याताः[९] । अथर्वाणोऽथनवन्तः । थर्वतिश्चरतिकर्मा । तत्प्रतिषेधः । तेषामेषा साधारणा भवति ॥१८॥

अङ्गिरसो नः पितरो नवग्वा अथर्वाणो भृगवः सोम्यासः ।
तेषां वयं सुमतौ यज्ञियानामपि भद्रे सौमनसे[१०] स्याम[११] ॥

अङ्गिरसो नः पितरः । नवगतयो नवनीत[१२]गतयो वा । अथर्वाणो भृगवः । सोम्याः सोमसम्पादिनः । तेषां वयम् । [१३]सुमतौ कल्याण्यां मतौ । यज्ञियानामपि चैषाम् । भद्रे भन्दनीये । भाजनवति वा । कल्याणे मनसि । स्यामेति ।

माध्यमि[१४]को देवगण इति नैरुक्ताः । पितर इत्याख्यानम् ।

अथाप्यृषयः स्तूयन्ते ॥ १९ ॥

सूर्यस्येव वक्षथो ज्योतिरेषां समुद्रस्येव महिमा गभीरः ।
वातस्येव प्रजवो नान्येन स्तोमो वसिष्ठा अन्वेतवे [१५]वः ॥

---

१. N. 4. 21.

२. RV. X. 15. 1; AV. 18. 1. 44; VS. 19. 49.

३. Quoted by SRV. VI. 75. 10. p. ii. 890.

४. प्राणमुन्नीयुः C 4, C 5, C 7, M 3, Mi, W 1, W 2, W 3.

५. माध्यमको C 4, C 5, C 7, M 3, Mi, W 1, W 2, W 3.

६. Cf. BD. VI. 155:
अत्र स्तूयते मध्यमो यमः ।

७. N. 3. 17.

८. N. 4. 21.

९. N. 3. 17.

१०. सौमनसे Roth.

११. RV. X. 14. 6; AV. 18. 1. 58.

१२. Quoted by SRV. I. 62. 4. p. i. 306.

१३. सुमतौ is placed between मतौ and यज्ञियानाम् C 4, C 5, C 7, M 3, Mi, W 1, W 2, W 3.

१४. माध्यमको C 4, C 5, C 7, M 3, Mi, W 1, W 2, W 3.

१५. RV. VII. 33. 8.

इति यथा ।

आप्त्या आप्नोतेः । तेषामेष निपातो भवत्यैन्द्र्यामृचि ॥ २० ॥

स्तुषेय्यं पुरुवर्पसमृभ्वमिनतममाप्त्यमाप्त्यानाम् ।
आ दर्षते शवसा सप्त दानून्प्र साक्षते प्रतिमानानि भूरि[1] ॥

स्तोतव्यम् । बहुरूपम् । उरुभूतम् । ईश्वरतमम् । आप्तव्यम् । आप्तव्यानाम् । आदृणाति । यः । शवसा बलेन । सप्तदातॄनिति वा । सप्तदानवानिति वा । प्रसाक्षते । प्रतिमानानि । बहूनि । साक्षतिराप्नोतिकर्मा[2] ॥ २१ ॥

अथातो मध्यस्थानाः स्त्रियः । तासामदितिः प्रथमागामिनी भवति । अदितिर्व्याख्याता[3] । तस्या एषा भवति ॥ २२ ॥

दक्षस्य वादिते जन्मनि व्रते राजाना मित्रावरुणा विवाससि ।
अतूर्तपन्थाः पुरुरथो[4] अर्यमा सप्तहोता विषुरूपेषु जन्मसु[5] ॥

दक्षस्य वादिते जन्मनि । व्रते कर्मणि[6] । राजानौ[7] । मित्रावरुणौ । परिचरसि । विवासतिः परिचर्यायाम् ।

हविष्माँ[8] आविवासति[9] ।

इत्याशास्तेर्वा । अतूर्तपन्था अत्वरमाणपन्थाः । बहुरथः[10] । अर्यमादित्यः । अरीन्नियच्छति । सप्तहोता । सप्तास्मै रश्मयो रसानभिसन्नामयन्ति । सप्तैनमृषयः स्तुवन्तीति वा । विषमरूपेषु जन्मसु । कर्मसूदयेषु ।

आदित्यो दक्षः[11] । इत्याहुः । आदित्यमध्ये च स्तुतः । अदितिर्दाक्षायणी ।

अदितेर्दक्षो अजायत दक्षाद्वदितिः परि[12] । इति च ।

---

१. RV. X. 120. 6; AV. 20. 107. 9.

२. Quoted by SRV. X. 120. 8. p. IV. 399.

३. N. 4. 22, 23.

४. तुरुरथो C 7.

५. RV. X. 64. 5.

६. कर्मणि व्रते C 4, C 5, C 7, M 3, Mi, W 1, W 2, W 3. & SRV. X. 64. 5. p. IV. 194.

७. Quoted SRV. loc. cit.

८. हविष्मानाविवासति C 1, C 2, C 3, C 6, M 1, M 4, S; Roth.

९. RV. I. 12. 9; SV. 2. 196; VS. 6. 23.

१०. लघुरथः C 2.

११. The quotation is untraced. Durga attributes it to the *devatā-statvavidaḥ* *i. e.* persons who know the reality of deity.

१२. RV. X. 72. 4.

तत्कथमुपपद्यते । समानजन्मानौ स्यातामिति । अपि वा देवधर्मेणेतरेतरजन्मानौ स्याताम् । इतरेतरप्रकृती[1] ।

अग्निरप्यदितिरुच्यते[2] । तस्यैषा भवति ॥ २३ ॥

यस्मै त्वं सुद्रविणो ददाशो[4]ऽनागास्त्वमदिते सर्वताता ।
यं भद्रेण शवसा चोदयासि प्रजावता राधसा ते स्याम[3] ॥

यस्मै त्वं सुद्रविणो ददासि । अनागास्त्वम् । अनपराधत्वम्[5] । अदिते । सर्वासु कर्मततिषु । आग आङ्पूर्वाद्गमेः । एन एतेः । किल्बिषं किल्भिदम् । सुकृतकर्मणो भयम्[6] । कीर्तिमस्य भिनत्तीति वा । यं भद्रेण । शवसा बलेन । चोदयसि । प्रजावता च राधसा [धनेन[7]] ते वयमिह स्यामेति ।

सरमा सरणात्[8] । तस्या एषा भवति ॥ २४ ॥

किमिच्छन्ती सरमा प्रेदमानड् दूरे ह्यध्वा जगुरिः पराचैः ।
कास्मेहितिः का परितक्म्यासीत्कथं रसाया अतरः पयांसि[9] ॥

किमिच्छन्ती सरमेदं प्रानट्[10] । दूरे ह्यध्वा ! जगुरिर्जङ्गम्यतेः । पराञ्चनैः[11] अञ्चितः । का तेऽस्मास्वर्थहितिरासीत् । किं परितकनम् । परितक्म्या रात्रिः[12] । परित एनां तक्म । तक्मेत्युष्णनाम । तकत इति सतः । कथं रसाया अतरः पयांसीति । रसा नदी रसतेः शब्दकर्मणः[13] । कथं रसानि तान्युदकानीति वा ।

देवशुनीन्द्रेण[14] प्रहिता पणिभिरसुरैः समूदे । इत्याख्यानम् ।

सरस्वती व्याख्याता । तस्या एषा भवति ॥ २५ ॥

---

१. Quoted by SRV. X. 72. 4. p. IV. 225.

२. Cf. BD. IV. 18.

३. RV. I. 94. 15.

४. ददाशो C 4, C 5, C 7, M 3, Mi, W 1, W 2, W 3.

५. अनपराधित्वम् C 4, C 5, C 7, M 3, Mi, W 1, W 2, W 3.

६. सुकृतकर्मणो भयम् is omitted by Durga.

७. Omitted by BK, C 4, C 5, C 7, Kn, M 3, Mi, R 8, W 1, W 2, W 3.

८. Cf. Quoted by SRV. I. 62. 3. p. i. 305.

९. RV. X. 108. 1.

१०. प्रापद् C 4, C 5, C 7, M 3, Mi, W 1, W 2, W 3; SRV. X. 108. 1. p. IV. 361.

११. Quoted by SRV. I. 63. 4. p. i. 312.

१२. Quoted by SRV. I. 116. 15. p. i. 519.

१३. Quoted by SRV. I. 112. 12. p. i. 490; cf. also. V. 53. 9. p. ii. 618.

१४. Durga adds the following:

वाग्वै सरमेति हि विज्ञायते ।

पा॒व॒का न॒: सर॑स्वती॒ वाजे॑भिर्वा॒जिनी॑वती ।
य॒ज्ञं व॑ष्टु धि॒यावसुः[1] ॥

पावका नः सरस्वती । अन्नैरन्नवती । यज्ञं वष्टु धियावसुः कर्मवसुः[2] ।

तस्या एषापरा भवति ॥ २८ ॥

म॒हो अर्ण॒: सर॑स्वती॒ प्र चे॑तयति के॒तुना॑ ।
धियो॒ विश्वा॒ वि रा॑जति[3] ॥

महदर्णः सरस्वती प्रचेतयति प्रज्ञापयति केतुना कर्मणा प्रज्ञया वा । इमानि च सर्वाणि प्रज्ञानान्य[4]भिविराजंति । वागर्थेषु[5] विधीयते । तस्मान्माध्यमिकां वाचं मन्यन्ते । वाग्व्याख्याता[6] । तस्या एषा भवति ॥ २७ ॥

यद्वाग्वद॑न्त्यविचेत॒नानि॒ राष्ट्री॑ दे॒वानां॑ निष॒साद॑ म॒न्द्रा ।
चत॑स्र॒ ऊर्जं॑ दुदुहे॒ पयां॑सि॒ क्व॑ स्विदस्याः पर॒मं ज॑गाम[7] ॥

यद्वाग्वदन्ति । अविचेतनान्यविज्ञातानि । राष्ट्री देवानां निषसाद [मन्द्रा[8]] मदना । चतस्रोऽनुदिश ऊर्जं दुदुहे पयांसि । क्व स्विदस्याः परमं जगामेति । यत्पृथिवीं गच्छतीति वा । यदादित्यरश्मयो हरन्तीति वा[9] ।

तस्या एषापरा भवति ॥ २८ ॥

दे॒वीं वाच॑मजनयन्त दे॒वास्तां वि॒श्वरू॑पाः प॒शवो॑ वदन्ति ।
सा नो॑ म॒न्द्रेष॒मूर्जं॒ दुहा॑ना धे॒नुर्वाग॒स्मानुप॒ सुष्टु॒तैतु[10] ॥

देवीं वाचमजनयन्त देवाः । तां सर्वरूपाः[11] पशवो वदन्ति । व्यक्तवाचश्चाव्यक्तवाचश्च । सा नो मदनान्नं[12] च रसं च दुहाना धेनुर्वागस्मानुपैतु सुष्टुता[13] ।

१. RV. I. 3. 10; SV. 1. 189; VS. 20. 84.

२. Quoted by SRV. I. 3. 10. p. i. 39.

३. RV. I. 3. 12; VS. 20 86.

४. भूतान्यभि० C 4, C 5, C 7, M 3, Mi, W 1, W 2, W 3.

५. Quoted by SRV. I. 3. 12. p. i. 40.

६. N. 2. 23.

७. RV. VIII. 100. 10.

८. Omitted by BK, C 1, C 5, C 7, Ku, M 3, Mi, R 8, W 1, W 2, W 3.

९. Quoted by SRV. VIII. 100. 10. p. iii. 589.

१०. RV. VIII. 100. 11.

११. विश्वरूपा: SRV. VIII. 100. 11. p. iii. 590.

१२. मननान्नं C 4, C 5, C 7, M 3, Mi, W 1, W 3.

१३. Quoted by SRV. loc. cit.

अनुमति[1] राकेति देवपत्न्याविति नैरुक्ताः। पौर्णमास्याविति याज्ञिकाः।

या पूर्वा पौर्णमासी सानुमतिः। योत्तरा सा राका[2]। इति विज्ञायते।

अनुमतिरनुमननात्। तस्या एषा भवति ॥ २९ ॥

अन्विदनुमते त्वं मन्यासै शं च नस्कृधि ।
क्रत्वे दक्षाय नो हिनु[3] प्र ण आयूंषि तारिषः[4] ॥

अनुमन्यस्वानुमते। त्वं सुखं च नः कुरु। अन्नं च नोऽपत्याय धेहि। प्रवर्धय च न आयुः[5]।

राका रातेर्दानकर्मणः। तस्या एषा भवति ॥ ३० ॥

राकामहं[6] सुहवां सुष्टुती हुवे शृणोतु नः सुभगा बोधतु त्मना ।
सीव्यत्वपः सूच्याच्छिद्यमानया ददातु वीरं शतदायमुक्थ्यम्[7] ॥

राकामहं सुह्वानां सुष्टुत्या ह्वये। शृणोतु नः सुभगा। बोधत्वात्मना। सीव्यत्वपः प्रजननकर्म। सूच्याच्छिद्यमानया। सूची सीव्यतेः। ददातु वीरम्। शतप्रदम्। उक्थ्यं वक्तव्यप्रशंसम्।

सिनीवाली कुहूरिति देवपत्न्याविति नैरुक्ताः। अमावास्ये इति याज्ञिकाः।

या पूर्वामावास्या सा सिनीवाली। योत्तरा सा कुहूः[8]। इति विज्ञायते।

सिनीवाली सिनमन्नं भवति। सिनाति भूतानि। वालं पर्व वृणोतेः। तस्मिन्नन्नवती। वालिनी वा। वालेनेवास्या[9]मणुत्वाच्चन्द्रमाः सेवितव्यो[10] भवतीति वा।

तस्या एषा भवति ॥ ३१ ॥

सिनीवालि पृथुष्टुके या देवानामसि स्वसा ।
जुषस्व हव्यमाहुतं प्रजां देवि दिदिड्ढि नः[11] ॥

---

१. अनुमती Roth & S'ivadatta.

२. AB. VII. 11. 2; GB. II. 1. 10; Ṣaḍ. B. IV. 6; cf. KB. III. 1. KS. XII. 8: या पूर्वा पौर्णमासी सानुमतिर्योत्तरा सा राका। Schroeder's ed. vol. i. p. 170.

३. Durga reads: इषं च तोकाय नो हिनु

४. VS. 34. 8; cf. AV. 7. 20. 2:

अन्विदनुमते त्वं मंससे शं च नस्कृधि ।
जुषस्व हव्यमाहुतं प्रजां देवि ररास्व नः॥

५. आयूः C 4, C 5, C 7, M 3, Mi, W1, W 2, W 3.

६. शाकामहं C 7.

७. RV. II. 32. 4; AV. 7. 48. 1.

८. AB. VII. 11. 3; GB. II. 1. 10; Ṣaḍ. B. IV. 6; cf. KB. III. 1. KS. XII. 8: या पूर्वामावस्या सा सिनीवाली योत्तरा सा कुहूः। Schroeder's ed. vol. i. p. 170.

९. वालेनैव० Roth.

१०. सेतव्यो C 4, C 5, C 7, M 3, Mi, W 1, W 2, W 3.

११. RV. II. 32. 6, AV. 7. 46. 1; VS. 34. 10.

सिनीवालि । पृथुजघने । स्तुकः[1] स्त्यायतेः संघातः । पृथुकेशस्तुके । पृथुष्टुते वा[2] । या त्वं देवानामसि स्वसा । स्वसा सु असा । स्वेषु सीदतीति वा[3] । जुषस्व हव्यमदनम्[4] । प्रजां च देवि दिशं[5] नः ।

कुहूर्गूहतेः । क्वाभूदिति वा । क्व सती हूयत इति वा । क्वाहुतं हविर्जुहोतीति वा[6] ।

तस्या एषा भवति ॥ ३२ ॥

कु॒हूम॒हं सु[7]कृतं॑ विद्म॒नाप॑सम॒स्मिन्य॒ज्ञे सु॒हवां॒ जोह॑वीमि ।
सा नो॑ ददा॒तु श्रव॑णं पि॒तॄणां॑ तस्यै॑ ते देवि ह॒विषा॑ विधेम[8] ॥

कुहूमहं सुकृतं विदितकर्माणमस्मिन्यज्ञे सुह्वानामाह्वये । सा नो ददातु श्रवणं पितृणाम् । पित्र्यं धनमिति वा । पित्र्यं यश इति वा । तस्यै ते देवि हविषा विधेमेति व्याख्यातम् ।

यमी व्याख्याता[9] । तस्या एषा भवति ॥ ३३ ॥

अ॒न्यमू॒ षु त्वं य॑म्य॒न्य उ॒ त्वां परि॑ ष्वजाते॒ लिबु॑जेव वृ॒क्षम् ।
तस्य॑ वा॒ त्वं मन॑ इ॒च्छा स वा॒ तवाधा॑ कृणुष्व सं॒विदं॒ सुभ॑द्राम्[10] ॥

अन्यमेव हि त्वं यमि । अन्यस्त्वां परिष्वङ्क्ष्यते । लिबुजेव वृक्षम् । तस्य वा त्वं मन इच्छ । स वा तव । अधानेन कुरुष्व संविदम् । सुभद्रां कल्याणभद्राम् ।

यमी यमं चकमे । तां प्रत्याचचक्षे[11] । इत्याख्यानम् ॥ ३४ ॥

उर्वशी व्याख्याता[12] । तस्या एषा भवति ॥ ३५ ॥

---

१. स्तुकः स्त्यायतेः is omitted by Durga.

२. पृथुकेशस्तुका पृथुष्टुतिर्वा C 4, C 5, M 3, Mi, W 1, W 2, W 3; ...पृथुष्टुकिर्वा C 7; पृथुकेशस्तुके पृथुस्तुके वा Roth.

३. स्वसा...सीदतीति वा is omitted by Durga.

४. °माहुतम् C 4, C 5, M 3, Mi, W 1, W 2, W 3; °मादनम् C 7.

५. दिशि C 4, C 5, C 7 M 3, Mi, W 1, W 2, W 3.

६. क्वाहुतं हविर्जुहोतीति वा is omitted by Durga.

७. सुवृतं C 1, C 2, C 3, C 6, M 1, M4, S; Roth & S'ivadatta.

८. MS. IV. 12. 6. Cf. AV. 7. 47. 1:

कुहूं दे॒वीं सु॒कृतं॑ विद्म॒नाप॑सम॒स्मिन् य॒ज्ञे
सु॒हवा॑ जोहवीमि ।
सा नो॑ र॒यिं वि॒श्ववा॑रं॒ नि य॑च्छा॒द् ददा॑तु
वी॒रं श॒तदा॑यमु॒क्थ्य॑म् ॥

९. N. 10. 19.

१०. RV. X. 10. 14; cf. AV. 18. 1. 16.

११. प्रत्याचचक्षेत्याख्यानम् S'iva.

१२. N. 5. 13.

विद्युन्न या पतन्ती दविद्योद्भरन्ती मे अप्या काम्यानि ।
जनिष्ठो अपो नर्यः सुजातः प्रोर्वशी तिरत दीर्घमायुः ॥

विद्युदिव या । पतन्त्यद्योतत[2] । हरन्ती मे अप्या काम्यानि । उदकान्यन्तरिक्षलोकस्य । यदा नूनमयं जायेताद्भ्योऽध्यप इति । नर्यो मनुष्यो नृभ्यो हितः । नरापत्यमिति वा । सुजातः सुजाततरः । अथोर्वशी प्रवर्धयते दीर्घमायुः ।

पृथिवी व्याख्याता[3] । तस्या एषा भवति ॥ ३६ ॥

बळित्था पर्वतानां खिद्रं बिभर्षि पृथिवि ।
प्र या भूमिं प्रवत्वति मह्ना जिनोषि महिनि[4] ॥

सत्यं त्वं पर्वतानां मेघानां खेदनं छेदनं [भेदनं] बलमत्र धारयसि पृथिवि । प्रजिन्वसि या भूमिम् । प्रवणवति । महत्त्वेन । महतीत्युदकवतीति वा ।

इन्द्राणी । इन्द्रस्य पत्नी । तस्या एषा भवति ॥ ३७ ॥

इन्द्राणीमासु नारिषु सुभगामहमश्रवम् ।
नह्यस्या अपरं चन जरसा मरते पतिः ।
विश्वस्मादिन्द्र उत्तरः[6] ॥

इन्द्राणीमासु नारिषु सुभगामहमशृणवम् । न ह्यस्या अपरामपि समां जरयां[7] म्रियते[8] पतिः । सर्वस्माद् य इन्द्र उत्तरस्तमेतद् ब्रूमः ।

तस्या एषापरा भवति ॥ ३८ ॥

नाहमिन्द्राणि रारण सख्युर्वृषाकपेर्ऋते ।
यस्येदमप्यं हविः प्रियं देवेषु गच्छति ।
विश्वस्मादिन्द्र उत्तरः[9] ॥

नाहमिन्द्राणि रमे । सख्युर्वृषाकपेर्ऋते । यस्येदमप्यं हविः । अप्सु शृतम् । अद्भिः संस्कृतमिति वा । प्रियं देवेषु निगच्छति[10] । सर्वस्माद् य इन्द्र उत्तरस्तमेतद् ब्रूमः ।

---

१. RV. X. 95. 10.

२. पतन्तं M 3.

३. N. 1. 13, 14.

४. RV. V. 84. 1.

५. Omitted by BK, C 4, C 5, C 7, Kn, M 3, Mi, R 8, W 1, W 2, W 3.

६. RV. X. 86. 11; AV. 20. 126. 11.

७. जरयां M 3, W 2.

८. म्रियेते M 3.

९. RV. X. 86. 12; AV. 20. 126. 12.

१०. नियच्छति is given as a variant by Durga.

गौरी रोचतेः। ज्वलतिकर्मणः। अयमपीतरो गौरो वर्ण एतस्मादेव। प्रशस्यो भवति।

तस्या एषा भवति ॥ ३९ ॥

गौरीर्मिमाय सलिलानि तक्षत्येकपदी द्विपदी सा चतुष्पदी।
अष्टापदी नवपदी बभूवुषी सहस्राक्षरा परमे व्योमन् ॥

गौरीर्निर्मिमाय सलिलानि। तक्षती कुर्वती। एकपदी मध्यमेन। द्विपदी मध्यमेन चादित्येन च। चतुष्पदी दिग्भिः। अष्टापदी दिग्भिश्चावान्तरदिग्भिश्च। नवपदी दिग्भिश्चावान्तरदिग्भिश्चादित्येन च। सहस्राक्षरा बहूदका। परमे व्यवने।

तस्या एषापरा भवति ॥ ४० ॥

तस्याः समुद्रा अधि वि क्षरन्ति तेन जीवन्ति प्रदिशश्चतस्रः।
ततः क्षरत्यक्षरं तद्विश्वमुप जीवति ॥

तस्याः समुद्रा अधिविक्षरन्ति। वर्षन्ति मेघाः। तेन जीवन्ति दिगाश्रयाणि भूतानि। ततः क्षरत्यक्षरमुदकम्। तत्सर्वाणि भूतान्युपजीवन्ति।

गौर्व्याख्याता। तस्या एषा भवति ॥ ४१ ॥

गौरमीमेदनु वत्सं मिषन्तं मूर्धानं हिङ्ङकृणोन्मातवा उ।
सृक्वाणं घर्ममभि वावशाना मिमाति मायुं पयते पयोभिः ॥

गौरन्वमीमेद्वत्सम्। मिषन्तमनिमिषन्तम्। आदित्यमिति वा। मूर्धानमस्याभिहिङ्ङकरोन्मननाय। सृक्वाणं सरणम्। घर्मं हरणम्। अभिवावशाना मिमाति मायुम्। प्रप्यायते पयोभिः। मायुमिवादित्यमिति वा।

वागेषा माध्यमिका। घर्मधुगिति याज्ञिकाः।

धेनुर्धयतेर्वा। धिनोतेर्वा। तस्या एषा भवति ॥ ४२ ॥

१. RV. I. 164. 41; cf. AV. 9. 10. 21.

२. गौरीर्मिमाय SRV. I. 164. 41. p. i. 715.

३. Quoted by SRV. loc. cit.

४. RV. I. 164. 42; AV. 9. 10. 22; 13. 1. 42.

५. Quoted by SRV. I. 164. 42. p. i. 716.

६. N. 2. 5.

७. RV. I. 164. 28; cf. AV. 9. 10. 6.

८. गौरन्नमीमे० W 2.

९. इषन्तम० W 2; निमिषन्तम० C 1, C 2, C 3, C 6, M 1, M 4, S; C 4, C 5, W 1, W 3, and Roth.

उप॑ ह्वये सु॒दुघां॑ धे॒नुमे॒तां सु॒हस्तो॑ गो॒धुगु॒त दो॑हदेनाम् ।
श्रेष्ठं॑ स॒वं स॑वि॒ता सा॑विषन्नो॒ऽभीद्धो॑ घ॒र्मस्तदु॒ षु प्र वो॑चम् ॥

उपह्वये सुदोहनां धेनुमेताम् । कल्याणहस्तो गोधुगपि च दोग्ध्येनाम् । श्रेष्ठं सवं सविता सुनोतु न इति । एष हि श्रेष्ठः सर्वेषां सवानां यदुदकं यद्वा पयो यजुष्मत् । अभीद्धो घर्मः । तं सु प्रब्रवीमि ।

वागेषा माध्यमिका । घर्मधुगिति याज्ञिकाः ।

अघ्न्याहन्तव्या भवति । अघघ्नीति वा । तस्या एषा भवति ॥ ४३ ॥

सू॒य॒व॒साद्भग॑वती॒ हि भू॒या अथो॑ व॒यं भग॑वन्तः स्याम ।
अ॒द्धि तृण॑मघ्न्ये विश्व॒दानीं॒ पिब॑ शु॒द्धमु॑द॒कमा॒चर॑न्ती ॥

सूयवसादिनी भगवती हि भव । अथेदानीं वयं भगवन्तः स्याम । अद्धि तृणमघ्न्ये । सर्वदा पिब च शुद्धमुदकमाचरन्ती ।

तस्या एषापरा भवति ॥ ४४ ॥

हि॒ङ्कृ॒ण्व॒ती व॑सुप॒त्नी॒ वसू॑नां व॒त्सम॒िच्छन्ती॒ मन॑सा॒भ्यागा॑त् ।
दु॒हाम॒श्विभ्यां॒ पयो॑ अ॒घ्न्येयं सा व॑र्धतां मह॒ते सौभ॑गाय ॥

इति सा निगदव्याख्याता ।

पथ्या स्वस्तिः । पन्था अन्तरिक्षम् । तन्निवासात् ।

तस्या एषा भवति ॥ ४५ ॥

स्व॒स्तिरिद्धि प्रप॑थे॒ श्रेष्ठा॒ रेक्ण॑स्वत्य॒भि या वा॒ममेति॑ ।
सा नो॑ अ॒मा सो अर॑णे॒ नि पा॑तु स्वा॒वे॒शा भ॑वतु दे॒वगो॑पा ॥

स्वस्तिरेव हि प्रपथे श्रेष्ठा । रेक्णस्वती धनवती । अभ्येति या । वसूनि वननीयानि । सा नोऽमा गृहे । सा निरमणे । सा निर्गमने पातु । स्वावेशा भवतु । देवी गोप्त्री देवान्गोपायत्विति । देवा एनां गोपायन्त्विति वा ।

उषा व्याख्याता । तस्या एषा भवति ॥ ४६ ॥

---

१. RV. I. 164. 26; AV. 7. 73. 7; 9. 10. 4.

२. सुदुघां C 4, C 5, C 7, M 3, Mi, W 1, W 2, W 3.

३. RV. I. 164. 40; AV. 7. 73. 11; 9. 10. 20.

४. सुयवसादिनी SRV. I. 164. 40. p. i. 715; & Roth.

५. Quoted by SRV. loc. cit.

६. RV. I. 164. 27; AV. 7. 73. 8; 9. 10. 5.

७. Quoted by SRV. X. 59. 7. p. iv. 172.

८. RV. X. 63. 16.

९. N. 2. 18.

अपोषा अनसः सरत्संपिष्टादह बिभ्युषी।
नि यत्सीं शिश्नथद्वृषा[१] ॥

अपासरदुषाः। अनसः संपिष्टान्मेघाद् बिभ्युषी। अनो वायुरनितेः। अपि वोपमार्थे स्यात्। अनस इव शकटादिव। अनः शकटम्[२]। आनद्धमस्मिञ्चीवरम्। अनितेर्वा स्यात्। जीवनकर्मणः। उपजीवन्त्येनत्। मेघोऽप्यन एतस्मादेव[२]। यन्निरशिश्नथत्। वृषा वर्षिता मध्यमः।

तस्या एषापरा भवति ॥ ४७ ॥

एतदस्या अनः शये सुसंपिष्टं विपाश्या।
ससार सीं परावतः[३] ॥

एतदस्या अन आशेते सुसंपिष्टम्। इतरदिव। विपाशि विमुक्तपाशि। ससारोषाः। परावतः प्रेरितवतः। परागताद्वा।

इळा व्याख्याता[४]। तस्या एषा भवति ॥ ४८ ॥

अभि न इळा यूथस्य माता स्मन्नदीभिरुर्वशी वा गृणातु।
उर्वशी वा बृहद्दिवा गृणानाभ्यूर्ण्वाना प्रभृथस्यायोः[६]।
सिषक्तु न ऊर्जव्यस्य पुष्टेः[७] ॥

अभिगृणातु न इळा। यूथस्य माता। [सर्वस्य माता।][८] स्मदभि नदीभिः। उर्वशी वा गृणातु। उर्वशी[९] वा। बृहद्दिवा महद्दिवा[१०]। गृणाना। अभ्यूर्ण्वाना। प्रभृथस्य प्रभृतस्य। आयोरयनस्य [मनुष्यस्य][१२] ज्योतिषो वोदकस्य वा। सेवतां नोऽन्नस्य पुष्टेः[११]।

रोदसी। रुद्रस्य पत्नी। तस्या एषा भवति ॥ ४९ ॥

---

१. RV. IV. 30. 10.

२. The passage अनः शकटम्...एतस्मादेव is omitted by Durga.

३. RV. IV. 30. 11.

४. N. 8. 7.

५. ऽस्मन्न० S'ivadatta.

६. ०स्यायोः C 7, M 3.

७. RV. V. 41. 19.

८. Omitted by BK, C 4, C 5, C 7, Kn, M 3, Mi, R 8, W 1, W 2, W 3; सर्वस्य माता सहचरतीभिर्नदीभिः is added on the margin in C 7.

९. उर्वशा C 7.

१०. Quoted by SRV. X. 64. 10. p. iv. 195.

११. Cf. SRV. V. 41. 19. p. ii. 582.

१२. Omitted by BK, C 4, C 5, C 7, Kn, M 3, Mi, R 8, W 1, W 2, W 3.

रथं नु मारुतं वयं श्रवस्युमा हुवामहे ।
आ यस्मिन्तस्थौ सुरणानि बिभ्रती सचा मरुत्सु रोदसी ॥

रथं क्षिप्रं मारुतं [मेघं[2]] वयं श्रवणीयमाह्वयामहे[3] । आ यस्मिन्तस्थौ सुरमणीयान्युदकानि बिभ्रती सचा मरुद्भिः सह रोदसी रोदसी ॥५०॥

॥ इत्येकादशोऽध्यायः ॥

[[1]श्येनो व्याख्यात [2]आदाय [3]स्वादिष्ठया [4]सोमं मन्यते [5]यत्त्वा देव [6]नवोर्नवः [7]परं मृत्यो [8]त्वेषमित्था [9]प्र वो मह [10]उदु ज्योतिर्धाता[11] ददातु [12]सोमस्या[13]थातो मध्यस्थाना देवगणा [14]आ विद्युन्मद्भि[15]रा रुद्रासो [16]विष्टी शमी [17]विरूपास [18]उदीरतामवरेऽ[19]ङ्गिरसो नः [20]सूर्यस्येव [21]स्तुषेय्यम[22]थातो मध्यस्थानाः स्त्रियो [23]दक्षस्य [24]यस्मै त्वं [25]किमिच्छन्ती [26]पावका नो [27]महो अर्णो [28]यद्वाग्वदन्ती [29]देवीं [30]वाचमन्विदनुमते [31]राकामहं [32]सिनीवालि [33]कुहूमहमन्य[34]मू-[35]र्वशी [36]विद्युन्न [37]वल्लित्थेन्[38]द्राणीं [39]नाहमिन्द्राणि [40]गौरीर्मिमाय [41]तस्याः समुद्रा [42]गौरमीमेदु[43]प ह्वये [44]सूयवसाद्भि[45]क्रूणवती [46]स्वस्तिरि[47]द्धिपोपा [48]एतदस्या [49]अभि नो [50]रथं नु मारुतमिति पञ्चाशत् ॥][4]

॥ इत्युत्तरषट्के पञ्चमोऽध्यायः ॥

॥ इति निरुक्त एकादशोऽध्यायः समाप्तः ॥

---

१. RV. V. 56. 8.

२. Omitted by BK, C 4, C 5, C 7, Kn, M 3, Mi, R 8, W 1, W 2, W 3.

३. आह्वयामः C 4, C 5, C 7, M 3, Mi, W 1, W 2, W 3.

४. Small figure within brackets represents the corresponding section of the eleventh chapter of the *Nirukta*.

अथ द्वादशोऽध्यायः

अथातो द्युस्थाना देवताः । तासामश्विनौ प्रथमागामिनौ भवतः । अश्विनौ यद्व्यश्नुवाते सर्वम् । रसेनान्यः[1] । ज्योतिषान्यः । अश्वैरश्विनावित्यौर्णवाभः ।

तत्कावश्विनौ । द्यावापृथिव्यावित्येके । अहोरात्रावित्येके । सूर्याचन्द्रमसावित्येके[2] । राजानौ पुण्यकृतावित्यैतिहासिकाः[3] । तयोः काल ऊर्ध्वमर्धरात्रात्प्रकाशीभावस्यानुविष्टम्भम् । अनुतमोभागो हि मध्यमो ज्योतिर्भाग आदित्यः ।

तयोरेषा भवति ॥ १ ॥

वसातिषु स्म चरथो[4]ऽसितौ पेत्वाविव ।

कदेदमश्विना युवमभि देवाँ अगच्छतम्[5] ॥

इति सा निगदव्याख्याता[6] ।

तयोः समानकालयोः समानकर्मणोः संस्तुतप्राययोरसंस्तवेनैषोऽर्धर्चो भवति । वासात्यो अन्य उच्यते । उषः पुत्रस्त्वन्य[7] इति ।

तयोरेषापरा भवति ॥ २ ॥

इहेह जाता समवावशीतामरेपसा तन्वा३ नामभिः स्वैः ।

जिष्णुर्वामन्यः सुमखस्य सूरिर्दिवो अन्यः सुभगः पुत्र ऊहे[8] ॥

---

१. Cf. S'B. IV. 1. 5. 16.
इमे ह वै द्यावापृथिवी प्रत्यक्षमश्विनाविमे हीदं सर्वमाश्नुवाताम् ।

२. Cf. BD. VII. 126; Quoted by SRV. I. 92. 1; 112. 1; 181. 4; 184. 3; X. 106. 5. pp. i. 416, 486, 764, 771; IV. 354.

३. Quoted by SRV. I. 89. 3. p. i. 396.

४. चरतो M 3.

५. The quotation is not traced.

६. S'ivadatta adds the following passage after व्याख्याता as the text in some of the MSS., which have however not been specified.

वसातिषु स्म चरथो वसातयो रातयो वसन्ते स्मा इतरेतरा तयोः । वक्तेर्वा वहतेर्वा । सितौ पेत्वाविव । अपेत्वा वृत्रहणं सुरातयोः ॥

७. त्वान्यः Roth.

८. RV. I. 181. 4.

इह चेह[1] च जातौ संस्तूयेते[2] पापेनालिप्यमानया तन्वा नामभिश्च स्वैः। जिष्णुर्वामन्यः सुमहतो बलस्येरयिता मध्यमः। दिवोऽन्यः सुभगः पुत्र ऊह्यन आदित्यः[3]।

तयोरेषापरा भवति ॥ ३ ॥

प्रातर्युजा वि बोधयाश्विनावेह गच्छताम् ।
अस्य सोमस्य पीतये[4] ॥

प्रातर्योगिनौ विबोधयाश्विनाविहागच्छतामस्य सोमस्य पानाय ।

तयोरेषापरा भवति ॥ ४ ॥

प्रातर्यजध्वमश्विना हिनोत न सायमस्ति देवया अजुष्टम् ।
उतान्यो अस्मद्यजते वि चावः पूर्वःपूर्वो यजमानो वनीयान्[5] ॥

प्रातर्यजध्वमश्विनौ प्रहिणुत न सायमस्ति देवेज्या अजुष्टमेतत् । अप्यन्योऽस्मद्यजते वि चावः । पूर्वःपूर्वो यजमानो वनीयान्वनयितृतमः।

तयोः कालः सूर्योदयपर्यन्तः। तस्मिन्नन्या देवता ओप्यन्ते ।

उषा वष्टेः कान्तिकर्मणः । उच्छतेरितरा माध्यमिका । तस्या एषा भवति ॥५॥

उषस्तच्चित्रमा भरास्मभ्यं वाजिनीवति ।
येन तोकं च तनयं च धामहे[6] ॥

उषस्तत् [चित्रं[7]] चायनीयं [मंहनीयं[8]] धनमाहर । अस्मभ्यमन्नवति । येन पुत्रांश्च पौत्रांश्च दधीमहि[9] ।

तस्या एषापरा भवति ॥ ६ ॥

---

१. इहेह SRV. I. 181. 4. p. i. 764.

२. संस्तूयेथे SRV. loc. cit.

३. Quoted by SRV. loc. cit.

४. RV. I. 22. 1.

५. RV. V. 77. 2.

६. RV, I. 92. 13; SV. 2. 1081; VS. 34. 33.

७. Omitted by BK, C 4, C 5, C 7, Kn, M 3, Mi, R 8, W 1, W 2, W 3.

८. Omitted by BK, C 4, C 5, C 7, Kn, M 3, Mi, R 8, W 1, W 2, W 3; and SRV. I. 92. 13. p. i. 415.

९. Quoted by SRV. loc. cit.

एता उ त्या उषसः केतुमक्रत पूर्वे अर्धे रजसो भानुमञ्जते ।

निष्कृण्वाना आयुधानीव धृष्णवः प्रति गावोऽरुषीर्यन्ति मातरः ॥

एतास्ता उषसः केतुमकृषत प्रज्ञानम् । एकस्या एव पूजनार्थे बहुवचनं स्यात् । पूर्वेऽर्धेऽन्तरिक्षलोकस्य समञ्जते भानुना । निष्कृण्वाना आयुधानीव धृष्णवः । निरित्येष समित्येतस्य स्थाने[2] ।

एमीदेषां निष्कृतं जारिणीव[3] । इत्यपि निगमो भवति ।

प्रति यन्ति । गावो गमनात् । अरुषीरारोचनात् । मातरो भासो निर्मात्र्यः ।

सूर्या सूर्यस्य पत्नी । एषैवाभिसृष्टकालतमा । तस्या एषा भवति ॥ ७ ॥

सुकिंशुकं शल्मलिं विश्वरूपं हिरण्यवर्णं सुवृतं सुचक्रम् ।

आ रोह सूर्ये अमृतस्य लोकं स्योनं पत्ये वहतुं कृणुष्व[5] ॥

सुकाशनं[6] शल्मलं सर्वरूपम् । अपि वोपमार्थे स्यात् । सुकिंशुकमिव शल्मलिमिति । किंशुकं क्रंशतेः प्रकाशयतिकर्मणः । शल्मलिः सुशरो भवति । शरवान्वा । आरोह सूर्ये अमृतस्य लोकमुदकस्य । सुखं पत्ये वहतुं कुरुष्व ।

सविता सूर्यां प्रायच्छत्सोमाय राज्ञे प्रजापतये वा[7] । इति च ब्राह्मणम् ।

वृषाकपायी वृषाकपेः पत्नी । एषैवाभिसृष्टकालतमा । तस्या एषा भवति ॥८॥

वृषाकपायि रेवति सुपुत्र आदु सुस्नुषे ।

घसत्त इन्द्र उक्षणः प्रियं काचित्करं हविर्विश्वस्मादिन्द्र उत्तरः ॥

वृषाकपायि रेवति सुपुत्रे मध्यमेन सुस्नुषे माध्यमिकया वाचा । स्नुषा साधुसादिनीति वा । साधुसानिनीति वा । स्वपत्यं तत्सनोतीति वा ।

प्राश्नातु त इन्द्र उक्षण एतान्माध्यमिकान्त्संस्त्यायान् । उक्षण उक्षतेर्वृद्धिकर्मणः । उक्षन्त्युदकेनेति वा । प्रियं कुरुष्व सुखाचयकरं हविः [सुखकरं हविः][9] । सर्वस्माद् य इन्द्र उत्तरस्[10]तमेतद्ब्रूम आदित्यम् ।

---

१. RV. I. 92. 1; SV. 2. 1105.

२. Quoted by SRV. I. 2. 6; III. 58. 9. pp. i. 32; ii. 328.

३. RV. X. 34. 5.

४. Quoted by SRV. I. 92. 1. p. i. 410.

५. RV. X. 85. 20; cf. AV. 14. 1. 61.

६. सुकासनं M 3.

७. Cf. AB. IV. 7. 1; cf. KB. XVIII. 1.

८. RV. X. 86. 13, AV. 20. 126. 13.

९. Omitted by BK, C 4, C 5, C 7, Kn, M 3, Mi, R 8, W 1, W 2, W 3. & SRV. X. 86. 13. p. IV. 269.

१०. The entire passage. वृषाकपायि रेवति...इन्द्र उत्तरः is quoted by SRV. loc. cit. The intervening words स्वपत्यं...उक्षन्त्युदकेनेति वा are omitted.

सरण्यूः सरणात् । तस्या एषा भवति ॥ ९ ॥

अपा॑गूहन्न॒मृतां॒ मर्त्ये॑भ्यः कृ॒त्वी सव॑र्णामददु॒र्विव॑स्वते ।
उ॒ताश्विना॑वभर॒द्यत्तदासी॒दज॑हादु॒ द्वा मि॑थु॒ना स॑र॒ण्यूः ॥[1]

अपा[2]गूहन्नमृतां मर्त्येभ्यः कृत्वी सवर्णामददुर्विवस्वते । अप्यश्विनावभरत् यत्तदासीत् । अजहाद् द्वौ मिथुनौ सरण्यूः ।

मध्यमं च माध्यमिकां च वाचमिति नैरुक्ताः । यमं च यमीं चेत्यैतिहासिकाः ।

तत्रेतिहासमाचक्षते[3] । त्वाष्ट्री सरण्यूर्विवस्वत आदित्याद्यमौ मिथुनौ जनयाञ्चकार[4] । स सवर्णामन्यां प्रतिनिधायाश्वं रूपं कृत्वा प्रदुद्राव[5] । स विवस्वानादित्य आश्वमेव रूपं कृत्वा तामनुसृत्य संबभूव[6] । ततोऽश्विनौ जज्ञाते[7] । सवर्णायां मनुः[8] । तदभिवादिन्येषर्ग्भवति ॥ १० ॥

त्वष्टा॑ दुहि॒त्रे व॑ह॒तुं कृ॑णो॒तीती॒दं विश्वं॒ भुव॑नं॒ समे॑ति ।
य॒मस्य॑ मा॒ता प॑र्यु॒ह्यमा॑ना म॒हो जा॒या विव॑स्वतो ननाश ॥[9]

त्वष्टा दुहितुर्वहनं करोतीति [इदं विश्वं भुवनं समेति][10] । इमानि च सर्वाणि भूतान्यभिसमागच्छन्ति । यमस्य माता पर्युह्यमाना महतो जाया विवस्वतो ननाश । रात्रिरादित्यस्य । आदित्योदयेऽन्तर्धीयते ॥ ११ ॥

सविता व्याख्यातः[11] । तस्य कालो यदा द्यौरपहततमस्काकीर्णरश्मिर्भवति । तस्यैषा भवति ॥ १२ ॥

विश्वा॑ रू॒पाणि॒ प्रति॑ मुञ्चते क॒विः प्रासा॑वीद्भ॒द्रं द्वि॒पदे॒ चतु॑ष्पदे ।
वि नाक॑मख्यत्सवि॒ता वरे॑ण्योऽनु॑ प्र॒याण॑मु॒षसो॒ वि रा॑जति ॥[12]

सर्वाणि प्रज्ञानानि प्रतिमुञ्चते मेधावी । कविः क्रान्तदर्शनो भवति । कवतेर्वा । प्रसुवति भद्रं द्विपाद्भ्यश्च चतुष्पाद्भ्यश्च । व्य[13]चिख्यपन्नाकं सविता वरणीयः । प्रयाणमनू[14]षसो विराजति ।

---

१. RV. X. 17. 2.

२. अप्यगूहन् C 1, C 2, C 3, C 6, M 1, M 4, S; Roth & S'ivadatta.

३. Cf. BD. VII. 7.

४. Cf. op. cit. VI. 162, 163.

५. Cf. op. cit. VII. 1.

६. Cf. op. cit. VII. 3, 4.

७. Cf. op. cit. VII. 6.

८. Cf. op. cit. VII. 2.

९. RV. X. 17. 1; AV. 3. 31. 5; 18. 1. 53.

१०. Omitted by BK, C 4, C 5, C 7, Kn, M 3, Mi, R 8, W 1, W 2, W 3.

११. N. 10. 31.

१२. RV. V. 81. 2; VS. 12. 3.

१३. व्यक्षपन्नाकं W 2.

१४. ०मनुषसो M 3; ०मुषसो C 4, C 5, C 7, Mi, W 1, W 2, W 3.

अघोरामः सावित्रः[1] । इति पशुसमाम्नाये[2] विज्ञायते ।

कस्मात्सामान्यादिति । अधस्तात्तद्वेलायां[3] तमो भवत्येतस्मात्सामान्यात् । अधस्ताद्रामोऽधस्तात्कृष्णः । कस्मात्सामान्यादिति । अग्निं चित्वा न रामामुपेयात्[4] । रामा रमणायोपेयते न धर्माय[4] । कृष्णजातीयैतस्मात्सामान्यात्[4] ।

कृकवाकुः सावित्रः[5] । इति पशुसमाम्नाये[6] विज्ञायते ।

कस्मात्सामान्यादिति[7] । कालानुवादं परीत्य । कृकवाकोः पूर्वं शब्दानुकरणं वचेरुत्तरम् ।

भगो व्याख्यातः[8] । तस्य कालः प्रागुत्सर्पणात् । तस्यैषा भवति ॥ १३ ॥

प्रा॒त॒र्जितं॒ भग॑मु॒ग्रं हु॑वेम व॒यं पु॒त्रमदि॑ते॒र्यो वि॑ध॒र्ता ।
आ॒ध्रश्चि॒द्यं मन्य॑मानस्तु॒रश्चि॒द्राजा॑ चि॒द्यं भगं॑ भ॒क्षीत्याह॑ ॥[9]

प्रातर्जितं भगमुग्रं ह्वयेम वयं पुत्रमदितेर्यो विधारयिता सर्वस्य । आध्रश्चिद्यं मन्यमान आढ्यीं[10]लुर्दरिद्रः । तुरश्चित् । तुर इति यमनाम । तरतेर्वा । त्वरतेर्वा । त्वरया तूर्णगतिर्यमः । राजा चिद्यं भगं भक्षीत्याह ।

अन्धो भग इत्याहुरनुत्सृप्तो न दृश्यते । प्राशित्रमस्याक्षिणी निर्जघान[11] । इति च ब्राह्मणम् ।

जनं भगो गच्छति[12] । इति [वा[13]] विज्ञायते[14] ।

जनं गच्छत्यादित्य उदयेन ।

---

१. TS. V. 5. 22. 1.
२. VS. 24. 1—40.
३. ०द्वेडायां Roth.
४. Cf. Vāsiṣṭha Dh. Sūt. XVIII. 17, 18: अथापि यमगीतान्श्लोकानुदाहरन्ति । नाग्निं चित्वा रामामुपेयात् । कृष्णवर्णा या रामा रमणायैव न धर्मायेति । Cf. also Karka on Pāraskara gṛhya sū. I. 4: तथा च यास्काचार्यः—रामा रमणायोपेयते न धर्मायेति ।...तथा चाह—अग्निं प्रथमं चित्वा न रामामुपेयादिति । Cf. Vis'varūpācārya in his *Bālakriḍā* on Yājñavalkya I. 56: कृष्णवर्णीया रामा रमणायैवोपेयत इति ब्राह्मणवादः । Cf. KS. XXII. 7: अग्निं चित्वा प्रथमं चित्वा न रामामुपेयात् ।
५. VS. 24. 35; TS. V. 5. 18. 1.
६. VS. 24. 1—40.
७. सामानादिति M 3.
८. N. 3. 16.
९. RV. VIII. 41. 2; VS. 34. 35; cf. AV. 3. 16. 2.
१०. आढ्याडु: Roth.
११. Cf. KB. VI. 13: तद् भगाय परिजहुः । तस्याक्षिणी निर्जघान । तस्मादाहुरन्धो भग इति । cf. S'B. I. 7. 4. 6: तद् भगाय दक्षिणत आसीनाय पर्याजहुः । तद् भगोऽवेक्षां चक्रे । तस्याक्षिणी निर्ददाह ।...तस्मादाहुरन्धो भग इति । Cf. GB. II. 1. 2: तस्मादाहुरन्धो वै भग इति ।
१२. Cf. MS. I. 6. 12: जनं भगोऽगच्छत् ।
१३. Omitted by BK, C 4, C 5, C 7, Kn, M 3, Mi, R 8, W 1, W 2, W 3.
१४. Omitted by Roth.

सूर्यः सर्तेर्वा । सुवतेर्वा[1] । [2]स्वीर्यतेर्वा । तस्यैषा भवति ॥ १४ ॥

उदु त्यं जातवेदसं देवं वहन्ति केतवः ।
दृशे विश्वाय सूर्यम्[3] ॥

उद्वहन्ति तं जातवेदसं रश्मयः केतवः । सर्वेषां भूतानां दर्शनाय सूर्यमिति[4] । [कमन्यमादित्यादेवमवक्ष्यत् ।][5]

तस्यैषापरा भवति ॥ १५ ॥

चित्रं देवानामुदगादनीकं चक्षुर्मित्रस्य वरुणस्याग्नेः ।
आप्रा द्यावापृथिवी अन्तरिक्षं सूर्य आत्मा जगतस्तस्थुषश्च[6] ॥

चायनीयं देवानामुदगमदनीकम् । ख्यानं मित्रस्य वरुणस्याग्नेश्च । आपूपुरद् द्यावापृथिव्यौ चान्तरिक्षं च महत्त्वेन [तेन[7]] । सूर्य आत्मा जङ्गमस्य च स्थावरस्य च ।

अथ यद्रश्मिपोषं पुष्यति तत्पूषा भवति[8] ।

तस्यैषा भवति ॥ १६ ॥

शुक्रं ते अन्यद्यजतं ते अन्यद्विषुरूपे अहनी द्यौरिवासि ।
विश्वा हि माया अवसि स्वधावो भद्रा ते पूषन्निह रातिरस्तु[9] ॥

शुक्रं ते अन्यत् । लोहितं ते अन्यत् । यजतं ते अन्यत् । यज्ञियं ते अन्यत् । विषमरूपे ते अहनी कर्म द्यौरिव चासि । सर्वाणि प्रज्ञानान्यवसि । अन्नवन् । भाजनवती ते पूषन्निह दत्तिरस्तु ।

तस्यैषापरा भवति ॥ १७ ॥

---

१. Cf. PMbh. vol. II. p. 86: सूसर्तिभ्यां सर्तेरूत्वं सुवतेर्वा रुडागमः । सरणाद्वा सुवति वा कर्मणीति सूर्यः ।

२. Cf. BD. VII. 128. (B).

३. RV. I. 50. 1; AV. 13. 2. 16; 20. 47. 13; SV. 1. 31; VS. 7. 41; 8. 41; 33. 31.

४. Cf. SRV. I. 50. 1. p. i. 248: उद्वहन्ति तं जातवेदसं देवमश्वाः केतवो रश्मयो वा सर्वेषां भूतानां संदर्शनाय सूर्यम् ।

५. Omitted by BK, C 4, C 5, C 7, Kn, M 3, Mi, R 8, W 1, W 2, W 3.

६. RV. I. 115. 1; AV. 13. 2. 35; 20. 137. 14.

७. Omitted by BK, C 4, C 5, C 7, Kn, M 3, Mi, R 8, W 1, W 2, W 3.

८. Cf. BD. ii. 63.

९. RV. VI. 58. 1; SV. 1. 75.

पथस्पथः परिपतिं वचस्या कामेन कृतो अभ्यानळर्कम् ।
स नो रासच्छुरुधश्चन्द्राग्रा[१] धियंधियं सीषधाति प्र पूषा[२] ॥

पथस्पथः । अधिपतिम् । वचनेन । कामेन कृतः । अभ्यानळर्कम्[३] । अभ्यापन्नोऽर्कमिति वा । स नो ददातु चायनीयाग्राणि धनानि । कर्मकर्म च नः प्रसाधयतु पूषेति ।

अथ यद्विषितो भवति तद्विष्णुर्भवति । विष्णुर्विशतेर्वा । व्यश्नोतेर्वा[४] ।

तस्यैषा भवति ॥ १८ ॥

इदं विष्णुर्वि चक्रमे त्रेधा नि दधे पदम् ।
समूळ्हमस्य पाँसुरे[५] ॥

यदिदं किं च तद्विक्रमते विष्णुः । त्रिधा निधत्ते पदम् । [त्रेधाभावाय[६] ।] पृथिव्यामन्तरिक्षे दिवीति शाकपूणिः । समारोहणे विष्णुपदे गयशिरसीत्यौर्णवाभः । समूळ्हमस्य[८] [पाँसुरे[९]] प्यायनेऽन्तरिक्षे पदं न दृश्यते । अपि वोपमार्थे स्यात् । समूळ्हमस्य[१०] पाँसुल[११] इव पदं न दृश्यत इति । पाँसवः पादैः सूयन्त इति वा । पन्नाः शेरत इति वा । पंसनीया[१२] भवन्तीति वा[१३] ॥ १९ ॥

विश्वानरो व्याख्यातः[१४] । तस्यैष निपातो भवत्यैन्द्र्यामृचि ॥ २० ॥

विश्वानरस्य वस्पतिमनानतस्य शवसः ।
एवैश्च चर्षणीनामूती हुवे रथानाम्[१५] ॥

विश्वानरस्यादित्यस्य । अनानतस्य । शवसो महतो बलस्य । एवैश्च कामैरयनैरवनैर्वा । चर्षणीनां मनुष्याणाम् । ऊत्या च पथा[१६] रथानाम् । इन्द्रमस्मिन्यज्ञे ह्वयामि ।

---

१. रसच्छु° Roth.

२. RV. VI. 49. 8; VS. 34. 42.

३. अभ्यानडर्कम् C 1, C 2, C 3, C 6, M 4, S; Roth & S'ivadatta.

४. Cf. BD. ii. 69.

५. RV. I. 22. 17; AV. 7. 26. 4.

६. Omitted by BK, C 4, C 5, C 7, Kn, M 3, Mi, R 8, W 1, W 2, W 3.

७. Cf. BD. ii. 64.

८. समूढमस्य C 1, C 2, C 3, C 6, M 4,

९. अप्यायने SRV. I. 22. 17. p. i. 120.

१०. Omitted by SRV. loc. cit. For the reading of the longer recension, see note ८.

११. पांसुर SRV. loc. cit.

१२. पिंसनीया: C 4, C 5, C 7, M 3, Mi, W 1, W 2, W 3.

१३. The passage: विष्णुर्विशतेर्वा...... भवन्तीति वा is quoted by SRV. loc. cit.

१४. N. 7. 21.

१५. RV. VIII. 68. 4; SV. 1. 364.

१६. यथा Roth.

वरुणो व्याख्यातः[१] । तस्यैषा भवति ॥ २१ ॥

येना पावक चक्षसा भुरण्यन्तं जनाँ अनु ।
त्वं वरुण पश्यसि[२] ॥

भुरण्युरिति क्षिप्रनाम । भुरण्युः शकुनिः । भूरिमध्वानं नयति[३] । स्वर्गस्य लोकस्यापि वोळ्हा[४] । तत्संपाती[५] भुरण्युः । अनेन पावकख्यानेन । भुरण्यन्तं जनाँ अनु । त्वं वरुण पश्यसि । तत्ते वयं स्तुम इति वाक्यशेषः ।

अपि वोत्तरस्याम्[६] ॥ २२ ॥

येना पावक चक्षसा भुरण्यन्तं जनाँ अनु ।
त्वं वरुण पश्यसि[७] ॥

वि द्यामेषि रजस्पृथ्वहा मिमानो अक्तुभिः ।
पश्यञ्जन्मानि सूर्य[८] ॥

व्येषि[९] द्याम् । रजश्च । पृथु महान्तं लोकम् । अहानि च मिमानोऽक्तुभी रात्रिभिः सह । पश्यञ्जन्मानि जातानि सूर्य ।

अपि वा पूर्वस्याम् ॥ २३ ॥

येना पावक चक्षसा भुरण्यन्तं जनाँ अनु ।
त्वं वरुण पश्यसि[१०] ॥

प्रत्यङ् देवानां विशः प्रत्यङ्ङुदेषि मानुषान् ।
प्रत्यङ् विश्वं स्वर्दृशे[११] ॥

---

१. N. 10. 3.

२. RV. I. 50. 6; AV. 13. 2. 21; 20. 47. 18; VS. 33. 32.

३. नयन्ति M 3.

४. वोढा C 1, C 2, C 3, C 6, M 4, S; & S'ivadatta.

५. The passage भुरण्युः शकुनिः...तत्संपाती is omitted in W 2; but added on the margin.

६. Cf. SRV. I. 50. 6. p. i. 250: तत्ते वयं स्तुम इति वाक्यशेषोऽपि वोत्तरस्यामन्वयस्तेन व्येषि ।

७. RV. I. 50. 6.

८. RV. I. 50. 7; AV. 13. 2. 22; 20. 47. 19.

९. वेषि C 4. C 5, C 7, M 3, Mi, W 1, W 2, W 3.

१०. RV. I. 50. 6.

११. RV. I. 50. 5; AV. 13. 2. 20; 20. 47. 17.

प्रत्यङ्ङिदं सर्वम् । [उदेषि । प्रत्यङ्ङिदं ज्योतिरुच्यते[1] । प्रत्यङ्ङिदं सर्वम्][2] (इदम्[3]) अभिविपश्यसीति ।

अपि वैतस्यामेवं[4] ॥ २४ ॥

येना पावक चक्षसा भुरण्यन्तं जनाँ अनु ।
त्वं वरुण पश्यसि[5] ॥

तेन नो जनानभिविपश्यसि ।

केशी केशा रश्मयः । तैस्तद्वान्भवति । काशनाद्वा[6] । [प्रकाशनाद्वा ।][7]

तस्यैषा भवति ॥ २५ ॥

केश्य१ग्निं केशी विषं केशी बिभर्ति रोदसी ।
केशी विश्वं स्वर्दृशे केशीदं ज्योतिरुच्यते[8] ॥

केश्यग्निं च विषं च । विषमित्युदकनाम । विष्णातेः । [विपूर्वस्य स्नातेः शुद्ध्यर्थस्य ।][9] विपूर्वस्य वा सचतेः । द्यावापृथिव्यौ च धारयति । केशीदं सर्वमिदमभिविपश्यति । केशीदं ज्योतिरुच्यत इत्यादित्यमाह ।

अथाप्येते इतरे ज्योतिषी केशिनी उच्येते । धूमेनाग्नी । रजसा च मध्यमः[10] ।

तयोरेषा[11] साधारणा भवति ॥ २६ ॥

त्रयः केशिन ऋतुथा वि चक्षते संवत्सरे वपत एक एषाम् ।
विश्वमेको अभि चष्टे शचीभिर्ध्राजिरेकस्य ददृशे न रूपम्[12] ॥

---

१. प्रत्यङ्ङिदं ज्योतिरुच्यते is omitted by Durga.

२. उदेषि...सर्वम् is omitted by BK, C 4, C 5, C 7, Kn, M 3, Mi, R 8, W 1, W 2, W 3.

३. Omitted by C 1, C 2, C 3, C 6, M 1, M 4, R 2, R 3, R 5, S.

४. °मिव W 2.

५. RV. I. 50. 6.

६. Cf. BD. ii. 65:

प्रकाशं किरणैः कुर्वंस्तेनैनं केशिनं विदुः ।

७. Omitted by BK, C 4, C 5, C 7, Kn, M 3, Mi, R 8, W 1, W 2, W 3.

८. RV. X. 136. 1.

९. Omitted by BK, C 4, C 5, C 7, Kn, M 3, Mi, R 8, W 1, W 2, W 3.

१०. Cf. BD. i. 94; ii. 65.

११. तेषामेषा C 1, C 2, C 3, C 6, M 1, M 4, R 2, R 3, R 5, S.

१२. RV. I. 164. 44; AV. 9. 10. 26.

त्रयः केशिन ऋतुथा विचक्षते । कालेकालेऽभिविपश्यन्ति । संवत्सरे वपत एक एषाम् । इत्यग्निः पृथिवीं दहति । सर्वमेकोऽभिविपश्यति कर्मभिरादित्यः । गतिरेकस्य दृश्यते न रूपं मध्यमस्य ।

अथ यद् रश्मिभिरभिप्रकम्पयन्नेति तद् वृषाकपिर्भवति । वृषाकम्पनः ।

तस्यैषा भवति ॥ २७ ॥

पुनरेहि वृषाकपे सुविता कल्पयावहै ।
य एष स्वप्ननंशनोऽस्तमेषि पथा पुनः ।
विश्वस्मादिन्द्र उत्तरः ॥

पुनरेहि वृषाकपे सुप्रसूतानि वः कर्माणि कल्पयावहै । य एष स्वप्ननंशनः । स्वप्नान्नाशयति । आदित्य उदयेन । सोऽस्तमेषि पथा पुनः । सर्वस्माद् य इन्द्र उत्तरस्तमेतद् ब्रूम आदित्यम् ।

यमो व्याख्यातः । तस्यैषा भवति ॥ २८ ॥

यस्मिन्वृक्षे सुपलाशे देवैः संपिबते यमः ।
अत्रा नो विश्पतिः पिता पुराणाँ अनु वेनति ॥

यस्मिन्वृक्षे सुपलाशे स्थाने वृतक्षये वा । अपि वोपमार्थे स्यात् । वृक्ष इव सुपलाश इति । वृक्षो व्रश्चनात् । पलाशं पलाशनात् । देवैः संगच्छते यमः । रश्मिभिरादित्यः । तत्र नः सर्वस्य पाता वा पालयिता वा पुराणाननुकामयेत ।

अज एकपादजन एकः पादः । एकेन पादेन पातीति वा । एकेन पादेन पिबतीति वा । एकोऽस्य पाद इति वा ।

एकं पादं नोत्खिदति ।

इत्यपि निगमो भवति । तस्यैष निपातो भवति वैश्वदेव्यामृचि ॥ २९ ॥

---

१. The whole passage त्रयः...मध्यमस्य is quoted by SRV. I. 164. 44. p. i. 716.

२. Cf. BD. ii. 67.

३. कल्पयावहै Roth.

४. RV. X. 86. 21; AV. 20. 126. 21.

५. Omitted by W 2.

६. नाशयसि Roth & SRV. X 86. 21. p. iv. 271.

७. The passage सुप्रसूतानि...पथा पुनः is quoted by SRV. loc. cit.

८. N. 10. 19.

९. RV. X. 135. 1.

१०. पलाशदनात् M 3; पलाशं पलाशनात् is omitted by Durga.

११. AV. 11. 4. 21.

पावीरवी तन्यतुरेकपादजो दिवो धर्ता सिन्धुरापः समुद्रियः ।
विश्वे देवासः शृणवन्वचांसि मे सरस्वती सह धीभिः पुरंध्या[1] ॥

पविः शल्यो भवति । यद्विपुनाति कायम्[2] । तद्वत् । पवीरमायुधम् । तद्वानिन्द्रः पवीरवान् ।

अतितस्थौ पवीरवान्[3] ।

इत्यपि निगमो भवति । तद् देवता वाक्पावीरवी । पावीरवी च दिव्या वाक् । तन्यतुस्तनित्री वाचोऽन्यस्याः । अजश्चैकपाद् दिवो धारयिता । सिन्धुश्च । आपश्च समुद्रियाश्च[4] । सर्वे च देवाः । सरस्वती च सह पुरन्ध्या स्तुत्या । प्रयुक्तानि धीभिः कर्मभिर्युक्तानि । शृण्वन्तु वचनानीमानीति ।

पृथिवी व्याख्याता[5] । तस्या एष निपातो भवत्यैन्द्राग्न्यामृचि ॥ ३० ॥

यदिन्द्राग्नी परमस्यां पृथिव्यां मध्यमस्यामवमस्यामुत स्थः ।
अतः परि वृषणावा हि यातमथा सोमस्य पिबतं सुतस्य[6] ॥

इति सा निगदव्याख्याता ।

समुद्रो व्याख्यातः[7] । तस्यैष निपातो भवति पावमान्यामृचि ॥ ३१ ॥

पवित्रवन्तः परि वाचमासते पितैषां प्रत्नो[8] अभि रक्षति व्रतम् ।
महः समुद्रं वरुणस्तिरो दधे धीरा इच्छेकुर्धरुणेष्वारभम्[9] ॥

पवित्रवन्तो रश्मिवन्तो माध्यमिका[10] देवगणाः पर्यासते [माध्यमिकां वाचम्][11] । मध्यमः[12] पितैषां प्रत्नः[13] पुराणोऽभिरक्षति व्रतं कर्म । महः समुद्रं वरुणस्तिरोऽन्तर्दधाति । अथ धीराः शक्नुवन्ति धरुणेषूदकेषु कर्मण आरभमारब्धुम्[14][15] ।

---

१. RV. X. 65. 13.

२. Cf. SRV. X. 65. 13. p. iv. 201: पविः शल्यो भवति...कायमित्यादि निरुक्तमनुसंधेयम् ।

३. RV. X. 60. 3. Durga remarks: निर्वचनस्यास्यामृच्युत्तरे पादे सम्यक् पाठोऽन्वेष्यः ।

४. च is omitted & added between धारयिता and सिन्धुः in M 3.

५. N. 1. 13, 14; cf. 9. 31; 11. 36.

६. RV. I. 108. 10.

७. N. 2. 10.

८. प्रज्ञो W 2.

९. RV. IX. 73. 3.

१०. माध्यमकाः C 7. M 3.

११. Omitted by BK, C 4, C 5, C 7, Kn, M 3, Mi, R 8, W 1, W 2, W 3.

१२. Omitted by Roth.

१३. प्रज्ञो W 2.

१४. आरम्भम् M 3.

१५. आरब्धम् W 2.

अज एकपाद् व्याख्यातः[1] । पृथिवी व्याख्याता[2] । समुद्रो व्याख्यातः[3] । तेषामेष निपातो भवत्यपरस्यां बहुदेवतायामृचि ॥ ३२ ॥

उत नोऽहिर्बुध्न्यः शृणोत्वज एकपात्पृथिवी समुद्रः ।
विश्वे देवा ऋतावृधो हुवानाः स्तुता मन्त्राः कविशस्ता अवन्तु[4] ॥

अपि च नोऽहिर्बुध्न्यः शृणोतु । अजश्चैकपात्पृथिवी च समुद्रश्च सर्वे च देवाः । ऋतवृधो वा । यज्ञवृधो वा । हूयमाना गीर्भिः स्तुताः । मन्त्राः कविशस्ताः । अवन्तु । मेधाविशस्ताः ।

दध्यङ् प्रत्यक्तो ध्यानमिति वा । प्रत्यक्तमस्मिन्ध्यानमिति[5] वा ।

अथर्वा व्याख्यातः[6] । मनुर्मननात्[7] । तेषामेष निपातो भवत्यैन्द्र्यामृचि[8] ॥ ३३ ॥

याम॑थर्वा मनुष्पिता दध्यङ् धियमत्नत ।
तस्मिन्ब्रह्माणि पूर्वथेन्द्र उक्था समग्मतार्चन्ननु स्वराज्यम्[9] ॥

यामथर्वा च । मनुश्च[10] पिता मानवानाम् । दध्यङ् च । धियमतनिषत । तस्मिन्ब्रह्माणि कर्माणि पूर्वेन्द्र उक्थानि[11] च संगच्छन्ताम् । अर्चन्योऽनूपास्ते स्वाराज्यम् ॥ ३४ ॥

अथातो द्युस्थाना देवगणाः । तेषामादित्याः प्रथमागामिनो भवन्ति । आदित्या व्याख्याताः[12] । तेषामेषा भवति ॥ ३५ ॥

इमा गिर आदित्येभ्यो घृतस्नूः सनाद्राजभ्यो जुह्वा जुहोमि ।
शृणोतु मित्रो अर्यमा भगो नस्तुविजातो वरुणो दक्षो अंशः[13] ॥

घृतस्नूर्घृतप्रस्नाविन्यः[14] । घृतप्रस्नाविण्यः । [घृतसानिन्यः । घृतसारिण्यः][15] इति वा । आहुतीरादित्येभ्यश्चिरं जुह्वा जुहोमि । [चिरं जीवनाय ।][15] चिरं राजभ्य इति वा । शृणोतु न इमा गिरो मित्रश्चार्यमा च भगश्च बहुजातश्च धाता दक्षो वरुणोऽंशश्च । अंशोऽंशुना व्याख्यातः ।

---

१. N. 12. 29.

२. N. 12. 30.

३. loc. cit.

४. RV. VI. 50. 14; VS. 34. 53.

५. ०स्मिन्ध्यानमिति C 4, C 5, C 7, M 3, Mi, W 1, W 2, W 3.

६. N. 11. 18.

७. ०मरणात् M 3.

८. Cf. BD. iii. 121.

९. RV. I. 80. 16.

१०. मनुष्य M 3.

११. तस्मिन्कर्मणि ब्रह्माणीन्द्र उक्थानि C 4, C 5, C 7, M 3, Mi, W 1, W 2, W 3.

१२. N. 2. 13.

१३. RV. II. 27. 1; VS. 34. 54.

१४. ०प्रस्नाविन्यः C 6, C 7; S'ivadatta.

१५. Omitted by BK, C 4, C 5, C 7, Kn, M 3, Mi, R 8, W 1, W 2, W 3.

सप्त ऋषयो व्याख्याताः । तेषामेषा भवति ॥ ३६ ॥

सप्त ऋषयः प्रतिहिताः शरीरे सप्त रक्षन्ति सदमप्रमादम् ।
सप्तापः स्वपतो लोकमीयुस्तत्र जागृतो अस्वप्नजौ सत्रसदौ च देवौ[3] ॥

सप्त ऋषयः प्रतिहिताः शरीरे । रश्मय आदित्ये । सप्त रक्षन्ति सदमप्रमादम् । संवत्सरमप्रमाद्यन्तः । सप्तापनास्त एव स्वपतो लोकमस्तमितमादित्यं यन्ति । तत्र जागृतोऽस्वप्नजौ सत्रसदौ च देवौ वाय्वादित्यौ । इत्यधिदैवतम् ।

अथाध्यात्मम् । सप्त ऋषयः प्रतिहिताः शरीरे । षडिन्द्रियाणि विद्या सप्तम्यात्मनि । सप्त रक्षन्ति सदमप्रमादम् । शरीरमप्रमाद्यन्ति । सप्तापनानीमान्येव स्वपतो लोकमस्तमितमात्मानं यन्ति । तत्र जागृतोऽस्वप्नजौ सत्रसदौ च देवौ प्राज्ञश्चात्मा तैजसश्च । इत्यात्मगतिमाचष्टे ।

तेषामेषापरा भवति ॥ ३७ ॥

तिर्यग्बिलश्चमस ऊर्ध्वबुध्नो यस्मिन्यशो निहितं विश्वरूपम् ।
अत्रासत ऋषयः सप्त साकं ये अस्य गोपा महतो बभूवुः ॥

तिर्यग्बिलश्चमस ऊर्ध्वबन्धन ऊर्ध्वबोधनो वा । यस्मिन्यशो निहितं विश्वरूपम् । अत्रासत ऋषयः सप्त सहादित्यरश्मयः । ये अस्य गोपा महतो बभूवुः । इत्यधिदैवतम् ।

अथाध्यात्मम् । तिर्यग्बिलश्चमस ऊर्ध्वबन्धन ऊर्ध्वबोधनो वा । यस्मिन्यशो निहितं विश्वरूपम् । अत्रासत ऋषयः सप्त सहेन्द्रियाणि । यान्यस्य गोप्तॄणि महतो बभूवुः । इत्यात्मगतिमाचष्टे ।

देवा व्याख्याताः । तेषामेषा भवति ॥ ३८ ॥

देवानां भद्रा सुमतिर्ऋजूयतां देवानां रातिरभि नो नि वर्तताम् ।
देवानां सख्यमुप सेदिमा वयं देवा न आयुः प्र तिरन्तु जीवसे[10] ॥

१. N. 10. 26.

२. सत्रसदौ च देवौ Roth.

३. VS. 34. 55.

४. अत्र C 4, C 5, C 7, M 3, Mi, W 1, W 2, W 3.

५. Cf. AV. 10. 8. 9. The accent of this stanza marked by Roth and S'ivadatta differs from that of the AV.

६. सर्वरूपम् C 1, C 2, C 3, C 6, M 1, M 4, S; Roth & S'ivadatta.

७. सर्वरूपम् C 1, C 2, C 3, C 6, M 1, M 4, S; Roth & S'ivadatta.

८. गोप्त्रीणि C 4, C 5, C 7, M 3, Mi, W 1, W 2, W 3.

९. N. 7. 15.

१०. RV. I. 89. 2; VS. 25. 15.

देवानां वयं [सुमतौ][1] कल्याण्यां मतौ । ऋजुगामिनाम् । ऋतुगामिनामिति[2] वा । देवानां दानमभि नो निवर्तताम् । देवानां सख्यमुपसीदेम वयम् । देवा न आयुः प्रवर्धयन्तु चिरं जीवनाय[3] ।

विश्वेदेवाः सर्वदेवाः[4] । तेषामेषा भवति ॥ ३९ ॥

ओमासश्चर्षणीधृतो विश्वे देवास आ गत ।
दाश्वांसो दाशुषः सुतम्[4] ॥

अवितारो[8] वा । अवनीया वा । मनुष्यधृतः सर्वे च देवा इहागच्छत । दत्तवन्तः । दत्तवतः सुतमिति ।

तदेतदेकमेव[5] वैश्वदेवं गायत्रं तृचं दशतयीषु विद्यते । यत्तु किंचिद् बहुदैवतं तद् वैश्वदेवानां स्थाने युज्यते[6] । यदेव विश्वलिङ्गमिति[7] शाकपूणिः । अनत्यन्तगतस्त्वेष उद्देशो भवति ।

बभ्रुरेको[9] ।

इति दश द्विपदा अलिङ्गाः[10] । भूतांशः काश्यपः[11] आश्विनमेकलिङ्गम्[12] । अभितष्टीयं[13] सूक्तमेकलिङ्गम्[14] ।

साध्या देवाः साधनात् । तेषामेषा भवति ॥ ४० ॥

यज्ञेन यज्ञमयजन्त देवास्तानि धर्माणि प्रथमान्यासन् ।
ते ह नाकं महिमानः सचन्त यत्र पूर्वे साध्याः सन्ति देवाः[15] ॥

यज्ञेन यज्ञमयजन्त देवाः । अग्निनाग्निमयजन्त देवाः[16] ।

अग्निः पशुरासीत् । तमालभन्त । तेनायजन्त[17] । इति च ब्राह्मणम् ।

---

१. Omitted by BK, C 4, C 5, C 7, Kn, M 3, Mi, R 8, W 1, W 2, W 3.

२. ऋजु° W 2.

३. Quoted by SRV. I. 89. 2. p. i. 395.

४. RV. I. 3. 7; VS. 7. 33; 33. 47.

५. °मिव C 4, C 5, C 7, M 3, Mi, W 1, W 2, W 3.

६. Cf. BD. ii. 128, 132, 133.

७. The term विश्वलिङ्गम् is used in BD. iii. 43.

८. Cf. SRV. I. 3. 7. p. i. 38.

९. RV. VIII. 29. 1.

१०. बभ्रुरेक...अलिङ्गाः is placed after आश्विनमेकलिङ्गम् in C 4, C 5, C 7, M 3, Mi, W 1, W 2, W 3; is omitted by Durga.

११. भूतांशः काश्यपः is the seer of RV. X. 106.

१२. Cf. BD. VIII. 18; cf. Sarvānu. VIII. 21.

१३. अभितष्टियं M 3.

१४. RV. III. 38.

१५. RV. I. 164. 50; X. 90. 16; AV. 7. 5. 1; VS. 31. 16.

१६. Quoted by SRV. I. 164. 50. p. i. 719.

१७. Cf. AB. i. 16. 36, 38-40; TS. V. 7. 26. 1: अग्निः पशुरासीत् । तेनायजन्त ।

तानि धर्माणि प्रथमान्यासन् । ते ह नाकं महिमानः संसेव्यन्त । यत्र पूर्वे साध्याः सन्ति देवाः साधनाः । द्युस्थानो देवगण इति नैरुक्ताः । पूर्वं देवयुगमित्याख्यानम् ।

वसवो यद् विवसते सर्वम् । अग्निर्वसुभिर्वासव इति समाख्या । तस्मात्पृथिवीस्थानाः । इन्द्रो वसुभिर्वासव इति समाख्या । तस्मान्मध्यस्थानाः । वसव आदित्यरश्मयो विवासनात् । तस्माद् द्युस्थानाः ।

तेषामेषा भवति ॥ ४१ ॥

सुगा वो देवाः सदनैमकर्म य आजग्मुः सवनैमिदं जुषाणाः ।
जक्षिवांसः पपिवांसश्च विश्वेऽस्मे धत्त वसवो वसूनि ॥

स्वागमनानि वो देवाः सुपथान्यकर्म य आगच्छत सवनानीमानि । जुषाणाः खादितवन्तः । पीतवन्तश्च । सर्वेऽस्मासु धत्त वसवो वसूनि ।

तेषामेषापरा भवति ॥ ४२ ॥

ज्मया अत्र वसवो रन्त देवा उरावन्तरिक्षे मर्जयन्त शुभ्राः ।
अर्वाक्पथ उरुज्रयः कृणुध्वं श्रोता दूतस्य जग्मुषो नो अस्य ॥

ज्मया अत्र वसवोऽरमन्त देवाः । ज्मा पृथिवी । तस्यां भवा उरौ चान्तरिक्षे मर्जयन्त गमयन्त रमयन्त । शुभ्राः शोभमानाः । अर्वाञ्च एनान्पथो बहुजवाः कुरुध्वम् । शृणुत दूतस्य जग्मुषो नोऽस्याग्नेः ।

वाजिनो व्याख्याताः । तेषामेषा भवति ॥ ४३ ॥

शं नो भवन्तु वाजिनो हवेषु देवताता मितद्रवः स्वर्काः ।
जम्भयन्तोऽहिं वृकं रक्षांसि सनेम्यस्मद्युयवन्नमीवाः ॥

---

१. समसेवन्त C 1, C 2, C 3, C 6, M 3, Mi, R 2, R 3, R 5, S.

२. द्युस्थाणो Roth.

३. सुपथा अकर्म Durga & S'ivadatta.

४. सवनमिदं Roth.

५. Cf. TS. i. 4. 44. 2; cf. AV. 7. 97. 4: सुगा वो देवाः सदना अकर्म य आजग्म सवने मा जुषाणाः । वहमाना भरमाणाः स्वा वसूनि वसुं घर्मं दिवमा रोहतानु ॥ Cf. VS. 8. 18: सुगा वो देवाः सदना अकर्म य आजग्मेदꣳ सवनं जुषाणाः । भरमाणा वहमाना हवींषि अस्मे धत्त वसवो वसूनि स्वाहा ॥

६. अत्र Roth.

७. RV. VII. 39. 3.

८. रमयन्त is omitted in M 3, but is added on the margin; also omitted by Durga.

९. सर्वा M 3.

१०. N. 2. 28.

११. RV. VII. 38. 7; VS. 9. 16; 21. 10.

सुखा नो भवन्तु वाजिनो ह्वानेषु देवतातौ यज्ञे। मितद्रवः सुमितद्रवः। स्वर्काः स्वञ्चना इति वा। स्वर्चना इति वा। स्वर्चिष इति वा। जम्भयन्तोऽहिं च वृकं च रक्षाँसि च। क्षिप्रमस्मद्यावयन्तु। अमीवा देवाश्वा इति वा।

देवपत्न्यो देवानां पत्न्यः। तासामेषा भवति ॥ ४४ ॥

देवानां पत्नीरुशतीरवन्तु नः प्रावन्तु नस्तुजये वाजसातये।
याः पार्थिवासो या अपामपि व्रते ता नो देवीः सुहवाः शर्म यच्छत ॥

देवानां पत्न्य उशत्योऽवन्तु नः। प्रावन्तु नः। [तुजये] अपत्यजननाय चान्नसंसननाय च। याः पार्थिवासो या अपामपि व्रते कर्मणि ता नो देव्यः सुहवाः शर्म यच्छन्तु शरणम्।

तासामेषापरा भवति ॥ ४५ ॥

उत ग्ना व्यन्तु देवपत्नीरिन्द्राण्य१ग्नाय्यश्विनी राट्।
आ रोदसी वरुणानी शृणोतु व्यन्तु देवीर्य ऋतुर्जनीनाम् ॥

अपि च ग्ना व्यन्तु देवपत्न्यः। इन्द्राणीन्द्रस्य पत्नी। अग्नाय्यग्नेः पत्नी। अश्विन्यश्विनोः पत्नी। राड् राजते। रोदसी रुद्रस्य पत्नी। वरुणानी च वरुणस्य पत्नी। व्यन्तु देव्यः कामयन्तां य ऋतुकालो जायानां य ऋतुकालो जायानाम् ॥ ४६ ॥

॥ इति द्वादशोऽध्यायः ॥

---

१. ०वयन् C 4, C 5, C 7, M 3, Mi, W 1, W 2, W 3.

२. तापामे०. M 3.

३. RV. V. 46. 7; AV. 7. 49. 1.

४. Omitted by BK, C 4, C 5, C 7, Kn, M 3, Mi, R 8, W 1, W 2, W 3.

५. कर्मणि व्रते M 3.

६. RV. V. 46. 8.

७. Quoted by SRV. V. 46. 8, p. ii, 602.

[[1]अथातो द्युस्थाना [2]वसातिषु स्मे[3]हेह जाता [4]प्रातर्युजा [5]प्रातर्यजध्व[6]मुषस्तच्चित्र[7]मेता उत्याः [8]सुकिंशुकं [9]वृषाकपाय्य[10]पागूहं[11]स्त्वष्टा दुहित्रे [12]सविता [13]विश्वारूपाणि [14]प्रातर्जितं[15]मुदुत्यं [16]चित्रं [17]शुक्रं ते [18]पथस्पथ [19]इदं विष्णु[20]र्विश्वानरो व्याख्यातो [21]विश्वानरस्य [22-25]येना पावकेति चतुष्कं [26]केश्यऽग्नि [27]त्रयः केशिनः [28]पुनरेहि [29]यस्मिन्वृक्षे [30]पावीरवी [31]यदिन्द्राग्नी [32]पवित्रवन्त [33]उत नोऽहि[34]र्य[35]मथर्वाथातो द्युस्थाना देवगणा [36]इमा गिरः [37]सप्त ऋषय[38]स्तिर्यग्बिलो [39]देवानां भद्रौ[40]मासो [41]यज्ञेन [42]सुगा वो देवा [43]उमया अत्र [44]शं नो भवन्तु [45]देवानां पत्नीरु[46]ग्ना व्यन्त्विति षट्चत्वारिंशत् ॥][1]

॥ इत्युत्तरषट्के षष्ठोऽध्यायः ॥

॥ इति निरुक्ते द्वादशोऽध्यायः समाप्तः ॥

॥ इति दैवतं काण्डमुत्तरार्धं च समाप्तम् ॥

---

1. Small figure within brackets represents the corresponding section of the twelfth chapter of the *Nirukta*.

अथ परिशिष्टम्।

अथ त्रयोदशोऽध्यायः।

अथेमा अतिस्तुतय इत्याचक्षते। अपि वा संप्रत्यय एव स्यात्। माहाभाग्याद् देवतायाः। सोऽग्निमेव प्रथममाह।

त्वम॑ग्ने द्युभि॒स्त्वमा॑शुशु॒क्षणि॑ः। इति यथैतस्मिन्सूक्ते।

न॒ हि त्वदा॒रे नि॒मिष॑श्च॒ नेशे॑। इति वरुणस्य।

अथैषेन्द्रस्य ॥ १ ॥

यद्याव॑ इन्द्र ते श॒तं श॒तं भूमी॑रु॒त स्युः।

न त्वा॑ वज्रिन्त्स॒हस्रं॒ सूर्या॒ अनु॒ न जा॒तम॑ष्ट॒ रोद॑सी ॥

यदि त इन्द्र शतं दिवः शतं भूमयः प्रतिमानानि स्युर्न त्वा वज्रिन्त्सहस्रमपि सूर्या न द्यावापृथिव्यावप्यभ्यश्नुवीतामिति।

अथैषादित्यस्य ॥ २ ॥

---

१. MS. Wilson 475 dated Saṃvat 1443 (=1387 A. D.), which gives Durga's comm. on ch. 7–12 of the *Nirukta*, does not contain the *paris'iṣṭa*. Another MS. (Mill. 142.) of Durga's comm. on both parts of the *Nirukta* ends with ch. 12th which is finished on f. 123. (355). The colophon is as follows: sic. समाप्तग्रन्थः This MS. is dated 1839 A. D. & does not contain the *paris'iṣṭa*.

२. The 13th ch. is written continuously: ॥ श्री ६ ॥ ॐ अथेमा etc. in M 1; with simply ॐ in M 4, C 2; with ॥ ६ ॥ in C 6 and S. C 1 is incomplete; and C 3 separates the 13th ch. from the previous part; the numbering of the leaves which contain the 13th is from the beginning of the MSS. of the shorter recension, M 3, C 5, W 2 and Mi, write the 13th ch. continuously, with श्री or ॐ at the beginning. C 4 separates the 13th & begins ॐनमो गणेशाय; W 1 separates & begins: श्री गणेशाय नमः ॥; W 3 separates & begins: ॐनमो यास्काय ॥.

३. महाभाग्याद् Mi; Roth.

४. RV. II. 1. 1.

५. RV. II. 28. 6.

६. RV. VIII. 70. 5.

७. ०ज्ञं. C 3.

यदुदञ्चो वृषाकपे गृहमिन्द्राजगन्तन।
क१स्य पुल्वघो मृगः कमगञ्जनयोपनो विश्वस्मादिन्द्र उत्तरः[2] ॥

यदुदञ्चो वृषाकपे गृहमिन्द्राजगमत। क स्य पुल्वघो मृगः। क स बह्वादी मृगः। मृगो[3] मार्ष्टेर्गतिकर्मणः। कमगमद्देशं जनयोपनः। सर्वस्माद्य इन्द्र उत्तरस्तमेतद्ब्रूम आदित्यम्।

अथैषादित्यरश्मीनाम्[4] ॥ ३ ॥

वि हि सोतोरसृक्षत नेन्द्रं[6] देवममंसत।
यत्रामदद्वृषाकपिरर्यः पुष्टेषु मत्सखा विश्वस्मादिन्द्र उत्तरः[5] ॥

व्यसृक्षत हि प्रसवाय। न चेन्द्रं देवममंसत। यत्रामाद्यद्वृषाकपिः[7] । अर्य ईश्वरः[8]। पुष्टेषु पोषेषु। मत्सखा मम सखा। मदनसखा। ये नः सखायस्तैः सहेति वा। सर्वस्माद्य इन्द्र उत्तरस्तमेतद्ब्रूम आदित्यम्। अथैषाश्विनोः[10] ॥ ४ ॥

सृण्येव जर्भरी तुर्फरीतू नैतोशेव तुर्फरी पर्फरीका।
उदन्यजेव जेमना मदेरू ता मे जराय्वजरं मरायु[11][12] ॥

सृण्येवेति द्विविधा सृणिर्भवति। भर्ता च हन्ता च। तथाश्विनौ चापि भर्तारौ। जर्भरी भर्तारावित्यर्थः। तुर्फरीतू हन्तारौ। नैतोशेव तुर्फरी पर्फरीका। नितोशस्यापत्यं नैतोशम्। नैतोशेव तुर्फरी क्षिप्रहन्तारौ। उदन्यजेव जेमना मदेरू। उदन्यजेवेत्युदकजे इव। रत्ने सामुद्रे चान्द्रमसे[13] वा। जेमने जयमने। जेमना मदेरू। ता मे जराय्वजरं[14] मरायु। एतज्जरायुजं शरीरं शरदमजीर्णम्।

अथैषा सोमस्य[15] ॥ ५ ॥

---

१. कमगं जनयोपनो. Mi, C 3, C 4.

२. RV. X. 86. 22.

३. Identical with the explanation given in N. 1. 20.

४. Quoted SRV. X. 86. 22. p. iv. 271.

५. RV. X. 86. 1.

६. Quoted in N. 1. 4. to illustrate the use of the particle *na*.

७. यत्रामतद्वृषा०. C 5; यत्रामाद्यद्वृषा०. M 1, M 3.

८. ०मद्यद्वृषा. C 3.

९. ईश्वरः Mi; omitted by C 4.

१०. Omitted by Durga.

११. RV. X. 106. 6.

१२. SRV. X. 106. 6. p. iv. 354.

१३. चान्द्रमसीति वा M 3, Mi, W 2, C 4, C 5; चान्द्रमसेति वा. B.

१४. जराद्यजरं M 3, Mi, W 2, C 4, C 5.

१५. This entire section together with 6th 7th and 8th is omitted by the commentary attributed to Durga.

तरत्स मन्दी धावति धारा सुतस्यान्धसः।
तरत्स मन्दी धावति ॥

तरति स पापं सर्वं मन्दी यः स्तौति धावति गच्छत्यूर्ध्वां गतिम्। धारा सुतस्यान्धसः। धारयाभिषुतस्य सोमस्य मन्त्रपूतस्य वाचा स्तुतस्य। अथैषा यज्ञस्य ॥ ६ ॥

चत्वारि शृङ्गा त्रयो अस्य पादा द्वे शीर्षे सप्तहस्तासो अस्य।
त्रिधा बद्धो वृषभो रोरवीति महो देवो मर्त्याँ आ विवेश ॥

चत्वारि श्रृङ्गेति[4] वेदा वा एत उक्ताः। त्रयोऽस्य पादा इति सवनानि त्रीणि। द्वे शीर्षे प्रायणीयोदयनीये। सप्त हस्तासः सप्त छन्दाँसि। त्रिधा बद्धस्त्रेधा बद्धो मन्त्रब्राह्मणकल्पैः। वृषभो रोरवीति। रोरवणमस्य सवनक्रमेण ऋग्भिर्यजुर्भिः सामभिर्यदेनमृग्भिः शंसन्ति[5] यजुर्भिर्यजन्ति सामभिः स्तुवन्ति। महो देव इत्येष हि महान्देवो यद्यज्ञो मर्त्याँ आविवेशेति। एष हि मनुष्यानाविशति[6] यजनाय। तस्योत्तरा भूयसे निर्वचनाय[7] ॥ ७ ॥

स्वर्यन्तो नापेक्षन्त आ द्यां रोहन्ति रोदसी।
यज्ञं ये विश्वतोधारं सुविद्वाँसो वितेनिरे ॥

स्वर्गच्छन्त ईजाना वा नेक्षन्ते। तेऽमुमेव लोकं गतवन्तमीक्षन्तमिति[9]। आ द्यां रोहन्ति रोदसी। यज्ञं ये विश्वतोधारं सर्वतोधारं सुविद्वांसो वितेनिर इति। अथैषा[10] वाचः प्रवल्हितेव ॥ ८ ॥

चत्वारि वाक्परिमिता पदानि तानि विदुर्ब्राह्मणा ये मनीषिणः।
गुहा त्रीणि निहिता नेङ्गयन्ति तुरीयं वाचो मनुष्या वदन्ति[11] ॥

---

१. RV. IX. 58. 1.

२. SRV. IX. 58. 1. p. iii. 664.

३. RV. IV. 58. 3.

४. शृङ्गे. C 3. cf. SRV. IV. 58. 3. p. ii. 492.

५. शंसति. C 3.

६. मनुष्याणा०. M 3.

७. Cf. Gopatha Brāh. I. 2. 16. It appears that the passage in the Nirukta is an adaptation of the Brāhmaṇa.

The stanza is quoted by Patañjali in the introductory part of the *Mahābhāṣya* and is interpreted with reference to grammar i. e. 4, horns are the four parts of speech, noun, verb, preposition & particle; 3 feet are the 3 tenses; seven hands are the seven cases and so on.

Cf. S'abara on *Mīmāṃsā I. 2. 46.* Cf. also Kumārila in his *Tantra-vārtika* on the same sūtra.

८. AV. 4. 14. 4; VS. 17. 68.

९. गतवन्त ईक्षन्त W 2, C 5; C 4 reads इच्छन्त, a क्ष being added on the margin.

१०. The commentary attributed to Durga is resumed on the 13th ch. from अथैषा etc.

११. RV. I. 164. 45.

चत्वारि वाचः परिमितानि पदानि । तानि विदुर्ब्राह्मणा ये मेधाविनः । गुहायां त्रीणि निहितानि नार्थं वेदयन्ते । गुहा गूहतेः । तुरीयं त्वरतेः । कतमानि तानि चत्वारि पदानि । ओंकारो महाव्याहृतयश्चेत्यार्षम् । नामाख्याते चोपसर्गनिपाताश्चेति वैयाकरणाः । मन्त्रः कल्पो ब्राह्मणं चतुर्थी व्यावहारिकीति याज्ञिकाः । ऋचो यजूंषि सामानि चतुर्थी व्यावहारिकीति नैरुक्ताः । सर्पाणां वाग्वयसां क्षुद्रस्य सरीसृपस्य चतुर्थी व्यावहारिकीत्येके[1] । पशुषु तूणवेषु[2] मृगेष्वात्मनि चेत्यात्मप्रवादाः । अथापि ब्राह्मणं भवति । सा वै वाक्सृष्टा चतुर्धा व्यभवत् । एष्वेव लोकेषु त्रीणि पशुषु तुरीयम् । या पृथिव्यां साग्नौ सा रथन्तरे । यान्तरिक्षे सा वायौ सा वामदेव्ये । या दिवि सादित्ये सा बृहति[3] सा स्तनयित्नौ[4] । अथ पशुषु ततो या वागत्यरिच्यत तां ब्राह्मणेष्वदधुः । तस्माद्ब्राह्मणा उभयीं वाचं वदन्ति[5] या च देवानां या च मनुष्याणाम्[6] । इति । अथैषाक्षरस्य ॥ ९ ॥

ऋचो अक्षरे परमे व्योमन्यस्मिन्देवा अधि विश्वे निषेदुः ।
यस्तन्न वेद किमृचा करिष्यति य इत्तद्विदुस्त इमे समासते[7] ॥

ऋचो अक्षरे परमे व्यवने यस्मिन्देवा अधिनिषण्णाः[8] सर्वे । यस्तन्न वेद किं स ऋचा करिष्यति । य इत्तद्विदुस्त इमे समासत इति विदुष उपदिशति । कतमत्तदेतदक्षरम् । ओमित्येषा वागिति शाकपूणिः । ऋचश्च ह्यक्षरे परमे व्यवने धीयन्ते नानादेवतेषु च मन्त्रेषु । एतद्ध वा एतदक्षरं यत्सर्वां त्रयीं विद्यां प्रतिप्रति[9] । इति च ब्राह्मणम् ॥ १० ॥

आदित्य इति पुत्रः शाकपूणेः[10] । एषर्ग्भवति यदेनमर्चन्ति प्रत्यृचः[11] सर्वाणि भूतानि तस्य यदन्यन्मन्त्रेभ्यस्[12]तदक्षरं भवति । रश्मयोऽत्र देवा उच्यन्ते य एतस्मिन्नधिनिषण्णा इत्यधिदैवतम् ।

अथाध्यात्मम् । शरीरमत्र ऋगुच्यते यदेनेनार्चन्ति प्रत्यृचः[11] सर्वाणीन्द्रियाणि तस्य यदविनाशिधर्म तदक्षरं भवति । इन्द्रियाण्यत्र देवा उच्यन्ते यान्य[13]स्मिन्नात्मन्येकं भवन्तीत्यात्मप्रवादाः ॥ ११ ॥

---

१. Cf. S'B. IV. 1. 3. 15, 16.

२. तूणवे M 3, W 2, Mi, C 4.

३. बृहती. M 3.

४. स्तन इत्वावथ M 3, C 3; स्तनयित्वाथ Mi, C 4; स्तनयित्वावथ M 1, M 4, C 2, C 5, C 6, W 1, W 2, W 3; R, B. and Gune in the Bhand. comm. vol. p. 50.

५. Cf. PMbh. i. 1. 1. p. i. 3.

६. Cf. MS. I. 11. 5. Also cf. KS. XIV. 5, where also this quotation occours with small variants.

७. RV. I. 164. 39.

८. अधिनिषण: C 3.

९. KB. 6. 12.

१०. शाकपूणिः Mi, W 2, C 4, C 5.

११. प्रत्यूचं M 3, W 2, C 4, C 5.

१२. ०न्मात्रेभ्य० M 3, Mi, W 2, C 4, C 5.

१३. यान्यस्मिन्नधिनिषणानीत्यात्मप्रवादः M 3, W 2, C 3, C 4, C 5; यान्यस्मिन्नधिषणानी० Mi; यान्यस्मिन्नात्मन्नेकं M 1; यान्यस्मिन्नधिनिषणानीत्यात्मप्रवादाः B; यान्यस्मिन्नेकं भवन्तीत्यात्मप्रवादाः is another variant given in B.

अक्षरं न क्षरति। न क्षीयते वा[1]। अक्षयं भवति। वाचोऽक्ष इति वा। अक्षो यान[2]स्याञ्जनात्। तत्प्रकृतीतरद्वर्तनसामान्यादिति । अयं मन्त्रार्थचिन्ताभ्यूहोऽभ्यूळ्हः। अपि श्रुतितोऽपि तर्कतः[3]। न तु पृथक्त्वेन मन्त्रा निर्वक्तव्याः। प्रकरणश एव तु निर्वक्तव्याः[4]। न ह्येषु प्रत्यक्षमस्त्यनृषेरतपसो वा[5]। पारोवर्यवित्सु तु खलु वेदितृषु भूयोविद्यः प्रशस्यो भवतीत्युक्तं पुरस्तात्[6]। मनुष्या वा ऋषिषूत्क्रामत्सु देवानब्रुवन्। को न ऋषिर्भविष्यतीति। तेभ्य एतं तर्कमृषिं प्रायच्छन्मन्त्रार्थचिन्ताभ्यूहमभ्यूळ्हम्। तस्माद्यदेव[7] किंचानूचानोऽभ्यूहत्यार्षं तद्भवति[8] ॥ १२ ॥

हृदा तष्टेषु मनसो जवेषु यद्ब्राह्मणाः संयजन्ते सखायः ।
अत्राह त्वं वि जहुर्वेद्याभिरोहब्रह्माणो वि चरन्त्यु त्वे[9] ॥

हृदा तष्टेषु मनसां[10] प्रजवेषु[11] यद्ब्राह्मणाः संयजन्ते समानाख्याना ऋत्विजः। अत्राह त्वं विजहुर्वेद्याभिर्वेदितव्याभिः प्रवृत्तिभिः। ओहब्रह्माण ऊहब्रह्माणः। ऊह एषां ब्रह्मेति वा। सेयं विद्या श्रुतिमतिबुद्धिः। तस्यास्तपसा पारमीप्सितव्यम्। तदिदमायुरिच्छता न निर्वक्तव्यम्। तस्माच्छन्दस्सु शेषा उपेक्षितव्याः। अथागमो यां यां देवतां निराह तस्यास्तस्यास्ताद्भाव्यमनुभवत्य[12]नुभवति ॥ १३ ॥[13]

---

१. वाक्क्षरं M 1, C 3; वाक्षर M 4, C 2, C 6, W 1, W 3; Roth.

२. पादामस्यां M 3, Mi, W 2, C 4, C 5.

३. तर्किंतो C 3.

४. Cf. N. 1. 20; 2. 4.

५. Cf. BD. VIII. 129. न प्रत्यक्षमनृषेरस्ति मन्त्रम्। Cf. also उव्वट on RVP. तथा चोक्तं। नहि प्रत्यक्षमस्त्यनृषेर्मंत्र इति.

६. N. 1. 16.

७. ०देवं B.

८. Cf. Kumārila Bhaṭṭa, *Tantravārtika*. Benares ed. p. 132. or I. 3. 7.

बहुकालाभ्यस्तवेदतदर्थज्ञानाहितसंस्काराणां वेदनियतमार्गानुसारिप्रतिभानां नोन्मार्गेण प्रतिभानं सम्भवतीत्याश्रित्योच्यते यदेव किं चानूचानोऽभ्यूहत्यार्षं तद्भवतीति।

९. RV. X. 71. 8.

१०. मनसां प्रजवेषु is missing in M 1, added on the margin in a different handwriting.

११. SRV. X. 71. 8. p. iv. 222.

१२. Roth does not repeat अनुभवति, which should be done as the evidence of Mss. shows. Mss. of both recensions without any exception repeat *anubhavati* which is a sure indication that the chapter is concluded.

१३. M 4, has the colophon: sic. ॥ इति १३ ध्याय: ॥; C 2, has the colophon: sic. ॥ इति निरुक्ते उत्तरषट्के सप्तमोऽध्याय: ॥ ६ ॥ शुभं भवतु ॥

S & C 6, have the Colophon: sic. ॥ इति निरुक्ते उत्तरषट्के सप्तमोध्याय: ॥; Mss. of the shorter recension have the following colophon: । १३ । प्रथम: पाद: । M 3; C 5, W 2, W 3; ॥ १३ ॥ त्रयोदशाध्यायस्य प्रथम: पाद: ॥ C 4, W 1; sic. ॥ त्रयोदशोध्याये प्रथम: पाद: ॥

In the introduction to his commentary on the Ṛgveda, Sāyaṇa describes the Nirukta as follows: तद्व्याख्यानं च समाम्नाय: समाम्नात इत्यारभ्य तस्यास्तस्यास्ताद्भाव्यमनुभवत्य-

व्याख्यातं दैवतं यज्ञाङ्गं च । अथात ऊर्ध्वमार्गगतिं व्याख्यास्यामः ।

सूर्य आत्मा ।

इत्युदितस्य हि कर्मद्रष्टा । अथैतदनुप्रवदन्ति । अथैतं महान्तमात्मानमेषर्गणः प्रवदति ।

इन्द्रं मित्रं वरुणमग्निमाहुः । इति ।

अथैष महानात्मात्मजिज्ञासयात्मानं प्रोवाच ।

अग्निरस्मि जन्मना जातवेदाः[11] ।

अहमस्मि प्रथमजा इत्येताभ्याम् ॥ १४[13] ॥

अग्निरस्मि जन्मना जातवेदा घृतं मे चक्षुरमृतं म आसन् ।

अर्कस्त्रिधातू रजसो विमानोऽजस्रो घर्मो हविरस्मि नाम[11] ॥

नुभवत्यत्यन्तैर्द्वादशभिरध्यायैर्यास्को निर्ममे । This shows that by the time of Sāyaṇa, the 13th section was regarded as an integral part of the Nirukta. That this was Sāyaṇa's genuine belief is further supported by his frequent quotations from these sections.

Madhusūdana Sarasvatī (C. 1560 A. D.) writes in his com. on the *Mahimnastotra*, s'loka 7 भगवता यास्केन 'समाम्नायः समाम्नातः इत्यादि त्रयोदशाध्यायात्मकं निरुक्तमारचितम् ।

A summary of the thirteen sections is added as follows:— अथेमा यद्यावो यदुदञ्चो त्रि हि सोतोः सृण्येव तरस्स चत्वारि शृङ्गा स्वर्यन्तश्चत्वारि वागृचो अक्षर आदित्य इत्यक्षरं न क्षरति हंदा तष्टेषु त्रयोदश ॥ M 4, C 2, C 6, S. C 2 include this summary in that of the following 37 sections given at the end of the last section of the next chapter. Although according to the colophon of C 2 the 13th ch. comes to an end, yet no summary of its contents is made. This shows that, in reality, the 13th ch. is not ended.

१. M 1 begins with ॐ but it does not begin every ch. with ॐ. M 4 begins with ॐ, and every ch. is commenced with ॐ. The text is not written continuously but is separated from the previous part in C 6.

२. See N. 7–12. chapters.

३. See N. 13. 1–13.

४. Fragment of RV. I. 115. 1.

५. कर्मद्रष्टा M 3, C 5, See. Bib. Ind. IV. 368.

६. Cf. N. 7. 18.

७. ०मेषर्गणः Bib. Ind.

८. प्रवदन्ति M 1, M 4, C 2, C 3, C 6, S; R. B. Bib. Ind.

९. RV. I. 164. 46.

१०. रश्मि C 3.

११. RV. III. 26. 7.

१२. ARS. 1. 9; TB. 2. 8. 8. 1; TA. 9. 10. 6; TU. 3. 10. 6; Nṛp. U. 2. 4.

१३. ॥ १४ ॥ १ ॥ M 1; ॥ १४ ॥ C 2, C 3; ॥ १ ॥ M 4, C 6, S; ॥ १ ॥ of the second pāda M 3, C 4, C 5, W 1, W 3; W 2 places the figure ॥ १४ ॥ although the words इति प्रथमः पादः are written after the 13th section. Mi has the figure ॥ १ ॥ १४ ॥. This will indicate the method used by various Mss. in numbering the following sections.

१४. धर्मो R. See Bib. Ind. IV. 368.

अहमस्मि प्रथमजा ऋतस्य पूर्वं देवेभ्यो अमृतस्य नाम[1] ।
यो मा ददाति स इदेवमावद[2] अहमन्नमन्नमदन्तमद्मि[3] ॥

इति स ह ज्ञात्वा प्रादुर्बभूव । एवं तं व्याजहारायन्तमात्मानमध्यात्मजमन्तिकमन्यस्मा आचक्ष्वेति ॥ १५[6] ॥

अपश्यं गोपामनिपद्यमानमा च परा च पथिभिश्चरन्तम् ।
स सध्रीचीः स विषूचीर्वसान आ वरीवर्ति भुवनेष्वन्तः[7] ॥

आवरीवर्ति भुवनेष्वन्तरिति । अथैष महानात्मा सत्त्वलक्षणस्तत्परं तद्ब्रह्म तत्सत्यं तत्सलिलं तदव्यक्तं तदस्पर्शं तदरूपं तदरसं तदगन्धं तदमृतं तच्छुक्लं तन्निष्ठो भूतात्मा । सैषा भूतप्रकृतिरित्येके । तत्क्षेत्रं तज्ज्ञानात्[9] क्षेत्रज्ञमनुप्राप्य निरात्मकम्[10] । अथैष महानात्मा त्रिविधो भवति । सत्त्वं रजस्तम इति । सत्त्वं तु मध्ये विशुद्धं तिष्ठति । अभितो रजस्तमसी इति कामद्वेषस्तम इत्यविज्ञातस्य विशुध्यतो विभूतिं कुर्वतः क्षेत्रज्ञपृथक्त्वाय कल्पते । प्रतिभातिलिङ्गो महानात्मा तमोलिङ्गो विद्या प्रकाशलिङ्गस्तमः । अपि निश्चयलिङ्ग आकाशः ॥ १६[11] ॥

आकाशगुणः शब्दः[12] । आकाशाद्वायुर्द्विगुणः स्पर्शेन । वायोर्ज्योतिस्त्रिगुणं रूपेण । ज्योतिष आपश्चतुर्गुणा रसेन । अद्भ्यः पृथिवी पञ्चगुणा गन्धेन । पृथिव्या भूतग्रामस्थावरजङ्गमाः । तदेतदहर्युगसहस्रं[13] जागर्ति । तस्यान्ते सुषुप्स्यन्नङ्गानि प्रत्याहरति । भूतग्रामाः पृथिवीमपि यन्ति । पृथिव्यपः । आपो ज्योतिषम् । ज्योतिर्वायुम् । वायुराकाशम् । आकाशो मनः । मनो विद्याम् । विद्या महान्तमात्मानम् । महानात्मा प्रतिभाम् । प्रतिभा प्रकृतिम् । सा स्वपिति युगसहस्रं[14] रात्रिः । तावेतावहोरात्रावजस्रं परिवर्तेते । स कालस्तदेतदहर्भवति ।

युगसहस्रपर्यन्तमहर्यद्ब्रह्मणो विदुः ।
रात्रिं युगसहस्रान्तां तेऽहोरात्रविदो जनाः[15] ॥ इति ॥ १७[16] ॥

---

१. नाभिः M 1, M 4, C 2, C 6, W 1, S. cf. SV. See. Bib. Ind. loc. cit.

२. इदेवमावा M 1, M 4, C 2, C 6, S. Roth, B; इवेदमावाद C 3, see Bib, Ind. loc. cit.

३. ARS. I. 9; TB. 2. 8. 8. 1; TA. 9. 10. 6; TU. 3. 10. 6; Nrp. U. 2. 4.

४. व्याजहारायतम etc. R. ते व्याजहारायन्तम॰ L.

५. ॰मभ्यात्म॰ R.

६. ॥ २ ॥ M 4, C 6, S; ॥ २ ॥ of the second pāda M 3, C 4, C 5, W 1, W 3; ॥ २ ॥ १५ ॥ Mi, ॥ १५ ॥ M 1, C 2, C 3; W 2.

७. RV. I. 164. 31; X. 177. 3.

८. Missing in the text but added on the margin in a different handwriting in M 1.

९. तदज्ञाना॰ Roth. see Bib. Ind. IV. 370.

१०. निरात्मजम् M 1, Roth. see Bib. Ind. loc. cit.

११. ॥ ३ ॥ M 4, C 6, S; ॥ ३ ॥ of the second pāda, M 3, C 4, C 5, W 1, W 3; ॥ ३ ॥ १६ ॥ Mi; ॥ १६ ॥ M 1, C 2, C 3; W 2.

१२. Cf. Manu. I. 75.

१३. Cf. Bh. Gītā. VIII. 16-19.

१४. Omitted by M 1.

१५. Cf. Bh. Gītā. VIII. 17; cf. Manu i. 73; cf. BD. VIII. 98.

१६. ॥ ४ ॥ M 4, C 6, S; ॥ ४ ॥ of the second pāda M 3, C 4, C 5, W 1, W 3; ॥ ४ ॥ १७ ॥ Mi; ॥ १७ ॥ M 1, C 2, C 3; W 2.

तं परिवर्तमानमन्योऽनुप्रवर्तते । स्रष्टा द्रष्टा विभक्तातिमात्रोऽहमिति गम्यते । स मिथ्यादर्शनेदं पावकं महाभूतेषु चिरोण्वाकाशाद्वायोः प्राणश्चक्षुश्च[1] वक्तारं च तेजसोऽद्भ्यः स्नेहं पृथिव्या मूर्तिः । पार्थिवाँस्त्वष्टौ गुणान्विद्यात्[2] । त्रीन्मातृतस्त्रीन्पितृतः । अस्थिस्नायुमज्जानः पितृतः । त्वङ्मांसशोणितानि मातृतः । अन्नपानमित्यष्टौ । सोऽयं पुरुषः सर्वमयः सर्वज्ञानोऽपि क्लृप्तः ॥ १८[3] ॥

स यद्यनुरुध्यते तद्भवति । यदि धर्ममनुरुध्यते[4] तद्देवो भवति । यदि ज्ञानमनुरुध्यते तदमृतो भवति । यदि काममनुरुध्यते संच्यवते । इमां योनिं संदध्यात्[5] । तदिदमत्र मतम् । श्लेष्मा रेतसः संभवति । श्लेष्मणो रसः । रसाच्छोणितम् । शोणितान्माँसम् । माँसान्मेदः । मेदसः स्नावा । स्नाव्नोऽस्थीनि । अस्थिभ्यो मज्जा । मज्जातो रेतः । तदिदं योनौ रेतः सिक्तं पुरुषः संभवति । शुक्रातिरेके[6] पुमान्भवति । शोणितातिरेके स्त्री भवति । द्वाभ्यां समेन नपुंसको भवति । शुक्रेण भिन्नेन[7] यमो भवति । शुक्रशोणितसंयोगान्मातृपितृसंयोगाच्च । तत्कथमिदं शरीरं परं संयम्यते । सौम्यो भवति । एकरात्रोषितं कललं भवति । पञ्चरात्राद् बुद्बुदाः । सप्तरात्रात्पेशी । द्विसप्तरात्रादर्बुदः । पञ्चविंशतिरात्रः स्वस्थितो घनो भवति । मासमात्रात्कठिनो[8] भवति । द्विमासाभ्यन्तरे शिरः संपद्यते । मासत्रयेण ग्रीवाव्यादेशः । मासचतुष्केण त्वग्व्यादेशः । पञ्चमे मासे नखरोमव्यादेशः । षष्ठे मुखनासिकाक्षिश्रोत्रं च संभवति । सप्तमे चलनसमर्थो भवति । अष्टमे बुध्याध्यवस्यति । नवमे सर्वाङ्गसंपूर्णो भवति ।

मृतश्चाहं पुनर्जातो जातश्चाहं पुनर्मृतः ।
नाना योनिसहस्राणि मयोषितानि यानि वै[9] ॥
आहारा विविधा भुक्ताः पीता नानाविधाः स्तनाः ।
मातरो विविधा दृष्टाः पितरः सुहृदस्तथा[10] ॥
अर्वाङ्मुखः पीड्यमानो जन्तुश्चैव समन्वितः ।
सांख्यं योगं समभ्यस्येत्पुरुषं वा पञ्चविंशकम्[11] ॥ इति ।

ततश्च दशमे मासे प्रजायते । जातश्च वायुना स्पृष्टो[12] न स्मरति जन्ममरणम् । अन्ते च शुभाशुभं कर्मैतच्छरीरस्य[13] प्रामाण्यम् ॥ १९[14] ॥

---

१. प्राणं चक्षुश्च M 3, C 4, C 5, W 1, W 2, W 3, Mi

२. See Bib. Ind. IV. 372.

३. ॥ ५ ॥ M 4, C 6, S; ॥ ५ ॥ of the second pāda M 3, C 4, C 5, W 1, W 3; ॥ ५ ॥ १५ ॥ Mi; ॥ १५ ॥ M 1, C 2, C 3; W 2.

४. धर्मोऽनु० Bib. Ind. loc. cit.

५. ०दभन्नवतम् M 3, Mi, W 1, W 2, C 4; ०दभन्नमतम् C 5.

६. Cf. AB. ii. 5. 5; iii. 3. 13. see Bib. Ind. IV. 373.

७. शुक्रभिन्नेन M 1, M 4, C 2, C 3, C 6, S, R, see Bib. Ind. IV. 373.

८. कठिणो R.

९. Cf. the *Garbhopaniṣat.* 4.

१०. „

११. Untraced.

१२. स्पृष्टस्तन्न. M 1, M 4, C 2, C 3, C 6, S, R. B.

१३ The passage: रसाच्छोणितम्...शुभाशुभं कर्म is almost identical with the *Garbhopaniṣat.* 2–4.

१४. ॥ ६ ॥ M 4, C 6, S; ॥ ६ ॥ of the second pāda M 3, C 4, C 5, W 1, W 3; ॥ ६ ॥ १९ ॥ Mi, ॥ १९ ॥ M 1, C 2, C 3; W 2.

अष्टोत्तरं संधिशतमष्टाकपालं शिरः संपद्यते । षोडश वपापलानि । नव स्नायुशतानि । सप्त शतं पुरुषस्य मर्मणाम् । अर्धचतस्रो रोमाणि कोट्यः । हृदयं ह्यष्टकपालानि । द्वादशकपालानि जिह्वा । वृषणौ ह्यष्टसुपर्णौ । तथोपस्थगुदपाय्वेतन्मूत्रपुरीषं कस्मादाहारपानसिक्तत्वादनुपचितकर्माणावन्योन्यं जयेते इति । तं विद्याकर्मणी समन्वारभेते पूर्वप्रज्ञा च । महत्यज्ञानतमसि मग्नौ जरामरणक्षुत्पिपासाशोकक्रोधलोभमोहमदभयमत्सरहर्षविषादेर्ष्यासूयात्मकैर्द्वन्द्वैरभिभूयमानः सोऽस्मादार्जवं जवीभावानां तन्निर्मुच्यते । सोऽस्मात्पाद्मं महाभूमिकावच्छरीराण्निमेषमात्रैः प्रकाय प्रकृतिरधिपतीय तैजसं शरीरं कृत्वा कर्मणोऽनुरूपं फलमनुभूय तस्य संक्षये पुनरिमँल्लोकं प्रतिपद्यते ॥ २०[६] ॥

अथ ये हिंसामाश्रित्य विद्यामुत्सृज्य महत्तपस्तेपिरे चिरेण वेदोक्तानि वा कर्माणि कुर्वन्ति ते धूममभिसंभवन्ति । धूमाद्रात्रिम् । रात्रेरपक्षीयमाणपक्षम् । अपक्षीयमाणपक्षाद् दक्षिणायनम् । दक्षिणायनात्पितृलोकम् । पितृलोकाच्चन्द्रमसम् । चन्द्रमसो वायुम् । वायोर्वृष्टिम् । वृष्टेरोषधयश्चैतद्भूत्वा तस्य संक्षये पुनरेवेमँल्लोकं प्रतिपद्यते ॥ २१[९] ॥

अथ ये हिंसामुत्सृज्य विद्यामाश्रित्य महत्तपस्तेपिरे ज्ञानोक्तानि वा कर्माणि कुर्वन्ति तेऽर्चिरभिसंभवन्ति । अर्चिषोऽहः । अह्न आपूर्यमाणपक्षम् । आपूर्यमाणपक्षादुदगयनम् । उदगयनाद्देवलोकम् । देवलोकादादित्यम् । आदित्याद्वैद्युतम् । वैद्युतान्मानसम् । मानसः पुरुषो भूत्वा ब्रह्मलोकमभिसंभवन्ति । ते न पुनरावर्तन्ते । शिष्टा दन्दशूका यत इदं न जानन्ति तस्मादिदं वेदितव्यम् । अथाप्याह ॥ २२ ॥[१०]

न तं विदाथ य इमा जजानान्यद्युष्माकमन्तरं बभूव ।
नीहारेण प्रावृता जल्प्या चासुतृप उक्थशासश्चरन्ति[११] ॥

न तं विद्यया विदुषो यमेवं विद्वाँसो वदन्ति । अक्षरं ब्रह्मणस्पतिमन्यद्युष्मा-

---

१. ततो M 1, C 2, C 3, C 6.

२. पाद्येत॰ M 3, Mi, C 4, C 5, W 1, W 2.

३. कर्मणा M 3, Mi, C 4, C 5, W 1, W 2; see Bib. Ind. IV. 375.

४. ॰दार्जवजवी॰ M 1, M 4, C 2, C 3, C 6, S; B.

५. सोऽस्मात्पाद्मम्महा॰ M 3, Mi, W 1, W 2, W 3, C 4, C 5.

६. ॥ ९ ॥ M 4, C 6, S; ॥ ९ ॥ of the second pāda M 3, C 4, C 5, W 1, W 3; ॥ ७ ॥ २० ॥ Mi; ॥ २० ॥ M 1, C 2, C 3; W 2.

७. तस्य संक्षये is omitted by M 3, Mi, W 1, W 2, W 3, C 4, C 5.

८. पुनरिमँल्लोकं L.

९. ॥ ८ ॥ M 4, C 6, S; ॥ ८ ॥ of the second pāda M 3, C 4, C 5, W 1, W 3; ॥ ८ ॥ २१ ॥ Mi; ॥ २१ ॥ M 1, C 2, C 3; W 2.

१०. ॥ ९ ॥ M 4, C 6, S; ॥ ९ ॥ of the second pāda M 3, C 4, C 5, W 3; ॥ ९ ॥ २२ ॥ Mi; ॥ २२ ॥ M 1, C 2, C 3; W 2. The इति द्वितीयः पादः ॥ ९ ॥ २२ ॥ W 1.

११. RV. X. 82. 7; VS. 17. 31; TS. 4. 6. 2. 2; Ks. 18. 1; Ms. 2. 10 3: 135. 1.

कमन्तरमन्यदेषामन्तरं वभूवेति । नीहारेण प्रावृतास्तमसा जल्प्या[1] चासुतृप उक्थशासः प्राणं सूर्यं यत्पथगामिन[2]श्चरन्ति । अविद्वाँसः क्षेत्रज्ञमनुप्रवदन्ति । अथाहो विद्वाँसः क्षेत्रज्ञोऽनुकल्पते । तस्य तपसा सहाप्रमादमेति । अथासख्यो भवति । तेनासन्ततमिच्छेत् । तेन सख्यमिच्छेत् । एष हि सखा श्रेष्ठः संजानाति भूतं भवद्भविष्यदिति । ज्ञाता कस्मात् । ज्ञायते[3]: । सखा कस्मात् । सख्यतेः । सह भूतेन्द्रियैः शेरते । महाभूतानि सेन्द्रियाणि । प्रज्ञया कर्म कारयतीति । तस्य यत्त[4]पः प्रतिष्ठाशीलमुपशम आत्मा ब्रह्मेति स ब्रह्मभूतो भवति । साक्षिमात्रो व्यवतिष्ठतेऽबन्धो ज्ञानकृतः ॥

अथात्मनो महतः प्रथमं भूतनामधेया[5]न्यनुक्रमिष्यामः ॥ २३ ॥[6]

हंसः । घर्मः । यज्ञः । वेनः । मेधः[10] । कृमिः । भूमिः[11] । विभुः । प्रभुः । शंभुः । राभुः । वधकर्मा । सोमः[12] । भूतम्[13] । भुवनम्[13] । भविष्यत्[13] । आपः[14] । महत्[15] । व्योम[16] । यशः[17] । महः[13] । स्वर्णीकम्[13] । स्मृतीकम्[13] । स्वृतीकम्[13] । सतीकम्[13] । सतीनम्[13] । गहनम्[13] । गभीरम्[13] । गह्वरम्[13] । कम्[18] । अन्नम्[13] । हविः[13] । सद्म[19] । सदनम्[13] । ऋतम्[20] । योनिः[21] । ऋतस्य योनिः[13] । सत्यम्[13] । नीरम्[22] । हविः[13] । रयिः[23] ।

---

१. जल्या M 3, Mi, C 4, C 5, W 1, W 3.

२. पथगामिन्यः M 3.

३. जानतेः C 5, C 4, W 2; जायतेः M 1, M 4, C 2, C 3, C 6, S; R. see Bib. Ind. IV. 380.

४. यत्तपः M 3.

५. ०धेयान्युत्क्रमिष्यामः R.

६. ॥ १० ॥ M 4, C 6, S; ॥ १० ॥ of the second pāda M 3, C 4, C 5, W 3; ॥ १० ॥ २३ ॥ Mi; ॥ २३ ॥ M 1, C 2, C 3; W 2; ॥ १ ॥ of the third pāda W 1.

७. Cf. Ngh. synonym of day. I. 9; synonym of sacrifice III. 17.

८. Ngh. III. 17.

९. Synonym of wise, Ngh. III. 15; synonym of sacrifice, Ngh. III. 17.

१०. Synonym of wise, Ngh. III. 15.

११. Synonym of earth, Ngh. I. 1.

१२. Ngh. V. 5.

१३. Synonym of water, Ngh. I. 12.

१४. Synonym of atmosphere, Ngh. I. 3; of water, I 12; terrestrial deities, V. 3.

१५. Synonym of water, Ngh. I. 12; of great, III. 3.

१६. Synonym of atmosphere, Ngh. I. 3; of quarter, I. 6; of water, I. 12.

१७. Synonym of water, Ngh. I 12; of food, II. 7; of wealth II. 10.

१८. Synonym of water, Ngh. I. 12; of happiness, III. 6.

१९. Synonym of water, Ngh. I. 12; of battle, II. 17; of house, III. 4.

२०. Synonym of wealth, Ngh. II. 10; of truth, III. 10.

२१. Synonym of water, Ngh. I. 12; of house, III. 4.

२२. See note १३. Omitted by M 3, C 4, C 5, W 1, W 2, W 3.

२३. Synonym of water, Ngh. I. 12; of wealth, II. 10.

सत्[1] । पूर्णम्[1] । सर्वम्[2] । अक्षितम्[1] । बर्हिः[3] । नाम[1] । सर्पिः[1] । अपः[4] । पवित्रम्[5] । अमृतम्[6] । इन्दुः[1] । हेम[6] । स्वः[7] । सर्गाः[8] । शम्बरम्[9] । अम्बरम्[10] । वियत्[11] । व्योम[12] । बर्हिः[3] । धन्व[11] । अन्तरिक्षम्[11] । आकाशम्[11] । आपः[13] । पृथिवी[14] । भूः[15] । स्वयम्भूः[11] । अध्वा[16] । पुष्करम्[11] । सगरः[17] । समुद्रः[11] । तपः[18] । तेजः[19] । सिन्धुः[20] । अर्णवः । नाभिः । ऊर्ध्वः[21] । वृक्षः । तत् । यत् । किम् । ब्रह्म[22] । वरेण्यम् । हंसः । आत्मा । भवन्ति[23] । वर्धन्ति[24] । अध्वानम् । यद्वाहिष्ठ्या[25] । शरीराणि । अव्ययं[26] च संस्कुरुते । यज्ञः । आत्मा । भवति । यदेनं तन्वते ।

अथैतं महान्तमात्मानमेतानि सूक्तान्येता ऋचोऽनुप्रवदन्ति ॥ २४[27] ॥

सोमः पवते जनिता मतीनां जनिता दिवो जनिता पृथिव्याः ।
जनिताग्नेर्जनिता सूर्यस्य जनितेन्द्रस्य जनितोत विष्णोः[28] ॥

१. Synonym of water, Ngh. I. 12.

२. सवम् B. see १.

३. Synonym of atmosphere, Ngh. I. 3; of water, I. 12; terrestrial diety, V. 2.

४. Synonym of water Ngh. I. 12; of action, II. 1.

५. Synonym of water, Ngh. I. 12; of pure, IV. 2.

६. Synonym of gold, Ngh. I. 2; of water, I. 12.

७. Synonym of water, Ngh. I. 12; of sacrifice, III. 17; atmospheric deity, V. 4.

८. Synonym of water, Ngh. I. 12; of celestial deity, V. 5.

९. Synonym of water, Ngh. I. 12, of strength, II. 9.

१०. Synonym of atmosphere, Ngh. I. 3; of near, II. 16.

११. Synonym of atmosphere, Ngh. I. 3.

१२. Synonym atmosphere, Ngh. I. 3; of quarter, I. 6; of water, Ngh. I. 12.

१३. Synonym of water, Ngh. I. 12.

१४. Cf. Ngh. I. 1; synonym of atmosphere, I. 2; terrestrial deity, V. 1; atmospheric deity V. 4; celestial deity V. 5.

१५. Synonym of earth, Ngh. I. 1; of atmosphere, I. 3.

१६. अध्व. B. and Bib. Ind. see ११.

१७. सगरं M 3, C 4, C 5, W 1, W 2, W 3, see ११.

१८. Synonym of flame, Ngh. I. 17.

१९. Synonym of flame, Ngh. I. 17; of water, I. 12.

२०. Cf. Ngh. I. 13.

२१. Omitted by च. छ. ज. Mss., see Bib. Ind. IV. 381. ऊर्ध्वः R. synonym of night, Ngh. I. 7.

२२. Synonym of water, Ngh. I. 12; of food, II. 7; of wealth, II. 10.

२३. भवति R. Bib. Ind.

२४. वधन्त्यध्वानम् R.

२५. यद्वाहिष्या R.

२६. अव्ययं संस्कुरुते M 3, C 4, C 5; अव्ययं च सङ्कुरुते W 2, Mi; see Bib. Ind. IV. 381.

२७. ॥ ११ ॥ M 4, C 6, S; ॥ ११ ॥ of the second pāda M 3, C 4, C 5, W 3; ॥ ११ ॥ २४ ॥ Mi; ॥ २४ ॥ M 1, C 2, C 3; W 2; ॥ २ ॥ of the third pāda W 1.

२८. RV. IX. 96. 5.

सोमः पवते जनयिता मतीनां जनयिता दिवो जनयिता पृथिव्या जनयिताग्नेर्जनयिता सूर्यस्य जनयितेन्द्रस्य जनयितोत विष्णोः ॥ २५[1] ॥

ब्रह्मा देवानां पदवीः कवीनामृषिर्विप्राणां महिषो मृगाणाम्।
श्येनो गृध्राणां स्वधितिर्वनानां सोमः पवित्रमत्येति रेभन्[2] ॥[3]

ब्रह्मा देवानामिति। एष हि ब्रह्मा भवति। देवानां देवनकर्मणामादित्यरश्मीनाम्। पदवीः कवीनामिति। एष हि पदं वेत्ति। कवीनां कवीयमानानामादित्यरश्मीनाम्[4]। ऋषिर्विप्राणामिति। एष हि ऋषिणो[5] भवति। विप्राणां व्यापनकर्मणामादित्यरश्मीनाम्। महिषो मृगाणामिति। एष हि महान्भवति। मृगाणां मार्गणकर्मणामादित्यरश्मीनाम्। श्येनो गृध्राणामिति। श्येन आदित्यो भवति। श्यायतेर्गतिकर्मणः। गृध्र आदित्यो भवति। गृध्यतेः स्थानकर्मणः। यत एतस्मिंस्तिष्ठति। स्वधितिर्वनानामिति। एष हि स्वयं कर्माण्यादित्यो धत्ते। वनानां वननकर्मणामादित्यरश्मीनाम्। सोमः पवित्रमत्येति रेभन्निति। एष हि पवित्रं रश्मीनामत्येति। स्तूयमान एष एवैतत्सर्वमक्षरम्। इत्यधिदैवतम्।

अथाध्यात्मम्। ब्रह्मा देवानामिति। अयमपि ब्रह्मा भवति। देवानां देवनकर्मणामिन्द्रियाणाम्। पदवीः कवीनामिति। अयमपि पदं वेत्ति। कवीनां कवीयमानानामिन्द्रियाणाम्[6]। ऋषिर्विप्राणामिति। अयमपि ऋषिणो[7] भवति। विप्राणां व्यापनकर्मणामिन्द्रियाणाम्। महिषो मृगाणामिति। अयमपि महान्भवति। मृगाणां मार्गणकर्मणामिन्द्रियाणाम्। श्येनो गृध्राणामिति। श्येन आत्मा भवति। श्यायतेर्ज्ञानकर्मणः। गृध्राणीन्द्रियाणि। गृध्यतेर्ज्ञानकर्मणः। यत एतस्मिंस्तिष्ठन्ति[8]। स्वधितिर्वनानामिति। अयमपि स्वयं कर्माण्यात्मनि धत्ते। वनानां वननकर्मणामि-

1. This is the reading of the Mss. of the shorter recension; those of the longer recension read the text as follows:

सोमः पवते। सोमः सूर्यः प्रसवनात्। जनिता मतीनां प्रकाशकर्मणामादित्यरश्मीनाम्। दिवो द्योतनकर्मणामादित्यरश्मीनाम्। पृथिव्याः प्रथमनकर्मणामादित्यरश्मीनाम्। अग्नेर्गतिकर्मणामादित्यरश्मीनाम्। सूर्यस्य स्वीकरणकर्मणामादित्यरश्मीनाम्। इन्द्रस्यैश्वर्यकर्मणामादित्यरश्मीनाम्। विष्णोर्व्याप्तिकर्मणामादित्यरश्मीनाम्। इत्यधिदैवतम्।

अथाध्यात्मम्। सोम आत्मा। अप्येतस्मादेवेन्द्रियाणां जनितेत्यर्थः। अपि वा सर्वाभिर्विभूतिभिर्विभूतत आत्मा। इत्यात्मगतिमाचष्टे॥ २५॥

२. ॥ १२ ॥ M 1, C 6, S; ॥ १२ ॥ of the second pāda M 3, C 4, C 5, W 3; ॥ १२ ॥ २५ ॥ Mi; ॥ २५ ॥ M 1, C 2, C 3; W 2; ॥ ३ ॥ of the third pāda W 1.

३. RV. IX. 96. 6; VS. 37. 7. TA. 10. 10. 4.

४. कवीयमाणाना° ख. ग. ऊ. see Bib. Ind. IV. 383.

५. ह्यृषिणा. ग. हि ऋषिणा. ख. ऊ. loc. cit.

६. कवीयमाणा° loc. cit.

७. अयमप्यृषिणो. Bib. Ind. IV. 384; B.

८. °तिष्ठति. Bib. Ind. loc. cit.

न्द्रियाणाम् । सोमः पवित्रमत्येति रेभन्निति । अयमपि पवित्रमिन्द्रियाण्यत्येति । स्तूयमानोऽयमेवैतत्सर्वमनुभवति । इत्यात्मगतिमाचष्टे[1] ॥ २६[2] ॥

तिस्रो वाचं ईरयति प्र वह्निर्ऋतस्य धीतिं ब्रह्मणो मनीषाम् ।
गावो यन्ति गोपतिं पृच्छमानाः सोमं यन्ति मतयो वावशानाः[3] ॥

वह्निरादित्यो भवति । स तिस्रो वाचः प्रेरयति । ऋचो यजूंषि सामान्यृतस्यादित्यस्य कर्माणि ब्रह्मणो मतानि । एव एवैतत्सर्वमक्षरम् । इत्यधिदैवतम् ।

अथाध्यात्मम् । वह्निरात्मा भवति । स तिस्रो वाच ईरयति [प्रेरयति[4] ।] विद्यामतिबुद्धिमताम्तस्यात्मनः कर्माणि ब्रह्मणो मतानि । अयमेवैतत्सर्वमनुभवति । इत्यात्मगतिमाचष्टे ॥ २७[5] ॥

सोमं गावो धेनवो वावशानाः सोमं विप्रा मतिभिः पृच्छमानाः ।
सोमः सुतः पूयते अज्यमानः सोमे अर्कास्त्रिष्टुभः सं नवन्ते[6] ॥

एत एव सोमं गावो धेनवो रश्मयो वावँश्यमानाः[7] कामयमाना आदित्यं यन्ति । एवमेव सोमं विप्रा रश्मयो मतिभिः पृच्छमानाः कामयमाना आदित्यं यन्ति । एवमेव सोमः सुतः पूयते अज्यमानः । एतमेवार्काश्च त्रिष्टुभश्च संनवन्ते । तत एतस्मिन्नादित्य एकं भवन्ति । इत्यधिदैवतम् ।

अथाध्यात्मम् । एत एव सोमं गावो धेनव इन्द्रियाणि वावश्यमानानि कामयमानान्यात्मानं यन्ति । एवमेव सोमं विप्रा इन्द्रियाणि मतिभिः पृच्छमानानि कामयमानान्यात्मानं[8] यन्ति । एवमेव सोमः सुतः पूयते अज्यमानः । इममेवात्मा च[9] सप्त ऋषयश्च संनवन्ते । तान्येतस्मिन्नात्मन्येकं[10] भवन्ति । इत्यात्मगतिमाचष्टे ॥ २८[11] ॥

---

१. इति is omitted by Roth.

२. ॥ १३ ॥ M 4, C 6, S; ॥ १३ ॥ of the 2nd pāda M 3, C 4, C 5, W 3; ॥ १३ ॥ २६ ॥ Mi; ॥ २६ ॥ M 1, C 2, C 3; W 2; ॥ ४ ॥ of the 3rd pāda W 1.

३. RV. IX. 97. 34.

४. प्रेरयति is omitted M 3, C 4, C 5, Mi, W 1, W 2, W 3.

५. ॥ १४ ॥ M 4, C 6, S; ॥ १४ ॥ of the 2nd pāda. M 3, C 4, C 5, W 3; ॥ १४ ॥ २७ ॥ Mi; ॥ २७ ॥ M 1, C 2, C 3, W 2; ॥ ५ ॥ of the 3rd pāda. W 1.

६. RV. IX. 97. 35.

७. वावाश्य० ख. ग. झ. see Bib Ind. IV. 386.

८. कामयमानान्यात्मानं omitted by M 3, C 4, C 5.

९. तानीमान्येत० M 3, C 4, C 5, W 1, W 2, W 3, Mi; Bib. Ind.

१०. ०त्मन्नेकं C 5.

११. ॥ १५ ॥ M 4, C 6, S; ॥ १५ ॥ of the 2nd pāda. M 3, C 4, C 5, W 3; ॥ १५ ॥ २८ ॥ Mi; ॥ २८ ॥ M 1, C 2, C 3, W 2; ॥ ६ ॥ of the 3rd pāda. W 1.

अक्रान्त्समुद्रः प्रथमे विधर्मञ्जनयन्प्रजा भुवनस्य राजा ।
वृषा पवित्रे अधि सानो अव्ये बृहत्सोमो वावृधे सुवान इन्दुः ॥

अत्यक्रमीत्समुद्र आदित्यः परमे व्यवने वर्षकर्मणा जनयन्प्रजा भुवनस्य राजा सर्वस्य राजा। वृषा पवित्रे अधि सानो अव्ये बृहत्सोमो वावृधे सुवान इन्दुः। इत्यधिदैवतम् ।

अथाध्यात्मम् । अत्यक्रमीत्समुद्र आत्मा परमे व्यवने ज्ञानकर्मणा जनयन्प्रजा भुवनस्य राजा सर्वस्य राजा । वृषा पवित्रे अधि सानो अव्ये बृहत्सोमो वावृधे सुवान इन्दुः । इत्यात्मगतिमाचष्टे ॥ २९[३] ॥

महत्तत्सोमो महिषश्चकारापां यद्गर्भोऽवृणीत देवान् ।
अदधादिन्द्रे पवमान ओजोऽजनयत्सूर्ये ज्योतिरिन्दुः ॥

महत्तत्सोमो महिषश्चकारापां यद्गर्भोऽवृणीत देवानामाधिपत्यम् । अदधादिन्द्रे पवमान ओजः । अजनयत्सूर्ये ज्योतिरिन्दुरादित्यः । इन्दुरात्मा ॥ ३०[६] ॥

विधुं दद्राणं समने बहूनां युवानं सन्तं पलितो जगार ।
देवस्य पश्य काव्यं महित्वाद्या ममार स ह्यः समान ॥

विधुं विधमनशीलम् । दद्राणं दमनशीलम् । युवानं चन्द्रमसम् । पलित आदित्यो गिरति । सद्यो म्रियते । स दिवा समुदिता । इत्यधिदैवतम् ।

अथाध्यात्मम् । विधुं विधमनशीलम् । दद्राणं दमनशीलम् । युवानं महान्तम् । पलित आत्मा गिरति । रात्रौ म्रियते । रात्रिः समुदिता । इत्यात्मगतिमाचष्टे ॥ ३१[९] ॥

साकञ्जानां सप्तथमाहुरेकजं षळिद्यमा ऋषयो देवजा इति ।
तेषामिष्टानि विहितानि धामशः स्थात्रे रेजन्ते विकृतानि रूपशः ॥

---

१. RV. IX. 97. 40.

२. महत्सोमो. Bib. Ind.

३. ॥ १६ ॥ M 4, C 6, S; ॥ १६ ॥ of the 2nd pāda M 3, C 4, C 5, W 3; ॥ १६ ॥ २९ ॥ Mi; ॥ २९ ॥ M 1, C 2, C 3, W 2; ॥ ७ ॥ of the 3rd pāda. W 1.

४. RV. IX. 97. 41.

५. देवानाधिपत्य° Roth; च. छ. ज. See Bib. Ind. IV. 387.

६. ॥ १७ ॥ M 4, C 6, S; ॥ १७ ॥ of the 2nd pāda. M 3, C 4, C 5, W 3; ॥ १७ ॥ ३० ॥ Mi; ॥ ३० ॥ M 1, C 2, C 3, W 2; ॥ ८ ॥ of the 3rd pāda. W 1.

७. RV. X. 55. 5; AV. 9. 27, 9.

८. द्रमनशीलम् M 3, C 4, C 5, Mi; W 1, W 2, W 3.

९. ॥ १८ ॥ M 4, C 6, S; ॥ १८ ॥ of the 2nd pāda. M 3; C 4, C 5, W 3, ॥ १८ ॥ ३१ ॥ Mi; ॥ ३१ ॥ M 1, C 2, C 3, W 2; ॥ ९ ॥ of the 3rd pāda W 1.

१०. RV. I. 164. 15; AV. 9. 25. 16.

सहजातानां षण्णामृषीणामादित्य[1]ः सप्तमः । तेषा[2]मिष्टानि वा कान्तानि वा क्रान्तानि वा गतानि वा मतानि वा नतानि वा । अद्भिः सह संमोदन्ते । यत्रैतानि सप्तऋषीणानि ज्योतीँषि तेभ्यः पर आदित्यः । तान्येतस्मिन्नेकं भवन्ति । इत्यधिदैवतम् ।

अथाध्यात्मम् । सहजातानां षण्णामिन्द्रियाणामात्मा सप्तमः । तेषामिष्टानि वा कान्तानि वा क्रान्तानि वा गतानि वा मतानि वा नतानि वा । अन्नेन सह संमोदन्ते । यत्रेमानि सप्तऋषीणानीन्द्रियाण्येभ्यः पर आत्मा । तान्येतस्मिन्नेकं भवन्ति । इत्यात्मगतिमाचष्टे ॥ ३२[3] ॥

स्त्रियः सतीस्ताँ उ मे पुंस आहुः पश्यदक्षण्वान्न वि चेतदन्धः ।
कविर्यः पुत्रः स ईमा चिकेत यस्ता विजानात्स पितुष्पितासत्[4] ॥

स्त्रिय एवै[5]ताः शब्दस्पर्शरूपरसगन्धहारिण्यस्ता अमुं पुंश[6]ब्दे निराहारः प्राण इति पश्यन्कष्टान्न विजानात्यन्धः । कविर्यः पुत्रः स इमा जानाति । यः स ई[7]मा जानाति स पितुष्पितासत् । इत्यात्मगतिमाचष्टे ॥ ३३[8] ॥

सप्तार्धगर्भा[9] भुवनस्य रेतो विष्णोस्तिष्ठन्ति प्रदिशा विधर्मणि ।
ते धीतिभिर्मनसा ते विपश्चितः परिभुवः परि भवन्ति विश्वतः ॥

सप्तैतानादित्यरश्मीनयमादित्यो गिरति । मध्यस्थानोर्ध्वशब्दः । ये[10]न्यास्मि-

---

1. See Roth's edition. p. 195.

2. From तेषामिष्टानि... to आचष्टे, the whole passage is taken from 10. 26.

3. ॥ १९ ॥ M 4, C 6, S; ॥ १९ ॥ इति द्वितीयः पादः M 3, C 4; ॥ १९ ॥ of the 2nd pāda. C 5, W 3; ॥ १९ ॥ ॥ ३२ ॥ Mi; ॥ ३२ ॥ M 1, C 2, C 3, W 2; ॥ १० ॥ of the 3rd pāda. W 1.

4. RV. I. 164. 16; AV. 9. 25. 16.

5. एवेति ताः M 1, M 4, C 2, C 3, C 6, S; R. च. छ. ज. See Bib. Ind. IV. 391.

6. पुंशब्देन. Bib. Ind. IV. 391.

7. ईमा. loc. cit.

8. ॥ २० ॥ M 4, C 6, S; ॥ १ ॥ of the 3rd pāda M 3, C 4; ॥ २० ॥ इति द्वितीयः पादः C 5, W 3; ॥ २० ॥ ३३ ॥ Mi; ॥ ३३ ॥ M 1, C 2, C 3, W 2; ॥ ११ ॥ ३३ ॥ इति तृतीयः पादः W 1.

9. RV. I. 164. 36; AV. 9. 28. 7.

10. यत एतास्मिंस्तिष्ठति M 1, M 4, C 2, C 3, C 6, S; R; यत एतस्मिंस्तिष्ठति च. छ. ज. (see Bib. Ind. IV. 392); यान्यास्मिंस्तिष्ठन्ति Bib. Ind. & Bom. The text preserved in Mss. of both recensions is corrupt. The correct reading can however be restored, for the commentary relating to soul *i. e.* the passage following अथाध्यात्मम् supplies evidence for the text preceeding the same. A comparison of these two parts shows that the same words are repeated, except that इन्द्रियाणि corresponds to rays & actions, आत्मा to the sun and इदम् is used in the latter whereon अदस् is used in the former. From this comparison, it is clear that the passage should be यान्येतास्मिंस्तिष्ठन्ति । I have adopted the reading of the Mss. of the shorter recension, because it is closer to the suggested restoration than the other.

स्तिष्ठति तानि धीतिभिश्च मनसा च विपर्ययन्ति परिभुवः परिभवन्ति सर्वाणि कर्माणि वर्षकर्मणा । इत्यधिदैवतम् ।

अथाध्यात्मम् । सप्तेमानीन्द्रियाण्ययमात्मा गिरति मध्यस्थानोर्ध्वेशब्दः । यान्यस्मिंस्तिष्ठन्ति तानि धीतिभिश्च मनसा च विपर्ययन्ति परिभुवः परिभवन्ति सर्वाणीन्द्रियाणि[1] ज्ञानकर्मणा । इत्यात्मगतिमाचष्टे ॥ ३४[2] ॥

न वि जा॑नामि॒ यदि॑वे॒दमास्मि॑ नि॒ण्यः संन॑द्धो॒ मन॑सा चरा॑मि[3] ।

न[4] विजानामि यदि वेदमस्मि निण्यः संनद्धो मनसा चरामि । न हि ज्ञान[5]-न्बुद्धिमतः[6] परिवेदयन्तेऽयमादित्योऽयमात्मा ॥ ३५[7] ॥

अपा॒ङ् प्राङे॑ति स्व॒धया॑ गृभी॒तोऽम॑र्त्यो॒ मर्त्ये॑ना॒ सयो॑निः ।
ता शश्व॑न्ता विषू॒चीना॑ वि॒यन्ता॒ न्य१॒न्यं चि॒क्युर्न नि चि॑क्युर॒न्यम् ॥

अपाञ्चयति प्राञ्चयति स्वधया गृभीतो ऽमर्त्य आदित्यो मर्त्येन चन्द्रमसा[9] सह । तौ शश्वद्गामिनौ विश्वगामिनौ बहुगामिनौ वा । पश्यत्यादित्यं न चन्द्रमसम् । इत्यधिदैवतम् ।

अथाध्यात्मम् । अपाञ्चयति प्राञ्चयति स्वधया गृभीतोऽमर्त्य आत्मा मर्त्येन

---

१. सर्वाणि कर्माणि वर्षकर्मणे० M 3; सर्वाणि कर्माणि ज्ञानकर्मणे० C 5.

२. ॥ २१ ॥ M 4, C 6, S; ॥ २ ॥ of the 3rd pāda M 3, C 4, ॥ १ ॥ of the 3rd pāda, C 5, W 3 ; ॥ २१ ॥ ३४ ॥ Mi; ॥ ३४ ॥ M 1, C 2, C 3, W 2; ॥ १ ॥ of the 4 th pāda, W 1.

३. RV. I. 164. 37; AV. 9. 28. 5. The Mss. of the longer recension except M 1 and C 6, add the second hemistich of the stanza also, *i. e.* यदा मागन् प्रथमजा ऋतस्यादिद्वाचो अश्नुवे भागमस्याः । Even the first hemistich is not fully given in C 6, which writes only न वि जानामि and then adds: अर्धर्चः ।.

४. The text is corrupt. I have again adopted the text of the shorter recension for it alone has any pretension of being a comment on the vedic quotation. The passage: न विजानामि...चरामि is omitted by all Mss. of the longer recension.

५. विजानन् M 1, M 4, C 2; विजानान् C 6, S; R; L.

६. ०मतः पुष्टिः पुत्रः परिवेदयन्ते. C 4; ०मतः पुत्रः परिवेदयन्ते M 1, M 4, C 2, C 6, S, R; Bib. Ind; Bom; L.

७. ॥ २२ ॥ M 4, C 6, S; ॥ ३ ॥ of the 3rd pāda M 3, C 4; ॥ २ ॥ of the 3rd pāda C 5, W 3; ॥ २२ ॥ ३५ ॥ Mi; ॥ ३५ ॥ M 1, C 1, C 3, W 2; ॥ ३ ॥ of the 4th pāda W 1.

८. RV. I. 164. 38; AV. 9. 28. 6.

९. मनसा Bib. Ind. IV. 395, which is obviously a mistake. मनसा be associated with आत्मा only as is done in the explanation, relating to soul, and not with the sun. The editor adopts the same reading in both the parts of the comm. which are intended to contrast each other.

मनसा सह। तौ शश्वद्गामिनौ विश्वगामिनौ बहुगामिनौ वा। पश्यत्यात्मानं न मनः। इत्यात्मगतिमाचष्टे ॥ ३६[1] ॥

तदिदा॑स॒ भुव॑नेषु॒ ज्येष्ठं॒ यतो॑ ज॒ज्ञ उ॒ग्रस्त्वे॒षनृ॑म्णः।
स॒द्यो ज॑ज्ञा॒नो नि रि॑णाति॒ शत्रू॒ननु॒ यं विश्वे॒ मद॒न्त्यूमाः[2] ॥

तद्भवति भूतेषु भुवनेषु ज्येष्ठमादित्यं यतो जज्ञ उग्रस्त्वेषनृम्णो दीप्तिनृम्णः। सद्यो जज्ञानो निरिणाति शत्रूनिति। रिणातिः[3] प्रीतिकर्मा दीप्तिकर्मा वा। अनुमदन्ति यं विश्व ऊमाः। इत्यधिदैवतम्।

अथाध्यात्मम्। तद्भवति भूतेषु भुवनेषु ज्येष्ठमव्यक्तं यतो जायत उग्रस्त्वेषनृम्णो ज्ञाननृम्णः। सद्यो जज्ञानो निरिणाति शत्रूनिति। रिणातिः[3] प्रीतिकर्मा दीप्तिकर्मा वा। अनुमदन्ति यं सर्वे ऊमाः। इत्यात्मगतिमाचष्टे ॥ ३७[4] ॥

को अ॒द्य यु॑ङ्क्ते धु॒रि गा ऋ॒तस्य॒ शिमी॑वतो भा॒मिनो॑ दुर्हृणा॒यून्।
आ॒सन्नि॑षून्हृ॒त्स्वसो॑ मयो॒भून्य ए॑षां भृ॒त्यामृ॒णध॒त्स जी॑वात्[5] ॥

क आदित्यो धुरि गा युङ्क्ते। रश्मीन्कर्मवतो भानुमतो दुराधर्षानसून्यसुनवन्तीषूनिषुणवन्ति[6] मयोभूनि सुखभूनि। य इमं संभृतं वेद कथं स जीवति। इत्यधिदैवतम्।

अथाध्यात्मम्। क आत्मा धुरि गा युङ्क्ते। इन्द्रियाणि कर्मवन्ति[7] भानुमन्ति[8] दुराधर्षानसून्यसुनवन्तीषूनिषुणवन्ति मयोभूनि सुखभूनि। य इमं[9] संभृतं[10] वेद चिरं जीवति। इत्यात्मगतिमाचष्टे ॥ ३८[11] ॥

क ई॑षते तु॒ज्यते॒ को बि॑भाय॒ को मं॑सते॒ सन्त॒मिन्द्रं॒ को अन्ति॑।
कस्तो॒काय॒ क इभा॑यो॒त रा॒येऽधि॑ ब्रवत्त॒न्वे॒३ को जना॑य[12] ॥

---

१. ॥ २३ ॥ M 4, C 6, S; ॥ ४ ॥ of the 3rd pāda M 3, C 4; ॥ ३ ॥ of the 3rd pāda C 5, W 3; ॥ २३ ॥ ३६ ॥ Mi; ॥ ३६ ॥ M 1, C 1, C 3, W 2; ॥ ३ ॥ of the 4th pāda W 1.

२. RV. X. 120. 1.

३. निरिणाति M 3, C 4, C 5, Mi, W 1, W 2, W 3; Bib. Ind.

४. ॥ २४ ॥ M 4, C 6, S; ॥ ५ ॥ of the 3rd pāda M 3, C 4; ॥ ४ ॥ of the 3rd pāda C 5, W 3; ॥ २४ ॥ ३७ ॥ Mi; ॥ ३७ ॥ M 1, C 1, C 3, W 2; ॥ ४ ॥ of the 4th pāda W 1.

५. RV. I. 84. 16.

६. °सूनसूनवन्ती°. ख. ग. ङ. see Bib. Ind. IV. 397.

७. कर्मवतो M 1, M 4, C 2, C 6, 4; R, च. छ. ज. see op. cit. 398.

८. भानुवन्ति M 3; भानुवतो M 1, M 4, C 2, C 6, S; R, च. छ. ज. see loc. cit.

९. इमानि M 3, W 1, W 2, W 3, C 4, C 5, Mi; Bib. Ind.

१०. संभृतानि M 3, W 1, W 2, W 3, C 4, C 5, Mi; Bib. Ind.

११. ॥ २५ ॥ M 4, C 6, S; ॥ ६ ॥ of the 3rd pāda M 3, C 4; ॥ ५ ॥ of the 3rd pāda C 5, W 3; ॥ ५ ॥ of the 4th pāda W 1; ॥ २५ ॥ ३८ ॥ Mi; ॥ ३८ ॥ M 1, C 1, C 3, W 2.

१२. RV. I. 84. 17.

क एव गच्छति को ददाति को बिभेति को मंसते सन्तमिन्द्रम्। कस्तोकायापत्याय महते च नो रणाय रमणीयाय दर्शनीयाय ॥ ३९[1] ॥

को अ॒ग्निमी॑ट्टे ह॒विषा॑ घृ॒तेन॑ स्रु॒चा य॑जाता ऋ॒तुभि॑र्ध्रु॒वेभि॑ः।
कस्मै॑ दे॒वा आ व॑हाना॒शु होम॒ को मं॑सते वी॒तिहो॑त्रः सुदे॒वः[2] ॥

क आदित्यं पूरयति[3] हविषा च घृतेन च स्रुचा यजाता ऋतुभिर्ध्रुवेभिरिति। कस्मै देवा आवहानाशु होमार्थान्को मंसते वीतिहोत्रः सुदेवः कल्याणदेवः। इत्यधिदैवतम्।

अथाध्यात्मम्। क आत्मानं पूरयति[3] हविषा च घृतेन च स्रुचा यजाता ऋतुभिर्ध्रुवेभिरिति। कस्मै देवा आवहानाशु होमार्थान्को मंसते[4] वीतिहोत्रः सुप्रज्ञः कल्याणप्रज्ञः। इत्यात्मगतिमाचष्टे ॥ ४०[5] ॥

त्वम॒ङ्ग प्र शं॑सिषो दे॒वः श॑विष्ठ॒ मर्त्य॑म्।
न त्वद॒न्यो म॑घवन्नस्ति मर्डि॒तेन्द्र॒ ब्रवी॑मि ते॒ वच॑ः[6] ॥

त्वमङ्ग प्रशंसीर्देवः शविष्ठ मर्त्यं न त्वदन्योऽस्ति मघवन्पाता वा पालयिता वा जेता वा सुखयिता[7] वा। इन्द्र ब्रवीमि ते वचः स्तुतियुक्तम्[8] ॥ ४१[9] ॥

द्वा सु॑प॒र्णा स॒युजा॒ सखा॑या समा॒नं वृ॒क्षं परि॑ षस्वजाते।
तयो॑र॒न्यः पिप्प॑लं स्वा॒द्वत्त्यन॑श्नन्न॒न्यो अ॒भि चा॑कशीति[10] ॥

द्वौ द्वौ प्रतिष्ठितौ सुकृतौ धर्मकर्तारौ[11]। दुष्कृतं पापं परिसारकमित्याचक्षते। सुपर्णा सयुजा सखायेत्यात्मानं [दुरात्मानं[12]] परमात्मानं प्रत्युत्तिष्ठति। शरीर

1. ॥ २६ ॥ M 4, C 6, S; ॥ ७ ॥ of the 3rd pāda M 3, C 4; ॥ ६ ॥ of the 3rd pāda C 5, W 3; ॥ ६ ॥ of the 4th pāda W 1; ॥ २६ ॥ ३९ ॥ Mi; ॥ ३९ ॥ M 1, C 1, C 3, W 2.

2. RV. I. 84. 18.

3. पूजयति M 3, C 4, C 5, W 1, W 2, W 3, Mi.

4. संसते R.

5. ॥ २७ ॥ M 4, C 6, S; ॥ ८ ॥ of the 3rd pāda M 3, C 4; ॥ ७ ॥ of the 3rd pāda C 5, W 3, ॥ ७ ॥ of the 4th pāda W 1; ॥ २७ ॥ ४० ॥ Mi; ॥ ४० ॥ M 1, C 1, C 3, W 2.

6. RV. I. 84. 19.

7. सुखयिता is repeated in C 5.

8. इति स्तुतिसंयुक्तम् M 3, W 1, W 2, W 3, Mi, C 4; इति स्तुतिसंप्रयुक्तम् C 5.

9. ॥ २८ ॥ M 4, C 6, S; ॥ ९ ॥ इति तृतीयः पादः M 3, C 4; ॥ ८ ॥ of the 3rd pāda C 5, W 3; ॥ ८ ॥ of the 4th pāda W 1; ॥ २८ ॥ ४१ ॥ Mi; ॥ ४१ ॥ M 1, C 1, C 3, W 2.

10. RV. I. 164. 20; AV. 9. 26. 10.

11. Cf. SRV. I. 164. 20. p. i. 704.

12. Omitted by MSS. of the shorter recension M 3, Mi, W 1, W 2, W 3, C 4, C 5.

एव तज्जायते वृक्षम् । ऋक्षं[1] शरीरम् । वृक्षे[2] पक्षौ प्रतिष्ठापयति । तयोरन्यद्भुक्त्वा-[3]न्यदनश्नन्नन्यां सरूपतां सलोकतामश्नुते । य एवं वेदानश्नन्नन्योऽभिचाकशीतीति[4] । इत्यात्मगतिमाचष्टे ॥ ४२ ॥[5]

[आ याहीन्द्र पथिभिरीळितेभिर्यज्ञमिमं नो भागधेयं जुषस्व ।[6]
तृप्तां जुहुर्मातुलस्येव योषा भागस्ते पैतृष्वसेयी वपामिव ॥

आगमिष्यन्ति शक्रो देवतास्ताभिमिस्तीर्थैभिः शक्रप्रतरैरीळितेभिरिमिस्तीर्थैर्यज्ञमिमं नो यज्ञभागमग्नीषोमभागाविन्द्रो जुषस्व । तृप्तामेवं मातुलयोगकन्या भागं सर्तकेव सा या देवतास्तास्तत्स्थाने शक्रं निदर्शनम्[7] ॥][8]

विप्रं विप्रासोऽवसे देवं मर्तास ऊतये ।
अग्निं गीर्भिर्हवामहे ॥[9]

विप्रं विप्रासो ऽवसे विदुः । [वेदं[10]] विन्दतेर्वेदितव्यम् । विमलं[11] शरीरं वायुना । विप्रस्तु पद्मनिलयं[12] हृदिस्थितमकारसंहारितमुकारं[13] पूरयन्[14]मकारनिलयं गमयति[15] । विप्रं प्राणेषु विन्दुः[16] सिक्तं विकसितं वह्नितेजः प्रभुं[17] कनकं[18] पद्मेष्वमृतशरीरममृतजातस्थितममृतवादममृतमुखं[19][20][21] वदन्ति । अग्निं गीर्भिर्हवामहे । अग्निं संबोधयेत् । अग्निः सर्वा देवताः[22] । इति । तस्योत्तरा भूयसे निर्वचनाय ॥ ४३ ॥

१. रक्षशरीरं M 1, M 4, C 2, C 3, C 6, C 7, S; R. Bib. Ind.

२. वृक्षं M 1, M 4, C 2, C 3, C 6, C 7, S; R. Bib. Ind.

३. ०रन्यो भुक्त्वा० Mi; ०रन्यद्भुक्त्वान्नम० M 1, M 4, C 2, C 3, C 6, C 7, S; Bib. Ind. ०रन्यद्भुक्त्वान्नम० R.

४. वेदान्नमन० M 1, M 4, C 2, C 3, C 6, C 7, S; R; विद्वानन० Bib. Ind.

५. ॥ १ ॥ of the 4th pāda M 3, C 5; ॥ १ ॥ ४४ ॥ Mi.

६. RVKh. VII. 55. 8.

७. निदर्शितम् Bib. Ind.

८. The entire section is omitted by MSS. of the shorter recension: M 3, Mi, W 1, W 2, W 3, C 4, C 5.

९. RV. VIII. 11. 6.

१०. Omitted by M 3, Mi, W 1, W 2, W 3, C 4, C 5.

११. विमलशरीरेण. M 1, M 4, C 2, C 3, C 6, C 7, S; R; Bib. Ind.

१२. हृत्पद्मनिलयस्थितमकारसंहितमुकारं M1, M 4, C 2, C 3, C 6, C 7, S; R; Bib. Ind.

१३. ०मकारं M 3.

१४. पूरयेत् M 1, M 4, C 2, C 3, C 6, C 7, S; R; Bib. Ind.

१५. गतं M 1, M 4, C 2, C 3, C 6, C 7, S; R; Bib. Ind.

१६. बिन्दुसिक्तं M 1, M 4, C 2, C 3, C 6, C 7, S; Bib. Ind; बिन्दुसिक्तं R.

१७. प्रभं M 1, etc.

१८. कनकपद्म०. M 1, etc.

१९. परमेष्वरमृत० M 3.

२०. ०वाचा० Mi, M 3; M 1 etc.

२१. मुखे. M 1 etc.

२२. KS. XII. 1. p. 162.

हंसः शुचिषद्वसुरन्तरिक्षसद्धोता वेदिषदतिथिर्दुरोणसत् ।
नृषद्वरसदृतसद्व्योमसदब्जा गोजा ऋतजा अद्रिजा ऋतम्[1] ॥

हंसं[2] इति हंसाः सूर्य[3]रश्मयः । परमात्मा परं ज्योतिः । पृथिव्याप्तेति[4] व्याप्तं सर्वं व्याप्तं वननकर्मा[5]भ्यासेनादित्यमण्डलेनेति । त्यजतीति[6] लोकः । त्यजतीति[6] हंसः[7] । त्यजन्तीति[8] हंसाः । [परमहंसाः[9]] परमात्मा सूर्यरश्मिभिः प्रभूतगंभीत[10]वसतीति । त्रिभिर्वसतीति वा । वह्नि[11]र्वसं[12]तीति वा । रश्मि[13]भिर्वसतीति वा । सुवर्णरेताः पूषा[14] गर्भाः । रिफि[15]रिति रिफता च[16]मकुटिलानि कुटन्ता रेफ[17]न्तान्त[18]रिक्षं चरे[19]दर्थेति । अन्तरिक्षं चर[20]तीति दिवि । भूमिगमनं[21] वा । स्वर्भानुः[22] सुप्रसूतो[23] (होता[24]) । होतादित्यस्यगता भवन्ति । अतिथिर्दुरोणसत् । स्र[25]वन्ति सर्वे रसा[26]श्चिकीर्षयन्ति रश्मि[27]भिश्चिकीर्षयन्तीति वा । [वह्निर्विकर्षयति[28] ।] नैतं[29] भवतीत्यश्वगोजा अद्रिगोजा धन[30]गोजा सर्व[31]गोजातिर्ऋच इति तेजो बहुजो शब्दो भवति । निगमो निगम[32]व्यो भवत्यृषि[33]निर्वचनाय ॥ ४४ ॥

---

१. RV. IV. 40. 5; VS. 10. 24; 12. 14.

२. हंसेति MSS. of the shorter recension.

३. सूर्यरश्मिभिः C 5.

४. पृथिवी व्याप्तेति. M 1, etc.

५. वननकर्मणानभ्या०. M 1, etc.

६. त्ययतीति M 1, etc.

७. हंसयन् M 1, M 4, etc.

८. त्यजतीति C 5; त्ययतीति M 1, M 4, C 2, C 3, C 6, C 7, S; R; Bib. Ind.

९. Omitted by M 3, Mi, W 1, W 2, W 3, C 4, C 5.

१०. ०गभीर० M 1, M 4 etc.

११. वह्निर्वसतीति वा comes after रश्मि... वा in M 1, M 4, etc.

१२. वसन्तीति वा C 5.

१३. रश्मिर्व० M 1, M 4, etc.

१४. पुरुषाः M 3, Mi, W 1, W 2, W 3, C 4.

१५. रिभेति रिभन्ता M 1, M 4, etc.; रिभीरिति रेकता M 3.

१६. वन० M 1, M 4, C 2, C 3, C 6, C 7. S; R; Bib. Ind.

१७. रिफन्ता० Mi; रिभन्ता० M 1, etc.

१८. अन्तरिक्षात् Mi ; अन्तरिक्षा M 1, M 4, etc.

१९. चरत्पथान्तरिक्षा, M 1, M 4, etc.

२०. चरदिति M 1, M 4, अन्तरिक्षा चरदिति R.

२१. भुवि M 1, M 4, etc.

२२. सुभानुः M 1, M 4, etc.

२३. सुप्रभूतो M 1, M 4, etc.

२४. Omitted by M 1, M 4, etc.

२५. द्रवन्ति Mi, C 4, W 1, W 2, W 3; सर्वे दुरोणसद् द्रवं, M 1, M 4, etc.

२६. विकर्षयति. M 1, M 4, etc.

२७. रश्मिर्विकर्षयति वह्निः० M 1, M 4, etc.

२८. Omitted by M 3, Mi, W 1, W 2, W 3, C 4, C 5.

२९. वननं M 1, M 4, etc.

३०. धरित्रिगोजा M 1, M 4, etc.

३१. ऋतगोजाः इत्यृतेति C 5; सर्वगोजा ऋतगोजा ऋतजो, Mi; सर्वे गोजा ऋतजा बहुशब्दा भवन्ति. M 1, M 4, etc.

३२. निगन्तव्यो Mi; निगमव्यति. M 1, M 4, etc.

३३. भवत्यृषे M 1, M 4, etc.

त्र्यम्बकं यजामहे सुगन्धिं पुष्टिवर्धनम्।
उर्वारुकमिव बन्धनान्मृत्योर्मुक्षीय मामृतात्[1]॥

त्र्यम्बको रुद्रः। तं त्र्यम्बकं यजामहे। [सुगन्धिम्[2]] सुगन्धिं सुष्ठुगन्धिं पुष्टिवर्धनं पुष्टिकारकमिव। उर्वारुकमिव [फलं[3]] बन्धनादारोधनान्मृत्योः सकाशान्मुञ्चस्व मां कस्मादित्येषापरा[4] भवति॥ ४५॥

जातवेदसे सुनवाम सोममरातीयतो नि दहाति वेदः।
स नः पर्षदति दुर्गाणि विश्वा नावेव सिन्धुं दुरितात्यग्निः[5]॥

जातवेदस इति जातमिदं सर्वं सचराचरं स्थित्युत्पत्ति[6]प्रलयं[7]न्यायेन[8] (जातवेदस्या[9] वैवं[10] जातवेदसेऽर्चाय)[11] सुनवाम सोममिति। प्रसवायाभिषवाय[12] सोमं राजानममृतम्। अरातीयतो यज्ञार्थमनिस्सो[13] निर्दहति[14] निश्चयेन दहति भस्मीकरोति। सोमो ददादित्यर्थः। स नः पर्षदति दुर्गाणि (विश्वानि) दुर्गमाणि[15] स्थानानि नावेव सिन्धुम्। (नावा सिन्धुं)[11] यथा (यः[11]) कश्चित्कर्णधारो नावा[16] सिन्धोः[17] स्यन्दमानानां[18] नदीं जलदुर्गां महाकुलां[19] तारयति दुरितात्यग्निरिति[20] दुरितानि[21] तारयति। तस्यैषापरा भवति॥ ४६॥

[इदं तेऽन्याभिरसमानमद्भिर्याः काश्च सिन्धुं प्र वहन्ति नद्यः।
सर्पो जीर्णामिव त्वचं जहाति पापं सशिरस्कोऽभ्युपेत्य[22]॥

इदं तेऽन्याभिरसमानाभिर्याः काश्च सिन्धुं पतिं कृत्वा नद्यो वहन्ति। सर्पो जीर्णामिव सर्पस्त्वचं त्यजति। पापं त्यजन्ति। आप आप्नोतेः। तासामेषा भवति॥ १४॥ ३४॥][23]

---

१. RV. VII. 59. 12.
२. Omitted by M 3, Mi, W 1, W 2, W 3, C 4, C 5.
३. Omitted by M 3, Mi, W 1, W 2, W 3, C 4, C 5.
४. कस्मादित्येषापरा. R.
५. RV. I. 99. 1.
६. ०युत्पत्तिः M 3.
७. ०प्रलयं M 3.
८. ०न्यायेनाछाय M 1, M 4, C 2, C 3, C 6, C 7.
९. जातवेदस्या इदं जातं Mi.
१०. वैवं M 3.
११. The passage within brackets is omitted by M 2, M 4, C 2, C 3, C 6, C 7, S; R; Bib. Ind.
१२. प्रसवेनाभि०. M 1, M 4, etc.
१३. ०मितिस्सो M 1, M 4, etc.
१४. निदहाति C 5; निश्चयेन निदहाति M 1, M 4, निश्चये निदहाति R.
१५. दुर्गमनानि M 1, M 4, etc.
१६. नावेव M 1, M 9, etc.
१७. सिन्धुः Mi.
१८. स्यन्दमिमां Mi; स्यन्दनान्नदीं M 1, M 4, etc.
१९. महाकूलां. M 1, M 4, etc.
२०. दुरितान्य० M 1, M 4, C 2, C 3, C 6, C 7, S; R; Bib. Ind.
२१. तानि. M 1, M 4, C 2, etc.
२२. Untraced.
२३. The whole section is omitted by M 3, Mi, C 4, C 5, W 1, W 2, W 3.

शतं जीव शरदो वर्धमानः शतं हेमन्ताञ्छतमु वसन्तान् ।
शतमिन्द्राग्नी सविता बृहस्पतिः शतायुषा हविषेमं पुनर्दुः[1] ॥

शतं जीव शरदो वर्धमानः । इत्यपि निगमो भवति । शतमिति शतं दीर्घमायुः । मरुतो मां[2] वर्धयन्ति । शतमेव[3] शतमात्मानं[4] भवति । [शतमनन्तं भवति । शतमैश्वर्यं भवति ।][5] शतमिति शतं दीर्घमायुः ॥ ४७ ॥

मा ते राधांसि मा त ऊतयो वसोऽस्मान्कदा चना दभन् ।
विश्वा च न उप मिमीहि मानुष वसूनि चर्षणिभ्य आ[6] ॥

मा च ते धनानि[7] मा च ते कदाचन[8] सरिषुः[9] सर्वाणि प्रज्ञानान्युपमानय[10] । मनुष्यहितोऽयमादित्योऽयमात्मा[11] । अथैतदनुप्रवदति[12] । अथैनं[13] महान्तमात्मानमे-र्षिगणः[14] प्रवदति । वैश्वकर्मणो[15] देवानां नु वयं जाना नासदासीन्नो सदासीत्तदानीम्[16] । इति च । सैषात्मजिज्ञासा । सैषा सर्वभूतजिज्ञासा । ब्रह्मणः सार्ष्टिं[17] सरूपतां सलोकतां गमयति य एवं वेद ।

नमो[18] ब्रह्मणे । नमो महते भूताय । नमो यास्काय । ब्रह्मशुक्लमसीय ब्रह्मशुक्लमसीय ॥ ४८ ॥

॥ इति परिशिष्टम् ॥

---

१. RV. X. 161. 4; AV. 3. 11. 4; 7. 53. 2; 20. 96. 9.

२. एना M 1, M 4, C 2, C 3, C 6, C 7, S; R; Bib. Ind.

३. शतमेनमेव M 1, M 4, C 2, C 3, C 6, C 7, S; R; Bib. Ind.

४. शतात्मानं M 1, M 4, C 2, C 3, C 6, C 7, S; R ; Bib. Ind.

५. The passage within brackets is omitted by M 3, Mi, W 1, W 2, W 3, C 4, C 5.

६. RV. I. 84. 20.

७. धामानि M 1, M 4, C 2, C 3, C 6, C 7, S; R; Bib. Ind.

८. कदा चिन. M 1, M 4, C 2, etc.

९. सर्षुः C 5.

१०. प्रज्ञान्युपमानय M 3; प्रज्ञानान्युपमानाय M 1, M 4, etc.

११. मनुष्याहितो MSS. of the longer recension.

१२. ०प्रवदन्ति M 1, M 4, etc.

१३. अथैतं M 1, M 4, etc.

१४. ०मेषर्गण: M 1, M 4, etc.

१५. विश्वकर्मणो Mi, वैश्वकर्मणे M 1, M 4, etc.

१६. RV. X. 129. 1.

१७. सारिष्टं C 5, M 1, M 4, etc.

१८. In the MSS. of the longer recension, M 1, M 4, C 2, C 3, C 6, C 7, S, the line runs thus: नमो ब्रह्मणे महते भूताय नमः पारस्कराय नमो यास्काय । ब्रह्मशुक्लमसीय etc. This is ignored by Roth. The evidence of the MSS. of both the recensions shows that this passage should form an integral part of the last section. The section should be ended after ब्रह्मशुक्लमसीय, the repetition of this word indicates that the section comes to an end here, but not after य एवं वेद.

APPENDIX I

APPENDIX I

Relation OF THE NIRUKTA TO THE FOLLOWING texts.

(1)	Taittirīya Saṃhitā.	तैत्तिरीयसंहिता ।
(2)	Maitrāyaṇī Saṃhitā.	मैत्रायणीसंहिता ।
(3)	Kāṭhaka Saṃhitā.	काठकसंहिता ।
(4)	Aitareya Brāhmaṇa.	ऐतरेयब्राह्मणम् ।
(5)	Kauṣītaki Brāhmaṇa.	कौषीतकिब्राह्मणम् ।
(6)	Ṣaḍviṃs'a Brāhmaṇa.	षड्विंशब्राह्मणम् ।
(7)	Taittirīya Brāhmaṇa.	तैत्तिरीयब्राह्मणम् ।
(8)	S'atapatha Brāhmaṇa.	शतपथब्राह्मणम् ।
(9)	Mantra Brāhmaṇa.	मन्त्रब्राह्मणम् ।
(10)	Daivata Brāhmaṇa.	दैवतब्राह्मणम् ।
(11)	Gopatha Brāhmaṇa.	गोपथब्राह्मणम् ।
(12)	Aitareya Āraṇyaka.	ऐतरेयारण्यकम् ।
(13)	Taittirīya Āraṇyaka.	तैत्तिरीयारण्यकम् ।
(14)	Sarvānukramaṇī and Vedārthadīpikā of Ṣaḍgurus'iṣya.	सर्वानुक्रमणी षड्गुरुशिष्यस्य वेदार्थदीपिका च ।
(15)	Bṛhat Sarvānukramaṇikā.	बृहत्सर्वानुक्रमणिका ।
(16)	Ṛgveda Prātis'ākhya.	ऋग्वेदप्रातिशाख्यम् ।
(17)	Atharva Veda ,,	अथर्ववेदप्रातिशाख्यम् ।
(18)	Vājasaneya ,,	वाजसनेयप्रातिशाख्यम् ।
(19)	Taittirīya ,,	तैत्तिरीयप्रातिशाख्यम् ।
(20)	Bṛhaddevatā.	बृहद्देवता ।
(21)	Aṣṭādhyāyī of Pāṇini.	अष्टाध्यायी ।
(22)	Arthas'āstra of Kauṭalya.	कौटल्यस्यार्थशास्त्रम् ।
(23)	Mahābhāṣya of Patañjali.	महाभाष्यम् ।
(24)	Pūrva Mīmāṃsā.	पूर्वमीमांसा ।
(25)	Sarvadars'anasaṃgraha.	सर्वदर्शनसंग्रहः ।

THE NIRUKTA.	THE TAITTIRĪYA SAṂHITĀ.
1. 5: वायुर्वा त्वा मनुर्वा त्वा ।	I. 7. 7. 2: वायुर्वा त्वा मनुर्वा त्वा ।
1. 15: उरु प्रथस्व ।	I. 1. 8. 1; I. 2. 12. 2; VI. 2. 7. 3: उरु प्रथस्व ।
ओषधे त्रायस्वैनम् ।	I. 2. 1. 1; I. 3. 5. 1; VI. 3. 3. 2: ओषधे त्रायस्वैनम् ।
स्वधिते मैनं हिंसीः ।	I. 2. 1. 1; I. 3. 5. 1; VI. 3. 3. 2: स्वधिते मैनं हिंसीः ।
एक एव रुद्रोऽवतस्थे न द्वितीयः ।	I. 8. 6. 1: एक एव रुद्रो न द्वितीयाय तस्थे ।
अग्नये समिध्यमानायानुब्रूहीति ।	VI. 3. 7. 1: अग्नये समिध्यमानायानुब्रूहीत्याह ।
2. 17: यदवृणोत्तद् वृत्रस्य वृत्रत्वमिति विज्ञायते ।	II. 4. 12. 2: स इमाँल्लोकानवृणोद् यदिमाँल्लोकानवृणोत्तद्वृत्रस्य वृत्रत्वम् ।
4. 17: सुविते मा धाः ।	I. 2. 10. 2: सुविते मा धाः ।
4. 21: नाभ्या सन्नद्धा गर्भा जायन्त इत्याहुः ।	VI. 1. 7. 2: यदबद्धमवदध्यात् । गर्भाः प्रजानां परापातुकाः स्युः । बद्धमवदधाति । गर्भाणां धृत्यै । निष्टर्क्यं बध्नाति प्रजानां प्रजननाय ।
अथापि शंयुर्बार्हस्पत्य उच्यते । तच्छंयोरावृणीमहे गातुं यज्ञाय गातुं यज्ञपतये ।	II. 6. 10. 2–3: शंयोरावृणीमह इत्याह । शंयुमेव बार्हस्पत्यं भागधेयेन समर्धयति । गातुं यज्ञाय गातुं यज्ञपतय इत्याह ।
5. 11: यमक्षितिमक्षितयः पिबन्ति......... यथा देवा अंशुमाप्याययन्ति ।	II. 4. 14. 1: यमादित्या अंशुमाप्याययन्ति यमक्षितमक्षितयः पिबन्ति ।
6. 8: सा मे सत्याशीर्देवेषु ।	III. 2. 7. 2: सा मे सत्याशीर्देवेषु ।
7. 24: अग्निर्वा इतो वृष्टिं समीरयति धामच्छद्दिवि[खलु वै] भूत्वा वर्षति मरुतः सृष्टां वृष्टिं नयन्ति यदा[खलु वै] असावादित्योऽग्निं रश्मिभिः पर्यावर्ततेऽथ वर्षति ।	II. 4. 10. 2: अग्निर्वा इतो वृष्टिमुदीरयति मरुतः सृष्टां नयन्ति यदा खलु वा असावादित्यो न्यङ् रश्मिभिः पर्यावर्ततेऽथ वर्षति धामच्छदिव खलु वै भूत्वा वर्षति ।
8. 22: आत्मा वै प्रयाजा आत्मा वा अनुयाजाः ।	VI. 1. 5. 4: आत्मा वै प्रयाजाः प्रजानुयाजाः ।
10. 5: यदरोदीत्तद्रुद्रस्य रुद्रत्वम् । इति हारिद्रविकम् ।	I. 5. 1. 1: सोऽरोदीत् । यदरोदीत्तद्रुद्रस्य रुद्रत्वम् ।

THE NIRUKTA.	THE TAITTIRĪYA SAṂHITĀ.
11. 33: कुहूमहं सुकृतं विद्मनापसमस्मिन्यज्ञे सुहवां जोहवीमि ।	III. 3. 11. 4: कुहूमहं सुभगां विद्मनापसमस्मिन्यज्ञे सुहवां जोहवीमि ।
सा नो ददातु श्रवणं पितॄणां तस्यास्ते देवि हविषा विधेम ॥	सा नो ददातु श्रवणं पितॄणान्तस्यास्ते देवि हविषा विधेम ।
12. 13: अधोरामः सावित्रः ।	V. 5. 22. 1: अधोरामः सावित्रः ।
......कृकवाकुः सावित्रः ।	V. 5. 18. 1: कृकवाकुः सावित्रः ।
12. 41: अग्निः पशुरासीत् । तमालभन्त । तेनायजन्त । इति च ब्राह्मणम् ।	V. 7. 26. 1: अग्निः पशुरासीत् । तेनायजन्त । स एतं लोकमजयत्

THE NIRUKTA.	THE MAITRĀYAṆĪ SAṂHITĀ.
1. 5: वायुर्वा त्वा मनुर्वा त्वा ।	I. 11. 6. Vol. I. p. 168: वायुर्वा त्वा मनुर्वा त्वा ।
1. 15: उरु प्रथस्व ।	I. 1. 9: उरु प्रथस्व ।
1. 15: ओषधे त्रायस्वैनम् ।	I. 2. 1; III. 9. 3: ओषधे त्रायस्वैनम् ।
स्वधिते मैनं हिंसीः । इत्याह हिंसन् ।	I. 2. 1; III. 9. 3: स्वधिते मैनं हिंसीरिति ।
असंख्याता सहस्राणि ये रुद्रा अधि भूम्याम् ।	II. 9. 9: असंख्याता सहस्राणि ये रुद्रा अधि भूम्याम् ।
अग्नये समिध्यमानायानुब्रूहीति ।	I. 4. 11: अग्नये समिध्यमानायानुब्रूहि ।
2. 14: न वा अमुं लोकं जग्मुषे किं च नाकम् ।	III. 3. 1: न वै तत्र किं चन जग्मुषे कम् ।
3. 4: तस्मात् पुमान्दायादः । अदायादा स्त्री । इति विज्ञायते । तस्मात् स्त्रियं जातां परास्यन्ति न पुमांसम् । इति च ।	IV. 6. 4: अथ यत्स्थालीं रिञ्चन्ति न दारुमयं तस्मात् पुमान्दायादः । स्त्र्यदायादाथ यत्स्थालीं परास्यन्ति न दारुमयं तस्मात् स्त्रियं जातां परास्यन्ति न पुमांसम् । अथ स्त्रिय एवातिरिच्यन्ते ।
	IV. 7. 9: यदेषातिरिच्यते तस्मात् स्त्रियः पुंसोऽतिरिच्यन्ते । तस्मात् स्त्रियं जातां परास्यन्ति न पुमांसम् ।
3. 20: नेमे देवा नेमेऽसुराः ।	I. 11. 9: नेमे देवा आसन्नेमेऽसुराः ।
3. 21: ग्नास्त्वाकृन्तन्नपसोऽतन्वत ।	I. 9. 4: ग्नास्त्वाकृन्तन्नपसोऽतन्वत ।
कृत्तिवासाः पिनाकहस्तोऽवततधन्वा ।	I. 10. 4: पिनाकहस्तः कृत्तिवासा अवततधन्वा ।
4. 6: एकतो द्वितस्त्रित इति त्रयो बभूवुः ।	IV. 1. 9: सोऽपोऽङ्गारेणाभ्यपातयत्तत एकतोऽजायत द्वितीयं ततो द्वितस्तृतीयं ततस्त्रितः ।

THE NIRUKTA.	THE MAITRĀYAṆĪ SAṂHITĀ.
4. 17: सुविते मा धाः ।	I. 2. 7: सुविते मा धाः ।
नवेन पूर्वं दयमानाः स्याम ।	IV. 13. 8: नवेन पूर्वं दयमानाः स्याम ।
4. 21: तच्छंयोरावृणीमहे गातुं यज्ञाय गातुं यज्ञपतये ।	IV. 13. 10: तञ्शंयोरावृणीमहे गातुं यज्ञाय गातुं यज्ञपतये ।
5. 5: तं मरुतः क्षुरपविना व्ययुः ।	I. 10. 14: तं मरुतः क्षुरपविना व्ययुः ।
5. 11. अध्रिगो शमीध्वं सुशमि शमीध्वं शमीध्वमध्रिगो ।	IV. 13. 4: अध्रिगो शमीध्वं सुशमि शमीध्वमध्रिगो ।
6. 16: तं मेदस्तः प्रति पचताग्रभीष्टाम् ।	IV. 13. 9: तं मेदस्तः प्रतिपचताग्रभीष्टाम् ।
7. 13: इन्द्राय वृत्रघ्ने ।	II. 2. 11: इन्द्राय वृत्रघ्न एकादशकपालम् ।
इन्द्राय वृत्रतुरे ।	इन्द्राय वृत्रतुरा एकादशकपालम् । ...यद्वृत्रघ्ने......यद्वृत्रतुरे...।
इन्द्रायाँहोमुचे ।	II. 2. 10: इन्द्रायाँहोमुचा एकादशकपालम् ।
7. 17: अथापि ब्राह्मणं भवति । अग्निः सर्वा देवता इति ।	I. 4. 14: अग्निर्वै सर्वा देवताः ।
7. 19: यत्तज्जातः पशूनविन्दत[इति] तज्जातवेदसो जातवेदस्त्वम् । इति ब्राह्मणम् ।	I. 8. 2: यज्जातः पशूनविन्दत तज्जातवेदसो जातवेदस्त्वम् ।
तस्मात्सर्वानृतूनपशवोऽग्निमभिसर्पन्ति । इति च ।	तस्मात्सर्वानृतूनपशवोऽग्निमभिसर्पन्ति ।
7. 23: अथापि वैश्वानरीयो द्वादशकपालो भवति ।	II. 1. 2: अग्नये वैश्वानराय द्वादशकपालं निर्वपेत् ।
असौ वा आदित्योऽग्निर्वैश्वानरः ।	II. 1. 2: असौ वा आदि ३ त्योऽग्निर्वैश्वानरः ।
अयमेवाग्निर्वैश्वानर इति शाकपूणिः ।	II. 1. 2: अग्निर्वैश्वानरः ।
7. 24: अग्निर्वा इतो वृष्टिं समीरयति धामच्छद्दिवि [खलु वै] भूत्वा वर्षति मरुतः सृष्टां वृष्टिं नयन्ति । यदा [खलु वै] असावादित्योऽग्निं रश्मिभिः पर्यावर्ततेऽथ वर्षति ।	II. 4. 8: अग्निर्वा इतो वृष्टिमीट्टे मरुतोऽमुतश्च्यावयन्ति तां सूर्यो रश्मिभिर्वर्षति ।
8. 19: देवेभ्यो वनस्पते हवींषि हिरण्यपर्ण प्रदिवस्ते अर्थम् । प्रदक्षिणिद्रशनया नियूय ऋतस्य वक्षि पथिभी रजिष्ठैः ॥	IV. 13. 7: देवेभ्यो वनस्पते हवींषि हिरण्यपर्ण प्रदिवस्ते अर्थम् । प्रदक्षिणिद्रशनया नियूय ऋतस्य वक्षि पथिभी रजिष्ठैः ॥
8. 20: वनस्पते रशनया नियूय पिष्टतमया वयुनानि विद्वान् । वह देवत्रा दिधिषो हवींषि प्र च दातारममृतेषु वोचः ॥	वनस्पते रशनया नियूय पिष्टतमया वयुनानि विद्वान् । वहा देवत्रा दिधिषो हवींषि प्र च दातारममृतेषु वोचः ॥

THE NIRUKTA.	THE MAITRĀYAṆĪ SAṂHITĀ.
8. 20: स्वाहाकृतयः । स्वाहेत्येतत्सु आहेति वा । स्वा वागाहेति वा ।	I. 8. 1. तं स्वा वागभ्यवदज्जुहुधीति...स्वाहा । इति स्वा ह्येनं वागभ्यवदत्तत्स्वाहाकारस्य जन्म ।
8. 22: ऋतवो वै प्रयाजाः ।	I. 4. 12: ऋतवो वै प्रयाजाः ।
9. 42: देवी जोष्ट्री...वीतां यज ।	IV. 13. 8.
9. 43: देवी ऊर्जाहुती...वीतां यज ।	IV. 13. 8.
12. 13: कृकवाकुः सावित्रः ।	III. 14. 15: कृकवाकुः सावित्रः ।
12. 14: जनं भगो गच्छति ।	I. 6. 12: जनं भगोऽगच्छत् ।

THE NIRUKTA.	THE KĀṬHAKA SAṂHITĀ.
1. 5: वायुर्वा त्वा मनुर्वा त्वा ।	XIII. 14: वायुर्वा त्वा मनुर्वा त्वा ।
1. 10: सु विदुरिव ।	VIII. 3: न वै सु विदुरिव ।
सु विज्ञायेते इव ।	VI. 2: सु विज्ञायेते इव ।
1. 14: प्रथनात्पृथिवीत्याहुः ।	VIII 2: यदप्रथत तत्पृथिवी ।
1. 15: उरु प्रथस्व ।	I. 8: उरु प्रथस्व ।
ओषधे त्रायस्वैनम् ।	II. 1: ओषधे त्रायस्वैनम् ।
स्वधिते मैनं हिंसीः ।	II. 1: स्वधिते मैनं हिंसीः ।
2. 14: न वा अमुं लोकं जग्मुषे किं च नाकम् ।	XXI. 2: न वा अमुं लोकं जग्मुषे किञ्च नाकम् ।
3. 4: तस्मात्स्त्रियं जातां परास्यन्ति न पुमांसम् ।	XXVII. 9: तस्मात्स्त्रियं जातां परास्यन्ति न पुमांसम् ।
3. 21: ग्नास्त्वाकृन्तन्नपसोऽतन्वत ।	IX. 9: ग्नास्त्वाकृन्तन्नपसोऽतन्वत ।
कृत्तिवासाः पिनाकहस्तोऽवततधन्वा ।	IX. 7: कृत्तिवासाः पिनाकहस्तोऽवततधन्वा ।
4. 6: एकतो द्वितस्त्रित इति त्रयो बभूवुः ।	XXXI. 7: सोऽपोऽङ्गारेणाभ्यपातयत्तत एकतोऽजायत द्वितीयं ततो द्वितस्तृतीयं ततस्त्रितः ।
4. 17: सुविते मा धाः ।	II. 8: सुविते मा धाः ।
नवेन पूर्वं दयमानाः स्याम ।	XIX. 13: नवेन पूर्वं दयमानाः स्याम ।
5. 5: तं मरुतः क्षुरपविना व्ययुः ।	XXXVI. 8: देवा वै वृत्रस्य मर्म नाविन्दँस्तं मरुतः क्षुरपविना व्ययुः ।
7. 13: इन्द्रायाँहोमुच इति ।	X. 9: इन्द्रायाँहोमुच एकादशकपालम् ।
7. 24: अग्निर्वा इतो वृष्टिं समीरयति धामच्छद्दिवि [खलु वै] भूत्वा वर्षति मरुतः सृष्टां वृष्टिं नयन्ति यदा [खलु वै] असावादित्योऽग्निं रश्मिभिः पर्यावर्ततेऽथ वर्षति ।	XI. 10: अग्निर्वा इतो वृष्टिमुदीरयति धामच्छदिव भूत्वा वर्षति मरुतस्सृष्टां वृष्टिं नयन्ति । यदासा आदित्योऽर्वाङ् रश्मिभिः पर्यावर्ततेऽथ वर्षति ।

THE NIRUKTA.	THE KĀṬHAKA SAṂHITĀ.
8. 4: आप्रीभिराप्रीणातीति च ब्राह्मणम् ।	XXVI. 9: स एता आप्रीरपश्यत्ताभिरात्मानमाप्रीणीत ।
8. 19: देवेभ्यो वनस्पते हवींषि हिरण्यपर्ण प्रदिवस्ते अर्थम् । प्रदक्षिणिद्रशनया नियूय ऋतस्य वक्षि पथिभी रजिष्ठैः ॥	XVIII. 21: देवेभ्यो वनस्पते हवींषि हिरण्यपर्ण प्रदिवस्ते अर्थम् । प्रदक्षिणिद्रशनया नियूय- र्तस्य वक्षि पथिभी रजिष्ठैः ॥
8. 20: वनस्पते रशनया नियूय पिष्टतमया वयुनानि विद्वान् । वह देवत्रा दिधिषो हवींषि प्र च दातारममृतेषु वोचः ॥	वनस्पते रशनयाभिधाय पिष्टतमया वयुनानि विद्वान् । वहा देवत्रा दिधिषो हवींषि प्र च दातारममृतेषु वोचः ॥
स्वाहाकृतयः । स्वाहेत्येतत्सु आहेति वा । स्वा वागाहेति वा ।	VI. 1: स्वा वागैद्द जुहुधीति स इतः पर्यमृष्ट तत्स्वाहेत्यजुहोत्तस्मादेषैवमाहुतिस्स्वा ह्येनं वागैद्द ।
8. 22: प्राणा वै प्रयाजाः प्राणा वा अनुयाजाः । आत्मा वै प्रयाजा आत्मा वा अनुयाजाः ।	XXVI. 9: प्राणा वै प्रयाजाः । XXIII. 9: आत्मा वै प्रयाजाः प्रजानुयाजाः ।
9. 42: देवी जोष्ट्री...वीतां यज ।	XIX. 13.
9. 43: देवी ऊर्जाहुती...वीतां यज ।	XIX. 13.
10. 5: यदरुदत्तद्रुद्रस्य रुद्रत्वम् ।	XXV. 1: यत्समरुजत्तद्रुद्रस्य रुद्रत्वम् ।
11. 29: या पूर्वा पौर्णमासी सानुमतिः । योत्तरा सा राका ।	XII. 8: या पूर्वा पौर्णमासी सानुमतिर्योत्तरा सा राका ।
11. 31: या पूर्वामावास्या सा सिनीवाली । योत्तरा सा कुहूः ।	या पूर्वामावास्या सा सिनीवाली योत्तरा सा कुहूः ।
12. 13: अग्निं चित्वा न रामामुपेयात् । रामा रमणायोपेयते न धर्माय ।	XXII. 7: अग्निं चित्वा प्रथमं चित्वा न रामामुपेयात् । द्वितीयं चित्वा नान्येषां स्त्रियस्तृतीयं चित्वा न कांचन ।

THE NIRUKTA.	THE AITAREYA BRĀHMAṆA.
1. 8: तद् यदाभिर्वृत्रमशकद्धन्तुं तच्छक्करीणां शक्करीत्वमिति विज्ञायते ।	V. 7. 3: यदिमाँल्लोकान्प्रजापतिः सृष्ट्वेदं सर्वमशक्नोद् यदिदं किंच तच्छक्कर्योऽभवंस्तच्छक्करीणां शक्करीत्वम् ।
1. 16: एतद् वै यज्ञस्य समृद्धं यद् रूपसमृद्धं यत्कर्म क्रियमाणमृग्यजुर्वाभिवदतीति च ब्राह्मणम् ।	I. 4. 9: एतद् वै यज्ञस्य समृद्धं यद् रूपसमृद्धं यत् कर्म क्रियमाणमृगभिवदति ।
2. 24: विश्वामित्रः सर्वमित्रः ।	XXIX. 4. 18: तदु वैश्वामित्रम् । विश्वस्य ह वै मित्रं विश्वामित्र आस । विश्वं हास्मै मित्रं भवति ।

THE NIRUKTA.	THE AITAREYA BRĀHMAṆA.
3. 17: अङ्गारेष्वङ्गिराः ।	XIII. 10. 2: येऽङ्गारा आसंस्तेऽङ्गिरसोऽभवन् ।
4. 27: पंचर्तवः संवत्सरस्येति च ब्राह्मणं हेमन्तशिशिरयोः समासेन ।	I. 1. 14: पंचर्तवो हेमन्तशिशिरयोः समासेन । तावान्संवत्सरः ।
4. 27: षष्टिश्च ह वै त्रीणि च शतानि संवत्सरस्याहोरात्रा इति च ब्राह्मणं समासेन ।	II. 17. 2: त्रीणि च वै शतानि षष्टिश्च संवत्सरस्याहानि ।
4. 27: सप्त च वै शतानि विंशतिश्च संवत्सरस्याहोराघ्रा इति च ब्राह्मणं विभागेन ।	II. 17. 4: सप्त च वै शतानि विंशतिश्च संवत्सरस्याहोरात्राः ।
5. 11: अध्रिगो शमीध्वं सुशमी शमीध्वं शमीध्वमध्रिगविति ।	II. 7. 11: अध्रिगो शमीध्वं सुशमि शमीध्वं शमीध्वमध्रिगा ३ उ इति ।
7. 5. 8: तिस्र एव देवता इति नैरुक्ताः ।	II. 17. 17: तिस्रो देवता अन्वाह । II. 17. 17: त्रयो वा इमे त्रिवृतो लोका एषामेव...
7. 5: अग्निः पृथिवीस्थानो वायुर्वेन्द्रो वान्तरिक्षस्थानः सूर्यो द्युस्थानः ।	V. 32. 1; तेभ्योऽभितप्तेभ्यस्त्रीणि ज्योतीँष्यजायंत । अग्निरेव पृथिव्या अजायत वायुरंतरिक्षादादित्यो दिवः ।
7. 8: अथैतान्यग्निभक्तीनि । अयं लोकः प्रातःसवनं वसन्तो गायत्री त्रिवृत् स्तोमो रथन्तरं साम ये च देवगणाः समाम्नाताः प्रथमे स्थाने ।	II. 32. 1: अग्निरिति प्रातःसवनस्य चक्षुषी... III. 13. 1: प्रजापतिर्वै...छंदांसि...व्यभजत् स गायत्रीमेवाग्नये...प्रातःसवनेऽभजत् । IV. 29. 1: अग्निर्वै देवता प्रथममहर्वहति त्रिवृत् स्तोमो रथंतरं साम गायत्री छंदः.... यत्प्रथमे पदे देवता निरुच्यते । यदयं लोकोऽभ्युदितो यद्राथंतरं यद्गायत्रं...एतानि वै प्रथमस्याह्नो रूपाणि । VIII. 12. 4: ...त्वा गायत्रेण छंदसा त्रिवृता स्तोमेन रथन्तरेण साम्ना रोहन्तु ।
7. 10: अथैतानीन्द्रभक्तीनि । अन्तरिक्षलोको माध्यन्दिनं सवनं ग्रीष्मस्त्रिष्टुप् पञ्चदशः स्तोमो बृहत्साम ये च देवगणाः समाम्नाता मध्यमे स्थाने ।	II. 32. 1: इन्द्र इति माध्यंदिनस्य । III. 13. 1: त्रिष्टुभमिन्द्राय...माध्यंदिने । IV. 31. 1: इन्द्रो वै देवता द्वितीयमहर्वहति । पञ्चदशः स्तोमो बृहत् साम त्रिष्टुप् छन्दः... यन्मध्ये पदे देवता निरुच्यते । यदंतरिक्षमभ्युदितं यद्बार्हतं यत्त्रैष्टुभं...एतानि वै द्वितीयस्याह्नो रूपाणि । VIII. 12. 4: रुद्रास्त्वा त्रैष्टुभेन छंदसा पंचदशेन स्तोमेन बृहता साम्ना रोहन्तु ।

THE NIRUKTA.	THE AITAREYA BRĀHMAṆA.
7. 11: अथैतान्यादित्यभक्तीनि। असौ लोकस्तृतीयसवनं वर्षा जगती सप्तदशः स्तोमो वैरूपं साम ये च देवगणाः समाम्नाता उत्तमे स्थाने...।	II. 32. 1: सूर्य इति तृतीयसवनस्य।
	III. 13. 1: जगतीं विश्वेभ्यो देवेभ्य आदित्येभ्यस्तृतीयसवने।
	V. 1. 1: विश्वे वै देवा देवतास्तृतीयमहर्वहन्ति। सप्तदशः स्तोमो वैरूपं साम जगती छंदः...यदुत्तमे पदे देवता निरुच्यते यदसौ लोकोऽभ्युदितो यद्वैरूपं यज्जागतं...एतानि वै तृतीयस्याह्नो रूपाणि।
	VIII. 12. 4: आदित्यास्त्वा जागतेन छंदसा सप्तदशेन स्तोमेन वैरूपेण साम्ना रोहन्तु।
7. 11: शरदनुष्टुबेकविंशः स्तोमो वैराजं सामेति पृथिव्यायतनानि।	V. 4. 1: एकविंशः स्तोमो वैराजं सामानुष्टुप् छंदः...यद्वैराजं यदानुष्टुभं...प्रथमस्याह्नो रूपम्।
	VIII. 12. 4: विश्वे त्वा देवा आनुष्टुभेन छंदसैकविंशेन स्तोमेन वैराजेन साम्ना रोहन्तु।
7. 11: हेमन्तः पंक्तिस्त्रिणवः स्तोमः शाक्वरं सामेत्यन्तरिक्षायतनानि।	V. 6. 1: त्रिणवः स्तोमः शाक्वरं साम पंक्तिश्छंदः...यच्छाक्वरं यत्पांक्तं...द्वितीयस्याह्नो रूपम्।
	VIII. 12. 4: आप्त्याश्च देवाः पांक्तेन छंदसा त्रिणवेन स्तोमेन शाक्वरेण साम्ना रोहन्तु।
7. 11: शिशिरोऽतिछंदास्त्रयस्त्रिंशः स्तोमो रैवतं सामेति द्युभक्तीनि।	V. 12. 1: त्रयस्त्रिंशः स्तोमो रैवतं सामातिछंदाश्छंदः...यद्रैवतं यदतिछंदा...तृतीयस्याह्नो रूपम्।
	VIII. 12. 4: मरुतश्च त्वांगिरसश्च देवा अतिछंदसा छंदसा त्रयस्त्रिंशेन स्तोमेन रैवतेन साम्ना रोहन्तु।
7. 12: पंक्तिः पञ्चपदा।	V. 19. 6: पञ्चपदा पंक्तिः...
7. 17: अथापि ब्राह्मणं भवति। अग्निः सर्वा देवताः। इति	I. 1. 4. अग्निर्वै सर्वा देवताः।
7. 23: तामनुकृतिं होताग्निमारुते शस्त्रे वैश्वानरीयेण सूक्तेन प्रतिपद्यते।	XII. 3. 4: स वैश्वानरीयेणाग्निमारुतं प्रत्यपद्यत।
7. 23: अथापि वैश्वानरीयो द्वादशकपालो भवति।	VII. 9. 1: सोऽग्नये वैश्वानराय द्वादशकपालं पुरोळाशं निर्वपेत्।

THE NIRUKTA.	THE AITAREYA BRĀHMAṆA.
7. 26: मातरिश्वा वायुः।	X. 6. 7: प्राणो मातरिश्वा।
8. 4: आप्रीभिराप्रीणातीति च ब्राह्मणम्।	II. 4. 1: आप्रीभिराप्रीणाति।
8. 22: प्राणा वै प्रयाजाः प्राणा वा अनुयाजा इति च ब्राह्मणम्।	I. 11. 3: प्राणा वै प्रयाजाः प्रजानं
	1. 17. 14: प्राणा वै प्रयाजानुयाजास्ते य इमे शीर्षन् प्राणास्ते प्रयाजा येऽवाञ्चस्तेऽनुयाजाः।
8. 22: यस्यै देवतायै हविर्गृहीतं स्यात् तां मनसा ध्यायेद् वषट् करिष्यन्।	III. 8. 1: यस्य देवतायै हविर्गृहीतं स्यात् तां ध्यायेद् वषट् करिष्यन्।
11. 29: या पूर्वा पौर्णमासी सानुमतिः। योत्तरा सा राकेति विज्ञायते।	VII. 11. 2: या पूर्वा पौर्णमासी सानुमतिः। योत्तरा सा राका।
11. 31: या पूर्वामावास्या सा सिनीवाली योत्तरा सा कुहूरिति विज्ञायते।	VII. 11. 3: या पूर्वामावास्या सा सिनीवाली। योत्तरा सा कुहूः।
12. 8: सविता सूर्यां प्रायच्छत् सोमाय राज्ञे प्रजापतये वा। इति च ब्राह्मणम्।	IV. 7. 1: प्रजापतिर्वै सोमाय राज्ञे दुहितरं प्रायच्छत् सूर्यां सावित्रीम्।
12. 41: अग्निनाग्निमयजन्त देवाः। अग्निः पशुरासीत्। तमालभन्त। तेनायजन्त। इति च ब्राह्मणम्।	I. 16. 36: यदग्निनाग्निमयजन्त।
	I. 16. 38: तेऽग्नेऽग्निनाग्निमयजन्त।
	I. 16. 39: तेऽग्नेऽग्निनाग्निमयजन्त।
	I. 16. 12: रक्षांसि वा एनं तर्ह्यालभन्ते।
	I. 16. 40: सैषा स्वर्ग्याहुतिर्यदग्न्याहुतिः।

THE NIRUKTA.	THE KAUṢĪTAKI BRĀHMAṆA.
1. 8: तद् यदाभिर्वृत्रमशकद्धन्तुं तच्छक्वरीणां शक्वरीत्वमिति विज्ञायते।	XXIII. 2: एताः शक्वर्य एताभिर्वा इन्द्रो वृत्रमशकद्धन्तुं तद्याभिर्वृत्रमशकद्धन्तुं तस्माच्छक्वर्यः।
1. 9: पर्याया इव त्वदाश्विनम्।	XVII. 4: पर्याया इव त्वदाश्विनम्।
4. 27: षष्टिश्च ह वै त्रीणि च शतानि संवत्सरस्याहोरात्रा इति च ब्राह्मणं समासेन।	III. 2: त्रीणि वै षष्टिशतानि संवत्सरस्याह्नां तत्सामिधेनीभिः संवत्सरस्याहान्याप्नोति।
6. 31: अदन्तकः पूषेति च ब्राह्मणम्।	VI. 13: तस्मादाहुरदन्तकः पूषा करम्भभाग इति ते देवा ऊचुः।
7. 5. 8: तिस्र एव देवता इति नैरुक्ताः।	VIII. 8: ता वै तिस्रो देवताः।
7. 5: यथा पृथिव्यां मनुष्याः पशवो देवा इति	I. 1: अस्मिन् वै लोके उभये देवमनुष्या आसुः।

THE NIRUKTA.	KAUṢĪTAKI BRĀHMAṆA.
7. 8: अथैतान्यग्निभक्तीनि । अयं लोकः प्रातःसवनं वसन्तो गायत्री त्रिवृत् स्तोमो रथन्तरं साम ।	VIII. 9: गायत्र्यावाग्नेय्यौ गायत्रोऽयं लोकः...।
	XII. 4: गायत्री प्रातःसवनं वहति ।
	XIV. 1: अग्निर्ज्योतिः...तदिमं लोकं लोकानामाप्नोति प्रातःसवनं यज्ञस्य ।
	XIV. 3: अस्मिँल्लोके गायत्रोऽयमग्निरध्यूढः ।
	XIV. 5: अग्नेरग्रे प्रातःसवनमासीत् ।
	XXII. 1: प्रथममहरयमेव लोक आयतनेनाग्निर्गायत्री त्रिवृत्स्तोमो रथन्तरं साम...
ये च देवगणाः समाम्नाताः प्रथमे स्थाने ।	प्रथमे पदे सदेवम् ।......
	प्रथमस्याह्नो रूपमिमं लोकं...गायत्री छन्दस्त्रिवृतं स्तोमं रथन्तरं साम प्राचीं दिशं वसन्तमृतूनां वसून्देवान्देवजातमग्निमधिपतिम् ॥ १ ॥
7. 10: अथैतानीन्द्रभक्तीनि । अन्तरिक्षलोको माध्यन्दिनं सवनं ग्रीष्मस्त्रिष्टुप् ।	VIII. 9: त्रिष्टुभा सौम्यौ त्रैष्टुभोऽन्तरिक्षलोकः...
	XIV. 1: इन्द्रो ज्योतिः...तदन्तरिक्षलोकं लोकानामाप्नोति माध्यंदिनं सवनं यज्ञस्य ।
	XIV. 3: त्रैष्टुभेऽन्तरिक्षलोके त्रैष्टुभो वायुरध्यूढः ।
	XIV. 5: इन्द्रस्य माध्यन्दिनं सवनम् ।
	XXII. 2: द्वितीयमहरन्तरिक्षलोकं आयतनेनेन्द्रस्त्रिष्टुप् ।
पञ्चदशः स्तोमो बृहत्साम ये च देवगणाः समाम्नाता मध्यमे स्थाने ।	पञ्चदशः स्तोमो बृहत्साम...मध्यमे पदे सदेवम् ...अन्तरिक्षलोकं द्वितीयेनाह्नाप्नुवन्ति त्रिष्टुभं छन्दः पञ्चदशं स्तोमं बृहत्साम दक्षिणां दिशं ग्रीष्ममृतूनां मरुतो देवान्देवजातमिन्द्रमधिपतिम् ॥
	XVI. 1: बलं वै वीर्यं त्रिष्टुब्बलमेव तद्वीर्यं यजमाने दधाति ।
अथास्य कर्म रसानुदानं वृत्रवधो या च का च बलकृतिरिन्द्रकर्मैव तत् ।	XXII. 2: यद्वै प्रत्यक्षमस्पृष्टं तत्कुर्वद्धतवद्व्रजवद्वृत्रहवद्वृषण्वदुद्वद्विवत्स्थितम् ।
7. 11: अथैतान्यादित्यभक्तीनि । असौ लोकस्तृतीयसवनं वर्षा जगती ।	VIII. 9: जगत्यौ वैष्णव्यौ जागतोऽसौ लोकः...
	XIV. 1: सूर्यो ज्योतिः...तदमुं लोकं लोकानामाप्नोति तृतीयसवनं यज्ञस्य ।

THE NIRUKTA.	KAUṢĪTAKI BRĀHMAṆA.
	XIV. 3: जागतेऽमुष्मिँल्लोके जागतोऽसावादित्योऽध्यूढः ।
	XVI. 1; XXX. 1:...आदित्यानां तृतीयसवनम् ।
7. 11: सप्तदशः स्तोमो वैरूपं साम ये च देवगणाः समाम्नाता उत्तमे स्थाने ।	XXII. 3: तृतीयमहरसावेव लोक आयतनेन वरुणो जगती सप्तदशः स्तोमो वैरूपं साम... उत्तमे पदे सदेवम् ।
	XXII. 5: यथा वै...अमुं लोकं तृतीयेनाह्नाप्नुवन्ति जगतीं छन्दः सप्तदशं स्तोमं वैरूपं साम प्रतीचीं दिशं वर्षा ऋतूनामादित्यान्देवान्देवजातं वरुणमधिपतिम् ।
शरदनुष्टुबेकविंशस्तोमो वैराजं सामेति पृथिव्यायतनानि ।	XXII. 9: चतुर्थेनाह्नाप्नुवन्त्यनुष्टुभं छन्द एकविंशं स्तोमं वैराजं सोमोदीचीं दिशं शरदमृतूनां...बृहस्पतिं च चन्द्रमसं चाधिपती।
हेमन्तः पंक्तिस्त्रिणवस्तोमः शाक्वरं सामेत्यन्तरिक्षायतनानि ।	XXIII. 3: पञ्चमेनाह्नाप्नुवन्ति पंक्तिं छन्दस्त्रिणवं स्तोमं शाक्वरं साम...हेमन्तमृतूनां मरुतो देवान्देवजातं रुद्रमधिपतिम् ।
7. 12: पंक्तिः पञ्चपदा ।	XI. 2: अथ वै पंक्तेः पञ्चपदानि ।
	I. 3, 4. XIII. 2; XIX. 4. 7: पञ्चपदा पंक्तिः ।
7. 23: अथापि वैश्वानरीयो द्वादशकपालो भवति।	IV. 3: द्वादशकपालमसौ वै वैश्वानरः ।
7. 23: असौ वा आदित्योऽग्निर्वैश्वानरः । इति ।	IV. 3: असौ वै वैश्वानरो योऽसौ तपति ।
7. 24: अस्ति हि सौर्य एककपालः...।	V. 8: अथ यत्सौर्य एककपालः ।...
7. 17: समुद्राद्ध्येषोऽद्भ्य उदेति । इति च ब्राह्मणम् ।	XXV. 1: समुद्राद्ध्येषोऽद्भ्य उदेति ।
8. 4: आप्रीभिराप्रीणातीति च ब्राह्मणम् ।	X. 3: आप्रीभिराप्रीणाति...तमस्यैताभिराप्रीभिराप्रीणाति तद्यदाप्रीणाति तस्मादाप्रियो नाम ।
8. 22: ऋतवो वै प्रयाजा ऋतवोऽनुयाजाः । इति च ब्राह्मणम् । पशवो वै प्रयाजाः पशवोऽनुयाजाः । इति च ब्राह्मणम् ।	III. 4: ऋतवो वै प्रयाजा ऋतूनेव तत्प्रीणाति । ......पशवो वै प्रयाजाः ।
प्राणा वै प्रयाजाः प्राणा वा अनुयाजाः । इति च ब्राह्मणम् ।	VII. 1: प्राणा वै प्रयाजा अपाना अनुयाजाः । X. 3: प्राणा वै प्रयाजा अपाना अनुयाजाः ।
10. 32: आदित्योऽपि सवितोच्यते ।	VII, 6: असौ वै सविता योऽसौ तपति ।

THE NIRUKTA.	THE KAUṢĪTAKI BRĀHMAṆA.
11. 29: या पूर्वा पौर्णमासी सानुमतिः । योत्तरा सा राकेति विज्ञायते ।	iii. 1: पूर्वां पौर्णमासीमुपवसेदिति पैङ्ग्यमुत्तरामिति कौषीतकम् ... उत्तरां पौर्णमासीमुपवसेत् । अनिर्ज्ञाय पुरस्तादमावास्यायां चन्द्रमसं यदुपवसति तेन पूर्वां प्रीणाति यद्यजते तेनोत्तरामुत्तरामुपवसेत् । उत्तरामु ह वै समुद्रो विजते सोममनु...
11. 31: या पूर्वामावास्या सा सिनीवाली । योत्तरा सा कुहूरिति विज्ञायते ।	
12. 8: सविता सूर्यां प्रायच्छत् सोमाय राज्ञे प्रजापतये वेति ब्राह्मणम् ।	xviii. 1: अथ यत्र ह तत् सविता सूर्यां प्रायच्छत् सोमाय राज्ञे यदि वा प्रजापतेः ।
12. 14: अन्धो भग इत्याहुरनुत्सृप्तो न दृश्यते प्राशित्रमस्याक्षिणी निर्जघानेति च ब्राह्मणम् ।	vi. 13: तद् भगाय परिजह्रुस्तस्याक्षिणी निर्जघान तस्मादाहुरन्धो भग इति ।

THE NIRUKTA.	THE ṢADVIMṢ'A BRĀHMAṆA.
7. 17: अथापि ब्राह्मणं भवति । अग्निः सर्वा देवताः । इति ।	iii. 7: अग्निर्वै सर्वा देवताः ।
11. 29: या पूर्वा पौर्णमासी सानुमतिः । योत्तरा सा राकेति विज्ञायते ।	IV. 6: या पूर्वा पौर्णमासी सानुमतिः । योत्तरा सा राका ।
11. 31: या पूर्वामावास्या सा सिनीवाली । योत्तरा सा कुहूरिति विज्ञायते ।	IV. 6: या पूर्वामावास्या सा सिनीवाली । योत्तरा सा कुहूः ।......पुष्ये चानुमतिर्ज्ञेया सिनीवाली तु द्वापरे । खार्वायां तु भवेद्राका कृतपर्वे कुहूर्भवेत् । [नूतने ?] चानुमतिं विद्याद् यस्मिन् दृश्येत् सा सिनीवाली । राकायां तु सम्पूर्णश्चन्द्रस्तु कुहूर्न दृश्येत् ।

THE NIRUKTA.	THE TAITTIRĪYA BRĀHMAṆA.
1. 15: ऊरु प्रथस्वेति प्रथयति ।	III. 2. 8. 4: उरु प्रथस्व ।
1. 15: अथापि जानन्तं संप्रेषयति । अग्नये समिध्यमानायानुब्रूहीति ।	III. 3. 7. 1: अग्नये समिध्यमानायानुब्रूहीत्याह ।
3. 8: सोऽदेवानसृजत तत् सुराणां सुरत्वम् । असोरसुरानसृजत तदसुराणामसुरत्वमिति विज्ञायते ।	II. 3. 8. 2: तेनासुनाऽसुरानसृजत । तदसुराणामसुरत्वम् । II. 3. 8. 4: दिवा देवत्राऽभवत् । तदनु देवानसृजत । तद्देवानां देवत्वम् ।
3. 20: नक्षत्राणि नक्षतेर्गतिकर्मणः ।	I. 5. 2. 5, 6: अमुँ स लोकं नक्षते । तन्नक्षत्राणां नक्षत्रत्वम् । देवगृहा वै नक्षत्राणि ।... यानि वा इमानि पृथिव्याश्चित्राणि तानि नक्षत्राणि ।
3. 20: नेमानि क्षत्राणि ।	II. 7. 18. 3: न वा इमानि क्षत्राण्यभूवन्निति । तन्नक्षत्राणां नक्षत्रत्वम् ।

The Nirukta.	The S'atapatha Brāhmaṇa.
1. 7: दक्षिणा दक्षतेः समर्धयतिकर्मणः । व्यृद्धं समर्धयतीति ।	II. 2. 2. 2. p. 146: स एष यज्ञो हतो न ददक्षे । तं देवा दक्षिणाभिरदक्षयंस्तद्यदेनं दक्षिणाभिरदक्षयंस्तस्माद् दक्षिणा नाम ।... अथ समृद्ध एव यज्ञो भवति तस्माद् दक्षिणा ददाति ।
1. 15: प्रथनात्पृथिवीत्याहुः ।	VI. 1. 3. 7. p. 505: तद् भूमिरभवत् । तामप्रथयत् । सा पृथिव्यभवत् ।
1. 15: ओषधे त्रायस्वैनम् ।	III. 1. 2. 7: ओषधे त्रायस्वेति वज्रो वै क्षुरः । तथो हैनमेष वज्रः क्षुरो न हिनस्ति । अथ क्षुरेणाभिनिदधाति ।
स्वधिते मैनँ हिंसीः । इत्याह हिंसन् ।	III. 1. 2. 7: स्वधिते मैनꣳहिंसीरिति वज्रो वै क्षुरः । तथो हैनमेष वज्रः क्षुरो न हिनस्ति । The passage is repeated in III. 6. 4. 10. and III. 8. 2. 12. verbatim reading परशुः and असिः for क्षुरः respectively.
अग्नये समिध्यमानायानुब्रूहीति ।	II. 5. 2. 9: अथाध्वर्युरेवाह । अग्नये समिध्यमानायानुब्रूहीति ।
2. 6: अथाप्यस्यैको रश्मिश्चन्द्रमसं प्रति दीप्यते ...आदित्यतोऽस्य दीप्तिर्भवति । सुषुम्णः सूर्यरश्मिश्चन्द्रमा गन्धर्वः ।	IX. 4. 1. 9: सुषुम्ण इति । सुयज्ञिय इत्येतत् सूर्यरश्मिरिति सूर्यस्येव हि चन्द्रमसो रश्मयश्चन्द्रमा गन्धर्वस्तस्य नक्षत्राण्यप्सरस इति चन्द्रमा ह गन्धर्वः ।
2. 10: समुद् द्रवन्त्यस्मादापः । समभिद्रवन्त्ये-नमापः ।	XIV. 2. 2. 2. p. 1035: अयं वै समुद्रो योऽयं पवत एतस्माद्वै समुद्रात्सर्वे देवाः सर्वाणि भूतानि समुद्द्रवन्ति ।
3. 4: अङ्गादङ्गात्संभवसि हृदयादधिजायसे । आत्मा वै पुत्रनामासि स जीव शरदः शतम् ॥	XIV. 9. 4. 8. p. 1106: स यामिच्छेत् । कामयेत मेति तस्यामर्थं निष्ठाप्य मुखेन मुखं संधायोपस्थमस्या अभिमृश्य जपेदङ्गादङ्गात्स-म्भवसि हृदयादधि जायसे । स त्वमङ्गकषायो-ऽसि दिग्धविद्धामिव मादयेति ।
3. 16: तथा पशुः पश्यतेः ।	VI. 2. 1. 4: यदपश्यत्तस्मादेते पशवस्तेष्वे-तमपश्यत्तस्माद्वेवैते पशवः ।
4. 21: अथापि शंयुर्बार्हस्पत्य उच्यते । तच्छं-योरावृणीमहे गातुं यज्ञाय गातुं यज्ञपतये ।	I. 9. 1. 24–27: अथ शम्योराह । शम्यु-र्ह वै बार्हस्पत्यः ।...तच्छंयोरावृणीमहे... गातुं यज्ञाय गातुं यज्ञपतयऽइति ।

THE NIRUKTA.	THE S'ATAPATHA BRĀHMAṆA.
4. 27: पञ्चर्तवः संवत्सरस्येति च ब्राह्मणं हेमन्तशिशिरयोः समासेन ।	I. 7. 2. 8: पञ्चर्तवः संवत्सरस्य । and also in XII. 3. 2. 1.
षष्टिश्च ह वै त्रीणि च शतानि संवत्सरस्याहोरात्रा इति च ब्राह्मणं समासेन ।	XII. 3. 2. 3: त्रीणि च वै शतानि षष्टिश्च संवत्सरस्य रात्रयः ।...अत्र तत्समं त्रीणि च शतानि षष्टिश्च संवत्सरस्याहानि ।
सप्त च वै शतानि विंशतिश्च संवत्सरस्याहोरात्रा इति च ब्राह्मणं विभागेन ।	XII. 3. 2. 4: सप्त च वै शतानि विंशतिश्च संवत्सरस्याहोरात्राणि ।
6. 31: पूषेत्यपरम् । सोऽदन्तकः । अदन्तकः पूषा । इति च ब्राह्मणम् ।	I. 7. 4. 7: तत्पूष्णे पर्योजहुस्तत्पूषा प्राश तस्य दतो निर्जघान तथेन्नूनं तदास तस्मादाहुरदन्तकः पूषेति ।
7. 5: अग्निः पृथिवीस्थानो वायुर्वेन्द्रो वान्तरिक्षस्थानः सूर्यो द्युस्थानः ।	XI. 2. 3. 1: तद् देवान् सृष्ट्वा...व्यारोचयदस्मिन्नेव लोकेऽग्निं वायुमन्तरिक्षे दिव्येव सूर्यम् ।
7. 14: अग्निः कस्मात् । अग्रणी भवति । अग्रं यज्ञेषु प्रणीयते ।	II. 2. 4. 2: तद्वाऽएनमेतदग्रे देवानामजनयत । तस्मादग्निरग्निर्ह वै नामैतद्यदग्निरिति स जातः पूर्वः प्रेयाय यो वै पूर्व एत्यग्रऽएतीति वै तमाहुः सोऽएवास्याग्निता ।
	VI. 1. 1. 11: सोऽग्निरसृज्यत स यदस्य सर्वस्याग्रमसृज्यत तस्मादग्निरग्निर्ह वै तमग्निरित्याचक्षते ।
7. 17: अथापि ब्राह्मणं भवति । अग्निः सर्वा देवताः ।	I. 6. 2. 8: सोऽग्निमेव प्राप्य संबभूव...सर्वा विद्याः सर्वं यशः सर्वमन्नाद्यं सर्वां श्रीम् ।
7. 23: अथासावादित्य इति पूर्वे याज्ञिकाः ।	IX. 3. 1. 25: स यः स वैश्वानरोऽसौ स आदित्यः ।
अथापि वैश्वानरीयो द्वादशकपालो भवति ।	VI. 6. 1. 5: वैश्वानरो द्वादशकपालः ।
7. 24: बहुभक्तिवादीनि हि ब्राह्मणानि भवन्ति । पृथिवी वैश्वानरः । संवत्सरो वैश्वानरः । ब्राह्मणो वैश्वानरः ।	XIII. 3. 8. 3: इयं(पृथिवी) वै वैश्वानरः । V. 2. 5. 15; VI. 6. 1. 5. संवत्सरो वैश्वानरः ।
7. 26: मातरिश्वा वायुः ।	VI. 4. 3. 4: अयं वै वायुर्मातरिश्वा योऽयं पवते ।
8. 10: उषासानक्ता । उषाश्च नक्ता च ।	VI. 7. 2. 3: अहोरात्रे वै नक्तोषासा ।
8. 22: छन्दांसि वै प्रयाजाश्छन्दांस्यनुयाजा इति च ब्राह्मणम् ।	I. 3. 2. 9: छन्दोभ्यस्तद् गृह्णाति । अनुयाजेभ्यो हि तद् गृह्णाति । छन्दांसि ह्यनुयाजाः ।
ऋतवो वै प्रयाजा ऋतवोऽनुयाजा इति च ब्राह्मणम् ।	I. 3. 2. 8: ऋतुभ्यस्तद् गृह्णाति । प्रयाजेभ्यो हि तद् गृह्णाति । ऋतवो हि प्रयाजाः ।

THE NIRUKTA.	THE S'ATAPATHA BRĀHMAṆA.
8. 22: प्राणा वै प्रयाजाः प्राणा वा अनुयाजा इति च ब्राह्मणम्।	XI. 2. 7. 27: प्राणा वै प्रयाजाः। अपाना अनुयाजाः।
9. 20: उरु मे कुर्वित्यब्रवीत्। तदुलूखलमभवत्। उरुकरं वै तत्तदुलूखलमित्याचक्षते परोक्षेणेति च ब्राह्मणम्।	VII. 5. 1. 22: उरु मे करदिति तस्मादुरुकरम्। उरुकरं ह वै तदुलूखलमित्याचक्षते परोक्षम्।
9. 24: पितुरित्यन्ननाम।	I. 9. 2. 20: अन्नं वै पितुः।
9. 26: आप आप्नोतेः।	VI. 1. 1. 9: यदाप्नोत्तस्मादापः।
10. 5: यदरोदीत्तद्रुद्रस्य रुद्रत्वमिति हारिद्रविकम्।	IX. 1. 1. 6: सोऽरोदीत्तस्य यान्यश्रूणि प्रास्कन्दंस्तान्यस्मिन्मन्यौ प्रत्यतिष्ठन्त्स एव शतशीर्षा रुद्रः समभवत्।
10. 7: अग्निरपि रुद्र उच्यते।	V. 2. 4. 13: यो वै रुद्रः सो अग्निः।
10. 8: तद् यदेनं प्राणैः समैन्धंस्तदिन्द्रस्येन्द्रत्वम्। इति विज्ञायते।	VI. 1. 1. 2: एष एवेन्द्रस्तानेष प्राणान्मध्यत इन्द्रियेणैन्द्ध यदैन्द्ध तस्मादिन्ध इन्धो ह वै तमिन्द्र इत्याचक्षते।
10. 26: विश्वकर्मा...सर्वमेधे सर्वाणि भूतानि जुहवांचकार। स आत्मानमप्यन्ततो जुहवांचकार।	XIII. 7. 1. 1: तदैक्षत न वै तपस्यानन्त्यमस्ति हन्ताहं भूतेष्वात्मानं जुहवानि भूतानि चात्मनीति। तत्सर्वेषु भूतेष्वात्मानं हुत्वा भूतानि चात्मनि...सर्वमेधे सर्वान्मेधान्हुत्वा सर्वाणि भूतानि...पर्येति।
10. 31: सविता सर्वस्य प्रसविता।	I. 1. 2. 17: सविता वै देवानां प्रसविता।
12. 14: अन्धो भग इत्याहुरनुत्सृप्तो न दृश्यते। प्राशित्रमस्याक्षिणी निर्जघान। इति च ब्राह्मणम्।	I. 7. 4. 6: तद् भगाय दक्षिणत आसीनाय पर्याजह्रुः। तद् भगोऽवेक्षांचक्रे। तस्याक्षिणी निर्ददाह।...तस्मादाहुरन्धो भग इति।

THE NIRUKTA.	THE MANTRA BRĀHMAṆA.
1. 15: ओषधे त्रायस्वैनम्।	I. 6. 5: ओषधे त्रायस्वैनम् ओषध इति। दर्भरूप उषधिर्देवता।
स्वधिते मैनं हिंसीः। इत्याह हिंसन्।	I. 6. 6: स्वधिते मैनं हिंसीः। स्वधित इति। स्वधितिर्देवता।

The following 2 stanzas are quoted by Sāyanācārya in the introductory remarks of his commentary on the Mantra Brāhmaṇa.

स्थाणुरयं भारहारः किलाभूदधीत्य वेदं न विजानाति योऽर्थम्।
योऽर्थज्ञ इत् सकलं भद्रमश्नुते नाकमेति ज्ञानविधूतपाप्मा॥
यदधीतमविज्ञातं निगदेनैव शब्द्यते।
अनग्नाविव शुष्कैधो न तज्ज्वलति कर्हिचित्॥
Cf. N. 1. 18.

Daivata Brāhmaṇa of the Sāmaveda

III. Khaṇḍa

The Nirukta.

N. 7. 12: गायत्री गायतेः स्तुतिकर्मणः । त्रिगमना वा विपरीता । गायतो मुखादुदपतदिति च ब्राह्मणम् । उष्णिगुत्स्नाता भवति । स्निह्यतेर्वा स्यात्कान्तिकर्मणः। उष्णीषिणी वेत्यौपमिकम् । उष्णीषं स्नायतेः । ककुप् ककुभिनी भवति । ककुप् च कुब्जश्च कुजतेर्वोब्जतेर्वा । अनुष्टुबनुष्टोभनात् । गायत्रीमेव त्रिपदां सतीं चतुर्थेन पादेनानुष्टोभतीति च ब्राह्मणम् । वृहती परिवर्हणात् । पङ्क्तिः पञ्चपदा । त्रिष्टुप् स्तोभत्युत्तरपदा । का तु त्रिता स्यात् । तीर्णतमं छन्दः । त्रिवृद्वज्रस्तस्य स्तोभतीति वा । यत्त्रिरस्तोभत्तत्त्रिष्टुभस्त्रिष्टुप्त्वमिति विज्ञायते ॥ १२ ॥

Khaṇḍa III.

अथातो निर्वचनम् । १ । गायत्री गायतेः स्तुतिकर्मणः । २ । गायतो मुखादुदपतदिति ह ब्राह्मणम् । ३ । उष्णिगुत्स्नानात्स्निह्यतेर्वा कान्तिकर्मणोऽपि वोष्णीषिणी वेत्यौपमिकम् ।४। ककुप् ककुद्रूपिणीत्यौपमिकम् । ५ । ककुप् च कुब्जश्च कुजतेर्वोब्जतेर्वा । ६ । अनुष्टुबनुष्टोभनात् । ७ । अन्वस्तोभदिति ह ब्राह्मणम् । ८ । पिपीलिका पेलतेर्गतिकर्मणः । ९ । पिपीलिका-मध्येत्यौपमिकम् । १० । बृहती वृंहतेर्वृद्धिकर्मणः ।११। विराड् विरमणाद्विराजनाद्वा ।१२। पङ्क्तिः पञ्चिनी पञ्चपदा । १३ । त्रिष्टुप् स्तोभ इत्युत्तरपदा । १४ । का तु त्रिता स्यात्तीर्णतमं छन्दो भवति । १५ । त्रिवृद्वज्रस्तस्य स्तोभमित्यौपमिकम् । १६ ।

N. 7. 13: जगती गततमं छन्दः । जलचरगतिर्वा । जल्गल्यमानोऽसृजदिति च ब्राह्मणम् । विराड्विराजनाद्वा विराधनाद्वा विप्रापणाद्वा । विराजनात्संपूर्णाक्षरा विराधनादूनाक्षरा विप्रापणादधिकाक्षरा । पिपीलिकामध्येत्यौपमिकम् । पिपीलिका पेलतेर्गतिकर्मणः ।

जगती गततमं छन्दो जज्जगतिर्भवति क्षिप्रगतिर्जज्मला(?) कुर्वन्नसृजतेति ह ब्राह्मणम् । १७ । This passage is cited by Guṇe in Bhand. Comm. Vol. p. 51.

The Nirukta.

1. 16: एतद् वै यज्ञस्य समृद्धं यद् रूपसमृद्धं यत् कर्म क्रियमाणमृग्यजुर्वाभिवदतीति च ब्राह्मणम् ।

2. 10: समुद्द्रवन्त्यस्मादापः । समभिद्रवन्त्येनमापः ।

4. 27: त्र्यृतुः संवत्सरः ।

Gopatha Brāhmaṇa.

II. 2. 6; p. 171: एतद्वै यज्ञस्य समृद्धं यद्रूपसमृद्धं यत्कर्मक्रियमाणमृग्यजुर्वाभिवदति ।

I. 1. 7; p. 7: तद् यत्समवद्रवन्त तस्मात् समुद्र उच्यते ।

I. 5. 5: त्रयो वा ऋतवः संवत्सरस्य ।

THE NIRUKTA.	GOPATHA BRĀHMAṆA.
4. 27: षष्टिश्च ह वै त्रीणि च शतानि संवत्सरस्याहोरात्रा इति च ब्राह्मणं समासेन । सप्त च वै शतानि विंशतिश्च संवत्सरस्याहोरात्राः ।	I. 5. 5; p. 119: त्रीणि च ह वै शतानि षष्टिश्च संवत्सरस्याहोरात्राणि ।...सप्त च ह वै शतानि विंशतिश्च संवत्सरस्याहानि च रात्रयश्च ।
7. 8: अथैतान्यग्निभक्तीनि । अयं लोकः प्रातःसवनं वसन्तो गायत्री त्रिवृत् स्तोम रथन्तरं साम ।	I. 1. 29; p. 21: किं दैवतमिति । ऋचामग्निर्देवतम् । तदेव ज्योतिर्गायत्रं छन्दः पृथिवीस्थानम् ।
	I. 1. 17; p. 13: तस्य प्रथमया...पृथिवीमग्निम्...गायत्रं छन्दस्त्रिवृतं स्तोमं...वसन्तमृतुम्......।
	I. 2. 24; p. 62: पृथिवी वा ऋचामायतनमग्निर्देवता गायत्रं छन्दः......।
	II. 3. 12; p. 199: अथातः...प्रातःसवनम् ......स आग्नेय्या गायत्र्याज्यं प्रत्यपद्यत ।
	II. 3. 10; p. 196: पुरस्तात् प्रातःसवने ...उक्थं...शस्त्वा चतुरक्षरम्......चतुरक्षरं तदष्टाक्षरं संपद्यते । अष्टाक्षरा वै गायत्री गायत्रीमेवैतत् ।
	II. 3. 16; p. 202: गायत्रं हि प्रातःसवनं ...परिदधाति ।......अयं वै लोकः प्रातःसवनम् । तस्य...पञ्चोक्थानि ।
7. 10: अथैतानीन्द्रभक्तीनि । अन्तरिक्षलोको माध्यन्दिनं सवनं ग्रीष्मस्त्रिष्टुप् पञ्चदश स्तोमो बृहत्साम ।	I. 1. 29: यजुषां वायुर्दैवतम् । तदेव ज्योतिस्त्रैष्टुभं छन्दोऽन्तरिक्षं स्थानम् ।
	I. 1. 18: तस्य द्वितीयया...अन्तरिक्षम् ।
	I. 1. 17: वायुं...त्रैष्टुभं छन्दः पञ्चदशं स्तोमं ...ग्रीष्ममृतुम् ।
	I. 2. 24: अन्तरिक्षं वै...आयतनं वायुर्देवता त्रैष्टुभं छन्दः......।
	II. 3. 10: माध्यन्दिने...त्रिष्टुभमेवैतत् ।
	II. 3. 12: तं माध्यन्दिने पवमाने...स ऐन्द्रया त्रिष्टुभा मरुत्वतीयं प्रत्यपद्यत ।
	II. 4. 4: ऐन्द्रं हि त्रैष्टुभं माध्यन्दिनँ सवनम् ।...अन्तरिक्षलोको माध्यन्दिनं सवनम् ...पञ्चोक्थानि माध्यन्दिनस्य सवनस्य ।

THE NIRUKTA.	GOPATHA BRĀHMAṆA.
7. 11: अथैतान्यादित्यभक्तीनि । असौ लोकस्तृतीयसवनं वर्षा जगती सप्तदशः स्तोमः ।	I. 1. 29: साम्नामादित्यो दैवतम् तदेव ज्योतिर्जागतं छन्दो द्यौः स्थानम् ।
	I. 1. 19: तस्य तृतीयया...दिवमादित्यं...जागतं छन्दः सप्तदशं स्तोमं...वर्षा ऋतुम्...।
	I. 2. 24: द्यौर्वै...आयतनमादित्यो देवता जागतं छन्दः......।
	II. 3. 10: तृतीयसवने...जगतीमेवैतत् ।
	II. 4. 18: जागतं हि तृतीयसवनम्...असौ वै लोकस्तृतीयसवनम् ।
7. 12: पङ्क्तिः पञ्चपदा ।	I. 3. 8: अथ यः पङ्क्तिं पञ्चपदाम् ।
	I. 3. 10: अथ या पङ्क्तिः पञ्चपदा ।
	1. 4. 24: इति होवाच पञ्चपदा पङ्क्तिः ।
7. 17· अथापि ब्राह्मणं भवति । अग्निः सर्वा देवता इति ।	II. 1. 12: अग्निर्वै सर्वा देवताः ।
7. 23: अयमेवाग्निर्वैश्वानर इति शाकपूणिः ।	I. 2. 20: ब्राह्मणो ह वा इममग्निं वैश्वानरं बभार । सोऽयमग्निर्वैश्वानरः...। अथायमीक्षतेऽग्निर्जातवेदा ब्राह्मणद्वितीयो ह वा अयमिदमग्निर्वैश्वानरो ज्वलति ।
8. 22: यस्यै देवतायै हविर्गृहीतं तां मनसा ध्यायेद् वषट्करिष्यन् ।	II. 3. 4: यस्यै देवतायै हविर्गृहीतं स्यात् तां मनसा ध्यायन् वषट्कुर्यात् ।
11. 29: या पूर्वा पौर्णमासी सानुमतिः। योत्तरा सा राकेति विज्ञायते ।	II. 1. 10: या पूर्वा पौर्णमासी सानुमतिर्योत्तरा सा राका ।
11. 31: या पूर्वामावास्या सा सिनीवाली योत्तरा सा कुहूरिति विज्ञायते ।	या पूर्वामावास्या सा सिनीवाली योत्तरा सा कुहूः ।
12. 14: अन्धो भग इत्याहुः ।	II. 1. 2: तस्मादाहुरन्धो वै भग इति ।

THE NIRUKTA.	THE AITAREYA ĀRAṆYAKA.
4. 27: सप्त च वै शतानि विंशतिश्च संवत्सरस्याहोरात्रा इति च ब्राह्मणं विभागेन ।	III. 2. 1: सप्त च वै शतानि विंशतिश्च संवत्सरस्याहोरात्राः ।

THE NIRUKTA.	THE TAITTIRĪYA ĀRAṆYAKA.
2. 11: तद् यदेनांस्तपस्यमानान् ब्रह्म स्वयम्भ्वभ्यानर्षत्त ऋषयोऽभवन् । तदृषीणामृषित्वमिति विज्ञायते ।	II. 9: तपस्यमानान्ब्रह्म स्वयंभ्वभ्यानर्षत्त ऋषयोऽभवन् । तदृषीणामृषित्वम् ।

THE NIRUKTA.	SARVĀNUKRAMAṆĪ.
N. 1. 2: कर्मसंपत्तिर्मन्त्रो वेदे ।	Paribhāṣā 1. न ह्येतज्ज्ञानमृते श्रौतस्मार्तकर्मप्रसिद्धिः ।
N. 1. 15: अथापीदमन्तरेण मन्त्रेष्वर्थप्रत्ययो न विद्यते...स्वार्थसाधकं च ।	मन्त्राणां ब्राह्मणार्षेयच्छन्दोदैवतविद्याजनाध्यापनाभ्यां श्रेयोऽधिगच्छति ।
N. 1. 20: नास्मै कामान्दुग्धे वाग्दोह्यान्देवमनुष्यस्थानेषु ।	
N. 2.10,11: cf.	61. 98: बृहस्पते द्वादशार्ष्टिषेणो देवापिर्वृष्टिकामो देवांस्तुष्टाव ।
N. 2. 11: ऋषिर्दर्शनात्	paribhāṣā 2. 4: यस्य वाक्यं स ऋषिः ।
N. 2. 24: स विश्वामित्रो नदीस्तुष्टाव गाधा भवतेति ।	18. 33: प्र पर्वतानां सप्तोना संवादो नदीभिर्विश्वामित्रस्योत्तितीर्षोः ।
N. 5. 13: उर्वश्यप्सरा...तस्या दर्शनान्मित्रावरुणयो रेतश्चस्कन्द ।	I. 166. p. 12....मित्रावरुणयोर्दीक्षितयोरुर्वशीमप्सरसं दृष्ट्वा वासतीवरे कुम्भे रेतोऽपतत् ।
N. 7. 1: तद्यानि नामानि प्राधान्यस्तुतीनां देवतानां तद्दैवतमित्याचक्षते.	paribhāṣā 2. 5: या तेनोच्यते सा देवता ।
N. 7. 1: यत्काम ऋषिर्यस्यां देवतायामार्थपत्यमिच्छन्स्तुतिं प्रयुङ्क्ते तद्दैवतः स मन्त्रो भवति ।	paribhāṣā 2. 7: अर्थेप्सव ऋषयो देवताश्छन्दोभिरुपाधावन् ।
N. 7. 3: एवमुच्चावचैरभिप्रायैर्ऋषीणां मन्त्रदृष्टयो भवन्ति ।	
N. 7. 3: एवमक्षसूक्ते द्यूतनिन्दा च कृषिप्रशंसा च ।	56. 34: प्रावेपाः पञ्चूना मौंजवान्वाक्षोऽक्षकृषिप्रशंसा चाक्षकितवनिन्दा च सप्तमी जगती ।
N. 7. 4: माहाभाग्याद्देवताया एक आत्मा बहुधा स्तूयते । एवमस्यात्मनोऽन्ये देवाः प्रत्यङ्गानि भवन्ति...आत्मजन्मान आत्मैवैषां रथो भवत्यात्माश्व आत्मायुधमात्मेषव आत्मा सर्वं देवस्य ।	paribhāṣā 2. 14: एकैव वा महानात्मा देवता. । pari° 2. 16: स हि सर्वभूतात्मा. pari° 2. 18: तद्विभूतयोऽन्या देवताः pari° 2. 12: तत्तत्स्थाना अन्यदेवतास्तद्विभूतयः ।
N. 7. 5: तिस्र एव देवता इति नैरुक्ताः । अग्निः पृथिवीस्थानः । वायुर्वेन्द्रो वान्तरिक्षस्थानः । सूर्यो द्युस्थानः ।......अपि वा कर्मपृथक्त्वात्...अपि वा पृथगेव स्युः पृथग्घि स्तुतयो भवन्ति तथाभिधानानि ।	paribhāṣā. 2. 8: तिस्र एव देवताः क्षित्यन्तरिक्षद्युस्थाना अग्निर्वायुः सूर्य इति । pari° 2. 13: कर्मपृथक्त्वाद्धि पृथगभिधानस्तुतयो भवन्ति ।
N. 7. 12: छन्दांसि छादनात्	paribhāṣā. 2. 6: यदक्षरपरिमाणं तच्छन्दः

THE NIRUKTA.	VEDĀRTHA DĪPIKĀ.
N. 2. 10. अन्तरिक्षं कस्मात् । अन्तरा क्षान्तं भवत्यन्तरेमे इति वा । शरीरेष्वन्तरक्षयमिति वा ।	Ved. dīp. 2. 8; p. 60: भूमिस्वर्गयोरंतरा मध्येऽमूर्ततयानुपलंभादंतरा क्षांतमित्येवमंतरिक्षम् ।
N. 2. 11. ऋषिर्दर्शनात् ।	Ved. dīp. 2. 4; p. 60: उक्तं च । ऋषिर्दर्शनादिति ॥
	Ved. dīp. 1. 1; p. 57: अर्तेः सनोतेश्च ऋषिशब्दो निरुच्यते ।
N. 7. 12: छन्दांसि छादनात् ।	Ved. dīp. 1. 1; p. 57: छन्दः पापेभ्यश्छादनात् ।
N. 9. 32. कण्टकः कन्तपो वा कृन्ततेर्वा कण्टतेर्वा स्याद्गतिकर्मण उद्गततमो भवति ।	Ved. dīp. 1. 2; p. 58: कण्टकाः पीडकाः कण्टयन्तीति निरुक्तिः ।

THE NIRUKTA.	R. PRĀTIS'ĀKHYA.
1. 1: तद्यान्येतानि चत्वारि पदजातानि नामाख्याते चोपसर्गनिपाताश्च तानीमानि भवन्ति ।	12. 5: 699: नामाख्यातमुपसर्गो निपातश्च चत्वार्याहुः पदजातानि शाब्दाः ।
भावप्रधानमाख्यातं सत्त्वप्रधानानि नामानि ।	12. 5: 700–701: तन्नाम येनाभिदधाति सत्त्वं तदाख्यातं येन भावं स धातुः ॥
	12. 8: 707: क्रियावाचकमाख्यातम्...सत्त्वाभिधायकं नाम...।
1. 3: न निर्बद्धा उपसर्गो अर्थान्निराहुरिति शाकटायनो नामाख्यातयोस्तु कर्मोपसंयोगद्योतका भवन्ति । उच्चावचाः पदार्थाः...तद्य एषु पदार्थः प्राहुरिमे तं नामाख्यातयोरर्थविकरणम् । आ...प्र परा...अभि...प्रति... अति सु...निर्दुर्...न्यव...उद्...सम्...व्यप ...अनु...अपि...उप...परि...अधि...।	12. 8: 707: उपसर्गो विशेषकृत् । 12. 6: 702–703: प्राभ्यापरानिर्दुरनुव्युपापसंपरिप्रतिन्यत्यधिसूदवापि । उपसर्गा विंशतिरर्थवाचकाः सहेतराभ्याम्...॥
1. 4: अथ निपाता...पदपूरणाः ।	12. 8: 707: निपातः पादपूरणः ।
1. 9: अथ ये प्रवृत्तेऽर्थेऽमिताक्षरेषु ग्रन्थेषु वाक्यपूरणा आगच्छन्ति पदपूरणास्ते मिताक्षरेष्वनर्थकाः...।	12. 9: 708: निपातानामर्थवशान्निपातनादनर्थकानामितरे च सार्थकाः । नेयंत इत्यस्ति संख्येह वाङ्मये मिताक्षरे चाप्यमिताक्षरे च ये ॥
1. 17: पदप्रकृतिः संहिता ।	2. 1: 105: संहिता पदप्रकृतिः ।

THE NIRUKTA.	ATHARVA-VEDA PRATIS'ĀKHYA.
1. 1: तद्यान्येतानि चत्वारि पदजातानि नामाख्याते चोपसर्गनिपाताश्च तानीमानि भवन्ति ।	1. 1: चतुर्णां पदजातानां नामाख्यातोपसर्गनिपातानां सन्ध्यपद्यौ गुणौ प्रातिज्ञम् ।
	The following verses are cited by the commentator in the begining of the fourth chapter (see J. A. O. S. vol. 7. p. 591): समासावग्रहविग्रहान्पदे यथोवाच छन्दसि शाकटायनः । तथा वक्ष्यामि चतुष्टयं पदं नामाख्यातोपसर्गनिपातानाम् ॥
भावप्रधानमाख्यातम् । सत्त्वप्रधानानि नामानि ।	II. 1: आख्यातं यत्क्रियावाचि नाम सत्त्वाख्यमुच्यते । निपाताश्चादयः सर्वे उपसर्गास्तु प्रादयः ॥
cf. N. 1. 3.	II. 17: प्रपराणिसमादुर्णिरवाधिपरिवीनि च । अत्यभ्यपिसूदपा य उपानुप्रतिविंशतिः ॥

THE NIRUKTA.	THE VĀJA. PRĀTIS'ĀKHYA.
1. 1: तद्यान्येतानि चत्वारि पदजातानि नामाख्याते चोपसर्गनिपाताश्च तानीमानि भवन्ति ।	8. 52: तच्चतुर्धा नामाख्यातोपसर्गनिपाताः ।
1. 1: भावप्रधानमाख्यातं सत्त्वप्रधानानि नामानि ।	8. 54–55: क्रियावाचकमाख्यातमुपसर्गो विशेषकृत् ।
1. 3: नामाख्यातयोस्तु कर्मोपसंयोगद्योतका भवन्ति ।...आ...प्र...अधि...।	सत्त्वाभिधायकं नाम निपाताः पादपूरणाः ॥
1. 4: अथ निपाता...ऽपि पदपूरणाः ॥	VI. 24: परोपापावप्रतिपर्यन्वप्यध्याङ्प्रसन्निर्दुरुन्निविस्वभि ।

THE NIRUKTA.	THE TAITTIRĪYA PRĀTIS'ĀKHYA.
1. 3: आ...प्र परा...अभि...प्रति...अति सु ...निर्दुर्...न्यव...उद्...सम्...व्यप..... अनु...अपि...उप...परि...अधि...।	1. 15: आप्रावोपाभ्यधिप्रतिपरिविनीत्युपसर्गाः ॥

THE NIRUKTA.	BṚHADDEVATĀ.
N. 1. 1: भावप्रधानमाख्यातम् ।	Bṛh. D. II. 121: भावप्रधानमाख्यातम् ।
N. 1. 1: पूर्वापरीभूतं भावमाख्यातेनाचष्टे ।	Bṛh. D. I. 44: यः पूर्वापरीभूत इहैक एव । ...आख्यातशब्देन तमर्थमाहुः ॥
N. 1. 2: षड् भावविकारा भवन्तीति वार्ष्यायणिर्जायतेऽस्ति विपरिणमते वर्धतेऽपक्षीयते विनश्यतीति ।	Bṛh. D. II. 121: षड् विकारा भवन्ति ते । जन्मास्तित्वं परीणामो वृद्धिर्हानं विनाशनम् ॥

THE NIRUKTA.	THE BṚHADDEVATĀ.
N. 1. 4: अथ निपाता उच्चावचेष्वर्थेषु निपतन्ति । अप्युपमार्थेऽपि कर्मोपसंग्रहार्थेऽपि पदपूरणाः ।	Bṛh. D. II. 89: उच्चावचेषु चार्थेषु निपाताः समुदाहृताः । कर्मोपसंग्रहार्थे च क्वचिच्चौपम्यकारणात् ॥
N. 1. 4: तेषामेते चत्वार उपमार्थे भवन्तीति। इवेति...नेति...चिदिति...न्विति ।	Bṛh. D. II. 91: इव न चिन्नु चत्वार उपमार्था भवन्ति ते ।
N. 1. 5: अगस्त्य इन्द्राय हविर्निरूप्य मरुद्भ्यः संप्रदित्सांचकार। स इन्द्र एत्य परिदेवयांचक्रे।	Brh. D. IV. 48–50: स तानभिजगामाशु निरुप्यैन्द्रं हविस्तदा । मरुतश्चाभितुष्टाव सूक्तैस्त्वन्निवति च त्रिभिः ॥ महश्चिदिति चैवेन्द्रं सहस्रमिति चैतया । निरुप्तं तद्धविश्चैन्द्रं मरुद्भ्यो दातुमिच्छति ॥ विज्ञायावेक्ष्य तद्भावम् इन्द्रो नेति तमब्रवीत् ।
N. 1. 6: न नूनमस्ति नो श्वः कस्तद्वेद यदद्भुतम् । अन्यस्य चित्तमभि संचरेण्यमुताधीतं विनश्यति ॥	Bṛh. D. IV. 50–51: न श्वो नाद्यतनं ह्यस्ति वेद कस्तद्यदद्भुतम् ॥ कस्यचित्त्वर्थसंचारे चित्तमेव विनश्यति ।
N. 1. 9: पदपूरणास्ते मिताक्षरेष्वनर्थकाः कमीमिद्विति ।	Bṛh. D. II. 90–91: मिताक्षरेषु ग्रन्थेषु पूरणार्थास्त्वनर्थकाः । कमीमिद्विति विज्ञेया ये त्वनेकार्थकाश्च ते ॥
N. 1. 20: तद् यदन्यदैवते मन्त्रे निपतति नैघण्टुकं तत् ।	Bṛh. D. I. 18: मन्त्रेऽन्यदैवतेऽन्यानि निगद्यन्तेऽत्र कानिचित् ।
N. 2. 2: अथ तद्धितसमासेष्वेकपर्वसु च... प्रविभज्य निर्ब्रूयात्। दण्ड्यः पुरुषो...दण्डमर्हतीति ।	Bṛh. D. II. 106: विग्रहान्निर्वचः कार्यं समासेष्वपि तद्धिते । प्रविभज्यैव निर्ब्रूयाद् दण्डार्हो दण्ड्य इत्यपि ॥
N. 2. 10: देवापिश्चार्ष्टिषेणः शन्तनुश्च कौरव्यौ भ्रातरौ बभूवतुः । स शन्तनुः कनीयानभिषेचयांचक्रे ।	Bṛh. D. VII. 155–157: आर्ष्टिषेणस्तु देवापिः कौरव्यश्चैव शन्तनुः । भ्रातरौ कुरुषु त्वेतौ राजपुत्रौ बभूवतुः ॥ ज्येष्ठस्तयोस्तु देवापिः कनीयांश्चैव शन्तनुः । त्वग्दोषी राजपुत्रस्तु ऋष्टिषेणसुतोऽभवत् ॥ राज्येन छन्दयामासुः प्रजाः स्वर्गं गते गुरौ । स मुहूर्तमिव ध्यात्वा प्रजास्ताः प्रत्यभाषत ॥
	VIII. 1: न राज्यमहमर्हामि नृपतिर्वोऽस्तु शन्तनुः । तथेत्युक्त्वाभ्यषिञ्चंस्ताः प्रजा राज्याय शन्तनुम् ॥
देवापिस्तपः प्रतिपेदे । ततः शन्तनो राज्ये द्वादश वर्षाणि देवो न ववर्ष ।	VIII. 2–6: ततोऽभिषिक्ते कौरव्ये वनं देवापिराविशत् । न ववर्षाथ पर्जन्यो राज्ये द्वादश वै समाः ॥

THE NIRUKTA.	THE BṚHADDEVATĀ.
तमूचुर्ब्राह्मणा अधर्मस्त्वया चरितः । ज्येष्ठं भ्रातरमन्तरित्याभिषेचितं तस्मात्ते देवो न वर्षतीति । स शन्तनुर्देवापिं शिशिक्ष राज्येन । तमुवाच देवापिः पुरोहितस्तेऽसानि याजयानि च त्वेति ।	ततोऽभ्यगच्छद्देवापिं प्रजाभिः सह शन्तनुः । प्रसादयामास चैनं तस्मिन्धर्मव्यतिक्रमे ॥ शिशिक्ष चैनं राज्येन प्रजाभिः सहितस्तदा । तमुवाचाथ देवापिः प्रह्वं तु प्राञ्जलिस्थितम् ॥ न राज्यमहमर्हामि त्वग्दोषोपहतेन्द्रियः । याजयिष्यामि ते राजन् वृष्टिकामेज्यया स्वयम् ॥ ततस्तं तु पुरोऽधत्त आर्त्विज्याय स शन्तनुः । स चास्य चक्रे कर्माणि वार्षिकाणि यथाविधि ॥
N. 2. 12: पुरोहितः पुर एनं दधति ।	
N. 2. 17: अहिरयनात् । एत्यन्तरिक्षे । अयमपीतरोऽहिरेतस्मादेव निर्ह्रसितोपसर्ग आहन्तीति ।	Bṛh. D. V. 166: अहिराहन्ति मेघान् स एति वा तेषु मध्यमः ।
N. 2. 18: उषाः कस्मात् । उच्छतीति । सत्या रात्रेरपरः कालः ।	Bṛh. D. III. 9: तम उच्छत्युषाः ।
N. 2. 23: तत्र सरस्वतीत्येतस्य नदीवद्देवतावच्च निगमा भवन्ति ।	Bṛh. D. II. 135–136: सरस्वतीति द्विविधमृक्षु सर्वासु सा स्तुता । नदीवद्देवतावच्च तत्राचार्यस्तु शौनकः । नदीवन्निगमाः षट् ते सप्तमो नेत्युवाच ह ।
N. 2. 24: विश्वामित्र ऋषिः सुदासः पैजवनस्य पुरोहितो बभूव...स वित्तं गृहीत्वा विपाट्छुतुद्र्योः संभेदमाययौ ।...स विश्वामित्रो नदीस्तुष्टाव गाधा भवतेति । अपि द्विवदपि बहुवत् ।	Bṛh. D. IV. 106; 107: पुरोहितः सन्निज्यार्थं सुदासा सह यन्नृषिः । विपाट्छुतुद्र्योः संभेदं शमित्येते उवाच ह ॥ प्रवादास्तत्र दृश्यन्ते द्विवद्बहुवदेकवत् ।
N. 5. 13: उर्वश्यप्सराः...तस्या दर्शनान्मित्रावरुणयो रेतश्चस्कन्द ।	Bṛh. D. V. 149: तयोरादित्ययोः सत्रे दृष्ट्वाप्सरसमुर्वशीम् । रेतश्चस्कन्द तत्कुम्भे न्यपतद्वासतीवरे ॥
N. 5. 14: सर्वे देवाः पुष्करे त्वाधारयन्त ।	Bṛh. D. V. 155: सर्वत्र पुष्करं तत्र विश्वे देवा अधारयन् ।
N. 6. 5: शकटं शाकिनी गावो जालमस्यन्दनं वनम् । उदधिः पर्वतो राजा दुर्भिक्षे नव वृत्तयः ॥	Bṛh. D. VI. 138: शकटं शाकिनी गावः कृषिरस्यन्दनं वनम् । समुद्रः पर्वतो राजा एवं जीवामहे वयम् ॥
N. 6. 31: करूळती...पूषेति...सोऽदन्तकः । अदन्तकः पूषेति च ब्राह्मणम् ।	Bṛh. D. IV. 139: करूळतीति पूषोक्तोऽदन्तकः स इति श्रुतेः ।
N. 7. 1: यत्काम ऋषिर्यस्यां देवतायामार्थपत्यमिच्छन्स्तुतिं प्रयुङ्क्ते तद्दैवतः स मन्त्रो भवति ।	Bṛh. D. I. 6: अर्थमिच्छन्नृषिर्देवं यं यमाहायमस्त्विति । प्राधान्येन स्तुवन्भक्त्या मन्त्रस्तद्देव एव सः ॥
N. 7. 3: एवमुच्चावचैरभिप्रायैरृषीणां मन्त्रदृष्टयो भवन्ति ।	Bṛh. D. I. 3: तद्धितांस्तदभिप्रायानृषीणां मन्त्रदृष्टिषु । विज्ञापयति विज्ञानं कर्माणि विविधानि च ॥

THE NIRUKTA.	THE BṚHADDEVATĀ.
N. 7. 4: माहाभाग्याद्देवताया एक आत्मा बहुधा स्तूयते । एकस्यात्मनोऽन्ये देवाः प्रत्यङ्गानि भवन्ति ।	Bṛh. D. I. 73; 74: तेषामात्मैव तत्सर्वं यद्यद्भक्तिः प्रकीर्त्यते ॥ तेजस्त्वेवायुधं प्राहुर्वाहनं चैव यस्य यत् ॥
N. 7. 4: आत्मैवैषां रथो...आत्मायुधं... आत्मा सर्वं देवस्य ।	Bṛh. IV. 143: आयुधं वाहनं चापि स्तुतौ यस्येह दृश्यते । तमेव तु स्तुतं विद्यात्तस्यात्मा बहुधा हि सः ॥
N. 7. 5: तिस्र एव देवताः...अग्निः पृथिवीस्थानो वायुर्वेन्द्रो वान्तरिक्षस्थानः सूर्यो द्युस्थानः ।	Bṛh. I. 69: अग्निरस्मिन्नथेन्द्रस्तु मध्यतो वायुरेव च । सूर्यो दिवीति विज्ञेयास्तिस्र एवेह देवताः ॥
N. 7. 8: अयं लोकः प्रातःसवनं वसन्तो गायत्री त्रिवृत्स्तोमो रथंतरं साम ये च देवगणाः समाम्नाताः प्रथमे स्थाने ।...अथास्य कर्म वहनं च हविषामावाहनं च देवतानां यच्च किंचिद्दार्ष्टिविषयिकमग्निकर्मैव तत् । अथास्य संस्तविका देवा इन्द्रः सोमो वरुणः पर्जन्य ऋतवः । आग्नावैष्णवं हविर्न त्वृक्संस्तविकी दशतयीषु विद्यते । अथाप्याग्नापौष्णं हविर्न तु संस्तवः ।	Bṛh. D. I. 115–116: लोकोऽयं यच्च वै प्रातःसवनं क्रियते मखे । वसन्तशरदौ चर्तू स्तोमोऽनुष्टुबथो त्रिवृत् ॥ गायत्री चैकविंशश्च यच्च साम रथंतरम् । I. 119–120: देवतावाहनं चैव वहनं हविषां तथा ॥ कर्म दृष्टे च यत्किंचिद् विषये परिवर्तते । I. 117–118: इन्द्रेण च मरुद्भिश्च सोमेन वरुणेन च । पर्जन्येनर्तुभिश्चैव विष्णुना चास्य संस्तवः ॥ अस्यैवाग्नेस्तु पूष्णा च साम्राज्यं वरुणेन च । देवतामर्थतत्त्वज्ञो मन्त्रैः संयोजयेद्धविः ॥ असंस्तुतस्यापि सतो हविरेकं निरुप्यते ।
N. 7. 10: अन्तरिक्षलोको माध्यंदिनं सवनं ग्रीष्मस्त्रिष्टुप्पञ्चदशस्तोमो बृहत्साम...। अथास्य कर्म रसानुप्रदानं वृत्रवधो या च का च [चिद् Shorter recension] बलकृतिरिन्द्रकर्मैव तत् । अथास्य संस्तविका देवा अग्निः सोमो वरुणः पूषा बृहस्पतिर्ब्रह्मणस्पतिः पर्वतः कुत्सो विष्णुर्वायुः । अथापि मित्रो वरुणेन संस्तूयते पूष्णा रुद्रेण च सोमो ऽग्निना [वायुना Shorter recension] च पूषा वातेन च पर्जन्यः ॥	Bṛh. D. I. 130–131: छन्दस्त्रिष्टुप् च पङ्क्तिश्च लोकानां मध्यमश्च यः । एतेष्वेवाश्रयो विद्यात् सवनं मध्यमं च यत् ॥ ऋतू च ग्रीष्महेमन्तौ यच्च सामोच्यते बृहत् । शक्करीषु च यद्गीतं नाम्ना तत्साम शाक्करम् ॥ II. 6: रसादानं तु कर्मास्य वृत्रस्य च निबर्हणम् । स्तुतेः प्रभुत्वं सर्वस्य बलस्य निखिला कृतिः ॥ II. 2–5: संस्तुतश्चैव पूष्णा च विष्णुना वरुणेन च । सोमवाय्वग्निकुत्सैश्च ब्रह्मणस्पतिनैव च ॥ बृहतस्पतिना चैव नाम्ना यश्चापि पर्वतः । कासुचित्केचिदित्याहुर्निपाताः स्तुतिषु स्तुताः । मित्रश्च श्रूयते देवो वरुणेन सहासकृत् । रुद्रेण सोमः पूष्णा च पुनः पूषा च वायुना ॥ वातेनैव च पर्जन्यो लक्ष्यतेऽन्यत्र वै क्वचित् ।

THE NIRUKTA.	THE BṚHADDEVATĀ.
N. 7. 11: असौ लोकस्तृतीयसवनं वर्षा जगती सप्तदशस्तोमो वैरूपं साम......चन्द्रमसा वायुना संवत्सरेणेति संस्तवः ।......शरदनुष्टुबेकविंशस्तोमो वैराजं सामेति पृथिव्यायतनानि । हेमन्तः पङ्क्तिस्त्रिणवस्तोमः शाक्वरं सामेत्यन्तरिक्षायतनानि ।	Bṛh. D. II. 13: असौ तृतीयं सवनं लोकः साम च रैवतम् । वैरूपं चैव वर्षाश्च शिशिरोऽथ ऋतुस्तथा ॥ II. 14: त्रयस्त्रिंशश्च यः स्तोमः क्लृप्त्या सप्तदशश्च यः । छन्दश्च जगती नाम्ना तथातिछन्दसश्च याः । II. 15: एतस्यैव तु विज्ञेया देवाः संस्तविकास्त्रयः ॥ II. 16: चन्द्रमाश्चैव वायुश्च यं च संवत्सरं विदुः ॥ I. 116: गायत्री चैकविंशश्च यच्च साम रथंतरम् । साध्याः साम च वैराजमाप्याश्च वसुभिः सह ॥ cf. I. 131.
N. 7. 13: देवताः...सूक्तभाजः......ऋग्भाजश्च...काश्चिन्निपातभाजः ।	Bṛh. D. I. 17: देवतानामधेयानि मन्त्रेषु त्रिविधानि तु । सूक्तभाञ्ज्यथवर्ग्भाञ्जि तथा नैपातिकानि तु ॥
N. 7. 14: अग्निः कस्मात् । अग्रणीर्भवति । अग्रं यज्ञेषु प्रणीयते । अङ्गं नयति संनममानः ।	Bṛh. D. II. 24: जातो यदग्रे भूतानामग्रणीरध्वरे च यत् । नाम्ना संनयते वाङ्गं स्तुतोऽग्निरिति सूरिभिः ॥
N. 7. 18: यस्तु सूक्तं भजते यस्मै हविर्निरुप्यतेऽयमेव सोऽग्निः । निपातमेवैते उत्तरे ज्योतिषी एतेन नामधेयेन भजेते ।	Bṛh. D. I. 78: निरुप्यते हविर्यस्मै सूक्तं च भजते च या । सैव तत्र प्रधानं स्यान्न निपातेन या स्तुता ॥
N. 7. 19: जातवेदाः...जातानि वेद । जातानि वैनं विदुः । जाते जाते विद्यत इति वा जातवित्तो वा जातधनो जातविद्यो वा जातप्रज्ञानः ।	Bṛh. D. I. 92: यद्विद्यते हि जातः सञ्जातैर्यद्वात्र विद्यते । II. 30: भूतानि वेद यज्जातो जातवेदाथ कथ्यते । यच्चैष जातविद्योऽभूद्वित्तं जातोऽधिवेत्ति वा ॥ II. 31: विद्यते सर्वभूतैर्हि यद्वा जातः पुनः पुनः ।
N. 7. 23: रोहात्प्रत्यवरोहश्चिकीर्षितस्तामनुकृतिं होताग्निमारुते शस्त्रे वैश्वानरीयेण सूक्तेन प्रतिपद्यते...तत आगच्छति मध्यस्थाना देवता रुद्रं च मरुतश्च ततोऽग्निमिहस्थानमत्रैव स्तोत्रियं शंसति ।	Bṛh. D. I. 102–103: रोहात्प्रत्यवरोहेण चिकीर्षन्नाग्निमारुतम् । शस्त्रं वैश्वानरीयेण सूक्तेन प्रतिपद्यते ॥ ततस्तु मध्यमस्थाना देवतास्त्वनुशंसति । रुद्रं च मरुतश्चैव स्तोत्रियेऽग्निमिमं पुनः ॥

THE NIRUKTA.	THE BṚHADDEVATĀ.
N. 7. 23: अथापि वैश्वानरीयो द्वादशकपालो भवति।......अथापि छान्दोमिकं सूक्तं सौर्यवैश्वानरं भवति ।......अथापि हविष्पान्तीयं सूक्तं सौर्यवैश्वानरं भवति । cf. 7. 24.	Bṛh. D. II. 16–17: केचित्तु निर्वपन्त्यस्य सौर्यवैश्वानरं हविः ॥ सौर्यवैश्वानरीयं हि तत्सूक्तमिव दृश्यते ।
N. 7. 24: आदित्यरश्मयस्ते यदामुतोऽर्वाञ्चः पर्यावर्तन्ते ।	Bṛh. D. II. 8–9:...सूर्यस्यैव तु पत्नयः ॥ अमुतोऽर्वाङ्निवर्तन्ते प्रतिलोमास्तदाश्रयाः ।
N. 8. 1: द्रविणोदाः कस्मात् । धनं द्रविणमुच्यते...बलं वा द्रविणं...तस्य दाता द्रविणोदाः ।	Bṛh. D. II. 25: द्रविणं धनं बलं वापि प्रायच्छद्येन कर्मणा । तत्कर्म दृष्ट्वा कुत्सस्तु प्राहैनं द्रविणोदसम् ॥
N. 8. 2: तत्को द्रविणोदाः । इन्द्र इति क्रौष्टुकिः । स बलधनयोर्दातृतमः ।..................	Bṛh. D. III. 61: तमाहुरिन्द्रं दातृत्वादेके तु बलवित्तयोः ॥
अयमेवाग्निर्द्रविणोदा इति शाकपूणिः । आग्नेयेष्वेव हि सूक्तेषु द्राविणोदसाः प्रवादाः भवन्ति।	Bṛh. D. III. 65: द्रविणोदोऽग्निरेवायं द्रविणोदास्तदोच्यते । आग्नेयेष्वेव दृश्यन्ते प्रवादा द्रविणोदसः ॥
N. 8. 2: अग्निरोजसा बलेन मथ्यमानो जायते तस्मादेनमाह सहसस्पुत्रं सहसः सूनुं सहसो यहुम् ।	Bṛh. D. III. 62: जायते च बलेनायं मथ्यत्यृषिभिरध्वरे ॥ III. 64:...दृश्यते सहसो यहो ॥
ऋत्विजोऽत्र द्रविणोदस उच्यन्ते । हविषो दातारस्ते चैनं जनयन्ति। ऋषीणां पुत्रो अधिराज एष इत्यपि निगमो भवति ।	Bṛh. D. III. 63–64: हवींषि द्रविणं प्राहुर्हविषो यत्र जायते । दातारश्चर्त्विजस्तेषां द्रविणोदास्ततः स्वयम् ॥ ऋषीणां पुत्र इत्येषाम्...।
N. 8. 3: एष हि वनानां पाता वा पालयिता वा ।	Bṛh. D. III. 26: अयं वनानां हि पतिः पाता पालयतीति वा ।
N. 8. 5: नपादित्यननन्तरायाः प्रजाया नामधेयम् ।	Bṛh. D. II. 27: अनन्तरां प्रजामाहुर्नपादिति कृपण्यवः ।
N. 8. 6: नराशंसो यज्ञ इति कात्थक्यः । नरा अस्मिन्नासीनाः शंसन्ति । अग्निरिति शाकपूणिः । नरैः प्रशस्यो भवति ।	Bṛh. D. II. 28:...यज्ञे यच्छस्यते नृभिः । स्तुवन्त्याप्रीषु तेनेमं नराशंसं तु कारवः ॥ III. 2–3: नराशंसमिहैके तु अग्निमाहुरथेतरे । नराः शंसन्ति सर्वेऽस्मिन्नासीना इति वाध्वरे ॥ एतमेवाहुरन्येऽग्निं नराशंसोऽध्वरे ह्ययम् । नरैः प्रशस्य आसीनैराहुश्चैवर्त्विजो नरः ॥
N. 8. 10: नक्तेति रात्रिनाम । अनक्ति भूतान्यवश्यायेन । अपि वा नक्ताव्यक्तवर्णा ।	Bṛh. D. III. 9:...नक्तानक्तीमां हिमबिंदुभिः । अपि वाव्यक्तवर्णेति नञ्पूर्वांश्चेरिदं भवेत् ॥

THE NIRUKTA.	THE BṚHADDEVATĀ.
N. 8. 13: त्वष्टा तूर्णमश्नुत इति नैरुक्ताः। त्विषेर्वा स्याद्दीप्तिकर्मणस्त्वक्षतेर्वा स्यात्करोतिकर्मणः।	Bṛh. D. III. 16: त्विषितस्त्वक्षतेर्वा स्यात्तूर्णमश्नुत एव वा। कर्मसूत्तारणो वेति...॥
N. 8. 14: माध्यमिकस्त्वष्टेत्याहुर्मध्यमे च स्थाने समाम्नातोऽग्निरिति शाकपूणिः।	Bṛh. D. III. 25: त्वष्टा रूपविकर्ता च योऽसौ माध्यमिके गणे।
N. 8. 22: तान्येतान्येकादशाप्रीसूक्तानि। तेषां वासिष्ठमात्रेयं वाध्र्यश्वं गार्त्समदमिति नाराशंसवन्ति। मैधातिथं दैर्घतमसं प्रैषिकमित्युभयवन्ति। अतोऽन्यानि तनूनपात्वन्ति।	Bṛh. D. II. 154–157: अत्रैव प्रैषसूक्तं स्यात्...। तेषां प्रैषगतं सूक्तं यच्च दीर्घतमा जगौ॥ मेधातिथौ यदुक्तं च त्रीण्येवोभयवन्ति तु। ऋषौ गृत्समदे यच्च वाध्र्यश्वे च यदुच्यते॥ नराशंसवदत्रेश्च ददर्श च यदौर्वशः। तनूनपादगस्त्यश्च जमदग्निश्च यज्जगौ॥ मेधातिथेर्ऋचां यास्तु प्रोक्ता द्वादश देवताः॥
N. 9. 23: मुद्गलो भार्म्यश्व ऋषिर्वृषभं च द्रुघणं च युक्त्वा संग्रामे व्यवहृत्याजिं जिगाय।	Bṛh. D. VIII: 12: आजावनेन भार्म्यश्व इन्द्रासोमौ तु मुद्गलः। अजयद्वृषभं युक्त्वा ऐन्द्रं च द्रुघणं रथे॥
N. 9. 40: शुनासीरौ। शुनो वायुः। शु एत्यन्तरिक्षे। सीर आदित्यः सरणात्।	Bṛh. D. V. 8: वायुः शुनः सूर्य एवात्र सीरः शुनासीरौ वायुसूर्यौ वदन्ति। शुनासीरं यास्क इन्द्रं तु मेने सूर्येन्द्रौ तौ मन्यते शाकपूणिः॥
N. 10. 5: यदरुदत्तद्रुद्रस्य रुद्रत्वमिति काठकम्। यदरोदीत्तद्रुद्रस्य रुद्रत्वमिति हारिद्रविकम्।	Bṛh. D. II. 34: अरोदीदन्तरिक्षे यद्विद्युद्वृष्टिं ददन्नृणाम्। चतुर्भिर्ऋषिभिस्तेन रुद्र इत्यभिसंस्तुतः॥
N. 10. 8: इन्द्र इरां दृणाति।	Bṛh. D. II. 36: इरां दृणाति यत्काले मरुद्भिः सहितोऽम्बरे। रवेण महता युक्तस्तेनेन्द्रमृषयोऽब्रुवन्॥
N. 10. 10: पर्जन्यस्तृपेराद्यन्तविपरीतस्य तर्पयिता जन्यः परो जेता वा जनयिता वा प्रार्जयिता वा रसानाम्।	Bṛh. D. II. 37–38: यदिमां प्रार्जयत्येको रसेनाम्बरजेन गाम्। कालेऽत्रिरौर्वशश्चर्षी तेन पर्जन्यमाहतुः॥ तर्पयत्येष यल्लोकाञ्जन्यो जनहितश्च यत्। परो जेता जनयिता यद्वामेयस्ततो जगौ॥
N. 10. 12: ब्रह्मणस्पतिर्ब्रह्मणः पाता।	Bṛh. D. II. 40: पातारं ब्रह्मणस्तेन शौनहोत्रः स्तुवञ्जगौ।
N. 10. 27: तार्क्ष्यः...तीर्णेऽन्तरिक्षे क्षियति। तूर्णमर्थं रक्षत्यश्नोतेर्वा।	Bṛh. D. II. 58: स्तीर्णेऽन्तरिक्षे क्षियति यद्वा तूर्णं क्षरत्यसौ।...तार्क्ष्यं तेनैवमुक्तवान्॥
N. 10. 42: देवतानामधेयान्यनुक्रान्तानि। सूक्तभाञ्जि हविर्भाञ्जि।	Bṛh. D. I. 17: देवतानामधेयानि मन्त्रेषु त्रिविधानि तु। सूक्तभाञ्ज्यथवर्गभाञ्जि तथा नैपातिकानि तु॥

THE NIRUKTA.	THE BṚHADDEVATĀ.
N. 10. 44: योऽहिः स बुध्न्यो बुध्नमन्तरिक्षं तन्निवासात् ।	Bṛh D. V. 166: योऽहिः स बुध्न्यो बुध्ने हि सोऽन्तरिक्षेऽभिजायते ।
N. 11. 5: चन्द्रमाश्चायन्द्रमति । चन्द्रो माता चान्द्रं मानमस्येति वा ।	Bṛh. D. VII. 129 (B): चारु द्रमति वा चायंश्चापानीयो दमत्युत ।
N. 11. 6: मृत्युर्मारयतीति सतो मृतं च्यावयतीति वा ।	Bṛh. D. II. 60. यत्तु प्रच्यावयत्येति घोषेण महता मृतम् । तेन मृत्युमिमं सन्तं स्तौति मृत्युरिति स्वयम् ॥
N. 11. 16: ऋभुर्विभ्वा वाज इति सुधन्वन आङ्गिरसस्य त्रयः पुत्रा बभूवुः ।	Bṛh. D. III. 83: सुधन्वन आङ्गिरसस्यासन्पुत्रास्त्रयः पुरा । ऋभुर्विभ्वा च वाजश्च शिष्यास्त्वष्टुश्च तेऽभवन् ॥
N. 12. 1: तत् कावश्विनौ । द्यावापृथिव्यावित्येके । अहोरात्रावित्येके । सूर्याचन्द्रमसावित्येके ।	Bṛh. D. VII. 126: सूर्याचन्द्रमसौ तौ हि प्राणापानौ च तौ स्मृतौ । अहोरात्रौ च तावेव ख्यातां तावेव रोदसी ॥
N. 12. 14: सूर्यः सर्तेर्वा सुवतेर्वा स्वीर्यतेर्वा ।	Bṛh. D. VII. 128 (B): सूर्यः सरति भूतेषु सु वीरयति तानि वा ।
N. 12. 16: अथ यद्रश्मिपोषं पुष्यति तत्पूषा भवति ।	Bṛh. D. II. 63: पुष्यन् क्षितिं पोषयति प्रणुदन् रश्मिभिस्तमः ।
N. 12. 18: अथ यद्विषितो भवति तद्विष्णुर्भवति । विष्णुर्विशतेर्वा व्यश्नोतेर्वा ।	Bṛh. D. II. 69: विष्णातेर्विशतेर्वा स्याद्वेवेष्टेर्व्याप्तिकर्मणः । विष्णुर्निरुच्यते सूर्यः सर्वं सर्वान्तरश्च यः ॥
N. 12. 25: केशी केशा रश्मयस्तैस्तद्वान्भवति । काशनाद्वा प्रकाशनाद्वा ।	Bṛh. D. II. 65: कृत्वा सायं पृथग्याति भूतेभ्यस्तमसोऽत्यये । प्रकाशं किरणैः कुर्वंस्तेनैनं केशिनं विदुः ॥
N. 12. 27: अथ यद्रश्मिभिरभिप्रकम्पयन्नेति तद्वृषाकपिर्भवति वृषाकम्पनः ।	Bṛh. D. II. 67: वृषैष कपिलो भूत्वा यन्नाकमधिरोहति । वृषाकपिरसौ तेन विश्वस्मादिन्द्र उत्तरः ॥ रश्मिभिः कम्पयन्नेति वृषा वर्षिष्ठ एव सः ॥
N. 12. 40: यत्तु किंचिद्बहुदैवतं तद्वैश्वदेवानां स्थाने युज्यते ।	Bṛh. D. II. 133: पादं वा यदि वार्धर्चमृचं वा सूक्तमेव वा । वैश्वदेवं वदेत्सर्वं यत्किंचिद्बहुदैवतम् ॥

THE NIRUKTA.	PĀṆINI'S AṢṬĀDHYĀYĪ.
Cf. 1. 3.	I. 4. 83–97.
1. 3: आ इत्यर्वागर्थे ।	I. 4. 89: आङ् मर्यादावचने ।
अभीत्याभिमुख्यम् ।	I. 4. 91: अभिरभागे ।
अति सु इत्यभिपूजितार्थे ।	I. 4. 95: अतिरतिक्रमणे च ।
	I. 4. 94: सुः पूजायाम् ।
अपीति संसर्गम् ।	I. 4. 96: अपिः पदार्थसंभावनान्ववसर्गगर्हासमुच्चयेषु ।
उपेत्युपजनम् ।	I. 4. 87: उपोधिके च ।
परीति सर्वतोभावम् ।	I. 4. 88: अपपरी वर्जने ।
अधीत्युपरिभावमैश्वर्यं वा ।	I. 4. 97: अधिरीश्वरे ।
1. 17: परः संनिकर्षः संहिता ।	I. 4. 109: परः संनिकर्षः संहिता ।

THE NIRUKTA.	THE ARTHAS'ASTRA OF KAUṬILYA.
N. 1. 1: तद्यान्येतानि चत्वारि पदजातानि नामाख्याते चोपसर्गनिपाताश्च तानीमानि भवन्ति...	II. 10: 28, p. 72: वर्णसंघातः पदम् । तच्चतुर्विधं नामाख्यातोपसर्गनिपाताश्चेति ।
भावप्रधानमाख्यातम् ।	अविशिष्टलिङ्गमाख्यातं क्रियावाचि ।
सत्त्वप्रधानानि नामानि ।	तत्र नाम सत्त्वाभिधायि ।
N. 1. 3:...नामाख्यातयोस्तु कर्मोपसंयोगद्योतका भवन्ति ।	क्रियाविशेषिताः प्रादय उपसर्गाः ।
N. 1. 4: अथ निपाता उच्चावचेष्वर्थेषु निपतन्ति...	अव्ययाश्चादयो निपाताः ।

THE NIRUKTA.	THE UṆĀDI SŪTRAS
1. 7: दक्षिणा दक्षतेः ।	II 50: द्रुदक्षिभ्यामिनन् ।
1. 13: प्रथनात्पृथिवीत्याहुः ।	I. 150: प्रथेः षिवन् संप्रसारणं च ।
1. 18: स्थाणुस्तिष्ठतेः । अर्थोऽर्तेः ।	II 4: उषिकुषिगर्तिभ्यः स्थन् ।
1. 20: भीमो बिभ्यत्यस्मात् । भीष्मोऽप्येतस्मादेव ।	I. 147: भियः षुग्वा ।
2. 2: तत्राप्येकेऽल्पनिष्पत्तयो भवन्ति । तद्यथैतदूतिर्मृदुः पृथुः पृषतः कुणारुमिति ।	I. 29: प्रथिम्रदिभ्रस्जां संप्रसारणं सलोपः । III. 111: पृषिरंजिभ्यां कित् ।
2. 5. गौरिति पृथिव्या नामधेयम् । यद् दूरं गता भवति । यच्चास्यां भूतानि गच्छन्ति ।	II. 67: गमेर्डोः ।

2. 6: वृक्षो व्रश्चनात् ।	III. 66: स्रुवश्चिकृत्यृषिभ्यः कित् ।
2.18: रात्रिः कस्मात्...रातेर्वा स्यात्। दानकर्मणः।	IV. 67: राशदिभ्यां त्रिप् ।
2. 27: अश्वः कस्मात् । अश्नुतेऽध्वानम् ।	I. 151: अशूप्रुषिलटिकणिखटिविशिभ्यः क्वन् ।
3. 5: श्मश्रु लोम । श्मनि श्रितं भवति ।	V. 28: श्मनि श्रयतेर्डुन् ।
3. 10: तळित्... ताडयतीति सतः ।	I. 100: ताडेर्णिलुक्च ।
3. 21: स्त्रियः स्त्यायतेरपत्रपणकर्मणः ।	IV. 165: स्त्यायतेर्ड्रट् ।
4. 10: लक्ष्मी...लक्षणाद्वा ।	III. 160: लक्षेर्मुट्च ।
4. 17: रयिरिति धननाम । रातेर्दानकर्मणः ।	II. 66: रातेर्डैः ।
7. 24: घृतमित्युदकनाम । जिघर्तेः सिञ्चतिकर्मणः ।	III. 89: अंजिघृसिभ्यः क्तः ।
8. 2: बलं वा द्रविणं यदेनेनाभिद्रवन्ति ।	II. 50: द्रुदक्षिभ्यामिनन् ।
9. 27: आप आप्नोतेः ।	II. 58: आप्नोतेर्ह्रस्वश्च ।
10. 5: रुद्रः...रोदयतेर्वा ।	II. 22: रोदेर्णिलुक्च ।
10. 4: इन्दुरिन्धेरुनत्तेर्वा ।	I. 13: उन्देरिच्चादेः ।
11. 30: राका रातेर्दानकर्मणः ।	III. 40: कृदाधारार्चिकलिभ्यः कः । *

THE NIRUKTA.	THE MAHĀBHĀṢYA OF PATAÑJALI.
1. 1: अपि वाहननादेव स्युः ।	Vol. III. p. 274: आहत्य तृचो यच्छाब्रम् ।
तद्यान्येतानि चत्वारि पदजातानि नामाख्याते चोपसर्गनिपाताश्च तानीमानि भवन्ति ।	1. 1. 1. Vol. I. p. 3: चत्वारि शृङ्गाणि चत्वारि पदजातानि नामाख्यातोपसर्गनिपाताश्च ।
	चत्वारि वाक्परिमिता पदानि चत्वारि पदजातानि नामाख्यातोपसर्गनिपाताश्च ।
भावप्रधानमाख्यातम् । सत्त्वप्रधानानि नामानि ।	V. 3. 2. Vol. II. p. 418: क्रियाप्रधानमाख्यातं भवति ।...द्रव्यप्रधानं नाम ।

---

* Cf. *Annals of the Bhandarkar Institute*, vol. IV. part 2. pp. 119-120. The passage in *the Annals* is full of inaccuracies. The reference on p. 119 to Uṇādi I. 156; I. 158; II. 235 is wrong; the correct reference being I. 150; I. 147; II. 67 respectively The quotation of the sūtras is wrong on the same page: अश्रुप्रुषि etc. should read अशूप्रुषि. On. p. 120. रारादिभ्यां मिप् IV. 67. should read राशदिभ्यां त्रिप् । The passages of the Nirukta are also inaccurately quoted: On p. 119 the derivation of लक्ष्मीः is quoted as लक्ष्मीर्लक्षणाद्वा । But the passage in the Nirukta 4. 10. is the following: लक्ष्मीर्लाभाद्वा । लक्षणाद्वा । The reference of this passage is wrongly given as 4. 9. On p. 120 रात्रिः रातेवास्याद दानकर्मणः (sic.) should read रात्रिः कस्मात् ।...रातेर्वा स्यात् । दानकर्मणः । (N. 2. 18). Similarly N. 3. 5. श्मश्रु श्मर्निश्रितं भवति (sic.) should read श्मश्रु लोम । श्मनि श्रितं भवति ।

THE NIRUKTA.	THE MAHĀBHĀṢYA OF PATAÑJALI.
गौरश्वः पुरुषो हस्तीति ।	1. 1. 1. Vol. 1. p. 1, 5: गौरश्वः पुरुषो हस्ती शकुनिर्मृगः etc.
इन्द्रियनित्यं वचनमौदुम्बरायणः ।	1. 4. 4. Vol. 1. p. 356: एकैकवर्णवर्तित्वाद्वाच उच्चरितप्रध्वंसित्वाच्च वर्णानाम् । एकैकवर्णवर्तिनी वाक् । न द्वौ युगपदुच्चारयति । ...उच्चरितप्रध्वंसिनः खल्वपि वर्णाः । उच्चरितः प्रध्वस्तः ।
	1. 1. 1. Vol. 1. p. 6: किं पुनर्नित्यः शब्द आहोस्वित्कार्यः ।
1. 2: व्याप्तिमत्त्वात्तु शब्देन संज्ञाकरणं व्यवहारार्थं लोके ।	1. 1. 6. Vol. 1. p. 105: अर्थगत्यर्थः शब्दप्रयोगः । अर्थं संप्रत्याययिष्यामीति शब्दः प्रयुज्यते ।
	1. 1. 9. Vol. 1. p. 175: शब्देनोच्चारितेनार्थो गम्यते । गामानय दध्यशानेत्यर्थ आनीयतेऽर्थश्च भुज्यते ।
1. 2: षड् भावविकारा भवन्तीति वार्ष्यायणिः । जायतेऽस्ति विपरिणमते वर्धतेऽपक्षीयते विनश्यतीति ।	1. 3. 1; Vol. 1. p. 258: षड् भावविकारा इति ह स्माह भगवान् वार्ष्यायणिः । जायतेऽस्ति विपरिणमते वर्धतेऽपक्षीयते विनश्यतीति ।
1. 3: न निर्बद्धा उपसर्गा अर्थान्निराहुरिति शाकटायनः ।	1. 3. 1. Vol. I. p. 256: क्रियाविशेषक उपसर्गः ।
नामाख्यातयोस्तु कर्मोपसंयोगद्योतका भवन्ति ।	2. 1. 1. Vol. I. p. 365: उपसर्गाश्च पुनरेवमात्मका यत्र कश्चित्क्रियावाची शब्दः प्रयुज्यते तत्र क्रियाविशेषमाहुः ।
अति सु इत्यभिपूजितार्थे । निर् दुर् इत्येतयोः प्रातिलोम्यम् ।	2. 2. 1. Vol. I. p. 416: एतदेव च सौनागैर्विस्तरतरकेण पठितम् । स्वती पूजायाम् । स्वती पूजायामिति वक्तव्यम् ।... दुर्निन्दायाम् ।
सम् इत्येकीभावम् ।	2. 1. 3. Vol. I. p. 393: समेकत्ववाची ।
परि इति सर्वतोभावम् ।	5. 1. 1. Vol. 2. p. 343: परिः सर्वतोभावे वर्तते ।
अधि इत्युपरिभावम् ।	1. 3. 1. Vol. 1. p. 256: अधिरुपरिभावे वर्तते ।
1 4: आचार्य आचारं ग्राहयति ।	1. 1. 3. Vol. I. p. 38: आचार्याचारात् संज्ञासिद्धिः । आचार्याचारात् संज्ञासिद्धिर्भविष्यति ।
1. 6: अद्यास्मिन् द्यवि । द्युरित्यह्नो नामधेयम् ।	5. 3. 1. Vol. II. p. 407: अन्यस्मिन्नहन्यन्येद्युः । etc.

THE NIRUKTA.	THE MAHĀBHĀṢYA OF PATAÑJALI.
1. 7: मंहतेर्दानकर्मणः ।	6. 1. 1. Vol. III. p. 16: मंहतिर्दानकर्मा ।
दक्षिणा दक्षतेः समर्धयतिकर्मणः । व्यृद्धं समर्धयतीति ।	5. 1. 2. Vol. II. p. 356: सर्वे ते दक्षिणा समृध्या इति । दक्षेर्वृद्धिकर्मणो दक्षिणा ।
1. 9: अक्षि चष्टेः । अनक्तेरित्याग्रायणः ।	Cf. 3. 2. 2. Vol. II. p. 119: अश्नुतेऽनेनेत्यक्षि ।
	Vol. III. p. 408: अंक्तेऽक्षिणी इत्युच्यते ।
1. 12: तत्र नामान्याख्यातजानीति शाकटायनो नैरुक्तसमयश्च ।	3. 3. 1. Vol. II. p. 138: नाम च धातुजमाह निरुक्ते । नाम खल्वपि धातुजम् । एवमाहुर्नैरुक्ताः । व्याकरणे शकटस्य च तोकम् । वैयाकरणानां च शाकटायन आह धातुजं नामेति ।
1. 15: अथापीदमन्तरेण मन्त्रेष्वर्थप्रत्ययो न विद्यते ।	I. 1. 9. Vol. I. p. 175: अर्थस्यासंभवात् । इह व्याकरणेऽर्थे कार्यस्यासंभवः ।
	1. 1. 9. Vol. I. p. 176: मन्त्राद्यर्थमिति चेत्तन्न ।
अथाप्यविस्पष्टार्था भवन्ति ।	2. 1. 1. Vol. I. p. 363: बहवो हि शब्दा येषामर्था न विज्ञायन्ते । जर्भरी तुर्फरी तु ।
1. 17: परः सन्निकर्षः संहिता ।	1. 4. 4. Vol. I. p. 354: परः सन्निकर्षः संहिता ।
	8. 3. 1. Vol. III. p. 430: परः सन्निकर्षः संहिता इत्युच्यते ।
1. 18: यद्गृहीतमविज्ञातं निगदेनैव शब्द्यते । अनग्नाविव शुष्कैधो न तु ज्वलति कर्हिचित् ॥	1. 1. 1. Vol. I. p. 2: यदधीतमविज्ञातं निगदेनैव शब्द्यते । अनग्नाविव शुष्कैधो न तज्ज्वलति कर्हिचित् ॥
1. 19: उत त्वः पश्यन्न...उशती सुवासाः ॥	1. 1. 1. Vol I. p. 4: उत त्वः पश्यन्न ...उशती सुवासाः ।
अप्येकः पश्यन्न पश्यति वाचमपि च शृण्वन्न शृणोत्येनामित्यविद्वांसमाहार्धम् । अप्येकस्मै तन्वं विसस्र इति स्वमात्मानं विवृणुते ।...जायेव पत्ये कामयमाना सुवासा ऋतुकालेषु सुवासाः...	अपि खल्वेकः पश्यन्नपि न पश्यति वाचम् । अपि खल्वेकः शृण्वन्नपि न शृणोत्येनाम् । अविद्वांसमाहार्धम् । उतो त्वस्मै तन्वं विसस्रे । तनुं विवृणुते । जायेव पत्ये उशती सुवासाः । जायेव पत्ये कामयमाना सुवासाः स्वमात्मानं विवृणुत एवं वाग्वाग्विदे स्वमात्मानं विवृणुते ।

THE NIRUKTA.	THE MAHĀBHĀṢYA OF PATAÑJALI.
2. 1: अथाप्युपधालोपो भवति जग्मतुर्जग्मुरिति ।	6. 1. 1. Vol. III. p. 17: उपधालोपस्यावकाशः......जग्मतुः जग्मुः । जघ्नतुः जघ्नुः ।
2. 1: अथाप्याद्यन्तविपर्ययो भवति स्तोका रज्जुः सिकतास्तर्किति ।	1. 1. 2. Vol. I. p. 31: कृतेस्तर्कुः । कसेः सिकताः हिंसेः सिंहः ।
2. 2: शवतिर्गतिकर्मा । कम्बोजेष्वेव भाष्यते ...विकारमस्यार्येषु भाषन्ते शव इति । दातिर्लवनार्थे प्राच्येषु । दात्रमुदीच्येषु ।	1. 1. 1. Vol. I. p. 9: शवतिर्गतिकर्मा । कम्बोजेष्वेव भाषितो भवति । विकार एनमार्या भाषन्ते शव इति ।...दातिर्लवनार्थे प्राच्येषु । दात्रमुदीच्येषु ।
2. 18: रातेर्वा स्याद्दानकर्मणः ।	Vol. III. p. 36: रातेर्दानकर्मणः ।
2. 21: मेहतीति सतः ।...उपरता आप इति वा ।	Vol. III. p. 16: मिहेर्मेघः । मेघश्च कस्माद्भवति । अपो ददाति ।
3. 1: अपत्यं कस्मात् ।...नानेन पततीति वा ।	5. 1. 2. Vol. II. p. 356: पुत्रा अपत्यमित्यपतनादपत्यम् ।
3. 9: धनं कस्मात् । धिनोतीति सतः ।	5. 1. 2. Vol. II. p. 356: धनमिति धिनोतेर्धनम् ।
3. 16: आदित्योऽत्र जार उच्यते । रात्रेर्जरयिता ।	3. 3. 1. Vol. II. p. 146: जरयन्तीति जाराः । जीर्यन्ति तैर्जाराः ।
3. 18: सिंहः सहनात् । हिंसेर्वा स्याद् विपरीतस्य ।	3. 1. 6. Vol. II. p. 87: हिंसेः सिंहः ।
3. 21: स्त्रियः स्त्यायतेः ।	1. 2. 3. Vol. I. pp. 245-6: ननु च लोकेऽपि स्त्यायतेरेव स्त्री...स्त्यायत्यस्यां गर्भ इति ।
4. 9: तितउ परिपवनं भवति ततवद्वा तुन्नवद्वा तिलमात्रतुन्नमिति वा ।	I. 1. 1. p. 4: तितउ परिपवनं भवति ततवद्वा तुन्नवद्वा ।
4. 10: सक्तुमिव...वाचि ॥ सक्तुमिव परिपवनेन पुनन्तः । सक्तुः सचतेर्दुर्धावो भवति कसतेर्वा स्याद्विपरीतस्य विकसितो भवति । यत्र धीरा मनसा वाचमकृषत प्रज्ञानं धीराः प्रज्ञानवन्तो ध्यानवन्तः । तत्र सखायः सख्यानि संजानते । भद्रैषां लक्ष्मीर्निहिताधि वाचीति ।...लक्ष्मीर्लाभाद्वा लक्षणाद्वा लप्स्यनाद्वा लाञ्छनाद्वा लषतेर्वा स्यात्प्रेप्साकर्मणो लग्यतेर्वा स्यादाश्लेषकर्मणो लज्जतेर्वा स्यादश्लाघाकर्मणः ।	1. 1. 1. p. 4: सक्तुमिव......वाचि ॥ सक्तुः सचतेर्दुर्धावो भवति । कसतेर्वा विपरीताद्विकसितो भवति ।...धीरा ध्यानवन्तो मनसा प्रज्ञानेन वाचमकृत वाचमकृषत। अत्रा सखायः सख्यानि जानते । अत्र सखायः सन्तः सख्यानि जानते । सायुज्यानि जानते ।...। भद्रैषां लक्ष्मीर्निहिताधि वाचि । एषां वाचि भद्रा लक्ष्मीर्निहिता भवति । लक्ष्मीर्लक्षणाद्भासनात्परिवृढा भवति ।

THE NIRUKTA.	THE MAHĀBHĀṢYA OF PATAÑJALI
4. 15: कन्या कमनीया भवति ।	3. 2. 3. Vol. II. p. 134: कम्रा कन्या कमना ।
5. 26: काकुदं तालवित्याचक्षते जिह्वा कोकुवा सास्मिन्धीयते । जिह्वा कोकुवा कोकूयमाना वर्णान्नुदतीति...... 5. 27: सुदेवो असि...सुषिरामिव ॥ सुदेवस्त्वं कल्याणदेवः कमनीयदेवो वा भवसि वरुण यस्य ते सप्त सिंधवः...यस्य ते सप्त स्रोतांसि तानि ते काकुदमनुक्षरन्ति सूर्मिः कल्याणोर्मिः स्रोतः सुषिरमनु यथा ।	1. 1. 1. p. 4. सुदेवो...सुषिरामिव ॥ सुदेवो असि वरुण सत्यदेवो असि यस्य ते सप्त सिन्धवः सप्त विभक्तयोऽनुक्षरन्ति काकुदम् । काकुदं तालु । काकुर्जिह्वा सास्मिन्नुद्यत इति काकुदम् । सूर्म्यं सुषिरामिव । तद्यथा शोभनामूर्मिं सुषिरामग्निरन्तः प्रविश्य दहत्येवं तव सप्तसिंधवः सप्तविभक्तयस्ताल्वनुक्षरन्ति । तेनासि सत्यदेवः ।
9. 11: रथो रंहतेः...रममाणोऽस्मिंस्तिष्ठतीति वा ।	Vol. I. p. 327: रमन्तेऽस्मिन्रथ इति ।
9. 15: अहिरिव भोगैः परिवेष्टयति बाहुम् ।	Vol. II. p. 340: अथवा भोगशब्दः शरीरवाच्यपि दृश्यते । तद् यथा । अहिरिव भोगैः पर्येति बाहुम् । अहिरिव शरीरैरिति गम्यते ।
13. 7: चत्वारि शृङ्गा त्रयो...मर्त्याँ आविवेश । चत्वारि शृङ्गेति वेदा वा एत उक्तास्त्रयोऽस्य पादा इति सवनानि त्रीणि द्वे शीर्षे प्रायणीयोदयनीये सप्त हस्तासः सप्त छन्दांसि त्रिधा बद्धस्त्रेधा बद्धो मन्त्रब्राह्मणकल्पैर्वृषभो रोरवीति । रोरवणमस्य सवनक्रमेण ऋग्भिर्यजुर्भिः सामभिर्यदेनमृग्भिः शंसन्ति यजुर्भिर्यजन्ति सामभिः स्तुवन्ति । महोदेवेत्येष हि महान्देवो यद्यज्ञो मर्त्याँ आविवेशेत्येष हि मनुष्यानाविशति यजनाय ।	1. 1. 1. p. 3: चत्वारि शृङ्गा......मर्त्याँ आविवेश । चत्वारि शृङ्गाणि चत्वारि पदजातानि नामाख्यातोपसर्गनिपाताश्च । त्रयो अस्य पादास्त्रयः काला भूतभविष्यद्वर्तमानाः । द्वे शीर्षे द्वौ शब्दात्मानौ नित्यः कार्यश्च । सप्त हस्तासो अस्य सप्त विभक्तयः त्रिधा बद्धस्त्रिषु स्थानेषु बद्ध उरसि कण्ठे शिरसीति । वृषभो वर्षणात् । रोरवीति शब्दं करोति । कुत एतत् । रौतिः शब्दकर्मा । महो देवो मर्त्याँ आविवेशेति । महान्देवः शब्दः । मर्त्या मरणधर्माणो मनुष्याः । तानाविवेश ।
13. 9: चत्वारि वाक्परिमिता......मनुष्या वदन्ति ॥ चत्वारि वाचः परिमितानि पदानि तानि विदुर्ब्राह्मणा ये मेधाविनो गुहायां त्रीणि निहितानि नार्थं वेदयन्ते । गुहा गूहतेस्तुरीयं त्वरतेः । कतमानि तानि चत्वारि पदानि ।... नामाख्याते चोपसर्गनिपाताश्चेति वैयाकरणाः ।	1. 1. 1. p. 3: चत्वारि वाक्परिमिता... मनुष्या वदन्ति । चत्वारि वाक्परिमिता पदानि चत्वारि पदजातानि नामाख्यातोपसर्गनिपाताश्च । तानि विदुर्ब्राह्मणा ये मनीषिणः । मनसः ईषिणो मनीषिणः । गुहा त्रीणि निहिता नेङ्गयन्ति । गुहायां त्रीणि निहितानि नेङ्गयन्ति । न चेष्टन्ते । न निमिशन्तीत्यर्थः । तुरीयं वाचो मनुष्या वदन्ति । तुरीयं ह वा एतद्वाचो यन्मनुष्येषु वर्तते । चतुर्थमित्यर्थः । चत्वारि ।

THE NIRUKTA.	THE PŪRVA MĪMĀṂSĀ.
1. 1: तत्रैतन्नामाख्यातयोर्लक्षणं प्रदिशन्ति भावप्रधानमाख्यातम् ।	2. 1. 1: भावार्थाः कर्मशब्दास्तेभ्यः क्रिया प्रतीयेत । एष ह्यर्थो विधीयते ॥
1. 1: तद्यत्रोभे भावप्रधाने भवतः	2. 1. 2: सर्वेषां भावोऽर्थ इति चेत् ।
1. 1: पूर्वापरीभूतं भावमाख्यातेनाचष्टे व्रजति पचतीति ।	2. 1. 4: येषां तूत्पत्तावर्थे स्वे प्रयोगो न विद्यते तान्याख्यातानि तस्मात्तेभ्यः प्रतीयेताश्रितत्वात्प्रयोगस्य ।
1. 1. उपक्रमप्रभृत्यपवर्गपर्यन्तं मूर्त्तं सत्त्वभूतं सत्त्वनामभिर्व्रज्या पक्तिरिति ।	2. 1. 3: येषामुत्पत्तौ स्वे प्रयोगे रूपोपलब्धिस्तानि नामानि तस्मात्तेभ्यः पराकांक्षा भूत्वा स्वे प्रयोगे ।
	Cf.
1. 1: इन्द्रियनित्यं वचनमौदुम्बरायणः ॥	1. 1. 6: कर्मैके तत्र दर्शनात् ।
	1. 1. 7: अस्थानात् ।
	1. 1. 8: करोतिशब्दात् ।
	1. 1. 9: सत्त्वान्तरे यौगपद्यात् ।
	1. 1. 10: प्रकृतिविकृत्योश्च ।
	1. 1. 11: वृद्धिश्च कर्तृभूम्नास्य ।
	1. 1. 12: समं तु तत्र दर्शनम् ।
	1. 1. 13: सतः परमदर्शनं विषयानागमात् ।
	1. 1. 14: प्रयोगस्य परम् ।
	1. 1. 15: आदित्यवद् यौगपद्यम् ।
	1. 1. 16: वर्णान्तरमविकारः ।
	1. 1. 17: नादवृद्धिपरा ।
	1. 1. 18: नित्यस्तु स्याद्दर्शनस्य परार्थत्वात् ।
	1. 1. 19: सर्वत्र यौगपद्यात् ।
	1. 1. 20: संख्याभावात् ।
	1. 1. 21: अनपेक्षत्वात् ।
1. 15: अनर्थका हि मन्त्राः ।	1. 2. 1: आम्नायस्य क्रियार्थत्वादानर्थक्यमतदर्थानां तस्मादनित्यमित्युच्यते ।
	1. 2. 39: अनित्यसंयोगान्मन्त्रानर्थक्यम् ।
1. 15: नियतवाचो युक्तयो नियतानुपूर्व्या भवन्ति ।	1. 2. 32: वाक्यनियमात् ।
1. 15: अथापि ब्राह्मणेन रूपसंपन्ना विधीयन्ते ।	1. 2. 33: बुद्धशास्त्रात् ।
	1. 2. 34: अविद्यमानवचनात् ।
1. 15: अथाप्यनुपपन्नार्था भवन्ति । ओषधे त्रायस्वैनम् । स्वधिते मैनं हिंसीः ।	1. 2. 35: अचेतनार्थसंबन्धात् ।

THE NIRUKTA.	THE PŪRVA MĪMĀṂSĀ OF JAIMINI.
1. 15: अथापि विप्रतिषिद्धार्था भवन्ति ।	1. 2. 36: अर्थविप्रतिषेधात् ।
1. 15: अथाप्यविस्पष्टार्था भवन्ति ।	1. 2. 38: अविज्ञेयात् ।
1. 16: अर्थवन्तः शब्दसामान्यात् ।	1. 2. 40: अविशिष्टस्तु वाक्यार्थः ।
	1. 3. 30: प्रयोगचोदनाभावादर्थैकत्वमविभागात् ।
1. 16: यथो एतन्नियतवाचो......लौकिकेष्वप्येतत् ।	1. 2. 44: अविरुद्धं परम् ।
1. 16: उदितानुवादः स भवति ।	1. 2. 41: गुणार्थेन पुनः श्रुतिः ।
	1. 2. 45: संप्रैषे कर्मगर्हानुपालम्भः संस्कारत्वात् ।
1. 16: यथो एतद्विप्रतिषिद्धार्था......लौकिकेष्वप्येतत् ।	1. 2. 47: गुणादविप्रतिषेधः स्यात् ।
1. 16: यथो एतदविसष्टार्था......	1. 2. 49: सतः परमविज्ञानम् ।

Sarvadars'anasamgraha.

THE NIRUKTA.	THE PĀṆINIDARS'ANA.
1. 1: तद्यान्येतानि चत्वारि पदजातानि नामाख्याते चोपसर्गनिपाताश्च तानीमानि भवन्ति ।	p. 140. ननु नामाख्यातभेदेन पदद्वैविध्यप्रतीतेः कथं चातुर्विध्यमुक्तमिति चेन्मैवं प्रकारान्तरस्य प्रसिद्धत्वात् । तदुक्तं प्रकीर्णके । द्विधा कैश्चित् पदं भिन्नं चतुर्धा पञ्चधापि वा । अपोद्धृत्यैव वाक्येभ्यः प्रकृतिप्रत्ययादिवदिति ॥ कर्मप्रवचनीयेन वै पञ्चमेन सह पदस्य पञ्चविधत्वमिति हेलाराजो व्याख्यातवान् । कर्मप्रवचनीयास्तु... ...उपसर्गेष्वेवान्तर्भवंतीत्यभिसन्धाय पदचातुर्विध्यं भाष्यकारेणोक्तं युक्तमिति विवेक्तव्यम् ॥
1. 1: भावप्रधानमाख्यातम् ।	p. 144. भाववचनो धातुरिति...क्रियावचनो धातुरिति...
1. 1: गौरश्वः पुरुषो हस्तीति ।	p. 135. गौरश्वः पुरुषो हस्ती शकुनिरित्यादयः......
1. 3: नामाख्यातयोस्तु कर्मोपसंयोगद्योतका भवन्ति ।	p. 140: कर्मप्रवचनीयास्तु क्रियाविशेषोपजनितसंबन्धावच्छेदहेतव इति संबन्धविशेषद्योतनद्वारेण क्रियाविशेषद्योतनादुपसर्गेष्वेवान्तर्भवन्ति ।

Note.—The references are to the pages of *Sarvadars'anasamgraha* edited in Bib. Ind. published at Calcutta in 1858. The system of Pāṇini is discussed in the 13th section of the Sarvadars'a. pp. 135–147 in this edition.

Additions.

P. 4. line 9:–Devarāja says that Mādhava does not read शव: but शिवम् and शापम् as synonyms of water. शिवम् occurs in the Veda as a synonym of water, but as शिवम् is used in the spoken language (*bhāṣā*) in the sense of water, the adoption of शिवम् is not quite appropriate. शापम् is extremely obscure. It has never been used as a synonym of water by ancient teachers. It may however be explained in the following way:—शपन्त्यनेनेति शापम्...हस्ते ह्युदकमादाय शपन्ति मुनय इति श्रूयते ।

P. 9. l. 11:–For शव as a synonym of बल cf. S'B. 9. 4. 4. 3. p. 738: बलं वै शवः ।

P. 10. l. 8:–उस्रा-इळा are quoted as synonyms of cow by S'abara in his commentary on the *Pūrvamīmāṃsā.* on X. 4. 32. p. 492. (Jivananda's edition.)

P. 11. l. 2:–Satyavratasāmas'rami attributes the reading स्रंसति to Devarāja (see p. 236. Bib. Ind. edition). This is incorrect for Devarāja really reads स्रंसते see p. 240. *op. cit.*

P. 25. l. 1:–All the accented Mss. and printed editions of the *Nighaṇṭu* put the *udātta* accent on the *ya* of रथर्यति which occurs in RV. IX. 3. 5 and does not bear any *udātta.* रथर्यतः occurs in RV. VIII. 101. 2 also without the *udātta.* रथर्यसि is found in RV. X. 37. 3 and is accented on the syllable *ya* because it occurs in a subo rdinate clause.

P. 26. l. 1:–शुनासीरौ bears a double accent in the Nighaṇṭu. As an example of *devatā-dvandva* compound it should have a double accent. It occurs once only in RV. IV. 57. 5 and is accented on the first syllable only शुनासीरौ although it is clear that it is a *devatā-dvandva* compound. The form शुनासीरा occurs in RV. IV. 57. 8. and is also accented on the first syllable only.

P. 27. l. 8:–With Yāska's definition of a noun and a verb, cf. Bhartṛhari, *Vākyapadīya.*

2. 346: क्रियाप्रधानमाख्यातं नाम्नां सत्त्वप्रधानता ।
चत्वारि पदजातानि सर्वमेतद्विरुध्यते ॥

P. 28. l. 1-2:–The passage पूर्वापरीभूतं...पर्यन्तं is quoted by S'abara in his commentary on the *Pūrvamīmāṃsā* 1. 1. 5. p. 15, with the remark: शास्त्रकारा अप्येवमाहुः ।

P. 29 l. 1:-cf. Bhartṛhari, *Vākyapadīya*, 2. 347:

वाक्यस्य बुद्धौ नित्यत्वमर्थयोगं च लौकिकम् ।
दृष्ट्वा चतुष्ट्वं नास्तीति वार्त्ताक्षौदुम्बरायणौ ॥

P. 30. l. 13:-आचारं ग्राहयति is quoted by Kṣīrasvāmin in his *Amaraṭīkā*, p. 114. 7.

Cf. *Vāyu Purāṇa, 59. 29-30. pp. 200-1.*

वृद्धा ह्यलोलुपाश्चैव आत्मवन्तो ह्यदम्भकाः ।
सम्यग्विनीता ऋजवस्तानाचार्यान् प्रचक्षते ॥
स्वयमाचरते यस्मादाचारं स्थापयत्यपि ।
आचिनोति च शास्त्रार्थान् यमैः संनियमैर्युतः ॥

Cf. Āpastam. Dh. Sū. 14:-यस्माद्धर्मानाचिनोति स आचार्यः । cf. S'abara on 1. 3. 13: आचार्यो वेदोऽभिप्रेतः । आचिनोत्यस्य बुद्धिम् ।

l. 14: cf. Pāṇini, 8. 2. 101: चिदिति चोपमार्थे...।

P. 40. l. 18-19:-The two lines are quoted by Kumārila Bhaṭṭa in his commentary *Tantravārtika* p. 213, reading अधीतं for गृहीतं ।

P. 41. l. 5-6:-Cf. Vis'varūpācārya in the *Bālakrīḍā* p. 83: अप्येकस्मै वाग् विस्रब्धमात्मानमर्पयति । जायेव पत्ये उशती कामयमाना सुवासा ऋतुकालेष्विति ।

l. 15:-दैवताध्यात्मे is a variant for देवताध्यात्मे ।

P. 42. l. 4:-Cf. S'abara, 8. 2. 53. vol. 2. p. 252: अपि च पृणातेः पर्वशब्दः । पृणातिश्च दाने प्रसिद्धः ।

P. 44. l. 4:-अप्यक्षरवर्णसामान्यान्निर्ब्रूयात् is quoted by Kumārila Bhaṭṭa in the *Tantravārtika* p. 214.

l. 10:-तत्त्वा यामि is a fragment of RV. I. 24. 11.

P. 45. l. 3:-Quoted by Kumārila Bhaṭṭa *op. cit.* p. 146: तथा चोक्तम् । शवतिर्गतिकर्मा । कम्बोजेष्वेव दृष्टः ।

l. 9:-अक्रूरो ददते मणिमिति looks like a quotation.

P. 48. l. 23:-Roth reads ध्वंसन॰ for ध्वसन॰.

P. 50. l. 10:-Cf. *Mahābhārata, Ādiparvan,* (Kumbhakoṇa ed.) 63. 49:

यं यं कराभ्यां स्पृशति जीर्णं स सुखमश्नुते ।
पुनर्युवा च भवति तस्मात्तं शन्तनुं विदुः ॥

In तनोऽस्त्विवति, तनो can be either in the vocative or in the genitive. If in the former, the reading should be तनो अस्त्विवति, if the latter, it should read तनोरस्त्विवति. The case is undoubtedly vocative.

P. 51. l. 14:-The quotation is found in KS. 21. 2, Vol. II. p. 39; Cf. MS. 3. 3. 1, Vol. III. p. 32.

P. 52. l. 15:-इन्द्रशत्रुः । Cf. *Nāradas'ikṣāvivarṇam.* i. 4: इन्द्रशत्रुर्मेघ उच्यते । इन्द्रः शब्दः शातयिताऽस्येति बहुव्रीहिः ।

P. 56. l. 11:-For काल cf. *Vāyu Purāṇa* 32. 30. p. 105: कालः कलयते सदा । cf. *Sus'ruta Sūtra Sthāna, chapter* VI. p. 22: स सूक्ष्मामपि कलां न लीयत इति कालः । संकलयति कालयति वा भूतानीति कालः । Nirnaya sagar ed. with the com. of Dalhaṇa.

P. 57. footnote 4:-Add, N. X. 31.

P. 58. l. 4:-Following the method of the Saṃhitā text, शुष्मेभि should be read शुष्मेभी ।

P. 60. l. 18:-Roth reads अमूर्या. Accent is wrong.

P. 60. footnote 11:-The quotation is from KS. XXVII. 9. Vol. II. p. 149.

P. 61. l. 18 as well as footnote 14:-The quotation is attributed to the *S'ruti* of the Bhāllavis by Vis'varūpācārya in his commentary, the *Bālakrīḍā* on *Yājñavalkyasmṛti* p. 61.

P. 63. l. 2:-Cf. S'aṅkara on the *Vedānta Sūtra* 1. 4. 12: कैश्चित्तु देवाः पितरो गन्धर्वा असुरा रक्षांसि च पञ्च पञ्चजना व्याख्याताः । अन्यैश्च चत्वारो वर्णा निषादपञ्चमाः परिगृहीताः ।

l. 6:-बाहू is a variant for बाहुः ।

P. 65. l. 19:-तत्सख इन्द्रः शुष्णं जघानेति looks like a quotation.

P. 69. l. 1:-The Mss. which mark accent on the quotation have changed the accent. The correct accent should be ब्राह्मणवद् वृषलवत् ।

P. 76. l. 11:-Roth reads एनेन for अनेन.

P. 79. l. 17:-आदित्यादश्वो निस्तष्ट इति seems to be a quotation.

P. 85. l. 18:-The quotation is identical with MS. IV. 13. 10.

P. 95. l. 9:-The quotation is found in MS. I. 10. 14; KS. XXXVI. 8.

P. 96. l. 16:-For the quotation, see *Āp. S'raut. Sū.* XII. 19. 6.

Footnote 16-add, RVKH. XVII. 7.

P. 99. l. 5:-Roth reads तच्छब्दवत्वात् for शब्दवत्वात् ।

P. 99. footnote 2:-Omit VS. 5. 7. The quotation is found in TS. II. 4. 14. 1.

Foot note 5:-Omit VS. 5. 7. Add, cf. AV. VII. 81. 6; cf. TS. II. 4. 14. 1.

P. 100. footnote 12:-Durga's quotation is identical with KS. IX. 4; MS. I. 10. 2, except the last line, which reads in the KS. as follows:—यदेकस्यापि धर्मण्येतत्तदवयजामहे ॥ स्वाहा । The same is given in the MS. as follows:—तदेकस्यापि चेतसि तदेकस्यापि धर्मणि । तस्य सर्वस्यांहसो ऽवयजनमसि ।

P. 120. l. 15:-S'ivadatta reads ऊरु for उरु. It is evidently a mistake.

P. 121. l. 8:-All the Mss. and printed editions read आस्कन्नं. There is no evidence therefore to question the genuineness of आस्कन्नं but as it qualifies स्कन्ध, it should have been आस्कन्नः for स्कन्ध is used in the masculine gender only and never in the neuter. Should this be taken as evidence in support of स्कन्ध being also used in the neuter or a slip on the part of Yāska?

P. 136. l. 19:-S'ivadatta adds च after आग्नावैष्णवं ।

P. 141. l. 18:-जातवेदस्यं is a variant.

P. 150. l. 8:-The text reads याचन्ति. The root याच् is used in the *Ātmanepada* in classical Sanskrit. Probably a fine distinction is made in this passage i. e. the solicitation is not meant for one's self but for others, hence the *parasmaipada* is used.

P. 168. l. 3:-धामानि त्रयाणि is not correct. It should be either (1) धामानि त्रीणि or (2) धामत्रयम्. In my opinion, the text is corrupt.

P. 178. l. 20:-Some critics think that the correct reading should be जामि and not अजामि. This view is erroneous. It is clear, these critics have not understood the passage. The word जामि is used in the sense of tautology. Some scholars are of opinion that the recurrence of an identical expression in a stanza is tautology. Others think that the recurrence of the same expression in a verse (*pāda*) is tautology. Another school of thought holds that if there is even a very slight difference (in the expression), it is the negation of tautology. यथा कथा च विशेषोऽजामि भवतीत्यपरम् । It is clear therefore that अजामि and not जामि is the correct reading.

P. 181. l. 14:-S'ivadatta reads सरस्वन् without any justification.

P. 186. l. 3-4:-जरायु is used in the masculine gender in the third but in the neuter gender in the fourth line. (जरायु जरया etc.) The word can be used in both genders but it does not look consistent to use the same word in two different genders in practically the same sentence.

P. 193. l. 14:-S'ivadatta reads स्वर्चिभिः although the same word in Durga's commentary in the same edition is printed as स्वर्चिभिः। I think, S'ivadatta confounds the Vedic word स्वर्चि with the classical स्वर्चिस्।

P. 194. l. 4:-S'ivadatta reads इति after उदन्यवे।

P. 204. l. 13 and 16:-S'ivadatta reads ऽस्मन्नदीभि॰ and ऽस्मदभिनदीभि॰.

P. 206. l. 6:-S'ivadatta reads अनुत्तमो while Durga seems to favour अनुतमो.

P. 216. l. 7:S'ivadatta adds च after धारयिता.

P. 225. l. 16:-The reading of the text is ईक्षन्तमिति. I suggest ईक्षन्त इति।

P. 227. l. 1:-S'ivadatta reads अक्षयो which is wrong. It should have been अक्षयं.

P. 230. l. 4:-S'ivadatta reads अन्नं पानमि॰.

P. 231. l. 5:-All Mss. read मम्रौ which does not give any sense. I suggest मम्रो.

P. 231. l. 14:-The reading of the text is प्रतिपद्यते but as the subject is ये I suggest प्रतिपद्यन्ते।